Roger Ebert's
ovie Yearbook
2010

Other Books by Roger Ebert

An Illini Century

A Kiss Is Still a Kiss

Two Weeks in the Midday Sun:
A Cannes Notebook

Behind the Phantom's Mask

Roger Ebert's Little Movie Glossary

Roger Ebert's Movie Home Companion
annually 1986–1993

Roger Ebert's Video Companion
annually 1994–1998

Roger Ebert's Movie Yearbook
annually 1999–2007, 2009

Questions for the Movie Answer Man

Roger Ebert's Book of Film: An Anthology

Ebert's Bigger Little Movie Glossary

I Hated, Hated, Hated This Movie

The Great Movies

The Great Movies II

Your Movie Sucks

Roger Ebert's Four-Star Reviews—1967–2007

Awake in the Dark: The Best of Roger Ebert

Scorsese by Ebert

With Daniel Curley
The Perfect London Walk

With Gene Siskel
The Future of the Movies: Interviews with Martin Scorsese,
Steven Spielberg, and George Lucas

DVD Commentary Tracks
Citizen Kane
Dark City
Casablanca
Floating Weeds
Crumb
Beyond the Valley of the Dolls

Roger Ebert's Movie Yearbook 2010

**Andrews McMeel
Publishing, LLC**

Kansas City • Sydney • London

Roger Ebert's Movie Yearbook 2010
copyright © 1999, 2000, 2001, 2002, 2003,
2004, 2005, 2006, 2007, 2008, 2009, 2010
by Roger Ebert.
For information write
Andrews McMeel Publishing, LLC,
an Andrews McMeel Universal company,
1130 Walnut Street,
Kansas City, Missouri 64106.

ISSN: 1532-8147
ISBN-13: 978-0-7407-8536-8
ISBN-10: 0-7407-8536-2

10 11 12 13 14 MLT 10 9 8 7 6 5 4 3 2 1

www.andrewsmcmeel.com

All the reviews in this book originally appeared
in the *Chicago Sun-Times*.

This book is dedicated
to Robert Zonka, 1928–1985.
God love ya.

ATTENTION: SCHOOLS AND BUSINESSES

Andrews McMeel books are available at quantity discounts with bulk purchase for educational, business, or sales
promotional use. For information, please write to: Special Sales Department, Andrews McMeel Publishing, LLC,
1130 Walnut Street, Kansas City, Missouri 64106.

Contents

Introduction

As you know, my life has undergone a fundamental change since I had surgery in the summer of 2006. The surgery was a success, and I am at present cancer free, but the result was a loss of my ability to speak. My first-grade report card had this notation: *Talks too much.* Well, I don't any longer.

This disability has ended my days on television, but it came with a silver lining. The focus of my work life has always been seeing movies and reviewing them, and that hasn't changed. In the early days of my recovery, my wife, Chaz, brought me a DVD of a movie she thought I might enjoy, *The Queen,* with Helen Mirren. She was correct. I took out a yellow legal pad and wrote my first review in a few months.

My illness involved more surgeries in an attempt to restore my speech, which were unsuccessful. What was constant were the movies. I attended as many as possible, watched more on DVD, and was soon up to form again. Indeed, I seem to be more productive than ever; as I write this in autumn 2009, I've already reviewed 211 reviews this year, as well as Great Movie essays, Questions for the Movie Answer Man, interviews, and entries in the blog I started writing in the spring of 2008.

People ask if my writing has changed since my illness. Not that I am aware of. But it has become more necessary. From the age of sixteen, I've been a newspaperman, and that has always been my first love. Television was unexpected. Now I am writing more than ever for the *Chicago Sun-Times* and my Web site. Because I've always been very verbal, this writing has become a form of speech. I take particular pleasure in writing a review because I am expressing myself as fully as possible, and the rest of the time I'm afraid I come across as the village idiot, holding up conversations while trying to scribble down notes.

What else has changed? I remember a day in 2008 when I was at a screening of the new Indiana Jones movie and realized how happy I was—how much I loved movies. I was still in a wheelchair during a rehabilitation process, and all hell was breaking loose on the screen, and I loved every moment of it, even the obvious special effects.

Something has improved. I have more time now to review films out of the mainstream: more foreign films, documentaries, smaller indie productions, revivals. I've always tried to cover those areas, but now I have more time. And opportunity. Some of the best films I've seen this year, like *Silent Light; You, the Living; Munyurangabo; Tulpan;* and *Departures* (filmed in Mexico, Sweden, Africa, Kazakhstan, and Japan) were films that might have flown under my radar.

I also find myself valuing the human qualities of a film. Serious illness focuses the mind on human mortality and draws idiotic entertainments like *Transformers: Revenge of the Fallen* into focus. What can anybody learn from such a film? Paul Cox, a director who has never made a film without human values, once said the experience of film should not make you less of a person than you were before it began.

Movie critics have an immediate consolation after undergoing such films. We can write our reviews. There are few things tastier than revenge, freshly brewed.

We missed a year of the *Yearbook* while I was sick, filling the gap with a collection of all my four-star reviews. The 2009 *Yearbook* doubled back and picked up everything published since the 2007 edition. Now here is 2010, which, depending on how you count, is the twenty-second or twenty-third annual volume. This one means a lot to me.

My thoughts go back to the original *Movie Home Companion* and to Donna Martin, the Andrews McMeel editor who conceived it and later persuaded me to switch to the *Yearbook* format. My sincere thanks to her, and to Dorothy O'Brien, who has been the book's valued editor at Andrews McMeel in recent years. Also to Sue Roush, my editor at Universal Press Syndicate, and to Laura Emerick, Miriam Dinunzio, Darel Jevens, Teresa Budasi, Thomas Conner, and all the other heroes at the *Chicago Sun-Times*, and Jim Emerson, John Barry, and the webstaff at rogerebert.com. Many others are thanked in the acknowledgments.

In autumn 2006, the University of Chicago Press published *Awake in the Dark,* a survey of my forty years of writing about the movies. My Andrews McMeel book *I Hated, Hated, Hated This Movie* inspired a sequel in spring 2007, *Your Movie Sucks.* As for the Great Movies books, there may be a volume three by the time you read this, and I'm already a dozen essays into volume four.

ROGER EBERT

Acknowledgments

My editor is Dorothy O'Brien, tireless, cheerful, all-noticing. My friend and longtime editor Donna Martin suggested the yearbook approach to the annual volume. The design is by Cameron Poulter, the typographical genius of Hyde Park.

My thanks to production editor Christi Clemons Hoffman, who renders Cameron's design into reality. John Yuelkenbeck at Coleridge Design is the compositor who has worked diligently on the series for years. I have been blessed with the expert and discriminating editing of Laura Emerick, Miriam DiNunzio, Darel Jevins, Jeff Johnson, and Teresa Budasi at the *Chicago Sun-Times*; Sue Roush at Universal Press Syndicate; and Michelle Daniel and David Shaw at Andrews McMeel Publishing. For much advice and counsel, thanks to Jim Emerson and John Barry of www.rogerebert.com.

Many thanks are also due to Marsha Jordan at WLS-TV. My gratitude goes to Carol Iwata, my expert personal assistant, and to Gregory Isaac, who is a computer whiz and invaluable aide-de-camp. I must also thank those who have given me countless observations and corrections, including Peter Debruge, Jana J. Monji, and Troylene Ladner.

And special thanks and love to my wife, Chaz, who was always at my side during a difficult illness, helped see three books through the press during that time, and was a cheerleader for this one. I am so grateful to her as we once again, relieved, enter a period of good health.

ROGER EBERT

Key to Symbols

★★★★ A great film
★★★   A good film
★★   Fair
★   Poor

G, PG, PG-13, R, NC-17:
Ratings of the Motion Picture
Association of America

G   Indicates that the movie is
suitable for general audiences

PG   Suitable for general audiences
but parental guidance is
suggested

PG-13 Recommended for viewers
13 years or above; may contain
material inappropriate for
younger children

R   Recommended for viewers
17 or older

NC-17 Intended for adults only

141 m. Running time

2008   Year of theatrical release

☞   Refers to "Questions for the
Movie Answer Man"

Reviews

A

Across the Universe ★ ★ ★ ★
PG-13, 133 m., 2007

Jim Sturgess (Jude), Evan Rachel Wood (Lucy), Joe Anderson (Max), Dana Fuchs (Sadie), Martin Luther McCoy (JoJo), T. V. Carpio (Prudence), Bono (Dr. Robert), Eddie Izzard (Mr. Kite). Directed by Julie Taymor and produced by Matthew Gross, Jennifer Todd, and Suzanne Todd. Screenplay by Dick Clement and Ian La Frenais.

Here is a bold, beautiful, visually enchanting musical where we walk INTO the theater humming the songs. Julie Taymor's *Across the Universe* is an audacious marriage of cutting-edge visual techniques, heartwarming performances, 1960s history, and the Beatles songbook. Sounds like a concept that might be behind its time, but I believe in yesterday.

This isn't one of those druggy 1960s movies, although it has what the MPAA shyly calls "some" drug content. It's not grungy, although it has Joe Cocker in it. It's not political, which means it's political to its core. Most miraculous of all, it's not dated; the stories could be happening now, and in fact they are.

For a film that is almost wall-to-wall music, it has a full-bodied plot. The characters, mostly named after Beatles songs, include Lucy (the angelic Evan Rachel Wood), who moves from middle America to New York; Jude (Jim Sturgess), a Liverpool ship welder who works his way to New York on a ship; and Lucy's brother Max (Joe Anderson), a college student who has dropped out (I guess). They now all share a pad in Greenwich Village with their musician friends, the Hendrixian JoJo (Martin Luther McCoy), the Joplinesque Sadie (Dana Fuchs), and the lovelorn Prudence (T. V. Carpio), who has a thing for Max, although the curious cutting of one scene suggests she might have lesbian feelings as well.

Jude and Lucy fall in love, and they all go through a hippie period on Dr. Robert's Magic Bus, where the doctor (Bono) and his bus bear a striking resemblance to Ken Kesey's magical mystery tour. They also get guidance from Mr. Kite (Eddie Izzard), having been some days in preparation. But then things turn serious as Max goes off to Vietnam, and the story gets swept up in the antiwar movement.

Yet when I say "story," don't start thinking about a lot of dialogue and plotting. Almost everything happens as an illustration to a Beatles song. The arrangements are sometimes familiar, sometimes radically altered, and the voices are all new; the actors either sing or synch, and often they find a mood in a song that we never knew was there before. When Prudence sings "I Wanna Hold Your Hand," for example, I realized how wrong I was to ever think that was a happy song. It's not happy if it's a hand you are never, never, never going to hold.

Julie Taymor, famous as the director of *The Lion King* on Broadway, is a generously inventive choreographer, such as in a basic training scene where all the drill sergeants look like G. I. Joe, a sequence where inductees in jockey shorts carry the Statue of Liberty through a Vietnam field, and cross-cutting between dancing to Beatles clone bands at an American high school prom and in a Liverpool dive bar. There are underwater sequences that approach ballet, a stage performance that turns into musical warfare, strawberries that bleed, rooftop concerts, and a montage combining crashing waves with the Detroit riots.

But all I'm doing here is list making. The beauty is in the execution. The experience of the movie is joyous. I don't even want to know about anybody who complains they aren't hearing "the real Beatles." Fred Astaire wasn't Cole Porter, either. These songs are now more than forty years old, some of them, and are timeless, and hearing these unexpected talents singing them (yes, and Bono, Izzard, and Cocker, too) only underlines their astonishing quality.

You weren't alive in the 1960s? Or the '70s, or '80s? You're like the guy on the IMDb message board who thought the band was named the *Beetles*, and didn't even get it when people made Volkswagen jokes because he hadn't heard of VW Beetles either. All is forgiven. Jay Leno has a Jaywalking spot for you. Just about anybody else is likely to enjoy *Across the Universe.*

I'm sure there were executives who thought it was suicidal to set a "Beatles musical" in "the Vietnam era." But this is a movie that fires its songs like flowers at the way we live now. It's the kind of movie you watch again, like listening to a favorite album. It was scheduled for the Toronto Film Festival, so was previewed (as several Toronto films were) for critics in major cities. I was drowning in movies and deadlines, and this was the only one I went to see twice.

Now do your homework and rent the DVD of *A Hard Day's Night* if you've never seen it. The thought that there are readers who would get this far in this review of this film and never have seen that film is unbearably sad. Cheer me up. Don't let me down (repeat three times).

Adoration ★ ★ ★
R, 101 m., 2009

Arsinee Khanjian (Sabine), Devon Bostick (Simon), Scott Speedman (Tom), Rachel Blanchard (Rachel), Noam Jenkins (Sami), Kenneth Walsh (Morris). Directed by Atom Egoyan and produced by Egoyan, Simone Urdl, and Jennifer Weis. Screenplay by Egoyan.

Atom Egoyan is fascinated by the way life coils back on itself. He uses coincidences and chance meetings not as plot devices but as illustrations of the ways we are linked across generations and national boundaries. His characters are often not completely connected to where they find themselves, and they bring along personal, sometimes secret, associations. These often reflect much larger realities in the outer world.

Adoration circles around a central event or nonevent. A report is read about a woman who falls in love with a man from the Middle East. His family is in Israel, he says, although I am not sure that is true. She becomes pregnant. He is unhappy at first but later overjoyed. They seem deeply in love. He wants her to fly to meet his parents in Bethlehem. For business reasons, he must take a later flight.

In an age of terrorism, this triggers alarms, but not for her. What becomes of these people and the flight is not for me to relate now. We see them only in flashbacks. The story presents more than one way they possibly did meet. The film is about other people in their lives—before, and after, they met. It is also about how these other people think about what they did and didn't do.

The buried issues involve nationalism, religion, and prejudice. But this is not a message film. It is about people trying to find their way through emotional labyrinths. We are not always sure what these are, or what really happened, or what these people really feel about it, or their motives. Neither are they. *Adoration* isn't confusion; it's about confused people. Most movies make it easy for us. The central characters know what they want, and we understand.

Here there is the illusion that we are feeling our way along with these people. The most important connection, although we don't realize it for a while, is a Toronto high school drama teacher named Sabine (Arsinee Khanjian, Egoyan's muse). She reads a story about the original air travel incident as an exercise in French class. Why that story? An exercise in comprehending spoken French. And something more . . .

A student named Simon (Devon Bostick) transforms this into a first-person story, with his mother as the pregnant woman and his father as the treacherous fiancé. Simon's parents are dead, and he lives with his Uncle Tom (Scott Speedman). Sabine encourages him to read his story to the class as if it were true—as an acting exercise, she says. The story is picked up in Internet chat rooms involving Simon's high school friends.

I don't want to say too much about what is real or imagined here, and nothing at all about the secret connection the teacher Sabine is hiding. Egoyan contrives meetings between Sabine and Tom with two rather brilliant sequences that keep us guessing even while played out in full view. And there are flashbacks to the couple in Simon's story and to his actual parents, played by the same actors, so that, as it frequently does in Egoyan's films, reality takes on uncertain implications.

Throbbing beneath are ideas about terrorism, about Israeli-Palestinian feelings, about Muslims in Canada, and about the role of the Internet in creating factoids that might as well be real. Statements are made involving these subjects, but they're all suspended in an incomplete resolution; the movie withholds closure. There are areas only suggested: the boy's anger at his father, the use of the original story to him, the circumstances of two deaths, the placing of blame.

Some viewers may find the film confusing; I found it absorbing. One problem with reviewing an Egoyan film is that you find yourself struggling to describe a fractured plot line and what characters (and we) may believe at one point and not later. This can be confusing and unsatisfactory. Yet the film presents emotions that are clear. Why does Egoyan weave a tangled web? Because his characters are caught in it. Our lives consist of stories we tell ourselves about our lives. They may be based on reality, but not necessarily, and maybe they shouldn't always be. If you couldn't do a little rewriting, how could you stand things?

Adventureland ★ ★ ★
R, 107 m., 2009

Jesse Eisenberg (James Brennan), Kristen Stewart (Em Lewin), Martin Starr (Joel Schiffman), Bill Hader (Bobby), Kristen Wiig (Paulette), Ryan Reynolds (Mike Connell), Margarita Levieva (Lisa P.). Directed by Greg Mottola and produced by Ted Hope, Anne Carey, and Sidney Kimmel. Screenplay by Mottola.

It is a truth of twenty-somethings that if you have a crappy summer job with other twenty-somethings, the way to take your mind off work is daydreaming of sex with your workmates. You are trapped there together, eight or ten hours a day for three months, right, so what else is there to make you dance to unheard melodies?

Take James. Here he is, all set to move to New York, and his dad loses his job and he's forced to take a job at a shabby Pittsburgh amusement park. All of the rides look second-hand, all of the games are rigged, and all of the prizes look like surplus. Your job is to encourage customers even more luckless than you are to throw baseballs at targets that are glued down, while inflamed with hopes of taking home a Big Ass Panda. That's what Bobby the owner calls them when he instructs you, "Nobody *ever* wins a Big Ass Panda."

Director Greg Mottola, who made the rather wonderful *Superbad*, is back now with a sweeter story, more quietly funny, again about a hero who believes he may be a virgin outstaying his shelf life. Jesse Eisenberg, from *The Squid and the Whale*, plays James, who has a degree in Renaissance studies. (The movie is set in the 1980s, and there may still be a few jobs around.) He's out of his element at Adventureland; Bobby has to coach him to fake enthusiasm when he announces the horse race game, where you advance your horse by rolling balls into holes. His performance reminded me uncannily of my last visit to Dave & Buster's.

Most of the male employees in the park lust for Lisa P. (Margarita Levieva), whose Adventureland T-shirt unfortunately advertises Rides Rides Rides. James is much more interested in Em (Kristen Stewart), who is quieter and deeper (Games Games Games). She's smart, quirky, and seems more grown-up than the others. A quick rapport springs up, despite her edge on James in sexual experience. She thinks he's kinda sweet. They talk about subjects that require more than one sentence.

This romance takes fragile bloom while Mottola, also the screenwriter, rotates through a plot involving James's friends, one of whom expresses his devotion by hitting him in the netherlands every time he sees him. We cut often to the owner, Bobby, and his wife, Paulette (Kristen Wiig), who are lovebirds and have firm ideas about how every job at the park should be performed, which doesn't endear them to the employees because they're usually right. Oh, and then there's Connell (Ryan Reynolds), the good-looking maintenance man, who is married, and why am I telling you that?

As the summer lurches between deadly boredom and sudden emergencies (someone wins a Big Ass Panda), James and Em grow closer. This is absorbing because they reveal themselves as smarter than anyone else realizes. From his earlier work, I expected to like Eisenberg. What surprised me was how much I admired Kristen Stewart, who in *Twilight* was playing below her grade level. Here is an actress ready to do important things. Together, and with the others, they make *Adventureland* more real and more touching than it may sound.

I worked two summers at Crystal Lake Pool in Urbana. I was technically a lifeguard and got free Cokes, but I rarely got to sit in the lifeguard chair. As the junior member of the staff, I was assigned to Poop Patrol, which involved plunging deep into the depths with a flyswatter and a bucket. Not a lot of status when you were applauded while carrying the bucket to the men's room. ("No spilling!" my boss, Oscar Adams, warned me.) But there was another lifeguard named Toni and—oh, never mind. I don't think she ever knew.

Alexandra ★ ★ ★ ½
NO MPAA RATING, 91 m., 2008

Galina Vishnevskaya (Alexandra), Vasily Shevtsov (Denis), Raisa Gichaeva (Malika). Directed by Alexander Sokurov and produced by Andrei Sigle. Screenplay by Sokurov.

It is as simple as this. An old lady is helped on board an armored military train and journeys all night to visit a remote Russian army outpost. The soldiers seem to know about her and her visit, and after a couple of local boys apparently try to "guide" her away from her suitcase, two soldiers in uniform turn up and escort her to the base.

We already know a lot about her. We know she is opinionated, proud, stubborn, and not afraid to express her opinion. She marches through the heat and dust into the base and is guided to her "hotel," a room with two cots in a barracks made of tents. Other information is revealed, slowly. Her name is Alexandra (Galina Vishnevskaya). She is here to visit her grandson, Denis. He is a captain in the army.

The base is located in Chechnya. It is a Muslim republic, occupied by the Russians, who are sullenly disliked. On the base, discipline seems informal, the soldiers lax. When Denis (Vasily Shevtsov) turns up, she is appalled by the state of his uniform and advises him to wash up. She also sniffs disapprovingly at other soldiers, tells helpers "Don't pull my arm" and "Don't push me!" and that she is perfectly capable of taking care of herself.

The next day she wanders the base so early that no one seems to be around, and that was when I remembered a similar scene in Bergman's *Wild Strawberries,* about an old man who dreams of wandering a deserted town. There are other parallels between the two films, but Bergman's is about an old man discovering himself, and *Alexandra* is about an old woman being discovered. She is a transformative presence.

The film was written and directed by Alexander Sokurov, maker of the remarkable *Russian Ark*—remember that one, in which he used only one uninterrupted shot to tour the Hermitage Museum? He follows the woman as she talks her way past a guarded checkpoint and wanders into town to find the market. She is tired and hot. It must be 100 degrees. She meets Malika (Raisa Gichaeva), a woman about her age, who gives her a seat in her booth, is friendly, and gives her cigarettes and cookies knowing that they will go to Russian soldiers. Then she invites Alexandra home to her flat in a building missing a big chunk because of bombs or shells. The two old women bond, and their conversation is the essence of the film.

If the locals do not like the Russians, the Russians do not like their duty. They can't see the point of it. They are not wanted, they will never be wanted, so why are they forced to stay? These conclusions aren't said in so many words, but they permeate the film. And notice the way some locals look at her with pointed dislike and some soldiers simply stare at her, perhaps because she is the only woman on the base and reminds them of grandmothers, mothers, sisters, girlfriends—the whole world outside their existence.

Alexandra is not a sweet little old lady. The fact that she is played by Vishnevskaya, who once ruled the Russian opera, may supply a hint of where she gets her confidence, her imperious manner. But when she hugs her grandson, when he braids her hair, when she says he "smells like a man" and she loves that smell, we get a window into her youth and her memories. Remarkable, how little Sokurov tells us, while telling us so much.

The color strategy of the movie is part of its effect. It is drab, brown, unsaturated. Reds and greens are pale, sometimes not even visible. Everything is covered with dust.

Brighter colors would add vitality to the base, but that would be wrong. The point is that for the soldiers it's a dead zone, life on hold, a cheerless existence. And this plainspoken old woman reminds them of a lifetime they are missing.

Alien Trespass ★ ★
PG, 90 m., 2009

Eric McCormack (Ted Lewis/Urp), Jenni Baird (Tammy), Robert Patrick (Vern), Dan Lauria (Chief Dawson), Jody Thompson (Lana Lewis). Directed by R. W. Goodwin and produced by Goodwin and James Swift. Screenplay by Steven P. Fisher.

Alien Trespass is a sincere attempt to make a film that looks like one of those 1950s B movies where a monster from outer space terrorized a small town, which was almost always in the desert. Small, to save on extras and travel. In the desert, because if you headed east from Hollywood that's where you were, and if you headed west you were making a pirate picture.

The movie is in color, which in the 1950s was uncommon, but otherwise it's a knowing replication of the look and feel of those pictures, about things with jaws, tentacles, claws, weapons that shot sparks, and eyes that shot laser beams at people, only they weren't known as laser beams but as Deadly Rays. Facing them are plucky locals, dressed in work clothes from Sears, standing behind their open car doors and looking up to watch awkward special effects that are coming—coming!—this way!

The movie doesn't bend over backward to be "bad." It tries to be the best bad movie that it can be. A lot of its deliberate badness involves effects some viewers might not notice. For example: bad back projection in shots looking back from the dashboard at people in the front seat. In the 1950s, before CGI, the car never left the sound stage, and in the rear window they projected footage of what it was allegedly driving past. Since people were presumed not to study the rear window intently, they got away with murder. In *Casablanca*, Rick and Ilsa drove from the Champs-Elysées to the countryside instantly.

The plot: Astronomer Ted Lewis (Eric McCormack) and his sexpot wife, Lana (Jody Thompson), are grilling cow-sized steaks in the backyard when something shoots overhead and crashes in the mountains. The sexpot wife is an accurate touch: The monster genre cast pinups like Mamie Van Doren and Cleo Moore, who were featured on the posters with Deadly Rays shooting down their cleavage.

Ted goes to investigate. When he returns, his body has been usurped by Urp, an alien. Urp means well. He needs help to track down another alien who arrived on the same flying saucer, named the Ghota, which has one eye, enough to qualify it as a BEM, or a Bug-Eyed Monster. The Ghota consumes people in order to grow, divide, and conquer. Sort of like B.O.B. in the new *Monsters vs. Aliens*, which is *also* a send-up of 1950s BEM movies. So far, Todd Haynes's *Far from Heaven* (2002) is the only movie ever made in tribute to a *great* movie of the 1950s.

The Ghota is battled by Urp and his plucky new buddy Tammy (Jenni Baird), a local waitress who is a lot more game than Lana. As nearly as I can recall, in the 1950s good girls were never named Lana and bad ones were never named Tammy. There are also hapless but earnest local cops (Robert Patrick and Dan Lauria) and an assortment of Threatened Townspeople. Also great shots of the Lewis family home, separated from the desert by a white picket fence, surrounded by the age-old story of the shifting, whispering sands.

Alien Trespass, directed by R. W. Goodwin (*The X Files* on TV) from a screenplay by Steven P. Fisher, is obviously a labor of love. But why? Is there a demand for cheesy 1950s sci-fi movies not met by the existing supply? Will younger audiences consider it to be merely inept, and not inept with an artistic intention? Here is a movie more suited to Comic-Con or the World Science Fiction Convention than to your neighborhood multiplex.

If you must see a science fiction movie about a threat from beyond Earth, there's one right now that I think is great: *Knowing*. If you're looking for a *bad* sci-fi movie about a threat, etc., most of the nation's critics mistakenly believe it qualifies. How can you lose? "From beyond the stars—a mysterious force strikes terror into the hearts of men!"

Alvin and the Chipmunks ★ ★
PG, 91 m., 2007

Jason Lee (Dave Seville), David Cross (Ian), Cameron Richardson (Claire), voice of Justin Long (Alvin), voice of Jesse McCartney (Theodore), voice of Matthew Gray Gubler (Simon). Directed by Tim Hill and produced by Ross Bagdasarian Jr., Janice Karman, and Steve Waterman. Screenplay by John Vitti, Will McRobb, and Chris Viscardi.

The most astonishing sight in *Alvin and the Chipmunks* is not three singing chipmunks. No, it's a surprise saved for the closing titles, where we see the covers of all the Alvin & C albums and CDs. I lost track after ten. It is inconceivable to me that anyone would want to listen to one whole album of those squeaky little voices, let alone ten. "The Chipmunk Song," maybe, for its fleeting novelty. But "Only You"?

There are, however, Alvin and the Chipmunks fans. Their latest album rates 4.5/5 at the iTunes store, where I sampled their version of "Only You" and the original by the Platters, and immediately downloaded *The Platters' Greatest Hits*. I imagine people even impatiently preorder the Chipmunks, however, which speaks highly for the drawing power of electronically altered voices by interchangeable singers. This film is dedicated to Ross Bagdasarian Sr., "who was crazy enough" to dream them up. I think the wording is about right.

Despite the fact that the film is set in the present, when the real (or "real") Chipmunks already have a back catalog bigger than Kimya Dawson's, the movie tells the story of how they become rock stars and almost get burned out on the rock circuit. Jason Lee stars as Dave Seville, who accidentally brings them home in a basket of muffins, discovers they can talk, and is soon shouting "Alvin!" at the top of his lungs, as Chipmunk lore requires that he must.

David Cross plays Ian, the hustling tour promoter who signs them up and takes them on the road, where they burn out and he suggests they start lip-synching with dubbed voices. Now we're getting into Alice in Wonderland territory, because of course they *are* dubbed voices in the first place. Indeed the metaphysics of dubbing dubbed chipmunks

who exist in the real world as animated representations of real chipmunks is . . . how did this sentence begin?

That said, whatever it was, *Alvin and the Chipmunks* is about as good as a movie with these characters can probably be, and I am well aware that I am the wrong audience for this movie. I am even sure some readers will throw it up to me that I liked the Garfield movie better.

Yes, but Garfield didn't sing, and he was dubbed by Bill Murray. My duty as a reporter is to inform you that the chipmunks are sorta cute, that Jason Lee and David Cross manfully play roles that require them, as actors, to relate with empty space that would later be filled with CGI, and that at some level the movie may even be doing something satirical about rock stars and the hype machine.

I was also grateful that Alvin wears a red sweater with a big "A" on it as an aid to identification, since otherwise all the chipmunks seem to be identical, like mutant turtles or Spice Girls. It doesn't much matter which one is Theodore and which one is Simon, although Simon is always the one who seems a day late and a walnut short.

American Gangster ★ ★ ★ ★
R, 157 m., 2007

Denzel Washington (Frank Lucas), Russell Crowe (Det. Richie Roberts), Chiwetel Ejiofor (Huey Lucas), Cuba Gooding Jr. (Nicky Barnes), Josh Brolin (Det. Trupo), Ted Levine (Lou Toback), Armand Assante (Dominic Cattano), Carla Gugino (Laurie Roberts). Directed by Ridley Scott and produced by Scott and Brian Grazer. Screenplay by Steven Zaillian, based on an article by Mark Jacobson.

Apart from the detail that he was a heroin dealer, Frank Lucas's career would be an ideal case study for a business school. *American Gangster* tells his success story. Inheriting a crime empire from his famous boss, Bumpy Johnson, he cornered the New York drug trade with admirable capitalist strategies. He personally flew to Southeast Asia to buy his product directly from the suppliers, used an ingenious importing scheme to get it into the United States, and sold it at higher purity and lower cost than anyone else was able to. At the end, he was worth more than $150 million, and got a reduced sentence by cutting a deal to expose three-quarters of the NYPD narcotics officers as corrupt. And he always took his mom to church on Sunday.

Lucas is played by Denzel Washington in another one of those performances where he is affable and smooth on the outside yet ruthless enough to set an enemy on fire. Here's a detail: As the man goes up in flames, Frank shoots him to put him out of his agony. Now that's merciful. His stubborn antagonist in the picture is a police detective named Richie Roberts (Russell Crowe), who gets a very bad reputation in the department. How does he do that? By finding $1 million in drug money—*and turning it in*. What the hell kindofa thing is that to do, when the usual practice would be to share it with the boys?

There is something inside Roberts that will not bend, not even when his powerful colleague (Josh Brolin) threatens him. He vows to bring down Frank Lucas, and he does, although it isn't easy, and his most troubling opposition comes from within the police. Lucas, the student of the late Bumpy, has a simple credo: Treat people right, keep a low profile, adhere to sound business practices, and hand out turkeys on Thanksgiving. He can trust the people who work for him because he pays them very well, and many of them are his relatives.

In the movie, at least, Lucas is low-key and soft-spoken. No rings on his fingers, no gold around his neck, no spinners on his hubcaps, quiet marriage to a sweet wife, a Brooks Brothers image. It takes the authorities the longest time to figure out who he is because they can't believe an African-American could hijack the Harlem drug trade from the Mafia. The Mafia can't believe it either, but Frank not only pulls it off, he's still alive at the end.

When it was first announced, Ridley Scott's movie was inevitably called the black *Godfather*. Not really. For one thing, it tells two parallel stories, not one, and it really has to because without Richie Roberts there would be no story to tell, and Lucas might still be in business today. But that doesn't save us from a stock female character who is becoming increasingly tiresome in the movies, the wife (Carla Gugino) who wants Roberts to choose between his job and his family. Their obligatory scenes together are recycled from a dozen or a hundred other plots, and although we sympathize with her (will they all be targeted for assassination?), we grow restless during her complaints. Roberts's domestic crisis is not what the movie is about.

It is about an extraordinary entrepreneur whose story was told in a *New York Magazine* article by Mark Jacobson. As adapted into a (somewhat fictionalized) screenplay by Steve Zaillian (*Schindler's List*), Lucas is a loyal driver, bodyguard, and coat holder for Bumpy Johnson (who has inspired characters in three other movies, including *The Cotton Club*). He listens carefully to Johnson's advice, cradles him when he is dying, takes over, and realizes the fatal flaw in the Harlem drug business: The goods come in through the Mafia after having been stepped on all along the way.

So he flies to Thailand, goes upriver for a face-to-face with the general in charge of drugs, and is rewarded for this seemingly foolhardy risk with an exclusive contract. The drugs will come to the United States inside the coffins of American casualties, which is apparently based on fact. It's all arranged by one of his relatives.

In terms of his visible lifestyle, the story of Frank Lucas might as well be the story of J. C. Penney, except that he hands out turkeys instead of pennies. Everyone in his distribution chain is reasonably happy because the product is high-quality, the price is right, and there's money for everyone. Ironically, an epidemic of overdoses occurs when Lucas's high-grade stuff is treated by junkies as if it's the usual weaker street strength. Then Lucas starts practicing what marketing experts call branding: It becomes known that his *Blue Magic* offers twice the potency at half the price, and other suppliers are forced off the streets by the rules of the marketplace, not turf wars.

This is an engrossing story, told smoothly and well, and Russell Crowe's contribution is enormous (it's not his fault his wife complains). Looking like a care-worn bulldog, his Richie Roberts studies for a law degree, remains inviolate in his ethical standards, and just keeps plugging away, building his case. The film ends (this isn't a spoiler, I hope) not with a *Scarface*-style shootout, but with Frank and Richie sitting down for a long, intelligent conversation, written by Zaillian to show two smart men who both know what the score is. As I hinted above: less *Godfather* than *Wall Street,* although for that matter a movie named *American Gangster* could have been made about Kenneth Lay.

American Teen ★ ★ ★
PG-13, 95 m., 2008

Featuring Hannah Bailey, Colin Clemens, Megan Krizmanich, Geoff Haase, Mitch Reinholt, Jake Tusing, and Ali Wikalinska. A documentary directed by Nanette Burstein and produced by Nanette Burstein, Jordan Roberts, Eli Gonda, and Chris Huddleston.

American Teen observes a year in the life of four high school seniors in Warsaw, Indiana. It is presented as a documentary, and indeed these students and their friends and families are all real people, and these are their stories. But many scenes seem suspiciously staged. Why would Megan, the "most popular" girl in school, allow herself to be photographed spreading toilet paper on a lawn and spray-painting "FAG" on the house window of a classmate? Is she really that unaware? She's the subject of disciplinary action in the film; why didn't she tell the school official she only did it for the movie?

Many questions like that occur while you're watching *American Teen,* but once you make allowance for the factor of directorial guidance, the movie works effectively as what it wants to be: a look at these lives, in this town ("mostly middle-class, white, and Christian"), at this time.

The director is Nanette Burstein, whose credits include the considerable documentaries *On the Ropes* and *The Kid Stays in the Picture.* She spent a year in Warsaw, reportedly shot one thousand hours of footage, and focused on four students who represent segments of the high school population.

Megan Krizmanich is pretty, on the school council, a surgeon's daughter, "popular," but sometimes considered a bitch. She dreams of going to Notre Dame, as her father, a brother, and a sister did. She seems supremely self-confident until late in the film, when we learn about a family tragedy that her mother blames for her "buried anger."

Colin Clemens, with a Jay Leno chin, is the basketball star. His dad has a sideline as an Elvis impersonator (pretty good, too). The family doesn't have the money to send him to college, so everything depends on winning an athletic scholarship, a fact he is often reminded of. He doesn't have a star personality but is a nice guy, funny.

Hannah Bailey is the girl who wants to get the hell out of Warsaw. She dreams of studying film in San Francisco. Her parents warn her of the hazards of life for a young girl alone in the big city, but she doesn't want to spend her life at a nine-to-five job she hates. "This is my life," she firmly tells her parents. She also goes into a deep depression when a boyfriend breaks up with her and misses so many days of school as a result that she is threatened with not graduating.

And Jake Tusing is the self-described nerd, member of the band, and compulsive video game player, who decorates his room with an astonishing array of stuffed, framed, or mounted animals. He has a bad case of acne, which is a refreshing touch, since so many movie teenagers seem never to be afflicted with that universal problem.

During this year, a guy will break up with his girl by cell phone. A topless photo of a girl will be circulated by Internet and cell phone to everyone in school, and, seemingly, in the world. Megan will make a cruel phone call to the girl. Romances will bloom and crash. Crucial basketball games will be played. And the focus will increasingly be on what comes next: college or work? Warsaw or the world?

Warsaw Community High School, with its sleek modern architecture, seems like a fine school, but we don't see a lot of it. Most of the scenes take place in homes, rec rooms, basements, fast-food restaurants, basketball games, and school dances (curiously, hardly anyone in the film smokes, although one girl says she does). We begin to grow familiar with the principals and their circles, and start to care about them; there's a certain emotion on graduation day.

American Teen isn't as penetrating or obviously realistic as her *On the Ropes,* but Nanette Burstein (who won the best directing award at Sundance 2008) has achieved an engrossing film. No matter what may have been guided by her outside hand, it is all in some way real, and often touching.

American Violet ★ ★ ★
PG-13, 103 m., 2009

Nicole Beharie (Dee Roberts), Tim Blake Nelson (David Cohen), Will Patton (Sam Conroy), Michael O'Keefe (Calvin Beckett), Xzibit (Darrell Hughes), Charles S. Dutton (Reverend Sanders), Alfre Woodard (Alma Roberts). Directed by Tim Disney and produced by Bill Haney. Screenplay by Haney.

You may recall the story from the news in 2000. The cops in a small Texas town arrested forty black people on drug charges in a sweep of a public housing project. They were working on a tip from a single informant, a former mental patient who had good reason to cooperate with them. Dee, a young mother of four, who was not found with drugs and had no history of drug use, was arrested primarily because she went outside to drag her little girl to safety. She, along with the others, is offered a plea bargain: If she pleads guilty, she gets probation. She refuses to plead guilty.

American Violet is clear about the motivation for such raids with little or no evidence. A guilty plea helps the district attorney build up a record as a crime fighter, even though he is the one who has committed the crime. A defendant who pleads guilty cannot continue to live in public housing and will always have a felony on her record. But if Dee caves in, she goes free and is reunited with her children. Her snaky ex-husband has snatched his kids and moved them in with his new girlfriend, who has a history of child abuse.

This is all based on an actual case (the names have been changed). This stuff happens all the time and is far from rare in Texas, a state with a shameful record of law enforcement practices. The movie occasionally intercuts commercials from the Gore-Bush campaign then under way, to no particular purpose except to remind me that as Texas governor, Bush commuted the sentence of only one of the 131 people put to death under his reign, even though public defenders presented no defense at all for 41 of them and a

third of their defense attorneys were later disbarred or sanctioned.

American Violet stars Nicole Beharie, a recent Juilliard graduate in her second role, as Dee Roberts. It is a stunning performance: She is small, vulnerable, fearful for her children, but damned if she will plead guilty to a crime she did not commit. She stands firm even as her mother, Alma (Alfre Woodard), begs her to take the plea; Alma argues the harsh racial realities of their small town. When Dee vows to stay in jail, she attracts the attention of the ACLU, which sends a lawyer named David Cohen (Tim Blake Nelson) down to defend her. Because he needs a local partner, he persuades the lawyer Sam Conroy (Will Patton), himself a former DA, to join him; Sam refuses at first but agrees out of guilt because he knows full well how the system works.

The DA is Calvin Beckett (Michael O'Keefe), a man of whom it can fairly be said that he has no interest at all in whether the people he has arrested are guilty. How would it look in an election year if he went around dropping drug charges? And now the stage is set for a docudrama that may have an outcome we already know but is a loud lesson about truth, justice, and the Texas Way. I know I'll hear complaints from Texans of a certain stripe. They won't see this film. They know all they want about the ACLU from their favorite broadcasters.

Some critics have found *American Violet* to be too mainstream, too agenda-driven, too much like made-for-TV, not enough "suspense." Say what? Dee is innocent, her lawyers are putting themselves at risk because of their outrage, and the DA is a heartless scofflaw. If the movie tries to have fun concealing that, it's jerking our chain.

What worked for me was the strength of the performances, beginning with Nicole Beharie as the convincing heroine. Alfre Woodard in attack mode is formidable; Tim Blake Nelson underplays as a determined, methodical lawyer, not a showboat, and Will Patton in some ways steals the show as a good man who has done bad in the past, knows it, and is trying to make up. As Beckett, Michael O'Keefe is rock-solid as a man who has more important things on his mind than justice.

American Violet, it's true, is not blazingly original cinema. Tim Disney's direction and the screenplay by Bill Haney are meat and potatoes, making this story clear, direct, and righteous. But consider the story. How would you feel if this happened to you? What if cases like this were to lead to disregard of due process of law at even the highest levels? I wish I could convince . . . hell, never mind. I can't. That district attorney? Still in office.

America the Beautiful ★ ★ ★
R, 106 m., 2008

A documentary written, directed, and narrated by Darryl Roberts and produced by Michele G. Bluthenthal, Roderick Gatlin, and Stela Georgieva.

The documentary *America the Beautiful* is not shrill or alarmist, nor does it strain to shock us. Darryl Roberts, its director and narrator, speaks mostly in a pleasant, low-key voice. But the film is pulsing with barely suppressed rage, and by the end I shared it. It's about a culture "saturated with the perfect," in which women are taught to seek an impossible physical ideal, and men to worship it.

It opens with shots of a pretty girl named Gerren Taylor, who looks terrific in the skimpiest of bikinis and draws admiration at a topless pool party, although she keeps her top on. Gerren is twelve. Her life as a fashion model began when a woman handed her a card for a modeling agency. She is tall, has a good figure and a model's "walk," and an ambitious mother named Michelle.

Roberts will follow her career in a film that's also a general look at the media-driven worship of women whom the average woman may never resemble (or, if they have any sense, feel the need to). To establish the world Gerren enters, he calmly assembles facts and observations: (1) "Three minutes of looking at a fashion magazine makes 90 percent of women of all ages feel depressed, guilty, and shameful"; (2) three years after the introduction of television to the Fiji Islands, the culture's rate of teenage bulimia went from zero to 11 percent; (3) a model who is six feet tall and weighs 130 pounds is told she must lose fifteen pounds; (4) the "average woman" in those crypto-feminist Dove soap ads became "average" only after complex makeup and photo retouching.

Roberts watches as Gerren becomes, for a season, a sensational success. Her appeal is based largely on her age. Celebrity magazines are fascinated by a twelve-year-old who models adult fashions, and she conquers Fashion Week in New York. But a year later her novelty has worn off, she is rejected by the same casting directors who selected her earlier, and after learning her hips are "too wide" for Milan, she and her mother seek success in London and Paris. After becoming a cover girl and overnight success, Gerren and her mom, who seem to live prudently, are essentially broke. Yes, she gets paid in London: She gets to keep the clothes she wears.

Their quest leads to an unsettled personal life for the young girl. During an argument with her mother over wearing a padded bra to school, Gerren sobs that her mom is ruining her high school years, but those years are impacted in ways she doesn't yet understand. Her sensible Los Angeles middle school principal finds she has become a classroom problem and asks her to sign a "behavior contract." Insulted, Michelle moves her daughter to a more "understanding" school in Santa Monica, and finally opts for home schooling.

Talking to models about the profession that drives them to starvation, Roberts is tentative and quiet as he asks things like, "Do you ever think this might have an impact on your . . . health?" The one time his voice lifts in anger is after a photographer fights with an African-American woman who refuses to wear makeup that will lighten her skin by four or five shades. Roberts, black himself, listens incredulously as the photographer berates the model for being ignorant, "unable to listen," and "knowing nothing" about beauty, fashion, and society. The "problem" of the model's dark skin tone is simply one manifestation of the "problems" all women are told they have if they don't match the fashion ideal. Roberts knows women like the model, and the photographer doesn't, but as the man with the camera, the photographer ordains himself with authority.

Roberts has a powerful message here, but he includes too much material not really necessary for his story. We could have done without his own experiences on a Web site named beautifulpeople.net, where applicants are rated on a sliding scale to discover if they're beautiful enough to qualify. We don't need still more standard footage of Paris Hilton, Britney Spears, and other plastic creatures. Even more unnecessary is an interview with celebrity-gossip journalist Ted Casablanca, whose four-letter language earns an R rating for a film that might rescue the lives of some girls age twelve and up.

But *America the Beautiful* carries a persuasive message and is all the more effective because of the level tone Roberts adopts. The cold fact is that no one can look like a supermodel and be physically healthy. And in a film filled with astonishments, one of the most stunning is that designers like their models the skinnier the better because—are you ready for this?—they save money on the expensive fabrics they use.

Angels and Demons ★ ★ ★
PG-13, 138 m., 2009

Tom Hanks (Professor Robert Langdon), Ewan McGregor (Camerlengo Patrick McKenna), Ayelet Zurer (Dr. Vittoria Vetra), Stellan Skarsgård (Commander Richter), Pierfrancesco Favino (Ernesto Olivetti), Nikolaj Lie Kaas (Assassin), Armin Mueller-Stahl (Cardinal Strauss). Directed by Ron Howard and produced by Howard, Brian Grazer, and John Calley. Screenplay by David Koepp and Akiva Goldsman, based on the novel by Dan Brown.

Since *Angels and Demons* depends on a split-second schedule and a ticking time bomb that could destroy the Vatican, it's a little distracting when the Camerlengo, a priest entrusted with the pope's duties between papacies, breaks into the locked enclave of the College of Cardinals and lectures them on centuries of church history.

These men, many of them elderly, may face death in minutes, which the Camerlengo knows. The commander of the Swiss Guard *thinks* he can evacuate the Vatican and the hundreds of thousands of faithful waiting in St. Peter's Square in fifteen minutes before an explosion vaporizes "a big chunk of Rome," but frankly, we in the audience think a lot of monsignors back home are going to receive promotions real soon.

Since very few plot details in the film are remotely plausible, including its desperate chase

across Rome, the history lesson is excusable. Having been told about the long war between the church and the Illuminati, and religion and science, we are grateful for the briefing, even if the cardinals already know most of the history. This kind of film requires us to be very forgiving, and if we are, it promises to entertain. *Angels and Demons* succeeds.

It's based on a novel that came before *The Da Vinci Code* in Dan Brown's oeuvre, but is set afterward. Professor Robert Langdon (Tom Hanks) is back at Harvard when he is summoned from a swimming pool by an emissary from the Vatican and flown to Rome to face a crisis. Earlier, we learned, a rare sealed vial of antimatter was stolen from the CERN Large Hadron Collider in Geneva, and a note taking credit comes from the Illuminati, a secret society that has long hated the church because of the days when it persecuted Galileo and other scientists.

A "popular and progressive" pope has just died. The cardinals have been summoned to elect his successor. Four of them, the *preferati*, the favorites to be the next pope, have been kidnapped. One will be executed at 8, 9, 10, and 11 p.m., until the battery on the antimatter vial runs out of juice at midnight, and the faithful will see more than a puff of white smoke above the Vatican. I don't recall if the Illuminati had any demands. Maybe it just wants revenge.

In that case, why hide the vial at the end of a trail that can be followed only by clues discovered or intuited by professor Langdon? Why not just blow up the place? What is the purpose of the scavenger hunt? Has it all been laboriously constructed as a test of professor Langdon's awesome knowledge? Are the Illuminati trying to get even after Langdon foiled Opus Dei, another secret society, in *The Da Vinci Code*?

I don't know, and, reader, there is no time to care. Langdon uses his knowledge of Illuminati symbols to follow the trail though four Rome churches. He has uncanny luck. He spots and correctly identifies every clue, even though they're very well hidden. Just as well because one dungeon overlooked or one statue pointing the wrong way, and he loses. For his companion he has the beautiful and brilliant Vittoria Vetra (Ayelet Zurer) from

CERN. Her father was murdered in the anti-matter theft. Her purpose is (a) to explain that the battery will indeed run down, (b) request her father's secret journals from Geneva, although they are never read, and (c) run along everywhere with Tom Hanks to provide him with urgent conversation.

Meanwhile, there is intrigue within the Vatican and lots of red herrings among all the red hats. The young Camerlengo (Ewan McGregor) joins the professor's desperate quest, as does the commander of the pope's protectors, the Swiss Guard (Stellan Skarsgard). Inside the conclave, Cardinal Strauss (Armin Mueller-Stahl) is in charge of the election. Because of his sinister mien (I love the phrase "sinister mien"), German accent, and absolutist views on church tradition, he seems set up to be a suspect, since the progressive pope's death may have been an inside job. (I forgot to mention that there has also been time to exhume the pontiff's remains and discover evidence of poisoning.)

All of this happens at breakneck speed, with little subtlety but with fabulous production values. The interiors of the Sistine Chapel, the Pantheon, churches, tombs, and crypts are rendered dramatically; the College of Cardinals looks both (a) very impressive and (b) like a collection of elderly extras from Cinecittà.

The film by no means tilts the conflict between science and religion one way or the other. The professor is not religious, indeed seems agnostic, but the church, on the other hand, is not portrayed as antiscience. Galileo would be happy that there is now a Vatican Observatory. If the Illuminati are indeed scientists, they would better employ themselves not avenging ancient deeds, but attacking modern fundamentalist cults.

The professor has a fascinating exchange with the Camerlengo, who asks him if he believes in God. He believes, he says, that the existence of God is beyond his mind to determine. "And your heart?" asks the priest. "My heart is not worthy." Agnostics and believers can both find something to agree with there; director Ron Howard does an even-handed job of balancing the scales.

So good, indeed, that even after Howard accused the church of refusing him access to Vatican locations, and although the depend-able William Donohue of the Catholic League has attacked his film, *Angels and Demons* received a favorable review from the official Vatican newspaper *L'Osservatore Romano*, which wrote it is a "harmless entertainment which hardly affects the genius and mystery of Christianity."

And come on, Ron: Would you *expect* the church to let you shoot a Dan Brown thriller in the Sistine Chapel? Get real.

Anita O'Day: The Life of a Jazz Singer ★ ★
NO MPAA RATING, 92 m., 2008

A documentary directed by Robbie Cavolina and Ian McCrudden and produced by Cavolina, McCrudden, and Melissa Davis.

Anita O'Day. In the 1940s and '50s, her name was routinely linked with Ella Fitzgerald, Billie Holiday, and Sarah Vaughan. If she is not as famous today, it isn't for a lack of talent. Perhaps it's that she spent most of her time singing and too much of it using heroin, and could not be bothered to focus on fame. She was good. I came home from this film and started downloading tracks into my iPod.

The film record of her career isn't as extensive as many other singers. She just didn't care about publicity. If you've seen her on a screen, it was probably in *Jazz on a Summer's Day,* the legendary doc about the 1958 Newport Jazz Festival. Standing in the sun that day, wearing a big floppy hat, a cocktail dress, and glass slippers—yes, glass slippers—she sang "Sweet Georgia Brown" as few songs have ever been sung; it is considered one of the best performances in jazz history.

She didn't even have all the tools for jazz singing. In a bold, cheeky interview she taped for *Anita O'Day: The Life of a Jazz Singer* not long before her death in 2006 at eighty-seven, she reveals that a bungled tonsillectomy left her minus her uvula, and prevented her from sustaining the vibrato necessary for proper jazz phrasing. Listening to her, I'd say she found a workaround.

Her life, she observes without regret or apology, was a "jazz life." That means she left home young, was hired by Gene Krupa the moment he heard her, toured with Krupa,

Woody Herman, and Stan Kenton, was addicted to heroin for fifteen years, did four months for marijuana possession, drank too much, was never without work, was usually broke, had four marriages and several abortions, had her longest relationship with a drummer and fellow addict she never married, recorded many albums with the premiere jazz label Verve, was on the charts, was a big hit touring Japan and Sweden, and—sorry, my vibrato just broke.

As remarkable as her life was, surviving it was her most astonishing accomplishment. It wasn't as tragic as Billie Holiday's, but that wasn't for lack of trying. After an overdose, she was once declared dead in an emergency room. You may think you're not eager to watch a woman in her mid-eighties remembering old times, but that would be before you heard her singing "The Nearness of You." This is one great dame. In her heyday, she had a fresh, perky Doris Dayish face, just the right slight overbite, and she looked smart when she was singing; she didn't smile a whole lot.

She was a serious musician. Listen to her discussing eighth notes and why they work for her. Her alto voice could sound like an instrument, and she fit right in with a sax. She didn't sing over a band; her voice was one of its soloists. In duets, she was a collaborator. Oscar Peterson could play the piano about as fast as it could be played, and she once raced him to the end of a song, never dropped a syllable unless she intended to, and finished first. The film includes footage of her first hit with Krupa. It was a 1941 duet with Roy Eldridge and his trumpet. The pairing of a white singer and a black musician was dangerous in those days. Krupa kept the song in when he toured the South. O'Day doesn't seem particularly impressed by any chances they were taking. *Anita O'Day: The Life of a Jazz Singer* chooses from all the existing materials and is invaluable. It is also flawed. Too many performances are interrupted. The talking heads are infringed upon by graphics that hide a third of the screen. Hardly matters. Here was a great artist. She enjoyed her life. She didn't complain at the time, she didn't complain when she went cold turkey, she didn't complain in her eighties. We see an interview where Bryant Gumbel presses her about her disorderly life,

which was no secret. She doesn't bite. As if it's the most obvious thing in the world, she tells him, "That's the way it went down, Bryant."

Anvil! The Story of Anvil ★ ★ ★
NO MPAA RATING, 90 m., 2009

Featuring Steve "Lips" Kudlow, Robb Reiner, G5, Ivan Hurd, Tom Araya, Chris Tsangarides, Tiziana Arrigoni, Cut Loose, Mad Dog, Lars Ulrich, Lemmy, Scott Ian, Slash. A documentary directed by Sacha Gervasi and produced by Rebecca Yeldham.

This is the sound of optimism: "Everything on the tour went drastically wrong. But at least there was a tour for it to go wrong on." The optimist is Steve "Lips" Kudlow, lead guitarist in Anvil, a band you've never heard of. In 1973, he made a friend named Robb Reiner in Toronto, who had a drum set, and they vowed to make rock 'n' roll until they were old. Now they are old, at least for heavy metal rockers.

Anvil! The Story of Anvil is a documentary about the moderate rise and long, long fall of their band, where musicians in the two other slots came and went, but Lips and Robb rocked on. "How many bands stay together for thirty years?" asks Slash of Guns N' Roses, in a backstage interview. "You've got the Stones, the Who, U2—and Anvil." Yeah. And Anvil.

Anvil had one modestly successful album (*Metal on Metal*), is credited as an influence by lots of heavy metal bands, had bad management and lousy record labels, and was Canadian at a time (as now) when that didn't feel synonymous with heavy metal. "I was raised to be polite," says Reiner, after he fails at a job in telephone hard selling.

Reiner is also seen working on a demolition project. Kudlow drives a delivery truck carrying school meals, and explains the menu. One day maybe lamb stew and meat loaf. Then meat loaf and pizza. Then pizza and lamb stew. He burns with the original fire: The band will, will, will win the success it deserves.

There are still loyal fans. One, Tiziana Arrigoni of Sweden, books a European tour for them. This was the tour that went drastically wrong. They missed trains. Couldn't find the club in Prague. Weren't paid. Were invited to the Monsters of Transylvania, a heavy metal concert.

Lips shares the news that the venue seats 10,000: "I hear the mayor of Transylvania is going to be there!" The audience numbers 178.

The documentary, directed by Anvil fan (and *The Terminal* screenwriter) Sacha Gervasi, spends time in Toronto with Lips's and Robb's spouses, siblings, children. The wives are loyal but not optimistic. The rockers are good family men. They were apparently spared the heavy metal plague of heavy drugs, although there is a little weed in one shot.

Down and down they fall. They get the veteran producer Chris Tsangarides to cut their thirteenth album ("our best work"—Lips), but have to release it themselves. One CD finds its way to Japan, and they are invited to a Tokyo concert with a venue seating (an ominous omen) 10,000. They play at the un-heavy-metal hour of 9:45 a.m. How many people turn up?

I don't know if their music is any good. Their fans think so. The doc doesn't show one song all the way through. But they swore a pledge when they were fourteen, and they're still honoring it, and at fifty-one Lips knows he still has it and that Anvil will be back on the charts. Maybe there is hope for Susan Boyle.

Appaloosa ★ ★ ★
R, 115 m., 2008

Ed Harris (Virgil Cole), Viggo Mortensen (Everett Hitch), Renee Zellweger (Allison French), Jeremy Irons (Randall Bragg), Timothy Spall (Phil Olson), Lance Henriksen (Ring Shelton). Directed by Ed Harris and produced by Harris, Robert Knott, and Ginger Sledge. Screenplay by Knott and Harris, based on the novel by Robert B. Parker.

Appaloosa started out making me feel the same as I did during the opening chapters of Larry McMurtry's *Lonesome Dove* and its TV miniseries. At its center is a friendship of many years between two men who have seen a lot together and wish they had seen less. This has been called a Buddy Movie. Not at all. A buddy is someone you acquire largely through juxtaposition. A friend is someone you make over the years. Some friends know you better than you know yourself.

That would be true of Everett Hitch (Viggo Mortensen), who for years has been teamed up with Virgil Cole (Ed Harris). They make a living cleaning bad guys out of Western towns. Virgil wears a sheriff's badge, and Everett is his deputy, but essentially they're hired killers. They perform this job with understated confidence, hair-trigger instincts, a quick draw, and deadeye aim. They're hired by the town of Appaloosa to end its reign of terror under the evil rancher Randall Bragg (Jeremy Irons).

So already you've got an A-list cast. Harris plays a man of few words, many of them pronounced incorrectly, and steel resolve. Mortensen is smarter than his boss, more observant, and knows to tactfully hold his tongue when he sees the sheriff making mistakes, as long as they're not fatal. Irons plays the rancher as one of those narrow-eyed snakes who is bad because, gosh darn it, he's good at it. Then a lady comes into town on the stage.

This is Allison French (Renee Zellweger), a widow, she says. No, she hasn't come to Appaloosa to find work as a schoolmarm or a big-hearted whore (the two standard female occupations in Westerns). She plays the piano and the organ and dresses like a big-city lady in fancy frocks and cute bonnets. She inquires at the sheriff's office about where she might find respectable lodgings. Her budget is limited. She has one dollar.

Zellweger is powerfully fetching in this role. She wins the sheriff's heart in a split second, and he "explains" to the hotel clerk that Miss French will be staying there and will play the piano. Virgil Cole has practiced for a lifetime at avoiding the snares of females, but he's a goner. Everett looks at him quizzically. But you don't keep a friend if you criticize his women—too quickly, anyway. Is there anything about Allison to criticize? The movie has a ways to go.

Virgil and Everett reminded me immediately of Gus McCrae and Woodrow Call in *Lonesome Dove*, not only in their long-practiced camaraderie, but also in their conversations about women. So smitten is Virgil that he abandons his tumbleweed ways and starts building a house for the widow. Meanwhile, Bragg sends three boys into town, who get themselves killed. A showdown approaches, viewed warily by the town leaders. Phil Olson (Timothy Spall) is their spokesman, and who better than Spall? He is the master of telegraphing subdued misgivings.

No more of the plot. What is seductive about

Appaloosa is its easygoing rhythm. Yes, we know there will be a shoot-out; it can't be avoided. But there is also time for chicken dinners and hot pies and debates about the new curtains, and for Miss French to twinkle and charm and display canny survival instincts. What makes the movie absorbing is the way it harmonizes all the character strands and traits and weaves them into something more engaging than a mere 1-2-3 plot. I felt like I did in *Lonesome Dove*—that there was a chair for me on the porch.

The film has been directed by Ed Harris and bears absolutely no similarity, as you might have anticipated, to his *Pollock* (2000), the story of an alcoholic abstract expressionist. Harris as a director allows the actors screen time to live. They're not always scurrying around to fulfill the requirements of the plot. They are people before the plot happens to them—and afterward, too, those who survive. He has something to say here about hard men of the Old West and their naive, shy idolatry of "good" women.

Harris comes ready for the gunplay. He just doesn't think it's the whole point. The shootin' scenes are handled with economy. Everett observes that one shoot-out is over lickety-split, and Virgil tells him: "That's because we're good shots." At the end of the day, everything works out as I suppose it had to, and we're not all tied in emotional knots or existential dread. I know I want me another slice of that hot pie.

Arctic Tale ★ ★
G, 84 m., 2007

Queen Latifah (Narrator). A documentary directed by Sarah Robertson and Adam Ravetch and produced by Adam Leipzig and Keenan Smart. Narration written by Linda Woolverton, Mose Richards, and Kristin Gore.

Arctic Tale journeys to one of the most difficult places on Earth for animals to make a living, and shows it growing even more unfriendly. The documentary studies polar bears and walruses in the Arctic as global warming raises temperatures and changes the way they have done business since time immemorial.

Much of the footage in the film is astonishing, considering that it was obtained at frigid temperatures, sometimes underwater, and usually within attacking distance of large and dangerous mammals. We follow two emblematic characters, Nanu, a polar bear cub, and Seela, a newborn walrus. The infants venture out into their new world of blinding white and merciless cold, and learn to swim or climb onto solid footing, as the case may be. They also get lessons from their parents on stalking prey, defending themselves against predators, and presumably keeping one eye open while asleep.

The animals are composites of several different individuals, created in the editing room from footage shot over a period of ten years, but the editing is so seamless that the illusion holds up. The purpose of the film, made by a team headed by the married couple of director Sarah Robertson and cinematographer Adam Ravetch, is not to enforce scholarly accuracy but to create a fable of birth, life, and death at the edge of the world.

It is said that the landmark documentary *March of the Penguins* began life in France with a cute sound track on which the penguins voiced their thoughts. The magnificence of that film is explained in large part by Morgan Freeman's objective narration, which was content to describe a year in the lives of the penguins; the facts were so astonishing that no embroidery was necessary.

Arctic Tale, on the other hand, chooses the opposite approach. Queen Latifah narrates a story in which the large and fearsome beasts are personalized almost like cartoon characters. And the sound track reinforces that impression with song: As dozens of walruses huddle together on an ice floe, for example, we hear *We Are Family* and mighty blasts of walrus farts.

They might also have been singing "we are appearing in a family film." The movie might be enthralling to younger viewers, and the images have undeniable power for everyone. The dilemma the movie sidesteps is that being a polar bear or a walrus is a violent undertaking. In a land without vegetation, evolution has provided that animals survive by eating each other. (Not that there aren't carnivores, including man, in temperate climates.) In one bloodcurdling scene, Nanu's mother cautiously shepherds her cubs away from a male polar bear that would, yes, like to eat them. And the walrus with her baby is automatically issued (it seems) another female walrus, an "auntie," who volunteers to help protect the little family. This is all the more unselfish considering what happens to the auntie.

The film does not linger on scenes of killing or eating, preferring to make it clear that such events, and other tragedies, are happening not far offscreen. The eyes of little audience members are spared the gory details. But the comfy view of Arctic life, opening with two little bear cubs romping in the snow and snuggling under Mom for a snack, quickly descends into a struggle for survival.

It's hard enough for them to live in such an icy world but harder still when the ice melts. When ice grows scarce, so will polar bears and walruses, because although both species are accomplished swimmers, they are mammals and have to breathe and need to crawl up on ice floes. Queen Latifah's narration, coauthored by Al Gore's daughter, makes it clear that global warming is to blame. We see Nanu walking gingerly across ice that is alarmingly slushy, and we can only speculate about how that makes her feel.

The movie gives some attention to other northern life forms, including jellyfish, birds, and foxes who trail behind polar bears to eat the remains of their kills. We see no humans, not even the Inuit who assisted the filmmakers. I was reminded of the extraordinary 2002 film *The Fast Runner,* about the lives and loves of the Inuit, and of course of the classic Flaherty documentary *Nanook of the North* (1922). To live in this place is to constantly tempt death.

In the end, I'm conflicted about the film. As an accessible family film, it delivers the goods. But it lives in the shadow of *March of the Penguins.* Despite its sad scenes, it sentimentalizes. It attributes human emotions and motivations to its central animals. Its music instructs us how to feel. And the narration and overall approach get in the way of the visual material.

Ashes of Time Redux ★ ★
R, 93 m., 2008

Brigitte Lin (Murong Yin/Murong Yang), Leslie Cheung (Ouyang Feng), Maggie Cheung (Brother's Wife), Tony Leung Chiu Wai (Blind Swordsman), Jacky Cheung (Hung Qi), Tony Leung Ka Fai (Huang Yaoshi), Li Bai (Hung Qi's Wife), Carina Lau (Peach Blossom), Charlie Yeung (Young Girl). Directed by Wong Kar Wai and produced by Wong, Jeffrey Lau, and Jacky Pang Yee Wah. Screenplay by Wong, based on the novel by Louis Cha.

redux (adj.): Brought back; revived.

If Wong Kar Wai were a painter, he might sometimes create bold, bright swirls on his canvas, with something figurative swimming into view. That's my impression of *Ashes of Time Redux,* first released in 1994, now reduxed. I didn't see the first version, which the director considered unfinished, requiring fourteen years of additional thought. So far has Kar Wai's, or Wong's, art grown and deepened in the meantime (especially in the great *In the Mood for Love*) that I am not quite sure why he set himself the task. Apparently he could not forget it, although many of his admirers have.

I watched attentively. I was dazzled by the beauty of the palette and the fluidity of the camera, and it was good to see familiar Hong Kong stars like Brigitte Lin, Leslie Cheung, Maggie Cheung, Tony Leung Chiu Wai, and Tony Leung Ka Fai in younger days. I have had Chinese names explained to me a dozen times, about how the family name goes first and the first name goes last. It's just that I never know how to deal with names that are half-Chinese and half-Western. Surely it's not Lin Brigitte?

IMDb is no help because they use their arcane knowledge of every name on Earth, so if you follow them, your editor is always complaining, That's not how the *New York Times* has it. I decided to eliminate the middleman and go straight to the *Times* review, which alas does not include a cast listing and refers unhelpfully to "both Tony Leungs," although this time it is made easy because Tony Leung Chiu Wai plays the Blind Swordsman and Tony Leung Ka Fai does not.

While I was there I decided to find out how Manohla Dargis handled the plot, which is somewhat confusing. I respect her work. She attends to these things. Here is her plot description: "See, there's this swordsman . . ."

That's it. That's all of it. Oh, wait, she adds that "Mr. Cheung, as a desert dweller called Ouyang, is a broker for itinerant swordsmen and their prospective clients." She doesn't say which Mr. Cheung. Probably not the blind swordsman.

I'm sure wisenheimers on the blogs will write, "Did she really see it?" I'm dead certain she did. I know I've seen it, and that's about as far as I could get. If you attempt to finish her sentence, you will find yourself either (a) lost in a thicket of interlocking flashbacking confusion, or (b) forced to fall back on the old "evocation" strategy, in which you are elusive and poetic ("It is a humble little tavern in Chinese medieval times, but through its doors . . .").

Sometimes a director is too familiar with the material. He has internalized it until it all makes sense to him. I remember when we were collaborating on *Beneath the Valley of the Ultra-Vixens*, and Russ Meyer would start lecturing about what Junkyard Sal could or couldn't do until you'd swear she was a Greek goddess. "Junkyard Sal wouldn't do that!" Russ would thunder. Once I said, "Of course she would. I've got the typewriter." At least in Russ Meyer's cinema, characters could or couldn't do things. That's why he was an artist and never had to make porn movies, in which the characters can do only one thing, or you want your money back.

But I stray. I enjoyed *Ashes of Time Redux*, up to a point. It's great looking, and the characters all know what they would do, although we do not. Wong Kar Wai doesn't supply much of a plot with a narrative engine to pull us through. He adds section headings like Spring, Summer, Autumn, Winter (a direct quote from e.e. cummings), but that only helps you to think, "Oh, now I see! I don't understand it, but it's happening in winter!"

It's perfectly OK in a case like this to relax and enjoy the experience. It is a beautiful film and never boring, not with its swordfights and romantic angst. This is a lush and well-choreographed example of the wuxia genre, which I have just now found out about, although it reaches back centuries and involves stories about swordplay and the martial arts. "Wuxia" means a lot less typing than "swordplay and the martial arts," so I want you to remember it.

The Assassination of Jesse James by the Coward Robert Ford ★ ★ ★ ½
R, 160 m., 2007

Brad Pitt (Jesse James), Casey Affleck (Robert Ford), Sam Shepard (Frank James), Mary-Louise Parker (Zee James), Paul Schneider (Dick Liddil), Jeremy Renner (Wood Hite), Garret Dillahunt (Ed Miller), Zooey Deschanel (Dorothy Evans), Michael Parks (Henry Craig), Ted Levine (Sheriff Timberlake), Sam Rockwell (Charley Ford). Directed by Andrew Dominik and produced by Jules Daly, Dede Gardner, Brad Pitt, Ridley Scott, and David Valdes. Screenplay by Dominik, based on the novel by Ron Hansen.

Few things have earned me more grief from readers than my suggestion that in the sport of sex, Captain Renault of *Casablanca* plays for both teams. I think I will get less disagreement when I focus on the homosexual undertones of *The Assassination of Jesse James by the Coward Robert Ford*. Jesse (Brad Pitt) is certainly not gay, but the Coward (Casey Affleck) is so powerfully mesmerized by him that hero worship shades into lust. Since sex between them is out of the question, their relationship turns into a curiously erotic dance of death; it is clear to both of them (and to anyone reading the title) what must happen at the end, and they move together toward that event with almost trancelike inevitability.

The movie has the space and freedom of classic Western epics. Like *McCabe and Mrs. Miller* and *Days of Heaven*, it was photographed in the wide open spaces of western Canada, where the land is so empty it creates a vacuum, demanding men to become legends. Jesse James is such a man, a ruthless killer and attentive father and husband, glorified in the dime novels that Robert Ford memorizes. If Ford is a coward, what does that make James, who led his efficient gang in stagecoach and bank robberies that involved the deaths of unarmed men and women? Yes, but he did it with style, you see, and Ford is only a callow squirt.

The story begins in 1881, after Jesse's legend is already part of the mythology and the James Gang has only one robbery left to go. The gang members are Jesse's older brother Frank (Sam Shepard), the Coward's older brother Charley

17

Ford (Sam Rockwell), Jesse's cousin, Wood Hite (Jeremy Renner), and the outlaw Dick Liddil (Paul Schneider). Robert Ford, at nineteen, comes after them begging to be let in; his devotion is so intense that Jesse asks him at one point, "Do you want to be like me, or do you want to *be* me?"

The Coward is like a starstruck stalker, something all the gang members recognize. Why does Jesse tolerate him? Is there a buried message that James, having become a founding member of America's celebrity royalty, realizes that Robert is the price he has to pay? After their last train job, Frank has had enough and heads out. Jesse goes home to his wife (Mary-Louise Parker) and children, and unaccountably invites Robert to visit them. There are the usual lyrical passages of Jesse playing with his kids and loving his wife, and yet all the time he and the Coward have something deadly going on between them. If Robert cannot be the lover of his hero, what would be more intimate than to kill him?

In a quiet parlor one day in Jesse's home, Robert knows, and Jesse knows, and we know, that the time has come. Ford doesn't so much shoot him in the back as have the back presented to him for the purpose. If he did not pull the trigger at that moment, I think they would both feel an appointment had been missed. Does Jesse want to die? I think he is fascinated by the idea and flies too close to the flame.

The film was written and directed by Andrew Dominik, based on the novel by Ron Hansen. It is Dominik's second and has a great deal in common with his good first film, *Chopper* (2001). That was the story of Australia's most notorious prisoner, who at one point is stabbed by his best friend, ignores it, talks for a time, and then looks down at the blood pouring from him, as if disappointed in the other man. Both Chopper Read and Jesse James were savage murderers and both masochistically put themselves in harm's way.

Dominik filmed *Chopper* largely in prison, but here opens up his camera to the far horizons, showing how small a man might feel unless he did something to make his mark. The cinematography is by Roger Deakins, who in *No Country for Old Men* by the Coen brothers shows the modern West as also in need of hard, unforgiving men to stand up to the landscape. Brad Pitt embodies Jesse James's mythic stature as if long accustomed to it; Casey Affleck plays the kid like Mark David Chapman, a nobody killing the one he loves. The gang members are like sidemen for Elvis, standing by in subservience, keeping the beat, all except for Frank, whom Sam Shepard plays as the insider who understands it all.

There are things about men, horses, and horizons that are uniquely suited to the wide screen. We see that here. The Western has been mostly in hibernation since the 1970s, but now I sense it stirring in rebirth. We have a program to register the most-read reviews on my Web site, and for the month of September 2007 the overwhelming leader was not *Eastern Promises*, not *Shoot 'Em Up*, not *The Brave One*, but *3:10 to Yuma*. Now here is another Western in the classical tradition.

Yes, it is long, at 160 minutes. There is a sense that an epic must have duration to have importance. The time reaching ahead of us must be as generous as the landscape unfolding before us. On this canvas Dominik portrays his hero at a time when most men were so powerless, they envied Jesse James even for imposing his will on such as they.

Atonement ★ ★ ★ ★

R, 122 m., 2007

Keira Knightley (Cecilia Tallis), James McAvoy (Robbie Turner), Romola Garai (Briony, age eighteen), Brenda Blethyn (Grace Turner), Vanessa Redgrave (Older Briony), Saoirse Ronan (Briony, age thirteen), Patrick Kennedy (Leon Tallis). Directed by Joe Wright and produced by Tim Bevan, Eric Fellner, and Paul Webster. Screenplay by Christopher Hampton, based on the novel by Ian McEwan.

Atonement begins on joyous gossamer wings and descends into an abyss of tragedy and loss. Its opening scenes in an English country house between the wars are like a dream of elegance, and then a thirteen-year-old girl sees something she misunderstands, tells a lie, and destroys all possibility of happiness in three lives, including her own.

The opening act of the movie is like a breathless celebration of pure, heedless joy, a demonstration of the theory that the pinnacle of human happiness was reached by life in an English country house between the wars. Of course, that was more true of those upstairs than downstairs. We meet Cecilia Tallis (Keira Knightley), bold older daughter of an old family, and Robbie Turner (James McAvoy), their housekeeper's promising son, who is an Oxford graduate thanks to the generosity of Cecilia's father. Despite their difference in social class, they are powerfully attracted to each other, and that leads to a charged erotic episode next to a fountain on the house lawn.

This meeting is seen from an upstairs window by Cecilia's younger sister, Briony (Saoirse Ronan), who thinks she sees Robbie mistreating her sister in his idea of rude sex play. We see the same scene later from Robbie and Cecilia's point of view, and realize it involves their first expression of mutual love. But Briony does not understand, has a crush on Robbie herself, and as she reads an intercepted letter and interrupts a private tryst, her resentment grows until she tells the lie that will send Robbie out of Cecilia's reach.

Oh, but the earlier scenes have floated effortlessly. Cecilia, as played by Knightley with stunning style, speaks rapidly in that upper-class accent that sounds like performance art. When I hear it, I despair that we Americans will ever approach such style with our words that march out like baked potatoes. She is so beautiful, so graceful, so young, and Robbie may be working as a groundsman but is true blue, intelligent, and in love with her. They *deserve* each other.

But that is not to be, as you know if you have read the Ian McEwan best-seller that the movie is inspired so faithfully by. McEwan, one of the best novelists alive, allows the results of Briony's vindictive behavior to grow offstage until we meet the principals again in the early days of the war. Robbie has enlisted and been posted to France. Cecilia is a nurse in London, and so is Briony, now eighteen, trying to atone for what she realizes was a tragic error. There is a meeting of the three, only one, in London, that demonstrates to them what they have all lost.

The film cuts back and forth between the war in France and the bombing of London, and there is a single (apparently) unbroken shot of the beach at Dunkirk that is one of the great takes in film history, achieved or augmented with CGI although it is. (If it looks real, in movie logic it is real.) After an agonizing trek from behind enemy lines, Robbie is among the troops waiting to be evacuated in a Dunkirk much more of a bloody mess than legend would have us believe. In the months before, the lovers have written, promising each other the happiness they have earned.

Each period and scene in the movie is compelling on its own terms, and then compelling on a deeper level as a playing-out of the destiny that was sealed beside the fountain on that perfect summer's day. It is only at the end of the film, when Briony, now an aged novelist played by Vanessa Redgrave, reveals facts about the story, that we realize how thoroughly, how stupidly, she has continued for a lifetime to betray Cecilia, Robbie, and herself.

The structure of the McEwan novel and this film directed by Joe Wright is relentless. How many films have we seen that fascinate in every moment and then, in the last moments, pose a question about all that has gone before, one that forces us to think deeply about what betrayal and atonement might really entail?

Wright, who also directed Knightley in his first film, *Pride and Prejudice,* shows a mastery of nuance and epic, sometimes in adjacent scenes. In the McEwan novel he has a story that can hardly fail him, and an ending that blindsides us with its implications. This is one of the year's best films.

The Audition ★ ★ ★

NO MPAA RATING, 107 m., 2009

Featuring Jamie Barton, Kiera Duffy, Michael Fabiano, Disella Larusdottir, Ryan McKinny, Angela Meade, Nicholas Pallesen, Matthew Olenk, Alek Shrader, Ryan Smith, Amber Wagner, Conductor Marco Armiliato, General Manager Peter Gelb, and Brian Dickie of the Lyric Opera of Chicago, a judge. A documentary directed by Susan Froemke and produced by the Metropolitan Opera.

Attending the Metropolitan Opera's annual National Council Auditions must be one of the great pleasures of operagoing. From forty-five districts of the nation, hopeful young singers compete to advance to fifteen regionals, from which they advance to semifinals in New York, and ten become national finalists. Of these, five become grand winners after public performances with the Met's full orchestra. "I sang on the Met stage with their orchestra!" exults Ryan Smith, one of the singers. "That's enough!"

The Audition is a backstage and onstage documentary observing this process as it unfolded two years ago. A sad element in the film is the fact that Ryan Smith, blessed with a sunny presence and a magnificent tenor voice, died at thirty-one, since the film was made. Chosen for the Lyric's Ryan Opera Center ensemble, he was diagnosed with lymphoma soon after. He speaks briefly about himself; he's older than the other finalists and actually stopped singing for three years, he says, before telling his parents he was going to give it two years of his best effort. That was good enough. It doesn't get any better than winning at this level.

I am far from being a music critic, but I am an opera lover; we've had season tickets at Chicago's Lyric for twenty years, and my love of opera began when I was twenty and drove a rental Vespa to the Baths of Caracalla in Rome, where I was delighted to see elephants and camels under the stars and discover that the Italians sold *glace* during the performance.

It goes without saying that any singer making it to the national auditions is gifted. The film is centered on their performances, as we follow them up the final steps of their ascent. The Met has produced the film, allowed access to backstage, rehearsals, costume fittings, and so on, and (most interesting) allows us to listen in on some of the jury's deliberations; the judges include Brian Dickie of Chicago's own Lyric.

However, and this is a big however, what we eavesdrop on is almost entirely complimentary. A gingerly discussion on the sensitive topic of the weights of singers is only fleetingly followed. Visiting dressing rooms and rehearsals, we see only pleasant, smiling, sometimes nervous faces. I suppose we shouldn't expect fiascos, breakdowns, or temper tantrums—and at this level, maybe there were none. The American opera stars I've met, such as Sam Ramey, are absolutely down-to-earth. I doubt if Maria Callas would have been a delight at the National Council.

I suspect the director, Susan Froemke, may have had some inside information. As the winners are being announced, her camera stays focused on one of them as if she knows what's going to happen. Speaking of that camera, I wonder why she chose a wide lens if she was going to do so much panning; the stretching at the sides of shots becomes distracting.

As a documentary, *The Audition* isn't cutting-edge. As an introduction to a new generation of American opera stars and an opportunity to hear them sing, it is splendid.

August Rush ★ ★ ★
PG, 114 m., 2007

Freddie Highmore (Evan Taylor/August Rush), Keri Russell (Lyla Novacek), Jonathan Rhys Meyers (Louis Connelly), Terrence Howard (Richard Jeffries), Robin Williams (Wizard Wallace), William Sadler (Thomas Novacek), Leon G. Thomas III (Arthur). Directed by Kirsten Sheridan and produced by Richard Barton Lewis. Screenplay by Nick Castle and James V. Hart.

Here is a movie drenched in sentimentality, but it's supposed to be. I dislike sentimentality where it doesn't belong, but there's something brave about the way *August Rush* declares itself and goes all the way with coincidence, melodrama, and skillful tear-jerking. I think more sensitive younger viewers, in particular, might really like it.

The story is a very free modern adaptation of elements from *Oliver Twist*. We meet Evan Taylor (Freddie Highmore), an eleven-year-old who runs away from his orphanage rather than be placed with a foster family. He has been told that his parents are still alive and were musicians, and he believes that through the power of music he can find them again. Do you begin to see what I mean about sentimentality?

As it happens, his parents *were* musicians, and they met through their music. Lyla (Keri Russell) was a cellist, and Louis (Jonathan Rhys Meyers) an Irish rock singer, and in a flashback we see them meeting in Greenwich Village, falling in love at first sight, and making love so very discreetly that they remain safely within the PG rating. They promise to meet again, but Lyla's stage-door father

(William Sadler) forces her to leave town for career reasons and they have no way to contact each other. Young lovers, learn from the movies and always remember: *Exchange cell numbers!* Inevitably, she is pregnant (otherwise they wouldn't be Evan's parents, now would they be?), but her father tells her the baby died and ships Evan to an orphanage. Nothing must interfere with Lyla's career.

Back to the present. The runaway Evan sees some street musicians in Washington Square Park, picks up a guitar and, despite having had no training, turns out to be a naturally gifted musician. Another young musician (Leon G. Thomas III), who is not called the Artful Dodger but should be, hears Evan and takes him back to an abandoned theater, where he and other young lads live under the management of a character who is called the Wizard (Robin Williams), but could be called Fagin. He sends his little army out into the streets every day not as pickpockets but as buskers. Only in a movie like *August Rush* could the endless practical and legal problems suggested by this arrangement be considered plausible.

The Wizard, who dresses like a drugstore cowboy, spots Evan's talent and introduces him to the world as August Rush. August believes, really believes, that music has the power to bring people together, and finds a sympathizer when he comes upon a church choir where the preacher (Mykelti Williamson) turns out to have connections at Juilliard. And so, yes, August is discovered as a child genius, and quickly earns the right to conduct his own symphony at an outdoor concert in Central Park, where he proves himself an expert conductor and (gasp!) his mother is the cellist and his father is nearby, both of them still under the spell of their long-lost love, and . . .

I'm telling you, the ghost of Dickens would be applauding. The movie, directed by Kirsten Sheridan and written by Nick Castle and James V. Hart, pulls out all the stops, invents new ones, and pulls them out too. But it has a light-footed, cheerful way about its contrivances, and Freddie Highmore (*Finding Neverland*) is so open and winning that he makes August seem completely sincere. One touch of craftiness would sink the whole enterprise.

Another quality about the movie is that it seems to sincerely love music as much as August does. If you're going to lay it on this thick, you can't compromise, and Sheridan doesn't. I don't have some imaginary barrier in my mind beyond which a movie dare not go. I'd rather *August Rush* went the whole way than just be lukewarm about it. Yes, some older viewers will groan, but I think up to a certain age, kids will buy it, and in imagining their response I enjoyed my own.

Australia ★ ★ ★
PG-13, 165 m., 2008

Nicole Kidman (Lady Sarah Ashley), Hugh Jackman (Drover), David Wenham (Neil Fletcher), Bryan Brown (King Carney), Jack Thompson (Kipling Flynn), David Gulpilil (King George), Brandon Walters (Nullah). Directed by Baz Luhrmann and produced by Luhrmann, G. Mac Brown, and Catherine Knapman. Screenplay by Luhrmann, Stuart Beattie, Ronald Harwood, and Richard Flanagan.

Baz Luhrmann dreamed of making the Australian *Gone with the Wind*, and so he has, with much of *GWTW*'s lush epic beauty and some of the same awkwardness with a national legacy of racism. This is the sort of film described as a "sweeping romantic melodrama," a broad family entertainment that would never have been made without the burning obsession of its producers (Luhrmann for *Australia*, David O. Selznick for *GWTW*). Coming from a director known for his punk-rock *Shakespeare's Romeo + Juliet* and the visual pyrotechnics of *Moulin Rouge*, it is exuberantly old-fashioned, and I mean that as a compliment.

The movie is set in 1939. Hitler has invaded Poland. The armies of the free world will need beef. In England, Lady Sarah Ashley (Nicole Kidman) is alarmed by reports that her husband is philandering on his enormous cattle station, Faraway Downs, in northern Australia. She comes to see for herself but arrives to find him murdered. Now the owner of an expanse as large as some countries, she dresses as if for tea. The British long followed the practice of dressing in warm climates as if they were not, and Lady Ashley keeps up the standard.

Here is the situation she finds: Drover

(Hugh Jackman), named for his trade, is a rough-hewn free-standing cowboy who has never seen a woman anything like her. He runs cattle drives. She wants him to become manager of the station, but he's a rolling stone. At Faraway Downs, he drives with experienced Aborigine ranch hands, and has under his special protection the Aboriginal boy Nullah (Brandon Walters), who is eleven or twelve. Nullah's grandfather is King George (David Gulpilil, who played a boy about Nullah's age in *Walkabout* from 1971). He has been accused of the murder of Lady Ashley's husband and has fled to a mountaintop, from which he seemingly sees everything. Nullah is a beautiful boy, biracial, bright, and filled with insight, and he provides the narration for the film.

As *Australia* is essentially a Western, there must be an evil rancher with a posse of stooges, and there is: King Carney (Bryan Brown). He wants to add Faraway Downs to his empire. Much will depend on whether Carney or Faraway can be first to deliver cattle to the port city of Darwin. Lady Ashley, prepared to sell out to Carney, sees things that make her reconsider and determines to join Drover, Nullah, and a ragtag band on a cattle drive that will eventually lead into No Man's Land. Meanwhile, the delicate lady and the rugged Drover begin to fall in love, just like Scarlett O'Hara and Rhett Butler.

She grows to love the boy and emotionally adopts him. Nullah is under constant threat of being swept up by the local police, enforcing a national policy of "capturing" part-white Aboriginal children and taking them to missions where they can "have the black bred out of them" and trained to be servants. Incredibly, this practice was ended by Australia only in 1973. And you think we were slow to change.

All the elements are in place for a cross between *GWTW* and *Red River*, with an infusion of *Rabbit-Proof Fence* (2002) and World War II. Luhrmann, known for his close work with the camera, pulls back here to show the magnificent landscape and the enormity of the cattle drive. The cattle are supplied mostly by CGI, which explains how they can seem to stampede toward a high cliff. No doubt some will find this scene hokey, but it also provides the dramatic high point of the movie, with Nullah channeling the teachings of his grandfather.

It's a great scene, but it also dramatizes the film's uncertainty about race. Luhrmann is rightly contemptuous of Australia's "reeducation" policies; he shows Nullah taking pride in his heritage and paints the white enforcers as the demented racists they were. But *Australia* also accepts Aboriginal mystical powers lock, stock, and barrel, and that I think may be condescending.

Well, what do you believe? Can the Aboriginal people materialize wherever they desire? Become invisible? Are they telepaths? Can they receive direct guidance from the dead? Yes, certainly, in a spiritual or symbolic sense. But in a literal sense? The Australians, having for decades treated their native people as subhuman, now politely endow them with god-like qualities. I am not sure that is a compliment. What they suffered, how they survived, how they prevailed, and what they have accomplished they have done as human beings, just as we all must.

The film is filled with problems caused by its acceptance of mystical powers. If Nullah is prescient at some times, then why does he turn into a scared little boy who needs rescuing? The climactic events in the film require action sequences as thrilling as they are formulaic, as is the love story. Scarlett and Rhett were products of the same society. Lady Sarah and Drover meet across a divide that separates not only social class but lifestyle, education, and geography. Such a gap can be crossed, but not during anything so simple as a moonlit night with "Over the Rainbow" being played on a harmonica.

GWTW, for all its faults and racial stereotyping, at least represented a world its makers believed in. *Australia* envisions a world intended largely as fable, and that robs it of some power. Still, what a gorgeous film, what strong performances, what exhilarating images, and—yes, what sweeping romantic melodrama. The kind of movie that is a *movie*, with all the word promises and implies.

Awake ★ ★ ★
R, 78 m., 2007

Hayden Christensen (Clay Beresford), Jessica Alba (Sam Lockwood), Terrence Howard (Dr. Jack Harper), Lena Olin (Lilith Beresford),

Christopher McDonald (Dr. Larry Lupin), Sam Robards (Clay Beresford Sr.), Arliss Howard (Dr. Jonathan Neyer). Directed by Joby Harold and produced by Jason Kliot, John Penotti, and Joana Vicente. Screenplay by Harold.

Do not believe anything you hear about *Awake,* do not talk to anyone about it, and above all do not even *glance* at the poster or ads, which criminally reveal a crucial plot twist. This movie, which was withheld from critics and has scored a pitiful 13 percent on the Tomatometer from those few who were able to see it, is a surprisingly effective thriller. I went to a regular theater to see it Friday afternoon, knowing nothing about it except that the buzz was lethal, and sat there completely absorbed.

The movie involves a very, very rich young man named Clay Beresford (Hayden Christensen), who lives with his loving but dominating mother (Lena Olin) and fears to tell her about his engagement with the beautiful Samantha (Jessica Alba). But "the clock is ticking," he is warned by his friend and surgeon Jack Harper (Terrence Howard). Jack saved Clay in the ER after he had a massive heart attack, and now Clay's on the waiting list for a transplant. "Marry that girl," Jack advises him, and even invites him into the operating room for a trial run to explain how dangerous the surgery is.

This and other medical procedures are highly unlikely, and the heart transplant itself involves an improbably small team, a last-minute replacement as the anesthesiologist, and an uninvited visitor allowed to put on a surgical gown and observe. But accuracy is not the point. Suspense is. And from the moment Clay realizes he is not fully under anesthesia and can hear and feel everything that is happening, the movie had me. The character does a voice-over in which he tries to force his eyes open and signal that he's conscious, and then a series of unexpected developments take place, which I will not even begin to reveal.

Since the movie involves a plot that cannot be discussed, let me just say that I may be the slowest tomato on the meter, but I did not anticipate the surprises, did not anticipate them piling on after one another, got very involved in the gory surgical details, and found the supporting soap opera good, as such things go.

It involves a rich kid who believes he can never live up to his father, a mother who believes she cannot surrender her son, and the beautiful Jessica Alba coming between them. It also involves Clay's determination to have the transplant performed by Dr. Jack, his trusted friend, instead of his mother's candidate (Arliss Howard), who boasts, "I have had my hands inside presidents." He wrote the book on transplants and will be the next surgeon general. "Well, I hope Jack has read your book," Clay replies.

All preposterous, I know, but this edges us into a consideration of why we are at the movies in the first place, and what works and what does not work. I got involved. I felt real suspense. I thought Lena Olin gave a nuanced performance as the mother, who is deeper than we first think, and that the tension between her and Alba was plausible. And I thought the scenes where Clay imagines leaving his body, roaming the hospital, and having psychic conversations were well handled.

So maybe I'm wrong. It has happened before. *Awake,* written and directed by first-timer Joby Harold, clocks at only seventy-eight minutes, but that's the right length for what happens. The movie opened under a cloud on a weekend all other mainstream movies sidestepped, apparently because it was our duty to commence Christmas shopping. But I felt what I felt, and there you have it.

Away We Go ★ ★ ★ ½
R, 97 m., 2009

John Krasinski (Burt), Maya Rudolph (Verona), Jeff Daniels (Jerry), Maggie Gyllenhaal (LN), Allison Janney (Lily), Chris Messina (Tom), Catherine O'Hara (Gloria), Paul Schneider (Courtney), Carmen Ejogo (Grace), Jim Gaffigan (Lowell). Directed by Sam Mendes and produced by Edward Saxon, Marc Turtletaub, and Peter Saraf. Screenplay by Dave Eggers and Vendela Vida.

Burt and Verona are two characters rarely seen in the movies: thirty-something, educated, healthy, self-employed, gentle, thoughtful, whimsical, not neurotic, and really truly in love. Their great concern is finding the best place and way to raise their child, who is a bun still in the oven. For every character like this I've seen in the last twelve months, I've seen twenty, maybe thirty, mass murderers.

Sam Mendes's *Away We Go* is a film for nice people to see. Nice people also go to *Terminator: Salvation*, but it doesn't make them any nicer. The movie opened June 5, 2009, in New York and Los Angeles, and then rolled out after lukewarm reviews accusing Verona and Burt of being smug, superior, and condescending. These are not sins if you have something to be smug about and much reason to condescend. Are the supporting characters all caricatures or simply a cross-section of the kinds of grotesques we usually meet in movies? I use the term "grotesque" as Sherwood Anderson does in *Winesburg, Ohio*: a person who has one characteristic exaggerated beyond all scale with the others.

Burt (John Krasinski) and Verona (Maya Rudolph) live in an underheated shabby home with a cardboard window. "We don't live like grown-ups," Verona observes. It's not that they can't afford a better home, so much that they are stalled in an impoverished student lifestyle. Now that they're about to become parents, they can't keep adult life on hold.

Away We Go is about an unplanned odyssey they take around North America to visit friends and family and essentially do some comparison shopping among lifestyles. Her parents are dead, so they begin with his: Gloria (Catherine O'Hara) and Jerry (Jeff Daniels). The parents truly *are* self-absorbed, and have no wish to wait around to welcome their first grandchild. They're moving to Antwerp.

Verona is of mixed race, and Gloria asks her conversationally, "Will the baby be black?" Is this insensitive? Why? Parents on both sides of an interracial couple would naturally wonder, and the film's ability to ask the question is not racist, but matter-of-fact in an America slowly growing tolerant. In moments like that the married screenwriters, Dave Eggers and Vendela Vida (both novelists and magazine editors), reflect a society in which race is no longer the primary defining characteristic.

After the parents vote for Belgium, Burt and Verona head for Phoenix and a visit with her onetime boss Lily (Allison Janney) and her husband, Lowell (Jim Gaffigan). Lily is a monster, a daytime alcoholic whose speech is grossly offensive and whose husband and children are in shock. Burt and Verona flee to Madison, where Burt's childhood friend Ellen (Maggie Gyllenhaal) has changed her name to "LN" and become one of those rigid campus feminists who have banned human nature from their rule book.

Then to Montreal and friends from college, Tom and Munch (Chris Messina and Melanie Lynskey), who are unhappily convinced they're happy. And next down to Miami and Burt's brother (Paul Schneider), whose wife has abandoned her family. Not a single example of healthy parenting in the lot of them.

The almost perfect relationship of (the unmarried) Verona and Burt seems to survive inside a bubble of their own devising, and since they can blow that bubble anywhere, they, of course, find the perfect home for it, in a scene of uncommon sunniness. They have been described as implausibly ideal, but you know what? So are their authors, Eggers and Vida. Consider: Thirty-somethings. Two children. Novelists and essayists. He publishes *McSweeney's*; she edits *The Believer*.

They are playful and at the same time socially committed. Consider his wonderful project 826 Valencia, a nonprofit storefront operation in San Francisco, Chicago, Los Angeles, New York, Seattle, Boston, and Ann Arbor. It runs free tutoring and writing workshops for young people from six to eighteen. The playful part can be seen in San Francisco, where the front of the ground floor is devoted to a Pirate Store. Yes. With eye patches, parrots' perches, beard dye, peg legs, planks for walking—all your needs.

I submit that Eggers and Vida are admirable people. If their characters find they are superior to many people, well, maybe they are. "This movie does not like you," sniffs Tony Scott of the *New York Times*. Perhaps with good reason.

The Axe in the Attic ★ ★ ★

NO MPAA RATING, 110 m., 2008

A documentary written, produced, and directed by Ed Pincus and Lucia Small.

I had no idea what happened after Hurricane Katrina devastated New Orleans and the Gulf Coast. No idea. I read the papers and watched the news on TV, and I had no idea. I learned the things they like to report: how hard the wind blew, how many inches of rain fell, the early death toll, victims living on a bridge, the people sheltered and/or imprisoned in the Superdome. But then another big story came along, and the news moved on, and I didn't think about Katrina so much.

Ed Pincus and Lucia Small saw the pictures on TV and decided to do something. They took an HD camera and set off on a sixty-day road trip from their home state of Vermont to Louisiana. Along the way they interviewed refugees who had settled for the time being in Philadelphia, Cincinnati, smaller cities, and government-funded trailer parks. *The Axe in the Attic* is their story of that journey.

When they arrived in the disaster zone, the sights were overwhelming. Square miles, whole counties, were destroyed. Families were uprooted. A way of life was torn apart. And the people they met were outraged by the pathetic inadequacy of the response by the federal government. FEMA, the optimistically named Federal Emergency Management Agency, was a target of scorn.

Not only did FEMA set up a bewildering barricade of red tape, in many cases it treated the hurricane victims as if they were homeless by choice. The National Guard was no better; on the bridge, troops leveled weapons at the refugees. The reason was not hard to understand: Many of the refugees were black. It was as if the government was trying to drive them out of the city by bulldozing rebuilding efforts and blocking relief agencies from delivering food and water, which would "only encourage people to stay."

Not only blacks are angry. The film also listens to white victims, who are angry on their own behalf and in many cases on behalf of blacks they have seen targeted for abuse rather than aid. They didn't know, but I have learned from another new documentary, *I.O.U.S.A.,* that federal accountants uncovered massive theft and fraud of FEMA funds, which paid for cars, vacations, champagne, lap dances, and porno films.

The hurricane didn't merely destroy by wind and flood. Its waters were contaminated by chemicals, and even weeks later, returning citizens wear face masks. Any clothes that got wet had to be destroyed; they burned the skin.

One opinion about the victims was that instead of expecting government aid, they should have gotten jobs. This at a time when tens of thousands of jobs disappeared. The film talks with one man who has to walk two and a half hours each way to a low-paying factory job because he can't afford a bus pass. He asks Lucia Small for money to buy a pass. She is conflicted: "Documentary ethics say we shouldn't pay people." I say to hell with documentary ethics, buy the man a pass.

Her moral argument is part of an element of the film I could have done without: Small and Pincus, partners in filmmaking but not in life, devote too much time to themselves. Their arguments quickly lose our interest. The film should have allowed the victims to speak for themselves, instead of going off-topic to become the story of its own making.

All the same, this is a shattering documentary. The witnesses in it mourn the loss of their homes and possessions, but also their loss of a city. "In New Orleans, nobody ever locked a door," one woman says. She saw her friends every day. She is now living in Florida: "I don't know anyone. Saturday at the mall is their family day."

The title? After an earlier hurricane, many residents learned to keep an axe in the attic in case the waters rose so high they had to hack a hole in their roofs. "That's why you saw so many people on roofs." Another says: "They say we got a warning. They got a warning six years ago to strengthen the levees." Strange that a levee separating white and black neighborhoods gave way only on the black side.

B

Baghead ★ ½
R, 84 m., 2008

Ross Partridge (Matt), Steve Zissis (Chad), Greta Gerwig (Michelle), Elise Muller (Catherine). Directed by Mark Duplass and Jay Duplass and produced by John Bryant, Jay Duplass, and Mark Duplass. Screenplay by Mark Duplass and Jay Duplass.

The modestly named "mumblecore" movement in new American indies is not an earthquake like the French New Wave, more of a trembling in the shrubbery. *Baghead,* by the Duplass brothers, Mark and Jay, is an example. Mumblecore movies are very low budget, shot on video, in love with handheld QueasyCam effects, and more often than not shot in the woods, where locations and extras are not a problem. *The Blair Witch Project* was not really a mumblecore movie, according to Peter Debruge, whose *Variety* article was definitive in defining the genre, but it's an early example of a Do It Yourself in the Woods genre that doesn't really cry out for more titles. On the other hand, I am informed by Jim Emerson, editor of rogerebert.com, a mumblecore shot in the woods is a bonus: "Actually, they're more likely to be shot in the filmmakers' apartments."

If you walk out after ten or fifteen minutes, you will have seen the best parts of the film. It opens at an underground film festival, where the director of a $1,000 epic (*We Came Naked*) takes questions after his premiere. Knowledgeable festival veterans will smile at the questions: "What was your budget?" of course, and "Did you use improvisation?" Why the budget is such a matter of concern puzzles me, but the people who ask that obligatory question always nod gratefully for the answer.

Anyway, our heroes attend the screening and attempt to crash the after-party without invitations. Walking past the security guard while carrying on an animated cell phone conversation seems to work, but not when you lack a cell phone and try to fake it with your wallet. At their own after-after-party, the four protagonists decide, the hell with it— they'll make their own movie.

The heroes are Matt (Ross Partridge), leader of the pack; his longtime on-again, off-again girlfriend Catherine (Elise Muller); his buddy Chad (Steve Zissis); and Chad's date, Michelle (Greta Gerwig), who seems more attracted to Matt than Chad. This generates what can be generously described as sexual tension in the woods, although not by me.

Their location is a cabin eleven miles up a country road (this distance later becomes important). They settle down to write a screenplay about four people in a cabin in the woods (that is, themselves), who are threatened by a guy with a bag over his head. I guess it's a guy. Girls aren't that stupid. During the course of their creativity session, one of them is indeed frightened by a guy with a bag ever his head, and it apparently couldn't be one of the other three. This baghead appears again at such perfectly timed moments that he must have a copy of the (unwritten) screenplay.

Here's where I have my problem. How is an uninformed total outsider going to *happen* to be eleven miles out in the woods with a bag over his head, and just *happen* to stumble upon these four people who *happen* to be writing exactly such a story? I weary, yes, I weary. He is obviously simply a device to make the movie long enough to qualify as a feature, and the denouement will be one of stunning underwhelmingness.

The dialogue contains way too many cries of "Matt!" and "Catherine!" and "Chad!" and "Michelle!" and "Matt! Where are you, Matt?" and so forth. There are better movies to be seen. Thousands. Their budget was low. Yes, I think I sensed they used improvisation. The film had its premiere at Sundance 2008, where I assume they were all invited to their after-party. I hope someone slipped in making a cell phone call on his wallet.

Ballast ★ ★ ★ ★
NO MPAA RATING, 96 m., 2008

Micheal J. Smith (Lawrence), JimMyron Ross (James), Tarra Riggs (Marlee), Johnny McPhail (John). Directed by Lance Hammer and produced by Hammer and Nina Parikh. Screenplay by Hammer.

Ballast is the very life of life. It observes three good, quiet people as they sink into depression, resentment, and rebellion. Then it watches patiently, gently, as they help one another find their futures together. There is a bedrock reality to it that could not be fabricated. It was filmed on locations in the Mississippi Delta and uses actors who had never acted before, but who never step wrong. Few professional actors could convince us so deeply.

But already you are filing this film away to forget. You don't care about the Mississippi Delta. You want to go see real movie stars. You already have too much reality in your life. You are suspicious of words like "quiet," "patiently," "gently." The film's own director does a better sales job in writing his synopsis, where you will find words like "embattled," "act of violence," "emotionally devastated," "the fury of a bitter and longstanding conflict." Be honest. Now it sounds less threatening to you.

The film centers on two households side by side on an open flatland. A man named Lawrence (Micheal J. Smith) lives in the house next to his sister-in-law Marlee (Tarra Riggs) and her twelve-year-old son, James (JimMyron Ross). After the death of Lawrence's brother, they are not on speaking terms. They ran a roadside convenience store and gas station together, but now it stands closed, its gate padlocked, and Lawrence sits at home alone, a cigarette burning itself down in his fingers. James comes to visit him one day.

That's really all I should tell you. The events in this film arrive when they happen, how they happen, in the order that they happen. The plot doesn't have "surprises," just things we didn't expect to happen. *Ballast* doesn't take the point of view of any one character. It regards them all. Because they all know what has happened before the story opens, the film doesn't use artificial dialogue to fill us in. We find out everything in the course of events. You will see how it unfolds the way life does.

Let me talk about the actors. They *are* these characters, with all the abilities and problems of real life. Be honest. When I wrote "Mississippi Delta," you immediately thought of poor black people. You know you did. The race of these characters has no relevance to the story. Lawrence and Marlee are not poor. Hell, they

have a gas station and a store. They're having a hard time right now because the store is closed and they are sad and angry, but you can see from the insides of their houses that while they're far from rich, they have what they need and a little more. James has his own motor scooter.

There is not one single shred of "amateur" about these performances. Not the smallest hint. After a long casting process, the writer-director, Lance Hammer, brought them all together and they discussed their characters. Hammer described the general outline. They improvised potential scenes every day for two months. The Mike Leigh approach. They all agreed that they had the final form more or less right. They were never given a finished script. They didn't have to memorize dialogue because they knew it from inside out: who they were, how they would say these things, how they would feel, what they would do.

There is a fourth named character, their neighbor John (Johnny McPhail). He is their friend and will help them if he can. He is not a saintly do-gooder. He is a decent man, has done OK in life, is older, is tactful, doesn't butt in when he isn't needed. He is a good neighbor, not The Good Neighbor. Then there are some kids who are alarming influences on James. Have you ever known a twelve-year-old who didn't know kids who are bad influences? Of course, if your kid is a bad influence, it's those other kids who got him that way.

Life goes on from day to day. We grow more and more intensely absorbed. The film uses no devices to punch up tension, manufacture suspense, underline motives. When there is anger, we see it coming from a long way away, and we watch it take its time to subside. Ordinary life begins to stir because it must. There is an ending that in one sense we probably anticipated, but it's like very few endings. When it comes, we think: "Yes. It would be like that. Exactly like that. We don't even need to see their faces. We feel their hearts."

Especially in its opening scenes, *Ballast* is "slower" and "quieter" than we usually expect. You know what? So is life, most of the time. We don't wake up and immediately start engaging with plot points. But *Ballast* inexorably grows and deepens and gathers power and absorbs us. I always say I hardly ever cry at sad films, but I sometimes do, just a little, at films about good people.

Note: Lance Hammer won the award for Best Director at Sundance 2008.

Balls of Fury ★ ★ ½
PG-13, 90 m., 2007

Dan Fogler (Randy Daytona), Christopher Walken (Mr. Feng), George Lopez (Agent Rodriguez), Maggie Q (Maggie), Tom Lennon (Karl Wolfschtagg), James Hong (Master Wong), Robert Patrick (Sgt. Pete Daytona). Directed by Robert Ben Garant and produced by Tom Lennon, Roger Birnbaum, Gary Barber, and Jonathan Glickman. Screenplay by Garant and Lennon.

Ping-Pong is to tennis as foosball is to soccer. I know it's on cable now, with lots of controversy over slower balls and faster paddles, but it retains for me only memories of rainy days at summer camp. I have never lost all affection for the sport, however, and am careful to play it at least once every decade. Thus it was with great eagerness that I attended *Balls of Fury,* which is, I believe, the first movie combining Ping-Pong and kung-fu and costarring Maggie Q. How many could there be?

Dan Fogler is the star, playing Randy Daytona, who in his youth was a Ping-Pong phenom but has been reduced in his twenties to working as a lounge act in Vegas, bouncing the ball off a board while flanked by two babes. That kind of lounge entertainment reminds me of an annual banquet of the Chicago Newspaper Reporters Association, at which the entertainment consisted of a man who came onstage with twelve of those paddles that have a bouncing ball attached with a rubber band, kept all twelve balls going at once, and then, one by one, got all twelve in his mouth.

Randy Daytona, now grown pudgy and in the early stages of a Curly Howard hairstyle, is discovered in Vegas by Rodriguez (George Lopez), an FBI agent who wants him to get back into training so he can compete undercover in an illegal global Ping-Pong and martial arts tournament run by the evil criminal weapons dealer Mr. Feng (Christopher Walken). Walken plays the role with makeup that makes him look Asian and clothes that look recycled from the wallpaper in a Chinese restaurant. Back in the days of Charlie Chan, Asians were rightfully offended when Caucasian actors portrayed them, but I doubt there is an Asian alive who will begrudge Walken this particular role.

Daytona's assignment: Get back in shape under the tutelage of blind Master Wong (James Hong) and his niece, played by Maggie Q (*Mission: Impossible III*). How can you be blind and play Ping-Pong? If you can't see, what other option do you have? Daytona thrives under his lessons, learns deadly martial arts moves from Maggie Q, and then he's ready for Mr. Feng's bizarre tournament.

Don't expect me to explain the rules and purposes of the tournament, if it has any. I was preoccupied with observing the sheer absurdity of everything on the screen, including Daytona's old Ping-Pong archenemy Karl Wolfschtagg (cowriter Tom Lennon), who will be a star if World Wrestling Entertainment ever sanctions this sport. All he needs is a leather mask and some spurs.

At some point in my study of the press releases, I came across the usual claims about how Fogler and the other actors became experts at the game and did many of their own scenes. Pure baloney. There are Ping-Pong games in this movie where the balls move faster than a quark on Saturday night. Fermilab should show *Balls of Fury* in its training program.

Now what else can I tell you? Well, I received a nice letter from Greg Packnett of Madison, Wisconsin, who enjoyed my "extremely qualified recommendation" for *Rush Hour 3,* remembering that while camping near the Wisconsin Dells, "it was so hot and so humid, that the people I was with decided to go to *Rush Hour 3* just for an excuse to spend a few hours in air-conditioning." Substituting the movie title, here's the qualified recommendation Mr. Packnett enjoyed so much: "Once you realize it's only going to be so good, you settle back and enjoy that modest degree of goodness, which is at least not badness, and besides, if you're watching *Balls of Fury,* you obviously didn't have anything better to do anyway."

The Band's Visit ★ ★ ★ ★
PG-13, 86 m., 2008

Sasson Gabai (Tewfiq), Ronit Elkabetz (Dina), Saleh Bakri (Haled), Khalifa Natour (Simon), Imad Jabarin (Camal), Tarak Kopty (Iman). Directed by Eran Kolirin and produced by Eilon Ratzkovsky, Ehud Bleiberg, Yossi Uzrad, Koby Gal-Raday, and Guy Jacoel. Screenplay by Kolirin.

The eight men wear sky-blue uniforms with gold braid on the shoulders. They look like extras in an opera. They dismount from a bus in the middle of nowhere and stand uncertainly on the sidewalk. They are near a highway interchange, leading, no doubt, to where they'd rather be. Across the street is a small café. Regarding them are two bored layabouts and a sadly, darkly beautiful woman.

They are the Alexandria Ceremonial Police Orchestra, a band from Egypt. Their leader, a severe man with a perpetually dour expression, crosses the street and asks the woman for directions to the Arab Cultural Center. She looks at him as if he stepped off a flying saucer. "Here there is no Arab culture," she says. "Also no Israeli culture. Here there is no culture at all."

They are in a dorp in the middle of the Israeli desert, having taken the wrong bus to the wrong destination. Another bus will not come until tomorrow. *The Band's Visit* begins with this premise, which could supply the makings of a light comedy, and turns it into a quiet, sympathetic film about the loneliness that surrounds us all. Oh, and there is some comedy, after all.

The town they have arrived at is lacking in interest even for those who live there. It is seemingly without activity. The bandleader, named Tewfiq (Sasson Gabai), asks if there is a hotel. The woman, Dina (Ronit Elkabetz), is amused. No hotel. They communicate in careful, correct English—she more fluent, he weighing every word. Tewfiq explains their dilemma. They are to play a concert tomorrow at the opening of a new Arab Cultural Center in a place that has almost, but not quite, the same name as the place they are in.

Tewfiq starts out to lead a march down the highway in the correct direction. There is some dissent, especially from the tall young troublemaker Haled (Saleh Bakri). He complains that they have not eaten. After some awkward negotiations (they have little Israeli currency), the Egyptians are served soup and bread in Dina's café. It is strange how the static, barren, lifeless nature of the town seeps into the picture even though the writer-director, Eran Kolirin, uses no establishing shots or any effort at all to show us anything beyond the café—and later, Dina's apartment and an almost empty restaurant.

Dina offers to put up Tewfiq and Haled at her apartment, and tells the young layabouts (who seem permanently anchored to their chairs outside her café) that they must take the others home to their families. And then begins a long, quiet night of guarded revelations, shared isolation, and tentative tenderness. Dina is tough but not invulnerable. Life has given her little that she hoped for. Tewfiq is a man with an invisible psychic weight on his shoulders. Haled, under everything, is an awkward kid. They go for a snack at the restaurant, its barren tables reaching away under bright lights, and Dina points out a man who comes in with his family. A sometime lover of hers, she tells Tewfiq. Even adultery seems weary here.

When the three end up back at Dina's apartment, where she offers them wine, the evening settles down into resignation. It is clear that Dina feels tender toward Tewfiq, that she can see through his timid reserve to the good soul inside. But there is no movement. Later, when he makes a personal revelation, it is essentially an apology. The movie avoids what we might expect, a meeting of the minds, and gives us instead a sharing of quiet desperation.

As Dina and Tewfiq, Ronit Elkabetz and Sasson Gabai bring great fondness and amusement to their characters. She is pushing middle age; he is being pushed by it. It is impossible for this night to lead to anything in their future lives. But it could lead to a night to remember. Gabai plays the bandleader as so repressed, or shy or wounded, that he seems closed inside himself. As we watch Elkabetz putting on a new dress for the evening and inspecting herself in the mirror, we see not vanity but hope. And throughout the evening we note her assertion, her confidence, her easily assumed air of independence. Yet when she gazes into the man's eyes, she sighs with regret that as a girl she loved the Omar Sharif movies that played daily on Israeli TV, but play no more.

There are some amusing interludes. A band member plays the first few notes of a sonata he has not finished (after years). A band mate calls him "Schubert." A local man keeps solitary vigil by a pay phone, waiting for a call from the girl he loves. He has an insistent way of showing his impatience when another uses the phone. In the morning, the band reassembles and leaves. *The Band's Visit* has not provided any of the narrative payoffs we might have expected, but it has provided something more valuable: an interlude involving two "enemies," Arabs and Israelis, that shows them both as only ordinary people with ordinary hopes, lives, and disappointments. It has also shown us two souls with rare beauty.

Battle for Terra ★ ★ ★
PG, 85 m., 2009

With the voices of: Luke Wilson (Jim Stanton), Evan Rachel Wood (Mala), Brian Cox (General Hemmer), James Garner (Doron), Chris Evans (Stewart Stanton), David Cross (Giddy), Justin Long (Senn), Dennis Quaid (Roven). Directed by Aristomenis Tsirbas and produced by Keith Calder, Ryan Colucci, Jessica Wu, and Dane Allan Smith. Screenplay by Evan Spiliotopoulos.

Battle for Terra is a bewitchingly animated story about an invasion from outer space by aliens who threaten to destroy all life on the planet so they can claim it as their own. I know what you're thinking. Here's the surprise: The aliens are the human race. The inhabitants of Terra look like cute tadpoles, combined with features of mermaids and seahorses.

The planet Terra (so named by the Terrans) is one of the stars of the film. A world where nearly everything seems to be organic, it has a unique scale. Although a Terran is of considerable size, about as large as a human child of six of seven, the vegetation grows on a much larger scale, so that a hollow reed can be used for high-rise living. The civilization includes certain mechanical features (helicopter chairs,

ultralight aircraft), but seems very much a part of nature.

The thinking that went into this other world is typical of classic science fiction, both in its physical details and its sociological ones. The atmosphere is apparently dense enough that the Terrans can hover with a minimal effort by their tadpole tails. It can also support huge, friendly sky leviathans, who float among the clouds like peaceful whales. The planet is ruled by a well-meaning thought-control autocracy, which enforces strict conformity and discourages independent thought.

When a vast human vessel appears in the sky, the Terrans assume it is God. The bright, rebellious Mala (voice by Evan Rachel Wood) thinks otherwise. When her light aircraft is pursued by a human fighter plane, she lures it into a crash, then rescues its pilot, Jim Stanton (Luke Wilson). Helped by Jim's chirpy robot companion, Giddy (David Cross), she saves his life and builds a dome within which he can breathe oxygen.

Oxygen is the problem. The humans, exhausted after a generations-long voyage through the cosmos, intend to replace Terra's atmosphere with oxygen, thus providing a new Earth for themselves, but alas, killing all life forms on Terra. This gaiacide is directed by the militarist General Hemmer (Brian Cox), who brushes away Jim's arguments that the two races can peacefully coexist.

All leads to war, which was a disappointment to me, because a film that offers invention and originality reduces itself to essentially just another aerial battle with, however, some nice touches. Are kids taught to require combat at the end? Could they perhaps be trusted to accept a character-based resolution?

The movie contains a subtle level of sociopolitical commentary, involving the blind faith encouraged by the leaders on both sides, the questioning of orthodoxy by Mala and her friend Senn (Justin Long), and the nuke-the-enemy strategy of General Hemmer. The assumption that the Earthlings are gods shows the pitfalls of imposing a supernatural solution to a natural problem.

The animation is nicely stylized and the color palette well chosen, although the humans are so square-jawed they make Dick Tracy look like Andy Gump. The voice performances are persuasive. The obvious drawback is that the film is in 3-D. If you can find a theater showing it in 2-D, seek out that one. The 3-D adds nothing and diminishes the light intensity, as if imposing a slightly cloudy window between the viewer and a brightly colored wonderland. Take off the glasses to see how much you're losing.

Battle in Seattle ★ ★ ★
R, 99 m., 2008

Andre Benjamin (Django), Woody Harrelson (Dale), Martin Henderson (Jay), Ray Liotta (Mayor Tobin), Connie Nielsen (Jean), Michelle Rodriguez (Lou), Channing Tatum (Johnson), Jennifer Carpenter (Sam), Charlize Theron (Ella). Directed by Stuart Townsend and produced by Townsend, Kirk Shaw, Maxime Remillard, and Mary Aloe. Screenplay by Townsend.

Battle in Seattle takes the actual 1999 protests against a summit meeting of the World Trade Organization and uses them as a backdrop for a fictional story about characters swept up in the tumult. The result is not quite a documentary and not quite a drama, but interesting all the same. It uses the approach of Haskell Wexler's *Medium Cool,* but without the same urgency; Wexler's actors were plunged into the actual demonstrations at the 1968 Chicago Democratic Convention, and *Battle* is not as convincing.

Much of the story involves an unnecessary romantic attraction between Jay (Martin Henderson), leader of the protesters, and Lou (Michelle Rodriguez), a member of the movement. They have to have disputes about tactics and motivations, etc., while drawing closer together, and in this context, they're just a distraction.

More to the point is Dale, the cop played by Woody Harrelson, whose pregnant wife (Charlize Theron), a bystander, is caught up in the crowd and beaten by police. Dale asks for leave time, but is ordered back on the street by his commanding officer and releases his grief through rage. Harrelson's emotional arc in the film is convincing and effective.

But what to make of Jean, the TV newswoman (Connie Nielsen), who plunges with her cameraman into the thick of the fighting, ignores orders from her station, and becomes sympathetic? Yes, it happens (a lot of reporters during Hurricane Katrina vented their anger at FEMA). That's not the problem. What seems odd is that she always seems to be at the crossroads between the action and the film's subplots, is always there for dramatic moments on video, and most of the time is the only TV news presence in the movie. Street reporters and their cameramen (and women!) tend to congregate at the same hotspots.

Those glitches aside, the movie makes a case for the way the WTO punishes Third World nations, allows the dumping of surpluses that drive workers away from jobs, and is managed for the benefit of the fat-cat nations. Some of the disagreement about the big Wall Street bailout reflects anger about the way money protects itself; should there even be a *question* that the executives who steered their companies into bankruptcy should be stripped of their multimillion-dollar bonuses?

Most people have never quite understood why there are protests all over the world about the WTO. *Battle in Seattle* has a commendable prologue and some dialogue that helps explain, but for a very moving ground-level doc that makes it all crystal clear, you might want to rent *Life and Debt* (2001), which is a close-up portrait of the destruction of small Jamaican farmers and the exploitation of workers. Would you believe the WTO pushes Third World nations into establishing poverty-wage barbed-wire enclaves for multinational corporations, inside of which local laws and protections do not apply?

Becoming Jane ★ ★ ★
PG, 120 m., 2007

Anne Hathaway (Jane Austen), James McAvoy (Tom Lefroy), Julie Walters (Mrs. Austen), James Cromwell (Rev. Austen), Maggie Smith (Lady Gresham), Laurence Fox (Mr. Wisley). Directed by Julian Jarrold and produced by Graham Broadbent, Robert Bernstein, and Douglas Rae. Screenplay by Kevin Hood and Sarah Williams.

Jane Austen wrote six of the most beloved novels in the English language, we are informed at the end of *Becoming Jane,* and so she did. The key word is "beloved." Her admirers do not analyze her books so much as they just plain love them to pieces. When I was very sick last year, there was a time when I lost all interest in reading. When I began to feel a little better, perhaps strong enough to pick up a book, it was Austen's *Persuasion.* Who else? And I entered again the world of that firm, fine intelligence, finding the humors and ironies of human existence in quiet domestic circles two centuries ago.

Becoming Jane is a movie every Janeite will want to see, although many will not approve of it. The Jane Austen in the film owes a great deal more to modern romantic fancies than to what we know about the real Jane Austen, and if Austen had been as robust and tall in those days (circa 1795) as Anne Hathaway, the five-foot, eight-inch actress who plays her, she would have been considered an Amazon. Studying the only portrait drawn during her life, by her sister Cassandra, I think she looked more like Winona Ryder. But no matter. Patton was no George C. Scott.

My quarrel involves what this film thinks Jane is "becoming": a woman or a novelist? The action centers on a passionate romance between Jane at about twenty and a handsome, penniless young lawyer named Tom Lefroy (James McAvoy). What intimacies or decisions they arrive at, I will leave for you to discover, but surely few of Jane's contemporaries would have allowed themselves to be so bold. Jane, in any event, discovers love. And in the movie's sly construction, she also discovers a great deal of the plot of *Pride and Prejudice,* beginning with Mr. Lefroy as the original for Mr. Darcy. She even happily chances on what will become the novel's opening words: "It is a truth universally acknowledged, that a single man in possession of a good fortune must be in want of a wife."

Austen is already an author as the movie opens, although she will not for many years be a published one. We see her sitting at a beautiful desk in a beautiful chair, writing with a beautiful quill pen in a stylish script, and gazing out at a beautiful pastoral view, like an illustration for a Regency edition of the Levenger catalog.

Reader, it was not so. In her famous *A Room of One's Own,* Virginia Woolf writes: "A woman must have money and a room of her own if she is to write fiction." But Austen, a rector's daughter, had neither. Woolf writes: "The middle-class family in the early 19th century was possessed only of a single sitting room between them. If a woman wrote, she would have to write in the common sitting room. . . . Jane Austen wrote like that to the end of her days. 'How she was able to effect all this,' her nephew writes in his memoir, 'is surprising, for she had no separate study to repair to, and most of the work must have been done in the general sitting room, subject to all kinds of casual interruptions.'"

But in the movie, as always in the movies, writing flows easily and life is hard, when in reality life is hard and writing is harder. Jane learns this in one of the movie's best scenes, when she calls on Ann Radcliffe, one of the few women novelists then existing, who created the gothic novel.

The romance with Tom Lefroy is based on speculation in a recent biography by Jon Spence, but I suspect it has been much improved here. In her surviving letters to Cassandra, to whom she told everything, Jane mentions Mr. Lefroy the first time on January 9, 1796, and the last time on January 16 of the same year. Love could hardly have flowered so fast in those days, especially since rectors' daughters had to walk everywhere.

So followers of Austen will know they are watching a fiction. How good is it? Pretty good, in the same way that the movies based on Austen's books are good; in the movie version of Britain in those years, Laura Ashley seems to have dashed in to dress everyone, while Martha Stewart was in the kitchen. Hathaway is a stunning beauty, with big eyes and a dazzling smile, and James McAvoy as Mr. Lefroy seems to have modeled his dashing personality on Tom Jones, the hero of a scandalous novel he gives Jane, who much enjoys it.

Her parents are played by Julie Walters and James Cromwell, who have the good sense to stay under the blankets while indulging in hanky-panky that must not have been common in the vicarages of the day. And Maggie Smith plays the dowager Lady Gresham, one of those minor titled figures who believe they've been charged by heaven to pass judgment on everyone in the neighborhood, especially anyone who is young and has a breath of feeling.

Mr. Lefroy's problem is that he depends on an allowance from his uncle, who will cut him off cold should he marry a country girl. Austen has another suitor named Mr. Wisley (Laurence Fox), who has money but no charm or beauty. Austen feels keenly that she must help support her family but believes optimistically she can do so from her writings, still for the most part unwritten. Lefroy is desperate not to lose his allowance. Yet they are so much in love. But can they live in a dirt-floored cottage, with Jane plunging her fair skin into laundry water?

The way all of this plays out is acted warmly by the principals, and Eigil Bryld's photography (of Ireland) makes England look breathtakingly green and inviting. The director, Julian Jarrold (*Kinky Boots* and the TV version of *White Teeth*) is comfortable with the material, and it is comfortable with him. Maybe too comfortable. The coast is clear for the sequel, *What Jane Became*.

Bedtime Stories ★ ★ ½
PG, 95 m., 2008

Adam Sandler (Skeeter Bronson), Keri Russell (Jill), Guy Pearce (Kendall), Russell Brand (Mickey), Richard Griffiths (Barry Nottingham), Courteney Cox (Wendy), Lucy Lawless (Aspen), Teresa Palmer (Violet Nottingham), Jonathan Morgan Heit (Patrick), Laura Ann Kesling (Bobbi). Directed by Adam Shankman and produced by Jack Giarraputo, Andrew Gunn, and Adam Sandler. Screenplay by Matt Lopez and Tim Herlihy.

Bedtime Stories was not my cup of tea, or even the saucer. Fairness requires me to report, however, that it may appeal to, as they say, "kids of all ages." I am not a kid of any age and do not qualify, but this is a harmless and pleasant Disney comedy and one of only three family movies playing over the holidays. It will therefore win the box-office crown big time, with Adam Sandler crushing Tom Cruise, Brad Pitt, Cate Blanchett, Mickey Rourke, Samuel L. Jackson, Kate Winslet, and others not in harmless Disney comedies. *The Tale of Despereaux* and *Marley and Me* also qualify as family films, although some parents may be frightened by Marley the dog.

Sandler plays a hotel handyman named Skeeter, which is a name even more unwise than Hussein if you want your child to run for president. His dear old dad ran a family motel at the corner of Sunset and La Cienega, an unlikely story, and was bought out by Nottingham the hotel tycoon (Richard Griffiths), who erected a towering heap of rooms on the site and put Skeeter in charge of changing the lightbulbs. Now Skeeter is also in charge of the overnight maintenance work on his niece and nephew while his sister (Courteney Cox) looks for work in Arizona.

The kids (Laura Ann Kesling and Jonathan Morgan Heit) want to be told bedtime stories, and Skeeter spins some terrific ones—so terrific, the movie's budget seems to be the best-kept secret this season. Literally hundreds of special-effects technicians labored to visualize Skeeter's fantasies, which involve a zero-gravity battle in outer space, a cowboy with a bright red horse, a medieval king, a gladiator, and so on. The kids start providing their own output, the stories have a weird way of coming true in real life, Skeeter tries to slant them to affect future events, and, as you know from the poster, gumballs rain from above.

Intercut with this folderol are (a) Skeeter's rivalry with Nottingham's evil hotel manager (Guy Pearce) for the hand of Nottingham's daughter (Teresa Palmer); (b) an attempt to save an eco-friendly school run by his sister's best friend (Keri Russell); and (c) reaction shots by Bugsy, the kids' pet guinea pig, whose hyperthyroid eyes the size of half-dollars are not cute. Sort of sad, really. Almost scary.

There are some nice sight gags. One involves a misunderstanding about fire-retardant spray. Another involves Skeeter being bitten on the tongue by a bee. He cannot utter one intelligible word during a crucial presentation to Nottingham and is funny in his desperate attempts. His scruffy friend Mickey (Russell Brand) leaps to the rescue and translates. Mickey is also an employee at the hotel, although anyone looking like him would be barred from any prudent hotel and might excite the curiosity of city health inspectors.

And that's about it. The first family comedy starring Adam Sandler. Just what you're looking for. Sandler reprises once again his clueless, well-meaning nebbish who wants to be liked. Once again the character relates best to kids, perhaps because there is so much he can learn from them. Once again, the message is that you have to believe. Apparently it doesn't matter so much *what* you believe. Just the act of believing is sufficient. Then you can believe you want to see the sequel.

Note: Our Chicago publicist, a really nice guy, announced that any movie critic attending in pajamas would be presented with free popcorn and a soft drink. How could he have known that the 7:30 p.m. screening would take place during a snowstorm on the coldest night of the winter? One of the critics nevertheless wore his PJs and cashed in. It must be true what they're saying about salaries in hard times.

Bee Movie ★ ★

PG, 100 m., 2007

With the voices of: Jerry Seinfeld (Barry B. Benson), Renee Zellweger (Vanessa), Matthew Broderick (Adam Flayman), Chris Rock (Mooseblood), John Goodman (Layton T. Montgomery), Patrick Warburton (Ken), Kathy Bates (Janet Benson), Barry Levinson (Martin Benson), Oprah Winfrey (Judge Bumbleton), Ray Liotta (himself), Sting (himself). Directed by Steve Hickner and Simon J. Smith and produced by Jerry Seinfeld and Christina Steinberg. Screenplay by Seinfeld, Spike Feresten, Andy Robin, and Barry Marder.

From each according to his ability, to each according to his need.

—Karl Marx

Applied with strict rigor, that's how bee society works in Jerry Seinfeld's *Bee Movie,* and apparently in real life. Doesn't seem like much fun. You are born, grow a little, attend school for three days, and then go to work for the rest of your life. "Are you going to work us to death?" a young bee asks during a briefing. "We certainly hope so!" says the smiling lecturer to appreciative chuckles all around.

One bee, however, is not so thrilled with the system. His name is Barry B. Benson, and he is voiced by Seinfeld as a rebel who wants to experience the world before settling down to a

lifetime job as, for example, a crud remover. He sneaks into a formation of ace pollinators, flies out of the hive, has a dizzying flight through Central Park, and ends up (never mind how) making a friend of a human named Vanessa (voice by Renee Zellweger). Then their relationship blossoms into something more, although not very much more, given the physical differences. Compared to them, a Chihuahua and a Great Dane would have it easy.

This friendship is against all the rules. Bees are forbidden to speak to humans. And humans tend to swat bees (there's a good laugh when Barry explains how a friend was offed by a rolled-up copy of *French Vogue*). What Barry mostly discovers from human society is *gasp!* that humans rob the bees of all their honey and eat it. He and his best pal, Adam (Matthew Broderick), even visit a bee farm, which looks like forced labor of the worst sort. Their instant analysis of the human-bee economic relationship is pure Marxism, if only they knew it.

Barry and Adam end up bringing a lawsuit against the human race for its exploitation of all bees everywhere, and this court case (with a judge voiced by Oprah Winfrey) is enlivened by the rotund, syrupy-voiced Layton T. Montgomery (John Goodman), attorney for the human race, who talks like a cross between Fred Thompson and Foghorn Leghorn. If the bees win their case, Montgomery jokes, he'd have to negotiate with silkworms for the stuff that holds up his britches.

All of this material, written by Seinfeld and writers associated with his TV show, tries hard, but never really takes off. We learn at the outset of the movie that bees theoretically cannot fly. Unfortunately, in the movie, that applies only to the screenplay. It is really, really, really hard to care much about a platonic romantic relationship between Renee Zellweger and a bee, although if anyone could pull if off, she could. Barry and Adam come across as earnest, articulate young bees who pursue logic into the realm of the bizarre, as sometimes happened on *Seinfeld.* Most of the humor is verbal and tends toward the gently ironic rather than the hilarious. Chris Rock scores best, as a mosquito named Mooseblood, but his biggest laugh comes from a recycled lawyer joke.

In the tradition of many recent animated

films, several famous people turn up playing themselves, including Sting (how did he earn that name?) and Ray Liotta, who is called as a witness because his brand of Ray Liotta Honey profiteers from the labors of bees. Liotta's character and voice work are actually kind of inspired, leaving me to regret the absence of B. B. King, Burt's Bees, Johnny B. Goode, and the evil Canadian bee slavemaster Norman Jewison, who—oh, I forgot, he exploits maple trees.

Before the Devil Knows You're Dead ★ ★ ★ ★
R, 117 m., 2007

Philip Seymour Hoffman (Andy), Ethan Hawke (Hank), Albert Finney (Charles), Marisa Tomei (Gina), Rosemary Harris (Nanette), Bryan F. O'Byrne (Bobby), Amy Ryan (Martha). Directed by Sidney Lumet and produced by Michael Cerenzie, Brian Linse, Paul Parmar, and William S. Gilmore. Screenplay by Kelly Masterson.

Sidney Lumet's *Before the Devil Knows You're Dead* is such a superb crime melodrama that I almost want to leave it at that. To just stop writing right now and advise you to go out and see it as soon as you can. I so much want to avoid revealing plot points that I don't even want to risk my usual strategy of oblique hints. You deserve to walk into this one cold.

Yet that would prevent my praise, and there is so much to praise about this film. Let me try to word this carefully. The movie stars Philip Seymour Hoffman and Ethan Hawke as brothers—yes, brothers, because although they may not look related, they always feel as if they share a long and fraught history. Hoffman plays Andy, a payroll executive who dresses well and always has every hair slicked into place, but has a bad drug habit and an urgent need to raise some cash. Hawke plays Hank, much lower on the financial totem pole, with his own reasons for needing money; he can't face his little girl and admit he can't afford to pay for her class outing to attend *The Lion King*. Hank looks more like the addict, but you never can tell.

Andy suggests they solve their problems by robbing a jewelry store. And not just any jewelry store, but find out for yourself. He has it all mapped out as a victimless crime: They won't use guns, they'll hit early Saturday when the shopping mall doesn't have customers, the store's losses will be covered by insurance, and so on. Sounds good on paper, before everything goes wrong. And that's when the movie becomes intense and emotionally devastating.

These two brothers are capable of feeling emotions rare in modern crime films: grief and remorse. They cave in with regret. And they *still* need money; Andy learns that when you are heartbroken it is bad enough, but even worse when your legs may be broken, too. Meanwhile, their dozy father (Albert Finney) starts looking into the case himself, and that leads to a conversation with one son that Eugene O'Neill couldn't have written any better.

The movie fully establishes the families involved. Finney has been married forever to Rosemary Harris and still loves her to pieces. Hoffman is married to Marisa Tomei, who just keeps on getting sexier as she grows older so very slowly. Hawke is divorced from Amy Ryan, who would happily see him in jail for nonpayment of child support. And although the film opens with Hoffman and Tomei ecstatically making love in Rio (say what you will about the big guy, Hoffman looks to be an energetic and capable lover), their marriage is far from perfect.

The Japanese name some of their artists as Living Treasures. Sidney Lumet is one of ours. He has made more great pictures than most directors have made pictures, and found time to make some clunkers on the side. Here he takes a story that is, after all, pretty straightforward, and tells it in an ingenious style we might call "narrative interruptus." The brilliant debut screenplay by Kelly Masterson takes us up to a certain point, then flashes back to before that point, then catches us up again, then doubles back, so that it meticulously reconstructs how spectacularly and inevitably this perfect crime went wrong.

And it doesn't simply go wrong, it goes wrong with an aftermath we care about. This isn't a movie where the crime is only a plot, and dead bodies are only plot devices. Its story has deeply emotional consequences. That's why an actor with Albert Finney's depth is needed for an apparently supporting role. If he isn't there when he's needed, the whole film loses. As for

Hoffman and Hawke, so seemingly different but such intelligent actors, they pull off that miracle that makes us stop thinking of anything we know about them and start thinking only of Andy and Hank. This is a movie, I promise you, that grabs you and won't let you think of anything else. It's wonderful when a director like Lumet wins a Lifetime Achievement Oscar at eighty and three years later makes one of his greatest achievements. ☞

Before the Rains ★ ★ ½
PG-13, 98 m., 2008

Linus Roache (Henry Moores), Rahul Bose (T.K. Neelan), Nandita Das (Sajani), Jennifer Ehle (Laura Moores), John Standing (Charles Humphries), Leo Benedict (Peter Moores). Directed by Santosh Sivan and produced by Doug Mankoff, Andrew Spaulding, Paul Hardart, Tom Hardart, and Mark Burton. Screenplay by Cathy Rabin, based on the film *Red Roofs* by Danny Verete.

Before the Rains tells the kind of story that would feel right at home in a silent film, and I suppose I mean that as a compliment. It's a melodrama about adultery, set against the backdrop of southern India in 1937. There's something a little creaky about the production, especially in its frequent use of large crowds of torch-bearing men, who can be summoned in an instant at any hour of day or night to blaze a trail, search for a missing woman, or group in front of the house of a possibly guilty man.

The movie comes from the Merchant-Ivory group, long associated with films made in English and filmed in India. It's directed by Santosh Sivan, originally a cinematographer, whose masterpiece *The Terrorist* (1999) involved a young woman committed to being a suicide bomber. That's the most thoughtful and empathetic film I've seen about the mind of a person who arrives at such a decision. It involves an assassination attempt; this one is set against the tide of Indian nationalism.

But it's not really a political film. It's driven by lust, guilt, and shame of a melodramatic sort that was right at home in the silent era. That doesn't mean it's old-fashioned, but that it's broadly melodramatic. It centers on the

lives of a British landowner in India, his Indian right-hand man, and his affair with his beautiful young servant woman. Both the man and the woman are married, so there are problems in addition to the taboo against mixing the races and classes.

The man is Henry Moores (Linus Roache), who lives in a big, comfortable house with his wife, Laura (Jennifer Ehle), and young son, Peter (Leo Benedict). Next door lives his assistant, T.K. (Rahul Bose), who has abandoned his roots in the nearby village and cast his lot with the Brits. They run a tea plantation and discover cinnamon higher in the hills. That involves the construction of a road up a steep hillside that must zigzag its way to the top to avoid being washed away in the monsoons.

Laura and Peter are away at the beginning of the film, and Henry and his servant Sajani (Nandita Das) seek honey for their tea in a "sacred grove." They're seen by two talkative young boys and that leads, as it must, to tragedy. Laura and Benjamin return. Sajani is beaten by her husband, who has learned of her secret tryst (but not the identity of her partner). And that sets into motion a series of events involving whom she can trust, whom she can believe, and where she can turn.

This paragraph is a spoiler. Henry gives T.K. all the money he has on hand and asks him to send Sajani "away." T.K. reports, "I put her in a boat—for the North." But India is a big country, and the North is a distant destination for a woman in a small boat with one oarsman. Sajani, covered in blood, returns in the middle of the night to T.K.'s house, where Henry meets her. He's desperate. The village has reported her "missing," his wife is having suspicions, and when Sajani asks him, "Do you really love me?" he replies, "No." I think he says that for her own good. But she takes a handy pistol and kills herself.

It's in the details that a film reveals its origins. How does that pistol come into her hands? Henry gave it to T.K. in an early scene, and at the midnight meeting T.K. takes it out for no good reason and doesn't even seem to notice as he drops it where her hand can find it. All of this is explained in close-ups. Silent films knew just how to handle such prop deliveries.

Before the Rains is lushly photographed, as we would expect, by Sivan himself. It's told sincerely and with energy. It enjoys its period settings and costumes, and even its conventions. In a movie with plenty of room for it, there isn't a trace of cynicism. I am growing weary (temporarily, I think) of films that are cynical about themselves. Having seen several films recently whose characters have as many realities as shape-shifters, I found it refreshing to see a one-level story told with passion and romanticism.

But I can't quite recommend it. In a plot depending on concealment and secrecy, Henry and T.K. make all the wrong decisions, including a cover-up that almost seems designed to fail. And I didn't even mention the banker who pulls the plug on the financing of the road. That's part of the silent tradition, too: bankers who pull plugs.

Be Kind Rewind ★ ★ ½
PG-13, 101 m., 2008

Jack Black (Jerry), Mos Def (Mike), Danny Glover (Mr. Fletcher), Mia Farrow (Miss Falewicz), Melonie Diaz (Alma). Directed by Michel Gondry and produced by Georges Bermann and Julie Fong. Screenplay by Gondry.

whimsy (n.): Playfully quaint or fanciful behavior or humor.

Michel Gondry's *Be Kind Rewind* is whimsy with a capital W. No, it's WHIMSY in all caps. Make that all-caps italic boldface. Oh, never mind. I'm getting too whimsical. Maybe Gondry does, too. You'll have to decide for yourself. This is a movie that takes place in no possible world, which may be a shame, if not for the movie, then for possible worlds.

The place: Passaic, New Jersey. On a street corner stands a shop so shabby that only an art director could have designed it. This is Be Kind Rewind, a store that rents a skimpy selection of VHS tapes. Not a DVD in sight. It's owned by Mr. Fletcher (Danny Glover), who has convinced himself the store was the birthplace of Fats Waller (identified only as "some old-time jazz musician" on one Web site, which has plainly never heard of him). Behind in his rent, Mr. Fletcher faces eviction, and the store will be pulled down, no doubt to make way for Starbucks or Dunkin' Donuts.

Mr. Fletcher's faithful, long-suffering clerk is Mike (Mos Def), who is entrusted with the store while the owner goes undercover, hoping to scope out the success of the big competitor down the street, West Coast Video. Maybe it's because they rent DVDs? To be in the video rental business and not have heard of DVDs does not speak well for Mr. Fletcher's knowledge of the market, but then we suspect that when we see his store. I was once in a dirt-floored "store and bar" in a poor rural district of Ireland that had a stock of one (1) bottle of Guinness. Same idea.

One of the store's most loyal visitors and nuisances is Jerry (Jack Black), who works nearby in a garage. Paranoid about a power plant next door, he breaks in to sabotage it and is zapped with so much electricity he looks like a lightning strike during one of Victor Frankenstein's experiments. This does not turn him into a cinder, only magnetizes him, after which he visits the store and inadvertently erases all the tapes.

Crisis. What to do before Mr. Fletcher comes back? The tapes can't be replaced, because Mike and Jerry don't have the money and besides, how easy is it to get VHS tapes except on eBay? I take that back. Amazon lists six VHS tapes of *Ghostbusters,* one of the erased movies, for one (1) cent each. At that rate, you could build up a decent VHS library for a dollar. Anyway, the lads have a masterstroke: They will *reenact* the movies and rent them to unsuspecting customers like Miss Falewicz (Mia Farrow), who won't know the difference anyway. Costarring as their female leads in these movies is the fetching Alma (Melonie Diaz), who has the sexiest smile since Rosario Dawson.

The reenactments are not very skillful, to put it mildly, but they have the advantage, as Mike argues, of not taking up all your time because they're as short as twenty minutes. They explain that they import their versions from Sweden, which is why they call them *sweded.* You can see the works of Mike and Jerry on the Web, by the way, which might be about two-thirds as good as seeing the whole movie. One of the perhaps inevitable consequences of reenacting movies is that the exercise brings out all the latent manic excess within Jack Black, who when he is trying that hard reminds me of a dog I know named Mick Q. Broderick, who gets so excited when you come over you have to go to the dry cleaners after every visit.

Whether their scheme works, whether the store is saved, whether Hollywood considers their work homage or piracy, I will leave for you to discover. But you haven't read this far unless you hope to learn whether I would recommend the movie. Not especially. I felt positive and genial while watching it, but I didn't break out in paroxysms of laughter. It's the kind of amusing film you can wait to see on DVD. I wonder if it will come out on VHS?

Bella ★ ★ ★
PG-13, 91 m., 2007

Eduardo Verastegui (Jose), Tammy Blanchard (Nina), Manny Perez (Manny), Ali Landry (Celia), Angelica Aragon (Mother), Jaime Tirelli (Father), Ramon Rodriguez (Eduardo). Directed by Alejandro Monteverde and produced by Eduardo Verastegui, Leo Severino, Monteverde, and Denise Pinckley. Screenplay by Monteverde and Patrick Million.

Bella tells the story of two people who fall in love because of an unborn child. Winner of the Audience Award at Toronto 2006, it is a heart-tugger with the confidence not to tug too hard. It stars an actor named Eduardo Verastegui, whom I would describe as the next Antonio Banderas if I ever wrote clichés like that, which I do not. Tall, handsome, bearded, he plays Jose, the chef of his brother's Mexican restaurant in New York, until his life changes one day when his brother fires a waitress named Nina (Tammy Blanchard) for being late.

Jose and Nina are not a couple. All the same, he walks out of the kitchen, chases her into the subway, apologizes that his brother humiliated her in front of the staff, and finds out she was late because she is pregnant. Now what kind of a reason is that for being late? If I were in the habit of criticizing other critics, which I am not, I would quote Robert Koehler of *Variety,* who writes: "Nina, however, could easily have been to work on time, since her delay was due to her buying and using a home pregnancy test—something she rationally would have done after her shift was over." Uh,

huh. And if Mr. Koehler feared he was pregnant, which would he do first? Buy and use a home pregnancy test or review *Bella*? I don't trust a review written by some guy who's wondering if he's pregnant.

Jose and Nina walk and talk, have lunch, share memories, and go to a restaurant where the owner, a friend of Jose's, offers to hire them both. Along the way, Jose tries to convince her to have the child. He is motivated by reasons that are fully explained in early premonitions and later flashbacks, which I will not reveal. Perhaps the clincher on his argument is provided by a visit to his mother and father (Angelica Aragon and Jaime Tirelli), whose warmth is a contrast to Nina's own wretched past.

Counterpoint is provided by Jose's brother, Manny (Manny Perez), who apparently was not as affected by the sunshine in his childhood home. He's a martinet and perfectionist, a taskmaster, heartless, and (as it turns out) incompetent to run his own kitchen. His attitude toward Nina's pregnancy is about as abstract as Robert Koehler's. Compare them to a man who is *bearing* a child. Remember Arnold Schwarzenegger in *Junior,* the movie where he was pregnant and said that merely scooping out the center of a honeydew melon gave him a *you know.*

I have failed to convey the charm of the movie. Eduardo Verastegui, despite sporting a beard so thick and black it makes him look like a nineteenth-century anarchist, has friendly eyes, a ready smile, and a natural grace in front of the camera that will soon have fans shifting their Banderas pinups to the bottom drawer. And Tammy Blanchard fits comfortably into the role of a woman who wants to do the right thing but feels alone, friendless, and broke. All she needs is someone to trust and she melts.

There is also a lot of cooking in the movie. Jungles of cilantro are chopped. The restaurant's staff luncheon features quail in a mole sauce. Verastegui looks like he knows what he's doing in the kitchen. His IMDb profile says he likes cooking, which I believe, although that's usually the desperation answer by people who can't think of anything they like. You sense a little of that, indeed, in his profile's next two sentences: He has a golden retriever; he likes golden retrievers. He stops short of liking to cook golden retrievers.

The movie is not deep and profound, but it's not stupid. It's about lovable people having important conversations and is not pro-choice or pro-life but simply in favor of his feelings—and hers, if she felt free to feel them. The movie is a little more lightweight than the usual Audience Award winner at Toronto (this year: Cronenberg's *Eastern Promises*), but why not? It was the best-liked film at the 2006 festival, and I can understand that.

Beowulf ★ ★ ★
PG-13, 114 m., 2007

Ray Winstone (Beowulf), Anthony Hopkins (King Hrothgar), John Malkovich (Unferth), Robin Wright Penn (Queen Wealthow), Brendan Gleeson (Wiglaf), Crispin Glover (Grendel), Alison Lohman (Ursula), Angelina Jolie (Grendel's mother). Directed by Robert Zemeckis and produced by Zemeckis, Steve Starkey, and Jack Rapke. Screenplay by Neil Gaiman and Roger Avary.

In the name of the mighty Odin, what this movie needs is an audience that knows how to laugh. Laugh, I tell you, laugh! Has the spirit of irony been lost in the land? By all the gods, if it were not for this blasted infirmity that the Fates have rendered me, you would have heard from me such thunderous roars as to shake the very Navy Pier itself down to its pillars in the clay.

To be sure, when I saw *Beowulf* in 3-D at the giant-screen IMAX theater, there were eruptions of snickers here and there, but for the most part the audience sat and watched the movie, not cheering, booing, hooting, recoiling, erupting, or doing anything else unmannerly. You expect complete silence and rapt attention when a nude Angelina Jolie emerges from the waters of an underground lagoon. But am I the only one who suspects that the *intention* of director Robert Zemeckis and writers Neil Gaiman and Roger Avary was satirical?

Truth in criticism: I am not sure Angelina Jolie was nude. Oh, her character was nude, all right, except for the shimmering gold plating that obscured certain crucial areas, but was she Angelina Jolie? Zemeckis, who directed the wonderful *Polar Express*, has employed a much more realistic version of the same animation technology in *Beowulf*. We are not looking at flesh-and-blood actors but special effects that look uncannily convincing, even though I am reasonably certain that Angelina Jolie does not have spike-heeled feet. That's right: feet, not shoes.

The movie uses the English epic poem, circa AD 700, as its starting point and resembles the original in that it uses a lot of the same names. It takes us to the Danish kingdom of King Hrothgar (Anthony Hopkins), where the king and his court have gathered to inaugurate a new mead hall, built for the purpose of drinking gallons of mead. The old hall was destroyed by the monster Grendel, whose wretched life consists of being the ugliest creature on earth and destroying mead halls.

To this court comes the heroic Geatsman named Beowulf (Ray Winstone), who in the manner of a Gilbert and Sullivan hero is forever making boasts about himself. He is the very model of a medieval monster slayer. (A Geatsman comes from an area of today's Sweden named Gotaland, which translates, Wikipedia helpfully explains, as "land of the Geats.") When the king offers his comely queen, Wealthow (Robin Wright Penn), as a prize if Beowulf slays Grendel, the hero immediately strips naked, because if Grendel wears no clothes, then he won't, either. This leads to a great deal of well-timed Austinpowerism, which translates (Wikipedia does not explain) as "putting things in the foreground to keep us from seeing the family jewels." Grendel arrives on schedule to tear down the mead hall, and there is a mighty battle, which is rendered in gory and gruesome detail, right down to cleaved skulls and severed limbs.

Now when I say, for example, that Sir Anthony plays Hrothgar, or John Malkovich plays Beowulf's rival Unferth, you are to understand that they supply voices and the physical performances for animated characters who look more or less like they do. (Crispin Glover, however, does not look a thing like Grendel, and if you are familiar with the great British character actor Ray Winstone, you will suspect he doesn't have six-pack abs.) *Variety* reports that Paramount has entered *Beowulf* in the

Academy's best animated film category, which means nothing is really there, realistic as it may occasionally appear. I saw the movie in IMAX 3-D, as I said, and like all 3-D movies, it spends a lot of time throwing things at the audience: spears, blood, arms, legs, bodies, tables, heads, mead, and so forth. The movie is also showing in non-IMAX 3-D, and in the usual 2-D. Not bad for a one-dimensional story.

But I'm not complaining. I'm serious when I say the movie is funny. Some of the dialogue sounds like Monty Python. No, most of the dialogue does. "I didn't hear him coming," a wench tells a warrior. "You'll hear me," he promises. Grendel is ugly beyond all meaning. His battles are violent beyond all possibility. His mother (Jolie) is like a beauty queen in centerfold heaven. Her own final confrontation with Beowulf beggars description. To say the movie is over the top assumes you can see the top from here.

Now about the PG-13 rating. How can a movie be rated PG-13 when it has female nudity? I'll tell you how. Because Angelina Jolie *is not really there*. And because there are no four-letter words. Even Jolie has said she's surprised by the rating; the British gave it a 12A certificate, which means you can be a year younger and see it over there. But no, Jolie won't be taking her children, she told the BBC: "It's remarkable it has the rating it has. It's quite an extraordinary film, and some of it shocked me."

Here's the exact wording from the MPAA's code people: "Classified PG-13 for intense sequences of violence including disturbing images, some sexual material and nudity." How does that compare with a PG rating? Here's the MPAA's wording on *Bee Movie*: "Classified PG for mild suggestive humor and a brief depiction of smoking." I have news for them. If I were thirteen, Angelina Jolie would be plenty nude enough for me in this movie, animated or not. If I were twelve and British, who knows?

Bigger, Stronger, Faster ★ ★ ★ ½
PG-13, 106 m., 2008

A documentary directed by Christopher Bell and produced by Alex Buono, Tasmin Rawady, and Jim Czarnecki. Screenplay by Bell, Buono, and Rawady.

Midway through watching Chris Bell's *Bigger, Stronger, Faster,* I started to think about another film I'd seen recently. The Bell documentary is about the use of steroids in sports and bodybuilding. The other film is Darryl Roberts's *America the Beautiful,* about the guilt some women feel because they don't look like the models in fashion magazines. The steroid users want to be bigger. The weight-obsessed women want to be thinner. The Roberts doc focuses on Gerren Taylor, who at twelve achieved fame as a child who looked like an adult fashion model. A year later, she was dropped by those who cast for runway models, but she tried to make a comeback. At thirteen.

Bell is one of three brothers. They've all used steroids, and two still do. Mike ("Mad Dog") Bell had some success in pro wrestling but never as the star, always as the scripted loser. Wrestling has dropped him, but he's still in training, even though he's now "too old," he's told. "I was born to attain greatness," he tells Chris, "and I'm the only one that's holding myself back."

The third Bell brother, Mark ("Smelly") Bell, has promised his wife he will stop taking steroids after he achieves his dream of powerlifting seven hundred pounds. He attains it, but later tells Chris he will use steroids again. Chris tells him, "I'm afraid you'll lose your job, your wife, and yourself." Smelly replies, "If I lose my job and my wife, what else do I have but myself?" Both of Chris's brothers are remarkably frank in talking to him, as are his parents, who are "opposed to steroids" but are red-faced with cheering after Smelly lifts the weights.

Bell uses a clip from the movie *Patton,* in which the famous general addresses his troops: "Americans love a winner and will not tolerate a loser." That is the bottom line of *Bigger, Stronger, Faster.* We say we're opposed to steroids, but we're more opposed to losing. Steroids are not nearly as dangerous as amphetamines, he points out, but the United States is the only nation that *requires* its fighter pilots to use amphetamines. They may be harmful, but they work.

This movie is remarkable in that it seems to be interested only in facts. I was convinced that Bell was interviewing people who knew a lot about steroids, and the weight of scientific, medical, and psychological opinion seems to be that steroids are not particularly dangerous. Is the movie "pro-steroid"? Yes, but it is even more against the win-win mentality. We demand that our athletes bring home victories, and yet to compete on a level playing field, they feel they have to use the juice.

The movie goes against the drumbeat of anti-steroid publicity, news reports, and congressional hearings to say that steroids are not only generally safe but have been around longer and been used more widely than most people know. Bell and his brothers grew up pudgy in a Poughkeepsie family, were mesmerized by early heroes like Hulk Hogan, Rambo, and Conan the Barbarian, got into weight-lifting, and still have muscular physiques. They all used muscles as a powerful boost to their self-esteem.

But think for a second. *America the Beautiful* quotes this statistic: "Three minutes of looking at a fashion magazine makes 90 percent of women of all ages feel depressed, guilty, and shameful." I don't have similar statistics about bodybuilders, but I assume they study the muscle magazines with similar feelings. Those who cannot be too thin or too muscular are attracted to opposite extremes but use the same reasoning: By pursuing an ideal that is almost unattainable and may be dangerous to their health, they believe they will be admired, successful, the object of envy.

Bell interviews some bodybuilders who are over fifty, maybe sixty, and still "in training." The words "in training" suggest that a competition is approaching, but they're in training against themselves. Against their body's desire to pump less iron, eat different foods, process fewer proteins, and, in general, find moderation. Anorexia represents one extreme of this reasoning. At another extreme is Gregg Valentino, who has the world's largest biceps; they look like sixteen-inch softballs straining against his skin. He makes fun of himself: He walks into a club and no chick is gonna go for that, "but the dudes come over." There are men who envy him.

What's sad is that success in both fashion and bodybuilding is so limiting. For every Arnold Schwarzenegger, who used the Mr. Universe crown to catapult himself into movie and political stardom, there are hundreds, thousands who spend their lives "in training." When a model gets thin enough (few do, especially in their own minds), they must spend their lives staying that thin.

The question vibrating below the surface of both docs is, has America become maddened by the need for victory? When our team is in the World Series, do we seriously give a damn what the home run kings have injected? We are devout in Congress, but heathens in the grandstands. That is one of Bell's messages, and the other is that steroids have become demonized far beyond their actual danger to society. Which side do you vote on? Chris Bell marks his ballot twice: Steroids are not very harmful, but by using them, we reveal a disturbing value system.

Big Man Japan ★ ★ ★ ½
PG-13, 113 m., 2009

Hitosi Matumoto (Dai Sato), Riki Takeuchi (Jumpy Monster), Ua (Sato's Manager), Ryunosuke Kamiki (Baby Monster), Itsuji Itao (Smelly Monster). Directed by Hitoshi Matsumoto and produced by Akihiko Okamoto. Screenplay by Matsumoto and Mitsuyoshi Takasu.

Well, I guess this is the movie I've been asking for. Whenever I see a superhero epic, I'm always nagged by logical questions—like, when the Incredible Hulk becomes enormous, how do his undershorts also expand? *Big Man Japan* answers that question with admirable clarity. Before Big Man grows, workers winch an enormous pair of undershorts up on two poles, and he straddles the crotch. Then he expands to fill them. Had to be something like that.

The movie, which is very funny in an insidious way, takes the form of a slice-of-life documentary about Dai Sato (Hitosi Matumoto), the latest generation in a Tokyo dynasty of monster killers. He is a quiet, introverted, unhappy man, whose wife has left him and taken away their daughter. He lives alone in cluttered bachelor squalor. Nothing much happens, but he's always on call, and when the Department of Defense needs him, he has to rush to the nearest power plant, be zapped with massive bolts of electricity, and grow into a giant ready to battle the latest monster with his only weapon, a steel club.

These are some monsters. One has expanding cables for arms, embraces skyscrapers, pulls them out of the ground, and throws them over his back. Then he has to flick his comb-over back in place. One consists of a giant body and one foot, with which he jumps on things. One exudes an overpowering stink. One breathes fire and looks like Hellboy. One has a single giant eyeball on a long stem hanging from its crotch, and wields it like a bola.

These monsters come from who knows where, and when they die we see their souls take flight and ascend to heaven. Their battles take place in cities that look gloriously like phony special effects, and unlike most monster movies with terrified mobs, these streets and buildings do not have a single person visible.

In contrast with the action scenes, the movie takes the form of a downbeat doc about the nightmare of being Big Man. Dai Sato never gets time off. He isn't paid much. He raises cash from TV specials about his fights and selling advertising space among his tattoos. People hate him for stepping on things, soiling the environment, and disturbing the peace. His TV ratings are down. He wonders why his agent, a chain-smoking, cell phone–addicted woman, has a new car but he takes the train. His only company comes from professional geishas.

Matumoto plays the role absolutely on the straight and level. So do all of the human characters. He is as concerned about the practical problems of being a superhero as I am. The film takes, or seems to take, his dilemma with utter seriousness. Matumoto is also the writer and director, and it becomes clear that he is satirizing three genres: the personal documentary, monster movies, and reality TV. And he does this slyly, with a scalpel instead of a hatchet. Only the monsters are over the top, and are they ever. The weird thing is that thanks to CGI, some of them have worried, middle-aged human faces on their grotesque bodies.

Note: Something has been nagging you. That name Matumoto doesn't seem quite right. You would be correct. Hitosi Matumoto's real name is Hitoshi Matsumoto, but he misspells both names in the credits. Little joke. Think Ada Sadler. He's a popular Japanese comedian. I hope all his overseas viewers get the joke.

The Black Balloon ★ ★ ★
PG-13, 97 m., 2009

Rhys Wakefield (Thomas Mollison), Luke Ford (Charlie Mollison), Gemma Ward (Jackie Masters), Erik Thomson (Simon Mollison), Toni Collette (Maggie Mollison). Directed by Elissa Down and produced by Tristram Miall. Screenplay by Down and Jimmy Jack.

At the center of *The Black Balloon* is Toni Collette's performance as the mother of an autistic son. The way she meets this challenge opens a way to understand all the other characters. Her son, Charlie, can be sweet and lovable. He can also make life for his family all but unbearable. Collette, as his mother, Maggie, has been dealing with him for seventeen years and seems to have long ago made her peace with the fact that Charlie is who he is and is not going to change. As his mother, she loves him.

The film is concerned largely with how her other son, Thomas (Rhys Wakefield), exists with his brother. Tom is a military brat, used to new towns and new schools, affable but shy. He shares the burden of Charlie (Luke Ford), cares for him, loves him, but is ashamed of him. Thomas is at just that point in adolescence when he's acutely conscious of all his defects, and in teenage social terms, Charlie is a defect.

In an acutely embarrassing scene, Thomas is revealed during a swimming class as a sixteen-year-old who cannot swim. This makes him a target for other students, who like many teenagers are quick to mock. One girl is nice to him. This is Jackie (Gemma Ward), a tall blonde who quietly makes it clear that she likes Thomas. Thomas doesn't really know how to deal with this, but his first instinct is to try to hide Charlie from her. And a crisis is building at home; his mom is pregnant again, his dad, Simon (Erik Thomson), insists on bed rest for her, and when Simon is away the burden of running the household falls on Thomas.

The Black Balloon establishes this family with a delicate mixture of tenderness and pain. Charlie is not made into a cute movie creature. He cannot speak, he cannot control his rages, he can have instant, violent mood changes. He runs through the neighborhood in his underpants. He throws a tantrum in a supermarket. He rubs his feces into the carpet. Thomas is supposed to protect Charlie from himself and perform the damage control.

The story elements of *The Black Balloon* could have been manipulated to make the film false and cute. In some circles, that would be interpreted as upbeat. The film tries to be true. The uplift comes in how the family, and Jackie, respond to Charlie. Maggie and Simon are strongly bonded in a marriage that has survived Charlie. They have no time for nobility; they are focused on doing what needs to be done. Charlie is theirs and will not be stored in a "facility." Thomas agrees with this, but he has a breaking point.

It is Jackie who turns out to be special. Although Gemma Ward, who plays her, is a well-known model and this is her first substantial role, there is nothing of the professional model in her performance. She creates a spontaneously warm young woman who cares for Thomas, sympathizes with him, accepts Charlie without question, and helps Charlie accept himself.

Luke Ford's performance as Charlie is a convincing tour de force. You may recall him as Brendan Fraser's heroic son in *The Mummy: Tomb of the Dragon Emperor*. Rhys Wakefield, in his first feature role, is a good casting decision, suggesting inner turmoil without overacting. But it is Toni Collette who explains, without even seeming to try, why this family is still together at all.

Elissa Down, who directed and cowrote the film, reportedly has two autistic brothers. Her experience informs this story, particularly in the way enormous pressure is brought to bear on the family. Perhaps she wrote from experience about how the two parents begin with unconditional love; how rare to see a happy, long-surviving marriage in a movie, where so often the father is flawed. Rare, too, and a tribute to the Australian film industry, to see a film that doesn't allow star power to compromise its vision.

The mainstream cinema would no doubt be eager to employ Gemma Ward in a no-brainer teeny romcom. She made the right choice here and seems poised to follow the example of another onetime model, Nicole Kidman, in treating herself seriously and not getting lost in the soul-deadening life of a professional model.

Black Snake Moan ★ ★ ★
R, 116 m., 2007

Samuel L. Jackson (Lazarus), Christina Ricci (Rae), Justin Timberlake (Ronnie), S. Epatha Merkerson (Angela), John Cothran Jr. (R.L.). Directed by Craig Brewer and produced by John Singleton and Stephanie Allain. Screenplay by Brewer.

I had never really heard many half snorts before. Snorts, yes, and silence. But what do you make of an audience that has no idea how to react? *Black Snake Moan* is the most peculiar movie I've seen about sex and race and redemption in the Deep South. It may be the most peculiar recent movie ever except for *Road House,* but then what can you say about *Road House*? Such movies defy all categories.

The movie—I will try to be concise—stars Samuel L. Jackson as a broken-down blues musician and vegetable market gardener whose wife has just walked out. On the road leading to his property, he finds a battered young white girl, whose injuries hardly seem curable by the cough syrup he barters fresh vegetables for at the drugstore. The girl is Rae (Christina Ricci); it is no coincidence that Jackson's character is named Lazarus, and Lazarus determines to return her from near death or whooping cough, one or the other. No saint himself, he wants to redeem her from a life of sluttery.

His technique, with a refreshing directness, is to chain her to a radiator. Good thing he lives way out in the wilderness. Lazarus and Rae have no sex per se, but they do a powerful lot of slapping, cursing, and chain rattling, and the reaction of the blue-collar town on Market Day is a study. I think the point is that they somehow redeem each other through these grotesqueries, a method I always urge be used with extreme caution.

The performances are very good: hell-bent

for leather and better than the material deserves. There is much hysteria and snot. The writer-director, Craig Brewer, made that other splendid story of prostitution and redemption, *Hustle and Flow*, with its Oscar-winning song ("It's Hard Out Here for a Pimp"). In fact, I pretty much enjoyed the whole movie, with some incredulity and a few half snorts.

Both *Black Snake Moan* and *Hustle and Flow* are about neglected characters living on the fringe who find a healing in each other. Both movies use a great deal of music to illustrate the souls of their characters.

We sense that the girl has never been treated other than in a beastly manner, and that the man, having lost his wife, is determined not to allow sex to betray his instincts to do good. Yes, I think it is probably against the law to chain a drifter to a radiator, but in a sense these people exist outside the law, society, and common or any kind of sense. Their society consists of the usual locals who seem clueless and remarkably unobservant, leading to remarkable non sequiturs.

There is another woman, the middle-aged pharmacist Angela, played by the sweet S. Epatha Merkerson, to provide Lazarus an alternative to a life of sluts and tramps. But, as for Rae—well, I gather that when compulsive nymphomania passes a certain point, you're simply lost.

After Rae says good-bye to her boyfriend Ronnie (played by Justin Timberlake), who has enlisted in the service for cloudy reasons, she immediately falls to the ground and starts writhing as if under attack by fire ants. This is her way of conveying uncontrollable orgiastic need. A girl that needy, you'd approach like Miss RoboCop.

I love the way that both Samuel Jackson and Christina Ricci take chances like this, and the way Brewer creates characters of unbelievable forbearance, like Ronnie, who is in a more or less constant state of panic attacks and compulsion. And I like the understated way the rural Tennessee locations are used. You have never seen a movie like this before. Then again, you may not hope to. Some good blues music helps carry the day.

I heard some days after the screening that Jackson considers this his best performance. Well, maybe it is. He disappears into the role,

and a good performance requires energy, daring, courage, and intensity, which he supplies in abundance. Few actors could accomplish work at this level with this screenplay. As for Christina Ricci, she was the right actor for this role; she embodies this poor, mixed-up creature and lets you experience both her pain and her hope. Her work defines the boundaries of the thankless.

Blame It on Fidel ★ ★ ★ ½
NO MPAA RATING, 100 m., 2007

Julie Depardieu (Marie), Stefano Accorsi (Fernando), Nina Kervel (Anna), Benjamin Feuillet (Francois), Martine Chevallier (Grandmother), Olivier Perrier (Grandfather). Directed by Julie Gavras and produced by Sylvie Pialat. Screenplay by Gavras, based on the novel by Domitilla Calamai.

Anna is a privileged and happy child, until one day when her parents radically change their style of living. This does not suit her. Like all children, she is profoundly conservative—not in a political way, but by demanding continuity and predictability in her life. One day she lives in a big house with a lovely garden, and the next she and her little brother are suddenly yanked into a grotty flat filled with bearded, chain-smoking young men.

It is 1970 in Paris, at a time of social change. What has happened is that her middle-class parents have become radicalized. Her Spanish father, Fernando (Stefano Accorsi), sufferers from guilt because his family cooperates with Franco's fascist regime, but his sister and her husband are communists. After the husband is arrested and destined to who knows what terrors from the police, Fernando and his French wife, Marie (Julie Depardieu), go to Spain, help his sister and niece escape, and come home as left-wing activists. Their idealism causes them to move into more humble working-class quarters and join forces with a group of Chilean exiles working for the election of the reformer Salvador Allende.

Anna (Nina Kervel) understands all of this only dimly. What she knows is that her world is out of order and her parents are acting oddly. She loves going to a Catholic school but is taken out of the religion class. She loves comic books but is informed that Mickey

Mouse is a fascist. She doesn't like opening her bedroom door and seeing strangers at all hours of the day and night. She is very displeased, and young Kervel, who was around nine when the film was made, gives an astonishing performance, showing that in some ways she is more mature than her parents.

She has an instinctive logic that won't accept all their instructions. Lectured on *group solidarity,* she decides to practice it one day in school. When the nun asks a question and Anna knows the answer, she nevertheless raises her hand along with all the other students, who are wrong. She knows they are wrong, I think, and this is her way of pointing out a flaw in the solidarity theory. Another day she is more specific, asking innocently how group solidarity differs from the behavior of sheep.

In the scenes in which Anna figures, the film is shot almost exclusively from her eye level. This is particularly effective when her parents take her along on a political demonstration, and what she sees are blue jeans, running shoes, and tear gas. It is foolhardy to take a kid to a potentially violent demonstration and foolish of her parents to think she must be instantly radicalized. But they do love her, and so do her grandparents, and so do the nannies who seem to come and go. (One of them, a Cuban refugee, confides in Anna that the communists are barbarians.)

The movie involves the adult children of two famous filmmakers. Its director, Julie Gavras, is the daughter of the Greek director Costa-Gavras, who made *Z, State of Siege,* and other pro-revolutionary films. Interesting to speculate that the screenplay, although based on an Italian novel by Domitilla Calamai, may in some respects reflect the director's own girlhood. And Marie, Anna's mother, is played by Julie Depardieu, daughter of Gerard. Was Julie's father also mercurial, zealous, and changeable, but loving? And were the childhood homes of both women filled with wine-drinking strangers night after night?

It is a blessing that *Blame It on Fidel* doesn't pull back to answer such questions but focuses resolutely on the world as seen through nine-year-old eyes. Kids don't care if millions are starving in South America nearly as much as they care that three-course family meals have been replaced by weird-looking casseroles.

They don't care if there is a God or not nearly as much as they like the nun who teaches divinity class. They're not thrilled that their parents are away in Spain or Chile fighting evil; they want them at home every night. And no matter what Anna is told, she knows these things are true and will not be swayed.

The film contains a surprising amount of understated humor. It is not a grim portrayal of a harsh upbringing, but an affectionate portrait of parents who will be able to change the world before they will be able to change their daughter. Anna and her parents continue to love one another above all, and so this is not an angry film but a wry and observant one. It could have been worse for Anna; consider Sidney Lumet's *Running on Empty* (1988), about the family of radical underground members in hiding. Anna's parents haven't bombed anyone, although they do circulate a lot of petitions.

Blindness ★ ½
R, 120 m., 2008

Julianne Moore (Doctor's Wife), Mark Ruffalo (Doctor), Alice Braga (Woman with Dark Glasses), Danny Glover (Man with Black Eye Patch), Gael Garcia Bernal (Bartender/King of Ward Three). Directed by Fernando Meirelles and produced by Niv Fichman, Andrea Barata Ribeiro, and Sonoko Sakai. Screenplay by Don McKellar, based on the novel by Jose Saramago.

Blindness is one of the most unpleasant, not to say unendurable, films I've ever seen. It is a metaphor about a group of people who survive under great stress, but frankly, I would rather have seen them perish than sit through the final three-quarters of the film. Not only is it despairing and sickening, it's ugly. Denatured, sometimes overexposed, sometimes too shadowy to see, it is an experiment to determine how much you can fool with a print before ending up with mud, intercut with brightly lit milk.

In an unspecified city (Toronto, mostly), an unspecified cause spreads blindness through the population. First a driver goes blind at a traffic light. Then his eye doctor goes blind. And so on, until just about the entire population is blind, except for the doctor's wife. Three wards in a prison are filled with people who are quarantined; armed guards watch them. Then I guess the guards go blind. I am reminded of my Latin teacher, Mrs. Link, making us memorize a phrase every day: *Pone seram, prohibe. Sed quis custodiet ipsos custodes?* *

Many of the imprisoned survivors soon descend into desperation and hunger. The big problem is with Ward Three and its savage leader (Gael Garcia Bernal). Finding a gun, he confiscates all the food and sells it to Ward One in return for jewelry and sexual favors. Oddly enough, I don't recall Ward Two, unless Ward Three was Ward Two and I missed Ward Three, and who cares?

Oh, what an ordeal. Clothes falling off. Nude in the cold. People fighting, dying, and raping. Blundering around and tripping over things. Hitting their heads. Being struck by pipes they don't see coming, swung by people who don't know what they're swinging at. In the midst of the hellhole is the doctor's wife (Julianne Moore), who doesn't know why she can still see, but loyally stays with her husband.

Is she a symbol of a person with sight leading the blind against the evildoers? Ouch, I stumbled! Who put that there? Maybe that's what she is. In a film that doesn't even try to explain the blindness (not that it could), there's room for nothing but symbols and metaphors and the well-diversified group we identify with, which includes an Asian couple (Yusuke Iseya and Yoshino Kimura), the doctor and his wife (Mark Ruffalo and Moore), a wise old black man (Danny Glover), a single woman (Alice Braga), a boy (Mitchell Nye), and a dog (uncredited).

And the noise. Lordy! This is a sound track so aggressive I was cringing in my seat. No merciful slumber during this film. Metal clangs, glass shatters, bullets are fired, people scream, and the volume of these sounds seems cranked up compared to the surrounding dialogue, like they do with TV commercials. My eyes, ears, and patience were assaulted. My hands and feet, OK.

What a pedigree this film has. Directed by Fernando Meirelles. Based on the novel by Portugal's Jose Saramago, winner of the 1998 Nobel Prize. I learn he long resisted offers to make his book into a movie. Not long enough. It is my good fortune to be attending a screening tonight of the newly restored print of *The Godfather*. I'm looking forward to the peace and quiet.

Lock her up; put away the key. But who will guard the guards?

—Juvenal

Mrs. Link told me that someday, and that day may never come, I'd call upon that phrase to do a service for me.

Body of Lies ★ ★ ★
R, 129 m., 2008

Leonardo DiCaprio (Roger Ferris), Russell Crowe (Ed Hoffman), Mark Strong (Hani Salaam), Golshifteh Farahani (Aisha), Oscar Isaac (Bassam), Alon Aboutboul (Al Saleem), Simon McBurney (Garland). Directed by Ridley Scott and produced by Scott and Donald De Line. Screenplay by William Monahan, based on the novel by David Ignatius.

If you take a step back from the realistic locations and terse dialogue, Ridley Scott's *Body of Lies* is a James Bond plot inserted into today's headlines. The film wants to be persuasive in its expertise about modern spy craft, terrorism, the CIA, and Middle East politics. But its hero is a lone ranger who operates in three countries, single-handedly creates a fictitious terrorist organization, and survives explosions, gunfights, and brutal torture. Oh, and he falls in love with a local beauty. And, of course, he speaks Arabic well enough to pass for a local.

This is Roger Ferris (Leonardo DiCaprio), who seems to operate as a self-directed freelancer in the war against a deadly terrorist organization (obviously a double for al-Qaida). His brainstorm is to fabricate a rival terrorist organization out of thin air, fabricate a fictitious leader for it, create a convincing evidence trail, and use it to smoke out Al Saleem, the secretive leader of the real terrorists (a surrogate for Bin Laden). Why will Al Saleem risk everything to come out of hiding? Jealousy, I think. Guarding his turf.

I can imagine a similar story as told by John Le Carre, even right down to the local beauty.

Some of the characters seem worthy of Le Carre, especially Hoffman (Russell Crowe), Ferris's CIA handler, and Hani Salaam (Mark Strong), the brilliant and urbane head of Jordanian security. But Le Carre would never be guilty of such preposterous thriller-style action. Here we have a spy who doesn't come in from the cold, crossed with Jason Bourne.

The most intriguing aspect of Ferris's activities is his growing disillusionment with them. He feels one local comrade has been abandoned to death, and after he sets up an innocent architect to unwittingly play the head of the fictitious terrorist agency, he single-handedly tries to save his life from an inevitable attack. That Ferris survives this man's fate is highly unlikely. And it leads to a situation where his own life is saved by the last-second arrival of the cavalry.

The movie depends on two electronic wonderments. One is the ability of Ferris to maintain instant, effortless cell phone contact with Hoffman, back in Washington. Wearing one of those ear-mounted devices, he seems to keep up a running conversation with his boss, even during perilous situations (his boss is often distracted by taking care of his kids).

The other wonderment is aerial surveillance so precise it can see a particular man walking down a street. The surveillance POV is so stable it's hard to believe it originates from a fast-moving high-altitude spy plane. In discussing Ridley Scott's superior *Black Hawk Down* (2002), I questioned the infrared technology that allowed distant commanders to monitor troop movements on the ground. Many readers informed me that was based on fact. Perhaps the astonishing images in *Body of Lies* is accurate; if so, it's only another step to locating Bin Laden with an aerial eyeball scan.

Ferris's romance in Amman involves a pretty nurse named Aisha (Golshifteh Farahani), who cares for him after he nearly dies in a blast. (One nice touch: A surgeon removes something from his arm and explains, "Bone fragment. Not yours.") The movie is realistic in showing a Muslim woman's difficulties in dating a Westerner; spying eyes are everywhere. It is less realistic in establishing why they are willing to take such a risk, since they're allowed no meaningful conversations to create their relationship. Aisha obviously exists as a conve-

nience of the plot and to set up the film's overwhelmingly unlikely conclusion.

The acting is convincing. DiCaprio makes Ferris almost believable in the midst of absurdities; the screenplay by William Monahan, based on the novel by David Ignatius, portrays him as a man who grows to reject the Iraq war and the role of the CIA in it. Crowe, who gained fifty pounds for his role, always dangerous for a beer drinker, is a remorselessly logical CIA operative. And I particularly admired the work of Mark Strong as the suave Jordanian intelligence chief, who likes little cigars, shady nightclubs, and pretty women, but is absolutely in command of his job.

The bottom line: *Body of Lies* contains enough you can believe, or almost believe, that you wish so much of it weren't sensationally implausible. No one man can withstand such physical ordeals as Ferris undergoes in this film, and I didn't even mention the attack by a pack of possibly rabid dogs. Increasing numbers of thrillers seem to center on heroes who are masochists surrounded by sadists, and I'm growing weary of the horror! Oh, the horror!

Boogie Man: The Lee Atwater Story ★ ★ ★ ½
NO MPAA RATING, 86 m., 2008

Featuring Tucker Eskew, Howard Fineman, Ed Rollins, Michael Dukakis, Eric Alterman, Sam Donaldson, Tom Turnipseed, Terry McAuliffe, Robert Novak, Ishmael Reed, and Mary Matalin. A documentary directed by Stefan Forbes and produced by Forbes and Noland Walker.

When he was a little boy, Lee Atwater pulled an electric cord, and a fryer full of hot grease fell on his little brother Joe, killing him. "He said he heard those screams every single day for the rest of his life," a friend remembers. "He grew up in a world without mercy."

A plausible case can be made that Lee Atwater was the greatest single influence on American politics in the past forty years. He was instrumental in the elections of Ronald Reagan and George H. W. Bush. Karl Rove and Bush 43 were his protégés. It is universally acknowledged that he wrote the modern Republican playbook. "If he had lived," a friend believes, "Bill Clinton would never have been elected president." Atwater predicted before anyone else that Clinton would be the greatest threat to Bush 41. He took the Clintons' Whitewater investment, in which they lost their entire $28,000, and made it the target of a $70 million federal investigation, which produced little of interest except a campaign talking point.

The funny thing was, Atwater didn't much care if he was a Republican or a Democrat. It was only about winning. Looking for opportunities in college, he picked the Young Republicans because there were fewer of them and better opportunities for him. Ever since he managed a campaign for class president in high school, he found himself more at home behind the scenes. In the Young Republicans, he managed Karl Rove's campaign to lead the organization. Members of the YRs at the time believe Rove probably lost, but say Atwater stole the election and then placed the decision into the hands of Vice President George H. W. Bush, who decided in favor of Rove.

Soon he was inside the GOP national party. Having helped Reagan survive Iran-Contra, he more or less appointed himself Bush 41's campaign adviser. He created the infamous Willie Horton ads when Bush ran against Dukakis, and floated rumors that Dukakis was against the Pledge of Allegiance. Asked at the time about the labeling of Dukakis as unpatriotic, young Bush 43 said to call him that would be a "mis-adjective."

Even while running Bush 41's campaign, Atwater was never admitted to the Bush inner circle; Barbara Bush distrusted him, and he came close to being fired. Then Bush started winning primaries. Remembering that presidential year, the Republican strategist Mary Matalin says: "Bush was a wimp and a wuss. Atwater was a hick and a hack." Atwater perfected at that time the technique of the "push poll," where the question itself served to spread suspicion ("Do you believe Gov. Dukakis opposes saluting the flag?"). He and George W. Bush became fast friends soon after they met, Rove adopted his tactics, and Atwater's posthumous influence could be seen in the swift-boating of John Kerry.

Boogie Man: The Lee Atwater Story, a remarkable documentary directed by Stefan Forbes, uses interviews with Atwater's targets and, especially, his old comrades, to paint a remarkable portrait of Atwater, who was charming, funny, smart, and a good enough blues musician to play on David Letterman and cut an album with B. B. King. He was also tortured and driven, and a bipartisan backstabber. Ed Rollins, Atwater's White House boss at the time, says in the doc that Atwater leaked a false story to ABC that "top GOP sources" said Rollins was leading an undercover effort to smear Geraldine Ferraro. Atwater wanted to force Rollins out in a new Bush administration, he says. Rollins hated him. But when Atwater was dying, he begged Rollins to look after him. "They're trying to destroy me," he said.

Atwater was popular with many reporters because he was good for quotes and leaks (or "leaks") and denials that were outrageous but delivered with disarming charm. About Iran-Contra: "We don't discuss how we make sausage." About the Willie Horton ad: "I don't think a lot of Southerners even noticed there was a black man in that ad." He had a genius for creating language that voters would remember. Learning that Tom Turnipseed, a Democratic opponent to his South Carolina congressional candidate, had received shock therapy as a young man, Atwater gleefully translated: "They had to hook him up to jumper cables." This is a fascinating portrait of an almost likable rogue. You'd rather spend time with him than a lot of more upstanding citizens. It makes a companion piece to Oliver Stone's *W.*

Atwater's death by brain tumor at age forty was preceded by deathbed regrets. The film has heartbreaking footage of this boyishly handsome man turned by chemo and radiation into a feeble, bloated caricature of himself. On his deathbed, he called for a Bible and sent telegrams of apology to those he had offended, even Willie Horton. "He said what he had done was bad and wrong," Rollins remembers. "He was scared to death of the afterlife." Mary Matalin, who never trusted or approved of Atwater, says: "After he died they found the Bible still wrapped in its cellophane." She thinks he might have been spinning right to the end.

Unusually for a South Carolina boy, Atwater had absolutely no interest in sports. None, except for professional wrestling. He loved it because it was fake, and everyone knew it was fake, and that was the whole point.

Bottle Shock ★ ★ ★ ½
PG-13, 112 m., 2008

Alan Rickman (Steven Spurrier), Chris Pine (Bo Barrett), Bill Pullman (Jim Barrett), Rachael Taylor (Sam), Freddy Rodriguez (Gustavo Brambilia), Dennis Farina (Maurice), Bradley Whitford (Professor Saunders), Miguel Sandoval (Mr. Garcia), Eliza Dushku (Joe). Directed by Randall Miller and produced by J. Todd Harris. Screenplay by Jody Savin, Miller, and Ross Schwartz.

In 1976, the year of the American bicentennial, the tall ships sailed from Europe to America and back again. But a smaller event was, in its way, no less impressive. In a blind taste-testing held in France, the wines of California's Napa Valley defeated the best the French had to offer—and all the judges were French! A bottle of the winning American vintage, it is said, now rests on exhibit in the Smithsonian Institution.

Bottle Shock is a charming fictionalized version of the victory, "based," as they love to say, "on a true story." Shot in locations near the locale of *Sideways* but set much closer to the earth, it tells the story of a struggling vineyard named Chateau Montelena, deeply in debt with three bank loans. It's run by the hard-driving Jim Barrett (Bill Pullman), who despairs of his layabout, long-haired son Bo (Chris Pine).

Meanwhile, in Paris, we meet a British wine lover named Steven Spurrier (Alan Rickman), whose tiny wine shop is grandly named The Academy of Wine. We never see a single customer in the shop, only the constant visits of a neighboring travel agent, Maurice (Dennis Farina, in full Chicago accent). Maurice encourages Steven by praising his wines, which he samples freely while passing out business advice.

Spurrier (yes, a real man) has been hearing about the wines of California and has an inspiration: His grand-sounding "academy" will sponsor a blind taste test between the wines of the two countries. That he is able to gather a panel of expert judges says much for the confidence of the French, who should have realized it was a dangerous proposition.

In Napa, we meet two other major players: A pretty summer intern named Sam (Rachael Taylor) and an employee of Jim's named Gustavo Brambilia (Freddy Rodriguez—yes, another real character). Gustavo has wine in his bones, if such a thing is possible, and would go on to found a famous vineyard. The two boys raise cash by Gustavo's (partially true) ability to identify any wine and vintage by tasting it, and of course they both fall in love with Sam, who lives for the summer in a shack out of *The Grapes of Wrath.*

The outcome is predictable; anyone who cares even casually knows the Yanks won, but the director milks great entertainment, if not actual suspense, out of the competition. Much of its effect is due to the precise, quietly comic performance by Alan Rickman as Spurrier. "Why do I hate you?" asks Jim Barrett, who resists the competition. "Because you think I'm an asshole," Spurrier replies calmly. "Actually, I'm not an asshole. It's just that I'm British, and, well . . . you're not."

We see him navigating the back roads of Napa in a rented Gremlin, selecting wines for his competition and getting around U.S. customs by convincing twenty-six fellow air travelers to each carry a bottle back for him. That the momentous competition actually took place, that it shook the wine world to its foundations, that it was repeated twenty years later, is a story many people are vaguely familiar with. But *Bottle Shock* is more than the story. It is also about people who love their work, care about it with passion, and talk about it with knowledge. Did you know that a thirsty, struggling vine produces the best wines? It can't just sit there sipping water. It has to struggle—just like Chateau Montelena.

Note: Read the credits to find out how the movie fudges a few names, facts, and vineyards—and what happened to Gustavo.

The Bourne Ultimatum ★ ★ ★ ½
PG-13, 115 m., 2007

Matt Damon (Jason Bourne), Julia Stiles (Nicky Parsons), David Strathairn (Noah Vosen), Scott

Glenn (Ezra Kramer), Paddy Considine (Simon Ross), Edgar Ramirez (Paz), Albert Finney (Dr. Albert Hirsch), Joan Allen (Pam Lundy). Directed by Paul Greengrass and produced by Patrick Crowley, Frank Marshall, and Paul Sandberg. Screenplay by Tony Gilroy, Scott Z. Burns, and George Nolfi, based on the novel by Robert Ludlum.

Run, Jason, run. The Bourne films have taken chases beyond a storytelling technique and made them into the story. Jason Bourne's search for the secret of his identity doesn't involve me in pulsating empathy for his dilemma, but as a MacGuffin, it's a doozy. Some guy finds himself with a fake identity, wants to know who he really is, and spends three movies finding out at breakneck speed. And if the ending of *The Bourne Ultimatum* means anything at all, he may need another movie to clear up the loose ends.

That said, so what? If I don't care what Jason Bourne's real name is, and believe me, I sincerely do not, then I enjoy the movies simply for what they are: skillful exercises in high-tech effects and stunt work, stringing together one preposterous chase after another in a collection of world cities, with Jason apparently piling up frequent flier miles between them.

Ultimatum is a tribute to Bourne's determination, his driving skills, his intelligence in outthinking his masters, and especially his good luck. No real person would be able to survive what happens to him in this movie, for the obvious reason that he would have been killed very early in *The Bourne Identity* (2002) and never have survived to make *The Bourne Supremacy* (2004). That Matt Damon can make this character more convincing than the Road Runner is a tribute to his talent and dedication. It's not often you find a character you care about even if you don't believe he could exist.

This time Bourne is engaged in a desperate hunt through, alphabetically, London, Madrid, Moscow, New York, Paris, Tangier, and Turin, while secret CIA operatives in America track him by a perplexing array of high-tech gadgets and techniques. I know Google claims it will soon be able to see the wax in your ear, but how does the CIA pinpoint Bourne so precisely and yet fail again

and again and again to actually nab him? You'd think he was bin Laden.

And why do they want him so urgently? Yes, he is proof that the CIA runs a murderous secret extra-legal black-ops branch that violates laws here and abroad, but the response to that is: D'oh! The CIA operation, previously called Treadstone, is now called Blackbriar. That'll cover their tracks. It's like if you wanted to conceal the Ford plant you'd call it Maytag. Seeking a hidden meaning in the names, I looked up Treadstone on Wiktionary.com and found it is a "fictional top-secret program of the Central Intelligence Agency in the Jason Bourne book and movie series." Looking up Blackbriar, I found nothing. So they are hidden again from the Wik empire.

In his desperate run to find the people who are chasing him, Jason hooks up in Madrid with the CIA's Nicky Parsons (Julia Stiles), who is given several dozen words to say with somber gravity before Jason is off to Algiers and running through windows and living rooms in the Casbah; I think I recognized some of the same steep streets from *Pepe le Moko*, which is a movie about just staying in the Casbah and hiding there, a strategy by which Jason could have avoided a lot of property damage.

Of course there are sensational car chases, improbable leaps over high places, clever double-reverses, and lightning decisions. The crashes all look fatal, but Bourne survives (funny; I don't remember any air bags being deployed). Sometimes we cut back to CIA headquarters (although surely a secret CIA black-op would not be hidden in its own headquarters) and meet agent Pamela Lundy (Joan Allen), who suspects maybe there is something to be said on Jason's behalf, and her boss, Noah Vosen (David Strathairn), who must have inherited hatred of Bourne as part of the agency's institutional legacy, since he wasn't in the first two movies. And then finally, that shadowy nightmare figure in Bourne's flashbacks comes into focus and, in the time-honored tradition of the Talking Killer, explains everything instead of whacking him right then and there. After which there is another chase.

The director, masterminding formidable effects and stunt teams, is Paul Greengrass

(*United 93, Bourne Supremacy*), and he not only creates (or seems to create) amazingly long takes, but does it without calling attention to them. Whether they actually are unbroken stretches of film or are spliced together by invisible wipes, what counts is that they present such mind-blowing action that I forgot to keep track. There are two kinds of long takes: (1) the kind you're supposed to notice, as in Scorsese's *GoodFellas*, when the mobster enters the restaurant, and (2) the kind you don't notice because the action makes them invisible. Both have their purpose: Scorsese wanted to show how the world unfolded before his hero, and Greengrass wants to show the action without interruption to reinforce the illusion it is all actually happening. Most other long takes are just showing off.

But why, if I liked the movie so much, am I going on like this? Because the movie is complete as itself. You sit there, and the action assaults you, and using words to re-create it would be futile. What actually happens to Jason Bourne is essentially immaterial. What matters is that *something* must happen so he can run away from it, or toward it. Which leads us back to the MacGuffin theory.

Boy A ★ ★ ★½
R, 100 m., 2008

Andrew Garfield (Jack Burridge), Peter Mullan (Terry), Katie Lyons (Michelle), Shaun Evans (Chris). Directed by John Crowley and produced by Lynn Horsford, Nick Marston, and Tally Garner. Screenplay by Mark O'Rowe, based on the novel by Jonathan Trigell.

Eric was a preadolescent with a violent streak and the wrong kind of friend in Philip. Together, they murdered a girl about their age and were put on trial as Boy A and Boy B. They were essentially evil, the prosecutor argued, and deserved the maximum legal sentence. Philip died in prison. Now Eric, at twenty-four, has been paroled and given a new identity: Jack Burridge.

Boy A is based on a novel by Jonathan Trigell, possibly inspired by the real-life British case of two youths seen on a shopping mall's security video as they led away a child who was found dead. Such cases raise the question: Are children who murder indeed essentially evil, or can they heal and change over a period of years? Should society give them a second chance?

That is the fervent belief in this film of Terry (Peter Mullan), the rehabilitation counselor for the renamed Jack (Andrew Garfield). He lectures Jack that he must never, ever reveal his secret. He believes Jack has changed, but society doesn't believe it and will crucify him. So warned, Jack takes a delivery job with a Manchester firm and begins his new life.

Mullan and Garfield anchor the film—Mullan, that splendid Scots actor (*My Name Is Joe*), and Garfield, twenty-four, with his boyish face and friendly grin. When Jack is rebuilding his existence, Terry is his lifeline, who encourages him almost daily. At first the new job goes well. He makes a friend of his job partner, Chris (Shaun Evans). And Michelle (Katie Lyons), the secretary at the office, boldly asks, "Aren't you going to ask me out for a drink, then?"

He does, and they fall sweetly in love. He urgently wants to tell her his secret, but Terry forbids it. One day when Jack and Chris are driving a country road, they come upon a car crash and rescue a young girl from the wreckage. They're hailed as heroes and get their photo on the front page of the *Manchester Evening News*—Jack with his hat brim pulled low over his eyes.

A series of events eventually leads to Jack's exposure by a shameless London tabloid, which runs the photo and breathlessly boasts that they've found Boy A, the embodiment of evil, now free to walk the streets. Jack's life collapses, and he goes on the run. These scenes are the movie's most desperate, ending at Brighton, where he has a fairly improbable chance encounter with Michelle.

By now we have seen, in a pub brawl, that Jack is still capable of violence. In flashbacks, we see boyhood behavior leading up to the tragic murder. And Terry's own son, a layabout, resents his father's clear preference for Boy A. The whole alternative identity falls apart, and Jack/Eric is left homeless and wandering.

Well, should he be forgiven? Judeo-Christian tradition teaches that a boy becomes a man ("reaches the age of reason," Catholics say) at about twelve. Eric looks nine or ten

51

when he commits his crime. Mistreated at home by a drunken father, raped by his brother, bullied at school, he has much to resent, much cruelty to absorb. When we see him at twenty-four, we are inclined to believe he deserves a new chance.

The film, directed by John Crowley and written by Mark O'Rowe, paints an accurate portrait of working-class life in the north of England, the grimness of the streets contrasting with the beauty of the countryside. It is spoken with accents, Mullan's Scots the hardest to understand. He can speak standard English, but the accent is one of his tools. I've never had a problem with his speech because he is such great actor you can forget the words and listen to the music.

He and Andrew Garfield fit well together—both have faces you like on first sight, both have charm, both have warmth. Garfield, just now emerging as a talent to watch (*The Other Boleyn Girl*), inhabits Jack effortlessly, showing his hope, his fears, his nightmares, his doubt that he deserves his new life. And the movie poses the age-old question of forgiveness. At this moment in Chicago, children with handguns kill people. Can we say, "Father, forgive them, for they know not what they do?"

The Boy in the Striped Pajamas ★ ★ ★ ½
PG-13, 94 m., 2008

Asa Butterfield (Bruno), David Thewlis (Father), Vera Farmiga (Mother), Rupert Friend (Lieutenant Kotler), Jack Scanlon (Shmuel), Amber Beattie (Gretel), Sheila Hancock (Grandma), Richard Johnson (Grandpa), Jim Norton (Herr Liszt). Directed by Mark Herman and produced by David Heyman. Screenplay by Herman, based on the novel by John Boyne.

Mark Herman's *The Boy in the Striped Pajamas* depends for its powerful impact on why, and when, it transfers the film's point of view. For almost all of the way, we see events through the eyes of a bright, plucky eight-year-old. Then we begin to look out through the eyes of his parents. Why and when that transfer takes place gathers all of the film's tightly wound tensions and savagely uncoils them. It is not what happens to the boy, which I will not tell you. It is all that happens. All of it, before and after.

Bruno (Asa Butterfield) is a boy growing up in a comfy household in Berlin, circa 1940. His dad (David Thewlis) goes off to the office every day. He's a Nazi official. Bruno doesn't think about that much, but he's impressed by his ground-level view of his father's stature.

One day Bruno gets the unwelcome news that his dad has a new job, and they will all be moving to the country. It'll be a farm, his parents reassure him. Lots of fun. Bruno doesn't want to leave his playmates and his much-loved home. His grandma (Sheila Hancock) doesn't approve of the move either. There seems to be a lot she doesn't approve of, but children are made uneasy by family tension and try to evade it.

There's a big house in the country, surrounded by high walls. It looks too stark and modern to be a farmhouse. Army officials come and go. They fill rooms with smoke as they debate policy and procedures. Bruno can see the farm fields from his bedroom window. He asks his parents why the farmers are wearing striped pajamas. They give him one of those evasive answers that only drive a smart kid to find out for himself.

At the farm, behind barbed wire, he meets a boy about his age. They make friends. They visit as often as they can. The other boy doesn't understand what's going on any more than Bruno does. Their stories were told in a 2007 young adult's novel of the same name by John Boyne, which became a best-seller. I learn the novel tells more about what the child thinks he hears and knows, but the film is implacable in showing where his curiosity leads him.

Other than what *The Boy in the Striped Pajamas* is about, it almost seems to be an orderly story of those British who always know how to speak and behave. Those British? Yes, the actors speak with crisp British accents, which I think is actually more effective than having them speaking with German accents or in subtitles. It dramatizes the way the German professional class internalized Hitler's rule and treated it as business as usual. Charts, graphs, titles, positions, uniforms, promotions, performance evaluations.

How can ordinary professional people proceed in this orderly routine when their business is evil? Easier than we think. I still obsess about those few Enron executives who knew the entire company was a Ponzi scheme. I can't forget the Oregon railroader who had his pension stolen. The laughter of Enron soldiers who joked about killing grandmothers with their phony California "energy crisis." Whenever loyalty to the enterprise becomes more important than simple morality, you will find evil functioning smoothly.

There has not again been evil on the scale of 1939–45. But there has been smaller-scale genocide. Mass murder. Wars generated by lies and propaganda. The Wall Street crash stripped people of their savings, their pensions, their homes, their jobs, their hopes of providing for their families. It happened because a bureaucracy and its status symbols became more important than what it was allegedly doing.

Have I left my subject? I don't think so. *The Boy in the Striped Pajamas* is not only about Germany during the war, although the story it tells is heartbreaking in more than one way. It is about a value system that survives like a virus. Do I think the people responsible for our economic crisis were Nazis? Certainly not. But instead of collecting hundreds of millions of dollars in rewards for denying to themselves what they were doing, I wish they had been forced to flee to Paraguay in submarines.

Brand Upon the Brain! ★ ★ ★ ½
NO MPAA RATING, 95 m., 2007

Sullivan Brown (Young Guy Maddin), Gretchen Krich (Mother), Maya Lawson (Sis), Erik Steffen Maahs (Older Bruno), Katherine E. Scharhon (Chance Hale). Directed by Guy Maddin and produced by Amy E. Jacobson and Gregg Lachow. Screenplay by Maddin and George Toles.

Guy Maddin's new film *Brand Upon the Brain!* exists in the world Maddin has built by hand over several features that seem to be trying to reinvent the silent cinema. Flickering, high-contrast black-and-white images, shot in 8 mm, tell a phantasmagoric story that could be a collaboration between Edgar Allan Poe and Salvador Dali. It's an astonishing film:

weird, obsessed, drawing on subterranean impulses, hypnotic.

The film opens with a man named Guy Maddin in a rowboat. He is a housepainter, answering his mother's summons. She wants two fresh coats of paint on the family's lighthouse, an orphanage that is the only structure on the island of Black Notch.

Once Guy arrives on the island, he is cast back into flashbacks of the troubled childhood he had there with his sister and his sexually jealous mother. She stands fiercely atop the lighthouse, sweeping the island with a powerful searchlight and a phallic telescope, and issuing commands through an "aerophone," an invention of Guy's dad, which allows communication between any two people who love each other, although few seem to love the mother.

The plot, as it always does in a Maddin film, careens wildly in bizarre directions, incorporating material that seems gathered by the handful from silent melodrama. There is a murder mystery involving an orphan named Savage Tom, and an investigation by two teenage detectives named the Light Bulb Kids, who discover suspicious holes in the heads of some of the orphans.

Elements from mad scientist and black magic stories also creep into the plot, while the film hurtles headlong into an assault of stark images.

Guy Maddin, based in Winnipeg, Manitoba, is a pleasant, soft-spoken man who hardly seems a likely source for this feverish filmmaking. His world, his style, and his artistry are all completely original, even when they seem to be echoing old silent films. The echoes seem to come from a parallel universe. In films like *The Saddest Music in the World,* he creates haunting worlds that approach the edge of comedy but never quite tip over.

In a sense, you will enjoy *Brand Upon the Brain!* most if you are either an experienced moviegoer who understands (somehow) what Maddin is doing or a naive filmgoer who doesn't understand that he is doing anything. The average filmgoer might simply be frustrated and confused. For me, Maddin seems to penetrate to the hidden layers beneath the surface of the movies, revealing a surrealistic underworld of fears, fantasies, and obsessions.

53

The Brave One ★ ★ ★ ½
R, 122 m., 2007

Jodie Foster (Erica Bain), Terrence Howard (Sean Mercer), Naveen Andrews (David Kirmani), Nicky Katt (Detective Vitale), Mary Steenburgen (Carol). Directed by Neil Jordan and produced by Susan Downey and Joel Silver. Screenplay by Roderick Taylor, Bruce A. Taylor, and Cynthia Mort.

How many films have there been about victims of violence who turn into avengers? Charles Bronson made five. Kevin Bacon's *Death Sentence* was released two weeks ago. How are we supposed to respond to them? When Bronson's kill count got above fifty, why didn't the scales of justice snap? But now here is Jodie Foster, with a skilled costar and director, to give us a movie that deals, really deals, with the issues involved.

Foster is such a good actress in thrillers: natural, unaffected, threatened, plucky, looking like she means it. And Neil Jordan's *The Brave One* gives her someone strong to play against. Terrence Howard and Foster are perfectly modulated in the kinds of scenes it's difficult for actors to play, where they both know more than they're saying, and they both know it.

Foster plays Erica, a talk jock on a New York radio station. She's engaged to a doctor named David (Naveen Andrews), they're in Central Park late one night, they're mugged, he's killed, and she's badly injured. When Erica is discharged, she's shaking with terror. Her illusion of a safe city life is destroyed. And one day she buys a gun and practices on a shooting range where you can see fear turning into anger in her eyes.

Not long after, she's in a late-night convenience store (note: midnight strolls in Central Park rank second only to all-night stores in their movie crime rates). A holdup takes place, there's violence, she kills a guy to save her life, and she feels—well, how does she feel? Shaken, nauseous maybe, but certainly glad she's alive.

We've started with one of those admirable National Public Radio types whose voice is almost maddeningly sane and patient, and now we have a woman (narrating the movie, sometimes) who sounds more like she doesn't work upstairs over the saloon but she does own a piece of it. Erica has never seen herself as capable of killing, and now she grows addicted to it, offering herself as defenseless bait for criminals and then proving how terribly mistaken they were.

These are the general parameters of all vengeance movies. And often there's a cop on the case who grows curiously close to the killer. With Bronson, it was Vincent Gardenia. With Bacon, Aisha Tyler. With Foster, it's Terrence Howard, playing a detective named Mercer who is assigned to the original mugging, who chats with Erica, who observes there seem to be a lot of people in the city who would like to get even. "Yes," she says, "there must be a lot of us." Us. Curious word choice. Mercer hears it.

Now the movie becomes less about Erica's killings and more about how they make her feel. And about how she and Mercer begin to feel about each other—not in a romantic way, although that scent is in the air, but as smart, wary people who slowly come to realize they share knowledge they dare not admit they share.

Neil Jordan, the director (*The Crying Game, Michael Collins, Breakfast on Pluto, Mona Lisa, The Good Thief*), often makes movies about characters who are not who they seem, and about those who wonder if they can trust them. His characters are not deliberately deceptive but have been pushed into their roles by their lives and don't see a way out. Often you sense in them a desperate urge to confess.

That kind of psychological suspense is what makes *The Brave One* spellbinding. The movie doesn't dine out on action scenes, but regards with great curiosity how these two people will end up. The movie's conclusion has a slight aroma of a studio rewrite to it; I'm not saying Jordan and his writers did revise it, but that the strict logic of the story should lead in a different direction. Where did Hollywood get the conviction that audiences demand an ending that lets them off the hook? Foster doesn't let herself off the hook in *The Brave One*, and we should be as brave as she is.

Brick Lane ★ ★ ★ ½
PG-13, 101 m., 2008

Tannishtha Chatterjee (Nazneen), Satish Kaushik (Chanu), Christopher Simpson (Karim),

Naeema Begum (Shahana), Lana Rahman (Bibi), Zafreen (Hasina). Directed by Sarah Gavron and produced by Alison Owen and Christopher Collins. Screenplay by Abi Morgan and Laura Jones, based on the novel by Monica Ali.

Brick Lane tells a story we think we already know, but we're wrong: It has new things to say within an old formula. It begins with a young woman from Bangladesh, whose mother's suicide causes her father to arrange her marriage with a man now living in London, older than her, whom she has never met. Nazneen (Tannishtha Chatterjee) is a stunning beauty, seventeen when she marries Chanu (Satish Kaushik), who is fat, balding, and easily twenty years older. So this will be a story of her servitude to this beast, right?

Not exactly. Chanu is not a hateful man. He is not a fountain of warmth and understanding and has few insights into his wife, but he is an earnest citizen, a hard worker, and there is sometimes a twinkle in his eye. He likes to sing little songs to himself. The two have three children; their first, a son, is a victim of crib death. The next two are daughters, Shahana (Naeema Begum) and Bibi (Lana Rahman). Time passes. Sex for Nazneen is a matter of closing her eyes and dreaming of her village back home and the sister she receives regular letters from.

Her husband is so unwise as to take loans from the usurer who works their council flat in East London; these loans apparently can never quite be repaid and delay their dream of returning "home." Meanwhile, Chanu pursues his dream of becoming a properly educated Brit, which for him means familiarity with Thackeray, Hume, and other authors not much read anymore, alas, by Brits. He dreams such knowledge will win him a promotion at work, but it doesn't; he loses his job and starts working as a minicab driver. And Nazneen does what other women in the public housing estate do—she buys a sewing machine and does piece work, finishing blue jeans.

That's how Karim (Christopher Simpson) comes into her life—young, handsome, charming, the delivery man for the unfinished jeans. Yes, they fall in love, have sex, talk of her divorce and their marriage. Chanu walks into the flat at times when he must be blind not to understand what's happening—but he doesn't, or at least he doesn't say anything; his method is to remain jolly at all times, as if everything's fine. The performance by Kaushik makes him almost impossible to dislike, although he's no doubt an ordeal to live with.

Now comes the part of the story that caused controversy when Monica Ali's best-selling novel was announced for filming. The attacks of 9/11 take place, anti-Muslim sentiment increases in London, community meetings are held, Karim starts growing a beard and becomes more militant, and then Chanu, of all people, turns into a spokesman against extremist militancy and in favor of a faith based not in politics but in the heart.

His sentiment aroused so much opposition among Muslims in London that the novel could not be filmed on Brick Lane (the center of London's Bangladeshi population), but in fact what Chanu says is deeply felt and seems harmless enough. Without getting into the politics, however, let me say that the film's story surprised me by being less about the illicit love affair and more about the marriage, Nazneen's deepest feelings, and the two daughters—the young one docile, the older one scornful of her father.

"Tell him you don't want to go home," says Shahana. "I've never once heard you tell him what you really feel." But what Nazneen really feels is a surprise even to herself, and the final notes of the film are graceful and tender. Watching it, I was reminded of how many shallow, cynical, vulgar movies I've seen in this early summer season, and how few that truly engage in matters of the heart. *Brick Lane* is about characters who have depth and reality, who change and learn, who have genuine feelings. And it keeps on surprising us, right to the end.

Brideshead Revisited ★ ★ ★
PG-13, 135 m., 2008

Matthew Goode (Charles Ryder), Ben Whishaw (Sebastian Flyte), Hayley Atwell (Julia Flyte), Emma Thompson (Lady Marchmain), Michael Gambon (Lord Marchmain), Ed Stoppard (Bridey Flyte), Felicity Jones (Cordelia Flyte),

Greta Scacchi (Cara), Jonathan Cake (Rex Mottram). Directed by Julian Jarrold and produced by Kevin Loader, Robert Bernstein, and Douglas Rae. Screenplay by Andrew Davies and Jeremy Brock, based on the novel by Evelyn Waugh.

No love story can be wholly satisfying in which the crucial decisions are made by the mother of the loved woman; still less, when she is the mother of both the loved woman and the loved man, and believes she is defending their immortal souls. That is the dilemma in Evelyn Waugh's masterful novel *Brideshead Revisited,* made into an inspired TV miniseries in 1981 and now adapted into a somewhat less inspired film.

The story is told by Charles Ryder (Matthew Goode), who when we meet him is a famous painter, a guest on a postwar Atlantic crossing. On board he encounters Julia Mottram (Hayley Atwell), who, when she was Julia Flyte in the years between the wars, inflamed Charles with love. That he was previously, less ardently in love with her brother Sebastian (Ben Whishaw) was a complication. That he was a middle-class boy infatuated with the entire family—their inherited Marchmain title, their wealth, their history, their great mansion Brideshead—was in a way at the bottom of everything.

The novel begins during the war, when Charles is posted to Brideshead, requisitioned as a military headquarters. His memories come flooding back, bittersweet, mournful. Time rolls back to the autumn day at Oxford, when Charles has moved into his ground-floor rooms just in time for Sebastian to throw up through the open window. Sebastian is a dazzling youth, witty, beautiful, the center of a gay coterie. Charles is not his type, is apparently not even gay, but that for Sebastian is the whole point, and he takes the boy under his arm.

The friendship between Charles and Sebastian during a summer holiday at Brideshead is enchanted and platonic until a tentative but passionate kiss. Then Lady Julia comes into view, and during a later holiday in Venice, she and Charles fall in love—and Sebastian is shattered when he realizes it. To blame his disintegration on lost love would be too simple, however, because from being an alcoholic he rapidly progresses into self-destruction in the hashish and opium dens of Morocco, his youthful perfection turned into a ghastly caricature.

At the center of all of this is Lady Marchmain (Emma Thompson, in a superb performance). Of her son's proclivities she professes a certain vagueness. Of her daughter's love for Charles, she makes it clear that it is not the matter of his lower caste that is the problem (that could be lived with), but the fact that he is an atheist, and the Marchmains have been Roman Catholic from time immemorial.

This theme must have attracted Waugh because he was a Catholic convert and was fascinated by the division between Catholics and Protestants as a social, as well as a religious, issue. Catholicism was once a practice punishable by death in England, and no doubt hidden somewhere in the stones of Brideshead is an ancient "priest hole," used by aristocratic Catholic families to conceal a priest if royal troops came sniffing. Lady Marchmain (and Julia) are not casually Catholic, but believe firmly in the dogma of the Church, and that any unbaptized children would be forbidden the sight of God. Since Charles will not renounce his atheism, he loses Julia, although not before first going as an ambassador for Lady Marchmain to Sebastian—one of the film's best scenes.

There are two peculiar fathers in the film. Lord Marchmain (Michael Gambon), still officially married of course, lives in exile in a Venetian palazzo with his mistress, Cora (Greta Scacchi). Charles's father (Patrick Malahide) is a pronounced eccentric who lives embalmed in a London house and apparently prefers playing chess with himself than conversing with his son. He is a character from Dickens.

Charles is Dickensian in a way, too: the impecunious and parentless youth adrift in an unfamiliar social system. Matthew Goode plays him as a little bland, a mirror for the emotions he attracts. Ben Whishaw steals all of his scenes as Sebastian, the carefree ones and the doom-laden ones. Hayley Atwell, as Julia, could have been drawn a little more carefully. The actress does what she can, but why, really, does Julia marry the odious and insufferable Rex Mottram, who is nothing more than a marked-down Jay Gatsby?

The movie, while elegantly mounted and well-acted, is not the equal of the TV production, in part because so much material had to be compressed into such a shorter time. It is also not the equal of the recent film *Atonement,* which in an oblique way touches on similar issues, especially unrequited love and wartime. But it is a good, sound example of the British period drama; midrange Merchant-Ivory, you could say. And I relished it when Charles's father barely noticed that he had gone away to Oxford—or come back, for that matter.

Bride Wars ★ ★
PG, 90 m., 2009

Kate Hudson (Liv), Anne Hathaway (Emma), Kristen Johnston (Deb), Bryan Greenberg (Nate), Candice Bergen (Marion), Steve Howey (Daniel), Chris Pratt (Fletcher). Directed by Gary Winick and produced by Julie Yorn, Alan Riche, and Kate Hudson. Screenplay by Greg DePaul, Casey Wilson, and June Diane Raphael.

Is there anyone old enough to care about weddings and naive enough to believe *Bride Wars*? Here is a sitcom about consumerism, centering on two bubble-brained women and their vacuous fiancés, and providing them with not a single line that is smart or witty. The dialogue is fiercely on-topic, dictated by the needs of the plot, pounding down the home stretch in clichés, obligatory truisms, and shrieks.

Kate Hudson and Anne Hathaway, who play the would-be brides, are good actors and quick-witted women, here playing characters at a level of intelligence approximating HAL 9000 after he has had his chips pulled. No one can be this superficial and survive without professional care. Compare this film with the wonderful *Rachel Getting Married*, for which Hathaway won an Oscar nomination as Rachel's sister, and now see how she plays a prenuptial Stepford Wife.

I am sure there are women who will enjoy *Bride Wars,* as a man might enjoy a film about cars and Hooters girls. It's like a moving, talking version of *Brides* magazine. Hudson and Hathaway play Liv and Emma, girlhood friends who made a vow to realize their dreams of both getting married at the Plaza.

They're serious. They've been saving up the money for their big days for more than ten years. No daddies are around to fork over.

Liv is a lawyer and has perhaps made some money. Emma, without parents, is a schoolteacher. They both go to the most famous wedding planner in Manhattan (Candice Bergen) and, with *three months' notice,* are able to nail down dates at the Plaza for a June wedding. This is before Madoff forced the wholesale cancellation of reservations.

Do you have any idea what such weddings would cost, after flowers and table decorations, invitations, gowns, limos, a reception, dinner, music, the sweets table, the planner, the event room at the Plaza, and rooms for the wedding parties to get dressed? Plus tips? For enough room to get the bride and her bridesmaids whipped into shape, I think you could all squeeze into an Edwardian Park suite, 1,000 square feet with a king-sized bed, which next June 7 will go for $2,195. Family of the bride? Impecunious out-of-town relatives? Groom and his best men? Have them wait in the hallway.

At least there will be no expenses for a honeymoon, since neither couple ever discusses one. The movie is about the brides and their weddings, and that's that. The grooms are, in fact, remarkably inconsequential, spending a lot of time sitting on couches and watching their brides act out romantic and revenge fantasies. That's because after both weddings are scheduled for the same time, Emma and Liv forget their lifelong bonds of friendship, start feuding, and play practical jokes involving a deep orange suntan, blue-dyed hair, and a projected video from their bachelorette party. They end up in a cat fight in the aisle. Fortunately neither one thinks of introducing E. coli into the punch bowl.

Women and men have different visions of wedding ceremonies. This I know from *Father of the Bride* (1991), with Steve Martin and Diane Keaton as the parents. Martin envisions the swell ceremony he will provide for his daughter: lots of balloons in the backyard and him manning the barbecue grill. Keaton gently corrects him. Even at the time I reviewed the movie, there was a newspaper story about a father who offered his daughter the choice of a nice ceremony or a condo.

Bride Wars is pretty thin soup. The characters have no depth or personality, no quirks or complications, no conversation. The story twist is so obvious from the first shot of two characters talking that they might have well been waving handkerchiefs over their heads and signaling: "Watch this space for further developments." The whole story is narrated by Candice Bergen as the wedding coordinator, who might as well have been instructing us how to carve bars of Ivory Soap into little ducks.

Broken English ★ ★ ½
PG-13, 93 m., 2007

Parker Posey (Nora Wilder), Melvil Poupaud (Julien), Drea de Matteo (Audrey Andrews), Justin Theroux (Nick Gable), Gena Rowlands (Vivien Wilder-Mann), Peter Bogdanovich (Irving Mann), Tim Guinee (Mark Andrews), Josh Hamilton (Charlie Ross). Directed by Zoe Cassavetes and produced by Andrew Fierberg, Jason Kliot, and Joana Vicente. Screenplay by Cassavetes.

First shot, a close-up: Parker Posey. Next shots, mostly close-ups. She smokes, she regards her face in the mirror, she does her hair and gets ready to go to work. She captures perfectly that way women have of arming themselves against the merciless scrutiny of the world. Does any woman, looking in the mirror, think of herself as beautiful?

What Posey brings to this sequence is something I've often felt while watching her movies, even the incomprehensible ones like *Fay Grim*. She stands poised between serene beauty and throwing a shampoo bottle at the mirror. She always looks great, and she always seems dubious and insecure. She can make half her mouth curl into a reluctant smile. But when she fully smiles, she's radiant. She is well cast for *Broken English,* because her character, Nora Wilder, needs precisely that in-between quality.

In some seasons, she falls instantly in love. In others, she sinks into depression. The perfect man comes along and hurts her cruelly. The movie, written and directed by Zoe Cassavetes (daughter of director John Cassavetes and actress Gena Rowlands), is about a woman with a knack for trusting untrustworthy men. She dates an actor (Justin Theroux) and a nice nor-mal guy (Josh Hamilton), and both times confides to her closest friend, Audrey (Drea de Matteo), that this guy might be the one, and both times she is crushingly wrong.

Then at a party she meets Julien (Melvil Poupaud), a French guy who seems too good to be true. Maybe that's where the story breaks down, if only because he *is* too good to be true. It's like he went to a feminist training academy to learn how to treat a woman with gentleness, warmth, and perfect sexual tact. He has to return to Paris. *Quel dommage.* She says she will join him there.

Meanwhile, there are subplots. Audrey is unhappy after five years of marriage. Nora's mother (Gena Rowlands) has wise but worried advice (most women "at your age," she tells Nora, have been snapped up). Nora, who works as the VIP concierge in a Manhattan boutique hotel, works all day to make others happy and then drinks and smokes and mourns about her life to Audrey.

Is Julien the answer? After all, she doesn't even speak French (unlikely, as the VIP concierge in a boutique hotel, but there you have it).

The question clearly becomes, Will she go to Paris and find Julien? If the answer is no, that's a rotten way to treat your audience. If it's yes, your movie is over. So I'm not giving away anything if I point out that, from the point of view of plot dynamics, she must first fail to find Julien and then succeed. As I've pointed out before, some movies give themselves away.

OK. She's in Paris. All she has to do is call Julien. How could there be a problem? Read no further if you can't guess . . . that she loses his number. And that after moping about Paris and meeting an extraordinary number of nice guys, she has a Meet Cute with Julien, but he is sullen and angry because she is on her way to the airport and has been in Paris and did not even call him. Obviously, a perfect Idiot Plot setup, because one word would solve everything. But he glowers between Metro stops, and when he finally discloses what bothers him, she says, "It's really complicated." Which it is not. All together now, as we telepathically chant the four words she needs to say.

So what happens is, *Broken English* establishes a sympathetic character, gets Parker Posey to make her real, and then grinds her in the gears of a plot we cannot believe. Surely these people are complex enough to have their futures settled by more than a Meet Cute and an Idiot Plot that can only hold out for two minutes? When the credits roll, we ask, along with Peggy Lee, "Is that all there is?" There is a very good movie named *Before Sunset* that begins more or less where this one ends. Which tells you something right there.

Brothers at War ★ ★ ★
R, 110 m., 2009

Featuring Jake Rademacher, Captain Isaac Rademacher, Sergeant Joe Rademacher, Jenny Rademacher, Claus Rademacher, Mahmoud Hamid Ali, Edward Allier, Zack Corke, Danelle Fields, Ben Fisher, Kevin Keniston, Frank McCann, Brandon "Mongo" Phillips, and Robert Smallwood. A documentary directed by Jake Rademacher and produced by Rademacher and Norman S. Powell.

I've been waiting for this film since the early days of the war in Iraq. *Brothers at War* is an honest, on-the-ground documentary about the lives of Americans fighting there. It has no spin. It's not left or right. I don't recall if it even mentions President Bush. It's not pro- or antiwar, although obviously the two brothers fighting there support it. It is simply about men and women.

The film is about the men in the Rademacher family from Decatur, Illinois. Jake, the oldest, always planned to go into the military but didn't make it into West Point and found himself as an actor. Isaac, the next, graduated top of his class at West Point and married his classmate Jenny. Joe, next in line, enlisted and was top of his class at Army Ranger school. The brothers were very close growing up, but Jake sensed a distance growing as they came home on leave. He felt he could never know their experience.

What Jake decided to do was visit them in Iraq and film a documentary of them at work—easier because Sergeant Joe was assigned to Captain Isaac's unit. This sounds simple enough, but it involved investment, logistical problems, and danger under fire. The result is a film that benefits from an inside view, as Jake is attached to Isaac's group and

follows them for extended periods under fire in the Sunni Triangle and on patrol on the Syrian border. It is clear that the brothers are expert soldiers.

But this is not a war film. It is a life film, and its scenes filmed at home are no less powerful than those filmed in Iraq. Jenny Rademacher served in Kuwait and elsewhere, then has their child. Isaac is deployed to Iraq soon after, and when he returns home it's to a daughter who has never met him. Jake films the homecomings and departures of both brothers, attends family gatherings, and watches Isaac as he trains troops of the Iraqi Army. The filmmakers are often under fire, and a man is killed on one mission by a roadside bomb.

Jake's entree gives him access to many moments of the kind you never see on the news. Nicknamed "Hollywood" and such an accustomed daily sight that soldiers are not self-conscious around his camera, he listens in on small talk, shop talk, and gab sessions. He watches during meals. He walks along on a door-to-door operation. He looks at houses and roadsides in a way that recognizes they may harbor his death. He gives a stark idea of the heat, the dust, the desolate landscape.

I've reviewed many documentaries about Iraq. All of them have been antiwar. "Why don't you ever review a pro-war documentary?" readers asked me. The answer was simple: There weren't any. There still aren't, because no one in this film argues in favor of the war—or against it, either. What you hear is guarded optimism, pride in the work, loyalty to the service. This is deep patriotism. It involves risking your life for your country out of a sense of duty.

Every time he saw Isaac or Joe deployed, Jake says, he wondered if he would ever see them again. In filming his documentary, he feels he has walked a little way in their shoes. As is often the case among men, the brothers leave these things unspoken. But now Jake sees their war as more of a reality and less of an abstraction. He invites his audience to do the same.

The Brothers Bloom ★ ★ ½
PG-13, 109 m., 2009

Rachel Weisz (Penelope), Adrien Brody (Bloom), Mark Ruffalo (Stephen), Rinko

Kikuchi (Bang Bang), Maximilian Schell (Diamond Dog), Robbie Coltrane (The Curator), Ricky Jay (Narrator). Directed by Rian Johnson and produced by Ram Bergman, James D. Stern, and Wendy Japhet. Screenplay by Johnson.

Those con-man movies are best that con the audience. We should think at some point that everything is for real or, even better, that we can see through it when we can't. I offer as examples works by the master of the genre, David Mamet: *House of Games, The Spanish Prisoner,* and *Redbelt.*

Rian Johnson's new film *The Brothers Bloom* lets us in on the con and then fools us. It does that in an interesting way. It gives us Stephen (Mark Ruffalo) and Bloom (Adrien Brody), and I might as well get this out of the way: I don't know why they're called the "brothers" Bloom when that's the first name of one, and neither seems to have a family name. Maybe I missed something.

From childhood, Stephen fabricates con scenarios and creates the characters and scripts for his younger brother, Bloom, to join him in. When they're adults, Stephen's girlfriend Bang Bang (Rinko Kikuchi), who speaks extremely rarely, is mostly involved as a passive bystander, witness, validator, or sometimes more. For Stephen, life is a con and he's living it. For Bloom, the game is getting old.

They meet a promising mark named Penelope (Rachel Weisz) who is rich, beautiful, and lonely, even though most women who are rich and beautiful don't have a crushing problem with loneliness. She falls into a scheme fashioned by the brothers, and I will not specify which falls in love with her, but one does, and then . . . I have to watch my step here. The brothers are such perfectionists that they like to involve as many marks as they can. Let's leave it at that.

At a certain point we think we're in on the moves of the con, and then we think we're not, and then we're not sure, and then we're wrong, and then we're right, and then we're wrong again, and we're entertained up to another certain point, and then we vote with Bloom: The game gets old. Or is it Stephen who finds that out? Bloom complains, "I'm

tired of living a scripted life." We're tired on his behalf. And on our own.

The problem with the movie is that the cons have too many encores and curtain calls. We tire of being (rhymes with "perked") off. When an exercise seems to continue for its own sake, it should sense it has lost its audience, take a bow, and sit down. And even then, *The Brothers Bloom* has another twist that might actually be moving, if we weren't by this time so paranoid. As George Burns once said, "Sincerity is everything. If you can fake that, you've got it made." A splendid statement, and I know it applies to this movie, but I'm not quite sure how.

This is a period picture but a little hazy as to which period. It's the second feature by the thirty-five-year-old Rian Johnson, who made the acclaimed Sundance "originality" winner *Brick* in 2005. That was a film noir crime story transplanted to a California high school. Now we have *The Sting* visiting eastern Europe. *The Brothers Bloom* was filmed for a reported $20 million, which was chickenfeed if you consider the locations in Montenegro, Serbia, Romania, and the Czech Republic.

The acting is a delight. Rachel Weisz creates a New Jersey heiress who is delightfully ditzy. Ruffalo is sincere at all times, even when he's not. Adrien Brody is so smooth his logical contradictions slide right past: He makes them sound as if they *must* mean something. The enigmatic Bang Bang, who acts as an assistant to the brothers, never says a word but often seems as if she's about to. And Johnson wisely hired Ricky Jay, veteran of so many Mamet films, to provide a narration in that voice that suggests he knows a lot more than he's telling.

Johnson has a fertile imagination, a way with sly comedy, and a yearning for the fantastical. But he needs to tend to his nuts and bolts and meat and potatoes. The film is just too smug and pleased with itself; as a general rule, an exercise in style needs to convince us it cares about more than style. Lesson in point: *The Life Aquatic with Steve Zissou.* The movie is lively at times, it's lovely to look at, and the actors are persuasive in very difficult material. But around and around it goes, and where it stops, nobody by that point much cares.

The Bucket List ★
PG-13, 97 m., 2008

Jack Nicholson (Edward Cole), Morgan Freeman (Carter Chambers), Sean Hayes (Thomas), Rob Morrow (Dr. Hollins), Beverly Todd (Virginia Chambers). Directed by Rob Reiner and produced by Craig Zadan, Neil Meron, and Alan Greisman. Screenplay by Justin Zackham.

The Bucket List is a movie about two old codgers who are nothing like people, both suffering from cancer that is nothing like cancer, and setting off on adventures that are nothing like possible. I urgently advise hospitals: Do not make the DVD available to your patients; there may be an outbreak of bedpans thrown at TV screens.

The film opens with yet another voice-over narration by Morgan Freeman, extolling the saintly virtues of a white person who deserves our reverence. His voice takes on a sort of wonderment as he speaks of the man's greatness; it was a note that worked in *The Shawshank Redemption* and *Million Dollar Baby,* but not here, not when he is talking of a character played by Jack Nicholson, for whom lovability is not a strong suit.

Nicholson plays Edward, an enormously rich man of about seventy, who has been diagnosed with cancer, given a year to live, and is sharing a room with Carter (Freeman), about the same age, same prognosis. Why does a billionaire not have a private room? Why, because Edward owns the hospital, and he has a policy that all patients must double up, so it would look bad if he didn't.

This is only one among countless details the movie gets wrong. Doesn't Edward know that hospitals make lotsa profits by offering private rooms, "concierge service," etc.? The fact is, Edward and Carter must be roommates to set up their Meet Cute, during which they first rub each other the wrong way, and then have an orgy of male bonding. Turns out Carter has a "bucket list" of things he should do before he kicks the bucket. Edward embraces this idea, announces, "Hell, all I have is money," and treats Carter to an around-the-world trip in his private airplane, during which they will, let's see, I have the itinerary right here, visit the pyramids, the Taj Mahal, Hong Kong, the French Riviera, and the Himalayas.

Carter is faithfully married to his loving wife, Virginia (Beverly Todd), who is remarkably restrained about seeing her dying husband off on this madcap folly. She doesn't take it well, but I know wives who would call for the boys with butterfly nets. Edward, after four divorces, has no restraints, plenty of regrets, and uses his generosity to mask egotism, selfishness, and the imposition of his goofy whim on poor Carter. That his behavior is seen as somehow redemptive is perhaps the movie's weirdest fantasy. Meanwhile, the codgers have pseudo-profound conversations about the Meaning of It All, and Carter's superior humanity begins to soak in for the irascible Edward.

The movie, directed by Rob Reiner, is written by Justin Zackham, who must be very optimistic indeed if he doesn't know that there is nothing like a serious illness to bring you to the end of sitcom clichés. I've never had chemo, as Edward and Carter must endure, but I have had cancer, and believe me, during convalescence after surgery the *last* item on your bucket list is climbing a Himalaya. It's more likely to be topped by keeping down a full meal, having a triumphant bowel movement, keeping your energy up in the afternoon, letting your loved ones know you love them, and convincing the doc your reports of pain are real and not merely disguising your desire to become a drug addict. To be sure, the movie includes plenty of details about discomfort in the toilet, but they're put on hold once the trots are replaced by the globe-trotting.

Edward and Carter fly off on their odyssey, during which the only realistic detail is the interior of Edward's private jet. Other locations are created, all too obviously, by special effects; the boys in front of the pyramids look about as convincing as Abbot and Costello wearing pith helmets in front of a painted backdrop. Meanwhile, we wait patiently for Edward to realize his inner humanity, reach out to his estranged daughter, and learn all the other life lessons Carter has to bestow. All Carter gets out of it is months away from his beloved family, and the opportunity to be a moral cheering section for Edward's conversion.

I'm thinking, just once, couldn't a movie open with the voice-over telling us what a great guy the Morgan Freeman character was? Nicholson could say, "I was a rich, unpleasant, selfish jerk, and this wise, nice man taught me to feel hope and love." Yeah, that would be nice. Because what's so great about Edward, anyway? He throws his money around like a pig and makes Carter come along for the ride. So what?

There are movies that find humor, albeit perhaps of a bitter, sardonic nature, in cancer. Some of them show incredible bravery, as in Mike Nichols's *Wit*, with its great performance by Emma Thompson. *The Bucket List* thinks dying of cancer is a laff riot, followed by a dime-store epiphany. The sole redeeming merit of the film is the steady work by Morgan Freeman, who has appeared in more than one embarrassing movie but never embarrassed himself. Maybe it's not Jack Nicholson's fault that his role cries out to be overplayed, but it's his fate, and ours.

Bug ★ ★ ★ ½
R, 110 m., 2007

Ashley Judd (Agnes White), Michael Shannon (Peter Evans), Harry Connick Jr. (Jerry Goss), Lynn Collins (R.C.), Brian F. O'Byrne (Dr. Sweet). Directed by William Friedkin and produced by Michael Ohoven, Holly Wiersma, Malcolm Petal, and Kimberly C. Anderson. Screenplay by Tracy Letts, based on his play.

William Friedkin's *Bug* begins as an ominous rumble of unease and builds to a shriek. The last twenty minutes are searingly intense: A paranoid personality finds its mate, and they race each other into madness. For Friedkin, director of *The Exorcist*, it's a work of headlong passion.

Its stars, Ashley Judd and Michael Shannon, achieve a kind of manic intensity that's frightening not just in itself but because you almost fear for the actors. They're working without a net.

The film is based on a play by Tracy Letts, an actor and playwright at Chicago's Steppenwolf Theatre, that was a hit in Chicago and New York. In the film, we meet Agnes (Judd), a waitress in a honky-tonk lesbian bar, living in a shabby motel. Her violent ex-husband (Harry Connick Jr.), just out on parole, walks back into her life, still violent. At about the same time her gay friend, R.C. (Lynn Collins), drags in a stray with haunted eyes. This is the polite stranger named Peter (Shannon), who says he doesn't want sex or anything else, is attentive and courteous, and is invited by Agnes to spend the night even though he seems (to us) like the embodiment of menace.

The story involves this man's obsession with bugs that he believes infect his cells and may have been implanted by the government during his treatment for obscure causes after military service in the Gulf. We think he's crazy. Agnes listens and nods and doesn't want him to leave; she feels safer around him. He begins to seem weirder. This doesn't bother her. With mounting urgency, she begins to share his obsession with bugs, and together they hurtle headlong into a paranoid fantasy that ties together in one perfect conspiracy all of the suspicions they've ever had about anything. There is a scene we're not prepared for, in which they're peering into a cheap microscope and seeing whatever they think they see.

Peter is mad, and Agnes's personality seems to need him to express its own madness. Ashley Judd's final monologue is a sustained cry of nonstop breathless panic, twisted logic, and sudden frantic insight that is a kind of behavior very rarely risked in or out of the movies. It may not be Shakespeare, but it's not any easier.

Shannon, a member of the Red Orchid Theatre in Chicago, delivers his own nonstop, rapid-fire monologue of madness; he has a frightening speech that scares the audience but makes perfect sense to Agnes. His focus and concentration compares in some ways to Peter Greene's work in Lodge Kerrigan's frightening *Clean, Shaven*.

The film is lean, direct, unrelenting. A lot of it takes place in the motel room, which by the end has been turned into an eerie cave lined with aluminum foil, a sort of psychic air raid shelter against government emissions or who knows what else? "They're watching us," Peter says.

The thing about *Bug* is that we're not scared for ourselves so much as for the characters in the movie. Judd and Shannon bravely cast all restraint aside and allow themselves to be seen as raw, terrified, and mad. The core of the film involves how quickly Judd's character falls into sympathy with Shannon's. She seems like a potential paranoid primed to be activated, and yet her transformation never seems hurried and is always convincing.

For Friedkin, the film is a return to form after some disappointments like *Jade*. It feels like a young man's picture, filled with edge and energy. Some reviews have criticized *Bug* for revealing its origins as a play, since most of it takes place on one set. But of course it does. There is nothing here to "open up" and every reason to create a claustrophobic feel. Paranoia shuts down into a desperate focus. It doesn't spread its wings and fly.

Burn After Reading ★ ★ ★

R, 96 m., 2008

George Clooney (Harry Pfarrer), Frances McDormand (Linda Litzke), John Malkovich (Osborne Cox), Tilda Swinton (Katie Cox), Brad Pitt (Chad Feldheimer), Richard Jenkins (Ted Treffon), J. K. Simmons (CIA Boss), David Rasche (CIA Officer). Directed by Ethan Coen and Joel Coen and produced by Tim Bevan, Eric Fellner, Ethan Coen, and Joel Coen. Screenplay by Ethan Coen and Joel Coen.

The Coen brothers' *Burn After Reading* is a screwball comedy that occasionally becomes something more. The characters are zany, the plot coils upon itself with dizzy zeal, and the roles seem like a perfect fit for the actors—yes, even Brad Pitt, as Chad, a gum-chewing, fuzzy-headed physical fitness instructor. I've always thought of him as a fine actor, but here he reveals a dimension that, shall I say, we haven't seen before.

What do I mean by "something more"? There is a poignancy in the roles played by Frances McDormand and George Clooney, both looking for love in all the wrong places. She plays Linda Litzke, one of Chad's fellow instructors, and is looking for her perfect match on the Web. This despite her conviction that she's far from perfect. In a scene of astonishing frankness (using a body double, I think) she submits to a merciless going-over by a plastic surgeon, and decides to have some

work done on her thighs, abdomen, breasts, underarms, and eyes. "I've gotten about as far as this body can take me," she decides.

Clooney is a happily married man, if only he knew it, named Harry Pfarrer. (It's one of those Jack Lemmony kind of names that sound like a cough, but I don't remember anyone saying it in the movie.) Harry also looks for dates on the Web, and, in general terms, will happily date anyone. He and Linda meet and seem to like each other, and then Linda and Chad find a computer disc at the gym. They read it and find it belongs to a CIA man named Osborne Cox (John Malkovich), who has just been fired for alcoholism. Cox is married to Katie (Tilda Swinton), who is also having an affair with Harry. You see how it goes.

No need to describe the plot. It goes around and around and comes out here, there, everywhere. All nicely put together, of course, but as an exercise, not an imperative. The movie's success depends on the characters and the dialogue. Linda and Chad, who remind me a little of Rupert and Masha in *The King of Comedy*, try to peddle their disc to the Russian embassy. Anything to raise money for that plastic surgery. The CIA, baffled, gets involved. A gung-ho officer (David Rasche), confused but determined, reports to his CIA boss (J. K. Simmons, *Juno*'s dad). The boss doesn't have much dialogue, but every line is a punch line.

The Malkovich character is a right proper SOB, one of those drunks who thinks he's not an alcoholic because he prudently watches the second hand on the clock until it's precisely five o'clock. He's a snarky, shaved-headed, bow-tie-wearing misanthrope who would be utterly amazed if he knew how his files got into the hands of two peons at a gym.

As for Clooney, in one movie he's the improbably handsome, superintelligent hero, and in the next, he's the forlorn doofus. You wouldn't believe what he's constructing in his basement. The Coens say that this film completes their "idiot trilogy" with Clooney, after *O Brother, Where Art Thou?* (2000) and *Intolerable Cruelty* (2003). Clooney as an idiot? As to the manner born.

Frances McDormand is wonderful. Here she channels a little of the go-getter determination of her police chief in *Fargo*. She's innocent of deep thoughts, but nothing can stop her. From the first time I noticed her, in a great scene with Gene Hackman in *Mississippi Burning*, she has had that rare ability to seem correctly cast in every role.

This is not a great Coen brothers film. Nor is it one of their bewildering excursions off the deep end. It's funny, sometimes delightful, sometimes a little sad, with dialogue that sounds perfectly logical until you listen a little more carefully and realize all of these people are mad.

The movie is only ninety-six minutes long. That's long enough for a movie, but this time, I dunno, I thought the end felt like it arrived a little arbitrarily. I must be wrong, because I can't figure out what could have followed next. Not even the device in the basement would have been around for another chapter.

C

Cadillac Records ★ ★ ★
R, 108 m., 2008

Adrien Brody (Leonard Chess), Jeffrey Wright (Muddy Waters), Gabrielle Union (Geneva Wade), Columbus Short (Little Walter), Cedric the Entertainer (Willie Dixon), Emmanuelle Chriqui (Revetta Chess), Eamonn Walker (Howlin' Wolf), Mos Def (Chuck Berry), Beyonce Knowles (Etta James). Directed by Darnell Martin and produced by Andrew Lack and Sofia Sondervan. Screenplay by Martin.

An argument could be made that modern rock 'n' roll was launched not at Sun Records in Memphis, but at Chicago's Chess Records, 2120 S. Michigan Ave., and its earlier South Side locations since the late 1940s. The Rolling Stones even recorded a song named after the address. The great Chess roster included Muddy Waters, Howlin' Wolf, Etta James, Willie Dixon, Chuck Berry, and Little Walter. They first made Chicago the home of the blues, and then rhythm and blues, which, as they say, had a child and named it rock 'n' roll.

Cadillac Records is an account of the Chess story that depends more on music than history, which is perhaps as it should be. The film is a fascinating record of the evolution of a black musical style and the tangled motives of the white men who had an instinct for it. The Chess brothers, Leonard and Phil, walked into neighborhoods that were dicey for white men after midnight, packed firearms, found or were found by the most gifted musicians of the emerging urban music, and recorded them in a studio so small it forced the sound out into the world.

This movie sidesteps the existence of Phil Chess, now living in Arizona, and focuses on the enigmatic, chain-smoking Leonard (Adrien Brody). Starting with an early liaison with Muddy Waters, who in effect became his creative partner, he visited "race music" radio stations in the South with his artists and payola, found and/or created a demand, and gave his musicians shiny new Cadillacs but never a good look at their royalties. Muddy (Jeffrey Wright) was probably paid only a share of the money he earned, but the more ferocious

Howlin' Wolf (Eamonn Walker), seemingly less sophisticated, held on to his money, made his own deals, and incredibly even paid health benefits for the members of his band.

It is part of the legend that Muddy was nice, Howlin' was scary, and they disliked each other. In the film, they are guarded, but civil and fierce competitors. Walker plays the six-foot-six Wolf as a scowler who somehow from that height looks up at people under hooded eyes and appears willing to slice you just for the convenience. The real Howlin' Wolf must have been more complex; he couldn't read or write until he was past forty, but then he earned his high school equivalency diploma and studied accounting, an excellent subject for an associate of Leonard Chess.

Did Chess love the music? Brody's performance and the screenplay by director Darnell Martin leave that question a little cloudy. Certainly, he had good taste and an aggressive business instinct, and he didn't sit in an office in the Loop, but was behind the bar at the Macomba Lounge on Saturday nights in the 1950s, when some of his more alarming customers must have figured, hey, a white man that crazy, maybe it's not a good idea to mess with him.

Leonard was married but maintained a wall between his business and his family. Martin's movie speculates that later in his career he may have fallen in love with his new discovery Etta James (Beyonce Knowles). If so, romance didn't blind him to her gifts, and in a movie where the actors do most of their own singing, her performances are inspired and persuasive.

The Chess artists had an influence in more than one way on white rock singers. The Beach Boys' "Surfing USA" has the same melody as Chuck Berry's "Sweet Little Sixteen." Frank Zappa borrowed Howlin's favorite exclamation, "Great Googley Moogley!" The Rolling Stones, who acknowledged their Chicago influences, paid a pilgrimage to South Michigan Ave. and arranged a European tour for Chess stars, and Keith Richards talked Chuck Berry into the concert shown in the great doc *Hail! Hail! Rock and Roll* and played backup guitar.

Given the number of characters and the

time covered, Darnell Martin does an effective job of sketching the backgrounds of some of her subjects, and doesn't go out of her way to indict Leonard's business methods. (Did the singers know their Cadillacs were paid for from their own money?) There is a poignant scene where Leonard arranges the first meeting between Etta James and her white father (who was—are you ready for this?—Minnesota Fats), and a close look at the troubled but durable marriage of Muddy Waters and his wife, Geneva Wade (Gabrielle Union).

The casting throughout is successful. Columbus Short suggests the building inner torments of Little Walter, and Cedric the Entertainer plays the singer-songwriter Willie Dixon as a creator and synthesizer. Nobody can really play Chuck Berry, but Mos Def does a great duck walk.

Eamonn Walker, at six-foot-one, is five inches shy of the towering Howlin', but he evokes presence and intimidation. Sometimes I'm amazed at actors. Seeing Howlin' Wolf bring danger into the room in this film, you'd never guess Walker started as a dancer, was a social worker, acts in Shakespeare, and is married to a novelist. Could any of the regulars at 2120 S. Michigan Ave. have guessed they would be instrumental in creating a music that would dominate the entire world for the next fifty years?

The Cake Eaters ★ ★ ★
NO MPAA RATING, 95 m., 2009

Kristen Stewart (Georgia), Aaron Stanford (Beagle), Bruce Dern (Easy), Elizabeth Ashley (Marge), Jayce Bartok (Guy), Melissa Leo (Ceci), Miriam Shor (Stephanie). Directed by Mary Stuart Masterson and produced by Masterson, Allen Bain, Darren Goldberg, Elisa Pugliese, and Jesse Scolaro. Screenplay by Jayce Bartok.

Kristen Stewart has been in feature films since 2003, but this year, still only eighteen, she became a big star as a vampire's girlfriend in *Twilight*. Now comes her remarkable performance in *The Cake Eaters*, made two years ago, showing her as a very different kind of lover in a very different kind of film. It's the directorial debut of Mary Stuart Masterson, herself a fine actress (*Fried Green Tomatoes*).

Stewart plays Georgia, a high school student who has a degenerative muscular disease. It causes her to walk unsteadily, stand crookedly and, as Beagle tells her, talk like she's had a few beers. Beagle (Aaron Stanford) is the kid she meets at a flea market. She asks him to come over to her house that evening. Beagle says, uh . . . ah . . . yeah, sure. He has no problems with her condition; it's just that he's terrified of girls.

Beagle is going through a rough time emotionally. His mom has recently died after a long ordeal with cancer. His dad, Easy (Bruce Dern), is a good guy and in his corner. His brother, Guy (Jayce Bartok, writer of the screenplay), sat out the entire illness in New York, seeking success as a rock or folk star, and has returned just too late for the funeral. Beagle is enraged at him. Beagle cared for his mom the whole three years.

Georgia, as played by Stewart, is not looking for sympathy. She's looking for sex and is very forthright about that. When a hairdresser asks her if she isn't rushing things, she says simply, "I don't have a lot of time." Why did she choose Beagle? He's OK-looking, he's not bothered by her disability, you can see he's gentle, and perhaps she suspects she can get him to do what she wants.

Masterson and her cast make these characters, and others, into specific people and not elements in a docudrama. Nobody is a "type," certainly not Georgia's grandmother Marge (Elizabeth Ashley), the kind of woman you know once raised some hell and hasn't completely stopped. When Beagle happens to see his dad kissing Marge, so soon after the funeral, he's devastated. This creates enormous tension among all three men in the family and a connection between Beagle and Georgia they're not aware of.

Beagle is three or four years older than Georgia, but behind her in emotional development, I sense. He's very naive. Georgia's mother (Melissa Leo, this year's Oscar nominee) is suspicious of him but has no hint of her daughter's plans for the unsuspecting boy. And Beagle's father is reassuring: "My boy has no game in that area, I promise you."

So there are three simultaneous romances:

Beagle and Georgia, Easy and Marge, and I forgot to mention Guy, who has a local girl named Stephanie (Miriam Shor), furious at him because he proposed marriage and then left for New York without even saying good-bye.

You might think with all of these plot lines and colorful characters, the movie turns into a carnival. Not at all. I won't say why. I'll only say it all leaves us feeling good about most of them. Masterson, like many actors, is an assured director even in her debut; working with her brother Pete as cinematographer, she creates a spell and a tenderness, and pushes exactly as far as this story should go.

Canvas ★ ★ ★
PG-13, 100 m., 2007

Joe Pantoliano (John Marino), Marcia Gay Harden (Mary Marino), Devon Gearhart (Chris Marino), Sophia Bairley (Dawn). Directed by Joseph Greco and produced by Joe Pantoliano and Bill Erfurth. Screenplay by Greco.

Canvas is a serious film about mental illness and a sentimental heart-warmer, and it succeeds in both ways. It tells the story of a ten-year-old whose mother is schizophrenic and whose father is loyal and loving but stretched almost beyond his endurance. The portrayal of schizophrenia in the film has been praised by mental health experts as unusually accurate and sympathetic; the story of the boy and his dad is a portrait of love under enormous stress.

Writer-director Joseph Greco says the film, his first feature, was influenced by his own childhood with a schizophrenic mother. Even the father's determination to build a sailboat comes from Greco's own life. His film benefits from persuasive, moving performances from all three leads: Joe Pantoliano as John Marino, a construction worker; Marcia Gay Harden as Mary, his wife; and Devon Gearhart as their young son, Chris. There is also an affecting performance by Sophia Bairley as Dawn, a schoolmate who becomes Chris's friend and confidant.

As the film opens, Mary is just a little too demonstrative in her love for Chris, whom she possibly hasn't seen for a while. That night Chris is awakened by flashing blue lights through the window; his mother has had a panic attack, and his father and the police are bringing her back to the house. She is under medication, which doesn't seem to be working, and on another night, when she runs wild through a rainstorm, the police handcuff her "for her own safety," and she is committed to an asylum.

All of this is very hard on Chris, as cruel schoolmates taunt him about his crazy mother. When his father, desperate for distraction, begins to build a sailboat in the driveway, Chris begins to hear that his dad is crazy, too. He is a wise, solemn kid, but it all begins to get to him, especially when his mother inappropriately crashes his precious birthday party for a few friends in a local arcade.

The more movies I see, the more I wonder at what actors can do. Consider Joe Pantoliano. Famous for *The Sopranos*, established as a character actor playing gangster and comic types, known by everyone including himself as "Joey Pants," he has a role here that most people would never think of him for, and he brings it tenderness and depth. He still loves his wife and yearns for her return to health. He loves his son but isn't always perceptive enough of his needs. He spends money that he doesn't have on the boat. He has worked hard for twenty years and has a boss who isn't fair with him. Pantoliano brings to all of these dimensions a confidence and understanding that is a revelation; how many other actors are trapped by typecasting and have such unexplored regions within their talent?

Marcia Gay Harden finds a fine balance between madness and the temptations of overacting. Yes, she runs wild sometimes but always as a human being, not as a caricature. And as the son, Devon Gearhart, who is at the center of many of the crucial scenes, has an unaffected and natural sincerity that is effective and convincing. I have noticed recently several performances by children that have a simplicity and grace that adults can only envy.

The film's ending may be more upbeat than the characters could hope for in real life, but it doesn't cave in to neat solutions. One scene in particular looks like a manufactured happy ending until the camera pulls back and provides a context for it. *Canvas* is a heart-warmer, as I said, a touching story of these people for whom the only response to mental illness is love.

Cape of Good Hope ★ ★ ★

PG-13, 107 m., 2006

Debbie Brown (Kate), Eriq Ebouaney (Jean Claude), Nthati Moshesh (Lindiwe), Morne Visser (Morne), Quanita Adams (Sharifa), David Isaacs (Habib), Kamo Masilo (Thabo), Nick Boraine (Stephen van Heern). Directed by Mark Bamford and produced by Suzanne Kay Bamford and Genevieve Hofmeyr. Screenplay by Mark and Suzanne Kay Bamford.

In Cape Town, one of the most beautiful cities on Earth, we meet people who move uncertainly into their own futures. The iron curtain separating the races has lifted, and they are all (except one) citizens on equal footing, but Mark Bamford's *Cape of Good Hope* is a postapartheid film in which the characters are less concerned with politics than with matters of the heart. Of course, political and economic concerns drift in (they do regardless of whether we admit it), but the title is a good one, standing not only for that point at the bottom of Africa where the Indian and Atlantic oceans meet, but also for good hope itself, about love, choices, and the future.

The movie belongs to a genre that has been named "hyperlink cinema" by the critic Alissa Quart in *Film Comment*. She suggests the structure was invented by Robert Altman, and Altman certainly brought it into modern times and made it particularly useful for showing interlocking stories in a world where lives seem to crash into each other heedlessly. *Crash,* indeed, is an example of the genre, as are Altman's *The Player* and *Short Cuts,* and such films as *Traffic, Syriana, City of God, Amores Perros,* and *Nine Lives.*

Cape of Good Hope transports the hyperlink movie to South Africa, to show how lives previously divided by race and class now connect more unpredictably. Two women (one white, one Indian) work at an animal shelter with a refugee from the Congo. We meet an African maid and her mother and son, a white veterinarian, an older woman trying to fool herself into romance with a younger man, and others whose lives are more connected than they realize. Most of the hidden connections eventually have positive results; this is a movie with characters we care about, living ordinary lives with reasonable goals.

Kate (Debbie Brown) is the white woman who runs the animal shelter. She has never married, is having an affair with a married man. Her best friend is Sharifa (Quanita Adams), a Muslim woman who works with her at the shelter; Sharifa is married to Habib (David Isaacs), and they are a childless couple who argue over their inability to conceive a child. One day Kate meets young Thabo (Kamo Masilo), a boy who lives in a nearby African township. He has a clever dog named Tupac (when will the hyperlinks end?), and Kate hires him and his dog to entertain at the shelter's open house. Through Thabo we meet his mother, Lindiwe (Nthati Moshesh), the maid, and his grandmother, who is conspiring to marry Lindiwe to an elderly but affluent local minister. Oh, and Kate has dealings with a veterinarian named Morne (Morne Visser), who likes her, although she seems to prefer the detachment of an affair.

These characters are introduced briskly in their everyday lives against the backdrop of the Cape Town suburb of Hout Bay, one of those communities that are strung along the lower slopes of Table Mountain, which so benevolently looks down on rich and poor, happy and miserable.

For me, the most interesting character it overlooks is Jean Claude (Eriq Ebouaney, who played the title role in *Lumumba* and had a key role in Brian de Palma's *Femme Fatale*). He is a French-speaking refugee from the violence of the Congo who works at the animal shelter cleaning the cages. On Sundays, he volunteers at the Cape Town Observatory. As a volunteer, his official job is to sweep and clean, although he often engages young students in stories of the universe that leave them goggle-eyed. Jean Claude in fact has a Ph.D. in astronomy, but like the Beirut surgeon in *Yes* who works in London as a waiter, he cannot as a refugee find the employment he was trained for. There is a colossal irony when Jean Claude is fired by the head of the observatory because government policy dictates that such jobs should go to locals. "But I am not paid!" he points out. Nevertheless, he has to go.

Jean Claude meets Lindiwe and her son, Thabo, falls in love with her, is idolized by the boy, is an alternative to the loathed elderly minister. But if his application for Canadian citizenship comes through, will he have to leave her behind? Meanwhile, Kate continues to befriend Thabo, which leads her to an after-dark visit to a nearby African township where, as any city-smart person should know, she might not be entirely safe wandering the streets by herself. These stories are intercut, or hyperlinked, to reveal more and unexpected connections. Will Kate dump the married man and find room in her life for the veterinarian? Will Sharifa and her husband be able to conceive? Do Jean Claude and Lindiwe have a future? And what about the dog at the shelter who was trained to attack blacks? Will it learn to get along with all races in the new South Africa?

While we are absorbed in these stories, while some of the characters appeal enormously to us, we are at the same time being drawn subtly into the emerging South African multiracialism. What *Cape of Good Hope* argues, I think, is that we live in sad times if political issues define our lives. When politics do not create walls (as apartheid did), most people are primarily interested in their families, their romances, and their jobs. They hope to improve all three. The movie is about their hope.

The movie was directed by Mark Bamford; his wife, Suzanne Kay Bamford, cowrote and coproduced. At the Toronto festival, they told me they were Americans who were unable to interest Hollywood in the stories they wanted to tell. They moved to Cape Town "for one year" and are still there after four. Ironically, their screenplay for *Cape of Good Hope* attracted the interest of Hollywood, but the studios wanted to use an American cast to play the South Africans. That would have lost the particular local flavor that is one of the film's assets.

Cashback ★ ★ ½
R, 102 m., 2007

Sean Biggerstaff (Ben), Emilia Fox (Sharon), Shaun Evans (Sean), Michelle Ryan (Suzy), Stuart Goodwin (Jenkins), Michael Dixon (Barry). Directed and produced by Sean Ellis. Screenplay by Ellis.

You may have seen *Cashback* on cable. It was a nineteen-minute short subject from 2005 that was nominated for an Oscar, and maybe should have won, about a grocery store clerk who made time go faster by stopping it. All the other humans in the store froze in place, and the kid, an art student, was free to undress them for a life class right then and there (I think this is a federal offense).

The kid, named Ben, was played by Sean Biggerstaff, aka Oliver Wood, the Gryffindor Quidditch captain, in the first two Harry Potter films. The film was written and directed by Sean Ellis, a fashion photographer who was rumored to be making a feature about the same idea, and now has. With admirable thrift, he has included every minute of his original short; that was made possible because all the original actors were available.

What he has added is a lot of introspection for his hero, plus loneliness and self-analysis and so much soft-core nudity you'd think Russ Meyer was back in town. The MPAA's R rating cites "graphic nudity"; that means not only that they are nude, but that you can see that they are nude. The film itself is whimsical and gentle and actually a date movie, even if it's frank about the desire of a great many young people to see other young people as nature supplied them. No, really, they actually do feel that way, even if they are not old enough to get past the R rating, which may come as news to the MPAA.

As the film opens, Ben begins a voice-over narration that will last pretty much all the way through and, to begin with, replaces what his angry ex-girlfriend Suzy (Michelle Ryan) said when they broke up. Whatever she was saying involves a lot of the upper front teeth overlapping the lower lip. Ben is morose at the loss of Suzy, can't sleep at night, and goes on the midnight shift at Sainsbury's (oh, the film is set in England). Then he begins to freeze time. To tell you the truth, I am not sure if he actually stops time or only fantasizes that he does; the second possibility is probably more likely.

There's a checkout clerk at the store named Sharon (Emilia Fox), who has one of those faces that looks at yours and makes friends. Ben begins to think less about Suzy. The heart of the movie involves his courtship with Sharon, which is mostly conducted by Sharon. He hangs out with a posse of male friends (the usual assorted geek, playboy, and loser types), who advise him in love, a subject which for them seems largely theoretical.

Ben and Sharon spend a lot of time talking, and Ben in his voice-over spends a lot of time talking about them talking, and that's a breakthrough right there, because so many teen romances in the movies operate on the premise of love at first sight and do not realize that while you should like someone in order to make out with them, getting beyond second base requires actual dialogue.

The movie is lightweight, as it should be. It doesn't get all supercharged. Ben and Sharon, despite setbacks, are delighted to be admired by such wonderful partners, and we are happy for them. And that's about it. Even though this movie stops time, it did not require a science adviser.

Cassandra's Dream ★ ★
PG-13, 108 m., 2008

Ewan McGregor (Ian Blaine), Colin Farrell (Terry Blaine), Tom Wilkinson (Uncle Howard), Sally Hawkins (Kate), Hayley Atwell (Angela Stark). Directed by Woody Allen and produced by Letty Aronson, Stephen Tenenbaum, and Gareth Wiley. Screenplay by Allen.

Woody Allen's *Cassandra's Dream* is about two brothers, one single and modestly successful, one struggling but in a happy relationship, who are both desperate to raise money and agree to commit a crime together. The identical premise is used in Sidney Lumet's *Before the Devil Knows You're Dead,* which is like a master class in how Allen goes wrong.

The Lumet film uses actors (Ethan Hawke and Philip Seymour Hoffman) who don't look like brothers but feel like brothers. Allen's actors (Ewan McGregor and Colin Farrell) look like brothers but don't really feel related. Lumet's film involves family members in a crime that seems reasonable but goes spectacularly wrong. Allen has a family member propose a crime that seems spectacularly unreasonable and goes right, with, however, unforeseen consequences. One of the brothers in both movies is consumed with guilt. And so on.

Lumet seems comfortable with his milieu, middle-class affluence in a New York suburb. Allen's milieu is not and perhaps never will be the Cockney working class of London, and his actors seem as much tourists as he is. Nevertheless, they plug away, in a plot that is intrinsically absorbing at times even with so much going against it.

McGregor and Farrell play Ian and Terry Blaine, Ian a partner in his dad's restaurant, Terry a hard-drinking, chain-smoking garage mechanic. Terry at least seems comfortable with his life and his supportive girlfriend (Sally Hawkins), although he dreams of getting rich quick; he gambles unwisely at the dog tracks. Ian also wants cash, and not only for a fishy-sounding opportunity to invest in California hotels. While driving a classic Jaguar borrowed from the garage where his brother works, he meets a high-maintenance sexpot actress (Hayley Atwell) and presents himself as a "property speculator" far richer than he is.

The brothers share a dream to own a boat. Terry wins big at the track, enough to buy a rusty bilge bucket, fix it up, and have a great day sailing with their two girls. But then Terry loses big-time, owes ninety thousand pounds, and discovers that guys are after him to break his legs. That's when rich Uncle Howard (Tom Wilkinson) returns from China (or somewhere) to make a proposition. His business empire is built on fraud, a colleague is about to squeal, and Howard wants the boys to do him a favor and murder the man.

Wilkinson, always a cool persuader, couches this in terms of family loyalty. That convinces the boys not nearly as much as does their own desperation. What happens I will not detail. This stretch of the movie does work and involves us, but then the lads run smack into an ending that was, to me, completely possible but highly unsatisfactory. Its problem is its sheer blundering plausibility. Allen's great *Match Point* (2005), on the other hand, also about crime and social con games, had an ending that was completely implausible and sublimely satisfactory. Remember how that ring falls at the end? What is fiction for, if not to manipulate the possible?

Chandni Chowk to China ★ ★
NO MPAA RATING, 168 m., 2009

Akshay Kumar (Sidhu), Deepika Padukone (Sakhi/Meow Meow), Mithun Chakraborty

(Dada), Ranvir Shorey (Chopstick), Gordon Liu (Hojo), Roger Yuan (Chiang). Directed by Nikhil Advani and produced by Mukesh Talreja, Rohan Sippy, and Ramesh Sippy. Screenplay by Rajat Aroraa and Shridhar Raghavan.

Chandni Chowk is a historic marketplace in the walled city of old Delhi, so now you understand the title of *Chandni Chowk to China,* and because the plot is simplicity itself there is nothing else to understand but its origins. This is the first Bollywood movie to get a North American release from a major studio, and was chosen, I suspect, because it is a slapstick comedy containing a lot of kung fu. That, and maybe because it stars Akshay Kumar, described in the publicity as "the heartthrob of Indian cinema and current reigning king of Bollywood."

I would need to see Kumar in something other than this to understand his fame. He comes across here as a cross between Jerry Lewis and Adam Sandler, but less manic than Jerry and not as affable as Sandler. What I can understand is that his costar, Deepika Padukone, abandoned a promising start as a badminton champion to become a model and actress. She is breathtaking, which of course is standard in Bollywood, where all the actresses are either breathtaking or playing mothers.

The story plays as though it could be remade as a Sandler comedy with no changes except for length. When you go to a movie in India, you get your money's worth, in what takes the time of a double feature. As my Mumbai friend Uma da Cunha told me, big Bollywood movies give you everything: adventure, thrills, romance, song, dance, stunts, the works. In India, when you go to the movies, you go to *the movies. Chandni Chowk to China* plays at 168 minutes, having been shortened, I learn, for the American release. It would be safe to say few viewers will complain of its brevity.

Kumar stars as Sidhu, a lowly potato and onion chopper in his father's potato pancake stand. He adores his Dada (Mithun Chakraborty), despite the old man's propensity for kicking him so high over Delhi that he's a hazard to low-flying aircraft. As eager to please as a puppy, he has a gift for getting into trouble, but all that changes the day he finds the image of a god on one of his potatoes. This image, to my eye, makes the eBay portraits on grilled cheese sandwiches look like Norman Rockwells.

No matter. He exhibits the potato and collects donations, which are stolen by the nefarious Chopstick (Ranvir Shorey), while meanwhile, in China, a village is menaced by an evil hoodlum named Hojo (Gordon Liu), no relation to the U.S. pancake vendor. Two villagers happen upon Sidhu in Chandni Chowk and are convinced he is the reincarnation of the mighty kung fu warrior who saved them from bandits in times long past. Sidhu is soon lured to their village, being promised wealth and voluptuous pleasures, but is now expected to defeat Hojo, who uses his bowler hat as a flying guillotine and may plausibly be related to Odd Job.

Enter the ravishing Deepika Padukone, in a dual role of Sakhi and Meow Meow, an Indian home shopping network hostess and Chinese tigress. As you see the film, you may reflect that the opportunities of an Indian actress to achieve dramatic greatness are limited by the industry's practice in filming them only as spectacular beauties, preferably with the wind rippling their hair. Kissing in public is severely frowned upon in India, so that the greatest tension in all romances comes as a heroine is maybe, just maybe, *about* to kiss someone. This is always spellbinding and illustrates my maxim that it is less erotic to snoggle for sixty minutes than spend sixty seconds wondering if you are almost about to be snoggled.

I gather that Akshay Kumar usually plays more stalwart heroes, with the obligatory unshaven look, wearing his testosterone on his face. It's unlikely he could have become the heartthrob of Indian cinema playing doofuses like this. He becomes involved with both Sakhi and Meow Meow, whose surprise relationship might have been more surprising had they not been played by the same actress. There are lots of martial arts sequences, and of course several song-and-dance numbers, including an Indian rap performance. It's done with great energy but with a certain detachment, as if nothing really matters *but* the energy.

My guess is that *Chandni Chowk to China* won't attract many fans of kung fu—or Adam

Sandler, for that matter. The title and the ads will cause them to think for a second, an unacceptable delay for fanboys. The movie will appeal to the large Indian audiences in North America and to Bollywood fans in general, who will come out wondering why this movie of all movies was chosen as Hollywood's first foray into commercial Indian cinema. I don't know a whole lot about Bollywood, and even I could name some better possibilities.

Changeling ★ ★ ★ ½
R, 140 m., 2008

Angelina Jolie (Christine Collins), John Malkovich (Reverend Gustav Briegleb), Jeffrey Donovan (Captain J. J. Jones), Colm Feore (Chief James E. Davis), Jason Butler Harner (Gordon Northcott), Amy Ryan (Carol Dexter), Michael Kelly (Detective Lester Ybarra), Geoff Pierson (S. S. Hahn). Directed by Clint Eastwood and produced by Eastwood, Brian Grazer, Ron Howard, and Robert Lorenz. Screenplay by J. Michael Straczynski.

Clint Eastwood's *Changeling* made me feel sympathy, and then anger, and then back around again. It is the factual account of a mother whose little boy disappeared, and of a corrupt Los Angeles Police Department running wild. Angelina Jolie stars as Christine Collins, whose nine-year-old son, Walter, went missing in March 1928. Some months later, the LAPD announced her son had been found alive in DeKalb, Illinois.

There was a problem. Collins said the boy was not hers. The police, under fire for lawlessness and corruption, had positioned the case as an example of their good work. They were determined to suppress Collins's protest. Even though the returned boy was three inches shorter than Walter, was not recognized by his teacher and classmates, and had dental records that did not match, Collins was informed she was crazy and locked up in a psychiatric ward on the strength of a captain's signature.

If her "rediscovered son" was a poster boy for the cops, her disappearance became the cause of an early radio preacher named Gustav Briegleb (John Malkovich), who had been thundering against police corruption. Meanwhile, a determined detective named Lester Ybarra (Michael Kelly) was led to the buried bodies of twenty young boys on an isolated chicken ranch outside Winesville, California.

Eastwood's telling of this story isn't structured as a thriller, but as an uncoiling of outrage. It is clear that the leaders of the LAPD serve and protect one thing: its own tarnished reputation. Jolie joins many other female prisoners whose only crime was to annoy a cop. The institution drugs them, performs shock treatment, punishes any protest. Mental illness is treated as a crime. This is all, as the film observes, based on a true story.

Eastwood is one of the finest directors now at work. I often say I'm mad at Fassbinder for dying at thirty-three and denying us decades of his films. In a way, I'm also mad at Eastwood for not directing his first film until he was forty-one. We could not do without his work as an actor. But most of his greatest films as a director have come after *retirement age.* Some directors start young and get tired. Eastwood is only gathering steam.

Changeling is seen with the directness and economy of his mentor, Don Siegel. It has not a single unnecessary stylistic flourish. No contrived dramatics. No shocking stunts. A score (by Eastwood) that doesn't underline but observes. The film simply tells its relentless story and rubs the LAPD's face in it. This is the story of an administration that directed from the top down to lie, cheat, torture, extract false confessions, and serve and protect its image. In a way, it is prophetic.

The Los Angeles Police Department, perhaps in part because it is unlucky enough to exist in Los Angeles, has often had a dark image in recent movies. Consider *L.A. Confidential, Training Day, Lakeview Terrace.* Lots of movies involve corrupt cops, but no city's police department has been as dramatically portrayed. Yes, there are hero cops, but they're mavericks. Dirty Harry, for all his problems, might have admired this movie.

Jolie, Malkovich and Geoff Pierson, as a lawyer who takes Collins's case before the Police Board, are very good at what they do very well. The film's most riveting performance is by Jason Butler Harner as Gordon Northcott, the serial killer. The character could not be adequately described on the page. Harner's mesmerizing performance brings him to sinister life as a self-pitying weasel specializing in smarmy phony charm. He doesn't play a sick killer. He embodies one.

The screenplay by J. Michael Straczynski follows the factual outlines of the story while condensing, dramatizing, and inventing. A man like Northcott can never be explained, but much of his oddness may have emerged from his childhood. That, and his parents, are left out of the film. He didn't discover until a later murder trial that his real parents were his sister and his father. Surely he sensed something was very wrong.

This whole background of Northcott is wisely sidestepped by Eastwood; eerie as it is, it would have been a detour in the story's relentless progress. Northcott comes over in Harner's portrayal as a man like John Gacy, Ted Bundy, and Jeffrey Dahmer: irretrievably evil, inexplicable, unreachable from the sane world. You don't have to gnash your teeth to be evil. Profoundly creepy is more like it.

Jolie plays Christine Collins without unnecessary angles or quirks. She is a supervisor at the telephone company, she loves her son, they live in a nice bungalow, all is well. She reacts to her son's disappearance as any mother would. But as weeks turn into months, and after the phony "son" is produced, her anger and resolution swell up until they bring the whole LAPD fabrication crashing down. Malkovich as the minister is refreshing: not a sanctimonious grandstander who gets instructions directly from God, but a crusading activist. And one more thing: the phony boy's reason for pretending to be Walter. It almost makes you want to hug him. Almost.

Charlie Wilson's War ★ ★ ★
R, 97 m., 2007

Tom Hanks (Charlie Wilson), Julia Roberts (Joanne Herring), Philip Seymour Hoffman (Gust Avrakotos), Amy Adams (Bonnie Bach), Ned Beatty (Doc Long), Om Puri (President Zia). Directed by Mike Nichols and produced by Gary Goetzman. Screenplay by Aaron Sorkin, based on the book by George Crile.

Charlie Wilson's War is said to be based on fact, and I have no reason to doubt that. It stars Tom Hanks as Representative Charles Wilson, a swinging, hard-drinking, coke-using liberal Democrat from Texas who more or less single-handedly defeated the Russians in Afghanistan. Yes. The Soviets withdrew in 1989, the Berlin Wall fell, the Cold War was over, and Ronald Reagan got all the credit. How could Wilson's operation have taken place without anyone knowing? If Ollie North's activities could, why not these?

Here's how it all happened, told in a sharp-edged political comedy directed by Mike Nichols and written by Aaron (*The West Wing*) Sorkin. Charlie Wilson, whose personal life was, shall we say, untidy, was popular in the Second Congressional District of Texas because he never met a pork-barrel project he didn't like, especially if it meant federal funds for the Second Congressional District of Texas. Apart from that, nobody back home much cared that he was a good ol' boy who liked company in a hot tub and was rarely without a drink in his hand.

He had a soft spot for a right-wing Houston millionaire socialite named Joanne Herring (Julia Roberts), a sometime TV talk show hostess, who hated the commies and wanted them to stop killing the brave Afghans. She had some connections, since she was an honorary consul to Pakistan. She told Charlie the Afghans need weapons to shoot down Russian helicopters. Since he was on the Defense Appropriations Subcommittee, he was ideally placed to help them.

Problem was, the United States couldn't afford to have American-made weapons found in Afghanistan. Herring's solution: The Israelis had lots of shoulder-mounted Soviet-made antiaircraft weapons, which they could supply to the Afghans through the back channel of Pakistan. *What?* asks Charlie. Pakistan and Israel working together?

Herring arranges for Wilson to meet her personal friend President Zia, the military dictator of Pakistan, who hates the Russians as much as she does. Zia sends him on a heartbreaking tour of Pakistan's refugee camps for displaced Afghans. Charlie finds the one man in the CIA who can actually help him: the pot-bellied, chain-smoking, hard-drinking outsider Gust Avrakotos (Philip Seymour Hoffman, with a squirrelly little mustache). Gust knows just the Israeli for them to talk to.

They will need money. The United States was then supplying the Afghan freedom fighters with a useless $5 million a year, but Charlie was a master at glad-handing, elbow-bending, and calling in favors, and that amount was quietly raised to $1 billion a year, all secret, because it was CIA funding, you see. With the use of some personal diplomacy and a Texas belly-dancer flown from Houston to Cairo, Charlie pulls off the deal.

All true, they say. Mrs. Herring, who was earlier Mrs. King and later Mrs. Davis, even agrees. Check out her Web site: joanneherring. com. She grew up in a house modeled on Mount Vernon and looks not totally unlike Julia Roberts. What is remarkable about the collaboration of Nichols and Sorkin is that they make this labyrinthine scheme not only comprehensible but wickedly funny, as Charlie Wilson uses his own flaws and those of others to do a noble deed. Well, it was noble at the time, although unfortunately, the "freedom fighters" later became the Taliban, and some of those weapons were no doubt used against American helicopters. As the man says, you can plan plans, but you can't plan results.

You might think Tom Hanks was miscast as the lovable sinner. Dennis Quaid, maybe, or Woody Harrelson. But Hanks brings something unique to the role: He plays a man spinning his wheels, bored with the girls and parties, looking for something to bring meaning to his slog through the federal bureaucracy. He and Gust (a perfect name) are well-matched. "Do you drink?" he asks the CIA man on their first meeting. "Oh, God, yes." Gust has been fighting for years to budge the CIA on Afghanistan, and now the right congressman falls into his hands.

Nichols fills the edges of the screen with unforced humor. There are "Charlie's Angels," his congressional staff of buxom young women, all of them smart. There's Charlie's special assistant, Bonnie, played by the lovable, fresh-faced Amy Adams (*Junebug, Enchanted*), who cleans up after him, gives him good advice, keeps his schedule, and adores him. And there is the presence of Hoffman himself, a smoldering volcano of frustration and unspent knowledge. It's hard to see how Charlie could have ended the Cold War without him, and impossible to see how Gust and Bonnie could have ended it without Charlie. The next time you hear about Reagan ending it, ask yourself if he ever heard of Charlie Wilson.

Che ★ ★ ★ ½
R, 129 m., 2009

Benicio Del Toro (Che Guevara), Demian Bichir (Fidel Castro), Santiago Cabrera (Camillo Cienfuegos), Elvira Minguez (Celia Sanchez), Jorge Perugorria (Joaquin), Edgar Ramirez (Ciro Redondo), Victor Rasuk (Rogelio Acevedo), Catalina Sandino Moreno (Aleida Guevara). Directed by Stephen Soderbergh and produced by Benicio Del Toro and Laura Bickford. Screenplay by Peter Buchman and Benjamin A. van der Veen.

Che Guevara is conventionally depicted either as a saint of revolution or a ruthless executioner. Stephen Soderbergh's epic biography *Che* doesn't feel the need to define him. It is not written from the point of view of history, but from Guevara's own POV on a day-to-day basis in the process of overthrowing the Batista regime in Cuba and then failing to repeat his success in Bolivia. Both parts of the film are based on his writings, including a diary in Bolivia written in the field, day to day.

The film plays in two parts, named *The Argentine* and *Guerrilla*. It resists the temptation to pump up the volume, to outline Che (Benicio Del Toro) against the horizon, to touch conventional biographical bases. In Cuba, we join him in midstream. We learn that he is a doctor but not how and why he became one. It is a given that he is a revolutionary. He is a natural leader of men. Fidel Castro is his comrade, but the film does not show them in a detailed relationship; much of the time, they are apart.

There isn't an explanation of why he chose to secretly leave Cuba after the revolution, no reference to his time in the Congo, no explanation about why he chose Bolivia as his next field of operation, no reference to the political decisions he made as a young man motorcycling across South America (as described in the 2004 film *The Motorcycle Diaries*).

Che is all in the present tense. He has made an irrevocable decision to overthrow governments. He explains why in his descriptions of injustice; he identifies with peasants and not with his own ruling class, and although he is nominally a Communist, we do not hear discussion of theory and ideology. He seems completely focused on the task immediately before him. His method is to give voice to popular resentment against a dictator, win the support of the people, and demoralize opposing armies of unenthusiastic soldiers. He needs few men because he has a powerful idea behind him.

That method worked in Cuba and failed in Bolivia. Soderbergh's 258-minute film works as an arc: upward to victory, a pause with his family in Argentina, downward to defeat. The scenes in Argentina show him with his second wife, Aleida (Catalina Sandino Moreno), and children but do not engage in why he left them, how his wife really feels, how he feels about them. A wanted person, he has disguised himself so successfully that his children do not recognize him as he presides over the dinner table. His wife shared his political ideas but must have had deep feelings about a man who would leave his children to lead a revolutionary war in another country; but we don't hear them, and in a way it's a relief to be spared the conventional scenes of recrimination. It is all as it is.

That helps explain another peculiarity of the film. Surprising attention is given to Che meeting the volunteers who join his guerrilla bands. Names, embraces. But little effort is made to single them out as individuals, to develop complex relationships. Che enforces an inviolable rule: He will leave no wounded man behind. But there is no sense that he is *personally* emotionally involved with his men. It is *a man* he will not leave behind, not *this* man. It is the idea.

In Cuba, the rebels are greeted by the people of the villages, given food and cover, cheered on in what becomes a triumphal tour. In Bolivia there seems little sympathy. Villagers betray him. They conceal government troops, not his own. When he lectures on the injustice of the government medical system, his audience seems unresponsive. You cannot lead a people into revolution if they do not want to follow. Soderbergh shows U.S. military advisers working with the Bolivians but doesn't blame the United States for Che's failure. Che chose the wrong war at the wrong time and place.

In showing both wars, Soderbergh does an interesting thing. He doesn't structure his battle scenes as engagements with clear-cut outcomes. Che's men ambush and are ambushed. They trade fire with distant enemies. There is usually a cut to the group in the aftermath of battle, its casualties not lingered over. This is not a war movie. It is about one man's unrealistic compulsion to stay his course.

Soderbergh made the film himself, directing, photographing, editing. There is no fancy camera work; he looks steadily at Che's dogged determination. There are very few subjective shots, but they are effective; Che's POV during his last moments, for example. There is a lot of the countryside, where these men live for weeks at a time. The overwhelming impression is of exhaustion, and Guevara himself has malaria part of the time and suffered from asthma. There is nothing more powerful than an idea whose time has come, and more doomed than one whose time is not now.

Benicio Del Toro, one of the producers, gives a heroic performance, not least because it's self-effacing. He isn't foregrounded like most epic heroes. In Cuba he emerges in victory; in Bolivia he is absorbed in defeat and sometimes almost hard to recognize behind a tangle of beard and hair. He embodies not so much a personality as a will.

You may wonder if the film is too long. I think there's a good reason for its length. Guevara's experience in Cuba and especially Bolivia was not a series of events and anecdotes, but a trial of endurance that might almost be called mad.   ☞

Chéri ★ ★ ★ ½
R, 92 m., 2009

Michelle Pfeiffer (Lea de Lonval), Rupert Friend (Chéri), Kathy Bates (Charlotte Peloux), Felicity Jones (Edmee), Iben Hjejle (Marie-Laure). Directed by Stephen Frears and produced by Andras Hamori, Bill Kenwright, Thom Mount, and Tracey Seaward. Screenplay by Christopher Hampton, based on the novels *Chéri* and *The Last of Chéri* by Colette.

Near the beginning of Colette's novel *Chéri*, Lea gives her young lover a necklace with forty-nine pearls. We can imagine there is one pearl for every year of her age. Her lover is twenty-four years younger than she. Therefore, twenty-five. Six years pass. In a way, the movie is about how twenty-five and forty-nine are not the same as thirty-one and fifty-five. Colette tells us their tragedy is that they were destined to be the only perfect love in each other's lives, yet were not born on the same day.

The success of Stephen Frears's film *Chéri* begins with its casting. Michelle Pfeiffer, as Lea, is still a great beauty, but nearing that age when a woman starts counting her pearls. Rupert Friend, as her lover Chéri, is twenty-seven and looks younger—too young to play James Bond, although he was considered. They are both accomplished actors, which is important, because *Chéri* tells a story of nuance and insinuation, concealed feelings and hidden fears.

Lea is a courtesan, currently without court. She has a lot of money and lives luxuriously. Chéri is the son of a courtesan, Charlotte Peloux (Kathy Bates). She and Lea have been friends for years; courtesans may be rich and famous, but they cannot really talk freely with women not like themselves. Lea was constantly in the life of her friend's son, named Fred but called Chéri ("darling") by one and all. One day Madame Peloux comes to her and asks her to take in the boy. She does not quite say (as Lee Marvin tells a whore in *Paint Your Wagon*), "I give you the boy. Give me back the man," but she might as well have.

Chéri is far from a virgin, but he needs some reining in. It turns out he accepts Lea's saddle quite willingly. What begins as lovemaking quickly becomes love, and they float in a perfumed world of opulent comfort, Lea paying all the bills. The two things a courtesan cannot ever do are really fall in love, and reveal what she is really thinking. Lea fails at the first.

You need not be told what happens in the story, or how thoughtless and cruel Chéri can be when it suits him. Be content to know that Lea knows sooner and Chéri later that what they had was invaluable and irreplaceable. *Chéri* became Colette's most popular book because of its air of describing familiar lives

with detached regret, and that is the tone Frears goes for: This is not a tear-jerker, but a record of what can happen when people toy with their hearts.

How well I remember that day in 1983 when I walked across Blackfriars Bridge in London and came upon an obscure little used book shop, and inside discovered a set of the works of Colette, small volumes, bound in matching maroon leatherette with cloth bookmarks. I have been in awe of her writing ever since. When Donald Richie, the great authority on Japanese cinema, was moving to a smaller flat in Tokyo and had to perform triage on his library, he gave away Shakespeare, because he felt he had internalized him, but could not bring himself to give away Colette.

Colette, who was eighty-one when she died in 1954, is probably best known to you as the author of *Gigi*. After leaving an unfaithful first husband, Colette, already a successful author, supported herself as a music hall performer, knew many courtesans in the era of La Belle Epoque, had affairs with women, shocked *tout le monde* with the first onstage kiss between two women, married the editor of *Le Matin*, and was divorced at fifty-one after she had an affair with her twenty-year-old stepson. So *Chéri* is not entirely a work of the imagination.

Colette's many books are considered difficult to film because much of what happens is based on emotions rather than events. This is a challenge Frears and his screenwriter, the playwright Christopher Hampton, have accepted. The film is about how to behave when you live at a distance from your real feelings. It is fascinating to observe how Pfeiffer controls her face and voice during times of painful hurt. It is bad to feel pain, worse to reveal it; a courtesan has her pride.

The performances seem effective to me, including Bates as Charlotte, who like many an older prostitute plays a parody of her profession. Laugh, and the world laughs with you. The cinematography by Darius Khondji and costumes by Consolata Boyle are meticulous in evoking decadence. The most emotional moments at the end occur off-screen and are related by the narrator (Frears himself). That is as it should be. Some things don't happen to people. They happen about them.

The Children of Huang Shi ★ ★ ½
R, 125 m., 2008

Jonathan Rhys Meyers (George Hogg), Radha Mitchell (Lee Pearson), Chow Yun Fat (Jack Chen), Michelle Yeoh (Madame Wang), David Wenham (Barnes), Guang Li (Shi Kai). Directed by Roger Spottiswoode and produced by Arthur Cohn, Wieland Schulz-Keil, Peter Loehr, Jonathan Shteinman, and Martin Hagemann. Screenplay by James MacManus and Jane Hawksley.

George Hogg is a British journalist sent to China to cover the 1930s war involving Japanese invaders and communist and nationalist Chinese. It's surprising he survived a day. Inexperienced and naive, he journeys into unfamiliar territory and spends way too much time standing in full view and taking photos. Some of the photos have real news value, such as a series involving a Japanese massacre of civilians, but, of course, the Japanese capture him and the photos.

This leads to the first of two moments when Hogg (Jonathan Rhys Meyers) is seconds from death; an executioner's sword seems already slicing down from the sky when he's rescued by a Chinese nationalist named Chen (Chow Yun Fat). Later he's rescued again, by a beautiful British woman named Lee Pearson (Radha Mitchell), a brave heroine who roams the countryside on horseback by herself, bringing food and medical help to the countless displaced people who need it.

She had a civilian occupation before necessity thrust this mission upon her. Soon Hogg finds the same thing happens to him: Lee takes him to an orphanage, puts him in charge of sixty children, and tells him he must feed and educate them, and tend to their health. How can he do that? Hogg has no training, but Lee gives him no choice. He teaches himself.

All of this seems impossible, but Roger Spottiswoode's film is based on fact; there was a real George Hogg. After he stars in an embarrassing public demonstration of the usefulness of flea powder, Hogg travels by mule to a nearby city where Madame Wang (Michelle Yeoh) runs a business dealing in seed, grains, and perhaps other things. He convinces her

they are in business together: She gives him the seeds and shares in the harvest.

The scenes of Hogg making the orphanage into a functioning community transform the movie from an unlikely adventure into an absorbing life story. The filmmaking is careful but not original; one kid is a rebel, one kid is a quick learner, and so on, and there is a goat that bleats every time it is on the screen. Hogg and the children miraculously restore a rusty generator, coax crops from the stony soil, and hold English classes ("Table! Table! Chair! Chair!"), although I am not sure why twelve-year-old orphans in the middle of China in the late 1930s needed to learn English. Math, maybe?

Thrown out of their orphanage, Hogg and the orphans make an exhausting five-hundred-mile trek across snow-covered mountains to find refuge. When they finally reach their destination, they gaze in silence, and the goat gets one close-up when it doesn't bleat. During this stretch of film, Hogg has fallen in love with Lee, and we learn that Chen and Madame Wang have, as they say, a history. Other secrets are revealed, but they come a little too quickly after the film's leisurely middle passages.

The Children of Huang Shi tells an engrossing story of a remarkable man, but nevertheless it's underwhelming. Dramatic and romantic tensions never coil very tightly, as the film settles into a contented pace. The photography is awesome, especially scenes set in the Gobi desert, which yes, they travel across, although not the whole way, I'm sure. I'm pleased to have seen the film and it has a big heart, but that doesn't make it urgent viewing.

Note: The R rating is earned by some very mild, nonexplicit lovemaking, some violence, some drug content. Nothing so strong it would bother teenagers, who might enjoy this film more than I did.

Children of Men ★ ★ ★ ★
R, 109 m., 2007

Clive Owen (Theodore Faron), Julianne Moore (Julian Taylor), Michael Caine (Jasper Palmer), Chiwetel Ejiofor (Luke), Charlie Hunnam (Patric), Clare-Hope Ashitey (Kee), Peter Mullan

(Syd), Pam Ferris (Miriam). Directed by Alfonso Cuaron and produced by Marc Abraham, Eric Newman, Hilary Shor, Iain Smith, and Tony Smith. Screenplay by Cuaron, Timothy J. Sexton, David Arata, Mark Fergus, and Hawk Ostby, based on the novel by P. D. James.

It is above all the look of *Children of Men* that stirs apprehension in the heart. Is this what we are all headed for? The film is set in 2027, when assorted natural disasters, wars, and terrorist acts have rendered most of the world ungovernable, uninhabitable, or anarchic. Britain stands as an island of relative order, held in line by a fearsome police state. It has been eighteen years since Earth has seen the birth of a human child.

We see today on the news the devastation of Baghdad, the latest city that has fallen through the safety net of civilization. We remember the war zones of Beirut, Algiers, Belfast, Vietnam. Surely it could not happen here? For a time after 9/11 it seemed anarchy might be unloosed upon our world, but now we have domestic calm, however transient.

Watching *Children of Men,* which creates a London in ruins, I realized after a point that the sets and art design were so well done that I took it as a real place. Often I fear it will all come to this, that the rule of law and the rights of men will be destroyed by sectarian mischief and nationalistic recklessness. Are we living in the last good times?

There is much to be said about the story of *Children of Men,* directed by Alfonso Cuaron and based on a lesser-known novel by P. D. James, who usually writes about a detective. But the story, like the stories of *Metropolis, Nosferatu,* or *Escape from New York,* is secondary to the visual world we are given to regard. Guerrilla fighters occupy abandoned warehouses. The homeless live in hovels. Immigrants are rounded up and penned in cages. The utilities cannot be depended upon. There are, most disturbing of all, no children. Only dogs and cats remain to be cared for and cherished.

As the film opens, the TV news reports that the world's youngest person has been stabbed to death in Buenos Aires because he declined to give an autograph. Theo Faron (Clive Owen), the film's hero, watches the news in a café and then leaves with his paper cup in his hand. Seconds later, a bomb destroys the café. This is essential: Faron is terrified. He crouches, and fear freezes his face. This will not be like conventional action pictures where the hero never seems to fear death.

Owen's character, indeed, seems to be central to the film's mood. He is tired, depressed, fearful, pessimistic. So is everyone else. They will all grow old and die, and then there won't be anybody else. We could imagine an aging society in which everyone lived in condos and the world was a vast retirement haven, but who would till the fields? Can you imagine a retirement home in which the decrepit fight over cans of peaches?

Britain, as the last functioning nation, has closed its borders, is deporting anyone who is not a citizen, and is engaged in a war between the establishment and a band of rebels who support immigrant rights. Faron is kidnapped by this group, headed by Julian Taylor (Julianne Moore), who was once his lover; they lost a child. Her associate, Luke (Chiwetel Ejiofor, in another unexpected character), backs her up with muscle and wisdom. Interestingly, there seems to be no racial prejudice in this Britain; they don't care what color you are, as long as you were on board before they pulled up the life rope. Julian's group wants Faron's influence to get travel papers for Kee (Clare-Hope Ashitey) so the young woman can be smuggled out of the country and to refuge in a rumored safe haven. Kee is a key to the future; the movie's advertising tells you why, but I will not.

The center of the film involves the journey toward the coast that Faron and Kee undertake with Julian, Luke, and Miriam (Pam Ferris), who is both watchdog and nurse. Along the way they are pursued by homeland security troops, and there is a chase scene with one of the most sudden and violent moments I have ever seen in a film. Not all of the chases in all of the *Bournes* equal this one, shot in a single take by one camera, for impact.

Their journey involves a rest stop at the country hideaway of an aging hippie (Michael Caine), who has known Faron for years; we are reminded again of how sweet Caine can seem in a character, how solicitous and concerned. It is a small but perfect performance. The journey continues toward the coast, and then there is a running gun battle (in the middle of an existing battle) down ruined streets of rubble and death. Many of the shots are, or seem, uninterrupted; there is the sense that this city is not a set but extends indefinitely in every direction, poisoned and lethal.

Here again, the action scenes seem rooted in sweat and desperation. Too many action scenes look like slick choreography, but Cuaron and Owen get the scent of fear and death, and nobody does anything that is particularly impossible. Small details: Even in the midst of a firefight, dogs scamper in the streets. Faron's hand reaches out to touch and reassure the nearest animal, and I was reminded of Jack London's belief that dogs (not cats so much) see us as their gods. Apparently sterility affects only humans on Earth; when we are gone, will the dogs still tirelessly search for us?

I have been using Hitchcock's term "MacGuffin" too much lately, but there are times when only it will do. The lack of children and the possibility of children are the MacGuffins in *Children of Men,* inspiring all the action, but the movie significantly never tells us why children stopped being born, or how they might become possible again. The children-as-MacGuffin is simply a dramatic device to avoid actual politics while showing how the world is slipping away from civility and coexistence. The film is not really about children; it is about men and women and civilization, and the way that fear can be used to justify a police state.

I admire that plot decision. I would have felt let down if the movie had a more decisive outcome; it is about the struggle, not the victor, and the climax in my opinion is open-ended. The performances are crucial because all of these characters have so completely internalized their world that they make it palpable, and themselves utterly convincing.

Alfonso Cuaron (born in 1961 in Mexico City) is not new to enormous sets and vast scopes. He was the director of *Harry Potter and the Prisoner of Azkaban* (2004), and I have long admired his overlooked *Great Expectations* (1998) and *A Little Princess* (1995), both of which created self-contained worlds of their own. They were in English; he returned to

Spanish to make the worldwide hit *Y tu Mama Tambien* (2001).

Here he fulfills the promise of futuristic fiction; the characters do not wear strange costumes or visit the moon, and the cities are not plastic hallucinations but look just like today, except tired and shabby. Here is certainly a world ending not with a bang but a whimper, and the film serves as a warning. The only thing we will have to fear in the future, we learn, is the past itself. Our past. Ourselves.

Choke ★ ★ ½
R, 89 m., 2008

Sam Rockwell (Victor Mancini), Angelica Huston (Ida Mancini), Brad William Henke (Denny), Kelly Macdonald (Paige Marshall). Directed by Clark Gregg and produced by Johnathan Dorfman, Temple Fennell, Beau Flynn, and Tripp Vinson. Screenplay by Gregg, based on the novel by Chuck Palahniuk.

All the pieces are here, but you have to glue the kite together to make it fly. *Choke* centers on a character who is content to be skanky and despicable, and who does not reform although the plot seems to be pushing him alarmingly in that direction. His name is Victor, and he is a sex addict.

Yes. So much is without joy in his life that he would live, if he could, in a constant state of orgasm. He probably perks up when the TV ads warn about four-hour tumescence. He's the kind of guy who attends Sex Addicts Anonymous meetings and sneaks out halfway to have dirty sex. His comrade in arms is Denny, who is a compulsive masturbator. I believe he only puts on his pants so he can reach inside.

Victor is played by Sam Rockwell, who seems to have become the latter-day version of Christopher Walken—not all the time, but when you need him, he's your go-to guy for weirdness. Denny is played by Brad William Henke. The fact that he has his sight disproves many warnings.

In addition to sex, Victor's life centers on sadness and fake near-death experiences. He spends a commendable amount of time at a nursing home where his mother, Ida (Anjelica Huston), has absolutely no idea who he is, which makes two of them. She provided him with a corrosive childhood, when as a mother she resembled the criminal character she played in *The Grifters*.

When Victor is not at his mother's side, he works a con game as a sideline. Carefully choosing a new restaurant each time, he pretends to have swallowed a big bite and be choking to death. Inevitably someone will rush over and clutch him in the Heimlich maneuver, and it has been his experience that such Samaritans often insist on giving him money. There is an ancient belief that when you save someone's life, you are responsible for it. I forget whose ancient belief it is, but take my word for it.

His mother is assigned to a hospital bed and tended by Nurse Paige (Kelly Macdonald), whose utility to the mother saves her from Victor's instant ravaging, and who oddly enough has theories on the forefront of medical knowledge that may find a sex addict useful. This is fascinating to Victor, whose days are spent in costume as an eighteenth-century colonialist at a theme park, where I believe Paul Revere rides every hour on the hour. Maybe not.

The movie was written and directed by Clark Gregg, who adapted a novel by Chuck Palahniuk (*Fight Club*). Some stretches are very funny, although the laughter is undermined by the desperation and sadness of the situations. Victor is presented as not so much a zany screwball, more of a case study. The film makes a flywheel kind of progress toward its conclusion, feeling like it has arrived not at a resolution but at a rest stop. Still, one of the problems with sex addicts may be that they cannot get enough rest.

A Christmas Tale ★ ★ ★ ½
NO MPAA RATING, 151 m., 2008

Catherine Deneuve (Junon), Jean-Paul Roussillon (Abel), Anne Consigny (Elizabeth), Mathieu Amalric (Henri), Melvil Poupaud (Ivan), Hippolyte Girardot (Claude), Emmanuelle Devos (Faunia), Chiara Mastroianni (Sylvia), Laurent Capelluto (Simon). Directed by Arnaud Desplechin and produced by Pascal Caucheteux. Screenplay by Desplechin and Emmanuel Bourdieu.

A Christmas Tale skates on thin ice across a crowded lake, arrives safely on the far shore, and shares a cup of hot cocoa and marshmallows with Death. It stars Catherine Deneuve as a woman dying of liver cancer and considering a bone marrow transplant, which could also kill her. Because she is almost weirdly resigned to her fate and doesn't seem to worry much, her serenity prevents the film from being a procession into dirgeland.

What it is, instead, is a strangely encompassing collection of private moments among the members of a large family with a fraught history. Some of the moments are serious, some revealing, some funny, some simply wry in the manner of a *New Yorker* story about small insights into the lives of characters so special as to deserve to be in the story.

The family involves parents, children, grandchildren, spouses, a girlfriend, and others. I will not name all of them and their relationships because what use is that kind of information if you haven't seen them and don't know who I'm talking about? For example, Junon Vuillard (Catherine Deneuve) and her husband, Abel (Jean-Paul Roussillon), have had four children, each one arriving with a different emotional meaning, but even in explaining this the movie grows murky, like a cousin at a family reunion telling you who the great-aunts of the in-laws are.

More to the point is the quietly playful approach of the director, Arnaud Desplechin, who seems to be demonstrating that *A Christmas Tale* is a movie that could have been made in several different tones, and showing us how he would have handled each of them. That leads to a wide range of musical genres, mood swings from solemn to the ribald, and always the peculiarity of the Deneuve character's cheerful detachment from her fate. She's like someone preparing for a familiar journey.

Desplechin doesn't focus on her troubles with a grim intensity. Sometimes he seems to be looking for ways to distract himself. For example, he is obviously familiar with Hitchcock's greatest film, *Vertigo*, which has no themes in common with this one. If you happen to have a video on hand, go to twenty-five minutes and fifty-two seconds into it, and watch what follows in the art gallery, as Jimmy Stewart stealthily approaches Kim Novak from behind. While you're at it, watch the whole film.

When you're watching *A Christmas Tale*, Desplechin's homage to that scene is unmistakable. It's not a shot-by-shot transposition, nor is the score a literal lift from Bernard Herrmann. They're evocations, uncannily familiar. The proof is, you'll see exactly what I saw when I watched the film. Now why does Desplechin do that? For fun, I think. Just showing off, the way I sneaked some e.e. cummings lines into my Answer Man column this week, for no better reason than that I could. Of course, an homage has to work just as well if you don't know its source. In fact, it may work better because you're not distracted by the connection. But nothing like a little value-added, as the British say.

Here's another way Desplechin pleases himself. He begins with the happy fact that Catherine Deneuve and Marcello Mastroianni were the parents of Chiara Mastroianni. In *A Christmas Tale*, Mastroianni plays Deneuve's daughter-in-law, a little poke in the ribs because when they're in the same movie they are invariably playing mother and daughter. OK, so we know that.

But look where he goes with it. It's obvious that Chiara has a strong facial resemblance to her mother. Desplechin doesn't make any particular effort to make the point, although he can hardly avoid showing her full face sometimes. Here's what he does. He almost makes it a point to demonstrate how much Chiara looks like her father. Luckily, her parents, when they conceived her, were the two most beautiful people in the world.

When he films her in profile and from very slightly below and behind, we're looking at the essence of Mastroianni. The images burned into our memories from *La Dolce Vita* and elsewhere are of a sad, troubled man, resigned to disappointment and all the more handsome because of it. I always feel tender toward Mastroianni. No actor—no actor—was more loved by the camera. So here he is, and the character he is sad about is played by Catherine Deneuve. I imagine Desplechin and his cinematographer, Eric Gautier, discussing these shots sotto voce in a far corner of the sound stage.

The film must be packed with Desplechin's invisible self-indulgences. Those we can see allow us to see the movie smiling to itself. Mastroianni smoked all the time. So does his daughter here, the same moody way. Desplechin has Deneuve smoking long, thin cigarettes, like Virginia Slims. When was the last time you saw anyone smoking those in a movie? Every time you see one, it's a tiny distraction. I'll tell you when. The last time was also Deneuve. They are the cigarettes she really smokes.

For long stretches *A Christmas Tale* seems to be going nowhere in particular and using a lot of dialogue to do so. These are not boring stretches. The movie is 151 minutes long and doesn't feel especially lengthy. The actors are individually good. They work together to feel like a family. Subplots threaten to occupy the foreground. All the while, something is preparing itself beneath the surface. In the film's last scene (in the final two shots, as I recall) all the hidden weight of the film uncoils and pounces. It really was about something, and it knew it all the time.

I recommend you seek other reviews to orient you to the actual plot. These words have been sort of value-added. If you have *Vertigo*, arm yourself before you attend.

City of Ember ★ ★ ½
PG, 95 m., 2008

Saoirse Ronan (Lina Mayfleet), Harry Treadaway (Doon Harrow), Tim Robbins (Loris Harrow), Bill Murray (Mayor Cole), Martin Landau (Sul), Toby Jones (Barton Snode), Mackenzie Crook (Looper), Marianne Jean-Baptiste (Clary). Directed by Gil Kenan and produced by Tom Hanks and Gary Goetzman. Screenplay by Caroline Thompson, based on the novel by Jeanne Duprau.

City of Ember tells of a city buried deep within the Earth as a shelter for human survivors after something awful happened upstairs—I'm not clear exactly what. Might have involved radiation, since giant mutant bees, moles, and beetles are roaming around down there. The moles have evolved into obese creatures with slimy tentacles surrounding their fangs, the better to eat you with, my dear.

But stop me before I get warmed up. This is

a Boys' and Girls' Own Adventure, rousing and action-packed and short, and if the sets are interesting and cheesy at the same time, well, Ember is *supposed* to be a set, constructed by The Builders to resemble a village. The population seems to consist of maybe three hundred people, all of them English-speaking, and apparently only two of them black. I didn't spot any evident Asians or Latinos, but I wasn't able to take a complete head count when Mayor Bill Murray was addressing them all in the square.

The heroes are young Doon Harrow (Harry Treadaway) and Lina Mayfleet (Saoirse Ronan), the son of a single father and the daughter of a single mom. Her dad drowned in an escape attempt with Doon's dad, Loris (Tim Robbins). We learn that The Builders endowed Ember's first mayor with a box displaying our old friend, the Red Digital Readout, which counts down two hundred years, at which point I guess it's safe to return to the surface. Given the advanced state of RDR technology, one that clicks only once a year is risky; ya could start watchin' the dern thing for like eleven months and get to thinkin' its batteries were runnin' a little low there.

It is hopeless to try to understand everything that's thrown at us. Does the magic box *really* contain only a disintegrating list of instructions? After all that fancy clicking when it slides open? Did it really just get shoved on a back shelf after one mayor dropped it? Why did the clock start running again?

The people live on canned foods. The storerooms look about as big as at your average supermarket. Could you really store enough food for more than two hundred years in there? The subterranean world is illuminated by countless regulation light bulbs that dangle high above. How are they changed?

At one point, Doon and Lina get into a boat as small as a bathtub, survive two waterwheels that revolve on principles unclear to me, and hurtle down a water chute that suggests someone must have been watching the underground railway scene in *Indiana Jones and the Temple of Doom* real close there. Although Lina at one point uses a crayon to scribble a blue sky on a drawing, the movie gives no idea how she knows there is a sky and it is blue.

And so on. But to be fair, this movie would probably entertain younger viewers, if they haven't already been hopelessly corrupted by high-powered sci-fi on TV and video. It's innocent and sometimes kind of charming. The sets are entertaining. There are parallels in appearance and theme to a low-rent *Dark City*. And carrying the connection a little further, the uncredited narrator sounds a whole lot to me like Kiefer Sutherland, who did the voice-overs in the non-director's cut of *Dark City*. One strange aspect: There are no computers in this future world. Therefore, no e-mail. They have messengers wearing red vests who run around and tell people things. So you never accidentally copy your boss.

The Class ★ ★ ★ ★
PG-13, 128 m., 2009

Francois Begaudeau (Francois), Wei Huang (Wei), Esmeralda Ouertani (Esmeralda), Franck Keita (Souleymane), Carl Nanor (Carl), Arthur Fogel (Arthur). Directed by Laurent Cantet and produced by Carole Scotta, Caroline Benjo, Barbara Letellier, and Simon Arnal. Screenplay by Cantet, Francois Begaudeau, and Robin Campillo, based on the novel *Entre les Murs* by Francois Begaudeau.

The Class might have been set in any classroom in the Western world, and I believe most teachers would recognize it. It is about the power struggle between a teacher who wants to do good and students who disagree about what "good" is. The film is so fair that neither side is seen as right, and both seem trapped by futility.

In a lower-income melting pot neighborhood in Paris, Francois, the teacher, begins a school year with high hopes and a desire to be liked by his students. They are a multiethnic group of fifteen- and sixteen-year-olds, few of them prepared by the educational system to be promising candidates for Francois' hopes. None of them seems stupid, and indeed intelligence may be one of their problems: They can see clearly that the purpose of the class is to make them model citizens in a society that has little use for them.

The movie is bursting with life, energy, fears, frustrations, and the quick laughter of a classroom hungry for relief. It avoids lockstep plotting and plunges into the middle of the fray, helping us become familiar with the students, suggesting more than it tells, allowing us to identify with many points of view. It is uncannily convincing.

The reason for that, I learn, involves the method of the director, Laurent Cantet, one of the most gifted new French directors. He began with a best-selling autobiographical novel by a teacher, Francois Begaudeau. He cast Begaudeau as the teacher. He worked for a year with a group of students, improvising and filming scenes. So convincing is the film that it seems documentary, but all of the students, I learn, are playing roles and not themselves.

There is a resentful Arab girl, who feels she is being undervalued by the teacher. A high-spirited African boy, very intelligent, but prone to anger. An Asian boy, also smart, who has learned (from his family's culture, perhaps) to keep a low profile and not reveal himself. Others who are confederates, pals, coconspirators.

A lot of grief in the classroom has to do with the rote teaching of French. As the students puzzle their way through, I don't know, the passive pluperfect subjunctive or whatever, I must say I sided with them. Despite the best efforts of dedicated and gifted nuns, I never learned to diagram a sentence, something they believed was of paramount importance. Yet I have made my living by writing and speaking. You learn a language by listening and speaking. You learn how to write by reading. It's not an abstraction. Do you think the people who first used the imperfect tense felt the need to name it?

The title of the original novel translates as *Between the Walls,* and indeed the film stays for the most part within the classroom. We know from Jack London that the members of a dog pack intensely observe one another. There can only be one top dog, and there are always candidates for the job. A school year begins with the teacher as top dog. Whether it ends that way is the test of a good teacher. Do you stay on top by strict discipline? With humor? By becoming the students' friend? Through psychology? Will they sense your strategy? Sometimes I think the old British public school system was best: Teachers were eccentric cranks, famous for their idiosyncrasies, who baffled their students.

Cloverfield ★ ★ ★
PG-13, 80 m., 2008

Michael Stahl-David (Rob Hawkins), Mike Vogel (Jason Hawkins), Odette Yustman (Beth McIntyre), Lizzy Caplan (Marlena Diamond), Jessica Lucas (Lily Ford), T. J. Miller (Hud). Directed by Matt Reeves and produced by J. J. Abrams and Bryan Burk. Screenplay by Drew Goddard.

Godzilla meets the "queasy-cam" in *Cloverfield,* a movie that crosses the Monster-Attacks-Manhattan formula with *The Blair Witch Project.* No, Godzilla doesn't appear in person, but the movie's monster looks like a close relative on the evolutionary tree, especially in one close-up. The close-up ends with what appears to be a POV shot of the guy with the video camera being eaten, but later he's still around. Too bad. If he had been eaten but left the camera's light on, I might have been reminded of the excellent video of my colonoscopy.

The movie, which has been in a vortex of rumors for months, is actually pretty scary at times. It's most frightening right after something very bad begins to happen in lower Manhattan and before we get a good look at the monster, which is scarier as a vaguely glimpsed enormity than as a big reptile. At least I think it's a reptile, although it sheds babies by the dozens, and they look more like spiders crossed with crabs. At birth they are already fully formed and functioning, able to scamper all over town, bite victims, grab them in subway tunnels, etc. I guess that makes the monster a female, although Godzilla, you will recall, had a baby, and the fanboys are still arguing over its gender. (Hold on! I just discovered online that those are not its babies at all, but giant parasitic lice, which drop off and go looking for dinner.)

The film, directed by Matt Reeves, is the baby of producer J. J. Abrams, creator of TV's *Lost.* It begins with home video–type footage and follows the fortunes of six twenty-something yuppies. The lead character is Rob

(Michael Stahl-David), who is about to leave town for a job in Japan. At a farewell surprise party, Hud (T. J. Miller) takes over the camera and tapes friends wishing Rob well, including Jason (Mike Vogel) and the beautiful Lily (Jessica Lucas). Hud is especially attentive toward Marlena (Lizzy Caplan), who says she's just on her way to meet some friends. She never gets there. The building is jolted, the lights flicker, and everyone runs up to the roof to see all hell breaking loose.

The initial scenes of destruction are glimpsed at a distance. Then things heat up when the head of the Statue of Liberty rolls down the street. Several shots of billowing smoke clouds are unmistakable evocations of 9/11, and indeed, one of the movie's working titles was *1/18/08*. So the statute has run out on the theory that after 9/11 it would be in bad taste to show Manhattan being destroyed. So explicit are *Cloverfield's* 9/11 references that the monster is seen knocking over skyscrapers, and one high-rise is seen leaning against another.

The leaning high-rise contains Beth (Odette Yustman), whom Rob feels duty-bound to rescue from her forty-ninth-floor apartment near Central Park. The others all come along on this foolhardy mission (not explained: how, after walking all the way to Columbus Circle, they have the energy to climb forty-nine flights of stairs, Lily in her high heels). Part of their uptown journey is by subway, without the benefit of trains. They're informed by a helpful soldier that the last rescue helicopter leaving Central Park will "have wheels up at oh-six-hundred," prompting me to wonder how many helicopters it would take to rescue the population of Manhattan.

The origin of the monster goes unexplained, which is all right with me after the tiresome opening speeches in so many of the thirty or more Godzilla films. The characters speculate that it came from beneath the sea, or maybe from outer space, but incredibly not one of them ever pronounces the word "Godzilla," no doubt for trademark reasons. The other incredible element is that the camcorder's battery apparently lasts, on the evidence of the footage we see, more than seven hours.

The entire film is shot in queasy-cam

handheld style, mostly by Hud, who couldn't hold it steady or frame a shot if his life depended on it. After the sneak preview, I heard some fellow audience members complaining that they felt dizzy or had vertigo, but no one barfed, at least within my hearing. Mercifully, the movie is even shorter than its alleged ninety-minute running time; how much visual shakiness can we take? And yet, all in all, it is an effective film, deploying its special effects well and never breaking the illusion that it is all happening as we see it. One question, which you can answer for me after you see the film: Given the nature of the opening government announcement, how did the camera survive?

Confessions of a Shopaholic ★ ★ ½
PG, 112 m., 2009

Isla Fisher (Rebecca Bloomwood), Hugh Dancy (Luke Brandon), Joan Cusack (Jane Bloomwood), John Goodman (Graham Bloomwood), John Lithgow (Edgar West), Kristin Scott Thomas (Alette Naylor), Leslie Bibb (Alicia Billington), Fred Armisen (Ryan Koenig), Julie Hagerty (Hayley), Krysten Ritter (Suze Cleath-Stewart), Robert Stanton (Derek Smeath). Directed by P. J. Hogan and produced by Jerry Bruckheimer. Screenplay by Tracey Jackson, Tim Firth, and Kayla Alpert, based on the books by Sophie Kinsella.

I liked *Confessions of a Shopaholic* about as much as I disliked *Sex and the City*. Both are about clueless women, but this one knows it. *SATC* is about women searching for love in most of the wrong places, and *Shopaholic* is about a woman searching for happiness in the places that are absolutely right for her: Prada, Gucci, Macy's, Barneys, Saks, and on down the avenue.

The plotting is on automatic pilot. It needs Chesley B. Sullenberger III. There is not a single unanticipated blip in the story arc. But here's what sort of redeems it: It glories in its silliness, and the actors are permitted the sort of goofy acting that distinguished screwball comedy. We get double takes, slow burns, pratfalls, exploding clothes wardrobes, dropped trays, tear-away dresses, missing maids of honor, overnight fame, public disgrace, and not, amazingly, a single obnoxious cat or dog.

At the center of this maelstrom is a genuinely funny comedienne named Isla Fisher. She reminded me of Lucille Ball, and not only because she's a redhead. She does one of the most difficult things any actress can do, which is physical comedy: walk into doors, drop trays, fall into people, go ass over teakettle. She plays a Perfect Ditz in the sense of the Perfect Storm, carrying all before her. Give her a fan and twenty seconds of tango lessons, and get off the floor.

It is to the credit of the director, P. J. Hogan of *My Best Friend's Wedding*, that he gives Fisher freedom and yet modulates it, so her character's earnest desire to please shines through. It was the same on *I Love Lucy*. Lucy wasn't a klutz because she was trying to look funny. She was a klutz because she was trying not to.

Fisher plays Rebecca Bloomwood, the only child of blue-collar parents (Joan Cusack and John Goodman), who has been reborn as a Most Preferred Customer through the miracle of credit cards. She begins with a narration describing the nearly erotic bliss she feels while shopping, and we follow her through store after store in an endless cycle of accessorizing outfits, and then buying outfits to match the accessories. It's like the dilemma of the ten hot dogs and eight buns: You can never come out even at the end.

She dreams of working for a famous fashion magazine but stumbles, literally, into a money management magazine published by the same company. How does this woman who knows nothing about money or its management get the job? By impressing the editor (Hugh Dancy) with her eccentric brilliance. Everything she does that's wrong turns out right. Also she benefits from a brave roommate, Suze (Krysten Ritter), who plays the Ethel Mertz role: coconspirator and occasional voice of reason.

Meanwhile, the villainous bill collector Derek Smeath (Robert Stanton) is on her trail, hints that breaking her legs is not out of the question, and eventually has one of the funnier scenes in the movie. After she gains (highly improbable) international fame overnight on the basis of her writing, it would

destroy her, she fears, to be unmasked. Whether it does or not, I leave it to your experience of cinematic plotting to determine.

Look, *Confessions of a Shopaholic* is no masterpiece. But it's funny, Isla Fisher is a joy, and—of supreme importance—it is more entertaining to a viewer with absolutely no eagerness to see it (like me) than *Sex and the City* was. Also, no movie can be all bad where the heroine attends a Shopaholics Anonymous meeting and meets a former Chicago Bulls star.

Constantine's Sword ★ ★ ★
NO MPAA RATING, 95 m., 2008

A documentary directed by Oren Jacoby and produced by Jacoby, James Carroll, Michael Solomon, and Betsy West. Screenplay by Carroll and Jacoby, based on the book by Carroll.

James Carroll speaks calmly and thoughtfully, and comes across as a reasonable man. He is our companion through *Constantine's Sword*, a film about the misalliance of church and state. In terms of screen presence, he is the opposite of one of his interview subjects, the Reverend Ted Haggard of Colorado Springs. To look upon Haggard's face is to wonder what he is really thinking because his mouth seems locked in an enormous smile ("Fiery-eyed and grinning maniacally, Mr. Haggard suggests a Paul Lynde caricature of a fire-and-brimstone preacher." —Stephen Holden, *New York Times*)

Carroll went to Colorado to interview Haggard and others about the alleged infiltration of the Air Force Academy by evangelical Christians. He also speaks with an academy graduate, Mikey Weinstein, who brought suit against the academy alleging that his cadet son, Casey, was the focus of officially sanctioned anti-Semitism. One academy chaplain, we learn, lectured new cadets on their duty to proselytize those who had not found Jesus.

For Haggard, that is the exercise of free speech. For Weinstein and Carroll, it is another chapter of the long-running history of Christianity's crusade against the Jews. Not long after, Carroll finds himself standing on the bridge in Rome where the Emperor Constantine is said to have had a vision of the cross of Jesus, with the words, "In this sign, you shall conquer." The linking of Christianity with the state began then and there, Carroll believes.

The film is a ninety-five-minute distillation of Carroll's best-seller *Constantine's Sword: The Church and the Jews* and is concerned with medieval anti-Semitism, the questionable record of Pius XII on Nazism, the Crusades, the wars in Vietnam and Iraq, and his own life as a former Catholic priest, the son of an Air Force general, an antiwar protestor, and still a practicing Catholic. That is too much ground to cover, but *Constantine's Sword* does an engrossing job of giving it a once-over. Perhaps it is the calm in Carroll's voice and the measured visual and editing style of the director, Oren Jacoby, that create an evocative journey out of what is really a hurtle through history.

Carroll has a lot of stories to tell us: Haggard and the explosion of evangelicalism ("a new megachurch of two-thousand-plus members comes into being every other day"); Constantine and the conversion of Rome from paganism; the Middle Ages and the crusaders who warmed up with the massacre of ancient Jewish cities in Germany; Edith Stein, a Jewish woman who became a Catholic nun and saint and a victim of Auschwitz; the Jewish family that has lived for centuries in the same district in Rome and supplied the popes with all their tableware for 150 years; and his own father, who was a strategist during the Cuban Missile Crisis.

Each topic is intrinsically interesting, even if the film sometimes seems short of visuals to illustrate it. There are too many shots of Carroll on the road, going places and looking at things. There isn't a lot new about his revisionist history of Christianity, but there is a lot that is not widely known, including the fact that the present pope has overturned the reforms of Vatican II and returned to the Mass a prayer for the conversion of the Jews. How much do we appreciate the Muslim prayers for *our* conversion? Or do they want us?

I've read over the years about the Air Force Academy controversy but didn't realize how deeply the academy's culture is embedded in evangelical zealotry. A similar controversy developed at the University of Colorado about an evangelical football coach's training sermons. Does religion belong in such contexts? In the academy's dining room, which seats thousands, every place setting for a week included a flyer promoting Mel Gibson's *The Passion of the Christ.* If those in charge of the academy did not understand instinctively why allowing that is an unacceptable crossing of the boundary between church and state, they should not have been allowed high office.

But I ramble. So does the movie, in an insidiously fascinating way. Perhaps it benefits by lacking a clear agenda and not following a rigid outline. Carroll is a man of limitless curiosity about his subjects, the kind of conversationalist you urge to keep on talking. As for Rev. Haggard, some months after his interview was filmed, he resigned as president of the National Association of Evangelicals, describing himself as a "liar and hypocrite" after his affair with a onetime male prostitute was revealed. I wonder how widely he was smiling then.

Control ★ ★ ★ ½
R, 121 m., 2007

Sam Riley (Ian Curtis), Samantha Morton (Debbie Curtis), Alexandra Maria Lara (Annik Honore), Joe Anderson (Hooky), James Anthony Pearson (Bernard Sumner), Toby Kebbell (Rob Gretton), Craig Parkinson (Tony Wilson), Harry Treadaway (Stephen Morris). Directed by Anton Corbijn and produced by Corbijn, Orian Williams, and Todd Eckert. Screenplay by Matt Greenhalgh, based on *Touching from a Distance* by Deborah Curtis.

Ian Curtis was one of those introverted teenagers who gaze sadly upon their own destiny. In his cramped bedroom in Macclesfield, England, his schoolboy's desk holds files labeled for poems, novels, and so on. The files are filled not so much with his work as with his dreams. He lies on his back on his narrow bed, smokes, ponders, listens to music. He would become the object of cult veneration as lead singer of the late-1970s band Joy Division, and he would commit suicide at twenty-three. There are times when we almost think that was his plan.

Control, one of the most perceptive of rock music biopics, has been made by two people who knew him very well. It is based on a memoir by his wife, Deborah (Samantha Morton), a teenager when they married, and directed by the photographer Anton Corbijn, whose early photos helped establish Curtis's image as young, handsome, and sorrowful. The title of Deborah's book, *Touching from a Distance,* could describe all his relationships.

There is irony in the band name Joy Division, because Ian seems to experience little joy and much inner division, as an almost passive participant in his own career. Listen to the two albums the band made, and you hear his lead vocals as relentless complaints against—what? The melancholy that prevents him from feeling the emotions expressed by his words?

The movie is quietly, superbly photographed and acted. It is in black and white and gray, of course, and we sense Ian was a man who dreamed in shadows, not colors. He is played by Sam Riley, who makes him seem always alone. There is a lot of performance footage, but Riley sees Ian not so much performing as functioning. His bandmates sometimes look at him with that inward expression people get when they wonder if they have enough gas to get to the next gas station.

Ian's marriage is, of course, a focus of the film, since his wife was not only its source but also a coproducer. He was clearly not ready for marriage. She was younger but more balanced and competent. Ian had an affair with Annik Honore (Alexandra Maria Lara), a Belgian, and the movie deals with that straight-on, not painting her as a home-wrecker but as another of the enablers Ian used. For him, I suspect, love meant not so much what he felt for a woman as what she felt for him.

Early in the film, Ian and Deborah attend a Sex Pistols concert, and Ian has his ideas altered about what a band is and what music is. His stage style with a microphone resembles a shy, introverted Johnny Rotten. We meet key players in the pivotal Manchester music scene of the period, including the entrepreneur Tony Wilson (Craig Parkinson), immortalized in Michael Winterbottom's *24 Hour Party People,* a film about the same time and place.

Ian Curtis suffered from epilepsy, a condition I'm not sure he fully understood. It seems to have come upon him around twenty, and sometimes during a stage performance we see him moving spasmodically and wonder if performing triggers episodes. Unlike epilepsy

as experienced by, say, Prince Myshkin in Dostoyevsky's *The Idiot,* Ian's does not seem to involve a transition through an ecstatic state. He grows agitated, blanks out, regains consciousness, is confused and depressed. His body has betrayed him.

The extraordinary achievement of *Control* is that it works simultaneously as a musical biopic and the story of a life. There's no rags-to-riches cliché mongering because, for Ian, even the riches were sackcloth. And since his early death is so well-known, the movie consists of a progression, not a progress. The emotional monitor is always Deborah, patient, loyal, worried; Morton, who is thirty, is absolutely convincing as a plucky teenage bride. The shots with which Corbijn leads up to and out of Ian's suicide are meticulously modulated. They do not sensationalize or romanticize. They look on from a certain distance, as we do, as everyone did, while this life moved helplessly toward its close.

Was Ian Curtis bipolar? I'm not an expert, but the movie led me to feel that he was not and that lithium, say, would not have helped him. His discontent was not a disease but a malaise, not manic-depression but more like the state described in "The Anatomy of Melancholy" by Robert Burton:

All my joys to this are folly,
Naught so sweet as melancholy.

Coraline ★ ★ ★
PG, 101 m., 2009

With the voices of: Dakota Fanning (Coraline Jones), Teri Hatcher (Mother/Other Mother), John Hodgman (Father/Other Father), Ian McShane (Mr. Bobinsky), Jennifer Saunders (Miss Spink), Dawn French (Miss Forcible), Robert Bailey Jr. (Wybie Lovat). Directed by Henry Selick, and produced by Claire Jennings and Mary Sandell. Screenplay by Selick, based on the novel by Neil Gaiman.

The director of *Coraline* has suggested it is for brave children of any age. That's putting it mildly. This is nightmare fodder for children, however brave, under a certain age. I know kids are exposed to all sorts of horror films via video, but *Coraline* is disturbing not for gory images but for the story it tells. That's rare in itself: Lots of movies are good at severing limbs but few at telling tales that can grab us down inside where it's dark and scary.

Even more rare is that Coraline Jones (Dakota Fanning) is not a nice little girl. She's unpleasant, complains, has an attitude, and makes friends reluctantly. Nor does she meet sweet and colorful new pals in her adventure, which involves the substitution of her parents by ominous doubles with buttons sewn over their eyes. She is threatened with being trapped in their alternate world, which is reached by an alarming tunnel behind a painted-over doorway in her own house.

Not that Coraline's own parents are all that great. They're busy, distracted, bickering, and always hunched over their computers. They hardly hear her when she talks. That's why she recklessly enters the tunnel and finds her Other Mother and Other Father waiting with roast chicken and a forced cheerfulness. All she needs to stay there is to have buttons sewn into her own eye sockets.

Coraline is the new film by Henry Selick, who made *The Nightmare Before Christmas* and again combines his mastery of stop-motion and other animation with 3-D. The 3-D creates a gloomier image (take off the glasses and the screen is bright), but then this is a gloomy film with weird characters doing nasty things. I've heard of eating chocolate-covered insects, but not when they're alive.

The ideal audience for this film would be admirers of film art itself, assuming such people exist. Selick creates an entirely original look and feel, uses the freedom of animation to elongate his characters into skeletal specters looming over poor Coraline. Her new friend Wybie (Robert Bailey Jr.) is a young hunchback whose full name is Wyborn, and it doesn't take Coraline long to wonder why his parents named him that.

Other Mother and Other Father (voices by Teri Hatcher and John Hodgman, who are also Mother and Father) essentially want to steal Coraline from her real but distracted parents and turn her into some kind of a Stepford Daughter. Their house, which looks like Coraline's own, has two old ladies (Jennifer Saunders and Dawn French) in the basement, boarders who seem in retirement from subtly

hinted careers in the adult entertainment industry. The upstairs boarder is Mr. Bobinsky (Ian McShane), a sometime vaudevillian who has a troupe of trained mice. One of the rooms of the house has insects bigger than Coraline who act as living furniture.

It's more or less impossible, for me anyway, to be scared by 3-D animation. The process always seems to be signaling, "I'm a process!" I think it's harder to get involved in a story when the process doesn't become invisible. I hear from parents who say, "My kids didn't even notice the 3-D!" In that case, why have it in the first place?

Kids who will be scared by the story may not all be happy to attend, 3-D or not. I suspect a lot of lovers of the film will include admirers of Neil Gaiman, whose Hugo Award–winning novel inspired Selick's screenplay. Gaiman is a titan of graphic novels, and there's a nice irony that one of his all-words books has been adapted as animation.

I admire the film mostly because it is good to look at. Selick is as unconventional in his imagery as Gaiman is in his writing, and this is a movie for people who know and care about drawing, caricature, grotesquery, and the far shores of storytelling. In short, you might care little about a fantasy, little indeed about this story, and still admire the artistry of it all, including an insidious score by Bruno Coulais, which doesn't pound at us like many horror scores, but gets under our psychic fingernails.

Credit is due to those who backed this film. I'm tired of wall-to-wall cuteness like *Kung Fu Panda* and wonder if Selick's approach would be suited to films for grown-ups adapted from material like stories by August Derleth or Stephen King. And perhaps I didn't make it clear that it's fine with me that Coraline is an unpleasant little girl. It would be cruelty to send Pippi Longstocking down that tunnel, but Coraline deserves it. Maybe she'll learn a lesson.

Crossing Over ★ ★ ½
R, 114 m., 2009

Harrison Ford (Max Brogan), Ray Liotta (Cole Frankel), Ashley Judd (Denise Frankel), Jim Sturgess (Gavin Kossef), Cliff Curtis (Hamid

Baraheri), Alice Braga (Mireya Sanchez), Alice Eve (Claire Sheperd), Justin Chon (Yong Kim), Summer Bishil (Taslima Jahangir), Ogechi Egonu (Alike). Directed by Wayne Kramer and produced by Frank Marshall. Screenplay by Kramer.

We spend a lot of time talking about the American Dream and have too much suspicion about those who want to live it. Feelings against immigrants are so freely expressed even in polite society that you'd think they all came here for the free lunch. *Crossing Over* creates a mosaic, too simplistic to be sure, of recent arrivals who came here for admirable reasons and will be valuable citizens if they get the chance. Most of them will, anyway. Some were damaged goods at home and have not traveled well.

It is hard to immigrate to this country legally and potentially fatal to do it illegally. That's why I speculate we get some of the best and the brightest; it takes determination, ambition, and skill to get into America either way. Many of those who arrive want to improve themselves, and in the process they will improve us.

I've been taking a lot of cabs the last couple of years, and I've noticed something. Most of the drivers are obviously immigrants, from India, Pakistan, Africa, the Philippines, the Middle East, and the Americas. Without a single exception they all have their car radios tuned to the same station, the best station we have, National Public Radio. It tells you something.

Crossing Over borrows the structure of *Crash* to tell interlocking stories about several immigrants, their problems, and their families. All of their lives connect in some way, if only through U.S. immigration officials. *Crash* wove its pattern fairly naturally. *Crossing Over* seems to strain, with too many characters, too many story strands, and too much of an effort to cover the bases. We meet immigrants new and established, legal and illegal, from Mexico, Nigeria, Bangladesh, Iran, England, Korea, and Australia. It feels like a list.

The connecting links are two immigration officers played by Harrison Ford and Cliff Curtis, an adjudicator (Ray Liotta), and an immigration defense attorney (Ashley Judd). The

stories involve a Mexican woman separated from her child in a raid; an Iranian family, well established, which is about to be naturalized; a Muslim teenager who attracts an FBI investigation by reading an outspoken (but legitimate) paper about 9/11 in class; a Korean teenager (Justin Chon) who is being pressured to join a Korean gang; an Australian would-be actress; an atheist Jew from the United Kingdom who poses as a teacher whose presence is needed in a Hebrew school; and a little Nigerian orphan who has been stranded in a holding center and will be sent back to Africa and danger.

Some of these stories are fascinating and some are heartbreaking, but together they seem too contrived. It's too neat the way they mingle, like the traffic on freeway interchanges seen in overhead shots that separate the passages. I was especially moved by Ford's involvement with the Mexican woman (Alice Braga), who is hauled away pleading with him to retrieve her child from the babysitter. He plays a decent man whose conscience won't let him forget, and he ends up uniting the child with grandparents in Mexico. And there's more to it than that. It's hard for him to leave his job at work.

Harrison Ford supplies the strong central strand in the story, but sometimes it grows so implausibly melodramatic we're distracted. Ashley Judd's character provides insights in the way our legal system handles immigration, and the Australian actress (Alice Eve) shows what she is willing to do for the venal official (Liotta) who happens to be Judd's husband. There is a contrast between an Iranian father who thinks of himself as a good Muslim, and a daughter (Summer Bishil) who thinks of herself as a good Muslim and a good American.

Yes, the film is "flawed"—that prissy film critic's complaint. If you're looking for plausibility and resist manipulation, you'll object to it. But sometimes movies are intriguing despite their faults, and you want to keep on watching. This one is like that.

The Curious Case of Benjamin Button ★ ★ ½
PG-13, 167 m., 2008

Brad Pitt (Benjamin Button), Cate Blanchett (Daisy), Taraji P. Henson (Queenie), Julia

Ormond (Caroline), Jason Flemyng (Thomas Button), Elias Koteas (Mr. Gateau), Tilda Swinton (Elizabeth Abbott). Directed by David Fincher and produced by Cean Chaffin, Kathleen Kennedy, and Frank Marshall. Screenplay by Eric Roth, based on a short story by F. Scott Fitzgerald.

The Curious Case of Benjamin Button is a splendidly made film based on a profoundly mistaken premise. It tells the story of a man who is old when he is born and an infant when he dies. All those around him, everyone he knows and loves, grow older in the usual way, and he passes them on the way down. As I watched the film, I became consumed by a conviction that this was simply *wrong.*

Let me paraphrase the oldest story I know: In the beginning there was nothing, and *then* God said, "Let there be light." Everything comes after the beginning, and we all seem to share this awareness of the direction of time's arrow. There is a famous line by e.e. cummings that might seem to apply to Benjamin Button: "and down he forgot as up he grew."

But no, it involves the process of forgetting our youth as we grow older.

We begin a movie or novel and assume it will tell a story in chronological time. Flashbacks and flash-forwards, we understand. If it moves backward through a story (Harold Pinter's *Betrayal*), its scenes reflect a chronology seen out of order. If a day repeats itself (Harold Ramis's *Groundhog Day*), each new day begins with the hero awakening and moving forward. If time is fractured into branching paths (*Synecdoche, New York*), it is about how we attempt to control our lives. Even time-travel stories always depend on the inexorable direction of time.

Yes, you say, but Benjamin Button's story is a fantasy. I realize that. It can invent as much as it pleases. But the film's admirers speak of how deeply they were touched, what meditations it invoked. I felt instead: Life doesn't work this way. We are an observer of our passage and so are others. It has been proposed that one reason people marry is that they desire a witness to their lives. How could we perform that act of love if we were aging in opposite directions?

The movie's premise devalues any relationship, makes futile any friendship or romance, and spits, not into the face of destiny, but backward into the maw of time. It even undermines the charm of compound interest. In the film, Benjamin (Brad Pitt) as an older man is enchanted by a younger girl (Cate Blanchett). Later in the film, when he is younger and she is older, they make love. This is presumably meant to be the emotional high point. I shuddered. NO! NO! What are they *thinking* during sex? What fantasies apply? Does he remember her as a girl? Does she picture the old man she loved?

Pitt will, of course, be nominated for best actor and may deserve it because of his heroic struggle in the performance. Yes, he had to undergo much makeup, create body language, and perform physically to be manipulated by computers. He portrays the Ages of Man with much skill. That goes with the territory. But how did he prepare *emotionally*? What exercises would the Method suggest? You can't go through life waving good-bye. He is born looking like a baby with all the infirmities of old age. He grows younger, until he resembles Brad Pitt, and then a younger Brad Pitt, and then—we do not follow him all the way as he recedes into the temporal distance.

The film was directed by David Fincher, no stranger to labyrinths (*Zodiac, Fight Club*). The screenplay is by Eric Roth, who wrote *Forrest Gump* and reprises the same approach by having his hero's condition determine his life experience. To say, however, that Roth "adapted" the original short story by F. Scott Fitzgerald would be putting it mildly. Fitzgerald wrote a comic farce, which Roth has made a forlorn elegy. Roth's approach makes Benjamin the size of a baby at birth. Fitzgerald sardonically but consistently goes the other way: The child is born as an old man, and grows smaller and shorter until he is finally a bottle-fed baby. Not much is said about Benjamin's mother, which is a pity, because he is five feet eight at birth, and I wonder how much pushing *that* required.

I said the film is well-made, and so it is. The actors are the best: Taraji P. Henson, Julia Ormond, Elias Koteas, Tilda Swinton. Given the resources and talent here, quite a movie might have resulted. But it's so hard to *care* about this story. There is no lesson to be learned. No catharsis is possible. In Fitzgerald's version, even Benjamin himself fails to comprehend his fate. He's born as a man with a waist-length beard who can read the encyclopedia, but in childhood plays with toys and throws temper tantrums, has to be spanked, and then disappears into a wordless reverie. *Benjamin* rejects these logical consequences because, I suspect, an audience wouldn't sit still for them.

According to the odds makers at Movie City News, *The Curious Case of Benjamin Button* is third among the top five favorites for Best Picture. It may very well win. It expends Oscar-worthy talents on an off-putting gimmick. I can't imagine many people wanting to see it twice. There was another film this year that isn't in the "top five," or listed among the front-runners at all, and it's a profound consideration of the process of living and aging. That's Charlie Kaufman's *Synecdoche, New York*. It will be viewed and valued decades from now. You mark my words. ☞

D

Dan in Real Life ★ ★ ★
PG-13, 93 m., 2007

Steve Carell (Dan Burns), Juliette Binoche (Marie), Dane Cook (Mitch Burns), John Mahoney (Poppy Burns), Dianne Wiest (Nana), Emily Blunt (Ruthie Draper), Alison Pill (Jane Burns), Brittany Robertson (Cara Burns). Directed by Peter Hedges and produced by Jon Shestack and Brad Epstein. Screenplay by Pierce Gardner and Hedges.

Steve Carell of *The 40-Year-Old Virgin* has a personality, or maybe it is a lack of personality, that is growing on me. He is content to exist on the screen without sending wild semaphores of his intentions, his uniqueness, and how funny he is. He's an everyman like a very (very) low-key Jack Lemmon. That makes him right for a romantic comedy like *Dan in Real Life,* during which he isn't expected to go over the top, but be just romantic and funny enough, you see, to let the situation work on its own terms.

He plays Dan Burns, a newspaper advice columnist whose wife died four years before. He's raising three girls on his own, two teenagers and a preteen, and he must be doing a good job because they treat him like a slightly slow brother. At Thanksgiving, he takes them all to Rhode Island, where his parents (John Mahoney and Dianne Wiest) own a vast, rambling brown-shingled beach house you probably couldn't touch for $20 million. Since Mahoney's big job is wearing an apron in the kitchen, it's hard to see him as a guy owning that kind of real estate. Maybe he inherited. Also on hand is Dan's brother, Mitch (Dane Cook).

Dan goes into town in the afternoon and runs into Marie (Juliette Binoche) in a bookstore. They begin one of those conversations that threaten to continue for a lifetime. It's not love at first sight, but it's intrigue, approval, and yearning. She supplies her phone number. That evening, brother Mitch brings his girlfriend home to the brown castle and, yes, it's Marie.

That's the setup, and the movie deals with how to fit all those conflicting emotions into the house. Good thing it's big enough for lots of secret conversations on the move; the fact that social rules forbid them to declare their growing love makes Marie and Dan feel all the more like blurting it out, and Binoche is superb at looking upon her new man with the regret she'd feel for a puppy she can't adopt.

The movie's director and cowriter, Peter Hedges, made the overlooked little treasure *Pieces of April,* a 2003 Sundance hit, also about a Thanksgiving family reunion (which oddly enough, also involved a family named Burns). His plot this time is less fraught, maybe because enormous stakes are not involved; Mitch and Marie are not desperately in love, Dan and Marie hardly know each other, and social awkwardness is the most difficult hurdle between here and happiness. That's why the movie's so soothingly pleasant.

Yes, there are some loud moments and big laughs, some of them involving the three girls, who seem to be enduring simultaneous hormonal yearnings, but Mahoney and Wiest keep a steady hand on the tiller, and the fireplaces and arts and crafts furniture exert a calming influence. Juliette Binoche also has much to do with the film's charm. French but eloquent in English, she fills a place that Ingrid Bergman used to inhabit in the cinema: Able to be very serious, very sweet, and very beautiful, she has the gravitas to make this story seem more important than a mere game of switching partners.

If the film has a flaw, and I'm afraid it does, it's the Sondre Lerche songs on the sound track. They are too foregrounded and literal, either commenting on the action or expounding on associated topics. In such a laid-back movie, they're in our face. The songs are on the Web site, if you doubt me. But I got over the music and had a good enough time, although something tells me this is the kind of movie that will inspire countless queries from moviegoers asking me where that house is. I'll save the trouble: I tried to find out but couldn't. It looks real enough and not digital, but there's not a single exterior photo of it on the official Web site.

Darfur Now ★ ★ ★
PG, 99 m., 2007

Featuring Don Cheadle, George Clooney, Hejewa Adam, Pablo Recalde, Ahmed Mohammed Abakar, Luis Moreno-Ocampo, Adam Sterling. A documentary written and directed by Ted Braun and produced by Cathy Shulman, Don Cheadle, and Mark Jonathan Harris.

We all know, having absorbed it from the mediasphere, that genocide is taking place in Darfur, but we do not all know where Darfur is. Africa, yes, vaguely, we realize. Something to do with Sudan. But where or what is Sudan? If it accomplishes nothing else, *Darfur Now* locates Sudan on the map (tenth largest nation on Earth, just below Egypt—boy, are we dumb) and tells us Darfur is its western region, almost the size of France. The region is landlocked in central Africa, bordered by Libya, Chad, and the Central African Republic. More than that, the film provides faces for the people of the region.

One of them is Hejewa Adam, who wears an automatic rifle over her shoulder. She was a peaceful villager until government-backed Janjaweed (Arab fighters on horseback) killed her three-month-old son. Now she is a fighter who sees no other option. Another person on the ground is Ahmed Mohammed Abakar, a farmer forced off his land, who has become a refugee leader. And we meet Pablo Recalde, in charge of distributing food from the world to Darfur, where much of it is stolen by the Janjaweed.

It would appear that the function of the Janjaweed is to destroy the villages of Darfur, remove the people from their (subsistence level) agriculture, and starve them. That is because they are not the same as other Sudanese. It is instructive that Darfur and the Sudan were independent entities living in relative peace before they were arbitrarily cobbled together by the nineteenth-century British-dominated Egyptian government, one of many African "nations" created by European colonial powers with no regard to local history, languages, or tribal identity.

Outside Darfur a key player is Luis Moreno-Ocampo, a prosecutor for the International Criminal Court at The Hague, who seeks to prosecute the Sudan for genocidal crimes but finds opposition because many important nations, China included, value their oil trade with the Sudan and care little about impoverished Darfur. Meanwhile, a quarter of a million have starved and perhaps two or three million have lost their homes or lands.

Cut to California, where the admirable Don Cheadle, joined by George Clooney, leads a movement to inspire American and European intervention. Cheadle learned about genocide firsthand while making *Hotel Rwanda*. And we meet Adam Sterling, a student who begins a movement to divest California of its investments in the Sudan. It is successful, and Governor Arnold Schwarzenegger gladly signs such a bill into law, although its impact may be more symbolic than economic. Washington remains aloof from the issue, apart from the speeches of involved senators.

All of this you will learn and see in *Darfur Now*. It is not a compelling documentary (too much exposition, not enough on-the-spot reality), but it is instructive and disturbing. Darfurians like Hejewa Adam await the arrival of "the Americans" to save her land. Perhaps she should announce that she is building a nuclear program.

The Darjeeling Limited ★ ★ ★ ½
R, 91 m., 2007

Owen Wilson (Francis), Adrien Brody (Peter), Jason Schwartzman (Jack), Amara Karan (Rita), Camilla Rutherford (Alice), Wally Wolodarsky (Brendan), Waris Ahluwalia (The Chief Steward), Barbet Schroeder (The Mechanic), Irrfan Khan (The Father), Bill Murray (The Businessman), Anjelica Huston (Patricia), Natalie Portman (Girlfriend). Directed by Wes Anderson and produced by Anderson, Roman Coppola, Lydia Dean Pilcher, and Scott Rudin. Screenplay by Anderson, Coppola, and Jason Schwartzman.

Three brothers in crisis and desperation meet in India in *The Darjeeling Limited*, a movie that meanders so persuasively it gets us meandering right along. It's the new film by Wes Anderson, who after *Rushmore* and *The Royal Tenenbaums* made *The Life Aquatic with Steve*

Zissou. Of that peculiar film I wrote: "My rational mind informs me that this movie doesn't work. Yet I hear a subversive whisper: Since it does so many other things, does it have to work, too? Can't it just *exist*? 'Terminal whimsy,' I called it on the TV show. Yes, but isn't that better than no whimsy at all?" After a struggle with my inner whisper, I rated the movie at 2.5 stars, which means, "Not quite."

I quote myself so early in this review because I feel about the same way about *The Darjeeling Limited,* with the proviso that this is a better film, warmer, more engaging, funnier, and very surrounded by India, that nation of perplexing charm. The brothers, who have not been much in contact, have a reunion after one is almost killed in a motorcycle crash, and they take a journey on a train so wonderful I fear it does not really exist. (It is the fancy of the art director.)

The reunion is convened by Francis (Owen Wilson), whose head bandages make him look like an extra from *The Mummy.* Having nearly died (possibly intentionally), he now embraces life and wants to Really Get to Know his younger brothers. They are Peter (Adrien Brody), poised to divorce a wife he doesn't love when she announces she is pregnant; and Jack (Jason Schwartzman), who dials all the way home to eavesdrop on his former girlfriend's answering machine.

They travel with a mountain of Louis Vuitton luggage, which means the movie will no doubt play this year's Louis Vuitton Hawaii International Film Festival. Francis has an assistant, Brendan (Wally Wolodarsky), whose office is next to the luggage in the baggage car, from which he issues forth a daily itinerary from the computer and printer he has brought along. The document is encased in plastic by the laminating machine he has also brought along. Insisting on this schedule is typical of Francis; he expects without question that his brothers will comply.

Francis is the compulsive type, which is why his younger brothers find it hard to be in the same room with him. They got enough of that from their mother. He announces that their train journey of reconciliation will be enriched by visits to all the principal holy places along the way. They are also enriched by their careless purchase of obscure medica-

tions that contain little magical mystery tours of their own.

One of the film's attractions for me was its Indian context; Anderson and his actors made a trip through India while he was writing the screenplay. It avoids obvious temptations to exoticism by surprising us; the stewardess on the train, for example, speaks standard English and seems American. This is Rita (Amara Karan). She comes round offering them a sweet lime drink, which is Indian enough, but later, when Jack sticks his head out a train window, he sees her head sticking out, too, as she puffs on a cigarette. Soon they are in each other's arms, not very Indian of her.

Anderson uses India not in a touristy way but as a backdrop that is very, very there. Consider a lengthy scene where the three brothers share a table in the diner with an Indian man who is a stranger. Observe the performance of the stranger. As an Indian traveling in first class, he undoubtedly speaks English, but they do not exchange a word. He reads his paper. The brothers talk urgently and openly about intimacies and differences. He does not *react* in any obvious way. His unperturbed presence is a reaction in itself. There is a concealed level of performance: They probably know he can understand them, and he probably knows they know this. There he sits, a passive witness to their lives. It is impossible to imagine this role played any better. He raises the level of the scene to another dimension.

The casting of the three brothers is also a good fit. Their personalities jostle each other in a family sort of way; they're replaying old tapes. Then they have unplanned adventures as a result of the obscure medications and end up off the train and in the "real" India with all of that luggage. But Anderson doesn't have them discover each other, which would be a cliché; instead, they burrow more deeply inside their essential natures. Then Francis springs a surprise: Their journey will end with a meeting with their mother (Anjelica Huston), who for some years has been a nun in an Indian religious order. Her appearance and behavior is our catalyst for understanding the brothers.

I said the movie meanders. It will therefore inspire reviews complaining that it doesn't fly straight as an arrow at its target. But it doesn't have a target, either. Why do we have to be the cops and enforce a narrow range of movie requirements? Anderson is like Dave Brubeck, whom I'm listening to right now. He knows every note of the original song, but the fun and genius come in the way he noodles around. And in his movie's cast, especially with Owen Wilson, Anderson takes advantage of champion noodlers.

Note: If you like this movie's whimsy and observant human comedy, there is a great Indian writer you must discover, and his name is R. K. Narayan.

The Dark Knight ★ ★ ★ ★
PG-13, 152 m., 2008

Christian Bale (Bruce Wayne),Michael Caine (Alfred), Heath Ledger (Joker), Gary Oldman (James Gordon), Aaron Eckhart (Harvey Dent), Maggie Gyllenhaal (Rachel Dawes), Morgan Freeman (Lucius Fox). Directed by Christopher Nolan and produced by Nolan, Charles Roven, and Emma Thomas. Screenplay by Christopher Nolan and Jonathan Nolan.

Batman isn't a comic book anymore. Christopher Nolan's *The Dark Knight* is a haunted film that leaps beyond its origins and becomes an engrossing tragedy. It creates characters we come to care about. That's because of the performances, because of the direction, because of the writing, and because of the superlative technical quality of the entire production. This film, and to a lesser degree *Iron Man*, redefine the possibilities of the "comic book movie."

The Dark Knight is not a simplistic tale of good and evil. Batman is good, yes; the Joker is evil, yes. But Batman poses a more complex puzzle than usual: The citizens of Gotham City are in an uproar, calling him a vigilante and blaming him for the deaths of policemen and others. And the Joker is more than a villain. He's a Mephistopheles whose actions are fiendishly designed to pose moral dilemmas for his enemies.

The key performance in the movie is by the late Heath Ledger, as the Joker. Will he become the first posthumous Oscar winner since Peter Finch? His Joker draws power from the actual inspiration of the character in the silent classic *The Man Who Laughs* (1928). His clown's makeup more sloppy than before, his cackle betraying deep wounds, he seeks revenge, he claims, for the horrible punishment his father exacted on him when he was a child. In one diabolical scheme near the end of the film, he invites two ferry-loads of passengers to blow up the other before they are blown up themselves. Throughout the film, he devises ingenious situations that force Batman (Christian Bale), Commissioner Gordon (Gary Oldman), and District Attorney Harvey Dent (Aaron Eckhart) to make impossible ethical decisions. By the end of the film, the whole moral foundation of the Batman legend is threatened.

Because these actors and others are so powerful, and because the movie does not allow its spectacular special effects to upstage the humans, we're surprised how deeply the drama affects us. Eckhart does an especially good job on Harvey Dent, whose character is transformed by a horrible fate into a bitter monster. It is customary in a comic book movie to maintain a certain knowing distance from the action, to view everything through a sophisticated screen. *The Dark Knight* slips around those defenses and engages us.

Yes, the special effects are extraordinary. They focus on the expected explosions and catastrophes, and have some superb, elaborate chase scenes. The movie was shot on location in Chicago, but it avoids such familiar landmarks as Marina City, the Wrigley Building, or the skyline. Chicagoans will recognize many places, notably LaSalle Street and Lower Wacker Drive, but director Nolan is not making a travelogue. He presents the city as a wilderness of skyscrapers, and a key sequence is set in the still-uncompleted Trump Tower. Through these heights the Batman moves at the end of strong wires, or sometimes actually flies, using his cape as a parasail.

The plot involves nothing more or less than the Joker's attempts to humiliate the forces for good and expose Batman's secret identity, showing him to be a poseur and a fraud. He includes Gordon and Dent on his target list, and contrives cruel tricks to play with the fact that Bruce Wayne once loved, and Harvey Dent now loves, Assistant D.A. Rachel Dawes (Maggie Gyllenhaal). The tricks are more cruel than he realizes, because the Joker doesn't know Batman's identity. Heath Ledger has a good deal of dialogue in the movie, and a lot of it isn't the usual jabs and jests we're familiar with: It's psychologically more complex, outlining the dilemmas he has constructed and explaining his reasons for them. The screenplay by Christopher Nolan and his brother Jonathan (who first worked together on *Memento*) has more depth and poetry than we might have expected.

Two of the supporting characters are crucial to the action and are played effortlessly by the great actors Morgan Freeman and Michael Caine. Freeman, as the scientific genius Lucius Fox, is in charge of Bruce Wayne's underground headquarters and makes an ethical objection to a method of eavesdropping on all of the citizens of Gotham City. His stand has current political implications. Caine is the faithful butler Alfred, who understands Wayne better than anybody and makes a decision about a crucial letter.

Nolan also directed the previous, and excellent, *Batman Begins* (2005), which went into greater detail than ever before about Bruce Wayne's origins and the reasons for his compulsions. Now it is the Joker's turn, although his past is handled entirely with dialogue, not flashbacks. There are no references to Batman's childhood, but we certainly remember it, and we realize that this conflict is between two adults who were twisted by childhood cruelty—one compensating by trying to do good, the other by trying to do evil. Perhaps they instinctively understand that themselves.

Something fundamental seems to be happening in the upper realms of the comic book movie. *Spider-Man II* (2004) may have defined the high point of the traditional film based on comic book heroes. A movie like the new *Hellboy II* allows its director free rein for his fantastical visions. But now *Iron Man* and even more *The Dark Knight* move the genre into deeper waters. They realize, as some comic book readers instinctively do, that these stories touch on deep fears, traumas, fantasies, and hopes. And the Batman legend, with its origins in film noir, is the most fruitful one for exploration. In his two Batman movies, Nolan has freed the character to be a canvas for a broader scope of human emotion. For Bruce

Wayne is a deeply troubled man, let there be no doubt, and if ever in exile from his heroic role, it would not surprise me what he finds himself capable of doing. ☞

Dark Streets ★ ★
R, 83 m., 2008

Gabriel Mann (Chaz), Bijou Phillips (Crystal), Izabella Miko (Madelaine), Elias Koteas (Lieutenant), Michael Fairman (Nathaniel). Directed by Rachel Samuels and produced by Andrea Balen, Claus Clausen, and Glenn M. Stewart. Screenplay by Wallace King, based on the play *City Club* by Glenn Stewart.

Dark Streets is the kind of film you can appreciate as an object, but not as a story. It's a lovingly souped-up incarnation of the film noir look, contains well-staged and performed musical numbers, and has a lot of cigarettes, tough tootsies, bad guys, and shadows. What it doesn't have is a story that pulls us along or a hero that seems as compelling as some of the supporting characters.

The hero is Chaz (Gabriel Mann), who has inherited a nightclub from his secretive father, who was a power magnate. Night after night, he sits in the club, smoking and regarding his stage shows. Too many nights after nights. The most noticeable thing about Chaz is his pencil-thin mustache. OK, so it's the 1930s, and actors like William Powell and Clark Gable had mustaches like that and played good guys, but somehow don't you associate the style more with snaky villains and riverboat gamblers? A very young man wearing such a mustache is trying to tell us something we don't want to know.

His club feels more like a set than a business. The whole film feels that way: as if the sets, actors, and dialogue are self-consciously posing as classic film noir instead of sinking into the element. Look at a film like *Dark City*, which is obviously made of sets but feels like noir to its very bones. Here, the moment Bijou Phillips and Izabella Miko appear on the screen, they exude: *I'm the dame in a movie nightclub!*

That's not to say they're not good. In fact, they're surprisingly good, especially in the club's jazz-based production numbers, where they sing and dance and are sultry and entertaining. It's wrong of me, but I'm always a little startled when someone like Bijou or Paris Hilton turns out to be talented, because it's wrong that's not what they're famous for.

It's difficult to imagine how Chaz's smallish club, even though it does good business, can afford to stage those production numbers, which, although not Vegas in scope, are at least comparable to those on a big-time cruise ship. I'm reminded of Broadway musicals where six extras play the audience in *42nd Street*. Other details seem out of scale. If Chaz's dad really was a power tycoon, shouldn't the offices of this vast monopoly be more impressive than some gold stenciling on the glass of an office door? I think the power blackouts that keep shutting down the city may be intended to remind us of Enron's deliberate California blackouts, but that plot thread leads nowhere.

The movie is directed by Rachel Samuels, with a screenplay by Wallace King, based on Glenn Stewart's play *City Club*. Since it plays more like the book for a musical, maybe she should have just gone ahead and made it a musical. That would have forgiven the lapses in logic, explained the sets and production numbers, and shrugged off problems of scale. And it would have built on the movie's strength (not just the performances but a nice sound track presence by Etta James, B. B. King, Natalie Cole, and others). You'd still need to make Chaz more formidable. At least in a musical, he doesn't need to be Robert De Niro.

The Day the Earth Stood Still ★ ★
PG-13, 103 m., 2008

Keanu Reeves (Klaatu), Jennifer Connelly (Helen Benson), Kathy Bates (Secretary of Defense), John Cleese (Professor Barnhardt), Jaden Smith (Jacob Benson), Jon Hamm (Michael Granier). Directed by Scott Derrickson and produced by Paul Harris Boardman, Gregory Goodman, and Erwin Stoff. Screenplay by David Scarpa.

SPOILER WARNING: *The Day the Earth Stood Still* need not have taken its title so seriously that the plot stands still along with it. There isn't much here you won't remember from the 1951 classic, even if you haven't seen it. What everyone knows is that a spaceship lands on Earth, a passenger named Klaatu steps out and is shot, and then a big metal man named Gort walks out and has rays shooting from its eyes, and the army opens fire.

That movie is at No. 202 in IMDb's top 250. Its message, timely for the nuclear age, was that mankind would be exterminated if we didn't stop killing one another. The message of the 2008 version is that we should have voted for Al Gore. This didn't require Klaatu and Gort. That's what I'm here for. Actually, Klaatu is nonpartisan and doesn't name names, but his message is clear: Planets that can sustain life are so rare that the aliens cannot allow us to destroy life on this one. So they'll have to kill us.

The aliens are advanced enough to zip through the galaxy yet have never discovered evolution, which should have reassured them life on Earth would survive the death of mankind. Their space spheres have landed all over the planet, and a multitude of species have raced up and thrown themselves inside, and a Department of Defense expert intuits: "They're arks! What comes next?" The defense secretary (Kathy Bates) intones: "A flood." So this is the first sci-fi movie based on intelligent design, except the aliens plan to save all forms of life *except* the intelligent one.

All this is presented in an expensive, good-looking film that is well-made by Scott Derrickson, but to no avail. As is conventional in such films, the fate of the planet narrows down to a woman, a child, and Klaatu. Jennifer Connelly plays Helen Benson, a Harvard scientist who is summoned by the government to advise it on the glowing sphere in Central Park. She has to leave behind her beloved little Jacob (Jaden Smith), her late husband's son by his first wife (more detail than we require, I think; just "her son" would have been fine). She meets Klaatu (Keanu Reeves), who looks human (and we already know why), but is a representative, or negotiator, or human-looking spokesthing, or something, for the aliens.

She discovers his purpose, takes him with her in her car, flees a federal dragnet, walks in the woods, introduces him to her brilliant scientist friend (John Cleese), lets him listen to a little Bach, tells him we can *change* if we're only given the chance, and expresses such love for Jacob that Klaatu is so moved he looks on dispassionately.

That's no big deal, because Klaatu looks on everything dispassionately. Maybe he has no passions. He becomes the first costar in movie history to elude falling in love with Jennifer Connelly. Keanu Reeves is often low-key in his roles, but in this movie, his piano has no keys at all. He is so solemn, detached, and uninvolved he makes Mr. Spock look like Hunter S. Thompson at closing time. When he arrives at a momentous decision, he announces it as if he has been rehearsing to say: "Yes, one plus one equals two. Always has, always will."

Jennifer Connelly and Kathy Bates essentially keep the human interest afloat. Young Jaden Smith is an appealing actor, but his character Jacob could use a good spanking, what with endangering the human race with a snit fit. Nobody is better than Connelly at looking really soulful, and I am not being sarcastic—I am sincere. There are scenes here requiring both actors to be soulful, and she takes up the extra burden effortlessly.

As for Bates, she's your go-to actress for pluck and plainspoken common sense. She announces at the outset that the president and vice president have been evacuated to an undisclosed location (not spelling out whether undisclosed to her or by her), and they stay there for the rest of the movie, not even calling her, although the president does make an unwise call to a military man. Make of this what you will. I suspect a political undertow.

One more detail. I will not disclose how the aliens plan to exterminate human life, because it's a neat visual. Let me just observe that the destruction of human life involves the annihilation of Shea Stadium, which doesn't even have any humans in it at the time. And that since the destruction begins in the mountains of the Southwest, yet approaches Shea from the East, the task must be pretty well completed by the time Jennifer Connelly needs to look soulful. And that Klaatu is a cockeyed optimist if he thinks they can hide out in an underpass in the park.

Death at a Funeral ★ ★ ★
R, 90 m., 2007

Matthew Macfadyen (Daniel), Rupert Graves (Robert), Alan Tudyk (Simon), Daisy Donovan (Martha), Kris Marshall (Troy), Andy Nyman (Howard), Jane Asher (Sandra), Keeley Hawes (Jane), Peter Vaughan (Alfie), Ewen Bremner (Justin), Peter Dinklage (Peter), Peter Egan (Victor). Directed by Frank Oz and produced by Sidney Kimmel, Share Stallings, Larry Makin, and Diana Phillips. Screenplay by Dean Craig.

When I was an altar boy, assisting at Requiem High Mass and planning how to spend my fifty-cent tip at the day-old pastry shop, funerals were sad affairs, with weeping and collapses and all that Latin. The only speaker was the priest, whose sermon reassured us that the Heavenly Father was reserving a space even now in the name of the faithful departed.

These days a lot of funerals have become vaudevillian, with readings, fond stories, laughter, favorite golden oldies, and everybody smiling about dear old Dad or whoever. If they don't send us off gently into that good night, neither do they rage, rage against the dying of the light (copyright Dylan Thomas, who raged plenty).

Frank Oz's *Death at a Funeral* finds its comedy in the peculiar human trait of being most tempted to laugh when we're absolutely not supposed to. Not that all of his characters are very amused. His story begins with the delivery of a casket to the British home of the mourning widow (Jane Asher) who lives with her son Daniel (Matthew Macfadyen) and his wife, Jane (Keeley Hawes), who hates living there so much she can hardly bear to remain even under the mournful circumstances. Not long after, a second casket is delivered, and we're off, and luckily we're all that's off.

Oz, working from a screenplay by Dean Craig, populates the funeral party with disasters waiting to happen. One of them involves Daniel's eulogy, which we see him rehearsing from three-by-five cards, which are a useful precaution if you forget your dad's name (priests always have a helpful memo tucked away in their breviary). Daniel is a prefailed novelist, which means he has not yet finished a novel in order to have it rejected. His despised brother, Robert (Rupert Graves), is a famed novelist living in Manhattan and is flying in just to make Daniel feel doubly miserable.

"Why do we only meet at funerals?" ask people who meet only at funerals. Simon

(Alan Tudyk), engaged to a family cousin named Martha (Daisy Donovan), has been dragged along specifically to meet Martha's father (Peter Egan), who is sure to hate him. Simon doesn't improve his chances when, for reasons I will not reveal, he finds himself naked and doing unidentifiable animal impressions. Simon makes a perfect bookend for old Uncle Alfie (Peter Vaughan), who seems astonished to find himself clothed, not to mention invited anywhere.

Every funeral has an uninvited guest, often a mislaid spouse, angry creditor, police detective, or child not recorded in the family Bible. This funeral has Peter Dinklage, who is becoming my favorite go-to actor for any movie that needs someone to go to. Like Rosie Perez, Danny De Vito, Queen Latifah, or Christopher Walken, he has that ability to make you brighten up and take notice, because with such a person on the screen, *something* interesting is bound to happen. Dinklage can look handsome in that menacing way that suggests he's about to dine out on your fondest hopes and dreams.

The movie is part farce (unplanned entrances and exits), part slapstick (misbehavior of corpses), and part just plain wacky eccentricity. I think the ideal way to see it would be to gather your most dour and disapproving relatives and treat them to a night at the cinema. If they are over a certain age and you have ever seen Polident in their bathrooms, be sure to supply them with licorice ropes.

Death Race ½★

R, 89 m., 2008

Jason Statham (Jensen Ames), Tyrese Gibson (Machine Gun Joe), Ian McShane (Coach), Joan Allen (Hennessey), Natalie Martinez (Case). Directed by Paul W. S. Anderson and produced by Anderson, Paula Wagner, and Jeremy Bolt. Screenplay by Anderson.

Hitchcock said a movie should play the audience like a piano. *Death Race* played me like a drum. It is an assault on all the senses, including common. Walking out, I had the impression I had just seen the video game and was still waiting for the movie.

The time is the near future, not that it matters. Times are bad. Unemployment is growing. A steelworker named Jensen Ames (Jason Statham) loses his job when the mill closes. He comes home to his loving wife and baby daughter, a masked man breaks in, the wife is killed, he is wounded, he is found guilty of his wife's murder and sentenced to the dreaded Terminal Island prison.

Treasure those opening scenes of drama, however brief they may be. The movie will rarely pause again. Prisons, we learn, are now private corporations, and Terminal raises money by pay-for-view Internet races. Its Death Race involves prisoners driving heavily armored cars bearing weapons such as machine guns, rocket launchers, and other inconveniences. If a prisoner wins five races, he gets his freedom.

But why, oh why, must I describe the rules of a Death Race? They hardly matter, nor will I take your time to tell you why Jensen Ames is enlisted to drive as the superstar Frankenstein, who wears a mask, so he could be anybody, which is the point. All of that is simply babble to set up the races.

In a coordinated visual and sound attack, mighty cars roar around the prison grounds, through warehouses, down docks, and so on, while blasting at each other, trying to avoid booby traps, and frequently exploding. Each car is assigned gimmicks like oil slicks and napalm, which can be used only once. Did I say this played like a video game? Jensen's archenemy is Machine Gun Joe (Tyrese Gibson), who is gay, which the plot informs us and thereafter forgets. Jensen's chief mechanic is Coach (Ian McShane), whose oily voice provides one of the film's best qualities. Natalie Martinez plays Case, Jensen's copilot, who screams, "Left turn! Left turn! NOW!"

And the warden of the prison is Hennessey, played by Joan Allen. Yes, that ethereal beauty, that sublime actress, that limitless talent, reduced to standing in an observation post and ordering her underlings to "activate weapons." She has a line of dialogue that employs both the f-word and the s-word and describes a possible activity that utterly baffles me. It is a threat, shall we say, that has never been uttered before and will never be uttered again. She plays her scenes with an icy venom that I imagine she is rehearsing to use in a chat with her agent.

Roger Corman is one of this film's producers, but *Death Race* is not a remake of his *Death Race 2000* (1975). That was a film about a cross-country race in which competitors were scored by how many people they ran over (one hundred points for someone in a wheelchair, seventy points for the aged, fifty points for kids, and so on). Sylvester Stallone played Machine Gun Joe. David Carradine played Frankenstein, but here he only plays the voice of one of the earlier (doomed) Frankensteins. Let us conclude that *Death Race* is not a brand that guarantees quality. That it will no doubt do great at the box office is yet another sign of the decline of the national fanboy mentality. ☞

December Boys ★ ★
PG-13, 105 m., 2007

Daniel Radcliffe (Maps), Christian Byers (Spark), Lee Cormie (Misty), James Fraser (Spit), Sullivan Stapleton (Fearless), Victoria Hill (Teresa), Jack Thompson (Bandy McAnsh), Teresa Palmer (Lucy), Ralph Cotterill (Shellbank), Kris McQuade (Mrs. McAnsh), Frank Gallacher (Father Scully). Directed by Rod Hardy and produced by Richard Becker. Screenplay by Marc Rosenberg, based on the novel by Michael Noonan.

In Australia, the height of summer arrives, of course, in December, which is not how *December Boys* gets its name. The title comes because four boys at the height of adolescence all have December birthdays, and so the nuns at their orphanage have arranged a special treat: a holiday at the seaside. After that summer, nothing will ever be the same again, an observation the movie should use on its posters. Hang on; it is on the posters.

The lads go to stay with a salty old sea dog named Bandy McAnsh (Jack Thompson) and his sickly wife, Mrs. McAnsh (Kris McQuade). He has retired from the navy and they have settled here, their eyes to the sea, their backs to the barren landscape. This is in about 1960, years and years before anyone will think of soaking T-shirts in a soup of red dirt and selling them as Red Dirt Shirts.

The boys are Misty, the narrator (Lee Cormie), Spark (Christian Byers), Spit (James

Fraser), and Maps (Daniel Radcliffe, in his first major post-Potter role). *Variety*, the showbiz bible, cuts to the chase in the opening words of its review: "Destined to be forever known as 'Harry Potter Gets Laid.'" As orphans, the boys (all except for Maps) are as eager to be adopted as puppies in an animal shelter. They meet a circus couple and decide they would make ideal parents. Fearless (Sullivan Stapleton) is a daredevil motorcycle rider, and his girlfriend, Teresa (Victoria Hill), is a French babe who has brought topless sunbathing to Australia years ahead of schedule.

The other three boys all wag their tails and try to seem adoptable. But Maps has his eye on another prize, a girl named Lucy (Teresa Palmer). As they have a flirtation and qualify the movie for *Variety*'s rewrite of the title, I was so forcibly reminded of another one that I wished I were seeing it instead. That would be *Flirting* (1991), where Thandie Newton and Noah Taylor play students at nearby Australian single-sex boarding schools and create the most tender and realistic love (not sex) scene I can remember. They set a high mark, which I'm afraid Maps and Lucy do not approach in a seduction that is by the numbers, only Lucy counts by twos.

She also gives Maps his first puff on a cigarette. The sight of Harry Potter smoking is a little like Mickey Mouse lighting up, but the period detail is accurate, and Radcliffe is convincing as the young man; he proves he can move beyond the Harry role, which I guess is the objective of this movie, but I am not sure that it proves he has star power—not yet, anyway, unless his costar, so to speak, is Harry Potter.

There are some elements in the film that baffle me, one of them being an underwater appearance by the Virgin Mary. I guess we might expect such a manifestation in some movies about Catholic orphans, but not in one so chockablock with mortal sins. To balance her, there is the earthy wisdom of Father Scully (Frank Gallacher), who escorts the lads on their holiday and gives them sales talks on being adopted, as if they were opposed to the idea. He knows the good Catholic couple, the McAnshes, and is their friend in need.

The movie is based on a novel by Michael Noonan, unread by me, which is described as "young adult fiction" by Amazon. Its young and adult elements fit together awkwardly, however, and it is hard to reconcile the storybook qualities of the first sequences with what the MPAA catalogues as PG-13-rated "sexual content, nudity, underage drinking, and smoking," and parents of younger Radcliffe fans will describe as "ohmigod." There seem to be two movies going on here at the same time, and *December Boys* would have been better off going all the way with one of them.

Dedication ★ ★
R, 93 m., 2007

Billy Crudup (Henry Roth), Mandy Moore (Lucy Reilley), Dianne Wiest (Carol), Bob Balaban (Arthur Planck), Bobby Cannavale (Don Meyers), Christine Taylor (Allison), Tom Wilkinson (Rudy Holt). Directed by Justin Theroux and produced by Daniela Taplin Lundberg, Galt Niederhoffer, and Celine Rattray. Screenplay by David Bromberg.

Henry Roth, the hero of *Dedication,* is a writer who does one thing correctly: He talks like he's taking dictation from himself. "Life is nothing but the occasional burst of laughter rising above the interminable wail of grief," he informs us, which may be true enough, but does little to set the mood for a romantic comedy.

Henry (Billy Crudup), possibly named after the author of *Call It Sleep,* threatens, like the real Roth, to become a one-book wonder. He writes children's books, which it is not in his nature to do because he hates children along with the rest of the human race. What kind of man goes out of his way to tell children that there is no Santa Claus?

He has written a best-seller, *Marty the Beaver,* with his collaborator, Rudy (Tom Wilkinson), an illustrator. Then Rudy dies, which is not a spoiler, but it might be a spoiler to reveal that he stays around for the rest of the movie in the form of a ghost. This strands Henry without his only friend. Henry, you understand, is a very odd man with a lot of problems, which seem less like a consistent syndrome than a collection of random neurotic tics.

For example, he is as attached to an old towel as Linus is to his security blanket. When he is having anxiety attacks, which are frequent, nothing will calm him but to put weights on his chest. And he manifests various forms of obsessive-compulsive behavior.

We meet his editor, Planck (Bob Balaban), who sits behind his desk looking mournful at the prospect of there being no further adventures of Marty the Beaver. He orders Henry to team up with another illustrator, Lucy (Mandy Moore), this despite Henry's inability to allow anyone into his life for purposes of collaboration on Marty the Beaver or anything else. And it's at about that point that *Dedication* jumps *onto* the rails and follows a familiar rom-com pathway: Will these two completely incompatible people work out their differences and eventually fall in love? What are the odds, considering they have the lead roles in the movie? Have we spent all that money only to see Mandy Moore's occasional laughter fading off into an interminable wail of grief? I think not.

The movie is a first-time directorial effort by Justin Theroux, a splendid actor, son of the writer Phyllis, nephew of the novelist Paul. He might have done better to have adapted something by them. My candidate for a novel begging to be filmed: Paul's *Chicago Loop,* about a respectable businessman who leads a macabre secret life. Instead, he began with a first screenplay by David Bromberg, which plays like a serve-yourself buffet of bits and pieces cobbled from other movies.

Billy Crudup and Mandy Moore are immensely likable actors. We like them so much we regret having to see them in this story, even though occasionally they slip into a cranny of it and seem to create their own private outtakes. Consider, for example, Crudup's explanation of why any woman should be overjoyed to share life with such a basket case as he. True, such a life wouldn't be boring, but remember the ancient Chinese curse (are there no modern Chinese curses?), "May you live in interesting times."

Maybe I would like *Dedication* more if I had not seen its separate elements time and again. Once Henry and Lucy have been handcuffed together by the plot, for example, I know with a certainty that they will end up in love. But I also know the screenplay structure requires a false dawn before the real dawn. There must be an element that threatens their obligatory happiness. And there is, in the person of Jeremy (Martin Freeman), her former lover, now back in the picture. And there must be a private problem of her own to balance Henry's peculiarities. And there is, in the person of her mother (Dianne Wiest), who wants to evict her, raising the specter that she will move in with the Wrong Person.

In a movie of unlikelihoods, the most problematical is Balaban, as the publisher, offering Lucy $200,000 on the side as a bonus to do all she can to make Henry function again. If there was money like that in children's books, Marty the Beaver would have a lot of new little friends.

Defiance ★ ★ ½
R, 136 m., 2009

Daniel Craig (Tuvia Bielski), Liev Schreiber (Zus Bielski), Jamie Bell (Asael Bielski), Alexa Davalos (Lilka Ticktin), Allan Corduner (Shimon Haretz), Mark Feuerstein (Isaac Malbin), Mia Wasikowska (Chaya). Directed by Edward Zwick and produced by Zwick and Pieter Jan Brugge. Screenplay by Zwick and Clayton Frohman, based on the book *Defiance: The Bielski Partisans* by Nechama Tec.

Defiance is based on the true story of a group of Jews in Belarus who successfully defied the Nazis, hid in the forest, and maintained a self-contained society while losing only about 50 of their some 1,200 members. The "Bielski Partisans" represented the war's largest and most successful group of Jewish resisters, although when filmmakers arrived on the actual locations to film the story, they found no local memory of their activities and, for many reasons, hardly any Jews. Edward Zwick's film shows how they survived, governed themselves, and faced ethical questions, and how their stories can be suited to the requirements of melodrama.

This story has all the makings of a deep emotional experience, but I found myself oddly detached. Perhaps that's because most of the action and principal characters are within the group. The Nazis are seen in large part as an ominous threat out there somewhere in the forest, like "Those We Don't Speak Of" in M. Night Shyamalan's *The Village*. Do I require a major Nazi speaking part for the film to work? No, but the drama tends to focus on issues, conflicts, and romances within the group, and in that sense could be a very good reality show but lacks the larger dimension of, say, *Schindler's List*.

What the film comes down to is a forest survival story with a few scenes of Nazis trying to find and destroy them and a few battle scenes, which furnish the trailer and promise more of an action film. The survival story may contain omens for our own time. In the most fearsome of future scenarios, we may all have to survive in the wilderness, and we should be so lucky to have the Bielski brothers to help us. They were farmers, strong, fierce, skilled in survival skills, pragmatic.

The brothers are Tuvia Bielski (Daniel Craig), Zus Bielski (Liev Schreiber), and Asael (Jamie Bell). After they flee from genocide into the forest, others come hoping to join them, and word of their encampment spreads through the refugee underground. Tuvia decides early on that they must take in all Jews, even the helpless ones who cannot contribute; Zus, a firebrand, is less interested in saving Jews than killing Nazis, which he reasons will save more Jews. This conflict—between helping our side or harming theirs—is seen even today in the controversy over the invasion of Gaza, with Israel playing the role of the Bielski settlement.

The refugees sort out into leadership and support roles, feed their growing group largely by stealing food, establish such institutions as a hospital, a court, and even a tannery. Romance blossoms, which is common in life but indispensable in a movie, and there are tender scenes that are awfully warmly lit and softly scored, under the circumstances. Craig and Schreiber bring conviction to their roles, differing so sharply that they even come to blows before the younger brother leaves to join the Russians (who hate Jews every bit as much as the Nazis do).

Early in the film there's a scene where a feckless middle-aged man named Shimon Haretz (Allan Corduner) hopes to join the group and is asked what he does. He thinks maybe he's an intellectual. This is no use to the partisans, although he is allowed to stay. At the time of the story, the region was largely agrarian and peasant, and many were skilled craftsmen, artisans, and laborers. I thought, I'm also an . . . intellectual. Of what use would I be in the forest? The film works in a way as a cautionary tale. Most of us live in a precarious balance above the bedrock of physical labor. Someday we may all be Shimon Haretz.

The best performance, because it's more nuanced, is by Liev Schreiber. His Zus Bielski is more concerned with the big picture, more ideological, more driven by tactics. Daniel Craig is very effective as Tuvia, the group leader, but his character, perhaps of necessity, is concerned primarily with the organization, discipline, and planning of the group. A farmer, he becomes an administrator, chief authority, and court of last resort.

As a Nazi observes, not without admiration, the Bielskis set up a self-sustaining village in the wilderness. Their situation is more precarious because they are surrounded by anti-Semites not only from Germany but also from Russia and Poland. They cooperate with Soviet forces from necessity but cannot delude themselves. Their efforts prevailed, and today there are thousands who would not have been born if they had not succeeded. ☞

Delirious ★ ★ ★ ½
NO MPAA RATING, 107 m., 2007

Steve Buscemi (Les Galantine), Michael Pitt (Toby Grace), Alison Lohman (K'Harma Leeds), Gina Gershon (Dana), Elvis Costello (Himself). Directed by Tom DiCillo and produced by Robert Salerno. Screenplay by DiCillo.

If he had not been an actor, Steve Buscemi could have been a paparazzo. But then, you can keep saying that about Buscemi. If he had not been an actor, he could have been an incompetent kidnapper (*Fargo*), or a cynical journalist (*Interview*), or a gangster (Tony Blundetto on *The Sopranos*), or a coffeehouse owner (*Art School Confidential*), or a fanatic record collector (*Ghost World*), or a drunk (*Trees Lounge*), or a director (which he was on *Trees Lounge, Interview,* and *Lonesome Jim*). Here's an actor who has 104 movie and TV roles listed on IMDb, and he could have been any of those characters.

There is a needy intensity about so many of his characters. As infants, before they could speak, they were already mentally saying, "I'm walkin' here! I'm walkin' here!" They insist on their space in a world that has never welcomed them, and that is a definition of paparazzi. "This is my spot!" they scream as they block off a foot of sidewalk to take one of countless millions of photographs of pitiful blond starlets emerging from limousines they screwed their way into.

Their dream is that one big picture. One like the shot that everybody has seen of Sophia Loren gazing in amusement at Jayne Mansfield's wayward neckline. More often, however, Buscemi's paparazzo in *Delirious* gets shots like Goldie Hawn having lunch or Elvis Costello not wearing his hat. For him, a big score is getting a photo of a star leaving the hospital after penile surgery. My advice: Take every shot you have of every actor leaving a hospital and say he just had penile surgery. How will it sound if he denies it?

Delirious, by writer-director Tom DiCillo, has a special quality because it does not make paparazzi a target but a subject. It *sees* Les, the name of the Buscemi character, whose name itself tells you what you need to know about him. It watches him work, it goes home with him, it listens while he espouses his paparazzi code to a new friend named Toby (Michael Pitt). Toby is a homeless street kid, sincere and maybe a little simple, but willing to work for free because he, perhaps alone among all the city's inhabitants, looks up to Les. But Toby is a handsome kid with a future, and his name tells his story, too: "to be." One of the first to figure that out is, appropriately, a casting director (Gina Gershon).

Les at first tells Toby to get lost. Then he takes mercy on him and allows him to be an unpaid assistant. He brings him home to his apartment, a cubby hole in a shabby building, and lets him sleep in the closet. And he teaches him the ropes, which is maybe the first time Les has actually articulated them for himself.

Their story centers on the starlet du jour, K'Harma Leeds (Alison Lohman), which, if you know what "karma" means, suggests she will sometimes be a lead, although not a speller. She's blond, pretty, clueless, thinks Toby is cute, and is a sitting duck for Les. She even invites Toby to a party. He asks if he can bring along a friend, and Les is such a bad strategist he actually starts taking pictures at the party instead of waiting to insinuate himself. He's like a fisherman so eager to reel in the line that he can't wait to hook a fish.

This is the best DiCillo movie I've seen, and he's made some good ones (*Box of Moonlight, The Real Blonde*). His second film was *Living in Oblivion* (1995), a generally well-reviewed story about the making of an indie film (with Buscemi playing the director), which DiCillo insists is *not* about the making of his first film, *Johnny Suede* (1991), starring the young Brad Pitt. He insists that over and over and over again.

What *Delirious* has is knowledge of overnight celebrities and those who feed on them, and insights into the self-contempt of the feeders. So much depends on Buscemi's performance here, and he has lived in the world of paparazzi targets. Just as in *Interview,* he was able to draw on the experience of doing countless publicity interviews. Buscemi plays Les not with disdain, as he might have, but with sympathy for a guy trying to get famous by taking photos of the famous; he is the flea on the flea. And Michael Pitt brings a touching innocence to his role as the flea on the flea on the flea. As for Alison Lohman, she just plain nails K'Harma, especially in a music video scene.

Note: The word "paparazzi" comes from the nickname "Paparazzo," for a celebrity photographer in Fellini's La Dolce Vita, *which didn't merely give us the name but almost invented the concept.*

Departures ★ ★ ★ ★
PG-13, 130 m., 2009

Masahiro Motoki (Daigo Kobayashi), Ryoko Hirosue (Mika, his wife), Tsutomu Yamazaki (Ikuei Sasaki), Kazuko Yoshiyuki (Tsuyako Yamashita), Takashi Sasano (Shokichi Hirata), Kimiko Yo (Yuriko Kamimura). Directed by Yojiro Takita and produced by Yasuhiro Mase, Toshiaki Nakasawa, and Toshihisa Watai. Screenplay by Kundo Koyama, based on the novel *Coffinman* by Shinmon Aoki.

"Death is for the living and not for the dead so much." This observation from the mourner of a dead dog in Errol Morris's *Gates of Heaven* strikes me as simple but profound. It is the insight inspiring *Departures,* the lovely Japanese movie that won this year's Oscar for best foreign film.

The story involves a young man who apprentices to the trade of "encoffinment," the preparation of corpses before their cremation. As nearly as I can recall, there is no discussion of an afterlife. It is all about the living. There is an elaborate, tender ceremony carried out before the family and friends of the deceased, with an elegance and care that is rather fascinating.

The hero is a man who feels he is owed a death. The father of Daigo (Masahiro Motoki) walked out on his mother when the boy was six, and ever since Daigo has hated him for that abandonment. Now about thirty, Daigo is a cellist in a small classical orchestra that goes broke. He and his wife, Mika (Ryoko Hirosue), decide to move back to a small town in the north of Japan and live in his childhood home, willed to him by his recently departed mother. He finds no work. He answers a want ad for "departures," which he thinks perhaps is from a travel agency.

The company serves clients making their final trip. Daigo is shocked to discover what the owner (Tsutomu Yamazaki) does; he cleans and prepares bodies, and painstakingly makes them up to look their best. The ritual involves undressing them behind artfully manipulated shrouds in front of the witnesses. The boss is a quiet, kind man, who talks little but exudes genuine respect for the dead.

Daigo doesn't tell his wife what he does. They need the money. His job is so low-caste that an old friend learns of it and snubs him. The clients are generally grateful; one father confesses cheerfully that the process freed him to accept the true nature of his child.

A lot is said about the casting process for a movie. Director Yojiro Takita and his casting director, Takefumi Yoshikawa, have surpassed themselves. In a film with four principal roles, they've found actors whose faces, so very human, embody what *Departures* wants to say about them. The earnest, insecure young man. The wife who loves him but is repulsed by the notion of him working with the dead. The boss, oracular, wise, kind. The office manager, inspirational but with an inner sadness. All of these faces are beautiful in a realistic, human way.

The enterprise of undertaking is deadly serious but has always inspired a certain humor, perhaps to mark our fears. The film is sometimes humorous, but not in a way to break the mood. The plot involves some developments we can see coming, but they seem natural, inevitable. The music is lush and sentimental in a subdued way, the cinematography is perfectly framed and evocative, and the movie is uncommonly absorbing. There is a scene of discovery toward the end with tremendous emotional impact. You can't say it wasn't prepared for, but it comes as a devastating surprise, a poetic resolution.

Some of the visual choices are striking. Observe the way Takita handles it when the couple are given an octopus for their dinner and are surprised to find it still alive. See how vividly Daigo recalls a time on the beach with his dad when he was five or six, but how in his memory his father's face is a blur. And how certain compositions suggest that we are all in waiting to be encoffined.

In this film, Kore-Eda's *After Life*, and, of course, Kurosawa's great *Ikiru*, the Japanese reveal a deep and unsensational acceptance of death. It is not a time for weeping and the gnashing of teeth. It is an observation that a life has been left for the contemplation of the survivors.

Diminished Capacity ★ ★

NO MPAA RATING, 89 m., 2008

Matthew Broderick (Cooper), Alan Alda (Uncle Rollie), Virginia Madsen (Charlotte), Louis C.K. (Stan), Jimmy Bennett (Dillon), Dylan Baker (Mad Dog McClure), Bobby Cannavale (Lee Vivyan), Jim True-Frost (Donny Prine), Lois Smith (Belle). Directed by Terry Kinney and produced by Celine Rattray, Galt Niederhoffer, and Daniel Taplin Lundberg. Screenplay by Sherwood Kiraly, based on his novel.

Diminished Capacity is a mild pleasure from one end to the other, but not much more. Maybe that's enough, serving as a reminder that movie comedies can still be about ordinary people and do not necessarily have to feature vulgarity as their centerpiece. Yes, I'm still hurting from the *The Love Guru* nightmare.

Dim Cap, as Uncle Rollie shortens the phrase, is about Cooper, a Chicago political columnist (Matthew Broderick), and his Uncle Rollie (Alan Alda), who are both suffering from memory loss. With Cooper, who was banged against a wall in somebody else's bar fight, the impairment is temporary. With Uncle Rollie, it may be progressing; his sister, Belle (Lois Smith), who is Cooper's mother, asks Cooper to come home and help her talk Rollie into a mental health facility. It's easy for Cooper to get away since he's just been fired from his newspaper job (at the *Tribune*, as you can tell from countless hints, although the paper is mysteriously never mentioned).

Cooper drives to his small hometown to find his mother overseeing Rollie, who has a big new project: He has attached fishing lines to an old-fashioned typewriter, so that every time he gets a bite, a letter gets typed. He searches the resulting manuscripts for actual words and combines them into poetry. Well, if monkeys can do it, why not fish?

The plot deepens. Uncle Rollie treasures a baseball card given him by his grandfather. The card features Frank Schulte, who played right field for the 1908 Chicago Cubs, and I don't need to tell you what the Cubs did in 1908. It may be the only card of its kind in existence, and Cooper and his mom realize that if Rollie sold it, all of his unpaid bills would be behind him. Meanwhile, Cooper has run into his old girlfriend Charlotte (Virginia Madsen), who has split with her husband; they slowly rekindle their romance. And what with one thing and another Charlotte and her son drive with Cooper and Rollie back to Chicago for a big sports memorabilia convention. They're trailed by the fiendish, rifle-toting hometown drunk Donny Prine (Jim True-Frost), who wants to steal the card.

Matthew Broderick has two light comedies in release this summer; the other is *Finding Amanda,* where he goes to Vegas to try to rescue his niece from a life of sin. In both films he reminded me of his amiability and quietly meticulous comic timing. He and Madsen find the right note for two old lovers who are casually renewing their romance.

The convention provides the movie's big set piece, as our heroes meet a nice baseball card dealer named Mad Dog McClure (Dylan Baker) and a crooked one named Lee Vivyan (Bobby Cannavale). It is Mad Dog who levels Lee with a withering curse: "You're bad for the hobby!" Baker and Cannavale more or less walk away with the scenes at the sports convention.

There is, of course, a duel over the invaluable card, and a fight, and a highly improbable showdown on a catwalk far above the convention arena, and a bit part for Ernie Banks, and a big kiss between Cooper and Charlotte, and it's all very nice, but not a whole lot more. The film is a coproduction of Chicago's Steppenwolf Theater, directed by veteran actor Terry Kinney, and inspired by Sherwood Kiraly's novel. Kinney shows himself a capable director, but isn't the material a little lightweight for Steppenwolf?

The Diving Bell and the Butterfly ★ ★ ★ ★
PG-13, 112 m., 2007

Mathieu Amalric (Jean-Dominique Bauby), Emmanuelle Seigner (Celine Desmoulins), Marie-Josee Croze (Henriette Durand), Anne Consigny (Claude), Patrick Chesnais (Dr. Lepage), Niels Arestrup (Roussin), Max von Sydow (Papinou). Directed by Julian Schnabel and produced by Kathleen Kennedy and Jon Kilik. Screenplay by Ronald Harwood.

The Diving Bell and the Butterfly is a film about a man who experiences the catastrophe I most feared during my recent surgeries: "locked-in syndrome," where he is alive and conscious but unable to communicate with the world. My dread I think began when I was a boy first reading Edgar Allan Poe's "The Premature Burial" at an age much too young to contemplate such a possibility. At least the man in the film can see and hear; the hero of Dalton Trumbo's *Johnny Got His Gun* is completely locked inside his mind.

The film is based on a real man and the book he astonishingly succeeded in writing although he could blink only his left eye. The man was Jean-Dominique Bauby (Mathieu Amalric), who was the editor of *Elle*, the French fashion magazine, when he had his paralyzing stroke. A speech therapist (Marie-Josee Croze) suggests a system of communication: They will arrange the alphabet in the order of most frequently used letters, and he will choose a letter by blinking. By this method, word by word, blink by blink, he dictated his memoir, *The Diving Bell and the Butterfly*, published in 1997, shortly before he died.

It was a superhuman feat, but how could it be filmed? The director is the artist Julian Schnabel, who has made two previous films about artists creating in the face of determined obstacles: *Basquiat* (1996), about a New York graffiti artist, and *Before Night Falls* (2000), about the persecuted Cuban poet Reinaldo Arenas. His solution, arrived at with screenwriter Ronald Harwood, is to show not merely the man in the bed, but to show what he sees and those around him and his memories and fantasies. This is not an easy way out because everything in the film is resolutely filtered through the consciousness of the locked-in man.

The result is not what you could call inspirational, because none of us would think to be in such a situation and needing inspiration. It is more than that. It is heroic. Here is the life force at its most insistent, lashing out against fate with stubborn resolve. And also with lust, hunger, humor, and all of the other notes that this man once played so easily. We see flashbacks to his children, to his mistress, to his fantasies. We see those around him now. And in a gravely significant scene, we see him meeting with his old father (Max von Sydow), who, Andrew Sarris notes, "gets off what may be the single most French line of all time," which is, "Having a mistress is no excuse for leaving the mother of your children; the world has lost its values."

Celine, the mother of his children and his former partner (played by Emmanuelle Seigner), remains loyal to him and even helps him communicate with another woman who also is a former lover (the male libido is indomitable). And all of the other women around him, including his nurse, his assistant, and a fantasy lover, are loving and patient and assure him that he is in some way the same vital man, filled with eagerness, lust, and brilliance. It is just that now it expresses itself one blink at a time.

The lead performance by Mathieu Amalric exists in two ways, as the unmoving man in bed and the vital man in his memories and fantasies. In that way it is fundamentally different from Daniel Day-Lewis's work in *My Left Foot*, about a man who could move only a toe. At least he could lurch and groan and cry. Both films find the inevitable solution to their challenge and the right actors to meet them.

Janusz Kaminski, the cinematographer, is in large part responsible for freeing the film from its own dangers of being locked in. From the cloudy opening POV shots of Jean-Dominique regaining consciousness, Kaminski fills the screen with life and beauty, so that it's not at all as depressing as it sounds. At the end we are left with the reflection that human consciousness is the great miracle of evolution, and all the rest (sight, sound, taste, hearing, smell, touch) are simply a toolbox that consciousness has supplied for itself. Maybe it would even be better to be Trumbo's Johnny than never to have been conscious at all.

Doubt ★ ★ ★ ★
PG-13, 104 m., 2008

Meryl Streep (Sister Aloysius), Philip Seymour Hoffman (Father Flynn), Amy Adams (Sister James), Viola Davis (Mrs. Miller), Joseph Foster II (Donald Miller), Alice Drummond (Sister Veronica), Audrie Neenan (Sister Raymond). Directed by John Patrick Shanley and produced by Scott Rudin. Screenplay by Shanley, based on his play.

A Catholic grade school could seem like a hermetically sealed world in 1964. That's the case with St. Nicholas in the Bronx, ruled by the pathologically severe principal Sister Aloysius, who keeps the students and nuns under her thumb and is engaged in an undeclared war with the new parish priest. Their issues may seem to center on the reforms of Vatican II, then still under way, with Father Flynn (Philip Seymour Hoffman) as the progressive, but for the nun, I believe it's more of a power struggle. The pope's infallibility seems, in her case, to have descended to the parish level.

Some will say the character of Sister Aloysius, played without a hint of humor by Meryl Streep, is a caricature. In my eight years of

Catholic school not a one of the Dominican nuns was anything but kind and dedicated, and I was never touched, except by Sister Ambrosetta's thunking forefinger to the skull in first grade. But I clearly remember being frightened by Sister Gilberta, the principal; being sent to her office in second or third grade could loosen your bowels. She never did anything mean. She just seemed to be able to.

Sister Aloysius of *Doubt* hates all inroads of the modern world, including ballpoint pens. This is accurate. We practiced our penmanship with fountain pens, carefully heading every page *JMJ*—for Jesus, Mary, and Joseph, of course. Under Aloysius's command is the sweet young Sister James (Amy Adams, from *Junebug*), whose experience in the world seems limited to what she sees out the convent window. Gradually during the autumn semester, a situation develops.

There is one African-American student in St. Nicholas, Donald Miller (Joseph Foster II), and Father Flynn encourages him in sports and appoints him as an altar boy. This is all proper. Then Sister James notes that the priest summons the boy to the rectory alone. She decides this is improper behavior and informs Aloysius, whose eyes narrow like a beast of prey. Father Flynn's fate is sealed.

But *Doubt* is not intended as a docudrama about possible sexual abuse. Directed by John Patrick Shanley from his Pulitzer- and Tony-winning play, it is about the title word, *doubt*, in a world of certainty. For Aloysius, Flynn is certainly guilty. That the priest seems innocent, that Sister James comes to believe she was mistaken in her suspicions, means nothing. Flynn knows a breath of scandal would destroy his career. And that is the three-way standoff we watch unfolding with precision and tension.

Something else happens. The real world enters this sealed parochial battlefield. Donald's mother (Viola Davis) fears her son will be expelled from the school. He has been accused of drinking the altar wine. Worse, being given it by Father Flynn. She appeals directly to Sister Aloysius, in a scene as good as any I've seen this year. It lasts about ten minutes, but it is the emotional heart and soul of *Doubt*. Viola Davis goes face-to-face with the preeminent film actress of this generation, and it is a confrontation of two equals that generates terrifying power.

Doubt. It is the subject of the sermon Father Flynn opens the film with. Doubt was coming into the church and America in 1964. Would you still go to hell if you ate meat on Friday? After the assassination of Kennedy and the beginnings of Vietnam, doubt had undermined U.S. certainty in general. What could you be sure of? What were the circumstances? The motives? The conflict between Aloysius and Flynn is the conflict between old and new, between status and change, between infallibility and uncertainty. And Shanley leaves us doubting.

I know people who are absolutely certain what conclusion they should draw from this film. They disagree. *Doubt* has exact and merciless writing, powerful performances, and timeless relevance. It causes us to start thinking with the first shot, and we never stop. Think how rare that is in a film.

The Duchess ★ ★ ★ ½
PG-13, 109 m., 2008

Keira Knightley (Georgiana), Ralph Fiennes (William Cavendish), Charlotte Rampling (Lady Spencer), Dominic Cooper (Charles Grey), Hayley Atwell (Bess Foster), Simon McBurney (Charles Fox), Aidan McArdle (Richard Sheridan). Directed by Saul Dibb and produced by Gabrielle Tana and Michael Kuhn. Screenplay by Dibb, Jeffrey Hatcher, and Anders Thomas Jensen, based on a book by Amanda Foreman.

Much is made in Britain of the fact that Georgiana, the Duchess of Devonshire (1757–1806), was the great-great-great-great-aunt of Diana, Princess of Wales. I wouldn't know where to start in counting my own great-great-great-great-aunts, but the Brits have an obsession with genealogy, and then too both women married men who were fabulously wealthy, had several enormous houses, and kept a mistress, and both women had lovers. The difference is, Georgiana was more interesting.

She was married off by her mother at sixteen to William Cavendish, the fifth Duke of Devonshire, a man who loved his dogs more than her. She was treated like chattel, valued only for her breeding ability, raped by the duke at least once, and became the most famous woman in England, save for Queen Charlotte, whose husband was merely mad. Georgiana was an outspoken liberal, a supporter of the American and French revolutions, a campaigner for one Whig prime minister (Charles Fox) and the lover of another (Charles Grey, whose daughter she bore). She was a feminist who dared to speak publicly on politics, although she accepted that women did not have the vote.

The Duchess is a handsome historical film, impeccably mounted, gowned, wigged, and feathered, where a husband and wife spend hours being dressed in order to appear at dinner to argue about whether the mutton is off. With Keira Knightley playing the duchess and Ralph Fiennes playing her husband, such a conversation is a minefield. The man has no conversation, addresses her primarily to issue instructions, and is obsessed with the production of a male heir, who would have much to inherit, including the grandest private house in London, and Chatsworth, in Derbyshire, the favorite of all British country houses. I have visited Chatsworth, and I was in awe. At today's prices, not even Bill Gates could live like the Devonshires.

For a woman to be duchess of such a private kingdom, to be immersed in politics, to be a beauty, a wit, a fashion leader, and a feisty scrapper with an appetite for better sex than the duke provisioned, Georgiana must have been extraordinary. I am not sure *The Duchess* quite does her justice. Yes, her marital views were flexible. She disliked but tacitly accepted the duke's numerous adulteries. She made only one close female friend, Lady Elizabeth Foster (Hayley Atwell), and the duke rogered her, too. Georgiana was enraged not only because of his infidelity but also for being robbed of her friend. Later they made it up, and she accepted Bess and her three sons into their household, referring to William as "our husband."

There was a reason for Bess's betrayal, and it wasn't lust. Her cruel husband had banned her from ever seeing her sons again, and William was powerful enough to reunite her with them. Later, he is quite prepared to prevent Georgiana from ever seeing their four children. Women had no rights even to their offspring. The Whigs, although behind the curve, were clearly the party of the future; the Tories supported the status quo.

The duke, duchess, and even Lady Elizabeth are capable of behaving according to the rules governing their class in even the most inflammatory situations. They often act as if on stage, and they are. When Lady Spencer (Charlotte Rampling), Georgiana's mother, says her affair with Grey is the talk of London, why should she be surprised? Every conversation in this film takes place in the presence of at least two servants.

I deeply enjoyed the film, but then I am an Anglophile. I imagine the behavior of the characters will seem exceedingly odd to some viewers. Well, it is. William is a right proper bastard without normal feelings—a monster. How do you make love with the fifth Duke of Devonshire? You close your eyes and think of the sixth Duke of Devonshire. Georgiana puts up with more than we can imagine. When we see her tender and playful in the company of Earl Grey, it is a refreshing change. We do not see William and Bess bedding each other, and just as well. We hear them.

This is not one of those delightful movies based on a Jane Austen novel. It is about hard realists, constrained in a stifling system and using whatever weapons they can command. It is rather fascinating on that level, although I would have loved to learn more about what the Whigs at that formal dinner *really* thought about Charles Fox's vision of the rights of man and the abolition of the slave trade.

Note: Yes, the famous tea is named after Earl Grey. It is my second favorite, after Lapsang Souchong, which has an aroma stirring nostalgia for fresh tar in autumn.

The Duchess of Langeais ★ ★ ★ ½
NO MPAA RATING, 138 m., 2008

Jeanne Balibar (Antoinette de Langeais), Guillaume Depardieu (Armand de Montriveau), Bulle Ogier (Princesse de Blamont-Chauvry), Michel Piccoli (Vidame de Pamiers), Barbet Schroeder (Duc de Grandlieu), Anne Cantineau (Clara de Serizy). Directed by Jacques Rivette and produced by Martine Marignac and Maurice Tinchant. Screenplay by Pascal Bonitzer and Christine Laurent, based on the novel by Honore de Balzac.

The lovers in *The Duchess of Langeais* never consummate their love, but it consummates them. The film is about two elegant aristocrats whose stubborn compulsions eat them alive. They're bullheaded to the point of madness. Their story is told with a fair amount of passion, but it's interior passion, bottled up, carrying them to a point far beyond what either one expects or desires.

The director is Jacques Rivette, one of the founders of the French New Wave, here giving himself over to a deliberate style that intensifies the impact of his fairly simple story. He begins in the 1820s with Armand, the marquis of Montriveau (Guillaume Depardieu), a general whose battlefield exploits have made him a national hero. At a ball, Armand sees the celebrated Antoinette, the duchess of Langeais (Jeanne Balibar), and approaches her with unmistakable designs. She agrees to be visited by him. At his own door that evening, he exalts to himself: "The duchess of Langeais is my mistress!" That she is married never really figures in the story; her husband exists only as a throwaway line, and when she eventually locks herself up with a cloistered order of nuns, who knows if he was even consulted? (Now there's a conversation-stopper: Q: "How is your wife, Duke?" A: "Still cloistered with those nuns.")

The relationship between Armand and Antoinette takes place mostly at arm's length, on sofas in her rooms, which follow one after another, leading us more deeply into her chamber of secrets. Through these rooms and others, the characters walk on hardwood floors, their sharp footfalls creating a harsh counterpoint to their words of yearning and rejection. The marquis desires to possess the duchess. Such is only natural for a national hero. She does not intend to be touched, but refuses in such an alluring way that he is left with hope. Their conversations take months, during which the marquis gradually loses his temper, starts shouting at her, and one night even has her abducted and taken to his rooms, where he threatens to brand her with a red-hot iron.

If he were a rapist, all would be over, but he is not. What's her game, anyway? She invites him back again and again, makes it clear she

109

will always be home to him after eight, and teases him by demanding more stories about his journey across the burning sands of the desert. After the end of each episode, she rises and goes to attend a ball. We see her at one of these affairs, where she could not be more remote and disdainful of the company if she were an automaton.

The story is eventually one of merciless teasing. The duchess has an aged relative, played by the great Michel Piccoli, who warns her: "Avoid, my dear duchess, getting too coquet with such a man." Armand is an eagle, he says, and will lose patience and snatch her away to his aerie. Still she leads Armand on. He asks to kiss the hem of her garment.

"I think so much of you," she says. "I will give you my hand."

He kisses it through the hem and asks, "Will you always think so much of me?"

"Yes, but we will leave it at that."

Adapted from a novel by Balzac, the movie makes much use of intertitles, one of which reads: "If the previous scene is the civil period of this sentimental war, the following is the religious one." I assume these are Balzac's words. The film opens with religion, as Armand recognizes her singing voice in the invisible choir of the cloistered convent on Majorca. It ends there, too, as one of his comrades unforgettably says (and read no further to avoid inescapable conclusions), "She was a woman. Now she is nothing. Let's tie a ball to each foot and throw her into the sea."

Will you like this film? The everyday moviegoer will find it as impenetrable as its heroine. But if you vibrate to nuances of style, if you enjoy tension gathering strength beneath terrible restraint, if you admire great acting, then you will. You might also notice Rivette's subtle design touches, with furniture, costumes, and candles.

Guillaume Depardieu, son of Gerard, plays the marquis as a tall, physically imposing figure who is gradually made the psychological captive of the duchess. And Jeanne Balibar, as Antoinette, makes the heroine into a real piece of work. Surely she knows she is driving this man mad and destroying herself. Why does she persist? Because she cannot help herself? Or because, sadistically, she knows that she can?

Duplicity ★ ★ ★
PG-13, 125 m., 2009

Julia Roberts (Claire Stenwick), Clive Owen (Ray Koval), Tom Wilkinson (Howard Tully), Paul Giamatti (Richard Garsik). Directed by Tony Gilroy and produced by Jennifer Fox, Kerry Orent, and Laura Bickford. Screenplay by Gilroy.

Julia Roberts and Clive Owen generate fierce electricity in *Duplicity*, but we (and they) don't know if it's romantic or wicked. They're Claire and Ray, government spies (she CIA, he MI6) who meet on assignment in Dubai; she sleeps with him, then steals his secret documents. They both enter the private sector, working for the counterespionage departments of competing shampoo giants. At stake: the formula for a top-secret product that, when revealed, does indeed seem to be worth the high-tech games being played to steal and protect it.

The movie resembles *Mad* magazine's Spy vs. Spy series, elevated to labyrinthine levels of complexity. Nothing is as it seems or even as it seems to seem; triple-crosses are only the warm-up. What's consistent through all of the intrigues is the (certain) lust and (possible) love between them. The theory is, they'll scheme together to steal the formula, sell it in Switzerland, split millions, and spend the rest of their lives spying on each other under the covers.

They're both such incurable operatives that neither one can trust the other. We're not even sure they trust themselves. They play an emotional cat-and-mouse game, cleverly scripted by director Tony Gilroy (*Michael Clayton*) to reflect classic romcoms; both actors seem to be channeling Cary Grant.

Claire and Ray seem to have hollow hearts. Can they, in their trade, sincerely love anyone? Knowing all the tricks, they know the other one knows them, too. This removes some of the romantic risk from the story, replacing it with a plot so ingenious that at the end we know more or less what happened, but mostly less. That's fun but deprives Roberts of her most winning note, which is lovability.

This isn't a two-hander; Gilroy uses his supporting cast for key roles. Tom Wilkinson and Paul Giamatti play the two enemy soap tycoons, both consumed by desperate intensity. Carrie Preston steals a scene from Roberts with her hilarious role as a company travel agent who may have been seduced by Ray but bubbles over about how glad she is that it happened. Roberts is amusingly inscrutable as she listens.

Duplicity is entertaining, but the complexities of its plot keep it from being really involving: When nothing is as it seems, why care?

The fun is in watching Roberts and Owen fencing with dialogue, keeping straight faces, trying to read each other's minds. That, and admiring the awesome technology that goes into corporate espionage. I don't understand why Wall Street executives deserve millions, but I can see why these two might. All the money they hope to steal, added together, wouldn't amount to an annual bonus for one of the bankruptcy masterminds.

E

Eagle Eye ★ ★
PG-13, 118 m., 2008

Shia LaBeouf (Jerry Shaw), Michelle Monaghan (Rachel Holloman), Rosario Dawson (Agent Zoe Perez), Michael Chiklis (Secretary Callister), Anthony Mackie (Major Bowman), Billy Bob Thornton (Agent Thomas Morgan). Directed by D. J. Caruso and produced by Alex Kurtzman, Roberto Orci, Patrick Crowley, and Edward L. McDonnell. Screenplay by John Glenn, Travis Wright, Hillary Seitz, and Dan McDermott.

SPOILER WARNING: The word "preposterous" is too moderate to describe *Eagle Eye.* This film contains not a single plausible moment after the opening sequence, and that's borderline. It's not an assault on intelligence. It's an assault on consciousness. I know, I know. I liked *The Mummy: Tomb of the Dragon Emperor,* but that film intended to be absurd. *Eagle Eye* has real cars and buildings and trains and CNN and stuff, and purports to take place in the real world.

You might like it, actually. Lots of people will. It involves relentless action: chases involving planes, trains, automobiles, buses. Hundreds of dead. Enough crashes to stock a junkyard. Lots of stuff being blowed up real good. Two heroes who lack any experience with violence but somehow manage to stick up an armored car at gunpoint, walk on board an unguarded military transport plane, and penetrate the ultrasecret twenty-ninth-floor basement of the Pentagon.

They are Jerry and Rachel (Shia LaBeouf and Michelle Monaghan). Both are ordinary Chicagoans until they start getting commands from a mysterious female voice on their cell phones. Now try to follow this: Whatever force is behind the voice has control of every cell phone and security camera in the nation. "They" can control every elevated train and every stoplight. Can observe the traffic and give precise driving instructions. Can control the movements of cranes in junkyards, the locations of garbage barges, and arrange for a rendezvous on a dirt road in an Indiana country field. Oh, and when a guy drives down the road to meet them in a van, They can instruct them to warn the guy that if he walks away he will be killed. If They don't want him dead, then why do They kill him—since the situation clearly reflects Their power?

We haven't even arrived at the Pentagon yet, and already the audience is chuckling at the impossibilities. I won't even get started on the air cargo container, the syringes inside, and the on-time recovery of the heroes after they give themselves shots. Turns out the syringes were in a briefcase that the heroes survived incredible death and destruction to pick up, and it isn't even needed after the plane takes off. I won't give it away, but the only thing They really need is an attribute of Jerry's. So here's an idea that would save billions of dollars and hundreds of lives: Why not get a couple of no-neck guys from the West Side to kidnap Jerry, haul him on board a private jet, and transport him to Them?

OK, OK. Enough with the implausibilities. This whole movie is a feature-length deus ex machina, and if you don't know what that is, look it up, because you're going to need it to discuss *Eagle Eye.* And yet, I think I'll use the tricky star-rating system to give it two stars. Now why would I give it two instead of, oh, say, one star? Both *because* of the elements I've complained about, and *in spite* of the elements I've complained about.

Let me explain. If you're looking for a narrative that makes much sense, *Eagle Eye* lacks one. It's essentially a lot of CGI and stunt work, all stuck together in a row. Shia LaBeouf is a good young actor, but you wouldn't discover that here. I barely had time to observe that he resembles an underweight John Cusack when he was off and running, as Jerry and Rachel became elements in effects scenes. The movie obviously intends to resemble and inspire a video game, and at that it is slick. I look forward to professor David Bordwell's students using their clickers to work out the average shot length. I'm predicting less than three seconds. So to summarize, *Eagle Eye* is great at all the things I object to, and I admit it. But I didn't enjoy it.

Earth ★ ★ ★

G, 99 m., 2009

A documentary directed by Alastair Fothergill and Mark Linfield and produced by Sophokles Tasioulis and Alix Tidmarsh. Screenplay by Fothergill, Linfield, and Leslie Megahey.

Made between 1948 and 1960, Walt Disney's *True Life Adventures* won three Oscars for best documentary feature, and several others won in the since-discontinued category of two-reel short features. Now the studio has returned to this admirable tradition with *Earth*. It's a film that younger audiences in particular will enjoy.

To be sure, Disney didn't produce the film. It is a feature-length compilation from the splendid BBC and Discovery channel series *Planet Earth*, utilizing the big screen to make full use of its high-def images. The feature's original narrator, Patrick Stewart, has been replaced by James Earl Jones.

What we see is astonishing. Polar bear cubs tumble their way to the sea. Birds of paradise make displays of ethereal beauty. Storks fly above the Himalayas. Elephants trek exhausted across a bone-dry desert. Humpback whales swim three thousand miles to their summer feeding grounds off Antarctica. A predator cat outruns a springbok. Ducklings leap from their nest to fly and plummet to the ground—a learning experience.

The most poignant sequence in the film shows a polar bear, lost at sea and searching for ice floes in a time of global warming, finally crawling ashore exhausted and starving. Desperate for food, he hopelessly attacks a herd of walruses, fails, and slumps dying to the earth; nearby walruses are indifferent.

In the tradition of such favorites of my childhood as Disney's *The Living Desert* and *The Vanishing Prairie*, the narration provides these animals with identities. It opens with a mother polar bear and two cubs. The desperate polar bear is identified as their father, although I will bet a shiny new dime that the authors of the narration have absolutely no evidence of its paternal history. I'm not complaining; in a film like this, that goes with the territory.

The film is filled with unexpected facts. Did you know the fir trees beginning at the northern tree line circle the globe with an almost unbroken forest, harbor almost no birds and mammals because they are not edible, and supply more of the planet's oxygen than the rain forests? Or that baby whales have to be taught to breathe?

Earth is beautiful and worthwhile. At its pre-opening press screening, cosponsored by the Lincoln Park Zoo in Chicago, we were supplied not with free popcorn but tiny evergreens to take home and plant.

Eastern Promises ★ ★ ★ ★

R, 96 m., 2007

Viggo Mortensen (Nikolai Luzhin), Naomi Watts (Anna Khitrova), Vincent Cassel (Kirill), Armin Mueller-Stahl (Semyon), Sinead Cusack (Helen), Jerzy Skolimowski (Stepan). Directed by David Cronenberg and produced by Robert Lantos and Paul Webster. Screenplay by Steve Knight.

David Cronenberg's *Eastern Promises* opens with a throat slashing and a young woman collapsing in blood in a drugstore and connects these events with a descent into an underground of Russians who have immigrated to London and brought their crime family with them. Like the Corleone family, but with a less wise and more fearsome patriarch, the Vory V Zakone family of the Russian Mafia operates in the shadows of legitimate business—in this case, a popular restaurant.

The slashing need not immediately concern us. The teenage girl who hemorrhages is raced to a hospital and dies in childbirth in the arms of a midwife named Anna Khitrova (Naomi Watts). Fiercely determined to protect the helpless surviving infant, she uses her Russian-born family (Sinead Cusack and Jerzy Skolimowski) to translate the dead girl's diary, and it leads her to a restaurant run by Semyon (Armin Mueller-Stahl), the head of the Mafia family. Her father begs her to go nowhere near that world.

Semyon has a vile son named Kirill (Vincent Cassel) and a violent but loyal driver and bodyguard, Nikolai (Viggo Mortensen). And the gears of the story shift into place when the diary, the midwife, and the crime family become interlocked.

Eastern Promises is no ordinary crime thriller, just as Cronenberg is no ordinary director. Beginning with low-rent horror films in the 1970s because he could get them financed, Cronenberg has moved film by film into the top rank of directors, and here he wisely reunites with Mortensen, star of their *History of Violence* (2005). No, Mortensen is not Russian, but don't even think about the problem of an accent; he digs so deeply into the role you may not recognize him at first.

Naomi Watts, playing an Anglicized second-generation immigrant, has no idea at first what she has gotten herself into and why the diary is of vital importance to these people. All she cares about is the baby, but she learns fast that the baby's life and her own are both at great risk. In fact, her entry into that world has driven a wedge into it that sets everybody at odds and challenges long-held assumptions.

The screenplay is by Steve Knight, author of the powerful film *Dirty Pretty Things* (2002), about a black market in body parts. It was set in London and had scarcely a native-born Londoner in it. He's fascinated by the worlds within the London world. Here, too. And his lines of morality are more murkily drawn here, as allegiances and loyalties shift, and old emotions turn out to be forgotten, but not dead.

Mortensen's Nikolai is the key player, trusted by Semyon. We are reminded of Don Corleone's trust in an outsider, Tom Hagen, over his own sons, Sonny and Fredo. Here Semyon depends on Nikolai more than Kirill, who has an ugly streak that sometimes interferes with the orderly conduct of business. Anna (Watts) senses she can trust Nikolai, too, even though it is established early that this tattooed warrior is capable of astonishing violence. At a time when movie "fight scenes" are as routine as the dances in musicals, Nikolai engages in a fight in this film that sets the same kind of standard that *The French Connection* set for chases. Years from now, it will be referred to as a benchmark.

Cronenberg has said he's not interested in crime stories as themselves. "I was watching *Miami Vice* the other night," he told Adam Nayman of Toronto's *Eye Weekly*, "and I realized I'm not interested in the mechanics of the mob but criminality and people who live in a state of perpetual transgression—that is interesting to me." And to me, as well. What the director and writer do here is not unfold a plot, but flay the skin from a hidden world. Their story puts their characters to a test: They can be true to their job descriptions within a hermetically sealed world where everyone shares the same values and expectations, and where outsiders are by definition the prey. But what happens when their cocoon is broached? Do they still possess fugitive feelings instilled by a long-forgotten babushka? And what if they do?

"Just don't give the plot away," Cronenberg begged in that interview. He is correct that it would be fatal, because this is not a movie of what or how, but of *why*. And for a long time, you don't see the why coming. It's that way with stories about plausible human beings, which is why I prefer them to stories about characters who are simply elements in fiction. There was a big surprise in *A History of Violence* that pretty much everybody entering the theater already knew. I have studied the trailer of *Eastern Promises*, and it doesn't give away a hint of its central business.

So let's leave it that way and simply regard the performances. I write little about casting directors because I can't know what really goes on, and of course directors make the final choice for key roles. But whatever Deirdre Bowen and Nina Gold had to do with the choices in this movie, including what might seem the unlikely choice of Mortensen, was pitch-perfect. The actors and the characters merge and form a reality above and apart from the story, and the result is a film that takes us beyond crime and London and the Russian Mafia and into the mystifying realms of human nature.

Easy Virtue ★ ★ ★
PG-13, 96 m., 2009

Jessica Biel (Larita), Colin Firth (Mr. Whittaker), Kristin Scott Thomas (Mrs. Whittaker), Ben Barnes (John), Kris Marshall (Furber), Kimberley Nixon (Hilda), Katharine Parkinson (Marion). Directed by Stephan Elliott and produced by Joseph Abrams, James D. Stern, and Barnaby Thompson. Screenplay by Elliott and Sheridan Jobbins, based on the play by Noel Coward.

Unusually for a play by Noel Coward, love has a struggle conquering all in *Easy Virtue,* a subversive view of British country house society between the wars. That era has been described as the most blessed in modern history (assuming you were upstairs and not down), but not here, where the Whittaker family occupies a moldering pile in the countryside. It is said that nothing in a country house should look new. Nothing in this one looks as if it were ever new.

To his ancestral seat, a fresh young man named John (Ben Barnes) brings his great love, Larita (Jessica Biel), to meet his hostile mother (Kristin Scott Thomas), his shambling father (Colin Firth), and his unfortunate sisters Marion (Katharine Parkinson) and Hilda (Kimberley Nixon), one snobbish, the other fawning. Perhaps the innocent John never realized how toxic his mother and elder sister were until Larita arrived to attract their poison.

Larita is an auto racer, the recent winner of the Monaco Grand Prix. It's worth remembering that in the 1920s racing drivers and pilots were admired almost like astronauts (see Shaw's *Man and Superman*), and females were goddesses. Yet Larita, an American unschooled in the labyrinth of the British upper crust, earnestly hopes to make her alliance with John a success. She does everything an American girl is taught to do, even supervising the preparation of what may be the first edible meal ever served in the stately home (all-purpose 1920s Brit recipe: "Cook until dead").

Scott Thomas and Firth are old hands at their characters, the one brittle and unpleasant, the other depressed, disillusioned, and unhappily wed. Ben Barnes is your prototypical fresh young man. Jessica Biel will surprise some with her skill; she takes to Coward as if to the manner (if not manor) born. She has certainly left her work in *The Texas Chainsaw Massacre* (2003) far behind. She makes Larita independent and able, yet capable of a love more sincere than the feckless John can comprehend. She would be the best thing that ever happened to him, and the story is essentially about whether he can get that through his head.

Mr. and Mrs. Whittaker are both more nuanced than the clichés they first seem. She has her urgent reasons for wishing her son to marry elsewhere. He is a member of that generation where most of the best and brightest died in the trenches of France—including, we learn, all of the men under his command. The matriarch clings desperately to the shreds of her fading family. Her husband retreats into dotty distraction and a studied casual evasiveness that masks despair.

Easy Virtue is being presented, and was no doubt intended by Coward, as a comedy. As we'd expect, the dialogue has an edgy wit, although it has no ambitions to be falling-down funny. Here is the *Odd Couple* formula applied in a specific time and place that make them feel very odd indeed.

The Edge of Heaven ★ ★ ★ ★

NO MPAA RATING, 122 m., 2008

Baki Davrak (Nejat Aksu), Nursel Kose (Yeter Ozturk), Nurgul Yesilcay (Ayten Ozturk), Patrycia Ziolkowska (Lotte Staub), Hanna Schygulla (Susanne Staub), Tuncel Kurtiz (Ali Aksu). Directed by Fatih Akin and produced by Andreas Thiel, Klaus Maeck, and Akin. Screenplay by Akin.

The best approach is to begin with the characters, because the wonderful, sad, touching movie *The Edge of Heaven* is more about its characters than about its story. There is a reason for that: This is one of those films of interlocking narrative strands, called a hyperlink movie, but the strands never link. True, they link for us because we possess crucial information about the characters—but they never link for the characters because they lack that information. I liked it that way.

There is an old man named Ali (Tuncel Kurtiz) in Bremen, Germany. He is from Turkey. He has a smile that makes you like him. Think of Walter Matthau. One day (as is his habit, I suspect), he goes to visit a prostitute. This is a middle-aged Turkish woman named Yeter (Nursel Kose), who works from the doorway of a brothel. Yeter is heard speaking by a group of Turkish men, who assume she is Muslim and tell her they will kill her unless she quits the business. Ali makes her an offer: He will pay her to move in with him on a permanent basis. She accepts.

Spoiler warning, I suppose, although this segment of the film is titled "Yeter's Death." Ali gets drunk, he hits her, she falls, she's dead, he's in prison. She was heartbroken in life because her daughter, Ayten (Nurgul Yesilcay), had been long out of touch with her. Yeter's body is shipped back to Istanbul, where we meet Ali's son, Nejat (Baki Davrak). Nejat is a professor at a German university but makes it his business to track down Yeter's daughter and somehow make reparation. In this process he moves back to Istanbul and buys a German-language bookstore from a man who is homesick for Germany.

Back and forth, between Turkey and Germany, the strands tangle. We meet Yeter's daughter, who is a member of a militant group. Deeply in trouble with the authorities, she flees to Germany, where she is befriended and taken home by a young woman named Lotte (Patrycia Ziolkowska). The two fall quickly and passionately in love. For reasons we will leave to them, Ayten ends up in a Turkish prison, Lotte goes to Istanbul to try to help her, and . . . well, nevermind.

You must also meet Lotte's mother, Susanne, who is played by the magnificent Hanna Schygulla, the legendary German actress, best known for her Fassbinder films. She is not pleased with her daughter's romance but in the end goes to Istanbul so that she, too, can try to help Ayten. In Turkey she meets Nejat and ends up living in the same room that her daughter had rented from him.

One of the deepest pleasures of going to the movies for many years is that we can watch actors age and ripen and understand what is happening to ourselves. Hanna Schygulla was once a sexpot in Fassbinder's *The Bitter Tears of Petra von Kant* (1972), and was a commanding star in his great film *The Marriage of Maria Braun* (1979). She was Fassbinder's most important acting talent and his muse, and has appeared in eighty-two films or TV projects. She was a young vixen once, then a sultry romantic lead, and now she is a plumpish woman of sixty-five. My own age, it occurs to me. But *what* a woman of sixty-five! Not a second of plastic surgery. She wears every year as a badge of honor. And here she is so tactful, so warm, so quietly spoken, so glowing, that she all but possesses the film, and we love her for her years and her art.

All this time, while perhaps thinking such thoughts, we are waiting for the penny to drop. Surely some combination of these people will discover how they are connected? But they never do. Maybe that requires a spoiler warning, too, because we are so accustomed to all the stories converging at the end of a hyperlink film. Not this time. The characters are related in theme, but not in plot.

Fatih Akin, who wrote and directed, made the powerful *Head-On* (2004), which in a very different way was about being Turkish and feeling dispossessed or threatened. Here he gives us three parents, a son, and two daughters, all of whose lives are affected, even governed, by the fact that some are Turks, some German. Religion doesn't really enter into it so much, except in inspiring Yeter's retirement. Akin's purpose, I think, is a simple one: He wants us to meet these people, know them, sympathize with them. Even old Ali is not so very evil; he had no intention to murder Yeter, and who among us, drunk or sober, has never unwisely done shameful things? My hand is not raised.

What happened to me during *The Edge of Heaven* was that I did care about the characters. I found them fascinating. They were not overwritten and didn't spend too much time explaining or justifying themselves. They just got on with their lives, and their lives got on with them, all the time swimming in the seas of two different cultures, two different sets of possibilities. Even the authorities are not the villains in the film.

Now if five, or four, of the characters found out how they were connected, what difference would that make? We are all connected, if only we could stand tall enough, see widely enough, and understand adequately. Mere plot points are meaningless. Fatih Akin wants us to realize that, I believe, and he also wants us to understand his creatures, who are for the most part good people, have good intentions, make mistakes, suffer for their errors, and try to soldier on, as do we all.

Eight Miles High ★ ★ ½
NO MPAA RATING, 114 m., 2008

Natalia Avelon (Uschi Obermaier), Matthias Schweighofer (Rainer Langhans), David Scheller

(Dieter Bockhorn), Alexander Scheer (Keith Richards), Victor Noren (Mick Jagger). Directed by Achim Bornhak and produced by Eberhard Junkersdorf and Dietmar Guntsche. Screenplay by Bornhak and Olaf Kraemer.

She was Germany's uber-groupie, a small-town Bavarian girl who lucked her way onto a magazine cover, became a famous model, slept with Jimi Hendrix and Mick Jagger, and had something a little more than that with Keith Richards. Along the way she was also involved with a radical commune, was on the cover of *Playboy*, traveled the world with a wealthy playboy in the bus he constructed for her, and gave a face to the word "Eurotrash." Whew.

Uschi Obermaier was a real woman. She slept her way to what looked like the top to her, but she was fiercely independent, rejected all offers of marriage, walked out on contracts to indulge her free spirit, and lived the life all groupies dream about (I guess). Then she told all in her autobiography, *High Times*. The distance "eight miles" has been added to the movie title no doubt in reference to the Byrds' song.

Critics have pretty much hated this film, although some have been kind ("deliciously dumb, reasonably well-made" —Andrew O'Hehir, Salon). It has much to be kind about. Natalia Avelon plays Uschi with a disdain for bras and blouses, her radical boyfriend has more hair than Angela Davis, her playboy boyfriend leaps about with the frenzied excitement of a forty-something hippie, and the impersonators of Jagger and Richards sometimes look a little like the real thing, in the right shadows, at certain angles. Jimi Hendrix is only cited.

The movie presents the surfaces of Obermaier's life, but never really lets us understand who she was. Avelon has a face for the role that is maddeningly unrevealing; sometimes she pouts, sometimes she's happy, sometimes she's pensive, sometimes she's out to lunch. As Rainer Langhans, the real-life leader of a Berlin commune, Matthias Schweighofer reflects a quality I noticed in a few real-life 1960s leftist radicals I knew: He's like a strict, scolding mother, lecturing those in his charge to correct their flawed ideas. That he and Uschi are "in love" is, I think, an ideological

decision for both. He's not comfortable with her celebrity, and she's not happy to be lectured. Although her modeling is accepted by the commune as a source of funds, they don't think she's really sincere in her worship of the cause, nor is she.

David Scheller is more interesting as the real-life Dieter Bockhorn, who ran a night-club in Hamburg, which he often closed to throw wild parties for his friends. Uschi has seen photos of him cavorting with African dancers, responds to his invitation to see the world, travels by bus with him for, I dunno, several years, it seems like. In those carefree years lots of hippies were drawn to India, and so are they, using a newspaper headline to convince a maharaja they are a prince and princess. She offers to throw them a wedding, and does, with a brass band, horses, elephants, costumed dancers, and all you can eat. Uschi, opposed to marriage, is told by Dieter that the ceremony "isn't really real," and going along with it is like a favor. Later, she pouts, "But I think it was real for him."

Now, what can I say about this biopic? Well, it's deliciously dumb and reasonably well-made, for starters. It has few human insights, and those of the most obvious kind. But it is not boring. That goes for something. If Uschi Obermaier comes across as shallow and heedless, well, maybe she was. This is not a role for an actress who radiates intelligence, like Tilda Swinton. The story of Uschi's life would not easily support depth and thoughtfulness, especially not with the amount of weed around.

There are some nice moments. She breaks up with Keith Richards, but later meets him by accident on a Mexican beach, and they find they're still in love. But he is getting married, and observes, "Seems like we're always meeting at the wrong end of the stick." Nice line. It seems doubtful that Jagger would come sniffing around Berlin without a bodyguard, but if you see Uschi in this movie, you may sympathize. The real Uschi, I learn from Wiki, was thin and slender. Not Avelon. She possesses a matched set of expensive breasts.

By the way, do not confuse this Uschi with my old pal Uschi Digard, the Russ Meyer supervixen from the late 1960s and early 1970s, although like Obermaier she became a diamond merchant and jewelry designer. She was from Sweden, was as famous a model as Obermaier, although not in French *Vogue*, and was all real. "Silicone," Russ believed, "spoils the fun," although he was later forced to relax his vigilance. It's an evocative name, Uschi. Makes me think of mashing ice cream.

El Camino ★ ★ ★
NO MPAA RATING, 87 m., 2009

Leo Fitzpatrick (Elliot), Christopher Denham (Gray), Elisabeth Moss (Lily), Wes Studi (Dave), Richard Gallagher (Matthew), Amy Hargreaves (Sissy). Directed by Erik S. Weigel and produced by Fran Giblin and Jason Noto. Screenplay by Weigel and Salvatore Interlandi.

El Camino is a pure American road movie, freed of the requirements of plot, requiring only a purpose and a destination. It is so pure that it involves two men and a woman, all in their twenties, all in the same station wagon, and there is *not* a romantic triangle. All three have different needs in life, and have joined only for this journey.

They meet for the first time when their friend Matthew (Richard Gallagher) dies. Elliot (Leo Fitzpatrick) and Matthew were in foster care together. Lily (Elisabeth Moss) was his former girlfriend. Gray (Christopher Denham) met him and felt an immediate bond. After the funeral, Gray and Lily decide to steal Matthew's ashes and scatter them in Mexico. Elliot insists on going along, and he will pay. That's the deal maker.

What did Matthew really mean to them? The movie lacks the usual heart-spilling confessions. All three are reticent, revealing themselves in elliptical asides. Nor do they spill the beans about their own lives. They pound on, mile after mile, North Carolina to Mexico, one cheap motel after another, lots of cigarettes, desultory talk, honky-tonk bars, a fight, unhappy telephone calls.

Road movies require colorful people along the way. This one has a couple. Wes Studi plays a self-employed man who repairs their car, invites them to dinner, has strong political opinions (not the ones you might expect), and contempt for Gray's cynicism. Amy Hargreaves plays an older woman in a bar who smiles at Gray and ends up listening to his introspections. And no, she's not a hooker; she's lonely and nice.

Mystery surrounds Elliot. Flashbacks suggest a confused childhood. We have no idea where he lives now, what he does, where he gets his money. I first saw the gawky Leo Fitzpatrick in the breakthrough movie *Kids* (1995), which also introduced Rosario Dawson, Chloe Sevigny, Justin Pierce, and Jon Abrahams. Fitzpatrick is gawky no more. He only gradually sheds his funeral suit and tie, tends to lean forward thoughtfully, gives the impression of not saying a lot of things that he could.

We begin to wonder what ashes will be scattered: only Matthew's, or perhaps the ashes of the false starts and undirected lives of the living? There are moments of self-discovery along the way, but not underlined with fraught dialogue or painfully intense acting. All three characters seem to be focusing mostly on themselves. In the way this confounds our road movie expectations, it becomes quietly absorbing.

The film is elegantly shot by Till Neumann in rarely seen 2.35:1 widescreen, good for the big boat they're driving in and for the landscape they're driving through. This is the opposite of queasy-cam, and it makes sense that one of those thanked by the filmmakers is the contemplative Terrence Malick (another is Gus Van Sant, himself a master of uncertain journeys). At the end, one of the characters has a next destination in mind. The other two seem prepared to simply move away from, not toward, their lives until now—and that, too, is in keeping with the tone. At a time of life when everything is still tentative, there's insight in a film that doesn't force them into corners.

El Cantante ★ ★
R, 116 m., 2007

Marc Anthony (Hector Lavoe), Jennifer Lopez (Puchi), John Ortiz (Willie Colon), Manny Perez (Eddie). Directed by Leon Ichaso and produced by Julio Caro, Jennifer Lopez, Simon Fields, and David Maldonado. Screenplay by Ichaso, David Darmstaedter, and Todd Anthony Bello.

This bulletin just in: If you use cocaine or heroin, you are very likely to become addicted, and if you become addicted, there are usually two choices: (1) get clean, or (2) die. The math is clear and has been proven in countless biopics about addicted musicians. The presumption in many of the pictures is that artists somehow need drugs because they are so talented they just can't stand it, or because of the "pressure" they're under, or because they need to be high all the time and not just on the stage, or because people won't leave them alone, or because they feel insecure or unworthy.

All lies. They are addicted because they are addicted. They got addicted by starting to take the stuff in the first place. It's chemistry. At some point, they don't use to get high, but to stop feeling sick. It is a sad, degrading existence, interrupted by flashes of feeling "OK." George Carlin once asked, "How does cocaine make you feel?" And he answered: "It makes you feel like having some more cocaine."

El Cantante, the life and death story of Hector Lavoe (Marc Anthony), the godfather of salsa, retraces the same tired footsteps of many another movie druggie before him. He lies, cheats, disappoints those who love him, and finally dies, although even the movie loses patience with the dying process and cuts out before getting to his years with AIDS (from an infected needle). All along the way, he is enabled and berated in equal measure by his wife and sometime manager, Puchi (Jennifer Lopez), who is our guide to his story in black-and-white flashbacks.

The end of the movie is a foregone conclusion, and Hector's inexorable descent is depressing, although interrupted by many upbeat musical numbers. Indeed, there seem to be two films here: a musical, with Anthony doing a terrific job of covering Lavoe's music, and a drugalogue. The sound track would be worth having. But there is nothing special about Lavoe's progress toward the grave: just the same old same old.

Lavoe was a gifted musician in Puerto Rico who moved to New York, changed his name from Perez, partnered with the great trombonist Willie Colon (who could have borrowed the leftover Perez), and began to blend Latin genres, jazz, and a dash of rock into something that was known as salsa and became very big. We sense the excitement of the new music in Anthony's stage performances, where he is backed by orchestras full of gifted musicians (Colon is played by John Ortiz), and where his moves project the joy of the music.

But always in the wings, looking worried, is Puchi. She loves the guy and his music, but not his drugs, and they have ceaseless arguments about his drug use, sometimes punctuated by her own. These period sequences are intercut with a modern-day Puchi, looking not a day older, remembering her life with Hector and reciting the litany of his fall from life. Since Puchi lived until 2002, she must have learned something about drugs, if only to stop, but her memories mostly take the form of puzzled complaints: That was a great night, but then . . . he went out and scored, used, passed out, etc., etc. They have a child, who functions as an afterthought in a few scenes, but mostly they roast in their private hell.

If you're a fan of Lavoe and salsa, or Lopez and Anthony, you'll want to see the movie for what's good in it. Otherwise, you may be disappointed. The director (Leon Ichaso) and his cowriters haven't licked a crucial question: Why do we need to see this movie and not just listen to the music?

Elegy ★ ★ ★
R, 108 m., 2008

Penelope Cruz (Consuela), Ben Kingsley (David Kepesh), Dennis Hopper (George O'Hearn), Patricia Clarkson (Carolyn), Peter Sarsgaard (Kenneth Kepesh), Deborah Harry (Amy O'Hearn). Directed by Isabel Coixet and produced by Tom Rosenberg, Gary Lucchesi, and Andre Lamal. Screenplay by Nicholas Meyer, based on a novel by Philip Roth.

Ben Kingsley, who can play just about any role, seems to be especially effective playing slimy intellectuals. *Elegy* is a film that could have been made for him, although by the time it's over, Penelope Cruz has slipped away with it and transformed Kingsley's character in the process. It's nicely done.

Kingsley plays David Kepesh, a professor of literature whose classroom manner seems designed to seduce the young student of his choice from each new class. He narrates the film and is not shy about describing his methods. To stay out of trouble, he waits until the semester is over and the grades have been given, and then throws a party at his book- and art-filled apartment, where he singles out his prey and dazzles her with flattering insights, intellectual bravado, and an invitation to meet sometime—just for coffee or a drink and conversation, you know.

His target this semester is the lithesome Consuela, played by Penelope Cruz as a Cuban-American who is old enough to know better but discerning enough to see that there may really be something to old Kepesh after all. The professor appoints himself her tutor to all the mysteries of life, art, New York, music, and sex. And for a while they mesh and enjoy each other.

But David grows obsessed with jealousy, convinced Consuela is seeing someone else— younger, of course, and more handsome and virile. He even accidentally drops in at a dance he knows she's attending to check up on her. His distrust spoils everything because she cannot abide not being trusted.

And then—the movie takes a dramatic turn, which I will not reveal, even though it contains all the deepest emotions and real feelings of the story. And in these scenes, Cruz is quietly powerful and very true. You understand why the Spanish director, Isabel Coixet, chose Cruz instead of, say, a nineteen-year-old. An actress needs depth and the experience of life to play these scenes, and Cruz has them.

The film is based on a novel by Philip Roth, who has just about exhausted my desire to read his stories about young babes falling for older, wiser intellectuals like, say, Philip Roth. I was reading his Library of America volume about Zuckerman recently and finally just put it down and said to the book: Sorry, Phil, but I cannot read one more speech founded on the f-word. I don't object to the f-word itself, but sorry, I've simply been overserved.

That *Elegy* is not simply a fantasy about the horny old rascal and the comely maid is to its credit. That it sees Manhattan clearly as a setting is also an advantage, since it is a place where we believe things like this are likely to happen. And then there is a wealth of supporting characters, notably Carolyn (Patricia Clarkson), no spring chicken, who has been

David's mistress for years. She can't believe there's another woman in his life and launches a barrage of f-words, but she makes the character real and poignant. I also liked Dennis Hopper as George, the old pal he has coffee with, who attempts to bring sanity into David's behavior, but despairs. And Peter Sarsgaard, as David's son, with problems of his own and a father who has become not only an embarrassment but, worse, an irrelevancy.

The movie is not great. I'm not sure why. Maybe the payoff plays too much like a payoff. Consuela asks David to do something I think we might be better off hearing about, instead of seeing. I'm not sure. The movie is obviously going for a big emotional charge at the end and might have been more effective with a quieter one. But you decide.

The 11th Hour ★ ★
PG, 91 m., 2007

A documentary directed by Leila Conners Petersen and Nadia Conners and produced by Leonardo DiCaprio, Chuck Castleberry, Brian Gerber, and Petersen. Screenplay by Petersen, Conners, and DiCaprio.

I agree with every word in this tedious documentary. As you can guess from the title, *The 11th Hour* sounds a warning that we have pretty much depleted the woodpile of planet Earth and, to keep things running, have been reduced to throwing our furniture on the fire. It is a devastating message.

Once there was a time when Earth existed on current energy. This year's sunlight fell on this year's crops, feeding and warming this year's human beings. With the exploitation of coal and oil, however, we have set fire to millions of years of stored energy as fast as we can, and the result is poisonous pollution, global warming, and planetary imbalance. What lies at the end of this suicidal spending spree? Stephen Hawking paints a future in which Earth resembles Venus, with a temperature of 482 degrees Fahrenheit. There would still be rain, however, although unfortunately of sulfuric acid.

Earth is cartwheeling out of balance. Did you know, as I learned in the new issue of *Discover*, that while fish stocks disappear from the oceans, their place is being taken by an unimaginably huge explosion of jellyfish— literally brainless creatures with a lifestyle consisting of eating? Sounds like us.

The 11th Hour gathers a group of respected experts to speak from their areas of knowledge about how we are despoiling our planet and what we might possibly do to turn things around. We don't have much time. The architects John Todd and Bruce Mau explain how we could build "green" buildings that would use solar energy, consume their own waste, and function much like a tree. There is no reason why every home (every newly built one, for sure) could not have solar panels on the roof to help heat, light, and cool itself. Well, one reason actually: The energy companies would resist any effort to redirect their own gargantuan subsidies toward eco-friendly homeowners.

We hear of the destruction of the forests, the death of the seas, the melting of the poles, the trapping of greenhouse gases. And in another forthcoming documentary, *In the Shadow of the Moon,* about the surviving astronauts who walked on the moon, we see their view of Earth from 250,000 miles away; it strikes us what an awfully large planet this is to be wrapped in such a thin and vulnerable atmosphere.

All of this is necessary to know. But are we too selfish to do anything about it? Why isn't everybody buying a hybrid car? They can get up to a third more fuel mileage. They are getting cheaper as gas grows more expensive. And here's the kicker: *They can go faster* because they have two engines. So you ask people if they're getting a hybrid, and they squirm and say, gee, they dunno, they'd rather stick to the old way of going slower, spending more on gas, and destroying the atmosphere. If booze companies advertise for responsible drinking and tobacco companies warn of health hazards, why don't gas companies ask you to buy a hybrid?

Some of these facts are in *The 11th Hour,* others are offered by me, and the point is: We more or less know all this stuff anyway. So does the movie motivate us to act on it? Not really. After I saw Al Gore's *An Inconvenient Truth,* my next car was a hybrid. After seeing *The 11th Hour,* I'd be thinking more about my next movie.

The film sidesteps one of the oldest laws of television news and documentaries: *Write to the picture!* When Gore's film tells you something, it shows you what it's talking about. Too much of the footage of *The 11th Hour* is just standard nature photography, as helicopter-cams swoop over hill and dale and birds look unhappy and ice melts.

This is intercut with fifty experts, more or less, who talk and talk and talk. The narrator and coproducer is Leonardo DiCaprio, who sounds like he's presenting a class project. Everyone is seen as talking heads, so we see them talk, then get some nature footage, then see them talk some more, until finally we're thinking, enough already; I get it. "A bore," Meyer the hairy economist once told the private eye Travis McGee, "is anyone who deprives you of solitude without providing you with companionship." This movie, for all its noble intentions, is a bore. Rent *An Inconvenient Truth* instead. Even if you've already seen it.

Elizabeth: The Golden Age ★ ★ ½
PG-13, 114 m., 2007

Cate Blanchett (Elizabeth I), Geoffrey Rush (Sir Francis Walsingham), Clive Owen (Sir Walter Raleigh), Samantha Morton (Mary, Queen of Scots), Abbie Cornish (Elizabeth Throckmorton), Jordi Molla (Philip II), Rhys Ifans (Robert Reston). Directed by Shekhar Kapur and produced by Tim Bevan, Eric Fellner, and Jonathan Cavendish. Screenplay by Michael Hirst and William Nicholson.

Elizabeth: The Golden Age is weighed down by its splendor. There are scenes where the costumes are so sumptuous, the sets so vast, the music so insistent, that we lose sight of the humans behind the dazzle of the production. Unlike *Elizabeth* (1998), by the same director, Shekhar Kapur, this film rides low in the water, its cargo of opulence too much to carry.

That's despite the return of the remarkable Cate Blanchett in the title role. Who else would be so tall, regal, assured, and convincing that these surroundings would not diminish her? We believe she is a queen. We simply cannot care enough about this queen. That Blanchett could appear in the same Toronto Film Festival playing Elizabeth and Bob Dylan, both splendidly, is a wonder of acting. But the film's screenplay, by Michael Hirst and William Nicholson, places her in the center of history that is baldly simplified, shamelessly altered, and pumped up with romance and action.

We see her kingdom threatened by two Catholics, Mary, Queen of Scots (Samantha Morton), who stood next in line to the throne, and Philip II of Spain (Jordi Molla), who was building a great armada to invade England. Elizabeth's treasury is depleted, her resources strained, her attention diverted by the arrival in her court of the dashing Sir Walter Raleigh (Clive Owen). He has just returned from the New Land with two gifts: the territory of Virginia, which he has named after her in honor of her virginity, and tobacco, which she smokes with great delight. Elizabeth was indeed by all accounts a virgin, but in 1585, when the story is set, she would have been over fifty and her virginity more or less settled. The film sidesteps the age issue by making her look young, sensuous, and fragrant, and yearning for a man such as Raleigh.

This Sir Walter, he is a paragon. He would have been thirty-two in 1585. Despite his shabby attire and rough-hewn manners, he uses brash confidence to rise in Elizabeth's esteem, and he becomes her trusted adviser and a mastermind of British military strategy. The film deals with the famous 1588 defeat of the armada with Raleigh at its center, commanding ships to be set afire and aimed to ram the Spanish vessels. He swings from ropes, brandishes his sword, saves himself by plunging into the sea, and in general proves himself a master swashbuckler, especially since history teaches us that the real Raleigh was ashore the whole time and played no role in the battles.

In the court, he is also a swordsman, seducing and impregnating Elizabeth's favorite lady-in-waiting, Elizabeth Throckmorton (Abbie Cornish). When Elizabeth hears this news, Blanchett rises to full fury in an awesome example of regal jealousy. She desired Raleigh for herself, of course, although there is no evidence that, in life, she had such feelings for him.

Some of the film's best scenes involve Mary, played by Samantha Morton as a heroic and devout woman who goes to the executioner's ax with dismay but royal composure. Elizabeth's own crisis of conscience over Mary's death is also well-played, but the film is far more interested by romantic intrigue and sea battles. I think it undervalues the ability of audiences to get involved in true historical drama instead of recycled action clichés.

Reviewing the earlier film, I suggested that Shekhar Kapur was perhaps influenced by the rich colors and tapestries of his native India. Here he seems carried away by them. There are scenes where the elaborate lace on Elizabeth's costume is so detailed and flawless that we don't think about the character, we wonder how long Blanchett must have had to stand there while holding the pose and not ruffling anything.

Can there be a third Elizabeth film? Of course there can. She lived until 1603, and some of her greatest glories were ahead of her. Shakespeare was active in London from the 1580s, although it was with Elizabeth's successor, James I, that his company enjoyed its great royal favor. No matter. With the same cavalier attitude to history as this second film, we could be talking about *Elizabeth and Shakespeare in Love*.

Elsa & Fred ★ ★ ½
PG, 106 m., 2008

China Zorrilla (Elsa), Manuel Alexandre (Alfredo), Blanca Portillo (Cuca), Roberto Carnaghi (Gabriel), Jose Angel Egido (Paco), Gonzalo Urtizberea (Alejo). Directed by Marcos Carnevale and produced by Jose Antonio Felez. Screenplay by Carnevale, Lily Ann Martin, and Marcela Guerty.

Elsa and I have one big thing in common. We both love the famous scene in Fellini's *La Dolce Vita* when Anita Ekberg and Marcello Mastroianni wade in the waters of the Trevi Fountain in Rome at dawn. That shared love is almost but not quite enough to inspire a recommendation from me for *Elsa & Fred*, which is a sweet but inconsequential romantic comedy.

Alfredo (Manuel Alexandre) has been a widower for seven months. He has been moved into a new apartment in Madrid by his shrill daughter, Cuca (Blanca Portillo). What would make him happier would be if she would stop micromanaging his life. His dog, Bonaparte, is better company. Through a Meet Cute involving a fender bender, he meets Elsa (China Zorrilla), an Argentinean neighbor in the same building.

They are both lonely, both looking for companionship. Alfredo is seventy-eight. Elsa says she is seventy-seven. Can you believe everything she says? On her wall there is a photograph of Ekberg in the great Fellini scene. When she was young, Elsa tells Fred, she was a ringer for Ekberg—often mistaken for her. Now she is no longer young, but she begins to take on beauty in the eyes of her new admirer, and tentatively they begin a romance.

The structure of the film, directed by Marcos Carnevale of Argentina, is foreordained. They will flirt, grow closer, spat, make up, grow even closer, and then time will inexorably exact some sort of toll. All of those things happen right on schedule, although the two actors give them a bittersweet appeal. Subplots involving a business deal and old secrets from the past are fitfully interesting. More entertaining are such stunts as how they deal with the bill in an expensive restaurant.

Spoiler warning: But what I really loved was the film's last act, when Alfredo fulfills Elsa's lifelong dream. He flies her to Rome for the first visit of her life, and after seeing all the other sights, they do indeed wade in the Trevi Fountain at dawn, in a scene photographed to remind us vividly of the Fellini original. This scene held me spellbound. It is true that Elsa no longer resembles Ekberg, if she ever did. But in her mind she does, and old Alfredo looks like young Marcello, and none of us look as we wish we did, but all of us can dream.

Enchanted ★ ★ ★

PG, 108 m., 2007

Amy Adams (Giselle), Patrick Dempsey (Robert Phillip), James Marsden (Prince Edward), Timothy Spall (Nathaniel), Idina Menzel (Nancy Tremaine), Rachel Covey (Morgan Phillip), Susan Sarandon (Queen Narissa). Directed by Kevin Lima and produced by Barry Josephson and Barry Sonnenfeld. Screenplay by Bill Kelly.

It's no surprise to me that Amy Adams is enchanting. She won my heart in *Junebug* (2005), where she told her clueless husband: "God loves you just the way you are, but he loves you too much to let you stay that way." You should have seen *Junebug* by now, which means you will not be surprised by how fresh and winning Amy Adams is in *Enchanted*, where her role absolutely depends on effortless lovability.

She's so lovable, in fact, she starts life as an animated princess in a Disney-style world. The birds, flowers, chipmunks, and cockroaches even love her and do her bidding. Listen, if you could employ the roaches of the world, you'd have a hell of a workforce. The princess is named Giselle, she has a beautiful singing voice, and although she resists singing "Someday, My Prince Will Come," I think she's always humming it to herself.

One day her prince does come. This is Prince Edward (James Marsden), and it is love at first sight, and there are wedding bells in the air before the wicked Queen Narissa (Susan Sarandon) puts the kibosh on romance by banishing Giselle to a place as far as possible from this magical kingdom. That would be Times Square. It is so very far, indeed, that the movie switches from animation to real-life and stays there. But the animated prologue does a good job of setting the stage, so that we understand the ground rules of what will essentially be a live-action story playing by Disney animation rules.

What results is a heart-winning musical comedy that skips lightly and sprightly from the lily pads of hope to the manhole covers of actuality, if you see what I mean. I'm not sure I do. Anyway, Prince Edward follows her to New York, along with his manservant Nathaniel (Timothy Spall in full Jeeves sail) and her chipmunk. But do not rush to the conclusion that Giselle and Edward find love in Gotham, because there is the complication of Robert (Patrick Dempsey), the handsome single dad she meets. He's raising a daughter named Morgan (Rachel Covey), and Morgan of course likes her on the spot when she ends up living with them as a homeless waif from an unimaginable place.

Not so welcoming is Nancy (Idina Menzel), who already fills the girlfriend slot in Robert's life. She's nice enough, but can she hold her ground against a movie princess? Not in a PG-rated world. So the romance and the adventure play out in ways that would be familiar enough in an animated comedy, but seem daring in the real world. First we get animation based on reality (*Beowulf*), and now reality based on animation.

The movie has a sound background in Disney animation, starting with director Kevin Lima (*Tarzan, A Goofy Movie*) and including the music by Alan Menken and lyrics by Stephen Schwartz, who composed for *Pocahontas* and *The Hunchback of Notre Dame*. More important, it has a Disney willingness to allow fantasy into life, so New York seems to acquire a new playbook.

We know, for example, that there are bugs in Manhattan. Millions of them, in a city where the garbage left overnight on the sidewalk must seem like a never-ending buffet. But when Giselle recruits roaches to help her clean Robert's bathtub—well, I was going to say, you'll never think of roaches the same way again, but actually, you will. I am reminded of *Joe's Apartment* (1996), which used five thousand real roaches, and of which I wrote: "That depresses me, but not as much as the news that none of them were harmed during the production."

Anyway, the roach scene is soon over, and the scheming begins, much aided by Sarandon's evil queen, who fears the specter of her son Edward marrying the unworthy Giselle. I am not sure that Robert and Morgan fully understand from whence Giselle comes, but they respond to the magic in her, and so do we.

Encounters at the End of the World ★ ★ ★ ★
G, 99 m., 2008

Directed and narrated by Werner Herzog and produced by Henry Kaiser. Screenplay by Herzog.

Read the title of *Encounters at the End of the World* carefully, for it has two meanings. As he journeys to the South Pole, which is as far as you can get from everywhere, Werner Herzog also journeys to the prospect of man's oblivion. Far under the eternal ice, he visits a curious tunnel whose walls have been decorated by various mementos, including a frozen fish that is far away from its home waters. What might travelers from another planet think of these souvenirs, he wonders, if they visit long after all other signs of our civilization have vanished?

Herzog has come to live for a while at the McMurdo Research Station, the largest habitation on Antarctica. He was attracted by underwater films taken by his friend Henry Kaiser, which show scientists exploring the ocean floor. They open a hole in the ice with a blasting device, then plunge in, collecting specimens, taking films, nosing around. They investigate an undersea world of horrifying carnage, inhabited by creatures so ferocious we are relieved they are too small to be seen. And also by enormous seals who sing to one another. In order not to limit their range, Herzog observes, the divers do not use a tether line, so they must trust themselves to find the hole in the ice again. I am afraid to even think about that.

Herzog is a romantic wanderer, drawn to the extremes. He makes as many documentaries as fiction films, is prolific in the chronicles of his curiosity, and here moseys about McMurdo chatting with people who have chosen to live here in eternal day or night. They are a strange population. One woman likes to have herself zipped into luggage and performs this feat on the station's talent night. One man was once a banker and now drives an enormous bus. A pipe fitter matches the fingers of his hands together to show that the second and third are the same length—genetic evidence, he says, that he is descended from Aztec kings.

But I make the movie sound like a travelogue or an exhibit of eccentrics, and it is a poem of oddness and beauty. Herzog is like no other filmmaker, and to return to him is to be welcomed into a world vastly larger and more peculiar than the one around us. The underwater photography alone would make a film, but there is so much more.

Consider the men who study the active volcanoes of Antarctica and sometimes descend into volcanic flumes that open to the surface—although they must take care, Herzog observes in his wondering, precise narration, not to be doing so when the volcano erupts. It happens that there is another movie opening now that also has volcanic tubes (*Journey to the Center of the Earth*). Do not confuse the two. These men play with real volcanoes.

They also lead lives revolving around monster movies on video, a treasured ice-cream machine, and a string band concert from the top of a Quonset hut during the eternal day. And they have modern conveniences of which Herzog despairs, like an ATM machine, in a place where the machine, the money inside it, and the people who use it, must all be airlifted in. Herzog loves these people, it is clear, because like himself they have gone to such lengths to escape the mundane and test the limits of the extraordinary. But there is a difference between them and Timothy Treadwell, the hero of *Grizzly Man,* Herzog's documentary about a man who thought he could live with bears and not be eaten, and was mistaken. The difference is that Treadwell was a foolish romantic, and these men and women are in this godforsaken place to extend their knowledge of the planet and of the mysteries of life and death itself.

Herzog's method makes the movie seem like it is happening by chance, although chance has nothing to do with it. He narrates as if we're watching movies of his last vacation—informal, conversational, engaging. He talks about people he met, sights he saw, thoughts he had. And then a larger picture grows inexorably into view. McMurdo is perched on the frontier of the coming suicide of the planet. Mankind has grown too fast, spent too freely, consumed too much, and the ice is melting and we shall all perish. Herzog doesn't use such language, of course; he is too subtle and visionary. He is nudged toward his conclusions by what he sees. In a sense, his film journeys through time as well as space, and we see what little we may end up leaving behind us. Nor is he depressed by this prospect, but only philosophical. We came, we saw, we conquered, and we left behind a frozen fish.

His visit to Antarctica was not intended, he warns us at the outset, to take footage of "fluffy penguins." But there are some penguins in the film, and one of them embarks on a journey that haunts my memory to this moment, long after it must have ended.

Note: Herzog dedicated this film to me. I am deeply moved and honored. The letter I wrote to him from the 2007 Toronto Film Festival is in the Essays chapter.

Enlighten Up! ★ ★ ★

NO MPAA RATING, 82 m., 2009

Featuring Nick Rosen, Norman Allen, B. K. S. Iyengar, Pattabhi Jois, Gurusharananda, Cyndi Lee, Alan Finger, Dharma Mittra, Shyamdas, Sharon Gannon, David Life, Joseph Alter, David Gordon White, Diamond Dallas Page, Madan Kataria. A documentary directed and produced by Kate Churchill. Screenplay by Churchill and Jonathon Hexner.

An unemployed journalist and a documentary filmmaker spend six months traveling far enough to circle the globe, and they discover that the secret of yoga is the same as how to get to Carnegie Hall: practice, practice, practice. Apart from that, apparently, there is no secret at all to yoga. At least, they don't find a yogi who will admit to one.

Kate Churchill and her subject, Nick Rosen, travel from New York to Boulder to California to Hawaii, and then on to India. Nick practices under masters ranging from the legendary Yogacharya B. K. S. Iyengar, ninety-one, named by *Time* as one of the one hundred most influential people in the world, to Diamond Dallas Page, named by *Pro Wrestling Illustrated* as the most hated wrestler of the year (1999).

All of these teachers, young and old, male and female, Eastern and Western, refuse to define or even really name the ultimate state one hopes to reach. When you get there, you will know it. You will find it within yourself. You just have to do it. Practice does not make perfection, but it makes improvement. One must not focus on the destination but on the journey. Live in the moment. Live in eternity. Find God. Let the body flow into a yoga position as light fills a diamond (Iyengar). Your reward will be tits and ass (Diamond Dallas).

This was all fine with me because I wasn't much interested in arriving at ultimate answers, and neither, it must be said, is Nick Rosen. He does, however, log a lot of miles and has a particularly interesting time in India. He practices fervently. His body assumes positions on which, unlike a diamond, the sun don't shine. He begins as a skeptic about the spiritual side of yoga, and ends the same way, and doesn't find any yogis who try to proselytize him.

Instead, they offer variations of "Just do it!" Nick just does it, and at the end of his trial he tells Kate that he feels good, sleeps better, is stronger, has an improved digestive system, and in theory a better sex life (in practice, he tells her, "I haven't been alone with a woman for months—except you").

He also has better breath control, an area of particular interest to me. Once at Rancho La Puerta I was taking a yoga class, and we were all told to close our eyes and emit the sound "ahhhhhhh." I did so. When I opened my eyes, everyone was staring at me. "You sustained that three times as long as anyone else in the room," the yoga instructor told me. "In fact, I've never seen anyone holding out that long." Chaz theorized it had something to do with my ability to keep talking without letting anyone get a word in edgeways.

Enlighten Up! may prove a disappointment to anyone seeking to discover the secrets of yoga, or have their own beliefs confirmed. Apparently it does all come down to practice. Some seem addicted to it, which seems a shame to me, because a discipline should be a path to a fuller life, not an alternative. If you spend the rest of your life practicing yoga, well, that's what you did with the rest of your life. It's healthier than sinning, but that's about the best you can say.

And yet this is an interesting movie, and I'm glad I saw it. I enjoyed all the people I met during Nick's six-month quest. Most seemed cheerful and outgoing, and exuded good health. They smiled a lot. They weren't creepy true believers obsessed with converting everyone. They seemed happy with where they were, and they assumed Nick wanted to be there, too. And for the most part they seem to live contented lives, although Diamond Dallas advises yoga as a way to meet chicks, and (a sharp shake of the wind chime, please) that man will never find tranquillity who has not divested himself of subterfuge in meeting chicks.

Kate Churchill's role is intriguing. At the outset she tells us she's a yoga practitioner who thought there would be a documentary in recruiting a novice and exposing that person to yoga, then filming what happened. She obviously hopes Nick will take to yoga more than he does, and sounds wistful in her off-camera questions. Is he beginning to find something more in it? Does he have a favorite teacher? Has his appreciation deepened?

Nick is an affable man who goes along with her plan. Recently downsized, he has little better to do than be flown around the world to yoga experiences. But he's not cut out to practice, practice, practice, and he's so laid back that few sparks fly. This is a peaceful kind of film, not terribly eventful, but I suppose we wouldn't want a yoga thriller. Relax. Let it happen. Or not.

Evening ★ ½
PG-13, 117 m., 2007

Claire Danes (Young Ann), Toni Collette (Nina), Vanessa Redgrave (Ann Lord), Patrick Wilson (Harris), Hugh Dancy (Buddy), Natasha Richardson (Constance), Mamie Gummer (Lila), Eileen Atkins (Nurse), Meryl Streep (Older Lila), Glenn Close (Lila's mother). Directed by Lajos Koltai and produced by Jeffrey Sharp. Screenplay by Susan Minot and Michael Cunningham, based on a novel by Minot.

There are few things more depressing than a weeper that doesn't make you weep. *Evening* creeps through its dolorous paces as prudently as an undertaker. Upstairs, in the big Newport mansion, a woman is dying in a Martha Stewart bedroom. She takes a very long time to die, because the whole movie is flashbacks from her reveries. This gives us time to reflect on deep issues, such as, who is this woman?

Everybody in the film knows her, and eventually we figure out that she is Ann (Vanessa Redgrave), once the young sprite played in the flashbacks by Claire Danes. I know I must be abnormally obtuse to be confused on this question, but I persisted in thinking she might be the aged form of Lila, who as a young girl (Mamie Gummer) is getting married as the movie opens (it opens in a flashback, then flashes forward to the bed where it is flashing back from). How could I make such a stupid error? Because the mansion she is dying in looks like the same mansion Lila was married from, so I assumed old Lila was still living there. Maybe it's a different mansion. Real estate confuses me.

There are two grown daughters hanging around at the bedside: Constance (Natasha Richardson) and Nina (Toni Collette). But you can't figure out who they are from the flashbacks, because neither has been born yet. However, the flashbacks devote a great deal of time to examining how Lila has had a crush on Harris (Patrick Wilson), a young doctor and wedding guest whose mother was the family's housekeeper. Lila's brother Buddy (Hugh Dancy) has also had a lifelong crush on Harris, but his love dare not speak its name. Ann is Lila's best friend and maid of honor, and she also falls in love with Harris.

Lila is scheduled to be married on the morrow to the kind of a bore who (I'm only guessing) would be happy as the corresponding secretary of his fraternity. She does not love him. She loves Harris. I already said that. But what makes this Harris so electrifying? Search me. If he is warm, witty, and wonderful on the inside, those qualities are well-concealed by his exterior, which resembles a good job of aluminum siding: It is unbending and resists the elements.

Oh, but I forgot: Harris has one ability defined in my *Little Movie Glossary*. He is a Seeing-Eye Man. Such men are gifted at pointing out things to women. Man sees, points, woman turns, and *now* she sees, too, and smiles gratefully.

Harris is a very highly evolved Seeing-Eye Man. Not once but twice he looks at the heavens and sees a twinkling star. "That's our star," he says, or words to that effect. "See it there?" He points. Young Ann looks up at the billions and billions of stars, sees their star, and nods gratefully. Director Lajos Koltai cuts to the sky, and we see it, too. Or one just like it.

In the upstairs bedroom, old Ann dies very slowly, remembering the events of the long-ago wedding night and the next morning. Out of consideration for us, her reveries are in chronological order, even including events at which she was not present, like before she arrived at the house. She is attended by a nurse with an Irish accent (Eileen Atkins), who

sometimes prompts her: "Remember a happy time!" Dissolve to Ann's memory of a happy time. It is so mundane that if it qualifies as a high point in her life, it compares with Paris Hilton remembering a good stick of gum.

What horrors have I overlooked? Oh, the Plunge. Family tradition at weddings requires all male guests to plunge from a high rock into the sea. This inevitably leads to shots of the barren ocean, and cries of, "Buddy? Buddy?" But I'm not giving anything away because Buddy is good for no end of cries of "Buddy?" in this movie. At one point, he needs a doctor, and they remember that Harris is a doctor, and start shouting "Harris! Harris!" in the forest, having absolutely no reason to suppose Harris is within earshot.

Buddy inevitably is an alcoholic whose family members are forever moving the wine bottle out of his reach. He has to get drunk as an excuse to kiss Harris. This is pathetic. Buddy should grow up, bite the bullet, and learn that it takes no excuse to get drunk.

Later on, women in the flashbacks get pregnant and deliver the children who will puzzle us in the flash forwards, and there is one of those poignant chance encounters in Manhattan in the rain, where two old lovers meet after many years and have hardly anything to say. You know the kind of poignant encounter I'm thinking of. All too well, I imagine.

Everlasting Moments ★ ★ ★ ★
NO MPAA RATING, 131 m., 2009

Maria Heiskanen (Maria Larsson), Mikael Persbrandt (Sigfrid Larsson), Jesper Christensen (Sebastian Pedersen), Callin Ohrvall (Maja Larsson). Directed by Jan Troell and produced by Thomas Stenderup. Screenplay by Niklas Radstrom, based on a story by Agneta Ulfsater Troell.

Rarely is there a film that evokes our sympathy more deeply than *Everlasting Moments*. It is a great story of love and hope, told tenderly and without any great striving for effect. It begins in Sweden in 1911 and involves a woman, her daughter, her husband, a camera, and the kindness of a stranger. It has been made by Jan Troell, a filmmaker whose care for these characters is instinctive.

The woman is named Maria Larsson. She lives with her husband, Sigfrid, in Malmo, a port city at the southern tip of Sweden. They eventually have seven children. "Sigge" is a laborer on the docks who takes the pledge time and again at the Temperance Society but falls back into alcoholism. He is a loving and jovial man when sober, but violent when he is drunk, and the children await his homecomings with apprehension.

The movie is not really about Sigge. It is about Maria, who is a strong woman, resilient, complex. She raises the children, works as a house cleaner, copes with the family's poverty. Once, when newly married, she won a camera in a lottery. Now she finds it and takes it to a photo shop to pawn it and buy food. There she meets Sebastian Pedersen, and he finds an undeveloped plate still in the camera. He develops it, and something about the photograph or Maria causes him to say he will buy the camera, but she must hold it for him and continue to take pictures.

Maria is not sophisticated and may have little education, but she is a deep and creative woman and an instinctively gifted photographer. She has no theory, but her choices of subjects and compositions are inspired. And perhaps Mr. Pedersen inspires her, too. He is much older and always polite and proper with her, but over a time it becomes clear that they have fallen in love.

No, the film is not about how she leaves her drunken husband and becomes a famous photographer. It is about how her inner life is transformed by discovering that she has an artistic talent. She continues to be committed to Sigge by a bond deeper than marriage or obligation. But she tentatively takes steps toward personal independence that were rare in that time. When Sigge goes to fight in the war, she supports the family by taking marriage photographs.

Maria Heiskanen, who plays Maria, makes her a shy woman who is almost frightened to take a larger view of herself. She is strong when she needs to be but unaccustomed to men like Mr. Pedersen, who treat her as something more than she conceives herself. One of the film's mysteries is how clearly she defines her marriage to Sigge, which endures, even though she fully feels the possibilities that Sebastian never quite offers. Mikael Persbrandt makes Sigge not a bad man but powerless over alcohol. His labor is back-breaking. And look at the tact of Jesper Christensen as Sebastian, who loves Maria from the moment he sees her but wants to protect her from the problems that could bring. The movie is intensely observant about these gradations of love.

Everlasting Moments reflects the great self-assurance of Jan Troell, whose work includes such masterpieces as *The Emigrants, The New Land,* and *Hamsun.* All of his films are about lives striving toward greater fullness. He respects work, values, and feelings. He stands apart from the frantic hunger for fashionable success. After I saw this film, I looked through a few of the early reviews of it and found critics almost startled by its humanism. Here is Todd McCarthy of *Variety:* "Beholding Troell's exquisite images is like having your eyes washed, the better to behold moving pictures of uncorrupted purity and clarity."

The story comes from the heart. Troell, who showed *Everlasting Moments* at Telluride 2008, adapted it from a novel by his wife, Agneta, who based it on one of her own family members, Maria Larsson. Maria lived this life and took some of the photographs we see. The film is narrated by her daughter, Maja Larsson (Callin Ohrvall), and in my imagination I hear Maja telling the story to Agneta, for Jan was born in Malmo, and the dates work out that they might both have known her well and always thought hers was a story worth telling.

Every Little Step ★ ★ ★
PG-13, 96 m., 2009

A documentary directed and produced by James D. Stern and Adam Del Deo.

Every Little Step is a documentary about the casting process starting in 2006 for a Broadway revival of *A Chorus Line,* a musical that has been running somewhere in the world since its premiere in 1975 and inspired Richard Attenborough's 1985 film. The musical is about seventeen dancers who audition for their roles. The doc honors countless more who auditioned but were not chosen.

As I watched the film, one thought above all others was inspired: These people must love dancing to the point of abandon to submit themselves to this ordeal. Dancers must be in physical shape as good as most pro athletes and better than many. In fact, they *are* professional athletes, because although what they perform in is art, what they do is demanding physical work.

Often starting as young children, they practice, rehearse, and at some point forgo ordinary lives to submerge themselves in this process. It's the same with Olympians. They train and condition and focus and sacrifice. They turn up by the hundreds for auditions (the shots of the lineup outside the open call in Manhattan would make a doc in themselves). To get a call-back means they are superbly talented. Even then, the odds are they won't be chosen. Then it's back to more painstaking preparation, another job done for the paycheck, more dreams, more lines, more auditions, and usually more disappointments.

What we sense in the film is the camaraderie among these hopeful dancers. They've all been through the process before, all have been disappointed before, all know better than anyone else what it takes, all believe the best candidates don't always win the jobs.

The stakes are so high that to be one of the judges must cause restless dreams. Among them are Bob Avian, Michael Bennett's fellow choreographer in the 1975 production, and a vivacious force of nature named Baayork Lee, a dancer who played Connie, many people's favorite character, in that production. She handles the lineups, leads routines, and is, in her presence and energy, a testimony that it is possible to survive and find joy in this world.

I was reminded of *The Audition,* a film I saw last month, about the Metropolitan Opera's annual National Council Auditions. The art forms are different; the ordeals are the same. Then we buy our tickets and attend, and make dinner plans, and worry about parking, and chat at intermission, and admire what we see, when admiration is not adequate. We should be kneeling on concrete to remind ourselves what dues these artists pay.

Exiled ★ ★ ½
R, 100 m., 2007

Nick Cheung (Wo), Roy Cheung (Cat), Josie Ho (Jin), Lam Set (Fat), Francis Ng (Tai), Anthony Wong (Blaze), Simon Yam (Boss Fay). Directed and produced by Johnnie To. Screenplay by Szeto Kam-yuen, Yip Tin-shing, and Milkyway Creative Team.

The opening scene in *Exiled* lacks only a score by Ennio Morricone to be a spaghetti Western. A fistful of knuckles raps on a door. No answer. Again. Again. The door opens. The man knocking asks for "Mr. Wo." A woman replies, "Not here. Wrong house." The routine is repeated again, for this is indeed the house of Mr. Wo (Nick Cheung), and the woman is his wife, Jin (Josie Ho).

The setting is the Chinese offshore island of Macao, in 1988, right before the Portuguese turned it over to the Chinese. Although all of the characters are Asian, the streets and buildings, mostly Portuguese architecture, look as Mexican as Chinese, and the plot and action look more spaghetti than noodles.

The two men who have turned up at Wo's house have been sent from Hong Kong to kill him. They are Blaze (Anthony Wong) and Fat (Lam Set). Then two more men turn up, and we discover they hope to protect him. They are Cat (Roy Cheung) and Tai (Francis Ng). A high-angle shot shows them staked out at perimeters of a sun-drenched square, smoking cigars. Nobody else is on the streets. Jin looks warily out a window sometimes.

All of this moves slowly ("suspensefully" would be stretching it), and then all hell breaks loose. Wo comes home and everyone starts shooting, and then, if there are survivors (draw your own conclusions), they all help Mrs. Wo set her house straight and sit down to a big meal, using chopsticks to extend their boarding-house reach. They were recently all shooting at each other, but they were childhood friends, and so after business comes pleasure.

Out of this meal comes a plot involving a ton of gold and the prospects of Boss Fay (Simon Yam), the Hong Kong godfather who wants Wo dead. A great deal more shooting goes on, and what we in the filmcrit biz are pleased to call "martial arts choreography." Well, it is choreography, damn it, when you move with agile and daring grace in ways the human body was not built for.

At this point I am tempted to begin a plot

description, about who shoots who, and with what, and why. But we can only get a couple thousand words on a page, and if my editors are wise, they will allow me nowhere near that much, even if it would be enough. So let me simply say that enormous numbers of gangsters shoot enormous numbers of bullets at each other, and they're all lousy shots or they'd all soon be dead, while in fact, after a long time, only most of them are.

And don't you love that shot where a guy rolls on the floor from behind one thing to behind another thing, while shooting with both hands? Try it sometime. Both hands fully outstretched with firing guns, and you can roll fast enough to avoid being hit. No using your feet to push, because they never do. They just roll, like a carpet.

Johnnie To, the director, is highly respected in this genre, and I suppose he does it about as well as you'd want it to be done, unless you wanted acting and more coherence. He's compared to John Woo and Andrew Lau. So there you are. I have not made a study of the genre, which has many subtleties and conventions, but I admire *Exiled* for moving and building fluently. I have quoted Dr. Johnson so often that my editors have given up asking me, "What's his first name, and what is he a doctor of?" As faithful readers will know, it was Dr. Johnson who said, of a dog standing on its hind legs, "It is not done well, but one is surprised to find it done at all." So there you are again.

The Express ★ ★ ★
PG, 129 m., 2008

Dennis Quaid (Ben Schwartzwalder), Rob Brown (Ernie Davis), Omar Benson Miller (Jack Buckley), Clancy Brown (Roy Simmons), Charles S. Dutton (Pops Davis). Directed by Gary Fleder and produced by John Davis. Screenplay by Charles Leavitt, based on a book by Robert Gallagher.

The Express is involving and inspiring in the way a good movie about sports almost always is. The formula is basic and durable, and when you hitch it to a good story, you can hardly fail. Gary Fleder does more than that in telling the story of Ernie Davis (the "Elmira Ex-

press"), the running back for Syracuse who in 1961 became the first African-American to win the Heisman Trophy. Davis was drafted by pro football, but then leukemia was discovered; he never played a pro game and died in 1963. He was twenty-three.

Set during Syracuse's undefeated 1959 season (actually two years before the season Davis won the Heisman), the movie shows him as the MVP at the Cotton Bowl in Dallas. He was informed he could be present to receive his trophy but could not attend the banquet in a segregated venue. Most of his teammates boycotted the banquet. Most. I'd like to talk today with the few who didn't.

The film remembers a time when black players were unwelcome in the South. It shows racist fans screaming at him and throwing beer cans at the West Virginia and Texas games. He had to enter the hotels by back doors and sleep in servants' quarters. This all took place well within the lifetimes and memories of many people. Jackie Robinson joined the Brooklyn Dodgers in 1949, but the Dodgers didn't play in the South. Davis was far from the first black star on a college team; Jim Brown preceded him at Syracuse, and how well I remember cheering beside my dad as we watched J. C. Caroline play for the University of Illinois in 1953–54. He was an All-American, but I recall the uproar when a barbershop in Champaign refused to cut his hair.

What makes *The Express* special is that it focuses not only on football but also on the relationship Davis had with his coach, Ben Schwartzwalder (Dennis Quaid). Schwartzwalder, who beat out fifty other schools (including Notre Dame) to recruit Davis, wasn't a racist by the standards of that time, which is to say he was a racist by today's standards. Not overtly, but as Quaid subtly shows in his performance, the coach had a certain mental distance from African-Americans. He promised Davis he would develop his awesome ability, and he did. In the process, getting to know Davis was part of a fundamental development of Schwartzwalder's attitude. They both became better men because of their friendship. The film is about football, but that relationship is its deeper subject.

The heroic athlete achieving his dreams

and dying too soon is an enduring movie archetype; remember *Brian's Song* (1971). Because we walk into these films knowing the hero will die, every scene takes on an added significance. Rob Brown plays Davis as a focused young man with a strong family behind him, confident, not intimidated or obsessed by racism, open to everyone (he became the first African-American member of the predominantly Jewish fraternity Sigma Alpha Mu). The movie deals in expected ways with his life off the field and concentrates on his playing.

There is a lot of football in the movie. It's well presented, but there is the usual oddity that it almost entirely shows success. I may have missed it, but I don't remember a single time when Davis is caught behind the line of scrimmage, fumbles, or drops a pass. We see these stars as our surrogates, and we don't enjoy watching ourselves fail.

The key supporting performance is by Omar Benson Miller (*Miracle at St. Anna*) as Buckley, Davis's black friend on the team, who advises him of situations Buckley has already experienced. The resonating Charles S. Dutton plays the grandfather who raised Davis. They reinforce him through some hostility to the team newcomer at first, but mercifully the team lacks a stereotyped racist; the emphasis under Schwartzwalder is so intensely on winning that anything else is unthinkable—if not for reasons of mortality, then for hard reality.

I'm a fall guy for movies like this. Yes, I see the formula grinding away, as it actually must, because Davis's real life corresponds to it. I can't remember a film about an untalented athlete, and not many about losing teams (they always win in the end). In the final analysis, it's not how you play the game that counts, but whether you win or lose.

F

The Fall ★ ★ ★ ★
R, 117 m., 2008

Catinca Untaru (Alexandria), Lee Pace (Roy Walker), Justine Waddell (Nurse Evelyn), Daniel Caltagirone (Governor Odious), Leo Bill (Charles Darwin), Sean Gilder (Walt Purdy), Julian Bleach (Indian Mystic), Marcus Wesley (Otta Benga), Robin Smith (Luigi). Directed and produced by Tarsem. Screenplay by Dan Gilroy, Nico Soultanakis, and Tarsem, based on the 1981 screenplay for *Yo Ho Ho,* by Valeri Petrov.

Tarsem's *The Fall* is a mad folly, an extravagant visual orgy, a free fall from reality into uncharted realms. Surely it is one of the wildest indulgences a director has ever granted himself. Tarsem, for two decades a leading director of music videos and TV commercials, spent millions of his own money to finance it, filmed it for four years in twenty-eight countries, and has made a movie that you might want to see for no other reason than because it exists. There will never be another like it.

The Fall is so audacious that when *Variety* calls it a "vanity project," you can only admire the man vain enough to make it. It tells a simple story with vast romantic images so stunning I had to check twice, three times, to be sure the film actually claims to have *absolutely no* computer-generated imagery. None? What about the Labyrinth of Despair, with no exit? The intersecting walls of zig-zagging staircases? The man who emerges from the burning tree? Perhaps the trick words are "computer-generated." Perhaps some of the images are created by more traditional kinds of special effects.

The story framework for the imagery is straightforward. In Los Angeles, circa 1915, a silent movie stuntman has his legs paralyzed while performing a reckless stunt. He convalesces in a half-deserted hospital, its corridors of cream and lime stretching from ward to ward of mostly empty beds, their pillows and sheets awaiting the harvest of World War I. The stuntman is Roy (Lee Pace), pleasant in appearance, confiding in speech, happy to make a new friend of a little girl named Alexandria (Catinca Untaru). She has broken

her arm falling from a tree while picking oranges in a nearby grove; an elbow brace holds it sticking sideways from her body, and in that hand she carries an old cigar box everywhere, with her treasures.

Roy tells a story to Alexandria, involving adventurers who change appearance as quickly as a child's imagination can do its work. We see the process. He tells her of an "Indian" who has a wigwam and a squaw. She does not know these words and envisions an Indian from a land of palaces, turbans, and swamis. The verbal story is input from Roy; the visual story is output from Alexandria.

The story involves Roy (playing the Black Bandit) and his friends, a bomb-throwing Italian anarchist, an escaped African slave, an Indian (from India), and Charles Darwin and his pet monkey Otis. Their sworn enemy, Governor Odious, has stranded them on a desert island, but they come ashore (riding swimming elephants, of course) and wage war on him. One scene shows the governor's towering private carriage, pulled by hundreds of slaves, while others toil on its wheels like human hamsters. The governor is protected by leather-clad warriors with helmets shaped like coal scuttles.

Roy draws out the story for a personal motive; after Alexandria brings him some communion wafers from the hospital chapel, he persuades her to steal some morphine tablets from the dispensary. Paralyzed and having lost his great love (she is the princess in his story), he hopes to kill himself. There is a wonderful scene of the little girl trying to draw him back to life.

Either you are drawn into the world of this movie or you are not. It is preposterous, of course, but I vote with Werner Herzog, who says if we do not find new images, we will perish. Here a line of bowmen shoots hundreds of arrows into the air. So many of them fall into the back of the escaped slave that he falls backward and the weight of his body is supported by them, as on a bed of nails, dozens of foot-long arrows. There is a scene of the monkey Otis chasing a butterfly through impossible architecture. When the monkey is shot, I was touched by the death of the lovable little simian.

At this point in reviews of movies like *The Fall* (not that there are any), I usually announce that I have accomplished my work. I have described what the movie does, how it looks while it is doing it, and what the director has achieved. Well, what has he achieved? *The Fall* is beautiful for its own sake. And there is a sweet charm from the young Romanian actress Catinca Untaru, who may have been dubbed for all I know, but speaks with the innocence of childhood, working her way through tangles of words. She regards with equal wonder the reality she lives in and the fantasy she pretends to. It is her imagination that creates the images of Roy's story, and they have a purity and power beyond all calculation. Roy is her perfect storyteller, she is his perfect listener, and together they build a world.

Note: The R rating should not dissuade bright teenagers from this celebration of the imagination.

Fanboys ★ ½
PG-13, 90 m., 2009

Sam Huntington (Eric), Christopher Marquette (Linus), Dan Fogler (Hutch), Jay Baruchel (Windows), Kristen Bell (Zoe). Directed by Kyle Newman and produced by Evan Astrowsky, Dana Brunetti, Matthew Perniciaro, and Kevin Spacey. Screenplay by Ernest Cline and Adam F. Goldberg.

A lot of fans are basically fans of fandom itself. It's all about them. They have mastered the *Star Wars* or *Star Trek* universes or whatever, but their objects of veneration are useful mainly as a backdrop to their own devotion. Anyone who would camp out in a tent on the sidewalk for weeks in order to be first in line for a movie is more into camping on the sidewalk than movies.

Extreme fandom may serve as a security blanket for the socially inept, who use its extreme structure as a substitute for social skills. If you are Luke Skywalker and she is Princess Leia, you already know what to say to each other, which is so much safer than having to ad lib it. Your fannish obsession is your beard. If you know absolutely all the trivia about your cubbyhole of pop culture, it saves you from having to know anything about any-

thing else. That's why it's excruciatingly boring to talk to such people: They're always asking you questions they know the answer to.

But enough about my opinions; what about *Fanboys*? Its primary flaw is that it's not critical. It is a celebration of an idiotic lifestyle, and I don't think it knows it. If you want to get in a car and drive to California, fine. So do I. So did Jack Kerouac. But if your first stop involves a rumble at a *Star Trek* convention in Iowa, dude, beam your ass down to Route 66.

The movie, set in 1999, involves four *Star Wars* fanatics and, eventually, their gal pal, who have the notion of driving to Marin County, breaking into the Skywalker Ranch, and stealing a copy of a print of *Star Wars Episode 1: The Phantom Menace* so they can see it before anyone else. This is about as plausible as breaking into the U.S. Mint and stealing some money so you can spend it before anyone else.

Fanboys follows in the footsteps of *Sex Drive* by allowing one of its heroes to plan a rendezvous with an Internet sex goddess. To avoid revealing any plot secrets in this movie, I will recycle my earlier warning: In a chat room, don't be too hasty to believe Ms. Tasty.

This plot is given gravitas because one of the friends, Linus (Christopher Marquette), is dying of cancer. His buddy Eric (Sam Huntington) is in favor of the trip because, I dunno, it will give Linus something to live for, I guess. The other fanboys are Hutch (Dan Fogler), who lives in his mother's garage/coach house, and Windows (Jay Baruchel), who changed his name from MacOS. Just kidding. Windows, Hutch, and Linus work in a comic book store, where their favorite customer is Zoe (Kristen Bell). She's sexy *and* a *Star Wars* fan. How cool is that? She's almost better than the date who turns into a pizza and a six-pack when the deed is done.

The question of Linus's cancer became the subject of a celebrated Internet flame war last summer, with supporters of *Fanboys* director Kyle Newman running Anti-Harvey Web sites opposing Harvey Weinstein's alleged scheme to cut the subplot out of the movie. The subplot survived, but it's one of those movie diseases that is mentioned occasionally so everyone can look solemn, and then dropped when the ailing Linus dons a matching black camouflage outfit and scales the Skywalker Ranch walls with a grappling hook.

Fanboys is an amiable but disjointed movie that identifies too closely with its heroes. Poking a little more fun at them would have been a great idea. They are tragically hurtling into a cultural dead end, mastering knowledge that has no purpose other than being mastered, and too smart to be wasting their time. When a movie's opening day finally comes and fanboys leave their sidewalk tents for a mad dash into the theater, I wonder who retrieves their tents, sleeping bags, portable heaters, and iPod speakers. Warning: Mom isn't always going to be there to clean up after you. ☞

Fast and Furious ★ ½
PG-13, 107 m., 2009

Vin Diesel (Dominic Toretto), Paul Walker (Brian O'Conner), Michelle Rodriguez (Letty), Jordana Brewster (Mia Toretto), John Ortiz (Campos), Laz Alonso (Fenix). Directed by Justin Lin and produced by Neil Moritz, Michael Fottrell, and Vin Diesel. Screenplay by Chris Morgan.

Fast and Furious is exactly and precisely what you'd expect. Nothing more, unfortunately. You get your cars that are fast and your characters that are furious. You should. They know how to make these movies by now. Producer Neil Moritz is on his fourth, and director Justin Lin on his second in a row. Vin Diesel and other major actors are back from *The Fast and the Furious* (2001). All they left behind were two definite articles.

This is an expertly made action film, by which I mean the special effects are good and the acting is extremely basic. The screenplay rotates these nouns through various assortments of dialogue: Race. Driver(s). Nitro. Meth. Sister. FBI. Border. Dead. Mexico. Murder. Prison. Traffic violations. Tunnel. Muscle car. Import. Plymouth. Funeral. Helicopter(s). Toretto. Ten seconds. Corona. Cocaine.

The plot. Dom Toretto (Vin Diesel) has been in the Dominican Republic for the last six years but now returns to America, where he is a wanted man. Probable charges: vehicular homicide, murder, smuggling, dating an FBI agent's sister. Reason for return: Letty (Michelle Rodriguez), the girl he loved, has been killed.

After Toretto's arrest all those years ago, he was allowed to escape by FBI agent Brian O'Conner (Paul Walker), for reasons explained in this film. Now Brian is back, on a task force to track down Toretto and the leader of a drug cartel.

This provides a scaffolding on which to hang the body of the movie, which involves a series of chase scenes, fights, explosions, and sexy women who would like to make themselves available to Toretto, to no avail. He is single-minded.

The pre-title chase scene is pretty amazing. Toretto and his group team up in four racing vehicles to pursue a truck hauling not one, not two, not three, but *four* enormous tanks of gasoline. Their method: Toretto drives close behind fourth tank, girl climbs out of sun roof, stands on hood, leaps to ladder on back of tank, climbs on top, runs to front of tank, leaps down, uncouples tank from third one. The reason the girl does this while Toretto drives is, I guess, well, you know what they say about women drivers.

Ever seen a truck hauling four enormous gas containers? I haven't. On a narrow mountain road? With a sudden, steep incline around a curve, when it narrows to one lane? Not me. Why are they going to this trouble? So their buddies can have free gas for a street race that night in L.A. I say let them buy their own damn gas. The race is down city streets with ordinary traffic on them. Then the wrong way on an expressway. Not a cop in sight. Where are the TV news choppers when you want them? This would get huge ratings.

I dunno. I admire the craft involved, but the movie leaves me profoundly indifferent. After three earlier movies in the series, which have been transmuted into video games, why do we need a fourth one? Oh. I just answered my own question. ☞

Fay Grim ★ ★
R, 118 m., 2007

Parker Posey (Fay Grim), Jeff Goldblum (Fulbright), James Urbaniak (Simon Grim), Saffron Burrows (Juliet), Liam Aiken (Ned Grim), Elina Lowensohn (Bebe), Leo Fitzpatrick

(Carl Fogg), Chuck Montgomery (Angus James), Thomas Jay Ryan (Henry Fool). Directed by Hal Hartley and produced by Hartley, Michael S. Ryan, Martin Hagemann, Jason Kliot, and Joana Vicente. Screenplay by Hartley.

Hal Hartley's *Fay Grim* stars Parker Posey and Jeff Goldblum in a search for a mysterious terrorist named Henry Fool. This man, we learn, has been part of intrigues involving Chile, Iraq, Israel, France, Germany, Russia, England, China, and the Vatican (where the pope *threw a chair at him*). All in the last seven years.

Posey plays the title character, a mom from Queens whose son gets in trouble at school for showing around a hand-cranked toy movieola with pornographic images. Who mailed him the device? Could it have something to do with her brother Simon (James Urbaniak), a Nobel Prize–winning poet who has been jailed for helping Henry Fool escape the United States? Or with Henry Fool (Thomas Jay Ryan) himself? Enter Fulbright (Goldblum) and Fogg (Leo Fitzpatrick), CIA agents searching for Henry's missing confessions. Soon Fay is caught up in an international intrigue.

But a peculiar intrigue it is, because Hartley's style seems determined to dampen our interest in the plot. Working with a usually tilting camera, he photographs his characters taking part in lugubrious and maddening dialogue of bewildering complexity. And he minimizes the action, which mostly takes place offscreen.

When a man leaps from a hotel roof, for example, we don't see what happens, but we hear a crash. When a man is hit by a car, we don't see it happen, but Hartley cuts to a staged and unconvincing shot of him rolling off the car's hood. Shoot-outs are handled with montages of still images.

The result is that we feel deliberately distanced from the film. It is not so much an exercise in style as an exercise in search of a style. The story doesn't involve us because we can't follow it, and we doubt if the characters can either. But am I criticizing Hartley, a leading indie filmmaker, for not making a more conventional thriller, with more chases and action scenes? Not at all. I am criticizing him for failing to figure out what he wanted to do instead, and delivering a film that is tortured in its attempt at cleverness and plays endlessly.

Parker Posey and Jeff Goldblum labor at their characters, and are often fun to watch. But in the absence of a screenplay that engages them, they have to fall back on their familiar personalities and quirks. They bring more to the movie than it brings to them.

Fay Grim is the sequel to *Henry Fool*, Hartley's 1998 film, which won the screenwriting prize at Cannes. In that one, Henry first motivated Simon to become a poet and didn't seem involved in intrigues. He was an enigma with no purpose other than being enigmatic. Now we find out much more about Henry, but it all seems arbitrary and made up on the spot.

As for Hartley's tilted camera, tilt shots have traditionally been used to create a heightened sense of danger; the characters can hardly hold onto the screen. Here they're used for scenes of stultifying dialogue and seem more like a desperate attempt to add interest to flat material. I like it better when style seems to emerge from a story (as in *The Third Man*) than when it feels trucked in from the outside.

Note: Much is made of the fact that Henry's confessions may be encrypted. It is ironic, therefore, that the key encryption simply involves initials that are seen upside down and need to be turned over? But see if you can figure out how Fay finds the blind antiques dealer who can explain it all to her. Kind of a coincidence?

Fear(s) of the Dark ★ ★ ½
NO MPAA RATING, 85 m., 2008

With the voices of: Aure Atika, Arthur H, Guillaume Depardieu, Nicole Garcia, Christian Hincker, Lino Hincker, Melaura Honnay, Amelie Lerma, Florence Maury, Amaury Smets, Brigitte Sy, Laurent Van Der Rest, Charlotte Vermeil, and Andreas Vuillet. Directed by Blutch, Charles Burns, Marie Caillou, Pierre di Sciullo, Lorenzo Mattotti, and Richard McGuire, and produced by Valerie Schermann and Christophe Jankovic. Screenplay by Blutch, Burns, di Sciullo, Jerry Kramsky, Michel Pirus, and Romain Slocombe.

Ideally, a film should flow smoothly into the mind, with no elbows sticking out. From the time some months ago when I first heard of *Fear(s) of the Dark,* I was annoyed by the *(s)*. This is ridiculous, I know. Such a detail has nothing to do with the quality of a movie. But let me ask you: What does *(s)* do for you? Or *Peur(s) du Noir* in French? Less than nothing? Yes.

Oh, well. The film is an anthology by six animators. It involves untitled shorts, punctuated by segments by the graphic artist Blutch featuring an aristocrat holding savage hounds straining at a leash. Each time a hound breaks free, it leaps upon the next story, and occasionally a victim. Some of the stories are pretty good, especially Charles Burns's tale involving a nasty and vaguely humanoid insect that burrows under the skin. The sight of the creature trapped in a jar is unsettling. The story reminded me of Guillermo del Toro's *Cronos* (1993), and indeed he is cited on the Web site as a champion of this film.

Richard McGuire has an effective haunted house story that reminded me a little of *Ugetsu* in the way it uses spirits who seem to possess the space the hero wanders into. Japanese echoes stir also in a story by Marie Caillou, about a bug-eyed young girl who is a student trapped in a nightmare.

Despite the title and the ads, this is not really a horror movie but more of a demonstration of the skills of the animators. The segments are like calling cards. Younger horror movie fans will not much identify with it. The hateful hounds don't supply a linking device so much as a separation. And although I admired most of the animation, during the film I found myself reminded of the four ghostly episodes of the classic Japanese ghost story anthology *Kwaidan* (1964), so hauntingly beautiful, which combined live action with frankly employed sound stage sets.

Note: Guillaume Depardieu's voice-over work here represents one of the final credits for the son of Gerard and Elisabeth Depardieu, who died October 13, 2008, of pneumonia at thirty-seven. Born into French acting royalty, he had a sad life, including a 2003 suspended sentence for an armed threat, and a leg amputation resulting from a motorcycle accident. His most interesting film was Pola X *(1999), an exceedingly strange modern adaptation of Herman Melville's* Pierre.

Feast of Love ★ ★

R, 102 m., 2007

Morgan Freeman (Harry), Greg Kinnear (Bradley), Radha Mitchell (Diana), Jane Alexander (Esther), Alexa Davalos (Chloe), Toby Hemingway (Oscar), Selma Blair (Kathryn), Stana Katic (Jenny), Billy Burke (David), Fred Ward (Bat), Sherilyn Lawson (Doctor). Directed by Robert Benton and produced by Gary Lucchesi, Tom Rosenberg, and Richard S. Wright.

Morgan Freeman returns in *Feast of Love* as a wise counselor of the troubled and heartsick. Apart from his great films, of which there are many, this is almost his standard role, although he also seems to spend a lot of time playing God. Most of his insights seem not merely handed down the mountain, but arriving as a successful forward pass. At the beginning of the film, he gives us the ground rules: "They say that when the Greek gods were bored, they invented humans. Still bored, they invented love. That wasn't boring, so they tried it themselves. And then they invented laughter—so they could stand it."

The Greek gods had one thing going for them. They were immutable. Zeus was always Zeus and Hera was always Hera, and they were always in character, always Zeuslike and Heraesque. In *Feast of Love,* however, Freeman plays a professor named Harry who is forced to contend with confused lovers who don't know, or can't reveal, their own hearts.

He lives in Portland, Oregon, in a long and happy marriage with Esther (Jane Alexander). Spare hours are spent in Jitters coffee shop, where his coffee cup is an omnipresent prop and useful timing device; sips punctuate his wisdom. The shop is owned by Bradley (Greg Kinnear), who thinks he is in love with his wife, Kathryn (Selma Blair). But he is living in a fool's paradise, as Harry easily sees one evening when they all go to a bar after a women's softball game.

"I saw two women fall in love with one another tonight," he tells Esther when he gets home. Yes, he watched as Jenny (Stana Katic), a shortstop on the opposing team, put a quarter in the jukebox, a hand on Kathryn's leg, and whispered, "From now on, that will be our song." Harry is bemused: "Bradley was sitting right there, and he didn't see a thing."

Bradley has blindness when it comes to women. He brings home a dog for Kathryn's birthday present, although she has told him time and again that she hates and fears dogs. Maybe there is a clue to their incompatibility when, during a forced visit to the animal shelter, she named this particular dog "Bradley."

This Bradley, he's a pushover. Next he falls in love with a Realtor named Diana (Radha Mitchell), who walks into his shop on a rainy day. She smokes organic cigarettes. Those are the ones that kill you but don't support Big Tobacco. She's having a heartless, purely physical affair with the studly David (Billy Burke), whom she has not quite broken up with. Bradley doesn't see this.

Meanwhile, Oscar (Toby Hemingway), the counterman in the coffee shop, falls in love with a girl who walks in one day and makes her love for him clear. This is Chloe (Alexa Davalos), who is good and true, but Oscar has problems of his own. He lives with his father, Bat (Fred Ward), a drunk who staggers around so comically he looks like he thinks he's in a silent comedy and lurks in the bushes brandishing a knife. No movie can be very good that contains Fred Ward's worst performance (it's the fault of the character, to be sure).

Have I left out any combinations? Only the doctor (Sherilyn Lawson) who bandages Bradley's finger after he cuts himself as punishment for losing Diana. All of these scenarios unwind under the thoughtful gaze of Harry, who returns with his nightly reports to Esther. They have had a wounding personal loss—an esteemed son, dead of an overdose. But Esther seems content to sit at home alone until such intervals as Harry can free himself from his coffee shop, park bench, and other counseling stations.

There are some good things in the movie. Some scenes play well as self-contained episodes. The city of Portland is beautifully evoked. Jane Alexander and Morgan Freeman make a couple we love. Greg Kinnear raises fecklessness to an art. And there is a lot more nudity than you'd expect, if you like that sort of thing.

All of these stories are woven into a tapestry by director Robert Benton, working from a screenplay by Allison Burnett, which is based on the novel by Charles Baxter. Benton has made better movies about doomed marriages (*Kramer vs. Kramer*), but this one has no organic reality because it depends on three artifices: (1) the clockwork success and failure of relationships, (2) the need for Harry as a witness, (3) the lickety-split time span that compresses the action so much it loses emotional weight. Harry is always looking on as if he already knows how every story will turn out. We're looking on in exactly the same way.

Fighting ★ ★ ★
PG-13, 105 m., 2009

Channing Tatum (Shawn MacArthur), Terrence Howard (Harvey Boarden), Luis Guzman (Martinez), Zulay Henao (Zulay Valez), Brian White (Evan Hailey), Altagracia Guzman (Lila). Directed by Dito Montiel and produced by Kevin Misher. Screenplay by Montiel and Robert Munic.

I like the way the personalities are allowed to upstage the plot in *Fighting*, a routine three-act fight story that creates uncommonly interesting characters. Set in the streets of Manhattan, Brooklyn, and the Bronx, involving a naive kid from Alabama and a mild-mannered hustler from Chicago, it takes place in a secret world of street fighting for high cash stakes. Do rich guys really bet hundreds of thousands on a closed-door bare-knuckle brawl? I dunno, but it's cheaper than filming a prize-fight arena.

Channing Tatum plays Shawn, whose dad was a wrestling coach near Birmingham. Terrence Howard plays Harvey, whom everybody seems to know. Shawn is a hot-tempered kid not doing very well at selling shoddy merchandise on the sidewalks. Harvey is soft-spoken, with a gentle voice and an almost passive personal style even though he works as an illegal fight promoter. He sees Shawn in a fight, recruits him, and lines up fights with $5,000, $10,000 and finally $100,000 purses.

He does this with stunning speed, even though at the first fight no one has ever seen Shawn before. The movie offers that and other problems of plausibility and logic, but I don't care about them because the director, Dito

Montiel, doesn't. Possibly hired to make a genre picture, he provides the outline and requirements, and then focuses on his characters. Terrence Howard's Harvey is the most intriguing: He's too laid back to be in the profession, so philosophical that he even faces what seems to be his own inevitable murder with calm resignation. He knows his world, is known in it, moves through it, yet seems aloof from it.

Channing Tatum, convincing as a former school athlete (which he was), quickly agrees to the fights, even against terrifying opponents. But *Fighting* invests much more feeling in his tentative relationship with Zulay (Zulay Henao), a single mom who works as a waitress in a private club where the private fight world hangs out. He approaches her like a well-raised southern boy would, politely, respectfully.

This arouses greater interest because of the screen presence of Zulay Henao, who sidesteps countless hazards suggested by her character and makes her sweet, sensuous, and perceptive. And then look at Altagracia Guzman as Lila, playing Zulay's elder relative (grandmother?), who was a great audience favorite as she guarded her beloved from the threat of a male predator. The way her talent is employed in the film is an ideal use of a supporting actress.

Listen also to the dialogue by Robert Munic and Montiel, which is far above formula boilerplate and creates the illusion that the characters might actually be saying it in the moment. An extended flirtation between Zulay and Shawn isn't hurried through for a bedroom payoff, but grows sweeter and more tender the longer it continues. This scene illustrates my theory that it is more exciting to wonder if you are about to be kissed than it is to be kissed.

Fighting is not a cinematic breakthrough, but it is much more involving than I thought it would be. The ads foreground the action, no doubt because that's what sells. The film transcends the worldview that produced the ad campaign and gives audiences a well-crafted, touching experience. Sometimes you can feel it when an audience is a little surprised by how deeply they've become involved.

Filth and Wisdom ★ ★

NO MPAA RATING, 81 m., 2008

Eugene Hutz (A.K.), Holly Weston (Holly), Vicky McClure (Juliette), Richard E. Grant (Professor Flynn), Stephen Graham (Harry Beechman), Inder Manocha (Sardeep). Directed by Madonna and produced by Nicola Doring. Screenplay by Madonna and Dan Cadan.

Aren't we all way beyond being shocked by sexual fetishes simply because they exist? Haven't we all stopped thinking, "Ohmigod! That's a guy in drag!" or "Ohmigod! That's a dominatrix!" or "Ohmigod! She's tattooed!" or having any kind of reaction to body piercing, which no longer even qualifies as a fetish, except when practiced on body areas we are unlikely to see anyway?

We live in a time, a sad time, I think, when some fetishes are even marketed to children. Consider the dominatrix Barbie doll. Of course, films that are *about* sexual fetishes can be fascinating. Remember *Secretary,* about S&M, or *The Crying Game,* about transvestism, or *Kissed,* about necrophilia. All very good films. But in simply observing the fact of a fetish, the old frisson is gone. I mention this because Madonna still gets intrigued, I guess, simply by regarding a stripper sliding down a pole.

Filth and Wisdom, Madonna's directing debut, is a pointless exercise in "shocking" behavior, involving characters in London so shallow that the most sympathetic is the lecherous Indian dentist (Inder Manocha) who is supposed to be a villain, maybe. The central character is A.K. (Eugene Hutz), a rock singer who moonlights as a male dominator and will dress up like a ringmaster and whip you if you pay the big bucks. He is a fountain of wise little axioms, of which one is actually profound: "The problem with treating your body like a cash register is that you always feel empty."

A.K. is the landlord for flatmates Holly (Holly Weston) and Juliette (Vicky McClure), and also their unpaid adviser, who steers Holly into stripping at a lap-dance sleaze pit. Madonna thinks it's funny, or sad, or something, that Holly is not too good at hanging upside-down from the pole and erotically sliding down it.

I saw my first strip show at the old Follies Burlesque on South State Street one day after I moved to Chicago, and I interviewed the immortal Tempest Storm when she appeared here. The strippers at that time performed slowly and seductively, and it was a "tease." Today's strippers leap on stage already almost naked and perform contortions that gotta hurt. Some are so gifted they can get one boob going clockwise and the other counterclockwise.

Ugh. They're erotic only to men who enjoy seeing women humiliate themselves. I was but a callow youth from a small town amid the soy fields, but, reader, I confess I idealized some of them. I haven't attended a strip show in years and years, and for that I am grateful. Oh, there was that time we were in Bangkok and saw the show with the Ping Pong balls. Who could think of sex during such a skillful display?

But I wander. *Filth and Wisdom* also places a blot on the record of Richard E. Grant, who brought snarkiness to perfection in *Withnail and I* and *How to Get Ahead in Advertising*. Here he's made to play an elderly, blind, gay, depressed poet who is smiling on the outside, and you know the rest. For what purpose? To help Madonna fill the endless eighty-one-minute running time with characters we don't care about, who don't care about one another except when dictated to by the screenplay, in a story nobody cares about. This is a very deeply noncaring movie. I liked Hutz when he sang. I imagine Gene Shalit ate his heart out when he saw Hutz's moustache.

Finding Amanda ★ ★ ½
R, 90 m., 2008

Matthew Broderick (Taylor Peters), Brittany Snow (Amanda), Steve Coogan (Jerry), Maura Tierney (Lorraine Mendon), Peter Facinelli (Greg). Directed by Peter Tolan and produced by Richard Heller and Wayne Allan Rice. Screenplay by Tolan.

A quietly perfect scene in *Finding Amanda* involves Taylor, the hero, arriving at a Las Vegas casino. Without overstating the case, the film makes it clear that Taylor is well-known here: The doorman, the bellboy, even the room maid greet him by name. That may be one of the danger signals of a gambling addiction.

Another one may be taking a check from out of the middle of your wife's checkbook.

Taylor (Matthew Broderick) is indeed an addicted gambler. He claims to be recovering. Hasn't placed a bet since . . . earlier today. He is also, over a longer span of time, a recovering alcoholic and drug addict. He works as a well-paid writer for a TV sitcom that everybody seems to agree is terrible and lives in a comfortable home with his comely wife, Lorraine (Maura Tierney), who is fed up to here with his gambling and has called an attorney.

That sets the stage for the central drama of the film. Taylor's twenty-year-old niece, Amanda (Brittany Snow) has left home, gone to Vegas and become a "dancer," which, we learn, is a euphemism for "stripper," which is a euphemism for "hooker." The girl's mother is begging him to intervene. Taylor is happy to oblige, since it means a trip to Vegas, where even the room maid, etc.

And so commences a peculiar film that is really two films fighting to occupy the same space. The first film, the one of the "quietly perfect scene," is about Taylor, his addictions, his emotions, and Jerry (Steve Coogan), a host at the casino. The second film, which has no perfect scenes, is about his niece, her life, and her boyfriend, Greg (Peter Facinelli). If there were more of the first story line and less of the second, this would be a better film. If there were none of the second story line, it might really amount to something. But there we are.

Broderick is splendid as the gambler. He knows, as many addicts do, that the addictive personality is very inward, however much acting-out might take place. He plays Taylor as a man constantly taking inventory of himself: How does he feel? Could he feel better? Can he take a chance? Does he feel lucky? Will one little bet, or drink, really hurt? How about two? Taylor evolves as a sympathetic man, one to be pitied (as his wife knows, although she is running low on pity). He is likable, intelligent, decent, really does hope to help his niece, and has several monkeys scrambling for space on his back.

Brittany Snow (Amber Von Tussle in *Hairspray*) does what she can with the role of Amanda as written, but that's just the problem: how it's written. She has it all figured out how she can have a nice car, house, clothes,

139

and boyfriend while hooking, which her old job at the International House of Pancakes did not make possible. Why she felt she had to move to Vegas to work at IHOP remains unexplained. Also unexplained, in my mind, is how she became a hooker (her "explanation" is harrowing and intended as heartbreaking, but sounds more like the story of someone looking for trouble). There is also the matter of the boyfriend, Greg. I know such men exist and someone has to date them, but why Amanda? This guy is such a scummy lowlife, he gives pimps a bad name. Why does she support him and endure his blatant cheating?

You will not find a convincing answer in this film. What you will find is a nicely modulated performance by Steve Coogan (*24-Hour Party People*) as Jerry, the casino's host, who knows Taylor from way back, extends him credit against his better judgment, knows an addictive gambler when he sees one and is looking at one. He makes Jerry not the heavy and not the comic foil, but an associate in a circular process of betting and losing and winning a little and betting and losing a lot, and so on. How Taylor's luck changes, and what happens, is for me entirely believable.

Finding Amanda will be followed closely in theaters by *Diminished Capacity,* a film starring Broderick as a newspaper columnist who goes to his hometown to help his uncle (Alan Alda). Broderick is just right in both films, acting his way under, over, around, and occasionally straight through the material. Now we need him in a better screenplay.

Fired Up ★
PG-13, 89 m., 2009

Nicholas D'Agosto (Shawn Colfax), Eric Christian Olsen (Nick Brady), Sarah Roemer (Carly), Molly Sims (Diora), Danneel Harris (Bianca), David Walton (Dr. Rick), Adhir Kalyan (Brewster), AnnaLynne McCord (Gwyneth), Juliette Goglia (Poppy), Philip Baker Hall (Coach Byrnes), Hayley Marie Norman (Angela). Directed by Will Gluck and produced by Matthew Gross, Peter Jaysen, and Charles Weinstock. Screenplay by Freedom Jones.

After the screening of *Fired Up,* one of my colleagues grimly observed that *Dead Man* was a better cheerleader movie. That was, you will recall, the 1995 Western starring Johnny Depp, Robert Mitchum, Billy Bob Thornton, and Iggy Pop. I would give almost anything to see them on a cheerleading squad. Here is a movie that will do for cheerleading what *Friday the 13th* did for summer camp.

The story involves two callow and witless high school football players, Shawn and Nick, who don't want to attend summer football training camp in the desert. They also want to seduce the school cheerleaders, so they decide to attend cheerleading camp, ha ha. Their high school is in Hinsdale, Illinois, whose taxpayers will be surprised to learn the school team trains in the desert just like the Cubs, but will be even more surprised to learn the entire film was shot in California. And they will be puzzled about why many of the cheers involve chants of the letters *F!U!*—which stand for *Fired Up,* you see.

Oh, is this movie bad. The characters relentlessly attack one another with the forced jollity of minimum-wage workers pressing you with free cheese samples at the supermarket. Every conversation involves a combination of romantic misunderstandings, double entendres, and flirtation that is just sad. No one in the movie has an idea in their bubbly little brains. No, not even Philip Baker Hall, who plays the football coach in an eruption of obligatory threats.

The plot involves a cheerleading competition along the lines of the one in *Bring It On* (2000), the *Citizen Kane* of cheerleader movies. That movie involved genuinely talented cheerleaders. This one involves ungainly human pyramids and a lot of uncoordinated jumping up and down. Faithful readers will recall that I often ask why the bad guys in movies wear matching black uniforms. They do in this one, too. The villains here are the Panther cheerleading squad. How many teams play in all black?

I could tell you about Carly, Bianca, Gwyneth, Poppy, and the other sexy cheerleaders, but I couldn't stir myself to care. There is an old rule in the theater: If the heroine coughs in the first act, she has to die in the third. In this movie, the cutest member of the squad is Angela (Hayley Marie Norman). She also has the nicest smile and the best personality and is on screen early and often, so I kept expecting her big scene, but no: She seems destined to be the cheerleader's cheerleader, pepping them up, cheering them on, smiling, applauding, holding up the bottom of the pyramid, laughing at funny lines, encouraging, bouncing in sync, and projecting with every atom of her being the attitude *You go, girls!* You've got a problem when you allow the most intriguing member of the cast to appear in that many scenes and never deal with her. That is not the movie's fatal flaw, however. Its flaw is that I was thinking about things like that.

Flanders ★ ★ ★
NO MPAA RATING, 91 m., 2007

Adelaide Leroux (Barbe), Samuel Boidin (Demester), Henri Cretel (Blondel), Jean-Marie Bruveart (Briche), David Poulain (Leclercq), Patrice Venant (Mordac), David Legay (Lieutenant), Inge Decaesteker (France). Directed by Bruno Dumont and produced by Jean Brehat and Rachid Bouchareb. Screenplay by Dumont.

It was W. G. Sebold who said that animals and men gaze at each other across a gulf of mutual incomprehension. Here is a film that crouches on the screen like a great, sullen beast. It is impossible to embrace, impossible to dismiss. I do not know what it is thinking, how it perceives life. But the film is not about animals. It is about men and women, inarticulate to the point of silence, putting one weary foot ahead of another in a march toward sadness.

Flanders, by Bruno Dumont, won the Jury Prize at Cannes 2007. His *L'Humanite* won it in 1999. Both films require a special kind of viewer. I wrote of *L'Humanite* that it is "for those few moviegoers who approach a serious movie almost in the attitude of prayer." But we do not approach *Flanders* as if attending a religious service. We are its pastor, helpless to console it. It stands wet and lonely outside our church of the human race.

The movie takes place in a pale, cold season, February or March, in that rural area of Belgium that saw some of the most brutal fighting of World War I. It takes place in the present day, when the tractor's plow turns up with the earth some white, chalky stuff that

might once have been bones. It is primarily about Barbe (Adelaide Leroux), a thin, unsmiling girl; Demester (Samuel Boidin), a passive farm worker; and Blondel (Henri Cretel), also a farm worker, so limited that he accepts Demester's blank silence as companionship.

Demester leans on a fence, staring at the fields. Barbe comes to stand next to him. "Did you get your letter?" she asks. He did, calling him to war. "You go on Monday?" He nods. "Shall we?" He nods. They walk across the fields, bed down in a hedgerow, and have sex with the efficiency of hedgehogs. It is not as good for her as it is for him because, we do not need to be told, it has never been good for either of them.

A group gathers in a rural tavern. They do not even get drunk. They drink their beer dutifully. Demester refuses to agree that he and Barbe are "a couple." She leaves the table and picks up Blondel. That will show him. But Demester does not much react, Blondel does not seem to have won anything, Barbe does not seem to think she has made much of a point.

Demester, Blondel, and other locals are trucked away to be sent to an unnamed war in an unnamed land. They commit atrocities and are themselves the victims of unspeakably horrible experiences. Demester, who survives, returns. Barbe, in the meantime, has had an abortion, spent time in a mental hospital, and is back on the farm. They have sex again. "I love you," Demester says. They are the saddest words in the movie.

This film has a few tangible pleasures, such as some somber shots of Demester walking far away in a field. Its achievement is theoretical. It wants to depict lives that are without curiosity, introspection, and hope. I watched with mournful restlessness. I admire it more today than yesterday when I saw it. I will never "like" it. I can imagine showing it to a film class and confronting the uncertain eyes of the students: What forlorn "masterpiece" had I forced upon them? How would I defend it?

I would say Dumont takes them about as far as they will ever want to go in the direction of human emptiness. Or maybe his film takes them nowhere, but simply occupies a place. It is *Waiting for Godot* without dialogue or the expectation of Godot. It is Bressonian, but demonstrates how Bresson is sublime and

Dumont is implacably stolid. Consider Dumont's character of Barbe and then, if you have the chance, watch Bresson's miraculous *Mouchette*. You want to console Mouchette. You want to regard Barbe from across a room, wondering how her personality displaces so little karma.

The actors are all locals, unprofessional, but fully equal to Dumont's barren designs for them. I recall when Emmanuel Schotte, the star of Dumont's much more involving *L'Humanite,* won the best actor award at Cannes and all of my friends agreed that in his acceptance speech the actor seemed *exactly* the same as his character. Is that acting? Perhaps it is one goal of acting.

Gene Siskel sometimes said a film should be more interesting than a documentary of the same actors having lunch. I would be interested in seeing Adelaide Leroux and Samuel Boidin having lunch together, or even having sex together. It is unutterably depressing to reflect they might seem the same as here. If this is life, then death, I think, is no parenthesis.

Note: I give it three stars because I don't want to discourage anyone who finds this description intriguing. On my Web site is a place for readers to vote. Consult their rating carefully. My reviews of L'Humanite *and* Mouchette *are online.*

Flash of Genius ★ ★ ★
PG-13, 120 m., 2008

Greg Kinnear (Robert Kearns), Lauren Graham (Phyllis Kearns), Dermot Mulroney (Gil Previck), Alan Alda (Gregory Lawson). Directed by Marc Abraham and produced by Gary Barber, Roger Birnbaum, and Michael Lieber. Screenplay by Philip Railsback, based on the *New Yorker* article by John Seabrook.

Why do corporations tend to be greedy? I suspect it's because their executives are paid millions and millions to maximize profits, minimize salaries, and slash benefits that cut into the bottom line. Sometimes this can be taken to comic-opera extremes, as when the (now) convicted thief David Radler was stealing millions from the *Sun-Times* and actually turned off the escalators to save on electricity. I guess that helps explain why the Ford Motor Co., followed by Chrysler, stole the secret of the intermittent windshield wiper from a little guy named Robert Kearns.

Why bother? Why not just pay the guy royalties? Simple: Because Ford thought it could get away with it. He was only a college professor. They had teams of high-priced lawyers with infinite patience. They risked having the legal fees cost them more than the patent rights, but what the hell. You can't go around encouraging these pipsqueaks.

I am aware that I sound just like a liberal, but at this point in history, I am sick and tired of giant corporations running roughshod over decent people—cutting their wages, polluting their work environment, cutting or denying them health care, forcing them to work unpaid overtime, busting their unions, and other crimes we have never heard George Bush denounce while he was cutting corporate taxes. I'm sure lower taxes help corporations to function more profitably. But why is that considered progress when many workers live in borderline poverty and executives have pissing contests over who has the biggest stock options?

But enough. I have *Flash of Genius* to review. Yes, I am agitated. I am writing during days of economic meltdown, after Wall Street raped Main Street while the Bush ideology held it down. Believe me, I could go on like this all day. But consider the case of Robert Kearns, played here touchingly by Greg Kinnear. He was a professor of engineering, a decent, unremarkable family man, and had a *Eureka!* moment: Why did windshield wipers only go on and off? Why couldn't they reflect existing conditions, as the human eyelid does?

Working in his basement, Kearns put together the first intermittent wiper from off-the-shelf components and tested it in a fish tank. He patented it in 1967. He demonstrated it to Ford but wouldn't tell them how it worked until he had a deal. After Ford ripped it off and reneged on the deal, he sued in 1982. Thirteen years later, he won thirty million dollars in a settlement where the automakers didn't have to admit deliberate theft.

Flash of Genius tells this story in faithful and often moving detail. If it has a handicap, it's that Kearns was not a colorful character—more of a very stubborn man with tunnel vision. He alienates his family, angers his business partner (Dermot Mulroney), and sorely tries the patience of his lawyer (Alan Alda), whom he is not afraid to accuse of incompetence. Was his victory worth it? The movie asks us to decide. For Robert Kearns, as depicted in this movie, it was. If he had not been obsessively obstinate, Ford would have been counting its stolen dollars.

The movie covers events taking place from 1953 to 1982. The wiper was hard to perfect. There are some gaps along the way, and we don't get to know his wife (Lauren Graham) and his family very well, nor perhaps does he. He calls his kids his "board of directors," but they mostly resign, only to return loyally in the end. Alda gives the film's strongest performance. Kinnear, often a player of light comedy, does a convincing job of making this quiet, resolute man into a giant-slayer.

Todd McCarthy of *Variety* notices an odd fact: Right to the end, Kearns always drove Fords. He remained loyal. I remember those days. You were a Ford, a Dodge, a Cadillac, or a Studebaker family, and that's what you remained. It was nice when sensible wipers were added to the package. Thanks, professor.

Food, Inc. ★ ★ ★ ½
PG, 94 m., 2009

A documentary directed by Robert Kenner and produced by Kenner and Elise Pearlstein.

The next time you tuck into a nice T-bone, reflect that it probably came from a cow that spent much of its life standing in manure reaching above its ankles. That's true even if you're eating it at a pricy steakhouse. Most of the beef in America comes from four suppliers.

The next time you admire a plump chicken breast, consider how it got that way. The egg-to-death life of a chicken is now six weeks. They're grown in cages too small for them to move, in perpetual darkness to make them sleep more and quarrel less. They're fattened so fast they can't stand up or walk. Their entire lives they are trapped in the dark, worrying.

All of this is overseen by a handful of giant corporations that control the growth, processing, and sale of food in this country. Take Monsanto, for example. It has a patent on a custom gene for soybeans. Its customers are *forbidden*

to save their own soybean seed for use next year. They have to buy new seed from Monsanto. If you grow soybeans outside their jurisdiction but some of the altered genes sneak into your crop from your neighbor's fields, Monsanto will investigate you for patent infringement. They know who the outsiders are and send out inspectors to snoop in their fields.

Food labels depict an idyllic, pastoral image of American farming. The sun rises and sets behind reassuring red barns and white frame farmhouses, and contented cows graze under the watch of the Marlboro Cowboy. This is a fantasy. The family farm is largely a thing of the past. When farmland comes on the market, the corporations outbid local buyers. Your best hope of finding real food grown by real farmers is at a local farmers' market. It's not entirely a matter of "organic" produce, although usually it is. It's a matter of food grown nearby, within the last week.

Remember how years ago you didn't hear much about E. coli? Now it seems to be in the news once a month. People are even getting E. coli poisoning from spinach and lettuce, for heaven's sake. Why are Americans getting fatter? A lot of it has to do with corn syrup, which is the predominant sweetener. When New Coke failed and Coke Classic returned, it wasn't to the classic recipe; Coke replaced sugar with corn sweeteners.

Cattle have been trained to eat corn instead of grass, their natural food. The Marlboro Cowboys should be riding through cornfields. Corn, in fact, is an ingredient in 80 PERCENT of supermarket products, including batteries and Splenda. Processing concentrates it. You couldn't eat enough corn kernels in a day to equal the calories in a bag of corn chips. Corn syrup can be addictive. Also fat and salt. A fast food meal is a heart attack in a paper bag. Poor families can't afford to buy real food to compete with the cost of $1.00 burgers and $1.98 "meals."

If this offends you, try to do something about it. The Texas beef growers sued Oprah. She won in court because she had the money to fight teams of corporate lawyers. You don't. Consider Carol Morrison, who refused to seal her chicken houses off from the daylight and opened them to the makers of this documentary. Morrison's chickens are not jammed into

143

cages, but we see chickens that are unable to stand up. A giant chicken processor canceled her contract and refused to do any more business with her. She was getting sick of how she treated chickens, anyway.

Good food is not a cause limited to actresses on talk shows. Average people are getting concerned. Amazingly, Wal-Mart signed up with Stonyfield Farm. Consumer demand. When you hear commentators complaining about how the "government is paying farmers to not grow food," understand that "farmers" are corporations, and that the government is buying their surpluses to undercut local farmers around the world. The farmers who grew Bermuda onions are just about out of business because of the dumping of American onions. "Socialized agriculture" benefits megacorporations, which are committed to the goals of most corporations: maximizing profits and executive salaries.

This doesn't read one thing like a movie review. But most of the stuff I discuss in it, I learned from the new documentary *Food, Inc.*, directed by Robert Kenner and based on the recent book *The Omnivore's Dilemma* by Michael Pollan. I figured it wasn't important for me to go into detail about the photography and the editing. I just wanted to scare the bejesus out of you, which is what *Food, Inc.* did to me.

It's times like these I'm halfway grateful that after surgery I can't eat regular food anymore, and have to live on a liquid diet out of a can. Of course, it contains soy and corn products, too, but in a healthy form. They say your total cholesterol level shouldn't exceed your age plus one hundred. Mine is *way* lower than that. And I don't have to tip.

The Foot Fist Way ★ ★

R, 87 m., 2008

Danny McBride (Fred Simmons), Mary Jane Bostic (Suzie Simmons), Ben Best (Chuck "The Truck" Wallace), Spencer Moreno (Julio Chavez), Carlos Lopez IV (Henry Harrison), Jody Hill (Mike McAlister). Directed by Jody Hill and produced by Erin Gates, Jody Hill, Robbie Hill, and Jennifer Chikes. Screenplay by Jody Hill, Danny McBride, and Ben Best.

The hero of *The Foot Fist Way* is loathsome and reprehensible and isn't a villain in any traditional sense. Five minutes spent in his company, and my jaw was dropping. Ten minutes, and I realized he existed outside any conventional notion of proper behavior. Children should not be allowed within a mile of this film, but it will appeal to *Jackass* fans and other devotees of the joyously ignorant.

The hero is named Fred Simmons. He's played by Danny McBride with a cool confidence in the character's ability to transgress all ordinary rules of behavior. Fred runs a Tae Kwan Do studio. He has the instincts of a fascist. His clients are drilled to obey him without question, to always call him "sir," to respect him above all others. Some of his clients are four years old. He uses profanity around them (and to them) with cheerful oblivion.

To a boy about nine years old, named Julio, he explains, "People are shit. The only person that you can trust is me, your Tae Kwan Do instructor." Julio needs consoling after he's disrespected by little Stevie, who is maybe a year younger. To teach Stevie respect, Fred beats him up. Yes. There are several times in the movie when Fred pounds on kids. He doesn't pull his punches. Most people in the audience will wince and recoil. I did. Others will deal with that material by reasoning that the fight stunts are faked and staged, their purpose is to underline Fred's insectoid personality, and "it's only a movie."

Which side of that fence you come down on will have a lot to do with your reaction. A zero-star rating for this movie could easily (in my case, even rapturously) be justified, and some fanboys will give it four. In all fairness it belongs in the middle. Certainly *The Foot Fist Way* doesn't like Fred; it regards him as a man who has absorbed the lingo of the martial arts but doesn't have a clue about its codes of behavior. He's as close to a martial arts practitioner as Father Guido Sarducci is to a Catholic priest. And the movie is often funny; I laughed in spite of myself.

Fred's offensiveness applies across a wide range of behavior. He is insulting to his wife's dinner guests, tries to kiss and maul students in his office, and asks one young woman who studies yoga: "Have you ever heard of it saving anyone from a gang-rape type of situation?"

He has found very few friends. He introduces his students to his buddy from high school, Mike McAllister (Jody Hill, the director), who has a fifth-degree black belt and a penetrating stare that seems rehearsed in front of a mirror.

Fred and Mike worship above all others Chuck "The Truck" Wallace (Ben Best, the cowriter), a movie star whose credits include the intriguingly titled *7 Rings of Pain 2*. When Chuck appears at a nearby martial arts expo, Fred asks him to visit his studio's "testing day," and then invites him home and shows him the master bedroom ("the wife and I will bunk on the couch"). That he assumes a movie star will want to spend the night is surprising, although perhaps less so when The Truck gets a look at Fred's wife, Suzie (Mary Jane Bostic). Fred leaves the two of them together while he teaches a class and is appalled when he returns to find Suzie and The Truck bouncing on the couch. What does he expect? Suzie has photocopies of her boobs and butt in "work papers from the office," and excuses her behavior at a party by saying, "I got really drunk—Myrtle Beach drunk."

McBride's performance is appallingly convincing as Fred. Despite all I've written, Fred comes across as a person who might almost exist in these vulgar times. McBride never tries to put a spin on anything, never strains for laughs. He says outrageous things in a level, middle-American monotone. He seems convinced of his own greatness, has no idea of his effect on others, and seems oblivious to the manifest fact that he is very bad at Tae Kwan Do. He is a real piece of work.

I cannot recommend this movie, but I can describe it, and then it's up to you. If it sounds like a movie you would loathe, you are correct. If it doesn't, what can I tell you? What it does, it does well, even to its disgusting final scene.

Note: The title is a translation of Tae Kwan Do.

Four Christmases ★ ★
PG-13, 82 m., 2008

Vince Vaughn (Brad), Reese Witherspoon (Kate), Robert Duvall (Howard), Jon Favreau (Denver), Mary Steenburgen (Marilyn), Dwight Yoakam (Pastor Phil), Tim McGraw (Dallas), Kristin Chenoweth (Courtney), Jon Voight (Creighton), Sissy Spacek (Paula). Directed by Seth Gordon and produced by Roger Birnbaum, Gary Barber, and Jonathan Glickman. Screenplay by Matt R. Allen, Caleb Wilson, Jon Lucas, and Scott Moore.

So here's the pitch, boss. *Four Christmases*. We star Reese Witherspoon and Vince Vaughn as a happily unmarried couple whose parents are divorced and remarried, and since nobody is talking to one another, they have to visit all four households on Christmas.

Why don't they just invite everybody over to their house or rent a private room at Spago?

No, no. They usually don't go to Christmas with *anyone*. They usually tell their parents they're out of cell phone contact, breast-feeding orphans in Guatemala.

Both of them?

They're really in Fiji. But their flight is canceled because of heavy fog. They're interviewed on TV, and now everybody knows they're still in town, and they have to make the rounds.

How long will this take to establish?

We introduce them, they go to the airport, they're on TV, *ba-bing, ba-bing, ba-bing.*

Cut two ba-bings. What's next?

First stop, Vince's dad. We'll get Robert Duvall. Mean old snake. Both of Vince's brothers are like extreme duel-to-the-death cage fighters. They beat the crap out of Vince, while ol' dad sits in his easy chair and verbally humiliates him.

Who are the brothers?

Jon Favreau and Tim McGraw.

Jon Favreau as a cage fighter?

He got a trainer.

Does McGraw sing?

That would slow down the family fight.

What about Reese?

Wait until she gets to her mom. Wait until we get to both moms. Her mom is Mary Steenburgen. She's sex hungry. His mom is Sissy Spacek. She's in love with Vince's best friend.

Those are both good actresses.

Right, but they can handle this. Jon Voight for her dad. He lives on Lake Tahoe. Perfect for Christmas.

What's his problem?

145

He lends the picture gravitas.

The audience, does it laugh while his brothers beat the crap out of Vince?

That's what we're hoping.

Tell me something else that's funny.

Two babies that urp on everyone.

That's funny?

OK, they projectile vomit.

A little better.

Also, we have Dwight Yoakam as Pastor Phil.

Spare me the religious details. All I want to know is, does Yoakam sing?

Nope.

We got two gold record singers and they don't sing?

So? We got five Oscar-winning actors and they don't need to act much. There *can't* be any singing, boss. If McGraw doesn't sing, then Yoakam doesn't sing. It's in the contract. A most-favored-nations clause.

Most-favored-nations would not even remotely apply here. That is insane.

There ain't no sanity clause.

4 Months, 3 Weeks and 2 Days ★ ★ ★ ★

NO MPAA RATING, 113 m., 2008

Anamaria Marinca (Otilia), Laura Vasiliu (Gabita), Alex Potocean (Adi), Vlad Ivanov (Mr. Bebe). Directed by Cristian Mungiu. Produced by Mungiu and Oleg Mutu. Screenplay by Mungiu.

Gabita is perhaps the most clueless young woman to ever have the lead in a movie about her own pregnancy. Even if you think Juno was way too clever, two hours with Gabita will have you buying a ticket to Bucharest for Diablo Cody. This is a powerful film and a stark visual accomplishment, but no thanks to Gabita (Laura Vasiliu). The driving character is her roommate, Otilia (Anamaria Marinca), who does all the heavy lifting.

The time is the late 1980s. Romania still cringes under the brainless rule of Ceausescu. In Cristian Mungiu's *4 Months, 3 Weeks and 2 Days,* Gabita desires an abortion, which was then illegal, not for moral reasons, but because Ceausescu wanted more subjects to rule. She turns in desperation to her roommate, Otilia,

who agrees to help her and does. Helps her so much, indeed, she does everything but have the abortion herself. In a period of twenty-four hours, we follow the two friends in a journey of frustration, stupidity, duplicity, cruelty, and desperation, set against a background of a nation where if it weren't for the black market, there'd be no market at all.

For Gabita, the notion of taking responsibility for her own actions is completely unfamiliar. We wonder how she has survived to her current twentyish age in a society that obviously requires boldness, courage, and improvisation. For starters, she convinces Otilia to raise money for the operation. Then she asks her to go first to meet the abortionist. Then she neglects to make a reservation at the hotel the abortionist specifies. That almost sinks the arrangement: The abortionist has experience suggesting that hotel will be a safe venue and suspects he may be set up for a police trap. His name, by the way, is Mr. Bebe (Vlad Ivanov), and no, *bebe* is apparently not Romanian for "baby," but it looks suspicious to me.

The movie deliberately levels an unblinking gaze at its subjects. There are no fancy shots, no effects, no quick cuts, and Mungiu and his cinematographer, Oleg Mutu, adhere to a rule of one shot per scene. That makes camera placement and movement crucial, and suggests that every shot has been carefully prepared. Even shots where the ostensible subject of the action is half-visible, or not seen at all, serve a purpose, by insisting on the context and the frame. Visual is everything here; the film has no music, only words or silences.

Otilia is heroic in this context; she reminds me a little of the ambulance attendant in the 2005 Romanian film *The Death of Mr. Lazarescu,* who drove a dying man around all night insisting on a hospital for him. Otilia grows exasperated with her selfish and self-obsessed friend, but she keeps on trying to help, even though she has problems of her own.

One of them is her boyfriend, Adi (Alex Potocean), who is himself so self-oriented that we wonder if Otilia is attracted to the type. Even though she tries to explain that she and Gabita have urgent personal business, he insists on Otilia coming to his house to meet his family that night. He turns it into a test of her love. People who do that are incapable of understanding that to compromise would be a proof of their own love.

The dinner party she arrives at would be a horror show even in a Mike Leigh display of social embarrassment. She's jammed at a table with too many guests, too much smoking, too much drinking, and no one who pays her the slightest attention. As the unmoving camera watches her, we wait for her to put a fork in somebody's eye. When she gets away to make a phone call, Adi follows her and drags her into his room, and then Adi's mother bursts in on them and we see who Adi learned possessiveness from.

When the friends finally find themselves in a hotel room with the abortionist, the result is as unpleasant, heartless, and merciless as it could possibly be. I'll let you discover for yourself. And finally there is a closing scene where Otilia and Gabita agree to never refer to this night again. Some critics have found the scene anticlimactic. I think it is inevitable. If I were Otilia, I would never even see Gabita again. I'd send over Adi to collect my clothes.

Filmmakers in countries of the former Soviet bloc have been using their new freedom to tell at last the stories they couldn't tell then. *The Lives of Others*, for example, was about the East German secret police. And in Romania, the era has inspired a group of powerful films, including the aforementioned *Mr. Lazarescu, 12:08 East of Bucharest* (2006), and *4 Months*, which won the Palme d'Or at Cannes 2007, upsetting a lot of American critics who admired it but liked *No Country for Old Men* more.

The film has inspired many words about how it reflects Romanian society, but obtaining an illegal abortion was much the same in this country until some years ago, and also in Britain, as we saw in Leigh's *Vera Drake*. The fascination of the film comes not so much from the experiences the friends have, however unspeakable, but in who they are, and how they behave and relate. Anamaria Marinca gives a masterful performance as Otilia, but don't let my description of Gabita blind you to the brilliance of Laura Vasiliu's acting. These are two of the more plausible characters I've seen in a while.

Fred Claus ★ ★
PG, 114 m., 2007

Vince Vaughn (Fred Claus), Paul Giamatti (Santa Claus), Miranda Richardson (Annette Claus), John Michael Higgins (Willie), Elizabeth Banks (Charlene), Rachel Weisz (Wanda), Kathy Bates (Mama Claus), Kevin Spacey (Clyde), Ludacris (DJ Donnie). Directed by David Dobkin and produced by Dobkin, Joel Silver, and Jessie Nelson. Screenplay by Dan Fogelman.

Know how a character in one movie can be so terrific another movie is spun off just to take advantage? That happened with Ma and Pa Kettle, who had small roles in *The Egg and I*, which led to their very own series. But enough of today's seminar on the history of cinema. What I'm wondering is whether a *scene* can inspire a spin-off.

I'm thinking of the best scene in *Fred Claus*, which takes place at a twelve-step support group for brothers of famous people. Maybe it's called Recovering Siblings Anonymous. Fred Claus (Vince Vaughn), who has suffered all of his life in the shadow of his beloved younger brother, Santa Claus, sits in the circle and shares. Also at the meeting are Roger Clinton, Frank Stallone, and Stephen Baldwin, and I'm not spoiling a laugh, because it's what they say that is so funny.

I'm thinking, too bad Billy Carter didn't live to steal this movie. But there are plenty more brothers to go around. Neil Bush comes to mind. How about Clint Howard, although he's been doing well lately? Or Jeffrey Skilling of Enron, now serving twenty-four years while his brother Tom is the popular and respected Chicago weatherman? This could be a movie like the Fantastic Four, where the brothers form a team. Tom Skilling screws up the weather forecast at the North Pole after Clint Howard feeds him bad info from a garbled headset at Santa's Mission Control, and Neil Bush saves the day by arranging for an executive pardon.

If you at least chuckled during my pathetic attempt at humor, that's more than may happen during long stretches of *Fred Claus*, which has apparently studied *Elf* and figured out everything that could have gone wrong with its fish-out-of-water Christmas fable. The movie

147

begins centuries ago in the Black Forest, when Mr. and Mrs. Claus and their first son, Fred, welcome a new bundle of joy: Nicholas Claus. Fred vows that he will be the bestest big brother little Nicky could ever hope for, but alas, Nicholas is such a paragon that you can't get over him, you can't get around him, and all Fred can do is go under him, in a bitter and undistinguished life. Think about it. What does Santa (Paul Giamatti) need with a brother? He's one-stop shopping.

It gets worse. Nicholas Claus becomes a saint. And it turns out, in a development previously unreported by theologians, that if you're a saint, that means both you and your family live forever. Yes! So Fred has to be St. Nick's brother forever and ever after. And this sad old planet would benefit, according to the Catholic count, by at least ten thousand immortal saints, although the Church reassures us with some confidence that they are all in heaven.

Flash forward to, yes, Chicago. Vince Vaughn should earn some kind of grace just for bringing this production to his hometown. He is in love with a meter maid (Rachel Weisz), who has moved here from London, which explains her accent if not her job choice. Fred stays pretty much out of touch with his famous kid brother, until he gets in a financial squeeze and has to call Santa for a $50,000 loan to open an off-track betting parlor across from the Chicago Mercantile Exchange—not a bad idea, actually.

The action moves to the North Pole and involves the flint-hearted Clyde Northcutt (Kevin Spacey), who is cracking down on cost overruns at the Pole, for whom, I'm not sure. That leads to turmoil among the elves, and Fred at last finds his role in life, but see for yourself.

The movie wants to be good-hearted but is somehow sort of grudging. It should have gone all the way. I think Fred Claus should have been meaner if he was going to be funnier, and Santa should have been up to something nefarious, instead of the jolly old ho-ho-ho routine. Maybe Northcutt could catch Santa undercutting his own elves by importing toxic toys from China, and Fred could save the lives of millions of kids by teaming up with Shafeek Nader.

Free for All! ★ ★ ★
NO MPAA RATING, 93 m., 2008

A documentary directed, written, and produced by John Wellington Ennis.

I'm getting tired of being angry about the 2004 presidential election. It is now clear enough that it may have been stolen. The vote totals in Ohio are particularly suspect. Florida in 2000 you know all about. But did you ever seriously focus on Ohio 2004?

You perhaps have vague memories of a controversy about polling machines. And confused voters. And how the chairman of George Bush's Ohio campaign was the secretary of state in charge of overseeing the election. And how the state awarded a $100 million contract for voting machines to Diebold, whose chairman attended a strategy session at Bush's Texas ranch, hosted a $1,000-a-plate dinner for Bush in his mansion, and told the press he would do whatever he could to ensure that Bush won Ohio.

You may have missed some details. Such as that Kenneth Blackwell, the GOP secretary of state/campaign manager, decreed (1) that a vote not cast in your precinct would not be counted; (2) that all precinct lines be redrawn; (3) that the new precincts would be explained on the secretary/chairman's Web site, which unfortunately was six months behind in being updated. Some voters actually found their way to the right place, such as a school gym, but didn't know that as many as four precincts were voting there, so that mathematically three of four were in the wrong lines and voted in the wrong precinct. Of course the Republicans efficiently informed their mailing and e-mail list members of correct voting sites.

These details and others are alleged in a new documentary named *Free for All!* by John Wellington Ennis, who traveled to Ohio in 2006 to see how the gubernatorial election (Blackwell against Democrat Ted Strickland) was going. Turns out it was not going well. In a state newly energized to correct voting irregularities, Blackwell lost to Strickland, winning only 37 percent of the vote. What a turnaround in two years.

The doc is engrossing, even enraging. It's

essentially a narration by Ennis, illustrated with video, stills, news footage, photos, and standard talking-head interviews. It doesn't have the visual liveliness of the Michael Moore docs that clearly influenced it. There is too much Ennis, whose I-can't-believe-this tone of voice wears out its welcome. But he has a lot to say. There's no easy way to summarize, so let me quote:

That the world got the official Ohio election results from a Web site made by the same Web designer smearing Bush's opponent (i.e., Mike Connell, a man instrumental in the Swift Boat attacks) wasn't the only suspect thing in election night. The Web servers for the election results in Ohio were suddenly moved in the middle of the night from Ohio to Tennessee. The entire business of reporting these numbers on the Web, where media and the rest of America take them from, was being run by this far-right partisan Web company. The same company hosted Bush's own Web site, and GOP.com, OhioGOP.com, Newt.com, and so on.

Would you trust an election supervised by Bush's campaign manager and reported by a site designed by the Swift Boat guy? Strange thing: All the exit polls showed Kerry winning Ohio, but then Bush pulled ahead late in the evening. If Bush had lost Ohio, he would have lost the election.

Friday the 13th ★ ★
R, 91 m., 2009

Jared Padalecki (Clay Miller), Amanda Righetti (Whitney Miller), Arlen Escarpeta (Lawrence), Danielle Panabaker (Jenna), Travis Van Winkle (Trent), Aaron Yoo (Chewie), Derek Mears (Jason Voorhees). Directed by Marcus Nispel and produced by Michael Bay, Andrew Form, Brad Fuller, and Sean Cunningham. Screenplay by Damian Shannon and Mark Swift.

Friday the 13th is about the best *Friday the 13th* movie you could hope for. Its technical credits are excellent. It has a lot of scary and gruesome killings. Not a whole lot of acting is required. If that's what you want to find out, you can stop reading now.

OK, it's just us in the room. You're not planning to see *Friday the 13th,* and you wonder

why anyone else is. Since the original movie came out in 1980, there were ten more films—sequels, retreads, fresh starts, variations, whatever. Now we get the 2009 *Friday the 13th,* which is billed as a "remake" of the original.

That it is clearly not. Let me test you with a trick question: How many kids did Jason kill in the first movie? The answer is none, since Mrs. Voorhees, his mother, did all of the killings in revenge on the camp counselors who let her beloved son drown in Crystal Lake.

Mrs. Voorhees is decapitated at the end of number one and again in the new version, so the new movie is technically a remake up until that point—but the decapitation, although preceded by several murders, comes *before* this movie's title card, so everything after that point is new.

It will come as little surprise that Jason still lives in the woods around Crystal Lake and is still sore about the decapitation of his mom. Jason must be sore in general.

So far in the series, he has been drowned, sliced by a machete in the shoulder, hit with an ax in the head, supposedly cremated, aped by a copycat killer, buried, resurrected with a lightning bolt, chained to a boulder and thrown in the lake again, resurrected by telekinesis, drowned again, resurrected by an underwater electrical surge, melted by toxic waste, killed by the FBI, resurrected through the possession of another body, returned to his own body, thrown into hell, used for research, frozen cryogenically, thawed, blown into space, freed to continue his murder spree on Earth 2, returned to the present, faced off against Freddy Krueger of *A Nightmare on Elm Street,* drowned again with him, and made to emerge from Crystal Lake with Freddy's head, which winks.

I know what you're thinking. No, I haven't seen them all. Wikipedia saw them so I didn't have to. The question arises: Why does Jason continue his miserable existence, when his memoirs would command a seven-figure advance, easy? There is another question. In the 1980 movie, twenty years had already passed since Jason first went to sleep with the fishes. Assuming he was a camper aged twelve, he would have been thirty-two in 1980, and in 2009 he is sixty-one. That helps explain why one of my fellow critics at the screening was wearing an AARP T-shirt.

SPOILER WARNING: At the end of this film, Jason is whacked with an ax and a board, throttled with a chain, and dragged into a wood chipper, although we fade to black just before the chips start to fly, and we are reminded of Marge Gunderson's immortal words. The next day brings a dawn, as one so often does, and two survivors sit on the old pier with Jason's body wrapped and tied in canvas. Then they throw him into Crystal Lake. Anyone who thinks they can drown Jason Voorhees for the fifth time is a cockeyed optimist.

Note: In my research, I discovered that the scientific name for fear of Friday the 13th is "paraskavedekatriaphobia." I envision a new franchise: Paraskavedekatriaphobia: A New Beginning, Paraskavedekatriaphobia: Jason Lives, Paraskavedekatriaphobia: Freddy's Nightmare, *etc.*

Frost/Nixon ★ ★ ★ ★
R, 122 m., 2008

Frank Langella (Richard Nixon), Michael Sheen (David Frost), Oliver Platt (Bob Zelnick), Sam Rockwell (James Reston Jr.), Kevin Bacon (Jack Brennan), Rebecca Hall (Caroline Cushing), Toby Jones (Swifty Lazar), Matthew Macfadyen (John Birt), Patty McCormack (Pat Nixon), Andy Miller (Frank Gannon), Kate Jennings Grant (Diane Sawyer), Eve Curtis (Sue Mengers). Directed by Ron Howard and produced by Howard, Tim Bevan, Eric Fellner, and Brian Grazer. Screenplay by Peter Morgan, based on his play.

Strange, how a man once so reviled has gained stature in the memory. How we cheered when Richard M. Nixon resigned the presidency! How dramatic it was when David Frost cornered him on TV and presided over the humiliating confession he had stonewalled for three years. And yet how much more intelligent, thoughtful, and, well, presidential, he now seems, compared to the occupant of the office from 2001 to 2009.

Nixon was thought to have been destroyed by Watergate and interred by the Frost interviews. But wouldn't you trade him in a second for Bush? The confession wrung out of him by Frost acted as a catharsis. He admitted what

everyone already knew, and that freed him to get on with things, to end his limbo at San Clemente, to give other interviews, to write books, to be consulted as an elder statesman. Indeed, to show his face in public.

Ron Howard's *Frost/Nixon* is a somewhat fictionalized version of the famous 1977 interviews, all the more effective in taking the point of view of the outsider, the "lightweight" celebrity interviewer, then in his own exile in Australia. Precisely because David Frost (Michael Sheen) was at a low ebb professionally and had gambled all his money on the interviews, his point of view enhances and deepens the shadows around Nixon (Frank Langella). This story could not have been told from Nixon's POV, because we would not have cared about Frost.

The film begins as a fascinating inside look at the TV news business and then tightens into a spellbinding thriller. Early, apparently inconsequential scenes (Frost as a "TV star," Frost picking up a woman on an airplane, Frost partying) are crucial in establishing his starting point. He was scorned at the time for even presuming to interview Nixon. He won the interview for two reasons: He paid the expresident $600,000 from mostly his own money, and he was viewed by Nixon and his advisers as a lightweight pushover.

And so he seems during the early stages of the interviews (the chronology has been much foreshortened for dramatic purposes). Nixon sidetracks Frost, embarks on endless digressions, evades points, falls back on windy anecdotes. Frost's team grows desperate. Consisting of an experienced TV newsman, Bob Zelnick (Oliver Platt), and a researcher, James Reston Jr. (Sam Rockwell), they implore him to interrupt Nixon, to bear down hard, to keep repeating questions until he gets an answer. Frost was a man accustomed to being nice to Zsa Zsa Gabor. He doesn't have to be nice to Nixon. He has hired Nixon.

I can't be sure how much of the film's relationship between the two men is fictionalized. I accept it as a given in the film, because this is not a documentary. The screenplay, by Peter Morgan, is based on his award-winning London and Broadway play, which also starred Langella and Sheen. What Morgan suggests is that even while he was out-fencing Frost, two things were going on deep within Nixon's mind: (1) a need to confess, which may have been his buried reason for agreeing to the interviews in the first place, and (2) an identification with Frost and even sympathy for him. Nixon always thought of himself as the underdog, the outsider, the unpopular kid. "You won't have Nixon to kick around anymore," he told the press when his political career apparently ended in his loss of the 1962 California gubernatorial election.

Now look at Frost. Although he had a brilliant early career in England, which Nixon may not have been very familiar with, he is shown in the film as a virtual has-been, exiled to Australia. You can count on Nixon and his agent Swifty Lazar (Toby Jones) to know that Frost had failed to find financial backing, was paying Nixon out of his own pocket, and would be ruined if he didn't get what he clearly needed. Then factor in Nixon's envy of Frost's popularity and genial personality. In one revealing moment, Nixon confides he would do anything to be able to attend a party and just relax around people. Nixon also questions him closely about his "girlfriends." Frost represented Nixon's vulnerabilities, his shortcomings, and even some of his desires.

This all sets the stage for the (fictionalized) scene that is the crucial moment in the story. A drunken Nixon calls Frost late at night. The next day, he doesn't remember the call, but like an alcoholic after a blackout, he has an all too vivid imagination of what he might have said. At that day's interview, he's not only playing their chess game with a hangover but has sacrificed his queen.

Frank Langella and Michael Sheen do not attempt to mimic their characters but to embody them. There's the usual settling-in period, common to all biopics about people we're familiar with, when we're comparing the real with the performance. Then that fades out, and we've been absorbed into the drama. Howard uses authentic locations (Nixon's house at San Clemente, Frost's original hotel suite), and there are period details, but the film really comes down to these two compelling, intense performances, these two men with such deep needs entirely outside the subjects of the interviews. All we know about the real Frost and the real Nixon is almost beside the point. It all comes down to those two men in that room while the cameras are rolling.

Frownland ★ ★ ★ ½
NO MPAA RATING, 106 m., 2008

Dore Mann (Keith Sontag), Paul Grimstad (Charles), Mary Wall (Laura), David Sandholm (Sandy), Carmine Marino (Carmine), Paul Grant (Exam Man). Directed by Ronald Bronstein and produced by Marc Raybin. Screenplay by Bronstein.

Frownland is a movie like a shriek for help. It centers on an extraordinary performance that plays like an unceasing panic attack. To call it uncompromising is to wish for a better word. It doesn't ask us to like its central character; after all, no one in the film does. I don't think he likes himself.

The character is named Keith (Dore Mann). He is in his late twenties, a chain-smoker, a shabby dresser, a door-to-door salesman for dubious coupon booklets benefiting multiple sclerosis. His girlfriend, Laura (Mary Wall), arrives sobbing at his tiny room, sleeps with her face to the wall, sticks him with a pushpin.

I feel sympathy for Keith, but I wouldn't want to spend time with him. He has a punishing manner of speech that involves starting sentences again and again, blurting out impassioned and inarticulate appeals, overwhelming his listeners. You can see his jaw working as he gathers the courage to speak again. He is constantly wiping his face with his hand. He makes his only friend desperate to get rid of him. His flatmate is jobless and can't pay his share. Keith's room is a single bed on the left and a row of kitchen implements on the right, with a two-foot aisle between.

His flatmate, Charles (Paul Grimstad), agrees to pay the electric bill, but Keith doesn't trust him. This sets up a devastating verbal assault from Charles—who, in fact, never pays the bill. His "friend" Sandy (David Sandholm) doesn't want him to visit and tricks him into leaving. When he fails at his hopeless door-to-door job, his boss, Carmine (Carmine Marino), who drives a crew of salesmen in his van, asks him how he'd like to walk home. His very way of speaking to people invites a "no."

One curiosity is that the film leaves Keith for

151

an extended scene involving Charles taking a test for a job application. I can see how the idea of testing people might apply to Keith, but otherwise this plays as a digression. Then we return to Keith with a harrowing scene where he is mocked by drunks at a disco. Incredibly, even here, Mann's work never goes over the top. We believe at every moment that this suffering creature is really feeling what he seems to feel, really saying what he needs to say. It is easy to imagine the performance going wrong, but it doesn't.

Now, why would you want to see this picture? Most readers of this review probably wouldn't. I'm writing for the rest of us. It is a rebirth of the need for expression that inspired the American independent movement in the first place, fifty years ago. It was written, directed, and edited by Ronald Bronstein, who had a crew of one cameraman, one soundman, and one grip. It has not been picked up for distribution; he is distributing it himself at shrines to outsider cinema (Facets Cinematheque in Chicago, the IFC Center in New York).

Yet the film has gained a foothold. It won a special jury prize at the important SXSW Festival in Austin. It won a Gotham Award from the Independent Feature Project in New York. It has been nominated for an Indie Spirit Award. To give you an idea of the challenge it presents, the *New York Times* praised it, but it was hated by *Film Threat*, "Hollywood's indie voice."

Such reactions are inspired by Dore Mann's performance, which in intensity equals Peter Greene's work in Lodge Kerrigan's *Clean, Shaven* (1993). Indeed, Kerrigan is one of the champions of the film. What Dore Mann does is not caricature, not "performance," not contrived. It is full throttle all the way with insecurity, needfulness, loneliness, mistrust, desperation, self-hate, apology, and despair.

Frownland has been described as a test for audiences. There will be walk-outs. But it doesn't set out to alienate its viewers; its only purpose is to do justice to Keith by showing him as he is. I will not forget him.

Frozen River ★ ★ ★ ★

R, 97 m., 2008

Melissa Leo (Ray Eddy), Misty Upham (Lila Littlewolf), Charlie McDermott (T.J.), Mark Boone Jr. (Jacques Bruno), Michael O'Keefe (Trooper Finnerty), James Reilly (Ricky). Directed by Courtney Hunt and produced by Heather Rae and Chip Hourihan. Screenplay by Hunt.

Sometimes two performances come along that are so perfectly matched that no overt signals are needed to show how the characters feel about each other. That's what happens between Melissa Leo and Misty Upham in *Frozen River,* playing two mothers who live without male support in shabby house trailers on the U.S.-Quebec border: Mohawk territory.

Leo plays Ray Eddy, whose husband left his car at a Mohawk bingo parlor and disappeared, perhaps on the bus to Atlantic City. He is an addicted gambler and has taken all the money they were saving to buy a better trailer. Ray scrapes by on a part-time job at the Yankee One Dollar store, and until payday, her kids, fifteen and five, are dining on popcorn and Tang.

Upham plays Lila Littlewolf, a Mohawk who works at the bingo hall and lives alone; her mother-in-law has "stolen" her one-year-old. The two women meet after Lila finds the keys in the husband's abandoned car and drives it away, and Ray follows her home: "That's my car." Lila says she knows a smuggler who will give her two thousand dollars for it, no questions asked. She knows a lot more than that, which is how Ray finds them both in the business of smuggling aliens across the border into the United States. This involves the two women in making hazardous car trips across the ice of a frozen river, dealing with unsavory types on both sides, and carrying Chinese and Pakistanis in the trunk.

Frozen River, a debut film written and directed by Courtney Hunt, never steps wrong. It resists all temptations to turn this plot into some kind of a thriller and keeps it grounded on the struggle for economic survival. The winner of the Grand Jury Prize at Sundance 2008, it is one of those rare independent films that knows precisely what it intends and what the meaning of the story is.

Ray Eddy is a heroine in her life. She refuses all offers by her son T.J. (Charlie McDermott) to drop out of school and get a job. She begs for full-time work at the store. She never set out to smuggle humans (she's tricked into it), but once she gets into it, she finds it pays well. She has no particular feelings about the people in the car trunk and throws away the Pakistani's precious duffel bag because it "might contain poison gas, and I don't want to be responsible for that."

T.J. watches solemnly and knows the real story: His dad has run off on them, there is no food, he is responsible for his little brother, the men are coming to collect the TV set. For Lila, life is sad; she perches on a freezing night in a tree outside her mother-in-law's window for glimpses of her baby and shares Pringles with the watchdog. She has Ray count the money in all of their deals because she can't see the bills.

Do these two women bond? This is not a story of bonding. It is a story of need. They hardly have a conversation that isn't practical and immediate, and theory and sentiment are beyond them. Neither actress is afraid to seem cold and detached. That we know their inner feelings is a tribute to the film. I don't know how Courtney Hunt came by her knowledge of this world, but it feels exact and familiar. Even the scenes with a state trooper (Michael O'Keefe) are played quietly and with a certain sympathy. But notice the grim realism of a scene at a topless bar (also in a house trailer).

And there is an awesome, terrifying beauty in their journeys across the ice. "I've seen semis make it," Lila says. The Mohawk reservation on the American side provides a kind of sanctuary for smugglers—although the tribal elders are wise to her and won't let her own a car. Ray's status as a white woman gives them a kind of immunity—for a while. The way the trooper approaches the case is matter-of-fact and humane.

In detail after detail, *Frozen River* is the story of two lives in economic emergency, and two women who are brave and resourceful and ready to do what is necessary. It doesn't play sides. It isn't about illegal aliens or smuggling. It's about replacing popcorn and Tang with a meal at the Chopper and some nice TV dinners. That it climaxes on Christmas Eve doesn't even seem contrived, just sad.

Fugitive Pieces ★ ★ ★ ½
R, 108 m., 2008

Stephen Dillane (Jakob), Rade Sherbedgia (Athos), Rosamund Pike (Alex), Ayelet Zurer (Michaela), Robbie Kay (Young Jakob), Ed

Stoppard (Ben), Rachelle Lefevre (Naomi). Directed by Jeremy Podeswa. Produced by Robert Lantos. Screenplay by Podeswa, based on the novel by Anne Michaels.

"To live with ghosts requires solitude."

So says the hero of *Fugitive Pieces*, a Canadian writer who as a child in Poland saw the Nazis murder his parents and drag away his sister. Rescued by a Greek archaeologist who was miraculously working on a dig near his hiding place, the boy is taken to safety on the man's home island in Greece, and eventually fate and a teaching position take them to Toronto. Having been gripped by the big silent eyes of the boy Jakob (Robbie Kay), we now meet him as an adult (Stephen Dillane). Both he and his savior, Athos (Rade Sherbedgia), are committed to recording the past so it will be saved from oblivion.

But it is his own past Jakob is most concerned about losing. He obsessively returns to his memories of his parents and sister, especially the tragic event he glimpsed from his hiding place behind some wallpaper. There are moments when he focuses on his lovely mother and we wonder if they ever happened; has desire augmented his memories? In the present, he is married to Alex (Rosamund Pike). He relentlessly tells her about the importance of not forgetting (one Holocaust survivor, he tells her, kept a photograph hidden under her tongue for three months; its discovery would have brought death). Alex encourages him to live sometimes in the present, but then she finds in his diary that he fears she is stealing that past away. "It makes your brain explode," she says, "his obsession with these details."

She walks out, and that triggers the thoughts about living in solitude. The line and all the poetic narration in the film come from the novel by Anne Michaels that inspired it. Jakob shares the original Toronto apartment he moved into with Athos, who grows older and, if such a thing is possible, kinder; such saints are rare. "You must try to be buried in ground that will remember you," he says, and that leads to Jakob's return to the Greek island, where he divides his year with Toronto.

There are neighbors in Toronto, Yiddish-speaking, whose son, Ben (Ed Stoppard), grows up and introduces the adult Jakob to another woman, a museum curator named Michaela (Ayelet Zurer). This woman is too good to be true, but then, for such a morose and fearful person, Jakob is blessed with wonderful people in his life. He takes her to Greece, he feels love, he begins to free himself from his ghosts.

Such a summary barely captures the qualities of *Fugitive Pieces*, written and directed by Jeremy Podeswa (*The Five Senses, Into the West*). He doesn't tell, he evokes, with the nostalgic images of his cinematographer, Gregory Middleton, the understated melancholy of the score by Nikos Kypourgos and the seamless time transitions of his editor, Wiebke von Carolsfeld. The film glides between the past and different periods in Jakob's later life, as it tries to show this man whose love for his family has essentially frozen him at the time he last saw them. He tortures himself: If he hadn't run away, would his sister have returned to their home? After being taken by the Nazis? Not likely.

There are other harrowing scenes, showing the Nazi occupation of the Greek island and the heroism of Athos in protecting Jakob and doing risky favors for neighbors. But the film is not about the Holocaust so much as it is about memory, how we use it, how we must treasure it, how we must not be enslaved by it. The lushly photographed earth tones of the Toronto scenes indeed almost evoke a storehouse for the past, and its shadows are finally burned away by the sunshine of Greece.

Since the film premiered in September 2007 at Toronto, more than one viewer has talked in wonder about its comforting qualities. For a film about the Holocaust, it is gentler than we might expect. A lot of that quality is caused by the face and presence of Rade Sherbedgia, an actor whose name you may not know although you have probably seen him many times. Some people have a quality of just smiling at you and making things heal. He does. And Stephen Dillane's worried, haunted face gives him the right person to work on, if only Athos, too, were not so absorbed in the past. If *Fugitive Pieces* has a message, it is that life can heal us, if we allow it.

G

The Gates ★ ★ ★
NO MPAA RATING, 98 m., 2007

A documentary directed by Antonio Ferrera and Albert Maysles and produced by Ferrera, Maureen Ryan, and Vladimir Yavachev.

Many people missed the point of the Gates, those 7,500 frames flowing with orange curtains that were installed along the pathways of Central Park in 2005. The point was not to look at them, but to use them, to walk through them and under them. One New York park board member, opposed to the proposal by artists Christo and Jeanne-Claude, said the addition of the Gates to the park "would be like Picasso painting *Guernica* on top of *The Last Supper*," demonstrating that he did not grasp the difference between a painting and a frame. He might have saved himself embarrassment by consulting *A Pattern Language* by Christopher Alexander, the most important architect alive, who would have had something to say about gates, entrances, exits, doors, portals, and views.

Entrances have everything to do with what we feel about what we are entering. All buildings until the birth of modern architecture knew this, and you can see it in church doors, temple gates, city walls, shop entrances, and cottage doorsteps. Now the doors of a modern building are likely to be a continuation of the same hostile slab of glass or steel that makes the rest of the building sterile and aloof. There will be no place to rest for a moment, inside or out, and no shelf to rest a burden on, and no decorative details to declare, "This is not just any place you are entering, but this honorable place." I believe even criminals feel differently about the judges they encounter inside an old courthouse than inside a new one.

My wife and I walked under the Gates and beneath the curtains. Thousands of others were doing the same. Many of them no doubt made the same journey daily, scarcely thinking of it. Certainly our walk was enriched by trees, grass, shrubbery, ponds, views. But now the Gates, by framing those sights, gave them a new aspect and importance. Not "grass on a hill," but *this* view of a grassy hill. Not a pond, but *look* at the pond. A frame of any sort values what it encloses. And as we walked, we felt subtly ceremonial. We were not walking, but *walking through the gates*. People walked a little more slowly, and sometimes had little smiles, and talked less on their cell phones, and perhaps felt more *there*.

The Gates, a documentary by Antonio Ferrera and Albert Maysles, records the struggle starting in 1979 as Christo and Jeanne-Claude tried to get planning permission to install their gates (for only two weeks, but you'd think they were planning to leave them forever). This despite the fact that the artists were going to pay for it all themselves. One mayor after another, perhaps too timid to support duh artz, said no. Bloomberg said yes, instantly. So, I believe, would have Chicago's Mayor Daley, whose wrought-iron fences and islands of flowers and neoclassical columns and Millennium Park declare, "This is a city worthy of such pomp and formality, such beauty and pride." Those who say Daley has the mentality of a bungalow owner have no idea of the pride a bungalow owner can take in his home. Maybe they live in high-rises where committees buy hideously tortured iron and dump it in the lobby.

The documentary is pretty much what you'd expect: Two decades of ignorant contempt, followed by the city finding it was really surprisingly fond of the Gates. How far do you think our beloved Chicago sidewalk cows would have gotten among the philistines of fifty years ago? Why does London cling to manifestly impractical red pillar boxes for its postal system, pillars that look like bright red Victorian fire hydrants? Because they're fun, that's why.

Christo and Jeanne-Claude age during the film, their hair turning gray (or red, in her case), but they never stop campaigning. It must have seemed so simple to them: Hey, people, lighten up! Don't be afraid of fancy and imagination! They actually had to use two high-powered lawyers, Scott Hodes of Chicago and Theodore W. Kheel of New York, to argue the case in favor of their gift to the city. The one thing lacking is a good sit-down chat with Christopher Alexander, explaining why cities require more, not less, attention to human feelings that cannot be reasoned away.

Get Smart ★ ★ ★ ½
PG-13, 110 m., 2008

Steve Carell (Maxwell Smart), Anne Hathaway (Agent 99), Dwayne Johnson (Agent 23), Alan Arkin (The Chief), Terence Stamp (Siegfried), James Caan (The President). Directed by Peter Segal and produced by Andrew Lazar, Charles Roven, Alex Gartner, and Michael Ewing. Screenplay by Tom J. Astle and Matt Ember.

The closing credits of *Get Smart* mention Mel Brooks and Buck Henry, creators of the original TV series, as "consultants." Their advice must have been: "If it works, don't fix it." There have been countless comic spoofs of the genre founded by James Bond, but *Get Smart* (both on TV and now in a movie) is one of the best. It's funny, exciting, preposterous, great to look at, and made with the same level of technical expertise we'd expect from a new Bond movie itself. And all of that is very nice, but nicer still is the perfect pitch of the casting.

Steve Carell makes an infectious Maxwell Smart, the bumbling but ambitious and unreasonably self-confident agent for CONTROL, a secret U.S. agency in rivalry with the CIA. His job is to decipher overheard conversations involving agents of KAOS, its Russian counterpart. At this he is excellent: What does it mean that KAOS agents discuss muffins? That they have a high level of anxiety, of course, because muffins are a comfort food. Brilliant, but he misses the significance of the bakery they're also discussing—a cookery for high-level uranium.

Smart is amazingly promoted to field agent by The Chief (Alan Arkin, calm and cool) and teamed with the beautiful Agent 99 (Anne Hathaway, who never tries too hard but dominates the screen effortlessly). They go to Russia, joining with Agent 23 (Dwayne Johnson, once known as The Rock). Their archenemy is waiting for them; he's Siegfried (Terence Stamp), a cool, clipped villain.

And that's about it, except for a series of special effects sequences and stunt work that would truly give envy to a James Bond producer. *Get Smart* is an A-level production, not a cheapo rip-off, and some of the chase sequences are among the most elaborate you can imagine—particularly a climactic number involving planes, trains, and automobiles. Maxwell Smart, of course, proves indestructible, often because of the intervention of Agent 99; he spends much of the center portion of the film in free fall without a parachute, and then later is towed behind an airplane.

The plot involves a KAOS scheme to nuke the Walt Disney concert hall in Los Angeles, during a concert being attended by the U.S. president. The nuclear device in question is concealed beneath the concert grand on the stage, which raises the question, since you're using the Bomb, does its location make much difference, give or take a few miles?

It raises another question, too, and here I will be the gloom-monger at the festivities. Remember right after 9/11, when we wondered if Hollywood would ever again be able to depict terrorist attacks as entertainment? How long ago that must have been, since now we are blowing up presidents and cities as a plot device for Maxwell Smart. I'm not objecting, just observing. Maybe humor has a way of helping us face our demons.

The props in the movie are neat, especially a Swiss Army–style knife that Maxwell never quite masters. The locations, many in Montreal, are awesome; I learned with amazement that Moscow was not one of them but must have been created on a computer. The action and chase sequences do not grow tedious because they are punctuated with humor. I am not given to quoting filmmakers in praise of their own work in press releases, but director Peter Segal does an excellent job of describing his method: "If we plan a fight sequence as a rhythmic series of punches, we would have a 'bump, bump, bam' or a 'bump, bump, smack.' We can slot in a punch line instead of a physical hit. The rhythm accentuates the joke and it becomes 'bump, bump, joke' with the verbal jab as the knockout or a joke, immediately followed by the last physical beat that essentially ends the conversation."

Yes. And the jokes actually have something to do with a developing story line involving Anne Hathaway's love life, the reason for her plastic surgery, and a love triangle that is right there staring us in the face. One of the gifts of Steve Carell is to deliver punch lines in the middle of punches and allow both to seem real enough, at least within the context of the movie. James Bond could do that, too. And in a summer with no new Bond picture, will I be considered a heretic by saying *Get Smart* will do just about as well? 🖙

Ghosts of Girlfriends Past ★ ★
PG-13, 100 m., 2009

Matthew McConaughey (Connor Mead), Jennifer Garner (Jenny Perotti), Michael Douglas (Uncle Wayne), Breckin Meyer (Paul Mead), Lacey Chabert (Sandra Volkom), Robert Forster (Sergeant Volkom), Anne Archer (Vondra Volkom), Emma Stone (Allison Vandermeersh). Directed by Mark Waters and produced by Jon Shestack and Brad Epstein. Screenplay by Jon Lucas and Scott Moore.

Remember *Harry, the Rat with Women*? This time his name is Connor Mead, but he's still a rat. A modern Scrooge who believes marriage is humbug, he is taught otherwise by the ghosts of girlfriends past, present, and future, and one who spans all of those periods. Just like Scrooge, he's less interesting after he reforms.

Matthew McConaughey plays Connor as a rich and famous *Vanity Fair* photographer whose ambition is to have sex with every woman he meets, as soon as possible. Sometimes this leads to a logjam. Impatient to sleep with his latest quarry, a model who just allowed an apple to be shot off her head with an arrow, Connor actually arranges an online video chat session to break up with three current girlfriends simultaneously, but is bighearted enough to allow them to chat with one another after he logs off.

Connor appears on the eve of the wedding of his younger brother Paul (Breckin Meyer), who lives in the mansion of their late Uncle Wayne (Michael Douglas), a structure designed roughly along the lines of Versailles. (Actually, it's Castle Hill, in Ipswich, Massachusetts, built by the Crane family of Chicago, whose toilets you may have admired.) Connor is attending the wedding only to warn against it; he has a horror of getting hitched and extols a lifetime of unrestrained promiscuity.

The movie is apparently set in the present. I mention that because every woman Connor meets knows all about his reputation for having countless conquests, and yet is nevertheless eager to service him. These days, I suspect a great many of those women, maybe all of them, would view him primarily as a likely carrier of sexually transmitted diseases. To be fair, in a fantasy scene, his used condoms rain from the heavens, an event not nearly as thought-provoking as the raining frogs in *Magnolia.*

Attending the wedding is Jenny (the lovely Jennifer Garner, from *Juno*), who was his first girlfriend and the one he should have married. The ghost of Uncle Wayne materializes as a spirit guide and takes Connor on a guided tour of his wretched excess, after which he bitterly regrets his loss of Jenny, leading to a development which I do not have enough shiny new dimes to award to everyone who can predict it.

Michael Douglas is widely said to have modeled his hair, glass frames, and general appearance on the noted womanizer Bob Evans, but actually he reminded me more of Kirk Douglas playing Bob Evans. It's an effective performance either way you look at it.

The potential is here for a comedy that could have been hilarious. But the screenplay spaces out some undeniably funny lines in too much plot business, and Matthew McConaughey, while admirably villainous as a lecher, is not convincing as a charmer. Just this weekend a new Michael Caine movie is opening, which makes me remember his Alfie, a performance that is to lechers as Brando is to godfathers.

Maybe the movie's problem runs a little deeper. It's not particularly funny to hear women described and valued exclusively in terms of their function as disposable sexual partners. A lot of Connor's dialogue is just plain sadistic and qualifies him as that part of an ass it shares with a doughnut.

Ghost Town ★ ★ ★
PG-13, 102 m., 2008

Ricky Gervais (Bertram Pincus), Tea Leoni (Gwen), Greg Kinnear (Frank Herlihy), Billy

Campbell (Richard), Kristen Wiig (Surgeon), Dana Ivey (Marjorie Pickthall), Aasif Mandvi (Dr. Prashar). Directed by David Koepp and produced by Gavin Polone. Screenplay by Koepp and John Kamps.

Why do I think Ricky Gervais is so funny in *Ghost Town*? Because he doesn't want to appear funny. He wants to appear aggravated. He plays a character named Bertram Pincus, who does not suffer fools gladly. When you consider everyone to be a fool, that can be a heavy cross to bear. Gervais, a British actor whose work on television is legion, has at last found a leading role in a feature, and it's a good one.

Bertram Pincus is not a happy camper. He is a dentist, a profession in which he finds delight in preventing patients from talking with him. He is unmarried, friendless, a loner, meticulous, obtuse, at times ridiculous. When a birthday cake is laid on for a friendly colleague in his office, he sneaks out. To join in the celebration would make his skin crawl. He is nasty to innocent bystanders.

He does all of this in a British accent, almost between clenched teeth, and reminds me a little of Terry-Thomas at full flood: an unmitigated bounder wrapped in propriety. He is about to have his moat breached. This assault is set in motion when a bus flattens Frank Herlihy (Greg Kinnear). Frank's death turns out to be linked to Bertram's colonoscopy. As you can imagine, Bertram is a man who considers a colonoscopy a grievous violation of privacy.

Bertram is technically dead for seven minutes during the procedure. (Don't put yours off; this is a microscopically rare phenomenon.) That makes him sort of half-dead, half-alive after he recovers, and as a result he can see both living people and ghosts. This puts him in urgent demand among the ghosts, who yearn to communicate with their loved ones and need him as a medium. The most desperate ghost he encounters is Frank, who was having an affair with his yoga instructor but now deeply regrets it and wants to communicate with his wife, Gwen (Tea Leoni).

Never mind about the plot details, which spin out in more or less obligatory fashion. Focus instead on Tea Leoni, lovable down to her toenails, and Frank, cursed by having to live (or die, that is) enveloped in guilt and gloom. Bertram recoils when a stranger approaches him. He is even more inconvenienced by ghosts. And he is the last man on earth who would attract Gwen, or be attracted by her, so of course he and Gwen find themselves falling in love, causing unspeakable frustration for Frank.

Ghost Town is a lightweight rom-com elevated by its performances. It is a reminder that the funniest people are often not comedians but actors playing straight in funny roles. Consider Cary Grant in *Topper* (1937), the obvious inspiration for David Koepp, who directed and cowrote *Ghost Town* with John Kamps. Because both Gervais and Kinnear seem so urgent in their desires, and because Tea Leoni has a seemingly effortless humor and grace, this material becomes for a while sort of enchanting.

Yes, it is required that the plot have some of its characters living happily ever after, and that requires some dialogue that is, excuse me, corny. I suppose it comes with the territory. There is poignancy in a subplot involving Dana Ivey as a woman who wants to communicate with her daughters, and indeed a whole crowd of ghosts hoping to send messages to the other side. We have this comforting notion of our deceased loved ones smiling down benevolently from heaven. Now that they're getting a good look at us, they're probably tearing out their hair.

Gigantic ★ ★ ½
R, 98 m., 2009

Paul Dano (Brian Weathersby), Zooey Deschanel (Harriet Lolly), Ed Asner (Mr. Weathersby), Jane Alexander (Mrs. Weathersby), John Goodman (Al Lolly), Sean Dugan (Gary Wynkoop), Brian Avers (Larry Arbogast). Directed by Matt Aselton and produced by Christine Vachon and Mindy Goldberg. Screenplay by Aselton and Adam Nagata.

On the basis of *Gigantic*, Matt Aselton can make a fine and original film. This isn't quite it, but it has moments so good all you wish for is a second draft. Nor is it ever boring. You can't say that about a lot of debuts. I suspect he was trying too hard to be terrific and not hard enough to get organized.

His hero, Brian Weathersby (the willfully bland Paul Dano), is a young and feckless mattress salesman. He was a late son in a tribe of unconventional brothers. When they all get together with Dad (Ed Asner) in the family's cottage in the woods, Dad bonds with him by consuming hallucinogenic mushrooms. How Brian would know he was hallucinating is a good question, because much of his life unfolds on the border of reality.

The Swiss mattress showroom occupies a vast upper floor of a warehouse. Into this space one day marches Al Lolly (John Goodman), a big man with a painful back problem. Brian shows him the high-end $14,000 mattress, which uses real horsehair, which is a big deal in the mattress universe. The mattress also inspires an inspection by Al's daughter Harriet (Zooey Deschanel), a beautiful girl with startling blue-green eyes. Although you might expect to find her on magazine covers, she is as inward as Brian; they speak in minimalist murmurs, as when she asks if he feels like having sex with her, and he confides that he does. Later he tells a friend that he doesn't know if he likes her or not. More accurately, probably, he doesn't know if he liked being jolted out of his lifelong dubiousness.

Ever since he was a little boy, Brian has been obsessed with the idea of adopting a Chinese baby. He doesn't understand why; he just is. Harriet might upset that dream in some obscure way. She invites him to her home, and he enters into a strange world ruled by Al Lolly, a rich, opinionated eccentric, who is driven everywhere flat on his back in the rear of a Volvo station wagon. The great open spaces of their apartment have been decorated by spending a great deal of money on a limited selection of furniture.

Brian's life is complicated by a berserk madman who ambushes him with assaults. This man seems imaginary, until Brian receives facial wounds that don't go away. To summarize: A loser mattress salesman with a peculiar father meets a beautiful lost girl with an eccentric millionaire father, and is attacked by a loony while trying to evade love and adopt a Chinese baby. Does this sound like a screenplay or a contest entry? In the UK it would be described as too clever by half, and "clever" is not a compliment over there.

The strange thing is, the characters are interesting. You could make a movie about them. That Brian's very sane mother is played by Jane Alexander is an example of how well the film is cast. The delicate relationship between Harriet and Brian is beautifully played by Deschanel and Dano, but the movie jars us out of it with bizarre sidetracks such as a scene set in a massage parlor; it's intended as funny but is finally a toss-up between odd and sad.

Gigantic is an example of a certain kind of "Sundance movie" made after the ship has sailed. The pendulum is swinging back toward the more classical forms of filmmaking. It's not enough to add, "Oh—and this homeless guy keeps attacking him." If you want a homeless guy, do something meaningful with him, as Mike Leigh did in *Happy-Go-Lucky*. Wackiness for its own sake is not a substitute for humor or much of anything else.

And yet look at the things here that are really good: the conversation between Brian and Harriet in the doctor's waiting room. The way the parents take to the Chinese baby. The way John Goodman modulates his performance to make Al Lolly a character and not a caricature. The way Harriet falls asleep on the $14,000 mattress, and what they say after she wakes up. Matt Aselton's next film might be a marvel.

Girl Cut in Two ★ ★ ★ ½
NO MPAA RATING, 114 m., 2008

Ludivine Sagnier (Gabrielle Deneige), Benoit Magimel (Paul Gaudens), Francois Berleand (Charles Saint-Denis), Mathilda May (Capucine Jamet), Caroline Silhol (Genevieve Gaudens), Marie Bunel (Marie Deneige), Valeria Cavalli (Dona Saint-Denis). Directed by Claude Chabrol and produced by Patrick Godeau. Screenplay by Chabrol and Cecile Maistre.

Claude Chabrol's *Girl Cut in Two* plays like a triangular romantic comedy until we discover that all three of the lovers are hurtling headlong to self-destruction. Even then it is comedic, in that macabre, Hitchcockian way that takes a certain delight in the flaws of mankind. It's a crime movie, as most of Chabrol's sixty-nine films have been, and at first the crime seems to be adultery. He doesn't leave it at that.

At the center of everything is Gabrielle Deneige (Ludivine Sagnier), a peppy young blonde who does the weather at the local TV station. Her mother runs a bookstore in Lyon and holds an autographing for the best-selling author Charles Saint-Denis (Francois Berleand). Also at the event is a spoiled local rich kid, Paul Gaudens (Benoit Magimel). These two men are going to bring her to a lot of grief.

But notice how nimbly Chabrol glides through his establishing scenes, and how adroitly he introduces other characters (the lecherous TV boss, the spoiled kid's bitchy mother, Gabrielle's sensible mother, the author's femme fatale agent). The story hums along in efficient although absorbing confidence, seeming to show us Gabrielle trapped between Saint-Denis and Paul, who both vow that they love her. Is this what the title means? Surely we won't really see her cut in two? Well, yes and no.

Hitchcock in *Psycho* made a point in the opening scenes that the film was Janet Leigh's story, that she was a woman with a secret, and that the story would be about that secret. Then she checked into the motel. Gabrielle doesn't disappear from *Girl Cut in Two*, but the film will be about a lot more than her romantic problems. It is important that she seem young, naive, and unguarded, so that we can watch both men trying to seduce her with unwholesome motives.

Chabrol and DePalma are often cited as the directors most influenced by Hitchcock. Consider the scene in this film where Saint-Denis takes Gabrielle to an exclusive private club and asks her to follow him down a corridor. For what purpose? We know it must be sexual, but Chabrol never shows us. This is the Hitchcock technique of building curiosity by deferring action. (Bomb explodes under table equals action. Bomb is under table but it doesn't explode equals suspense.) I was also reminded of the brothel client's little lacquered box in Bunuel's *Belle de Jour*. By never showing us what it contains, he generates enormous erotic curiosity.

The men are odd and interesting. Francois Berleand's Charles is an old rake, hair and beard trimmed to the same length, expertly seductive, a good actor, but devious. Does he really consider his wife a saint? What precisely is his relationship with his agent, who looks like an up-market Vampira? As for Paul, he's such a vain, preening, foppish creature that Gabrielle should see right through him— which she does, in fact. Paul's mother, Genevieve (Caroline Silhol), a rich widow, has a monologue that is hypnotizing, expertly delivered and . . . make up your own mind. The three central characters are in an emotional fencing match, and Gabrielle lacks a mask.

The plot was probably inspired by an actual event, which I will not mention because you may be familiar with it. In any event, Chabrol's insidious style is more absorbing than the plot, as it should be. Chabrol, at seventy-eight, is one of four living members of the French New Wave. The others: Jean-Luc Godard (seventy-seven), Eric Rohmer (eighty-eight), Jacques Rivette (eighty). They've all made films within the last two years and are said to be in preproduction on new projects. And they said it would never last.

The Girlfriend Experience ★ ★ ★ ★
R, 77 m., 2009

Sasha Grey (Chelsea), Chris Santos (Chris), Peter Zizzo (Wealthy Client). Directed by Steven Soderbergh and produced by Mark Cuban, Gregory Jacobs, and Todd Wagner. Screenplay by Brian Koppelman and David Levien.

This film is true about human nature. It clearly sees needs and desires. It is not universal, but within its particular focus it is unrelenting. Steven Soderbergh's *The Girlfriend Experience* is about a prostitute and her clients. In such a relationship, the factor of money makes the motives fairly direct on both sides.

In the language of escort advertising, "GFE" promises a "girlfriend experience." Sometimes sex may not even be involved, although it is implicitly permitted. A man seeking a girlfriend experience offers to pay for companionship, conversation, another human being in his life. The women offering a GFE are acting a role, but in some ways it can be a therapeutic one. We know what sexual surrogates do. A "girlfriend" may be playing a human surrogate.

The film involves a woman named Chelsea and the men in her life. She has been living with one of them for eighteen months, and in a way he may be a boyfriend experience. He doesn't seem much more meaningful to her than a client. The other men are of various ages and backgrounds, but they all have one thing in common: They are wealthy, and Chelsea is not inexpensive. Typically they take her to an expensive restaurant and then a luxury hotel. They may send a limousine for her.

We listen to them talking. We watch them talking. Most of them want to talk about what she does for a living. There is the polite fiction that she is talking about other men, hypothetical men, and not the one she is with. They like to give her advice about how to invest her money and who to vote for (the story takes place during the 2008 campaign). Each one has some reason for thinking he is somehow special. Set during the run-up to the stock market crash, it shows both sides more interested in investing than sex.

These men don't want a girlfriend experience. They want a boyfriend experience. They want to feel as if they're on a date. They will be listened to. Their amazing comments will be smiled at. Their hair will be tousled. They will be kidded. They have told Chelsea about their wives and children, and she remembers their names. They can kiss her. There is no illusion that they are leaving their wives, and none that she wants them to. She simply empowers them to feel younger, more looked up to, more clever than they are.

What draws a powerful man to pay for a woman outside of marriage? It's not the sex. In fact, sex is the beard, if you know what I mean. By paying money for the excuse of sex, they don't have to say: "I am lonely. I am fearful. I am growing older. I am not loved. My wife is bored with me. I can't talk to my children. I'm worried about my job, which means nothing to me." Above all, they are saying: "Pretend you like me."

The film was written by Brian Koppelman and David Levien. Believe it or not, the same two wrote the screenplay for Soderbergh's *Ocean's Thirteen*. I imagine the three of them sitting around on the *Ocean's* set and asking, "What could we be doing instead of this?"

Chelsea is played by Sasha Grey. She is twenty-one. Since 2006, according to IMDb, she's made 161 porn films, of which only the first title can be quoted here: *Sasha Grey Superslut*. No, here's another, which makes me smile: *My First Porn No. 7*. I haven't seen any of them, but now I would like to see one, watching very carefully, to see if she suggests more than one level.

Grey wasn't hired because of her willingness to have sex on the screen; there's no explicit sex in the movie, and only fleeting nudity. I suspect Soderbergh cast her because of her mercenary approach to sex—and her acting talent, which may not be ready for Steppenwolf but is right for this film. She owns her own agency and Web site, manages other actresses, has a disconnect between herself and what she does for a living. So does Chelsea.

The film is intent on her face. It often looks over the shoulder of her clients. She projects precise amounts of interest and curiosity, but conceals real feelings. It is a transaction, and she is holding up her end. Notice the very small nods and shakes of her head. Observe her word choices as she sidesteps questions without refusing to answer them. When her roommate/boyfriend insists on knowing the name of one of her clients, she is adroit in her reply.

Once she allows her mask to slip: a surprising moment when she reveals what she may feel. Sasha Grey perfectly conveys both her hope and her disappointment, keeping both within boundaries. You wonder how a person could look another in the eye and conceal everything about themselves. But the financial traders who are her clients do it every day. Their business is not money, but making their clients feel better about themselves. ☞

The Golden Compass ★ ★ ★ ★
PG-13, 114 m., 2007

Nicole Kidman (Mrs. Coulter), Dakota Blue Richards (Lyra), Daniel Craig (Lord Asriel), Sam Elliott (Lee Scoresby), Eva Green (Serafina

Pekkala), Christopher Lee (First High Councilor), Tom Courtenay (Farder Coram), Derek Jacobi (Magisterial Emissary), Ben Walker (Roger), Simon McBurney (Fra Pavel), Ian McKellen (Iorek Byrnison), Ian McShane (Ragnar Sturlusson), Freddie Highmore (Pantalaimon), Kathy Bates (Hester), Kristin Scott Thomas (Stelmaria). Directed by Chris Weitz and produced by Bill Carraro and Deborah Forte. Screenplay by Weitz, based on the novel by Philip Pullman.

The Golden Compass is a darker, deeper fantasy epic than the *Lord of the Rings* trilogy, *The Chronicles of Narnia,* or the Potter films. It springs from the same British world of quasi-philosophical magic but creates more complex villains and poses more intriguing questions. As a visual experience, it is superb. As an escapist fantasy, it is challenging. Teenagers may be absorbed and younger children may be captivated; some kids in between may be a little conflicted, because its implications are murky.

They weren't murky in the original 1995 novel, part of the His Dark Materials trilogy by Philip Pullman, a best-seller in Britain, less so here. Pullman's evil force, called the Magisterium in the books, represents organized religion, and his series is about no less than the death of God, whom he depicts as an aged, spent force. This version by New Line Cinema and writer-director Chris Weitz (*About a Boy*) leaves aside religion and God, and presents the Magisterium as sort of a Soviet dictatorship, or Big Brother. The books have been attacked by American Christians over questions of religion; their popularity in the United Kingdom may represent more confident believers whose reaction to other beliefs is to respond, rather than suppress.

For most families, such questions will be beside the point. Attentive as I was, I was unable to find anything anti-religious in the movie, which works above all as an adventure. The film centers on a young girl named Lyra (Dakota Blue Richards), in an alternative universe vaguely like Victorian England. An orphan raised by the scholars of a university not unlike Oxford or Cambridge, she is the niece of Lord Asriel (Daniel Craig), who entrusts her with the last surviving Alethiometer, or

Golden Compass, a device that quite simply tells the truth. The Magisterium has a horror of the truth because it represents an alternative to its thought control; the battle in the movie is about no less than man's preservation of free will.

Lyra's friend Roger (Ben Walker) disappears, one of many recently kidnapped children, and Lyra hears rumors that the Magisterium has taken them to an Arctic hideaway. At her college, she meets Mrs. Coulter (Nicole Kidman), who suspiciously offers her a trip to the North aboard one of those fantasy airships that look like they may be powered by steam. And the adventure proper begins.

I should explain that in this world, everyone has a spirit, or demon, which is visible, audible, and accompanies them everywhere. When they are with children, these spirits are shape shifters, but gradually they settle into a shape appropriate for the adult who matures. Lyra's is a chattering little creature who can be a ferret, mouse, fox, cat, even a moth. When two characters threaten each other, their demons lead the fight.

Turns out the Magisterium is experimenting on the captured children by removing their souls and using what's left as obedient servants without free will. Lyra challenges this practice, after taking the advice of the grizzled pilot Lee Scoresby (Sam Elliott) to find herself an armored bear. She enlists the magnificent bear Iorek, who must duel to the death with the top bear of the North. She also finds such friends as a flying witch named Serafina (Eva Green) and some pirate types named Gyptians, whose lifestyle resembles seafaring gypsies.

The struggle involves a mysterious cosmic substance named Dust, which embodies free will and other properties the Magisterium wants to remove from human possibility. By "mysterious," I mean that Dust appears throughout the movie as a cloud of dancing particles, from which emerge people, places, and possibilities, but I have no idea under which rules it operates. Possibly it represents our human inheritance if dogma did not interfere.

As Lyra, Dakota Blue Richards is a delightful find, a British-American schoolgirl who was twelve when she was discovered in an audition involving a total of ten thousand girls. She is pretty, plucky, forceful, self-possessed, charismatic, and just about plausible as the mistress of an armored bear and the protector of Dust. Nicole Kidman projects a severe beauty in keeping with the sinister Mrs. Coulter (had Pullman heard about our girl Ann when he wrote his book?), and Daniel Craig and Sam Elliott (with his famous moustache never more formidable) give her refined and rough surfaces to play against.

The cast is jammed with the usual roll call of stage and screen greats, some of them in person, some of them voice-over talent: Christopher Lee, Tom Courtenay, Derek Jacobi, Simon McBurney, Ian McKellen, Ian McShane, Kathy Bates, Kristin Scott Thomas. The British fantasy industry has become a bigger employer even than the old Hammer horror films. And why is it, by the way, that such tales seem to require British accents?

I realize this review itself may be murky because theological considerations confuse the flow. Let me just say that I think *The Golden Compass* is a wonderfully good-looking movie, with exciting passages and a captivating heroine in Lyra. That the controversy surrounding it obscures its function as a splendid entertainment. That for adults it will not be boring or too simplistic. And that I still don't understand how they know what the symbols on the Golden Compass represent, but it certainly seems articulate.

Gomorrah ★ ★ ★ ★

NO MPAA RATING, 136 m., 2009

Marco Macor (Marco), Ciro Petrone (Piselli/Ciro), Salvatore Abruzzese (Toto), Toni Servillo (Franco), Carmine Paternoster (Roberto), Gianfelice Imparato (Don Ciro), Maria Nazionale (Maria), Salvatore Cantalupo (Pasquale). Directed by Matteo Garrone and produced by Domenico Procacci. Screenplay by Garrone, Maurizio Braucci, Ugo Chiti, Gianni Di Gregorio, Massimo Gaudioso, and Roberto Saviano, based on the book by Saviano.

It is all so sordid. *Gomorrah* is a film about Italian criminals killing one another. One death after another. Remorseless. Strictly

business. The question arises: How are there enough survivors to carry on the business? Another question: Why do willing recruits submit themselves to this dismal regime?

The film is a curative for the romanticism of *The Godfather* and *Scarface*. The characters are the foot soldiers of the Camorra, the crime syndicate based in Naples that is larger than the Mafia but less known. Its revenues in one year are said to be as much as $250 billion—five times as much as Madoff took years to steal. The final shot in the film suggests the Camorra is invested in the rebuilding of the World Trade Center. The film is based on fact, not fiction.

Gomorrah, which won the grand prize at Cannes 2008 and the European Film Award, is an enormous hit in Europe. It sold five hundred thousand tickets in France, which at ten dollars a pop makes it a blockbuster. There was astonishment that the Academy passed it over for foreign film consideration. I'm not so surprised. The Academy committee more often goes for films that look good and provide people we can care about. *Gomorrah* looks grimy and sullen and has no heroes, only victims.

That is its power. Here is a movie about the day laborers of crime. Somewhere above them are the creatures of the $250 billion, so rich, so grand, so distant, with no apparent connection to crime. No doubt New York and American officials sat down to cordial meals with Camorra members while deciding the World Trade contracts and were none the wiser.

Roberto Saviano, who wrote the best-seller that inspired the movie, went undercover, used informants, even (I learn from John Powers on NPR) worked as a waiter at their weddings. His book named names and explained exactly how the Camorra operates. Now he lives under twenty-four-hour guard, although as the Roman poet Juvenal asked, "Who will guard the guards?"

Matteo Garrone, the director, films in the cheerless housing projects around Naples. "See Naples and die" seems to be the inheritance of children born here. We follow five strands of the many that Saviano unraveled in his book, unread by me. There is an illegal business in the disposal of poisonous waste. A fashion industry that knocks off designer lines and works from sweatshops. Drugs, of course. And then we meet teenagers who think they're tough and dream of taking over locally from the Camorra. And kids who want to be gangsters when they grow up.

None of these characters ever refer to *The Godfather*. The teenagers know De Palma's *Scarface* by heart. Living a life of luxury, surrounded by drugs and women, is perhaps a bargain they are willing to make even if it costs their lives. The problem is that only the death is guaranteed. No one in this movie at any time enjoys any luxury. One of them, who delivers stipends to the families of dead or jailed Camorra members, doesn't even have a car and uses a bicycle. The families moan that they can't make ends meet, just like Social Security beneficiaries.

Garrone uses an unadorned documentary style, lean, efficient, no shots for effect. He establishes characters, shows their plans and problems, shows why they must kill or be killed—often, be killed because of killing. Much is said about trust and respect, but little is seen of either. The murders, for the most part, have no excitement and certainly no glamour—none of the flash of most gangster movies. Sometimes they're enlivened by surprise, but it is the audience that's surprised, not the victims, who often never know what hit them.

The actors are skilled at not being "good actors," if you know what I mean. There is no sizzle. Only the young characters have much life in them. Garrone directs them to reflect the bleak reality of their lives, the need and fear, the knowledge that every conversation could be with their eventual killer or victim. Casual friendship is a luxury. Families hold them hostage to their jobs. The film's flat realism is correct for this material.

You watch the movie with growing dread. This is no life to lead. You have the feeling the men at the top got there laterally, not through climbing the ladder of promotion. The Camorra seems like a form of slavery, with the overlords inheriting their workers. The murder code and its enforcement keep them in line: They enforce their own servitude.

Did the book and the movie change things? Not much, I gather. The film offers no hope. I like gangster movies. *The Godfather* is one of

the most popular movies ever made—most beloved, even. I like them as movies, not as history. We can see here they're fantasies. I'm reminded of mob bosses like Frank Costello walking into Toots Shor's restaurant in that fascinating documentary *Toots*. Everyone was happy to see him—Jackie Gleason, Joe DiMaggio, everyone. At least they knew who he was. The men running the Camorra are unknown even to those who die for them.

Gone Baby Gone ★ ★ ★ ½
R, 115 m., 2007

Casey Affleck (Patrick Kenzie), Michelle Monaghan (Angie Gennaro), Morgan Freeman (Jack Doyle), Ed Harris (Remy Bressant), John Ashton (Nick Poole), Amy Ryan (Helene McCready), Amy Madigan (Bea McCready), Titus Welliver (Lionel McCready). Directed by Ben Affleck and produced by Alan Ladd Jr., Sean Bailey, and Dan Rissner. Screenplay by Affleck and Aaron Stockard, based on the novel by Dennis Lehane.

Boston seems like the most forbidding city in crime movies. There are lots of movies about criminals in Los Angeles, Chicago, New York, and points between, but somehow in Boston the wounds cut deeper, the characters are angrier, their resentments bleed, their grudges never die, and they all know everybody else's business. The novelist Dennis Lehane captured that dour gloom in his books inspiring *Mystic River* and now *Gone Baby Gone*. What would it take to make his characters happy?

This is his fourth story involving Patrick Kenzie (Casey Affleck) and Angie Gennaro (Michelle Monaghan), lovers and business partners who are private investigators specializing in tracking down deadbeats. Approached by clients who have deadly matters on their minds, Patrick and Angie protest that they're just garden-variety PIs, don't carry guns, aren't looking for heavy lifting. Then somehow they end up with crucifixion murders, kidnapped babies, and, always, people who are not who or what they seem.

This could become a franchise, if we didn't start grinning at their claims to be basically amateurs. In *Gone Baby Gone*, Ben Affleck, in his debut as a director, assumes we haven't read the four novels, approaches Patrick and Angie head-on, and surrounds them with a gallery of very, very intriguing characters. He has his brother Casey and Monaghan play babes in a deep, dark woods, their youth and inexperience working for them as they wonder about what veteran cops don't question. The result is a superior police procedural and something more—a study in devious human nature.

I know, the title sounds like the movie should star Bill Haley and the Comets. But there is a rough authenticity from the first shots, especially when we meet a woman named Bea McCready (Amy Madigan) and her husband, Lionel (Titus Welliver), who don't think the cops are doing enough to track down her four-year-old niece. They think people who know the neighborhood and don't wear badges might find out more. They're right.

The police investigation is being led by Jack Doyle (Morgan Freeman) of the police Crimes Against Children task force, who, unlike a standard movie cop, doesn't resent these outsiders but suggests they work with his men Remy Bressant (Ed Harris) and Nick Poole (John Ashton). Not likely, but good for the story, as the trail begins in the wreckage of a life being lived by the little girl's single mother, Helene (Amy Ryan). She is deep into drugs, which she takes whenever she can sober up enough, and there seems to be a connection between her supplier and a recent heist of a pile of drug money.

Enough about the plot. What I like about the movie is the way Ben Affleck and his brother, both lifelong Bostonians, understand the rhythm of a society in which people not only live in each other's pockets, but are trying to slash their way out. This movie and *The Assassination of Jesse James* . . . announce Casey's maturation as an actor, and this movie also proves, after her film *The Heartbreak Kid*, that Michelle Monaghan should not be blamed for the sins of others.

And when you assemble Morgan Freeman, Ed Harris, Amy Madigan, and Amy Ryan as sidemen, the star soloists can go out for a cigarette and the show goes right on. One reason crime movies tend to be intrinsically interesting is that the supporting characters

have to be riveting. How far would Jason Bourne get in a one-man show?

There are some secrets and concealed motives in *Gone Baby Gone*, but there always are in any crime movie without name tags saying "Good Guy" and "Bad Guy." What distinguishes the screenplay by Ben Affleck and Aaron Stockard, which departs from the novel in several ways, is (a) how well-concealed the secrets are, and (b) how much perfect sense they make when they're revealed. I am grateful when a movie springs something on me and I feel rewarded, not tricked.

I also like the way that certain clues are planted in plain view. We can see or hear them just fine. It's that we don't know they're clues. No glowering close-ups or characters skulking in a corner to give the game away. That's a tribute to the writing—and the acting, which doesn't telegraph anything. Actors talk about how well they like to get to know their characters. Sometimes it's better if they take them at face value and find out more about them along with the rest of us.

There are dark regions below the surface of the story. Was the child taken by a pedophile? There's a suspect, all right, but maybe he's too obvious. Certainly Helene, the mother, is no help. She's so battered by drugs and drink that she's hardly quite sure if a conversation is taking place. It's amazing the little girl made it to four; her aunt and uncle must have had a lot to do with that. The unspoken assumption is that somewhere a clock is ticking, and the longer the child remains missing, the more likely she will be found dead or never be found at all. And here are these two kids, skip tracers who have lives and destinies depending on them.

Gonzo: The Life and Work of Dr. Hunter S. Thompson ★ ★ ★ ½
R, 121 m., 2008

Johnny Depp (Narrator). A documentary directed by Alex Gibney and produced by Gibney, Graydon Carter, Jason Kliot, Joana Vicente, Eva Orner, and Alison Ellwood. Screenplay by Gibney.

In all the memories gathered together in *Gonzo: The Life and Work of Dr. Hunter S. Thompson*, there was one subject I found conspicuously missing: the fact of the man's misery. Did he never have a hangover? The film finds extraordinary access to the people in his life, but not even from his two wives do we get a description I would dearly love to read, on what he was like in the first hour or two after he woke up. He was clearly deeply addicted to drugs and alcohol, and after a stupor-induced sleep he would have awakened in a state of withdrawal. He must have administered therapeutic doses of booze or pills or *something* to quiet the tremors and the dread. What did he say at those times? How did he behave? Are the words "fear and loathing" autobiographical?

Of course, perhaps Thompson was immune. One of the eyewitnesses to his life says in wonderment, "You saw the stuff go in, and there was no discernible effect." I don't think I believe that. If there was no discernible effect, how would you describe his behavior? If he had been sober all his life, would he have hunted wild pigs with a machine gun? Thompson was the most famous (or notorious) inebriate of his generation, but perhaps he really was one of those rare creatures who had no hangovers, despite the debaucheries of the day(s) before. How much did he consume? A daily bottle of bourbon, plus wine, beer, pills of every description.

The bottom line is, he got away with it, right up until his suicide, which he himself scripted and every one of his friends fully expected. As a journalist, he got away with murder. He reported that during a presidential primary Edward Muskie ingested Ibogaine, a psychoactive drug administered by a "mysterious Brazilian doctor," and this information, which was totally fabricated, was actually picked up and passed along as fact. Thompson's joke may have contributed to Muskie's angry tantrums during the 1972 Florida primary. No other reporter could have printed such a lie, but Thompson was shielded by his legend: He could print anything. "Of all the correspondents," says Frank Mankiewicz, George McGovern's 1972 campaign manager, "he was the least factual, but the most accurate."

He was an explosive, almost hypnotic, writer, with a savage glee in his prose. I remember eagerly opening a new issue of *Rolling Stone* in the 1970s and devouring his work. A great deal of it was untrue, but it dealt in a kind of exalted super-truth, as when he spoke of Richard Nixon the vampire roaming the night in Washington. Thompson had never heard of objectivity. In 1972 he backed George McGovern as the Democratic nominee, and no calumny was too vile for him to attribute to McGovern's opponents in both parties. I suppose readers were supposed to know that and factor it into the equation.

This documentary by Alex Gibney (*Taxi to the Dark Side, No End in Sight*) is remarkable, first of all, for reminding us how many pots Hunter dipped a spoon in. He rode with the Hells Angels for a year. Ran for sheriff of Pitkin County, home of Aspen, and lost, but only by 204 to 173. Covered the 1972 and 1976 presidential primaries in a way that made him a cocandidate (in the sense of codependent). Had a baffling dual personality, so that such as McGovern, Jimmy Buffett, Tom Wolfe, and his wives and son remember him fondly but say that he could also be "absolutely vicious."

He taught himself to write by typing Fitzgerald's *The Great Gatsby* again and again, we're told. How many times? we ask ourselves skeptically. Was that part of the fantastical legend? Nobody in the film was around while he was doing it. He became famous for writing about "the edge" in his Hells Angels book— that edge of speed going around a curve that you could approach, but never cross without wiping out and killing yourself. He did a lot of edge riding on his motorcycle and never wiped out. He said again and again that the way he chose to die was by his own hand, with a firearm, while he was still at the top. He died that way, using one of his twenty-two firearms, but "he was nowhere near the top," says Sondi Wright, his first wife.

He started to lose it after Africa, says Jann Wenner, who ran his stuff in *Rolling Stone*. He went to Zaire at great expense to cover the Rumble in the Jungle for the magazine, got hopelessly stoned, missed the fight (while reportedly in the hotel pool), and never filed a story. "After Africa," says Sondi, "he just couldn't write. He couldn't piece it together." He did some more writing, of course, such as a heartfelt piece after 9/11. But he had essentially disappeared into his legend, as the outlaw of Woody Creek, blasting away with his weapons, making outraged phone calls, getting impossibly high. Certainly he made an impression on his time like few other journalists ever do; the comparison would be with H. L. Mencken.

This film gathers interviews from a wide and sometimes surprising variety of people (Pat Buchanan, Jimmy Carter, Hells Angel Sonny Barger). It has home movies, old photos, TV footage, voice recordings, excerpts from files about Thompson. It is narrated by Johnny Depp, mostly through readings from Thompson's work. It is all you could wish for in a doc about the man. But it leaves you wondering, how was it that so many people liked this man who does not seem to have liked himself? And what about the hangovers?

Goodbye Solo ★ ★ ★ ★
NO MPAA RATING, 91 m., 2009

Souleymane Sy Savane (Solo), Red West (William), Carmen Leyva (Quiera), Diana Franco Galindo (Alex), Lane "Roc" Williams (Roc), Mamadou Lam (Mamadou). Directed by Ramin Bahrani and produced by Bahrani and Jason Orans. Screenplay by Bahrani and Bahareh Azimi.

Two actors. One from Africa. The other who was a bodyguard for Elvis. Who but Ramin Bahrani would find these men and pair them in a story of heartbreaking depth and power? Bahrani is the new great American director. He never steps wrong. In *Goodbye Solo* he begins with a situation that might unfold in a dozen different ways and makes of it something original and profound. It is about the desire to help and the desire to not be helped.

In Winston-Salem, North Carolina, a white man around seventy gets into the taxi of an African immigrant. He offers him a deal. For $1,000, paid immediately, he wants to be driven in ten days to the top of a mountain in Blowing Rock National Park, to a place so windy that the snow falls up. He says nothing about a return trip. The driver takes the money but is not happy about this fare. He asks some questions and is told to mind his own business.

Now look at these actors. They aren't playing themselves, but they evoke their characters so fully that they might as well be. Red West plays William, the white man. His face is

a map of hard living. He was a Marine and a boxer. He became a friend of Elvis in high school. He was his bodyguard and driver from 1955—a charter member of the "Memphis Mafia." He split with Elvis after breaking the foot of the cousin who was bringing Elvis drugs and telling him he would work his way up to his face.

Souleymane Sy Savane plays Solo, the taxi driver. He is from the Ivory Coast, although the character is from Senegal. Savane was a flight attendant for Air Afrique. Solo is studying for just such a job. Solo lives in Winston-Salem, is married to a Mexican-American woman, adores the woman's young daughter, and acts as her father. William's face was made to look pissed off. Solo's face was made to smile. We are not speaking of an odd couple here. We're speaking of human nature. You can't learn acting like this.

Bahrani worked with these actors for months. Savane drove a taxi in Winston-Salem. Red West spent a lifetime rehearsing William (although in real life he is said to be kind and friendly). Bahrani and his cinematographer, Michael Simmonds, discussed every shot. Although *Goodbye Solo* is an independent film in its heart and soul, it is a classical film in its style. It is as pure as something by John Ford. Only its final shot might call attention to itself—but actually, we aren't thinking about the shot, we're thinking about what has happened, and why.

Don't get the idea the whole film takes place in the taxi. It takes place in Winston-Salem, a city it wears with familiarity because Bahrani was born and raised there. We feel the rhythms of Solo's life. Of his relationship with his wife, Quiera (Carmen Leyva), and their pride in her daughter, Alex (Diana Franco Galindo). Like many taxi drivers, Solo knows where you can find drugs or a sexual partner. But he isn't a pusher or a pimp; he's a one-man service industry, happy to help.

The film sees cars being repaired in front yards, a few customers at a downtown movie theater on a weekday night, a lonely motel room, a bar. The next few times William calls a cab, he begins to notice the driver is always Solo. What's up with that? With almost relentless good cheer, Solo insinuates himself into William's life—becomes his chauffeur, his protector, his adviser, even for a few nights his roommate and almost his friend. It occurred to me that Red West may have performed similar functions for Elvis, another man pointed to doom.

Neither William nor Solo ever once speaks about their real subject, about what William seems to be about to do. It hangs in the air between them. Alex, the stepdaughter, comes to love old William, who has the feel of a grandfather about him. But no, Alex is not one of those redeeming movie children. She doesn't understand everything and brings in an innocence that Solo and William both respect.

Goodbye Solo is not finally about what William and Solo do. It is about how they change, which is how a great movie lifts itself above plot. These two lives have touched, learned, and deepened. Not often do we really *care* this much about characters. We sense they're not on the automatic pilot of a plot. They're feeling their way in life. This is a great American film.

This is Bahrani's third feature, after *Man Push Cart* (2005) and *Chop Shop* (2007). His films are about outsiders in America: a Pakistani who operates a coffee-and-bagel wagon in Manhattan, Latino kids who scramble for a living in an auto parts bazaar in the shadow of Shea Stadium. Now a Senegalese who wants to help an American whose weathered face belongs in a Western. Bahrani, whose parents immigrated from Iran, felt like an outsider when he was growing up in Winston-Salem: "There were blacks, whites and my brother and me." He loves the city, and you can tell that in this film. He is curious about people, and you can tell that from all his films. He told me he asks the same question of all of his characters: How do you live in this world?

A film like this makes me wonder if we are coming to the end of the facile, snarky indie films. We live in desperate times. We are ready to respond to films that ask that question. How do you live in this world? Bahrani knows all about flashy camera work, tricky shots, visual stunts. He teaches film at Columbia. But like his fellow North Carolinian David Gordon Green, he is drawn to a more level gaze, to a film at the service of its characters and their world. Wherever you live, when this film opens, it will be the best film in town. ☞

Good Luck Chuck ★

R, 96 m., 2007

Dane Cook (Charlie Logan), Jessica Alba (Cam Wexler), Dan Fogler (Stu), Lonny Ross (Joe). Directed by Mark Helfrich and produced by Barry Katz and Mike Katz. Screenplay by Josh Stolberg.

Here is the dirty movie of the year, slimy and scummy, and among its casualties is poor Jessica Alba, who is a cutie and shouldn't have been let out to play with these boys. *Good Luck Chuck* layers a creaky plot device on top of countless excuses to show breasts, sometimes three at a time, and is potty-mouthed and brain-damaged.

It stars the potentially likable Dane Cook as the lovelorn Charlie Logan, leading me to wonder why, in the same week when Michael Douglas plays a flywheel named Charlie, that name seems to fit so well with characters who are two slices short of a pizza. Young Charlie, who is not called "Chuck" except in the title, is hexed by an eleven-year-old goth girl at a spin-the-bottle party. Because he fights off her enthusiastic assault, she issues this curse: Every woman he falls in love with will leave him and immediately find the man of her dreams.

Charlie grows up to become a dentist. His best friend is still the short, chubby, curly-haired Stu (Dan Fogler). The naming rule here is, Charlie for hero, Stu for best friend, and if there's a villain, he should be referred to only by his last name, which must have a Z or W in it, or a hissing sound. Stu, obsessed by breasts, has grown up to become a plastic surgeon, and so loves his craft that he has purchased Pam Anderson's former breast implants and keeps them in an oak display case, where they look surprisingly small, more like ice packs for insignificant wounds. One peculiarity of the dentist and the plastic surgeon is that they have adjacent offices with an adjoining door, so that Charlie can pop over to Stu's and offer a layman's opinion on his latest boob job.

Anyway, Charlie, who has been unlucky in love, meets Cam (Jessica Alba), who works at a seaquarium and loves penguins so much she might herself be willing to sit on one of their eggs all winter. Apart from being beautiful and friendly, her character trait is that she's a klutz, so physically dangerous she might even step on her own toes. Whatever she touches, she breaks, knocks over, turns on, or damages.

Although he's in love with Cam, Charlie is distracted by the seduction attempts of dozens of beautiful women because a rumor has spread all over town that if they sleep with him, they'll find the husband of their dreams. Stu does some follow-through research and finds out the rumor is true. Funny thing is, the women who crowd Charlie's waiting room all look as if they have come through the connecting door after enhancement by Stu. Charlie connects with so many of them that at one point the screen splits into sixteen separate copulation scenes, just to keep up.

You see Charlie's problem. Cam, a nice girl, doesn't want to date him because he's such a "sport." And Charlie realizes that if he ever sleeps with her, she'll immediately leave him for the man of her dreams. How will this paradox be resolved? By putting us through the agony of an automatic plot device, that's how.

The startling thing about the movie is how juvenile it is. Stu, in particular, is a creepy case of arrested development. Consider the whole scenario he stages with a fat woman who might break Charlie's hex. She's not only fat, she has pimples all over, and yes, we get a close-up of them. There is a word for this movie, and that word is ick.

Goya's Ghosts ★ ★ ★
R, 114 m., 2007

Javier Bardem (Brother Lorenzo), Natalie Portman (Ines/Alicia), Stellan Skarsgård (Francisco Goya), Randy Quaid (King Carlos IV), Jose Luis Gomez (Tomas Bilbatua). Directed by Milos Forman and produced by Saul Zaentz. Screenplay by Forman and Jean-Claude Carriere.

Milos Forman's *Goya's Ghosts* is an extraordinarily beautiful film that plays almost like an excuse to generate its images. Like the Goya prints being examined by the good fathers of the Inquisition in the opening scene, the images stand on their own, resisting the pull toward narrative, yet adding up to a portrait of grotesque people debased by their society. The priests lament Goya's negative portrait of Spain, which shows remarkable prescience on their part, since they're condemning in 1772 prints that were not created by the painter until 1799.

In fiction, fooling around with historical accuracy is allowed, and *Goya's Ghosts* indulges itself. Many of the characters did indeed exist, but I wonder if they really performed many of their actions in this film. The events concern not only the Spanish artist (Stellan Skarsgard) but Brother Lorenzo (Javier Bardem), one of the Inquisition's priests, and Ines Bilbatua (Natalie Portman), the beautiful young daughter of a local merchant.

Goya uses Ines as a model for the angels he paints for churches. He is also a court painter, engaged in a portrait of Queen Maria Luisa (Blanca Portillo) and a portrait commissioned by Lorenzo, who recognizes his genius. When Ines is spotted by Inquisition spies declining a dish of pork in a tavern, she is hauled in, accused of Judaism, and tortured until she confesses her "sin." Her father (Jose Luis Gomez) goes to Goya to ask him to intervene with Lorenzo, and all their lives are intertwined.

The Holy Office of the Inquisition referred to torture "as being put to the question." The theory was that God would give you strength to tell only the truth. Ines's father's theory is that people will confess to anything if they are tortured, an insight that has never gone out of style. The father persuasively argues this point with Lorenzo, in a scene that *Variety* unkindly compares to Monty Python. Fifteen years pass; Napoleon conquers Spain and abolishes the Inquisition; Lorenzo, having fled, signs on to the principles of the French Revolution and surfaces as a prosecutor for Napoleon. His job includes jailing the former Inquisitor General (Michael Lonsdale). Meanwhile, Ines is finally released from the dungeons, where she had a daughter, who . . .

Enough of this plot. It's filled with so much melodrama, coincidence, and people living their lives against the backdrop of history that Victor Hugo would feel overserved. There are so many dramatic incidents, indeed, that it's hard to figure out who the central figure is supposed to be. Lorenzo gets top billing, but they're all buffeted by the winds of fate. I didn't feel the strong identification with anyone that I had with Forman's *Amadeus,* but as

169

consolation I was able to watch enraptured at a visual portrait of a time and place.

Consider an early scene. Footmen for King Carlos IV (Randy Quaid, and very good, too) throw an animal corpse in a field to attract vultures. Then the king shoots them, like pigeons. He also bags some rabbits, but Maria Luisa thinks she'd prefer the vultures for dinner. Other set pieces show the extraordinary cruelty of the dungeons, the obscene magnificence of the royal residences, the bawdiness of the taverns, the boldness of the bordellos, and streets teeming with life in the midst of death.

The actors invest their characters with surprising depth, considering how the plot has to keep so many story lines afloat. Skarsgard makes Goya into a man with a wonderful smile, an affable manner, and the confidence of an artist who stands outside the rules. Bardem, without making too much a point of it, shows an ambitious man, not enthusiastically evil but capable of the occasional vileness, who can convince himself he is both an Inquisitor for the church and a prosecutor for the emperor (the same job, really).

Natalie Portman, in a triple role, plays a beautiful young girl, a haggard torture victim, and a vulnerable prostitute, all with fearless conviction. And Randy Quaid has a smaller role as the king but is an inspired if unexpected casting choice, as in a scene where he performs on a violin and almost bashfully confesses he composed the piece himself.

Much of the depth of the film comes from the sound design of Leslie Shatz; we hear precision in the ways vast church doors open and close, we hear far-off bells and echoing interiors, and the sound of shoulders being dislocated is understated but persuasive. And the cinematography of Javier Aquirresarobe is, well, painterly—look at the compositions, the colors, and especially the shading.

Now I must tell you that *Goya's Ghosts* got cruel reviews when it opened late last fall in Europe. I don't make a habit of reviewing reviews, but the advance word on this picture was impossible to avoid ("Creaks along like an anemic snail" —Derek Malcolm; "Close to a disaster" —*Telegraph;* "Dull as dishwater" —Neil Smith). Sometimes I wonder if critics aren't reviewing the film they would have preferred rather than the one the director preferred.

I doubt that Forman and the legendary screenwriter Jean-Claude Carriere lacked the ability to tell a conventional story. I think the clue to their purpose is right there in the opening scene of the Goya drawings. Look carefully, and you may find something in the film to remind you of most of them. *Goya's Ghosts* is like the sketchbook Goya might have made with a camera.

Grace Is Gone ★ ★ ★
PG-13, 85 m., 2007

John Cusack (Stanley Phillips), Shelan O'Keefe (Heidi Phillips), Grace Bednarczyk (Dawn Phillips), Alessandro Nivola (John Phillips). Directed by James C. Strouse and produced by John Cusack, Grace Loh, Galt Niederhoffer, Daniela Taplin Lundberg, and Celine Rattray. Screenplay by Strouse.

John Cusack can project such tenderness and kindness. He doesn't often play roles that give him the chance, but when he does (*Say Anything, High Fidelity, Being John Malkovich*), he knows how to do it. His character, Stanley Phillips, in *Grace Is Gone* is one of his most vulnerable and is the key to the movie's success.

He is a suburban dad with two young daughters and a wife in the military. He supports the war in Iraq and would be there himself if he didn't have bad eyes. One day two Army officers come to his door, and he won't invite them in, as if reluctant to admit the news they've come to tell him. His wife has been killed in the war.

The girls are Heidi (Shelan O'Keefe), twelve years old, and Dawn (Grace Bednarczyk), who is eight. He sits them down in the living room to break the news and finds that he simply cannot. Instead, in a crazy evasion he improvises on the spur of the moment, he announces they will get in the car and drive to Enchanted Gardens, a Florida theme park they like. Heidi, who is very smart, thinks this sounds fishy: He's pulling them out of school to go on an unannounced holiday? Dawn doesn't ask any questions.

The trip involves the usual cookie-cutter roadside chain eateries and the usual interstate highway sameness, although it is punctuated by a stop to visit his brother (Alessandro Nivola), a layabout who rouses himself at the sight of Stanley to start attacking the war. Stanley won't be baited. He shares his secret, begs it be kept a secret, and loads the girls back in the car.

Enchanted Gardens, as it turns out, is not quite enchanted enough to be the right setting for breaking the bad news, which Heidi has more or less intuited on her own. But there does come a time on the beach when the truth must be told, and he does it gently and with love. That's what the movie is really about, anyway: not the war, but Stanley's love for his daughters.

There have been many scenes where mothers told children about the deaths of their fathers, but none where the roles are reversed, as in *Grace Is Gone*. The movie comes as a quiet revelation. Every time a news program features the faces and names of U.S. troops killed in Iraq, I feel a little shock when they show a woman. It doesn't seem right. Getting killed in the war doesn't seem right for anyone, of course, but you know what I mean.

Grace Is Gone is not a great movie, simply functional, but Cusack gives a great performance. The film somehow doesn't live up to his work. It wasn't shot on video (and for that matter, good video these days can look great), but the screen looks dingy and some life seems to be faded from it.

The story drags its feet a little, too, considering we know where they're going and what must happen when they get there. And a possible political confrontation between the two brothers is so adroitly sidestepped that the movie, although probably antiwar, never really declares itself. All we have is a father who has lost his wife, and two girls who have lost their mother. The way Cusack handles that, it's enough.

Gran Torino ★ ★ ★ ½
R, 116 m., 2008

Clint Eastwood (Walt Kowalski), Bee Vang (Thao Lor), Ahney Her (Sue Lor), Christopher Carley (Father Janovich). Directed by Clint Eastwood and produced by Robert Lorenz and Bill Gerber. Screenplay by Nick Schenk.

I would like to grow up to be like Clint Eastwood. Eastwood the director, Eastwood the actor, Eastwood the invincible, Eastwood the old man. What other figure in the history of the cinema has been an actor for fifty-three years, a director for thirty-seven, won two Oscars for direction, two more for Best Picture, plus the Thalberg Award, and at seventy-eight can direct himself in his own film and look meaner than hell? None, that's how many.

Gran Torino stars Eastwood as an American icon once again—this time as a cantankerous, racist, beer-chugging retired Detroit autoworker who keeps his shotgun ready to lock and load. Dirty Harry on a pension, we're thinking, until we realize that only the autoworker retired; Dirty Harry is still on the job. Eastwood plays the character as a man bursting with energy, most of which he uses to hold himself in. Each word, each scowl, seems to have broken loose from a deep place.

Walt Kowalski calls the Asian family next door "gooks" and "chinks" and so many other names he must have made it a study. How does he think this sounds? When he gets to know Thao, the teenage Hmong who lives next door, he takes him down to his barber for a lesson in how Americans talk. He and the barber call each other a Polack and a Dago and so on, and Thao is supposed to get the spirit. I found this scene far from realistic and wondered what Walt was trying to teach Thao. Then it occurred to me Walt didn't know it wasn't realistic.

Walt is not so much a racist as a security guard, protecting his own security. He sits on his porch defending the theory that your right to walk through this world ends when your toe touches his lawn. Walt's wife has just died (I would have loved to meet *her*), and his sons have learned once again that the old bastard wants them to stay the hell out of his business. In his eyes they're overweight meddlers working at meaningless jobs, and his granddaughter is a self-centered greed machine.

Walt sits on his porch all day long, when he's not doing house repairs or working on his prized 1972 Gran Torino, a car he helped assemble on the Ford assembly line. He sees a lot. He sees a carload of Hmong gangstas trying to enlist the quiet, studious Thao into their thuggery. When they threaten Thao to make him try to steal the Gran Torino, Walt catches him red-handed and would just as soon shoot him as not. When Thao's sister, Sue (Ahney Her, likable and sensible), comes over to apologize for her family and offer Thao's services for odd jobs, Walt accepts only reluctantly. When Sue is threatened by some black bullies, Walt's eyes narrow, and he growls and gets involved because it is his nature.

What with one thing and another, his life becomes strangely linked with these people, although Sue has to explain that the Hmong are mountain people from Vietnam who were U.S. allies and found it advisable to leave their homeland. When she drags him over to join a family gathering, Walt casually calls them all "gooks" and Sue a "dragon lady," they seem like awfully good sports about it, although a lot of them may not speak English. Walt seems unaware that his role is to embrace their common humanity, although he likes it when they stuff him with great-tasting Hmong food and flatter him.

Among actors of Eastwood's generation, James Garner might have been able to play this role, but my guess is, he'd be too nice in it. Eastwood doesn't play nice. Walt makes no apologies for who he is, and that's why, when he begins to decide he likes his neighbors better than his own family, it means something. *Gran Torino* isn't a liberal parable. It's more like out of the frying pan and into the melting pot. Along the way, he fends off the sincere but very young parish priest (a persuasive Christopher Carley), who is only carrying out the deathbed wishes of the late Mrs. Kowalski. Walt is a nominal Catholic. Hardly even nominal.

Gran Torino is about two things, I believe. It's about the belated flowering of a man's better nature. And it's about Americans of different races growing more open to one another in the new century. This doesn't involve some kind of grand transformation. It involves starting to see the gooks next door as people you love. And it helps if you live in the kind of neighborhood where they *are* next door.

If the climax seems too generic and preprogrammed, too much happening fairly quickly, I like that better than if it just dribbled off into sweetness. So would Walt. ☞

The Great Buck Howard ★ ★ ★ ½
PG, 90 m., 2009

John Malkovich (Buck Howard), Colin Hanks (Troy Gable), Emily Blunt (Valerie Brennan), Steve Zahn (Kenny), Griffin Dunne (Jonathan Finerman), Ricky Jay (Gil Bellamy), Tom Hanks (Mr. Gable). Directed by Sean McGinly and produced by Tom Hanks and Gary Goetzman. Screenplay by McGinly.

Is there anyone better than John Malkovich at barely containing his temper? He gravitates toward characters who do not suffer fools lightly, and that would include the Great Buck Howard, who once was Johnny Carson's favorite guest. Buck was dropped from Johnny's guest list and now tours the provinces, taking his magic act from small stages to smaller ones, but he still has his dignity.

"I LOVE this town!" he shouts with outstretched arms in Akron, and Akron still loves him. He is famous for his "signature effect," in which his evening's fee is given to an audience member and he uses his psychic powers to find it. He has never failed, and no one has ever discovered how he does it.

Buck was named "the Great" by Carson and still maintains a facade of greatness, even in front of Troy (Colin Hanks, Tom's son), his newly hired road manager. Malkovich invests him with self-importance and yet slyly suggests it's not all an act; you believe at some level Buck really does love that town, and also when he says, as he always does, "I LOVE you people!"

The story is told from Troy's point of view. His father (Tom Hanks) fervently wants him to enter law school, but he wants to test showbiz, and this is his first contact with any degree of fame. He never penetrates the Great Buck Howard's facade (and neither do we), but he sure does learn a lot about showbiz, some of it intimately from Valerie (Emily Blunt), a new PR person hired for Buck's spectacular new illusion in Cincinnati. Troy learns to carry bags, open doors, deal with local reps, and supply mineral water, not distilled ("I'm not an iron," Buck crisply tells Troy's eventual replacement).

We see Buck as Troy does, as an impenetrable mystery. Buck is far from forgotten (he guests on shows hosted by Regis Philbin and Kelly Ripa, Jon Stewart, and Martha Stewart, all playing themselves). He can still fill a room, even if it's a smaller room. His manager, Gil (Ricky Jay, who always seems to know the inside odds), even gets him a Las Vegas booking.

What happens there, and how it happens, is perceptive about showbiz and even more perceptive about Buck and his "signature effect."

Well, how *does* he find the person in the room holding the money—every time? Rumors are common that he uses a hidden spotter, whispering into a mike hidden in his ear. When Troy tells him this, Buck invites two doctors on stage to peer into his ears, then turns his back to the room and covers his head with a black cloth. Does he still find the money?

If he does, it can't be because of psychic powers, can it? I firmly believe such illusions are never the result of psychic powers, but I am fascinated by them anyway. The wisdom of this film, directed and written by Sean McGinly, is to never say. Troy practically lives with the man and doesn't have a clue. He's asked if Buck is gay, and he replies truthfully, "I don't know. I've never seen him with anybody." Colin Hanks is affecting as a man young enough and naive enough to be fascinated by whatever it is Buck represents. Emily Blunt is sweetly kind to him. No one else could have played Buck better than Malkovich. I LOVE this guy.

I've read one review that complains we never meet the real Buck Howard. Of course we don't. There may *be* no real Buck Howard. But the film is funny and perceptive in the way it shows the humiliations for a man with Buck's tender vanity. The ladies singing on stage. The many who have no idea who he is. Being bumped off the news by Jerry Springer. Being bumped off Jay Leno for Tom Arnold. Distilled water.

Note: McGinly's screenplay is based on his observations as road manager for the Amazing Kreskin, to whom the film is dedicated.

The Great Debaters ★ ★ ★ ★
PG-13, 127 m., 2007

Denzel Washington (Melvin B. Tolson), Forest Whitaker (James Farmer Sr.), Nate Parker (Henry Lowe), Jurnee Smollett (Samantha Booke), Denzel Whitaker (James Farmer Jr.), Jermaine Williams (Hamilton Burgess), Gina Ravera (Ruth Tolson), John Heard (Sheriff Dozier), Kimberly Elise (Pearl Farmer). Directed by Denzel Washington and produced by Todd Black, Joe Roth, Kate Forte, Washington, and Oprah Winfrey. Screenplay by Robert Eisele.

The Great Debaters is about an underdog debate team that wins a national championship, and some critics have complained that it follows the formula of all sports movies by leading up, through great adversity, to a victory at the end. So it does. How many sports movies, or movies about underdogs competing in any way, have you seen that end in defeat? It is human nature to seek inspiration in victory, and this is a film that is affirming and inspiring and re-creates the stories of a remarkable team and its coach.

The team is from little Wiley College in Marshall, Texas, an African-American institution in the heart of the Jim Crow South of the 1930s. The school's English professor, Melvin Tolson (Denzel Washington), is a taskmaster who demands the highest standards from his debate team, and they're rewarded with a national championship. That's what the "sports movie" is about, but the movie is about so much more, and in ways that do not follow formulas.

There are, for example, Tolson's secret lives. Dressed in overalls and work boots, he ventures out incognito as an organizer for a national sharecropper's union. He's a dangerous radical, the local whites believe, probably a communist. But he's organizing both poor whites and blacks, whose servitude is equal. He keeps his politics out of the classroom, however, where he conceals a different kind of secret: He is one of America's leading poets. Yes, although the movie barely touches on it, Tolson published long poems in such magazines as the *Atlantic Monthly,* and in 1947 was actually named poet laureate of Liberia. Ironic, that his role as a debate coach would win him greater fame today.

He holds grueling auditions and selects four team members: Henry Lowe (Nate Parker), who drinks and fools around but is formidably intelligent; Hamilton Burgess (Jermaine Williams), a superb debater; James Farmer Jr. (Denzel Whitaker), a precocious fourteen-year-old who is their researcher; and Samantha Booke (Jurnee Smollett), the substitute and only female debater they've heard of. Tolson drills them, disciplines them, counsels them, and leads them to a string of victories that results in a triumph over Harvard, the national champion.

We get a good sense of the nurturing black community that has produced these students, in particular James Farmer Sr. (Forest Whitaker), a preacher (young Denzel Whitaker, as his son, is no relation, and not named after Washington, for that matter). James Jr. would go on to found the Congress of Racial Equality (CORE). Tolson drives his team on long road trips to out-of-town debates, and one night traveling late, they have the defining emotional experience of the film: They happen upon a scene where a white mob has just lynched a black man and set his body afire. They barely escape with their own lives. And daily life for them is fraught with racist peril; especially for Tolson, who has been singled out by the local sheriff as a rabble-rouser. These experiences inform their debates as much as formal research.

The movie is not really about how this team defeats the national champions. It is more about how its members, its coach, its school and community believe that an education is their best way out of the morass of racism and discrimination. They would find it unthinkable that decades in the future, serious black students would be criticized by jealous contemporaries for "acting white." They are black, proud, single-minded, and focused, and it all expresses itself most dramatically in their debating.

The debates themselves have one peculiarity: The Wiley team always somehow draws the "good" side of every question. Since a debate team is supposed to defend whatever position it draws, it might have been intriguing to see them defend something they disbelieve, even despise. Still, I suppose I understand why that isn't done here; it would have interrupted the flow. And the flow becomes a mighty flood, in a powerful and impassioned story. This is one of the year's best films.

Note: In actual fact, the real Wiley team did beat the national champions, but from USC, not Harvard. Screenwriter Robert Eisele explains, "In that era, there was much at stake when a black college debated any white school, particularly one with the stature of Harvard. We used Harvard to demonstrate the heights they achieved."

Great World of Sound ★ ★ ★
R, 106 m., 2007

Pat Healy (Martin), Kene Holliday (Clarence), Robert Longstreet (Layton), Rebecca Mader (Pam), John Baker (Shank), Tricia Paoluccio (Gloria). Directed by Craig Zobel and produced by David Gordon Green, Melissa Palmer, Richard A. Wright, and Zobel. Screenplay by George Smith and Zobel.

If you've ever wondered about how some of those would-be stars get on *American Idol,* here is a film about some who don't. *Great World of Sound* is a movie about an outfit that buys ads in the papers offering free auditions to new talent, and then tries to sell them a "professional recording session" that will produce a CD allegedly distributed to radio stations and record companies.

To some degree, this offer is real. To a very small degree. We actually even see one of the clients in the "professional" studio. But the real point is to get the hopefuls to show their "commitment" by "investing" $3,000 in their "futures." We follow two of the Great World salesmen on their odyssey through the cheap motels and fast-food grease pits of the South: Martin (Pat Healy), a neat, introverted worrywart, and Clarence (Kene Holliday), an ebullient African-American who, after spending three years on the streets of Houston, is happy to have this job or any job.

In a way, the movie resembles Albert and David Maysles's great documentary *Salesman* (1968), about door-to-door Bible salesmen. The salesmen in both films are led to expect much larger rewards than are possible. But *Great World* has another dimension: Although Martin and Clarence are fictional characters, many (but not all) of those who come to audition aren't in on the joke. They think it's a real audition: In that sense, they're as exploited in real life as in the story. (Director Craig Zobel says he got releases from everybody after the fact.)

Some of the performers make you wonder how they deluded themselves that they had talent. But one, a young African-American girl, sings her "New National Anthem," which is so good I think it should be recorded for real. Oddly enough, Martin likes it, too, and commits the con man's cardinal sin: investing in his own scam.

The movie resembles *Boiler Room* and *Glengarry Glen Ross* in how the recruiters of the salesmen tell expansive stories about how successful they have become. It's a little heartbreaking, however, how moderate the "riches" are that they promise their recruits. If they work hard and do good business, the salesmen are told, they can hope to clear $1,000 a month. Shank (John Baker), the head of the enterprise, adds a bit of stagecraft at one point, dialing his bank on a speaker phone and hearing his current balance read aloud. It was, as I recall, something like $13,000. Not millions.

The drama in the film arises as Martin has a crisis of conscience, while Clarence has a crisis of fear that he might be back on the streets soon. Watching them work the marks is fascinating, when one is dubious and the other desperate. *Great World of Sound,* a Sundance hit, is Zobel's first film, a confident, surehanded exercise focusing on the American Dream turned nightmare.

Grindhouse ★ ★ ½

A double feature of:

Planet Terror ★ ★

Death Proof ★ ★ ★

R, 191 m., 2007

Rose McGowan (Cherry Darling/Pam), Kurt Russell (Stuntman Mike), Freddy Rodriguez (Wray), Rosario Dawson (Abernathy), Josh Brolin (Dr. William Block), Vanessa Ferlito (Arlene), Marley Shelton (Dakota Black), Jordan Ladd (Shanna), Jeff Fahey (JT), Sydney Tamiia Poitier (Jungle Julia), Michael Biehn (Sheriff Hague). Directed by Robert Rodriguez, Eli Roth, Quentin Tarantino, Edgar Wright, and Rob Zombie and produced by Elizabeth Avellan, Rodriguez, Eli Roth, Gabriel Roth, Erica Steinberg, and Tarantino. Screenplay by Rodriguez and Tarantino.

Quentin Tarantino's *Death Proof* and Robert Rodriguez's *Planet Terror* play as if *Night of the Living Dead* and *Faster, Pussycat! Kill! Kill!* were combined on a double bill under the parentage of the dark sperm of vengeance.

Together the two separate feature-length stories combine into *Grindhouse,* a deliberate attempt by the two directors to re-create the experience of a double feature in a sleazy B-house. Scratches and blemishes mar the prints, frames or even whole reels are purportedly missing, and the characters have the shallow simplicity of action figures entirely at the disposal of special effects. They are separated by a group of four trailers for still more B-minus pictures.

This evocation of a grindhouse may have existed somewhere, sometime, but my moviegoing reaches back to before either director was born, and I have never witnessed a double bill and supporting program much like the one they have created. No, not even in half-forgotten Chicago theaters like the McVickers, Roosevelt, Shangri-La, Monroe, Loop, or Parkway. Not even while trying specifically to find "Dog of the Week" candidates for Spot the Wonder Dog to bark at. And it must be said that when it comes to fabricating bad movies, Rodriguez and Tarantino have a failure of will. To paraphrase Manny Farber, you can catch them trying to shove art up into the crevices of dreck.

I can imagine the pitch meeting at which the two directors told Harvey and Bob Weinstein why they had to make this double-header. In that room were the most skilled conversational motormouths I've met, and I mean that as a compliment. If Tarantino tells you about the last time he ate an Italian beef sandwich, you want to film it in 70 mm. But let's face it. The fundamental reason young males went to schlock double features in the golden age was in the hope of seeing breasts or, lacking that, stuff blowed up real good. Now that the mainstream is showing lots of breasts and real big explosions, there is no longer a market for bad movies showing the same thing.

I recall a luncheon at Cannes thrown by the beloved schlockmeister Sam Arkoff of American International Pictures. "Sam!" said Rex Reed, after seeing Arkoff's new film *Q,* about a Quetzalcoatl that swooped down on Wall Street to gobble up stockbrokers. "What a surprise! Right in the middle of all that schlock, a great Method performance by Michael Moriarty!" Arkoff blushed modestly. "The schlock was my idea," he said.

So, OK, *Grindhouse* is an attempt to re-create

a double feature that never existed for an audience that no longer exists. What's the good news? Tarantino's *Death Proof*, which I liked better, splits into two halves involving quartets of women, most of them lesbians, who are targeted by Stuntman Mike (Kurt Russell), who uses his "death-proof" car as a murder weapon. The movie ends with a skillful scene involving a deadly highway game and a duel between two cars. That and another highway massacre are punctuated by long—too long—passages of barroom dialogue. The movie has two speeds—pause and overdrive.

Rodriguez's *Planet Terror* recycles the durable *Living Dead* formula: A band of the healthy fight off shuffling bands of zombies. I have written before about my weariness with zombies, who as characters are sadly limited. What distinguishes Rodriguez's picture is the extraordinary skill of the makeup, showing us oozing wounds, exploding organs, and biological horrors. The movie wants to be as repulsive and nauseating as possible. The plot, involving go-go dancers and an action-packed doctor, is a clothesline for gore, explosions, bodily mayhem, and juicy innards on parade.

Both directors are eager to work in as many references as possible, verbal and visual, to their favorite movies; Russ Meyer seems quoted a lot. The backgrounds are papered with more vintage movie posters than you'd expect to find in a Texas saloon, except maybe in Austin. There are also various cultural references. For example, deejay Jungle Julia's listeners recite lines from "Stopping by the Woods on a Snowy Evening," but you would be wrong to think that is a reference to a poem by Robert Frost. No, according to IMDb.com, it refers to Don Siegel's thriller *Telefon* (1977), where the words were "used as a posthypnotic signal to activate Russian sleeper agents."

Grindhouse is both impressive and disappointing. From a technical and craft point of view it is first-rate; from its standing in the canons of the two directors, it is minor. And I wonder what the point is when two of Tarantino's women are obsessed with *Vanishing Point* (1971), a movie Tarantino obviously treasures. It explains the appearance in the movie of a 1970 Dodge Challenger, but is an explanation really necessary? Hell, I had a '57 Studebaker Golden Hawk, and it spoke for itself. We feel like the dialogue is movie-buff jargon overheard in a Park City saloon.

My own field of expertise in this genre is the cinema of Russ Meyer, and I was happy to see QT's closing homage to the tough girls and the beaten stud in *Faster, Pussycat! Kill! Kill!* (1965), which John Waters has named as the greatest film of all time. One heroine even copies Tura Satana's leather gloves, boots, and ponytail. I may have spotted, indeed, the most obscure quotation from Meyer. In an opening montage of his *Beyond the Valley of the Dolls* (1970), there is a brief, inexplicable shot of a boot crushing an egg. Rodriguez uses the same composition to show a boot crushing a testicle. So the cinema marches on.

After failing in theaters as a double bill, *Grindhouse* was split by the Weinsteins into two shorter films. The Tarantino, then lengthened by the director, played at Cannes, where Harvey Weinstein admitted at a press conference that, for daring to release the combined films at a running time over three hours, he received a "public spanking." Now that might have made a movie.

The Grocer's Son ★ ★ ★

NO MPAA RATING, 96 m., 2008

Nicolas Cazale (Antoine Sforza), Clotilde Hesme (Claire), Daniel Duval (Monsieur Sforza), Jeanne Goupil (Madame Sforza), Liliane Rovere (Lucienne), Paul Crauchet (Pere Clement), Stephan Guerin-Tillie (Francois Sforza). Directed by Eric Guirado and produced by Milena Poylo and Gilles Sacuto. Screenplay by Guirado and Florence Vignon.

The term "coming of age" always seems to apply to teenagers. But you can come of age in your twenties, thirties, or forties, or maybe never. I define it as beginning to value other people for who they are, rather than what they can do for you.

Antoine (Nicolas Cazale) is thirty-ish, lives in a cluttered room in Paris, and left home ten years ago promising never to return to the village where his parents ran the only grocery store. His father has a heart attack, and that forces him to go to the hospital for a reunion with his brother and mother, whom he has avoided. She comes home to his room to spend the night, and what with one thing and another he reluctantly returns to the village to help her with the business.

That means taking over his father's daily route with a van packed with groceries, produce, and provisions. He already knows the route—probably learned it going along as a kid. It takes him through the painterly landscape of Provence, stopping at particular homes or crossroads where old people depend on the service. A popular item seems to be tinned peas. Antoine is not the model of friendliness. He curtly advises one old-timer to pay his tab and rejects his father's long-standing arrangement to barter with another for eggs.

Madame Sforza, his mother (Jeanne Goupil), is a sunny woman with a lovely smile and wisely doesn't push him too hard. His brother, Francois (Stephan Guerin-Tillie), visits, and they fight, as usual. And there is another visitor. This is Claire (Clotilde Hesme), who lives across the hall from him in Paris. "And this would be my room?" she asks Madame Sforza. "You're not sleeping with Antoine?" she asks. "We don't sleep together," Claire explains. "That's good," the mother says. "Rare, but good."

It is clear that his mother is curious about the exact relationship between Antoine and Claire, who is taking a correspondence course to be admitted to a Spanish university. The two young people obviously like each other and would be a good match, but Antoine is too self-centered and selfish to open himself to her. Nor is he any good with customers, he is informed by his Paris friend Hassan, who also runs a grocery. Antoine seems to find it difficult to release the words "Thank you."

You can probably guess the trajectory of the story. But it's not really the destination that makes this a charmer; it's the journey there, mostly by grocery van. The side of the truck opens and is propped up to display the goods inside. When the side falls down and flattens old Lucienne (Liliane Rovere), who is none too pleased with Antoine's prices anyway, she walks out to the van at the next visit wearing a bowl on her head.

The film was directed and co-written by Eric Guirado, who reportedly followed and observed country grocers on their routes. He works gently. The summer unfolds slowly. Claire goes back to Paris. The father arrives from Paris. The countryside is calm and seductive. The mother soldiers on, keeping the store open late "to help people." And Antoine comes of age. That's all the film is, apart from having humor, warmth, kindness, insight, and scenery. That's enough.

H

Hairspray ★ ★ ★ ½
PG, 115 m., 2007

Nikki Blonsky (Tracy Turnblad), John Travolta (Edna Turnblad), Queen Latifah (Motormouth Maybelle), Michelle Pfeiffer (Velma Von Tussle), Christopher Walken (Wilbur Turnblad), Zac Efron (Link Larkin), Brittany Snow (Amber Von Tussle), Amanda Bynes (Penny Pingleton), James Marsden (Corny Collins), Elijah Kelley (Seaweed), Allison Janney (Prudy Pingleton). Directed by Adam Shankman and produced by Craig Zadan and Neil Meron. Screenplay by Leslie Dixon, based on the 1988 screenplay by John Waters and the 2002 musical stage play by Mark O'Donnell and Thomas Meehan.

Hairspray is just plain fun. Or maybe not so plain. There's a lot of craft and slyness lurking beneath the circa-1960 goofiness. The movie seems guileless and rambunctious, but it looks just right (like a Pat Boone musical) and sounds just right (like a golden oldies disc) and feels just right (like the first time you sang "We Shall Overcome" and until then it hadn't occurred to you that we should).

It bounces out of bed with Tracy Turnblad (Nikki Blonsky), a roly-poly bundle of joy, whose unwavering cheerfulness shines on the whole picture. "Good morning, Baltimore!" she sings, as she dances through a neighborhood where everyone seems to know and love her, even the garbagemen who let her ride on the roof of their back loader. She's like a freelance cheerleader.

At school she links up with best friend Penny Pingleton (Amanda Bynes), whose name is undoubtedly a tribute to Penny Singleton, who played Dagwood's Blondie. They live for the moment when the minute hand crawls with agonizing slowness to the end of the school day, and they can race home and dance along with *The Corny Collins Show*, the local teenage TV danceathon. In those days every local market had a show like that. Maybe Dick Clark plowed them under. I miss their freshness and naïveté.

Corny (James Marsden) is well named, as he presides over a posse of popular kids known as his Council. Tracy longs to be on the Council. The star of the show and head of the Council is Amber Von Tussle (Brittany Snow), whose mother, Velma (Michelle Pfeiffer), manages the station and enforces an all-white policy for the show, except for the monthly Negro Day organized by Maybelle (Queen Latifah), owner of a record shop.

All of this is recycled from the original 1988 John Waters film, which made Ricki Lake a star, and from the Broadway musical made from it, but it's still fresh the third time around. It's a little more innocent than Waters would have made it, but he does his part by turning up in a cameo role as a flasher (look quick and you see Ricki Lake and Pia Zadora, too). The plot involves Tracy's instinctive decency as she campaigns to integrate the program, endangering her campaign to get on the Council.

Tradition requires her mother, Edna, to be played by a man in drag: Divine in the film, Harvey Fierstein in the musical, and this time, John Travolta, who may be wearing a fat suit but still moves like the star of *Saturday Night Fever*. Tracy's father, Wilbur, is played by Christopher Walken, who has a hairpiece surely borrowed from his store, which is named "Hardy Har Har" and sells jokes and novelties. Oh, how I miss the Whoopee Cushion.

The plot wheels right along while repairing one outpost of Baltimore racism, and what's remarkable is that some fairly serious issues get discussed in song and dance. Tracy is sent to detention one day and learns a whole new style of dancing from the black students there and takes it to TV, reminding me of the days when TV preachers thought Elvis was the spawn of Satan. Now they look like him. Call in today for your "free" healing water.

The point, however, is not the plot but the energy. Without somebody like Nikki Blonsky at the heart of the picture, it might fall flat, but everybody works at her level of happiness, including her teen contemporaries Zac Efron, Taylor Parks, and Elijah Kelley (the last two Maybelle's children), and the usual curio-shop window full of peculiar adults (Jerry Stiller, Paul Dooley). You know the story, you've seen the movie and heard all about the musical, and you think you know what to expect. But the movie seems to be happening right now, or right then, and its only flaw as a period picture is that there aren't enough Studebakers in it.

Hamlet 2 ★ ★ ★
R, 92 m., 2008

Steve Coogan (Dana Marschz), Joseph Julian Soria (Octavio), Elisabeth Shue (Elisabeth Shue), Skylar Astin (Rand), Phoebe Strole (Epiphany), Marshall Bell (Mr. Rocker), Catherine Keener (Dana's Wife), David Arquette (Gary the Boarder), Amy Poehler (Cricket Feldstein), Shea Pepe (The Critic). Directed by Andrew Fleming and produced by Eric D. Eisner, Leonid Rozhetskin, and Aaron Ryder. Screenplay by Fleming and Pam Brady.

The problem with a sequel to *Hamlet* is that everybody interesting is dead by the end. That doesn't discourage Dana Marschz, a Tucson high school drama teacher, from trying to save the school's theater program with a sequel named *Hamlet 2*. The shop class builds him a time machine, and he brings back the dead characters, plus Jesus, Einstein, and the very much alive Hillary Clinton. Music is by the Tucson Gay Men's Chorus.

Hamlet 2 stars the British comedian Steve Coogan, who with this film and *Tropic Thunder* may develop a fan base in America. He's sort of a gangling, flighty, manic Woody Allen type, but without the awareness of his neurosis. Oh, he knows he has problems. He's a recovering alcoholic, so broke he and his wife have to take in a boarder, and when his drama class is thrown out of the school lunchroom they have to meet in the gym during volleyball practice.

Anyone who has ever been involved in high school theatrical productions will recognize a few elements from *Hamlet 2*, here much exaggerated. There are the teacher's pets who usually play all the leads. The rebellious new student who's sort of an ethnic Brando. The pitiful costumes. The disapproving school board, which wants to discontinue the program. The community uproar over the shocking content (gay men singing "Rock Me, Sexy Jesus"?). The ACLU lawyer, named Cricket

(Amy Poehler), who flies to the rescue but seems to have a tendency toward anti-Semitism. And above all the inspired, passionate, more than slightly mad drama teacher.

Mr. Marschz (to pronounce it, you have to sort of buzz at the end) has seen too many movies like *Dead Poets Society* and *Mr. Holland's Opus*, and tries to inspire his students with his bizarre behavior. This takes little effort, especially after he starts wearing caftans to school because his wife (Catherine Keener) thinks he's impotent because jockey shorts cut off his circulation. Principal Rocker (Marshall Bell) is his unremitting enemy, and Octavio (Joseph Julian Soria) is the brilliant but rebellious student (he comes across as street tough but is headed for Brown). Rand (Skylar Astin) and Epiphany (Phoebe Strole) are his special pets, now feeling left out.

And then there is Elisabeth Shue. Yes, the real Elisabeth Shue, Oscar nominee for *Leaving Las Vegas*. When Dana goes to the hospital for treatment of his broken f-you finger, he tells the nurse she looks like his favorite actress, Elisabeth Shue. "That's because I am Elisabeth Shue," she says, explaining that she got tired of all the BS in showbiz and decided to help people by becoming a nurse. She agrees to visit his class. You can imagine the questions she gets.

Chaotic rehearsals and legal maneuvers by Cricket succeed in getting the play staged—not in the school, but in an abandoned railroad shed. Some of the characters may have the same names as characters in *Hamlet,* but that's about as far as the resemblance goes. No danger of plagiarism charges. The Gay Men's Chorus is very good, Dana himself not so good in the role of Jesus, moon-walking on the water.

Much depends on the verdict of my favorite character in the movie, the critic of the high school paper (Shea Pepe), a freshman who is about five feet tall. Having eviscerated Dana's previous production, he helpfully gives him advice (he should stop remaking movies like *Erin Brockovich* and do something original). *Hamlet 2* is original, all right. But will the kid like it?

The movie is an ideal showcase for the talents of Coogan, whom you may remember from *A Cock and Bull Story* (2005), the film

179

about a film of *Tristram Shandy,* where only one person involved in the production had ever read the book. He is a TV legend in the UK, but not so uber-Brit that he doesn't travel well. He seems somewhat at home in Tucson, which, let it be said, has got to be a nicer town than anybody in this movie thinks it is.

Hancock ★ ★ ★
PG-13, 92 m., 2008

Will Smith (John Hancock), Charlize Theron (Mary Embrey), Jason Bateman (Ray Embrey), Eddie Marsan (Red), Jae Head (Aaron Embrey), David Mattey (Man Mountain). Directed by Peter Berg and produced by Akiva Goldsman, Michael Mann, Will Smith, and James Lassiter. Screenplay by Vy Vincent Ngo and Vince Gilligan.

I have been waiting for this for years: a superhero movie where the actions of the superheroes have consequences in the real world. They always leave a wake of crashed cars, bursting fire hydrants, exploding gas stations, and toppling bridges behind them, and never go back to clean up. But John Hancock, the hero of *Hancock,* doesn't get away with anything. One recent heroic stunt ran up a price tag of seven million dollars, he's got hundreds of lawsuits pending, and when he saves a stranded whale by throwing it back into the sea, you can bet he gets billed for the yacht it lands on.

Hancock, the latest star showcase for Will Smith, has him playing a Skid Row drunk with superpowers and a super hangover. He does well, but there are always consequences, like when he saves a man whose car is about to be struck by a train, but causes a train wreck. What he needs is a good PR man. Luckily, the man whose life he saved is exactly that. He's Ray Embrey (Jason Bateman, the adopting father in *Juno*), and Ray has a brainstorm: He'll repay Hancock by giving him a complete image makeover. If this sounds like a slapstick comedy, strangely enough it isn't. The movie has a lot of laughs, but Smith avoids playing Hancock as a goofball and shapes him as serious, thoughtful, and depressed.

Embrey the PR whiz brings Hancock home to dinner to meet his wife, Mary (Charlize

Theron), and son, Aaron (Jae Head). The first time she meets him, Mary gives Hancock an odd, penetrating look. Also the second time, and also the third time. OK, OK, already: We get it. One odd, penetrating look after another. They have some kind of a history, but Hancock doesn't know about it, and Mary's not talking.

She has a lot to keep quiet about, although thank goodness she eventually opens up, or the movie wouldn't have a second half. I will not reveal what she says, of course, because her surprise is part of the fun. I am willing to divulge some of the setup, with Ray coaching Hancock to start saying "thank you" and "you did a good job here," and stop flying down out of the sky and crushing $100,000 cars. Ray also gets him a makeover: Gone is the flophouse wardrobe, replaced by a slick gold and leather costume, and Hancock gets a shave, too. Does it himself, with his fingernails.

He appeared some eighty years ago in Miami, as far as he knows. He doesn't know very far. He has no idea where his powers came from, or why he never grows any older. He can fly at supersonic speeds, stop a speeding locomotive, toss cars around, and in general do everything Superman could do, but not cleanly, neatly, or politely. Part of his reform involves turning himself in to the law and serving a prison term, although the chief of police has to summon him from prison to help with a bank hostage crisis. (In prison, there's a guy named Man Mountain who must not read the papers, or he would never, ever try to make Hancock his victim.)

It's not long after the bank hostage business that Mary reveals her secret, Hancock starts asking deep questions about himself, and the movie takes an odd, penetrating turn. This is the part I won't get into, except to say that the origin stories of superheroes consistently underwhelm me, and Hancock's is one of the most arbitrary. Even Mary, who knows all about him, doesn't know all that much, and I have a shiny new dime here for any viewer of the movie who can explain exactly how Hancock came into being.

Not that it matters much anyway. I guess he had to come into being *somehow*, and this movie's explanation is as likely as most, which is to say, completely preposterous. Still, *Hancock* is a lot of fun, if perhaps a little top-heavy with stuff being destroyed. Will Smith makes the character more subtle than he has to be, more filled with self-doubt, more willing to learn. Jason Bateman is persuasive and helpful on the PR front, and it turns out Charlize Theron has a great deal to feel odd and penetrating about.

The Hangover ★ ★ ★ ½
R, 100 m., 2009

Bradley Cooper (Phil), Ed Helms (Stu), Zach Galifianakis (Alan), Heather Graham (Jade), Justin Bartha (Doug), Jeffrey Tambor (Sid). Directed by Todd Phillips and produced by Phillips and Dan Goldberg. Screenplay by Jon Lucas and Scott Moore.

Now this is what I'm talkin' about. *The Hangover* is a funny movie, flat out, all the way through. Its setup is funny. Every situation is funny. Most of the dialogue is funny almost line by line. At some point we actually find ourselves caring a little about what happened to the missing bridegroom—and the fact that we almost care is funny, too.

The movie opens with bad news for a bride on her wedding day. Her fiancé's best buddy is standing in the Mohave Desert with a bloody lip and three other guys, none of whom is her fiancé. They've lost him. He advises her there's no way the wedding is taking place.

We flash back two days to their road trip to Vegas for a bachelor party. Her future husband, Doug (Justin Bartha), will be joined by his two friends, the schoolteacher Phil (Bradley Cooper) and the dentist Stu (Ed Helms). Joining them will be her brother, Alan (Zach Galifianakis), an overweight slob with a Haystacks Calhoun beard and an injunction against coming within two hundred feet of a school building.

The next morning, Doug will be missing. The other three are missing several hours: None of them can remember a thing since they were on the roof of Caesars Palace, drinking shots of Jagermeister. They would desperately like to know: How in the hell do you wake up in a $4,200-a-night suite with a tiger, a chicken, a crying baby, a missing tooth, and a belly button pierced for a diamond dangle? And when you give your parking check to the doorman, why does he bring around a police car? And where is Doug?

Their search provides a structure for the rest of the movie, during a very long day that includes a fact-finding visit to a wedding chapel, a violent encounter with a small but very mean Chinese mobster, a sweet hooker, an interview with an emergency room doctor, and an encounter with Mike Tyson, whose tiger they appear to have stolen, although under the circumstances he is fairly nice about it. There is never an explanation for the chicken.

Despite these events, *The Hangover* isn't simply a laff riot. I won't go so far as to describe it as a character study, but all three men have profound personality problems, and the Vegas trip works on them like applied emergency therapy. The dentist is rigidly ruled by his bitchy girlfriend. The schoolteacher thinks nothing of stealing the money for a class trip. And Alan . . .

Well, Zach Galifianakis's performance is the kind of breakout performance that made John Belushi a star after *Animal House*. He is short, stocky, wants to be liked, has a yearning energy, was born clueless. It is a tribute to Galifianakis's acting that we actually believe he is sincere when he asks the clerk at the check-in counter: "Is this the real Caesar's palace? Does Caesar live here?"

The film is directed by Todd Phillips, whose *Old School* and *Road Trip* had their moments but didn't prepare me for this. The screenplay is by Jon Lucas and Scott Moore, whose *Ghosts of Girlfriends Past* certainly didn't. This movie is *written*, not assembled out of off-the-shelf parts from the Apatow Surplus Store. There is a level of detail and observation in the dialogue that's sort of remarkable: These characters aren't generically funny, but specifically funny. The actors make them halfway convincing.

Phillips has them encountering a mixed bag of weird characters, which is standard, but the characters aren't. Mr. Chow (Ken Jeong), the vertically challenged naked man they find locked in the trunk of the police car, is strong, skilled in martial arts, and really mean about Alan being fat. He finds almost anything a fat man does to be hilarious. When he finds his clothes and his henchmen, he is not to be trifled with. Jade (Heather Graham), a stripper, is forthright: "Well, actually I'm an escort, but stripping is a good way to meet clients." She isn't the good-hearted cliché, but more of a sincere young woman who would like to meet the right guy.

The search for Doug has them piecing together clues from the ER doctor, Mike Tyson's security tapes, and a mattress that is impaled on the uplifted arm of one of the Caesars Palace statues. The plot hurtles through them. If the movie ends somewhat conventionally, well, it almost has to: Narrative housecleaning requires it. It began conventionally, too, with uplifting music and a typeface for the titles that may remind you of *My Best Friend's Wedding*. But it is not to be. Here is a movie that deserves every letter of its R rating. What happens in Vegas stays in Vegas, especially after you throw up.   ☞

The Happening ★ ★ ★
R, 91 m., 2008

Mark Wahlberg (Elliot Moore), Zooey Deschanel (Alma Moore), John Leguizamo (Julian), Betty Buckley (Mrs. Jones), Ashlyn Sanchez (Jess), Spencer Breslin (Josh). Directed by M. Night Shyamalan and produced by Shyamalan, Sam Mercer, and Barry Mendel. Screenplay by Shyamalan.

If the bee disappears from the surface of the Earth, man would have no more than four years to live.

—Albert Einstein

An alarming prospect, and all the more so because there has been a recent decline in the honeybee population. Perhaps it is comforting to know that Einstein never said any such thing—less comforting, of course, for the bees. The quotation appears on a blackboard near the beginning of M. Night Shyamalan's *The Happening,* a movie that I found oddly touching. It is no doubt too thoughtful for the summer action season, but I appreciate the quietly realistic way Shyamalan finds to tell a story about the possible death of man.

One day in Central Park people start to lose their trains of thought. They begin walking backward. They start killing themselves. This

behavior spreads through Manhattan, and then all of the northeastern states. Construction workers throw themselves from scaffolds. Policemen shoot themselves. The deaths are blamed on a "terrorist attack," but in fact no one has the slightest clue, and New York City is evacuated.

We meet Elliot Moore (Mark Wahlberg), a Philadelphia high school science teacher; the quote was on his blackboard. We meet his wife, Alma (Zooey Deschanel), his friend Julian (John Leguizamo), and Julian's daughter, Jess (Ashlyn Sanchez). They find themselves fleeing on a train to Harrisburg, Pennsylvania, although people learn from their cell phones that the plague, or whatever it is, may have jumped ahead of them.

Now consider how Shyamalan shows the exodus from Philadelphia. He avoids all the conventional scenes of riots in the train station, people killing one another for seats on the train, etc., and shows the population as quiet and apprehensive. If you don't know what you're fleeing, and it may be waiting for you ahead, how would you behave? Like this, I suspect.

Julian entrusts his daughter with Elliot and Alma, and goes in search of his wife. The train stops permanently at a small town. The three hitch a ride in a stranger's car and later meet others who are fleeing, from what or to what, they do not know. Elliot meets a man who talks about a way plants have of creating hormones to kill their enemies, and he develops a half-baked theory that man may have finally delivered too many insults to the grasses and the shrubs, the flowers and the trees, and their revenge is in the wind.

By now the three are trekking cross-country through Pennsylvania, joined by two young boys, whom they will eventually lose. They walk on, the wind moaning ominously behind them, and come to the isolated country home of Mrs. Jones (Betty Buckley), a very odd old lady. Here they eat and spend the night, and other events take place, and Elliot and Alma find an opportunity to discuss their love and reveal some secrets and speculate about what dread manifestation has overtaken the world.

Too uneventful for you? Not enough action? For me, Shyamalan's approach was more effective than smash-and-grab plot-mongering. His use of the landscape is disturbingly effective. The performances by Wahlberg and Deschanel bring a quiet dignity to their characters. The *strangeness* of starting a day in New York and ending it hiking across a country field is underlined. Most of the other people we meet, not all, are muted and introspective. Had they been half-expecting some such "event" as this, whatever its description?

I know I have. For some time the thought has been gathering at the back of my mind that we are in the final act. We have finally insulted the planet so much that it can no longer sustain us. It is exhausted. It never occurred to me that vegetation might exterminate us. In fact, the form of the planet's revenge remains undefined in my thoughts, although I have read of global deserts and starvation, rising sea levels and the ends of species.

What I admired about *The Happening* is that the pace and substance of its storytelling allowed me to examine such thoughts, and to ask how I might respond to a wake-up call from nature. Shyamalan allows his characters space and time as they look within themselves. Those they meet on the way are such as they might indeed plausibly meet. Even the television and radio news is done correctly, as convenient clichés about terrorism give way to bewilderment and apprehension.

I suspect I'll be in the minority in praising this film. It will be described as empty, uneventful, meandering. But for some it will weave a spell. It is a parable, yes, but it is also simply the story of these people and how their lives and existence have suddenly become problematic. We depend on such a superstructure to maintain us that one or two alterations could leave us stranded and wandering through a field, if we are that lucky.   ☞

Happy-Go-Lucky ★ ★ ★ ★
R, 118 m., 2008

Sally Hawkins (Poppy), Eddie Marsan (Scott), Alexis Zegerman (Zoe), Samuel Roukin (Tim). Directed by Mike Leigh and produced by Simon Channing Williams. Screenplay by Leigh.

Mike Leigh's *Happy-Go-Lucky* is the story of a good woman. As simple as that. We first see

Poppy pedaling her bike through London and smiling all the time to herself. She stops at a bookshop and tries to cheer up the dour proprietor. No, that isn't right. She doesn't want to change him, just infect him with her irrepressible good nature. She may not even be aware of how she operates. Then her bike is stolen. She takes that right in stride.

Poppy (Sally Hawkins) is one of the most difficult roles any actress could be assigned. She must smile and be peppy and optimistic at (almost) all times, and do it naturally and convincingly, as if the sunshine comes from inside. That's harder than playing Lady Macbeth. Sally Hawkins has been in movies before, including Leigh's *Vera Drake* and Woody Allen's *Cassandra's Dream*, but this is her star-making role. She was named best actress at Berlin 2008. I will deliberately employ a cliché: She is a joy to behold.

At first, that seems to be all there is to it. The movie will be about Poppy and her job as an elementary school teacher, and the lessons she is taking in flamenco dancing, and her flatmate Zoe, and her sister Suzy, and how she starts to feel about Tim, the school counselor who comes to assist her with a troubled little boy. That would almost be enough. But *Happy-Go-Lucky* is about a great deal more and goes very much deeper.

As she works with the little boy, we see that she's not at all superficial but can listen, observe, empathize, and find the right note in response. In another scene, which may not seem to fit but is profoundly effective, she comes across a homeless man in the shadows under a rail line, and talks with him. He's one of those people who chants the same thing, ferociously, over and over. She listens to him, speaks with him, asks if he's hungry. She is not afraid. She's worried about him. I think he's aware of that, and it soothes him. It is possible nobody has spoken to him in days or weeks.

So we get these glimpses into Poppy's deeper regions. Then she decides to take driving lessons and meets Scott, the instructor. He is played brilliantly by Eddie Marsan, an English comedian who as an actor often finds morose, worrywart roles. Consider him as the pessimistic Jewish father in *Sixty Six*. Scott is an angry man. Oddly for a driving instructor, he seems to channel road rage. His system for

183

helping her remember the rearview mirror and the two side mirrors involves naming them after fallen angels. He screams at her. No one could drive with Scott at their side.

Any other person would quit working with Scott after one lesson. Not Poppy. Does she think she can help him? Their relationship descends into an extraordinary scene during which we suddenly see right inside both of them and understand better what Poppy's cheerfulness is all about. We also see Scott's terrifying insecurity and self-loathing; Marsan is spellbinding.

This is Mike Leigh's funniest film since *Life Is Sweet* (1991). Of course, he hasn't ever made a *completely* funny film, and *Happy-Go-Lucky* has scenes that are not funny, not at all. There are always undercurrents and oddness. His films feel as if they're spontaneously unfolding; he has a vision of his characters that is only gradually revealed. He almost always finds remarkable performances, partly because he casts actors, not stars, and partly because he and the actors rehearse for weeks, tilting the dialogue this way and that, contriving back stories, finding out where the characters came from before the movie began, predicting where they will go after it's over.

I had seen Sally Hawkins in movies before. She was the rich girl who went to the private clinic in *Vera Drake*. No role could be more different than Poppy. Leigh, who spent years working for the stage, was able to imagine her as Poppy, a role very few women could play. Maybe Meryl Streep could sustain that level of merriness, but then, what can't she do? And now I must ask, what can't Hawkins do? There are countless ways she might have stepped wrong. But she breezes in on her bicycle and engages our deepest sympathy. Poppy has a gift, as I said, for not running but standing there, reading the situation, understanding other people, and acting helpfully. And by that I do not mean she cheers them up.

Harry Potter and the Order of the Phoenix ★ ★ ½
PG-13, 138 m., 2007

Daniel Radcliffe (Harry Potter), Rupert Grint (Ron Weasley), Emma Watson (Hermione Granger), Helena Bonham Carter (Bellatrix Lestrange), Michael Gambon (Albus Dumbledore), Brendan Gleeson (Mad-Eye Moody), Gary Oldman (Sirius Black), Alan Rickman (Severus Snape), Maggie Smith (Minerva McGonagall), Imelda Staunton (Dolores Umbridge). Directed by David Yates and produced by David Barron and David Heyman. Screenplay by Michael Goldenberg, based on the novel by J. K. Rowling.

Whatever happened to the delight and, if you'll excuse the term, magic in the Harry Potter series? As the characters grow up, the stories grow, too, leaving the innocence behind and confusing us with plots so labyrinthine that it takes a Ph.D. from Hogwarts to figure them out. *Harry Potter and the Order of the Phoenix* still has much of the enchantment of the earlier films, but Harry no longer has as much joy. His face is lacking the gosh-wow-this-is-really-neat grin. He has internalized the secrets and delights of the world of wizards and is now instinctively using them to save his life.

An early scene illustrates this change. Harry and his cousin Dudley are attacked by dementors and in desperation he uses a secret spell to defeat them. But that earns the disapproval of his superiors at Hogwarts, and he is threatened with expulsion, because the spell is not to be used in public around Muggles. What is it, like a secret Masonic grip? When you're about to get your clock stopped by dementors and you know the spell, what are you expected to do? Fall over passively and get demented?

There comes a time, which I fear is approaching as we near the end of the series, that Harry and his friends will grow up and smell the coffee. They weren't trained as magicians for fun. And when they eventually arrive at some apocalyptic crossroads, as I fear they will, can the series continue to live in PG-13 land? The archvillain Voldemort is shaping up as the star of nightmares.

Harry (Daniel Radcliffe) has reason to fear that playtime is long behind. As a wizard chosen in childhood for his special powers, he has reason to believe Voldemort has returned and will have to be dealt with. The Ministry of Magic, like many a government agency, is hidebound in outdated convictions and considers Harry's warning to be heresy—and at Hogwarts, a fierce new professor of the dark arts, Dolores Umbridge (Imelda Staunton), has been installed to whip Harry into line.

Her enemies include Harry's protector, Dumbledore (Michael Gambon, looking as shabby as a homeless headmaster). Hermione (Emma Watson) and Ron (Rupert Grint) join Harry in fomenting resistance to Umbridge (rhymes with "umbrage"), and soon they are mapping clandestine schemes to defend Dumbledore. Their plots, alas, seem more serious than the mischief Harry and friends would have thought up in earlier days. Yes, I know time passes, and the actors are seven years older than when they started filming. But if a kid starts watching Potter movies with this film, would he guess they used to be a little more whimsical?

By now, if we know anything at all about the Potter series, it's that nothing is as it seems, and the most unlikely characters have occult connections. Yes, but so many surprises have popped out of the hat that a veteran Potter watcher can almost, by a process of elimination, figure out who will surprise us next. For Harry, like many another leader before him, it is time to leave the nest and begin to work in the world. For the first time since we saw platform 9¾ at King's Cross, the city of London has a major role now, as Harry and sidekicks fly down the Thames and swoop past Big Ben.

That causes me to wonder, what is the practical connection between the world of magic and the world of Muggles? Will Harry, or should Harry, become a world leader? Can wands and spells be of use in today's geopolitical turmoil? Or are Hogwarts grads living in a dimension of their own? All will be told, I guess, in the final book in J. K. Rowling's series, and then the retail book industry will be back on its own again.

These things said, there is no denying that *Order of the Phoenix* is a well-crafted entry in the Potter series. The British have a way of keeping up production values in a series, even when the stories occasionally stumble. There have been lesser James Bond movies, but never a badly made one. And the necessary use of CGI here is justifiable because what does magic create, anyway, other than real-life CGI without the computers?

And as for the cast, the Potter series has turned into a work-release program for great British actors mired in respectable roles. Imelda Staunton is perfect here as the Teacher from Hell. Helena Bonham Carter looks like the double for all three of Macbeth's witches. And then take a roll call: Robbie Coltrane, Ralph Fiennes (in the wings as Voldemort), Michael Gambon, Brendan Gleeson, Richard Griffiths, Jason Isaacs, Gary Oldman, Alan Rickman, Fiona Shaw, David Thewlis, Emma Thompson, Warwick Davis, Julie Walters, and the incomparable Maggie Smith.

My hope, as we plow onward through Potters No. 6 and No. 7, is that the series will not grow darker still. Yet I suppose even at the beginning, with those cute little mail owls, we knew the whimsy was too good to last. Now that Harry has experienced his first kiss, with Cho Chang (Katie Leung), we can only imagine what new opportunities lie ahead. Agent 009.75?

The Haunting in Connecticut ★ ★
PG-13, 92 m., 2009

Virginia Madsen (Sara Campbell), Kyle Gallner (Matt Campbell), Martin Donovan (Peter Campbell), Amanda Crew (Wendy), Elias Koteas (Reverend Popescu). Directed by Peter Cornwell and produced by Paul Brooks, Daniel Farrands, Wendy Rhoads, and Andrew Trapani. Screenplay by Adam Simon and Tim Metcalfe.

The Haunting in Connecticut isn't based on just any old true story. No, it's based on *the* true story. That would be the case of the Snedeker family, who in the 1970s moved into a ghost-infested house in Southington, Connecticut, and had no end of distress. We know their story is true because it was vouched for by Ed and Lorraine Warren, the paranormal sleuths, who also backed up Bill Ramsey, a demonic werewolf who bit people, *The Amityville Horror*, and the story of Jack and Janet Smurl, who inspired the movie *The Haunted*.

Even so, I doubt it's "based on." More likely it was "loosely inspired by" a story. At the end of the movie, the Snedeker house is consumed by flames, and yet we're told before the credits that it was restored, rehabbed, and lived in happily ever after. So much for any hopes of a sequel. Of course, *Amityville* inspired a prequel, so I may not be safe. I don't believe a shred of this movie is true. Ray Garton, the author of *In a Dark Place,* a book including the case, observed that the Snedekers couldn't get their stories straight. When he reported this to the investigators, Wikipedia says, he was instructed to "make the story up" and "make it scary."

But what does that matter if all you're looking for is a ghost story? *The Haunting in Connecticut* is a technically proficient horror movie, well acted by good casting choices. We have here no stock characters, but Virginia Madsen and Martin Donovan in a troubled marriage, Kyle Gallner as their dying son, and Elias Koteas as a grim priest. They make the family, now known as the Campbells, about as real as they can be under the circumstances.

The movie has an alarming score and creepy photography, and a house that doesn't look like it has been occupied since the original inhabitants . . . died, let's say. So all the elements are there, and one of my fellow critics said he "screamed like a girl three times," although he is rather known for doing so. There are two scream-able elements: (1) surprises and (2) specters.

The surprises are those moments when a hand, a face, a body, a body part, or (usually) a cat leaps suddenly into the frame, and you jump in your seat and then say, "Aw, it was only a cat." Or a face, a body part, a vampire bat, etc. The specters involve some ghostly apparitions that may or may not be physical. There are so many of them that the movie, set in Connecticut but filmed in Canada, has credits for "ghost coordinators" in both Vancouver and Winnipeg. Having seen Guy Maddin's brilliant *My Winnipeg,* I believe the ghosts coordinate themselves there.

Matt, the Campbell's son, is dying of cancer and must be driven many miles for his radiation treatments. Madsen, playing his mother, makes an "executive decision" to buy a house in the distant town so Matt, with radiation burns and nausea, doesn't have to drive so far. She gets a really good deal. Let me ask you something. If you found a terrific price on a three-story Victorian mansion with sunporches, lots of bedrooms, original woodwork, and extensive grounds in Connecticut, and it hadn't been lived in since events in the 1920s, how willing would *you* be to laugh off those events?

If the movie has a flaw, and it does, it's too many surprises. Every door, window, bedroom, hallway, staircase, basement area, attic, and crawl space is packed with surprises, so that it is a rare event in the house that takes place normally. The Campbells are constantly being surprised, so often they must be tuckered out at day's end from all of that running, jumping, and standing real still.

But I must not be too harsh, because surprises are what a movie like this trades in. I also thought Elias Koteas did a great job as the priest, who was not a ghostbuster in a Roman collar but a fellow radiation patient who never looked like he was confident good would win out in the end. (It is noteworthy that the Catholic Church does what it can to discourage exorcism, even though it could have done a lot of business in the boom times after *The Exorcist.*)

So. A preposterous story, so many scares they threaten to grow monotonous, good acting and filmmaking credits, and what else? Oh, what's with the ectoplasm? Didn't Houdini unmask that as a fraud? And the Amazing Randi? And what's it doing still being treated as real in *the* true story?

The Heartbreak Kid ★ ★

R, 108 m., 2007

Ben Stiller (Eddie Cantrow), Malin Akerman (Lila), Michelle Monaghan (Miranda), Jerry Stiller (Eddie's father), Rob Corddry (Mac), Carlos Mencia (Uncle Tito), Stephanie Courtney (Gayla), Ali Hillis (Jodi), Kathy Lamkin (Lila's Mom). Directed by Bobby Farrelly and Peter Farrelly and produced by Ted Field and Bradley Thomas. Screenplay by Scott Armstrong and Leslie Dixon, based on the screenplay by Neil Simon and the short story *A Change of Plan* by Bruce Jay Friedman.

The premise of *The Heartbreak Kid* is that a man marries a woman who quickly becomes unbearable to him. The problem is that she just as quickly becomes unbearable to us. Perhaps it is a tribute to Malin Akerman, who plays the new bride, named Lila, that she gets the job done so well; after a point, we cringe when she appears on the screen.

Nor do we have much sympathy for her new

husband, Eddie, played by Ben Stiller. Eddie is a shallow, desperate creature, driven by his hungers, always looking as if he'd like to gnash the flesh of those who oppose him. So here we have a marriage between two unpleasant people, and into these jaws of incompatibility is thrown the person of Miranda (Michelle Monaghan), a sweet girl who deserves better.

The movie is a remake of Elaine May's splendid 1972 comedy, written by Neil Simon, much revised by May. Her movie starred Charles Grodin as a passive-aggressive social climber, May's own daughter Jeannie Berlin as his alarming first wife, and Cybill Shepherd as the WASP goddess on a Florida beach whom he falls in love with on his honeymoon. That film was better in every way, not least because it did not require the Lila character to be revealed as a potty-mouthed sexual predator.

The plot outlines are the same. Man ends his prolonged bachelorhood with an unwise marriage, discovers on honeymoon (then to Florida, now to Mexico) that she has Big Problems. After she collapses with an ugly sunburn, he meets the real girl of his dreams on the beach, and they fall in love while he neglects to mention that he is married.

As Neil Simon and Elaine May knew, this is a good comic situation. As the Farrelly brothers do not know, there are certain kinds of scenes that are deal breakers, rupturing the fabric of comedy and becoming just simply, uncomfortably unpleasant. They have specialized in over-the-top transgressive comedy (*There's Something About Mary*), but always before with characters who could survive their sort of acid bath. Here the characters are made to do and say things that are outside their characters and maybe outside any characters.

Consider the question of the parents of the newlywed. Lila's mother (Kathy Lamkin) is revealed as a very overweight fatso, with the implication that Lila will eventually balloon to such a size. But what's so great about Eddie's father (Jerry Stiller), a vulgarian with an orange toupee, who sees women as throwaway commodities, advises his son to get all the sex he can, anywhere he can, and ends up in a Las Vegas hot tub with a blonde (Kayla Kleevage, yes, Kayla Kleevage) whose breasts are so big they bring the show to a halt the same way a three-legged woman might? There is also an example of a

"Mexican Folklore Dance" that involves a donkey with unappetizing sexual equipment. The Farrellys' overkill breaks the fabric of their story.

There are small moments of real humor. The hair on the head of the first child of Eddie's best pal (Rob Corddry), for example. Lila's showdown between a deviated septum and a shrimp. The suspicions that Miranda's cousin (Danny McBride) has about Eddie. The way Eddie is vilified in the speeches after the wedding of a former girlfriend. More of that and less of peeing on poisonous jellyfish might have helped. But the film is a squirmy miscalculation of tone.

Hellboy II: The Golden Army ★ ★ ★ ½
PG-13, 120 m., 2008

Ron Perlman (Hellboy), Selma Blair (Liz Sherman), Doug Jones (Abe Sapien), Jeffrey Tambor (Tom Manning), Luke Gross (Prince Nuada), John Hurt (Trevor Bruttenholm), Seth McFarlane (Johann Kraus [voice]), Anna Walton (Princess Nuala). Directed by Guillermo del Toro and produced by Lawrence Gordon, Mike Richardson, and Lloyd Levin. Screenplay by del Toro, based on the comic book by Mike Mignola.

Imagine the forges of hell crossed with the extraterrestrial saloon on Tatooine and you have a notion of Guillermo del Toro's *Hellboy II: The Golden Army*. In every way the equal of his original *Hellboy* (2004), although perhaps a little noisier, it's another celebration of his love for bizarre fantasy and diabolical machines. The sequel bypasses the details of Hellboy's origin story but adds a legend read to him as a child by his adoptive father (John Hurt), in which we learn of an ancient warfare between humans and, well, everybody else: trolls, monsters, goblins, the Tooth Fairy, everybody.

There was a truce. The humans got the cities and the trolls got the forests. But humans have cheated on our end of the deal by building parking lots and shopping malls, and now Prince Nuada (Luke Gross) defies his father, the king, and hopes to start the conflict again. This would involve awakening the Golden Army: seventy times seventy slumbering mechanical warriors. Standing against this decision is his twin sister, Princess Nuala (Anna Walton).

And so on. I had best not get bogged down in plot description, except to add that Hellboy (Ron Perlman) and his sidekicks fight for the human side. His comrades include Abe Sapien (Doug Jones), sort of a fish-man, the fire-generating Liz Sherman (Selma Blair), a Teutonic adviser named Johann Kraus (Seth McFarlane), and of course Princess Nuala. Tom Manning (Jeffrey Tambor) from the secret center for extrasensory perception tags along but isn't much help except for adding irrelevancies and flippant asides.

Now that we have most of the characters onstage, let me describe the sights, which are almost all created by CGI of course, but how else? There's a climactic showdown between Hellboy and the prince, with the Golden Army standing dormant in what looks like the engine room of hell. Enormous interlocking gears grind against each other for no apparent purpose, except to chew up Hellboy or anything else that falls into them. Lucky they aren't perfectly calibrated.

There are also titanic battles in the streets of Manhattan, involving gigantic octo-creatures and so on, but you know what? Although they're well done, titanic battles in the streets of Manhattan are becoming commonplace in the movies these days. What was fascinating to me was what the octo-creature transformed itself into, which was unexpected and really lovely. You'll see.

The towering creatures fascinated me less, however, than some smaller ones. For example, swarms of tens of thousands of calcium-eaters, who devour humans both skin and bone and are the source of the Tooth Fairy legend. They pour out of the walls of an auction house and attack the heroes, and in my personal opinion Hellboy is wasting his time trying to shoot them one at a time.

I also admired the creativity that went into the Troll Market (it has a secret entry under the Brooklyn Bridge). Here I think del Toro actually was inspired by the Tatooine saloon in *Star Wars,* and brings together creatures of fantastical shapes and sizes, buying and selling goods of comparable shapes and sizes. It would be worth having the DVD just to study the market a frame at a time, discovering what secrets he may have hidden in there. The movies only rarely give us a genuinely new kind of place to look at; this will become a classic.

There are, come to think of it, other whispers of the *Star Wars* influence in *Hellboy II.* Princess Nuala doesn't have Princess Leia's rope of hair (just ordinary long blond tresses), but she's not a million miles distant from her. And Abe Sapien looks, moves, and sort of sounds so much like C3PO that you'd swear the robot became flesh and developed gills. I also noticed hints of John Williams's *Star Wars* score in the score by Danny Elfman, especially during the final battle. Not a plundering job, you understand, more of an evocation of mood.

What else? Two love stories, which I'll leave for you to find out about. And the duet performance of a song that is rather unexpected, to say the least. And once again a strong performance by Ron Perlman as Hellboy. Yes, he's CGI for the most part, but his face and voice and movements inhabit the screen figure, and make him one of the great comic heroes. Del Toro, who preceded *Hellboy II* with *Pan's Labyrinth* (2006) and the underrated *Blade II* (2002) is warming up now for *Doctor Strange* and *The Hobbit.* He has an endlessly inventive imagination and understands how legends work, why they entertain us, and that they sometimes stand for something. For love, for example. ☞

Hell Ride ★

R, 83 m., 2008

Larry Bishop (Pistolero), Michael Madsen (The Gent), Eric Balfour (Comanche), Vinnie Jones (Billy Wings), Dennis Hopper (Eddie Zero). Directed by Larry Bishop and produced by Michael Steinberg, Larry Bishop, and Shana Stein. Screenplay by Bishop.

I read an article the other day saying the average age of motorcyclists is going up. Judging by *Hell Ride,* the average age of motorcycle gang members is approaching the Medicare generation, not that many will survive to collect the benefits. Some of the "plot" involves revenge for the torching of the girlfriend of the gang president. That took place in the bicentennial year of 1976, which was, let's see, thirty-two years ago. By the time they kill the guy who did it, he's a geezer with so many chin whiskers they can barely cut his throat.

The movie was written and directed by Larry Bishop, who also stars as Pistolero, president of an outlaw club named the Victors. Bishop starred in a motorcycle movie named *The Savage Seven* in 1968, which was, let's see, forty years ago. He was also in *The Devil's 8, Angels Unchained,* and *Chrome and Hot Leather.* It's a wonder he doesn't have a handicapped placard for his hog.

In between searching for a killer, he leads a gang whose members are sort of hard to tell apart, except for The Gent (Michael Madsen), so called because instead of leathers he wears a ruffled formal shirt under a tux jacket with his gang colors stitched on the back. Why does he do that? The answer to that question would require character development, and none of the cast members develop at all. They spring into being fully created and never change, like Greek gods.

There are cameo roles for two icons of biker movies, Dennis Hopper and David Carradine, who play old-timers—that is, contemporaries of the other gang members. Madsen, at fifty, may be the youngest cast member, and also brings along expertise in doing The Walk. That would be the scene made famous from *Reservoir Dogs* and a zillion other movies where three or four tough guys lope along in unison away from something that is about to blow up and don't flinch when it does.

Wait a minute. Maybe the guy who gets blown up was the killer and not the grizzled old-timer. I dunno. The enemy gang of the Victors are the 666ers, but I couldn't tell them apart except for the close-ups of the colors on their backs, which had the disadvantage of not showing their faces. There is a character named Deuce, but I don't know why. Or maybe he is a gang.

The movie was executive-produced by Quentin Tarantino. Shame on him. He intends it no doubt as another homage to grindhouse pictures, but I've seen a lot of them, and they were nowhere near this bad. *Hell's Angels on Wheels,* for example: pretty good.

All these guys do is shoot one another and roll around in bars with naked girls with silicone breasts—who don't seem to object to the bikers' smelly grime. The girls look about twenty-five, tops, but the only reference to age in the movie is when a biker names his bike after the horse Trigger, and is asked, "How old is Trigger in horse-bike years?" Quick—whose horse was Trigger? Can anyone under twenty-five answer? OK, then: Silver? Champion? Topper?

Henry Poole Is Here ★ ★ ★ ½
PG, 101 m., 2008

Luke Wilson (Henry Poole), Radha Mitchell (Dawn), Adriana Barraza (Esperanza), George Lopez (Father Salazar), Cheryl Hines (Meg), Richard Benjamin (Dr. Fancher), Morgan Lily (Millie), Rachel Seiferth (Patience), Beth Grant (Josie). Directed by Mark Pellington and produced by Tom Rosenberg, Gary Lucchesi, Richard Wright, Gary Gilbert, and Tom Lassally. Screenplay by Albert Torres.

Henry Poole Is Here achieves something that is uncommonly difficult. It is a spiritual movie with the power to emotionally touch believers, agnostics, and atheists—in that descending order, I suspect. It doesn't say that religious beliefs are real. It simply says that belief is real. And it's a warmhearted love story.

It centers on a man named Henry Poole (Luke Wilson), who has only one problem when he moves into a house. He is dying. Then he acquires another problem. His neighbor Esperanza (Adriana Barraza) sees the face of Jesus Christ in a stain on his stucco wall. Henry Poole doesn't see the face, and indeed neither do we most of the time, even if we squint. It's a hit-or-miss sort of thing.

Wilson plays Henry as hostile and depressed. Well, he has much to be depressed about. "We hardly ever see this disease in the States," the doctor tells him. "It steamrolls through your system." Patience (Rachel Seiferth), the nearly blind checkout girl at the supermarket, gives him dietary hints when she notices he buys mostly vodka and frozen pizza. Although her glasses are half an inch thick, she's observant: "Why are you sad and angry all the time?"

Henry starts hearing voices in his backyard. There is a rational reason for this. He is being secretly recorded by Millie (Morgan Lily), the five-year-old who lives next door on the other side from Esperanza. Millie's mother is the lovely Dawn (Radha Mitchell), who apologizes for her daughter, brings cookies, and also notices how sad and angry Henry is. He is especially angry with Esperanza, warning her to stay out of his yard and stop praying to his bad stucco job. But she has seen Jesus and cannot be stopped. She brings in Father Salazar (George Lopez), who explains that the church does not easily declare miracles but keeps an open mind.

There are more details, which I must not reveal, including certain properties of the wall. I will observe that the director, Mark Pellington, uses some of the most subtle special effects you've probably seen for some time to fine-tune the illusion that the face of Christ is really there, or really not there. I will now think of this movie every time I drive through the Fullerton Avenue underpass of the Kennedy Expressway in Chicago, where since April 2005 people have said they can see the Virgin Mary in a wall stain. There are always flowers there.

The thing is, certain miraculous events take place, and the people involved believe it is because they touched Henry's wall. Patience the checkout girl even quotes the formidable intellectual Noam Chomsky, who, she informs Henry, said some things cannot be explained by science. One critic of this film believes it is antiscience and pounds you over the head to believe. Not at all. It is simply that Chomsky is right, as any scientist will tell you. What do I believe? I believe science can eventually explain everything, but only if it gets a whole lot better than it is now and discovers realms we do not even suspect. You could call such a realm God. You could, of course, call it anything you wanted; it wouldn't matter to the realm.

Another critic, or maybe it is the same critic, believes the movie is a Hollywood ploy to reach the Christian market. Not at all. Esperanza sees Jesus because the face of Jesus is ready in her mind, supplied by holy cards and paintings. You might see the face of Uncle Sam. No one knows what Jesus looked like. It is also strange that the Virgin's appearances always mirror her holy card image. People from biblical lands at that time would have been a

good deal darker and shorter. The movie gets that right: The image is so low on the wall that Jesus must have stood less than five feet tall.

But I stray, and I do injustice to this film. I fell for it. I believed the feelings between Henry and Dawn. I cared about their tenderness and loneliness. I thought Millie was adorable. I thought Father Salazar had his head on straight. I loved Esperanza's great big heart. And I especially admired the way that Henry stuck to his guns. He doesn't believe there's a face on his stucco, and that's that. And no, he doesn't undergo a deathbed conversion. That's because . . . but find out for yourself.

He's Just Not That Into You ★ ★
PG-13, 129 m., 2009

Ben Affleck (Neil), Jennifer Aniston (Beth), Drew Barrymore (Mary), Jennifer Connelly (Janine), Kevin Connolly (Conor), Bradley Cooper (Ben), Ginnifer Goodwin (Gigi), Scarlett Johansson (Anna), Justin Long (Alex). Directed by Ken Kwapis and produced by Nancy Juvonen. Screenplay by Abby Kohn and Marc Silverstein, based on the book by Greg Behrendt and Liz Tuccillo.

Ever noticed how many self-help books are limited to the insight expressed in their titles? You look at the cover, you know everything inside. The rest is just writing. I asked Amazon to "surprise me" with a page from inside the best-seller *He's Just Not That Into You,* and it jumped me to page 17, where I read: "My belief is that if you have to be the aggressor, if you have to pursue, if you have to do the asking out, nine times out of 10, he's just not that into you."

I personally would not be interested in a woman who needed to buy a book to find that out. Guys also figure out that when she never returns your calls and is inexplicably always busy, she's just not that into you. What is this, brain surgery? I have tried, but I cannot imagine what was covered in the previous sixteen pages of that book. I am reminded of the book review once written by Ambrose Bierce: "The covers of this book are too far apart."

The movie version of *He's Just Not That Into You* dramatizes this insight with comic vignettes played by actors who are really too good for this romcom. Jennifer Aniston in particular has a screen presence that makes me wonder why she rarely takes on the kinds of difficult roles her costars Jennifer Connelly, Scarlett Johansson, and Drew Barrymore have played. There are depths there. I know it.

The movie takes place in modern-day Baltimore, where those four, and Ginnifer Goodwin, play women who should ask themselves: Is he really that into me? Aniston, for example, plays Beth, who has been living for years with Neil (Ben Affleck), who is perfect in every respect except that he is disinclined to marry her. "We're happy just the way we are," he argues. The old "if it's not broke, don't fix it" routine. But if a woman knows her loved one won't ever want to marry her, it's her heart that's broke, and there is only one way to fix it. There are even evolutionary theories to explain this.

Gigi (Goodwin), on the other hand, doesn't have a perfect boyfriend, or any at all, and sits by her phone like a penguin waiting for the damn egg to hatch. Why hasn't that dreamy guy who asked for her number called back? Maybe, just maybe, it's because he doesn't want to. I haven't read the book, but I know that much. There was once a girl I didn't call, and she mailed me a book titled *The Dance-Away Lover*. How did I instinctively know the book was about me? Why did I know everything in it without having to read it? Because the book was intended for her, that's why.

Janine (Connelly) is married to Ben (Bradley Cooper), who doesn't share her ideas about home decoration, which are that you always make the more expensive choice. Not a lot of guys are into that. If you get one who is, he may make it a general policy and decide to trade you in for an advanced model. Look for a guy who treats you not as an acquisition but as an angel of mercy, the answer to the prayers of the rat he knows he is.

Mary (Barrymore) is surrounded by great guys, but they're all gay. They're from that subspecies of gay men who learned everything they know about life from Bette Davis. This is true even if they've never seen one of her movies. Then there's Anna (Johansson), who is courted fervently by Conor (Kevin Connolly), who would marry her in a second, except she's "committed" to a married man, who

is committed to not marrying her, which is maybe what she likes about him, along with getting the right to constantly be the wronged one in a relationship she, after all, freely walked into.

The problem with most of the movie's women is that they are only interested in (a) the opposite sex, (b) dating, and (c) marriage. Maybe that's because the screenplay only has so much time. But a movie about one insecure woman talking to another can be monotonous, unless you're a masochist looking to share your pain. If you consider a partner who has no more compelling interests than a, b, or c, you're shopping for boredom.

There is one superb monologue in the movie, by Drew Barrymore, who complains that she is driven crazy by the way guys always seem to be communicating in another medium. She calls at home but he doesn't pick up. She calls on his cell, and he e-mails her. She texts him. He Twitters back and leaves coded hints on MySpace. She tries snail mail. He apparently never learned how to open one. She yearns for the days when people had one telephone and one answering machine, and a guy had either definitely called you, or he had not.

This is a very far from perfect movie, and it ends on an unsatisfactory note. Stop reading *now* because I am going to complain that most of the stories have happy endings. Not in the real world, they don't. In the real world, the happy endings come only with a guy who's really into you. I should write a self-help book: *If Some Guy Says He Loves You, Check It Out.*

Hitman ★ ★ ★
R, 110 m., 2007

Timothy Olyphant (Agent 47), Dougray Scott (Mike Whittier), Olga Kurylenko (Nika), Robert Knepper (Yuri Marklov), Ulrich Thomsen (Mikhail Belicoff), Michael Offei (Jenkins). Directed by Xavier Gens and produced by Pierre-Ange le Pogam, Charles Gordon, and Adrian Askarieh. Screenplay by Skip Woods.

This may only be my quirky way of thinking, but if you wanted to move through the world as an invisible hit man responsible for more than one hundred killings on six continents, would you shave your head to reveal the bar code tattooed on the back of your skull? Yeah, not me, either. But Agent 47 has great success with this disguise in *Hitman,* which is a better movie than I thought it might be.

Agent 47 (Timothy Olyphant) has no name because he was raised as an orphan from birth by a shadowy organization named the Agency, which is "known to all governments" and performs assassinations for hire. He was trained in all the killing skills and none of the human ones, which is why the young woman Nika (Olga Kurylenko) is such a challenge for him. A prostitute held in slavery by the drug-dealing brother of the Russian premier, she follows him, obeys him, offers herself to him, and although he remains distant, he cannot remain indifferent.

Agent 47 is in Russia on a job: assassinate Belicoff (Ulrich Thomsen), the premier. This he thinks he does. Yet Belicoff appears in public almost immediately after the hit, alive and speaking. How did this happen? An Interpol agent named Mike (Dougray Scott) is just as puzzled: "My man doesn't miss."

How it happens is not my business to tell you, but I will say that Agent 47 is betrayed by the Agency and finds himself being pursued by both Interpol and the Russian secret police. As he and Nika move from St. Petersburg to Moscow, there is one shoot-out after another, close escapes, daring leaps into the void, high-tech booby traps, and so on.

The movie, directed by Xavier Gens, was inspired by a best-selling video game and serves as an excellent illustration of my conviction that video games will never become an art form—never, at least, until they morph into something else or more.

What I found intriguing about the movie was the lonely self-sufficiency of Agent 47, his life without a boyhood, his lack of a proper name, his single-purpose training. When Nika comes into his life he is trained to guard against her, but he cannot because she is helpless, needy, depends on him, and is a victim like himself. So he takes her along with him (which only increases her danger) while not making love. You know what? I think he may be a virgin trained to make war, not love.

To the degree the movie explores their relationship, it is absorbing. There is also intrigue

at the highest levels of Russian politics, as the moderate Belicoff is apparently targeted for death. All of that is well done. Other scenes involve Agent 47 striding down corridors, an automatic weapon in each hand, shooting down opponents who come dressed as Jedi troopers in black. These scenes are no doubt from the video game. The troopers spring into sight, pop up, and start shooting, and he has target practice. He also jumps out of windows without knowing where he's going to land, and that feels like he's cashing in a chip he won earlier in the game.

If you want to see what Agent 47 might have seemed like without the obligatory video game requirements, I urge you to rent Jean-Pierre Melville's *Le Samourai* (1967), which is about a lone-wolf assassin in Paris (Alain Delon). He, too, works alone, is a professional, cuts off his emotions, seems lonely and cold. But the movie is about him, not his killing score.

The key producer on *Hitman* was Adrian Askarieh, who told *Variety* he doesn't consult or collaborate with the makers of a video game he has purchased for filming, but instead focuses on the characters and situation. Wise. To the degree he doesn't try to reproduce the aim-and-shoot material, he has a movie here. To the degree Olyphant and Kurylenko can flesh out their characters, they do.

The movie is rated R, despite reports that the studio demanded edits to trim down the violence. It has a high body count, but very little blood and gore. I wish it had less. It's the people we care about in movies, not how many dead bodies they can stack up. *Hitman* stands right on the threshold between video game and art. On the wrong side of the threshold, but still, give it credit.

Honeydripper ★ ★ ★ ½
PG-13, 123 m., 2008

Danny Glover (Tyrone Purvis), Lisa Gay Hamilton (Delilah Purvis), Yaya DaCosta (China Doll), Charles S. Dutton (Maceo Green), Gary Clark Jr. (Sonny Blake), Mable John (Bertha Mae Spivey), Vondie Curtis Hall (Slick), Stacy Keach (Sheriff Pugh). Directed by John Sayles and produced by Maggie Renzi. Screenplay by Sayles.

John Sayles's *Honeydripper* is set at the intersection of two movements that would change American life forever: the civil rights movement, and rhythm and blues. They may have more to do with each other than you might think, although that isn't his point. He's more concerned with spinning a ground-level human comedy than searching for pie in the sky. His movie is rich with characters and flowing with music.

The time, around 1950. The place, Harmony, Alabama. The chief location, the Honeydripper Lounge, which serves a good drink but is feeling the competition from a juke joint down the road. The proprietor, Pine Top Purvis (Danny Glover), is desperately in debt. The wife, Delilah (Lisa Gay Hamilton), is causing him some concern: Will she get religion and disapprove of his business? The best friend, Maceo (Charles S. Dutton), is a sounding board for his problems. The nightmare, the local sheriff (Stacy Keach), is a racist, but doesn't go overboard like most. Club characters: blues singer (Mable John) and her man (Vondie Curtis Hall).

Into Harmony one day comes a footloose young man named Sonny, played by Gary Clark Jr., in real life a rising guitar phenom. He drifts into the Honeydripper looking for a job or a meal and carrying something no one has ever seen before: a homemade electric guitar carved out of a solid block of wood. Pine Top has no work for him, and the youth is soon arrested by the sheriff (his crime: existing while unemployed) and put to work picking cotton for a crony.

Meanwhile, in desperation, Pine Top books the great Guitar Sam out of New Orleans and puts up posters all over town. Sure, he can't afford him, but the plan is, Guitar Sam will bring in enough business on one Saturday night to pay his own salary and also the lounge's worst bills. Pine Top finds out what real desperation is when Guitar Sam doesn't arrive on the train. He wonders if the kid with the funny guitar can play a little. After all, no one in Harmony knows what Guitar Sam really looks like.

Now all the pieces are in place for an unwinding of local race issues, personal issues, financial issues, and some very, very good music, poised just at that point when the blues were turning into rhythm and blues, which after all is what rock and roll is only an alias for. Because after all, yes, the kid can play a little. More than a little.

John Sayles has made nineteen films, and none of them is a two-character study. As the writer of his own work, he instinctively embraces the communities in which they take place. He's never met a man who was an island. Everyone connects, and when that includes black and white, rich and poor, young and old, there are lessons to be learned, and his generosity to his characters overflows into affection.

Danny Glover is well cast to stand at the center of this story. A tall, imposing, grave presence as Pine Top, he is not so much a music lover as a survivor. This is his last chance to save the Honeydripper and his means of making a living. And Gary Clark Jr. is the right man to be told: Tonight, you are Guitar Sam. He may be a prodigy, but he is broke, scared, young, and far from home. So this isn't one of those showbiz stories where a talent scout is in the audience, but a story where the audience looks at him with great suspicion until his music makes them smile.

As for the sheriff's role: As I suggested, lots of Alabama sheriffs were more racist than he is, which is not a character recommendation, but means that he isn't evil just to pass the time and would rather avoid trouble than work up a sweat. At that time, in that place, he was about the best you could hope for. Within a few more years, the Bull Connors would be run out of town, one man would have one vote, and the music of the African-American South would rule the world. That all had to start somewhere. It didn't start on Saturday night at the Honeydripper, but it didn't stop there, either.

Hotel for Dogs ★ ★ ½
PG, 100 m., 2009

Emma Roberts (Andi), Jake T. Austin (Bruce), Kyla Pratt (Heather), Lisa Kudrow (Lois), Kevin Dillon (Carl), Don Cheadle (Bernie), Johnny Simmons (Dave), Troy Gentile (Mark). Directed by Thor Freudenthal and produced by Lauren Shuler Donner, Jonathan Gordon, Ewan Leslie, and Jason Clark. Screenplay by Leslie, Jeff Lowell, Bob Schooley, and Mark McCorkle, based on the book by Lois Duncan.

Hotel for Dogs is a sweet, innocent family movie about stray dogs that seem as well-trained as Olympic champions. Friday, the Jack Russell terrier who's the leader of the pack, does more acting than most of the humans and doesn't even get billing. I know, because I searched for one, hoping to mention him by name and call him a good doggie.

What can Friday do? Let himself up and down from a fire escape landing, using a pulley-and-counterweight system. Find his masters anywhere in the city. Steal hot dogs and possibly a whole gyros wheel. Get out of his collar and back in again. Outrace dogs five times his size in a sprint down city streets. And join dozens of other dogs in mastering these abilities: feeding himself, using a doggie fire hydrant, sitting on a toilet, running on a treadmill, activating a bone-throwing mechanism. I'm only scratching the surface.

Friday belongs to Andi (Emma Roberts) and Bruce (Jake T. Austin), a brother and sister in foster care. He is kept a secret from their foster parents, two obnoxious would-be rock musicians (Lisa Kudrow and Kevin Dillon). The kids saved him from the streets, and he has been their secret pal through three years and five foster homes. One day he leads them into an abandoned downtown hotel occupied by two dogs he makes friends with, and soon the kids find themselves running an unofficial animal shelter.

In this they're assisted by Dave (Johnny Simmons) and Heather (Kyla Pratt), two Nickelodeon-cute employees at a pet shop, which they can apparently abandon on a moment's notice to use the store's van on rescue missions. Since they can't possibly care for all those dogs, little Bruce rigs up Rube Goldberg devices to automate the tasks. There's even an automatic door knocker to send the dogs into frenzies of barking and jumping. Good exercise, although sooner or later these dogs will get wise to it.

Don Cheadle plays the dedicated social worker in charge of the kids, who bails them out when they get in trouble with cops and meany attendants at the animal pound. He even has a big speech on the Dog Hotel steps, during which I did my best not to think of *Hotel Rwanda*. What I thought instead was, Marley could learn a lot from these dogs.

Hot Rod ★ ★ ★
PG-13, 88 m., 2007

Andy Samberg (Rod Kimble), Isla Fisher (Denise), Jorma Taccone (Kevin Powell), Bill Hader (Dave), Danny R. McBride (Rico), Ian McShane (Frank Powell), Sissy Spacek (Marie Powell), Will Arnett (Jonathan), Chris Parnell (Barry Pasternak). Directed by Akiva Schaffer and produced by John Goldwyn and Lorne Michaels. Screenplay by Pam Brady.

Rod Kimble, the hero of *Hot Rod,* is Evel Knievel on a moped. He leads a life resembling an episode of *Jackass.* Not a day passes without him attempting a harebrained stunt, and failure doesn't discourage him because he knows in his heart that he is destined to become world famous.

Rod is played by Andy Samberg from *Saturday Night Live,* who on the basis of this film, I think, could become a very big star. With a trusting face, a gigantic smile, and an occasional Burt Reynolds mustache, he has the innocence of many great comedians, who always seem surprised at the way their schemes turn out; like Buster Keaton, he springs up after every disaster, ready for more, hoping to get rich, win the girl, be universally acclaimed, and so on.

Samberg is one of the first comedy stars spawned by the Internet. With his Berkeley buddies Jorma Taccone and Akiva Schaffer, he made short films that became enormously popular on the net and was signed by *SNL,* which also took Taccone and Schaffer aboard as writers. They're still together; Schaffer is the director of *Hot Rod,* and Taccone costars as Kevin, Rod's half brother and half-willing sidekick for his stunts.

Samberg is twenty-seven, but he looks about seventeen in the film and lives at home with his mom (Sissy Spacek) and stepdad (Ian McShane). He has been told of the daring heroism of his father, now deceased, and dreams of emulating him. But he can't even outmaneuver his stepfather, who routinely defeats him in fights. This does not involve abuse, but a ferocious rivalry between the two. When his mom breaks the news that his stepdad needs a heart transplant they can't afford, Rod is devastated. That means he loses any hope of defeating him in hand-to-hand combat.

Rod vows to raise the necessary $50,000 so that he can save his stepfather's life and then reduce him to a pulp. Some of his attempts at moneymaking are painful; hired as an entertainer at a children's party, he is hung upside-down and turned into a human piñata. His daredevil show involving the municipal swimming pool also turns out badly.

All his publicity efforts add up to an attempt to jump over fifteen buses (the real Evel Knievel once jumped fourteen buses, although close study of his career indicates he crashed about as often as Rod Kimble). To prepare for his jump, Rod begins a training regime, leading to a tumble down a hill that—well, see for yourself.

The movie is funny, I think, because it is sincere. It likes Rod. It doesn't portray him as a maniacal goofball, but as an ambitious kid who really thinks, every single time, that he will succeed. In creating this aura of sincerity, *Hot Rod* benefits from Sissy Spacek's performance: She plays the mom absolutely straight, without inflection, as if she were not in a comedy. That's the only right choice; supporting characters are needed to reinforce Rod, not compete with him.

Rod's would-be girlfriend Denise (Isla Fisher) is, of course, going with another guy, but Rod persists in the belief that his inevitable fame will win her over, as if girls are searching for guys with his job description (Knievel had to kidnap his own first wife, but, to be fair, he wasn't yet a daredevil). All of these characters and some of the conflicts are familiar from other movies, but *Hot Rod* puts a nice spin on them. It's funny pretty much all the way through, even in the final showdown between Rod and his stepdad. I have seen countless movie fights that stagger the imagination, but this one goes over the top and comes down on the other side. Just what Rod would like to do someday.

The Hottest State ★ ★

R, 117 m., 2007

Mark Webber (William Harding), Catalina Sandino Moreno (Sara Garcia), Ethan Hawke (Vince), Laura Linney (Jesse), Michelle Williams (Samantha), Sonia Braga (Mrs. Garcia), Jesse Harris (Dave Afton), Daniel Ross (Young Vince), Anne Clarke (Young Jesse). Directed by Ethan Hawke and produced by Yukie Kito and Alexis Alexanian. Screenplay by Hawke, based on his novel.

As a topic of fiction, the only things I have against young love are youth and romance. There has to be something more. Who would care about Romeo and Juliet if it hadn't been for their unfortunate misunderstanding? There has to be comedy, or tragedy, or suspense, or personality quirks, or *something* more than the fact that Young Person A loves Young Person B. This also applies to Old People A&B.

Ethan Hawke's *The Hottest State*, which he wrote, directed, and costars in, is based on his 1996 "semiautobiographical" novel, and therefore inspired in some way by his similarities to his hero: comes to New York from Texas, wants to be an actor, falls in love, etc. I would perhaps have enjoyed the movie more if it had been a "semibiographical" novel, based on *both* the boy and the girl. When his hero stands in the street reciting beneath her window from *Romeo and Juliet* (and he does), surely the point is not his gauche behavior but her failure to pour water on him.

The movie involves William (Mark Webber) and Sara Garcia (Catalina Sandino Moreno, from *Maria, Full of Grace*). She is a Latina from a wealthy background in Connecticut, cutting out any hope of culture clash, since Latinas will not have been unknown to him in Texas, although at least her background provides her with an interesting mother (Sonia Braga). William, we learn in flashbacks, is himself the product of young love that did not end well between a distant father (played by Hawke) and a mother (Laura Linney) whose realistic advice could be borrowed from Olympia Dukakis in *Moonstruck* (in place of sympathizing with William, she reminds him that in the long run he will be dead, and his heartbreak won't matter so much).

William and Sara meet in a bar, like each other, find out they're both in the arts, and play at boyfriend and girlfriend. Then they take a vacation to Mexico, seem to fall truly in love, finally have sex, and then when they meet next in New York she has decided she doesn't want him, or anyone, as a lover. Which breaks his heart and causes him to paste grieving messages on his windows, which she can see from hers. (Romantic tip: When a lover tells you they don't want to see you "or anyone," they already have someone else in mind.)

If the stakes were higher, all of this might matter more. But William and Sara have not interested us as themselves, and don't seem to interest each other as much as they like the romantic roles they're playing. Will the world be different, or their lives irrevocably changed, if they break up? I don't think so. Their tree falls in the forest, and nobody cares except the termites.

I admired Hawke's directorial debut, *Chelsea Walls* (2001), ever so much more than this movie because it was about more interesting people and more interesting love; it was set in the Chelsea Hotel, which, when people get beyond a certain threshold of "interesting," may be the only hotel in New York that will accept them. In *The Hottest State*, Hawke uses fairly standard childhood motivations for his unhappiness and reveals too little real interest in the Sara character. Why *did* she seem to fall in love and then announce she didn't want to see him anymore? From her point of view, I mean. In fact, the best angle on this whole story might be from her point of view.

Hounddog ★ ★
R, 93 m., 2007

Dakota Fanning (Lewellen), Cody Hanford (Buddy), Robin Wright Penn (Stranger Lady), David Morse (Daddy), Piper Laurie (Grammie), Afemo Omilami (Charles), Jill Scott (Big Mama Thornton). Directed by Deborah Kampmeier and produced by Kampmeier, Scott Franklin, Raye Dowell, Terry Leonard, Roberta Hanley, Jen Gatien, and Lawrence Robins. Screenplay by Kampmeier.

Dakota Fanning takes an impressive step forward in her career, but that's about the only good thing about *Hounddog*. The reigning child star, now fourteen, handles a painful and complex role with such assurance that she reminds me of Jodie Foster in *Taxi Driver*. But

her character is surrounded by a swamp of worn-out backwoods Southern clichés that can't be rescued even by the other accomplished actors in the cast.

She plays Lewellen, a barefoot tomboy who lives in a shack with her father (David Morse), a slovenly drunk and self-pitying whiner. Next door is Grammie (Piper Laurie), who keeps house well but is a hard-drinking slattern. Lewellen prowls the woods and frequents the swimming hole with her best friend, Buddy (Cody Hanford), as they trade awkward kisses and examine each other's private parts with great curiosity.

The poverty of her family is indicated by the usual marker: rusting trucks in the lawn. Her father operates a tractor, which during a rainstorm is struck by lightning. This hurls him to the ground and makes him even more dramatically loony. He is seized by anxiety that his daughter will abandon him, and one night he walks into the local tavern seeking her, having failed to notice that he is stark naked. The pool players prod him with their cues. Lewellen stalks in and drags him home.

Somehow amid this chaos the young girl succeeds in being playful and high-spirited, until she is raped by an older teenager. She grows silent and morose, even comatose, and one night is visited by dozens of (imaginary?) snakes, who crawl in through her bedroom window and perform a function, whether demonic or healing, that is understood by her friend and protector Charles (Afemo Omilami), a black man who works in the stables of the local gentry. He brings her back to health and lectures her about making people treat her with respect.

Moving around the edges of the story is a character known in the credits as Stranger Lady (Robin Wright Penn). Her identity and function are left unclear, except for the fact that it will be immediately obvious to any sentient viewer exactly who she is. It has been some time since I quoted from Ebert's Little Movie Glossary, but the Stranger Lady perfectly fits the Law of Economy of Characters, which teaches us that whenever an important star appears in a seemingly unexplained role, that character will represent the solution to a plot question.

Now about *Hounddog*. Lewellen is a passionate fan of Elvis and has some small local fame for her Elvis impersonations. Her life may be transformed when she hears Charles and his friends, including Jill Scott as Big Mama Thornton, performing in the rhythm and blues tradition that inspired Elvis. Lewellen is obsessed with the news that Elvis will be performing in a local concert and is cruelly tricked when she thinks she can get a ticket. One moonlit night, Elvis himself drives past in a pink Cadillac and blows her a kiss. Yes. Elvis would have driven himself to the concert, alone, down back roads, of course.

Hounddog is assembled from the debris of countless worn-out images of the Deep South, and is indeed beautifully photographed. But the writer-director, Deborah Kampmeier, has become inflamed by the imagery and trusts it as the material for a story, which seems grotesque and lurid. David Morse's Daddy, well-played as the character may be, is a particularly dreary presence, pitiful instead of sympathetic. Having seen so many of these fine actors in other roles, my heart goes out for them. Still, the discovery here is the remarkable Dakota Fanning, opening the next stage in her career and doing it bravely, with presence, confidence, and high spirits.

House of the Sleeping Beauties ★
NO MPAA RATING, 99 m., 2009

Vadim Glowna (Edmond), Angela Winkler (Madame), Maximilian Schell (Kogi), Birol Unel (Mister Gold), Mona Glass (Secretary), Marina Weiss (Maid). Directed by Vadim Glowna and produced by Glowna and Raymond Tarabay. Screenplay by Glowna, based on the novella by Yasunari Kawabata.

House of the Sleeping Beauties has missed its ideal release window by about forty years. It might—*might*—have found an audience in that transitional period between soft- and hard-core, when men would sit through anything to see a breast, but even then, I dunno. It's discouraging to see a movie where the women sleep through everything. They don't even have the courtesy to wake up and claim to have a headache.

I know I am being disrespectful to what is obviously intended to be a morose meditation about youth, age, men, women, children, mothers, hookers, johns, life, death, and the endless possibilities I thought of at sixteen when I heard that song "Behind the Green Door." The movie has been inspired by a 1961 novella by Yasunari Kawabata, who explores the now-obsolete Japanese theory that a woman should be seen but not heard. Even then, they were supposed to wake up sometimes and speak submissively.

The film centers on five scenes in which Edmond, a dying man in his sixties (Vadim Glowna, the director), lies in bed next to sleeping nude women of about twenty, all breathtakingly beautiful, and utters a mournful interior soliloquy about his age, their perfection, his mother, a childhood sexual experience, and his own misery. This is an intensely depressing experience for Edmond and for us, intensified by his robotic smoking habit. Sometimes he shakes a woman or slaps her on her butt, but if anything is going to wake her up, his breath will.

Surrounding these scenes is a plot more intriguing than they deserve, involving Edmond's old friend Kogi (Maximilian Schell), who advised him to visit the brothel in the first place. Kogi is concerned that Edmond is depressed by the death of his wife and young daughter in an auto accident. This happened fifteen years ago. I think the human ability to heal ourselves is such that, after fifteen years, you can expect to be sad and deeply regretful, but if you are still clinically depressed, you need medical attention.

It is also a wonder that this shambling sad sack and secret drinker is still apparently the head of a big corporation and has a full-time driver for his stretch BMW. Here is one tycoon who could definitely not be played by Michael Douglas. We've seen ultrarich Masters of the Universe before, but now we get the first Masturbator of the Universe.

The brothel is a one-bedroom operation supervised by Madame (Angela Winkler), a handsome woman of a certain age, who explains that the women have been "prepared" to sleep the whole night through, and the man is invited to sleep next to them (sleeping pills provided) and feast his eyes, or perhaps caress, but no funny business like sticking his finger in her mouth. Since Madame goes away all night, there's no telling what could happen to these helpless women, of course.

Do you find this premise anything but repugnant? It offends not only civilized members of both sexes, but even dirty old men, dramatizing as it does their dirtiness and oldness. Obvious questions arise, but, no, Madame will not explain why the women sleep so soundly, and the house rules strictly forbid any contact with the women outside the house. How does she find the women? Who are they? Why do they seem to sleep peacefully instead of as if they are drugged? How do they keep their hair and makeup impeccable? Why don't they snore?

Does Edmond get up to nastiness? There is a close-up of his tumescence, which looks younger and healthier than the rest of him, but no explicit sex. It hardly matters; the film is intended as allegory, although I am unsure what the allegory teaches us. Perhaps the message is: "You see what can happen to you if you direct and star yourself in a movie like this."

How to Lose Friends and Alienate People ★ ★ ★ ½
R, 110 m., 2008

Simon Pegg (Sidney Young), Kirsten Dunst (Alison Olsen), Megan Fox (Sophie Maes), Jeff Bridges (Clayton Harding), Gillian Anderson (Eleanor Johnson), Danny Huston (Lawrence Maddox). Directed by Robert B. Weide and produced by Stephen Woolley and Elizabeth Karlsen. Screenplay by Peter Straughan, based on the memoir by Toby Young.

When a film begins with the proud claim that it was "inspired by real events," the word "inspired" usually translates as "heavily rewritten from." I can't remember if How to Lose Friends and Alienate People even makes the claim. But it could fairly claim to be "inspired by real events so much more outrageous than anything in this movie that you wouldn't believe it."

I have been a follower of the real Toby Young for years. He is much more preposterous than "Sidney Young," the hero of this film, which is based on Toby's memoir. He first came to fame in the early '90s as coeditor of *Modern Review,* a British magazine devoted to

fierce criticism of everything but itself. The magazine ended in tabloid headlines after Young shut it down and traded savage insults with his coeditor, the equally famous Julie Burchill, who had left her husband and announced she was a lesbian. Young went on to fail sensationally as a writer for *Vanity Fair* and as a Hollywood screenwriter. He is currently back in London as drama critic for the *Spectator.* If I were a producer, I would hire security to keep him away from my opening nights or any other nights. However, I gather that, at forty-five, he has settled down a little.

I'm fond of British eccentrics. Consider Young's Wiki entry. He is the son of a baron, could legally call himself "the Honorable," studied at Oxford, Harvard, and Cambridge, went on to become Britain's favorite drunk since Jeffrey Bernard, and was described by *Private Eye* magazine as looking like "a peeled quail's egg dipped in celery salt." He has starred in West End comedies, one based on his book. He is a very funny writer, often providing inspiring material for himself. His father, a sociologist, created the term "meritocracy." The son defined demeritocracy. He's the kind of man you might enjoy having dinner with, but you wouldn't risk staying for dessert.

How to Lose Friends and Alienate People is "based on" his tumultuous employment at *Vanity Fair* magazine, where, yes, he really did send a strip-o-gram to the office on Bring Your Daughter to Work Day ("a regrettable mistake"). He blew through deadlines, vomited on people, wrecked parties, brushed with libel, suggested offensive story ideas, alienated the very celebrities he was paid to celebrate, and pulled off the neat trick of being shunned by most of the publicists in America.

How to Lose Friends and Alienate People is possibly the best movie that could be made about Toby Young that isn't rated NC-17. It stars Simon Pegg, who was born to play Young, just as Peter O'Toole was destined to play Jeffrey Bernard. On Young's first day at work at *Sharp's* magazine, he wears a T-shirt emblazoned: "Young, Dumb & Full of ——." (No dashes in the movie.) His editor, Clayton Harding (Jeff Bridges), hires him after he tries to sneak into a *Sharp's* party carrying a famous pig. I've known editors that tolerant.

When a reporter at the *Sun-Times* tried to hurl a chair through the editor's office window, the editor quietly asked him, "Any complaints about the interior decorating, Paul?" Full disclosure: That was the same editor who hired me. The rest of the story: The window was made of unbreakable plastic, and the chair rebounded, striking the reporter.

Back to the movie. Harding puts up with incredible behavior by Young, which can only be explained by drink, drugs, spectacularly bad judgment, lust, rampaging ambition, or a need to be the center of attention, however appalled. There is one woman at the office who can tolerate him. This is Alison Olsen (Kirsten Dunst), who writes the captions on photos (an important job at *Sharp's*). Young is too blinded by a fifteen-minutes-of-fame sexpot named Sophie (Megan Fox) to give Alison the time of day. Meanwhile, Alison is being manhandled by another editor, the unsavory and back-stabbing Maddox (Danny Huston, as oily as his old man could be).

What you'd expect from the upward-bound-young-man formula would be a Machiavellian schemer. What you get in *How to Lose Friends* is a flywheel who embarrasses his magazine at every opportunity. Why? He detests the celebrity culture he has been hired to write about and has some half-baked idea that he is attacking it through acts of self-destruction.

In a boring old world, such people are to be prized. I have met only one man I would back to be more outrageous than Toby Young, even though he is handicapped by not using drugs. His name is Jay Robert Nash. Those who know him would agree with me. He once walked into a saloon in a tiny mountain town in Colorado, where cowboys were not only drinking around the fire but had tethered their horses outside, and serenaded them with "Rhinestone Cowboy," and *meant well* by it. I saw this. It should be said that both Nash and Young are good fathers and nice men. I can't speak for Crosby and Stills.

Hunger ★ ★ ★ ½
NO MPAA RATING, 92 m., 2009

Michael Fassbender (Bobby Sands), Liam Cunningham (Father Dominic Moran), Stuart Graham (Raymond Lohan), Brian Milligan (Davey Gillen), Liam McMahon (Gerry Campbell). Directed by Steve McQueen and produced by Laura Hastings-Smith and Robin Gutch. Screenplay by McQueen and Enda Walsh.

It was a desperate business, and *Hunger* is a desperate film. It concerns the fierce battle between the Irish Republican Army and the British state, which in 1981 led to a hunger strike in which ten IRA prisoners died. The first of them was Bobby Sands, whose agonizing death is seen with an implacable, level gaze in the closing act of the film.

If you do not hold a position on the Irish Republican cause, you will not find one here. *Hunger* is not about the rights and wrongs of the British in Northern Ireland, but about inhuman prison conditions, the steeled determination of IRA members such as Bobby Sands, and a rock and a hard place. There is hardly a sentence in the film about Irish history or politics, and only two extended dialogue passages: one a long debate between Sands and a priest about the utility or futility of a hunger strike, the other a doctor's detailed description to Sands's parents about the effect of starvation on the human body.

There is not a conventional plot to draw us from beginning to end. Instead, director Steve McQueen, an artist who employs merciless realism, strikes three major chords. The first involves the daily routine of a prison guard (Stuart Graham), who is emotionally wounded by his work. The second involves two other prisoners (Brian Milligan and Liam McMahon), who participate in the IRA prisoners' refusal to wear prison clothes or bathe. The third involves the hunger strike.

This is clear: Neither side will back down. Twice we hear Prime Minister Margaret Thatcher describing the inmates of the Maze prison in Belfast as not political prisoners but criminals. The IRA considers itself political to the core. The ideology involved is not even mentioned in the extraordinary long dialogue scene, mostly in one shot, between Sands and a priest (Liam Cunningham) about whether a hunger strike will have the desired effect. The priest, worldly, a realist, on very civil terms with Sands, never once mentions suicide as a sin; he discusses it entirely in terms of its usefulness.

Sands thinks starvation to death will have an impact. The priest observes that if it does, Sands will by then be dead. His willingness to die reflects the bone-deep beliefs of Irish Republicans; recall the Irish song lyric, "And always remember, the longer we live, the sooner we bloody well die."

Sands's death is shown in a tableaux of increasing bleakness. It is agonizing, yet filmed with a curious painterly purity. It is alarming to note how much weight the actor Michael Fassbender lost; he went from 170 to 132 pounds. His dreams or visions or memories toward the end, based on a story he told the priest, would have been more effective if handled much more briefly.

Did the hunger strike succeed? After the remorseless death toll climbed to ten, Thatcher at last relented, tacitly granting the prisoners political recognition, although she refused to say so out loud. She was called the Iron Lady for a reason. Today there is peace in Northern Ireland. The island nation is still divided. Bobby Sands is dead. The priest has his conclusions, the dead man has his, or would if he were alive.

I

I Am Legend ★ ★ ★
PG-13, 114 m., 2007

Will Smith (Robert Neville), Alice Braga (Anna), Dash Mihok (Alpha Male), Charlie Tahan (Ethan), Salli Richardson (Zoe), Willow Smith (Marley). Directed by Francis Lawrence and produced by Akiva Goldsman, James Lassiter, David Heyman, and Neal Moritz. Screenplay by Mark Protosevich and Goldsman, based on the novel by Richard Matheson.

The opening scenes of *I Am Legend* have special effects so good that they just about compensate for some later special effects that are dicey. We see Manhattan three years after a deadly virus has killed every healthy human on the island, except one. The streets are overgrown with weeds, cars are abandoned, the infrastructure is beginning to collapse. Down one street a sports car races, driven by Robert Neville (Will Smith), who is trying to get a good shot at one of the deer roaming the city. He has worse luck than a lioness who competes with him.

Neville has only his dog to keep him company. He lives barricaded inside a house in Greenwich Village, its doors and windows sealed every night by heavy steel shutters. That's because after dark the streets are ruled by bands of predatory zombies—hairless creatures who were once human but have changed into savage, speechless killers with fangs for teeth. In his basement, Neville has a laboratory where he is desperately seeking a vaccine against the virus, which mutated from a cure for cancer.

The story is adapted from a 1954 sci-fi novel by Richard Matheson, which has been filmed twice before, as *The Last Man on Earth* (1964), starring Vincent Price, and *The Omega Man* (1971), starring Charlton Heston. In the original novel, which Stephen King says influenced him more than any other, Neville cultivated garlic and used mirrors, crosses, and sharpened stakes against his enemies, who were like traditional vampires, not super-strong zombies. I am not sure it is an advance to make him a scientist, arm him, and change the nature of the creatures; Matheson developed a kind of low-key realism that was doubly effective.

In *I Am Legend*, the situation raises questions of logic. If Neville firmly believes he is the last healthy man alive, who is the vaccine for? Only himself, I guess. Fair enough, although he faces a future of despair, no matter how long his cans of Spam and Dinty Moore beef stew hold out; dogs don't live forever. And how, I always wonder, do human beings in all their infinite shapes and sizes, mutate into identical pale zombies with infinite speed and strength?

Never mind. Given its setup, *I Am Legend* is well-constructed to involve us with Dr. Neville and his campaign to survive. There is, however, an event that breaks his spirit, and he cracks up—driving out at night to try to mow down as many zombies with his car as he can before they kill him. He is saved with a bright light by a young woman named Anna (Alice Braga), who is traveling with a boy named Ethan (Charlie Tahan).

He takes them home and she explains they are trying to get to a colony of survivors in Vermont. Neville doubts that such a colony exists. I doubt that she and the boy would venture through Manhattan to get there. Yes, she has doubtless heard his nonstop taped voice on all AM frequencies, asking to be contacted by any other survivors. But we have seen every bridge into Manhattan blown up in a quarantine of the island, so how did they get there? Boat? Why go to the risk?

Never mind again because Anna and the boy import dramatic interest into the story when it needs it. And director Francis Lawrence generates suspense effectively, even though it largely comes down to the monster movie staple of creatures leaping out of the dark, gnashing their fangs, and hammering at things. The special effects generating the zombies are not nearly as effective as the other effects in the film; they all look like creatures created for the sole purpose of providing the film with menace, and have no logic other than serving that purpose.

I Am Legend does contain memorable scenes, as when the island is being evacuated, and when Neville says good-bye to his wife and daughter (Salli Richardson and Willow Smith), and when he confides in his dog (who is not computer-generated—most of the time, anyway). And if it is true that mankind has one hundred years to live before we destroy our planet, it provides an enlightening vision of how Manhattan will look when it lives on without us. The movie works well while it's running, although it raises questions that later only mutate in our minds.

Illegal Tender ★ ★ ½
R, 105 m., 2007

Rick Gonzalez (Wilson Jr.), Wanda De Jesus (Millie DeLeon), Dania Ramirez (Ana), Jessica Pimentel (Young Millie), Manny Perez (Wilson DeLeon Sr.), Antonio Ortiz (Randy), Tego Calderon (Choco). Directed by Franc Reyes and produced by John Singleton. Screenplay by Reyes.

Even as the teenage girlfriend of a South Bronx drug dealer, Millie DeLeon is the investment adviser you'd want on your account. Without telling him, Millie invests his profits in Microsoft. This was in the late 1980s. "I only made one mistake," she tells her son years later. "I didn't buy enough."

What she bought, however, was enough to turn $2 million into a fortune, and as the story jumps forward twenty years, Millie (Wanda De Jesus) is living in an elegant suburban home, and one of her sons, Wilson DeLeon Jr. (Rick Gonzalez), is attending Danbury College, pulling down 4.0 grades, and is in love with a student named Ana (Dania Ramirez). He also dotes on his kid brother, Randy (Antonio Ortiz), who is by a different father, because Wilson DeLeon Sr. got gunned down in a Mob grudge on the day he was born.

They lead a life both comfortable and dangerous, as Millie realizes in the supermarket one day when she is spotted by a hit woman from her past. In a panic, she races home, tells the boys to start packing because they're moving again, and sets a revenge tragedy into motion.

Illegal Tender was written and directed by Franc Reyes, who is fascinated by the zero degrees of separation between low and high finance. Reyes's first film was *Empire* (2002),

about another young South Bronx kingpin who is fascinated by the lifestyle of a flashy Wall Street wunderkind. His protagonist this time comes closer to making an escape, but the bad guys from her boyfriend's past have long memories and more reasons than we think for wanting her and her family dead.

My advice to her would be twofold: Move to a suburb a lot farther away from the Bronx than Connecticut, and do not give your son his father's name with a "junior" tacked on. How many Wilson DeLeon Jr.s can there be who are not the offspring of *the* Wilson DeLeon?

Never mind. This movie is based on drama, not logic. Otherwise, four or five hit men would not come calling in broad daylight and open fire at the outside of the DeLeon house. Hit men are supposed to be cleverer than that, no? And is it possible they could all, every last one, be wiped out by a fortyish housewife and her son whose entire gun experience consists of shooting three cans off a rock in only about eleven shots? And all before the cops arrive? A running gun battle in a rich suburb usually gets a pretty quick response.

We're not thinking a lot about things like that, however, because the dynamic of the picture circles Wanda De Jesus and her passionate performance as a mother who wants to protect her family. The other main strand is how Wilson Jr. evolves in a short time from Joe College to his father's son. This journey takes him back to Puerto Rico and a search for his father's past.

"How come you speak such good Spanish?" the kingpin asks him. "I'm Puerto Rican," he says. "Yeah," says the kingpin, "but most Puerto Ricans from New York speak lousy Spanish." I wanted Wilson Jr. to explain, "Plus, I got a four-point average in Spanish at school."

Like *Empire, Illegal Tender* has the potential to be a better film than it is. Franc Reyes obviously wants to make a rags-to-riches story about a Puerto Rican kid from the streets who climbs the American financial ladder, and almost equally obviously doesn't want to sell it to Hollywood as a guns-and-drugs picture. I urge him to just go ahead and do it. The film's producer, John Singleton, whose own life has taken him from South Central to the top in Hollywood, would probably support him.

And if it's true that Reyes has his act so together that he shot this good-looking picture in only twenty-eight days, he could do it at the right price.

As it is, *Illegal Tender* works as a melodrama, and it benefits enormously from the performance of Wanda De Jesus. She isn't a big movie star, but is so good that she's cast by them and works with them in major roles; she costarred with Clint Eastwood in his *Blood Work*, has been cast in major roles by such as Michael Mann, Laurence Fishburne, and Joel Schumacher, is all over *CSI: Miami*, and has real screen presence. She sells us her character and her concerns, and with this screenplay, she has her work cut out for her.

I Love You, Man ★ ★ ★ ½
R, 104 m., 2009

Paul Rudd (Peter Klaven), Jason Segel (Sydney Fife), Rashida Jones (Zooey), Andy Samberg (Robbie), J. K. Simmons (Oz), Jane Curtin (Joyce), Jon Favreau (Barry), Jaime Pressly (Denise). Directed by John Hamburg and produced by Hamburg and Donald De Line. Screenplay by Hamburg and Larry Levin.

I would like to have a friend like Sydney Fife. I think a lot of guys would. Even though it's funny, charming, and lighthearted, that may be the basic appeal of *I Love You, Man*. Sydney represents the freedoms most men hesitate to give themselves, maybe through fear of ending up alone, arrested, or locked inside behavior that looks fun when you're young but crazy when you're older. The great thing about Sydney is that he lives your fantasies so you don't have to yourself.

Peter needs a Sydney (Jason Segel) in his life. He has been told this by Zooey (Rashida Jones), the girl he plans to marry. She would, however, have preferred a less extreme case than *this* Sydney. Peter (Paul Rudd) is a Realtor who is hopelessly, even touchingly, clueless when it comes to seeming the least bit cool. One of those really nice guys who, when the chips are down, has no idea where to look, what to say, how to move, or how to extricate himself gracefully from an impossible situation. He gets along great with women but has no male best friend, and actually needs to find one to be best man at his wedding.

Because this is a romcom, various obligatory scenes are necessary; Peter goes shopping for a best friend on some man-dates with guys met on the Internet, with predictable results. The movie feels locked into formula until the appearance of Sydney, met while scarfing free food at Peter's open house for the home of Lou Ferrigno. Jason Segel brings sunshine into the movie; we like his character even more quickly than Peter does.

Sydney lives in a little frame cottage a block up the street from the Venice Beach boardwalk. This house was cheap in, oh, say, the Depression. Now it only looks cheap. We never see its interior; Sydney escorts Peter directly to his "man cave," a converted garage in the backyard where he keeps all his toys: drum set, guitars, music system, flat-screen TV, movie posters, lava lamps, weird souvenirs, recliner chairs, wet bar, fridge, wall hangings, even an area dedicated to . . . well, never mind.

Jason Segel plays Sydney as a man thoroughly comfortable within his own skin, an unapologetic hedonist who uses his intelligence as a comic weapon. Essentially, the whole movie is based on the fact that he is able to create an actually plausible, human best friend. Incredibly, this is the first time I'm aware of seeing him in a movie. I apparently saw him in *SLC Punk!* and *Slackers* (zero stars), but never saw his recent *Forgetting Sarah Marshall*. I think he's a natural for Walter Matthau, and both Segel and Rudd would be perfect for a SoCal retread of the classic British one-upmanship comedy *School for Scoundrels*.

Rudd is also very good and very funny, using delicate timing to create a man who is never quite right for the room. Observe his attempts to look loose and casual. He even pulls off sincere scenes with the lovely Rashida Jones, and sincerity, as we know, is the downfall of many a romcom and almost all buddy movies. I believe my Little Movie Glossary even contains an entry about an obligatory moment in all buddy movies in which one of the characters says, you guessed it, "I love you, man."

John Hamburg, who cowrote and directed, populates his film with many other gifted comedy actors, including J. K. Simmons as

Peter's father, Jane Curtin as his mother, Andy Samberg as his gay brother, and Jon Favreau and Jaime Pressly as a married couple from hell—their own. Lou Ferrigno finds the right note as the client about to fire his Realtor, who has asked himself the question, "How many people want to buy a mansion in Beverly Hills with a statue of the Incredible Hulk in the garden?"

I Love You, Man is above all just plain funny. It's funny with some dumb physical humor, yes, and some gross-out jokes apparently necessary to all buddy movies, but also funny in observations, dialogue, physical behavior, and Sydney Fife's observations as a people watcher. I heard a lot of *real* laughter from a preview audience, not the perfunctory laughter at manufactured payoffs. You feel good watching the movie. That's what comedies are for, right? Right?   ☞

Imagine That ★ ★ ½
PG, 107 m., 2009

Eddie Murphy (Evan Danielson), Thomas Haden Church (Johnny Whitefeather), Yara Shahidi (Olivia Danielson), Nicole Ari Parker (Trish), Ronny Cox (Tom Stevens), Martin Sheen (Dante D'Enzo), DeRay Davis (John Strother). Directed by Karey Kirkpatrick and produced by Ed Solomon and Lorenzo di Bonaventura. Screenplay by Solomon and Chris Matheson.

Eddie Murphy's new family comedy is a pleasant and unassuming fantasy in which a high-powered investment adviser gets advice from his daughter's imaginary friends. We never see the friends, but we see a great deal of the daughter, and it's a charming performance from newcomer Yara Shahidi.

She plays Olivia, seven years old, who doesn't see nearly enough of her daddy. He is Evan Danielson (Murphy), who is competing for a big promotion at his Denver investment firm. Olivia is being raised by his former wife, Trish (Nicole Ari Parker), who insists it is time for the child to spend some quality time with her father.

Evan is not well equipped to handle this, or much of anything else apart from his job. He can't find babysitters, takes the kid to the office, and to his horror discovers she has drawn with water paints all over his notes and charts for a crucial meeting. It does not go well. He's upstaged by Johnny Whitefeather (Thomas Haden Church), a Native American who evokes the great spirits and Indian legends to convince the clients the force is with him.

In response, Murphy does one of his semicomic riffs, desperately improvising advice from the stories Olivia told him about her drawings. He returns to his office expecting to be fired, but, amazingly the advice turns out to be solid gold. But how did he do that? What did Olivia know? She knew what a fairy princess told her, and she can see her imaginary world when she has her precious blue blankie over her head. Evan doesn't know what else to do, so he starts turning to Olivia for more investment tips, and she's right again and again.

The movie is amusing without ever being break-out funny—except for one scene, loudly appreciated by the kiddies in the audience, when he makes pancakes and Olivia insists he eat them covered with gobs of ketchup, mustard, chocolate sauce, and hot sauce. Kids may not get all the verbal jokes, but playing with food, they understand.

Murphy stays interestingly in character, not going over the top. He does his usual rapid-fire dialogue and desperate invention, but more sanely than usual. The film is really about the father-daughter relationship, and Murphy comes through as sincere, confused, lonely, and with a good heart.

The key to the chemistry between them is Yara Shahidi's work as the daughter. Apparently she really is seven, and her previous experience is limited to three episodes of *In the Motherhood*. She's a natural. I never caught her trying to be "cute." She played every scene straight and with confidence, and she's filled with personality. I've been noticing recently how good the child actors are in movies. Maybe they grow up inputting acting from TV. I wonder why not all young actors can bring this gift with them into adulthood. To paraphrase e.e. cummings: And down they forgot as up they grew.

The third major role, by Thomas Haden Church, is an interesting invention: an Indian con man, trading on his background to score points in the boardroom, steamrolling the clients with his people's lore. This is funny. Is it offensive? Not when we find out more about Johnny Whitefeather.

So all of these elements are present in the film and supply nice moments, but director Karey Kirkpatrick, the writer of animated films such as *Chicken Run* and *Over the Hedge,* never brings them to takeoff velocity. They rest on the screen, pleasant, amusing, but too predictable for grown-ups and not broad enough for children. I couldn't believe *Imagine This* counts on one of the most exhausted clichés in the movies, the parent making a dramatic late entrance to a child's big concert.

Still, think about this: If the investment gurus of Wall Street had turned to their kids for advice, we might not be in such a mess.

I'm Not There ★ ★ ★ ½
R, 135 m., 2007

Christian Bale (Jack/Pastor John), Cate Blanchett (Jude), Marcus Carl Franklin (Woody), Richard Gere (Billy), Heath Ledger (Robbie), Ben Whishaw (Arthur), Charlotte Gainsbourg (Claire), David Cross (Allen Ginsberg), Bruce Greenwood (Keenan Jones), Julianne Moore (Alice Fabian), Michelle Williams (Coco Rivington). Directed by Todd Haynes and produced by James D. Stern, John Sloss, John Goldwyn, and Christian Vachon. Screenplay by Haynes and Oren Moverman.

I'm Not There is an attempt to consider the contradictions of Bob Dylan by building itself upon contradictions. Maybe that's the only way to do it. If you made a biopic with Dylan played by the same actor all the way through, it might become the portrait of a shape-shifting schizophrenic. Todd Haynes's approach is to create six or seven Dylans, depending on how you count, and use six actors to play them. This way each Dylan is consistent on his own terms, and the life as a whole need not hold together.

There are so many Bob Dylans that it is difficult to sort out which ones you admire, and which you despise. I spent years disliking Dylan on the basis of the 1967 D. A. Pennebaker documentary *Don't Look Back,* and then underwent a conversion after seeing Martin Scorsese's 2005 doc *No Direction Home: Bob Dylan.* But what was either film but the portrait of a possible Dylan? No considerable artist since B. Traven has spent more effort concealing his tracks and covering his trail, and at the end of the day we are left with the music, which is all the artist really owes us.

If you are not much familiar with Dylan, this film is likely to confuse or baffle. If, like me, you know both of the documentaries well, have read some of the legends, have seen him in concert, and have been colonized by some of his songs, you are likely to respond with a wry admiration for the enormous risks Todd Haynes has taken here. As in his very different previous film, *Far from Heaven,* he is essentially remaking cinema to reveal what it is really trying and achieving. *Far from Heaven* exposed the gay subtext of 1950s Douglas Sirk melodramas, and *I'm Not There* shows how the other docs of Dylan have imposed consistency upon an elusive and mercurial person. What Haynes does is take away the reassuring segues that argue everything flows and makes sense, and show what's really chaos under the skin of the film.

He achieves that here by casting six actors in the role of Bob Dylan (real name Robert Allen Zimmerman, so the disguises begin before the movie). One of the actors is a young African-American boy (Marcus Carl Franklin) who claims to be Woody Guthrie; a second is Jack, a Greenwich Village folksinger (Christian Bale); a third is Robbie (Heath Ledger), appearing in a Hollywood film, who settles down, gets married, and has kids; a fourth is Jude (Cate Blanchett), a hero who alienated his fans by switching from acoustic to electric guitar and from folk to folk-rock; a fifth is an actor (Richard Gere) appearing in a Western about Billy the Kid; a sixth is a Dylan (Ben Whislaw) submitting to a contentious interview about his career, and then we double back to Christian Bale again, who plays either a seventh or a transformation of the first, Pastor John, a born-again Christian.

No effort is made to explain how these Dylans are connected, which is the point, I think. Dylanologists will recognize scenes inspired by specific moments in the singer's career and even specific shots on film; Blanchett is uncanny at embodying the Dylan of *Don't Look Back.* Bale is on target as the young Dylan who traveled from Minneapolis to Greenwich Village and reinvented himself as the heir to Woody Guthrie, but even then there may be deception; a 2000 documentary named *The Ballad of Ramblin' Jack* argues that Dylan was a copycat of Guthrie's original heir, Ramblin' Jack Elliott. Arlo Guthrie credits Ramblin' Jack with teaching him his father's music.

Dylan did appear in Sam Peckinpah's *Pat Garrett and Billy the Kid*, although not as Billy. He did convert to Christianity. Point by point, you can connect the Dylans in the film to chapters in the singer's life. And there is no difficulty in recognizing that a folksinger named Alice Fabian (Julianne Moore) represents Joan Baez, who felt betrayed by the young talent she had opened doors for. And that Claire (Charlotte Gainsbourg) represents Dylan's wife, Sara. And Allen Ginsberg (David Cross) is named Allen Ginsberg, so no problem there.

By creating this kaleidoscope of Dylans, Haynes makes a portrait not of the singer but of our perceptions. There is a parallel in Oliver Stone's *JFK*, which I think was intended not as a solution of the Kennedy assassination but as a record of our paranoia about it. And there is another work that seems relevant: Francois Girard's brilliant 1993 film *32 Short Films About Glenn Gould*, which uses actors to re-create a series of real and imagined scenes in the life of the reclusive Canadian pianist.

Coming away from *I'm Not There*, we have, first of all, heard some great music (Dylan surprisingly authorized use of his songs, both his own recordings and performed by others). We've seen six gifted actors challenged by playing facets of a complete man. We've seen a daring attempt at biography as collage. We've remained baffled by the Richard Gere cowboy sequence, which doesn't seem to know its purpose. And we have been left not one step closer to comprehending Bob Dylan, which is as it should be.

In Bruges ★ ★ ★ ★
R, 107 m., 2008

Colin Farrell (Ray), Brendan Gleeson (Ken), Ralph Fiennes (Harry), Clemence Poesy (Chloe), Jeremie Renier (Erik), Thekla Reuten (Marie), Jordan Prentice (Jimmy). Directed by Martin McDonagh and produced by Graham Broadbent and Pete Czernin. Screenplay by McDonagh.

You may know that Bruges, Belgium, is pronounced *broozh*, but I didn't, and the heroes of *In Bruges* certainly don't. They're Dublin hit men, sent there by their boss for two weeks after a hit goes very wrong. One is a young hothead who sees no reason to be anywhere but Dublin; the other, older, gentler, more curious, buys a guide book and announces: "Bruges is the best-preserved medieval city in Belgium!"

So it certainly seems. If the movie accomplished nothing else, it inspired in me an urgent desire to visit Bruges. But it accomplished a lot more than that. This film debut by the theater writer and director Martin McDonagh is an endlessly surprising, very dark human comedy, with a plot that cannot be foreseen but only relished. Every once in a while you find a film like this that seems to happen as it goes along, driven by the peculiarities of the characters.

Brendan Gleeson, with that noble shambles of a face and the heft of a boxer gone to seed, has the key role as Ken, one of two killers for hire. His traveling companion and unwilling roommate is Ray (Colin Farrell), who successfully whacked a priest in a Dublin confessional but tragically killed a little boy in the process. Before shooting the priest, he confessed to the sin he was about to commit. After accidentally killing the boy, he reads the notes the lad made for his own confession. You don't know whether to laugh or cry.

Ken and Ray work for Harry, apparently a Dublin crime lord, who for the first two-thirds of the movie we hear only over the phone, until he materializes in Bruges and turns out to be a worried-looking Ralph Fiennes. He had the men hiding out in London, but that wasn't far enough away. Who would look for them in Bruges? Who would even look for Bruges? Killing the priest was business, but "blowing a kid's head off just isn't done."

The movie does an interesting thing with Bruges. It shows us a breathtakingly beautiful city without ever seeming to be a travelogue. It uses the city as a way to develop the characters. When Ken wants to climb an old tower "for the view," Ray argues, "Why do I have to climb up there to see down here? I'm already down here." He is likewise unimpressed by glorious paintings, macabre sculptures, and picturesque canals, but is thrilled as a kid when he comes upon a film being shot.

There he meets two fascinating characters: First he sees the fetching young blonde Chloe (Clemence Poesy, who was Fleur Delacour in *Harry Potter and the Goblet of Fire*). Then he sees Jimmy (Jordan Prentice), a dwarf who figures in a dream sequence. He gets off on a bad footing with both, but eventually they're doing cocaine with a prostitute Jimmy picked up and have become friends, even though Ray keeps calling the dwarf a "midget" and having to be corrected.

Without dreaming of telling you what happens next, I will say it is not only ingenious but almost inevitable the way the screenplay brings all of these destinies together at one place and time. Along the way, there are times of great sadness and poignancy, times of abandon, times of goofiness, and that kind of humor that is *really funny* because it grows out of character and close observation. Colin Farrell in particular hasn't been this good in a few films, perhaps because this time he's allowed to relax and be Irish. As for Brendan Gleeson, if you remember him in *The General,* you know that nobody can play a more sympathetic bad guy.

Martin McDonagh is greatly respected in Ireland and England for his plays; his first film, a short named *Six Shooter* starring Gleeson, won a 2006 Oscar. In his feature debut, he has made a remarkable first film, as impressive in its own way as *House of Games,* the first film by David Mamet, whom McDonagh is sometimes compared with. Yes, it's a "thriller," but one where the ending seems determined by character and upbringing rather than plot requirements. Two of the final deaths are, in fact, ethical choices. And the irony inspiring the second one has an undeniable logic, showing that even professional murderers have their feelings.

The Incredible Hulk ★ ★ ½
PG-13, 114 m., 2008

Edward Norton (Bruce Banner), Liv Tyler (Betty Ross), Tim Roth (Emil Blonsky), Tim Blake Nelson (Samuel Sterns), Ty Burrell (Dr. Samson), William Hurt (General Ross), Lou Ferrigno (Voice of Hulk). Directed by Louis Leterrier and produced by Avi Arad, Kevin Feige, and Gale Anne Hurd. Screenplay by Zak Penn and Edward Norton, based on the Marvel comic books by Stan Lee and Jack Kirby.

The Incredible Hulk is no doubt an ideal version of the Hulk saga for those who found Ang Lee's *Hulk* (2003) too talky or, dare I say, too thoughtful. But not for me. It sidesteps the intriguing aspects of Hulkdom and spends way too much time in, dare I say, noisy and mindless action sequences. By the time the Incredible Hulk had completed his hulk-on-hulk showdown with the Incredible Blonsky, I had been using my Timex with the illuminated dial way too often.

Consider the dilemma of creating a story about the Hulk, who is one of the lesser creatures in the Marvel Comics stable. You're dealing with two different characters: mild-mannered scientist Dr. Bruce Banner and the rampaging, destructive Hulk, who goes into frenzies of aggression whenever he's annoyed, which is frequently, because the army is usually unloading automatic weapons into him. There is even the interesting question of whether Dr. Banner is really conscious inside the Hulk. In the Ang Lee version, he was, more or less, and confessed to Betty Ross: "When it happens, when it comes over me, when I totally lose control . . . I like it." In this 2008 version by Louis Leterrier, the best Banner can come up with is that being the Hulk is like a hyperthyroid acid trip, and all he can remember are fragments of moments.

It's obvious that the real story is the tragedy that Bruce Banner faces because of the Hulk-inducing substance in his blood. If Banner never turned into the Hulk, nobody would ever make a movie about him. And if the Hulk were never Banner, he would be like Godzilla, who tears things up real good but is otherwise, dare I say, one-dimensional.

The Ang Lee version was rather brilliant in the way it turned the Hulk story into matching sets of parent-child conflicts: Betty Ross (Jennifer Connelly) was appalled by her father the general (Sam Elliott), and Bruce Banner (Eric Bana) suffered at the hands of his father, a scientist who originally created the Hulk genes and passed them along to his child. (Nick Nolte had nice scenes as the elder Dr. Banner.)

In the new version, Betty (Liv Tyler) still has big problems with her father the general (William Hurt); she's appalled by his plans to harness the Hulk formula and create a race of super-soldiers. In both films, Banner (Ed Norton) and Ross are in love but don't act on it because the Hulk business complicates things way too much, although I admit there's a clever moment in *Hulk* 2008 when Bruce interrupts his big chance to make love with Betty because when he gets too excited, he turns into the Hulk, and Betty is a brave girl but not that good of a sport.

Consider for a moment General Ross's idea of turning out Hulk soldiers. They would be a drill sergeant's worst nightmare. When they weren't Hulks, why bother to train them? You'd only be using them in the fullness of their Hulkdom, and *then* how would you train them? Would you just drop thousands of Ed Nortons into enemy territory and count on them getting so excited by free fall that they became Hulks? (This transformation actually happens to Banner in *Hulk* 2008, by the way.)

So. What's to like in *The Incredible Hulk?* We have a sound performance by Ed Norton as a man who desperately does not want to become the Hulk and goes to Brazil to study under a master of breath control in order to curb his anger. And we have Liv Tyler in full, trembling sympathy mode. Banner's Brazilian sojourn begins with an astonishing shot: From an aerial viewpoint, we fly higher and higher above one of the hill cities of Rio, seeing hundreds, thousands, of tiny houses built on top of one another, all clawing for air. This is the *City of God* neighborhood, and as nearly as I could tell, we were looking at the real thing, not CGI. The director lets the shot run on longer than any reasonable requirement of the plot; my bet is, he was as astonished as I was, and let it run because it was so damned amazing.

The scenes involving Banner in Brazil are well conceived, although when he accidentally contaminates a bottled soft drink with his blood, the movie doesn't really deal with the consequences when the drink is consumed in the United States. The contamination pro- vides General Ross with his clue to Banner's whereabouts, and army troops blast the hell out of the City of God; all through the movie, the general deploys his firepower so recklessly that you wonder if he has a superior, and if he ever has to account for the dozens, hundreds, thousands, who die while his guys are blasting at the Hulk with absolutely no effect.

Enter Emil Blonsky (Tim Roth), a marine General Ross recruits because he's meaner and deadlier than anyone else. Blonsky leads the chase in Rio. Later, Banner's research associate Dr. Samuel Sterns (Tim Blake Nelson) is forced to inject Blonsky with a little Hulkie juice, setting up a titanic rooftop battle in Harlem between Hulk and Blonsky. And this battle, as I have suggested, pounds away relentlessly, taking as its first victim our patience. *Iron Man,* the much better spiritual partner of this film, also ended with a showdown between an original and a copycat, but it involved two opponents who knew who they were and why they were fighting. When you get down to it, as a fictional creature, the Incredible Hulk is as limited as a bad drunk. He may be fun to be around when he's sober, but when he drinks too much, you just feel sorry for the guy. ☞

Indiana Jones and the Kingdom of the Crystal Skull ★ ★ ★ ½
PG-13, 124 m., 2008

Harrison Ford (Indiana Jones), Cate Blanchett (Irina Spalko), Karen Allen (Marion Ravenwood), Ray Winstone (George "Mac" McHale), John Hurt (Professor Oxley), Jim Broadbent (Dean Stanforth), Shia LaBeouf (Mutt Williams). Directed by Steven Spielberg and produced by Frank Marshall. Screenplay by David Koepp.

Indiana Jones and the Kingdom of the Crystal Skull. Say it aloud. The very title causes the pulse to quicken, if you, like me, are a lover of pulp fiction. What I want is goofy action— lots of it. I want man-eating ants, swordfights between two people balanced on the backs of speeding jeeps, subterranean caverns of gold, vicious femme fatales, plunges down three waterfalls in a row, and the explanation for flying saucers. And throw in lots of monkeys.

The Indiana Jones movies were directed by Steven Spielberg and written by George Lucas and a small army of screenwriters, but they exist in a universe of their own. Hell, they created it. All you can do is compare one to the other three. And even then, what will it get you? If you eat four pounds of sausage, how do you choose which pound tasted the best? Well, the first one, of course, and then there's a steady drop-off of interest. That's why no Indy adventure can match *Raiders of the Lost Ark* (1981). But if *Crystal Skull* (or *Temple of Doom* from 1984 or *Last Crusade* from 1989) had come first in the series, who knows how much fresher it might have seemed? True, *Raiders of the Lost Ark* stands alone as an action masterpiece, but after that the series is *compelled* to be, in the words of Indiana himself, "same old same old." Yes, but that's what I *want* it to be.

Crystal Skull even dusts off the Russians, so severely underexploited in recent years, as the bad guys. Up against them, Indiana Jones is once again played by Harrison Ford, who is now sixty-five but looks a lot like he did at fifty-five or forty-six, which is how old he was when he made *Last Crusade*. He has one of those Robert Mitchum faces that don't age; it only frowns more. He and his sidekick, Mac McHale (Ray Winstone), are taken by the cool, contemptuous Soviet uber-villainess Irina Spalko (Cate Blanchett) to a cavernous warehouse to seek out a crate he saw there years ago. The contents of the crate are hyper-magnetic (lord, I love this stuff) and betray themselves when Indy throws a handful of gunpowder into the air.

In ways too labyrinthine to describe, the crate leads Indy, Mac, Irina, and the Russians far up the Amazon. Along the way they've gathered Marion Ravenwood (Karen Allen), Indy's girlfriend from the first film, and a young biker named Mutt Williams (Shia LaBeouf), who is always combing his ducktail haircut. They also acquire Professor Oxley (John Hurt), elderly colleague from the University of Chicago, whose function is to read all the necessary languages, know all the necessary background, and explain everything.

What happens in South America is explained by the need to create (1) sensational chase sequences and (2) awe-inspiring specta-

cles. We get such sights as two dueling jeep-like vehicles racing down parallel roads. Not many of the audience members will be as logical as I am and wonder who went to the trouble of building *parallel* roads in a rain forest. Most of the major characters eventually find themselves at the wheels of both vehicles; they leap or are thrown from one to another, and the vehicles occasionally leap right over each other. And that Irina, she's something. Her Russian backups are mostly just atmosphere, useful for pointing their rifles at Indy, but she can fight, shoot, fence, drive, leap, and kick, and keep on all night.

All leads to the discovery of a subterranean chamber beneath an ancient pyramid, where they find an ancient city made of gold and containing . . . but wait, I forgot to tell you they found a crystal skull in a crypt. Well, sir, it's one of thirteen crystal skulls, and the other twelve are in that chamber. When the set is complete, amazing events take place. Professor Oxley carries the thirteenth skull for most of the time, and finds it repels man-eating ants. It also represents one-thirteenth of all knowledge about everything, leading Irina to utter the orgasmic words, "I want to *know!*" In appearance, the skull is a cross between the aliens of the special edition of Spielberg's *Close Encounters of the Third Kind* and the hood ornaments of 1950s Pontiacs.

What is the function of the chamber? "It's a portal—to another dimension!" Oxley says. Indy is sensible: "I don't think we wanna go that way." It is astonishing that the protagonists aren't all killed twenty or thirty times, although Irina will become The Woman Who Knew Too Much. At his advanced age, Professor Oxley tirelessly jumps between vehicles, survives fire and flood and falling from great heights, and would win on *American Gladiators*. Relationships between certain other characters are of interest, since (a) the odds against them finding themselves together are astronomical, and (b) the odds against them *not* finding themselves together in this film are incalculable.

Now what else can I tell you, apart from mentioning the blinking red digital countdown, and the moving red line tracing a journey on a map? I can say that if you liked the other Indiana Jones movies, you will like this one, and that if you did not, there is no talking to you. And I can also say that a critic trying to place it in a hierarchy with the others would probably keep a straight face while recommending the second pound of sausage.

The Informers ★ ★ ½
R, 98 m., 2009

Billy Bob Thornton (William Sloan), Kim Basinger (Laura Sloan), Winona Ryder (Cheryl Moore), Mickey Rourke (Peter), Jon Foster (Graham Sloan), Amber Heard (Christie), Austin Nichols (Martin), Lou Taylor Pucci (Tim Price), Brad Renfro (Jack), Chris Isaak (Les Price), Mel Raido (Bryan Metro), Rhys Ifans (Roger). Directed by Gregor Jordan and produced by Marco Weber. Screenplay by Bret Easton Ellis and Nicholas Jarecki, from the novel by Ellis.

The Informers is about dread, despair, and doom, and its characters are almost all about to be hit with more reasons for dread and despair, and a shared doom. It takes place in the Los Angeles showbiz drug subculture circa 1983, when AIDS didn't have a name and cocaine looked like the answer to something. It demonstrates the eerie ways that music and movies connect people from vastly different lives in a subterranean way where desire is the common currency.

What do they desire? Drugs, sex, power, wealth, and fame or its proximity. These things have made their lives hollow daily punishments, treatable only by oblivion. One character, in a moment of desperate need, says, "All I want is someone to tell me what is good, and someone to tell me what is bad." Hemingway told him, if he had been listening: "What is moral is what you feel good after, and what is immoral is what you feel bad after."

As nearly as I can recall, none of the characters ever feels happy. They're all pitiful, some are evil, the rest are helpless. There may be a few who are bystanders, like the anchorwoman, but even she's guilty of sleeping with a married studio chief primarily because of who he is. Almost everyone in this film is connected by sexual partners, sometimes in ways they never suspect.

The film, based on work by Bret Easton Ellis, takes place in his usual world of hedonistic excess. It tells many interweaving stories and is skillfully cast with actors who embody precisely what their roles call for. What common needs can link characters played by Billy Bob Thornton, Kim Basinger, Mickey Rourke, Winona Ryder, Lou Taylor Pucci, Amber Heard, Chris Isaak, Jon Foster, Brad Renfro, and Rhys Ifans? See paragraph two.

The scenes cycle through parties, famous restaurants, studio offices, TV news sets, Mulholland Drive, beaches, and beds. A lot of beds, often populated by bisexual threesomes. Thornton is the studio head, Basinger is his pill-popping wife, Ryder is the newswoman. Basinger uses a male prostitute who is one of the threesomes. Thornton's children despise him.

There is a wasted rock singer in the film (Mel Raido) who thinks he might once have lived in L.A. He vaguely realizes at times where he is and what he is doing. A father (Isaak) who takes his son to Hawaii, suspects the kid might be gay, approves when he invites a girl to dinner, then tries to pick her up. A wasted night clerk (Brad Renfro) who hopes to be an actor, ends up being victimized by his loathsome uncle (Rourke) into possibly (not certainly) committing a monstrous act. A young girl (Heard) who sleeps with anyone, more or less out of indifference.

There is no hope in this world. No frogs falling from the sky. I have met a few people like this and imagine they tend to meet one another. Their humanity has been burnt right out. Bret Easton Ellis is sometimes described as the poet of beautiful blond people whose lives are devoted to making themselves and others miserable. True enough. The most intimate, and startling, scene between Thornton and Basinger involves him requesting something disgusting (not sexual) and her providing it, while they're both preoccupied with whether they can ever live together again, or even want to. The fact that this service she provides takes place without discussion suggests the numbness of their souls.

If *The Informers* doesn't sound to you like a pleasant time at the movies, you are right. To repeat: dread, despair, and doom. It is often, however, repulsively fascinating, and has been directed by Gregor Jordan as a soap opera from hell, with good sets and costumes.

If he finds no depths in the characters, well, what depths are there? What you see is what you get. Sometimes less than that. Some viewers of *The Informers* criticize it for lacking a third act, but these lives are all two-act plays.

Note: Brad Renfro, who once played Huck Finn, died of a heroin overdose on January 15, 2008. He was twenty-five. He is actually very good here, in a role he possibly never dreamed of playing.

Inkheart ★ ★

PG, 105 m., 2009

Brendan Fraser (Mo Folchart), Paul Bettany (Dustfinger), Helen Mirren (Elinor Loredan), Jim Broadbent (Fenoglio), Andy Serkis (Capricorn), Eliza Hope Bennett (Meggie), Rafi Gavron (Farid), Sienna Guillory (Resa). Directed by Iain Softley and produced by Softley, Cornelia Funke, and Diana Pokorny. Screenplay by David Lindsay-Abaire, based on the novel by Funke.

I never knew reading was so dangerous. No child seeing *Inkheart* will ever want to be read to again, especially if that child loves its mother, as so many do. Here is a film about a man named Mo who, when he reads aloud, has the power of liberating fictional characters into the real world. The drawback is that real people are trapped within the same book. Tit for tat. A law of physics must apply.

The film opens with its best scene, for me, anyway: the professional book buyer Mo (Brendan Fraser) and his twelve-year-old daughter, Meggie (Eliza Hope Bennett), poking through an open-air book market. As always I was trying to read the titles on the spines. Not realizing that *Inkheart* is based on a famous fantasy novel, I had the foolish hope the movie might be about books. No luck. Wait till you hear what it's about.

At the edge of the market is a dark little bookstore presided over by a dark little man. As Mo prowls its aisles, he hears the faint chatter of fictional characters calling to him. (Dictionaries must be almost impossible to shut up.) Sixth sense leads him to discover, on an obscure shelf, the novel *Inkheart,* in the format of a Penguin mystery from the 1950s. He buys it, slips it into his pocket, and the two of them are followed by a mysterious skulking man.

We discover this is the very book Mo was reading when his wife, Meggie's mother (Sienna Guillory), was sucked into its pages, and that is the true story, Meggie, of how your mom suddenly disappeared when you were little. Yeah, right, Dad. At the same time, various demonic creatures were liberated from the book's pages. They have now set up shop in a mountaintop castle and are conspiring to command Mo's power now that he has discovered their book again. Do they want to return to its pages, or be reunited with old chums in the real world? And how do you get a mortgage to buy a castle when you're a demonic creature and your résumé mentions only fictional adventures in an out-of-print book? The banks must have been lending carelessly there awhile back.

Mo and Meggie take refuge in a cliffside mansion occupied by her great-aunt Elinor (Helen Mirren). Mansion? Looks to me like a dreamy tourist hotel from a Merchant-Ivory production. Elinor is a nasty scold who always wears a turban, the reliable standby of the actress tired of having her hair fussed over every second. I hope good Dame Helen passed this tip along to young Eliza Hope Bennett, who shows every sign of becoming an accomplished actress.

The movie now descends into the realm of your basic good guys vs. wrathful wraiths formula, with pitched battles and skullduggery. The villains are Dustfinger (Paul Bettany) and the ambitious Capricorn (Andy Serkis), and there is always the threat of Mo and Meggie being transmogrified into the pages of the book. There they'd at least have the company of the missing mom and the shabby author Fenoglio (Jim Broadbent), who wrote the novel within *Inkheart,* and apparently was only set free to rise up one level, to the novel containing his novel. Thanks for nothing.

Lots of screams, horrible fates almost happening, close scrapes, cries for help, special effects, monomania, quick thinking, pluck, fear, and scrambling. You know the kinds of stuff. I learn there are two more novels in this series by Cornelia Funke, both of which will remain just as unread by me as the first. It is hard to guess what they will involve, however, because this one closes with a curiously cobbled-together ending that seems to solve everything, possibly as a talisman against a sequel.

In Search of a Midnight Kiss ★ ★ ★ ½
NO MPAA RATING, 100 m., 2008

Scoot McNairy (Wilson), Sara Simmonds (Vivian), Brian Matthew McGuire (Jacob), Katy Luong (Min), Twink Caplan (Wilson's Mom), Nic Harcourt (Radio DJ). Directed by Alex Holdridge and produced by Seth Caplan and Scoot McNairy. Screenplay by Holdridge.

Let's begin with the actors. Sara Simmonds is a pretty girl, and Scoot McNairy is a good-looking guy. But neither one is improbably attractive. In their story, which begins before sunset and ends after sunrise, if you get my drift, they're no Julie Delpy and Ethan Hawke. If they were, they wouldn't be looking for a date on the afternoon of December 31. Simmonds and McNairy look, act, speak, and have thoughts that uncannily resemble life: We believe these could be real people. Yes, Delpy and Hawke are real people, too, but not anyone we'd ever hope to be.

McNairy plays Wilson, who begins New Year's Eve on an unpromising note by masturbating before a Photoshopped computer image of his roommate's girlfriend. He is discovered by the roommate and the girlfriend. Awkward. Min (Katy Luong) claims she's sort of flattered. Jacob (Brian Matthew McGuire) decides Wilson clearly needs a date and suggests a posting on Craigslist. "Misanthrope seeks misanthrope," Wilson bitterly types. He gets a call from Vivian (Simmonds). She is interviewing candidates because she doesn't want to spend the Eve with a loser.

In the sidewalk café where Wilson's audition begins, Vivian comes across as a furiously smoking, aggressive put-down artist. She claims she's seventeen, then accuses Wilson of being a mental statutory rapist, then says she's twenty-seven. Their conversation goes sort of OK after that, and she gives him until 6 p.m. before she calls in another candidate.

At this point we think their date will be very short and blood may be shed. Then begins a long day's journey through the night, choreographed with delicacy, some humor, some pathos by writer-director Alex Holdridge, and photographed in glorious black-and-white by

Robert Murphy. Taking the subway, they wander around downtown L.A., including the Sheridan Square area haunted by abandoned and shuttered movie palaces. On the stage of one of them, Vivian, who wants to be an actress, dreams of reopening all the theaters and re-creating a golden age. Wilson, who moved to L.A. three months ago from Texas, had a screenplay, of course, but it was lost when his laptop was stolen.

Black-and-white is the correct medium for this material. Holdridge finds locations that, paradoxically, look just like Los Angeles, but like no part of the city you've ever seen before. A decaying business district is no place to begin a date, but Wilson, who has warmed up, even finds romance in a sign painted on an old building: *Los Angeles Sanitary District—1927*.

They talk. I wouldn't call it flirting. Both are painfully earnest. They reveal secrets. You might be able to guess one of them. They talk about her abusive redneck ex-boyfriend, and they go together to steal her possessions out of her ex-apartment. She accuses Wilson of planning to have sex on their first date and asks, "You're carrying a condom, aren't you?" He denies it. She discovers he's carrying five. He can explain it. In a sense, he's carrying them for his roommate.

The night unfolds and the movie never steps wrong. We increasingly admire the quality of the acting: Both actors take their characters through a difficult series of changes, without ever seeming to try or be aware of it. We sense them growing closer. We also sense they were not created for each other. We sense those things because they do, too.

The story is obviously influenced by Richard Linklater's *Before Sunrise* and *Before Sunset*. He is thanked in the end credits. Anne Walker, producer of this film, also produced *Sunrise*. But *In Search of a Midnight Kiss* isn't an homage or a recycling job. It's a film with its own organic existence, its own reason for being. It is ultimately a very true and moving story. I came to care about Wilson and Vivian. I hope they had a happy new year.

The International ★ ★ ★
R, 118 m., 2009

Clive Owen (Louis Salinger), Naomi Watts (Eleanor Whitman), Armin Mueller-Stahl

(Wilhelm Wexler), Brian F. O'Byrne (The Consultant). Directed by Tom Tykwer and produced by Charles Roven, Richard Suckle, and Lloyd Phillips. Screenplay by Eric Warren Singer.

Not since the days of silent movies have bankers as a group been cast so ruthlessly as villains. They used to wear waxed mustaches and throw widows and orphans out into the storm. Now the mustaches are gone. "Banker" has been incorporated into the all-embracing term "Wall Street." The bankers in *The International* broker arms deals, sell missiles under the counter, and assassinate anyone who gets too snoopy. First they throw you out into the storm, then they blow you up.

Whether this is a fair portrait is not the purpose of a movie review to determine. It is accurate of the bankers on view here, and given the face of Armin Mueller-Stahl, once familiar as a good guy, now enjoying a new career as a ruthless villain. His bank, based in Luxembourg, as so many schemes are, has been assassinating Nosy Parkers for getting too close to their operations, which involve investing in African rebels and nuclear weaponry, and arming both sides of the Israeli-Palestinian conflict.

Does it seem to you that a bank with headquarters in Luxembourg is asking for it, just as a nice girl shouldn't rent a room in a whorehouse? In the opening scenes we meet the Interpol agent Louis Salinger (Clive Owen), keeping watch in Berlin as his partner meets with an insider of the bank. The partner is killed by mysterious means, and that, as they say, makes it personal. Salinger is joined by Eleanor Whitman (Naomi Watts), a district attorney from Manhattan, for cloudy law enforcement reasons but excellent dramatic ones: It's great to have a plucky blonde in the plot.

The movie has a scene in it Hitchcock might have envied, a gun battle ranging up and down the ramps of the Guggenheim Museum in New York. Why there? Because the visuals are terrific. After Salinger and Whitman follow their quarry there, how do dozens of the bank's killers turn up? Because they're needed. Why do assassination squads in the movies always dress in matching uniforms? Makes them easier to identify. You don't ask

questions like that. You simply enjoy the magnificent absurdity of the scene. (It was filmed, by the way, on an enormous interior set in Germany.)

A lot of the remainder of the movie involves dialogue and plotters skulking around colorful international locales including even Istanbul, that traditional setting for intrigue. I found the unfolding of the plot sort of fascinating. The ads will no doubt play up the shoot-out, but you may be relieved to discover this isn't another hyperkinetic exercise in queasy-cammery. It's more interested in demonstrating that a bank like this transcends national boundaries and corrupts everyone it deals with.

How does it do this? With money. As David Mamet so usefully informs us: "Everybody needs money. That's why they call it money." In the film, everything is secondary to the bank's profits, and an Italian political candidate, not unlike Berlusconi, is shot during a speech. Why the bank, so efficient, isn't better at going after Salinger and Whitman isn't hard to explain: They're needed for the whole movie. The Berlusconi type has a big dialogue scene in which he explains, succinctly and objectively, how banks, armies, and governments interact. Apparently our Wall Street was a babe in the woods, being motivated merely by arrogance, avarice, and ego.

I enjoyed the movie. Clive Owen makes a semi-believable hero, not performing too many feats that are physically unlikely. He's handsome and has the obligatory macho stubble, but he has a quality that makes you worry a little about him. I like heroes who *could* get killed. Naomi Watts wisely plays up her character's legal smarts and plays down the inevitable possibility that the two of them will fall in love.

The director is Tom Tykwer (*Run, Lola, Run*). Here he's concerned not merely with thriller action but with an actual subject: the dangers of a banking system that operates offshore no matter where your shoreline is. We're gradually getting it into our heads that in the long run your nuclear capability may not be as important as your bank balance. Banks are not lending much money these days, but if you want to buy some warheads, they might take a meeting.

213

Interview ★ ★ ★
R, 86 m., 2007

Steve Buscemi (Pierre Peders), Sienna Miller (Katya), Michael Buscemi (Robert Peders), Tara Elders (Maggie), Molly Griffith (Waitress). Directed by Steve Buscemi and produced by Gijs van de Westelaken and Bruce Weiss. Screenplay by Buscemi and David Schechter.

The Washington correspondent for a news-weekly is assigned to interview a celebrity sex icon, to his disgust and eventually to hers. Pierre (Steve Buscemi) has never seen a performance by Katya (Sienna Miller) and has done so little homework he hardly knows anything about her except that he loathes the very idea of such a woman. Katya has processed so many interviews that she's sick of them, turns up an hour late, and is not so much surprised that Pierre knows nothing about her as astonished that he has the nerve to try to fake the interview.

Such things happen. I once went to talk to Burt Lancaster about a movie named *Castle Keep*. The interview lasted four minutes. "You didn't like the picture, did you?" he asked. No, I said. "Then we have nothing to talk about, do we?" He walked out. Years later, I had a perfectly pleasant interview with Lancaster; stars just get ground down by the publicity process.

Interview was directed and cowritten by Buscemi, who plays the impatient newsman so well you can almost sense his toes curling in his shoes. Katya is apparently intended to be a Paris Hilton type. She plays the dumb sex kitten to perfection but has hidden levels of intelligence, insight, and game-playing. I've found over the years that most famous "dumb starlets" are smart. If they were really dumb, they would be unknown.

The Pierre character makes the mistake of condescending to Katya, insulting her, and making it clear he'd rather be in Washington covering a breaking story. The interview crashes, they walk out, and then paparazzi stalking Katya push Pierre into traffic, he gets a cut on his head, and she insists on taking him to her nearby apartment.

That's act one. Act two turns into a two-hander with them talking, drinking, smoking, doing some cocaine, flirting, dueling, insulting,

and playing nasty head games. This formula is familiar enough; think of Neve Campbell and Dominic Chianese in James Toback's *When Will I Be Loved* (2004) and Ethan Hawke and Uma Thurman in Richard Linklater's *Tape* (2001), not to mention the Burtons in Mike Nichols's *Who's Afraid of Virginia Woolf?* (1966).

Why did it need to be done again? The original director on this project was Theo van Gogh, a Dutch director murdered in the street by an Islamic assassin who disapproved of one of his films. Van Gogh had planned to remake it in English with Miller and Buscemi, so the film went ahead. Buscemi handles it skillfully, using van Gogh's method of filming with three simultaneous video cameras. He and Miller are especially good at making plausible shifts in emotional speed. Will they sleep together or strangle each other? Are they really sharing their darkest, most shameful secrets? Which is the better actor? Which, for that matter, is the better interviewer?

A subtext of the film is that both actors most certainly know the types they're playing and are fed up with them, enough to put a cutting edge on their characters. Miller has known vacuous bimbos and can occasionally play one on TV, perhaps for her own amusement because celebrity journalists are so pathetically hungry for bimbo sound bites. Buscemi has doubtless encountered countless interviewers from hell.

If I have a problem with the movie, it's the too-neat O. Henry ending. I would have rather plunged deeper into the fearful waters they tread. A perfectly realistic movie on such a situation would have been fascinating, but here it has been adjusted, alas, to the requirements of the audience. Why do people get so angry at movies that end in mystery and unresolved wounds, like *Lost in Translation?* Why do they like it when a movie, however fascinating, goes on autopilot to wrap things up at the end?

What would really happen in this situation? The two characters would pass out, wake up with fearful hangovers, retain a blurred memory of the night before, not be sure if they slept together, hope to never see each other again, or shudder in shame if they did. Buscemi caught that dynamic in his perceptive debut film about alcoholism, *Trees Lounge*

(1996), and look at how perfectly Joey Lauren Adams's *Come Early Morning* (2006) portrays it with Ashley Judd. The problem with most stories about drinking all night and burrowing to the truth, however, is that if you can drink that much, you can't burrow, or if you can, it's not worth a damn.

Still, I found *Interview* kind of fascinating, especially in the ways Buscemi and Miller make their performances into commentaries on the types of characters they play. When actors are really turned loose to play actors, they can achieve merciless accuracy; see Naomi Watts portray a day in the life of an actress in Scott Coffey's *Ellie Parker* (2005). If all the world's a stage for the rest of us, for them it's a backstage.

In the Shadow of the Moon ★ ★ ★ ★
PG, 100 m., 2007

With Buzz Aldrin, Alan Bean, Eugene Cernan, Michael Collins, Jim Lovell, John Young, Charlie Duke, Edgar D. Mitchell, Harrison Schmitt, and Dave Scott. A documentary directed by David Sington and produced by Duncan Copp.

We think of the *Apollo* voyages to the moon more in terms of the achievement than the ordeal. On the night of July 20, 1969, we looked up at the sky and realized that men, who had been gazing at the moon since they were boys, had somehow managed to venture there and were walking on its surface.

Yes, but consider the journey. Three men were packed like sardines in a tiny space capsule ("Spam in a can," the Gemini astronauts called themselves) and sent on a 480,000-mile round trip in a vessel whose electrical wiring was so questionable it had already burned three of them alive on a test pad. The capsule sat atop a rocket that had a way of blowing up. They had no way of knowing where, on the moon, they would land, if they got there. Compared to them, Evel Knievel was a Sunday driver.

Yes, but they took their chances, and they made it. Six of the seven *Apollo* missions landed on the moon, and the saga of *Apollo 13* was a masterpiece of ingenuity in the face of catastrophe. Now here is a spellbinding documentary interviewing many of the surviving astronauts, older men now, about their memories of the adventure. One who is prominently missing is Neil Armstrong, first man on the moon, who says he was first only by chance, and gets too much attention. Gene Siskel sat next to him on an airplane once and thought to himself, "Here is a man who is very weary of being asked what it was like to walk on the moon." So they talked about other things.

Of the others, every one is still sharp and lively and youthful in mind, even often in body. I attended the Conference on World Affairs in Boulder, Colorado, several times with Rusty Schweickart and noticed that he tended to be on panels that were about everything but space exploration. Yet here, in front of the cameras, they open up in a heartfelt way. The most stunning moment reveals how desperately they wanted to be part of the missions: Gus Grissom, one of the three astronauts killed in the launch-pad fire, earlier told John Young he doubted the safety of the wiring in the 100 percent oxygen atmosphere of the capsule but didn't dare complain because he might be booted out of the program for a negative attitude.

When you were on the moon, they remember, you could blank out Earth by holding up your thumb in front of your face. Yet they were struck by how large the planet was, and how thin and fragile its atmosphere, floating in an infinite void and preserving this extraordinary thing, life. And below, we were poisoning it as fast as we could.

The interviews with the astronauts are intercut with footage that is new, in great part, and looks better than it has any right to do. A researcher for this production spent years screening NASA footage that was still, in many cases, in its original film cans and had never been seen. The film was cleaned up and restored, the color refreshed, and the result is beautiful and moving. The *Apollo* missions were, after all, the most momentous steps ever taken by mankind; our species, like all living things, has evolved to live and endure on the planet of its origin. Random life spores may have traveled from world to world by chance, but this was the first time any living thing looked up and said, "I'm going there." These astronauts are still alive, but as long as mankind survives, their journeys will be seen as the turning point—to what, it is still to be seen.

In the Valley of Elah ★ ★ ★ ★
R, 120 m., 2007

Tommy Lee Jones (Hank Deerfield), Charlize Theron (Detective Emily Sanders), Susan Sarandon (Joan Deerfield), James Franco (Sergeant Dan Carnelli), Jonathan Tucker (Mike Deerfield), Frances Fisher (Evie), Jason Patric (Lieutenant Kirklander), Josh Brolin (Chief Buchwald). Directed by Paul Haggis and produced by Patrick Wachsberger, Steven Samuels, Darlene Caamano Loquet, Haggis, and Larry Becsey. Screenplay by Haggis.

I don't know Tommy Lee Jones at all. Let's get that clear. I've interviewed him, and at Cannes we had one of those discussions at the American Pavilion. He didn't enjoy doing it, but he felt duty-bound to promote his great film *The Three Burials of Melquiades Estrada*. During my questions he twisted his hands like a kid in the principal's office. He remains a mystery to me, which is why I feel free to share some feelings about him. I'm trying to understand why he is such a superb actor.

Look at the lines around his eyes. He looks concerned, under pressure from himself, a man who has felt pain. Look at his face. It seems to conceal hurtful emotion. He doesn't smile a lot, but when he does, it's like clouds are lifting. Listen to his voice, filled with authority and hard experience. Notice when he speaks that he passes out words as if they were money he can't afford. Whether these characteristics are true of the private man, I have no way of knowing.

Paul Haggis's *In the Valley of Elah* is built on Tommy Lee Jones's persona, and that is why it works so well. The same material could have been banal or routine with an actor trying to be "earnest" and "sincere." Jones isn't trying to be anything at all. His character is simply compelled to do what he does and has a lot of experience doing it. He plays a Vietnam veteran named Hank Deerfield, now hauling gravel in Tennessee. He gets a call from the Army that his son Mike, just returned from a tour in Iraq, is AWOL from his squad at Fort Rudd. That sounds wrong. He tells his wife, Joan (Susan Sarandon), that he's going to drive down there and take a look into things. "It's a two-day drive," she says. He says, "Not the way I'll drive it."

He checks into a cheap motel. His investigations in the area of Fort Rudd take him into topless bars, chicken shacks, the local police station, the base military police operation, and a morgue where he's shown something cut into pieces and burned, and he IDs the remains as his son. Looking through his son's effects, he asks as a distraction if he can have his Bible while he's pocketing his son's cell phone. It's been nearly destroyed by heat, but a friendly technician salvages some video from it, filled with junk artifacts but still retaining glimpses of what it recorded on video: glimpses of hell.

To describe the many avenues of his investigation would be pointless and diminish the film's gathering tension. I'd rather talk about what Haggis, also the writer and coproducer, does with the performance. Imagine the first violinist playing a note to lead the orchestra into tune. Haggis, as director, draws that note from Jones, and the other actors tune to it. They include Charlize Theron as a city homicide detective, Jason Patric as a military policeman, Sarandon as Deerfield's wife, and various other police and military officers and members of Mike's unit in Iraq.

None of these characters are heightened. None of them behave in any way as if they're in a thriller. Other directors might have pumped them up, made them colorful or distinctive in some distracting way. Theron could (easily) be sexy. Patric could (easily) be a bureaucratic paper pusher. Sarandon could (easily) be a hysterical worrier, or an alcoholic, or push it any way you want to. You know how movies make supporting actors more colorful than they need to be, and how happily a lot of actors go along with that process.

Not here. Theron, who is actually the costar, so carefully modulates her performance that she even ignores most of the sexism aimed at her at the police station. Nor is there any hint of sexual attraction between her and anybody else, nor does she sympathize with Hank Deerfield and work on his behalf. Nor, for that matter, does she compete with him. She simply does her job and raises her young son.

I don't think there's a scene in the movie that could be criticized as "acting," with quotation marks. When Sarandon, who has already lost one son to the Army, now finds she has lost both, what she says to Jones over the telephone is filled with bitter emotion but not given a hint of emotional spin. She says it the way a woman would if she had held the same conversation with this man for a lifetime. The movie is about determination, doggedness, duty, and the ways a war changes a man. There is no release or climax at the end, just closure. Even the final dramatic gesture only says exactly what Deerfield explained earlier that it says, and nothing else.

That tone follows through to the movie's consideration of the war itself. Those who call *In the Valley of Elah* anti-Iraq-war will not have been paying attention. It doesn't give a damn where the war is being fought. Hank Deerfield isn't politically opposed to the war. He just wants to find out how his son came all the way home from Iraq and ended up in charred pieces in a field. Because his experience in Vietnam apparently had a lot to do with crime investigation, he's able to use intelligence as well as instinct. And observe how Theron, as the detective, observes him, takes what she can use, and adds what she draws from her own experience.

Paul Haggis is making good films these days. He directed *Crash* and wrote *Million Dollar Baby*, both Oscar winners, and was nominated as cowriter of *Letters from Iwo Jima*. He and his casting directors assembled an ideal ensemble for this film, which doesn't sensationalize but just digs and digs into our apprehensions. I have been trying to think who else could have carried this picture except Tommy Lee Jones, and I just can't do it. Who else could tell Theron's young son the story of David and Goliath (which took place in the Valley of Elah) and make it sound like instruction in the tactics of being brave?

Into the Wild ★ ★ ★ ★
R, 150 m., 2007

Emile Hirsch (Christopher McCandless), Marcia Gay Harden (Billie McCandless), William Hurt (Walt McCandless), Jena Malone (Carine McCandless), Catherine Keener (Jan Burres), Brian Dieker (Rainey), Vince Vaughn (Wayne Westerberg), Zach Galifianakis (Kevin), Kristen Stewart (Tracy), Hal Holbrook (Ron Franz).

Directed by Sean Penn and produced by Penn, Art Linson, and Bill Pohlad. Screenplay by Penn, based on the book by Jon Krakauer.

For those who have read Thoreau's *Walden*, there comes a time, maybe lasting only a few hours or a day, when the notion of living alone in a tiny cabin beside a pond and planting some beans seems strangely seductive. Certain young men, of which I was one, lecture patient girlfriends about how such a life of purity and denial makes perfect sense. Christopher McCandless did not outgrow this phase.

Jon Krakauer's *Into the Wild*, which I read with a fascinated dread, tells the story of a twenty-two-year-old college graduate who cashes in his law school fund and, in the words of Mark Twain, lights out for the territory. He drives west until he can drive no farther, and then north into the Alaskan wilderness. He has a handful of books about survival and edible wild plants, and his model seems to be Jack London, although he should have devoted more attention to that author's *To Build a Fire*.

Sean Penn's spellbinding film adaptation of this book stays close to the source. We meet Christopher (Emile Hirsch), an idealistic dreamer in reaction against his proud parents (William Hurt and Marcia Gay Harden) and his bewildered sister (Jena Malone). He had good grades at Emory; his future in law school was right there in his grasp. Why did he disappear from their lives, why was his car found abandoned, where was he, and why, why, why?

He keeps journals in which he sees himself in the third person as a heroic loner, renouncing civilization, returning to the embrace of nature. In centuries past such men might have been saints, retreating to a cave or hidden hermitage, denying themselves all pleasures except subsistence. He sees himself not as homeless, but as a man freed from homes.

In the book, Krakauer traces his movements through the memories of people he encounters on his journey. It was an impressive reporting achievement to track them down, and Penn's film affectionately embodies them in strong performances. These are people who take in the odd youth, feed him, shelter him, give him clothes, share their lives, mentor him—and

217

worry as he leaves to continue his quest, which seems to them, correctly, as doomed.

By now McCandless has renamed himself Alexander Supertramp. He is validated by his lifestyle choice. He meets people such as Rainey and Jan (Brian Dieker and Catherine Keener), leftover hippies still happily rejecting society, and Wayne (Vince Vaughn), a hard-drinking, friendly farmer. The most touching contact he makes is with Ron (Hal Holbrook), an older man who sees him clearly and with apprehension, and begins to think of him as a wayward grandson. Christopher lectures this man, who has seen it all, on what he is missing, and asks him to follow him up a steep hillside to see the next horizon. Ron tries, before he admits he is no longer in condition.

And then McCandless disappears from the maps of memory, into unforgiving Alaska. Yes, it looks beautiful. It is all he dreamed of. He finds an abandoned bus where no bus should be and makes it his home. He tries hunting, not very successfully. He lives off the land, but the land is a zero-tolerance system. From his journals and other evidence, Penn reconstructs his final weeks. Emile Hirsch plays him in a hypnotic performance, turning skeletal, his eyes sinking into his skull while they still burn with zeal. It is great acting, and more than acting.

This is a reflective, regretful, serious film about a young man swept away by his uncompromising choices. Two of the more truthful statements in recent culture is that we need a little help from our friends, and that sometimes we must depend on the kindness of strangers. If you don't know those two things and accept them, you will end up eventually in a bus of one kind or another. Sean Penn himself, fiercely idealistic, uncompromising, a little less angry now, must have read the book and reflected that there, but for the grace of God, went he. The movie is so good partly because it means so much, I think, to its writer-director. It is a testament like the words that Christopher carved into planks in the wilderness.

I grew up in Urbana, Illinois, three houses down from the Sanderson family—Milton and Virginia and their boys, Steve and Joe. My close friend was Joe. His bedroom was filled with aquariums, terrariums, snakes, hamsters, spiders, and butterfly and beetle collections. I

envied him like crazy. After college he hit the road. He never made a break from his parents, but they rarely knew where he was. Sometimes he came home, and his mother would have to sew $100 bills into the seams of his blue jeans. He disappeared in Nicaragua. His body was later identified as a dead Sandinista freedom fighter. From a nice little house surrounded by evergreens at the other end of Washington Street, he left to look for something he needed to find. I believe in Sean Penn's Christopher McCandless. I grew up with him.

The Invasion ★ ★
PG-13, 95 m., 2007

Nicole Kidman (Carol), Daniel Craig (Ben), Jeremy Northam (Tucker), Jackson Bond (Oliver), Jeffrey Wright (Dr. Galeano). Directed by Oliver Hirschbiegel and produced by Joel Silver. Screenplay by David Kajganich, based on the novel *The Body Snatchers* by Jack Finney.

The Invasion is the fourth, and the least, of the movies made from Jack Finney's classic science-fiction novel *The Body Snatchers*. Here is a great story born to be creepy, and the movie churns through it like a road company production. If the first three movies served as parables for their times, this one keeps shooting off parable rockets that fizzle out. How many references in the same movie can you have to the war in Iraq and not say anything about it?

Don Siegel's classic *Invasion of the Body Snatchers* (1956) was about alien pods that arrived on Earth, sucked up the essence of human hosts, and became duplicates of them—exact copies, except for what made them human. It was widely decoded as an attack on McCarthyism. Phil Kaufman's *Invasion of the Body Snatchers* (1978), inexplicably described by Pauline Kael as "the American movie of the year," was said to have something to do with Watergate and keeping tabs on those who are not like you. Abel Ferrara's *Body Snatchers* (1994), by far the best of the films, might have been about the spread of AIDS.

And *The Invasion*? One of the alien beings argues persuasively that if everyone were like them, there'd be no war in Iraq, no genocide in Darfur—no conflict in general, I guess, although they don't seem to have much of a position on global warming. I don't have a clue what the movie thinks, if anything, about Iraq, which is mentioned so frequently, but it may be a veiled attack on cults that require unswerving conformity from their members. Which cults? I dunno.

In all four movies, alien spores arrive on Earth from space. In the early films they take the form of pods, which look like very large brown snow peas. Some viewers complained after Kaufman's movie that they couldn't believe aliens could truck those pods all over San Francisco, to which the obvious reply is: Do you expect a movie titled *Invasion of the Body Snatchers* to be plausible?

In Oliver Hirschbiegel's new version, the spores piggy-back on a returning space shuttle that crashes and scatters debris from Dallas to Washington. Anyone who touches the debris gets the infection, which is then spread by touch and the exchange of vomit (in more ways than you might imagine). In Washington, a psychiatrist named Carol (Nicole Kidman) has a patient who complains, "My husband just . . . isn't my husband anymore." Versions of this line do duty in all four films. The pod people look like the people they occupy and have the same memories ("Remember Colorado?"), but they walk like mannequins with arthritis, except when they're running like zombies.

Carol's estranged husband, Tucker (Jeremy Northam), is a disease control expert who becomes infected and after four years suddenly wants to start spending time with their child, Oliver (Jackson Bond). Little Oliver texts his mom that his dad is different. Carol's current good friend is a doctor named Ben (Daniel Craig), who is one of many to notice a new "flu virus" that is spreading through the land.

His colleague, a researcher named Dr. Galeano (Jeffrey Wright), gets a sample of the virus, and in a performance that would be the envy of every scientist since Newton, gazes at it through a microscope and almost immediately explains what it is, how it reproduces, how it takes over when we fall asleep, and (apparently only a day or two later) how to defeat it with an antibody that can seemingly be manufactured so quickly and in such quantities that it can be sprayed from crop dusters.

By this point the movie has lost all coherence, not to mention flaunting a scene where a helicopter lands atop a towering skyscraper in Washington, where federal law decrees no building can be taller than the Capitol.

This may not be entirely Hirschbiegel's fault. Warner Bros. didn't approve of his original version and brought in the Wachowskis to rewrite it and James McTeigue (*V for Vendetta*) to direct their revisions. All three served time on the *Matrix* movies: just the team you'd want to add a little incomprehensible chaos.

The genius of the Ferrara version was to make his very sympathetic heroine a young girl on an Army base who can't get anyone to listen to her. You know how adults can be when kids claim they've seen aliens. The problem with this new version is that it caves in and goes for your basic car chase scenes (spinning tires, multiple crashes, car in flames, dozens of pod people hanging onto it, etc). If aliens are among us, we will not be saved by stunt driving.

Nicole Kidman, Daniel Craig, Jeremy Northam, little Jackson Bond, Jeffrey Wright, and other cast members do what they can with dialogue that can hardly be spoken, and a plot that we concede must be implausible but does not necessarily have to upstage the *Mad* magazine version. And the aliens themselves are a flop. Just like zombies, they're pushovers: easy to spot, slow-moving, not too bright, can be shot dead or otherwise disposed of. OK. Now we've had *Invasion of the Body Snatchers* twice, *Body Snatchers*, once and *Invasion* once. Somebody should register the title *Of The.*

I.O.U.S.A. ★ ★ ★ ½
PG, 85 m., 2008

Featuring David M. Walker, Robert Bixby, Paul Volker, Ron Paul, Warren Buffett, Paul O'Neill, and others. A documentary directed by Patrick Creadon and produced by Christine O'Malley and Sarah Gibson. Screenplay by Creadon, O'Malley, and Addison Wiggin.

A letter to our grandchildren, Raven, Emil, and Taylor:

I see you growing up into such beautiful

people, and I wish all good things to you as you make the leap into adulthood. But I have just seen a film named *I.O.U.S.A.* that snapped into sharp focus why your lives may not be as pleasant as ours have been. Chaz and I had the blessing of growing up in an optimistic, bountiful America. We never fully realized that we were paying for many of our comforts with your money.

Let me explain. There is something called the "national debt." In the movie's interviews with ordinary people, it has a hard time finding anyone who knows exactly what that is. Well, I've never exactly known, either. I thought I knew, but it never came up in conversation, and it became a meaningless abstraction, even though in 2009 the debt will pass nine *trillion* dollars. You might think of those as dollars our nation has spent without having them.

What will this mean to you? It will mean you will live in a country no longer able to pay for many of the services and guarantees we take for granted. In forty years, when you are still less than my age, it looks like the government will be able to pay for only three things: interest on the national debt, *some* Social Security, and *some* Medicare. It will not be able to afford any of the other functions it now performs.

How did we get into this situation? With a federal government that has been throwing bad money after good. Of all the presidents in the last century, the only one who was able to achieve a balanced budget and produce a surplus was Bill Clinton. He did that by bravely raising taxes and cutting spending. Our current president, George W. Bush, is now finishing up eight years of throwing around money like a drunken sailor. His fellow conservatives, like Rush Limbaugh, like to talk about "tax-and-spend Democrats." But they seem to be "don't-tax-and-spend-even-more Republicans."

Not that this film takes sides. It is nonpartisan and includes many Republicans who agree with its argument that the country is headed for disaster within the lifetimes of many now living. It centers on David M. Walker, until recently the U.S. comptroller general, and Robert Bixby, the head of the nonpartisan Concord Coalition, who have

been on a national Fiscal Wake-Up tour that will last until the November elections. They are trying to sound the alarm, but they speak to half-empty town halls and captive Rotarians and get pushed off the local news by a story of a man who swallowed a diamond.

I don't really believe this review will inspire enormous numbers of people to go see the film. But if they do, they'll find it accomplishes an amazing thing. It *explains* the national debt, the foreign trade deficit, the decrease in personal savings, how the prime interest rate works, and the weakness of our leaders. No, not only George W. Bush, but politicians of both parties who know if they vote against a tax cut they will be lambasted by their opponents and could lose their jobs. In the film we see President Bush asked about the debt and replying: "Ask the economists. I think I only got a B-minus in economics." Then he gives that little chuckle. "But I got an A-plus in cutting taxes."

Yes, he cut taxes while our spending mushroomed. What we have to do is bite the bullet and pay higher taxes while spending less. The war in Iraq is a much sexier issue. But no matter what happens in Iraq, the real crisis we face is the debt. The movie includes testimony by former Fed chairman Paul Volker, former treasury secretary Paul O'Neill, billionaire Warren Buffett, Congressman Ron Paul, and others on both sides of the fence who all agree: Don't buy what you can't pay for. Any politician who tries to win votes by promising to cut taxes is digging our country's grave.

Here's an interesting statistic. I remember when "Made in China" meant cheap and shabby merchandise. No longer. In the ranking of the trade imbalance among all the world's nations, China is first with the highest surplus, and the United States is last with the largest deficit. The Chinese now hold a huge chunk of our debt. If they ever call in the loan, it would destroy our economy. In the presidential debate earlier in the year, Ron Paul was a lonely voice talking about the debt; the others on both sides paid lip service to the problem and moved on.

So here's the bottom line, kids. The United States is probably going to go broke during your lifetimes. Actually, it's already broke, but getting deeper into debt allows it to keep running on thin air, like the Road Runner. My advice? Start savings accounts. Don't buy what you can't afford. Learn Chinese.

Iron Man ★ ★ ★ ★
PG-13, 126 m., 2008

Robert Downey Jr. (Tony Stark/Iron Man,) Terrence Howard (Colonel Rhodes), Jeff Bridges (Obadiah Stane/Iron Monger), Gwyneth Paltrow (Pepper Potts). Directed by Jon Favreau and produced by Ari Arad. Screenplay by Mark Fegus and Hank Ostby.

When I caught up with *Iron Man,* a broken hip had delayed me and the movie had already been playing for three weeks. What I heard during that time was that a lot of people loved it, that they were surprised to love it so much, and that Robert Downey Jr.'s performance was special. Apart from that, all I knew was that the movie was about a big iron man. I didn't even know that a human occupied it and halfway thought that the Downey character's brain had been transplanted into a robot, or a fate equally weird.

Yes, I knew I was looking at sets and special effects—but I'm referring to the reality of the illusion, if that makes any sense. With many superhero movies, all you get is the surface of the illusion. With *Iron Man,* you get a glimpse into the depths. You get the feeling, for example, of a functioning corporation. Consider the characters of Pepper Potts (Gwyneth Paltrow), Stark's loyal aide, and Obadiah Stane (Jeff Bridges), Stark's business partner. They don't feel drummed up for the occasion. They seem to have worked together for a while.

Much of that feeling is created by the chemistry involving Downey, Paltrow, and Bridges. They have relationships that seem fully formed and resilient enough to last through the whole movie, even if plot mechanics were not about to take them to another level. Between the two men, there are echoes of the relationship between Howard Hughes and Noah Dietrich in Scorsese's *The Aviator* (2004). Obadiah Stane doesn't come onscreen waving flags and winking at the camera to announce he is the villain; he seems adequately explained simply as the voice of reason at Stark's press conference. (Why did "Stark,"

during that scene, make me think of "raving mad"?) Between Stark and Pepper, there's that classic screen tension between "friends" who know they can potentially become lovers.

Downey's performance is intriguing and unexpected. He doesn't behave like most superheroes: He lacks the psychic weight and gravitas. Tony Stark is created from the persona Downey has fashioned through many movies: irreverent, quirky, self-deprecating, wisecracking. The fact that Downey is allowed to think and talk the way he does while wearing all that hardware represents a bold decision by the director, Jon Favreau. If he hadn't desired that, he probably wouldn't have hired Downey. So comfortable is Downey with Tony Stark's dialogue, so familiar does it sound coming from him, that the screenplay seems almost to have been dictated by Downey's persona.

There are some things that some actors can safely say onscreen, and other things they can't. The Robert Downey Jr. persona would find it difficult to get away with weighty, profound statements (in an "entertainment movie," anyway—a more serious film like *Zodiac* is another matter). Some superheroes speak in a kind of heightened, semiformal prose, as if dictating to *Bartlett's Familiar Quotations.* Not Tony Stark. He could talk that way and be Juno's uncle. *Iron Man* doesn't seem to know how seriously most superhero movies take themselves. If there is wit in the dialogue, the superhero is often supposed to be unaware of it. If there is broad humor, it usually belongs to the villain. What happens in *Iron Man,* however, is that sometimes we wonder how seriously even Stark takes it. He's flippant in the face of disaster, casual on the brink of ruin.

It's prudent, I think, that Favreau positions the rest of the characters in a more serious vein. The supporting cast wisely does not try to one-up him. Gwyneth Paltrow plays Pepper Potts as a woman who is seriously concerned that this goofball will kill himself. Jeff Bridges makes Obadiah Stane one of the great superhero villains by seeming plausibly concerned about the stock price. Terrence Howard, as Colonel Rhodes, is at every moment a conventional straight arrow. What a horror show it would have been if they were all tuned to

Tony Stark's sardonic wavelength. We'd be back in the world of *Swingers* (1996), which was written by Favreau.

Another of the film's novelties is that the enemy is not a conspiracy or spy organization. It is instead the reality in our own world today: Armaments are escalating beyond the ability to control them. In most movies in this genre, the goal would be to create bigger and better weapons. How unique that Tony Stark wants to disarm. It makes him a superhero who can think, reason, and draw moral conclusions, instead of one who recites platitudes.

The movie is largely founded on its special effects. When somebody isn't talking, something is banging, clanging, or laying rubber. The armored robotic suits utilized by Tony and Obadiah would upstage lesser actors than Downey and Bridges; it's surprising how much those two giant iron men seem to reflect the personalities of the men inside them. Everything they do is preposterous, of course, but they seem to be doing it, not the suits. Some of their moments have real grandeur—as when Tony tests his suit to see how high it will fly, and it finally falls back toward Earth in a sequence that reminded me of a similar challenge in *The Right Stuff*.

The art direction is inspired by the original Marvel artists. The movie doesn't reproduce the drawings of Jack Kirby and others, but it reproduces their feeling, a vision of out-scaled enormity, seamless sleekness, secret laboratories made not of nuts and bolts but of . . . vistas. A lot of big budget f/x epics seem to abandon their stories with half an hour to go and just throw effects at the audience. This one has a plot so ingenious it continues to function no matter how loud the impacts, how enormous the explosions. It's an inspiration to provide Tony with that heart-saving device; he's vulnerable not simply because Obadiah might destroy him, but because he might simply run out of juice.

That leaves us, however, with a fundamental question at the bottom of the story: Why must the ultimate weapon be humanoid in appearance? Why must it have two arms and two legs, and why does it matter if its face is scowling? In the real-world competitions between fighting machines, all the elements of design are based entirely on questions of how

well they allow the machines to attack, defend, recover, stay upright, and overturn their enemies. It is irrelevant whether they have conventional eyes, or whether those eyes narrow. Nor does it matter whether they have noses, because their oxygen supply is obviously not obtained by breathing. The solution to such dilemmas is that the armored suits look the way they do for entirely cinematic reasons. The bad iron man should look like a mean machine. The good iron man should utilize the racing colors of Tony Stark's favorite sports cars. It wouldn't be nearly as much fun to see a fight scene between two refrigerators crossed with the leftovers from a boiler room.

At the end of the day it's Robert Downey Jr. who powers the liftoff separating this from most other superhero movies. You hire an actor for his strengths, and Downey would not be strong as a one-dimensional mightyman. He is strong because he is smart, quick, and funny, and because we sense his public persona masks deep private wounds. By building on that, Favreau found his movie, and it's a good one.

Is Anybody There? ★ ★ ½
PG-13, 92 m., 2009

Michael Caine (Clarence), Bill Milner (Edward), Anne-Marie Duff (Mum), David Morrissey (Dad), Elizabeth Spriggs (Prudence), Leslie Phillips (Reg), Ralph Raich (Clive), Rosemary Harris (Elsie). Directed by John Crowley and produced by David Heyman, Marc Turtletaub, and Peter Saraf. Screenplay by Peter Harness.

Sir Michael Caine makes acting look as natural as running water. I have never sensed an ounce of egotism in his makeup. The videos he made to teach film acting are plain-spoken and practical. Of course, you need inspiration and talent. But what can he tell you about that? He tells you that you have to look out of the same eye all during a close-up. Or if you don't, that's what they mean by shifty-eyed.

Look at him here in *Is Anybody There?* Caine is seventy-six years old, but this is the first movie where he looks it. He doesn't give a damn. He's supposed to be old. That's why he has checked himself, reluctantly, into an old folks' home. It's called Lark Hall; it's close to the sea and inhabited by dotty seniors who have little to entertain them apart from territorial battles and simmering resentments.

He plays a retired magician named the Amazing Clarence, who drives up in a van painted like an ice cream wagon and almost runs down Edward (Bill Milner), who is about ten and whose parents run the operation. Edward likes living in Lark Hall because he's fascinated by ghosts, and he reasons that a home for the aged would be a good place to find some. He sneaks his tape recorder under the bed of a dying patient, hoping to capture some spirit manifestations.

The Amazing Clarence is spiteful, hostile, and unfriendly. Edward doesn't much notice. He's a force of nature and bowls over Clarence with his curiosity. The old magician is persuaded to put on a magic show for the other retirees; he pretends great reluctance, but I doubt it because if you're still tooling around the countryside in a van and doing one-night stands at seventy-six, it may be because you like to.

The rest of *Is Anybody There?* doesn't measure up to the Amazing Clarence and his young acolyte. Lark Hall seems less like a retirement home than a failed pilot for a sitcom, with old folks who behave in relentlessly obvious comic shtick. It reminded me nostalgically of *Mrs. Palfrey at the Claremont* (2005), with Joan Plowright and Anna Massey among the inhabitants of an establishment where the evening meals were an exercise in thrilling nonverbal communication. The folks in Lark Hall should spend more time eyeing one another and less time acting out.

I can't really recommend the film, unless you admire Caine as much as I do, which is certainly possible. Let's say I somehow found myself retired, and I was informed that the movie was shallow, clunky, and sitcomish, but that Michael Caine played an old magician named the Amazing Clarence in it. I would take the remnants of my latest Social Security check and hobble down to the theater, because my sixth sense would tell me Caine would be worth the price of admission. I would, however, demand a full refund if the Amazing Clarence didn't attempt at least one magic trick that went spectacularly wrong. Reader, the theater would be able to keep my money.

I Served the King of England ★ ★ ★
R, 118 m., 2008

Ivan Barnev (Young Jan Dite), Oldrich Kaiser (Old Jan Dite), Julia Jentsch (Liza), Martin Huba (Skrivanek), Marian Labuda (Walden), Milan Lasica (Professor), Josef Abrham (Hotelier Brandejs). Directed by Jiri Menzel and produced by Petr Dvorak, Helena Uldrichova, Dusan Kukal, Vit Komrzy, and Luba Feglova. Screenplay by Menzel, based on the novel by Bohumil Hrabal.

I first got to know the Czech director Jiri Menzel through his whimsical 1966 Oscar winner, *Closely Watched Trains*. Looking up my old review, I found a sentence that could also apply to his latest film: "If you're charged up emotionally, you'd better lie down for an hour or two before going to see it. It requires an audience at peace with itself."

Don't assume, however, that Menzel's *I Served the King of England* is a snoozer; for that matter, don't assume it has anything to do with the king of England. It's a film filled with wicked satire and sex both joyful and pitiful. But Menzel doesn't pound home his points. He skips gracefully through them, like his hero. He takes the velvet glove approach.

Here is a film with a hatred of Nazis and a crafty condemnation of communist bureaucracy and cronyism. It seems to be a comic tale of the long and somewhat uneventful life of Jan Dite, who worked as a waiter, bought a hotel with stolen postage stamps, and was jailed because he wasn't quick enough to figure out what the communists, when they came to power, really wanted from him. Even that story has a happy ending: He was sentenced to fifteen years, but because of an "amnesty," was released after only fourteen years and eleven months.

Menzel loves that kind of deadpan detail. In *Closely Watched Trains*, the hero's grandfather was crushed while trying to hypnotize the German army. *I Served the King of England* is a life story told by the old and gray Jan Dite (Oldrich Kaiser) about the adventures of the young and clueless Jan Dite (Ivan Barnev). The youth was easily impressed by uniforms, pomp, theatrical displays of grandness, hotel dining rooms jammed with chandeliers, mirrors, candles, curtains, finery. It all came together for him when he was hired as a waiter in Prague's grandest hotel.

Parts of his life story are told in the style of a silent film because Menzel, like all good directors, does not depend entirely on what the characters say. *I Served the King of England* could probably be enjoyed about as much without the English subtitles—although you'd want to keep the playful piano score, of course. The characters are like those in a Buster Keaton comedy: immediately evident, looking just as they should, absorbed by themselves, sometimes doing things simply to amuse themselves, exhibiting grace.

Jan Dite is in awe of the majestic headwaiter, who floats among the tables like a dancer in *Swan Lake*, all the while balancing a heavy tray stacked with meals. Jan treats him like a god. Where did the man learn such grandeur? He served the king of England. One day the man is tripped, drops a tray, and goes on a rampage. The other waiters agree: It was the only decent thing for him to do. Jan ascends to headwaiter, and "ascend" may be the correct word, since he is a very small man.

Menzel apparently sees the pecking order in the dining room as mirroring the Nazi Party's. Jan soon wants more than to serve; he wants to own and accumulate. He marries a fiercely Aryan woman who enlists in the German army, leaving him a box of rare stamps she has looted from the homes of Jews. He happily uses them to buy the hotel. Do we see a pattern here? Didn't the communists appropriate the Jewish wealth, factories, businesses, and art that were stolen by the Nazis?

There is a sequence where the hotel is used by the Nazis as a luxurious resort for a pool full of bodacious Aryan beauties whose duty is to become impregnated by soldiers on leave. How this works out I will leave for you to discover. You see the velvet glove slipping. A metaphor for the Jan Dite character runs through the film after he discovers to his amusement that anyone, even a millionaire, will stoop to pick up loose change from the sidewalk. Dite is a shallow man in a society that becomes a very deep hole.

We will not soon see a comedy like this made in America. Even if it were entirely translated into American characters and terms, audiences would wonder what it was about. We have lost the delight in the irony that Mark Twain and H. L. Mencken practiced. The movie must come to us bearing the answers to its questions. When I say "we," of course, I do not include anyone who has read this far. We would not ask: A Czech comedy? Sly? No appearance by the king of England? An iron fist inside the glove?

Many more things happen here than I have described, including Jan Dite's own sex life and the erotic image beloved by his wife. But enough, although I should add that the name Dite means "child."

I've Loved You So Long ★ ★ ★ ½
PG-13, 117 m., 2008

Kristin Scott Thomas (Juliette), Elsa Zylberstein (Lea), Serge Hazanavicius (Luc), Laurent Grevill (Michel), Frederic Pierrot (Faure), Lise Segur (P'tit Lys), Jean-Claude Arnaud (Papy Paul). Directed by Philippe Claudel and produced by Sylvestre Guarino. Screenplay by Claudel.

I've Loved You So Long begins with a situation similar to *Rachel Getting Married*. One sister is released from an institution for a homecoming with another sister who is not overjoyed to see her. Both of the sisters are believed responsible for a tragic death some years in the past. There are subtle questions about whether either one can be "trusted," even now. But the two films are otherwise completely different, and if you've seen one, you haven't seen the other.

Rachel is as American as apple pie. *I've Loved You So Long* is as French as *tarte de pomme*. Hackneyed expressions, but there you are. One of the most French elements in *Loved You* is Juliette, played by Kristin Scott Thomas. Yes, from *The English Patient*. One of those actors who can move effortlessly between English and French, like Jacqueline Bisset or, with a charming accent, Jeanne Moreau, who had a British mother.

French seems to agree with Scott Thomas. In her English-language roles, she sometimes seems a little cool, ever so slightly aloof. In French, she warms, is more free with emotions, more easily reaches joy and sorrow. Watch her here falling in love with the two adopted Vietnamese daughters of her sister, Lea (Elsa Zylberstein). It's a love that seems spontaneous and not faked.

She also comes home to her sister's husband, Luc (Serge Hazanavicius), and his father, Papy Paul (Jean-Claude Arnaud). Luc doesn't welcome her with open arms. He's nervous about her being with the children. Papy Paul has lost the power to speak and spends all of his time reading books. In an American movie, this trait might make his character eccentric, a practitioner of dark arts, or unnecessary. *Zut!* In France, he just likes to read.

The film explores the past at arm's length; everyone is afraid to discuss it except indirectly. No one dares ask her straight-out questions. Families are like that. There's an elephant in a lot of living rooms. At a dinner party that begins on a cheerful but somewhat uneasy note, one of the guests takes almost sadistic pleasure in asking Juliette questions it is clear she will not answer. This is social sadism in the guise of innocent curiosity.

One of the few in Juliette's corner is her probation officer (Frederic Pierrot), who understands, as the others do not, what Juliette has gone through and what fifteen years in prison really do to the human spirit. She has to learn to be released, to be free, to live her life without the unconscious air of someone afraid of being locked up again. Some people appear to be friends but only want to help her up to a point, for example, at her first job after prison.

Everything centers on Juliette. Her transgression was more unforgivable than what Rachel's sister did. Her feelings run even deeper. She has been away for longer and finds it more difficult to gather up the threads of life. This is one of Kristin Scott Thomas's most inspired performances. Maybe she could have been up for Academy consideration. Pity she speaks French.

I Want Someone to Eat Cheese With ★ ★ ★

NO MPAA RATING, 80 m., 2007

Jeff Garlin (James), Bonnie Hunt (Stella Lewis), Sarah Silverman (Beth), Amy Sedaris (Ms. Clark), Joey Slotnick (Larry), Gina Gershon (Mrs. Pilletti), David Pasquesi (Luca), Paul Mazursky (Charlie), Mina Kolb (Mrs. Aaron), Richard Kind (Herb Hope), Dan Castellaneta (Dick), Tim Kazurinsky (Bill Bjango), Steve Dahl (Father). Directed by Jeff Garlin and produced by Garlin, Erin O'Malley, and Steve Pink. Screenplay by Garlin.

Every fifteen or twenty times out of the gate, a Second City sketch will end not on a punch line, but on a moment of quiet insight and sympathy. *I Want Someone to Eat Cheese With*, a virtual reunion of Second City actors, is a comedy made from such moments. It is a minor movie, but a big-time minor movie, if you see what I mean. It celebrates its modesty, it becomes our friend, and we're surprisingly touched by it even though it doesn't rock us. If there is such a thing as a must-see three-star movie, here it is.

The film is the love child of Jeff Garlin, who plays Larry David's sidekick on *Curb Your Enthusiasm*. Garlin coproduces, writes, directs, and stars, surrounding himself with other Second City veterans going back even to the Golden Age, such as Mina Kolb and Paul Mazursky. He plays James, a thirty-nine-year-old actor in the current Second City troupe, living at home with his mother (Kolb) and spending long, lonely late hours stretched out on the hood of his car in the shadow of Wrigley Field, eating junk food from an all-night store. He has not had sex in five years, and confides this in a voice that suggests he wishes it had been six or seven.

Second City actors typically live in the city, not in an insular showbiz ghetto. They swim with the others in the underpaid but always busy Chicago theater scene. They have friends like Larry (Joey Slotnick), the clerk at the all-night store, who tries to prevent James from buying pudding and pound cake at midnight. And like Stella (Bonnie Hunt), a schoolteacher, who never exactly becomes his girlfriend, and whose students are informed on Career Day that, in Willy Wonka terms, "You are the chocolate river of your life." And like his mom, who is smart and loving and channels Kolb herself, rather than collapsing into stereotypes.

James obsesses with being cast for the title role of a new production of *Marty*. Yes, he'd be perfect for it. I wouldn't dream of telling you who gets the role, but Marty's mother is played by Gina Gershon. Yes, Gina Gershon. Meanwhile, James's manager, Herb Hope (Richard Kind), looks at him with that Richard Kind kind of pity and fires him, explaining he's doing him a favor.

James mopes about Chicago, mostly along the Old Town–Wrigley Field axis. He has empty hours to fill before, and especially after, his Second City gig. Leaving early from an Overeaters Anonymous meeting, he flees to an ice cream parlor, and behind the counter is Beth (Sarah Silverman). She is the one who wants someone to eat cheese with. Beth all but assaults James with her bold provocations, even taking him along to buy brassieres. Is this what he was really missing?

Like *Curb Your Enthusiasm,* which Garlin has directed on occasion, *I Want Someone to Eat Cheese With* has a conversational tone. Unlike too many movies made and populated by comedians, it has no striving for effect, no anxiety that we won't get the joke. It is a movie made by friends about friends, and we get to feel curiously as if they are our friends.

Sometimes they are. Tim Kazurinsky plays Bill Bjango, whose name alone stirs trains of thought, and there is a cameo role for talk jock Steve Dahl, who may not be a Second City alum but certainly provides air time for the troupe. Others such as Amy Sedaris and David Pasquesi have vivid supporting roles, funny, but in character. The movie feels like episodic television, not trying to score all its points at once because it knows these lives will go on and on, advancing, retreating, mixing, regretting, living. What do you want to do tonight, Marty? I dunno. What do you want to do?

J

The Jane Austen Book Club ★ ★ ★ ½
PG-13, 105 m., 2007

Kathy Baker (Bernadette), Maria Bello (Jocelyn), Emily Blunt (Prudie), Amy Brenneman (Sylvia), Hugh Dancy (Grigg), Maggie Grace (Allegra), Lynn Redgrave (Sky), Jimmy Smits (Daniel), Marc Blucas (Dean). Directed by Robin Swicord and produced by John Calley, Julie Lynn, and Diana Napper. Written by Swicord, based on the book by Karen Joy Fowler.

Jane Austen wrote six novels, which are pillars of English literature in spite of being delightful, wise, warm, and beloved. Robin Swicord's *The Jane Austen Book Club* centers on its six members, who meet over six months to discuss the novels, which seem to have an uncanny relevance to events in their own lives, just as the newspaper horoscope always seems to be about you. No, it is not necessary to have read the novels or seen all the Jane Austen movie adaptations, but that would add another dimension to this film.

What you need to know is that Austen is usually concerned about her heroine's struggle to find the right romantic partner for *her*, despite her rivals, class prejudice, her own diffidence, the blindness of her loved one, the obstinacy of her family, and economic necessities. You could say that Austen created "chick lit" and therefore "chick flicks." You could, but I would not, because I despise those terms as sexist and ignorant. As a man, I would hate to have my tastes condescended to as the opposite of chick lit, which, according to Gloria Steinem, is "prick lit." I read Jane Austen for a simple reason, not gender-related: I cannot put her down and often return to her in times of trouble.

Remarkable, that a woman who died at forty-one in 1817 should still be so popular, all her books in print in countless editions, inspiring movies that routinely win Oscars, the subject of Karen Joy Fowler's best-selling *The Jane Austen Book Club,* and her life the subject of another 2007 movie, *Becoming Jane.* One edition of her *Pride and Prejudice* ranks above two thousand on Amazon's best-selling fiction list, which is surprising if you reflect that there are at least nine other current editions of the same novel on sale. ("See all 8,882 search findings," Amazon offered, but I didn't have the nerve.)

The movie is a celebration of reading, and oddly enough that works, even though there is nothing cinematic about a shot of a woman (or the club's one male member) reading a book. Such shots are used as punctuation in the film, where they work like Ozu's "pillow shots," quiet respites from the action. The only drawback to them from my point of view was that all the characters seem to be reading standard editions—not a Folio Society subscriber among them.

The club is founded by Bernadette (Kathy Baker), a woman of (naturally) about sixty, who has been divorced (of course) six times. She thinks it will help console her friend Jocelyn (Maria Bello), who as the film opens is attending a funeral for her beloved Rhodesian ridgeback. Any woman who has an expensive service for her dog needs a man in her life. Or maybe not. Maybe she's got it figured out.

The club membership grows by adding other emotionally needy members. Prudie (Emily Blunt) is a miserable high school French teacher who was planning her first trip to France only to have her younger and distant husband (Marc Blucas) call it off for unspecified "business reasons." Sylvia (Amy Brenneman) is being divorced by Daniel (Jimmy Smits), despite her illusion that theirs is a happy marriage. Sylvia's lesbian daughter, Allegra (Maggie Grace), also has a romantic crisis going and is closeted from her mother, though not from us. Circling in Prudie's life is her mother (Lynn Redgrave), an ex-hippie pothead who is not a bit like Austen's formidable dowagers, except that she meddles.

And there is a male member of the club, Grigg (Hugh Dancy), whom Jocelyn wants to pair off with Sylvia, although he would like to pair off with Jocelyn, something she does not see because like many an Austen heroine she is blind! blind! to true love that is staring her right in the eyes. Grigg is not, shall we say, a born reader of Jane Austen; he prefers science fiction, although his tastes are admirable and he is forever promoting Ursula K. Le Guin.

These six meet at one another's houses, their discussions intercut with developments in their private lives, which they share, sometimes obliquely, at the meetings. In this process they demonstrate how great books can illuminate and counsel us all. The person who does not read is often under the impression that they're being picked on by fate. A reader knows it's necessary because of the story line.

Some will quibble and cavil that the movie is too contrived: six books, six members, six sets of problems, six, six, six (and sex, of course). Contrivance is actually part of the appeal. One of the reasons we return to Austen, Dickens, Trollope, and the estimable Mrs. Gaskell is that their novels are contrived. The structure and ultimate destination are easily foreseeable, but what's fascinating are their characters, how they think and talk, how colorful and urgent they are, and how blind! blind! they are to what they should surely do if only we could advise them.

I settled down with this movie as with a comfortable book. I expected no earth-shaking revelations and got none, and everything turned out about right in a clockwork ending that reminded me of the precision the Victorians always used to tidy up their loose ends. It is crucial, I think, that writer-director Swicord (author of the screenplays for *Little Women*, *Memoirs of a Geisha*, and *The Perez Family*) has created characters who really do seem to have read the books and talk like they have. And she has created a book club that, like all book clubs, is really about its members. Chick flick indeed! Guys, take your best buddy to see this movie. Tell him, "It's really cool, dude, even though there aren't any eviscerations."

JCVD ★ ★ ½
R, 92 m., 2008

Jean-Claude Van Damme (JCVD), Herve Sogne (Lieutenant Smith), Francois Damiens (Bruges), Norbert Rutili (Perthier), Olivier Bisback (Doctor), Karim Belkhadra (Vigile). Directed by Mabrouk El Mechri and produced by Sidonie Dumas. Screenplay by Frederic Benudis, El Mechri, and Christophe Turpin.

I remember the global high point of Jean-Claude Van Damme's career. That would have been at the 1992 Cannes Film Festival, when he and his *Universal Soldier* costar Dolph Lundgren got into a shoving match on the grand staircase leading up to the festival's Auditorium Lumiere. The festival's entrances are documented by every TV network in Europe and by a melee of paparazzi. Think how humiliating it was for their scuffle to be so widely seen. Doing research on the Web, I went to Lundgren's own site, only to find myself quoted: "Some said it was a publicity stunt. I say if you can do one thing and do it well, stick to it."

It says something peculiar about the nature of celebrity that on your own Web site you are still quoting a snarky remark about your sixteen-year-old publicity stunt. But wait. There may be hope. Here's a press release from early 2008: Lundgren insists he can "overcome scheduling difficulties" and reunite with Van Damme. "You know, I was thinking today, it would be great to make a movie with the '80s action Rat Pack—Jean Claude and a few others."

I'm trying to think of a few others. I remember it more as the Rat Whack. But that's just me. If my theme today is the fleeting passage of time, so is Van Damme's. The new film from the Muscles from Brussels is the surprisingly transgressive *JCVD*, which trashes his career, his personal life, his martial arts skills, his financial stability, and his image. He plays himself, trapped in a misunderstood hostage crisis, during which we get such a merciless dissection of his mystique that it will be hard to believe him as a Universal Soldier ever again. On the other hand, it will be easier to like him. This movie almost endearingly savages him.

Van Damme obviously was a good sport to make this movie, which is like every self-parodying Bruce Willis cameo rolled into one. The movie opens with a virtuoso single take in which Van Damme fights, chops, shoots, and kick-boxes his way down an endless street while dozens of stunt men topple from high places, cars explode, and at some point it becomes very funny. The CGI is so evident and the fights so choreographed that it confirms something I've long believed: The most difficult thing an action star does during a battle scene is to hit his marks.

Cut to Los Angeles, where the Muscles loses

a child custody battle. His ex-wife wins after his wee daughter tells the judge she gets teased by the kids at school after one of her daddy's movies plays on TV. In the real America, it would be incredibly cool to have JCVD as your dad. In Los Angeles, meanies from third grade would be gossiping that your dad had the wrong agent. "Tell him to sign with Morris," that Britneyette who thinks she's so cute would taunt.

Back home in Brussels after years abroad, JCVD has his card rejected at an ATM and goes into a bank to get some money. Alas, he walks in on a stickup, and the fanboys at the video store across the street call the cops and report he's the one committing the crime. Soon the police have the area surrounded, while behind the barricades a (smallish) crowd of his fans chants its support. It's like *Dog Day Afternoon* with hamsters.

The suspense in the hostage crisis is pretty much a dud, and the standoff ends as it must, but it's funny when JCVD's old parents tearfully implore him to release his prisoners and express concern about the turn his career has taken. Van Damme says worse things about himself than critics would dream of saying, and the effect is shockingly truthful. I sorta enjoyed myself. I could have done without the scene where he floats in anguished reverie, making Hamlet sound like an extrovert.

And that's that, except on Wikipedia I discovered that JCVD is "known throughout the French-speaking world" for his "picturesque aphorisms." Man, oh, man, they're picturesque, all right. I'm going to tack on a bunch and let the editors decide how many they have room for.

"You don't need a flash to photograph a rabbit that already has red eyes."

"If you work with a jackhammer during an earthquake, stop, otherwise you are working for nothing."

"If you phone a psychic and she doesn't answer the phone before it rings, hang up."

"My wife is not my best sexual partner, but she's good with the housework."

"Obviously I've taken drugs."

"When I walk across my living room from my chimney to my window, it takes me ten seconds, but for a bird it takes one second, and for oxygen zero seconds!"

"I am fascinated by air. If you remove the air from the sky, all the birds would fall to the ground. And all the planes, too."

"Air is beautiful, yet you cannot see it. It's soft, yet you cannot touch it. Air is a little like my brain."

Jellyfish ★ ★ ★
NO MPAA RATING, 78 m., 2008

Sarah Adler (Batya), Nikol Leidman (Little Girl), Gera Sandler (Michael), Noa Knoller (Keren), Ma-nenita De Latorre (Joy), Zharira Charifai (Malka). Directed by Etgar Keret and Shira Geffen and produced by Amir Harel, Ayelet Kait, Yael Fogiel, and Laetitia Gonzalez. Screenplay by Geffen.

Jellyfish tells the stories of three young women whose lives, for a change, do not interlock so much as coexist. It never quite explains why these three were chosen and not three others. I found that refreshing because with some films based on entwined lives, you spend more time untangling the plot than caring about it.

In *Jellyfish,* one character is a waitress for a wedding catering firm, another is a new bride, and the third is a home care worker for elderly women. To be sure, there is a mystical vision (or memory) at the end of the film, but I'm not sure I understand the logic behind it, and I don't think I require one. It inexplicably spans a generation but works just as it is.

The film is set in Tel Aviv, but it's not an "Israeli film." That's where it was made, but it's not about anything particularly Israeli. It could take place in countless cities, and it's not "about" anything at all, in the way of a message, a theme, or a revelation. What it offers is a portrait of some time in these lives, created with attentive performances and an intriguing way of allowing them to emerge a little at a time.

The film also gives us sharply defined supporting characters. The most enigmatic, sufficient to be the center of a movie of her own, is an angelic little girl who wanders up to Batya (Sarah Adler) at the beach. She has an inner tube around her middle, which she refuses to be parted from. There are no parents in sight. Batya takes the girl to the police, who aren't much interested. They advise her to care for her over the weekend, while they wait to see if a missing-persons report comes in.

That seems a strange police decision (are there no social agencies in Israel?), but it allows a scene where Batya takes the child to her catering job, and the little girl gets her fired, and in the process she meets a woman who is a freelance wedding photographer, and so on. The photographer is fired, too, and the women end up smoking on a loading dock, discussing turns of fate. Batya has problems, and water is one of their common themes: (a) the little girl seemingly emerged from the sea, and (b) the leak in her apartment ceiling has covered the floor with about four inches of water. A tenuous link, but there you have it.

Another lead character is Keren (Noa Knoller), who breaks her ankle in a particularly ignominious way at her own wedding: She's locked into a toilet cubicle and tries to climb over the door. She and her husband have to cancel their plans for a cruise, end up in a hotel room they hate, and what's worse, the elevator goes out, and at one point it seems that her husband might have bodily carried her up twelve flights of stairs. Maybe only six. Try that sometime. The husband meets a mysterious woman from the top-floor suite, and they spend way too much time together because they're both smokers. The woman says she is a writer, but there's more to it than that.

The most realistic, down-to-earth woman in the film is Joy (Ma-nenita De Latorre), from the Philippines, who works as a minder. Her latest client, dumped on her by the woman's actress daughter, is a short-tempered case study who shouts at her to speak Hebrew or German. The girl does speak English, which is enough in many situations around the world, is learning Hebrew as fast as she can, isn't being paid much, and has a good heart. She convinces the old woman to see her daughter as Ophelia in a decidedly peculiar *Hamlet* (it seems to be written not in iambic pentameter, but in chanted repetition).

These stories have as their justification the fact that they are intrinsically interesting. I think that's enough. *Jellyfish* won the Camera d'Or at Cannes 2007 for best first feature. Given all the temptations that lure gifted first-time filmmakers with three stories to tell, each story with its own story within it, I think director Etgar Keret and his codirector and writer, Shira Geffen, are commendable, since they bring it in at seventy-eight minutes. You can easily see how it could have overstayed its welcome, especially if it ever got around to explaining that little girl, and if she's who she seems to be in the dream or vision or hallucination or whatever. Rather than an explanation in a case like that, I prefer the vision to appear, make its impact, and leave unexplained.

Jerichow ★ ★ ★

NO MPAA RATING, 91 m., 2009

Benno Furmann (Thomas), Nina Hoss (Laura), Hilmi Sozer (Ali), Andre M. Hennicke (Leon), Claudia Geisler (Administrator), Marie Gruber (Cashier), Knut Berger (Policeman). Directed by Christian Petzold and produced by Florian Koerner von Gustorf and Michael Weber. Screenplay by Petzold.

In a district where unemployment and poverty are common, it may not seem like wealth to own a snack shop. But if you own a string of them, you've got it made. Ali owns a string. He also owns a beautiful blond wife, whom he acquired by paying off her debts, just like he got the snack shops and a shiny new Mercedes.

Yet Ali is not a happy man. Born in Turkey but raised in East Germany, he moans, "I am in a country where nobody wants me, with a wife I bought." He needs a friend. Also a driver, after he loses his license for drunk driving. He hires Thomas, who has troubles of his own: He has been dishonorably discharged from the German forces in Afghanistan, his wife has just died, his savings have been stolen in a settlement of a gambling debt, he was knocked out in the process, and he is homeless and broke. Sure, he'd like to be Ali's driver.

This is the setup for Christian Petzold's *Jerichow,* named for the East German locale. Petzold may ring a bell for you from last year's weirdly intriguing thriller *Yella,* about a woman on the lam from an abusive husband and hoping to embezzle a fortune in her new job. Yella was played by Nina Hoss, who plays

Ali's wife, Laura, here. She would be sexy if she didn't have that quality of edgy desperation. Ali (Hilmi Sozer), who looks a little like a Turkish Bob Hoskins, is a very untrusting man, convinced he is being cheated for an excellent reason: He is.

Thomas (Benno Furmann), who shows in one scene he is very confident with brutal hand-to-hand fighting, is the kind of man Ali is looking for—a collector, enforcer, spy, and dependent on Ali. He is also taller than Ali, younger, and better-looking, which doesn't escape Laura's attention. We can see trouble coming.

Ali likes to flash his money and hint at big plans, but he leads a narrow life. He and Laura live at the end of a forest road, next to the warehouse where they load a van with milk, soda, chips, and candy for daily deliveries. He is half-crazy with paranoia, sneaking around corners to catch his shop managers stealing. He also fears catching Laura and Thomas together, and when he makes a business trip to Turkey, is he almost setting them up?

It may not be that simple. Nothing in this movie may be that simple. Petzold doesn't make level-one thrillers, and his characters may be smarter than us or dumber. It's never just about the plot, anyway. It has to do with random accidents, dangerous coincidences, miscalculations, simple mistakes. And the motives are never simple.

It's easy to compare *Jerichow* with the films of *The Postman Always Rings Twice*, with the grimy gas station owner, the sexy wife, and the rugged drifter, but people have a way of not behaving according to their superficial qualities. And there may be something going on here about the complexities of being a stranger in a very strange land.

Jimmy Carter Man from Plains ★ ★ ★
PG, 126 m., 2007

A documentary written and directed by Jonathan Demme and produced by Demme and Neda Armian.

Jimmy Carter could be sitting in the shade watching his peanuts grow, but at eighty-three he maintains a ceaseless schedule of travel, speeches, talk show appearances, and meetings, most devoted to his obsession with peace in the Middle East. Jonathan Demme's new documentary, *Jimmy Carter Man from Plains,* shows a man whose beliefs, both political and religious, seem to reinvigorate him; he even carries his own luggage in airports and hotels.

Demme, a skilled documentarian as well as a considerable feature director (*The Silence of the Lambs, Philadelphia*), follows Carter in late 2006 on a tour to promote his newest book, *Palestine: Peace Not Apartheid.* The former president, who brokered the famous Camp David handshake between Israeli prime minister Menachem Begin and Egyptian president Anwar Sadat, believes there will never be peace in the region if the two sides do not talk and eventually agree, and throughout the tour he is picketed and challenged by pro-Israel demonstrators, who especially dislike his use of the word "apartheid." We get the feeling he might have chosen another word if he'd realized how that one would upstage rational discussion about his book.

The impression we get is that Carter is a man at peace with himself. He rarely raises his voice, doesn't get impatient with aides, is stern but not angry with interviewers who have not read his book. He and Rosalynn, his wife since 1946, read a verse from the Bible every night before bedtime, and sometimes he takes the pulpit at his local church; his brand of Christianity teaches him that he is his brother's keeper, and we see him building housing for the poor in the aftermath of Katrina. If he has differences with the current occupant of the White House, and he does, we have to sense them between the lines; he doesn't seize the opportunity of an omnipresent camera to make partisan speeches.

Watching the film, I recalled Demme's 1992 documentary *Cousin Bobby,* about his cousin Robert Castle, a white Episcopalian priest who had served an inner-city church in Harlem for many years. There are ways in which the cousin and President Carter are similar, including their sleeves-up, rigorous style of putting their faith into action. They don't want to build enormous architectural monuments to themselves, but help ordinary folks get on with their lives. Neither one will have any trouble squeezing through the eye of the needle.

The fact is that Jimmy Carter is an immensely good man, as far as I can tell from Demme's film and everything else I know about him. One reason to see this film might be to learn more about his views on the Middle East, but a better reason might be to observe how he attends to the privilege and responsibility of doing what he believes is the right thing. It cannot be a pleasure, the never-ending round of airports, buses, taxis, hotel rooms, and interviews. He doesn't make things easy on himself by accepting the use of private jets, and he waits in line along with everyone else. He doesn't accept fees for speeches. I think he flies first class more because of the Secret Service than his own insistence. I don't see any ego-gratification going on. He seems to believe he is doing his duty, and if I am ever eighty-three, or seventy-three, I hope I can find the same energy and dedication in my own little sphere.

I saw this film for the first time at the 2007 Toronto Film Festival. On the same day, I read a news story about the book *Dead Certain* by Robert Draper in which President George W. Bush confided some of his plans for retirement. Bush told Draper: "I'll give some speeches, to replenish the ol' coffers—I don't know what my dad gets—it's more than fifty to seventy-five thousand per speech. . . . Clinton's making a lot of money." In another interview, he noted Clinton's recent work with the United Nations and said that after he retired, "You won't catch me hanging around the U.N."

I wrote about that in my report from Toronto, closing with the reflection that everyone should choose the retirement plan that is right for them.

Journey to the Center of the Earth ★ ★
PG, 92 m., 2008

Brendan Fraser (Trevor Anderson), Josh Hutcherson (Sean), Anita Briem (Hannah). Directed by Eric Brevig and produced by Charlotte Huggins, Beau Flynn, and Cary Granat. Screenplay by Michael Weiss, Jennifer Flackett, and Mark Levin, inspired by the novel by Jules Verne.

There is a part of me that will always have affection for a movie like *Journey to the Center of the Earth*. It is a small part and steadily shrinking, but once I put on the 3-D glasses and settled into my seat, it started perking up. This is a fairly bad movie, and yet at the same time maybe about as good as it could be. There may not be an eight-year-old alive who would not love it. If I had seen it when I was eight, I would have remembered it with deep affection for all these years, until I saw it again and realized how little I really knew at that age.

You are already familiar with the premise, that there is another land inside of our globe. You are familiar because the Jules Verne novel has inspired more than a dozen movies and countless TV productions, including a series, and has been ripped off by such as Edgar Rice Burroughs, who called it Pellucidar and imagined that the earth was hollow and there was another world on the inside surface. (You didn't ask, but yes, I own a copy of *Tarzan at the Earth's Core* with the original dust jacket.)

In this version, Brendan Fraser stars as a geologist named Trevor, who defends the memory of his late brother, Max, who believed the center of the earth could be reached through "volcanic tubes." Max disappeared on a mysterious expedition, which, if it involved volcanic tubes, should have been no surprise to him. Now Trevor has been asked to spend some time with his nephew, Max's son, who is named Sean (Josh Hutcherson). What with one thing and another, wouldn't you know they find themselves in Iceland, and peering down a volcanic tube. They are joined in this enterprise by Hannah (Anita Briem), whom they find living in Max's former research headquarters near the volcano he was investigating.

Now begins a series of adventures, in which the operative principle is: No matter how frequently or how far they fall, they will land without injury. They fall very frequently and very far. The first drop lands them at the bottom of a deep cave, from which they cannot possibly climb, but they remain remarkably optimistic: "There must be a way out of here!" Sure enough, they find an abandoned mine shaft and climb aboard three cars of its miniature railway for a scene that will make you swear the filmmakers must have seen *Indiana*

Jones and the Temple of Doom. Just like in that movie, they hurtle down the tracks at breakneck speeds; they're in three cars, on three more or less parallel tracks, leading you to wonder why three parallel tracks were constructed at great expense and bother, but just when such questions are forming, they have to (1) leap a chasm, (2) jump from one car to another, and (3) crash. It's a funny thing about that little railway: After all these years, it still has lamps hanging over the rails, and the electricity is still on.

The problem of lighting an unlit world is solved in the next cave they enter, which is inhabited by cute little birds that glow in the dark. One of them makes friends with Sean and leads them on to the big attraction—a world bounded by a great interior sea. This world must be a terrible place to inhabit; it has man-eating and man-strangling plants, its waters harbor giant-fanged fish and fearsome sea snakes that eat them, and on the farther shore is a Tyrannosaurus rex.

So do the characters despair? Would you despair if you were trapped miles below the surface in a cave and being chased by its hungry inhabitants? Of course not. There isn't a moment in the movie when anyone seems frightened, not even during a fall straight down for thousands of feet, during which they link hands like skydivers and carry on a conversation. Trevor gets the ball rolling: "We're still falling!"

I mentioned 3-D glasses earlier in the review. Yes, the movie is available in 3-D in "selected theaters." Select those theaters to avoid. With a few exceptions (such as the authentic IMAX process), 3-D remains underwhelming to me—a distraction, a disappointment, and more often than not offering a dingy picture. I guess setting your story inside the earth is one way to explain why it always seems to need more lighting.

The movie is being shown in 2-D in a majority of theaters, and that's how I wish I had seen it. Since there's that part of me with a certain weakness for movies like this, it's possible I would have liked it more. It would have looked brighter and clearer, and the photography wouldn't have been cluttered up with all the leaping and gnashing of teeth. Then I could have appreciated the work of the plucky actors, who do a lot of things right in this movie, of which the most heroic is keeping a straight face.

Juno ★ ★ ★ ★
PG-13, 92 m., 2007

Ellen Page (Juno MacGuff), Michael Cera (Paulie Bleeker), Jennifer Garner (Vanessa Loring), Jason Bateman (Mark Loring), Allison Janney (Bren MacGuff), J. K. Simmons (Mac MacGuff), Olivia Thirby (Leah). Directed by Jason Reitman and produced by Lianne Halfon, John Malkovich, Mason Novick, and Russell Smith. Screenplay by Diablo Cody.

Jason Reitman's *Juno* is just about the best movie of the year. It is very smart, very funny, and very touching; it begins with the pacing of a screwball comedy and ends as a portrait of characters we have come to love. Strange, how during Juno's hip dialogue and cocky bravado, we begin to understand the young woman inside, and we want to hug her.

Has there been a better performance this year than Ellen Page's creation of Juno? I don't think so. If most actors agree that comedy is harder than drama, then harder still is comedy depending on a quick mind, utter self-confidence, and an ability to stop just short of going too far. Page's presence and timing are extraordinary. I have seen her in only two films, she is only twenty, and I think she will be one of the great actors of her time.

But don't let my praise get in the way of sharing how much fun this movie is. It is so very rare to sit with an audience that leans forward with delight and is in step with every turn and surprise of an uncommonly intelligent screenplay. It is so rare to hear laughter that is surprised, unexpected, and delighted. So rare to hear it coming during moments of recognition, when characters reflect exactly what we'd be thinking, just a moment before we get around to thinking it. So rare to feel the audience joined into one warm shared enjoyment. So rare to hear a movie applauded.

Ellen Page plays Juno MacGuff, a sixteen-year-old girl who decides it is time for her to experience sex, and enlists her best friend, Paulie (Michael Cera), in an experiment he is not too eager to join. Of course she gets pregnant, and after a trip to an abortion clinic that leaves her cold, she decides to have the child. But what to do with it? She believes she's too young to raise it herself. Her best girlfriend, Leah (Olivia Thirby), suggests looking at the ads for adoptive parents in the *Penny Saver*: "They have 'Desperately Seeking Spawn,' right next to the pet ads."

Juno informs her parents, in a scene that decisively establishes how original this film is going to be. It does that by giving us almost the only lovable parents in the history of teen comedies: Bren (Allison Janney) and Mac (J. K. Simmons). They're older and wiser than most teen parents are ever allowed to be, and warmer and with better instincts and quicker senses of humor. Informed that the sheepish Paulie is the father, Mac turns to his wife and shares an aside that brings down the house. Later, Bren tells him, "You know, of course, it wasn't his idea." How infinitely more human and civilized their response is than all the sad routine "humor" about parents who are enraged at boyfriends.

Mac goes with Juno to meet the would-be adoptive parents, Vanessa and Mark Loring (Jennifer Garner and Jason Bateman). They live in one of those houses that look like Martha Stewart finished a second before they arrived. Vanessa is consumed with her desire for a child, and Mark is almost a child himself, showing Juno "my room," where he keeps the residue of his ambition to be a rock star. What he does now, at around forty, is write jingles for commercials.

We follow Juno through all nine months of her pregnancy, which she pretends to treat as mostly an inconvenience. It is uncanny how Page shows us, without seeming to show us, the deeper feelings beneath Juno's wisecracking exterior. The screenplay by first-timer Diablo Cody is a subtle masterpiece of construction, as buried themes slowly emerge, hidden feelings become clear, and we are led, but not too far, into wondering if Mark and Juno might possibly develop unwise feelings about one another.

There are moments of instinctive, lightning comedy: Bren's response to a nurse's attitude during Juno's sonar scan, and her theory about doctors when Juno wants a painkiller during childbirth. Moments that blindside us with truth, as when Mac and Juno talk about

the possibility of true and lasting love. Moments that reveal Paulie as more than he seems. What he says when Juno says he's cool and doesn't even need to try. And the breathtaking scene when Juno and Vanessa run into each other in the mall, and the future of everyone is essentially decided. Jennifer Garner glows in that scene.

After three viewings I feel like I know some scenes by heart, but I don't want to spoil your experience by quoting one-liners and revealing surprises. The film's surprises, in any event, involve not merely the plot but insights into the characters, including feelings that coil along just beneath the surface so that they seem inevitable when they're revealed.

The film has no wrong scenes and no extra scenes, and flows like running water. There are two repeating motifs: the enchanting songs, so simple and true, by Kimya Dawson, and the seasonal appearances of Paulie's high school cross-country team, running past us with dogged consistency, Paulie often bringing up the rear, until his last run ends with Paulie, sweaty in running shorts, racing to Juno's room after her delivery.

Just Another Love Story ★ ★ ★ ½
NO MPAA RATING, 104 m., 2009

Anders W. Berthelsen (Jonas), Rebecka Hemse (Julia), Nikolaj Lie Kaas (Sebastian), Charlotte Fich (Mette), Dejan Cukic (Frank), Karsten Jansfort (Poul), Flemming Enevold (Overlaege Dichmann), Bent Mejding (Hr. Castlund). Directed by Ole Bornedal and produced by Michael Obel. Screenplay by Bornedal.

Apart from a little nudity, *Just Another Love Story* could have been inspired, almost shot by shot, from a 1940s film noir from RKO, when it would have started with Robert Mitchum dying on the sidewalk in the rain. This is a vigorous thriller from Denmark that tells the classic noir story of a flawed cop trapped between a good wife and a bad woman. The twist is, the woman doesn't know she's been bad, since she has amnesia. It gets better.

Jonas is a Copenhagen homicide scene photographer, happily married, two kids. One day his car stalls, another car slams into him, runs head-on into a third car, and flips into the ditch. The other driver, Julia, is critically injured. He visits her in the hospital and is greeted with joy by her family, who assumes he must be the Sebastian she told them about, the new fiancé she met in Vietnam. He had to return on a later flight.

At this point, if Jonas (Anders W. Berthelsen) had seen any noirs at all, he would say: "I don't know who Sebastian is, but my name is Jonas." He pauses for a fatal instant and is swept into another life. Because Julia (Rebecka Hemse) doesn't remember much and can't see well, she has no choice but to agree with her family that this is Sebastian. Her father gives him a blank check, her family embraces him, and Jonas topples into a double life.

Oh, but it's more than that. Most noirs are. One thing about them is that they're rigidly moralistic. If you cheat on your wife, you're going to pay for it. This is true even if your wife knows nothing about it, the other woman can scarcely be blamed, and you start out only trying to accommodate an accident victim and her worried family.

Ole Bornedal, the film's writer and director, works at a considerably quicker pace than traditional noirs and ingeniously introduces ironies and complications I will not even hint at. The closing scenes of the plot spring one surprise after another. They seem laid on thick, but we have to admit, given all that leads up to them, they make sense.

Just Another Love Story works in nice little touches. I liked Jonas's partner in photographing crime scenes, who deals with the violence and gore by laughing about it. There's a scene where a horrifying situation is described, and the guy shakes, he's chuckling so hard. Why is this shown? Well, if you photograph murder scenes, you deal with it the best you can. The whole movie flavors its plot with quirky observations and asides.

It's interesting that two of the best thrillers of the last several months, *Tell No One* and *Just Another Love Story,* have come from Europe. Both movies gain because they star actors unfamiliar to us. They gain because there's room in them for close observation of the characters. They gain most of all because they don't slow down the plot for unnecessary special effects scenes—fights, chases, things like that. Unless such scenes are necessary or very well-done, essentially they just put the plot on hold while the filmmakers flex their muscles. Here the plotting has all the muscle that's required.

K

King of California ★ ★ ★
PG-13, 93 m., 2007

Michael Douglas (Charlie), Evan Rachel Wood (Miranda), Willis Burks II (Pepper). Directed by Michael Cahill and produced by Alexander Payne, Michael London, Avi Lerner, and Randall Emmett. Screenplay by Cahill.

In *King of California*, Michael Douglas looks like Whiskers McCrazy. Why do people who look like this resent being treated as if they look like this? Security guards are attracted to him like bears to honey. Did it occur to anyone that the movie might have been funnier if he'd been groomed like the tycoons he's played in all those corporate roles, his hair slicked back like Pat Riley's?

To be sure, it would be hard to explain how his character, Charlie, got the wardrobe and the grooming in the institution he has just been discharged from, but that could be part of the fun: "I cut my hair in a mirror with a nail-clipper, and didn't you ever see one of those prison-break movies where they make Nazi uniforms out of old blankets?" He would be explaining that to his sixteen-year-old daughter, Miranda (Evan Rachel Wood), who has been living parentless at home for the last two years; her mother walked out some time ago, and she keeps child welfare off her back by convincing each set of authorities that she is actually with the other parent. That's a confusing sentence, but then it's an explanation intended to confuse.

Meanwhile, she works overtime at McDonald's, still somehow affords the cost of living in their increasingly run-down house, and acts like she is level-headed and competent, even if she's scared. She's unsettled that her strange father has reappeared, and it's obvious he is less prepared to make survival decisions than she is. He's manic-depressive, is my guess, and has been busy studying ancient documents that convince him a treasure in gold was buried by early Spanish conquistadors somewhere near where they are now, in Santa Clarita. He obtains a metal detector and enlists poor Miranda in an obsessive search that takes them through parking lots and down the sides of highways.

Their search is at first fruitless, but Charlie remains undaunted, and Miranda gamely goes along. There is something quietly hypnotic about his quest that begins to win her over into the delusion that he just possibly might be right. Of course, he could be wrong, too, but at least their mission gives them a purpose. Using the metal detector and surveying instruments, he convinces himself he has found the gold, which is now buried under the aisle of a Costco. Have you ever seen a guy like this using a metal detector in a Costco? I actually think I may have. Just field-testing it, maybe. Exploiting his daughter's talent as a minimum-wage employee, Charlie convinces her to get a job at the Costco and steal a key. And then, one dark night . . .

Well, yes, the plot of *King of California* is absurd. Maybe not so absurd to Charlie, however, whose quest is positioned as an assault on the bland conformity of society. What kind of a man, in possession of certain information that a fortune is buried under Costco, would be such a wimp that he wouldn't go after it? Douglas does an interesting thing with the role. He starts with our assumption that he is unbalanced, which of course he is, and then doesn't overact the looniness but simply focuses on the obsession. His unspoken assumption that Miranda shares his goal removes the need for him to convince her—at least in his mind.

The film, in its own off-center way, is worth seeing, if only because of the zealotry of the Douglas performance and the pluck of Evan Rachel Wood, nineteen when she made it, who since *Thirteen* (2003) has become a young star with a future. The first-time writer-director Michael Cahill doesn't exactly convince me that this film cried out to be his debut, as he follows into the strange places Charlie leads him. But at least he wants to work off the map and not turn out another standard study of angst, violence, or terminal hipness. We have not seen these characters before, which is a rare gift from a movie.

Charlie and Miranda make observations along the way about how things have changed, even in her young life. Some of them involve the family's old neighborhood, which they used to have to themselves before all those other home owners moved in and turned it into a suburb. "We used to be surrounded by nothing," he says. Her reply is that they still are, but now nothing has a population. I know how he feels every time I pass the yuppie restaurants on the stretch of Clark Street formerly dominated by the Last Stop Before Expressway Liquor Store.

There is a belief in this movie that a flywheel like Charlie is actually saner than the boring people around him. At least he embraces life and goes for the gold. But there is a name for his condition, and he quite possibly may have been discharged prematurely. No matter how his quest concludes, it will not be, for a mental health professional, a happy ending. But we are not professionals, and we enjoy him instead of diagnosing him. When you stand back a step from the movie, you admire Douglas and Wood for starting with potentially unplayable characters and playing them so well we actually care about a quest that, in a way, seems more designed for Abbott and Costello.

The King of Kong: A Fistful of Quarters ★ ★ ★
PG-13, 90 m., 2007

Featuring Steve Wiebe, Billy Mitchell, Walter Day, Nicole Wiebe, Todd Rogers, Steve Sanders, Doris Self. A documentary directed by Seth Gordon and produced by Ed Cunningham. Screenplay by Gordon.

Remember Donkey Kong? This would have been in the early 1980s, and you would have been standing in a video arcade, bar, truck stop, or bowling alley, trying to save the damsel in distress from the gorilla. It was voted the third best coin-operated arcade video game of all time (after Pac-Man and Galaga). Yes, and now it is 2007, and grown men still chase each other across the country in pursuit of the world-record Donkey Kong score.

The King of Kong: A Fistful of Quarters, a documentary that is beyond strange, follows two archenemies in their grim, long-term rivalry, which involves way more time than any human should devote to Donkey Kong. I am reminded of the butler's line in *A New Leaf* to Walter Matthau: "You are carrying on in your own lifetime, sir, a way of life that was extinct before you were born."

In this corner, the man in black, wearing a goatee and looking like a snake oil pitchman, is Billy Mitchell of Hollywood, Florida, in real life a hot sauce tycoon (Rickey's World Famous Sauces), who says he is the man who first retailed chicken wings in their modern culinary form in Florida. That was not enough for one lifetime. He also achieved the first perfect game in the history of Pac-Man, his high score on Donkey Kong stood unchallenged for twenty-five years, and in 1999 he was named Video Game Player of the Century. In 2004, Mitchell began a series of special commemorative labels on hot sauce bottles to honor major gaming events and their champions.

In the other corner, looking like your average neighbor, Steve Wiebe of Seattle, who got laid off at Boeing the very day he and his wife bought a new house. He has kids, he's likable, and he plays Donkey Kong on a machine in his garage, where we gather he spends hours and hours and hours. He's now working as a high school science teacher.

The referee: Walter Day, halfway between them in Iowa, who runs a Web site named Twin Galaxies, and is the chief scorekeeper of competitive gaming. Day's serenity was severely challenged when Wiebe mailed in a home videotape showing himself breaking Mitchell's famous record. In the world of Donkey Kong, this was as monumental as Barry Bonds beating Hank Aaron's record, except that Wiebe is the Hank Aaron of these two, if you see what I mean.

Mitchell fires back. He questions the record, the machine, the video, and Wiebe's character. Wiebe dips into his meager savings to go to Florida and challenge Mitchell head-on. Mitchell won't show. Or he does show at a few conventions and is easy to spot with his satanic wardrobe and pneumatic wife, but never quite turns up to play. He's glimpsed sometimes passing ominously in the background.

This isn't fun for these men. It's deadly serious. A world championship is at stake, and only gradually do we realize how very few people give a damn. Unlike recent docs about spelling bees, Scrabble, and crossword puzzles, there aren't large audiences in this film. Game players may turn up by the thousands at conventions, but apparently only a handful care much about Donkey Kong; it's like a big auto show vs. a parade of Model T's.

The documentary stares incredulously at the Machiavellian Mitchell, who seems to play the same role in the world of Donkey Kong as masked marauders do in pro wrestling. We hate this guy. Why won't he play Wiebe? What's with that tape he sends in that seems to show him beating Wiebe's record, but has some curious technical difficulties? Is this little world too heavily invested in Mitchell as its superstar? How long can Wiebe's wife remain patient and supportive of his lonely quest? Will Walter Day burn out and retire?

All questions to which you will find answers, sort of, in the film. I would never dream of giving away the ending. But I can give away what happened after the ending. This film premiered at the Tribeca Film Festival on May 5, 2007. Today I went to www.TwinGalaxies.com and discovered that on July 13, 2007, the twenty-fifth anniversary of his original record, "in front of an audience of hundreds," Billy Mitchell topped his own record by scoring 1,050,200 points. I have a sinking feeling that Steve Wiebe is out in the garage right now.

The Kite Runner ★ ★ ★ ★
PG-13, 120 m., 2007

Khalid Abdalla (Amir), Homayoun Ershadi (Baba), Shaun Toub (Rahim Khan), Atossa Leoni (Soraya), Said Taghmaoui (Farid), Zekiria Ebrahimi (Young Amir), Ali Danesh Bakhtyari (Sohrab), Ahmad Khan Mahmoodzada (Young Hassan), Nabi Tanha (Ali), Elham Ehsas (Young Assef). Directed by Marc Forster and produced by William Hornberg, Walter F. Parkes, Rebecca Yeldham, and E. Bennett Walsh. Screenplay by David Benioff, based on the novel by Khaled Hosseini.

How long has it been since you saw a movie that succeeds as pure story? That doesn't depend on stars, effects, or genres, but simply fascinates you with how it will turn out? Marc Forster's *The Kite Runner,* based on a much-loved novel, is a movie like that. It superimposes human faces and a historical context on the tragic images of war from Afghanistan.

The story begins with boys flying kites. It is the city of Kabul in 1978, before the Russians, the Taliban, the Americans, and the anarchy. Amir (Zekiria Ebrahimi) joins with countless other boys in filling the sky with kites; sometimes they dance on the rooftops while dueling, trying to cut other kite strings with their own. Amir's friend is Hassan (Ahmad Khan Mahmoodzada), the son of the family's longtime servant. He is the best kite runner in the neighborhood, correctly predicting when a kite will return to Earth and waiting there to retrieve it.

The boys live in a healthy, vibrant city, not yet touched by war. Amir's father, called Baba (Homayoun Ershadi), is an intellectual and secularist who has no use for the mullahs. His servant, Ali (Nabi Tanha), has been with the family for years, has become like family himself. And Baba, whose kindly eyes are benevolent, loves both boys.

There is a neighborhood bully named Assef (Elham Ehsas), jealous of Amir's kite, his skills, and his kite runner. And on a day that will shape the course of many lives, he and his gang track down Hassan, attack him, and rape him. Amir arrives to see the assault taking place and, to his shame, sneaks away. And then a curious chemistry takes place. Amir feels so guilty about Hassan that his feelings transform into anger, and he tries insulting his friend, even throwing ripe fruit at him, but Hassan is impassive. Then Amir tries to plant evidence to make Hassan seem to be a thief, but even after Hassan (untruthfully and masochistically) confesses, Baba forgives him. It is Hassan's father who insists he and his son must leave the home, over Baba's protests.

The film has opened with the modern-day Amir, now living in Los Angeles, receiving a telephone call from his father's friend Rahim Khan: "You should come home. There is a way to be good again." And then commences a remarkable series of old memories and new realities, of the present trying to heal the wounds of the past, of an adult trying to repair the damage he set in motion as a boy. For if he had not lied about Hassan, they would all be together in Los Angeles and the telephone call would not have been necessary.

Working from Khaled Hosseini's bestseller, Forster and his screenwriter, David Benioff, have made a film that sidesteps the emotional disconnects we often feel when a story moves between past and present. This is all the same story, interlaced with the fabric of these lives. There is also a touching sequence as Amir and his father, now older and ill, meet a once-powerful Afghan general and his daughter, Soraya (Atossa Leoni). For Amir and Soraya, it is instant love, but protocol must be observed, and one of the warmest scenes in the movie involves the two old men discussing the future of their children. I want to mention once again the eyes, indeed the whole face, of the actor Homayoun Ershadi, as Amir's father; here is a face so deeply good it is difficult to imagine it reflecting unworthy feelings.

What happens back in Afghanistan (and Pakistan) in the year 2000 need not be revealed here, but the scenes combine great suspense with deep emotion. One emblematic moment: a soccer game where the audience, all men and all oddly silent, are watched by guards with rifles. The film works so deeply on us because we have been so absorbed by its story, by its destinies, by the way these individuals become so important that we are forced to stop thinking of "Afghans" as simply a category in body counts on the news.

The movie is acted largely in English, although many (subtitled) scenes are in Dari, which I learn is an Afghan dialect of Farsi, or Persian. The performances by the actors playing Amir and Hassan as children are natural, convincing, and powerful; recently I have seen several such child performances, which adults would envy for their conviction and strength. Ahmad Khan Mahmoodzada, as Hassan, is particularly striking, with his serious, sometimes almost mournful face. (The boys in the film, who feared Afghan reprisals for appearing in the rape scene, were moved by Paramount to safety in the United Arab Emirates.)

One of the areas in which the movie succeeds is in its depiction of kite flying. Yes, it uses special effects, but they function to represent what freedom and exhilaration the kites represent to their owners. I remember my own fierce identification with my own kites as a child. I was up there; I was *represented*. Yet

there is a fundamental difference between the kite flyer (Amir) and the kite runner (Hassan). Perhaps that sad wisdom in Hassan's eyes comes from his certainty that all must fall to Earth, sooner or later.

This is a magnificent film by Marc Forster, who since *Monster's Ball* (2001) has made *Finding Neverland* (2004), *Stay* (2005), and *Stranger Than Fiction* (2006). All fine work, but *The Kite Runner* equals *Monster's Ball* in its emotional impact. Like *House of Sand and Fog* and *Man Push Cart*, it helps us to understand that the newcomers among us come from somewhere and are somebody.

Kit Kittredge: An American Girl ★ ★ ★ ½
G, 100 m., 2008

Abigail Breslin (Kit), Julia Ormond (Mrs. Kittredge), Chris O'Donnell (Mr. Kittredge), Max Thieriot (Will), Zach Mills (Stirling Howard), Joan Cusack (Miss Bond), Stanley Tucci (Jefferson J. Berk), Willow Smith (Countee), Madison Davenport (Ruthie Smithens), Jane Krakowski (Miss Dooley), Glenne Headley (Mrs. Howard), Wallace Shawn (Mr. Gibson). Directed by Patricia Rozema and produced by Elaine Goldsmith-Thomas, Lisa Gillan, Ellen L. Brothers, and Julie Goldstein. Screenplay by Ann Peacock, based on the stories by Valerie Tripp.

Considering that it is inspired by one of the dolls in the American Girl product line, *Kit Kittredge: An American Girl* is some kind of a miracle: an actually good movie. I expected so much less. I was waiting for some kind of banal product placement, I suppose, and here is a movie that is just about perfect for its target audience and more than that. It has a great look, engaging performances, real substance, and even a few whispers of political ideas, all surrounding the freshness and charm of Abigail Breslin, who was eleven when it was filmed.

The movie is set in Cincinnati at the dawn of the Great Depression; perfectly timed, it would appear, as we head into another one. Kit pounds furiously on the typewriter in her tree house, determined to become a girl reporter, while a big story is happening right downstairs in her family house: Its mortgage is about to be foreclosed. Her dad (Chris O'Donnell) has lost his car dealership and gone to Chicago seeking work, her mom (Julia Ormond) is taking in boarders, and there's local hysteria about muggings and robberies allegedly committed by hoboes.

Kit meets a couple of hoboes. Will (Max Thieriot) is about her age, and his sidekick Countee (Willow Smith) is a little younger. They live in the hobo camp down by the river, along with as nice a group of hoboes as you'd ever want to meet, and Kit tries selling their story and photos to the editor of the local paper (snarling Wallace Shawn). No luck. But other adventures ensue: She adopts a dog, her mom acquires chickens, Kit sells the eggs, and the new boarders are a colorfully assorted lot. And she sees such unthinkable sights as neighbors' furniture being moved to the sidewalk by deputies. Will that happen at her address?

The boarders include a magician (Stanley Tucci), a nurse (Jane Krakowski), the erratic driver (Joan Cusack) of a mobile library truck, and assorted others, eventually including even a monkey. Kit's mom hides her treasures in a lock box, but it is stolen, and unmistakable clues point to the hoboes. A footprint found under a window, for example, has a star imprint that exactly matches the boots found in Will's tent, and the sheriff names him the prime suspect. But hold on! Kit and her best friends, Stirling and Ruthie (Zach Mills and Madison Davenport), develop another theory, which would clear Will and implicate someone (dramatically lowered voice) a lot closer to home.

All of this (the missing loot, Kit's ambitions, Important Clues) is, of course, the very lifeblood of the Nancy Drew and Hardy Boys books, and Kit Kittredge not only understands that genre but breathes life into it. This movie, intelligently and sincerely directed by Patricia Rozema (Mansfield Park) does not condescend. It does not cheapen or go for easy laughs. It is as serious about Kit as she is about herself and doesn't treat her like some (indignant exclamation) dumb girl.

If you have or know or can borrow a girl (or a boy) who collects the American Girl dolls, grab onto that child as your excuse to see this movie. You may enjoy it as much as the kids

do—maybe more, with its period costumes, settings, and music. The kids may be astonished that banks actually foreclosed on people's homes in the old days (hollow laugh). And there may be a message lurking somewhere in the movie's tolerance of hoboes. The American Girl dolls have already inspired TV movies about Molly, Felicity, and Samantha. What's for sure is that if Kit Kittredge sets the tone for more upcoming American Girl movies, we can anticipate some wonderful family films.

Knowing ★ ★ ★ ★
PG-13, 122 m., 2009

Nicolas Cage (John Koestler), Rose Byrne (Diana Wayland), Chandler Canterbury (Caleb Koestler), Lara Robinson (Lucinda Embry/Abby Wayland), Ben Mendelsohn (Phil Beckman). Directed by Alex Proyas and produced by Proyas, Todd Black, Jason Blumenthal, and Steve Tisch. Screenplay by Proyas, Ryne Pearson, Juliet Snowden, and Stiles White.

Knowing is among the best science fiction films I've seen—frightening, suspenseful, intelligent, and, when it needs to be, rather awesome. In its very different way, it is comparable to the great Dark City, by the same director, Alex Proyas. That film was about the hidden nature of the world men think they inhabit, and so is this one.

The plot involves the most fundamental of all philosophical debates: Is the universe deterministic or random? Is everything in some way preordained, or does it happen by chance? If that question sounds too abstract, wait until you see this picture, which poses it in stark terms: What if we could know in advance when the earth will end?

Nicolas Cage, in another wound-up, edgy performance, plays Koestler, a professor of astrophysics at MIT. He votes for deterministic; as he tells his class, he believes "shit happens." His wife has died, and he's raising his young son, Caleb (Chandler Canterbury). A time capsule is opened at Caleb's grade school, containing the drawings of students in 1959 predicting the sights of 2009. But the sheet Caleb gets isn't a drawing; it's covered with rows of numbers. In a prologue, we've seen the girl with haunted eyes, Lucinda (Lara Robinson), who so intensely pressed the numbers into the paper.

What do these numbers mean? You already know from the TV ads, but I don't believe I should tell you. I'll write another article that will contain spoilers. Let me say that Koestler discovers almost by accident a pattern in the numbers, and they shake his scientific mind to its core. His obsession is scoffed at by his MIT colleague, a cosmologist named Beckman (Ben Mendelsohn), who warns Koestler against the heresy of numerology—the finding of imaginary patterns in numbers. Beckman's passionate arguments in the film, which are not technical yet are scientifically sound, raise the stakes. This is not a movie about psychic mumble-jumble; Koestler is a hard-headed scientist, too, or always thought he was, until that page of numbers came into his hands.

By "scientifically sound," I don't mean anyone at MIT is going to find the plot other than preposterous. So it is—but not while the movie is playing. It works as science fiction, which often changes one coordinate in an otherwise logical world just to see what might happen. For Koestler, it leads to a rejection of what he has always believed, to his serious consideration of the paranormal, and to his discovery of Diana (Rose Byrne), the daughter of little Lucinda who wrote down the numbers, and Abby, the granddaughter (Lara Robinson again).

He believes the two children are somehow instrumental in the developing scenario, and he bonds with Diana to protect them from evil Strangers in the woods—who are mostly kept far enough away in long shots to prevent them from seeming more Strange than they must. The logic of the story leads us to expect something really spectacular at the end, and I was not disappointed visually, although I have logical questions that are sort of beside the point.

With expert and confident storytelling, Proyas strings together events that keep tension at a high pitch all through the film. Even a few quiet, human moments have something coiling beneath. Pluck this movie, and it vibrates. Even something we've seen countless times, like a car pursuit, works here because of the meaning of the pursuit and the high stakes.

There are sensational special effects in the film, which again I won't describe. You'll know the ones I mean. The film is beautifully photographed by Simon Duggan, the Marco Beltrami score hammers or elevates when it needs to, and Richard Learoyd's editing is knife-edged; when he needs to hurtle us through sequences, he does it with an insistence that doesn't feel rushed.

You may have guessed from the TV ads that something very bad is unfolding for the earth, and you may ask, not unreasonably, how these two nice parents and their lovable kids can possibly have any effect on it. Ah, but that would be in a random universe, and *Knowing* argues that the universe is deterministic. Or . . . *does* it? Your papers will be due before class on Monday. ☞

Kung Fu Panda ★ ★ ★
PG, 91 m., 2008

With the voices of: Jack Black (Po), Dustin Hoffman (Master Shifu), Angelina Jolie (Tigress), Ian McShane (Tai Lung), Jackie Chan (Monkey), Seth Rogen (Mantis), Lucy Liu (Viper), David Cross (Crane), Randall Duk Kim (Oogway), James Hong (Mr. Ping), Michael Clarke Duncan (Commander Vachir), Dan Fogler (Zeng). Directed by John Stevenson and Mark Osborne and produced by Melissa Cobb. Written by Jonathan Aibel and Glenn Berger.

Kung Fu Panda is a story that almost tells itself in its title. It is so hard to imagine a big, fuzzy panda performing martial arts encounters that you intuit (and you will be right) that the panda stars in an against-all-odds formula, which dooms him to succeed. For the panda's target audience, children and younger teens, that will be just fine, and the film presents his adventures in wonderfully drawn Cinemascope animation. It was also shown in some IMAX venues.

The film stars a panda named Po (voice by Jack Black), who is so fat he can barely get out of bed. He works for his father, Mr. Ping (James Hong), in a noodle shop, which features Ping's legendary Secret Ingredient. How Ping, apparently a stork or other billed member of the avian family, fathered a panda is a mystery, not least to Po, but then the movie is filled with a wide variety of creatures who don't much seem to notice their differences.

They live in the beautiful Valley of Peace with an ancient temple towering overhead, up zillions of steps, which the pudgy Po can barely climb. But climb them he does, dragging a noodle wagon, because all the people of the valley have gathered up there to witness the choosing of the Dragon Warrior who will engage the dreaded Tai Lung (Ian McShane) in kung fu combat. Five contenders have been selected, the "Furious Five": Monkey (Jackie Chan), Tigress (Angelina Jolie), Mantis (Seth Rogen), Viper (Lucy Liu), and Crane (David Cross).

Tigress looks like she might be able to do some serious damage, but the others are less than impressive. Mantis in particular seems to weigh about an ounce, tops. All five have been trained (for nearly forever, I gather) by the wise Shifu, who with Dustin Hoffman's voice is one of the more dimensional characters in a story that doesn't give the others a lot of depth. Anyway, it's up to the temple master, Oogway (Randall Duk Kim), an ancient turtle, to make the final selection, and he chooses— yes, he chooses the hapless and pudgy Po.

The story then becomes essentially a series of action sequences, somewhat undermined by the fact that the combatants seem unable to be hurt, even if they fall from dizzying heights and crack stones open with their heads. There's an extended combat with Tai Lung on a disintegrating suspension bridge (haven't we seen that before?), hand-to-hand-to-tail combat with Po and Tai Lung, and, upstaging everything, an energetic competition over a single dumpling.

Kung Fu Panda is not one of the great recent animated films. The story is way too predictable and, truth to tell, Po himself didn't overwhelm me with his charisma. But it's elegantly drawn, the action sequences are packed with energy, and it's short enough that older viewers will be forgiving. For the kids, of course, all this stuff is much of a muchness, and here they go again.

L

Lady Chatterley ★ ★
NO MPAA RATING, 168 m., 2007

Marina Hands (Lady Connie Chatterley), Jean-Louis Coulloc'h (Parkin), Hippolyte Girardot (Sir Clifford), Helene Alexandridis (Mrs. Bolton), Helene Fillieres (Hilda). Directed by Pascale Ferran and produced by Gilles Sandoz. Screenplay by Roger Bohbot, Ferran, and Pierre Trividic, based on the novel *John Thomas and Lady Jane* by D. H. Lawrence.

Lady Chatterley is a kinder, gentler version of the story most people know as *Lady Chatterley's Lover*. It's based on an earlier version of D. H. Lawrence's once-scandalous novel that had the too-perfect title *John Thomas and Lady Jane*. While involving Lawrence's approval of transcendent lust, the film also has a great deal of time for flowers, running water, close-ups of hands, and long shots of trees. Also, of course, for the class struggle, lustful sex, and close attention to the genitals.

Let's begin with the genitals, or, as Groucho Marx called them, the netherlands. The story involves the young and fragrant Lady Connie Chatterley (Marina Hands) and her husband, Sir Clifford (Hippolyte Girardot), a wealthy mine owner who was paralyzed from the waist down in World War I. The movie's opening shot shows Connie waving good-bye from their country house as Clifford walks to his car and drives away, so we must assume they were married before the war. But Connie remains childless, and there is no heir to their estate.

Which leads us to questions involving the netherlands. Wandering the grounds lonely as a cloud, Connie comes upon the gamekeeper, Parkin (Jean-Louis Coulloc'h). He is sponging himself bare-chested, which inspires her (and us) to inspect her own naked body in a mirror. Life creeps along quietly at the country house, where Sir Clifford seems to observe a daily word limit, and the housekeeper, Mrs. Bolton (Helene Alexandridis), says little, wrings her hands, and has a look fraught with worry about, at a guess, everything.

But back to the netherlands. Connie and Parkin begin a love affair. Day after day she goes flower collecting in the woods, and they meet in his hut to make love on the floor. One day, as he is undressing, she says, "Turn around," and she (and we) gets a close-up of the netherlands flagpole. Later, after sex, she views him again and observes, "It's so funny, how now it's only a little bud." Which leads to the conclusion that her sex education with Sir Clifford must have been sadly limited, even before the war.

That may help explain why Clifford is satisfied to do without her all day every day and be content when she returns late with a handful of daffodils. She is a kind and dutiful wife, to be sure, and they spend quiet time reading, apparently always the same books. In other versions of the story, Clifford is enraged that Connie has been bagged by the gamekeeper, but here he seems almost willfully determined not to know. He would even understand if Connie were to become pregnant by another man (an Englishman, of "decent stock") to provide him with an heir, and she goes off with her sister for a month at the seaside, presumably to arrange this, although at the time she is already two months pregnant. Maybe three. Since Parkin is a strong, muscular man, Sir Clifford is about to be presented with the world's largest short-term baby.

All of this is shown with admittedly gorgeous photography, lyrical montages, and sylvan melodies. The film is spoken in French, directed by Pascale Ferran, although we are to understand that the characters are English. It won six Cesar awards, the French Oscars, including best film, best actress, most-promising actress, and best screenplay, and was nominated for four more. But not for best actor! Since Jean-Louis Coulloc'h takes the thankless role of Parkin and distinguishes it, that seems unfair.

I must also report that on www.rottentomatoes.com, the film is scoring an astonishing 100 percent favorable rating on the Tomatometer from those major critics the site deems "cream of the crop." Alas, my vote will spoil the perfect game, unless I am demoted to skim. Why do they love it so? They admire the way sex grows into true love, the gentleness and sweetness of the relationship, and that the film does not rush into sex but moseys there, in 168 minutes heavy with pastoral lyricism, and that Connie and Parkin learn to see, really see, the other person across the class divide.

So I am almost alone in my lack of enchantment, and yet even I feel some affection. Jean-Louis Coulloc'h is a fascinating Parkin. He's not a rough-hewn macho man, but a man who prefers to be left alone, a man whose mother said he was as much girl as boy, a tender lover, a brave partner, a tactful friend. And he seems real, not like a male model ready for underwear ads. He "looks a bit like Oliver Stone with a sleeker nose," writes my friend Lisa Nesselson, *Variety*'s Paris correspondent. Marina Hands is quiet, serene, daring, and beautiful, although David Noh, a good critic banished from the cream of the crop, not unfairly observes "one barely believes a single thought ever clouds Hands' porcelain brow."

All of the qualities its admirers see in the film are indeed there and visible, but I was not much moved. Lawrence wrote much better novels that inspired much better movies (*Sons and Lovers, Women in Love, The Rainbow, The Fox*). Most of them include some version of the full monty, which in a Lawrence film is like the toy in a box of Cracker Jack. Watching this film, I reflected that there are only so many boxes of Cracker Jack you can eat before you decide to hell with the toy.

La France ★ ★ ½
NO MPAA RATING, 102 m., 2008

Sylvie Testud (Camille), Pascal Greggory (Lieutenant), Guillaume Verdier (Cadet), Francois Negret (Jacques), Laurent Talon (Antoine), Pierre Leon (Alfred). Directed by Serge Bozon and produced by Philippe Martin and David Thion. Screenplay by Axelle Ropert.

Here is one of the strangest and most original war movies I've seen. Whether it is successful is a good question. *La France* centers on the story of Camille (Sylvie Testud), wife of a French soldier during World War I. She lives within a long walk of the Western Front, and after receiving an alarming letter from him, she boldly sets out to find him.

To do this, she cuts her hair and disguises herself as a boy. She encounters a group of about a dozen soldiers, who accept her as male, which is one of the first hints that the film will not be rigidly realistic. The men are led by a friendly lieutenant (Pascal Greggory). Their uniforms are ragged. After wounding Camille in the hand when they mistake her for an enemy, they find her a cast-off uniform with the smell of death about it. They explain they were separated from their main unit and are looking for it.

They engage in a long trek through forest and field. Sometimes distant guns are heard, but there are no signs of war except for a trench they walk down later in the film. The scenery is suspiciously pastoral, sylvan, and deserted for being so close to a war. At a time when, needless to say, we are not expecting it, the soldiers produce musical instruments and burst into song. Yes. Guitars, a banjo, an accordion, a clarinet, a violin, what may be a dulcimer. When marching, they show no sign of carrying these instruments, which mysteriously appear all four times they need to sing. At one point, they sing their way past a sentry.

Does Camille look like a teenage boy? Not to me. Testud has an angular face that is at least not soft and rounded, and she has pluck, as when she climbs a watchtower and kills a threatening lookout. But she looks like a girl. That the soldiers do not recognize this is consistent with their inability to fear that enemy troops might hear their songs. They are walking not through a war, but through a fantasy.

This is an intriguing idea, consistent with the moment when Camille's missing husband appears out of the woods and walks straight toward her. The film has had little action, except for a scene involving a farmer and his son who give them food and refuge. Refuge? Yes, these soldiers are deserters, looking for Belgium. Along the way they conduct deep, sad conversations about a soldier's life and tell a parable about a comrade named Pierre; they even read poetry. This must be the song and story squad.

I had a problem with the film's visual strategy. At least half of the scenes take place at night. No, not "day for night," but pitch-black night, where the soldiers appear and disappear from view. I learn from IMDb.com that the director, Serge Bozon, and his cinematographer (his sister Celine) employed a special film stock to get what they consider the "aquarium feeling" of the night scenes. Rather than seeing faces swimming out of the murk, I would rather have had a fair chance of seeing more of the characters.

Not that they are deeply developed. In keeping, I guess, with the decision to make a fantasy, they are all as consistent as the figures in a myth. They don't change. I can imagine deep, personal interaction, suspicion, revelation in the story of a disguised woman among men, but all of these characters seem swept along by the same narrative tide.

Yes, the music is intriguing and odd. The songs are more modern than the period, and have a certain bluegrass feel. There is no joy in their singing, but that is the point: These are sad, exhausted men. There is a point being made about war, in a very unexpected way. *La France* won the coveted Prix Jean Vigo as the best feature of 2007. It is inventive and unconventional, to be sure, and I credit Bozon for his daring, but personally I was not convinced.

Lake of Fire ★ ★ ★ ½
NO MPAA RATING, 152 m., 2007

Featuring Noam Chomsky, Alan M. Dershowitz, Nat Hentoff, Dallas Blanchard, Norma McCorvey, Peter Singer, Randall Terry, Frederick Clarkson, Bill Baird, Frances Kissling, Michael Griffin, and Paul Hill. A documentary written, directed, and produced by Tony Kaye.

Readers often complain about documentaries that don't tell "both sides." Those who care deeply about the issue of abortion in America, no matter which side they are on, may complain that this film tells the other side. This is a brave, unflinching, sometimes virtually unwatchable documentary that makes such an effective case for both pro-choice and pro-life that it is impossible to determine which side the filmmaker, Tony Kaye, stands on. All you can conclude at the end is that both sides have effective advocates, but the pro-lifers also have some alarming people on their team.

One of them is an earnest young man named Paul Hill, neat haircut, aviator glasses, who says we should execute all abortionists. He doesn't stop there. We should also execute all blasphemers. What is a blasphemer? he's asked. Well, he says, like people who say "God damn it." Anyone who says "God damn it" should be executed? "Yes," he says firmly. Later, he murders a Florida doctor who performed abortions. It's one of two murders in the film, which result in the death penalty, which pro-life advocates generally support.

Other pro-lifers buy property next to abortion clinics and build platforms so their supporters can climb onto them and shout over fences at young women entering the clinic. They consider abortion to be murder, plain and simple, and they are also against birth control and sex education, which have proven in recent years to reduce unplanned pregnancies and therefore abortions.

On behalf of their argument, Hill shows graphic footage of abortions and their consequences. The scene that shook me most deeply has a doctor sorting through a pan of blood, fluid, and body parts to be sure he has removed an entire fetus. Tiny hands and feet can clearly be seen. There is also a shot of what look like full-term babies stacked in a freezer, but something about the shot, and the method of storage, leads me to disbelieve it. Nevertheless, throughout the film we see more than enough to convince us that what is being aborted is often recognizably human.

The sanest voice of reason on the pro-life side is Nat Hentoff, the veteran left-wing writer for the *Village Voice*, described as a civil libertarian and an atheist. He argues from a logical, not religious, point of view that when a sperm and an egg unite, a human being is in the process of formation, and the process should not be interrupted. His dispassionate remarks, whether or not you agree with them, are a calm center in the middle of a strident storm.

Another key witness in the film is Norma McCorvey, who was the anonymous "Jane Roe" in the 1973 Supreme Court decision Roe v. Wade. She was a pro-choice activist for years, had her home and car shot at, felt a virtual prisoner in her house, and then there was an unanticipated development. The property next door was purchased by antiabortionists, she started to visit them, she found their office so calm and friendly that she was converted, and she now speaks at pro-life events. We also meet, anonymously, some of the young women who apply at abortion clinics and hear their stories. And we hear grim statistics: If abortion is made illegal again in America, the abortion rate will remain about the same as it was before Roe v. Wade, but the fatality rate will start climbing. Before the Supreme Court decision, the leading cause of death among young women, we're told, was not cancer, not heart disease, not accidents, but side effects of illegal abortions.

The film has been a life's work for Kaye, a British citizen, now fifty-five, who has been filming it on and off for seventeen years. He shoots in 35 mm widescreen, using black-and-white (color would be unbearable). His film is long at 152 minutes but doesn't seem long because at every moment something absorbing, disturbing, depressing, or infuriating is happening. True, he comes down on neither side of the debate. But what he shows inadvertently is how the tradition of freely exchanged ideas in America has been replaced by entrenched true believers who drown out voices of moderation.

Alan M. Dershowitz, the Harvard law professor, tells a parable in the film that seems to apply. A rabbi is asked to settle a dispute between a husband and wife. He hears the husband's view. "You're right," he tells him. He hears the wife's view. "You're right," he tells her. One of his students protests: "Rabbi, they both can't be right." The rabbi nods. "You're right," he says.

Lakeview Terrace ★ ★ ★ ★
PG-13, 110 m., 2008

Samuel L. Jackson (Abel Turner), Patrick Wilson (Chris Mattson), Kerry Washington (Lisa Mattson), Jay Hernandez (Javier Villareal). Directed by Neil LaBute and produced by James Lassiter and Will Smith. Screenplay by David Loughery and Howard Korder.

Neil LaBute's *Lakeview Terrace* is a film about a black cop who makes life hell for an interracial couple that moves in next door. It will inspire strong reactions among its viewers, including outrage. It is intended to. LaBute often creates painful situations that challenge a character's sense of decency. This time he does it within the structure of a thriller, but the questions are there all the same.

For example, the neighbor, Abel Turner, is a bitter racist. He has his reasons, but don't we all. It is one mark of a sociopath to try to cure his wounds by harming others. The decent person does not visit his obsessions and prejudices upon his neighbor but is enjoined to love him as he does himself. Since Turner (Samuel L. Jackson) may hate himself, of course that is a problem.

But take a step back. What if all the races were switched? If the neighbor were white, the husband next door black, his wife white? Same script. It would be the story of a sociopathic white racist. It might be interesting, but it would have trouble getting made. The casting of Jackson as the neighbor creates a presumption of innocence that some will hold onto longer than the story justifies. Don't think for a moment that LaBute doesn't know audience members will be thinking about that switch of identities. He wants us to. All of his films feature nasty people who challenge nasty thoughts or fears within ourselves. Is this movie racist for making the villain black, or would it be equally racist by making the villain white? Well? What's your answer?

Jackson, a Los Angeles police veteran, lives on Lakeview Terrace, a crescent of comfortable suburbia in the hills of the city. The lots are pie-shaped, so the houses are placed close together, but the lots open out into big back yards. Into the house next door, newcomers arrive: Chris Mattson (Patrick Wilson) and his wife, Lisa (Kerry Washington). They seem fairly recently married, happy. Turner starts slow, dropping some subtly hostile remarks, and then escalates his war on this couple. I will not describe his words and actions, except to say he pushes buttons that make the Mattsons first outraged, then fearful, then angry—at him and each other.

Take another step back. Mattson's father-in-law, a successful attorney, is cool and civil toward his daughter's white husband. Mattson's own parents, his wife observes, "are always making a point of telling me how much they love me." Why make that a special point? Because they do or because they don't? What do you think? Lisa's father asks Chris point-blank: "Are you planning to have children with my daughter?" Is he eager to become a grandfather? Doesn't sound like it.

Well, are they having kids? Lisa wants to get pregnant right now. Chris says, "We have an agreement to wait a while." Why wait a while? Because that makes sense while they're getting their feet on the ground? Or because he's ambivalent about his wife? You decide. Even if waiting does "make sense," are his feelings worthy of their marriage? Even while making a superb thriller, LaBute makes the film more than that. It deals with one of his themes, the difficult transition from prolonged adolescence to manhood, a journey Chris takes in the film. It is not easy. Many of the steps are contrary to his nature.

LaBute ingeniously poses moral choices in all of his films. In his first great picture, *In the Company of Men*, about a cruel office worker who plays a trick on a deaf woman, does the villain gain more pleasure by hurting her or forcing his passive male coworker to act against his own better nature? Both? Why does the coworker go along? Timidity? Buried aggression? Homoerotic feelings for his buddy? See?

On top of all these questions, LaBute constructs a tightly wound story that also involves crude male bonding at an LAPD bachelor party, sexual humiliation, attempted rape (not by Chris or Turner), a cat-and-mouse game with cell phones, and a violent conclusion during which we must decide if Chris is right about Turner, or wrong, or just discovering how to push *his* buttons. I'm surprised by the PG-13 rating.

It's a challenging journey LaBute takes us on. Some will find it exciting. Some will find it an opportunity for an examination of conscience. Some will leave feeling vaguely uneasy. Some won't like it and will be absolutely sure why they don't, but their reasons will not agree. Some will hate elements that others can't even see. Some will only see a thriller. I find movies like this alive and provoking, and I'm exhilarated to have my thinking challenged at every step of the way.

The effect is only intensified by the performances, especially by Jackson, who for such a nice man can certainly play vicious. Kerry Washington's character, in my mind, takes the moral high ground, although it's a little muddy.

Her beauty and vulnerability are called for. Patrick Wilson plays a well-meaning man who is challenged to his core and never thought that would happen. I think I know who is good and bad or strong and weak in this film. But here's the brilliance of it: I don't know if they do.

Note: Lake View Terrace is the name of the street where Rodney King was arrested and beaten. This film mentions King and uses the street name, but not the location.

Land of the Lost ★ ★ ★
PG-13, 93 m., 2009

Will Ferrell (Dr. Rick Marshall), Danny McBride (Will Stanton), Anna Friel (Holly Cantrell), Jorma Taccone (Chaka). Directed by Brad Silberling and produced by Jimmy Miller and Sid and Marty Krofft. Screenplay by Chris Henchy and Dennis McNicholas.

Land of the Lost is a seriously deranged movie. That's not to say it's bad, although some of its early critics consider it a hanging offense ("a pot of ersatz dinosaur piss"—Peter Keough, *Boston Phoenix*). Marshall Fine even apologizes for prematurely predicting that *Night at the Museum: Battle of the Smithsonian* would be "the most witless, humor-challenged movie of the summer." The release inspires fervent hatred, which with the right kind of movie can be a good thing. Amid widespread disdain, I raise my voice in a bleat of lonely, if moderate, admiration.

The film involves a gloriously preposterous premise, set in a series of cheerfully fake landscapes that change at the whim of the art director. How else to explain a primeval swamp within walking distance of a limitless desert? Or to explain a motel sign from another dimension that appears there, with all of the motel missing but plenty of water still in the pool? And dinosaurs walking the earth at the same time as early man, just like in *Alley Oop* and *The Flintstones*?

Will Ferrell plays Dr. Rick Marshall, a scientist who assures Matt Lauer of the *Today* show that he has discovered a way to solve the energy crisis by importing fossil fuels from a parallel dimension. Lauer informs him that respectable scientists think he's mad. Like who? "Stephen Hawking," Lauer says. Dr. Rick goes nuclear: "You promised you wouldn't mention that!"

Marshall has, in fact, invented a machine that will transport him to one of those other worlds, and he is encouraged to try it by the only scientist in the world who agrees with him, Holly Cantrell (Anna Friel), who was thrown out of Cambridge for saying so. For reasons far too complicated to enumerate, they are joined in their journey by a fireworks salesman and part-time guide to a mysterious cave named Will (Danny McBride). Their cave tour strangely includes a river that seems to originate in thin air and flow into an artificial mountain before sucking them into a vortex and depositing them in . . . the Land of the Lost.

There they become friends with Chaka (Jorma Taccone), who belongs to a tribe of Missing Links and offers convincing evidence that in his land the straightening of teeth had not been developed. Luckily, Holly speaks his language. Yes, speaks his language, indicating that the movie will do anything to get to the next scene.

There are many jokes about dinosaur manure, dinosaur urine, dinosaur intelligence, dinosaur babies, and dinosaurs' hurt feelings. Also blood-sucking insects, carnivorous trees, and the sound track from *A Chorus Line*. The use of the songs is utterly wacky, of course, which is why I liked it.

The movie is inspired by the 1974 TV series and has the same producers, Sid and Marty Krofft. The two will never be confused, but they share one thing in common: deliriously fake locations, props, and special effects. The dinosaurs are so obviously not really there in shots where they menace humans that you could almost say their shots are *about* how they're not really there. Confronted with such effects, the actors make not the slightest effort to appear terrified, amazed, or sometimes even mildly concerned. Some might consider that a weakness. I suspect it is more of a deliberate choice, and I say I enjoyed it.

I guess you have to be in the mood for a goofball picture like this. I guess I was. Marshall Fine says it's worse than *Night at the Museum*, but I've seen *Night at the Museum*, and Marshall, this is no *Night at the Museum*.

248

Lars and the Real Girl ★ ★ ★ ½
PG-13, 106 m., 2007

Ryan Gosling (Lars), Emily Mortimer (Karin), Paul Schneider (Gus), Kelli Garner (Margo), Patricia Clarkson (Dr. Dagmar), Nancy Beatty (Mrs. Gruner). Directed by Craig Gillespie and produced by John Cameron, Sarah Aubrey, and Sidney Kimmel. Screenplay by Nancy Oliver.

How do you make a film about a life-size love doll ordered through the Internet into a life-affirming statement of hope? In *Lars and the Real Girl* you do it with faith in human nature and with a performance by Ryan Gosling that says things that cannot be said. And you surround him with actors who express the instinctive kindness we show to those we love.

Gosling, who has played neo-Nazis and district attorneys, now plays Lars Lindstrom, a painfully shy young man who can barely stand the touch of another human being. He functions in the world and has an office job, but in the evening he sits alone in a cabin in the backyard of his family home. His mother died years ago, his depressive father more recently. Now the big house is occupied by his brother Gus (Paul Schneider) and pregnant sister-in-law, Karin (Emily Mortimer). She makes it her business to invite him to dinner, to share their lives, but he begs off with one lame excuse after another and sits alone in the dark.

One day a coworker at the office, surfing Internet porn, shows Lars a life-size vinyl love doll that you can order customized to your specifications. A few weeks later a packing crate is delivered to Lars, and soon his brother and sister-in-law are introduced to the doll. She is, they learn, named Bianca. She is a paraplegic missionary of Brazilian and Danish blood, and Lars takes her everywhere in a wheelchair. He has an explanation for everything, including why she doesn't talk or eat.

The movie somehow implies without quite saying that, although the doll comes advertised with "orifices," Lars does not use Bianca for sex. No, she is an ideal companion, not least because she can never touch him. With a serenity bordering on the surreal, Lars takes her everywhere, even to church. She is as real as anyone in his life can possibly be at this point in the development of his social abilities.

Gus is mortified. Karin is more accepting; she believes that, for Lars, any change is progress. They arrange for Lars and Bianca to start seeing Dagmar (Patricia Clarkson), a therapist, who advises them to allow Lars to live with his fantasy. Dagmar "treats" Bianca and confides in Lars. Nothing is said in so many words, but we sense that she thinks Bianca functions the way pets do with some closed-in people: The doll provides unconditional love, no criticism, no questions.

The miracle in the plot is that the people of Lars's community arrive at an unspoken agreement to treat Bianca with the same courtesy that Lars does. This is partly because they have long and sadly watched Lars closing into himself and are moved by his attempt to break free. The film, directed by Craig Gillespie and written by Nancy Oliver (*Six Feet Under*), wisely never goes for even one moment that could be interpreted as smutty or mocking. There are, to be sure, some moments of humor; you can't take a love doll everywhere without inspiring double takes. And Gus sometimes blurts out the real-world truths we are also thinking.

There are so many ways *Lars and the Real Girl* could have gone wrong that one of the film's fascinations is how adroitly it sidesteps them. Its weapon is absolute sincerity. It is about who Lars is and how he relates to this substitute for human friendship, and that is all it's about. It has a kind of purity to it. Yes, it's rated PG-13, and that's the correct rating, I believe. It could inspire conversations between children and their parents about masturbation, loneliness, acceptance of unusual people, empathy.

We all know a few people who walk into a socially dangerous situation, size it up, and instantly know what to say and how to set people at ease. My Aunt Martha could do that. She was a truth teller, and all some situations need is for someone to tell the truth instead of pussyfooting around embarrassments. Consider, in this film, the neighbor named Mrs. Gruner (Nancy Beatty). She rises to the occasion in a way both tactful and heroic. While Gus is worried about what people will think, Mrs. Gruner (and Karin and Dagmar) are more concerned with what Lars is thinking.

As we watch this process, we glimpse Lars's inner world, one of hurt but also hidden hope. Nine actors out of ten would have (rightly) turned down this role, suspecting it to be a minefield of bad laughs. Ryan Gosling's work here is a study in control of tone. He isn't too morose, too strange, too opaque, too earnest. The word for his behavior, so strange to the world, is serene. He loves his new friend, treats her courteously, and expects everyone else to give her the respect he does.

How this all finally works out is deeply satisfying. Only after the movie is over do you realize what a balancing act it was, what risks it took, what rewards it contains. A character says at one point that she has grown to like Bianca. So, heaven help us, have we. If we can feel that way about a new car, why not about a lonely man's way to escape from sitting alone in the dark?

Last Chance Harvey ★ ★ ★
PG-13, 92 m., 2009

Dustin Hoffman (Harvey Shine), Emma Thompson (Kate Walker), Eileen Atkins (Maggie), Liane Balaban (Susan), James Brolin (Brian), Kathy Baker (Jean). Directed by Joel Hopkins and produced by Tim Perell and Nicola Usborne. Screenplay by Hopkins.

Last Chance Harvey is a tremendously appealing love story surrounded by a movie not worthy of it. For Dustin Hoffman, after years of character roles (however good) and dubbing the voices of animated animals, it provides a rare chance to play an ordinary guy. For Emma Thompson, there is an opportunity to use her gifts for tact and insecurity. For both, their roles project warmth and need.

When the film gets out of their way and leaves them alone to relate with each other, it's sort of magical. Then the lumber of the plot apparatus is trundled on, and we wish it were a piece for two players. One subplot, scored with funny-bumpy-scary music, is entirely unnecessary. And even with the two stars on screen, there is too much reliance on that ancient standby, the Semi-Obligatory Lyrical Interlude.

But what's good is very good. Hoffman plays Harvey, a failed jazz pianist who has found success writing jingles for TV ads.

Thompson plays Kate, an airport interviewer for a British agency. Hoffman flies to London to attend his daughter's wedding, and in the space of twenty-four hours he learns that he has been fired and that his daughter would prefer her stepfather gave her away. At the same time, Thompson is ignored on a blind date and has to deal with a mother who fears her new neighbor is a vivisectionist.

They met briefly when Harvey was rude to her at the airport. The next day, when both are deep in misery, they find themselves the only two people in a pub. Harvey recognizes her, apologizes, and out of desperation tries to start a conversation. She resists. But notice the tentative dialogue that slowly allows them to start talking easily. It's not forced. It depends on his charm and her kindness.

Pitch perfect. But then the dialogue fades down and the camera pulls back and shows them talking and smiling freely, and the music gets happier, and there is a montage showing them walking about London with lots and lots of scenery in the frame. The movie indulges the Semi-OLI more than once; it uses the device as shorthand for scenes that should be fully transcribed. In *Before Sunrise* and *Before Sunset*, Richard Linklater sent Ethan Hawke and Julie Delpy talking all through a night in Vienna and all through a day in Paris, and never let them stop, and kept his camera close. Why didn't Joel Hopkins, the writer-director of *Last Chance Harvey*, try the same? He had the right actors.

He gets one thing right. They stay outdoors. Going to his hotel or her flat would set the stage for body language neither one is ready for. They avoid the issue by walking around London, although unfortunately Hopkins sends them mostly up and down the Victoria Embankment and the South Bank, so he can hold the Thames vista in the background. We get more montages of them walking and talking, as substitutes for listening to a conversation we've become invested in.

One subplot works well. After she starts him talking about why his relationship with his daughter failed, she tells him he *must* attend her wedding reception. He says she must go with him. He will buy her a dress. There is a gratuitous and offensive montage of her trying on dresses, including one frilly gown that looks perfect for a fancy dress ball in *Gone with the Wind*. Not only is this montage an exhausted cliché, they're in a hurry, remember? But when they get to the reception, Harvey is touching in a carefully worded speech.

The subplot that doesn't work involves Kate's mother (Eileen Atkins). She peers through the curtains at the suspicious neighbor, thinks she sees him carrying a body to the woodshed, and speed-dials her daughter every five minutes. Every time we cut to her, we get that peppy suspense music, as the movie confuses itself with light comedy.

Last Chance Harvey has everything it needs and won't stop there. It needs the nerve to push all the way. It is a pleasure to look upon the faces of Hoffman and Thompson, so pleasant, so real. Their dialogue together finds the right notes for crossing an emotional minefield. They never descend into tear-jerking or cuteness. They are all grown up and don't trust love nearly as much as straight talk. Hopkins deserves credit for creating these characters. Then he should have stood back and let them keep right on talking. Their pillow talk would have been spellbinding. ☞

The Last House on the Left ★ ★ ½
R, 100 m., 2009

Tony Goldwyn (John Collingwood), Monica Potter (Emma Collingwood), Sara Paxton (Mari Collingwood), Garret Dillahunt (Krug), Spencer Treat Clark (Justin), Riki Lindhome (Sadie), Aaron Paul (Francis), Martha MacIsaac (Paige). Directed by Dennis Iliadis and produced by Wes Craven, Sean Cunningham, and Marianne Maddalena. Screenplay by Adam Alleca and Carl Ellsworth, based on the 1972 film by Craven.

I have seen four films inspired by the same thirteenth-century folk ballad: Ingmar Bergman's *The Virgin Spring* (1960), Wes Craven's *The Last House on the Left* (1972), David DeFalco's *Chaos* (2005), and now Dennis Iliadis's remake of the 1972 film, also titled *The Last House on the Left*.

What I know for sure is that the Bergman film is the best. Beyond that, it is a confusion of contradictions. I gave the 1972 film 3½ stars, describing it as "a tough, bitter little sleeper of a movie that's about four times as good as you'd expect." I gave the 2005 film zero stars, describing it as "ugly, nihilistic and cruel—a film I regret having seen." What do I think about the latest story about a girl who goes walking in the woods, is raped and in some versions is killed, and whose attackers then seek shelter in the house of her parents, who realize who they are and take revenge?

Would I still admire 1972 today? Can I praise 2009 after savaging 2005? Isn't it all more or less the same material? Not quite. In the Bergman film, the father asks God's forgiveness for taking vengeance and says: "I promise You, God, here on the dead body of my only child, I promise you that, to cleanse my sins, here I shall build a church. On this spot. Of mortar and stone . . . and with these, my hands."

And such a church was built in the 1300s, and still stands at Karna in Sweden. No churches will be built because of the other films, no parents will ask forgiveness, and few members of the audience will think they should. These are in the horror genre, which once tried to scare the audience but now invites the audience to share the fear and pain of the characters. It is the one genre that can lead the box office without name stars, perhaps because its fans know that big stars very rarely appear in one (I'm not thinking of films where story is first but those in which graphic violence is first).

Horror films have connoisseurs, who are alert to gradations in violence. The well-informed critic "Fright" at the Web site Horror Movie a Day writes: "In the original, EVERYTHING was just so depraved, the rape barely stuck out as anything worse than the other things they endured. Not the case here, and so while some may cry foul that the movie is too toned down, I think it's a good decision." Not many unseasoned audience members will find the 2009 rape scene "toned down," and indeed I found it painful to watch. In the 2005 film, it was so reprehensibly and lingeringly sadistic I found it unforgivable. So now my job as a film critic involves grading rape scenes.

I don't think I can. I wrote that original *Last House* review thirty-seven years ago. I am not the same person. I am uninterested in being "consistent." I approach the new film as sim-

ply a filmgoer. I must say it is very well made. The rape scene appalled me. Other scenes, while violent, fell within the range of contemporary horror films, which strive to invent new ways to kill people so the horror fans in the audience will get a laugh.

This film, for example, which as I write has inspired only one review (by "Fright"), has generated a spirited online discussion about whether you can kill someone by sticking their head in a microwave. Many argue that a microwave won't operate with the door open. Others cite an early scene establishing that the microwave is "broken." The question of whether one *should* microwave a man's head never arises.

Let's set that aside and look at the performances. They're surprisingly good, and I especially admired the work of Monica Potter and Tony Goldwyn as the parents of one of two girls who go walking in the woods. It is no longer only the father who takes revenge; both parents work together, improvising, playing a deadly chess game in their own home, which they know better than the villains. We are only human, we identify with the parents, we fear for them, and we applaud their ingenuity.

There is also sound work by Krug (Garret Dillahunt), the convincingly evil leader of a pack of degenerates. He isn't just acting scary. He creates a character. And Sara Paxton, who has been acting since eight and was twenty when the movie was made, shows, as so many sexy young blondes do, that they are better than the bubblehead roles they are mostly given.

It is also true that director Dennis Iliadis and his cinematographer, Sharone Meir, do a smooth job of handling space and time to create suspense. The film is an effective representative of its genre, and horror fans will like it, I think, but who knows? I'm giving it a 2½ on the silly star rating system and throwing up my hands.

The Last Mistress ★ ★ ★ ½
NO MPAA RATING, 114 m., 2008

Asia Argento (Vellini), Fu'ad Ait Aattou (Ryno de Marigny), Roxane Mesquida (Hermangarde), Claude Sarraute (Marquise de Flers), Yolande Moreau (Comtesse d'Artelles),

Michael Lonsdale (Vicomte de Prony). Directed by Catherine Breillat and produced by Jean-Francois Lepetit. Screenplay by Breillat, based on the novel by Jules Barbey d'Aurevilly.

In *The Last Mistress,* a passionate and explicit film about sexual obsession, everything pauses for a scene depicting a wedding. It is 1835, in a church in Paris. Vows are exchanged between Ryno de Marigny, a notorious young libertine, and the high-born Hermangarde, whose wealth will be a great comfort to the penniless Ryno. The film opens with two gossipy old friends wondering why the Marquise de Flers would sacrifice her beloved granddaughter to this rake.

I wondered why time was devoted to the ceremony, in a film where Hermangarde speaks scarcely one hundred words and the great passion is between Ryno and his mistress of ten years, the disreputable Vellini. Then I realized it was an excuse to work in the Biblical readings ("requested by the bride and groom"—surely a modern touch?). The Gospel contains God's strictures about man and wife, divorce and adultery, letting no man put asunder, etc. The epistle is Paul to the Corinthians, venting his admonishments to women, who must always take second place, cover their heads in the sight of the Lord, obey their masters, and so on.

These readings enter the film precisely to be contradicted by Vellini (Asia Argento) in every atom of her being. Born out of wedlock to an Italian princess and a Spanish matador, she is technically wed to an English aristocrat but in fact is the most impetuous courtesan in Paris. When she overhears young Ryno (Fu'ad Ait Aattou) describe her as a "mutt," she permits herself the smallest smile before taking another lick of her ice cream (shaped like what we now call a torpedo).

Their relationship begins with her hatred, or what she convinces Ryno is her hatred; it inspires his uncontrollable desire and leads to a duel with her husband during which Ryno is nearly killed with a bullet near his heart. As he lingers near death, so inflamed is Vellini that she bursts into his bedchamber and licks the blood from his wound. The doctor growls about "infection," but never mind: She has been inspired by his sacrifice. Any man who would suffer that much for her love would surely suffer more.

The Last Mistress is the latest film from the French director Catherine Breillat, famous for the explicit eroticism of such films as *Fat Girl* and *Romance.* Here she makes an elegant period piece, with all the costumes, carriages, servants, chateaus, and mannered behavior we would expect, and then explodes its decorum with a fiery performance by Argento. Does she love her young prize, with his lips full as a woman's? Does he love her, with her two front teeth tilted inward like a vampire's? Love has nothing to do with it. They are in the grip of erotomania.

That in itself could be fairly routine, if it were not for the way Breillat frames her story. Understand that Ryno sincerely loves Hermangarde (Roxane Mesquida). Two days before the marriage, he says his formal farewell to Vellini, which is followed by helpless sex. Later the same night, he pays a courtesy call on the old Marquise de Flers (Claude Sarraute), who arranged the marriage and considers it her "masterpiece," so sure is she about Ryno.

Alas, she has been informed of his affair with Vellini and now asks for a confession. This he supplies in tender and earnest terms. Then she asks for details. These he supplies in lurid flashbacks. The marquise prides herself on being a liberated woman of the previous century. "Damn this herb tea!" she says. "A little port will warm us up." Soon she is stretched out full length in her chair, her feet propped on a divan, drinking in the details of his story.

It is Claude Sarraute's performance that I loved most of all in the film. I can easily imagine spending the night in the salon of this old lady and telling her everything she wants to hear. Her face is so intelligent, her manner so direct that my only fear would be to disappoint her. Astonished, I discover from *Variety* that Sarraute is a "distinguished journalist and commentator who last dabbled in acting more than fifty years ago." She gives dimension and meaning to Ryno's long story of powerless surrender.

Argento's performance is also remarkable. Dressed to flaunt her immorality (in one costume, she is the devil), she puffs on cigars, draws blood, follows the newlyweds to their remote coastal hideaway. Ryno hates himself for being unable to resist her. In one shot, Breillat fills the screen with naked flesh and two items of jewelry: his wedding ring and Vellini's bracelet in the shape of a serpent.

One of the old gossips is played by the immortal Michael Lonsdale, who predicted that Ryno would never be able to stay away from Vellini and takes some satisfaction in being proven right, but not as much as he takes in a properly roasted chicken. Of all the vices, he observes, gluttony lasts the longest and never disappoints. As for debauchery, poor Ryno is desperately overserved, and it is hard for us, even as he surrenders to devouring need, not to feel sorry for him.

Late Bloomer ★ ★ ★ ½
NO MPAA RATING, 83 m., 2008

Masakiyo Sumida (Sumida), Mari Torii (Nobuko), Naozo Horita (Take), Ariko Arita (Oba-chan), Sumiko Shirai (Aya). Directed by Go Shibata and produced by Toshiki Shima. Screenplay by Shibata.

I see so many references to Go Shibata's *Late Bloomer* as a thriller or horror film. That may be true, but it's beside the point. Here is a film about the despair and rage building up within a man whose body has betrayed him. It fearlessly regards the dark side of severe disability, and would be offensive if we didn't know it represents only this single character, who is going mad.

Sumida (Masakiyo Sumida) is dealing with what seems to be muscular dystrophy. He is aided by a care giver, has some sort of job at a disability center, speaks with a computerized voice, gets drunk regularly, and has a scrawny beard, tangled hair, and thick, permanently smudged eyeglasses. He uses an electric wheelchair. His pastimes are drinking, watching pornography, and going to underground rock concerts with his friend Take (Naozo Horita). On the whole, people seem happy to spend time with him, and he takes many meals with Take, who is a counselor.

In the ways that he can be, Sumida is a party animal. I remember a guy in his twenties who hung out at O'Rourke's in the 1970s. I think he had MS. He'd be warmly greeted when he came in. He liked to booze, too, but he was still

walking and knew he had his limit. He threw a party once. You should have seen his pad. Psychedelic posters, glo-lights, sound system cranked up high, a water bed, an open bar, pot. He braced his jaw as he spoke, but it wasn't hard to understand him. He was friendly with the girls. Once when we were wondering if he was getting any, a couple of girls who were regulars traded private little smiles.

The thing to realize when you see a person like that is: There's somebody at home! He doesn't automatically have a mental disability. It's OK to go ahead and say what's on your mind. You don't have to end every sentence with "Right?" and "OK?" and "You know what I mean?" so that he has to nod and nod and nod. It's easy to imagine how a man like Sumida, who might be a barfly even if he were unimpaired, could develop a lot of pent-up frustration.

A young woman named Nobuko (Mari Torii) volunteers to serve as his companion. Part of a school project. She's sweet and friendly, but not gifted with the unique abilities of a true care giver. She brightens his day. Then he begins to suspect she is seeing Take. Sumida tells a bedridden friend in a similar condition that he is in love. The friend warns him: Nothing good will come of that for you. Spare yourself.

And now *Late Bloomer* begins its journey into the pain and anger of Sumida's mind. What happens, you will discover. This is not a movie about the essential humanity of a good-hearted disabled person. Someone with MD can be as dangerous as someone without. There's somebody at home, all right, and he's hurting.

You have to meet the film's visual style halfway. It's shot in contrasty black and white, slo-mo, fast-mo, sometimes jagged cutting, sometimes an erratic handheld camera that suggests the jerky way Sumida must view the world. You watch for a while, and the movie is tough going. Then it takes hold, and you begin identifying with Sumida. He is a bad, bad man. You can sort of understand that.

La Vie En Rose ★ ★ ★ ★
PG-13, 140 m., 2007

Marion Cotillard (Edith Piaf), Sylvie Testud (Momone), Pascal Greggory (Louis Barrier),

Emmanuelle Seigner (Titine), Jean-Paul Rouve (Louis Gassion), Clotilde Courau (Anetta Gassion), Jean-Pierre Martins (Marcel Cerdan), Gerard Depardieu (Louis Leplee). Directed by Olivier Dahan and produced by Alain Goldman. Screenplay by Dahan and Isabelle Sobelman.

She was the daughter of a street singer and a circus acrobat. Her mother dumped her with her father, who dumped her with his mother, who ran a brothel. In childhood, diseases rendered her temporarily blind and deaf. She claimed she was cured by St. Therese, whose shrine the prostitutes took her to. One of the prostitutes adopted her until her father returned, snatched her away, and put her to work in his act. From her mother and the prostitute she heard many songs, and one day when his sidewalk act was doing badly, her father commanded her, "Do something." She sang "La Marseilles." And Edith Piaf was born.

Piaf. The French word for "sparrow." She was named by her first impresario, Louis Leplee. He was found shot dead not long after—possibly by a pimp who considered her his property. She stood four feet, eight inches tall, and so became "The Little Sparrow." She was the most famous and beloved French singer of her time—of the century, in fact— and her lovers included Yves Montand (whom she discovered) and the middleweight champion Marcel Cerdan. She drank too much, all the time. She became addicted to morphine and required ten injections a day. She grew old and stooped before her time and died at forty-seven.

Olivier Dahan's La Vie en Rose, one of the best biopics I've seen, tells Piaf's life story through the extraordinary performance of Marion Cotillard, who looks like the singer. The title, which translates loosely as "life through rose-colored glasses," is from one of Piaf's most famous songs, which she wrote herself. She is known for countless other songs, perhaps most poignantly for "Non, Je ne Regrette Rien" ("No, I Regret Nothing"), which is seen in the film as her final song; if it wasn't, it should have been.

How do you tell a life story so chaotic, jumbled, and open to chance as Piaf's? Her life did not have an arc but a trajectory. Joy and tragedy seemed simultaneous. Her loves were heartfelt but doomed; after she begged the boxer Cerdan to fly to her in New York, he was killed in the crash of his flight from Paris. Her stage triumphs alternated with her stage collapses. If her life resembled in some ways Judy Garland's, there is this difference: Garland lived for the adulation of the audience, and Piaf lived to do her duty as a singer. From her earliest days, from the prostitutes, her father, and her managers, she learned that when you're paid, you perform.

Oh, but what a performer she was. Her voice was loud and clear, reflecting her early years as a street singer. Such a big voice for such a little woman. At first she sang mechanically but was tutored to improve her diction and to express the meaning of her words. She did that so well that if you know what the words Non, je ne regrette rien mean, you can essentially feel the meaning of every other word in the song.

Dahan and his cowriter, Isabelle Sobelman, move freely through the pages of Piaf's life. A chronology would have missed the point. She didn't start here and go there; she was always, at every age, even before she had the name, the little sparrow. The action moves back and forth from childhood to final illness, from applause to desperation, from joy to heartbreak (particularly in the handling of Cerdan's last visit to her). This mosaic storytelling style has been criticized in some quarters as obscuring facts (quick: How many times was she married?). But think of it this way: Since there are, in fact, no wedding scenes in the movie, isn't it more accurate to see husbands, lovers, friends, admirers, employees, and everyone else as whirling around her small, still center? Nothing in her early life taught her to count on permanence or loyalty. What she counted on was singing, champagne, infatuation, and morphine.

Many biopics break down in depicting their subjects in old age, and Piaf, at forty-seven, looked old. Gene Siskel once referred to an actor's old-age makeup as making him look like a turtle. In La Vie en Rose there is never a moment's doubt. Even the hair is right; her frizzled, dyed, thinning hair in the final scenes matches the real Piaf in the videos I cite below. The only detail I can question is her resiliency after all-night drinking sessions. I once knew an alcoholic who said, "If I wasn't a drinker and I woke up with one of these hangovers, I'd check myself into the emergency room."

Then there are the songs, a lot of them. I gather from the credits that some are dubbed by other singers, some are sung by Piaf herself, and some, in parts at least, by Cotillard. In the video clips you can see how Piaf choreographed her hands and fingers, and Cotillard has that right, too. A singer who has been dead fifty years and sang in another language must have been pretty great to make it onto so many saloon jukeboxes, which is how I first heard her. Now, of course, she's on my iPod, and I'm listening to her right now. *Pour moi toute seule.*

Le Doulos ★ ★ ★ ½
NO MPAA RATING, 108 m., 1962 (rereleased 2008)

Jean-Paul Belmondo (Silien), Serge Reggiani (Maurice), Jean Dessailly (Inspector Clain), Fabienne Dali (Fabienne), Michel Piccoli (Nuttheccio), Monique Hennessy (Therese). Directed by Jean-Pierre Melville and produced by Georges de Beauregard and Carlo Ponti. Screenplay by Melville, based on the novel by Pierre Lesou.

Near the end of *Le Doulos,* Jean-Paul Belmondo reinterprets everything that has gone before, his words illustrated by flashbacks to the film we have seen. That is essentially a wink by the writer-director, Jean-Pierre Melville, suggesting that he was misleading us all along. This goes with his territory: "I take care never to be realistic," he said in a 1963 interview. Does it matter that what we're seeing is not necessarily what we're getting? Not at all. The movie is entirely about how it looks and feels.

I am an admirer of Melville; his *Bob le Flambeur* and *Le Samourai* are in my Great Movies collection. He helped introduce film noir to the New Wave generation and was such a lover of all things American that he renamed himself after Herman Melville. His heroes tend to drive Detroit cars that look huge on the streets of Paris; when one character in this film parks three spaces down from the car

of another, how can he *not* notice the twenty-footer and be tipped off the other guy is already there? Melville was also a fetishist of American men's clothing styles, he said, and you will scarcely see a beret in his films. Indeed, *le doulos,* which means "the finger man" in Parisian criminal slang, is the name for the small-brimmed fedora that most of the men wear.

The film is made of elements Melville said he came to love in the black-and-white American crime movies of the 1930s: shadows, night, trench coats, guns, tough guys, cigarettes, slinky dames, cocktail bars, crooked cops, betrayal, loot, and a plot shutting out the world and confining the characters within their own lives and space. It looks gorgeous in the newly restored 35 mm print by Rialto Pictures, which will no doubt issue it as a DVD.

The film opens with a newly released prisoner (Serge Reggiani) calling on a man who set up a diamond heist for him. He later has good reason to believe the Belmondo character fingered him, in a plot that leads through nightclubs, whisky bars (no wine for Melville), dark underpasses, and deserted suburban wastelands. There are three lovely lady friends, including Therese (Monique Hennessy), who is attached to Nuttheccio (Michel Piccoli), a shady nightclub owner. Belmondo ties her up and gags her, which is perhaps what she deserves, depending on what we choose to believe. (The movie drew some criticism for its treatment of women, leading Melville to defend himself: He did not mistreat the women; his characters did.)

To see both Belmondo and Piccoli in 1962 is to be reminded how early they embodied their distinctive screen presences: Piccoli, the balding, saturnine slickster with the five o'clock shadow, and Belmondo, the oily outlaw punk. One trick that Melville plays is to dress them, and others, in essentially identical trench coats and hats, and then shoot them in shadows or from behind, so that we are misled for a while about who we're watching. This, coupled with a habit that some of them have of straightening their hats before a mirror, perhaps suggests they are interchangeable, playing different games by the same rules. See, too, how meticulously Alain Delon treats his hat in *Le Samourai,* about a hit man who lives with a code as rigid as a samurai's. The Belmondo character here has a code, too, but he keeps it so concealed it doesn't do him much good.

The plot is, as I've suggested, baffling. I'll give a shiny new dime to anyone who understands Belmondo's illustrated lecture at the end. It is designed to explain that he is *not* the finger man everyone (and the film until then) thinks he is—but can he be believed? It really matters not, as we enjoy plunging into an underworld of deadly confusion.

Let the Right One In ★ ★ ★ ½
R, 114 m., 2008

Kare Hedebrant (Oskar), Lina Leandersson (Eli), Per Ragnar (Hakan), Henrik Dahl (Erik), Karin Bergquist (Yvonne), Peter Carlberg (Lacke). Directed by Tomas Alfredson and produced by John Nordling and Carl Molinder. Screenplay by John Ajvide Lindqvist, based on his novel.

I look at young people who affect the Goth look. I assume they want to keep a distance and make a statement. The leather can be taken off, the tattoos not so easily. It is relatively painless to pierce many body areas, not all. But what would it feel like to be pierced by a vampire's fangs? That would be more than a look, wouldn't it? And you wouldn't want to advertise yourself as a vampire.

Let the Right One In is a "vampire movie," but not even remotely what we mean by that term. It is deadly grim. It takes vampires as seriously as the versions of *Nosferatu* by F. W. Murnau and Werner Herzog do, and that is very seriously indeed. It is also a painful portrayal of an urgent relationship between two twelve-year-olds on the brink of adolescence. It is not intended for twelve-year-olds.

It opens with the reflection of Oskar (Kare Hedebrant) looking soberly out a window. He may remind you of the boy in Bergman's *The Silence,* looking out of the train window. They will both have much to be sober about. There will be many reflections in the film, not all from mirrors, but this is not one of those vampire stories that drags out the crosses and the garlic.

Oskar is lonely. His parents have separated, neither one wants him, he is alone a lot. He hangs around outside in the snowy Swedish night. One night he meets a kid named Eli (Lina Leandersson), who is about his age. Eli is lonely too, and they become friends. Oskar is at that age when he accepts astonishing facts calmly because life has given up trying to surprise him. Eli walks through the snow without shoes. Eli has a faint scent almost of a corpse. "Are you a vampire?" Oskar asks Eli. Yes. Oh. They decide to have a sleepover in his bed. Sex is not yet constantly on Oskar's mind, but he asks, "Will you be my girlfriend?" She touches him lightly. "Oskar, I'm not a girl." Oh.

Oskar is cruelly bullied at school by a sadistic boy who travels with a posse of two smaller thugs and almost drowns him in a swimming pool. At a time like this it is useful to have a vampire as your best pal. A girl vampire or a boy vampire, it doesn't really matter.

I have not even started to describe this film, directed by Tomas Alfredson and written by John Ajvide Lindqvist, based on his novel. I will not go into the relationship Eli has with an unsavory middle-aged man named Hakan (Per Ragnar). Maybe he is her familiar, maybe he just likes blood. Nor will I talk about the iron rod and the knife, or Oskar's horrible parents. I've already made it sound grim enough, and the fact is, there are some funny moments. Vampire-funny, you know. "Are you really my age?" Oskar asks Eli. "Yes. But I've been this age for a very long time."

Remove the vampire elements, and this is the story of two lonely and desperate kids capable of performing dark deeds without apparent emotion. Kids washed up on the shores of despair. The young actors are powerful in draining roles. We care for them more than they care for themselves. Alfredson's palette is so drained of warm colors that even fresh blood is black. We learn that a vampire must be invited into a room before it can enter. Now the title makes sense.

Note: Jeremy Knox of Film Threat likes the film as much as I do, but comes from a different place. He writes: "I'd even go so far as to say this would make a great date film. Women will melt watching this. Not only that, but it'd also make a fine film to show to the ten- to sixteen-year-old crowd. Little kids, especially girls, will love this. Yeah, there's some blood and one really quick shot of nudity, but just because they're young doesn't mean they're stupid. Kids will totally get this."

They'll get it, all right. In the neck.   ☞

Lights in the Dusk ★ ★ ★ ½
NO MPAA RATING, 78 m., 2008

Janne Hyytiainen (Koistinen), Maria Jarvenhelmi (Mirja), Ilkka Koivula (Lindholm). Directed and produced by Aki Kaurismaki. Screenplay by Kaurismaki.

More and more I am learning to love the films of Aki Kaurismaki, that Finnish master of the stories of sad and lonely losers. Like very few directors (such as Tati, Fassbinder, Keaton, Fellini), he has created a world all his own, and you can recognize it from almost every shot. His characters are dour, speak little, expect the worst, smoke too much, are ill-treated by life, are passive in the face of tragedy. Yes, and they are funny.

It is a deadpan humor. Kaurismaki never signals us to laugh, and at festivals there is rarely a roar of laughter, more often the exhalation people make when they are subduing a roar of laughter. His characters are lovable, but nobody seems to know that. *Lights in the Dusk* is the third film in his "loser trilogy," preceded by *Drifting Clouds,* the story of an unemployed couple hopelessly in debt, and *The Man Without a Past,* the story of a homeless man who has no idea who he is. How can I convince you these stories are deeply amusing? I can't. Take my word for it.

In *Lights in the Dusk,* everybody on the screen smokes more than ever, perhaps because it is the highlight of their day. We meet Koistinen (Janne Hyytiainen), a night watchman who says "I have no friends" because it is true: He has no friends. Well, there is the woman who runs the late-night hot dog stand. She is nice to him, but he is cold to her.

Koistinen is shunned at work by his fellow security guards. After three years, the manager cannot remember his name. People stare at him in restaurants. One night he is approached at his solitary table in a cafe by an attractive blonde who asks, "Is this seat taken?" He asks her why she sat there when the café is empty. "Because you looked like you needed company."

They date, if that is the word. They sit rigidly through a movie, almost silently through a dinner, and he stands in the corner at a disco. He invites her to dinner in his basement flat, which has large pipes running through it. He offers her a fresh bagel: "The roast is in the oven." She says, "Koistinen, I have to make a trip. My mother is ill." He asks, "When?" She says, "Right now," and stands up and leaves.

He protests to three bruisers that their dog has been tied outside a bar for days, without water. They take him offscreen and he returns beaten. Most of Kaurismaki's beatings are offscreen, mercifully. There is a plot behind all of his misfortune, which leads to jail time and then a cot in a homeless shelter. He disastrously tries to take action against those who have used him. The hot-dog girl seeks him out. The dog finds a new owner. There is a happy ending, lasting about thirty seconds.

It isn't what happens, it's how it happens. You'll have a hard time finding Kaurismaki in a theater in most cities (and states), but he's waiting for you on DVD. Put a Kaurismaki in your Netflix queue. Most any film will do. You will start watching it and feel strangely disoriented because none of the usual audience cues are supplied. You're on your own. You will watch it engrossed and fascinated right up until the very end, which will not feel much like an ending. You will for some reason feel curious to see another Kaurismaki film. If by any chance you dislike the film and turn it off, let it wait a day, and start it again. You were wrong.

The Limits of Control ★ ½
R, 116 m., 2009

Isaach De Bankole (Lone Man), Alex Descas (Creole), Jean-Francois Stevenin (French), Luis Tosar (Violin), Paz de la Huerta (Nude), Tilda Swinton (Blonde), Youki Kudoh (Molecules), John Hurt (Guitar), Gael Garcia Bernal (Mexican), Hiam Abbass (Driver), Bill Murray (American). Directed by Jim Jarmusch and produced by Stacey Smith and Gretchen McGowan. Screenplay by Jarmusch.

I am the man in *The Limits of Control.* I cannot tell you my name because the screenplay has not given me one. There's only room for so many details in 116 minutes. Call me The Man With No Name. I wander through Spain saying as little as possible, as Clint Eastwood did in films I enjoyed as a boy. Now I am a man, handsome, exotic, cool, impenetrable, hip, mysterious, quiet, coiled, enigmatic, passive, stoic, and hungry.

On my journey, I enter cafés and always specify the same order: "Two espressos, in two separate cups." In each café, I am met by a contact. I exchange matchboxes. The one I hand over is filled with diamonds. The one I am given contains a note on a small piece of paper, which I eat. I meet strange people. I do not know them. They know me. I am the one with two espressos in two separate cups. One is a beautiful young woman, always nude, whom I would like to get to know better, but not in this movie.

The writer and director of the film is Jim Jarmusch. I've seen several of his movies and even appeared in a couple. This one takes the cake. He is making some kind of a point. I think the point is that if you strip a story down to its bare essentials, you will have very little left. I wonder how he pitched this idea to his investors.

As an actor, my name is Isaach De Bankole. I have the opportunity to appear in scenes with actors who are known for the chances they take. Sometimes an actor like that will prove nothing except that he is loyal to his friends or a good sport. Bill Murray is appearing so frequently in such films I think it is time for him to star in a smutty action comedy. The other good sports include Tilda Swinton, Gael Garcia Bernal, John Hurt, and Paz de la Huerta, who is nude all the time. That's a good sport and a half.

My acting assignment was not so hard. I costarred with Mathieu Amalric in *The Diving Bell and the Butterfly*. He played a man whose movement was restricted to one eye. Now there was a tough assignment. I acted in Lars von Trier's *Manderlay*, where the locations were suggested by chalk lines on the floor of a sound stage. Not as much fun as Spanish cafés. I starred in the Quebec film *How to Make Love to a Negro Without Getting Tired*, and I played the negro, but I was the one who got tired.

So I'm not complaining. We actors enjoyed Spain. Often we would gather for a dinner of paella and sangria. One night Bill Murray

quoted Gene Siskel: "I ask myself if I would enjoy myself more watching a documentary of the same actors having dinner." We all sat and thought about that, as the night breeze blew warm through the town and a faraway mandolin told its tale.

We were pretty sure it would be a good-looking movie. Jarmusch was working with the cameraman Christopher Doyle, and they spent a lot of time discussing their palette, figuring their exposure and framing their compositions. That reminded me of a silent film named *Man with a Movie Camera*, which some people think is the best film ever made. It shows a man with a movie camera, photographing things. Was Jarmusch remaking it without the man and the camera?

Lions for Lambs ★ ★ ½

R, 88 m., 2007

Robert Redford (Dr. Stephen Malley), Meryl Streep (Janine Roth), Tom Cruise (Senator Jasper Irving), Michael Pena (Ernest Rodriguez), Derek Luke (Arian Finch), Andrew Garfield (Todd Hayes), Peter Berg (Lieutenant Colonel Falco). Directed by Robert Redford and produced by Redford, Matthew Michael Carnahan, Tracy Falco, and Andrew Hauptman. Screenplay by Carnahan.

Useful new things to be said about the debacle in Iraq are in very short supply. I'm not sure that's what *Lions for Lambs* intends to demonstrate, but it does, exhaustingly. Essentially, if I have this right, we should never have invaded Iraq, but now that we're there, (1) we can't very well leave, and (2) we can't very well stay, so (3) the answer is, stay while in the process of leaving.

The movie is a talkathon with a certain amount of military action. It could be presented about as well as a radio play. Directed by Robert Redford, it uses an all-star cast, which focuses attention away from the dialogue and toward the performances. Since I doubt that's what Redford intended, it doesn't speak well for the screenplay by Matthew Michael Carnahan. When a third of a movie involves a verbal duel between Tom Cruise and Meryl Streep, what are we supposed to do, not notice who's talking?

The movie follows three story lines, plus a flashback linking all of them. In Washington, a veteran journalist (Streep) sits down for an exclusive interview with a Republican senator (Cruise) who has presidential ambitions. In Los Angeles, a political science professor (Redford) sits down to discuss the purposes of life with a brilliant but disappointing student (Andrew Garfield). And in Afghanistan, two of the professor's former pupils (Michael Pena and Derek Luke) are involved in a firefight on a snowy mountain peak.

As it happens, they are involved in the very military strategy that the senator is touting to the journalist. It involves seizing the high ground in Afghanistan earlier in the season than the Taliban can get there, to control mountain passes and therefore prevent Taliban troop movements. The Cruise character presents this as a strategic breakthrough on a level with, I dunno, Nelson's rout of Napoleon. It's actually supposed to convince Streep the war can be won.

In Los Angeles, the promising student has just stopped caring, and the talk with his professor is designed to reignite his passion. He should get involved in his nation's politics—take an interest, take a stand. The flashback shows the two soldiers winning a classroom debate by calling the other side's bluff: They have enlisted in the military.

The movie is anti–Bush's war, I guess. The journalist makes better points than the senator, anyway. What the professor and his student think is hard to say, although they are very articulate in muddying the waters. As for the two enlistees, it is safe to assume that at the end of the film they are wondering whether their debate strategy was the right one.

There is a long stretch toward the beginning of the film when we're interested, under the delusion that it's going somewhere. When we begin to suspect it's going in circles, our interest flags, and at the end, while rousing music plays, I would have preferred the Peggy Lee version of "Is That All There Is?"

Little Ashes ★ ★ ★
R, 112 m., 2009

Javier Beltran (Federico García Lorca), Robert Pattinson (Salvador Dalí), Matthew McNulty (Luis Buñuel), Marina Gatell (Magdalena), Arly Jover (Gala). Directed by Paul Morrison and produced by Carlo Dusi, Jonny Persey, and Jaume Vilalta. Screenplay by Philippa Goslett.

It was a ripe time to live at the Students' Residence in Madrid and study at the School of Fine Arts. When he arrived from Catalonia in 1922, Salvador Dalí met the future poet Federico García Lorca and future filmmaker Luis Buñuel. Dalí was a case study, dressed as a British dandy of the previous century with a feminine appearance. No doubt he was a gifted painter. He was to become a rather loathsome man.

Little Ashes focuses on an unconsummated romantic attraction between Dalí (Robert Pattinson) and García Lorca (Javier Beltran), who in the flower of youthful idealism and with the awakening of the flesh began to confuse sexuality with artistry. Not much is really known about their romance, such as it was, but in the conservative Catholic nation of the time and given Dalí's extreme terror of syphilis, it seems to have been passionate but platonic.

It found release in their roles in the developing Surrealist movement, in which church, state, ideology, landowners, parents, authorities, and laws were all mocked by deliberately outlandish behavior. In 1929, Dalí wrote and Buñuel directed probably the most famous of all Surrealist works, the film *Un Chien Andalou* (*The Andalusian Dog*), with its notorious images of a cloud slicing through the moon and a knife slicing through a woman's eyeball. In a time before computer imagery, it was a real eyeball (belonging to a pig, not a woman, but small comfort to the pig).

By 1936, García Lorca was dead, murdered by Spanish fascists. The story is told in the film *The Disappearance of García Lorca* (1997). Buñuel fled Spain to Mexico, then later returned as one of the world's greatest filmmakers. Dalí betrayed his early talent, embraced fascism, Nazism, and communism, returned repentant to the church, and become an odious caricature of an artist, obsessed by cash. "Each morning when I awake," he said, "I experience again a supreme pleasure—that of being Salvador Dalí." Yes, but for a time he was a superb painter.

Little Ashes is a film that shows these personalities being formed. Because most audiences may not know much about Dalí, García Lorca, and Buñuel, it depends for its box-office appeal on the starring role of Robert Pattinson, the twenty-three-year-old British star of *Twilight*. He is the heartthrob of the teenage vampire fans of *Twilight* but here shows an admirable willingness to take on a challenging role in direct contrast to the famous Edward Cullen. Is it too much to hope that *Twilight* fans will be drawn to the work of García Lorca and Buñuel? They'd be on the fast track to cultural literacy.

Biopics about the youth of famous men are often overshadowed by their fame to come. *The Motorcycle Diaries*, for example, depended for much of its appeal on our knowledge that its young doctor hero would someday become Che Guevara. *Little Ashes* is interested in the young men for themselves.

It shows unformed young men starting from similar places but taking different roads because of their characters. García Lorca, who is honest with himself about his love for another man, finds real love eventually with a woman, his classmate Magdalena (Marina Gatell). Dalí, who presents almost as a transvestite, denies all feelings, and like many puritans ends as a voluptuary. Buñuel, the most gifted of all, ends as all good film directors do, consumed by his work. I am fond of his practical approach to matters. Warned that angry mobs might storm the screen at the Paris premiere of *Un Chien Andalou*, he filled his pockets with stones to throw at them.

The film is absorbing but not compelling. Most of its action is inward. The more we know about the three men the better. Although the eyeball-slicing is shown in the film, many audiences may have no idea what it is doing there. Perhaps Dalí's gradual slinking away from his ideals, his early embrace of celebrity, and his preference for self-publicity over actual achievement, makes better sense when we begin with his shyness and naivete; is he indeed entirely aware that his hair and dress are those of a girl, or has he been coddled in this way by a strict, protective mother who is hostile to male sexuality?

Whatever the case, two things stand out: He has the courage to present himself in quasi-

drag, and the other students at the Residence, inspired by the fever in the air, accept him as "making a statement" he might not have been fully aware of.

I have long believed that one minute of wondering if you are about to be kissed is more erotic than an hour of kissing. Although a few gay sites complain *Little Ashes* doesn't deliver the goods, I find it far more intriguing to find how repressed sexuality expresses itself, because the bolder sort comes out in the usual ways and reduces mystery to bodily fluids. Orgasms are at their best when still making big promises, don't you find?

Lola Montes ★ ★ ★ ½
NO MPAA RATING, 110 m., 1955 (rereleased 2008)

Martine Carol (Lola Montes), Peter Ustinov (Ringmaster), Anton Walbrook (King Ludwig I), Henri Guisol (Maurice), Lise Delamare (Mrs. Craigie), Paulette Dubost (Josephine), Oskar Werner (Student). Directed by Max Ophuls and produced by Albert Caraco. Screenplay by Ophuls.

One of the signs of a great director is his ability to sustain a consistent personal tone throughout a film. The work of certain directors can be recognized almost at once; a few hundred feet of Godard or Fellini are sufficient. Max Ophuls was such a director, and his *Lola Montes* has as much unity of tone as any film I can remember.

It is all of a piece from beginning to end: the mood, the music, the remarkably fluid camera movement, the sets, the costumes. It is a director's film. The actors are in Ophuls's complete control, an additional element in his examination of the romantic myth.

His story involves the infamous Lola Montes, "The Most Scandalous Woman in the World," the mistress of Franz Liszt and King Ludwig of Bavaria, of students and artists, of soldiers and ringmasters. We find her in a New Orleans circus, the star attraction in a review of her sensational career. Peter Ustinov, the ringmaster, narrates her past as Lola revolves on a platform. Later the customers will have their chance to spend a dollar and kiss her hand.

The device of the circus is as successful as it is daring. Using it to supply his narrative thread, Ophuls slides through a series of flashbacks with as much ease and psychological completeness as Welles exhibited in *Citizen Kane*. The structure of the film is terribly artificial—flashbacks suspended from a fantasy circus—and the style itself is a highly mannered romanticism. But it works; Ophuls understands and justifies his method.

He is not so successful, unfortunately, with the performance of the late Martine Carol in the title role. Famous in the 1950s as a sort of prototype Bardot, Miss Carol was a third-rate actress, and she comes across as wooden, shallow, not even very attractive.

Ophuls apparently needed Miss Carol's box-office name to help justify his $1.5 million budget (this was the most expensive French film to date when it was completed in 1955). He tries to make an advantage of her weakness by directing her almost as a doll; her function is to watch impassively while her lovers save her scenes. The best performance in the film is by Anton Walbrook as the deaf, touching old king. Peter Ustinov is typically excellent. Oskar Werner, as a young student, is not much better than ever.

Lola Montes was a commercial flop when Ophuls released it in 1955, shortened against his will. He died two years later, still engaged in a battle with the film's producers. An even more savagely butchered version was in circulation for a few years. Through the efforts of the *Village Voice*'s Andrew Sarris and other lovers of the film, a somewhat restored version was shown at the first New York Film Festival in 1963 and in an improved version in 1968. In reviews at the time, Sarris called it "the greatest film of all time."

Now, thanks to the discovery of additional footage and new digital technology, the film has finally been restored to Ophuls's original version, which was thought lost after the cuts in the 1950s. It showed for the third time at the 2008 New York Film Festival in October. It is now complete and looks better than at any time in its viewing history. In fact, it is breathtaking, an extravaganza of bright circus colors and Ophuls's fluid camera in wide-screen Cinemascope.

The Longshots ★ ★ ★
PG, 94 m., 2008

Ice Cube (Curtis Plummer), Keke Palmer (Jasmine Plummer), Tasha Smith (Claire), Jill Marie Jones (Ronnie), Dash Mihok (Cyrus), Miles Chandler (Damon), Matt Craven (Coach Fisher). Directed by Fred Durst and produced by Ice Cube, Matt Alvarez, and Nick Santora. Screenplay by Santora and Doug Atchison.

If I've seen one movie about a team of underdogs from a small town, I've seen a dozen. But I hadn't seen *The Longshots* before. It's based on the true story of eleven-year-old Jasmine Plummer, from the Chicago suburb of Harvey, who in 2003 became the first female to play quarterback in the Pop Warner football tournament.

Her story is remarkable, especially if you factor in her national wrestling title and her grades as an honor student. But the film is remarkable in other ways. It includes some of the expected elements of any film from this genre, but without the usual Hollywood supercharging. It's not all pumped up with flash and phoniness. Its stars play their characters with a quiet conviction, warm and touching. Its heroine is not the usual young girl who is required to be smarter and talk faster and correct adults in their faulty thinking. She has humility, shyness, and a certain sadness.

And that is all the more impressive because Jasmine is played by Keke Palmer, who seems absolutely convincing in the role. Yet consider that this is the same actress (thirteen when the movie was shot) who played Queen Latifah's niece in *Barbershop 2,* held her own in an exchange with Cedric the Entertainer in that film, has starred in Medea projects by Tyler Perry, and was the youngest actress ever nominated for best actress by the Screen Actors Guild.

That means this is real acting. Her Jasmine has *not* always wanted to play boys' football. In fact, she doesn't want to. But she has a good eye and a strong throwing arm, and is pushed into it by her Uncle Curtis (Ice Cube), who was a star years ago on the same team. Curtis has been unemployed since the town's factory closed, has no aim in life, loves his niece, and acts like a father to her because her own dad abandoned the family. He teaches her all he knows about quarterbacking, and more or less forces the coach (Matt Craven) to put her in a game. She's small but smart and quick, and soon her story is picked up by the press, and she quarterbacks the team into Pop Warner history.

Some facts have been changed. Harvey becomes Minton, Illinois, a small town with a sizable African-American population. Since the factory closed, Main Street has a lot of empty storefronts and there's not much civic spirit. But the team revives hope and pride. And Ice Cube and Keke Palmer create a believable uncle-niece relationship that is right down to the ground in honesty and sincerity.

It's also nice that the team accepts her pretty quickly. They like her, she plays well, and that's that. No practical jokes or hazing, although some of the other girls in school are jealous and snippy. Some of the best things about this film are what it doesn't do. The director, Fred Durst (lead singer for Limp Bizkit), and his writers, Nick Santora and Doug Atchison, are actually interested in these human beings, not in all the semi-obligatory clichés.

No team bully. No seemingly tragic injuries. Not many fans in the stands, although more trickle in when the team starts to win. There's a little romance between Curtis and a schoolteacher (Jill Marie Jones), but it's mostly low-key conversation. Jasmine's mother (Tasha Smith) runs the town diner and is not in personal crisis. The movie even lacks that old groaner, the scene where the kid spots a parent in the crowd and is suddenly inspired. And the ending will surprise you by being true to life.

The movie, in short, is absolutely sure what it wants to be, right down to the worn-out grass on the football field, so realistically photographed by Conrad W. Hall. Even the signs Jasmine's fans hold up look homemade, when a lot of teen sports movies seem to have employed sign painters. And Jasmine dresses exactly like an ordinary girl her age and doesn't seem to be auditioning for a role as an American Girl doll. The more the movie builds, the more it grows on you. And would you believe this? Keke Palmer was also born in Harvey.

The Love Guru ★
PG-13, 87 m., 2008

Mike Myers (Guru Pitka), Jessica Alba (Jane Bullard), Justin Timberlake (Jacques Grande), Romany Malco (Darren Roanoke), Meagan Good (Prudence), Omid Djalili (Guru Satchabigknoba), Ben Kingsley (Guru Tugginmypuddha), Verne Troyer (Cherkov). Directed by Marco Schnabel and produced by Michael De Luca and Mike Myers. Screenplay by Myers and Graham Gordy.

What is it with Mike Myers and penis jokes? Having created a classic funny scene with his not-quite-visible penis sketch in the first Austin Powers movie, he now assembles, in *The Love Guru*, as many more penis jokes as he can think of, none of them funny except for one based on an off-screen *thump*. He supplements this subject with countless other awful moments involving defecation and the deafening passing of gas. Oh, and elephant sex.

The plot involves an American child who is raised in an Indian ashram (never mind why) and becomes the childhood friend of Deepak Chopra. Both come to America, where Chopra becomes a celebrity, but Guru Pitka (Myers) seems doomed to anonymity. That's until Jane Bullard (Jessica Alba), owner of the Toronto Maple Leafs, hires him to reconcile her star player, Darren Roanoke (Romany Malco), with his estranged wife, Prudence (Meagan Good). Just at the time of the Stanley Cup play-offs, Prudence has left her husband for the arms and other attributes of star Los Angeles player Jacques "Le Coq" Grande (Justin Timberlake), said to have the largest whatjamacallit in existence.

And what *don't* they call it in *The Love Guru*? The movie not only violates the Law of Funny Names (usually not funny), but rips it from the Little Movie Glossary and tramples it into the ice. Yes, many scenes are filmed at the Stanley Cup finals, where we see much of the Maple Leafs' dwarf coach (Verne Troyer), also the butt of size jokes (you will remember him as Mini-Me in the Powers films). There is also a running gag involving the play-by-play commentators and occasional flashbacks to the guru's childhood in India, where he studied under Guru Tugginmypuddha (Ben Kingsley). One of the guru's martial arts involves fencing with urine-soaked mops. Uh-huh.

Myers, a Canadian, incorporates some Canadian in-jokes; the team owner's name,

Bullard, evokes the Ballard family of Maple Leaf fame. At the center of all of this is Guru Pitka, desperately trying to get himself on *Oprah* and finding acronyms in some of the most unlikely words. He has a strange manner of delivering punch lines directly into the camera and then laughing at them—usually, I must report, alone.

Myers is a nice man and has made some funny movies, but this film could have been written on toilet walls by callow adolescents. Every reference to a human sex organ or process of defecation is not automatically funny simply because it is naughty, but Myers seems to labor under that delusion. He acts as if he's getting away with something, but in fact all he's getting away with is selling tickets to a dreary experience. There's a moment of invention near the beginning of the film (his flying cushion has a back-up beeper), and then it's all into the Dumpster. Even his fellow actors seem to realize no one is laughing. That's impossible because they can't hear the audience, but it looks uncannily like they can, and do.

Love in the Time of Cholera ★ ½
R, 138 m., 2007

Javier Bardem (Florentino Ariza), Giovanna Mezzogiorno (Fermina Daza), Benjamin Bratt (Dr. Juvenal Urbino), Catalina Sandino Moreno (Hildebranda Sanchez), Hector Elizondo (Don Leo), Liev Schreiber (Lotario Thurgot), Fernanda Montenegro (Transito Ariza), Laura Harring (Sara Noriega), John Leguizamo (Lorenzo Daza). Directed by Mike Newell and produced by Scott Steindorff. Screenplay by Ronald Harwood, based on the novel by Gabriel García Márquez.

Small wonder that *One Hundred Years of Solitude,* Gabriel García Márquez's best novel, has never been filmed. Watching *Love in the Time of Cholera,* based on another of his great works, made me wonder if he is even translatable into cinema. Gabo's work may really live only there on the page, with his lighthearted badinage between the erotic and the absurd, the tragic and the magical. If you extract the story without the language, you are left with dust and bones but no beating heart.

Consider the story of *Love in the Time of Cholera.* A young man named Florentino (Javier Bardem) is struck by the thunderbolt of love when he first regards Fermina (Giovanna Mezzogiorno). Guarded by her fiercely watchful father (John Leguizamo), she finds ways to accept Florentino's love letters and his love, but when her father discovers what is going on, he ships her far away. Young love cannot survive forever at a distance, and Fermina, half-convinced by her father's ferocity that Florentino is beneath her, marries a successful man, a doctor named Juvenal Urbino (Benjamin Bratt). He is not a bad man, this doctor, and their marriage is not unhappy, and if Juvenal has a wandering eye, well, so did many men in South America of 150 years ago.

Florentino remains faithful to his first love, in spirit, if not in flesh. He makes love with many women, but he never loves them. That part of his heart is reserved forever for Fermina. Fifty years pass, the doctor dies, Florentino reappears to announce that his love is strong as ever, she wallops him, then she accepts him, and the decades are erased in their eyes, although not from their faces.

This is, perhaps, not a profound or classic story. Is it tragedy or soap opera? Ah, that's where Gabriel García Márquez has us. It is both, at the same time, and sad and funny, and there is foolishness in it, and drollery, and his prose dances over the contradictions. The British scandal rag *News of the World* (fondly known as *Screws of the World*) used to have a motto, "All human life is here," but it better applies to Gabo. He is said to have popularized the uniquely South American style of magic realism, but when I read him I feel no realism, only magic.

Now his delicate fantasy has been made concrete in this film. Characters who live in our imaginations have been assigned to actors, and places that exist in dreams have been assigned to locations. Yes, I know that's what all movies do with all stories, and most of the time it works. But not this time. I don't know when, watching a movie, I have been more constantly aware of the actors who were playing the roles. That's not a criticism but an observation.

Take, for example, Javier Bardem, because he is such a good actor. In *No Country for Old Men,* I completely lost sight of him in the character of the murderous Anton Chigurh. Now Chigurh is an absurd monstrosity, not really believable in any sense, but he *works* in the movie. Florentino Ariza is supposed to be believable, and in the book we care for him, but in the movie, why, that's Javier Bardem! And when he is an old man, why, that's Javier Bardem with all that makeup! Gene Siskel used to describe old-age makeup as making young actors look like turtles. The problem is not with bad old-age makeup, but with the impossibility of old-age makeup. Twenty or thirty years, yes, and then you're pushing it. Better take the solution of *The Notebook* and have two characters played by Rachel McAdams and Ryan Gosling when young, Gena Rowlands and James Garner when old. That way everyone can relax.

There is another problem with the movie, and it has to do with Mike Newell's direction. He is too bread-and-butter here. The story requires light footwork, a kind of dancing over the ice before it cracks, and Newell strides steadily onward. It does not matter much that the events all unfold right on time; they should seem to unfold themselves and be surprised that they have. Nothing should seem preordained, not even when Gabo uses leaps back and forth through time to let you know perfectly well what is coming. Good lord, you should think, it came to pass exactly as he said it would! Instead, you think, now her husband is going to die, and Florentino will reappear, and . . .

I'm wondering, as I started by saying, if what makes García Márquez so great a writer is his work's insistence on being read, not seen. The last internationally released film adaptation of his work, Arturo Ripstein's *No One Writes to the Colonel* (1999), played at Sundance and folded; the only country where it opened theatrically was Spain. Ruy Guerra's *Erendira* (1983) also barely opened. For an author whose *Solitude* has sold more than sixty million copies, that's not much of a record; some short stories have also been filmed, to little notice. I am told by the critic Jeff Schwager that Gabo himself has written the stories and screenplays for many Spanish-language films (IMDb lists thirty-eight!), but as none of them have leaped the language barrier with much ease, I wonder how successful they were.

Is there another great modern writer so hard to translate successfully into cinema? Saul Bellow? Again, it's all in the language. The only thing Saul and Gabo have in common is the Nobel Prize. Now that's interesting.

The Lucky Ones ★ ★ ★
R, 113 m., 2008

Tim Robbins (Fred Cheaver), Rachel McAdams (Colee Dunn), Michael Pena (T.K. Poole). Directed by Neil Burger and produced by Burger, Brian Koppelman, David Levien, and Rick Schwartz. Screenplay by Burger and Dirk Wittenborn.

Three soldiers, home on a month's leave from Iraq, find themselves on an odyssey from New York to Las Vegas in *The Lucky Ones*. That's the setup. The journey involves your standard rest stops: friendly diners, dubious mechanics, fervent church people, roadside hookers, redneck saloons, lonely motels, tornadoes, casinos, those sorts of things. This formula is fraught with pitfalls, but the characters and the actors redeem it with a surprising emotional impact.

Tim Robbins plays the father figure, a fiftysomething career army sergeant who received a back injury and is returning home to St. Louis. After a blackout shuts down JFK, he rents a car and ends up taking the others on board. Rachel McAdams plays Private Colee Dunn, who has a leg injury and is heading for Vegas to return a guitar belonging to her boyfriend, who was killed in the war. Michael Pena plays Sergeant T.K. Poole, injured by shrapnel in the groin, who wants to go to Vegas to find hookers who can reawaken his equipment before he meets his stateside girlfriend.

Don't laugh when I say this: These three resemble in broad outline the three returning servicemen in the classic *The Best Years of Our Lives* (1946). That film had an alcoholic older man returning to a loyal wife, one younger man returning to a sluttish wife, and another afraid to marry his girlfriend because he had lost his hands. Change one man to a woman, shuffle a little, and you see what I mean.

That doesn't mean the film is an "homage"; director and cowriter Neil Burger told me he hasn't seen the 1946 film. It means the underlying structure and character group is somewhat archetypal. What distinguished *Best Years* was its gravitas. What made *The Lucky Ones* so gratifying to me was anything but gravitas; these three characters are simply likable, warm, sincere, and often funny. The performances are so good they carry the film right along.

Consider the events during the road trip. They are far from original. Many road movies are *about* what happens on the road. In *The Lucky Ones*, the events are somewhat inconsequential backdrops to the three-way relationship and the sympathy we feel for the characters. Yes, there are some considerable payoffs at the end, although not exactly unforeseen. There are also some plot contrivances at the end that seem hauled in. I noted this but didn't much mind.

Rachel McAdams (*The Notebook, Mean Girls*) comes into her own here. Previously she has been seen mostly as a hot chick (the title of her worst film) or an idealized sweetheart. Here she is feisty, vulnerable, plucky, warm, and funny. This is her coming-of-age as an actress. She provides yet another lesson that you can't judge acting ability until you see an actor given a chance to really stretch. Watch the poignancy of the scene when she meets her boyfriend's family.

Michael Pena plays a type I recognize: young, earnest, prudent, brimming with unsolicited advice. The opposite of stereotypes. T.K. needs to grow up some more, of course. He is so obsessed with his groin injury because without sex, he says, he and his girlfriend have nothing in common. This is an upbeat film, which explains, I suppose, why the shrapnel after-effects could be cured not by a doctor but by a hooker. If he and his girl have only sex in common, maybe she could have done the healing freelance. Along the way, Pena's T.K. provides a nudging counterpoint.

Tim Robbins's army lifer is, above all, a decent man and honest enough to reveal how he received his back injury in less-than-heroic circumstances. We sense he's been shepherding younger soldiers for most of his career, and now, during his leave, he's doing it again. He is not stupid, but he isn't the brightest bulb

in the chandelier. He has a plan to finance his son's college tuition by winning in Vegas. This shows a touching but unwise fatherly love. Because we know how smart and quick Robbins is, it's uncanny how convincing he is as a steady and dependable calming hand.

Movies about the war in Iraq have not been popular—not even such a good one as *In the Valley of Elah,* with its Tommy Lee Jones performance. But as I wrote after seeing *The Lucky Ones* at Toronto, it is *not* an Iraq war movie. These three characters could be returning home from anywhere, for countless reasons. That might be a weakness in a film that wanted to make a statement about Iraq, but these three good and brave soldiers see the war in personal, not ideological, terms and the film clearly focuses on their personalities more than their experiences. There were some reviews from Toronto that seemed to focus on its departure from some theoretical, serious war film. I believe audiences will be moved by the characters. I was.

Lust, Caution ★ ★ ★
NC-17, 158 m., 2007

Tony Leung (Mr. Yee), Joan Chen (Mrs. Yee), Tang Wei (Wong Chia Chi [Mrs. Mak]), Chu Tsz-ying (Lai), Wang Leehom (Kuang Yu Min), Anupam Kher (Indian Jeweler). Directed by Ang Lee and produced by William Kong and Lee. Screenplay by James Schamus and Wang Hiu Ling.

Ang Lee's *Lust, Caution* is first languid, then passionate, as it tells the story of a young woman who joins a political murder plot and then becomes emotionally involved with her enemy. It begins at a 1942 mah-jongg game in Hong Kong, when erotic undertones become clearly audible to us, and then flashes back to Shanghai, 1938, during the Japanese occupation of China. One of the rich ladies at the game table is revealed to have been a college student and not really the wife of a wealthy (but unseen) tycoon.

The underlying plot gradually reveals itself. Too gradually, some will believe, unless the languor is necessary to create the hothouse atmosphere that survives in the midst of war. The mah-jongg game is taking place in the home of Mr. Yee (Tony Leung), whose wife (Joan Chen) is the hostess. Since coming from Shanghai, he has moved up in the collaborationist government, handles interrogations and tortures, and is repaid by status and access to such restricted items as nylon stockings, cigarettes, even diamonds. When Mr. Yee comes home in the middle of the game, he exchanges a significant look with Mrs. Mak (Tang Wei), who first joined the circle in Shanghai.

It's clear to us there's something secret and intimate between them. But who is this wealthy Mrs. Mak, who travels in a chauffeured car but whose husband is always away on business? The flashback reveals her as Wong Chia Chi, a young student who on summer vacation falls in with a group of radical Chinese patriots and takes a key role in their hope of assassinating one of the Chinese who are working with the Japanese. Her assignment: become Mr. Yee's lover.

This she did in Shanghai, but the war separated them before she was able to bring about an opportunity for Yee's murder (she is not expected to do it herself). A natural actress, she took easily to the roles of lover and rich woman. But she had some difficulty in sacrificing her virginity, which was necessary for her to convincingly play a married woman.

We do not see Mr. Yee at work, torturing his countrymen, but Leung is able to project the man's capability for menace and begins to do that in bed with her. Then commence the scenes that earned the film its NC-17 rating. They are not specifically hard-core in detail, but involve so many arcane and athletic sexual positions that the MPAA's injunction against the depiction of "thrusting" is left with their clothes on the floor.

When their sex drifts steadily into S&M, the nature of their relationship shifts. It is impossible to say that Wong Chia Chi/Mrs. Mak *likes* his tastes in pain and bondage, but they create a fearful intimacy that, for both of them, transcends their lives apart. And it is that tension, between private fascination and public danger, that gives the movie its purpose.

Failing to find the connecting link between such Ang Lee films as *Sense and Sensibility*, *Brokeback Mountain*, and *The Hulk*, I was quickly corrected by readers who said, obviously, all his films are about people trying to realize their essential natures despite the constraints of society. Readers, you were right. Here we have a woman who hates her lover enough to help kill him and yet is mesmerized by him. And a man whose official position would be destroyed by the exposure of this affair (especially if it were discovered whom Mrs. Mak really is). Yet the heart, as Pascal said, has its reasons. Mr. Yee and Mrs. Mak are just as transgressive as the *Brokeback* lovers, just as entranced by a form of sex that is frowned on by their societies.

There is not a frame of the film that is not beautiful, but there may be too many frames. Why does Ang Lee go into such depth and detail to establish this world, and why does he delay the film's crucial scenes? I don't know, but of course seeing the film the first time I didn't know that was what he was doing, and I grew restless before I grew involved. Asked to edit the sex scenes to avoid the dreaded NC-17 rating, Lee quite properly refused and was backed all the way by James Schamus, his cowriter and, significantly, head of Focus Features, which released the film.

The nature of the sex is Lee's subject, and he is too honest to suppress that. His moments of full frontal nudity avoid the awkwardness of most movie sex scenes in which the lovers, although alone, carefully mask their naughty bits. The scenes are not edited for erotic effect, it must be observed, but are treated in terms of their psychological meaning.

Film by film, Ang Lee, from Taipei out of the University of Illinois, has become one of the world's leading directors. This film was his second Golden Lion winner in three years at the Venice Film Festival. But it is not among his best films. It lacks the focus and fire that his characters finally find. Less sense, more sensibility.

Lymelife ★ ★ ★ ½
R, 95 m., 2009

Alec Baldwin (Mickey Bartlett), Kieran Culkin (Jimmy Bartlett), Rory Culkin (Scott Bartlett), Jill Hennessy (Brenda Bartlett), Timothy Hutton (Charlie Bragg), Cynthia Nixon (Melissa Bragg), Emma Roberts (Adrianna Bragg). Directed by Derick Martini and produced by Steven

Martini, Barbara DeFina, Jon Cornick, Alec Baldwin, Michele Tayler, and Angela Somerville. Screenplay by Derick Martini and Steven Martini.

Lymelife sometimes cuts to the tiny buildings and inhabitants of a model suburb, the kind you might find on display in a Realtor's office. Just as frequent are its shots of actual homes in a Long Island suburb, of the sort occupied by the Bartlett and Bragg families. The film is about the distance between the ideal and the real.

Unhappy suburban families are more familiar in the movies than real ones—perhaps because, as Tolstoy believed, all happy families are the same. The sickness of these two families emanates from the parents. Two are committing adultery with each other. A third has Lyme disease and regards life with fatigue and depression.

The movie isn't about Lyme disease, but it serves as a theme: "Isn't it amazing that your whole life can be changed by a bug the size of a pimple on your ass?" A tick has destroyed the spirit of Charlie Bragg (Timothy Hutton) and left his sluttish wife, Melissa (Cynthia Nixon), open to the predations of her business partner, Mickey Bartlett (Alec Baldwin). Mickey's wife, Brenda Bartlett (Jill Hennessy), knows what's going on but tries to stand above it.

Their children are directly affected, and much of the film is seen through the eyes of two kids around fifteen, Scott Bartlett (Rory Culkin) and Adrianna Bragg (Emma Roberts). In a film of good actors, these are two finely realized performances. Scott has an inarticulate crush on Adrianna and is wounded when he sees her with an older, more studly boy. Adrianna likes him—they've been lifelong friends—but likes to date "more mature" men, which at that age may mean seventeen. Both of them know what Mickey and Melissa are doing. Adrianna is cynical; he's betrayed.

But those are only the outlines of a tender, sometimes painful, sometimes blackly comic story. The film's characters are not types but particular people, and if the adults protect themselves in one way or another, the children are wide open. That includes Scott's older brother, Jimmy (Kieran Culkin), who is getting out while he can and has enlisted in the service. (The film has misplaced the Falkland Islands conflict in the 1970s, but how many even remember it? Nor was it a U.S. war.)

Rory Culkin's performance is the mainspring. Apart from the misfortune that they all look angelic, the Culkin family is rich in gifted actors. Here Rory plays a sexually inexperienced, bullied, sensitive kid, wounded by the loud arguments of his parents. His mother, played by Hennessy, is a strong, good woman, keeping a brave face for her kids, loathing her husband. He lives through his work (a new suburban home development), buys a new home for them without even mentioning it to her, and has sex with Melissa because she is there.

Now look at the Timothy Hutton character, the sick one. Exhausted, emasculated, hopeless, he stares at a blank television screen, watches unseen as his wife and Mickey have sex in the basement, develops a strange obsession with a deer he often sees in a forest near his house. Such a low-energy character might seem to offer little for an actor to "do," but Hutton brings the film a level of defeat and despair that shadows everything. They could all end up like him; Brenda wraps Scott's neck, wrists, and ankles with duct tape and searches his hair for ticks.

The film is by Derick Martini, written with his brother Steven. I met them at Toronto 1999, with their screenplay for the quirky indie *Goat on Fire and Smiling Fish*. This is their first feature—showing confidence enough, despite a heavyweight cast, to build carefully to their unexpectedly appropriate conclusion. Martini is especially good with Alec Baldwin, an actor whose power is used here to create an intense mano a mano with Jimmy. He and Hennessy are lacerating together in a scene of mutual hate.

A buried subject is parenting. There are two good parents here. Brenda has a warm scene with Scott the morning after his confirmation (and, she doesn't know, his first sexual experience); Adrianna, the young girl, who knows more about life than Scott, sees him with sympathy, and handles him with almost maternal care. Emma Roberts's performance is far deeper than the sexpot we first seem to see.

Lymelife doesn't have the sheer power of *The Ice Storm*, but it's not just another recycling of suburban angst. By allowing their characters complexity, the Martinis spill open those tiny model homes as thoroughly as a dropped Monopoly game.

M

Madagascar: Escape 2 Africa ★ ★ ★
PG, 88 m., 2008

With the voices of: Ben Stiller (Alex), Chris Rock (Marty), David Schwimmer (Melman), Jada Pinkett Smith (Gloria), Sacha Baron Cohen (King Julien), Cedric the Entertainer (Maurice), Andy Richter (Mort), Bernie Mac (Zuba), Alec Baldwin (Makunga), Sherri Shepherd (Alex's Mom), will.i.am (Moto Moto). Directed by Eric Darnell and Tom McGrath and produced by Mireille Soria and Mark Swift. Screenplay by Darnell, McGrath, and Etan Cohen.

These poor animals. First, they're hauled away from the comforts of the Central Park Zoo to be stranded on Madagascar. Then they find a crashed Cargo Cult airplane from WWII, tape the plane together, and try to fly it back home. Why would they rather be in New York? Can't get a cab in Madagascar? They all belong to separate species, but they're comfortable with diversity. These guys would have turned themselves in to Noah.

It doesn't look like that plane is gonna make it. That doesn't mean across the Atlantic from Africa. It means across Africa to the Atlantic. Do they (or their audience) realize Madagascar is *east* of Africa, in the Indian Ocean? How I know, I had a friend from Madagascar once. Beat me at chess.

Some people are probably wondering about the title *Madagascar: Escape 2 Africa,* because they think the animals escaped 2 Africa in the first place. Now shouldn't they be escaping 4rom Africa? So they take off, and (spoiler?) crash in Africa. Now they are faced with exactly the same dilemma as in the first film: Can wild animals survive in the wild?

They do a pretty funny job, which is the point. This is a brighter, more engaging film than the original *Madagascar.* I'll bet Dreamworks cofounder Jeffrey Katzenberg was hands-on. When he was at Disney, he made friends with a lion during the filming of *The Lion King.* He even appeared with it on a leash at the junket. He looked more relaxed than the members of the press. Usually at a junket, they're the ones who do the eating.

All of the original voice talents are back, doing their original characters. What an all-star cast: Ben Stiller, Chris Rock, David Schwimmer, Jada Pinkett Smith, Sacha Baron Cohen, Cedric the Entertainer, Andy Richter, Bernie Mac, Alec Baldwin, and will.i.am, who has one of those names like his mother was frightened during pregnancy by a typographer.

The look of *Madagascar: Escape 2 Africa* is open and sunlit. Better the wild savannah than the dense jungle. The action is thrilling (sacrifices to a volcano, a struggle for water), and there is a touching romance between Gloria the hippo and Melman the giraffe. I want to think Melman is not named after Larry (Bud) Melman, but I don't have the strength of character. Anyway, the prospect of a giraffe making love to a hippo is enough to set me writing limericks. Can it be done? I think it might be safer than a hippo making love to a giraffe.

So OK, kids, if you liked the first one, this is better. Your parents may like it, too, although they may have to dash out for just a second to see *Soul Men.*

Mad Money ★ ½
PG-13, 104 m., 2008

Diane Keaton (Bridget Cardigan), Queen Latifah (Nina Brewster), Katie Holmes (Jackie Truman), Ted Danson (Don Cardigan), Adam Rothenberg (Bob Truman). Directed by Callie Khouri and produced by James Acheson, Jay Cohen, and Frank DeMartini. Screenplay by Glenn Gers and John Mister.

There is something called "found poetry." The term refers to anything that was not written as poetry but reads as if it was. I would like to suggest a new category: found reviews. These are not really reviews but serve the same function. I found one just now, and after a struggle with myself, I have decided to share it with you. It is about *Mad Money,* a movie in which Diane Keaton, Queen Latifah, and Katie Holmes are lowly workers who team up to rob a Federal Reserve Bank.

I was noodling around Rotten Tomatoes, trying to determine who played the bank's security chief, and noticed the movie had not yet been reviewed by anybody. Hold on! In the "Forum" section for this movie, "islandhome" wrote at 7:58 a.m. January 8: "review of this movie . . . tonight i'll post." At 11:19 a.m. January 10, "islandhome" was finally back with the promised review. It is written without capital letters, flush-left like a poem, and I quote it spelling and all:

> hello sorry i slept when i got back
> well it was kinda fun
> it could never happen in the way it was
>   portraid
> but what ever its a movie
> for the girls most will like it
> and the men will not mind it much
> i thought it was going to be kinda like
>   how tobeat the high cost of living
> kinda the same them but not as much fun
> ill give it a 4 Out of 10

I read this twice, three times. I had been testing out various first sentences for my own review, but somehow the purity and directness of islandhome's review undercut me. It is so final. "for the girls most will like it / and the men will not mind it much." How can you improve on that? It's worthy of Charles Bukowski.

Anyway, here's how I was going to start out: *Mad Money* is astonishingly casual for a movie about three service workers who steal millions from a Federal Reserve Bank. There is little suspense, no true danger, their plan is simple, the complications are few, and they don't get excited much beyond some high-fives and hugs and giggles. If there was ever a movie where Diane Keaton would be justified in bringing back "la-di-da," this is that movie.

Keaton costars with Queen Latifah and Katie Holmes. She's set up as a rich wife whose husband (Ted Danson) gets downsized. They owe a mountain of debt, their house is being repossessed, and she thinks she might as well (gulp) get a job. The best she can do is emptying the garbage at the Federal Reserve.

That's when she spots a loophole in the bank's famous security system. She figures out a way to steal used bills on the way to the shredder and smuggle them out of the building stuffed into her bra and panties, and those of her partners in crime, Katie and the Queen. This system works. And the beauty is, the money isn't missed because it has supposedly already been destroyed. All they're doing is spending it one more time on its way to the shredder. A victimless crime, unless it brings down the economy, of course.

I would have gone on to observe that the movie makes it all look so easy and painless that it's a good thing it opens with a flash-forward showing them in a panic mode, so we know that sooner or later something exciting will happen. In the meantime, we get more scenes starring Ted Danson, with a hairstyle that makes him look alarmingly like a cross between David Cronenberg and Frankenstein's monster. And there's of course a chief of security who is constantly being outwitted. And so on.

Mad Money is actually a remake of a 2001 TV movie, I discovered on IMDb. Britain's Granada made it about a team of cleaners who pull the same scam on the Bank of England. Two character first names are the same (Bridget and Jackie), but the last name of the Keaton and Danson characters is changed from Watmore to Cardigan. Go figure. Or don't. The bottom line is, some girls will like it, the men not so much, and I give it 1½ stars out of 4.

Mamma Mia! ★ ★
PG-13, 98 m., 2008

Meryl Streep (Donna), Pierce Brosnan (Sam), Colin Firth (Harry), Stellan Skarsgård (Bill), Julie Walters (Rosie), Dominic Cooper (Sky), Amanda Seyfried (Sophie), Christine Baranski (Tanya). Directed by Phyllida Lloyd and produced by Judy Craymer and Gary Goetzman. Screenplay by Catherine Johnson, based on the stage musical.

I saw the stage version of *Mamma Mia!* in London, where for all I know it is now entering the second century of its run, and I was underwhelmed. The film version has the advantage of possessing Meryl Streep, Pierce Brosnan, Amanda Seyfried, Colin Firth, and Julie Walters—but they are assets stretched fairly thin. And there are the wall-to-wall songs by ABBA, if you like that sort of thing. I don't, not much, with a few exceptions.

But here's the fact of the matter. This movie wasn't made for me. It was made for the people who will love it, of which there may be a multitude. The stage musical has sold thirty million tickets, and I feel like the grouch at the party. So let me make that clear and proceed with my minority opinion.

The action is set on a Greek isle, where the characters are made to slide down rooftops, dangle from ladders, enter and exit by trapdoors, and frolic among the colorful local folk. The choreography at times resembles calisthenics, particularly in a scene where the young male population, all wearing scuba flippers, dance on the pier to "Dancing Queen" (one of the ABBA songs I do like).

It would be charity to call the plot contrived. Meryl Streep plays Donna, who runs a tourist villa on the island, where she has raised her daughter, Sophie (Seyfried), to the age of twenty. Sophie, engaged to Sky (Dominic Cooper), has never known who her father is. But now she's found an old diary and invited the three possible candidates to her forthcoming wedding. She'll know the right one at first sight, she's convinced. They are Sam (Pierce Brosnan), Bill (Stellan Skarsgard), and Harry (Colin Firth), and if you know the first thing about camera angles, shot choice, and screen time, you will quickly be able to pick out the likely candidate—if not for sperm source, then for the one most likely to succeed in one way or another.

Meryl Streep's character of course knows nothing of her daughter's invitations, but even so, it must be said she takes a long time to figure out why these particular men were invited. Wouldn't it be, like, obvious? She has earnest conversations with all three, two of whom seem to have been one-night stands; for them to drop everything and fly to Greece for her after twenty years speaks highly of her charms.

The plot is a clothesline on which to hang the songs; the movie doesn't much sparkle when nobody is singing or dancing, but that's rarely. The stars all seem to be singing their own songs, aided by an off-screen chorus of, oh, several dozen, plus full orchestration. Meryl Streep might seem to be an unlikely choice to play Donna, but you know what? She can play anybody. And she can survive even the singing of a song like "Money, Money, Money." She has such a merry smile, and seems to be actually having a good time.

Her two best friends have flown in for the occasion: Tanya (Christine Baranski, an often-married plastic surgery subject) and Rosie (Julie Walters, plainer and pluckier). With three hunks their age like Brosnan, Firth, and Skarsgard on hand, do they divvy up? Not exactly. But a lot of big romantic decisions do take place in just a few days.

The island is beautiful. Moviegoers will no doubt be booking vacations there. The energy is unflagging. The local color feels a little overlooked in the background; nobody seems to speak much Greek. And then there are the songs. You know them. You may feel you know them too well. Or maybe you can never get enough of them. Streep's sunshine carries a lot of charm, although I will never be able to understand her final decision in the movie—not coming from such a sensible woman. Never mind. Love has its way. ☞

Management ★ ★ ★
R, 93 m., 2009

Steve Zahn (Mike), Jennifer Aniston (Sue), Woody Harrelson (Jango), Fred Ward (Jerry), Margi Martindale (Trish). Directed by Stephen Belber and produced by Marty Bowen, Wyck Godfrey, and Sidney Kimmel. Screenplay by Belber.

Sometimes casting has everything to do with a movie. In the usual course of events, a high-powered company sales executive wouldn't have much to do with Mike, the hapless loser who works and lives at the Arizona motel where she plans to spend one night. But cast Steve Zahn as the loser and it becomes thinkable.

The sales rep is Sue, played by Jennifer Aniston, who is upward-bound, successful, sharply dressed, and reduced to spending her evenings in remote motels, playing games on her laptop. Sue is every woman Mike has ever wanted but has never had, which is easy because he wants all women and has never had any. He's a nice guy, often stoned, under the thumbs of his parents, who own the motel, and looks at her with the love-struck eyes of a wet puppy.

Why and how they end up in the laundry room doing the rumpy-pumpy on a dryer is something *Management* takes for granted.

Sometimes, apparently, high-powered Manhattan career women swoon in the presence of a guy who looks like he should be pumping their gas. His courtship technique is cute: He checks her in, carries her bags, brings her flowers, knocks again with the "customary" house bottle of champagne, uncorks it, gets two plastic-wrapped glasses from the bathroom, and struggles to say several coherent words in a row.

We can more or less predict where all of this will lead. Mike is obviously the fish out of water, so he must travel to New York to dramatize his unsuitability. Then Sue must travel to Washington, where she sees Jango (Woody Harrelson), a former punk rocker who has become a yogurt millionaire (for Harrelson, this is typecasting). Then Mike must follow her there.

He's not a stalker, you understand. He only wants to lick her hand, curl up at her feet, and be thrown a Milk Bone when he's been a good boy. It is Aniston's task to make us believe Sue might be won over by this, and because she succeeds, the movie works as a sweet romcom with some fairly big laughs.

What's nice is to see Zahn playing a guy who's not the dimmest bulb in the chandelier. For some reason he's often typecast as a stoner dimwit, maybe because he was so good at playing such roles early in his career. Here he's smart enough, just extremely socially challenged. Watch Aniston play off him with her pert intelligence; she could demolish him but is touched by his lack of defenses.

Fred Ward has a good role here as Mike's father, a perfectionist stuck with a slacker as an heir. Eventually he, too, is touched. That only leaves one question, which first-time writer-director Stephen Belber wisely doesn't mine for a subplot: Why did Sue's office travel manager book her into this motel?

Man in the Chair ★ ½
PG-13, 107 m., 2007

Christopher Plummer (Flash Madden), Michael Angarano (Cameron Kincaid), M. Emmet Walsh (Mickey Hopkins), Robert Wagner (Taylor Moss), Tracey Walter (Mr. Klein), Mitch Pileggi (Floyd), Joshua Boyd (Murphy White). Directed by Michael Schroeder and produced by Schroeder, Randy Turrow, and Sarah Schroeder. Screenplay by Michael Schroeder.

Man in the Chair is a movie about a high school student who enlists two movie industry veterans from old-folks' homes to help him with his project. And I mean old folks. Flash Madden (Christopher Plummer) claims to have been given his nickname by Orson Welles on the set of *Citizen Kane,* which means, if he was twenty-five at the time, he is ninety-one now. And Mickey Hopkins (M. Emmet Walsh), a writer, claims to have written *Queen Christina,* which, if he was twenty-five at the time, would make him ninety-nine.

Of course we know Mickey didn't write *Queen Christina* (or *Gone with the Wind,* another one of his "credits"), and the odds are against Flash's story, too. The chances are they are both lying, but the kid, Cameron (Michael Angarano) doesn't think of that, and neither does the writer-director, Michael Schroeder, although it might have made this a better movie.

What it is, instead, is a half-baked idea for a movie with way too many characters and subplots. Do we really need another lovable cheering section of characters (and character actors) who live at the Motion Picture Home and have individual headlined character traits? Do we need animal haters who catch and kill dogs as a business? Do we need the kid to have a mean father? Do we need him to have a competitor who bullies him at school? Do we need for old Flash to be such an alcoholic that to still be drinking like that at ninety-one must mean he only started at ninety?

The movie works so hard at juggling its clichés that it fails to generate interest in its story—which turns out to be not the skateboarding drama the kid had in mind, but a docudrama Flash sells him on about the mistreatment of old folks like Mickey. Then the animal subplot takes over as the old folks and the kid attack the cruel dog pound, uh-huh. And there is a stunt involving gasoline that is way too far over the top.

Christopher Plummer is a superb actor. I applauded him off-Broadway as the best Iago I have ever seen. No doubt there were aspects of the *idea* of this character that appealed to him, but did he measure its probability? And as for Mickey, M. Emmet Walsh, also a great character actor, has made a living looking moth-eaten and ramshackle, but good Lord, what they do to Mickey in this picture, it's a mercy his poor mother isn't alive to see it (if she were 25 when she had Mickey, she'd be 124 now).

I know an old writer. His name is William Froug, he lives in Florida, and if you look him up on Amazon you will see he is still writing brilliant and useful books about screenwriting and teleplays. He is not merely as sharp as a tack, he is the standard by which they *sharpen* tacks. If he had been advising the kid, the kid would have made a better movie, and if he had been advising the director of *Man in the Chair*, we would have been spared the current experience. Just because you're old doesn't mean you have to be a decrepit caricature. One thing that keeps Froug young is that, unlike Flash Madden, he almost certainly does not sit on an expressway overpass guzzling Jack Daniel's from a pint bottle.

Note: If flashbacks are meant to recall reality, it is unlikely that the slate on Citizen Kane *would have misspelled the name of Orson Welles.*

Man on Wire ★ ★ ★ ★
PG-13, 94 m., 2008

Featuring Philippe Petit, Paul McGill, Annie Allix, Ardis Campbell, Jean-Louis Blondeau, David Demato, Jean-Francois Heckel, Aaron Haskell, and David Frank. A documentary directed by James Marsh and produced by Simon Chinn.

I am afraid of heights. Now you know. That is one reason I was helplessly engrossed in *Man on Wire*, the story of how Philippe Petit crossed *eight times* on a tightwire between the two towers of the World Trade Center on August 7, 1974. Another reason is that the documentary, a hybrid of actual and restaged footage, is constructed like a first-rate thriller.

Early in the film, we see what we think is sadly familiar footage: construction workers and huge trucks and cranes at work in the footprint of one of the WTC towers. At first I thought this was a film of the cleanup after 9/11. As the scene develops, I realized I was watching an early stage in the construction of the towers. The film shows the towers growing, huge steel beams being lifted, the puzzle being put together. As it happens, 9/11 is not even mentioned in the film, which is the right decision, I think. *Man on Wire* is about the vanquishing of the towers by bravery and joy, not by terrorism.

We meet Philippe Petit, a French wire walker, magician, unicyclist, and street performer, who tells us he was sitting in a dentist's office when he saw a drawing of the proposed towers and knew he was destined to conquer them. He drew a pencil line between them. His wire. The film will follow his campaign, as he enlists an unlikely cadre of helpers, draws inspiration from his girlfriend, Annie, and becomes obsessed with those two magnets acting on his personality.

Man on Wire, directed by James Marsh (*Wisconsin Death Trip*), has access to all of Petit's film, video, and photographs of the assault on the towers. But there is more than that. Ingeniously using actors and restaging events, Marsh fleshes out the story with scenes that could never have been filmed, such as the episode when Petit and a partner crouched motionless under tarps on a beam near the top floor as a security guard nosed around. He has gathered a motley crew, including a pot-addled musician and an executive who actually works in an office in one tower. He trains these amateurs on how to rig a high wire. Properly, he hopes.

This new footage is integrated seamlessly into the old; I gave up trying to decide which was which by the look of the picture, although a few sequences (shadows climbing a staircase) are obviously CGI. Marsh is dealing with an event that is almost thirty-five years old, and when he shows the same people at two stages of their lives, I assume either the younger or the older one is the actor, but I couldn't always be sure which. Philippe Petit is himself, both now and then, speaking fluent English, excited, passionate, voluble.

Even as a child he liked to climb things. No telling why. He taught himself to walk on a wire, practiced endlessly, dreamed of conquering the clouds. He rehearsed on wire strung up in country fields. His first great feat was to walk on a wire between the two bell towers of Notre Dame. Then he walked between the towers of the Sydney Harbour Bridge in Australia. As the World Trade Center was growing, so were his ambitions.

He never just *walked* on a wire. He lay down, knelt, juggled, ran. Every wire presented its own problems, and in rehearsing for the WTC, he built a wire the same distance in France. To simulate the winds, the movements of the buildings and the torsion of the wire, he had friends jiggle his wire, trying to toss him off. His balance was flawless. He explains how a wire can move: up and down, sideways, laterally, and it can also sometimes twist.

The installation of a wire between the two towers was as complicated as a bank heist. He and his friends scouted the terrain, obtained false ID cards, talked their way into a freight elevator reaching to the top—above the level of the finished floors. Incredibly, they had to haul nearly a ton of equipment up there. You may have heard how they got the wire across and how they guy-wired it, but if you don't know, I won't tell you.

They did it, anyway. Their plan worked. And on the morning of that August 7, Petit took the first crucial step that shifted his weight from the building to the wire, and stood above a drop of 1,350 feet. Many people know he crossed successfully. I had no idea he went back and forth eight times, the police waiting on both sides. His friends shed tears as they remember it happening. It was dangerous, foolhardy, glorious. His assistants feared they could be arrested for trespassing, manslaughter, or assisting a suicide. Philippe Petit was arrested and found guilty. The charge: disturbing the peace. ☞

Margot at the Wedding ★ ★ ★
R, 93 m., 2007

Nicole Kidman (Margot), Jennifer Jason Leigh (Pauline), Zane Pais (Claude), Jack Black (Malcolm), John Turturro (Jim), Flora Cross (Ingrid), Ciaran Hinds (Dick), Halley Feiffer (Maisy). Directed by Noah Baumbach and produced by Scott Rudin. Screenplay by Baumbach.

I wonder if his family knew Noah Baumbach was taking notes? First in *The Squid and the Whale* and now with *Margot at the Wedding*, he puts an intelligent but alarming family under the microscope and finds creepy-squirmy things crawling around. Of course, there is no reason to be certain the family in either movie is inspired by his own. But given the degree of familiarity, there's no reason not to, either. Besides, the character Margot in this one is accused of storing up every family pain, humiliation, and embarrassment for recycling in her short stories. Isn't there a rule that if you bring a literary crime onstage in the first act, you have to commit it in the third?

The movie opens as Margot (Nicole Kidman) and her son, Claude (Zane Pais), are traveling by train to the wedding of Pauline (Jennifer Jason Leigh), the sister she is not on speaking terms with. Pauline still lives in the big family house up east. With a child of her own, the precocious Ingrid (Flora Cross), and another on the way, Pauline's planning to marry Malcolm (Jack Black), who can spend up to a week writing a letter to the editor and is growing a mustache that he hopes will look funny.

Margot, the writer, has deliberately not brought along her husband, Jim (John Turturro), because she has plans to meet Dick (Ciaran Hinds), her former and perhaps future lover, at a local book signing. Dick has a daughter, Maisy (Halley Feiffer), who is just at that age when she has power but not wisdom about sexuality. Maisy and Ingrid will bond and no doubt start a first draft of *Ingrid and/or Maisy at the Wedding.*

All of these characters gather with some apprehension for an outdoor wedding that may not have been planned out of the pages of *American Bride.* And Margot is brutal with Pauline, advising her that Malcolm is not worthy to be her husband. We're not sure. He seems extremely inward and eccentric, and possibly unemployable, but maybe he's just what a high-powered ball of nerves like Pauline needs, if not as a husband, then as a letter writer. He is certainly the only person on the horizon without a neurotic agenda.

It is never explained why the two sisters haven't been speaking, but I understand why. They are such equals that neither one has ever been able to gain the upper hand. All of their lifestyle choices seem intended as rebukes to each other. They've spent a lifetime both trying to stand on the same place and push the other away. There's no great painful event in the past, just the mutual feeling that each is complete without a sister. Notice the scene when Pauline challenges Margot to climb a tree.

On the other hand, they're able to be brutally truthful with each other, especially in conversations about their sexual desirability. What does it do to a woman when she spends years pushing off men who want to sleep with her and gradually finds there's no one to push? Where are male chauvinist pigs when you need them? Many of their conversations take place in front of the kids, who look like they are in training to become the next generation of dysfunctionality.

Writing about this movie from the Toronto festival, Jim Emerson had a great observation: "It's like a Neil LaBute picture cowritten by Jules Feiffer." Yes, and Elaine May might have done one of her ghost rewrites, so to speak. The characters are into emotional laceration for fun. They are verbal, articulate, self-absorbed, selfish, egotistical, cold, and fascinating. They've never felt an emotion they couldn't laugh at.

Which brings us full circle. *Margot at the Wedding* may not be based on Noah Baumbach's own family, but it demonstrates a way of looking at families that he must have learned somewhere. Both of his parents were writers and, to one degree or another, film critics; I remember Gene Siskel telling a friend at dinner that film critics eventually became critical of everything: "For example, your tie is hideous." In revenge, the friend went to Marshall Field's and asked to buy their ugliest tie. Two salesclerks helped him in a spirited debate to select the tie that qualified. My friend wore it the next time they met. Siskel identified the brand of the tie correctly and said: "If you like that tie, it shows you have better taste than 99 percent of men." So it goes with the family in this movie. All of its members are engaged in a mutual process of shooting each other down. Watching *Margot at the Wedding* is like slowing for a gaper's block.

Marley and Me ★ ★ ★
PG, 120 m., 2008

Owen Wilson (John Grogan), Jennifer Aniston (Jenny Grogan), Eric Dane (Sebastian Tunney), Alan Arkin (Arnie Klein), Kathleen Turner (Ms. Kornblut). Directed by David Frankel and produced by Gil Netter and Karen Rosenfelt. Screenplay by Scott Frank and Don Roos, based on the book by John Grogan.

The second greatest headline in the history of the *Onion* is "Millions of Pet Owners Demand to Know: 'Who's a Good Boy?'"

This line is not frequently used in the Grogan household. There is a reason for that. Marley is not a good boy. I'd love to have a dog around the house, but not Marley. We have, you know, stuff we like. Books, dishes, tables, chairs, rugs, curtains. You know how it is. Marley considers such objects to be food, playthings, or enemies.

There was a real Marley. He belonged to John and Jennifer Grogan and was the subject of a 2005 best-seller that has been adapted into this film. I hope the book earned enough to pay for Marley's overhead. Marley has the behavior pattern of a manic wrecking crew and the appetite of a science fiction monster, but you gotta love him. At least, the Grogans gotta love him. They may be as crazy as their dog. Here is a useful lesson. When you go to the pet lady and she shows you a group of Labrador puppies and one is cheaper than all the others, this is not the time to go bargain hunting.

Marley and Me is a cheerful family movie about a young couple starting out in life with a new house, new jobs, a new dog, and then three children, whom the dog doesn't eat or it wouldn't be rated PG. Owen Wilson and Jennifer Aniston play the Grogans as brave and resourceful. Every couple has to survive ups and downs in their marriage, but Louis XVI and Marie Antoinette might be alive today if they'd adopted Marley, he had eaten the crown jewels, and they'd fled the palace and abdicated.

You would think the dog would supply the playful, upbeat elements in this movie. Not exactly. Marley supplies the Sturm und Drang, 24-7. It is Grogan's professional life that supplies the fantasy. He gets a job as a cub reporter on a newspaper and is soon *ordered* by his editor (Alan Arkin) to become a columnist. "Nothing doing!" he says. He'd rather cover school board meetings and sewer inspectors. Arkin counters: "I'll double your salary!"

In today's newspaper world, this plays like escapist porn. Grogan would be ordered to carry a route on his way to work and Arkin would be replaced by Uncle Scrooge. But Grogan makes the canny decision to write a column about the dog, and it is a great success. Soon the column and the dog are beloved. Marley becomes as useful to Grogan as Slats Grobnik was to Mike Royko: always good for a column on a slow day. Come to think of it, Marley has all the earmarks of having been trained by Slats, starting out as a puppy by eating bar stools and spittoons.

This may be the first family film I've seen that will frighten more adults than children. The Marley kids, Conor, Patrick, and Colleen, all love Marley. Their parents are appalled. At one point, Jenny actually despairs and tells John that either the dog goes or she does. No, actually, she doesn't force him to choose. She's outta there. But she relents and returns to the doggie from hell. The thing about Marley, see, is that he has an uncanny way of knowing exactly when to pause in eating the garbage and gaze soulfully upon his masters with unconditional love.

When Marley is not on the screen, Wilson and Aniston demonstrate why they are gifted comic actors. They have a relationship that's not too sitcomish, not too sentimental, mostly smart and realistic. That's because she plays a newspaper reporter, too. Marley would have been a welcome break after a day in the riotous city rooms of the good old days. In today's city rooms, reporters hide in their cubicles praying to escape extermination. I say lock Scrooge in a cage and throw in Marley.   ☞

Married Life ★ ★ ★

PG -13, 90 m., 2008

Pierce Brosnan (Richard Langley), Chris Cooper (Harry Allen), Patricia Clarkson (Pat Allen), Rachel McAdams (Kay Nesbitt). Directed by Ira Sachs and produced by Steve Golin, Sachs, Sidney Kimmel, and Jawal Nga. Screenplay by Sachs and Oren Moverman, based on the novel *Five Roundabouts to Heaven* by John Bingham.

Remember the time businessmen were expected to drink martinis at lunch, and the time they were expected not to? Ira Sachs's *Married Life* begins with Harry taking Richard into his confidence at a martinis-and-cigarettes lunch that confirms the movie is set in 1949. Harry (Chris Cooper) is a buttoned-down, closed-in respectable type. Richard (Pierce Brosnan) is more easygoing. You can tell by the way they smoke. Harry is painfully earnest as he tells his friend that he plans to leave his wife for a much younger woman. The younger woman truly and deeply loves him. All his wife wants is sex.

Why does Harry share this information? I think he wants understanding and forgiveness from a man he respects. He has arranged for the young woman to join them at lunch. Here she comes now. She is Kay (Rachel McAdams). She has the bottle-blond hair and the bright red lipstick, the Monroe look. But don't get the wrong idea. She's a sweet kid, and she really does love Harry. The movie has a voice-over narration by Richard, but we don't need it to tell from the look in his eyes that Richard desires Kay, and that from the moment he sees her he wants to take her away from the dutiful Harry.

How dutiful is Harry? So devoted to his wife that he can't stand the thought of telling her he wants a divorce. He decides to take pity on her, spare her that pain, and murder her instead. Sort of a mercy killing. He's serious about this. He knows how devoted his wife is to him and how this news would shatter her, and he doubts she could stand it.

This story, which crosses film noir with the look and feel of a Douglas Sirk film, balances between its crime element and its social commentary: Everything Harry does is within the terms of a circa-1950 middle-class suburban marriage, with what we have been taught are all of its horrors. Marriage is always bad in these dark movies. I personally think it was better than in 1950s comedies, but then that's just me. We have the same problems, but we smoke less and use more jargon. And no generation thinks its fashions look funny, although Gene Siskel used to amuse himself by watching people walking down the street and thinking to himself, "When they left home this morning, they thought they looked good in that."

But enough. What about Harry's wife? She is Pat, played by Patricia Clarkson, who is so expert at portraying paragons of patient domestic virtue: so trusting, oblivious, or pre-occupied that she never thinks to question Harry's absences when he's seeing Kay. Richard observes all of this in a low-key, factual way; it's as if he's telling us the story over martinis. He even addresses us directly at times.

Will Harry really try to kill his wife? Many men have killed their wives for less, shall we call them, considerate motives. Sachs and his cowriter, Oren Moverman, have based their screenplay on the pulp novel *Five Round-abouts to Heaven* by John Bingham, who, I learn from the critic Keith Uhlich, was a British intelligence agent and the original for John Le Carre's character George Smiley. Smiley, however, would be the Richard character here, not the Harry. The story has been ported from the land of roundabouts to the land of four-way stops, all except for Richard, who is British and urbane, which with Harry possibly passes for trustworthy.

Pierce Brosnan is becoming a whole new actor in my eyes, after this film, *The Matador, Evelyn,* and *The Tailor of Panama*. It's the kiss of death to play James Bond, but at least it gives you a chance to reinvent yourself. Chris Cooper reinvents himself in every film; can this be the same actor from *Adaptation*? Here he seems so respectable. Rachel McAdams does a nice job of always seeming honest and sincere, even when she makes U-turns, but Patricia Clarkson, as always, has a few surprises behind that face that can be so bland, or scornful, or in between. Still housewives run deep.

There is so much passion in this story that it's a wonder how damped down it is. Nobody shouts. And we discover that Harry is not the only person in the story who can surprise us. The lesson, I think, is that the French have the right idea, and adultery is no reason to destroy a perfectly functioning marriage. But is the movie about marriage, or sex, or murder, or the murder plot, or what? I'm not sure. It deals all those cards, and fate shuffles them. You may not like it if you insist on counting the deck after the game and coming up with fifty-two. But if you get fifty-one and are amused by how the missing card was made to vanish, this may be a movie to your liking.

Martian Child ★ ★
PG, 106 m., 2007

John Cusack (David), Joan Cusack (Liz), Bobby Coleman (Dennis), Amanda Peet (Harlee), Sophie Okonedo (Sophie), Oliver Platt (Jeff), Richard Schiff (Lefkowitz). Directed by Menno Meyjes and produced by David Kirschner, Ed Elbert, and Corey Sienega. Screenplay by Seth Bass and Jonathan Tolins, based on a novel by David Gerrold.

"I'm not human," little Dennis says at one point in *Martian Child*. So he believes. The lonely orphan has convinced himself that he was not abandoned by his parents but arrived here from Mars. To protect himself against the sun, he walks around inside a cardboard box with a slit cut for his eyes and wears a weight belt around his waist to keep himself from drifting up into the sky. At no point during the film does anyone take mercy on the kid and explain that the sun is much more pitiless on Mars and the gravity much lower.

Still, this isn't a film about planetary science but about love. Dennis attracts the attention of a lonely science fiction writer named David (John Cusack), a widower who can't get the cardboard box out of his mind and goes back to the orphanage one day with some suntan cream. Eventually, almost against his own will, he asks Dennis to come home with him for a test run and decides to adopt him. The movie is the sentimental, very sentimental, story of how that goes.

Few actors in the right role can be sweeter or more lovable than John Cusack, and he is those things almost to a fault in *Martian Child,* which is so bland and safe that it might appeal more directly to children than adults. Cusack plays another widower in his much more affecting movie *Grace Is Gone*, and you wonder why he took two fairly similar roles so closely together.

This is not to say *Martian Child* lacks good qualities. Young Bobby Coleman plays Dennis as consistent, stubborn, and suspicious, and Amanda Peet has a warm if predictable role as the woman in David's life who starts out as best friend and ends up where female best friends often do, in his arms. But it is Joan Cusack, John's real-life sister playing his movie sister, whose contribution is most welcome, because she brings a little sassiness and cynicism to a film that threatens to drown in lachrymosity.

The movie leaves no heartstring untugged. It even has a beloved old dog, and you know what happens to beloved old dogs in movies like this. Or if you don't, I don't have the heart to tell you. And there is the standard board of supervisors in control of adoptions, which without exception in this genre adopts a policy against adoptive parents who are loving and loved, or who exhibit the slightest sign of being creative or unorthodox in any way. I suspect they would rather have a kid adopted by a mercenary than a science fiction writer, especially one who hasn't already ripped off Dennis's gravity belt and left him to float up into the sky, where it is very cold and even lonelier than inside a cardboard box.

Medicine for Melancholy ★ ★ ★ ½
NO MPAA RATING, 88 m., 2009

Wyatt Cenac (Micah), Tracey Heggins (Joanne). Directed by Barry Jenkins and produced by Justin Barber. Screenplay by Jenkins.

Medicine for Melancholy is nothing more or less than the story of a man and a woman spending twenty-four hours together. It has no other agenda, which is part of its charm. Haven't we all spent some interesting time together with a stranger, talking a little about our lives, sharing a certain communion, with no certainty that we will ever see them again?

Micah and Joanne are African-Americans in their late twenties who wake up next to each other in a bed in an expensive home on San Francisco's Nob Hill. They are hung over. They don't know each other's names. She wants to go home and forget. He persuades her to have breakfast. In a perhaps symbolic walk across a hill into a less posh neighborhood, he tries to cheer her up. It becomes clear that in a city with a 7 percent black population, he sees her as intriguing: a single, hip black woman in what he describes as the "indie world."

They talk. They take a taxi to her neighborhood—not to her door. She leaves her wallet in the cab. He discovers she is Joanne, not "An-

gela." He tracks her down on his bike. He kids her. They bike to an art gallery. Then they go through a couple of museums. They're getting to like each other.

Micah is interested in stereotypes. He observes that two black people spending Sunday at art museums does not fit the stereotype. Whose? His, I think. She asks what race has to do with it. He says his identity, in the eyes of the world, is as a black man. "That's what people see." Who would speculate he supplies and maintains upscale private aquariums? And Joanne? Her expensive condo in the Marina belongs to her lover, a white man now in London on business. He is an art curator, although Micah observes there is not a single artwork in the condo.

"Does it matter that he's white?" she asks. "Yes and no," Micah says. A good answer. The day does not continue their discussion of interracial dating. It becomes more of a test-drive of a possible life together. Neither seriously expects to lead such a life, but it's intriguing to play. At one point they go to Whole Foods. When a newly met couple go grocery shopping together, they're playing house.

Micah is concerned with demographics and residential patterns. He passionately loves San Francisco and has seen gentrification push out the populations and neighborhoods that gave it flavor. All men need a lecture topic when trying to impress a woman, and this is his. At one point the film drops in on a completely unrelated discussion group about housing policy; it's the sort of detour you might find in *Waking Life.*

The actors are effortlessly engaging. Tracey Heggins plays skittish at first, then warmer and playful. Is she having a better time than she usually has with her white lover? Yes. Well, maybe yes and no. She doesn't talk enough about him for us to be sure. Wyatt Cenac plays a smart charmer; the urban facts he cites are a reminder of his comedy alter ego, the "Senior Black Correspondent" on Jon Stewart's *The Daily Show.*

Medicine for Melancholy is a first, but very assured, feature by Barry Jenkins, who has the confidence to know the precise note he wants to strike. This isn't a statement film or a bold experiment in style; it's more like a *New Yorker* story that leaves you thinking, yes, I see how they feel. The film is beautifully photographed by James Laxton; much of the color is drained, making it almost black and white. The critic Karina Longworth writes: "I guessed that the entirety of the film had been desaturated 93 percent to match the racial breakdown, but in a recent interview, Jenkins said the level of desaturation actually fluctuates." The visual effect is right; McLuhan would call this a cool film.

Memories of Tomorrow ★ ★ ★ ½
NO MPAA RATING, 122 m., 2007

Ken Watanabe (Masayuki Saeki), Kanako Higuchi (Emiko Saeki), Kenji Sakaguchi (Naoya Ito), Kazue Fukiishi (Rie Saeki), Asami Mizukawa (Keiko Ikuno), Noritake Kinashi (Shigejuki Kizaki). Directed by Yukihiko Tsutsumi and produced by Sunao Sakagami and Tatsuo Kawamura. Screenplay by Uiko Miura and Hakaru Sunamoto, based on the novel by Hiroshi Ogiwara.

At first it's a matter of a missed word, a forgotten name. Then he forgets how to drive a familiar route. The advertising executive keeps his worries to himself, but he can't hide his problems, and eventually a doctor delivers a dread prognosis: early onset Alzheimer's. He is only forty-nine.

Memories of Tomorrow is the first movie I've seen about the disease that is told from the sick person's point of view, not that of family members. The director, Yukihiko Tsutsumi, often uses a subjective camera to show the commonplace world melting into bewildering patterns and meanings. The subject of the film, Saeki, is a high-octane ad executive with a young and eager team, and as a perfectionist, it depresses him to discover his own imperfections mounting. He forgets dates, times, business meetings. In one breathtaking scene, he gets lost in Tokyo's urban maze and takes instructions from a secretary over his cell phone while literally running back to his office.

The character is played by Ken Watanabe (*Batman, Memoirs of a Geisha, Letters from Iwo Jima*), and there is a personal element in his brave and painful performance. Watanabe is now forty-eight, and since he was thirty, I learn from the *Japan Times*, he has been fighting leukemia. His Saeki is just as determined to fight Alzheimer's and is much aided by his patient and courageous wife, Emiko (Kanako Higuchi), who writes notes naming everything in their house, prepares his daily schedule, and keeps up a brave front.

He holds on as long as he can, even accepting a lesser position and a smaller pension to stay with his company, but finally he must retire and return to a home where now it is his wife who goes out every morning to earn a salary. He has better days and worse days, and a day fraught with fear when he must make a speech at his daughter's wedding. He loses the text of his speech. "Just say anything," his wife whispers. "I'm here for you." She takes his hand.

She has the patience of a saint, but one day he physically hurts her. The director handles this painful moment with great visual tact, not showing it but instead cutting to the sudden darting of fish in an aquarium. And then his wife snaps, telling him with cold anger what a distant husband he has been, how flawed, how cruel.

The movie isn't structured like a melodrama but reflects a slow fading of the light. There are moments of almost unbearable sadness, as in what he reveals to a nurse at the end of a tour of a nursing home. And we observe the indifference of the company where he has been a salaryman all his life: Yes, thanks for your contribution; now go quietly, please, and don't let the clients know. Some films on Alzheimer's attempt to show an upside. I don't think there is an upside. At least with cancer you get to be yourself until you die.

The Merry Gentleman ★ ★ ★ ½
R, 99 m., 2009

Michael Keaton (Frank Logan), Kelly Macdonald (Kate Frazier), Tom Bastounes (Dave Murcheson), Bobby Cannavale (Michael), Darlene Hunt (Diane), Guy Van Swearingen (Billy Goldman), William Dick (Mr. Weiss). Directed by Michael Keaton and produced by Ron Lazzeretti, Steven A. Jones, and Tom Bastounes. Screenplay by Lazzeretti.

Good actors sometimes despair of finding worthy opportunities. They cheerlessly attend a premiere of their new film and think, "I could direct better than this dingbat." Sometimes they're right. I give you Michael Keaton, whose *Merry Gentleman* is original, absorbing, and curiously moving in ways that are far from expected. Michael Keaton once starred in *Jack Frost* as a boy's father imprisoned in a snowman. Think about that.

Keaton is one of the most intelligent men I have met in the acting profession, where you don't have much success these days if you're dumb. His mind is alive and present in many of his characters, and sometimes you get the impression the character is thinking, "I could say a lot more if the screenplay allowed me." What is uncanny about *The Merry Gentleman* is the way he implies that his character sometimes wishes he had said less.

Keaton plays Frank Logan, a Chicago hit man who is efficient and deadly, but suicidal. But no, this isn't a crime movie. Nothing as easy as that. It's a character study as Georges Simenon might have written, and Logan isn't the most important character. That is Kate Frazier, an abused wife newly employed in an office. A crime movie requires a skillful actress, but *The Merry Gentleman* requires a gifted one, and Keaton as director correctly places his focus on Kelly Macdonald, who played Josh Brolin's small-town wife in *No Country for Old Men*. Keaton wisely allows her to use a mid-Atlantic version of her Scots accent, because why not? She gets another aspect to her character for free.

These two first encounter each other through what is technically a Meet Cute, but they don't collide while entering a revolving door. Logan has just used a sniper scope to murder a man in an office window across the street. The job performed, he stands on the ledge of a rooftop and prepares to jump off. Kate, emerging from the street door of the building, looks up, sees him, and screams. He is startled and falls back onto the roof. He knows she has seen him. Now they will have to meet.

Is the movie about his intention to kill her before she can identify him? It's legitimate for us to think so. Although Logan goes through the motions of preparing for that, there is the possibility that he might have murdered for the last time. Yet how can we know? Kate reports the incident to the police, who file a rou-

tine report. Then the dead man is found, and a policeman named Murcheson (Tom Bastounes) realizes she must have seen the killer.

Murcheson, a recovering alcoholic, is immediately attracted to her. He invites her for "a coffee or something." Recovering from marriage, she is not eager to make a new friend. Murcheson, who is not a bad person, persists. Logan must realize the woman who saw him is dating the policeman on the case. There are other elements in play, but discover for yourself.

What is so good about the movie is the way Kate relates to these two men, who both hunger for care and sympathy. The screenplay is by Ron Lazzeretti, who writes dialogue of a very high order: subtle, cautious, aware. We understand this will not be a movie about a triangle and will not hurry to a neat conclusion. It will be about a worthwhile woman trying to relate to two difficult puppies left on her doorstep.

The Merry Gentleman isn't jolly. There are undercurrents of sadness and dread. Both men are frightened of their flaws. What will happen may be unforeseeable. Watch Keaton. His is a complex performance, evoking a damaged man who has, somewhere inside, ordinary emotions. As a director, he is attentive to the inner feelings of all three main characters, and it is there that a lot of the film really resides.

Of Lazzeretti I know little, except that he directed a feature in 1999 named *The Opera Lover,* and it also starred Tom Bastounes, an intriguing actor. I believe they met through Second City. Lazzeretti set out to write a film about humans, not genre stereotypes, and I suspect that's what attracted Keaton. The hit man–possible victim situation provides a reason for this unsocial man to need to meet her and adds potential suspense, but I was pleased the movie ended in the way it did.

Michael Clayton ★ ★ ★ ★
R, 119 m., 2007

George Clooney (Michael Clayton), Sean Cullen (Gene Clayton), Tom Wilkinson (Arthur Edens), Tilda Swinton (Karen Crowder), Sydney Pollack (Marty Bach), Michael O'Keefe (Barry Grissom), Ken Howard (Don Jefferies), Denis O'Hare (Mr.

Greer). Directed by Tony Gilroy and produced by Jennifer Fox, Kerry Orent, Sydney Pollack, and Steve Samuels. Screenplay by Gilroy.

George Clooney brings a slick, ruthless force to the title role of *Michael Clayton,* playing a fixer for a powerful law firm. He works in the shadows, cleaning up messes, and he is a realist. He tells clients what they don't want to hear. He shoots down their fantasies of "options." One client complains bitterly that he was told Clayton was a miracle worker. "I'm not a miracle worker," Clayton replies. "I'm a janitor."

Clooney looks as if he stepped into the role from the cover of *GQ*. It's the right look. Conservative suit, tasteful tie, clean shaven, every hair in place. Drives a leased Mercedes. Divorced, drives his son to school, has him on Saturdays. Has a hidden side to his life. Looks prosperous but lost his shirt on a failed restaurant and needs $75,000 or bad things might happen. Would certainly have $75,000 if he didn't frequent a high-stakes poker game in a back room in Chinatown. Not much of a personal life.

Clayton works directly with Marty Bach (Sydney Pollack), the head of the law firm; it's one of those Pollack performances that embody authority, masculinity, intelligence, and knowing the score. But one of Bach's top partners has just gone berserk, stripping naked in Milwaukee during a deposition hearing and running through a parking lot in the snow. This is Arthur Edens (Tom Wilkinson), who opens the film with a desperate voice-over justifying himself to Michael.

The video of the deposition is not a pretty sight. One of the people watching it in horror is Karen Crowder, the chief legal executive for one of Marty Bach's most important clients, a corporation being sued for poisonous pollution. Crowder is played by Tilda Swinton, who has been working a lot lately because of her sheer excellence; she has the same sleek grooming as Clayton, the power wardrobe, every hair in place. Thinking of Clooney, Pollack, Wilkinson, and Swinton, you realize how much this film benefits from its casting. Switch out those four and the energy and tension might evaporate.

The central reality of the story is that the corporation is guilty, it is being sued for billions, the law firm knows it is guilty, it is being paid millions to run the defense, and now Arthur Edens holds the smoking gun, and it's not quite all he's holding when he runs naked through the parking lot.

Enough of the plot. Naming the film after Michael Clayton is an indication that the story centers on his life, his loyalties, his being just about fed up. Arthur Edens is a treasured friend of his, a bipolar victim who has stopped taking his pills and now glows with reckless zeal and conviction. We meet Clayton's family, we get a sense of the corporate culture he inhabits, and we sense how controlling the risks of other people sends him to the poker tables to create and confront his own risks—sort of an antidote.

The legal-business-thriller genre has matured in the last twenty years, led by authors like John Grisham and actors like Michael Douglas. It involves high stakes, hidden guilt, desperation to contain information, and mighty executives blindsided by *gotcha!* moments. We're invited to be seduced by the designer offices, the clubs, the cars, the clothes, the drinks, the perfect corporate worlds in which sometimes only the restroom provides a safe haven.

I don't know what vast significance *Michael Clayton* has (it involves deadly pollution but isn't a message movie). But I know it is just about perfect as an exercise in the genre. I've seen it twice, and the second time, knowing everything that would happen, I found it just as fascinating because of how well it was all shown happening. It's not about the destination but the journey, and when the stakes become so high that lives and corporations are on the table, it's spellbinding to watch the Clooney and Swinton characters eye to eye, raising each other, both convinced the other is bluffing.

The movie was written and directed by Tony Gilroy, son of the director Frank D. Gilroy (*The Subject Was Roses*). It's the directing debut for Gilroy, who is a star screenwriter (all three *Bourne* pictures, *Extreme Measures, The Devil's Advocate, Proof of Life*). As a first-time director, his taste runs toward the classical style and not toward the Bourne shaky cam.

Working with the great cinematographer Robert Elswit (*Syriana; Good Night, and Good Luck; Magnolia*), he uses stable, brooding establishing shots, measured editing that underlines the tension in conversations, and lighting that separates the fluorescent sterility of Clayton's business world from the warmth of family homes and the eerie quiet of a field at dawn.

When he shows us Arthur Edens's loft, it has the same sort of chain-link enclosure that Gene Hackman's character had in *The Conversation,* and they are the same kinds of characters: paranoid, in possession of damaging evidence, not as well protected as they think. The thing about Michael Clayton is, he's better at knowing how well protected they are and what they think.

A Mighty Heart ★ ★ ★ ½
R, 100 m., 2007

Angelina Jolie (Mariane Pearl), Dan Futterman (Daniel Pearl), Archie Panjabi (Asra Nomani), Irrfan Khan (Captain), Will Patton (Randall Bennett), Denis O'Hare (John Bussey), Aly Khan (Omar Saeed Sheikh). Directed by Michael Winterbottom and produced by Brad Pitt, Dede Gardner, and Andrew Eaton. Screenplay by John Orloff, based on the memoir by Mariane Pearl.

A Mighty Heart begins with shots of the teeming streets of Karachi, Pakistan, a city with a population that seems jammed in shoulder-to-shoulder. Terrorists will emerge from this sea of humanity, kidnap the American journalist Daniel Pearl, and disappear. The film is about the desperate search for Pearl (Dan Futterman) before the release of the appalling video showing him being beheaded. It is told largely through the eyes of, and based on a memoir by, his widow, Mariane.

We know how the story is going to end. The real drama is played out with the natures of the people looking for him. They include his pregnant wife, a French radio journalist who conceals her grief behind a cool and calculating facade to help her husband's chances; their friend Asra (Archie Panjabi), whose apartment becomes a nerve center; a Pakistan security official (Irrfan Khan), whose uncertain position reflects the way his country accepts American money and harbors terrorists; an American agent (Will Patton), whose skills are

better adapted to American cities; and one of Pearl's bosses at the *Wall Street Journal* (Denis O'Hare), who offers encouragement without much reason.

Standing at the center of the story is Mariane Pearl, played by Angelina Jolie in a performance that is both physically and emotionally convincing. A few obvious makeup changes make her resemble the woman we saw so often on TV (curly hair, darker skin, the swelling belly), but Jolie's performance depends above all on inner conviction; she reminds us, as we saw in some of her earlier films like *Girl, Interrupted* (1999), that she is a skilled actress and not merely (however entertainingly) a tomb raider.

The movie, directed by the versatile British filmmaker Michael Winterbottom (*24 Hour Party People, The Road to Guantanamo*), is notable for what it leaves out. Although we do meet the possible suspect Omar Saeed Sheikh (Aly Khan), there are not any detailed scenes of Pearl with his kidnappers, no portrayals of their personalities or motivations, and we do not see the beheading and its video. That last is not just because of Winterbottom's tact and taste, but because (I think) he wants to portray the way Pearl has almost disappeared into another dimension. His kidnappers have transported him outside the zone of human values and common sense. We reflect that the majority of Muslims do not approve of the behavior of Islamic terrorists, just as the majority of Americans disapprove of the war in Iraq.

Many thrillers depend on action, conflict, triumph, and defeat. This one depends on impotence and frustration. The kidnappers cannot do more than snatch one unarmed man after he gets out of a taxi, and Pearl's friends are lost in a maze of clues, lies, gossip, and dead ends. The movie has been described as a "police procedural," but I saw it more as a stalemate.

Mariane Pearl reminds us in her book, and the movie reminds us, too, that some 230 other journalists have lost their lives since Pearl's kidnapping, most of them during the conflict in Iraq. That means they proportionately had a higher death rate than combat soldiers. That's partly because they are ill-prepared for the risks they take, and partly because they're targets. The Americans who complain about "negative" news are the ideological cousins of those who shoot at CNN crews. The news is the news, good or bad, and those who resent being informed of it are pitiful. More Americans are well informed about current sports and auto-racing statistics, I sometimes think, than anything else.

What is most fascinating about Mariane Pearl, in life and in this movie, is that she is not a stereotyped hysterical wife, weeping on camera, but a cool, courageous woman who behaves in a way best calculated to save her husband's life. Listen to her speak and sense how her mind works. While you experience the fear and tension that Winterbottom records, see also how she tries to use it and not merely be its victim.

What is best about *A Mighty Heart* is that it doesn't reduce the Daniel Pearl story to a plot, but elevates it to a tragedy. A tragedy that illuminates and grieves for the hatred that runs loose in our world, hatred as a mad dog that attacks everyone. Attacks them for what seems, to the dog, the best of reasons.

Milk ★ ★ ★ ★
R, 127 m., 2008

Sean Penn (Harvey Milk), Emile Hirsch (Cleve Jones), Josh Brolin (Dan White), James Franco (Scott Smith), Diego Luna (Jack Lira), Alison Pill (Anne Kronenberg), Lucas Grabeel (Danny Nicoletta). Directed by Gus Van Sant and produced by Dan Jinks and Bruce Cohen. Screenplay by Dustin Lance Black.

Sean Penn amazes me. Not long before seeing *Milk,* I viewed his work in *Dead Man Walking* again. Few characters could be more different, few characters could seem more real. He creates a character with infinite attention to detail and from the heart out. Here he creates a character who may seem like an odd bird to mainstream America and makes him completely identifiable. Other than the occasional employment of Harvey Milk's genitals, what makes him different? Some people may argue there is a gay soul, but I believe we all share the same souls.

Harvey Milk became in 1977 the first openly gay man elected to public office in America. Yes, but I have become so weary of the phrase "openly gay." I am openly heterosexual, but this is the first time I have ever said so. Why

can't we all be what we prefer? Why can't gays simply be gays and "unopenly gays" be whatever they want to seem? In 1977, it was not so. Milk made a powerful appeal to closeted gays to come out to their families, friends, and coworkers, so the straight world might stop demonizing an abstract idea. But so powerful was the movement he helped inspire that I believe his appeal has now pretty much been heeded, save in certain backward regions of the land that a wise gay or lesbian should soon deprive of their blessings.

Gus Van Sant's film begins with Harvey Milk at forty-eight, reflecting into his tape recorder about a personal journey that began at forty. At that watershed age he grew unsatisfied with his life and decided he wanted to really *do* something. A researcher at Bache & Co. and a Goldwater Republican, Milk became involved with a hippie theater company in Greenwich Village and began to edge the closet door ajar and wave out tentatively. He was in love with Scott Smith (James Franco), they moved to San Francisco, they opened a camera shop in the shadow of the Castro theater, and saw that even America's largest and most vocal gay community was being systematically persecuted by homophobic police.

Milk didn't enter politics as much as he was pushed in by the evidence of his own eyes. He ran for the Board of Supervisors three times before being elected in 1977. He campaigned for a gay rights ordinance. He organized. He acquired a personal bullhorn and stood on a box labeled "SOAP." He forged an alliance including liberals, unions, longshoremen, teachers, Latinos, blacks, and others with common cause. He developed a flair for publicity. He became a fiery orator. Already known as the Mayor of Castro Street, he won public office. It was a bully pulpit from which to challenge rabble-rousers like the gay-hating Anita Bryant.

Milk, from an original screenplay by Dustin Lance Black, tells the story of its hero's rise from disaffected middle-aged hippie to national symbol. Interlaced are his romantic adventures. He remained friendly with Scott Smith after they drifted apart because of his immersion in politics. He had a weakness for befriending wet puppies: at first, Cleve Jones (Emile Hirsch), who became another community organizer. Then Jack Lira (Diego Luna), a

Mexican-American who became neurotically jealous of Milk's political life. The prudent thing would have been to cut ties with Lira, but Milk was almost compulsively supportive.

His most fateful relationship was with Dan White, a seemingly straight member of the Board of Supervisors, a Catholic who said homosexuality was a sin and campaigned with his wife, kids, and the American flag. An awkward alliance formed between Milk and White, who was probably gay and used their areas of political agreement as a beard. "I think he's one of us," Milk confided. The only gay supervisor, Milk was also the only supervisor invited to the baptism of White's new baby. White was an alcoholic, all but revealed his sexuality to Milk during a drunken tirade, became unbalanced, resigned his position, wasn't allowed back on the board by Mayor George Moscone, and on November 27, 1978, walked into city hall and assassinated Milk and Moscone.

Milk tells Harvey Milk's story as one of a transformed life, a victory for individual freedom over state persecution, and a political and social cause. There is a remarkable shot near the end, showing a candlelight march reaching as far as the eyes can see. This is actual footage. It is emotionally devastating. And it comes as the result of one man's decisions in life.

Sean Penn never tries to show Harvey Milk as a hero and never needs to. He shows him as an ordinary man: kind, funny, flawed, shrewd, idealistic, yearning for a better world. He shows what such an ordinary man can achieve. Milk was the right person in the right place at the right time, and he rose to the occasion. So was Rosa Parks. Sometimes, at a precise moment in history, all it takes is for one person to stand up. Or sit down.

Millions (A Lottery Story) ★ ★ ★ ½
NO MPAA RATING, 101 m., 2008

Featuring Phylis Breth, Barb and Dwain Nelson, Donna Lange, Curtis Sharp, Susan and Donny Breth, and Lou Eisenberg. A documentary directed by Paul La Blanc and produced by La Blanc and Jordon Katon.

Millions (A Lottery Story) is not so much about six lottery winners as about six people

whom I watched with growing fascination and affection. What did I expect when the movie began? Former millionaires now on Skid Row, I suppose, contrasted with misers counting their compound interest and intercut with bizarre misadventures. What I found were people who, if I may say so, are utterly unfazed by their sudden wealth, and who have developed strategies for coping not with wealth or poverty, but with life. They all seem happy, and it has nothing to do with the lottery.

The movie follows four kitchen workers from a Minnesota high school and two New Yorkers who were once famous because they were the first to win $5 million at the dawn of the lottery and became the stars of television ads. The Minnesotans, sixteen altogether, split up $95,450,000 on a shared Powerball ticket, which works out to $5,965,625 apiece, a figure none of them ever once mentions.

They're from Holdingford, Minnesota, a town that Garrison Keillor himself once called "the Lake Wobegonest town in Minnesota." The town is so typical of his monologues that not only are the high schoolers' grades above average, but the interstate highway makes a four-mile detour just to avoid it. Of the four women we meet, all come from large families (I'm talking like eleven or sixteen kids), all worked hard on family dairy farms, many still keep dairy cattle as a second job, and none of them quit their jobs in the high school kitchen.

Phylis Breth is most eloquent about staying on the job. "These are my best friends, and I love my work." She is a dishwasher, and uses a little laugh to end many sentences. "I've got bad knees, I've had four surgeries, and this job keeps you going. On days when they serve mashed potatoes or cheese, it gets pretty hectic." Like some of the others, she bought a new house, not a mansion, just comfy, and she finally has what she long dreamed of, a refrigerator with an ice-cube maker. She still hits all the garage sales, pouncing on a two-dollar ice cream scoop.

Of the New Yorkers, who won in the early 1970s, Lou Eisenberg lives in retirement in West Palm Beach, in a very basic condo. All of his winnings are gone, and he gets by on Social Security and a small pension. But he has a girlfriend, knows people everywhere he goes, bets at the dog track daily. He spent every lottery check almost as it came in. Why didn't he invest for the future? "I never thought I would live to be seventy-six."

The other, Curtis Sharp, has also run through his winnings. Some of them went to invest in a company claiming to make an electric automobile that could run forever without ever being recharged. At one point the company was valued at "billions," he assures us, before the government came in and charged the organizer with selling fraudulent stock. Curtis still believes the guy was on the level: "Someday that investment is going to pay off." Having been a "drinker and fornicator," he moved to Nashville to buy a beer joint. Then he saw the light, found Jesus, and is a preacher.

The two of them became famous for their New York Lotto commercials. "A Jew and a black man," Lou says. "A good fit." Curtis was known for his bowler hats and collected one hundred. Before winning, Lou had owned a beauty shop, but something came over him one day, he developed panic attacks, and found he could not speak or look people in the eye. He got a job at $240 a week, screwing in lightbulbs. The Lotto saved him: "It was like a shot in the arm." It sure was. We see clips of him gabbing away on TV with Johnny Carson, Regis Philbin, Ted Koppel, Sammy Davis Jr.

There are times in this documentary that I was reminded of work by Errol Morris. The director, Paul La Blanc, has the same ear for the American vernacular and the same eye for obsessions. Take Phylis Breth, for example. Many women clean house for days before letting a camera crew into their homes, but let's say her housekeeping is not Wobegonian. But then we meet her daughter, Susan, the opposite. As she provides a tour of her orderly pantry shelves, ticking off "1994 pickles . . . last year's tomato juice," she proudly shows us that most of her preserves are in jars that originally held the retail version of the same substances. Her homemade salsa is in a salsa jar, for example, with the original label still on.

If there is one thing the Holdingford ladies are sure of, it's that their winnings will send their children through college. Apart from that, they carry on as before. Susan's husband,

Donny, is known as the "wood man," because if you have a fallen tree, he comes around and cuts it into firewood. With pride he shows a shed jammed with logs. They heat their home all winter with wood, in a climate that goes to thirty below. "I've burned wood all my life, and I will keep on burning wood as long as the good Lord lets me," he says.

Getting to know these people, I realized I knew others exactly like them. The women could come from my downstate Illinois family. Giving me a recipe once, my Aunt Mary said, "One tater for everybody, one for the pot, and one for fear of company." For fear. Perfect. I wrote it down as part of the recipe.

Miracle at St. Anna ★ ★ ★
R, 160 m., 2008

Derek Luke (Aubrey Stamps), Michael Ealy (Bishop Cummings), Laz Alonso (Hector Negron), Omar Benson Miller (Sam Train), Matteo Sciabordi (Angelo), John Leguizamo (Enrico), Joseph Gordon-Levitt (Tim Boyle), Valentina Cervi (Renata), Pierfrancesco Favino (Peppi Grotta). Directed by Spike Lee and produced by Roberto Cicutto and Luigi Musini. Screenplay by James McBride, based on his novel.

Spike Lee's *Miracle at St. Anna* contains scenes of brilliance, interrupted by scenes that meander. There is too much: too many characters, too many subplots. But there is so much here that is powerful that it should be seen no matter its imperfections. There are scenes that could have been lost to more decisive editing, but I found after a few days that my mind did the editing for me, and I was left with lasting impressions.

The story involves four African-American soldiers behind enemy lines in Italy in World War II. It's a story that needed telling. It begins with an old black man looking at an old John Wayne movie on TV and murmuring, "We fought that war, too." The next day he goes to work at the post office and does something that startles us. The movie will eventually explain who he is and why he did it. But in a way, we don't need that opening scene, and we especially don't need the closing scene, not the way it plays, when a man walks slowly toward a seated man on a beach. The problem is, the wrong man is doing the walking.

You may disagree. There is one "extraneous" scene that is absolutely essential. While in the Deep South for basic training, the four soldiers are refused service in a local restaurant, while four German POWs relax comfortably in a booth. Such treatment was not uncommon. Why should blacks risk their lives for whites who hate them? The characters argue about this during the movie, after boneheaded decisions and racist insults from a white officer. One has the answer: He's doing it for his country, for his children and grandchildren, and because of his faith in the future. The others are doing it more because of loyalty to their comrades in arms, which is what all wars finally come down to during battle.

Miracle at St. Anna has one of the best battle scenes I can remember, on a par with *Saving Private Ryan* but more tightly focused on a specific situation rather than encompassing a huge panorama. The four soldiers find themselves standing in a river, with a Nazi loudspeaker blasting the sultry voice of "Axis Sally," who promises them sexy women and racial equality in Germany. Their white superior officer orders artillery strikes on their position because he can't believe any blacks could possibly have advanced so far. Then the Nazis open fire. The visceral impact of the episode is astonishing.

The four who survive find themselves in a small hill village. They are Stamps (Derek Luke), cool and collected; Cummings (Michael Ealy), a skirt chaser; Negron (Laz Alonso), a Puerto Rican; and Train (Omar Benson Miller), a towering man with the gentle simplicity of a child. Train has picked up the head of a statue from Florence and carries it with him because he believes that it makes him invulnerable.

Among the Italians they meet are three important ones: Angelo (Matteo Sciabordi), a young boy whom Train saves from death; Renata (Valentina Cervi), a daring and attractive village woman; and Peppi (Pierfrancesco Favino), known as the Great Butterfly, who is a leader of the region's anti-Nazi partisans. All the characters and all the villagers are involved in another battle scene fought in the steep pathways and steps of the village. Both firefights are choreographed with immediate visceral effect.

The story of the bond between Train and the boy Angelo seems like material for a different movie. Yes, it involved me, but it seemed to exist on the plane of parable, not realism. It involved a shift of the emotions away from the surrounding action. The acting is superb. Omar Benson Miller (not actually as tall as the movie makes him seem) feels responsible for the boy because he saved his life, and the two form a bond across the language barrier. Matteo Sciabordi, in his first performance, is a natural the camera loves. I can imagine an entire feature based on these two, but I am not sure this story, seen this way, could have taken place in the reality of this film.

Another scene I doubted was an extended one involving a dance in the local church, music playing loudly, GIs standing illuminated in an open doorway, just as if they weren't behind enemy lines and the hills weren't possibly crawling with Nazis. The romantic developments during that scene would have seemed more at home in a musical.

In a sense, the scenes I complain about are evidence of Lee's stature as an artist. In a time of studios and many filmmakers who play it safe and right down the middle, Spike Lee has a vision and sticks to it. The scenes I object to are not evidence of any special perception I have. They're the kind of scenes many studio chiefs from the dawn of film might have singled out in the interest of making the film shorter and faster. But they're important to Lee, who must have defended them. And it's important to me that he did. When you see one of his films, you're seeing one of *his* films. And *Miracle at St. Anna* contains richness, anger, history, sentiment, fantasy, reality, violence, and life. Maybe too much. Better than too little.

The Mist ★ ★

R, 125 m., 2007

Thomas Jane (David Drayton), Marcia Gay Harden (Mrs. Carmody), Laurie Holden (Amanda Dumfries), Andre Braugher (Brent Norton), Toby Jones (Ollie), William Sadler (Jim

Grondin), Jeffrey DeMunn (Dan Miller), Frances Sternhagen (Irene), Alexa Davalos (Sally), Nathan Gamble (Billy Drayton). Directed by Frank Darabont and produced by Darabont and Liz Glotzer. Screenplay by Darabont, based on the story by Stephen King.

Combine (1) a mysterious threat that attacks a town and (2) a group of townspeople who take refuge together, and you have a formula apparently able to generate any number of horror movies, from *Night of the Living Dead* to *30 Days of Night*. All you have to do is choose a new threat and a new place of refuge, and use typecasting and personality traits so we can tell the characters apart.

In *The Mist*, based on a Stephen King story, a violent storm blows in a heavy mist that envelops that favorite King locale, a village in Maine. When the electric power goes out, David Drayton (Thomas Jane) and his young son, Billy (Nathan Gamble), drive slowly into town to buy emergency supplies at the supermarket. They leave Mom behind, which may turn out to be a mistake. Inside the store, we meet a mixed bag of locals and weekenders, including Brent Norton (Andre Braugher), the Draytons' litigious neighbor; Mrs. Carmody (Marcia Gay Harden), a would-be messianic leader; and the store assistant, Ollie (Toby Jones), who, like all movie characters named Ollie, is below average height and a nerd.

You may not be astonished if I tell you that there is Something Out There in the mist. It hammers on windows and doors and is mostly invisible until a shock cut that shows an insect the size of a cat, smacking into the store window. Then there are other things, too. Something with tentacles ("What do you think those tentacles are attached to?" asks David). Other things that look like a cross between a praying mantis and a dinosaur. Creatures that devour half a man in a single bite.

David and Mrs. Carmody become de facto leaders of two factions in the store: (1) the sane people, who try to work out plans to protect themselves, and (2) the doomsday apocalypse mongers, who see these events as payback for the sinful ways of mankind. Mrs. Carmody's agenda is a little shaky, but I think she wants lots of followers, and I wouldn't put the idea of human sacrifice beyond her. David advises

everybody to stay inside, although of course there are hotheads who find themselves compelled to go out into the mist for one reason or another. If you were in a store and man-eating bugs were patrolling the parking lot, would you need a lot of convincing to stay inside?

David proves a little inconsistent, however, when he leads a group of volunteers to the drugstore in the same shopping center to get drugs to help a burned man. There is a moral here, and I am happy to supply it: Never shop in a supermarket that does not have its own prescription department. There is another moral, and that is that since special effects are so expensive, it is handy to have a mist so all you need is an insect here, a tentacle there, instead of the cost of entire bug-eyed monsters doing a conga line.

The movie was written and directed by Frank Darabont, whose *The Shawshank Redemption* is currently number two on IMDb's all-time best movies list, and who also made *The Green Mile*. Both were based on Stephen King's work, but I think he picked the wrong story this time. What helps, however, is that the budget is adequate to supply the cardboard characters with capable actors and to cobble together some gruesome and slimy special effects.

Everyone labors away to bring energy to the clichés, including Toby Jones, who proves that a movie Ollie may have unsuspected resources. Thomas Jane is energetic in the thankless role of the sane leader, but Marcia Gay Harden—well, give her a break; it's not a plausible or playable role. I also grew tired of Andre Braugher's neighbor, who takes so much umbrage at imagined slights that he begins to look ominously like a plot device.

If you have seen ads or trailers suggesting that horrible things pounce on people, and they make you think you want to see this movie, you will be correct. It is a competently made Horrible Things Pouncing on People movie. If you think Frank Darabont has equaled the *Shawshank* and *Green Mile* track record, you will be sadly mistaken. If you want an explanation for the insect monsters (and this is not really giving anything away), there is speculation that they arrived through a rift in the space-time continuum. Rifts in space-time continuums are one of the handiest inventions of science fiction, so now you've got your complete formula: threat to town, group of townspeople, and rift. Be my guest.

Mister Lonely ★ ★
NO MPAA RATING, 112 m., 2008

Diego Luna (Michael Jackson), Samantha Morton (Marilyn Monroe), Denis Lavant (Charlie Chaplin), Anita Pallenberg (The Queen), James Fox (The Pope), Esme Creed-Miles (Shirley Temple), Richard Strange (Abraham Lincoln), Werner Herzog (Father Umbrillo). Directed by Harmony Korine and produced by Nadja Romain. Screenplay by Harmony Korine and Avi Korine.

I wish there were a way to write a positive two-star review. Harmony Korine's *Mister Lonely* is an odd, desperate film, lost in its own audacity, and yet there are passages of surreal beauty and preposterous invention that I have to admire. The film doesn't work, and indeed seems to have no clear idea of what its job is, and yet (sigh) there is the temptation to forgive its trespasses simply because it is utterly, if pointlessly, original.

All of the characters except for a priest played by Werner Herzog and some nuns live as celebrity impersonators. We can accept this from the Michael Jackson clone (Diego Luna), and we can even understand why when, in Paris, he meets a Marilyn Monroe impersonator (Samantha Morton), they would want to have a drink together in a sidewalk café. It's when she takes him home with her that the puzzlements begin.

She lives in a house with the pretensions of a castle in the Highlands of Scotland. It is inhabited by an extended family of celebrity impersonators, and they portray, to get this part out of the way, Charlie Chaplin (Denis Lavant), the Pope (James Fox), the Queen (Anita Pallenberg), Shirley Temple (Esme Creed-Miles), Abraham Lincoln (Richard Strange), Buckwheat, Sammy Davis Jr., and, of course, the Three Stooges. Now consider. How much of a market is there in the remote Highlands for one, let alone a houseful, of celebrity impersonators? How many pounds and pence can the inhabitants of the small nearby village be expected to toss into their hats? How would

it feel to walk down the high street and be greeted by such a receiving line? What are the living expenses?

But such are logical questions, and you can check credibility at the door. This family is not only extended but dysfunctional, starting with Marilyn and Charlie, who are a couple, although she says she thinks of Hitler when she looks at him, and he leaves her out in the sun to burn. Lincoln is foul-mouthed and critical of everyone, Buckwheat thinks of himself as foster parent of a chicken, and the Pope proposes a toast: They should all get drunk in honor of the deaths of their sheep.

Perhaps that's how they support themselves: raising sheep. However, there seem scarcely two dozen sheep, which have to be destroyed after an outbreak of one of those diseases sheep are always being destroyed for. They're shotgunned by the Three Stooges. Or maybe there are chickens around somewhere that we don't see. The chickens would probably be in the movie in homage to Werner Herzog, who famously hates chickens.

Now you are remembering that I mentioned Herzog and some nuns. No, they do not live on the estate. They apparently live in South America, where they drop sacks of rice on hungry villages from an altitude of about two thousand feet. Rinse well. When one of the nuns survives a fall from their airplane, she calls on all of the nuns to jump, to prove their faith in God. I would not dream of telling you if they do.

Herzog feels a bond with Korine, who was still a teenager when he wrote the screenplay for Larry Clark's great *Kids* (1995). Korine is visionary and surrealistic enough to generate admiration from Herzog, who also starred in his *Julien Donkey-Boy* (he plays a schizophrenic's father, who listens to bluegrass while wearing a gas mask). In addition to the chickens, *Mister Lonely* has another homage to Herzog, a shot of an airplane taking off, which you would have to be very, very familiar with the director's work to footnote.

Various melodramatic scenarios burrow to the surface. Marilyn is fraught with everything a girl can be fraught with. Lincoln has anger-management problems. The Pope insists he is not dead. Everyone works on the construction of a theater, in which they will present their show, expecting to—what? Stand in a spotlight and do tiny bits evoking their celebrities? Then fulsome music swells, and the underlying tragedy of human existence is evoked, and the movie is more fascinating than it has any right to be, especially considering how fascinating it is that it was made at all.

Mongol ★ ★ ★ ½
R, 126 m., 2008

Tadanobu Asano (Temudgin), Honglei Sun (Jamukha), Khulan Chuluun (Borte), Odnyam Odsuren (Young Temudgin), Amarbold Tuvshinbayar (Young Jamukha), Bayartsetseg Erdenabat (Young Borte), Amadu Mamadakov (Targutai). Directed by Sergei Bodrov and produced by Sergey Selyanov. Screenplay by Arif Aliyev and Bodrov.

Mongols need laws. I will make them obey—even if I have to kill half of them.
　　　　　　　　　　　　　　　—Genghis Khan

Sergei Bodrov's *Mongol* is a ferocious film, blood-soaked, pausing occasionally for passionate romance and more frequently for torture. As a visual spectacle, it is all but overwhelming, putting to shame some of the recent historical epics from Hollywood. If it has a flaw, and it does, it is expressed succinctly by the wife of its hero: "All Mongols do is kill and steal."

She must have seen the movie. That's about all they do in *Mongol.* They do not sing, dance, chant, hold summit meetings, have courts, hunt, or (with one exception) even cook or eat. They have no culture except for a series of sayings: "A Mongol does, or does not . . ." a long list of things, although many a Mongol seems never to have been issued the list, and does (or does not) do them anyway. As a result, the film consists of one bloody scene of carnage after another, illustrated by hordes of warriors eviscerating one another while bright patches of blood burst upon the screen.

At the center of the killing is invariably the khan, or leader, named Temudgin (Tadanobu Asano), who is not yet Genghis Kahn, but be patient: This film is the first of a trilogy.

The film opens with Temudgin (Odnyam Odsuren) at the age of nine, taken by his fa-

ther to choose a bride from the Merkit clan. This will settle an old score. But along the way they happen upon a smaller clan, and there Temudgin first sets eyes on ten-year-old Borte (Bayartsetseg Erdenabat), who informs him he should choose her as his bride. He agrees, and thus is forged a partnership that will save his life more than once.

Years pass, the two are married, and Borte (played as an adult by Khulan Chuluun) makes a perfect bride but one hard to keep possession of. She is kidnapped by another clan, bears the first of two children claimed by Temudgin despite reasons to doubt, and follows her man into a series of battles that stain the soil of Mongolia with gallons of blood.

It happens that I have seen another movie about Mongols that suggests they do more than steal and kill. This is the famous nine-hour, three-part documentary *Taiga* (1995) by Ulrike Ottinger, who lived with today's yurt dwellers, witnessed one of their trance-evoking religious ceremonies, observed their customs and traditions, and learned in great detail how they procure and prepare food. There is also a wrestling match that is a good deal more cheerful than the contests in *Mongol.* But you do not have the time for a nine-hour documentary on this subject, I suppose, nor does *Mongol.* The nuances of an ancient and ingeniously developed culture are passed over, and it cannot be denied that *Mongol* is relentlessly entertaining as an action picture.

It left me, however, with some questions. Many involve the survival of the young Temudgin. Having inherited all his father's enemies, he is captured more than once, and we actually see him being fed so he can grow tall enough to kill ("Mongols do not kill children"). His neck and hands are imprisoned in a heavy wooden yoke, and when he escapes, he has the energy to run for miles across the steppe. On another occasion, he falls through the ice of a lake, and the movie simply ignores the question of how he is saved, unless it is by Tengri, God of the Blue Sky. Yes, I think it was Tengri, who also appears as a wolf and saves him more than once. If you want to be Genghis Khan, it helps to have a god in your corner.

Finally Temudgin is imprisoned in a cell surrounded by a moat populated by savage dogs. No such arrangement can hold him, of course, and he leads his clan into yet another series of battles, as gradually it occurs to him that this is no way to live, and the Mongols need to be united under a strong leader who will enforce less anarchistic battle practices. It's at about that point the movie ends, and we reflect that Temudgin has to survive two more such films to become Genghis Khan. And we think our election campaigns run on too long.

Monsters vs. Aliens ★ ★ ½
PG, 96 m., 2009

With the voices of: Reese Witherspoon (Susan/Ginormica), Seth Rogen (B.O.B.), Hugh Laurie (Dr. Cockroach, Ph.D.), Will Arnett (The Missing Link), Kiefer Sutherland (Gen. W.R. Monger), Rainn Wilson (Gallaxhar), Stephen Colbert (President Hathaway), Paul Rudd (Derek Dietl). Directed by Rob Letterman and Conrad Vernon and produced by Lisa Stewart. Screenplay by Letterman, Maya Forbes, Wallace Wolodarsky, Jonathan Aibel, and Glenn Berger.

Monsters vs. Aliens is possibly the most commercial title of the year. How can you resist such a premise, especially if it's in 3-D animation? Very readily, in my case. I will say this first and get it out of the way: 3-D is a distraction and an annoyance. Younger moviegoers may think they like it because they've been told to, and picture quality is usually far from their minds. But for anyone who would just like to be left alone to SEE the darned thing, like me, it's a constant nudge in the ribs saying, *Never mind the story. Just see how neat I look.*

The film was made in Tru3D, the DreamWorks process that has been hailed by honcho Jeffrey Katzenberg as the future of the cinema. It is better than most of the 3-D I've seen (it doesn't approach the work on *The Polar Express* and *Beowulf*). But if this is the future of movies for grown-ups and not just the kiddies, saints preserve us. Billions of people for a century have happily watched 2-D and imagined 3-D. Think of the desert in *Lawrence of Arabia*. The schools of fish in *Finding Nemo*. The great hall in *Citizen Kane*.

Now, that flawless screen surface is threatened with a gimmick, which, let's face it, is intended primarily to raise ticket prices and make piracy more difficult. If its only purpose was artistic, do you think Hollywood would spend a dime on it? The superb MaxiVision process is available for $15,000 a screen, and the Hollywood establishment can't even be bothered to look at it. Why invest in the technology of the future when they can plunder the past?

Speaking of the past, *Monsters vs. Aliens* retreads some of the monsters that starred in actual 1950s B movies: a blob, the 50-foot woman, and no end of aliens with towering foreheads on their dome-shaped heads. Whether the average kid will get all of the connections is beside the point; if kids could accept Pokemon and the Teenage Mutant Ninja Turtles, these monsters are going to seem like masterpieces of manic personality.

The plot: On her wedding day, sweet Susan (Reese Witherspoon) is mutated by a meteorite; just as she walks down the aisle, she grows to (I learn) just an inch short of 50 feet, maybe because Disney wanted to respect the copyright. Her husband (Paul Rudd) was no match for her anyway, and now he really has small man complex. After she wreaks havoc with every step, the military names her Ginormica, no doubt sidestepping *Amazonia* so as not to offend the lesbian lobby. She's snatched by the feds and deposited in a secret government prison holding other monsters, who have been languishing since the 1950s. They're old enough that, if they escape, they could terrorize the subway on a senior pass.

Earth is invaded by a robot that has one big eyeball in the middle of its head, like a giant Leggs pantyhose container bred with an iSight camera. Gen. W.R. Monger (Kiefer Sutherland) and the president (Stephen Colbert) are helpless to deal with this threat, and in desperation release the monsters to save the earth. Springing, leaping, skittering or oozing into battle we have Ginormica at the head of an army including B.O.B., Insectosaurus, Dr. Cockroach, and The Missing Link.

With the exception of Susan, who is perky, these creatures have no personalities in the sense of the distinctive characters in DreamWorks' *Shrek* movies. Basically they express basic intentions, fears, and desires in terms of their physical characteristics. There is a lot of banging, clanging, toppling, colliding, and crumbling in the movie, especially when San Francisco is attacked by Gallaxhar, a squid that is the master of the robot. Conventional evolutionary guidelines are lost in the confusion.

I didn't find the movie rich with humor, unless frenetic action is funny. Maybe kids have learned to think so. Too bad for them. Think of the depth of *Pinocchio*. Kids in those days were treated with respect for their intelligence. *Monsters vs. Aliens* is also lacking in wit. What is wit? Well, for example, the spirit in which I am writing this review. The dictionary defines it as *analogies between dissimilar things, expressed in quick, sharp, spontaneous observations*. A weak point with the monsters, and way outside Gallaxhar's range.

I suppose kids will like this movie, especially those below the age of reason. Their parents may not be as amused, and if they have several children, may ask themselves how much it was worth for the kids to wear the glasses. Is there a child who would see this movie in 2-D (which has brighter colors than 3-D) and complain?

Moon ★ ★ ★ ½
R, 97 m., 2009

Sam Rockwell (Sam Bell), Kevin Spacey (Gerty), Dominique McElligott (Tess Bell). Directed by Duncan Jones and produced by Stuart Fenegan and Trudie Styler. Screenplay by Nathan Parker.

Is *Moon* evoking *2001*, or does its mining outpost on the far side of the moon simply happen to date back to the *2001* era (which was, of course, eight years ago)? I lean toward the second theory. After the mission carrying Dave Bowman disappeared beyond Jupiter, mankind decided to focus on the moon, where we were already, you will recall, conducting operations. The interior design of the new moon station was influenced by the *2001* ship, and the station itself was supervised by Gerty, sort of a scaled-down HAL 9000 that scoots around.

At some point in the future (we can't nail down the story's time frame), this station on the far side is manned by a single crew member, Sam Bell (Sam Rockwell). He's working out the final days of a three-year contract and

is close to cracking from loneliness. Talking to loved ones via video link doesn't satisfy. The station is largely automated; it processes lunar rock to extract helium-3, used to provide Earth with pollution-free power from nuclear fusion. My guess is, the station is on the far side because you don't want to go gazing at the Man in the Moon some night and see a big zit on his nose.

The station is large and well-appointed, and has entertainment resources and adequate supplies. Sam communicates frequently with the home office . . . and so does Gerty. Sam doesn't do any actual mining, but his human hands and brain are needed for repairs, maintenance, and inspection. One day he's outside checking up on something, and his lunar rover smashes up. He's injured and awakens in the station's medical facility. And that, I think, is all I need to say. A spoiler warning would mean secrets are revealed—and you'd look, wouldn't you, no matter what you say.

I want to take a step back and discuss some underlying matters in the film. In an age when our space and distance boundaries are being pushed way beyond the human comfort zone, how do we deal with the challenges of space in real time? In lower gravity, how do our bodies deal with loss of bone and muscle mass? How do our minds deal with long periods of isolation?

The *2001* vessel dealt with the physical challenges with its centrifuge. Dave and Frank had each other—and HAL. Sam is all on his own, except for Gerty, whose voice by Kevin Spacey suggests he was programmed by the same voice synthesizers used for HAL. Gerty seems harmless and friendly, but you never know with these digital devils. All Sam knows is that he's past his shelf date and ready to be recycled back to Earth.

Space is a cold and lonely place, pitiless and indifferent, as Bruce Dern's character grimly realized in Douglas Trumbull's classic *Silent Running*. At least he had the consolation that he was living with Earth's last vegetation. Sam has no consolations at all. It even appears that a new guy may have entered the orbits of his wife and daughter. What kind of a man would volunteer for this duty? What kind of a corporation would ask him to? We, and he, find out.

Moon is a superior example of that threatened genre, hard science fiction, which is often about the interface between humans and alien intelligence of one kind or other, including digital. John W. Campbell Jr., the godfather of this genre, would have approved. The movie is really all about ideas. It only seems to be about emotions. How real are our emotions, anyway? How real are we? Someday I will die. This laptop I'm using is patient and can wait.

Note: The capable director, Duncan Jones, was born Duncan Zowie Heywood Jones. Easy to understand if you know his father is David Bowie, rhymes with Zoe, not Howie. Jones a successful UK commercial director; this is his debut feature. ☞

Moscow, Belgium ★ ★ ★
NO MPAA RATING, 106 m., 2009

Barbara Sarafian (Matty), Jurgen Delnaet (Johnny), Johan Heldenbergh (Werner), Anemone Valcke (Vera), Sofia Ferri (Fien), Julian Borsani (Peter). Directed by Christophe van Rompaey and produced by Jean-Claude van Rijckeghem. Screenplay by van Rijckeghem and Pat van Beirs.

She backs up her car. His big truck runs into it. She should have looked first. A truck that size shouldn't have been in a parking lot. They get out and start screaming insults at each other. This is in a Flemish-speaking city in Belgium. We quickly learn that the f-word sounds exactly the same in English and Flemish.

Now here is the intriguing element. They are both livid with anger. Their insults escalate from their driving abilities to their genders. Women are bloodsuckers. Men are—never mind what men are. At some point, very subtle and hard to define, their insults turn into play. No, they don't start grinning. They still both seem angry. But they grow verbally inventive, and we sense, and they sense, a shift in the weather. It ends with him asking her out for coffee.

The buried emotions in this scene play out all through *Moscow, Belgium,* an uncommon comedy that is fairly serious most of the time. She is Matty (Barbara Sarafian), forty-one years old. He is Johnny (Jurgen Delnaet), in his late twenties. Matty's husband has walked out on her and her three kids. Johnny's girlfriend left him for some rich dude. Johnny has fallen helplessly in love with her, possibly because he has met his match in insults, possibly because a woman who can think that fast on her feet can—never mind what she can do.

Their working-class neighborhood of Ghent is named Moucou, with high rises, heavy traffic, rough bars. Johnny lives here in the sleeping compartment of his truck cab. He is friendly, has eyes that smile, hair she would probably love to take a brush to. Her hair is a slightly tidier mess. She has no desire to meet a man, especially one so much younger. Her husband, Werner (Johan Heldenbergh), an art teacher, left her for a little tart who was one of his students. One cradle robber is enough for her family.

Now about her kids. They are individuals intent on their own lives and indifferent to the fact that they are in a movie. Here's what I mean by that. Ever notice how in a lot of movies the family members are playing Family Members? The kids are arrayed around the dinner table smoothly fitting in their dialogue. Matty's kids are Vera, about seventeen, who regards her mother with weary insight; a younger daughter, Fien, who is going through a stage of reading everyone's Tarot cards and relating to you as if you're the Hanging Man or The Fool; and a still younger son, Peter, who is obsessed by airplanes. Johnny comes for dinner, but they're indifferent to him or, in Vera's case, tactfully withdrawn.

Werner turns up when he hears about his wife's young boyfriend, and they all share a family meal that I suspect owes something to Mike Leigh's family occasions of awkward, weird embarrassment. Matty has to choose: the faithless husband who is a handsome jerk, or the love-struck truck driver with a disturbing past and good reasons to never, ever drink again. The audience would advise her against both.

Underneath everything rolls the rhythm of Matty's real life. Men can come and go, but someone needs to put food on the table, do the shopping, be a parent. Matty has a job in the post office, where half the customers seem to know her. This is not the greatest job, but it's what she has. She understands Johnny's pride in his truck. It is all he has, but it is *his*. He can come and go with the freedom of a ranch hand. Werner, on the other hand, sometimes seems like one of the kids. Well, both men do. By the virtue of their continuity through family crises, women maintain a home, which serves as a powerful attraction.

The performances make these characters work. Barbara Sarafian, first seen in a long shot as she looks painfully hostile and withdrawn, is weather-beaten but attractive. Johnny must be the despair of his mother: an unkempt charmer who looks like trouble. Werner is a creep. The only grown-up in the movie is Vera. She puts her mother to an unexpected test, and Matty, after a double take, shows she has instinctive love for her daughter.

I will not be revealing a thing if I say we're not too sure Matty has made the right choice at the end. That's because neither choice would be the right choice. But notice how deeply the director, Christophe van Rompaey, has drawn us into these lives, how much we finally care, and with what sympathy all the actors enter into the enterprise.

Moving Midway ★ ★ ★
NO MPAA RATING, 98 m., 2008

Featuring Charlie Hinton Silver, Robert Hinton, Elizabeth "Sis" Cheshire, Al Hinton, Abraham Lincoln Hinton. A documentary directed by Godfrey Cheshire and produced by Cheshire, Jay Spain, and Vincent Farrell. Screenplay by Cheshire.

SPOILER WARNING: *Moving Midway* tells three stories, each one worthy of a film of its own. (1) It records the journey home to North Carolina of the film critic Godfrey Cheshire and his discovery of his family's secret history. (2) It documents the ordeal of moving a 160-year-old Southern plantation house to a new location miles away, not by road but overland. (3) It demolishes the myth of the Southern plantation.

Movie critics are always asked if they've ever wanted to make a movie of their own. A handful, like Peter Bogdanovich and Rod Lurie, have had success with features. Others, like Todd McCarthy, have made good documentaries. Godfrey Cheshire's first film follows the first rule of both kinds of films: Start with a strong story that you feel a personal connection with. His story grows stronger, and the connections deeper.

Like many critics (the Alabama-born Jonathan Rosenbaum comes to mind), Cheshire was a small-town boy who moved to the big city. First it was Raleigh, and now New York. In North Carolina, his youth revolved around Midway Plantation, outside of Raleigh, the family seat since 1848. In 2006 the ravages of progress overran Midway. It was boxed in by two expressways. Best Buy was across the street. Target and Home Depot were moving in. Godfrey's brother Charlie hired experts to jack up the house, put it on wheels, and move it to sixty or seventy acres deep into the country.

Godfrey went south to film this undertaking. It stirred family memories and stories about the ghosts many people thought they had seen in Midway. Then he heard from an NYU professor of African-American studies named Robert Hinton, who said he was related to the family; Hinton is the ancestral name. Robert was an African-American. Godfrey invited him to come to North Carolina, visit the house, and watch the move.

Hinton had written about a much-publicized North Carolina family reunion that reunited the black and white members of the same plantation family. Now he received an e-mail from a Brooklyn teacher named Al Hinton, who said his ninety-six-year-old grandfather, Abraham Lincoln Hinton, had some memories to share.

Abraham, visited by Godfrey and Robert, his mind clear as a bell, recalled his father, born in 1848, taking him past a big white two-story house and saying it was his birthplace. That was Midway. Oral tradition in the African-American branch of the family recorded that they were descended from a Hinton patriarch and a cook who was a black slave. There seems no doubt, both in genealogy and physical evidence: Every Hinton, white and black, has the same distinctive nose, which can clearly be seen in the portrait of their common ancestor.

Godfrey made these discoveries while filming, and Robert became coproducer. He considers the myth of the idyllic plantation as formed in works like *Birth of a Nation* and

Gone with the Wind, and demolished by *Roots.* Robert Hinton, whose slave ancestors constructed Midway and picked cotton there, is a succinct and sometimes droll observer. He surprises Godfrey by telling him he considers Midway part of his own heritage, and again when he says it doesn't bother him at all that the original land will be buried beneath a parking lot. Robert on Civil War reenactments: "I'm comfortable with the idea that they keep refighting it, as long as they keep losing it."

Invited by Al and Abraham to a Hinton family reunion, Godfrey finds he has more than one hundred African-American cousins, all of whom know exactly who they are descended from. "It is becoming clearer," he says, "that the South is a mixed-race society." Robert reveals to him: "I found after I came north that I was more comfortable with Southern whites than with young blacks up here." When Cheshire's lively mother, Sis, and the stately Abraham meet, they are instantly at ease, even kidding with each other. Not that Sis doesn't believe the slaves, by and large, were taken good care of.

This is a deceptive film. It starts in one direction and discovers a better one. Cheshire is a dry, almost dispassionate narrator, and that is good; preaching about his discoveries would sound wrong. Robert Hinton, whose feelings run deep, brings the story into focus: "I always wanted to meet a white Hinton. I was hoping I would hate him. The problem is, I like you, so I can't lay a lot of stuff on you." He is philosophical, but not resigned. There is a difference.

Meanwhile, at the new Shoppes of the Midway Plantation mall, there is a restaurant named Mingo's. That was the name of Midway's first slave. The local mayor, bursting with civic pride about the new development, explains how we have all moved on and outgrown the troubles of the past. The mayor is black. We are now in the twenty-first century.

Mr. Magorium's Wonder Emporium ★ ★ ★

G, 93 m., 2007

Dustin Hoffman (Mr. Edward Magorium), Natalie Portman (Molly Mahoney), Jason Bateman (Henry Weston), Zach Mills (Eric Applebaum), Ted Ludzik (Bellini the Bookbuilder). Directed by Zach Helm and produced by James Garavente and Richard N. Gladstein. Screenplay by Helm.

Mr. Magorium is 243 years old, he informs us. He has possibly survived so long by being incapable of boredom. Life for him is a daily adventure, which he shares with the children who pack into his magical toy store. And let's talk about the toy store first. If the movies consist of millions and millions of rooms, some of them indoors, some outdoors, some only in our minds, Mr. Magorium's Wonder Emporium is one of the most delightful. It is jammed to the ceilings and bursting the walls with toys that, in some cases, seem to be alive, and in most cases seem to be real *toys,* and not the extrusions of market research.

The emporium, a quaint old store squeezed in between two modern monoliths, has been run since time immemorial by Edward Magorium, who is played by Dustin Hoffman as a daffy old luv with a slight overbite, a hint of a lisp, a twinkle of the eyes, and boundless optimism. He is so optimistic he is looking forward to his next great experience, which will be death. And he dearly hopes that after he departs, the emporium will be taken over by young Molly Mahoney (Natalie Portman), who is his only employee, except for Bellini the Bookbuilder (Ted Ludzik), who does not seem quite real and possibly just operates in the basement as a freelancer.

Molly is not sure she is ready to shoulder such a responsibility, and her lack of self-confidence provides the conflict without which the movie would be left in search of a plot. She was once a prodigy at the piano, but her failure of nerve on the stage has spread into other areas of her life, and it is Edward's mission to correct that. Looking on (and narrating) is Eric (Zach Mills), a young boy who seems to live at the store as unofficial monitor of all activities.

One dark day an accountant shows up. This is Henry Weston (Jason Bateman), who has been assigned by ominous shadowy parties to look into the emporium's books, which seem to have fallen behind by roughly two centuries. The emporium is threatened with financial ruin, and even if it survives, will Molly care to take over? Because no one else but Molly will do, you see. She contains the same kind of magical spark that has allowed Edward to keep things humming along.

All of this perhaps sounds like a wonderful family movie, and to a degree it is, although the story arcs involving Molly and the accountant and the threats to the store are all recycled from countless other films. The plot is forever being upstaged by the emporium. We want to stop worrying about Molly's self-esteem and just play with more neat stuff. And is there ever any real doubt that there will be a happy ending? None. It's just that everybody has to pretend there is.

Hoffman has countless characters inside of him, and this is one of his nicest. Edward Magorium is very matter-of-fact about his great age, his astonishing store, and his decision that it is time to move on to the next life. He takes it all for granted. Portman, as Molly, doesn't think it's that simple, and she has the thankless task of holding out against the old man's certainty. The suspense, such as it is, will possibly enthrall kids up to a certain age, but their parents, once they get over the visual delights of the emporium, will be grateful the proceedings last only ninety-three minutes. That's about as long as this notion will carry us, or a little longer.

The first-time direction and screenplay are by Zach Helm, who wrote Marc Forster's metaphysical comedy *Stranger Than Fiction* (2006), with Will Ferrell as a tax man who starts hearing a voice in his head describing what he does all day, a little before he does it. Dustin Hoffman was in that movie, too, as an English professor who determines that the hero's life is being written by a novelist and uses his skills to figure out who it is. Helm has the kind of imagination that makes you want to see what he'll do next. And he has the taste or luck to have assembled production designer Therese DePrez, art director Brandt Gordon, and set decorator Clive Thomasson, without all of whom the emporium would not live up to its billing. This isn't quite the over-the-top fantasy you'd like it to be, but it's a charming enough little movie, and probably the younger you are, the more charming.

Mr. Woodcock ★ ★ ★

PG-13, 87 m., 2007

Billy Bob Thornton (Mr. Woodcock), Seann William Scott (John Farley), Susan Sarandon (Beverly Farley), Amy Poehler (Maggie Hoffman), Ethan Suplee (Nedderman). Directed by Craig Gillespie and produced by Bob Cooper. Screenplay by Michael Carnes and Josh Gilbert.

Billy Bob Thornton is in full *Bad Santa* mode in *Mr. Woodcock,* an uneasy comedy about an adult who returns home to discover his mother is planning to marry the gym teacher who made his high school days a living hell. The thing about Thornton is, he makes no compromises and takes no prisoners when he plays guys like Woodcock. He's a hateful jerk, and he means it. That makes the movie better, actually, than if we sensed a heart of gold under the crust, but it doesn't exactly make it funnier.

Woodcock uses his position in authority to pick on the weak and helpless in his gym classes, including the overweight, the stuttering, and those who are simply no good at physical education. He slams them with basketballs thrown at wounding velocity, he runs them around the gym for looking funny, he finds their weaknesses and mocks them. "It'll make men out of them," he explains. No, it won't. It'll make Woodcocks out of them.

Seann William Scott plays John Farley, the hometown boy who has gone out into the world and written a best-selling self-help book that, like most self-help books, tells you the same things your mother and Norman Vincent Peale told you, and charges for the privilege. Anyone read *The Secret* lately? Give me a break. Anyway, from what we learn about it, Farley's book recycles the usual slogans and meaningless platitudes and has made him a celebrity.

But all his adult wealth and fame turns to ashes when he discovers his mom, Beverly (Susan Sarandon), is dating Mr. Woodcock, and all his old fears come back. Give Thornton and the director, Craig Gillespie, full points for playing Woodcock as an uncompromising, insulting, tactless, hurtful, sadistic buttwipe. When Farley finally challenges him to a fight, his reply is: "You must like getting spanked, Farley. I guess it runs in the family." Ouch. That's even in the trailer.

I can imagine this as a softball comedy, but it's perversely more interesting as hardball. Take the Sarandon character. She's been alone for years, Woodcock is nice to her, she craves company and attention, and the guy apparently really does like her. Her son is making a rare visit home, but her life will go on, and she has to be free to make the best of it. That's better than making her an innocent victim.

I'm not sure, but I suspect that Woodcock's treatment of kids borders on the illegal, yet he's named Educator of the Year and doesn't seem to give a flying flatulency in a windstorm if everybody hates him. Will he be cruel to Beverly Farley? Hard to say, but that's what her son fears.

To laugh at parts of this film would indicate one has a streak of Woodcockism in oneself. But to gaze in stupefied fascination is perfectly understandable. That's what makes Thornton such a complex actor. He can play a tough coach like the one in *Friday Night Lights* as a three-dimensional human being and then make Mr. Woodcock into a monster. And hey, why, after all these years, hasn't Woodcock ever been promoted to a coaching position? Maybe because he likes to be a bully, and the football players might beat him bloody.

Anyway, all is resolved, one way or another, in a rather contrived ending that might have something to do with the film's three weeks of reshoots, as reported by Patrick Goldstein in the *LA Times* and documented on IMDb. I would have been happier if young John Farley had torn his positive thinking book to shreds, slammed Mr. Woodcock in the gut with a medicine ball, and told him to drop and give him fifty quick ones or he'd do it again.

The Mummy: Tomb of the Dragon Emperor ★ ★ ★
PG-13, 112 m., 2008

Brendan Fraser (Rick O'Connell), Jet Li (Emperor Han), Maria Bello (Evelyn O'Connell), Michelle Yeoh (Zi Juan), Luke Ford (Alex O'Connell), John Hannah (Jonathan Carnahan), Isabella Leong (Lin), Anthony Wong Chau-Sang (General Yang), Russell Wong (Ming Guo), Liam Cunningham (Mad Dog Maguire). Directed by Rob Cohen and produced by Sean Daniel, Bob Ducsay, James Jacks, and Stephen Sommers. Screenplay by Alfred Gough and Miles Millar.

Moviegoers who knowingly buy a ticket for *The Mummy: Tomb of the Dragon Emperor* are going to get exactly what they expect: There is a mummy, a tomb, a dragon, and an emperor. And the movie about them is all that it could be. If you think *The Mummy: Tomb of the Dragon Emperor* sounds like a waste of time, don't waste yours.

I, as it happens, have time to waste, and cannot do better than to quote from my review of *The Mummy* (1999): "There is hardly a thing I can say in its favor, except that I was cheered by nearly every minute of it. I cannot argue for the script, the direction, the acting, or even the mummy, but I can say that I was not bored and sometimes I was unreasonably pleased. There is a little immaturity stuck away in the crannies of even the most judicious of us, and we should treasure it."

I was not, however, pleased by *The Mummy Returns* (2001), although it inspired one of my funnier reviews. But *The Mummy: Tomb of the Dragon Emperor* is the best in the series and, from the looks of it, the most expensive. And once again it presents the spectacle of undead warriors who are awakened from the slumber of ages only to be defeated in battle—this time, by the skeletons of the slaves buried beneath the Great Wall after constructing it (which is a neat trick).

Rick O'Connell (Brendan Fraser) and his wife, Evelyn (Mario Bello), are back, having come out of retirement to race to the aid of their now-adult son Alex (Luke Ford), who has inadvertently awakened the mummy of the Dragon Emperor (Jet Li). In a prologue, we learn he was cursed by the sorceress Zi Juan (Michelle Yeoh), who incurred his wrath by spurning his love, and later, we learn, bearing the daughter of General Ming (Russell Wong). Both daughter and mother are immortal. So is the emperor, although it is a mixed blessing when you are immortal but mummified inside a thick cocoon of terracotta. Where's the benefit?

Now the emperor has awakened, and he unleashes his army of ten thousand slumbering warriors to feed his ambition to conquer the world, which is going to take more than ten thousand spear carriers, but he's operating on B.C. time. To counter him, the sleeping slave-skeletons are awakened by the sorceress and are sort of funny: One misplaces his head and screws it back on. The battle between these two sides is won by the side with the fewest missing heads.

Before that climactic event, however, Rick, Evelyn, Alex, and Evelyn's supercilious brother Jonathan (John Hannah) penetrate the underground city of the mummy, survive a perilous series of booby traps, and in several other ways remind us of Indiana Jones, the obvious inspiration for this series, which has little—no, nothing—to do with Boris Karloff's *The Mummy* (1932). They even make it into the Himalayas, and . . . could that be the lost city of Shangri-La?

The emperor is a shape-shifter, able to turn himself into a three-headed fire-breathing dragon, which coils, twists, turns, and somehow avoids scorching itself. He speaks in a low bass rumble, just like Imhotep, the mummy in the two earlier pictures, whose name continues to remind me of an Egyptian house of pancakes. But moving the action from Egypt to China allows a whole new set of images to be brought into play, and the movie ends by winking at us that the next stop will be Peru.

Now why did I like this movie? It was just plain dumb fun is why. It is absurd and preposterous, and proud of it. The heroes maintain their ability to think of banal clichés even in the most strenuous situations. Brendan Fraser continues to play Rick as if he is taking a ride at Universal Studios, but Maria Bello has real pluck as she uses a handgun against the hordes of terra-cotta warriors. The sacrifice of the sorceress in relinquishing not only her own immortality but that of her daughter permits love to bloom, although would you really want a bride who was four thousand years old, even if she was going to die?

Music Within ★ ★ ½
R, 93 m., 2007

Ron Livingston (Richard Pimentel), Melissa George (Christine), Michael Sheen (Art Honneyman), Yul Vazquez (Mike Stoltz), Rebecca De Mornay (Richard's Mother), Hector Elizondo (Dr. Ben Padrow). Directed by Steven Sawalich and produced by Sawalich and Brett Donowho. Screenplay by Bret McKinney, Mark Andrew Olsen, and Kelly Kennemer.

I have good things to write about *Music Within,* but I have some troubles with it, too. First, the good stuff: This is an entertaining, sometimes inspiring film about a man named Richard Pimentel (Ron Livingston), who serves in Vietnam and is almost completely deafened when a shell lands near him in battle. Returning to America, he receives not exactly expert treatment for his disability and is cast out into the world to find himself all but unemployable. Among the friends he makes in the disabled community is Art Honneyman (Michael Sheen), who has cerebral palsy but is a powerhouse of intelligence and wit.

The two of them experience firsthand the discrimination, sometimes unconscious, that the world inflicts on those who look, sound, or act differently. In one of the movie's most infuriating scenes, they are asked to leave a restaurant "because you're disturbing the other customers." How are they disturbing them? By being there. By existing. By Honneyman being twisted and in a wheelchair and talking awkwardly.

Pimentel's own experiences and what he sees happening to his friends inspire him to become a disability-rights activist, and although the movie doesn't quite say so, he must have been the driving force behind the Americans with Disabilities Act (1990) because no one else is mentioned. Taken just on these terms, the movie works, it's effective, and I believe audiences will respond to it.

My own feelings are a little more complex. They began forming in early childhood. Growing up in Urbana, Illinois, I was unknowingly at the center of a rehabilitation movement that formed after the Second World War. Thousands of returning vets were in wheelchairs. Unlike Pimentel, who is told in the film he doesn't qualify for veteran's college funds because he is deaf, many of them attended universities on the G.I. Bill.

The University of Illinois sits on a landscape flat as a pancake. Ideal for wheelchairs. The Urbana-Champaign community, starting in 1946, began to build ramps into buildings, adapt elevators and washrooms, make curb cuts, and equip buses with chair lifts. This was not done overnight, but the town became known as wheelchair-friendly. Our local TV sportscaster, Tom Jones, was in a wheelchair. Our wheelchair athletes, organized in a program by Dr. Tim

Nugent, helped launch wheelchair sports. During Vietnam, the loudest antiwar protester on campus was an SDS member named Rudy Frank who walked with so many braces he looked like Robocop. There was Ken Viste, my photo chief at the *Daily Illini*. He was in a chair, but that didn't keep him off the sidelines while shooting sports events. Disabled people were no big deal.

Things like that were happening all over the country, and I learned a little about them in 1962 when I went along as an aide on a tour of Southern Africa with eighteen wheelchair athletes, who demonstrated that life did not end with forms of paralysis. All of this was before Pimentel went to Vietnam.

The national disability-rights movement had many parents. Such men as Robert Burgdorf, Justin Whitlock Dart Jr., and Senator Bob Dole were instrumental. Remember Ron Kovic, who was born on the Fourth of July? Here in Chicago, my friend Marca Bristo founded Access Living to support the disabled who wanted to live independently. She lobbied relentlessly in city hall and Springfield. She was appointed chair of the National Council on Disability. No, she didn't create the Americans with Disabilities Act. But Google both her and Pimentel and decide for yourself who played a larger role in the movement.

What bothers me is that *Music Within* takes an individual story, an inspiring one, yes, and then thinks that's all there is to be told. It wasn't one guy who got mad. It was decades of struggle, decades of rejection, decades of streets that couldn't be crossed, stairs that couldn't be climbed, houses that couldn't be lived in, and customers who couldn't be bothered. Richard Pimentel was more a beneficiary of the disability rights movement than a pioneer. So why do I give the movie two and a half stars? Because what it does, it does sincerely and fairly well. Just remember that its hero stands for countless others.

Must Read After My Death ★ ★ ★
NO MPAA RATING, 76 m., 2009

A documentary directed, produced, and written by Morgan Dews.

Here is a cry from the grave. A woman who died some eight years ago at the age of eighty-nine left behind about fifty hours of audiotapes, two hundred home movies, and three hundred pages of documents, a record that all ended, thirty years before that, on the death of her husband. The cache was labeled, in bold marker on a manila envelope, *Must Read After My Death*. What an anguished story it tells, of a marriage from hell.

The woman was named Allis. Her grandson, Morgan Dews, has created this film from her archives and understandably represses her family name. She met her husband Charley when they were both married to others. What she wanted was a nice little house with a white picket fence, where she would bear his children, whether or not they were married, because she knew they would have beautiful children together. They were married, and until death did not part.

It was an "open marriage." Charley was away much of the year on business, often to Australia. They decided to exchange Dictaphone recordings, and later tape recordings, and Allis saved hours of taped telephone messages. Charley is forthright about his adventures with "interesting women" he has met in Australia, "good dancers" and obviously good at more than that, "but the international operators listen in." Allis tells only of one weekend affair. She says she thinks she "helped" the man rebuild his self-confidence.

Charley is such a perfect bastard. His dry voice objectively slices through everything. He speaks of love and travel arrangements in the same tone. When he's home, there is always fighting. Always. Not about sex; he sees the real problems in their marriage as housekeeping and finances. Allis says she was meant to be a good mother but was never a housekeeper. She speaks four languages, went to college, was married first to a European, did some kind of unspecified singing. We hear not a word about Charley's first marriage.

Charley and Allis have three sons and a daughter. Charley is relentless with them about their "chores." He's an alcoholic, and it seems to make him a perfectionist. He's tall, balding, handsome in that Harry Smith way. Allis is small, tidy, worried. There are tapes of screaming rages involving Charley and his sons; their daughter, Morgan's mother, not much heard, leaves home at sixteen, following the advice in Philip Larkin's famous poem about destructive families, "This Be the Verse": "Get out as early as you can."

The first line of that poem certainly describes the marriage of Charley and Allis. All four children are angry, miserable, neurotic in various ways. The family falls into the clutches of a psychiatrist named Lenn, who wrongly sends one son to a mental institution, diagnoses Charley as "the worst inferiority complex I've ever seen," and strews misery and anguish as freely as his advice. What we learn of the children later in life is that three of them, anyway, grew up into apparently happy married adults with children.

It was the family itself that was toxic. They needed to get out. Charley is hated by the children, and Allis thinks of herself as not meant for such a life. She and Charley never have a real talk about "open marriage," but it certainly suits good-time Charley, a man without a single moment of introspection in this film.

Home movies and now the ubiquitous videotape mean that everyday lives are now recorded with a detail not dreamed of earlier. We will never hear all of Allis's recordings and see all her images, but this distillation by Morgan Dews might have been what she had in mind when she stored away those records of pain. They act as her justification of her life, her explanation of the misery of her children. I watched this film horrified and fascinated. There is such raw pain here. Allis might have read or seen *Revolutionary Road* and by comparison envied that marriage.

There are things you will see here that will lead you to some conclusions. I will leave you to them. All I can say is that I believe the daughter's guess at the end is correct. We learn that after Charley died, Allis moved to her own small cottage in Vermont and "continued her volunteer work." She lived another thirty years. She never mentioned Charley again.

My Best Friend ★ ★ ★
PG-13, 95 m., 2007

Daniel Auteuil (Francois), Dany Boon (Bruno), Julie Gayet (Catherine), Julie Durand (Louise). Directed by Patrice Leconte and produced by Olivier Delbosc and Marc Missonnier. Screenplay by Leconte and Jerome Tonnerre.

My Best Friend tells the story of Francois, a man who has no friends at all. Who tells him that? All of his friends, at his birthday party. Once they get started on the subject, they bluntly confess they don't like him. No, not even his business partner. Don't like him and never have. Francois is stunned; obviously he never really knew what friendship was. He confused it with acquaintanceship, maybe, or partnership, or people he spent a lot of time with.

Francois is played by the sad-eyed Daniel Auteuil, one of the most familiar faces in French films (recently he starred in *Cache*, that intriguing film about the man who received anonymous videos of himself and his family). As an actor he is so flexible he can move from playing the sad-sack antiques dealer in this picture to playing Napoleon in the next film he made.

Here he is a man so alone and lonely that when he finds he has no friends, he is compelled at an auction to pay a small fortune he can't afford for a Greek vase whose owner commissioned it in memory of *his* best friend "and filled it with my tears." I am reminded of Daniel Curley's novel *A Stone Man, Yes,* with a title inspired by a man eternally chasing his love around a Greek vase; good enough for a stone man, yes, but not for one of flesh and blood.

Francois's partner, Catherine (Julie Gayet), doubts Francois's claims that he does indeed have a best friend. Appalled by how much he has put their company in debt, she makes him a bet. Unless he can produce a true and convincing best friend in ten days, he will have to give her the vase. Fair enough. But the search goes badly; his best friend at school, tracked down after many years, turns out always to have hated him.

One day Francois gets into the taxi of Bruno (Dany Boon), who has an opinion on everything. Francois is put off by the man's assurance and nonstop chattering, but when they meet again and again (coincidences are invaluable in movies), the driver begins to intrigue him, and eventually he hires Bruno as a tutor to teach him how to make friends. Of course the driver takes the job; there is nothing about human nature that the French do not think they know. The lessons are the stuff sitcoms are made of, and *My Best Friend* seems destined to be remade by Hollywood.

The film unfolds easily, with affection for the man no one likes, and at ninety-five minutes, it doesn't overstay its welcome. It was directed by Patrice Leconte, who makes intelligent films combining sympathy for his characters with a quick wit, a dark undertow, and a love of human peculiarity. He told me that on his tombstone he wanted the words: "This man loved to make movies." And he said: "I believe a filmmaker is like a chemist. You mix elements that have nothing to do with each other, and you see what will happen. Sometimes it blows up in your face."

Let me interrupt the flow of this review to mention some of his titles I think are extraordinarily good and the way they combine opposites: *Monsieur Hire* (shy bachelor and bold sex object), *The Hairdresser's Husband* (man obsessed with hairdressers and a hairdresser), *Ridicule* (a landowner and the king), *The Girl on the Bridge* (suicidal girl and circus knife thrower), *The Widow of Saint-Pierre* (condemned man and governor's wife), *The Man on the Train* (criminal and quiet loner), and *Intimate Strangers* (psychiatrist mistakes accidental visitor for client). Three of those titles have been on my annual Best Ten lists.

Certainly Francois and Bruno have nothing to do with each other. Or perhaps they do, but Francois with his blinders wouldn't notice it. As for Bruno, his lifelong obsession with facts and figures and dates is interesting; by knowing enough about the surface of the world to appear on a quiz show, he can avoid the depths.

These two men need each other. We know that. Patrice Leconte knows that. But do they know that? Thinking about the casting, if there's a Hollywood remake, I'm thinking Robert Downey Jr. as Francois and Adam Sandler as Bruno.

My Kid Could Paint That ★ ★ ★
PG-13, 83 m., 2007

Featuring Marla Olmstead, Mark Olmstead, Laura Olmstead, Amir Bar-Lev, Anthony Brunelli, Elizabeth Cohen, and Michael Kimmelman. A documentary produced and directed by Amir Bar-Lev.

The truth lurking beneath *My Kid Could Paint That* is that your kid *couldn't* paint that. The documentary considers the perplexing case of Marla Olmstead, a four-year-old girl from Binghamton, New York, who got a lot of publicity because at her age she was producing abstract paintings that sold for hundreds and then thousands of dollars, were awarded gallery shows, generated a firestorm in the art community, and were the subject of a controversial segment on *60 Minutes*.

The paintings are pretty good. They are as good as some, not most, abstract paintings. They play into the hands of those who dismiss abstract art as the process of applying paint to canvas with a technique that looks random and unconsidered. Some, not all, abstract art gains its importance not because of its intrinsic quality but because of its price. At $25, it looks like dribbles. At $25 million, it looks like a masterpiece.

The story as told by Mark, Marla's dad, an amateur painter himself, is that one day little Marla was on the kitchen table while he was painting, and she grabbed a brush and started painting, too. The child showed an instinctive feeling for color, pattern, composition, and texture, and because of her age and the abstract-art-debunking angle, she started to get worldwide publicity.

The problem was, no one had actually seen Marla creating a whole work from start to finish except, presumably, her parents. *60 Minutes* came to do a piece on the girl, put their equipment all over the house, and installed a secret camera in the basement ceiling. Through it, they were able to see Marla beginning a painting with urgent whispered instructions from her father. We never see him touch a brush to the painting, but on the other hand, the finished painting doesn't look like a "Marla," but like something any child could paint.

Is the little girl the star of a hoax by her family? Amir Bar-Lev, the maker of this film, says he doesn't know, and the film has an open ending. He grew quite close to the Olmsteads and at times worried that he was betraying their confidence. My own verdict as an outsider is, no, Marla didn't paint those works, although she may have applied some of the paint.

But it's more complicated than that. As I said, some of the paintings are pretty good.

People might pay hundreds if they were by a kid, but would they pay thousands unless they actually liked them? The irony may be that Mark Olmstead is a gifted painter who could never break into the closed circle of abstract art without a gimmick like Marla.

My favorite modern painter is Gillian Ayres, OBE. Ayres (born 1930) is a well-known British abstract expressionist whose huge canvases, often measuring several feet in their dimensions, look like finger painting because they are. With untrammeled exuberance, she paints in bright colors with a thick impasto. Chaz and I had not heard of her when we saw one of her paintings in a warehouse and simultaneously agreed we loved it. No, a kid couldn't paint that.

In the last analysis, I guess it all reduces to taste and instinct. Some paintings are good, says me, or says you, and some are bad. Some paintings could be painted by a child, some couldn't be.

My Life in Ruins ★ ½
PG-13, 95 m., 2009

Nia Vardalos (Georgia), Richard Dreyfuss (Irv), Alexis Georgoulis (Poupi), Rachel Dratch (Kim), Maria Adanez (Lena), Maria Botto (Lala), Harland Williams (Big Al), Alistair McGowan (Nico). Directed by Donald Petrie and produced by Michelle Chydzik Sowa and Nathalie Marciano. Screenplay by Mike Reiss.

Nia Vardalos plays most of *My Life in Ruins* with a fixed toothpaste smile, which is no wonder because her acting in the film feels uncomfortably close to her posing for a portrait. Rarely has a film centered on a character so superficial and unconvincing, played with such unrelenting sameness. I didn't hate it so much as feel sorry for it.

Vardalos plays Georgia, an American tour guide in Athens, in rivalry with Nico (Alistair McGowan), who always gets assigned the new bus with the well-behaved Canadians, while our girl gets the beater containing a group of walking human clichés who were old when *If It's Tuesday, This Must Be Belgium* was new. You got your loud Yankees, your boozy Aussies, your prowling Spanish divorcees, your ancient Brits, and, of course, your oblig-atory Jewish widower who is laughing on the outside and mourning on the inside.

These characters are teeth-gratingly broad and obvious, apart from Richard Dreyfuss, who brings life, maybe too much life, to Irv, who tells bad jokes even though he is old enough to have learned funnier ones. To him, I recommend the delightful Web site www.oldjewstellingjokes.com, where every single old Jew is funnier than he is. Irv, of course, eventually reveals a sentimental side and does something else that is required in the Screenplay Recycling Handbook. (Interested in reading it? Send in five dollars. I won't mail it to you, but thanks for the money. Rim shot, please.)

The central question posed by *My Life in Ruins* is, what happened to the Nia Vardalos who wrote and starred in *My Big Fat Greek Wedding*? She was lovable, earthy, sassy, plumper, more of a mess, and the movie grossed more than $300 million. Here she's thinner, blonder, better dressed, looks younger, and knows it. She's like the winner of a beauty makeover at a Hollywood studio. She has that "Don't touch my makeup!" look. And if anyone in Hollywood has whiter, straighter, more gleaming teeth, we'll never know it, because like most people they'll usually keep their lips closed.

To speculate on people's motives is risky and can be unfair. Let me gently suggest that when Nia Vardalos made *My Big Fat Greek Wedding* she was an unlikely, saucy movie star who didn't take herself seriously. She was also an incomparably better screenwriter than Mike Reiss, the autopilot sitcom veteran who cobbled together this lousy script.

Now she is rich, famous, and perhaps taking herself seriously after being worked over for one too many magazine covers. She has also made the mistake of allowing herself to be found in one of those situations that only happen in trashy romance novels. The driver of her bus is a surly Greek named Poupi (Alexis Georgoulis), who has a beard that looks inspired by the Smith Brothers. After he shaves it off, he emerges as an improbably handsome, long-locked Adonis of the sort that customarily only dates older women if he has reason to think they are rich. This romance is embarrassing.

There is, in short, nothing I liked about *My Life in Ruins,* except some of the ruins. The tourists are even allowed to consult the Oracle at Delphi. That scene reminded me of when Chaz and I visited an ancient temple at Ise in Japan. Outside the gates, monks sat on platforms inscribing scrolls. "You may ask anything you want," our guide told us. "Will there be peace in our time?" asked Chaz. The monk gave a look at our guide. Our guide said, "Ah . . . I think maybe better question be more like, 'How many monks live in temple?'"

Note: "Poupi" is pronounced "poopy." That would never get past the editor of a romance novel.

My Name Is Bruce ★ ★
R, 86 m., 2008

Bruce Campbell (Bruce Campbell), James J. Peck (Guan-Di), Taylor Sharpe (Jeff), Ted Raimi (Mills Toddner), Grace Thorsen (Kelly). Directed by Bruce Campbell and produced by Campbell and Mike Richardson. Screenplay by Mark Verheiden.

Many's the actor who has brooded in his trailer and pondered: "Maybe I could direct better than this idiot." With Bruce Campbell that is often true, with the exceptions of such directors as Sam Raimi, with whom he has worked eleven times, and the Coen brothers (four). You know you're in trouble when your top-user-rated title at IMDb is a video game, although the gameboys are such generous raters they place the game *Evil Dead: Regeneration* right above the film *Fargo.*

In that Coen brothers' film, Campbell played an uncredited soap opera actor on a TV set in the background, but that was as a favor, because he and the Coens have long been friends. They met him on *Crimewave* (1985), their first writing credit, which was directed by, no surprise, Sam Raimi. Campbell has appeared in horror and exploitation movies without number, has always provided what the role requires, has inspired fondness in the genre's fans, and has been in some movies where I've been the lonely voice protesting they are good, such as *Congo* (1995), which featured a martini-sipping gorilla, volcanoes, earthquakes, and the always economical scene in which an actor looks over his shoulder, sees something, screams, and the screen turns black.

Also please consult my review of *Bubba Ho-Tep* (2002). In that film, which is set in recent times, Elvis and JFK did not die but are roommates in an East Texas nursing home. Campbell plays Elvis. Ossie Davis plays JFK. "But you're black," Elvis observes. JFK nods: "After Lyndon Johnson faked my assassination, they dyed me."

You see that Bruce Campbell often returns value for money. And in that spirit, I welcome his first work as a director since *The Man with the Screaming Brain* (2005). He plays himself in a lampoon of his career, his movies, his genres, and everything else he stands for. Maybe it's only "one-note insider navel-gazing," writes one of its critics, but if the navel has been there, done that, and had unspeakable horrors wreaked onto it, the navel has paid its dues.

The plot involves a movie star helping to save Gold Lick, Oregon, from an ancient Chinese god named Guan-Di, played by James J. Peck, although that could be anybody inside the suit. I know Dave Prowse, who wore the Darth Vader suit, and a lot of good that did him. Guan-Di, the god of war, for reasons best known unto himself, inhabits a falling-apart shanty-board crypt in the decrepit local cemetery that looks like the set for a grade-school production of a haunted graveyard movie. His eyes are flaming coals. Hard to see the evolutionary advantage there.

Campbell depicts himself as a drunken slob behind on his alimony, a vain, egotistical monster, a phony, a poseur, and a man in flight from his most recent movie, *Cave Alien 2.* This movie would make the perfect lower half of a Bruce Campbell double feature. If you don't already know who Bruce Campbell is, it will set you searching for other Bruce Campbell films on the theory that they can't all be like this. Start with *Evil Dead II,* is my advice. Not to forget *Bubba Ho-Tep.* In fact, start with them before *My Name Is Bruce,* which is low midrange in the Master's ouvre.

My Sister's Keeper ★ ★ ★ ½
PG-13, 108 m., 2009

Cameron Diaz (Sara Fitzgerald), Abigail Breslin (Anna Fitzgerald), Alec Baldwin (Campbell

Alexander), Jason Patric (Brian Fitzgerald), Sofia Vassilieva (Kate Fitzgerald), Joan Cusack (Judge De Salvo), Heather Wahlquist (Aunt Kelly), Thomas Dekker (Taylor Ambrose), Evan Ellingson (Jesse Fitzgerald), David Thornton (Dr. Chance). Directed by Nick Cassavetes and produced by Mark Johnson, Chuck Pacheco, and Scott L. Goldman. Screenplay by Cassavetes and Jeremy Leven, based on the novel by Jodi Picoult.

My Sister's Keeper is an immediate audience grabber, as we learn that an eleven-year-old girl was genetically designed as a source of spare parts for her dying sixteen-year-old sister. Yes, it's possible: In vitro fertilization ensured a perfect match. And no, this isn't science fiction like Kazuo Ishiguro's novel *Never Let Me Go*, with its cloned human replacements. It's just a little girl subjected to major procedures almost from birth to help her sister live.

So far they have succeeded, and Kate (Sofia Vassilieva) is alive long after her predicted death at five. Her sister, Anna (Abigail Breslin), has donated blood, bone marrow, and stem cells, and now is being told she must donate one of her kidneys. She's had it. It dismays her to know she was conceived as an organ bank, and she wants her chance at a normal life without round trips to the operating room. She may be young but she's bright and determined, and she decides to file a lawsuit against her parents for "medical emancipation."

Hers would be a model family if not for her sister's death sentence. Her mom, Sara (Cameron Diaz), is a successful Los Angeles lawyer. Her dad, Brian (Jason Patric), is a fire chief. Her older brother, Jesse (Evan Ellingson), is a good student but feels ignored. Anna and Kate love each other dearly. But always there is Sara's relentless drive to keep her daughter alive. Like some successful attorneys, she also wants to win every case in her private life.

Anna goes to an attorney who boasts a 90 percent success rate in his TV ads. This is the polished Campbell Alexander (Alec Baldwin), who drives a Bentley convertible and is known for bringing his dog into courtrooms. Anna offers her savings of seven hundred dollars. This is far under his fee, but he listens and accepts the case.

Although *My Sister's Keeper*, based on the best-seller by Jodi Picoult, is an effective tear-jerker, if you think about it, it's something else. The movie never says so, but it's a practical parable about the debate between pro-choice and pro-life. If you're pro-life, you would require Anna to donate her kidney, although there is a chance she could die and her sister doesn't have a good prognosis. If you're pro-choice, you would support Anna's lawsuit.

The mother is appalled by the lawsuit. Keeping her daughter alive has been a triumph for her all of these years. The father is shocked, too, but calmer and more objective. He can see Anna's point. She has her own life to live, and her own love to demand. The performances don't go over the top, although they can see it from where they're standing. Cameron Diaz has the greatest challenge because her determination is so fierce, but she makes her love evident—more for Kate, it must be said, than for Anna and Jesse. Jason Patric, too, rarely gets sympathetic roles, and he embodies thoughtfulness and tenderness. The young actors never step wrong.

Nicely nuanced, too, is Alec Baldwin as the hotshot attorney. He doesn't have a posh office, and his photo is plastered on billboards, but he's not a fly-by-night, and he has a heart. He also has a sense of humor; in several supporting roles recently, he has stepped in with lines enriched by unexpected flashes of wit. Also navigating around clichés here is Joan Cusack as the judge. She takes that impossible case and convinces us she handles it about as well as possible. The enigma is the underdeveloped brother, Jesse, who runs away for three days.

We're never told what that was all about; in the film, it serves merely to distract us when Taylor (Thomas Dekker), Kate's fellow cancer patient, seems to disappear. The hospital romance between Taylor and Kate is one of the best elements of the movie, tender, tactful, and very touching.

The screenplay by Jeremy Leven and Nick Cassavetes (who directed) is admirable in trusting us to figure things out. Because it's obvious in one beautiful scene that Kate is wearing a wig, they didn't ask, "Will the audience understand that?" and add a jarring line. Routine courtroom theatrics are avoided. We learn of the verdict in the best way. We can see the wheels turning, but they turn well.

The Mysteries of Pittsburgh ★ ★
R, 95 m., 2009

Jon Foster (Art Bechstein), Peter Sarsgaard (Cleveland), Sienna Miller (Jane), Nick Nolte (Joe Bechstein), Mena Suvari (Phlox). Directed by Rawson Marshall Thurber and produced by Michael London and Jason Ajax Mercer. Screenplay by Thurber, based on the novel by Michael Chabon.

After that summer, nothing would ever be the same again. Where have we seen that movie before? Most recently in *Adventureland*, another movie set in 1980s Pittsburgh. If you think about it, after every summer nothing will ever be the same again. But *The Mysteries of Pittsburgh* has an unusually busy summer, in which a hero who is a blank slate gets scrawled all over with experiences.

The movie is all the more artificial because it has been made with great, almost painful, earnestness. It takes a plot that would have been at home in a 1930s Warner Bros. social melodrama, adds sexuality and a little nudity, and Bob's your uncle. It's based on a 1988 novel by Michael Chabon, still much read and valued, but to call it "inspired by" would be a stretcher. Hardly a thing happens that doesn't seem laid on to hurry along the hero's coming of age.

That hero is Art (Jon Foster), whose voice-over narration does not shy away from the obvious. He is the son of Joe Bechstein (Nick Nolte), a mobster of such stature that he has his own FBI shadows. Joe would like Art to follow him into the family business, but Art wants nothing to do with it. He'll become a broker, which in the 1980s was an honest trade. For the summer he takes a job at a vast surplus bookstore, where the minimum wage allows him to lose himself.

Life comes racing after him. Phlox (Mena Suvari), the store manager, pages him on the intercom for sex on demand in the stock room. At a party, he meets the winsome blonde Jane (Sienna Miller), whose boyfriend, Cleveland (Peter Sarsgaard), is both friendly and disturbing. These two mess with his mind: Jane although she doesn't mean to, Cleveland because he is a sadistic emotional manipulator. The first little "joke" Cleveland plays on Art should have sent Art running as

far from Cleveland as he could get. But Art is pathologically passive; the summer happens to him, but he can't be said to happen to it.

Complications from countless other movies. The fraught relationship with his father. Phlox's possessiveness. Jane's ambivalence. Cleveland's odd promotion of an emotional, if not at first sexual, ménage à trois. Then a crime-driven climax that arrives out of thin air and involves a very small world indeed. Finally a bittersweet closing narration that seems to tie up loose ends but really answers nothing about Art except whether he still lives in Pittsburgh.

Complicating this are some well-developed performances for such an underdeveloped screenplay. Peter Sarsgaard is intriguing as the seductive, profoundly screwy Cleveland. Mena Suvari is pitch-perfect in a finally thankless role. Nick Nolte, in expensive suits, hair slicked back, takes no nonsense as the hard mob boss. Sienna Miller is sweet but is never allowed to make clear why she is attracted to either man. Jon Foster, as the feckless protagonist, is the latest in a long line of manipulated male ingénues going back beyond Benjamin in *The Graduate*. This is a guy who hardly deserves the attention of the other characters in the story, with his closed-in, inarticulate, low self-esteem.

At the end, Art is supposed to have learned lessons in life from his "last summer before life begins." The melancholy likelihood is, however, that he learned nothing except the punch line to the old joke, "Don't do that no more." At summer's end he seems poised to graduate directly into the Lonely Crowd. There is an old word: nebbish. It is still a good word.

My Winnipeg ★ ★ ★ ★
NO MPAA RATING, 80 m., 2008

Darcy Fehr (Guy Maddin), Ann Savage (Mother), Amy Stewart (Janet Maddin), Louis Negin (Mayor Cornish), Brendan Cade (Cameron Maddin), Wesley Cade (Ross Maddin), Fred Dunsmore (Himself). Directed by Guy Maddin and produced by Jody Shapiro and Phyllis Laing. Screenplay by Maddin.

If you love movies in the very sinews of your imagination, you should experience the work of Guy Maddin. If you have never heard of him, I am not surprised. Now you have. A new Maddin movie doesn't play in every multiplex or city or state. If you hear of one opening, seize the day. Or search where obscure films can be found. You will be plunged into the mind of a man who thinks in the images of old silent films, disreputable documentaries, movies that never were, from eras beyond comprehension. His imagination frees the lurid possibilities of the banal. He rewrites history; when that fails, he creates it.

First, a paragraph of dry fact. Maddin makes films that use the dated editing devices of old movies: Iris shots, breathless titles, shock cutting, staged poses, melodramatic acting, recycled footage, camera angles not merely dramatic but startling. He uses these devices to tell stories that begin with the improbable and march boldly into the inconceivable. My paragraph is ending now, and you have seen how difficult it is to describe his work. I will end with two more statements: (1) Shot for shot, Maddin can be as surprising and delightful as any filmmaker has ever been, and (2) he is an acquired taste, but please, sir, may I have some more?

Consider his film *My Winnipeg*. The city fathers commissioned it as a documentary, to be made by "the mad poet of Manitoba," as a Canadian magazine termed him. Maddin has never left his hometown, although, judging by this film, it has left him. It has abandoned its retail landmarks, its sports traditions, and even the daily local soap opera, *Ledge Man*, which ran for fifty years and starred Maddin's mother. As every episode opened, a man was found standing on a ledge and threatening to jump, and Maddin's mother talked him out of it.

Is that true? It's as true as anything else in the film. My friend Tony Scott of the *New York Times* thought he should check out some of the facts in *My Winnipeg* but decided not to. Why should he doubt the film? I certainly believe that after a stable fire at the racetrack, terrified horses stampeded into a freezing river and were frozen into place—their heads rising from the ice for the rest of the winter, for skaters to picnic on. I believe there are two taxi companies, one serving streets, and the other back lanes shown on no map. I believe

Guy Maddin himself was born in the Winnipeg Arena during a game, nursed in the women's dressing room, and brought back a few days later for his first hockey match.

I also believe this because it is shown in the film: After Manitoba joined the hated (American-controlled) National Hockey League, the arena was enlarged to hold larger crowds. When the tragic decision was made to destroy the beloved arena by demolition, only the new parts collapsed, leaving the bones of the old arena still standing. "Demolition is one of our few growth industries," he says, acting as his own narrator.

Maddin was raised in this city, which he says has "ten times the sleepwalking rate" of any other. His childhood occurred in a house built as three white squares, one for his mother's beauty parlor, one for his aunt's family, one for his own. The scents of the parlor drifted up into his bedroom, and "every word of conversation swirled up out of that gynocracy." He attended a convent school named the Academy of the Super Vixens, ruled by "ever-opiating nuns."

Many of these facts are glimpsed through the windows of a train that seems headed out of town but never gets there. The narration is hallucinatory: "Old dreamy addresses, addresses, addresses, dreamy river forks. We see maps of the rivers fading into the fork of a woman's loin and back again." We are told that shadow-rivers flow beneath the visible ones. That the local madams were highly respected and streets were named after them and their brothels. That white-bearded Mayor Cornish (Louis Negin) personally judged the city's annual Golden Boy pageant, measuring biceps and thighs before scandal forced him out: too many Golden Boys on the city payroll!

I try to evoke, but I have failed! Failed! Disaster! I have tried to evoke the opiations of Guy Maddin, only to discover that the mother in the film is played by Ann Savage, star of *Detour*. Yes! A film in the Great Movies Collection of my Web site! Detour! Rocky road ahead! Savage! Maddin's father lies in state under a rug in the living room! Dead—not forgotten. Savage stepping around him! Watch your step. Savage! See this film!

N

National Treasure:
Book of Secrets ★ ★
PG, 104 m., 2007

Nicolas Cage (Ben Gates), Jon Voight (Patrick Gates), Harvey Keitel (Sadusky), Ed Harris (Jeb Wilkinson), Diane Kruger (Abigail Chase), Justin Bartha (Riley Poole), Bruce Greenwood (U.S. President), Helen Mirren (Emily Appleton). Directed by Jon Turteltaub and produced by Jerry Bruckheimer and Turteltaub. Screenplay by Cormac Wibberley and Marianne Wibberley.

National Treasure: Book of Secrets has without a doubt the most absurd and fevered plot since, oh, say, *National Treasure* (2004). What do I mean by fevered? What would you say if I told you that Mount Rushmore was carved only in order to erase landmarks pointing to a fabled City of Gold built inside the mountain? That the holders of this information involved John Wilkes Booth and a Confederate secret society named the Knights of the Golden Circle? And that *almost exactly the same people* who tracked down the buried treasure in the first movie are involved in this one?

Yes, even the same FBI agent and the same national archivist and Benjamin Franklin Gates (Nicolas Cage) and his father, Patrick Henry Gates (Jon Voight). They're famous now (one has written a best-seller), but they *never* discuss the coincidence that they are involved in an uncannily similar adventure. Yes, once again they are all trapped within the earth and dangling over a terrifying drop. And their search once again involves a secret document and a hidden treasure. No, this time it's not written in invisible ink on the back of the Declaration of Independence. It involves a missing page from Booth's diary, a coded message, an extinct language, and a book that each U.S. president hands over to his successor, which contains the truth about Area 51, the so-called moon landings, Nixon's missing eighteen minutes, the JFK assassination, and, let's see . . . oh, yeah, the current president would like to know what's on page 47, although if he is the only man allowed to look at the book, how does he know that he doesn't know what's on page 47?

I have only scratched the surface. The heroes of this tale have what can only be described as extraordinary good luck. Benjamin once again is an intuitive code breaker, who has only to look at a baffling conundrum to solve it. And what about their good fortune when they are on top of Mount Rushmore, looking for hidden signs, and Benjamin interprets an ancient mention of "rain from a cloudless sky" and passes out half-liter bottles of drinking water for everyone to sprinkle on the rock so the old marking will show up? It's not a real big mountain, but it's way too big for six people to sprinkle with Crystal Geyser. But, hey! After less than a minute of sprinkling, here's the mark of the spread eagle!

Compared to that, the necessity of kidnapping the president from his own birthday party and leading him into a tunnel beneath Mount Vernon is a piece of cake, even though it is never quite made clear how Benjamin knows about the tunnel. Oh, yeah: He has George Washington's original blueprints. For that matter, it's never explained why so many people over so many generations have spent so much time and money guarding the City of Gold. And why leave clues if they are designed never to be interpreted, and for that matter you don't want anyone to interpret them? And although lots of gold has been mined in South Dakota, how much would it take to build a *city*? Remember, all the gold in Fort Knox is only enough to fill Fort Knox, which is about as big as City Hall in the underground city.

Yes, I know, all of this is beside the point. That person who attends *National Treasure: Book of Secrets* expecting logic and plausibility is on a fool's mission. This is a Mouth Agape Movie, during which your mouth hangs open in astonishment at one preposterous event after another. This movie's plot plays tennis not only without a net, but also without a ball or a racket. It spins in its own blowback. And, no, I don't know what that means, but this is the kind of movie that makes you think of writing it.

I gotta say, the movie has terrific if completely unbelievable special effects. The actors had fun, I guess. You might, too, if you like goofiness like this. Look at the cast: Cage and Voight and Helen Mirren and Ed Harris and

Diane Kruger and Harvey Keitel and Justin Bartha and Bruce Greenwood. You could start with a cast like that and make one of the greatest movies of all time, which is not what happened here.

New in Town ★ ★
PG, 96 m., 2009

Renee Zellweger (Lucy Hill), Harry Connick Jr. (Ted Mitchell), J. K. Simmons (Stu Kopenhafer), Siobhan Fallon Hogan (Blanche Gunderson), Frances Conroy (Trudy Van Uuden). Directed by Jonas Elmer and produced by Paul Brooks, Darryl Taja, Tracey Edmonds, and Peter Safran. Screenplay by Kenneth Rance and C. Jay Cox.

We open on a gathering of the Scrappers Club, four women around a kitchen table pasting things into scrapbooks. The moment we hear one of them talking, we're not too surprised to find her name is Blanche Gunderson. Her sister Marge, the trooper, must have been the ambitious one. Not that Blanche isn't, just that she's relentlessly nice.

So are most of the folks in the small town of New Ulm, Minnesota, which is so cold in the winter that scrapping warms you up. Old Ulm (I know you were wondering) is the town on the Danube where Einstein was born. To this frigid outpost flies Lucy Hill, a high-powered exec from Miami, whose mission is to downsize the local food products plant more or less out of existence.

Lucy is the cute-as-a-button Renee Zellweger, so we know she's only kidding when she pretends to be a heartless rhymes-with-witch who hammers around on her stiletto heels and won't smile. That doesn't scare Blanche (Siobhan Fallon Hogan), Lucy's assistant, who invites her home for dinner ("We're only havin' meat loaf"). So uncannily does her accent resemble Marge in *Fargo* that I was trying to remember where I had heard it recently, doncha know?

The extra man at Blanche's table turns out to be Ted Mitchell (Harry Connick Jr.), the widowed dad of a thirteen-year-old girl, whom Blanche obviously thinks would be a great match for Lucy. That Ted, the union guy at the plant Lucy plans to downsize, is perhaps not a perfect match never even occurs to

Blanche, who like all Minnesotans and most Dakotans, is just plain nice. I mean that. I've been to Fargo. You should go sometime.

Ted doesn't seem nice at first, but then, jeez, he's originally from out of town, y'know. Ted and Lucy get in such a fight at the table that they both stalk out, which means they miss out on Blanche's famous tapioca pudding. Glossary Rule: Whenever a recipe is much discussed in the first act, it will be tasted in the third.

So firmly do we believe Lucy is visiting relatives of the *Fargo* cast that it's a surprise to learn *New in Town* was actually filmed in Winnipeg, which here looks nothing like the glittering metropolis in Guy Maddin's masterpiece. New Ulm consists of some houses, a VFW hall with a Friday fish fry, the food plant, and not a whole lot else except snow. But the people are friendly, hardworking, and proud of their plant, and soon Lucy softens, begins to like them, and reveals she was Renee Zellweger all along.

Because this is a romcom with no ambition in the direction of originality, Lucy is single, and Ted is the only eligible unmarried man in the cast, so do the math. The only remaining question is whether Lucy can save the plant, if you consider that much of a question. Am I giving too much away? This is the kind of movie that gives itself away. I've used that line before.

The real question is, do you like this sort of romcom? It's a fair example of its type, not good, but competent. The plant workers seem to function like the chorus in an opera, shutting down the line for Lucy's arias from a catwalk and moving as a unit with foreman Stu Kopenhafer (J. K. Simmons) always in the front. Simmons has grown a bushy beard and is wearing a fat suit (I hope), so you may not recognize him as Juno's dad. Let the bushy beard be a lesson: A bushy beard is the enemy of an actor's face unless he is playing Santa or attacking with a chainsaw.

The only question remaining after *New in Town* is, how come there's never a movie where a small-town girl leaves the snarly, greedy, job-ladder-climbing people behind and moves to the big city, where she is embraced by friendly folks, fed meat loaf and tapioca, and fixed up with Harry Connick Jr.?

Next Day Air ★ ★ ★
R, 90 m., 2009

Donald Faison (Leo), Mike Epps (Brody), Wood Harris (Guch), Omari Hardwick (Shavoo), Darius McCrary (Buddy), Yasmin Deliz (Chita), Mos Def (Eric), Emilio Rivera (Bodega), Cisco Reyes (Jesus), Debbie Allen (Ms. Jackson). Directed by Benny Boom and produced by Scott Aronson and Inny Clemons. Screenplay by Blair Cobbs.

Next Day Air is a bloody screwball comedy, a film of high spirits. It tells a complicated story with acute timing and clarity, and it gives us drug-dealing lowlifes who are almost poetic in their clockwork dialogue. By that I mean they not only use the words, they know the music.

Donald Faison stars in a cast of equals, as a pothead delivery man for the Next Day Air firm, who hurls around packages marked "Fragile!" as if he has never seen that word. Drifting in a cloud of weed, he delivers a package to the wrong apartment. Because it contains ten bricks of cocaine, this is a mistake, although perhaps not as fundamental as shipping it from L.A. to Philadelphia in the first place. FedEx and UPS have never lost anything of mine, but then, I've never shipped ten bricks of cocaine, which are likely to attract more attention than a signed copy of *Roger Ebert's Movie Yearbook 2009*.

The drugs are intended for a Latino couple (Cisco Reyes and Yasmin Deliz) and shipped by a cigar-smoking drug lord (Emilio Rivera) who is very annoyed when they are lost. He comes with his sidemen to pound some questions into Faison, who finally leads them to the apartment, where they find a gang of lousy bank robbers (Mike Epps, Wood Harris, Omari Hardwick) who got the shipment, and three men who plan to buy the drugs from them.

This puts, I dunno, nine or ten heavily armed men in a room of limited size. One reason the cops don't respond to the eventual gunfire is that the room simply couldn't hold them. Since a shotgun and an automatic rifle are included with their handguns and one of those gourmet carving knife sets, I'm not sure why the MPAA's R rating mentions "some violence." In the MPAA's coded terminology, the word "some" means "violence, but nothing to get too worked up about." I guess that's fair; there are none of those 3-D X-ray shots showing a bullet inching its way in slow motion through human organ meats.

A plot this complex, with so many characters to keep alive, could easily go astray. Indeed, I could make no sense of this week's *Perfect Sleep* despite a fulsome narration. But the director, Benny Boom, a music video director, knows what he's doing and skillfully intercuts the story strands. The first-time screenplay by Blair Cobbs has a lot of dire dialogue, very sunny, and presents the world's most inept bank robbers along with its most inept delivery man and most imprudent drug lord.

Nice surprise: Debbie Allen plays the manager of the delivery company, and gets a big laugh; no, not just because the audience sees she's Debbie Allen.

Nick and Norah's Infinite Playlist ★ ★
PG-13, 90 m., 2008

Michael Cera (Nick), Kat Dennings (Norah), Aaron Yoo (Thom), Rafi Gavron (Dev), Ari Graynor (Caroline), Alexis Dziena (Tris), Jonathan Wright (Lethario), Zachary Booth (Gary), Jay Baruchel (Tal). Directed by Peter Sollett and produced by Kerry Kohansky, Andrew Miano, Chris Weitz, and Paul Weitz. Screenplay by Lorene Scafaria, based on the novel by Rachel Cohn and David Levithan.

There is one merciful element to *Nick and Norah's Infinite Playlist*. The playlist is not infinite. The movie trudges around the Lower East Side of Manhattan in pursuit of a group of seventeen-somethings who are desperately seeking a mysterious band named Where's Fluffy. Clues are posted on the walls of toilet stalls, which are an unreliable source of information.

Nick and Norah have no relationship to the hero and heroine of *The Thin Man*, which I urgently advise you to watch instead of this film. That movie stars William Powell as a man who steadily drinks martinis and is never more than half-percolated. This one has a best friend character named Caroline (Ari Graynor) who drinks, I forget, I think it was banana daiquiris, and gets so drunk she ends up near Times Square in a toilet in the bus terminal, where she is fishing, not for Where's Fluffy clues, but for her gum, which fell into the toilet while she was vomiting. Didn't Ann Landers warn that this was one of the danger signals of alcoholism?

Nick and Norah are played by Michael Cera, best remembered as Juno's boyfriend, and Kat Dennings, best known for *The 40-Year-Old Virgin*, where she played anything but. They work well together, are appealing, and desperately require material as good as those films. Here they're not stupid; it's just that they're made to act stupidly. There's not much to recommend an all-night search through the dives of Manhattan for a lost friend who makes Britney Spears seem like a stay-at-home.

The two meet at a club, when Norah needs Nick to pose as her boyfriend to make her ex-boyfriend jealous. He is named Tal (Jay Baruchel). My first Chicago girlfriend was named Tal, which is Hebrew for "the morning dew." I don't think he knows that. So then, let's see, the plot requires an ex-girlfriend for Nick. This is Tris (Alexis Dziena), a blond vixen of the type that in most teeny movies is infinitely unattainable for nice kids like Nick.

Give Nick credit, he knows all about playlists. Tris has broken up with him as the movie opens, and he cuts many custom CDs for her in an attempt to win her back. These fall into the hands of Norah, who adores them, and What a Coincidence that Tris's ex is the very same guy she picked to play her pretend boyfriend. Ohmigosh. How Norah never previously saw Tris and Nick together is a good question since every character in this movie has built-in GPS equipment that allows them to stumble across any other character whenever the plot requires it.

I was relieved to observe that Nick doesn't drink as he pilots his battered Yugo around Manhattan. Ever notice how Yugos look like stretch Gremlins? People spot its bright yellow paint job and hail him, thinking it's a cab. This is impossible, since he doesn't have an illuminated sign for an Atlantic City casino on his roof.

Nick & Norah's Infinite Playlist lacks some of the idiocy of your average teenage romcom. But it doesn't bring much to the party. It sort of ambles along, with two nice people at the center of a human scavenger hunt. It's not much of a film, but it sort of gets you halfway there, like a Yugo.

Night at the Museum: Battle of the Smithsonian ★ ½
PG, 105 m., 2009

Ben Stiller (Larry Daley), Amy Adams (Amelia Earhart), Owen Wilson (Jedediah Smith), Hank Azaria (Kahmunrah/The Thinker), Christopher Guest (Ivan the Terrible), Alain Chabat (Napoleon Bonaparte), Ricky Gervais (Dr. McPhee), Steve Coogan (Octavius), Bill Hader (General Custer), Robin Williams (Teddy Roosevelt). Directed by Shawn Levy and produced by Levy, Chris Columbus, and Michael Barnathan. Screenplay by Robert Ben Garant and Thomas Lennon.

Don't trust me on this movie. It rubbed me the wrong way. I can understand, as an abstract concept, why some people would find it entertaining. It sure sounds intriguing: *Night at the Museum: Battle of the Smithsonian*. If that sounds like fun to you, don't listen to sourpuss here.

Oh, did I dislike this film. It made me squirmy. Its premise is lame, its plot relentlessly predictable, its characters with personalities that would distinguish picture books, its cost incalculable (well, $150 million). Watching historical figures enact the clichés identified with the most simplistic versions of their images, I found myself yet once again echoing the frequent cry of Gene Siskel: Why not just give us a documentary of the same actors having lunch?

One actor surpasses the material. That would be Amy Adams, as Amelia Earhart, because she makes Amelia sweet and lovable, although from what I gather, in real life that was not necessarily the case. I found myself looking forward to the upcoming biopic about Earhart with Hilary Swank. Over the closing credits, Bonnie Koloc could sing Red River Dave McEnery's "Amelia Earhart's Last Flight":

Just a ship out on the ocean, a speck against the sky,

Amelia Earhart flying that sad day;
With her partner, Captain Noonan, on
the second of July
Her plane fell in the ocean far away.

(Chorus)

There's a beautiful, beautiful field
Far away in a land that is fair,
Happy landings to you, Amelia Earhart,
Farewell, first lady of the air.

Sigh. Sort of floats you away, doesn't it? But then I crash-landed in the movie, where Amelia Earhart has to become the sidekick of Larry Daley (Ben Stiller), who has faked his résumé to get hired as a security guard and rescue his buddies from *Night at the Museum* (2006).

What has happened, see, is that the Museum of Natural History is remodeling. They're replacing their beloved old exhibits, like Teddy Roosevelt mounted on his horse, with ghastly new interactive media experiences. His friends are doomed to go into storage at the National Archives, part of the Smithsonian Institution. We see something of its sterile corridors stretching off into infinity; it looks just a little larger than Jorge Luis Borges's Library of Babel, and you remember how big *that* was.

However, Larry is able to manage one last night of freedom for them before the crates are filled with plastic popcorn. This is thanks to, I dunno, some kind of magic tablet of the villainous Pharaoh Kahmunrah (Hank Azaria). Among the resurrected are Teddy Roosevelt (Robin Williams), General Custer (Bill Hader), Ivan the Terrible (Christopher Guest), Octavius (Steve Coogan), and Albert Einstein (Eugene Levy). Also, the stuffed monkey from our first manned (or monkeyed) satellite, on a flight where the mission controller is played, of course, by Clint Howard, who has played mission controllers in something like half a dozen movies, maybe a dozen. When he gets a job, he already knows all of the lines. I could give you the exact number of the mission controllers he has played, but looking up Clint Howard's IMDb credits for a review of *Night at the Museum: Battle of the Smithsonian* seems like dissipation.

What is the motivation for the characters?

Obviously, the video game they will inspire. Wilbur Wright is here with the first airplane, and Amelia pilots the plane she went down in on that sad second of July. Rodin's Thinker (Hank Azaria) is somewhat distracted, his chin leaning on his hand, no doubt pondering such questions as: "Hey, aren't I supposed to be in the Musee Rodin in Paris?"

The reanimated figures are on three scales. Some are life-size. Some are larger-than-life-size, like the statue in the Lincoln Memorial on the National Mall. Some are the size of tiny action figures, and they're creepy, always crawling around and about to get stepped on. Nobody asks Abe Lincoln any interesting stuff like, "Hey, you were there—what did Dick Nixon really say to the hippies during his midnight visit to your memorial?"

I don't mind a good dumb action movie. I was the one who liked *The Mummy: Tomb of the Dragon Emperor*. But *Night at the Museum: Battle of the Smithsonian* is such a product. Like ectoplasm from a medium, it is the visible extrusion of a marketing campaign.

Nights in Rodanthe ★ ½

PG-13, 97 m., 2008

Richard Gere (Dr. Paul Flanner), Diane Lane (Adrienne Willis), Scott Glenn (Robert Torrelson), Christopher Meloni (Jack Willis), Viola Davis (Jean). Directed by George C. Wolfe and produced by Denise Di Novi. Screenplay by Ann Peacock and John Romano, based on the novel by Nicholas Sparks.

Nights in Rodanthe is what *Variety* likes to call a "weeper." The term is not often intended as praise. The movie attempts to jerk tears with one clunky device after another, in a plot that is a perfect storm of cliché and contrivance. In fact, it even contains a storm—an imperfect one.

The movie stars Richard Gere and Diane Lane, back again, together again, after *Unfaithful* (2002). I have no complaints about their work here. Admiration, rather, as they stay afloat in spite of the film's plot, location, voice-overs, and not-very-special effects. They are true movie stars and have a certain immunity against infection by dreck.

He plays Paul, a surgeon. She plays Adrienne, a mother of two, separated from her snaky husband. To help out a friend, she is taking care of a rustic inn on an island of the Outer Banks of North Carolina. He is the only weekend guest. He has booked it to "be by myself," he says, and also "to find someone to talk to." To summarize: These two beautiful, unhappy people are alone in a romantic beachfront inn. If the inn is really where it seems to be, on the edge of the water in a vast stretch of deserted, high-priced beach frontage, then it is not CGI and will soon be listed as *This Week* magazine's "steal of the week."

A hurricane is approaching. Hurricane warnings are issued just hours before it arrives. A grizzled old-timer at the local grocery wisely says it's gonna be real big. Adrienne stocks up on white bread. Having spent days watching CNN as little whirling twos and threes inched across the Gulf Coast, I would say this warning was belated. Paul doesn't evacuate because of some dialogue he is made to say. Adrienne doesn't because she promised her friend to look after the inn. They put up some shutters and have a jolly game of indoor basketball while tossing spoiled canned goods into a garbage can. "Ratatouille! Spam! Lard!"

The hurricane strikes. If it has a name, they don't know it. It blows off some shutters and cuts off the power. Do they face "certain death"? They cling to each other while sitting on the floor next to a bed. Then they cling to each other after getting into the bed. Have you ever made love during a hurricane that is shaking the house? I haven't. How did it go for you?

The hurricane bangs the shutters like *The Amityville Horror*. It must have no eye, so the wind only blows once. In the morning after the storm, the sun is shining and the inn is still standing. Remarkable, really, considering the photos from Galveston. It is a three- or four-story clapboard building, taller than it is wide, standing on stilts at the veritable water's edge. We see damage: a skateboard and a bike blown up. Some trees blown over. Just the most wonderful gnarly old piece of driftwood.

Reader, they fall in love. They deal with the real reason Paul came to Rodanthe, which I will say nothing about, except that it involves a grieving man who is well-played by Scott Glenn. Paul and Adrienne have found true love for the first time in their lives. Paul has an estranged son who has opened a clinic on a mountainside in Ecuador. He must go there.

They exchange letters. The mountainside has no telephones but excellent mail service. The letters serve the function of the notebook in the (much better) adaptation of Sparks's *Notebook*. These letters are read aloud in voice-overs that would not distinguish a soap opera. Does Paul find his son? Does Adrienne reunite with her snaky husband? Does her troubled and hostile teenage daughter turn into a honey bun from one scene to the next? Does the movie depend upon a deus ex machina to propel itself toward the lachrymose conclusion? Yes, no, yes, and yes.

Nobel Son ★ ★ ★
R, 110 m., 2008

Alan Rickman (Eli Michaelson), Bryan Greenberg (Barkley Michaelson), Shawn Hatosy (Thaddeus James), Mary Steenburgen (Sarah Michaelson), Eliza Dushku (City Hall), Bill Pullman (Max Mariner), Danny DeVito (George Gastner). Directed by Randall Miller and produced by Miller and Jody Savin. Screenplay by Savin and Miller.

When Alan Rickman portrays an egomaniacal, self-preening, heartless SOB, he seems to have found himself an autobiographical role. Since Rickman the human being (yes, there is such a thing) is kind, genial, and well-loved, he is in fact acting in *Nobel Son,* but who else could seem so utterly at home as a supercilious, snide, hurtful snake? I'm thinking maybe Richard E. Grant. The late Terry-Thomas, certainly. There isn't a long list.

Rickman plays a brilliant chemist named Eli Michaelson, the kind of man who, when he wins the Nobel Prize, those who know him best exclaim, "$#!t!" His wife loves her work as a forensic pathologist, perhaps because when she is disassembling the victim of a run-in with an auto crusher, she can imagine it is her husband. Eli belittles his son in all things. He considers his colleagues inferiors at best, insectoid at worst.

In *Nobel Son,* just when Eli is preparing to fly to Sweden and favor the crown with his presence, his son, Barkley (Bryan Greenberg), is kidnapped. The ransom: his $2 million prize money. I am reminded of the day I called my mother to tell her I had won the Pulitzer, and she said, "Oh, honey, does it pay anything?" She meant well. She just didn't see how I could make a living just . . . going to the movies, you know. Eli's inclination is to tell the kidnappers: "You keep my son, and I'll keep my money." Then a severed thumb arrives in the mail. Never a harbinger of good.

Nobel Son is a mercilessly convoluted version of a Twister, that genre in which the plot whacks us as if it's taking batting practice. I will not hint at anything that happens. I will simply observe that it's all entertaining. The plot by itself could have become tiresome; no audience enjoys spending all evening walking into stone walls. But the acting is another matter.

Rickman supplies the crown jewel in the cast, but Mary Steenburgen is no less amusing as his wife, Sarah. A woman can be married to a man like Eli only by being a masochist, insane, or in possession of a highly developed sense of sardonic irony. She doesn't talk like Alice Kramden on *The Honeymooners,* but you know what I mean. And Steenburgen's appearance is a pleasant surprise. She's so often cast as comic goofballs that it's good to be reminded that in a normal style and sensible clothes, she's a beauty and a charmer. This movie makes up for *Four Christmases.*

Shawn Hatosy plays the kidnapper, who gets up to more than we expect and less than he understands. Danny DeVito is a "recovering obsessive-compulsive" gardener, which is just as well because imagine how often you'd want to wash your hands in *that* line of work. Bill Pullman is a cop who thinks the whole setup stinks, and he's only sniffing at one corner of it.

These characters are, in order, Eli, Sarah, Barkley, Thaddeus, Max, and Gastner. All names right at home in a novel by Dickens. But then there's the brilliant writer played by Eliza Dushku, whom Barkley meets at a poetry reading. Her name is City Hall. Marry her, and every time you make a call from a bar it will sound important.

I have studiously avoided plot description because everything I said would be a lie or misleading. Assume these actors have not chosen this screenplay as a waste of their time. That would be *Four Christmases.* The plot is ingenious, the schemes are diabolical, and it is not every day that a character needs to inform us, "It is more cruel to eat the living than the dead," although now that I think about it, I agree. If you cannot follow every loop and coil of the plot, relax: Neither can the plot. At the end, by my calculations, the leftovers include one dead body and a hand without its thumb.

No Country for Old Men ★ ★ ★ ★
R, 123 m., 2007

Tommy Lee Jones (Sheriff Ed Tom Bell), Javier Bardem (Anton Chigurh), Josh Brolin (Llewelyn Moss), Woody Harrelson (Carson Wells), Kelly Macdonald (Carla Jean Moss), Garret Dillahunt (Deputy Wendell), Tess Harper (Loretta Bell). Direced by Ethan Coen and Joel Coen and produced by Coen, Coen, and Scott Rudin. Screenplay by Coen and Coen, based on the novel by Cormac McCarthy.

The movie opens with the flat, confiding voice of Tommy Lee Jones. He describes a teenage killer he once sent to the chair. The boy had killed his fourteen-year-old girlfriend. The papers described it as a crime of passion, "but he tolt me there weren't nothin' passionate about it. Said he'd been fixin' to kill someone for as long as he could remember. Said if I let him out of there he'd kill somebody again. Said he was goin' to hell. Reckoned he'd be there in about fifteen minutes."

These words sounded verbatim to me from *No Country for Old Men,* the novel by Cormac McCarthy, but I find they are not quite. And their impact has been improved upon in the delivery. When I get the DVD of this film, I will listen to that stretch of narration several times; Jones delivers it with a vocal precision and contained emotion that is extraordinary, and it sets up the entire film, which regards a completely evil man with wonderment, as if astonished that that such a merciless creature could exist.

The man is named Anton Chigurh. No, I don't know how his last name is pronounced. Like many of the words McCarthy uses, particularly in his masterpiece *Suttree,* I think it is employed like an architectural detail: The point is not how it sounds or what it means, but the brushstroke it adds to the sentence. Chigurh (Javier Bardem) is a tall, slouching man with lank black hair and a terrifying smile, who travels through Texas carrying a tank of compressed air and killing people with a cattle stun gun. It propels a cylinder into their heads and whips it back again.

Chigurh is one strand in the twisted plot. Ed Tom Bell, the sheriff played by Jones, is another. The third major player is Llewelyn Moss (Josh Brolin), a poor man who lives with his wife in a house trailer and one day, while hunting, comes across a drug deal gone wrong in the desert. Vehicles range in a circle like an old wagon train. Almost everyone on the scene is dead. They even shot the dog. In the back of one pickup are neatly stacked bags of drugs. Llewelyn realizes one thing is missing: the money. He finds it in a briefcase next to a man who made it as far as a shade tree before dying.

The plot will involve Moss attempting to make this $2 million his own, Chigurh trying to take it away from him, and Sheriff Bell trying to interrupt Chigurh's ruthless murder trail. We will also meet Moss's childlike wife, Carla Jean (Kelly Macdonald), a cocky bounty hunter named Carson Wells (Woody Harrelson), the businessman (Stephen Root) who hires Carson to track the money after investing in the drug deal, and a series of hotel and store clerks who are unlucky enough to meet Chigurh.

No Country for Old Men is as good a film as the Coen brothers, Joel and Ethan, have ever made, and they made *Fargo*. It involves elements of the thriller and the chase but is essentially a character study, an examination of how its people meet and deal with a man so bad, cruel, and unfeeling that there is simply no comprehending him. Chigurh is so evil he is almost funny sometimes; "He has his principles," says the bounty hunter, who has knowledge of him.

Consider another scene in which the dialogue is as good as any you will hear this year. Chigurh enters a rundown gas station in the middle of wilderness and begins to play a word game with the old man (Gene Jones) behind the cash register, who becomes very nervous. It is clear they are talking about whether Chigurh will kill him. Chigurh has by no means made up his mind. Without explaining why, he asks the man to call the flip of a coin. Listen to what they say, how they say it, how they imply the stakes. Listen to their timing. You want to applaud the writing, which comes from the Coen brothers, out of McCarthy.

The $2 million turns out to be easier to obtain than to keep. Moss tries hiding in obscure hotels. Scenes are meticulously constructed in which each man knows the other is nearby. Moss can run, but he can't hide. Chigurh always tracks him down. There seems to be a hole in the plot around here somewhere. Skip the next paragraph to avoid a spoiler.

Yes, the money briefcase has a transponder in it, but why does Chigurh have the corresponding tracker? If the men in the drug deal all killed each other and the man who unknowingly carried the transponder died under the tree, how did Chigurh come into the picture? I think it's because he set up the deal and planned to buy the drugs with the "invested" $2 million, end up with the drugs, and get the money back. That the actual dealers all killed each other in the desert and the money ended in the hands of a stranger was not his plan. That theory makes sense, or it would, if Chigurh were not so peculiar that it is hard to imagine him negotiating such a deal. "Do you have any idea," Carson Wells asks him, "how crazy you really are?"

Read safely again. This movie is a masterful evocation of time, place, character, moral choices, immoral certainties, human nature, and fate. It is also, in the photography by Roger Deakins, the editing by the Coens, and the music by Carter Burwell, startlingly beautiful, stark, and lonely. As McCarthy does with the Judge, the hairless exterminator in his *Blood Meridian* (Ridley Scott's next film), and as in his *Suttree,* especially in the scene where the river bank caves in, the movie demonstrates how pitiful ordinary human feelings are in the face of implacable injustice. The movie also loves some of its characters and pities them, and has an ear for dialogue not as it is spoken but as it is dreamed.

Many of the scenes in *No Country for Old Man* are so flawlessly constructed that you want them to simply continue, and yet they create an emotional suction, drawing you to the next scene. Another movie that made me

313

feel that way was *Fargo*. To make one such film is a miracle. Here is another.

No End in Sight ★ ★ ★ ★
NO MPAA RATING, 122 m., 2007

A documentary directed by Charles Ferguson and produced by Ferguson, Jenny Amias, Audrey Marrs, and Jessie Vogelson. Screenplay by Ferguson.

Remember the scene in *A Clockwork Orange* where Alex has his eyes clamped open and is forced to watch a movie? I imagine a similar experience for the architects of our catastrophe in Iraq. I would like them to see *No End in Sight,* the story of how we were led into that war and more than three thousand American lives and hundreds of thousands of other lives were destroyed.

They might find the film of particular interest because they would know so many of the people appearing in it. This is not a documentary filled with antiwar activists or sitting ducks for Michael Moore. Most of the people in the film were important to the Bush administration. They had top government or military jobs, they had responsibility in Iraq or Washington, they implemented policy, they filed reports, they labored faithfully in the service of U.S. foreign policy, and then they left the government. Some jumped, some were pushed. They all feel disillusioned about the war and the way the White House refused to listen to them about it.

The subjects in this film now feel that American policy in Iraq was flawed from the start, that obvious measures were not taken, that sane advice was disregarded, that lies were told and believed, and that advice from people on the ground was overruled by a cabal of neocon goofballs who seemed to form a wall around the president.

The president and his inner circle *knew*, just *knew*, for example, that Saddam had or would have weapons of mass destruction, that he was in league with al-Qaeda and bin Laden, and that in some way it was all hooked up with 9/11. Not all of the advice in the world could penetrate their obsession, and they fired the bearers of bad news.

It is significant, for example, that a Defense Intelligence Agency team received *orders* to find links between al-Qaeda and Saddam. That there were none was ignored. Key adviser Paul Wolfowitz's immediate reaction to 9/11 was "war on Iraq." Anarchy in that land was all but ensured when the Iraqi army was disbanded against the urgent advice of General Jay Garner, the American administrator, who was replaced by the neocon favorite Paul Bremer. That meant that a huge number of competent military men, most of them no lovers of Saddam, were rendered unemployed—and still armed. How was this disastrous decision arrived at? People directly involved said it came as an order from administration officials who had never been to Iraq.

Did Bush know and agree? They had no indication. Perhaps not. A national intelligence report commissioned in 2004 advised against the war. Bush, who apparently did not read it, dismissed it as guesswork—a word that seems like an ideal description of his own policies.

Who is Charles Ferguson, director of this film? Onetime senior fellow of the Brookings Institution, software millionaire, originally a supporter of the war, visiting professor at MIT and Berkeley, he was trustworthy enough to inspire confidence from former top officials. They mostly felt that orders came from the precincts of Vice President Cheney, that Cheney's group disregarded advice from veteran American officials, and in at least one case channeled a decision to avoid Bush's scrutiny. The president signed, but didn't read, and you can see the quizzical, betrayed looks in the eyes of the men and women in the film, who found that the more they knew about Iraq, the less they were heeded.

Although Bush and the war continue to sink in the polls, I know from some readers that they still support both. That is their right. And if they are so sure they are right, let more young men and women die or be maimed. I doubt they will be willing to see this film, which further documents an administration playing its private war games. No, I am distinctly not comparing anyone to Hitler, but I cannot help be reminded of the stories of him in his Berlin bunker, moving nonexistent troops on a map and issuing orders to dead generals.

No Reservations ★ ★

PG, 104 m., 2007

Catherine Zeta-Jones (Kate Armstrong), Aaron Eckhart (Nick Palmer), Abigail Breslin (Zoe), Patricia Clarkson (Paula), Bob Balaban (Therapist). Directed by Scott Hicks and produced by Sergio Aguero and Kerry Heysen. Screenplay by Carol Fuchs.

Here is a love story that ends "and they cooked happily ever after." It's the story of Kate, a master chef who rules her kitchen like a warden, and Nick, perhaps equally gifted, who comes to work for her and is seen as a rival. Since Kate is played by the beautiful Catherine Zeta-Jones and Nick by the handsome Aaron Eckhart, is there any doubt they will end up stirring the same pots and sampling the same gravies?

No Reservations also has something to do with how a woman "should" behave. Kate's restaurant is owned by Paula (Patricia Clarkson), who hauls Kate out front to meet her "fans" but wants her to stay in the kitchen when a customer complains. This is contrary to Kate's nature. She doesn't want to waste time glad-handing, but if anyone dares to complain about her pâté or her definition of "rare," she storms out of the kitchen, and soon the customer storms out of the restaurant. We've heard about male chefs throwing tantrums (I think it's required), but for Kate to behave in an unladylike manner threatens her job.

There's a subplot. Kate finds herself caring for round-eyed little Zoe (Abigail Breslin), the orphaned child of her sister. Kate has long since vowed never to marry or have children, so this is an awkward fit. But Zoe gets along fine with Nick, who lets her chop basil in the kitchen and tempts her with spaghetti, and soon she's playing matchmaker between the two grown-ups. From meeting in the refrigerator room for shouting matches, they progress to thawing the crab legs.

The movie is focused on two kinds of chemistry: of the kitchen and of the heart. The kitchen works better, with shots of luscious-looking food, arranged like organic still lifes. But chemistry among Nick, Kate, and Zoe is curiously lacking, except when we sense some fondness—not really love—between Zoe and her potential new dad.

Kate and Nick are required by the terms of the formula to be drawn irresistibly together, despite their professional rivalry. But I didn't feel the heat. There was no apparent passion; their courtship is so laid-back it seems almost like a theoretical exercise. For that matter, Kate treats little Zoe like more of a scheduling problem than a new adoptive daughter. The actors dutifully perform the rituals of the plot requirements but don't involve us (or themselves) in an emotional bond.

The movie is a remake of *Mostly Martha* (2002), a German film very much liked by many, unseen by me. Watching its trailer, I can't decide anything about the quality of the original film, but I do recognize many of the same scenes and even similar locations. *No Reservations* doesn't seem to reinvent it so much as recycle it.

There are some nice things in the film. Zeta-Jones is convincing as a short-tempered chef, if not as a replacement mom and potential lover. Clarkson balances on the tight wire a restaurant owner must walk. Bob Balaban, as Kate's psychiatrist, has a reserve that's comically maddening. Aaron Eckhart struggles manfully with an unconvincing character (is he really afraid to run his own kitchen?). We feel Abigail Breslin has the stuff to emerge as a three-dimensional kid if she weren't employed so resolutely as a pawn.

But *No Reservations*, directed by the usually superior Scott Hicks (*Shine, Hearts in Atlantis, Snow Falling on Cedars*), has too many reservations. It goes through the motions, but the characters seem to feel more passion for food than for one another.

Nothing but the Truth ★ ★ ★ ½

R, 106 m., 2009

Kate Beckinsale (Rachel Armstrong), Vera Farmiga (Erica Van Doren), Matt Dillon (Patton Dubois), Angela Bassett (Bonnie Benjamin), Alan Alda (Albert Burnside), David Schwimmer (Ray Armstrong), Floyd Abrams (Judge Hall). Directed by Rod Lurie and produced by Lurie, Bob Lari, and Marc Frydman. Screenplay by Lurie.

Alan Alda has a scene in *Nothing but the Truth* where he reads a dissenting Supreme Court opinion defending the right of journalists to protect confidential sources. I assumed the speech was genuine and was surprised to learn that the case inspiring the film was not heard by the Supreme Court. In fact the speech was written by Rod Lurie, the writer and director of the film, who would make an excellent Supreme if writing opinions were the only requirement. It was so soundly grounded in American idealism that I felt a patriotic stirring.

The film is obviously inspired by the case of Judith Miller, a *New York Times* reporter who served eighty-five days in prison for refusing to name her source in the Valerie Plame affair. That was the case in which Vice President Cheney's top aide blew the cover of a CIA agent in order to discredit the agent's husband, who investigated reports that Niger sold uranium to Saddam Hussein. He found no such evidence. The uranium story was part of the web of Bush-Cheney lies about WMDs that were used to justify the Iraq war.

The case is complicated, but if you know the general outlines, you can easily interpret Lurie's fictional story as a direct parallel to Miller/Valerie Plame/Joseph Wilson, though the names and specific details have been changed. In real life, Miller's reporting, accuracy, and objectivity were sharply questioned, and Lurie wisely sidesteps history to focus on the underlying question: Which is more important, the principle of confidentiality or national security? Trying to deal with the real Miller story would have trapped the film in a quicksand of complications.

I'm sure some readers are asking, why don't I just review the movie? Why drag in politics? If you are such a person, do not see *Nothing but the Truth*. It will make you angry or uneasy, one or the other. That Bush lied to lead us into Iraq is a generally accepted fact, and the movie regards a few of the consequences.

Lurie, however, has more on his mind than a political parable. The movie is above all a drama about the people involved, and his actors are effective at playing personalities, not symbols. Kate Beckinsale is Rachel Armstrong, the reporter for the *Capital Sun-Times*. Vera Farmiga is Erica Van Doren, the outed spy. Matt Dillon plays prosecutor Patton Dubois, obviously intended as U.S. prosecutor Patrick Fitzgerald, now so involved in the case

of our fascinating former Illinois governor. Alda is the high-priced Washington lawyer hired by the newspaper to defend Rachel. Angela Bassett is the newspaper's editor, under pressure to tart up coverage, trying to stand firm. And this is interesting: There is a wonderful performance by Floyd Abrams as the federal judge; in real life, he was Miller's attorney.

Armstrong and Van Doren are suburban Washington soccer moms whose children attend the same school. They know each other by sight. In possession of the leak, the reporter asks the agent point-blank if it is true, and the agent replies in terms Justice Scalia does not believe decent people use in public. It is a fierce scene.

Dubois, the prosecutor, calls Armstrong as a witness in his investigation of the leak, and she refuses to name her source. That begins her harrowing ordeal in jail, where eventually she has been behind bars longer than any sister prisoner. She will not tell, even though this decision estranges her husband (David Schwimmer), alienates her young son, and paints her as a heartless mother who places job above family.

How she is treated seems to go beyond reasonable punishment. Dillon, as Dubois, is positioned as the villain, but objectively he is only doing his job, and Dillon says he played the role as if he were the film's good guy. Alda comes on strong as a man not above boasting of his expensive Zegna suit, but grows so involved that he goes pro bono. The dire costs to both women are at the heart of things.

Lurie, who is a powerful screenwriter, is freed by fiction to do two very interesting things. (1) He presents the issues involved with great clarity. (2) He shows that a reporter's reasons for concealing a source may be more compelling than we guess. What is deeply satisfying about *Nothing but the Truth* is that the conclusion, which will come as a surprise to almost all viewers, is not a cheat, is plausible, and explains some unresolved testimony.

Nothing but the Truth is a finely crafted film of people and ideas, of the sort more common before the movie mainstream became a sausage factory. It respects the intelligence of the audience, it contains real drama, it earns its suspense, and it has a point to make. In the ordinary course of events, it would have had a high-profile release and plausibly won nominations. But the economic downturn struck down its distributor, the film missed its release window, and its life must be on DVD. It is far above the "straight-to-DVD" category, and I hope filmgoers discover that.   ☞

Notorious ★ ★ ★ ½
R, 122 m., 2009

Jamal "Gravy" Woolard (Notorious B.I.G.), Angela Bassett (Voletta Wallace), Derek Luke (Sean Combs), Anthony Mackie (Tupac Shakur), Antonique Smith (Faith Evans), Naturi Naughton (Lil' Kim). Directed by George Tillman Jr. and produced by Voletta Wallace, Wayne Barrow, Mark Pitts, Robert Teitel, and Trish Hofmann. Screenplay by Reggie Rock Bythewood and Cheo Hodari Coker.

He was known as Notorious B.I.G., a man-mountain of rap, but behind the image was Christopher Wallace, an overgrown kid who was trying to grow up and do the right thing. The image we know about. The film *Notorious* is more interested in the kid. He was born in Brooklyn, loved his mother—a teacher who was studying for a master's degree—got into street-corner drug dealing because he liked the money, performed rap on the street, and at twenty was signed by record producer Sean "Puffy" Combs. Four years later, he was dead.

Documentaries about B.I.G. have focused on the final years of his life. *Notorious* tells us of a bright kid who was abandoned by his father, raised by a mother from Jamaica who laid down the rules, and told the kids on the playground he would be famous someday. "You too fat, too black, and too ugly," a girl tells him. He just looks at her. He is sweet-tempered, even after being seduced into the street-corner crack business, but he sounds tough in his rap songs—he is tough, introspective, autobiographical, and a gifted writer.

His demo tape is heard by Sean Combs (Derek Luke), who is seen in the film as a good influence, in part perhaps because he's the executive producer. Combs draws a line between the street as a market and a place where he wants his artists to be seen. B.I.G. leaves the

drug business and almost overnight becomes a huge star, an East Coast rapper to match the West Coast artists such as Tupac Shakur.

Tupac was shot dead not long before B.I.G. was murdered, and the word was they died because of a feud between the East and West Coast dynasties and onetime friends B.I.G. and Tupac (Anthony Mackie). Another version, in Nick Broomfield's 2002 documentary *Biggie and Tupac,* is that both shootings were ordered by rap tycoon Suge Knight and carried out by off-duty LAPD officers in his hire. Broomfield produces an eyewitness and a bag man who says on camera that he delivered the money. The film, perhaps wisely, sidesteps this possibility.

Notorious is a good film in many ways, but its best achievement is the casting of Jamal Woolard, a rapper named Gravy, in the title role. He looks uncannily like the original, and Antonique Smith is a ringer for B.I.G.'s wife, Faith Evans. Woolard already knew how to perform but took voice lessons for six months at Juilliard to master B.I.G.'s sound. He performs a lot of music in the film, all of it plot-driven, sure to become a best-selling sound track. As an actor, he conveys the singer's complex personality: a mother's boy, a womanizer, an artist who accepts career guidance from his managers, a sentimentalist, an ominous presence.

The real B.I.G. may have had a harder side, but we don't see it here. Instead, director George Tillman Jr. and his writers, Reggie Rock Bythewood and Cheo Hodari Coker, craft an understated message picture in which B.I.G. eventually decides to accept responsibility for the children he has fathered, and as his mother, Voletta (Angela Bassett), urges him to do, become a man. Shortly before his death, he announces a new direction for his music.

Bassett doesn't play Voletta as a conventional grasping mamma. She believes in tough love and throws her son out of their apartment after she finds cocaine under the bed. Few actors are better at fierce resolve than Bassett, and she provides a baseline for her son's fall and eventual rise. The real Voletta is in the Broomfield documentary, where in 2002 she looks like . . . an older Angela Bassett.

George Tillman and his producing partner,

Robert Teitel, are Chicagoans who have, together and separately, been involved in some of the best recent films about African-American and minority characters: *Nothing Like the Holidays, Soul Food, Men of Honor,* both *Barbershop* pictures, *Beauty Shop.* None of these films is sanctimonious, none preaches, but in an unobtrusive way they harbor positive convictions. In *Notorious,* they show how talent can lift a kid up off the street corner but can't protect him in a culture of violence. The whole gangsta rap posture was dangerous, as B.I.G. and Tupac proved.

Note: Tupac: Resurrection, *an extraordinary 2002 documentary, uses hours of autobiographical tapes left behind by Shakur to allow him to narrate his own life story. He also proved his acting ability in* Gridlock'd, *Vondie Curtis-Hall's 1997 film where he costarred with Tim Roth.*

O

Ocean's Thirteen ★ ★ ½
PG-13, 122 m., 2007

George Clooney (Danny Ocean), Brad Pitt (Rusty Ryan), Matt Damon (Linus Caldwell), Andy Garcia (Terry Benedict), Don Cheadle (Basher Tarr), Bernie Mac (Frank Catton), Ellen Barkin (Abigail Spooder), Al Pacino (Willie Banks), Elliott Gould (Reuben Tishkoff). Directed by Steven Soderbergh and produced by Jerry Weintraub. Screenplay by Brian Koppelman and David Levien.

The genius of the past decays remorselessly into the routine of the present, and one example is the downfall of the caper picture.

The classic caper genre had rules set in stone. It began (1) with an impregnable fortress (vault, casino, museum, or even Fort Knox). Then we met (2) a group of men who hoped to impregnate it. There was (3) a setup about the defenses of the fortress, and (4) a chalk talk in which the mastermind told the others what they were going to do and how they were going to do it. This had the advantage of also briefing the audience, so that the actual caper could proceed in suspenseful silence while we understood what they were doing and why.

The modern caper movie, such as Steven Soderbergh's *Ocean's Thirteen,* dispenses with such tiresome exposition and contains mostly action and movie star behavior. Only the characters know what the plan is, and we are expected to watch in gratitude and amazement as they disclose it out of their offscreen planning and plotting. Fair enough, if it's done with energy and style. If, however, their plan involves elements that are preposterously impossible, I feel as if I'm watching one of Scrooge McDuck's schemes.

All of the *Ocean's* movies, including the long-ago Sinatra version (1960), are remade or inspired by a great French caper movie, Jean-Pierre Melville's *Bob le Flambeur* (*Bob the Gambler,* 1956), in which Bob actually laid down chalk lines in an open field to walk his accomplices through a raid on a casino. The movie is on DVD in the Criterion Collection;

see what you're missing now that the formula has been adapted for ADD sufferers.

Ocean's Thirteen begins as aging and beloved casino legend Reuben Tishkoff (Elliott Gould) plans to open his latest and greatest Vegas casino. Alas, he has taken for a partner the devious double-crosser Willie Banks (Al Pacino, very good), who swindles him out of the casino and lands him in the emergency room with shock and grief. Then Reuben's loyal friends (played by George Clooney, Brad Pitt, Don Cheadle, Bernie Mac, Matt Damon, etc.) gather at his bedside and vow to sabotage the opening of the new casino.

I don't know what kind of resources these rootless but glamorous men have, except that they are apparently unlimited. They manufacture trick card shufflers, sabotage the roulette wheels, and even give the man they think is the guru of casino ratings (David Paymer) something resembling the heartbreak of psoriasis. These plans are not explained; they are simply pulled out of the heroes' hats, or thin air.

To be sure, Soderbergh is a gifted director and (under a pseudonym) cinematographer, and he has a first-rate cast. Most of the audience will probably feel they got their money's worth, and that's the bottom line. But I grew impatient with the lickety-split pacing. This material is interesting enough that it needs care and attention, not the relentlessness of a slide show.

I know full well I'm expected to Suspend My Disbelief. Unfortunately, my disbelief is very heavy, and during *Ocean's Thirteen* the suspension cable snapped. I think that was when they decided to manufacture a fake earthquake to scare all the high-rollers on opening night. How did they plan to do this? Why, by digging under the casino with one of the giant tunnel-boring machines used to dig the Eurotunnel between France and England.

Yes, you can buy your own. There were originally eleven. One sold on eBay for around $7 million. A boring machine, I find, weighs about six hundred tons. How easy do you think it would be for a handful of Vegas slicksters to buy such a machine, transport it to America, move it cross-country, and use it to drill a tunnel under the Strip (which never sleeps), all the while removing untold tons of earth, rock, and sand without being noticed? And without causing earthquakes in all the other casinos they bored under?

I am reminded of that IMAX documentary about climbing Mount Everest. All I could think of was, if it's hard for the climbers, think about how hard it is for the guys carrying the big IMAX camera up the mountain. I wanted to see a doc about them. Now if you had a movie about smuggling a six-hundred-ton tunnel-boring machine under Vegas, *that* would be a caper.

Ocean's Thirteen proceeds with insouciant dialogue, studied casualness, and a lotta stuff happening, none of which I cared much about because the movie doesn't pause to make do develop the characters, who are forced to make do with their movie star personas. Take Don Cheadle, for example. After the magnificence of his performance in *Hotel Rwanda* and the subtle, funny, sad power of his leading role in Kasi Lemmons's upcoming *Talk to Me*, we get him hanging around in this picture looking like they needed him to get to thirteen. I guess he has to make movies like this to pay the mortgage. My advice? Rent. You have no idea the headaches of home ownership.

Of Time and the City ★ ★ ★ ½
NO MPAA RATING, 77 m., 2009

A documentary directed by Terence Davies and produced by Solon Papadopoulos and Roy Boutler. Screenplay by Davies.

The streets of our cities are haunted by the ghosts of those who were young here long ago. In memory we recall our own past happiness and pain. Terence Davies, whose subject has often been his own life, now turns to his city, Liverpool, and regrets not so much the joys of his youth as those he did not have. Central to these are the sexual experiences forbidden by the Catholic Church to which he was most devoted.

Liverpool was once a shipbuilding capital of the world, later a city broken by unemployment and crime, and now a recovering city named the European Capital of Culture in 2008. For many people, Liverpool's cultural contribution begins and ends with the Beatles, and Davies does little to update that view except to focus on its postwar architecture, which is grotesque, and its modern architecture, much improved, but still lacking the grandeur of the city's Victorian glory.

The way Davies and his cinematographer, Tim Pollard, regard heritage buildings and churches, their domes and turrets worthy of an empire, suggests that he, like me, prefers buildings that express a human fantasy and not an abstract idea. What is it that makes the Hancock magnificent and Trump Tower appalling? Not just the Trump's bright, shiny tin appearance, the busy proportions of its facade, or its see-through parking levels, but a lack of modesty and confidence. It insists too much. On the other hand, there is nothing modest about the grandiloquent civic structures of Liverpool, but their ornate cheekiness is sort of touching. They had no idea they were monuments to the end of an era.

In this city Davies was born into modest circumstances, was shaped and defined by the Church, was tortured by his forbidden homosexual feelings, and gradually grew to reject the Church and the British monarchy. He remembers a boy who put a hand on his shoulder "and I didn't want him to take it away." In his parish, Church of the Sacred Heart, "I prayed until my knees bled," but release never came.

These memories are mixed with those of the city, suggested with remarkable archival footage collated from a century: crowds in the streets and at the beach, factories, shipyards, faces, movie theaters, snatches of song, long-gone voices, an evocation of a city tuned in to the BBC for the Grand National, a long-gone horse and rider falling at the first hurdle, the wastelands surrounding new public housing, children and dogs at play, and, yes, the Beatles.

The sound track includes classical music and pop tunes, and the deep, rich voice of Davies, sometimes quoting poems that match the images. The film invites a reverie. It inspired thoughts of the transience of life. It reminded me sharply of Guy Maddin's *My Winnipeg* (2008), which combined old footage and new footage that looked even older into the portrait of a city that existed only in his imagination. I imagine the city fathers in both places were astonished by what their sons had wrought, although in Winnipeg they would have found a great deal more to amuse them.

O'Horten ★ ★ ★ ½
PG-13, 89 m., 2009

Baard Owe (Odd Horten), Espen Skjonberg (Trygve Sissener), Githa Norby (Mrs. Thogersen), Bjorn Floberg (Flo), Kai Remlov (Steiner Sissener), Henny Moan (Svea). Directed and produced by Bent Hamer. Screenplay by Hamer.

The thing about a deadpan comedy is it has to think. It must involve us in the lives of its characters so we can understand why they are funny while at the same time so distant. *O'Horten*, a bittersweet whimsy by the Norwegian director Bent Hamer, finds that effortless. It is about a retiring railroad engineer named Odd Horten. *Odd* is a common enough first name in Norway, but reflect that English is widely used in Scandinavia.

O'Horten is a quiet, reflective man, a pipe smoker who lives alone but is not lonely and sets his life by the railroad timetable. He is baffled by retirement. He's not sure when he should be anywhere. After the retirement party thrown by his fellow engineers, who sing him a "choo-choo-choo woo-woo-woo" song, he is uncertain. An evening begins on an inauspicious note when he is unable to get into a colleague's apartment, climbs a scaffolding in freezing weather, lets himself into someone else's window, and finds himself in conversation with a small boy.

O'Horten has his consolations. One is Mrs. Thogersen (Githa Norby), a sweet, silvery-haired widow who lives at the end of the Oslo–Bergen run. He is accustomed to overnighting in her arms. "So . . . this is the end?" she asks on his last run. Apparently so. It doesn't occur to him that they could rendezvous without him driving a train there.

Left to his own devices, O'Horten allows himself to be drawn into uncertain circumstances. There is the case of Trygve Sissener (Espen Skjonberg), a curious old man who informs O'Horten, "Ever since I was young, I have been able to see with my eyes closed." To prove it, he takes O'Horten on a drive through Oslo with a black hood pulled over his head. You would think this would be terrifying for an engineer who once hit a moose on the tracks, but no. He puffs his pipe, interested.

His Oslo resembles the macabre Stockholm of the director Roy Andersson, whose *Songs from the Second Floor* we showed at Ebertfest a few years ago. Inexplicable events seem to be a matter of course. Why, for example, would well-dressed businessmen slide on their fannies down an icy incline? O'Horten is probably wondering the same thing but doesn't inquire.

Odd is played by Baard Owe, a trim, fit man with a neat mustache, who may cause you to think a little of James Stewart, Jacques Tati, or Jean Rochefort. He has some regrets. He was never an Olympic ski jumper like his mother. Too afraid. He never really developed any hobbies. He has few friends. He was on the rails too much. He prides himself in perfection on the job but has no need for perfection in his life. At least a pipe smoker can always count on his pipe.

Once ★ ★ ★ ★
R, 85 m., 2007

Glen Hansard (Guy), Marketa Irglova (Girl), Hugh Walsh (Drummer), Gerry Hendrick (Guitarist), Alastair Foley (Bassist), Geoff Minogue (Eamon). Directed by John Carney and produced by Martina Niland. Screenplay by Carney.

I'm not at all surprised that my esteemed colleague Michael Phillips of the *Chicago Tribune* selected John Carney's *Once* as the best film of 2007. I gave it my Special Jury Prize, which is sort of an equal first; no movie was going to budge *Juno* off the top of my list. *Once* was shot for next to nothing in seventeen days, doesn't even give names to its characters, is mostly music with not a lot of dialogue, and is magical from beginning to end. It's one of those films where you hold your breath, hoping it knows how good it is and doesn't take a wrong turn. It doesn't. Even the ending is the right ending, the more you think about it.

The film is set in Dublin, where we see a street musician singing for donations. This is the Guy (Glen Hansard). He attracts an audience of the Girl (Marketa Irglova). She loves his music. She's a pianist herself. He wants to hear her play. She doesn't have a piano. He takes her to a music store where he knows the owner, and they use a display piano. She plays some Mendelssohn. We are in love with this movie. He is falling in love with her. He just sits there and listens. She is falling in love with him. She just sits there and plays. There is an unusual delay before we get the obligatory reaction shot of the store owner, because all the movie wants to do is sit there and listen, too.

This is working partly because of the deeply good natures we sense these two people have. They aren't "picking each other up." They aren't flirting—or, well, technically they are, but in that way that means "I'm not interested unless you're too good to be true." They love music, and they're not faking it. We sense to a rare degree the real feelings of the two of them; there's no overlay of technique, effect, or style. They are just purely and simply themselves.

Hansard is a professional musician, well known in Ireland as leader of a band named the Frames. Irglova is an immigrant from the Czech Republic, only seventeen years old, who had not acted before. She has the kind of smile that makes a man want to be a better person so he can deserve being smiled at.

The film develops their story largely in terms of song. In between, they confide their stories. His heart was broken because his girlfriend left him and moved to London. She takes him home to meet her mother, who speaks hardly any English, and to join three neighbors who file in every night to watch their TV. And he meets her child, which comes as a surprise. Then he finds out she's married. Another surprise, and we sense that in his mind he had already dumped the girl in London and was making romantic plans. He's wounded, but brave. He takes her home to meet his dad, a vacuum cleaner repairman. She has a Hoover that needs fixing. It's kismet.

He wants to record a demo record, take it to London, and play it for music promoters. She helps him, and not just by playing piano. When it comes down to it, she turns out to be levelheaded, decisive, take-charge. An ideal producer. They recruit other street musicians

for a session band, and she negotiates a rock-bottom price for a recording studio. And so on. All with music. And all with their love, and our love for their love, only growing. At one point he asks if she loves him, and she answers in Czech, and the movie doesn't subtitle her answer because if she'd wanted subtitles, she would have answered in English, which she speaks perfectly well.

Once is the kind of film I've been pestered about ever since I started reviewing again. People couldn't quite describe it, but they said I had to see it. I *had* to. Well, I did. They were right.

The Orphanage ★ ★ ★ ½
R, 106 m., 2007

Belen Rueda (Laura), Fernando Cayo (Carlos), Roger Princep (Simon), Geraldine Chaplin (Aurora), Mabel Rivera (Pilar), Montserrat Carulla (Benigna). Directed by Juan Antonio Bayona and produced by Guillermo del Toro, Alvaro Augustin, Joaquin Padro, and Mar Targarona. Screenplay by Sergio G. Sanchez.

Now here is an excellent example of why it is more frightening to await something than to experience it. *The Orphanage* has every opportunity to descend into routine shock and horror, or even into the pits with the slasher pictures, but it pulls the trigger only a couple of times. The rest is all waiting, anticipating, dreading. We need the genuine jolt that comes about midway to let us see what the movie is capable of. The rest is fear.

Hitchcock was very wise about this. In his book-length conversation with Truffaut, he used a famous example to explain the difference between surprise and suspense. If people are seated at a table and a bomb explodes, that is surprise. If they are seated at a table and you know there's a bomb under the table attached to a ticking clock, but they continue to play cards, that's suspense. There's a bomb under *The Orphanage* for excruciating stretches of time.

That makes the film into a superior ghost story, if indeed there are ghosts in it. I am not sure: They may instead be the experience or illusion of ghosts in the mind of the heroine, and since we see through her eyes, we see what she sees and are no more capable than she is of being certain. That means when she walks down a dark staircase, or into an unlit corridor or a gloomy room, we're tense and fearful, whether we're experiencing a haunted house or a haunted mind. And when she follows her son into a pitch-black cave, her flashlight shows only a thread of light through unlimited menace.

The movie centers on Laura (Belen Rueda), who as a young girl was raised in the orphanage before being taken away one day and adopted. Now in her thirties, she has returned with her husband, Carlos (Fernando Cayo), and their young son, Simon (Roger Princep), to buy the orphanage and run it as a home for sick or disabled children. She has memories here, most of them happy, she believes, but as images begin to swim into her mind and even her vision, she has horrifying notions about what might have happened to the playmates she left behind on that summer day thirty years ago.

Simon, too, seems disturbed, and since no other children have arrived, he creates imaginary playmates. One of them, a boy with a sack over his head, he shows in a drawing to his mother, who is startled because this very image exists in her own mind. Does that mean—well, what could it mean? Telepathy? Or the possibility that Simon, too, is the product of her imagination? The line between reality and fantasy is so blurred in the film that it may even be, however unlikely, that Simon exists and is imagining her.

It matters not for us because we are inside Laura's mind no matter what. And when a decidedly sinister "social worker" (Montserrat Carulla) turns up, he learns because of her that he is adopted and dying. He apparently runs away, even though he needs daily medication. His parents spend months searching for him, putting posters everywhere, convinced he is not dead. But many children may have died at the orphanage. The parents consult a psychic (Geraldine Chaplin), who possibly provides what people claim they want from a psychic (but really don't): the truth.

The film, a Spanish production directed by Juan Antonio Bayona and produced by Guillermo del Toro (*The Devil's Backbone, Pan's Labyrinth*), is deliberately aimed at viewers with developed attention spans. It lingers to create atmosphere, a sense of place, a sympathy with the characters, instead of rushing into cheap thrills. Photographed by Oscar Faura, it has an uncanny way of re-creating that feeling we get when we're in a familiar building at an unfamiliar time, and we're not quite sure what to say if we're found there, and we might have just heard something, and why did the lights go out? You may be capable of walking into any basement on Earth, but if you go down the stairs into the darkened basement of the house you grew up in, do you still . . . feel something?

OSS 117: Cairo, Nest of Spies ★ ★ ★
NO MPAA RATING, 99 m., 2008

Jean Dujardin (Hubert Bonisseur de la Bath), Berenice Bejo (Larmina El Akmar Betouche), Aure Atika (Princess Al Tarouk), Philippe Lefebvre (Jack Jefferson), Constantin Alexandrov (Setine). Directed by Michel Hazanavicius and produced by Eric Altmayer and Nicolas Altmayer. Screenplay by Jean-Francois Halim, based on the novels by Jean Bruce.

Well, to begin with, *OSS 117: Cairo, Nest of Spies* is a terrific title. Better than the film, but there you are. Watching it, I began to shape a review about how its hero, French agent 117, was influenced by James Bond out of Inspector Clouseau and Austin Powers (try not to picture that). But then I discovered from *Variety* that the character Agent 117 actually appeared in a novel in 1949; its author, Jean Bruce, wrote no less than 265 novels about him, qualifying for second place, I guess, behind Georges Simenon's Inspector Maigret. And the agent appeared in seven earlier movies.

The books and movies, I gather (not having read or seen any of them), were more or less straightforward action, so although Ian Fleming may have created 007 with a debt to 117, what he brought new to the table was the idea of comedy. And if the Bond movies are themselves quasi-serious on some level, Mike Myers went completely over the top with Austin Powers, inspiring the makers of this new film to try to make *him* seem laid-back.

323

Their agent is now the subject of a parody so far over the top that, well, it's not every day you see two spies fighting by throwing dead chickens at each other.

The movie stars Jean Dujardin as Agent 117 (real name: Hubert Bonisseur de la Bath), whom in 1955 is sent by the French secret service to Egypt to deflect the impending Suez crisis, bring peace among the Americans, Russians, and Egyptians, and settle the problems of the Arab world. No problem-o. Jean Dujardin, who looks more than a little like the young Sean Connery, is in a Bondian film that begins with an extreme action sequence, has titles based on the view through a roving gun sight, and cuts directly to Rome and 117 in a tuxedo, making out with a beauty garbed in satin, who tries to stab him in the back.

The movie travels familiar ground, with a nod as well to *Top Secret, Airplane!* and that whole genre. Even compared to them, it pushes things just a little—not too far, but toward the loony. For example, Agent 117's cover role in Cairo is as the owner of a wholesale chicken business. When he discovers that the chickens cluck and the roosters crow when the lights are on, but not when they're off, he has no end of fun playing with the light switch. This is a guy who's short some bulbs.

How stupid is he? Leaving Rome for Cairo, he meets his local contact, a lithesome beauty named Larmina El Akmar Betouche (Berenice Bejo) and on the trip from the airport complains about how much dust there is in the desert. Shown the Suez Canal, he congratulates the Egyptians for having the foresight to dig it four thousand years ago. He assures her that Arabic is a ridiculous language, and she is dreaming if she thinks millions of people speak it. And his sleep is interrupted one morning by a call to prayer from a muezzin in the tower of a nearby mosque. "Shut the **** up!" he bellows out the window, and then climbs the tower and silences the troublemaker.

The movie relishes its 1955 look, not just in the costumes and locations, but in such details as special effects and fight scenes. Remember hand-to-hand combat pre–Bruce Lee? No end of tables and chairs get trashed, while the distinctly Bondian musical score pounds away relentlessly. One nice 1950s touch: "Cigarette?" he's asked. "I'm trying to start," he replies.

For a parody, the movie is surprisingly competent in some of the action scenes, when the dim-witted hero turns out to have lightning improvisational skills. And there is an escape scene that develops in unforeseen ways. Dujardin is somehow able to play his clueless hero as a few degrees above the doofus level, mixing in a little suave seductiveness and then effortlessly drifting into charmingly crafted comments that are bold insults, if only he understood that.

My only problem is, there's a little too much of 117. Only ninety-nine minutes long, it nevertheless seems to go on more than necessary. There is a limit to how long such a manic pitch can be maintained. It's the kind of film that might seem funnier if you kept running across twenty minutes of it on cable. Yet I suppose that is not a fatal fault, and I have developed the same kind of affection for 117 that I have for Austin Powers. Who else would tell that lithesome beauty, "You're not a Lebanese reporter posted to Rome! You're actually the niece of Egypt's King Farouk!" It was the "Egypt's King Farouk" part that got me. Like she didn't know who he was. And like he didn't know Farouk had been deposed by Nasser. Well, that I can believe.

Outlander ★ ★
R, 115 m., 2009

Jim Caviezel (Kainan), Sophia Myles (Freya), Jack Huston (Wulfric), Ron Perlman (Gunnar), John Hurt (Rothgar). Directed by Howard McCain and produced by Chris Roberts. Screenplay by McCain and Dirk Blackman.

I am tempted to describe the plot of *Outlander* as preposterous, but a movie about an alien spaceship crashing into a Viking fjord during the Iron Age is *likely* to be preposterous. Two alien life forms survive the crash: Kainan and a monster known as "the Moorwen." Kainan, played by Jim Caviezel, looks exactly like a human being. The Moorwen looks like a giant, speedy, armored hippo-beetle with a toothy front end designed in the same forges of hell that produced the alien in *Alien*.

Kainan was returning from the Moorwen's home planet, which his race had terraformed, not quite wiping out all the Moorwens. The creatures counterattacked, wiping out most of Kainan's fellow settlers; what he doesn't realize is that one Moorwen was onboard ship when he blasted off. Kainan uses a handy device to pump the local Earth language (Viking, spoken in English) into his mind through his eyeball and soon encounters the nearest Viking village.

Having seen more than a few movies, we intuit that this village will contain a venerable king (Rothgar, played by John Hurt), his bodacious daughter (Freya, played by Sophia Myles), a jealous young warrior (Wulfric, played by Jack Huston), and a menacing dissident (Gunnar, played by Ron Perlman). There are also numerous villagers who stand around in the background looking intensely interested.

The village is suspicious of this strange "outlander." Then Vikings start to disappear in the forest, and Kainan realizes he has brought along a passenger. After he saves Rothgar from the Moorwen, he wins royal favor and organizes the village in a plan to lure the beast into a deep pit with stakes at the bottom and burn it alive.

I began my study of science fiction at the age of nine, with *Tom Corbett, Space Cadet*. I grew to love the authors who incorporated as much science as possible: Clarke, Asimov, Heinlein. They would have had questions about Kainan. For example, is he as human as he appears? It seems unlikely from a Darwinian point of view that two human species should evolve independently and contemporaneously on separate worlds. Even more so that they would share common sexual feelings and be able to mate, although that is precisely what Kainan and Freya propose.

But yes, their love flowers, against a backdrop of Arthurian romance. The Moorwen is the dragon, of course. And much depends on a sword mighty enough to pierce its armor. To forge this Excalibur, Kainan dives into the fjord and retrieves scrap steel from the wreckage of his ship, thus bringing the Iron Age to a quick close—in this village, anyway. The climax involves the usual violent and incoherent special effects scenes, after which Rothgar gives Kainan the hand of his daughter, and Kainan and Freya presumably retire to discover if separate evolutionary paths have outfitted them with compatible fixtures.

Outlander is interesting as a collision of genres: The monster movie meets the Viking saga. You have to give it credit for carrying that premise to its ultimate (if not logical) conclusion. It occurs to me, however, that the Moorwen had legitimate reason to be grieved. First Kainan's race appropriated the Moorwen planet for its own purposes, then it massacred the Moorwens, now it was picking off a survivor. Do you think genocide or colonialism are concepts to be found in *Outlander*? Not a chance. That's because Kainan is so human, and the Moorwens are, well, just not our sort.

Outsourced ★ ★ ★
PG-13, 102 m., 2007

Josh Hamilton (Todd Anderson), Ayesha Dharker (Asha), Asif Basra (Purohit N. Virajnarianan), Matt Smith (Dave), Larry Pine (Veteran Tourist). Directed by John Jeffcoat and produced by Tom Gorai. Screenplay by George Wing and Jeffcoat.

There is nothing in India more mysterious than the lovely land itself. The riot of colors, the careless jumble of the cities, the frequent friendliness and good humor of a people who are so different from us except that, often, they speak the same language. More or less.

Outsourced begins with an American sent to India to train the low-paid employees of a new call center for his company, American Novelty Products. It sells, he explains, "kitsch to redneck schmucks." His Indian assistant asks him, "Excuse me. What is 'redneck'? What is 'kitsch'? What is 'schmuck'?" And what are these products? American eagle sculptures. Wisconsin cheesehead hats. Branding irons for your hamburgers.

The American is named Todd (Josh Hamilton), although everyone hears it wrong and calls him "Mr. Toad." His assistant has a much more sensible name, Purohit N. Virajnarianan (Asif Basra). Although wages are low in India, Purohit will make 500,000 rupees as the new manager. That comes out to about $11,000, enough for him to realize a long-delayed marriage to his betrothed.

Todd is a stranger in a very strange land. Some of his experience reminded me of my own at the Calcutta and Hyderabad film

325

festivals. He wildly overtips a beggar woman at the airport. He finds himself riding in one of those three-wheeled open-air taxis. He makes the mistake of eating street food. He encounters new definitions of the acceptable (on a crowded bus, a young boy politely stands up to offer Todd his seat, then sits back down on his lap). He is constantly bombarded by offers to go here, go there, buy this, see that. Sometimes these offers are worth listening to, as when they lead him to a charming rooming house.

And what about the call center itself? It looks like a concrete-block storage hut, still under construction. Inside, Purohit oversees twelve or fifteen employees struggling with customer complaints.

Question: "I'm ordering my American eagle from India?" Answer: "It is not made here, sir. It is made in China."

Average length of a call: over twelve minutes. Todd's instructions: Get it down to six. Impossible. He starts with pep talks and lessons in pronunciation: "Say you are in Chicago. Pronounce it sha-CAW-ga." They obediently repeat, "Shy-CALL-go." But one employee seems ahead of the curve. This is the beautiful, helpful Asha (Ayesha Dharker), whom you may have seen in the title role of *The Terrorist* and the quite different role of Queen Jamillia in *Star Wars: Episode II—Attack of the Clones.*

She questions Todd during his classes, tells him he needs to know more about India, has a smile that dismisses his doubts. She becomes his teacher on such mysteries as Kali, the goddess of destruction. ("Sometimes it is good to destroy. Then things can start again.") And of course they fall in love, although it is not to be because she was promised in an arranged marriage at the age of four. "Then why are we here?" he asks her on a business trip, as they debate a position they find in a book at the Kama Sutra Hotel. "This is like a trip to Goa," she says, referring to the idyllic southern province of India, formerly Portuguese. In her mind, before a lifelong arranged marriage, one trip to Goa is permitted.

Outsourced is not a great movie, and maybe couldn't be this charming if it was. It is a film bursting with affection for its characters and for India. It never pushes things too far, never

stoops to cheap plotting, is about people learning to really see one another. There is a fundamental sweetness and innocence to it. Josh Hamilton, a veteran of more than forty movies, finds a defining role here, as an immensely amiable man. To look upon Ayesha Dharker is to like her. And in a time when the word "chemistry" is lightly bandied about, what they generate is the real thing. As in all Indian movies, there is no sex, but because this is a U.S. production, there is some kissing, and wow, it beats anything in the *Kama Sutra.*

Over Her Dead Body ★ ★
PG-13, 95 m., 2008

Eva Longoria Parker (Kate), Paul Rudd (Henry), Lake Bell (Ashley), Lindsay Sloane (Chloe), Stephen Root (Sculptor), Jason Biggs (Dan), William Morgan Sheppard (Father Marks). Directed by Jeff Lowell and produced by Paul Brooks, Scott Niemeyer, Peter Safran, and Norm Waitt. Screenplay by Lowell.

Why is nobody utterly in awe of ghosts in *Over Her Dead Body* and so many other ghost-coms? Here is a supernatural manifestation from another realm, and everybody treats it as a plot device. The movie even drags in a Catholic priest, who seems bewilderingly ignorant of his church's beliefs about ghosts (they don't exist) and treats the situation as an opportunity for counseling.

The setup: It's the wedding day of Henry and Kate (Paul Rudd and Eva Longoria). She's a Type A perfectionist who races manically around the reception venue, straightening place settings, adjusting decorations, and flying into a rage at the ice sculptor (Stephen Root) who has delivered an ice angel—without wings! She orders him to take it back and bring her one with wings, which, as everybody knows, all angels possess. He argues reasonably that you can't just stick wings on an ice sculpture. In a tragic accident involving the sculpture, Kate is killed.

Flash forward a decent amount of time and Henry, still in mourning, is informed by his sister, Chloe (Lindsay Sloane), that it's time for his life to begin again. He should start dating. He won't hear of it. He's still in love with Kate. She persuades him to visit Ashley (Lake Bell), a psychic she knows. He does so. Is she a real psychic? Sometimes. She begins to get vibes. So does he. Neither one needs to be psychic to realize they are falling in love with each other.

I guess it's all right for psychics (as opposed to psychiatrists) to date their clients, but Ashley seeks advice. She gets it from Dan (Jason Biggs), her partner in a catering business. Also from Father Marks (William Morgan Sheppard), who also doesn't know that his church doesn't believe in psychics. (Was he ordained by mail order? The Church teaches that consulting a psychic is a sin, although it doesn't totally rule out info from the other side, suggesting it could be disinformation from Satan.) Anyway, meanwhile . . . eek! The ghost of Kate appears, none too pleased that another woman has designs on her man. She intends to sabotage their romance.

What happens then? Kate looks completely real, although she has no material presence and can walk through walls, etc. I always wonder why walls are meaningless to such beings, but they never fall through floors. Do elevators go up without them? Never mind. The plot plays out as you would expect it to, as the amazing presence of a ghost is effortlessly absorbed into the formula plot. If it were me and a ghost, I'd put my personal agenda on hold and ask all sorts of questions about the afterlife. Wouldn't you?

Heaven, in this movie, is represented in the standard way: Everything is blindingly white, and everyone is garbed in white, even an angel (Kali Rocha) who has, by the way, no wings. Well, of course it doesn't. Being a pure spirit, it has no need to fly. Kate switches back to a conventional wardrobe for her sojourns here below. How would I depict heaven? As a featureless void with speaking voices. I haven't decided about subtitles.

Even in a movie with a ghost, the hardest thing to believe is a revelation that Dan makes to Ashley. They have worked together five years, and yet she is astonished. I will leave the revelation for you to discover, only adding that I believe it would be impossible for Dan to work five years in the catering industry without his secret being obvious to everyone.

Consider for a moment how this movie might play if it took itself seriously. Would it be better than as a comedy? I suspect so. Does the premise "her ghost turns up and fights the new romance" make you chuckle? Me neither. It's the kind of angle that could seem funny only at a pitch meeting. Not only have we been there, done that, we didn't want to go there, do that in the first place.

P

Paris 36 ★ ★ ½
PG-13, 120 m., 2009

Gerard Jugnot (Pigoil), Clovis Cornillac (Milou), Kad Merad (Jacky), Nora Arnezeder (Douce), Pierre Richard (Monsieur TSF), Bernard-Pierre Donnadieu (Galapiat), Maxence Perrin (Jojo), Elisabeth Vitali (Viviane). Directed by Christophe Barratier and produced by Nicolas Mauvernay and Jacques Perrin. Screenplay by Barratier.

Sometimes you get the feeling that if a movie had been made years ago, it would now be considered a classic. *Paris 36* is like that—an old-fashioned story set around a music hall. Cutting-edge, it's not. But if taken in the right spirit, enjoyable.

In the 1930s, in no particular neighborhood in Paris, an ancient music hall named the Chansonia wheezes along with performers who are past their sell-by dates. It's a time of social upheaval in France; the Popular Front, a left-wing coalition, has taken power, and the rise of Hitler is stirring up French right-wingers. The Chansonia's cast and crew are solidly socialist.

For Pigoil (Gerard Jugnot), the left-wing stage manager, things are going badly. The Chansonia's fascist landlord has padlocked the doors for rent in arrears, Pigoil and his friends are all out of work, his wife has left him, and a silence has fallen upon the neighborhood. The burden, he feels, rests on his shoulders. Jacky (Kad Merad), a man who wears a sandwich board for the theater but believes he can do impressions, becomes a supporter. Also Milou (Clovis Cornillac), a young radical, who helps him to reopen the doors again. But it is not enough to have the doors open; customers must use them.

The day is saved by the miraculous appearance of Douce (Nora Arnezeder), a chantoozie who is not only said to be a future star, but actually has the charisma to prove it. She's an overnight success, the show comes together, but the day is only apparently saved. The situation is fraught with complications. There is the problem of Pigoil's gifted young son Jojo (Maxence Perrin), an accordionist now in the custody of his faithless mother, and the schemes of the fascist landlord Galapiat (Bernard-Pierre Donnadieu).

Paris 36 takes place in a neighborhood known locally simply as the Faubourg (the street). Remarkably, I learn, this entire neighborhood—streets, facades, cafés—was built as a set outside Prague. It's one of those movie neighborhoods not crowded with extras. Like the street in Spike Lee's *Do the Right Thing*, it's a place where everyone knows one another; the street's a stage, and the neighbors are players on it. And they all know about Monsieur TSF (Pierre Richard), nicknamed after a French broadcasting station. He never leaves his room, but the jazz on his radio keeps everyone humming.

It is inevitable that the movie ends with a smashing song-and-dance number starring Douce and, of course, young Jojo. It's one of those numbers where the size of the cast (even including Pigoil) seems improbable. Not to mention the sound of the orchestra. The theater is too small to possibly support such a production, but never mind: Hey, gang, let's rent the old Chansonia and put on a show!

The movie otherwise lacks a certain energy, advances somewhat creakily through its plot, and contains mostly obligatory surprises. Still, it's pleasant and amusing. If I had seen it before I was born, I would have loved it.

Paul Blart: Mall Cop ★ ★ ★
PG, 87 m., 2009

Kevin James (Paul Blart), Jayma Mays (Amy), Keir O'Donnell (Veck Sims), Bobby Cannavale (Commander Kent), Stephen Rannazzisi (Stuart), Shirley Knight (Mom Blart), Raini Rodriguez (Maya Blart). Directed by Steve Carr and produced by Adam Sandler, Jack Giarraputo, Barry Bernardi, Todd Garner, and Kevin James. Screenplay by James and Nick Bakay.

Paul Blart: Mall Cop is a slapstick comedy with a hero who is a nice guy. I thought that wasn't allowed anymore. He's a single dad, raising his daughter with the help of his mom; he takes his job seriously; he may be chubby but he's brave and optimistic. And he's in a PG-rated film with no nudity except for a bra strap, and no jokes at all about bodily functions.

What's even more amazing, the movie isn't "wholesome" as a code word for "boring." It's as slam-bang preposterous as any R-rated comedy you can name. It's just that Paul Blart and the film's other characters don't feel the need to use the f-word as the building block of every sentence. They rely on the rest of the English language, which proves adequate.

Kevin James stars as Officer Blart, who looks like the result of an experiment combining the genomes of Jackie Gleason and Nathan Lane. He dreams of making it into the state police, and indeed is in great physical shape but tends to collapse because of hypoglycemia. He carries around little sugar packets the way some people pack nitro for angina. He's a veteran security officer at a giant mall in West Orange, New Jersey, which he patrols aboard a Segway, a vehicle he has so mastered that he can even go in reverse without looking.

It is Black Friday, the day after Thanksgiving, busiest shopping day of the year. He turns up pitifully hung over. Paul doesn't drink, but the night before, assaulted by hot sauce during a nacho-eating contest, he chugged a pitcher he mistakenly thought contained virgin margaritas. His behavior alienated a pretty mall salesclerk named Amy (Jayma Mays), and his heart has been broken, far from the first time.

The mall is seized by a tightly organized crew of thieves, and customers are ordered outside, but Blart was playing free video games and didn't notice. Now he's locked inside, the only person who might be able to save Amy, his daughter, Maya (Raini Rodriguez), and their fellow prisoners. Yes, it's a hostage situation, with the mall already surrounded by cops and a SWAT team. The plan of the thieves is sensationally stupid, guaranteed to call attention to their scheme, easy to thwart, and possibly inspired by watching *Dog Day Afternoon* while drunk.

Everything is a sitcom until Officer Blart goes into action in an astonishingly inventive cat-and-mouse chase past myriad product placements, all of which find uses. The movie even discovers a new angle on the old hiding-in-the-ventilation-shaft routine.

Paul Blart emerges as a hero and something

else: Kevin James illustrates how lighting and camera angles can affect our perception of an actor. In the early scenes, he's a fat schlub, but after he goes into action, the camera lowers subtly, the lighting changes, and suddenly he's a good-looking action hero, ready for business. He demonstrates what fat men have secretly believed for a long time. Should Daniel Craig someday retire, I am supporting Kevin James for the next James Bond.

The Perfect Holiday ★ ★ ½
PG, 96 m., 2007

Gabrielle Union (Nancy), Morris Chestnut (Benjamin), Charlie Murphy (J-Jizzy), Katt Williams (Delicious), Faizon Love (Jamal), Queen Latifah (Narrator), Terrence Howard (Mr. Bah-Humbug), Malik Hammond (John-John), Khail Bryant (Emily), Jeremy Gumbs (Mikey), Jill Marie Jones (Robin), Rachel True (Brenda). Directed by Lance Rivera and produced by Shakim Compere, Leifur B. Dagfinnsson, Mike Elliott, Joseph P. Genier, Queen Latifah, and Marvin Peart. Screenplay by Rivera, Marc Calixte, Nat Mauldin, and Jeff Stein.

The Perfect Holiday is a big-hearted romantic comedy based on Meet Cutes, mistaken identities, rebounding fibs, a Santa Claus operating under false pretenses, a nasty rapper, a three-hundred-pound elf, three cute kids, and Gabrielle Union, whose only Christmas wish is that a nice man would pay her a compliment. The movie's biggest suspension of disbelief involves Gabrielle Union having that problem.

She's Nancy, the beautiful mother of the three kids, divorced from a famous rapper named J-Jizzy (Charlie Murphy, Eddie's older brother). He's a Scrooge with no time for his kids, even though the oldest boy (Malik Hammond) keeps trying to bring his parents back together. When Nancy's daughter, Emily (Khail Bryant), overhears her mother's wish, she passes it on to a department store Santa, who is the aspiring songwriter Benjamin (Morris Chestnut). He sees Nancy and Emily together, knows just what to say to Nancy when they meet, and soon the two are deeply in love.

Only problems are, he doesn't know she's

the rapper's ex-wife, and she doesn't know he was Santa, doesn't really sell office supplies, and has a song contract with her ex-husband. Benjamin's lucky break is to write a lovely Christmas ballad, which J-Jizzy records after his manager (Katt Williams) explains that the song "I Love the Ho-Ho-Hos" just doesn't sound right. How this all works out involves the usual "rom-com" twists and turns, mistakes and misunderstandings, and despair before delight.

The movie has odd notions of record production. Although it clearly begins deep into Christmas season, there's time for J-Jizzy to record a holiday album, for his manager to disparage it, for them to discover Benjamin's song and record it, and for the album to be in stores before December 25. I suppose if the plot requires that, we have to go along.

One device that seems a little strange is the materialization throughout the movie of an odd couple made up of the Narrator (Queen Latifah) and Mr. Bah-Humbug (Terrence Howard). They observe the action, she tries to help out, he tries to spoil things, she gets all the best moments, and he hardly seems to know what his assignment is in the plot. They're supernatural, somehow. The presence of the Queen is a reminder of her movie *The Last Holiday*, a real charmer, and although she's a coproducer of *The Perfect Holiday*, those expecting a sequel to her best performance will be disappointed.

What isn't disappointing is the energy level throughout the picture, including appealing performances by Malik Hammond and Khail Bryant, the kids who essentially drive the plot. I also liked Faizon Love as Santa's elf and Benjamin's sidekick, and Jill Marie Jones and Rachel True have fun as Nancy's long-suffering girlfriends. There's not much that's original about the film, but it's played with high spirits and good cheer, there are lots of musical interludes, and it's pitched straight at families.

The Perfect Sleep ★ ½
R, 105 m., 2009

Anton Pardoe (Narrator), Roselyn Sanchez (Porphyria), Patrick Bauchau (Nikolai), Peter J. Lucas (Ivan), Tony Amendola (Dr. Sebastian), Sam Thakur (The Rajah). Directed by Jeremy Alter and produced by Alter, Keith Kjarval, and Anton Pardoe. Screenplay by Pardoe.

The Perfect Sleep puts me in mind of a flywheel spinning in the void. It is all burnished brass and shining steel, perfectly balanced as it hums in its orbit; yet because it occupies a void, it satisfies only itself and touches nothing else. Here is a movie that goes about its business without regard for an audience.

Oh, it is well-crafted, I grant you that. The cinematography contains fine compositions, looking down steeply on angled shadows and seeking down lost corridors. It has interiors that look like nineteenth-century landmarks of architecture just after the movers left with the furniture. It has grim men, a seductive woman, guns, knives, garrotes, scalpels, needles, cudgels, feet, fists, and baseball bats. It even has Patrick Bauchau, with the most insinuating voice since Orson Welles. But what in God's name is it about?

The Perfect Sleep does not lack explanation; in fact, the unnamed hero (Anton Pardoe) provides a narration that goes on and on and on, perhaps because the screenplay is by Anton Pardoe. He has returned to an unnamed city after ten years of fleeing men who would kill him, one who may be his father, a woman named Porphyria (Roselyn Sanchez), whom he loves and who has always loved him, a child he raised or fathered—or is an orphan, I'm unclear—an ambitious crime boss named The Rajah, a sinister physician named Dr. Sebastian (Tony Amendola), empty streets, wicked staircases, not many cars, and lots of streetlights.

It's all here. And after telling you so much about what's in it, wouldn't you think I could tell you the plot? I know the Narrator is back, he wants revenge, people want revenge on him, everybody is getting killed, and he personally is beaten, stabbed, kicked, thrown down stairs, skewered, hammered with karate, strangled, whipped, and shot point-blank in the head, and, what a guy, he just keeps on narrating, narrating, and narrating.

There are many unique ways of delivering mayhem in the film, some of them described in clinical detail by Dr. Sebastian while he is administering them. "Jugular . . . carotid? Carotid . . . jugular?" he debates with himself, his scalpel poised. At another point, he walks cheerfully up to two guys and stabs them in a lung apiece. Then he explains to them that they each have a collapsed lung. Dreadfully painful but not fatal.

He suggests it would be appalling for one to have two collapsed lungs. And he delivers this speech: "Our very biological structure promises us that, if it be now, 'tis not to come; if it be not to come, it will be now; if it be not now, yet it will come: Good sirs, the readiness is all." If this sounds like part of a famous speech, you are correct. I fancy the two collapsed lung guys are trying to remember where they heard it when he stabs them in the remaining two lungs. Now I know a lot about collapsed lungs, but I'm not entirely sure who Dr. Sebastian is.

Maybe it doesn't matter. Maybe if it did, the plot would give us a place to dig in our claws and hold on. The movie seems more interested in behavior. Many scenes take place in vast empty spaces like abandoned rehearsal halls or hotel function rooms. Major characters are discovered along an office corridor behind glass doors with their names stenciled on (more fun than captions). There are shadows on top of shadows. It's the film noir universe, all right. What does the title refer to? Perhaps to what you will enjoy during the film.

Perfume: The Story of a Murderer ★ ★ ★ ★
R, 145 m., 2007

Ben Whishaw (Jean-Baptiste Grenouille), Dustin Hoffman (Giuseppe Baldini), Alan Rickman (Antoine Richis), Rachel Hurd-Wood (Laura Richis), John Hurt (Narrator). Directed by Tom Tykwer and produced by Bernd Eichinger. Screenplay by Andrew Birkin, Eichinger, and Tykwer, based on the novel by Patrick Suskind.

Not only does *Perfume* seem impossible to film, it must have been almost impossible for Patrick Suskind to write. How do you describe the ineffable enigma of a scent in words? The audiobook, read by Sean Barrett, is the best audio performance I have ever heard; he snuffles and sniffles his way to greatness, and you almost believe he is inhaling bliss or the essence of a

stone. I once almost destroyed a dinner party by putting it on for "five minutes," after which nobody wanted to stop listening.

Patrick Suskind's famous novel involves a twisted little foundling whose fishwife mother casually births him while chopping off cod heads. He falls neglected into the stinking charnel house that was Paris three hundred years ago, and is nearly thrown out with the refuse. But Grenouille grows into a grim, taciturn survivor (Ben Whishaw) who possesses two extraordinary qualities: He has the most acute sense of smell in the world and has absolutely no scent of his own.

This last attribute is ascribed by legend to the spawn of the devil, but the movie *Perfume: The Story of a Murderer* makes no mention of this possibility, wisely limiting itself to vile if unnamed evil. Grenouille grows up as a tanner, voluptuously inhaling the world's smells, and eventually talks himself into an apprenticeship with Baldini (Dustin Hoffman), a master perfumer, now past his prime, whose shop is on an overcrowded medieval bridge on the Seine.

Mention of the bridge brings to mind the genius with which director Tom Tykwer (*Run, Lola, Run*) evokes a medieval world of gross vices, all-pervading stinks, and crude appetites. In this world, perfume is like the passage of an angel—some people think, literally. Grenouille effortlessly invents perfect perfumes, but his ambition runs deeper; he wants to distill the essence of copper, stone, and beauty itself. In pursuit of this last ideal he becomes a gruesome murderer.

Baldini tells him the world center of the perfume art is in Grasse, in southern France, and so he walks there. I was there once myself, during the Cannes festival, and at Sandra Schulberg's villa met *les nez de* Grasse, "the noses of Grasse," the men whose tastes enforce the standards of a global industry. They sat dressed in neat business suits around a table bearing a cheese, which they regarded with an interest I could only imagine. On the lawn, young folk frolicked on bedsheets strewn with rose petals. You really must try it sometime.

It is in the nature of creatures like Grenouille (I suppose) that they have no friends. Indeed he has few conversations, and they are rudimentary. His life, as it must be, is almost entirely

331

interior, so Tykwer provides a narrator (John Hurt) to establish certain events and facts. Even then, the film is essentially visual, not spoken, and does a remarkable job of establishing Grenouille and his world. We can never really understand him, but we cannot tear our eyes away.

Perfume begins in the stink of the gutter and remains dark and brooding. To rob a person of his scent is cruel enough, but the way it is done in this story is truly macabre. Still it can be said that Grenouille is driven by the conditions of his life and the nature of his spirit. Also, of course, that he may indeed be the devil's spawn.

This is a dark, dark, dark film, focused on an obsession so complete and lonely it shuts out all other human experience. You may not savor it, but you will not stop watching it, in horror and fascination. Ben Whishaw succeeds in giving us no hint of his character save a deep, savage need. And Dustin Hoffman produces a quirky old master whose life is also governed by perfume, if more positively.

Hoffman reminds us here again, as in *Stranger Than Fiction*, what a detailed and fascinating character actor he is—able to bring to the story of Grenouille precisely what humor and humanity it needs, and then tactfully leaving it at that. Even his exit is nicely timed.

Why I love this story, I do not know. Why I have read the book twice and given away a dozen copies of the audiobook, I cannot explain. There is nothing fun about the story, except the way it ventures so fearlessly down one limited, terrifying, seductive dead end and finds there a solution both sublime and horrifying. It took imagination to tell it, courage to film it, thought to act it, and from the audience it requires a brave curiosity about the peculiarity of obsession.

Persepolis ★ ★ ★ ★
PG-13, 95 m., 2008

Chiara Mastroianni (Marjane), Catherine Deneuve (Tadji [Mother]), Danielle Darrieux (Grandmother), Simon Abkarian (Ebi [Father]), Francois Jerosme (Uncle Anouche), Gabrielle Lopes (Young Marjane). Directed by Marjane Satrapi and Vincent Paronnaud and produced by Marc-Antoine Robert and Xavier Rigault.

Screenplay by Satrapi and Paronnaud, based on Satrapi's graphic novels.

I attended the Teheran film festival in 1972 and was invited to the home of my guide and translator to meet her parents and family. Over tea and elegant pastries, they explained proudly that Iran was a "modern" country, that they were devout Muslims but did not embrace the extremes of other Islamic nations, that their nation represented a new way. Whenever I read another story about the clerical rule that now grips Iran, I think of those people and millions of other Iranians like them, who do not agree with the rigid restrictions they live under—particularly the women. Iranians are no more monolithic than we are, a truth not grasped by our own zealous leader. Remember, on 9/11 there was a huge candlelight vigil in Teheran, in sympathy with us.

That was the Iran that Marjane Satrapi was born into in 1969, and it was the Iran that ended in the late 1970s with the fall and exile of the shah. Yes, his rule was dictatorial; yes, his secret police were everywhere and his opponents subjected to torture. But that was the norm in the Middle East and in an arc stretching up to the Soviet Union. At least most Iranians were left more or less free to lead the lives they chose. Ironically, many of them believed the fall of the shah would bring more, not less, democracy.

Satrapi remembers the first nine or ten years of her life as a wonderful time. Surrounded by a loving, independently minded family, living in a comfortable time, she resembled teenagers everywhere in her love for pop music, her interest in fashion, her Nikes. Then it all changed. She and her mother and her feisty grandmother had to shroud their faces from the view of men. Makeup and other forms of western decadence were forbidden. At her age she didn't drink or smoke, but God save any woman who did.

Satrapi, now living in Paris, told her life story in two graphic novels, which became best-sellers and have now been made into this wondrous animated film. The animation is mostly in black and white, with infinite shades of gray and a few guest appearances, here and there, by colors. The style is deliberately two-dimensional, avoiding the illusion of depth in current animation. This approach may sound spartan, but it is surprisingly involving, wrapping us in this autobiography that distills an epoch into a young woman's life. Not surprisingly, the books have been embraced by smart teenage girls all over the world, who find much they identify with. Adolescence is fueled by universal desires and emotions, having little to do with government decrees.

Marjane, voiced as a child by Gabrielle Lopes and as a teenager and adult by Chiara Mastroianni, is a sprightly kid, encouraged in her rambunctiousness by her parents (voiced by Catherine Deneuve and Simon Abkarian), and applauded by her outspoken grandmother (Danielle Darrieux). She dotes on the stories of her spellbinding Uncle Anouche (Francois Jerosme), who has been in prison and sometimes in hiding but gives her a vision of the greater world.

In her teens, with the Ayatollah Khomeini under full steam, Iran turns into a hostile place for the spirits of those such as Marjane. The society she thought she lived in has disappeared, and with it much of her freedom as a woman to define herself outside of marriage and the fearful restrictions of men. Sometimes she fast-talks herself out of tight corners, as when she is almost arrested for wearing makeup, but it is clear to her parents that Marjane will eventually attract trouble. They send her to live with friends in Vienna.

Austria provides her with a radically different society, but one she eventually finds impossible to live in. She was raised with values that do not fit with the casual sex and drug use she finds among her contemporaries there, and after going a little wild with rock and roll and acting out, she doesn't like herself, is homesick, and returns to Iran. But it is even more inhospitable than she remembers. She is homesick for a nation that no longer exists.

In real life, Marjane Satrapi eventually found a congenial home in France. I imagine Paris offered no less decadence than Vienna, but her experiences had made her into a woman more sure of herself and her values, and she grows into—well, the author of books and this film, which dramatize so meaningfully what her life has been like. For she is no heroine, no flag-waving idealist, no rebel, not always wise, sometimes reckless, but with strong family standards.

It might seem that her story is too large for one ninety-eight-minute film, but *Persepolis* tells it carefully, lovingly, and with great style. It is infinitely more interesting than the witless coming-of-age western girls we meet in animated films; in spirit, in gumption, in heart, Marjane resembles someone like the heroine in *Juno*—not that she is pregnant at sixteen, of course. While so many films about coming of age involve manufactured dilemmas, here is one about a woman who indeed does come of age, and magnificently.

Note: Persepolis *shared the jury prize at Cannes 2007 and has been selected by France as its official Oscar entry in the foreign-language category, a rare honor for any animated film.*

Pete Seeger: The Power of Song ★ ★ ★
NO MPAA RATING, 93 m., 2007

Featuring Pete Seeger, Toshi Seeger, Bob Dylan, Natalie Maines, Tom Paxton, Bruce Springsteen, David Dunaway, Bess Lomax Hawes, Joan Baez, Ronnie Gilbert, Jerry Silverman, Henry Foner, Eric Weissberg, Arlo Guthrie, Peter Yarrow, Mary Travers, Julian Bond, Tommy Smothers, and Bonnie Raitt. A documentary directed by Jim Brown and produced by Michael Cohl and William Eigen.

I don't know if Pete Seeger believes in saints, but I believe he is one. He's the one in the front as they go marching in. *Pete Seeger: The Power of Song* is a tribute to the legendary singer and composer who thought music could be a force for good, and proved it by writing songs that have actually helped shape our times ("If I Had a Hammer," "Turn, Turn, Turn") and popularizing "We Shall Overcome" and Woody Guthrie's unofficial national anthem, "This Land Is Your Land." During his long career (he is eighty-eight) he has toured tirelessly with song and stories, never happier than when he gets everyone in the audience to sing along.

This documentary, directed by Jim Brown, is a sequel of sorts to Brown's wonderful *The Weavers: Wasn't That a Time* (1982), which centered on the farewell Carnegie Hall concert of the singing group Seeger was long associated with. The Weavers had many big hits circa 1950 ("Goodnight Irene," "Kisses Sweeter Than Wine") before being blacklisted during the McCarthy years; called before the House Un-American Activities Committee and asked to name members of the Communist Party, Seeger invoked not the Fifth, but the First Amendment. The Weavers immediately disappeared from the playlists of most radio stations, and Seeger did not appear on television for seventeen years, until the Smothers Brothers broke the boycott.

But he kept singing, invented a new kind of banjo, did more for the rebirth of that instrument than anyone else, cofounded two folksong magazines, and with Toshi, his wife of sixty-two years, did more and sooner than most to live a "green" lifestyle, just because it was his nature. On rural land in upstate New York, they lived for years in a log cabin he built himself, and we see him still chopping firewood and working on the land. "I like to say I'm more conservative than Goldwater," Wikipedia quotes him. "He just wanted to turn the clock back to when there was no income tax. I want to turn the clock back to when people lived in small villages and took care of each other."

With access to remarkable archival footage, old TV shows, home movies, and the family photo album, Brown weaves together the story of the Seegers with testimony by admirers who represent his influence and legacy: Bruce Springsteen, Bob Dylan, Natalie Maines of the Dixie Chicks, Tom Paxton, Joan Baez, Arlo Guthrie, Peter Yarrow, Mary Travers, Julian Bond, and Bonnie Raitt. There is also coverage of the whole Seeger family musical tradition, including brother Mike and sister Peggy.

This isn't simply an assembly of historical materials and talking heads (however eloquent), but a vibrant musical film as well, and Brown has remastered the music so that we feel the real excitement of Seeger walking into a room and starting a sing-along. Unique among musicians, he doesn't covet the spotlight but actually insists on the audience joining in; he seems more choir director than soloist.

You could see that in 2004 at the Toronto Film Festival, in the "final" farewell performance of the Weavers, as he was joined on-stage by original group members Ronnie Gilbert and Fred Hellerman, who go back fifty-seven years together, and more recent members Erik Darling and Eric Weissberg. Missing from the original group was the late Lee Hays, who cowrote "If I Had a Hammer."

The occasion was the showing of an interim Brown doc, *Isn't This a Time,* a documentary about a Carnegie Hall "farewell concert" in honor of Harold Leventhal's fiftieth anniversary as an impresario. It was Leventhal who booked them into Carnegie Hall the first time in the late 1940s, and Leventhal who brought them back to the hall when the group's left-wing politics had made them victims of the show business blacklist. Although Seeger has sung more rarely in recent years, claiming his voice is "gone," he was in fine form that night in Toronto, his head as always held high and thrown back, as if focused in the future.

Sadly, for many people, Seeger is still associated in memory with the Communist Party USA. Although never a "card-carrying member," he was and is adamantly left-wing; he broke with the party in 1950, disillusioned with Stalinism, and as recently as this year, according to Wikipedia, apologized to a historian: "I think you're right. I should have asked to see the gulags when I was in the U.S.S.R."

What I feel from Seeger and his music is a deep-seated, instinctive decency, a sense of fair play, a democratic impulse reflected by singing along as a metaphor. I get the same feeling from Toshi, who coproduced this film and has coproduced her husband's life. How many women would sign on with a folksinger who planned to build them a cabin to live in? The portrait of their long marriage, their children and grandchildren, is one of the most inspiring elements in the film. They actually live as if this land was made for you and me.

Pierrot le Fou ★ ★ ½

NO MPAA RATING, 110 m., 1965 (rereleased 2007)

Jean-Paul Belmondo (Ferdinand), Anna Karina (Marianne). Directed by Jean-Luc Godard and produced by Georges de Beauregard. Screenplay by Godard, based on the novel *Obsession* by Lionel White.

Godard's *Pierrot le Fou* (1965) is the same film I liked so much when it opened here in 1968 and assigned a three-and-a-half-star rating. In fact, it is probably a better film, because it is being shown in a new 35 mm print. But while I once wrote of it as "Godard's most virtuoso display of his mastery of Hollywood genres," I now see it more as the story of silly characters who have seen too many Hollywood movies.

There was a point when it was revolutionary to show young lovers flaunting society, committing crimes thoughtlessly, and running hand in hand over hill and dale, beach and field. And then there was a point where it was postrevolutionary. Or maybe, to take a more optimistic view of the progress of cinema, prerevolutionary.

The film stars Jean-Paul Belmondo, then thirty-two, and Anna Karina, then twenty-five, as Ferdinand and Marianne, Ferdinand's baby-sitter and onetime girlfriend, who run away together from a party and from their spouses. First stop, Marianne's flat, when Ferdinand goes into the next room, sees a dead body, and returns to the living room. Later, she passes the body, which Godard shows us only by filming Belmondo's eyes watching her. Nice touch. And she sings a song. Then they hit the road in a series of stolen cars, supporting themselves by stickups.

It is so very boring when infatuation and sex have to take the place of a genuine interest in the other person, which Ferdinand discovers more quickly than Marianne, perhaps because that delightful and beautiful woman is mad. There are times when she wishes he were crazier and calls him "Pierrot," the name of a character from Italian stage comedy and opera who is a clown and a fool. "My name is Ferdinand," he tirelessly corrects her.

At the party they run away from there is a famous scene in which an older man with a cigar is seen standing against a wall. This is Samuel Fuller, the American director, playing himself and explaining, "My name is Samuel Fuller. I'm an American film director in Paris making an action picture." He is filmed in color; the rest of the party is filmed in bold tints. What does that mean? It means that we notice it and wonder what it means, which can be said for a lot of Godard's shots.

Barreling through the countryside, the cou-ple make use of old movies. During a dicey moment, Marianne remembers a Laurel and Hardy trick. She faces the guy with the gun, she looks up, he looks up, and she punches him in the stomach. There is also an auto robbery, involving a car on a turntable in a grease pit, that Keaton might have invented, less violently to be sure.

I was in full flood of admiration for Jean-Luc Godard in the 1960s. Seemed like everyone was. One year, they showed three of his films at the New York Film Festival. The thing was, he made shots that knew they were shots, and you watched them knowing they were shots, and they knew you were watching, and you were all in on it together.

There was a barnyard scene in *Weekend* (1968) where the camera rotated in a circle once, twice, and then rotated back the other way just a little, *to show that it knew, and you knew, that it was rotating.* How cool. And a tracking shot of an unbelievably long traffic jam, which remains one of the great shots, but great about what? I wrote in my review of that film: "At some point, we realize that the subject of the shot is not the traffic jam but the fact that the shot is so extended. 'Politics is a traveling shot,' Godard told us a few years ago, and now we know what he meant." Uh-huh.

Godard's early black-and-white films were masterpieces. Later, he needed to dial down. Still later, he disappeared into long and (for many) pointless stylistic video exercises that remained widely unseen. He still retained the ability to make much-debated films, like *Hail Mary* (1986), but he wasn't drawn that way. *Pierrot le Fou* stood at the tipping point between the great early films like *My Life to Live* and later films that were essentially about themselves, or adult children at play.

I closed my earlier review of *Pierrot le Fou* by writing: "Godard, a former film critic, once said that the only valid way to criticize a movie was to make one of your own. That is true of his own work, at least." To which I now add: But perhaps not entirely in the way he intended.

Pineapple Express ★ ★ ★ ½
R, 111 m., 2008

Seth Rogen (Dale Denton), James Franco (Saul Silver), Danny McBride (Red), Gary Cole (Ted

335

Jones), Rosie Perez (Carol), Amber Heard (Angie Anderson), Bill Hader (Private Miller), James Remar (General Bratt). Directed by David Gordon Green and produced by Judd Apatow and Shauna Robertson. Screenplay by Seth Rogen and Evan Goldberg.

David Gordon Green, that poet of the cinema, is the last person you'd expect to find directing a Judd Apatow male-buddy comedy about two potheads who start a drug war. But he does such a good job there's a danger he'll become in demand by mainstream Hollywood and tempted away from the greatness he showed in *George Washington* and *Undertow*. (I can imagine his agent hiding this review from him.)

Pineapple Express has all the elements you'd expect from the genre: male bonding, immature sexual desires, verbal scatology, formidable drug abuse, fight scenes, gunfire, explosions. Yawn? Not this time. It's a quality movie even if the material is unworthy of the treatment. As a result, yes, it's a druggie comedy that made me laugh.

The heroes are a process server named Dale (Seth Rogen) and his drug dealer, Saul (James Franco). Both are stoned in every single scene. Dale has a romance going with Angie (Amber Heard), who I hope is of legal age, although physical sex isn't necessarily involved. I think Dale is still at the age of emotional development where going all the way means asking a girl to go steady. Saul is even more pathetic, hiding in his apartment filled with electronic gizmos and merchandise.

Dale drops in on Saul one day to buy some weed, and Saul gives him a sample of a new product just imported by his connection. This is Pineapple Express, a blend of marijuana so sublime, he says, that even smoking it is a crime "like killing a unicorn." Dale gets high on the aroma alone. Floating away from Saul's after a hallucinatory conversation, he goes to serve a summons on Ted Jones (Gary Cole), the very man Saul gets his pot from.

Parked in front of the house for one last toke, Dale is horrified to see a squad car parked behind him and throws away the joint. Then he has a front-row seat to witness, through a huge glass wall, a man being shot dead by Ted and a female cop (Rosie Perez).

He speeds away, leaving Ted to find the joint, sample it, identify it, and know that the murder witness bought it from Saul. The buddies know Ted will make this connection and begin a desperate flight from Ted's incompetent hit men. This leads them into a funny stumble through a forest preserve, the loss of their car, and Dale's attempt to plausibly sit through dinner with Angie's parents (Ed Begley Jr. and Nora Dunn) while stoned, bleeding, torn, disheveled, and in need of being hosed down.

The critic James Berardinelli observes: "A lot of buddy films aren't fundamentally that different from romantic comedies. The relationships are often developed in the same fashion, only with male bonding replacing sexual chemistry." Does that make Dale and Saul gay, even if they're not aware of it? I think that describes the buddies in a lot of buddy movies produced by Judd Apatow, including the recent *Step Brothers*. Especially in the obligatory happy ending, there's a whole lot of hugging and chanting of "I love you, man!"

A third major character enters the scene when Dale and Saul visit Saul's buddy, Red (Danny McBride), who has already betrayed them to the hit men. All of this leads, don't ask how, to a full-scale war between Ted's men and a rival drug empire, "the Asians," who attack conveniently dressed in matching black uniforms, which makes them easy targets under the sunlamps of Ted's indoor pot farm. Many, many people die horribly, none more thoroughly than poor Rosie Perez.

Two teams have met to make this picture: the Apatow production line, and Green and his cameraman, Tim Orr, soundman Chris Gebert, actor Danny McBride, and others he met at the North Carolina School of the Arts. As always, even in their zero-budget first effort, they use widescreen compositions with graceful visual instincts, although you may be excused for not noticing them, considering what happens. The movie has the usual chase, this time between two squad cars, but to my amazement I found it exciting and very funny, especially the business about Saul's leg.

Pineapple Express is the answer to the question, "What would happen if a movie like this was made by a great director?" This question descends directly from those old rumors that

Stanley Kubrick was going to make a porn film. Give it a moment's thought. And I suspect Green of foiling Apatow's vow to include at least one penis in every one of his comedies. This time, it's not a penis but a finger, and a good thing, too.

Note: Despite a "warning," the movie is enthusiastically pro-pot. ☞

The Pink Panther 2 ★ ★
PG, 92 m., 2009

Steve Martin (Jacques Clouseau), Jean Reno (Ponton), Emily Mortimer (Nicole), Andy Garcia (Vincenzo), Alfred Molina (Pepperidge), Yuki Matsuzaki (Kenji), Aishwarya Rai Bachchan (Sonia), John Cleese (Dreyfus), Lily Tomlin (Mrs. Berenger). Directed by Harald Zwart and produced by Robert Simonds. Screenplay by Scott Neustadter, Michael H. Weber, and Steve Martin.

I was smiling all the way through the opening credits of *The Pink Panther 2*. They made me miss the golden age of credits, when you actually found out who the actors were going to be and maybe saw a little cartoon in the bargain: this time, one about the misadventures of the Pink Panther, of course. And then the names in the cast!

Imagine these appearing one after another: Steve Martin, Jean Reno, Emily Mortimer, Andy Garcia, Alfred Molina, Aishwarya Rai Bachchan, John Cleese, Lily Tomlin, Jeremy Irons, Johnny Hallyday . . . wait a minute! Aishwarya Rai Bachchan! That's the Indian actress Aishwarya Rai! The most beautiful woman in the world!

As the movie began, my smile faded. The actors are let down by the screenplay and direction, which don't really pop the supporting characters out into strong comic focus. Maybe the cast is simply too star-studded? There's sometimes the feeling they're being cycled onscreen by twos and threes, just to keep them alive.

Then there's the albatross of the Blake Edwards and Peter Sellers films. Edwards was a truly inspired director of comedies (*The Party, SOB, Victor/Victoria*). Peter Sellers was a genius who somehow made Inspector Clouseau seem as if he really were helplessly incapable of functioning in the real world, and somehow incapable of knowing that. Steve Martin is a genius, too, but not at being Inspector Clouseau. It seems more like an exercise.

The plot: "The Tornado" has stolen the Magna Carta, the Japanese emperor's sword, and the Shroud of Turin. Next may be the Pink Panther, the pink diamond that is, for some reason, the symbol of France's greatness and not merely an example of carbon under great pressure. Clouseau is chosen, despite the apoplectic agitation of Chief Inspector Dreyfus (John Cleese), to join an international police Dream Team to thwart the possible deed.

Also onstage is Clouseau's assistant, Nicole (Emily Mortimer), a fragrant rose; she and Jacques are so in love with each other they cannot even bring themselves to admit it. The Italian team member, Vincenzo (Andy Garcia), family name Doncorleone, moves on Nicole and tells Clouseau that Sonia (Aishwarya Rai) likes him. That creates a romcom situation that's sort of muted because of Jacques and Nicole's shyness, and because the film seems reluctant to foreground Sonia very much. Aishwarya Rai is breathtaking in Bollywood films, where they devote a great deal of expertise to admiring beauty, but here she's underutilized and too much in the background.

Molina plays Pepperidge, a Sherlockian type who claims to be a great deducer of clues. Clouseau takes one look at him and they start a deducing showdown, sort of funny. Reno is Ponton, Clouseau's associate inspector, whose considerable presence never really pays off. Yuki Matsuzaki, as the Japanese cop Kenji, seems to be projecting ideas about the character that were edited out or never written in. Tomlin is the departmental expert on P.C. behavior, whom Clouseau argues with ("But . . . blondes *are* dumb!").

Opportunities to better develop all of these characters are lost, and we're left with the sight and stunt gags, which are central to the Panther movies, of course, but feel recycled: This time, little kids are the kung fu experts, for example, instead of Cato.

Too many of the stunt gags are performed without payoffs; Buster Keaton, the master, always gave you reaction shots. When Clouseau is mistaken for the pope, for example, and seems to fall from his balcony to his death, why isn't there a crowd to contemplate the fallen Frenchman with his black moustache, maybe lurching to his feet, blessing them, and intoning *dov'e la toilette?* Or after Clouseau sets the restaurant on fire, why not make him struggle to get back inside, telling the firemen he insists on paying his check?

The first two Panther movies, *The Pink Panther* (1963) and *A Shot in the Dark* (1964), were a serendipitous coming together of Edwards and Sellers. Truth to tell, none of their others were as inspired. The moment had passed. And it still hasn't come back round again. Zut!

Pride and Glory ★ ★
R, 125 m., 2008

Edward Norton (Ray Tierney), Colin Farrell (Jimmy Egan), Jon Voight (Francis Tierney Sr.), Noah Emmerich (Francis Tierney Jr.), Jennifer Ehle (Abby Tierney). Directed and produced by Gavin O'Connor. Screenplay by O'Connor and Joe Carnahan.

Pride and Glory is the kind of film where you feel like you know the words and ought to be singing along. It follows the well-worn pathways of countless police dramas before it. We find a drug deal gone bad, corruption on the force, brother against brother, alcoholic dad who is both their father and their superior officer, family friend as a traitor, plus one dying wife and another one who is fed up. There's a stroke of originality: A baby seems about to be branded by a hot steam iron.

If you set this in New York, provide all the characters with strong ethnic identities, film under glowering skies, add a lot of dead bodies right at the start, and have characters shout at one another, all you'd have to do is change the names and hire different actors, and you could do this all again and again.

The setup: Four cops are killed in a drug bust gone wrong. They are under the command of Francis Tierney Jr. (Noah Emmerich). The moment you bring a Junior onstage, the formula requires a Senior, in this case played by Jon Voight as a high-maintenance boozer. Senior confronts his other son, Ray Tierney (Edward Norton), who has fled the streets for a low-risk assignment after Something Very Bad happened a few years ago, and persuades him to rejoin the tough guys: After all, he has to help out Junior.

Also involved is the Tierney brother-in-law, Jimmy Egan (Colin Farrell). Oh, and Junior's wife, Abby (Jennifer Ehle), is dying of cancer and has lost her hair to chemo. And Ray's wife, Tasha (Carmen Ejogo), has split with him and, in the tradition of all cop wives, accuses him of neglecting his family and, on Christmas, receiving a visit from a guy who would be the first one you would pick out of a lineup, whether or not you recognized him, because he looks like he has just done Something Very Bad.

The plot involves how and why the four cops were killed. This may not come as a shock to veteran filmgoers: There is a culture of corruption in the department, and one character is guilty, one is innocent, and one is conflicted in his loyalties. Once we know this, we know there will be a series of angry and desperate confrontations among the three, interlaced with violent face-downs with criminals, cops being slammed up against walls in the basement of headquarters, and Senior drinking even more because he is horribly confused about whether he values truth above family loyalty, and either one above loyalty to the department. Jon Voight is a fine actor, but putting him in a role like this is like hanging him out to dry.

My friend McHugh used to be fond of suddenly announcing, "Clear the bar! I want to drink by myself!" Such a moment supplies the sensationally bad ending to *Pride and Glory,* when one brother enters the bar where the other brother is drinking, flashes his badge, and tells everyone to scram. Why? So he and his brother can settle everything with a brutal fistfight. As we know, under the Macho Code, this means that after two people who love each other end up beaten and bloody, they will somehow arrive at a catharsis. How that solves this tangled web of loyalty, deceit, and corruption, I can't be exactly sure.

Private Property ★ ★ ★ ½
NO MPAA RATING, 95 m., 2007

Isabelle Huppert (Pascale), Yannick Renier (Francois), Jeremie Renier (Thierry), Kris

Cuppens (Jan), Raphaelle Lubansu (Anne), Patrick Descamps (Luc). Directed by Joachim Lafosse and produced by Joseph Rouschop. Screenplay by Lafosse and Francois Pirot.

I met her near the beginning, at Cannes, sitting on the lawn of a villa sloping down toward the sea. It was 1977, the year Isabelle Huppert made *The Lacemaker*. She was twenty-four, had already made more than a dozen features, starting at seventeen. She told me how that happened: "I walked up to the studio door in Paris, knocked, and said, 'I am here.'" She was. She has a quiet confidence that is almost terrifying.

At fifty-four, but looking no age at all in particular, she has made eighty-nine film and television projects. She works all the time. Everybody wants her. She told me: "When I need to escape, I get on a plane and fly to Chicago. It is my secret city. I go where I want, do what I want, nobody recognizes me, nobody can find me."

Now here she is in Joachim Lafosse's *Private Property*. She plays the divorced mother of twin sons, who treat her badly, which she allows. They live in a big country house outside a Belgian town, bought for them by her ex-husband when he left. The husband has remarried and has a child. She has started to date a man, and they talk about running a B&B somewhere. It is time for her to live her own life. Her sons don't think so.

They are Francois and Thierry, played by Yannick and Jeremie Renier, real-life brothers but not twins. Francois does odd jobs around the house and postpones his future; Thierry goes to school. The boys play games, they laze about, they are waited on hand and foot by their mother. Why should they leave? They have it good. They hate the new boyfriend and the fact that their mother is dating.

The film opens with Huppert, as Pascale, stripping and looking at herself intently in a mirror. Only Huppert could do this in quite the way she does. She is not presenting her nudity for examination; she is presenting her examination itself. One of the boys is watching her. If she realizes that (I think she does), it is a matter of indifference, as again later when she showers while another son is in the bathroom.

I don't think this is intended to signal incestuous feelings. I think it signals that too

many barriers have fallen between them, and she cannot reconstruct the walls that all parents need to put up sometimes. The architect Christopher Alexander believes every house that has enough room should have a "couple's domain," an area off-limits for the children. Good fences make good families. Meals, we assure ourselves, "are the one time the family can get together." In this family, they work as war. Pascale cooks, sets the table, serves the meal, and then sits down to hostility from Thierry and silent, withdrawn embarrassment from Francois.

She wants to keep peace. She does it by suppressing her own feelings. She knows what she wants, her freedom, but she can't take it. Will the boys still be there when they are thirty? They're stuck on Mom. We remember Huppert's great performance in Michael Haneke's *The Piano Teacher* (2001), which won her the best actress prize at Cannes ("unanimously," the jury specified). She played a fortyish woman who was still living with her mother, sleeping in the same bed, masochistically mutilating herself, then taking retribution in the sadistic manipulation of young men she had studied carefully. Both films draw on some of the same compulsions and inhibitions.

What draws us into *Private Property* is how so many things happen under the surface, never commented upon. At any given moment, we cannot say for sure what the characters fully feel, since they often act at right angles to their emotions. Lafosse said at film festival interviews that he was not even sure if the film was primarily about the mother. Is she simply carried along on the tide of her family? Are they drifting out to sea?

The story's ending is brought about by actions involving the house. I will not be more specific. But it is hard to see how those actions could provoke all that happens. Sometimes the pressure in a family builds so that something relatively inconsequential pulls everything apart. We are accustomed to films in which the characters have fairly specific motivations. Huppert is inspired in the way she withdraws from confrontations and expresses her wishes enough to provoke others, but never enough to realize them. An emotional balancing act showing such weakness takes a strong actress to pull it off.

The Promotion ★ ★
R, 85 m., 2008

Seann William Scott (Doug), John C. Reilly (Richard), Jenna Fischer (Jen), Lili Taylor (Laurie), Fred Armisen (Scott), Gil Bellows (Board Exec), Bobby Cannavale (Dr. Timm), Rick Gonzalez (Ernesto). Directed by Steve Conrad and produced by Steven A. Jones and Jessika Borsiczky Goyer. Screenplay by Conrad.

The Promotion is a human comedy about two supermarket employees who are always ill at ease. It's their state of being. I felt a little ill at ease watching it because I was never quite sure whether I was supposed to be laughing at them or feeling sorry for them. It's one of those off-balance movies that seems to be searching for the right tone.

The setting: a Chicago supermarket. The central characters: Doug (Seann William Scott), thirty-three, a loyal employee, and Richard (John C. Reilly), mid-thirties, a Canadian who has immigrated to America with his Scottish wife, Laurie (Lili Taylor), and their daughter. Doug is recently married to Jen (Jenna Fischer). When their supermarket chain decides to open a new store, the two men are in line for a promotion to store manager.

They both desperately desire and need this job. Doug has convinced his wife he's a "shoo-in," and they invest all of their savings in a nonrefundable deposit on a house. Richard is a recovering alcoholic and drug addict, now in AA, trying to prove he is a trustworthy husband and father. The two men fight for the job not in a slapstick way but in an understated, underhanded way that Doug feels bad about, Richard not so much. ("We're all just out here to get some food," Richard philosophizes. "Sometimes we bump into each other.")

The movie is unusually quiet and introspective for a comedy. Doug provides a narration, and Richard gets one of his own in the form of a self-help tape he obsessively listens to. Doug decides Richard is a "nice guy" and observes, "all Canadians are nice." That's before Richard fakes an injury to lodge a dreaded "in-store complaint" that could cost Doug his job.

Richard himself is on a self-destruct mission. Consider an episode when Doug hits a young black man who has thrown a bottle of Yoo-Hoo at him in the parking lot. Doug apologizes to a "community forum," backed up by a panel including Richard and the store's board of directors. He says something about a "few bad apples." Apology accepted. Afterward, however, when they're all standing around relieved, Richard tells one of the community leaders, "You are not a black apple to me." Explaining this digs him in deeper, until he's reduced to speechlessness. He has a gift for saying the wrong things at the wrong times.

Richard actually is nice at times, however. As a member of a motorcycle gang, he once watched his fellow members roar through a toll gate without paying, and then sheepishly told the collector, "I'll pay for them all." Doug empathizes with Richard, even to the point of defending him to the board, but he feels rotten inside: Having lied to his wife that he has the job, he finds a present of long-sleeve shirts they can't afford. He's afraid he's stuck in the ranks of the short-sleeve guys.

I was interested in the fates of these two men, but mildly. I was expected to laugh, but I only smiled. Some of the race-based situations made me feel uncomfortable. All of the characters, especially the straight-arrow chairman of the board (Gil Bellows), needed to be pushed further into the realms of comedy. More could have been done with the store's other employees. At the end of *The Promotion*, I wondered what the atmosphere was like on the set every day. How does it feel to make a movie where the characters don't seem sure who they are?

The Proposal ★ ★ ★
PG-13, 107 m., 2009

Sandra Bullock (Margaret Tate), Ryan Reynolds (Andrew Paxton), Mary Steenburgen (Grace Paxton), Craig T. Nelson (Joe Paxton), Betty White (Grandma Annie), Denis O'Hare (Mr. Gilbertson), Malin Akerman (Gertrude), Oscar Nunez (Ramone). Directed by Anne Fletcher and produced by David Hoberman and Todd Lieberman. Screenplay by Pete Chiarelli.

The Proposal is a movie about a couple who start out hating each other and end up liking each other. It's a funny thing about that. I started out hating the movie and ended up liking it.

It opens on a rather cheerless note, as the portrait of Margaret (Sandra Bullock), a tyrannical book editor, and Andrew (Ryan Reynolds), her long-suffering assistant. Known on office instant messages as The Witch, she terrorizes underlings, fires the man who wants her job, and orders Andrew to marry her.

How that happens is, she's a Canadian in danger of being deported, she imperiously ignored the law, and now she figures if she gets married she'll get her green card. They blackmail each other in their prenuptial hostage negotiations and fly off to Sitka, Alaska, to meet his folks. Sitka turns out to be a charming waterfront town, filled with chic little shops like the Fudgery, no fast-food stores or franchise chains, and a waterfront that looks less like a working fishing harbor than a tourist resort. Perhaps that's because the movie was filmed not in Alaska, but in Massachusetts and Rhode Island. Alaska might have been too real for this fantasy.

So I was sitting there cringing, knowing with uncanny certainty where the story was going. No movie begins with scenes of a man and a woman who are utterly incompatible unless it ends with them in love, unless perhaps it might be one about Hitler and Eleanor Roosevelt. They will fly to Alaska, she will be charmed by his family, she will be moved by the community spirit, she will love the landscape after the skyscraper towers of Manhattan, and they will have misadventures, probably involving unintended nudity and someone falling off a boat. So it is written.

But slowly, reluctantly, disbelievingly, they will start to warm up to each other. And it was about at that point when reluctantly, disbelievingly, I began to warm up to them. Bullock is a likable actress in the right roles, which she has been avoiding frequently since *Speed 2: Cruise Control* (1997), which I liked more than she did. She is likable here because she doesn't overdo it and is convincing when she confesses that she has warmed to his family's embrace— and who would not, since Andrew's mother is the merry Mary Steenburgen and his grandmother is the unsinkable Betty White. His father, Craig T. Nelson, is not quite so embraceable, but only because he is protective.

The key scene involves Steenburgen and White fitting Granny Annie's wedding dress for Bullock, and the presentation of a family heirloom. I don't care how much of a witch a woman is, when she sees herself in the mirror wearing her grandmother-in-law's gown, she's going to cave in. For that matter, Bullock was never that convincing as the office witch; she couldn't have touched Meryl Streep's work in *The Devil Wears Prada*.

The Proposal is much enhanced by all of the supporting performances. Betty White, at eighty-seven, makes her character eighty-nine and performs a Native American sunrise ceremony beside a campfire in the forest, which is not easy, especially in the Alaskan summer when the sun hardly sets. And look for a character named Ramone (Oscar Nunez), who will remind you of an element in *Local Hero*.

The Proposal recycles a plot that was already old when Tracy and Hepburn were trying it out. You see it coming from a great distance away. As it draws closer, you don't duck out of the way because it is so cheerfully done you don't mind being hit by it.

P2 ★ ★ ★

R, 98 m., 2007

Rachel Nichols (Angela Bridges), Wes Bentley (Thomas). Directed by Franck Khalfoun and produced by Alexandre Aja, Gregory Levasseur, Patrick Wachsberger, and Erik Feig. Screenplay by Aja, Khalfoun, and Levasseur.

If you have seen the ads for *P2*, or even heard about them, you know what the movie involves. A woman works late in the office on Christmas Eve, leaves after everyone else, descends to parking level P-2 to get her car, finds it won't start, and then meets the homicidal madman who is the overnight lot attendant. Yes, I know, it sounds like a formula slasher film, but it's actually done well, and in the current climate at least most Women in Danger films end up with Men in Danger. There were elements of *P2* that even reminded me a little of Jodie Foster's *Panic Room*—especially in complexities involving cell phones, alarms, spycams, and doors that are locked or unlocked.

The movie benefits from being played

about as straight as it can be, given the material. Rachel Nichols, as the endangered heroine, Angela, doesn't do stupid things or make obvious mistakes. And Wes Bentley, as Thomas, the lonely guy on overnight duty, doesn't froth at the mouth or cackle with insane zeal. Oh, he's insane, all right, but he's one of those insane lonely guys who can't understand why Angela doesn't want to share his Christmas dinner (turkey and trimmings, and even corn muffins!), even though he has stripped her to her negligee, chained her to the furniture, and has a savage dog lunging at her. He's just trying to be friends.

A movie like this depends on invention in the screenplay. You can't merely have the woman running around frantically while the guy pops up in the foreground with a standard horror movie swooshing sound. There has to be a little logic. And Angela thinks of most of the right things to do, even though most of the time she can't do them. In today's high-security climate, if you're locked in, you're locked in. One day when we have more time, I'll tell you about when I went for a winter stroll in London's Hyde Park and didn't know the gates were locked at six, and how it started snowing while I was trying to climb a slushy hill to get to a tree branch that I thought might allow me to drop over a six-foot fence with sharp spikes on the top, and how when I balanced on the tree and called for help to passers-by, they walked a little faster.

It's that kind of an evening for Angela. She does everything right, but it doesn't work. And when she somehow gets out a garbled call for help on 911, two cops turn up and *they* do everything right, too. Often in thrillers the cops are practically standing on a dead body and don't notice anything. But these guys are pros, they follow the ropes, they don't buy Thomas's story at face value, and *still* they don't save Angela. It's a lot more exciting that way.

This is, in case you haven't noticed, the best autumn for movies in years. There are a dozen, maybe two dozen, movies in current release that I would recommend over *P2*. Maybe four dozen. Maybe three dozen. But horror movies routinely *win the weekend* at the box office, and it is no small consolation that the customers who insist on their horror movie this weekend will see a well-made one.

It's such a good season that even the slashers are superior.

Public Enemies ★ ★ ★ ½
R, 140 m., 2009

Johnny Depp (John Dillinger), Christian Bale (Melvin Purvis), Marion Cotillard (Billie Frechette), Billy Crudup (J. Edgar Hoover), Stephen Dorff (Homer Van Meter), Stephen Lang (Charles Winstead), Branka Katic (Anna Sage). Directed by Michael Mann and produced by Mann and Kevin Misher. Screenplay by Mann, Ronan Bennett, and Ann Biderman, based on the book *Public Enemies: America's Greatest Crime Wave and the Birth of the FBI, 1933–34* by Bryan Burrough.

"I rob banks," John Dillinger would sometimes say by way of introduction. It was the simple truth. That was what he did. For the thirteen months between the day he escaped from prison and the night he lay dying in an alley, he robbed banks. It was his lifetime. Michael Mann's *Public Enemies* accepts that stark fact and refuses any temptation to soften it. Dillinger was not a nice man.

Here is a film that shrugs off the way we depend on myth to sentimentalize our outlaws. There is no interest here about John Dillinger's childhood, his psychology, his sexuality, his famous charm, his Robin Hood legend. He liked sex, but not as much as robbing banks. "He robbed the bankers but let the customers keep their own money." But whose money was in the banks? He kids around with reporters and lawmen, but that was business. He doesn't kid around with the members of his gang. He might have made a very good military leader.

Johnny Depp and Michael Mann show us that we didn't know all about Dillinger. We only thought we did. Here is an efficient, disciplined, bold, violent man, driven by compulsions the film wisely declines to explain. His gang members loved the money they were making. Dillinger loved planning the next job. He had no exit strategy or retirement plans.

Dillinger saw a woman he liked, Billie Frechette, played by Marion Cotillard, and courted her, after his fashion. That is, he took her out at night and bought her a fur coat, as he had seen done in the movies; he had no real adult experience before prison. They had sex, but the movie is not much interested. It is all about his vow to show up for her, to protect her. Against what? Against the danger of being his girl. He allows himself a tiny smile when he gives her the coat, and it is the only vulnerability he shows in the movie.

This is a very disciplined film. You might not think it was possible to make a film about the most famous outlaw of the 1930s without clichés and "star chemistry" and a film-class screenplay structure, but Mann does it. He is particular about the way he presents Dillinger and Billie. He sees him and her. Not them. They are never a couple. They are their needs. She needs to be protected because she is so vulnerable. He needs someone to protect in order to affirm his invincibility.

Dillinger hates the system, by which he means prisons, which hold people, banks, which hold money, and cops, who stand in his way. He probably hates the government, too, but he doesn't think that big. It is him against them, and the bastards will not, *cannot*, win. There's an extraordinary sequence, apparently based on fact, where Dillinger walks into the "Dillinger Bureau" of the Chicago Police Department and strolls around. Invincible. This is not ego. It is a spell he casts on himself.

The movie is well researched, based on the book by Bryan Burrough. It even bothers to try to discover Dillinger's speaking style. Depp looks a lot like him. Mann shot on location in the Crown Point jail, scene of the famous jailbreak with the fake gun. He shot in the Little Bohemia Lodge in the same room Dillinger used, and Depp is costumed in clothes to match those the bank robber left behind. Mann redressed Lincoln Avenue on either side of the Biograph Theater and laid streetcar tracks; I live a few blocks away and walked over to marvel at the detail. I saw more than you will; unlike some directors, he doesn't indulge in beauty shots to show off the art direction. It's just there.

This Johnny Depp performance is something else. For once, an actor playing a gangster does not seem to base his performance on movies he has seen. He starts cold. He plays Dillinger as a fact. My friend Jay Robert Nash says 1930s gangsters copied their styles from the way Hollywood depicted them; screenwriters like Ben Hecht taught them how they spoke. Dillinger was a big movie fan; on the last night of his life, he went to see Clark Gable playing a man a lot like him, but he didn't learn much. No wisecracks, no lingo. Just military precision and an edge of steel.

Christian Bale plays Melvin Purvis in a similar key. He lives to fight criminals. He is a cold realist. He admires his boss, J. Edgar Hoover, but Hoover is a romantic, dreaming of an FBI of clean-cut young accountants in suits and ties who would be a credit to their mothers. After the catastrophe at Little Bohemia (the FBI let Dillinger escape but killed three civilians), Purvis said to hell with it and made J. Edgar import some lawmen from Arizona who had actually been in gunfights.

Mann is fearless with his research. If I mention the Lady in Red, Anna Sage (Branka Katic), who betrayed Dillinger outside the Biograph when the movie was over, how do you picture her? I do, too. We are wrong. In real life she was wearing a white blouse and an orange skirt, and she does in the movie. John Ford once said, "When the legend becomes fact, print the legend." This may be a case where he was right. Mann might have been wise to decide against the orange and white and just break down and give Anna Sage a red dress.

This is a very good film, with Depp and Bale performances of brutal clarity. I'm trying to understand why it is not quite a great film. I think it may be because it deprives me of some stubborn need for closure. His name was John Dillinger, and he robbed banks. But there had to be more to it than that, right? No, apparently not.

The Punisher: War Zone ★ ★
R, 101 m., 2008

Ray Stevenson (Frank Castle), Dominic West (Billy Russo/Jigsaw), Julie Benz (Angela Donatelli), Doug Hutchison (Loony Bin Jim), Colin Salmon (Paul Budiansky), Wayne Knight (Microchip), Dash Mihok (Martin Soap), Stephanie Janusauskas (Grace). Directed by Lexi Alexander and produced by Gale Ann Hurd. Screenplay by Nick Santora, Art Marcum, and Matt Holloway, based on the Marvel comic books.

You used to be able to depend on a bad film being poorly made. No longer. *The Punisher: War Zone* is one of the best-made bad movies I've seen. It looks great, it hurtles through its paces, and it is well-acted. The sound track is like elevator music if the elevator were in a death plunge. The special effects are state of the art. Its only flaw is that it's disgusting.

There's a big audience for disgusting, and I confidently predict the movie will "win the weekend," if not very many hearts and minds. Here you will see a man's kidney ripped out and eaten, a chair leg pushed through a head via the eyeball, a roomful of men wiped out by the Punisher revolving upside-down from the chandelier and firing machine guns with both hands, a widow and her wee girl threatened with mayhem, heads sliced off, victims impaled and skewered, and the villain thrown into a machine that crushes glass bottles in much the same way concrete is mixed.

The glass-crushing machine caught my eye. Billy (Dominic West) is socked into it by the Punisher (Ray Stevenson) and revolves up to his neck in cutting edges while screaming many, many four-letter words, which, under the circumstances, are appropriate.

What confused me is that nearby in the same factory there is a conveyor belt carrying large lumps of hamburger or something. I expected Billy to emerge as ground round, but then I thought, how much ground glass can you really add to ground round? It's not often that you see meat processing and bottle crushing done in adjacent operations in the same factory. I was looking for the saltwater taffy mixer.

Billy survives his ordeal and announces to his henchmen, "From now on, my name is Jigsaw." This is after he has had operations, apparently lasting only minutes by the movie's time line, to stitch up his face with twine. He now looks like the exhibit in the entrance lobby of the Texas Chainsaw Museum, and one eye looks painfully introspective.

The movie is not heavy on plot. By my Timex Indiglo, there was no meaningful exposition at all during the first fifteen minutes, just men getting slaughtered. Then things slow down enough to reveal that the Punisher, aka Frank Castle, who avenged the murder of his family in an earlier film, has now killed a good guy who was father to little Grace (Stephanie Janusauskas) and husband to Angela (Julie Benz), who will Never Be Able to Forgive Him for What He's Done, nor should she, but she will.

The city, Montreal playing New York, has a small population, consisting only of good guys and bad guys and not much of anybody else. I'd get out, too. It's the kind of violence the president should fly over in Air Force One and regard sadly through the window. It goes without saying that the bad guys are unable to shoot the Punisher with their machine guns. That's consistent with the epidemic of malfunctioning machine guns in all recent super-violent films. Yet the Punisher kills a couple dozen hoodlums with his machine guns, while spinning upside-down under that chandelier.

Now pause to think with me. Everyone around the table is heavily armed. More armed men bust in through the door. The revolving Punisher is suspended in the center of the room. Because of the logic of the laws of physical motion, most of the time he is shooting away from any individual bad guy. How can they possibly miss hitting him? It's so hard these days, getting good help.

The Punisher: War Zone is the third in a series of Punisher movies. It follows *The Punisher* (1989), starring Dolph Lundgren, and *The Punisher* (2004), starring Thomas Jane and John Travolta. Since the second film has the same title as the first, it's hard to tell them apart, but why would you want to? My fellow critic Bill Stamets, settling down for the screening, shared with me that he watched the 2004 movie for his homework. I did my algebra.

Push ★ ½
PG-13, 111 m., 2009

Chris Evans (Nick Gant), Dakota Fanning (Cassie Holmes), Camilla Belle (Kira Hudson), Cliff Curtis (Hook Waters), Djimon Hounsou (Henry Carver). Directed by Paul McGuigan and produced by Bruce Davey, William Vince, and Glenn Williamson. Screenplay by David Bourla.

Push has vibrant cinematography and decent acting, but I'm blasted if I know what it's about. Oh, I understand how the characters are paranormals, and how they're living in a present that was changed in the past, among enemies who are trying to change the future. I know they can read minds and use telekinesis to move things. I know they're a later generation of a Nazi experiment gone wrong, and the U.S. Army wants them for super-soldiers.

But that's all simply the usual horsefeathers to set up the situation. What are they *doing*? The answer to that involves a MacGuffin that would have Hitchcock harrumphing and telling Alma, "Oh, dear, they really have allowed themselves to get carried away." The MacGuffin is a briefcase. Yes, like in *Pulp Fiction*, but this time we know what's in it. It's a drug or serum that (is the only thing that?) kills paranormals. And the Division desperately wants it.

I'm not sure if the Division is part of the army or against it. I know that the telekinetic Nick (Chris Evans) is hiding from it in Hong Kong, and that the Pusher Cassie (Dakota Fanning) finds him there and brings along the briefcase (I think), and that she's followed there by most of the other characters, including Kira (Camilla Belle) and the Division agent Henry (Djimon Hounsou), who is another Pusher. Pushing involves not drugs but Pushing into other people's minds.

Kira is said to be the only paranormal who ever survived the deadly serum. But why did they want her dead? And who are they? And why is it so urgent to find the briefcase, which contains a syringe filled with the serum? This is an especially perplexing question for me because when the syringe was being filled to kill Kira, it looked to me like the label on the bottle of medicine clearly said "B-12," an excellent curative for anemia, which none of the characters has a problem with.

Apart from the MacGuffin, the movie is wall to wall with the Talking Killer Syndrome. Never have more people pointed more guns at more heads and said more words without anyone getting shot. Even if they are telekinetic and can point the guns without holding them.

All of these people, and others, speak very earnestly about Pushing, and they plot to outwit and outthink enemy Pushers, and clearly they are in a lot deeper than the audience is ever likely to get. It's like you're listening to shop talk in a shop that doesn't make anything you've ever seen.

Dakota Fanning's Cassie claims at one point that she's "older than twelve," but I dunno. Her mother would probably not have allowed her to fly off to Hong Kong alone, wearing a miniskirt and with purple streaks in her hair, but her mother has been killed, which is part of her problem. She does get a little drunk, which provides the movie's only laugh. Dakota's real mother probably told her, "Dakota, honey, why don't you take the role and get to see Hong Kong?" If that's what happened, she has the best reason of anybody for being in this movie.

Q

Quantum of Solace ★ ★
PG-13, 105 m., 2008

Daniel Craig (James Bond), Olga Kurylenko (Camille), Mathieu Amalric (Dominic Greene), Judi Dench (M), Jeffrey Wright (Felix Leiter), Gemma Arterton (Agent Fields). Directed by Marc Forster and produced by Michael G. Wilson and Barbara Broccoli. Screenplay by Paul Haggis, Neal Purvis, and Robert Wade.

OK, I'll say it. Never again. Don't ever let this happen again to James Bond. *Quantum of Solace* is his twenty-second film, and he will survive it, but for the twenty-third it is necessary to go back to the drawing board and redesign from the ground up. Please understand: James Bond is not an action hero! He is too good for that. He is an attitude. Violence for him is an annoyance. He exists for the foreplay and the cigarette. He rarely encounters a truly evil villain. More often a comic opera buffoon with hired goons in matching jumpsuits.

Quantum of Solace has the worst title in the series save for *Never Say Never Again,* words that could have been used by Kent after King Lear utters the saddest line in all of Shakespeare: "Never! Never! Never! Never! Never!" The movie opens with Bond involved in a reckless car chase on the tollway that leads through mountain tunnels from Nice through Monte Carlo and down to Portofino in Italy, where Edward Lear lies at rest with his cat, Old Foss. I have driven that way many a time. It is a breathtaking drive.

You won't find that out here. The chase, with Bond under constant machine-gun fire, is so quickly cut and so obviously composed of incomprehensible CGI that we're essentially looking at bright colors bouncing off one another, intercut with Bond at the wheel and POV shots of approaching monster trucks. Let's all think together. When has an action hero ever, even once, been killed by machine-gun fire, no matter how many hundreds of rounds? The hit men should simply reject them and say, "No can do, Boss. They never work in this kind of movie."

The chase has no connection to the rest of the plot, which is routine for Bond, but it's about the movie's last bow to tradition. In *Quantum of Solace* he will share no cozy quality time with the Bond girl (Olga Kurylenko). We fondly remember the immortal names of Pussy Galore, Xenia Onatopp, and Plenty O'Toole, who I have always suspected was a drag queen. In this film, who do we get? Are you ready for this? Camille. That's it. Camille. Not even Camille Squeal. Or Cammy Miami. Or Miss O'Toole's friend, Cam Shaft.

Daniel Craig remains a splendid Bond, one of the best. He is handsome, agile, muscular, dangerous. Everything but talkative. I didn't count, but I think M (Judi Dench) has more dialogue than 007. Bond doesn't look like the urge to peel Camille has even entered his mind.

He blows up a hotel in the middle of a vast, barren, endless Bolivian desert. It's a luxury hotel, with angular W Hotel–style minimalist room furniture you might cut your legs on and a bartender who will stir or shake you any drink, but James has become a regular bloke who orders lager. Who are the clients at this highest of high-end hotels? Lawrence of Arabia, obviously, and millionaires who hate green growing things. Conveniently, when the hotel blows up, the filmmakers don't have to contend with adjacent buildings, traffic, pedestrians, skylines, or anything else. Talk about your blue screen. Nothing better than the azure desert sky.

Why is he in Bolivia? In pursuit of a global villain, whose name is not Goldfinger, Scaramanga, Drax, or Le Chiffre, but . . . Dominic Greene (Mathieu Amalric). What is Dominic's demented scheme to control the globe? As a start, the fiend desires to corner the water supply of . . . Bolivia. Ohooo! Nooo! This twisted design, revealed to Bond after at least an hour of death-defying action, reminds me of the famous laboratory mouse who was introduced into a labyrinth. After fighting his way for days through baffling corridors and down dead ends, finally, *finally,* parched and starving, the little creature crawled at last to the training button and hurled his tiny body against it. And what rolled down the chute as his reward? A licorice gum ball.

Dominic Greene lacks a headquarters on

the moon or on the floor of the sea. He operates out of an ordinary shipping warehouse with loading docks. His evil transport is provided by forklifts and pickup trucks. Bond doesn't have to creep out to the ledge of an underground volcano to spy on him. He just walks up to the chain-link fence and peers through. Greene could get useful security tips from Wal-Mart.

There is no Q in *Quantum of Solace,* except in the title. No Miss Moneypenny at all. M now has a male secretary. That Judi Dench, what a fox. Bond doesn't even size him up. He learned his lesson with Plenty. This Bond, he doesn't bring much to the party. Daniel Craig can play suave, and he can be funny, and Brits are born doing double entendre. Craig is a fine actor. Here they lock him down. I repeat: James Bond is not an action hero! Leave the action to your Jason Bournes. This is a swampy old world. The deeper we sink in, the more we need James Bond to stand above it.

R

Race to Witch Mountain ★ ★ ½
PG, 98 m., 2009

Dwayne Johnson (Jack Bruno), AnnaSophia Robb (Sara), Alexander Ludwig (Seth), Carla Gugino (Dr. Alex Friedman), Ciaran Hinds (Henry Burke), Garry Marshall (Dr. Donald Harlan), Tom Everett Scott (Matheson). Directed by Andy Fickman and produced by Andrew Gunn. Screenplay by Matt Lopez and Mark Bomback.

Before the sneak preview of *Race to Witch Mountain,* they had a little quiz show and gave away T-shirts. One question: "Who plays Jack Bruno?" Half the audience roared, "The Rock!" Not one lonely vote for Dwayne Johnson. The other famous movie "Rock" was born Roy Harold Scherer Jr. It's a name that stays in the mind.

I think Dwayne Johnson has a likable screen presence and is a good choice for an innocuous family entertainment like this, and also he once sent me some Hawaiian Macadamia Nut Brickle. I would have mailed it back because film critics are not supposed to accept gifts from movie stars, but I accidentally ate it first. What Johnson does here is provide a credible tough-guy action hero in a nonthreatening mode. He rules over chases, fights, explosions, and an Ooze Monster, yet never seems nasty, so the kids can feel safe around him.

Young audiences will like the kids in the movie, played by AnnaSophia Robb and Alexander Ludwig. And in using kids as the costars, the movie has its cake and eats it too, because Sara and Seth may look like they're fifteen or sixteen, but actually, you see, they're aliens whose flying saucer crash-landed and is being held at a secret government UFO facility inside Witch Mountain—so secret, the mountain is not shown on Google Maps. I suspected right away it was a mountain made for this movie because it is shaped like a sawed-off version of the mashed potato sculpture that Richard Dreyfuss kept sculpting in *Close Encounters of the Third Kind*—the one that resembled, you remember, the outcrop where the flying saucer landed.

Anyway, Dwayne Johnson plays a former driver for a Las Vegas mob boss who goes straight after he gets out of prison and starts driving a taxi. In his backseat one day, Sara and Seth materialize, explain they are aliens, and ask him to drive them to a remote desert location. They talk like an artificial intelligence program that got a D in English, although later they gradually start to sound more like Disney teenagers. They're later joined by Dr. Alex Friedman (Carla Gugino), an expert who was in Vegas lecturing to fanboys and girls at a combination UFO convention and costume party.

On their tail is a pursuit team of federal agents led by a hardnose named Burke (Ciaran Hinds). Burke moves in a caravan of three black SUVs with tinted glass, although when necessary he can materialize dozens of heavily armed SWAT team members. The chase leads deep into Witch Mountain, although not before the kids enter a buried chamber beneath a miner's shack and there obtain some kind of extraterrestrial cell phone extracted by Seth after plunging his arm up to the elbow into a pulsating mass of gelatinous goo.

Further details I will leave for your discovery. Since Seth and Sara only appropriated the bodies of human teenagers, I was left with a couple of questions. (1) Did they displace real teenagers, or only clone themselves? (2) They're cute, but what do they actually look like as aliens? Not quivering gobs of mucilaginous viscidity, I trust.

Rachel Getting Married ★ ★ ★ ★
R, 111 m., 2008

Anne Hathaway (Kym), Rosemarie DeWitt (Rachel), Bill Irwin (Paul), Tunde Adebimpe (Sidney), Mather Zickel (Kieran), Anna Deavere Smith (Carol), Anisa George (Emma), Debra Winger (Abby). Directed by Jonathan Demme and produced by Demme, Neda Armian, and Marc Platt. Screenplay by Jenny Lumet.

The rules say that critics don't discuss movies after screenings. After I saw Jonathan Demme's *Rachel Getting Married* for the second time, however, a friend asked: "Wouldn't you love to attend a wedding like that?" In a way, I felt I had. Yes, I began to feel absorbed in the experience. A few movies can do that, can slip you out of your mind and into theirs.

Rachel (Rosemarie DeWitt) does indeed get married. There is an engrossing plot involving her sister, Kym (Anne Hathaway). But I believe the film's deep subject is the wedding itself: how it unfolds, who attends, the nature of the ceremony, and what it has to observe about how the concept of "family" embraces others, and how our multicultural society is growing comfortable with itself.

The story centers on Kym (Hathaway), a recovering drug addict, who after being in and out of rehab for ten years is now several months into a treatment that seems to be working. She's given a day pass to attend her sister's wedding. Her family lives in a big old country house in Connecticut, filled with memories, family, future in-laws, and the friends of bride and groom. Sidney (Tunde Adebimpe), Rachel's intended, is a classical musician, and all kinds of music fills a film that has no formal score. The wedding party is what we call "diverse." I'm not going to identify characters by race because such a census would offend the whole spirit of the film. These characters love one another, and that's it.

Notice the visual strategy of Demme and his cinematographer, Declan Quinn. Some shots are dealt with in a traditional way (establishing, close-ups, etc). More shots plunge right into the middle of the characters; some may be hand-held, or maybe not, but for me they reproduced an experience we've all had. That's when we wander through a party looking first here and then there, noticing who is where and why, connecting threads, savoring. Sometimes we walk outside and look through doorways and windows. This visual approach is how they populate the film with a large number of characters, establish them, familiarize us, and don't pause for redundant identifications. We don't meet everyone at a wedding, but we observe everyone.

Consider in this context the former and present wives of the father, Paul (Bill Irwin). His first wife, Abby (Debra Winger), is the mother of Kym, Rachel, and a younger brother who drowned. She is of intense importance to Kym. Their private conversation is filmed in a traditional, powerful way, underlining dialogue and emotion. Then consider Paul's second wife, Carol (Anna Deavere Smith). She has limited dialogue and no big dramatic scenes. But without being obvious about it, Demme and Quinn make her very present. As we wander through the house and sit through the rehearsal dinner, the wedding, and the party, we are always aware of her.

This is exactly right and observant of the way a loved and comfortable "second wife" functions at an event where the bride's parents have higher billing. She knows everyone, watches everything, is pleased or concerned, stands quietly behind her husband, loves his daughters, smoothes the waves. To give her a foreground role would have been a mistake. But you will not forget her.

One of the reasons Smith works so well, as an unobtrusive soothing element, is typecasting. She *looks* like she would be the kind of person she plays. Whether she really is or not, I wouldn't know. But that's not the point of typecasting. Why have I given so much attention to a relatively minor character? Because she represents the film's approach to all the characters. When Robert Altman is thanked in the end credits, I imagine it is not only because he was Demme's friend, but because his instinct for ensemble stories was an example. Demme owes much to his editor, Tim Squyres, who also edited Altman's *Gosford Park*, another film that kept track of everyone at a big house party. That might have been the very reason he was hired.

Demme's achievement is shared with the original screenplay by Sidney Lumet's daughter, Jenny Lumet. This is her first writing credit, but the story might have felt like second nature to her. She is descended from artists; her grandparents on her mother's side were the singer Lena Horne and the jazz legend Louis Jordan Jones; her grandparents on her father's side were Baruch and Eugenia Lumet, an actress and an actor-director. Her father is the director Sidney Lumet, and her mother the writer Gail Lumet Buckley. The apple did not fall far from those trees. I don't have to be told that her life has included countless gatherings of the nature of Rachel's wedding. And although I do not know Sidney Lumet well, I know enough to say he is kind and warm; I suspect he was an inspiration for the character Paul, who can hear Carol even when she isn't talking.

Jenny Lumet has a sister, the sound editor Amy Lumet. That's interesting. Is the film autobiographical? I have no way of knowing. Demme demonstrates something he shares with Altman: He likes to be surrounded by his own extended family. The gray-bearded man who performs the ceremony is his cousin, Reverend Robert Castle, subject of Demme's doc *Cousin Bobby* (1992). His daughter Josephine is in the film. And so on. Apart from the story, which is interesting enough, *Rachel Getting Married* is like theme music for an evolving new age.

Rails & Ties ★ ★ ½
PG-13, 101 m., 2007

Kevin Bacon (Tom Stark), Marcia Gay Harden (Megan Stark), Miles Heizer (Davey Danner), Marin Hinkle (Renee), Eugene Byrd (Otis Higgs), Bonnie Root (Laura Danner). Directed by Alison Eastwood and produced by Robert Lorenz, Peer Oppenheimer, and Barrett Stuart. Screenplay by Micky Levy.

Sometimes there's a movie that has better things in it than the underlying material deserves. Alison Eastwood's *Rails & Ties* is a movie like that. I found the opening third tremendously intriguing and involving—I thought the emotions were so real they could be touched—but then the film lost its way and fell into the clutches of sentimental melodrama.

It opens on a railroad engineer going to work. This is Tom Stark (Kevin Bacon), and he not merely loves his job but feels a sense of duty about it that is part of the fiber of his being. He has been told he can take the day off because of bad news he has received about the health of his wife. But he wouldn't think of it. He follows the railroad book on all things, including life and death.

We meet his wife, Megan (Marcia Gay Harden), who is dying of cancer and filled with fear and grief, and she has some moments that are heartbreaking. She needs her husband, or maybe she needs a husband who could be emotionally available to her; Tom is

not there for her and hasn't been for years, pouring all of his passion into trains. At work, he's behind the throttle, and at home, he's tinkering with his elaborate model train layout.

We meet another mother and her young son. This is Laura Danner (Bonnie Root), who has big problems and has taken a lot of pills and parked her car on the tracks with her nine-year-old son, Davey (Miles Heizer), belted in next to her. Coming around a bend, Tom sees the car on the tracks but makes a snap judgment that an emergency stop might throw cars off the track and injure passengers. His co-engineer (Eugene Byrd) begs him to brake, but Tom knows the book, the book covers the situation, and the book says not to brake. Davey gets out of the car, tries to pull his mother free, and jumps aside just seconds before he would have been killed along with her.

"He didn't even *try* to stop!" Davey says over and over again. Tom Stark knows there will be a hearing but is confident he will get a pass because he was following the book. And all of that, up to there and for several more scenes, plays immediate and true. But then the movie veers into a more standard storytelling pattern. Because much of it is well done, for what it is, I won't reveal key details. But assume that in one way or another the boy has good reason to escape from a foster home, and that he finds a way to meet Tom and Megan Stark.

Yes, he feels anger toward the man. Perhaps some of it is displaced from his mom, whose decision to park on the tracks remains a troubling mystery to him. The way things work out, his visit to the Starks, which should have been over almost immediately, seems to extend indefinitely. And they begin to love each other.

This in itself is not an unworthy plot development, but somehow the urgency of Megan's early grief and Tom's early emotional stonewalling gets channeled into acceptable, safe, narrative strategies. We can relax. The story will steer us safely past unacceptable despair. There is even a scene involving the model train layout to clear the air because, yes, Davey likes trains about as much as Tom does. And then one development leads to another and everything leads up to a final scene and a final shot that I found myself rejecting emotionally.

I know in the real world that what happens

at the end of the movie is likely enough. But other outcomes are possible, and given the places the movie took me and the implicit promises it made, I found no release or closure in the ending. In a movie that detoured into emotional manipulation, I found myself, paradoxically, wanting more manipulation. When a movie jumps the tracks of implacable logic, you may regret it, but you go along with it because you have to. The last thing you want is for it to jump back on the tracks.

That is not to overlook the qualities of *Rails & Ties*, above all in the acting. Marcia Gay Harden has a scene by herself that defines hopelessness and desolation. Kevin Bacon makes it clear, without even seeming to try, why the railroad is his fortress and its rule book is his bible. And young Miles Heizer does such a good job with the nine-year-old that I repeat a recent observation: Have you noticed in a lot of movies how natural, convincing, and pure the performances of the child actors are?

Alison Eastwood (Clint's daughter) must be a good director, because she can place those qualities on the screen. I wish I knew more about the history of the Micky Levy screenplay—whether it went through rewrites, was steered in a wrong direction, was questioned. When the film premiered at Telluride and Toronto, there were some who doubted coincidences involving characters and trains. Those sorts of things go with the territory, and I find it interesting that the screenplay risked them. But there were fundamental decisions to be made about the lives and fates of these characters, and I think somehow the filmmakers lost the way—lost sight of the people inside the plot.

The Rape of Europa ★ ★ ★

NO MPAA RATING, 117 m., 2008

Joan Allen (Narrator). A documentary written, produced, and directed by Richard Berge, Nicole Newnham, and Bonni Cohen, based on the book by Lynn H. Nicholas.

We know the Nazis looted art from the nations they overran. Maybe we've seen *The Train* (1964) and know how one shipment was thwarted. But how many important paintings, sculptures, and other artworks would you say the Nazis made off with? Hundreds? Thousands?

The Rape of Europa, a startling documentary, puts the number rather higher: *one-fifth* of all the known significant works of art in Europe—millions. Incredibly, Hitler maintained shopping lists of art for every country he invaded and dispatched troops to secure (i.e., plunder) the works and ship them back to Germany. He had plans to build a monumental art museum in Linz, his Austrian birthplace, and was working on models of the structure even during his final days in the Berlin bunker. His right-hand man Goering was no less keen as a collector.

That Hitler was mad is well known. That he was mad about art, not so well. He was, in his youth, an ambitious painter and applied to an art school in Vienna but was rejected. The general outline of his early art career, somewhat fictionalized, can be seen in *Max*, a little-noticed 2002 film starring Noah Taylor as Hitler and John Cusack as a one-armed Jewish art dealer in Munich who befriends Hitler, his liquor deliveryman.

Hitler's art was not good (we see some landscape watercolors), and his taste in art was terrible. He had a weakness for heroic Nordic supermen and women in a style of uber-kitsch, and he believed modern art was Jewish and decadent. In addition to the artworks he looted, he ordered the destruction of countless others; not all of those Nazi bonfires consumed only books.

This absorbing documentary begins with one painting, Gustav Klimt's *Gold Portrait of Adele Bloch-Bauer,* which, like countless other paintings, was stolen from Jews, disappeared, and then mysteriously reappeared in galleries and museums in Europe and America with shadowy provenance. Maria Altmann, the niece of the man who commissioned the painting, waged a long legal battle to have possession returned to her and won; when the painting was later sold at auction, its price of $135 million set a record.

But until recently, many possessors of stolen artworks have chosen to ignore claims by their original owners, and only now is an international tracing operation under way. It is believed that countless priceless works languish in the shadows of private homes, discreetly kept out of sight. Work is only beginning on a central clearinghouse of information.

Many other works of sculpture and architecture were destroyed by the bombing raids of both sides, although an occasional exception was made; the city of Venice, for example was spared by American bombers. Much praise is given to the Monument Men, American art experts enlisted into the Army and deployed under the orders of Eisenhower to identify and protect the surviving heritage of liberated nations. In stark contrast, American bombs destroyed museums in Baghdad and throughout Iraq, and others were looted; no effort was made by our commanders to preserve the treasures.

Ratatouille ★ ★ ★ ★
G, 114 m., 2007

With the voices of: Patton Oswalt (Remy), Lou Romano (Linguini), Ian Holm (Skinner), Janeane Garofalo (Colette), Brian Dennehy (Django), Peter O'Toole (Anton Ego), Brad Garrett (Gusteau), Peter Sohn (Emile). Directed by Brad Bird and produced by John Lasseter. Screenplay by Bird, based on an original story by Jan Pinkava, Jim Capobianco, and Bird.

A lot of animated movies have inspired sequels, notably *Shrek*, but Brad Bird's *Ratatouille* is the first one that made me positively desire one. Remy, the earnest little rat who is its hero, is such a lovable, determined, gifted rodent that I want to know what happens to him next, now that he has conquered the summit of French cuisine. I think running for office might not be beyond his reach, and there's certainly something De Gaullean about his snout.

Remy is a member of a large family of rats (a horde, I think, is the word) who ply the trash cans and sewers of a Parisian suburb, just like good rats should. "Eat your garbage!" commands Remy's father, Django, obviously a loving parent. The rats are evicted from their cozy home in a cottage kitchen ceiling in a scene that will have rat haters in the audience cringing (and who among us will claim they don't hate rats more than a little?), and they are swept through the sewers in a torrential flood. Students of Victor Hugo will know that the hero Jean Valjean of *Les Miserables* found the Seine because he knew that every sewer must necessarily run downhill toward it, and indeed Remy washes up near the river, in view of the most famous restaurant in *tout la France*. This is the establishment of Auguste Gusteau, author of the best-seller *Anyone Can Cook*, a title that might not go over very well in France, which is why the book appears to be in English and might well be titled, *Anyone Can Cook Better Than the English*. (Famous British recipe: "Cook until gray.")

Remy (voice by Patton Oswalt) has always been blessed, or cursed, with a refined palate and a sensitive nose, and now he starts skulking around the kitchen of his culinary hero (voice by Brad Garrett). Alas, the monstrous food critic Anton Ego (Peter O'Toole) issues a scathing indictment of Gusteau's recent cooking, the chef dies in a paroxysm of grief, or perhaps it is not a paroxysm, but I like the word, and the kitchen is taken over by the sniveling little snipe Skinner (Ian Holm). Lowest of the low is Gusteau's nephew Linguini (Lou Romano), who must be hired, but is assigned to the wretched job of *plongeur*— literally, one who washes the dishes by plunging them into soapy water.

Linguini and Remy meet, somehow establish trust and communication, and when Linguini gets credit for a soup that the rat has saved with strategic seasonings, they team up. Remy burrows into Linguini's hair, is concealed by his toque, can see through its transparent sides, and controls Linguini by pulling on his hair as if each tuft were a joystick. Together, they astonish Paris with their genius.

All of this begins as a dubious premise and ends as a triumph of animation, comedy, imagination, and, yes, humanity. What is most lovable about Remy is his modesty and shyness, even for a rat. He has body language so expressive that many humans would trade for it. Many animated characters seem to communicate with semaphores, but Remy has a repertory of tiny French hand gestures, shrugs, and physical expressiveness. Does any other nationality have more ways of moving a finger and an eyebrow less than an inch while signaling something as complex as, "I would do anything for you, monsieur, but as you see,

I have only two hands, and these times we live in do not permit me the luxury of fulfilling such requests."

Brad Bird and his coproducer John Lasseter pretty clearly take over leadership in the animation field right now. Yes, Bird made *The Incredibles,* but the one that got away was his wonderful *The Iron Giant,* in which a towering robot was as subtle, gentle, and touching as Remy. His eye for detail is remarkable. Every prop and utensil and spice and ingredient in the kitchen is almost tangible, and I for one would never turn off the Food Channel if Remy hosted a program named *Any Rat Can Cook.*

This is clearly one of the best of the year's films. Every time an animated film is successful, you have to read all over again about how animation isn't "just for children" but "for the whole family" and even "for adults going on their own." No kidding!

The Reader ★ ★ ★ ½
R, 123 m., 2008

Kate Winslet (Hanna Schmitz), Ralph Fiennes (Michael Berg), David Kross (Young Michael Berg), Lena Olin (Rose Mather/Ilana Mather), Bruno Ganz (Professor Rohl). Directed by Stephen Daldry and produced by Anthony Minghella, Sydney Pollack, Donna Gigliotti, and Redmond Morris. Screenplay by David Hare, based on the novel by Bernhard Schlink.

The crucial decision in *The Reader* is made by a twenty-four-year-old youth, who has information that might help a woman about to be sentenced to life in prison but withholds it. He is ashamed to reveal his affair with this woman. By making this decision, he shifts the film's focus from the subject of German guilt about the Holocaust and turns it on the human race in general. The film intends his decision as the key to its meaning, but most viewers may conclude that *The Reader* is only about the crimes of the Nazis and the response to them by postwar German generations.

The film centers on a sexual relationship between Hanna (Kate Winslet), a woman in her midthirties, and Michael (David Kross), a boy of fifteen. That such things are wrong is beside the point; they happen, and the story is about how it connected with her earlier life and his later one. It is powerfully, if sometimes confusingly, told in a flashback framework, and powerfully acted by Winslet and Kross, with Ralph Fiennes coldly enigmatic.

The story begins with the cold, withdrawn Michael in middle age (Fiennes) and moves back to the late 1950s and a day when young Michael is found sick and feverish in the street and taken back to Hanna's apartment to be cared for. This day, and all their days together, will be obsessed with sex. Hanna makes little pretense of genuinely loving Michael, whom she calls "kid," and although Michael has a helpless crush on Hanna, it should not be confused with love. He is swept away by the discovery of his own sexuality. What does she get from their affair? Sex, certainly, but it seems more important that he read aloud to her: "Reading first. Sex afterwards." The director, Stephen Daldry, portrays them with a great deal of nudity and sensuality, which is correct, because for those hours, in that place, they are about nothing else.

One day Hanna disappears. Michael finds her apartment deserted, with no hint or warning. His unformed ego is unprepared for this blow. Eight years later, as a law student, he enters a courtroom and discovers Hanna in a group of Nazi prison guards being tried for murder. Something during this trial suddenly makes another of her secrets clear to him and might help explain why she became a prison guard. His discovery does not excuse her unforgivable guilt. Still, it might affect her sentencing. Michael remains silent.

The adult Michael has sentenced himself to a lonely, isolated existence. We see him after a night with a woman, treating her with remote politeness. He has never recovered from the wound he received from Hanna, nor from the one he inflicted on himself eight years after. She hurt him; he hurt her. She was isolated and secretive after the war; he became so after the trial. The enormity of her sin far outweighs his, but they are both guilty of allowing harm because they reject the choice to do good.

At the end of the film, Michael encounters a Jewish woman in New York (Lena Olin), who eviscerates him with her moral outrage. She should. But she thinks he seeks understanding for Hanna. Not so. He cannot forgive

353

Hanna's crimes. He seeks understanding for himself, although perhaps he doesn't realize that. In the courtroom he withheld moral witness and remained silent, as she did, as most Germans did. And as many of us have done or might be capable of doing.

There are enormous pressures in all human societies to go along. Many figures involved in the Wall Street meltdown have used the excuse, "I was only doing my job. I didn't know what was going on." President Bush led us into war on mistaken premises and now says he was betrayed by faulty intelligence. U.S. military personnel became torturers because they were ordered to. Detroit says it was only giving us the cars we wanted. The Soviet Union functioned for years because people went along. China still is.

Many of the critics of *The Reader* seem to believe it is all about Hanna's shameful secret. No, not her past as a Nazi guard. The earlier secret she essentially became a guard to conceal. Others think the movie is an excuse for soft-core porn disguised as a sermon. Still others say it asks us to pity Hanna. Some complain we don't need yet another "Holocaust movie." None of them think the movie may have anything to say about them. I believe the movie may be demonstrating a fact of human nature: Most people, most of the time, all over the world, choose to go along. We vote with the tribe.

What would we have done during the rise of Hitler? If we had been Jews, we would have fled or been killed. But if we were one of the rest of the Germans? Can we guess, on the basis of how most white Americans, north and south, knew about racial discrimination but didn't go out on a limb to oppose it? Philip Roth's great novel *The Plot Against America* imagines a Nazi takeover here. It is painfully thought-provoking and probably not unfair. *The Reader* suggests that many people are like Michael and Hanna and possess secrets that we would do shameful things to conceal. ☞

Recount ★ ★ ★

NO MPAA RATING, 115 m., 2008

Kevin Spacey (Ron Klain), John Hurt (Warren Christopher), Laura Dern (Katherine Harris), Tom Wilkinson (James Baker), Denis Leary (Michael Whouley), Ed Begley Jr. (David Boies), Bob Balaban (Ben Ginsburg). Directed by Jay Roach and produced by Kevin Spacey. Screenplay by Danny Strong.

Katherine Harris was a piece of work. The Florida secretary of state during the 2000 elections is not intended as the leading role in *Recount*, an HBO docudrama about that lamentable fiasco, but every time Laura Dern appears on the screen, she owns it. Watch her stride into a room of powerful men, pick up a little paper packet of sugar for her coffee, and shake it with great sweeping arm gestures as if she were a demonstrator in an educational film.

As much as anyone, Harris was responsible for George W. Bush being declared the winner of the state, and thus of the presidency. In a bewildering thicket of controversy about chads, hanging chads, dimpled chads, military ballots, voting machines, and nearsighted elderly voters, it was her apparent oblivion that prevented a meaningful recount from ever taking place. Don't talk to me about the Florida Supreme Court, the U.S. Supreme Court, or even the hero of the film, a Democratic Party strategist named Ron Klain (Kevin Spacey). They had a great influence on events, but it was Katherine Harris who created a shortage of time that ultimately had a greater effect than anything else.

And this is the fascinating part, the part that Laura Dern exploits until her performance becomes mesmerizing: Harris did it *without seeming to know what she was doing*. Although she was the head of Bush's Florida campaign, she bats her eyes in innocence while announcing a "firewall" isolating her office from anyone, Democrat or Republican, lest they affect her worship of the power of law. After that announcement, it is the merest detail that the film portrays two GOP strategists moving into her office and giving her suggestions. They include her when talking about what "we" have to do.

But even in the privacy of her office, she never quite seems to know what they are doing or why. She signals that her mind is operating in more elevated, more long-range dimensions. She sees it all as an adventure starring herself, and sometimes seems to be thanking her classmates for electing her homecoming queen. "Ten years ago," she tells her minders in a wondering voice, "I was teaching the chicken dance to seniors, and now I've been thrust into a political tempest of historical dimensions."

She sure has. *Recount,* an efficient and relentless enactment of the strategists on both sides of the Florida controversy, shows an accident that was waiting to happen. So confusing was the state's "butterfly ballot" (how such terms resound in memory) that large numbers of senior citizens from liberal districts apparently cast mistaken votes for Pat Buchanan, a right-wing independent. Buchanan himself went on CNN to doubt that his support was quite that strong in Palm Beach County. If their chads alone had been correctly punched, Al Gore might have been elected president. But a chad is a chad. And the film follows all the jaw-dropping developments that kept us so enthralled during that confusing season.

The point of view is largely Klain's, played as a weary and dogged idealist by Spacey. As the film opens and it looks like Gore will win the election, he turns down a job offer from Gore because he thinks he deserves better. Yet soon he is the engine behind the Democrats' legal challenges, persisting even more than Gore himself probably would have. "You know what's funny about all this?" he asks his teammate Michael Whouley (Denis Leary). "I'm not even sure I *like* Al Gore." Klain's GOP opponent is James Baker (Tom Wilkinson), written and played as a man who does what any reasonable politician would have done under the circumstances. Often enough these ultimate insiders seem to get most of their information from CNN; aides frequently run in and tell them to watch the TV, as when both supreme courts drop their bombshells.

You might assume the movie is pro-Gore and anti-Bush, but you would not be quite right. Dave Grusin's almost eerie score evokes a journey into uncharted territories and haunted lands, but that's as close as it comes to making a statement (other than the incredulity voiced by the losers). The Democratic Party figures portrayed in the film have been the loudest in protest, especially Warren Christopher (John Hurt), who was the first head of the Gore team, and is portrayed as a wimp ready to cave in to the GOP. Whether the film is fair to him, I cannot say.

Recount portrays a lot of Democrats as being in favor of an "orderly transition of power" at whatever cost, and a lot of Republicans as being in favor of winning, in an orderly transition or any other kind. At least, as an exhausted Warren Christopher says when all is over and his man has lost: "The system worked. There were no tanks in the streets." Of course, at that time he would not have been thinking of the streets of Baghdad.

Redacted ★ ★ ★ ½
R, 91 m., 2007

Patrick Carroll (Reno Flake), Rob Devaney (Lawyer McCoy), Izzy Diaz (Angel Salazar), Mike Figueroa (Sergeant Jim Vasquez), Ty Jones (Master Sergeant Jim Sweet), Kel O'Neill (Gabe Blix), Daniel Stewart Sherman (Specialist B. B. Rush). Directed by Brian De Palma and produced by Jennifer Weiss, Simone Urdl, Jason Kliot, and Joana Vicente. Screenplay by De Palma.

The rape and subsequent murders in *Redacted* actually happened, and we are told that director Brian De Palma found out about them on the Internet, in blogs and YouTube postings, and on American and Arabic sites. He fictionalizes them, as he must for legal reasons, but presents them in a way suggesting how he found them; the movie looks cobbled together largely from found Web footage. It's better photographed than much similar material on the Web, and edited to create a relentless momentum, but he wants us to feel as if we're discovering this material for ourselves.

So we would be forced to, if the movie's buried message is clear. *Redacted* is a word simply meaning "edited," and is often used by the military as a way of calling a simple act by an objective, and therefore defused, name. In a similar fashion, a "rendition" can be a kidnapping and torture. The film explains the origin of much of its footage by introducing us to a soldier named Angel Salazar (Izzy Diaz), who carries a digital video camera and thinks maybe he can make a documentary to get him into film school. A good plan, but if you notice that the movie is set in Samarra, you may recall the parable of the man whose best-laid plans went wrong there.

The story comes down to this: The soldiers of Alpha Company are manning a checkpoint. A car speeds past. They open fire, and a pregnant woman and her unborn child are killed. Two more hearts and minds not won over. In retribution, one of the company's members is killed by local militia. In response, the two men who fired on the car (Rush, played by Daniel Stewart Sherman, and the well-named Flake, played by Patrick Carroll) lead a nighttime raid during which a fifteen-year-old girl is raped, her family is murdered, and their house set afire. Company members are informed by Flake and Rush that if they don't keep quiet, they will die. There is no reason to doubt this.

Much of this action mirrors the events in an earlier De Palma film, *Casualties of War* (1989), in which Michael J. Fox played a Vietnam soldier who turned away from a rape. What is different in this film is the visual style, which informs us by its very nature that after the invention of the cheap video camera and the Internet, few actions can be assumed to be secret. De Palma uses the method to demonstrate how good (or neutral) soldiers can be turned into criminals or silent accomplices by a threat of violence from their comrades. How if you put men in a hellhole and arm them, and if they are predisposed to violence, they will not always follow the rules, or even remember them.

Redacted is a metaphor for what De Palma and others believe is the fatal flaw of our Iraq strategy: You cannot enforce "freedom" at gunpoint. Now that some 200,000 Iraqis have died in the war, for whatever reason and at whatever hands, it is hard to see how many of the rest would be as grateful for our presence as we are assured they are. This is something Angel Salazar finds out during the filming of his documentary, although unfortunately his key footage is redacted in a very direct way.

You may be vaguely aware of a controversy involving De Palma and some of his own footage that was "redacted." This involved the montage of "actual" photographs from Iraq that close the film. They were all actual at one point, but now some of them are staged, and others have been altered by having faces obscured by a black marker pen, lest the subjects' privacy be violated. Since they are dead, one doubts they would sue, but perhaps the black smudges make De Palma's point in another way.

The acting is curious. Some of it is convincing, and some of the rest is convincing in a different way: It convinces us that nonactors know they are being filmed and are acting and speaking slightly differently than they otherwise would. That makes some try to appear nicer, and others try to appear tougher or more menacing. That edge of inauthentic performance paradoxically increases the effect: Moments seem more real because they're not acted flawlessly.

The result of the film is shocking, saddening, and frustrating. The latest polls show that the great majority of the American public has withdrawn its approval from the war and its architects. Why should it be a mystery that the Iraqis do not love us? Did our mothers not ask us, "How would you feel if someone did that to you?" Yes, they are killing us, too, but they live there, and we went a great distance for our appointment in Samarra.

The name of the real girl, who was actually fourteen, was Abeer Qasim Hamza al-Janabi.

Redbelt ★ ★ ★

R, 98 m., 2008

Chiwetel Ejiofor (Mike Terry), Alice Braga (Sondra Terry), Emily Mortimer (Laura Black), Tim Allen (Chet Frank), Joe Mantegna (Jerry Weiss), Rodrigo Santoro (Bruno Silva), Max Martini (Joe Collins), Ricky Jay (Marty Brown). Directed by David Mamet and produced by Chrisann Verges. Screenplay by Mamet.

David Mamet's *Redbelt* assembles all the elements for a great Mamet film, but they're still spread out on the shop floor. It never really pulls itself together into the convincing, focused drama it promises, yet it kept me involved right up until the final scenes, which piled on developments almost recklessly. So gifted is Mamet as a writer and director that he can fascinate us even when he's pulling rabbits out of an empty hat.

The movie takes place in that pungent Mamet world of seamy streets on the wrong side of town, and is peopled by rogues and con men, trick artists and thieves, those who believe and those who prey on them. The cast is assembled from his stock company of actors whose very presence helps embody the atmosphere of a Mamet story, and who are almost always not what they seem, and then not even what they seem after that. He is fascinated by the deceptions of one confidence game assembled inside another.

At the center of a story, in a performance evoking intense idealism, is Mike Terry (Chiwetel Ejiofor), a martial arts instructor who runs a storefront studio on a barren city street. His is not one of those glass and steel fitness emporiums, but a throwback to an earlier time; the sign on his window promises jujitsu, and he apparently studied this art from those little pamphlets with crude illustrations that used to be advertised in the back pages of comic books. I studied booklets like this as a boy; apparently one embodies the philosophy of The Professor, a Brazilian martial arts master who is like a god to Mike.

Mike has few customers, is kept afloat by the small garment business of his wife, Sondra (Alice Braga), and is seen instructing a Los Angeles cop named Joe Collins (Max Martini). When you seem to be your studio's only instructor, the impression is fly-by-night, but there's a purist quality to Mike's dedication that has Joe completely convinced, and they both seriously believe in the "honor" of the academy.

Now commences a series of events it would be useless to describe, and which are eventually almost impossible to understand, involving a troubled lawyer (Emily Mortimer), a movie star (Tim Allen), the star's shifty manager (Joe Mantegna), and the world of a pay-TV fight promoter (Ricky Jay). All of these characters seem like marked-down versions of the stereotypes they're based on, and the pay-for-view operation feels more like local access cable than a big-bucks franchise.

In a bewildering series of deceptions, these people entrap the idealistic Mike into debt, betrayal, grief, guilt, and cynical disappointments, all leading up to a big televised fight sequence at the end that makes no attempt to be plausible and is interesting (if you are a student of such things) for its visual fakery. We've seen a lot of crowd scenes in which camera angles attempt to create the illusion of thousands of people who aren't really there, but *Redbelt* seems to be offering a crowd of hundreds (or dozens) who aren't really there. At a key point, in a wildly impossible development, the action shifts out of the ring, and the lights and cameras are focused on a man-to-man showdown in a gangway. The conclusion plays like a low-rent parody of a Rocky victory. The last shot left me underwhelmed.

So now you're wondering why you might want to see this movie at all. It might be because of the sheer art and craft of Mamet himself. For his dialogue, terse and enigmatic, as if in a secret code. For his series of "reveals" in which nothing is as it seems. For his lost world of fly-by-night operators. For his actors like Ricky Jay, who would be familiar with the term "suede shoe artist." For his bit parts for unexplained magicians. Especially for a sequence when Mike Terry, as baffled as we are, essentially asks for someone to explain the plot to him.

If you savor that sort of stuff, and I do, you may like *Redbelt* on its own dubious but seductive terms. It seems about to become one kind of movie, a conventional combination of con games and action, and then shadowboxes its way into a different kind of fight, which is about values, not strength. It's this kind of film: Some of the characters at the end, hauled in to provide a moral payoff, seem to have been airlifted from Brazil—which, in fact, they were.

Religulous ★ ★ ★ ½
R, 101 m., 2008

Bill Maher (Himself). A documentary directed by Larry Charles and produced by Jonah Smith, Palmer West, and Bill Maher. Screenplay by Maher.

I'm going to try to review Bill Maher's *Religulous* without getting into religion. Is that OK with everybody? Good. I don't want to fan the flames of a holy war.

The movie is about organized religions: Judaism, Christianity, Islam, Mormonism, TV evangelism, and even Scientology, with detours into pagan cults and ancient Egypt. Bill Maher, host, writer, and debater, believes they are all crazy. He fears they could lead us prayerfully into mutual nuclear doom. He doesn't get to Hinduism or Buddhism, but he probably doesn't approve of them either.

This review is going to depend on one of my own deeply held beliefs: It's not what the movie is about; it's how it's about it. This movie is about Bill Maher's opinion of religion. He's very smart, quick, and funny, and I found the movie entertaining, although sometimes he's a little mean to his targets. He visits holy places in Italy, Israel, Great Britain, Florida, Missouri, and Utah, and talks with adherents of the religions he finds there, and others.

Or maybe "talks with" is not quite the right phrase. It's more that he lines them up and shoots them down. He interrupts, talks over, slaps on subtitles, edits in movie and TV clips, and doesn't play fair. Reader, I took a guilty pleasure in his misbehavior. The people he interviews are astonishingly forbearing, even most of the truckers in a chapel at a truck stop. I expected somebody to take a swing at him, but nobody did, although one trucker walked out on him. Elsewhere in the film, Maher walks out on a rabbi who approvingly attended a Holocaust denial conference in Iran.

Maher had a Jewish mother and a Catholic father, and was raised as a Catholic until he was thirteen, when his father stopped attending services. He speaks with his elderly mother, who tells him: "I don't know why he did that. We never discussed it." He asks her what the family believed, before and after that event. "I don't know what we believed," she says. No, she's not confused. She just doesn't know.

Most everybody else in the film knows what they believe. If they don't, Maher does. He impersonates a Scientologist at London's Speakers' Corner in Hyde Park and says Scientology teaches that there was a race of thetans several trillion years old (older than the universe, which is only 13.73 billion years) and that we are born with thetans inside us, which can be detected by an E-Meter, on sale at your local Scientology center, and driven out by "auditing," which takes a long time and unfortunately costs money.

Many of Maher's confrontations involve logical questions about holy books. For example, did Jonah really live for three days in the belly of a large fish? There are people who believe it. Is the end of days at hand? A U.S. senator says he thinks so. Will the Rapture occur in our lifetimes? Widespread agreement. Mormons believe Missouri will be the paradise ("Branson, I hope," says Maher). There are even some people who believe Alaska has been chosen as a refuge for the saved after Armageddon. In Kentucky, Maher visits the Creation Museum, which features a diorama of human children playing at the feet of dinosaurs.

His two most delightful guests, oddly enough, are priests stationed in the Vatican. Between them, they cheerfully dismiss wide swathes of what are widely thought to be Catholic teachings, including the existence of hell. One of these priests almost dissolves in laughter as he mentions various beliefs that I, as a child, solemnly absorbed in Catholic schools. The other observes that when Italians were polled to discover who was the first person they would pray to in a crisis, Jesus placed sixth.

Maher meets two representations of Jesus. One is an actor at the Holy Land Experience theme park in Orlando. He stars in a reenactment of the Passion, complete with crown of thorns, wounds, a crucifix, and Roman soldiers with whips. I suppose I understand why Florida tourists would take snapshots of this ordeal, but when Jesus stumbles, falls, and is whipped by soldiers, I was a little puzzled why they applauded.

The other Jesus, Jose Luis de Jesus Miranda, believes he actually is the Second Coming— that is, Jesus made flesh in our time. He explains how the bloodline traveled from the Holy Land through Spain to Puerto Rico. He has one hundred thousand followers.

Why have I focused on the Christians? Maher also has interesting debates with Muslims about whether the Quran calls for the death of infidels. And he interviews an Israeli manufacturer who invents devices to sidestep the bans on Sabbath activity. Since the laws prohibit you from operating machines, for example, they've invented a "negative telephone." Here's how it works: All the numbers on the touch-pad are constantly engaged. All you do is insert little sticks into holes beside the numbers you *don't* want to work.

I have done my job and described the

movie. I report faithfully that I laughed frequently. You may very well hate it, but at least you've been informed. Perhaps you could enjoy the material about other religions and tune out when yours is being discussed. That's only human nature.

Rendition ★ ★ ★ ★
R, 120 m., 2007

Jake Gyllenhaal (Douglas Freeman), Reese Witherspoon (Isabella El-Ibrahimi), Omar Metwally (Anwar El-Ibrahimi), Peter Sarsgaard (Alan Smith), Meryl Streep (Corrinne Whitman), Alan Arkin (Senator Hawkins), Igal Naor (Abasi Fawal), Moa Khouas (Khalid El-Emin), Zineb Oukach (Fatima Fawal). Directed by Gavin Hood and produced by Steve Golin and Marcus Viscidi. Screenplay by Kelley Sane.

This is being done in our name. People who are suspected for any reason, or no good reason, of being terrorists can be snatched from their lives and transported to another country to be held without charge and tortured for information. Because the torture is conducted by professionals in those countries, our officials can blandly state "America does not torture." This practice, known as an "extraordinary rendition," was authorized, I am sorry to say, under the Clinton administration. After 9/11 there is reason to believe the Bush administration uses it frequently.

Gavin Hood's terrifying, intelligent thriller *Rendition* puts a human face on the practice. We meet Anwar El-Ibrahimi (Omar Metwally), an Egyptian-born American chemical engineer who lives in Chicago. He and his wife, Isabella (Reese Witherspoon), have a young son, and she is in advanced pregnancy with another child. After boarding a flight home from a conference in Cape Town, Anwar disappears from the airplane, his name disappears from the passenger list, and Isabella hears nothing more from him.

He was taken from the plane by the CIA, we learn. His cell phone received calls from a terrorist, or perhaps from someone else with the same name, or perhaps it was stolen or lost and used by somebody else. His background is clean, and he passes a lie detector test, but is hooded, flown to an anonymous country, and

placed in the hands of an expert torturer named Abasi Fawal (Igal Naor). His frantic wife is told he never got on the flight, although she later discovers his credit card was used for an in-flight duty-free purchase.

If there is one thing history and common sense teaches us, it is that if you torture someone well enough, they will tell you what they think you want to hear. As successful interrogation experts have patiently explained to Congress, much more useful information is obtained using the carrot than the stick. Yet Anwar is held naked in a dungeon, beaten, nearly drowned, shocked with electricity, kept sleepless, shackled. Does it occur to anybody that he is more likely to "confess" if he is not a terrorist than if he is?

The movie sets into motion a chain of events caused by the illegal kidnapping. Isabella, played by Reese Witherspoon with single-minded determination and love, contacts an old boyfriend (Peter Sarsgaard) who is now an aide to a powerful senator (Alan Arkin). Convinced the missing man is innocent, the senator intervenes with the head of U.S. intelligence (Meryl Streep). She responds in flawless neocon-speak, simultaneously using terrorism as an excuse for terrorism, and threatening the senator with political suicide. Arkin backs off.

Meanwhile, in the unnamed foreign country, we meet a CIA pencil pusher named Douglas Freeman (Jake Gyllenhaal), who has little experience in fieldwork but has taken over the post after the assassination of his boss. His job is to work with and "supervise" the torturer Abasi. This he does with no enthusiasm but from a sense of duty. He is not cut out for this kind of work, drinks too much, broods, and has discussions with Abasi, who is an intelligent man and not a monster.

How this all plays out has much to do with Abasi's daughter, Fatima (Zineb Oukach), who is secretly in love with a fellow student not approved of by her family. All these human strands, seemingly so separated, eventually weave into the same rope in a film that builds its suspense by the uncoiling of personalities.

It is now so well-established that America authorizes the practices shown in this film that when President Bush goes on television to blandly deny it, with his "Who, we?" little-boy innocence, I feel saddened. He may eventually be the last person to believe himself. What the film documents is that we have lost faith in due process and the rule of law, and have forfeited the moral high ground. Reading some of the reviews after I saw this film at the Toronto festival, I was struck by a comment by James Rocchi on Cinematical.com: "Anytime someone tells you that you can't make an omelet without breaking eggs, immediately demand to see the omelet."

Gavin Hood, the South African director of *Rendition,* first came into wide view with the wonderful *Tsotsi* (2005), which won the Academy Award for best foreign film. Now comes this big, confident, effective thriller with its politics so seamlessly part of its story. Next for him: *Wolverine,* based on the X-Men character. I hope we don't lose him to blockbusters. A film like *Rendition* is valuable and rare. As I wrote from Toronto: "It is a movie about the theory and practice of two things: torture and personal responsibility. And it is wise about what is right, and what is wrong."

Reprise ★ ★

R, 105 m., 2008

Espen Klouman Hoiner (Erik), Anders Danielsen Lie (Phillip), Viktoria Winge (Kari), Odd Magnus Williamson (Morten), Pal Stokka (Geir), Christian Rubeck (Lars). Directed by Joachim Trier and produced by Karin Julsrud. Screenplay by Eskil Vogt and Trier.

If there was ever a movie that seems written and directed by its characters, that movie is Joachim Trier's *Reprise.* Here is an ambitious and romantic portrait of two young would-be writers that seems made by ambitious and romantic would-be filmmakers. In the movie, the young heroes idolize Norway's greatest living writer, who tells one of them his novel is good and shows promise, except for the ending, where he shouldn't have been so poetic. The movie itself is good and shows promise, except for the ending, when Trier shouldn't have been so poetic. Not only does *Reprise* generate itself, it contains its own review.

The twenty-three-year-old heroes are Erik and Phillip. They seem to be awfully nice boys who have some growing-up to do. It opens

with the two of them simultaneously dropping the manuscripts of their first novels into a post box. Then an anonymous narrator takes over and describes some possible futures of the characters and their novels. We will be hearing a lot from that narrator, and he, along with Erik and Phillip and Phillip's girlfriend, Kari, remind us inescapably of Francois Truffaut's *Jules and Jim.*

The movie is set in Oslo, with a visit to Paris. I have been to Oslo, and it's nowhere near the gray arrangement of apartment blocks and perfunctory landscaping that we see in the movie. (Nor is it Paris.) I have met Norwegians, who are nowhere near the bland, narcissistic Erik and Phillip. The big problem with the movie is our difficulty in working up much real interest in the characters. They're not compelling. Even when Phillip becomes so obsessed with Kari that he has to be accommodated in a mental institution, and even after (back on the streets) he takes her to Paris on the exact anniversary of their first trip there, it's impossible to see him as passionate. His emotions never seem to be at full volume.

The high point, passion-wise, comes during their Paris trip. His mother has confiscated his photos of Kari, fearing they will trigger a relapse. So in Paris he poses her to take them again, Kari even helpfully hitching up her skirt to more closely match the original. They visit the same café (I think). Then they check into the same hotel and make love in (one assumes) much the same way.

The movie finds it necessary to do something I'm growing weary of: It depicts their love-making at greater length than depth. They're seen in profile, in dim lighting, with a sound track that reminded me of the Hondells ("First gear—it's all right. Second gear—hold on tight").

After their breathing reaches overdrive, they disengage and she soon enough says, "You don't still love me." That word *love* is such a troublemaker. For characters like those in the movie, it represents an attainment like feeling patriotic or missing your dog. It's a state not consuming, not transcendent, but obligatory.

I also wearied of Phillip's countdowns. At a party, he bets himself Kari will turn and look at him at "zero" when he counts down from "ten." He tempts fate on his bicycle, in traffic, by closing his eyes while counting down. It's the kind of numerology that was charming in *Me and You and Everyone We Know*, when the heroine imagines that the sidewalk stretching ahead of her represents the life span of herself and the guy she likes, and they're halfway to the corner. It was fanciful and fetching in that film, but disposable in this one—indeed, bordering on idiotic, because Phillip isn't that kind of person. For him the counting down not only seems to represent (a) something meaningful, but also (b) age-appropriate. If I were Kari, I'd jump ship at "seven," and actually she does tell Phillip, "I can't take it any more." Bonus points for taking it as long as she does.

Erik has a girlfriend, too, the seldom-seen (by his friends) Lillian, whom he pulls apart from because he fears she might not fit in with his friends, who therefore seldom see her. The characters meet in cafés, restaurants, one another's apartments, lakesides, and punk concerts. They take music very seriously, or say they do, but with fans like these, punk audiences would applaud politely.

Then there is the matter of their novels and the title of one of them, *Prosopopeia*. Well, Norway's greatest living writer thinks it's a good title, just as the book is a "good" book. You get the impression that, at his age, "great" would trigger a seizure. I never got any clear idea of what the novels were about, not even during a torturous television chat show that later triggers the greatest living writer's observation that TV is not the ideal medium for discussing literature. The cinema is an ideal medium for considering characters like those in *Reprise*, but you'd have to see *Jules and Jim* to find out why.

Rescue Dawn ★ ★ ★ ½

PG-13, 125 m., 2007

Christian Bale (Dieter Dengler), Steve Zahn (Duane), Jeremy Davies (Gene), Galen Yuen (Y.C.), Abhijati Muek Jusakul (Phisit), Chaiyan Lek Chunsuttiwat (Procet), Teerawat Ka Ge Mulvilai (Little Hitler). Directed by Werner Herzog and produced by Steve Marlton, Elton Brand, and Harry Knapp. Screenplay by Herzog.

When he was a child during World War II, Dieter Dengler had an attic room on a German hillside overlooking a valley. One day an American fighter plane roared past "only feet away," he recalled. The plane's canopy was down; he made eye contact with the pilot for a moment and instantly knew that he wanted to fly.

Werner Herzog's *Rescue Dawn*, based on Dengler's experiences, begins early in the Vietnam War, when Dengler is a U.S Navy pilot stationed on a carrier in the Gulf of Tonkin. At eighteen, he enlisted in order to get American citizenship—and to fly. Assigned to a secret illegal bombing mission over Laos, he is shot down, and the film involves his experiences as a prisoner of war, his escape, and his harrowing fight for survival in the jungle. He was one of only seven Americans to escape from a Viet Cong POW camp and live. Dengler (Christian Bale) scoffs at his flimsy bamboo "cell" until a fellow American tells him, "Don't you get it? It's the jungle that is the prison."

His ordeal includes torture in the camp (he is hung by his heels with an ants' nest fastened to his head) and an agonizing trek through the jungle, at first with a fellow American named Duane (Steve Zahn), then alone. Herzog makes no attempt to pump this story up into a thrilling adventure. There is nothing thrilling about dysentery, starvation, insect bites, and despair. The film heads instead into the trembling fear at Dengler's center.

This feature has been long on the mind of Herzog, who film for film is the most original and challenging of directors. He used the real Dieter Dengler in a 1997 documentary named *Little Dieter Needs to Fly*, in which he took Dengler back to the jungle and together they re-created his escape while Dengler provided a breathlessly intense narration.

Considering that Herzog made both films, it is perhaps not surprising that the "fictional" feature is more realistic than the documentary. With Herzog there is always free trade between fact and fantasy. *Little Dieter* shows Dengler obsessively opening and closing the doors and windows of his house to be sure he is not locked in. Not true, Herzog told me; the director added that detail for dramatic effect. Also in the doc, Dengler imagines himself being followed through the jungle by a bear, who came to represent "death, my only friend." That seems to be a fantasy, yet Herzog says it was real. But there is no bear in *Rescue Dawn.* Too hard to believe, is my guess.

The movie is, indeed, perhaps the most believable Herzog has made. For a director who gravitates toward the extremes of human behavior, this film involves extreme behavior, yes, but behavior forced by the circumstances. There is nothing in it we cannot, or do not, believe. I was almost prepared to compare it to the classic storytelling of a John Huston film when I realized it had crucial Herzogian differences.

One is the use of location. Asked long ago why he went to so much trouble to shoot *Aguirre, the Wrath of God* and *Fitzcarraldo* hundreds of miles into the rain forests of the Amazon, he said it involved "the voodoo of location." He felt actors, directors, cinematographers, and perhaps the film itself absorbed something from where the shooting took place. Even his vampire film *Nosferatu* (1990) sought out the same locations F. W. Murnau used in the silent 1922 original.

In *Rescue Dawn,* filmed in the jungles of Thailand, there is never the slightest doubt we are in the jungle. No movie stars creeping behind potted shrubbery on a back lot. The screen always looks wet and green, and the actors push through the choking vegetation with difficulty. We can almost smell the rot and humidity. To discuss the power of the performances by Bale, Zahn, and Jeremy Davies (another POW) would miss the point unless we speculated about how much of the conviction in their work came from the fact that they were really doing it in the hellish place where it was really done.

The other Herzog touch is the music. Herzog recoils from conventional scores that mirror the action. Here he uses not upbeat adventure music but brooding, introspective, doomy music by Klaus Badelt; classical and chamber performances; and passages by Popol Vuh, the German New Age band that supplied so much of the feeling in *Aguirre* and *Fitzcarraldo.*

Rescue Dawn opened in some markets on July 4. It is about a man who won the Distinguished Flying Cross and the Navy Cross (none of which it mentions). Given the times we live in, is it an upbeat, patriotic film? Not by intention. It is simply the story of this man. When he is finally greeted back aboard his aircraft carrier, there is no "mission accomplished" banner, and when he is asked for his words of advice for the cheering crew, he says: "Empty that which is full. Fill that which is empty. If it itches, scratch it."

Resurrecting the Champ ★ ★ ★
PG-13, 111 m., 2007

Samuel L. Jackson (Champ), Josh Hartnett (Erik), Kathryn Morris (Joyce), Alan Alda (Metz), Teri Hatcher (Flak), Rachel Nichols (Polly), David Paymer (Whitley), Dakota Goyo (Teddy). Directed by Rod Lurie and produced by Lurie, Mike Medavoy, Bob Yari, and Marc Frydman. Screenplay by Michael Bortman and Allison Burnett.

In the news business, there is an intoxication in making a big story your own. In *Zodiac,* a cartoonist strays off his beat and tries to solve a string of serial killings. In Rod Lurie's *Resurrecting the Champ,* a sportswriter stumbles on the story of a skid-row drunk who used to be a contender. Erik (Josh Hartnett) has been told by his editor he is sloppy and lazy, and when he comes upon Champ, it's like a gift from heaven. The former heavyweight boxer (Samuel L. Jackson) has just been beaten up by some young punks but harbors little resentment against them. He's talkative and tells Erik his story.

His real name, he says, is Bob Satterfield. At one time he was ranked number three. He even sparred with Marciano. Now he's a shambling mess, old, homeless, remembering past glories. A lot of boxers with his history would have had their brains scrambled, but Champ remembers the past in detail; alcohol is his problem. Erik senses what we reporters like to assure our editors is a "great story." We are not modest about reviewing our unwritten work.

Erik, separated from his wife (Kathryn Morris), has a son named Teddy (Dakota Goyo) whom he tells about all the celebrities he meets. All reporters meet celebrities, just like all detectives meet murderers, but you know you're a pitiful dad when you try name-dropping to impress a six-year-old. The home life doesn't supply many of the film's best scenes, but I like the newspaper office performance by Alan Alda, as Erik's editor. Have you noticed in recent movies that Alda has *finally* stopped looking so much like Hawkeye Pierce? It frees him up in his characters.

Jackson disappears into his role, completely convincing, but then he usually is. What a fine actor. He avoids pitfalls like making Champ a maudlin tearjerker, looking for pity. He's realistic, even philosophical, about his life and what happened to him. Hartnett is efficient enough in his role, but doesn't have enough edges and angles on him to be a sportswriter. Robert Downey Jr. for sportswriter, Josh Hartnett for movie critic.

There are developments in this movie that I don't want to hint at, especially since they surprised me, and you should have the same pleasure. They call into question, let us say, people's motives for doing things, and what happens when two people have the misfortune to find that their motives are a good fit.

So let us talk about the plight of the former boxer. Jackson obviously gave a lot of thought to the character, and invents him fresh instead of cobbling him together out of leftovers. A punch-drunk stumblebum would have been wearisome here, but you can see the intelligence in Champ's eyes, even despite the hair and makeup that make the sleek Jackson look like Alley Oop. He has a few words with Erik, sizes him up, and takes care of business. Apparently he has a better nose for suckers than for sucker punches.

He made me curious enough that I Wikipediaed Bob Satterfield and found out, yes, he was a real fighter, nicknamed the Bombardier, and was KO'd by the Raging Bull himself in a 1946 fight in Wrigley Field. He was a Chicago boy, Golden Gloves champ in 1941, fought Ezzard Charles and Archie Moore, won fifty, lost twenty-five, with four draws. This is more than Erik knows; he's never heard of Satterfield, but Satterfield is only too happy to fill him in. And Erik is right: It does make a great story. Does he remember everything with perfect accuracy? There is an old newspaper adage, now mostly abandoned: "Never check a good quote twice."

Revolutionary Road ★ ★ ★ ★
R, 119 m., 2009

Leonardo DiCaprio (Frank Wheeler), Kate Winslet (April Wheeler), Kathy Bates (Helen Givings), Michael Shannon (John Givings), Kathryn Hahn (Milly Campbell), David Harbour (Shep Campbell), Zoe Kazan (Maureen Grube), Dylan Baker (Jack Ordway), Jay O. Sanders (Bart Pollock), Richard Easton (Howard Givings). Directed by Sam Mendes and produced by John N. Hart, Scott Rudin, and Bobby Cohen. Screenplay by Justin Haythe, based on the novel by Richard Yates.

Life is what happens to you while you're busy making other plans.
—John Lennon

Revolutionary Road shows the American Dream awakened by a nightmare. It takes place in the 1950s, the decade not only of Elvis but of *The Man in the Gray Flannel Suit*. It shows a young couple who meet at a party, get married, and create a suburban life with a nice house, a manicured lawn, "modern" furniture, two kids, a job in the city for him, housework for her, and martinis, cigarettes, boredom, and desperation for both of them.

The Wheelers, Frank and April, are blinded by love into believing life together will allow them to fulfill their fantasies. Their problem is, they have no fantasies. Instead, they have yearnings—a hunger for something *more* than a weary slog into middle age. Billy Wilder made a movie in 1955 called *The Seven Year Itch* about a restlessness that comes into some marriages when the partners realize the honeymoon is over and they're married for good and there's an empty space at the center.

Frank (Leonardo DiCaprio) and April (Kate Winslet) can't see inviting futures for themselves. Frank joins the morning march of men in suits and hats out of Grand Central and into jobs where they are "executives" doing meaningless work—in Frank's case, he's "in office machines." He might as well be one. April suggests he just quit so they can move to Paris; she can support them as a translator at the American Embassy, and he can figure out what he really wants to do. Translating will not support their Connecticut lifestyle, but Paris! What about their children? Their children are like a car you never think about when you're not driving somewhere.

Frank agrees, and they think they're poised to take flight, when suddenly he's offered a promotion and a raise. He has no choice, right? He'll be just as miserable, but better paid. In today's hard times, that sounds necessary, but maybe all times are hard when you hate your life. Frank and April have ferocious fights about his decision, and we realize that April was largely motivated by her own needs. Better to support the neutered Frank in Paris with a job at the embassy, where she might meet someone more interesting than their carbon-copy neighbors and the "real estate lady," Helen Givings (Kathy Bates).

Helen makes a tentative request. Can she and her husband bring their son John (Michael Shannon) over for a meal? He's in a mental institution, and perhaps some time with a nice normal couple like the Wheelers would be good for him. John comes for dinner, and we discover his real handicap is telling the truth. With cruel words and merciless observations, he chops through their facade and mocks their delusions. It is a wrecking job.

Remember, this is the 1950s. A little after the time of this movie, *Life* magazine would run its famous story about the beatniks, "The Only Rebellion Around." There was a photo of a beatnik and his chick sitting on the floor and listening to an LP record of modern jazz that was cool and hip, and I felt my own yearnings. I remember on the way back from Steak 'n Shake one night, my dad drove slow past the Turk's Head coffeehouse on campus. "That's where the beatniks stand on tables and recite their poetry," he told my mom, and she said, "My, my," and I wanted to get out of that car and put on a black turtleneck and walk in there and stay.

The character John is not insane, just a beatnik a little ahead of schedule. He's an early assault wave from the 1960s, which would sweep over suburbia and create a generation its parents did not comprehend. What he does for the Wheelers is strip away their denials and see them clearly. Do you know these John Prine lyrics?

Blow up your TV, throw away your paper,
Go to the country, build you a home.
Plant a little garden, eat a lot of peaches,
Try an' find Jesus on your own.

Frank and April are played by DiCaprio and Winslet as the sad ending to the romance in *Titanic,* and all other romances that are founded on nothing more than . . . romance. They are so good, they stop being actors and become the people I grew up around. Don't think they smoke too much in this movie. In the 1950s everybody smoked everywhere all the time. Life was a disease, and smoking held it temporarily in remission. And drinking? Every ad executive in the neighborhood would head for the Wrigley Bar at lunchtime to prove the maxim: One martini is just right, two are too many, three are not enough.

The direction is by Sam Mendes, who dissected suburban desperation in *American Beauty,* a film that after this one seems merciful. The screenplay by Justin Haythe is drawn from the famous 1961 novel by Richard Yates, who has been called the voice of the postwar Age of Anxiety. This film is so good it is devastating. A lot of people believe their parents didn't understand them. What if they didn't understand themselves?

Revolver ½★
R, 115 m., 2007

Jason Statham (Jake Green), Ray Liotta (Dorothy Macha), Vincent Pastore (Zach), Andre Benjamin (Avi), Terence Maynard (French Paul), Andrew Howard (Billy), Mark Strong (Sorter), Francesca Annis (Lili Walker). Directed by Guy Ritchie and produced by Luc Besson and Virginie Silla. Screenplay by Ritchie.

Guy Ritchie's *Revolver* is a frothing mad film that thrashes against its very sprocket holes in an attempt to bash its brains out against the projector. It seems designed to punish the audience for buying tickets. It is a "thriller" without thrills, constructed in a meaningless jumble of flashbacks and flash-forwards and subtitles and mottos and messages and scenes that are deconstructed, reconstructed, and self-destructed. I wanted to signal the projectionist to put a gun to it.

The plot. What is the plot? Jason Statham

has spent seven years in jail between a con man in the cell on one side and a chess master on the other. Back on the street, he walks into a casino run by his old enemy Ray Liotta and wins a fortune at the table. Did he cheat or what? I dunno. Liotta sics some hit men on him. Then two mysterious strangers (Vincent Pastore and Andre Benjamin) materialize in Statham's life at just such moments when they are in a position to save it. Who, oh who, could these two men, one of whom plays chess, possibly be?

The movie begins with a bunch of sayings that will be repeated endlessly like mantras throughout the film. Chris Cabin at filmcritic.com thinks these have some connection with the Kabbalah beliefs of Ritchie and his wife, Madonna. I know zilch about the Kabbalah, but if he's right, and if Ritchie follows them, I would urgently warn other directors to stay clear of the Kabbalah. Judging by this film, it encourages you to mistake hopeless confusion for pure reason.

Oh, this film angered me. It kept turning back on itself, biting its own tail, doubling back through scenes with less and less meaning and purpose, chanting those sayings as if to hammer us down into accepting them. It employed three editors. Skeleton crew. Some of the acting is better than the film deserves. Make that all of the acting. Actually, the film stock itself is better than the film deserves. You know when sometimes a film catches fire inside a projector? If it happened with this one, I suspect the audience might cheer.

Rocket Science ★ ★ ★ ½
R, 101 m., 2007

Reece Daniel Thompson (Hal Hefner), Anna Kendrick (Ginny Ryerson), Nicholas D'Agosto (Ben Wekselbaum), Vincent Piazza (Earl Hefner), Margo Martindale (Coach Lumbly), Stephen Park (Judge Pete), Lisbeth Bartlett (Juliet Hefner), Denis O'Hare (Doyle Hefner). Directed by Jeffrey Blitz and produced by Effie T. Brown and Sean Welch. Screenplay by Blitz.

The high school hero of *Rocket Science* stutters, but all high school kids stutter. It's just that most of them don't do it with their voices. They stutter in the way they don't know how to present themselves, what to say next, how to talk their way out of embarrassment, when to make an approach to someone they have a crush on, or how to perform in class when everybody's looking at them. It's just that Hal Hefner (Reece Daniel Thompson) does it out loud.

That's why he seems to be an odd choice when Ginny Ryerson (Anna Kendrick) talks him into joining the school debate team. The movie opens when she loses her regular debate partner, Ben Wekselbaum (Nicholas D'Agosto). His meltdown is spectacular. In the middle of a debate, he is effortlessly speeding along at a zillion words a second (I learn debaters call this *spreading*) when suddenly he freezes. His mind goes blank and he can't think of a single thing to say. Who can't identify with that?

Ben drops off the team and starts beating himself up psychologically, and that's when Ginny recruits Hal. She has reasons of her own, which are revealed in the fullness of time, but oddly enough they're not the reasons we're expecting. *Rocket Science* is not a formula high school movie, is not about formula kids, and is funny in a way that makes you laugh but it still kinda hurts.

The movie's director, Jeffrey Blitz, must have learned a lot about overachieving kids and their occasional breakdowns while directing his first film, the suspenseful Oscar-nominated documentary *Spellbound* (2002), about the National Spelling Bee. He learned other things, too, like how when adolescent boys of a certain age think about anything but sex, it's a distraction.

Hal has too many hang-ups to develop much of a love life, but the kid who lives next door to Ginny obsesses on her, spies on her, steals her brassiere, and in general makes himself miserable. Meanwhile, does Ginny like Hal, does she feel sorry for him, or is she playing a cruel trick?

Hal has problems beside Ginny. His dad (Denis O'Hare) walks out of his marriage one day, after saying farewell to Hal and his older brother, Earl (Vincent Piazza), in the kind of speech a man might make before leaving for a better job. Then his mom (Lisbeth Bartlett) starts dating a nice Korean judge (Stephen Park), although she lacks certain interethnic instincts. "Is this some kind of an exotic

Korean dish?" she asks, "because it has a strange odor." The judge smiles. "It's tuna casserole."

The movie is not a slick repackaging of visual clichés from *Teen Vogue* (that one was *Bratz*) but instead seems to be in a plausible high school filled with students who act and look about the right age, even though they're a little older. The movie was shot in Baltimore, doubling for "Plainsboro High School" in New Jersey, and even spells Plainsboro correctly throughout, unlike "Carry Nation High School" in *Bratz,* which couldn't even spell its title. (This just in: *Carry* is an acceptable spelling for Ms. Nation's first name, but *Bratz* is, of course, a short form of "bratwurst.")

Hold on. I'm drifting back toward my review of *Spellbound.* The thing about *Rocket Science* is that its behavior, even its villainy, is within plausible margins. Ginny is a hateful "popular girl," but she isn't hateful beyond all reason. Hal's mother's new boyfriend is not a stereotyped interloper, but a nice guy who would be an improvement. And a lot of the laughs come in understated asides that reveal character.

The leads, Reece Daniel Thompson and Anna Kendrick (*Camp*), are early in what promise to be considerable careers. Kendrick can make you like her even when you shouldn't, and Thompson fine-tunes the pathos of his dilemma to slip comedy into moments that could be deadly.

I suspect a lot of high school students will recognize elements of real life in the movie (that's why it's rated R, to protect them from themselves) and that the movie will build a following. It may gross as little as *Welcome to the Dollhouse* or as much as *Clueless,* but whichever it does, it's in the same league.

RocknRolla ★ ★ ★
R, 117 m., 2009

Gerard Butler (One Two), Tom Wilkinson (Lenny Cole), Thandie Newton (Stella), Mark Strong (Archy), Idris Elba (Mumbles), Tom Hardy (Handsome Bob), Toby Kebbell (Johnny), Jeremy Piven (Roman), Ludacris (Mickey). Directed by Guy Ritchie and produced by Ritchie, Joel Silver, Susan Downey, and Steve Clark-Hall. Screenplay by Ritchie.

I'm looking at *RocknRolla* and I'm thinking, why make a movie about stealing a parcel of London real estate, when you could make a movie about stealing a trillion bucks of real estate? British gangsters may dress better than Wall Street overlords and be more colorful, but they just don't think big. After watching Richard S. Fuld, CEO of Lehman Brothers, squirm before the House Oversight and Government Reform Committee (HOG-REFORM) as he explained why he deserved $350 million for guiding his company into bankruptcy, I found it refreshing to watch hoodlums squirm because they might get *personally* kneecapped without even so much as a golden hang-glider.

Guy Ritchie's new movie is about some very hard cases from the London and Russian underworlds who are all trying to cheat one another, and about an accountant whom the term "femme fatale" has been hanging around waiting to describe. It's one of those rare circular con jobs where you can more or less figure out what's going on, and you can more or less understand why nobody else does, although at various times they all think they do, and at other times you're wrong. While they engage in these miscalculations, they act terrifically dangerous to one another—so smoothly you'd swear they were in the second year of a repertory tour.

You know who Tom Wilkinson is. You may not recognize him here, for reasons I won't describe because then you would. He's funny and terrifically dangerous as Lenny Cole, a gangster with the memory of a tax collector. He owns or has leveraged great swathes of London, including one swath urgently required by a Russian gangster named Uri Obamavich (Karel Roden), who comes to Cole. Now follow this attentively. One Two (Gerard Butler), Handsome Bob (Tom Hardy), and Mumbles (Idris Elba), whose parents may have been Dick Tracy fans, borrow $7 million from Cole to buy some land. Cole secretly owns the land and won't sell it to them, and arranges to steal the money back and demands to be paid. So he has the money and still has his land. Ken Lay would be proud.

But that's the simple part. Now Uri pays Cole $7 million to put the fix in on his own swath deal through Cole's tame London councilman, offering Cole his "good luck painting" as security. The femme fatale (Thandie Newton), Uri's accountant, sees a way to sidetrack the money herself. She hires One Two and Mumbles to steal Cole's $7 million, which she doesn't know was briefly their $7 million, from which they can pay $2 million to Cole and he won't kill them, but they lose the money and Cole doesn't have the $7 million to pay Uri, and meanwhile the invaluable "good luck painting" has been stolen, so at this point I'm not sure who has the money, maybe the femme fatale, but Cole needs it to give Uri, and Uri desperately needs it for harrowing reasons of his own, and the councilman needs it to save his career. Uri may not give a damn about his priceless painting, but Cole doesn't know that and sends Archy (Mark Strong) and Mickey (Ludacris) to find out who stole the painting, and—ohmigod!—it's in the hands of Cole's own stepson, the druggie rocknrolla Johnny Quid (Toby Kebbell), and Cole discovers that if there's anyone harder to deal with than a Russian mafioso, it's a druggie rocknrolla stepson.

Now don't go medieval on me because I gave away the whole plot, because (1) that's only the first time around the block, (2) right now you can't remember what I said, and (3) I may have gotten large parts of it wrong, although my fingers were bleeding from scribbling notes. The bottom line is, all these people chase the same money around with the success of doggie tail-biting, and it's a lot of fun, and it's not often in these con films that *everybody* is conning *everybody*, and they're all scared to death, and nobody knows which cup the pea is under.

RocknRolla (which is how they say *rock and roller* in the East End) isn't as jammed with visual pyrotechnics as Ritchie's *Lock, Stock and Two Smoking Barrels* (1998), but that's OK, because with anything more happening the movie could induce motion sickness. It never slows down enough to be really good and never speeds up enough to be the Bourne Mortgage Crisis, but there's one thing for sure: British actors love playing gangsters as much as American actors love playing cowboys, and it's always nice to see people having fun.

Role Models ★ ★ ★
R, 99 m., 2008

Seann William Scott (Wheeler), Paul Rudd (Danny), Christopher Mintz-Plasse (Augie), Jane Lynch (Sweeny), Bobb'e J. Thompson (Ronnie), Elizabeth Banks (Beth). Directed by David Wain and produced by Mary Parent, Scott Stuber, and Luke Greenfield. Screenplay by Wain, Paul Rudd, Ken Marino, and Timothy Dowling.

Role Models is the kind of movie you don't see every day, a comedy that is funny. The kind of comedy where funny people say funny things in funny situations, not the kind of comedy that whacks you with manic shocks to force an audible Pavlovian response.

Now that we've cleared the room by using "Pavlovian," let's enjoy *Role Models*. This is a fish-out-of-water plot with no water. The characters are all flopping around in places they don't want to be. Paul Rudd and Seann William Scott play Danny and Wheeler, teammates who drive a Minotaur-mobile super truck from school to school, touting a Jolt-like drink as the high-octane energy boost that will get you high without a jail sentence: "Just say no to drugs, and 'YES!' to Minotaur!"

They get in trouble and are assigned to community service. Sweeny (Jane Lynch), the woman in charge of the program, could have been your usual Nurse Ratched type, but instead she's a brilliant comic invention, a former big-time cokehead from the Village with tattoos on her arm. I don't know why, but I have always found it pleasing to hear a pretty middle-aged woman saying, "You can't bullshit a bullshitter."

Danny and Wheeler are assigned to be mentors in a Big Brother kind of program for young troublemakers. Here the film is inventive. The heroes are assigned a potty-mouth and a nerd, but not like any you've seen before. Danny gets Augie (Christopher Mintz-Plasse), whose life is entirely absorbed in a medieval fantasy game where bizarrely costumed "armies" do battle in parks with fake swords. There are mostly younger teenagers and lonely men with mountain-man beards. Sort of a combination of Dungeons and Dragons and pederasty. Wheeler draws Ronnie

(Bobb'e J. Thompson), a sassy rebel who looks about ten and hasn't had his growth yet. Not only does Ronnie know all the bad words, he can deliver them with the loud confidence of Chris Rock at full speed. Bobb'e J. Thompson will have his own show on Comedy Central before he's twenty-five.

So these two terrific young actors go through all the steps of a formula plot, but a formula plot works if you're laughing at the plot and not noticing the formula. There are nicely drawn supporting characters, including the pompous King Argotron (Ken Jeong). He rules this universe, and its members take him very, very seriously, even going so far as to fork-feed him and wipe his chin with a napkin at a pancake house.

Then there is Beth (Elizabeth Banks, Miri to Zack), Danny's girlfriend, who breaks up with him after he insults an Italian coffeehouse waitress. He shouts at her for calling a taller coffee a *vingt*. That's not Italian! (It's French, but she may have been saying *venti*.) Twenty ounces, you see. Anyway, Beth is sick of his anger and his dark moods. Augie helps to bring them back together after he accidentally gazes upon her "boobies." He is ecstatic. Earlier, he and Danny had started to bond for the first time when Danny told him: "Remember, for every man in the world, there are two boobies, more or less." A troubled young man needs all the encouragement he can get.

What's interesting about the fantasy medieval warfare is that the players take it with deadly seriousness. This is not a game. It is the game of their very lives. When they are tagged by a sword, they are dead, and what is unbearable is that they are still alive to know they are dead and listen to their enemies' scorn. The punishment is they can't play anymore. Oh, this is heavy stuff. Remember that story a few years ago about some college students who were playing a fantasy game in the tunnels and sewers beneath a campus, and a few of them got lost or killed, I forget which?

Everything is satisfactorily resolved in the end, as the formula requires. But since their problems were a little deeper than usual in this genre, our pleasure is increased a little. Not to the point where we're cheering, you understand. But to the point where we're thinking, hey, I sort of liked that.

I was mentioning little Ronnie's attitude. I like this exchange:

Ronnie: Suck it, *Reindeer Games*!
Danny: I'm not Ben Affleck.
Ronnie: You white, then you Ben Affleck.

Romance and Cigarettes ★ ★ ★ ★
R, 115 m., 2007

James Gandolfini (Nick Murder), Susan Sarandon (Kitty), Kate Winslet (Tula), Steve Buscemi (Angelo), Bobby Cannavale (Fryburg), Mandy Moore (Baby), Mary-Louise Parker (Constance), Aida Turturro (Rosebud), Eddie Izzard (Gene), Christopher Walken (Cousin Bo), Elaine Stritch (Mother). Directed by John Turturro and produced by John Penotti and Turturro. Screenplay by Turturro.

How did one of the most magical films of the 2005 festival season become one of the hardest films of 2007 to see? John Turturro's *Romance and Cigarettes* is the real thing, a film that breaks out of Hollywood jail with audacious originality, startling sexuality, heartfelt emotions, and an anarchic liberty. The actors toss their heads and run their mouths like prisoners let loose to race free.

The story involves a marriage at war between a Queens high-steel worker named Nick (James Gandolfini) and his tempestuous wife, Kitty (Susan Sarandon), who has found a poem he wrote to his mistress (Kate Winslet), or more accurately, to that part of her he most treasures. After Kitty calls him a whoremaster (the film is energetic in its vulgarity), they stage a verbal battle in front of their three grown daughters, and then he escapes from the house to do—what? To start singing along with Engelbert Humperdinck's "A Man Without Love," that's what.

He dances in the street and is joined by a singing chorus of garbage men, neighbors, and total strangers. What do I mean by "singing along"? That we hear the original recordings and the voices of the actors, as if pop music not only supplies the sound track of their lives, but they sing along with it. The strategy of weaving in pop songs continues throughout and is exhilarating, reminding me of Woody Allen's *Everyone Says I Love You.*

Gandolfini and Sarandon, who portray a

love that has survived but is battered and bitter, are surrounded by their "armies," as Nick describes them to a cop. She has their three young adult daughters (Mary-Louise Parker, Mandy Moore, and Aida Turturro), her cousin Bo (Christopher Walken), and the church choir director (Eddie Izzard). He has his work partner (Steve Buscemi) and of course his mistress, who works in a sex lingerie boutique.

Now that I have made this sound like farce, let me make it sound like comedy, and then romance. The dialogue, by Turturro, has wicked timing to turn sentences around in their own tracks. Notice how Nick first appeals to his daughters, then shouts, "This is between your mother and me!" Listen to particular words in a Sarandon sentence that twists the knife.

Observe a scene in Gandolfini's hospital room. He is being visited by his mother (Elaine Stritch) and Buscemi (eating the Whitman's Sampler he brought as a gift). She tells them both something utterly shocking about her late husband, in a monologue that is off the wall and out of the room and heading for orbit. Then observe Buscemi's pay-off reaction shot, which can be described as an expression of polite interest. I can draw your attention to the way he does that, the timing, the expression, but I can't do it justice. Actors who can give you what Stritch gives you, and who can give you Buscemi's reaction to it, should look for a surprise in their pay packet on Friday.

Now as to Winslet's mistress, named Tula. She is not a tramp, although she plays one in Nick's life. She actually likes the big lug, starting with his belly. She talks her way through a sex romp Russ Meyer would envy, and then is so tender to the big, sad guy that you wanna cry. Although the characters in this movie are familiar with vulgarity, they are not limited to it, and *Romance and Cigarettes* makes a slow, lovely U-turn from raucous comedy to bittersweet regret.

The movie got caught in its own turnaround as MGM and United Artists changed hands, was in limbo for a time, was picked up by Sony for DVD release (2008), and was at one time being distributed by Turturro.

So many timid taste mongers have been affronted by the movie that it's running 33 percent on the TomatoMeter, so let me run my own RebertoMeter, which stands at 100, and includes these quotes: "It's the most original picture by an American director I've seen this year, and also the most delightful" (Andrew O'Hehir, Salon); "More raw vitality pumping through *Romance and Cigarettes* than in a dozen perky high school musicals" (Stephen Holden, *New York Times*); "Turturro's energetic, stylish musical about love, sex, and death is such an outrageous film that it's almost impossible not to adore it" (Geoff Andrew, *Time Out London*); and "Four stars and both of my thumbs way up!" (me).

The Romance of Astrea and Celadon ★ ★ ½
NO MPAA RATING, 109 m., 2009

Andy Gillet (Celadon), Stephanie Crayencour (Astrea), Cecile Cassel (Leonide), Veronique Reymond (Galathee), Rosette (Sylvie), Rodolphe Pauly (Hylas), Jocelyn Quivrin (Lycidas). Directed by Eric Rohmer and produced by Philippe Liegeois and Jean-Michel Rey. Screenplay by Rohmer, based on the novel by Honore d'Urfe.

The French New Wave began circa 1958 and influenced in one way or another most of the good movies made ever since. Some of its pioneers (Melville, Truffaut, Malle) are dead, but the others (Godard, Chabrol, Rivette, Resnais, Varda), are still active in their late seventies and up, and Eric Rohmer, at eighty-eight, has only just announced that *The Romance of Astrea and Celadon* may be his last film.

It doesn't look like a typical Rohmer. He frequently gives us contemporary characters, besotted not so much by love as by talking about it, finding themselves involved in ethical and plot puzzles, at the end of which he likes to quote a proverb or moral. His films are quietly passionate and lightly mannered.

But then, so is *Astrea and Celadon,* even if it's set in fifth-century Gaul and involves shepherds, shepherdesses, druids, and nymphs. The story was told in a novel by Honore d'Urfe, marquis of Valromey and count of Chateauneuf, who published it in volumes between 1607 and 1627—running, I learn, some five thousand pages. The film version must therefore be considerably abridged at 109 minutes, although it leaves you wondering if the novel ran on like this forever.

The movie does rather run on, although it is charming and sweet, and perhaps too languid. It is about two lovers obsessed with love's codes of honor. That is, curiously, the same subject as Rivette's 2007 film *The Duchess of Langeais,* made when he was seventy-nine. The characters seem perversely more dedicated to debating the fine points than getting down to it. Rivette has them talking to one another; Rohmer has them fretting while separated.

The story is told in pastoral woodlands and pastures and along a river's banks. We meet the handsome Celadon (Andy Gillet) and the beautiful Astrea (Stephanie Crayencour), shepherds and in love, not long before a tragic misperception breaks Astrea's heart, and Celadon hurls himself into the river in remorse. Believed by Astrea to be dead, he is fished out by the statuesque nymph Galathee (Veronique Reymond) and her handmaidens and kept all but captive in her castle. He pines, sworn never to be seen by Astrea's eyes again, while the two lovers debate the loopholes in romantic love with their friends. They also debate such matters as whether the Trinity corresponds to the Roman gods and sing, quote poetry, and mostly seem to ignore sheep.

A druid priest convinces Celadon to disguise himself as a girl and infiltrate Astrea's inner circle, creating much suspense, mostly on my part, as I kept expecting Astrea to exclaim, "Celadon, do you actually think you can fool anyone with that disguise?" But they play by the rules, and then things pick up nicely when they break them.

This would not be the Rohmer film you would want to start with. I've seen most of his films, and my first was *My Night at Maud's* (1969), about a long conversation about everything but love—which is to say, about love. Rohmer, I think, delights in these dialogue passages as allowing him to see his characters more carefully than in your usual formula, where courtships seem to be conducted via hormonal aromas. Sometimes his approach is sexier. The knee in *Claire's Knee* (1970) fascinated me more than entire bodies in countless films. Why Rohmer decided to end with this film I cannot say. Perhaps after forty-five years of features, he had heard it all.

Roman de Gare ★ ★ ½
R, 103 m., 2008

Dominique Pinon (Pierre Laclos/Louis), Fanny Ardant (Judith Ralitzer), Audrey Dana (Huguette), Cyrille Eldin (Paul). Directed, written, and produced by Claude Lelouch.

Roman de Gare is French for what we call an "airport novel," but it's virtually the opposite. In a good airport novel, the plot plows you through safety-belt demonstrations, five-dollar "snacks," and lists of connecting flights. In *Roman de Gare,* the plot has a way of braking to a halt and forcing us to question everything that has gone before. What can we believe, and when can we believe it? Directed by Claude Lelouch, that inexhaustible middlebrow whose *A Man and a Woman* (1966) monopolized art house screens for months and months, it's so clever that finally that's all it is: clever.

It begins with a flash-forward to the end (or, as it turns out, not quite the end), featuring a famous novelist being questioned by the cops for murder. This is Judith Ralitzer, played by the elegant Fanny Ardant, Francois Truffaut's widow. She's idolized by the next character we meet, Huguette (Audrey Dana). We join her and her boyfriend, Paul (Cyrille Eldin), in a car on an expressway at 3 a.m. They're having a fight that seems to be about her smoking but is actually about their entire relationship, which ends when Paul abandons her at a highway café, taking with him her purse, money, keys, everything. What a lousy trick.

Watching this happen is a man (Dominique Pinon) drinking coffee in the café. He offers her a ride and keeps sipping his coffee until she agrees. The movie hints this is actually Jacques Maury, a pedophile who has escaped from prison. Nicknamed "The Magician," he performs magic tricks to entrance his victims. On the other hand, he may be Judith Ralitzer's ghost writer, as he claims. And what about a worried wife we meet talking to a cop? She thinks her husband, a schoolteacher, has abandoned her. Lelouch constructs a story in which this same man could be one, but not, *I think,* all of the above.

Dominique Pinon is a fascinating actor to watch. With a stepped-on face, a scrawny beard, and a low-key, insinuating manner, he is not blessed by the gods, but he seems able to fascinate women. As he and Huguette drive through the night, he drops the bombshell that he's the ghost writer of her favorite novelist. Then he says things that may synch with news reports of the Magician. All the time, he chews gum in lots of fast little chomps. I was going to say he looks like he's chewing his cud, but he's not like a cow; he's like an insect.

At this point, the movie had me rather fascinated. Turns out Huguette and Paul were driving to the country so she could introduce her parents to Paul for the first time. "Would you do me a huge favor?" she asks her new friend. She wants him to impersonate her fiancé. This leads us into a sly domestic comedy, when Huguette's mother wonders who this little man really is, and Huguette's daughter (who lives on the farm) takes him trout fishing; they're gone for hours, while Huguette reflects she knows nothing about the man except that he said he was a ghost writer and then he said he wasn't. And now the *real* Paul turns up at the farmhouse.

It's here that the movie goes wrong, starting with Huguette's method of facing this situation. Then we learn more about the novelist, her ghost writer, the wife with the missing husband, the cop she's talking to, one of his relatives, and magic tricks. I've invested countless words denouncing plots as retreads! Standard! Obligatory! Here's a plot that double-crosses itself at every opportunity. I should be delighted with it, especially since it visits two of my favorite places, Cannes and Beaune, home of a medieval hospital that made a deep impression on me. Lined up along the walls of an enormous arching room, the patients are bedded in alcoves with a clear view of the altar where Mass is celebrated; the Beaune cure is prayer.

Offshore from Cannes in her luxurious yacht, Judith floats with whomever the hell Dominique Pinon is playing now. He has unexpected plans for her next novel, leading to the question that generates the flash-forward at the beginning. The closing scenes of the movie are dominated by Fanny Ardant, who has the kind of sculptured beauty Truffaut must have recognized when he desired to make her his wife and his star.

When a movie like *Roman de Gare* works, it's ingenious, deceptive, and slippery. When it doesn't, it's just jerking our chains. I think I understand the alternative realities of the plot, and I concede the loose ends are tied up, sort of, but I didn't care. One of the characters played by Pinon would have been enough for this movie. I would have been interested in the escaped pedophile or the ghost writer. But not in both of them interchangeably, and that pesky missing husband. Come on, I'm thinking, give us a place to stand. Do we care about Huguette because her favorite novelist is a fraud, or because her daughter may be sleeping with the fishes?

Roman Polanski: Wanted and Desired ★ ★ ★ ½
NO MPAA RATING, 100 m., 2008

A documentary directed by Marina Zenovich and produced by Jeffrey Levy-Hinte and Lila Yacoub. Screenplay by Zenovich, Joe Bini, and P. G. Morgan.

The tragic story of Roman Polanski, his life, his suffering, and his crimes, has been told and retold until it assumes the status of legend. After the loss of his parents in the Holocaust, after raising himself on the streets of Nazi-controlled Poland, after moving to America to acclaim as the director of *Chinatown*, after the murder by the Manson Family of his wife and unborn child . . . what then?

He was arrested and tried for unlawful sexual intercourse with a thirteen-year-old girl, the least of several charges including supplying her with drink and drugs. Then he fled the country to avoid a prison sentence and still remains in European exile for that reason. That is what everybody remembers, and it is all here in Marina Zenovich's surprising documentary, *Roman Polanski: Wanted and Desired*.

But there is so much more, and the story she builds, brick by brick with eyewitness testimony, is about crimes against the justice system carried out by the judge in Polanski's case, Laurence J. Rittenband. So corrupt was this man that the documentary finds agreement among the three people (aside from Polanski) most interested in the outcome: the defense

371

attorney, Douglas Dalton; the assistant district attorney who prosecuted the case, Roger Gunson; and Samantha Gailey Geimer, who was the child involved.

Their testimony nails Rittenband as a shameless publicity seeker who was more concerned with his own image than arriving at justice. Who broke his word to attorneys on both sides. Who staged a fake courtroom session in which Gunson and Geimer were to go through the motions of making their arguments before the judge read an opinion he had already prepared. Who tried to stage such a "sham" (Gunson's term) a second time. Who juggled possible sentences in discussions with outsiders, once calling a Santa Monica reporter, David L. Jonta, into his chambers to ask him, "What the hell should I do with Polanski?" Who discussed the case with the guy at the next urinal at his country club. Who held a press conference while the case was still alive. Who was removed from the case on a motion by *both* prosecution and defense.

The most significant fact of the film is that the prosecutor Gunson, a straitlaced Mormon, agrees with the defender Dalton that justice was not served. Both break their silences for this film after many years, Gunson saying, "I'm not surprised that he left the country under those circumstances." Samantha Geimer, whose family asked at the time that Polanski not be prosecuted or jailed, came public in 1997 to forgive him, and now says she feels Rittenband was running the case for his own aggrandizement, "orchestrating some little show that I didn't want to be in." And in 2003, I learn from the *New York Times*, she published a statement concluding: "Who wouldn't think about running when facing a fifty-year sentence from a judge who was clearly more interested in his own reputation than a fair judgment or even the well-being of the victim?"

It is her own well-being that leaves her bitter about the judge and the press, when as a child she became the center of an international media circus. Finally, she says, "I just stayed in my room." Now an intelligent and well-spoken adult, she represents herself with quiet dignity.

Polanski's ordeal with the press began after the 1969 Manson murders. Before the case was

linked to Manson, Polanski was widely reported to be a Satanic drug addict who probably orchestrated the killings himself. That was a crushing irony for a man who had suffered so much as a child and had now lost so much as an adult.

Yes, what he did with the thirteen-year-old girl was very wrong. That there were mitigating circumstances should not concern us. He confessed his guilt in a plea bargain arranged by the judge and both attorneys. He turned up at Chino State Prison to serve a ninety-day "evaluation" sentence. When Chino agreed with the parole board and two court-appointed psychiatrists (one is in the film) that he should be given parole, Rittenband decided to ignore those opinions because he was getting a bad image, he complained in chambers, while trying to orchestrate the second of his sham sessions (Dalton calls them "like a mock trial").

Zenovich uses file footage of Polanski at the time, TV news bites, newspaper clippings, even scenes from Polanski's films (*Rosemary's Baby* made such an impact that some thought it was made under Satanic inspiration). There are no current interviews with Polanski himself—just older TV interviews. But she has achieved extraordinary access to the other still-living players in the case, and they all seem to be in agreement: Polanski is correct in saying the judge played with him as a cat might play with a mouse. The corruption in Rittenband's courtroom was worthy of *Chinatown*.

Note: On July 15, 2008, Polanski and Dalton asked the L.A. district attorney's office to review his case based on new evidence disclosed in the film, including alleged improper communication between a member of the prosecutor's office (not Gunson) and Rittenband.

Rudo y Cursi ★ ★ ★
R, 103 m., 2009

Gael Garcia Bernal (Tato), Diego Luna (Beto), Guillermo Francella (Batuta), Dolores Heredia (Elvira), Adriana Paz (Tona), Jessica Mas (Maya). Directed by Carlos Cuaron and produced by Alfonso Cuaron, Alejandro Gonzalez Inarritu, Guillermo del Toro, and Frida Torresblanco. Screenplay by Carlos Cuaron.

I am gradually discovering that soccer is superior to American football: quicker, more athletic, depending on improvisation more than planning. In South and Central America, where American baseball has been embraced, soccer is a way of life. A movie like *Rudo y Cursi* helps explain why: One day, peons on a banana plantation; the next day, playing for big bucks in Mexico City. Just bring your shorts, your shoes, your shirt, and your ability. No shoulder pads.

The movie is a rags-to-beeyaches comedy about two half brothers from a poor rural background who are spotted one day by a talent scout. Why was he even watching their small-town game on a vacant lot? He was stranded there, along with his disabled red sports convertible and his trophy squeeze, by a slow-moving auto shop. He sees them playing and offers them an audition, which hinges ironically on the ancient confusion between audience right and stage right.

This is not a deep movie, but it's a broad one. It reunites three talents who had an enormous hit with *Y Tu Mama Tambien* in 2001: the actors Gael Garcia Bernal and Diego Luna, and Carlos Cuaron, who wrote that film and writes and directs this one. Instead of trying to top themselves with life and poignancy, they wisely do something for fun.

Tato (Bernal) plays the accordion and dreams of a future as a musical star, although nothing about his singing and playing suggests much of a future. Beto (Luna) has a wife and kids and has recently been promoted to foreman of a banana-picking crew. He dreams of being a pro goalie in much the same way we all dream of being Susan Boyle, although without her talent.

Batuta (Guillermo Francella), the talent scout, is a smooth-talking slickster who considers himself a historian and philosopher of soccer. He is the film's narrator and shares the surprising news that soccer was invented by ancient Aztecs while kicking around the severed heads of their enemies. So much for the belief that it originated in China in about 200 B.C. I'm not surprised. To hear them tell it, everything originated in China in about 200 B.C.

The boys travel eagerly to Mexico City, leaving behind Beto's family, their mother, and their mother's assorted worthless husbands.

They pick up nicknames. Tato is "Cursi," meaning cornball. Beto is "Rudo," meaning rough-edged. They're dazzled by the bright lights, the big city, and, in Rudo's case, the joys of high-stakes poker. Tato realizes his fantasy of meeting a sexy spokesmodel he's worshipped on TV and tapes his first music video, which, on the basis of its outcome, seems likely to be the last.

Curiously, and wisely, there's not a lot of soccer action in the movie, although it goes without saying there's a Big Match. This isn't a sports movie but a human comedy, and it depends on the effortless chemistry between Luna and Bernal, who evoke, like real brothers, the ability to love and hate each other and push all the right buttons. We are happy for their sudden good fortune, but somehow doubtful it will amount to much; they want success, but not enough to commit their entire lives to the quest.

The movie is the first from the newly formed Cha Cha Cha Productions, a collaboration of the top Mexican directors Alejandro Gonzalez Inarritu (*Amores Perros*), Guillermo del Toro (*Pan's Labyrinth*), and Alfonso Cuaron (brother of Carlos and director of *Y Tu Mama Tambien*). It comes at the end of an exciting decade for the Mexican cinema, which because of its high quality and the growing indie, foreign, and Spanish-speaking markets in the United States, is finding significant success. *Rudo y Cursi* is the sort of high-level buddy movie every national cinema needs for export—along with its masterpieces, to be sure.

Rush Hour 3 ★ ★
PG-13, 91 m., 2007

Chris Tucker (Carter), Jackie Chan (Lee), Noemie Lenoir (Genevieve), Hiroyuki Sanada (Kenji), Yvan Attal (George), Jingchu Zhang (Soo Yung), Youki Kudoh (Jasmine), Max von Sydow (Reynard), Roman Polanski (Detective Revi). Directed by Brett Ratner and produced by Arthur Sarkissian, Roger Birnbaum, Jay Stern, Jonathan Glickman, and Andrew Z. Davis. Screenplay by Jeff Nathanson.

I like this movie about as much as it's possible to like a movie with a two-star rating. Given its materials, it couldn't have been much better, but it's every bit as good as it is, if you see what I mean. Once you realize it's only going to be so good, you settle back and enjoy that modest degree of goodness, which is at least not badness, and besides, if you're watching *Rush Hour 3,* you obviously didn't have anything better to do anyway.

The filmmakers didn't either, I guess. It has been six years since *Rush Hour 2,* and unless you believe that director Brett Ratner and his stars, Chris Tucker and Jackie Chan, spent all that time turning down offers for a sequel, it seems fairly likely that this is a case of returning once more with a bucket before the well runs dry. Tucker is again Carter, the motor-mouth LAPD cop who's always in trouble, and Chan is again Lee, the ace Hong Kong cop called in to partner with him. This is, you realize, a formula. A friend of mine (I think it is me) calls these Wunza Movies. You know, wunza L.A. cop and wunza cop from China, and neither wunza guy you want to mess with.

Curious how Carter is always being hauled in from a punishment gig like traffic cop and being assigned to super-important cases that will require him to investigate backstage at the Folies Bergere in Paris, etc. This time one of Lee's old pals, Ambassador Han, has been shot in L.A., probably by a Chinese Triad gang, who are getting to be as handy as the Mafia for movie plots. Lee, in town as the ambassador's bodyguard, runs after the shooter in one of those impossible Jackie Chan chase scenes; it used to be we were amazed by his stunts, but these days I find myself even more amazed that he can still run that far.

Lee partners with his old friend Carter, and they go to the hospital to question the ambassador's beautiful daughter, Soo Yung (Jingchu Zhang). This produces the movie's funniest line, by Carter: "Let's go to the gift shop and get her a little teddy bear." Soo Yung had possession of an envelope with key evidence her father was going to use in testimony before the World Court. The envelope is, of course, this movie's MacGuffin, and was stolen from Soo Yung at her karate academy.

The cops go there and have a battle with the world's tallest man (Sun Ming Ming). I think he's the same man who got married recently and was about twice as tall as his bride. Or maybe he's another tall guy—naw, it has to be the same guy. Yao Ming, the basketball player, is only seven feet six inches, and Sun Ming Ming is seven feet nine inches. When Jackie Chan engages him in kung fu, he has to call on some of his wall-climbing skills.

Anyway, the chase leads to Paris, where the fragrant Genevieve (Noemie Lenoir) appears. Her function in the film, apart from certain plot details, is—to appear, which she does to great effect. And soon Carter is backstage at the Folies Bergere, and all the time we know, just *know,* that the Eiffel Tower is in the background of so many shots for a reason.

Yes, there is a pursuit up and down the tower, with Jackie Chan doing the usual impossible things, although at fifty-three, he doesn't do all of his own stunts. What difference does it make? In these days of special effects, who can tell anyway? For years, I suspected that the only reason Jackie did the stunts himself was to provide footage for the shots during the closing credits, showing him waving cheerfully as he was taken to the hospital.

All of these events take place efficiently and I was amused, even in a dialogue sequence involving a "Mr. Yu" and a "Mr. Mee," in which "He's Mee" and "I'm Yu," and who's on first? If you are trapped in a rainstorm in front of a theater playing this picture, by all means go right in. You won't have a bad time, will feel affectionate toward Lee and Carter, and stay dry.

S

Sangre de Mi Sangre ★ ★ ★
NO MPAA RATING, 100 m., 2008

Jorge Adrian Espindola (Pedro), Armando Hernandez (Juan), Jesus Ochoa (Diego), Paola Mendoza (Magda), Eugenio Derbez (Anibal), Israel Hernandez (Ricardo), Leonardo Anzure (Simon). Directed by Christopher Zalla and produced by Benjamin Odell and Per Melita. Screenplay by Zalla.

Sangre de Mi Sangre, the grand jury prize winner at Sundance 2007, gives us wonderful actors struggling in a tangled web of writing. The film is built around two relationships, both touching, both emotionally true. But time after time, we're brought up short by absolute impossibilities and gaping improbabilities in the story. To give one example: A newly arrived Mexican immigrant struggles to find his father in New York City. All he has is the seventeen-year-old information that the man works in (or perhaps owns) a French restaurant. Working his way through the yellow pages listings of French restaurants, he successfully finds his father. Uh-huh.

Let's back up to earlier screenplay questions. We meet the hero, Pedro, as he escapes from Mexico by quickly scaling a fence along the U.S. border. Is it that easy to cross? Never mind; waiting on the other side (not miles away, or hidden) is a truck waiting to take immigrants to New York. Wouldn't U.S. customs patrols notice it, in full view in an urban area? Pedro is hustled inside, the doors are slammed, and the truck begins a 2,500-mile journey that can apparently be survived on half a taco and a small bottle of water. More surprising still is that no effort is made to charge Pedro for the trip. He rides free.

Pedro (Jorge Adrian Espindola) is young, earnest, trusting. On the journey he makes a friend of Juan (Armando Hernandez), and tells him his story: He hopes to find his father in New York and carries a letter to the old man from his mother. When Pedro wakes up at the end of the trip, Juan has already disappeared with the letter.

Juan is enterprising and decides to pose as Pedro; maybe it's true, as Pedro's mother claimed, that the father owned the restaurant where he earned money, which he sent home for several years. But why a French restaurant? Using the address on the envelope, Juan easily finds the shabby apartment of old Diego (Jesus Ochoa), who has never seen him and has no desire to acquire a son. But Juan is ingratiating and tells a convincing story; after all, he has read the letter and Diego refuses to.

Meanwhile, the *real* Pedro wanders the streets, remembering only his father's street address (still accurate after seventeen years). He enlists Magda, a hard-worn Mexican girl who does drugs, makes a living by her wits and her body, and wants nothing to do with Pedro. They nevertheless become confederates, picking up fifty dollars here or there by performing sex for men who want to watch.

At this point you're rolling your eyes and wondering how the grand jury at Sundance, or any jury, could have awarded such a story its prize. But you would have missed what makes the film special: the relationships. Juan does such a good job of playing Pedro that he convinces Diego he really is his son. And the real Pedro gets a quick series of lessons in surviving the mean streets and comes to care about (not for) Magda.

The truest of these relationships, paradoxically, is the false one. Jesus Ochoa, a much-honored Mexican actor, creates a heartbreaking performance as Diego, the "old man," as Juan always calls him. He was once in love in Mexico, left, sent money home, returned, and then (after apparently fathering the real Pedro) returned to New York seventeen years ago. Maybe he told his wife he owned a restaurant, or maybe she lied about that to her son. No matter. He is a dishwasher and vegetable slicer, who earns extra money by sewing artificial roses. He has money stashed away. He is big, burly, very lonely. He comes to care for this "son." And despite Juan's deception, Juan comes to care for him—almost, you could say, as a father.

Magda is a tougher case. She does not bestow her affection lightly, nor is the real Pedro attracted to prostitution as a way for them to earn money. But Zalla, the director, does a perceptive, concise job of showing us how

Magda lives on the streets and nearly dies. Magda and Pedro are together as a matter of mutual survival.

Pedro, Juan, and Diego have paths that must eventually cross, we think. See for yourself if they do. And try not to ask why the police, planning to break down a door by surprise, would announce their approach with five minutes of sirens. The story's conclusion is rushed and arbitrary, but so perhaps it has to be. *Sangre de Mi Sangre* (*Blood of My Blood*) is a film that stumbles through a maddening screenplay but nevertheless generates true emotional energy.

Savage Grace ★ ★ ½
NO MPAA RATING, 97 m., 2008

Julianne Moore (Barbara Daly), Stephen Dillane (Brooks Baekeland), Eddie Redmayne (Tony Baekeland), Elena Anaya (Blanca), Unax Ugalde (Jake), Hugh Dancy (Sam Green). Directed by Tom Kalin and produced by Iker Monfort, Katie Roumel, Pamela Koffler, and Christine Vachon. Screenplay by Howard Rodman, based on the book by Natalie Robins and Steven M. L. Aronson.

When a movie's story ends and words appear on the screen telling us what happened then, they are sometimes inspirational, sometimes triumphant, sometimes sad. But I don't think I've ever seen an outcome more pathetic than the one described at the end of *Savage Grace*. They describe the ultimate destiny of Tony Baekeland, whose misfortune it was to be the heir of a great fortune. His fate is all the more appalling because it hardly seems inevitable. He is a very disturbed young man, as who might not be after the life he led? But life took him to tragic extremes.

The movie tells the true story of the marriage of Barbara Daly (Julianne Moore) and Brooks Baekeland (Stephen Dillane), who glittered erratically in the social circles of the 1940s through the 1960s. Brooks's grandfather invented Bakelite, used in everything, we learn, from cooking utensils to nuclear bombs. By the third generation the fortune has produced Brooks, a vapid clotheshorse who nevertheless perhaps deserves better than a wife who is all pose and attitude, all brittle facade, deeply rot-

ten inside. Their son, Tony (Eddie Redmayne), who narrates much of the story, is raised as her coddled darling but feels little real love from either parent and grows into a narcissistic, hedonistic, inverted basket case.

Oh, but they all look so elegant! They know how to dress and how to behave (and misbehave) in the high society watering holes of New York (1950s), Paris (1960s), Majorca and London (into the 1970s). They are known everywhere, loved nowhere, except for a few hangers-on like Sam (Hugh Dancy), a gay "walker" who accompanies Barbara after Brooks has left.

It's not simply that Brooks has left. He left with Blanca (Elena Anaya), the Spanish beauty Tony brought home from the beach one day, only to watch his father seduce her from right under his nose. Tony is of indeterminate sexuality from the beginning and now tilts over into homosexuality, with such friends as Jake (Unax Ugalde), a pot-smoking beach creature. Sam, an art dealer, is also in the mix, and indeed mother, son, and walker all end up in bed together.

The tone of the film is set by Julianne Moore, in what I suppose must be described as a fine performance, although she has little enough to work with. Barbara was so shallow. She was all clothes and hair and endless cigarettes, and conversation that was never really adequate for the level she was aiming for. She also had a nasty habit of saying rude things to break up social events, and you can hardly blame Brooks for leaving—although he, too, was so lacking in ordinary human qualities.

Decadence, of course, is the word to describe this world, but nothing really prepares us for its final descent. I will not describe what happens at the end, except to say nothing has really prepared us for it. It's hard to take. Very hard. And then those stark white letters on the black background.

This is the first film in fifteen years by Tom Kalin, who made *Swoon* in 1992. That was about another famous scandal, the murder of Bobby Franks by Richard Loeb and Nathan Leopold Jr. Both films are about protagonists without ordinary moral values; they find the unacceptable to be thinkable, even a pleasure. Or a compulsion.

But what we miss in the film is insight into

Barbara and Brooks and Tony. In his letters and diaries, Tony makes a great effort toward understanding his life but doesn't come up with much. Living these lives, for these people, must have been sad and tedious, and so, inevitably, is their story and, it must be said, the film about it.

The Savages ★ ★ ★ ½
R, 113 m., 2007

Laura Linney (Wendy Savage), Philip Seymour Hoffman (Jon Savage), Philip Bosco (Lenny Savage), Gbenga Akinnagbe (Jimmy), Peter Friedman (Larry). Directed by Tamara Jenkins and produced by Anne Carey, Ted Hope, and Erica Westheimer. Screenplay by Jenkins.

The Savages seems a curious movie to be opening four days before Christmas, but maybe not: Christmas Day itself is said to be the top moviegoing day of the year, as families (a) seek something they can do together without having to talk, or (b) use them as an excuse to escape from the house. Not all holidays are by Norman Rockwell, and maybe some grown children will enjoy this touching, humorous film about an elderly father whose time has come to leave his "retirement community" and move into "assisted living" (which my Aunt Mary referred to as "assisted dying").

Wendy and Jon Savage (Laura Linney and Philip Seymour Hoffman) are sister and brother, she living in New York City, he living in Buffalo, she an aspiring playwright, he a professor and author of books about the theater. They are smart, articulate, and knowledgeable about drama, attributes that do them no good at all when they get a call from Sun City that their dad, Lenny (Philip Bosco), has started to write on the wall with his excrement.

After some reluctance, mostly on Jon's part, they fly to Arizona and find their dad shacked up with Doris, a girlfriend his age. I was reminded of a friend of mine whose eighty-five-year-old dad discovered Viagra and insisted on calling his son with daily reports on his sex life. My friend pleaded with him to spare the details. There are some things children desperately do not want to know. Doris spares

them the occasion for such reports, however, by suddenly passing away, and Jon and Wendy decide to move their father to Buffalo so he will be close to them. He is a hostile curmudgeon who probably moved to Arizona in the first place to get away from them, but now he's in no position to resist.

Writer-director Tamara Jenkins (*Slums of Beverly Hills*) doesn't sentimentalize this material; quite the opposite. Lenny remains Lenny to the best of his ability, which means a short temper, a foul vocabulary, and a constant state of irritation. We gather that he was not a joy to grow up with; indeed, the scars still borne by his children are such that they refer to their childhoods only obliquely. Whatever the relationship between their parents was like, it has left them unable to form liaisons of their own; Wendy is having a joyless affair with a married man, and Jon has a Polish girlfriend he refuses to marry even if it would save her from deportation back to Poland. That he weeps over his inability shows that he is aware of his emotional scars and fears to heal them.

There is a genre of movies set in old-folks' homes that resemble sitcoms, including colorful characters, lots of one-liners, and a pecking order. The nursing home they find for Lenny in Buffalo is the next step after such a place. It is essentially run by the caregivers who treat their clients something like misbehaving children. One who seems to care is a Nigerian immigrant named Jimmy (Gbenga Akinnagbe), who sympathizes with Jon and Wendy and shares lore about caring for the aged. Kristen Thomson played a similar character in Sarah Polley's *Away from Her*—the experienced nurse who knows what the family has gone through and will go through.

A movie like this depends on nuance and performance if it is not to descend entirely into soap opera. Jenkins knows that and is quietly insistent that we observe little moments and dropped words and exchanged glances. The resettling of Jon and Wendy's father causes the resettling of their own lives and forces them to examine memories they hoped were buried. Both Linney and Hoffman are so specific in creating these characters that we see them as people, not elements in a plot. Hoffman in particular shows how many disguises he has within his seemingly immutable presence; would you know it is the same actor here and in two other films this season, *Before the Devil Knows You're Dead* and *Charlie Wilson's War*?

The Savages confronts a day that may come in all of our lives. Two days, actually, the first when we are younger, the second when we are older. *Ballad of Narayama*, a great Japanese film, is about a community that decides when a person has outlived any usefulness and leaves that person on the mountain to die. It seems cruel, but even the dying seem to think it appropriate. Better than to have been healthy and strong once, and reduced to writing on the walls.

A Secret ★ ★ ★

NO MPAA RATING, 105 m., 2008

Cecile de France (Tania), Patrick Bruel (Maxime), Ludivine Sagnier (Hannah), Julie Depardieu (Louise), Mathieu Amalric (Francois), Nathalie Boutefeu (Esther), Yves Jacques (George), Valentin Vigourt (Francois [age seven]), Quentin Dubuis (Francois [age fourteen]). Directed by Claude Miller and produced by Yves Marmion. Screenplay by Miller and Natalie Carter, based on the novel by Philippe Grimbert.

Let's set aside for the moment the idea that the characters in *A Secret* are Jewish. If you were Catholic, Protestant, Muslim, Hindu, Buddhist, atheist, whatever, and the country had been occupied by ruthless forces determined to track you down and exterminate you, what would you do? How would you protect your family?

Would you put a sign on the door saying, "Please exterminate us first to demonstrate our moral courage and bring shame down upon you?" Or would you attempt to conceal your identity, change your name, obtain forged papers, move to a safe haven? It wouldn't take me long to puzzle that one out.

But what if something went horribly wrong with your plans? What if you survived but others died? Would you feel guilt? How would you deal with that? Would you blame yourself if there was nothing you could have done? What would you keep secret? What if a whole generation shared your feelings and fears?

In France during the Nazi occupation, hundreds of thousands of Jews were deported and killed. Some of the French were collaborators and prospered. Some of the French were in the Resistance and risked their lives as anti-Nazi terrorists. Most of the French kept their heads low and their opinions to themselves. Jews were included in all three categories. See Truffaut's 1980 film of the wartime theater in Paris, *The Last Metro*. After the war, astonishing numbers of French claimed to have been in the Resistance all along.

Claude Miller's *A Secret* is inspired by a French best-seller by Philippe Grimbert, who has the same family name as the family in his novel. More precisely, they share the family name Grinberg. As it became clear the Nazis would occupy vast areas of France, including Paris and Lyon, they changed it. After the war, they preserved their secret from those who had not known them before. During the war we sympathize with their decision. But by maintaining it, what torments did they feel?

This film is about the torments and how they were visited on later generations. It centers on the story of a teenager who is a disappointment to his parents because he has no skill at athletics. This is crushing to young Francois (Quentin Dubuis) and continues to haunt the adult Francois (Mathieu Amalric, star of *The Diving Bell and the Butterfly*). When he was fourteen, a family friend who lived across the courtyard (Julie Depardieu) told him some things he seemed to be the last to know.

This is a sad and lonely boy. He feels inadequate and unloved by his parents (Cecile de France and Patrick Bruel). In his fantasies, they were an ideal couple, hopelessly in love. In his solitude as a child (Valentin Vigourt), unable to join in the play of others, he imagines a brother who is taller, athletic, charming, and loved. His invisible companion is with him everywhere, even at the dinner table. His father is furious about the shadow brother.

Miller, a gifted veteran French director (*Class Trip, The Accompanist, The Little Thief*) and a French Jew born in 1942, seems to feel a special urgency in this material, as does Grimbert, the author of the book. They are telling a story less uncommon in France than it might seem. The film, they say, "is based on real people." People we care for, worry about, sympathize with, and pity. Who can cast the first stone?

The Secret Life of Bees ★ ★ ★ ½
PG-13, 110 m., 2008

Queen Latifah (August Boatwright), Dakota Fanning (Lily Owens), Jennifer Hudson (Rosaleen Daise), Alicia Keys (June Boatwright), Sophie Okonedo (May Boatwright), Nate Parker (Neil), Tristan Wilds (Zach Taylor), Hilarie Burton (Deborah Owens), Paul Bettany (T. Ray Owens). Directed by Gina Prince-Bythewood and produced by James Lassiter, Ewan Leslie, Joe Pichirallo, Lauren Shuler Donner, and Will Smith. Screenplay by Prince-Bythewood, based on the novel by Sue Monk Kidd.

As a realistic portrayal of life in rural South Carolina in 1964, *The Secret Life of Bees* is dreaming. As a parable of hope and love, it is enchanting. Should it have been painful or a parable? Parable, I think, so it will please those who loved the novel by Sue Monk Kidd.

One critic has described it as sappy, syrupy, sentimental, and sermonizing, and those are only the S's. The same review admitted it is also "wholesome and heartwarming," although you will never see "wholesome" used in a movie ad.

I go with heartwarming. There is such a thing as feeling superior to your emotions, but I trust mine. If I sense the beginnings of a teardrop in my eye during a movie, that is evidence more tangible than all the mighty weight of Film Theory. "The immediate experience," one of the wisest of critics called it. That's what you have to acknowledge. I watched the movie, abandoned history and plausibility, and just plain fell for it. If it had been a bad movie, it would have been ripe for vivisection. But it is not a bad movie.

Above all, it contains characters I care for, played by actors I admire. If a script doesn't get in the way, a movie like that just about has to work. Queen Latifah, who combines conviction, humor, and a certain majesty, plays August Boatwright, a woman about as plausible as a fairy godmother and so what. She lives outside town in a house painted the color of the Easter Bunny and gathers honey for a living. Famous honey, from happy bees. Living with her are her two sisters: June (Alicia Keys), a classical cellist and civil rights activist, and May (Sophie Okonedo), whom you don't want to startle with anything sad.

In a shack many miles away, fourteen-year-old Lily Owens (Dakota Fanning) lives with her cruel father (Paul Bettany). Her best friend and defender, the black housekeeper Rosaleen (Jennifer Hudson), endures the wrath of the father because she will not abandon Lily. One day Rosaleen is so bold as to attempt to register to vote and is beaten by racists in the nearby town. This results, of course, in her arrest. Lily helps her escape the town, and they set off on a journey to the town of Tiburon, which Lily knows about because of something she found in her late mother's possessions: the label for a honey jar.

As Lily helps Rosaleen flee from virtual slavery, it's impossible not to think about Huck and Jim, unless Political Correctness has prevented you from reading that greatest of all novels about black and white in America. From what little we see of the folks in Tiburon, they're as nice as the folks in Lily's hometown were mean.

They land on August's doorstep. She takes them in, over resistance from the militant June. And there the proper story begins, involving discoveries about the past, problems in the present, and hopes for the future. These are well-handled melodramatic events that would not benefit from being revealed here.

Dakota Fanning comes of age in this film and in the somewhat similar but less successful *Hounddog*. She's not a kid anymore. She has always been a good actress, and she is only growing deeper and better. I expect her to make the transition from child to woman with the same composure and wisdom that Jodie Foster demonstrated. Here she plays a plucky, forthright, and sometimes sad and needy young teen with the breadth this role requires and a depth that transforms it.

Then observe Sophie Okonedo, the London-born, Cambridge-educated actress who has no trouble at all playing a simple-minded, deeply disturbed country girl. The English have little trouble with Southern accents. Michael Caine explained it to me once. Has to do with Appalachia being settled by working-class Brits. Her May is the heart of the film, because her heart is so open. She has some delicate emotional transitions to traverse here and convinces us of them. Remember her in *Hotel Rwanda*?

The Alicia Keys character, June, is really too complex for a supporting role. In the workings of the story, she functions as an eye opener for Rosaleen, who has never guessed black women could be so gifted and outspoken. The three sisters live in an idyllic household that must have taken a powerful lot of honey sales, even then, to maintain. That isn't an issue. We believe it, because Queen Latifah as August beams watchfully on all before her, and nobody can beam like Latifah. If ever there was a woman born to be christened Queen, she's the one.

I have great affection for this film because it honors a novel that many people loved for good reasons. It isn't superior, nor does it dumb it down. It sees what is good and honors it. The South was most likely not like this in 1964. That was the year the Voting Rights Act and Civil Rights Act were passed. The Boatwright farm, as I said, is really a dream. But in those hard days, people needed dreams.

The Secret of the Grain ★ ★ ★ ½
NO MPAA RATING, 151 m., 2009

Habib Boufares (Slimane Beiji), Hafsia Herzi (Rym), Faridah Benkhetache (Karima), Abdelhamid Aktouche (Hamid), Bouraouia Marzouk (Souad), Hatika Karaoui (Latifa), Alice Houri (Julia). Directed by Abdellatif Kechiche and produced by Claude Berri. Screenplay by Kechiche.

A nineteen-year-old actress named Hafsia Herzi steps into the cinema in this film. I have a feeling it will be, like the first film of Isabelle Huppert, not simply a debut, but an announcement: "Here I am, and I am the real thing." She is the energy at the heart of a life-filled portrait of a big family of second-generation immigrants in a shabby French port city, a family that nourishes love, jealousy, discouragement, ambition, and a whole lot of dining and talking.

The Secret of the Grain is the wrong title for this movie. In France, where it was honored for best film, director, screenplay, and most promising actress, the title translates as "Fish Couscous." In England, it opened as *Couscous*. The only secret involving the grain is why it's so late being served. What were you expecting, Napoleon's toenails?

The wave of immigrants from former French colonies such as Tunisia, Morocco, and Algeria began in the late 1950s and continues, but most of the early arrivals are now grandparents, their offspring speaking only a few words of Arabic. We land in the middle of such a family, its patriarch the grave, taciturn Slimane Beiji (Habib Boufares). He's in the process of losing his job at a shipyard and negotiating uneasily between his first wife, Souad (Bouraouia Marzouk), and his lover, Latifa (Hatika Karaoui), who owns a little hotel. He has two sons, one always in lust, but saves his deepest affection for Latifa's daughter, Rym (Hafsia Herzi). We have to gather these facts from the others, because Slimane doesn't confide.

The Tunisian-born writer-director, Abdellatif Kechiche, isn't interested in a formal story, although he does provide a cliff-hanging third act. He wants us to see these people live. Early in the film, he has a dinner table scene of such virtuosity that we feel we know everyone, even those we haven't seen before. This scene only incidentally sets up plot points; its purpose is to show strong opinions, deep feelings, humor, and a sincere interest in the food. The cook is the first wife, renowned for her couscous; she always sends a plate home to Slimane, who lives in a little room in Latifa's hotel. She also, as a ritual, gives a plate from every meal to the nearest homeless man she can find.

Still waters run deep. Slimane reveals plans to use his severance pay to open a restaurant aboard a rusty ship in the harbor, serving Souad's couscous. His strongest supporter is Rym, and as she talks with Slimane and a group of old musicians who live at the hotel, and to her mother, she reveals herself as an instinctive actress who tells each what they need to hear. She never gets angry, never pushes too hard, and doesn't insist, but it's almost impossible to keep her from having her way.

The film arrives at a big free dinner thrown by Slimane for the town big shots, in hopes of getting planning permission for the restaurant. Here we see race and class discrimination in France; the big shots are happy to wine and dine for free, but in their minds immigrants are not . . . quite . . . French. The younger generation all seem quintessentially French to us, but what do we know?

There are two amazing dialogue scenes in the movie. One involves Rym pleading with her mother to attend Slimane's opening night, despite the couscous being prepared by the other woman. The other involves Alice Houri as Julie, who is married to Slimane's womanizing son and explains with astonishing passion why he is a liar, a worthless scumbag, and a failure as husband and father.

This verbal assault comes to poor Slimane as the latest in a series of disasters, including the delivery of the dinner. Help comes, not from an unexpected source, but certainly in an unexpected way. We leave the movie as we entered, in the middle of things. *The Secret of the Grain* never slows, always engages, may continue too long, but ends too soon. It is made of life itself. Hafsia Herzi has four more films in the can and two in production. Remember her name.

The Secrets ★ ★ ★ ½
NO MPAA RATING, 127 m., 2009

Fanny Ardant (Anouk), Ania Bukstein (Naomi), Michal Shtamler (Michelle), Adir Miller (Yanki), Guri Alfi (Michael). Directed by Avi Nesher and produced by Nesher and David Silber. Screenplay by Nesher and Hadar Galron.

Naomi is a great disappointment to her father. She is his student, the most learned, the most devout student of the respected old rabbi. But she hasn't learned the most important lesson: how to be a submissive woman, to submit herself to the will of her father and her future husband. Even worse, she wickedly thinks she could someday be a rabbi herself.

There are hints in *The Secrets* that she knows well how her father's beliefs worked in the life of her mother: "Often when I came into this kitchen, I found her weeping." Naomi submits to her father the rabbi but not to her father the man. The rabbi has decided that his student Michael will marry Naomi. Naomi has no feeling for this man: She knows more than he does, but he treats her as a silly girl and piously asserts his narrow view of a woman's role.

Naomi buys time. After the death of her mother, she postpones the wedding and convinces her father to let her spend some time in a seminary in a secluded town in Israel. Here she will come into her own as a natural spiritual leader, as a woman, and as someone who discovers the difference between convenient and romantic love.

Avi Nesher's *The Secrets,* a deeply involving melodrama, has all the devices to draw us into this story. In some ways it is a traditional narrative. But it is more. It is gently and powerfully acted. And it is thoughtful about its characters, so that even though they follow a somewhat predictable arc, they contain surprises for us. They keep thinking for themselves.

Naomi (Ania Bukstein) seems at first a subdued, intellectual young woman, who believes explicitly in her father's orthodoxy. But as she sees how it worked in her mother's life and is working in hers, she experiences the basic feminist insight: Why a man but not a woman? It fascinates me that in some religions, men subscribe so eagerly to a dogma that oppresses women, and some women agree with it. Naomi does not agree.

At the seminary, one of her roommates doesn't even think of agreeing. This is Michelle (Michal Shtamler), from Paris, with a chip on her shoulder. The two find themselves assigned to make daily meal deliveries to Anouk (Fanny Ardant), a very ill French woman, just released from prison and living in the town. Michelle discovers on the Internet that Anouk's sentence was for murder. The details of the crime are left murky, but the woman desperately wants to be cleansed and appeals to Naomi and Michelle to help her.

Their help for Anouk is the crux of the film. Even though she is not Jewish, Anouk seeks Jewish healing, and Naomi essentially acts as a rabbi in trying to help her. These scenes are the most moving in the film, involving a secret visit to an ancient cleansing pool, which, of course, is off-limits to women.

Through this process Naomi and Michelle grow close romantically, tension grows between Naomi and the loathsome Michael, Naomi's father reacts with towering rage, and the movie becomes an argument against some elements of his style of Judaism. It will help clarify for some viewers that Judaism incorporates beliefs that are not all in agreement.

The Secrets is, first of all, continuously absorbing, which most good films must be. The performances by the three leading actresses are compelling, although Ardant is required to sustain the note of fatal illness perhaps too long. There's a subplot involving a klezmer clarinetist that's delightful. And one about the older woman in charge of the seminary that evokes an earlier generation's beliefs about the limitations of women.

So *The Secrets* plays as a melodrama and much more: a film about religious and sexual intolerance, about reconciling opposed beliefs, about matching the fervor of feminism against religious patriarchy, and even in some ways a social comedy. It contains an object lesson for the whole genre involving romance and the battle of the generations: Such films can actually be serious about something.

Self-Medicated ★ ★ ★

R, 107 m., 2007

Diane Venora (Louise Eriksen), Michael Bowen (Dan Jones), Greg Germann (Keith McCauley), Monty Lapica (Andrew Eriksen), Kristina Anapau (Nicole), Matthew Carey (Aaron), William Stanford Davis (Gabe). Directed by Monty Lapica and produced by Tommy Bell and Lapica. Screenplay by Lapica.

The opening scene in Monty Lapica's *Self-Medicated* is a particularly chilling exercise in antisocial behavior. A car filled with out-of-control teenagers cruises the Strip in Las Vegas, shooting at tourists with paint guns. This is the sort of behavior, like using laser pointers illegally, that you hope doesn't leak out to numbskulls at large. One of the kids is Andrew (played by Lapica himself), who is usually high on street drugs, allegedly because he mourns the death of his beloved father.

As most drug counselors will advise you, drug abuse has to be seen separately from the "problems" that "inspire" it. The majority of drunks and druggies use today because they used yesterday, and that's why they will use again tomorrow. I remember a guy in O'Rourke's who said he was drinking "because it's Christmas." Informed that he had missed the mark by three days, he said, "OK, then, I'm drinking because it isn't Christmas."

Whatever his reasons, Andrew is out of control. He has walked out of school, he hates his pill-addicted mom (Diane Venora), and she can't get it together to really talk to him, let alone help him. So she makes a call and attendants from a "treatment center" pounce on him in the middle of the night and haul him away. This is staging an intervention big-time.

The film, said to be somewhat autobiographical, is critical both of Andrew and his treatment. Unlike portrayals you may have seen of the wise and useful Betty Ford or Hazelden centers, this (fictional) outfit in St. George, Utah, treats its patients as prisoners, adopts a good cop/bad cop counseling regime, and apparently plans to send patients to American Samoa to complete their "recovery" as forced labor. I am not making this up; it's inspired, I understand, by an actual treatment center, since shut down, although not the one Lapica attended.

The facility is more realistically portrayed than the one depicted in *One Flew Over the Cuckoo's Nest*, but this is a docudrama, not a fable. Andrew comes up against a counselor named Dan (Michael Bowen), who apparently loathes druggies and thinks his disgust will cure them. Another counselor named Keith (Greg Germann) has a kinder, gentler approach, but if Andrew hated school, it's nothing to how he feels about this place. As he checks in, he's already mentally escaping.

The title is a little misleading. Andrew and his mother are self-medicators, yes (her drugs are prescribed, but a middle-aged woman can often make that happen). But Andrew is also, in a way, self-treating. Alcoholics Anonymous, the most effective means of staying clean and sober, talks about "hitting bottom," and *Self-Medicated* plays like the story of Andrew throwing himself at the bottom and sticking. Eventually, if he's not entirely around the bend, a light will dawn.

Helping him see the light is Gabe, a man who lives on the streets (William Stanford Davis). From the man who has been there, who has nothing and therefore nothing to lose, Andrew senses he is gaining insights without any motive or spin. The same strength sits at the center of an AA meeting, where everyone is in the same boat and there is no captain.

On the basis of this film, Monty Lapica, at twenty-four, has a career ahead of him as a director, an actor, or both. He also has a life ahead of him, which the film does a great deal to make clear.

September Dawn no stars
R, 111 m., 2007

Jon Voight (Jacob Samuelson), Trent Ford (Jonathan Samuelson), Tamara Hope (Emily Hudson), Jon Gries (John D. Lee), Taylor Handley (Micah Samuelson), Lolita Davidovich (Nancy Dunlap), Dean Cain (Joseph Smith), Terence Stamp (Brigham Young). Directed by Christopher Cain and produced by Cain, Scott Duthie, and Kevin Matossian. Screenplay by Carole Whang Schutter and Cain.

On September 11, 1857, at the Mountain Meadows Massacre, a group of fanatic Mormons attacked and slaughtered a wagon train of about 120 settlers passing through Utah on their way to California. Can we all agree that the date has no significance? No, we cannot, because *September Dawn* is at pains to point out that on another September 11, another massacre took place, again spawned by religion.

But hold on. Where did I get that word "fanatic"? In my opinion, when anybody believes their religion gives them the right to kill other people, they are fanatics. Aren't there enough secular reasons for war? But there is no shortage of such religions, or such people. The innocent, open-faced Christians on the wagon train were able to consider settling California, after all, because some of their co-religionists participated in or benefited from the enslavement of Africans and the genocide of Native Americans.

Were there fanatics among those who ran the Salem Witch Trials or the Inquisition or the Crusades? Or the Holocaust? No shortage of them. Organized religion has been used to justify most of the organized killing in our human history. It's an inescapable fact, especially if you consider the Nazis and communists as cults led by secular gods. When your god inspires you to murder someone who worships god in a different way or under another name, you're barking up the wrong god. Football teams praying before a game reduce the same process to absurdity: What god worthy of the name cares which team wins?

The vast majority of the members of all religions, I believe and would argue, don't want to kill anybody. They want to love and care for their families, find decent work that sustains life and comfort, live in peace, and get along with their neighbors. It is a deviant streak in some humans, I suspect, that drives them toward self-righteous violence and uses religion as a convenient alibi.

That is true, wouldn't you agree, about Mormons, Christians, Muslims, Jews, Hindus, Buddhists, and so on? No, not all of you would agree, because every time I let slip the opinion that most Muslims are peaceful and nonviolent, for example, I receive the most extraordinary hate mail from those assuring me they are not. And in a Muslim land, let a newspaper express the opinion that most Christians and Jews are peaceful and nonviolent, and that newspaper office is likely to be burned down. The worst among us speak for the best.

Which brings us back to September 11, 1857, when a crazy Mormon zealot named Bishop Jacob Samuelson (Jon Voight) ordered the massacre of the visiting wagon train after first sending his spokesman, John D. Lee (Jon Gries), to lie that if they disarmed, they would be granted safe passage. Whether the leader of his church, Brigham Young (Terence Stamp), approved of this action is a matter of much controversy, denied by the church, claimed by *September Dawn*.

What a strange, confused, unpleasant movie this is. Two theories have clustered around it: (1) It is anti-Mormon propaganda in order to muddy the waters around the presidential campaign of Mitt Romney, or (2) it is not about Mormons at all, but an allegory about the 9/11/01 terrorists. Take your choice. The problem with allegories is that you can plug them in anywhere. No doubt the film would have great impact in Darfur.

My opinion is that there isn't anything to be gained in telling this story in this way. It generates bad feelings on all sides, and at a time when Mormons are at pains to explain they are Christians, it underlines the way that these Mormons consider all Christians to be "gentiles." The Mormons are presented in no better light than Nazis and Japanese were in Hollywood's World War II films. Wasn't there a more thoughtful and insightful way to consider this historical event? Or how about a different event altogether? What about the Donner Party? They may have been cannibals, but at least they were nondenominational.

If there is a concealed blessing, it is that the film is so bad. Jon Voight, that gifted and versatile actor, is here given the most ludicrous and unplayable role of his career, and a goofy beard to go along with it. Terence Stamp, as Brigham Young, comes across as the kind of man you'd find at the back of a cave in a Cormac McCarthy novel. The Christians are so scrubbed and sunny they could have been teleported in time from the Lawrence Welk program.

And isn't it sickening that the plot stirs in some sugar by giving us what can only be described as a horse whisperer? This movie needs human whisperers. And giving us a romance between the bishop's son and a pretty gentile girl? And another son of the bishop who dresses up like an Indian and goes batty at the scent of blood? And real Native Americans who assist the Mormons in their killing, no doubt thinking, well, we can get around to the Mormons later? I am trying as hard as I can to imagine the audience for this movie. Every time I make any progress, it scares me.

Seraphine ★ ★ ★

NO MPAA RATING, 126 m., 2009

Yolande Moreau (Seraphine), Ulrich Tukur (Wilhelm Uhde), Anne Bennent (Anne Marie), Genevieve Mnich (Madame Duphot), Nico Rogner (Helmut), Adelaide Leroux (Minouche), Serge Lariviere (Duval), Francoise Lebrun (Mere Superieure). Directed by Martin Provost and produced by Milena Poylo and Gilles Sacuto. Screenplay by Provost and Marc Abdelnour.

You might not look twice at her. Seraphine is a bulky, work-worn housecleaner who gets down on her knees in a roomy print dress and fiercely scrubs the floor. She slips away from work to steal turpentine from the church votive candles, blood from the butcher, and clay from the fields, and these she combines with other elements to mix the paints she uses at night, covering panels with fruits and flowers that seem to look at us in alarm.

Seraphine de Senlis, who died in a French mental institution in 1942, today has her paintings in many museums. She did not paint for money or fame, although she grew heady when they began to come. She painted because she was instructed to by her guardian angel. Sometimes while painting she would loudly sing in praise of the Holy Virgin. In this miraculous film we learn nothing of her low birth or early life; we see only her daily toil and nightly ecstasy.

Seraphine arrives from France as the year's most honored film, winner of seven Cesars from the French Academy, including best film and best actress. The actress is Yolande Moreau, who combines, as some people do, a plain face with moments of beauty. Notice her fleeting little smile of complicity as she steals fuel from candles before the Virgin. Moreau plays Seraphine as a straight-ahead charger, a little stooped, marching always with energy, plunging into work, not saying much, shy, but very much who she is. Her physical bearing tells us what we need to know about her mental state.

Her life is changed forever when Wilhelm Uhde (Ulrich Tukur) comes as a boarder to the home she works in; it offers a pastoral setting near Chantilly, and she observes that Uhde needs relief from stress. He's a famous German art critic and a Paris gallery owner, already well-known as an early champion of Picasso and Braque; he discovered Rousseau. He glimpses one of Seraphine's little paintings of apples, asks to see more, is convinced she is a primitive genius. (In the film, we appear to see her actual paintings.)

She observes everything, worries about Uhde, sees he is sad, offers him some of her homemade "power wine," tells him that when she is sad, she walks in the forest and touches the trees. We even see her climbing one, in her late fifties, for the view.

She lives in bitter poverty, hounded by her landlady, doing laundry for a few francs, doling out her coins at the local store to buy canvas and the paints she cannot mix herself. Uhde admires her work, which she cannot believe, gives her some money, makes her some promises, and then disappears: As a German, he flees France at the outset of World War I. Ten years after the war, he and his sister return to Senlis. He assumes Seraphine is dead. At a town hall exhibition by local artists, he sees a work that is unmistakably hers, but larger and more finished. He is overwhelmed, as many others would be.

Seraphine is not a rags-to-riches story. The director, Martin Provost, who wrote it with Marc Abdelnour, focuses intently on Seraphine's delusions, on the manic state that overtakes her at the prospect of fame and fortune, about how she hides far inside so that Uhde cannot reach her. I've seen many films hoping to understand the nature of great artists; one that comes close is *Vincent,* by Paul Cox. This is another. It "explains" nothing but feels everything. It reminded me of two other films: Bresson's *Mouchette,* about a poor girl victimized by a village, and Karen Gehre's *Begging Naked,* shown at Ebertfest this year, about a woman whose art is prized even as she lives in Central Park.

People like these are not entirely to be pitied. Their art is a refuge. All artists fall into a reverie state while working. Some experience a joy that obliterates their circumstances. The problem is that when they're not creating, they have to go right on living.

Serbis ★ ★ ½
R, 91 m., 2009

Gina Pareno (Nanay Flor), Jaclyn Jose (Nayda), Julio Diaz (Lando), Coco Martin (Alan), Kristofer King (Ronald), Dan Alvaro (Jerome), Mercedes Cabral (Merly), Roxanne Jordan (Jewel). Directed by Brillante Mendoza and produced by Ferdinand Lapuz. Screenplay by Armando Lao.

Although *Serbis* spends a great deal of time following its characters through the corridors and up and down the stairs of a shabby Filipino porno movie theater, we never get a clear idea of the interior layout. And the auditorium looks rather small considering the hulking exterior of the Family Theater. But maybe that's the idea, because the film is a labyrinth of lost and wandering lives.

An extended family runs this failing old theater, lives in it, too, and is even raising a cute little son. The movies on the screen are hetero, but nobody is watching. The dark seats and the bright corridors and staircases are home to gay hustlers and their clientele, everybody knows it, nobody cares, many of them seem to be waiting around for something to relieve their boredom. There is some gratitude when a goat gets loose inside the theater. How it climbed so high without being seen on the stairs is a good question; maybe it's a mountain goat.

Up and down the staff and customers go, like ants in a hill. We get to know the members of the Pineda family of Angeles City pretty well, especially Nayda (Jaclyn Jose), the daughter, whose son is the little boy, and whose mother, Nanay Flor (Gina Pareno), is due in court for her husband's divorce hearing. A strong matriarch, she fiercely wants to be rid of the man. And there is another worry: Merly (Mercedes Cabral), girlfriend of the cousin/projectionist Alan (Coco Martin), has announced she is pregnant, so there will be the expense of a wedding no one wants.

In a film so immersed in sex, there is little actual sex. *Serbis* (the word means "service") is about a closed world in which sex is a commodity and it's a buyer's market. Sexual encounters are hurried, hidden, and never lingered on by the camera of director Brillante Mendoza, who is more absorbed by faces, routine, work, and the passage of time. The body part that receives the most attention is the projectionist's butt, where there is a painful boil. His self-treatment for this affliction reportedly drew groans at the Cannes 2008 press screening, but it seems a quick and relatively painless solution, and I will file it away.

The film opens with a curious scene: Nayda bathes, dresses herself, and applies lipstick in front of a mirror, while telling her reflection, "I love you." Later there is a scene of her mother applying lipstick in preparation for her court appearance. Given the seedy surroundings, there is something touching about these two women preparing their faces to bravely face the world.

This is not a film most people will enjoy. Its qualities are apparent only if one appreciates cinematic style for itself. I enjoyed it because I got into Mendoza's visual use of the corridors and staircases and their life rhythms. Most people will find that annoying. Anyone hoping to see sex will be badly disappointed. Let's put it this way: If you see only one art film this month, this shouldn't be the one. If you see one every week, you might admire it.

Seven Pounds ★ ★ ★
PG-13, 100 m., 2008

Will Smith (Ben Thomas), Rosario Dawson (Emily Posa), Woody Harrelson (Ezra Turner), Michael Ealy (Ben's Brother), Barry Pepper (Dan). Directed by Gabriele Muccino and produced by Todd Black, James Lassiter, Jason Blumenthal, Steve Tisch, and Will Smith. Screenplay by Grant Nieporte.

I am fascinated by films that observe a character who is behaving precisely, with no apparent motivation. A good actor brings such a role into focus, as Will Smith does in the enigmatically titled *Seven Pounds*. Who is he, what does he want, why is he behaving so oddly for an IRS agent? And why won't he kiss Rosario Dawson when they both so obviously want that to happen?

As Ben Thomas, the man from the IRS, he can get in anywhere and ask any question. But surely the IRS doesn't require him to punch a nursing home supervisor for not allowing an old lady her bath? And why, after he intuits he is speaking to a blind man on the phone, is he so needlessly cruel to him? And why then does he follow the same man (Woody Harrelson) into a restaurant and engage him in conversation?

And why does he check into a fleabag hotel? Doesn't the IRS pay him a salary? And what favor does his lifelong friend Dan (Barry Pepper) owe him? And why is he looking for people who need their own favors? And so on. For much of the first hour of *Seven Pounds*, Ben Thomas acts according to a plan that seems perfectly clear, but only to himself. The reason it goes unexplained is that he has no need to explain it to himself and no way to explain it to anyone else.

I am reminded of a film you should see someday, Melville's *Le Samourai*, about a man who lies on a bed in a dark hotel room and smokes, and gets up, and pays meticulous attention to his appearance, and goes out into the night, and we have no idea who this man is. I find this more interesting than a movie about a man whose nature and objectives are made clear in the first five minutes in a plot that simply points him straight ahead.

Will Smith displays a rather impressive range of emotional speeds here. He can be a tough, merciless IRS man. He can bend the rules on some cases. He can have a candlelight dinner with a beautiful woman named Emily Posa (Dawson) and go home afterward. She can sense his deep sadness. He is angry with people sometimes, but he seems angriest of all at himself. It's quite a performance. And Dawson makes Emily not simply a woman confused, maybe offended, by his behavior, but a woman of instinctive empathy who does an emotional dance with him, following his lead when he needs to be treated like an IRS agent, or like a perfect gentleman, or like a man who needs understanding even if she doesn't know what she's supposed to understand.

I haven't even hinted about the hidden motives in this film. Miraculously, for once even the trailers don't give anything away. I'll tell you one thing: I may have made Ben sound like an angel, but he is very much flesh and blood, and none of his actions are supernatural. He has his reasons.

The director is Gabriele Muccino, who also directed Smith in *The Pursuit of Happyness*. He is effective at timing the film's revelations so that they don't come suddenly like a U-turn; they're revealed at the last necessary points in the story. Some people will find it emotionally manipulative. Some people like to be emotionally manipulated. I do, when it's done well.

17 Again ★ ★ ★
PG-13, 98 m., 2009

Zac Efron (Mike O'Donnell), Matthew Perry (Adult Mike), Leslie Mann (Scarlet), Thomas Lennon (Ned Gold), Michelle Trachtenberg (Maggie), Sterling Knight (Alex), Melora Hardin (Jane Masterson). Directed by Burr Steers and produced by Adam Shankman and Jennifer Gibgot. Screenplay by Jason Filardi.

Mike O'Donnell's wife wants a divorce, his kids are remote, he didn't get the job promotion he expects, and everything else in his life has gone wrong since that magic year when he was seventeen, a basketball star, in love, and looked like Zac Efron instead of Matthew Perry. He's obviously a case for treatment by a Body Swap Movie.

Revisiting the trophy case at his old high school, Mike encounters a janitor who, from the way he smiles at the camera, knows things beyond this mortal coil. If only Mike could go back to seventeen and not make all the same mistakes. In *17 Again*, he can. He falls into a Twilight Zone vortex and emerges as Zac Efron. They say be careful what you wish for, because you might get it. Mike should have been more specific. Instead of wishing to be seventeen again, he should have wished to go back twenty years in time.

Yes, he becomes himself trapped inside his own seventeen-year-old body. Same wife, same kids, same problems. As Old Mike was getting divorced, he'd moved in with his best friend, Ned (Thomas Lennon), and now he throws himself on Ned's mercy: Will Ned pose as his father, so Young Mike can be his son and help out his kids by enrolling in the same high school again? Ned, who is a software millionaire and middle-aged fanboy, agrees, especially after he falls helplessly in love with the high school principal, Jane (Melora Hardin).

Young Mike becomes the new best friend of his insecure son, Alex (Sterling Knight). Then he meets Alex's mom, Scarlet (Leslie Mann), who, of course, before the vortex was his wife, and before that his high school bride (Allison Miller). She thinks it's strange that he looks *exactly* like the boy she married at seventeen. He explains he is the son of an uncle, who I guess would have to be Old Mike's brother, so it's curious Old Scarlet never met him, but if she doesn't ask that, why should I?

In high school, Young Mike again becomes a basketball star, befriends Alex, and attempts to defend his Gothish daughter, Maggie (Michelle Trachtenberg), against the predations of her jerk boyfriend, who as a hot-rodding jock traveling with a posse is, of course, the *last* guy in school who would date, or be dated by, a moody girl who wears black.

I've seen Body Swaps before (Tom Hanks in *Big*). The first act of this movie seemed all retread. Then it started to dig in. There are twin romances; as Shakespeare demonstrated, one must be serious and the other farcical. Young Mike is still seriously in love with his wife, Old Scarlet, and she is powerfully attracted to this boy who's a double for her first love. She thinks that's wrong. He knows it isn't, but how can he explain?

Meanwhile, best buddy Ned courts Principal Masterson, who for the first time in his life has Taught Him What Love Means. Before her, ecstasy was owning Darth Vader's costume. I will not describe what happens the first time they go out to dinner, except to say that it's comic genius, perfectly played by Melora Hardin and Thomas Lennon.

I attended a screening held by a radio station, which attracted mainly teenage girls who left their boyfriends behind. When Zac Efron took off his T-shirt, the four in front of me squealed as if there were buzzers in their seats. Now that he's a little older, Efron has a Tom Cruiseish charm and a lot of confidence. Why Matthew Perry was cast as his adult self is hard to figure; does your head change its shape in twenty years?

17 Again is a pleasant, harmless PG-13 entertainment, with a plot a little more surprising and acting a little better than I expected. Mike is dispatched into that vortex by the bearded old janitor with a delighted smile. The janitor (Brian Doyle Murray) is quite a convenience, supplying vortexes when needed. If his smile reminds you of anyone, he's played by Bill Murray's brother. ☞

Sex and the City ★ ★
R, 145 m., 2008

Sarah Jessica Parker (Carrie Bradshaw), Kim Cattrall (Samantha Jones), Kristin Davis (Charlotte York), Cynthia Nixon (Miranda Hobbes), Chris Noth (Mr. Big), Jennifer Hudson (Louise), Candice Bergen (Enid Frick), David Eigenberg (Steve Brady), Evan Handler (Harry Goldenblatt), Jason Lewis (Smith Jerrod). Directed by Michael Patrick King and produced by King, Sarah Jessica Parker, John Melfi, and Darren Star. Screenplay by King, based on the novel by Candace Bushnell and the TV series.

I am not the person to review this movie. Perhaps you will enjoy a review from someone who disqualifies himself at the outset, doesn't much like most of the characters, and is bored by their bubble-brained conversations. Here is a 145-minute movie containing one (1) line of truly witty dialogue: "Her forties is the greatest age at which a bride can be photographed without the unintended Diane Arbus subtext."

That line might not reverberate with audience members who don't know who Diane Arbus was. But what about me, who doesn't reverberate with the names on designer labels? There's a montage of wedding dresses by world-famous designers. I was lucky I knew who Vivienne Westwood was, and that's because she used to be the girlfriend of the Sex Pistols' manager.

The movie continues the stories of the four heroines of the popular HBO series, which would occasionally cause me to pause in my channel surfing. They are older but no wiser, and all facing some kind of a romantic crossroads. New Line has begged critics not to reveal plot secrets, which is all right with me, because I would rather have fun with plot details. I guess I can safely say: Carrie (Sarah Jessica Parker) is in the tenth year of her relationship with Mr. Big (Chris Noth) when they sort of decide to buy a penthouse they name "Heaven on Fifth Avenue." Publicist Samantha (Kim Cattrall) has moved to Los Angeles, where her client Smith (Jason Lewis) has become a daytime TV star. Charlotte (Kristin Davis) and her husband, Harry (Evan Handler), have adopted a Chinese daughter. And Miranda (Cynthia Nixon) is in a crisis with her husband, Steve (David Eigenberg).

What with one thing and another, dramatic developments cause the four women to join each other at a luxurious Mexican resort, where two scenes take place that left me polishing my pencils to write this review. The girls go sunbathing in crotch-hugging swimsuits, and Miranda is ridiculed for the luxuriant growth of her pubic hair. How luxuriant? One of her pals describes it as *the National*

Forest, and there's a shot of the offending proliferation that popped the Smith Brothers right into my head.

A little later, Charlotte develops a tragic case of *turista* and has a noisy accident right there in her pants. This is a key moment, because Carrie has been so depressed she has wondered if she will ever laugh again. Her friends say that will happen when something really, really funny happens. When Charlotte overflows, Carrie and the others burst into helpless laughter. Something really, really funny has finally happened! How about you? Would you think that was really, really funny?

Sex and the City was famous for its frankness, and we expect similar frankness in the movie. We get it, but each *frank* moment comes wrapped in its own package and seems to stand alone from the story. That includes (1) a side shot of a penis, (2) sex in positions other than the missionary, and (3) Samantha's dog, which is a compulsive masturbator. I would be reminded of the immortal canine punch line ("because he can"), but Samantha's dog is a female. "She's been fixed," says the pet lady, "but she hasn't lost the urge." Samantha can identify with that. The dog gets friendly with every pillow, stuffed animal, ottoman, and towel, and here's the funny thing, she ravishes them male-doggy-style. I went to AskJeeves.com and typed in "How do female dogs masturbate?" and did not get a satisfactory answer, although it would seem to be: "Just like all dogs do, but not how male dogs also do."

On to Mr. Big, the wealthy tycoon and victim of two unhappy marriages, who has been blissfully living in sin with Carrie for ten years. I will supply no progress report on their bliss. But what about Mr. Big himself? As played by Chris Noth, he's so unreal he verges on the surreal. He's handsome in the Rock Hudson and Victor Mature tradition, and has a low, preternaturally calm voice that delivers stock reassurances and banal clichés right on time. He's so . . . passive. He stands there (or lies there) as if consciously posing as The Ideal Lover. But he's . . . kinda slow. Square. Colorless. Notice how, when an old friend shouts rude things about him at an important dinner, he hardly seems to hear them, or to know he's having dinner.

The warmest and most human character in

the movie is Louise (Jennifer Hudson), who is still in her twenties and hasn't learned to be a jaded consumerist caricature. She still believes in True Love, is hired as Carrie's assistant, and pays her own salary on the first day by telling her about a Netflix of designer labels (I guess after you wear the shoes, you send them back). Louise is warm and vulnerable and womanly, which does not describe any of the others.

All of this goes on for nearly two and a half hours, through New Year's Eve, Valentine's Day, and other bonding holidays. The movie needs a Thanksgiving bailout opportunity. But this is probably the exact *Sex and the City* film that fans of the TV series are lusting for. I know some nurses who are going to smuggle flasks of cosmopolitans into the theater on opening night and have a Gal Party. "Do you think that's a good idea?" one of them asked me. "Two flasks," I said.

Sex Drive ★ ★

R, 101 m., 2008

Josh Zuckerman (Ian), Clark Duke (Lance), James Marsden (Rex), Amanda Crew (Felicia), Alice Greczyn (Mary), Seth Green (Ezekiel). Directed by Sean Anders and produced by Bob Levy, Leslie Morgenstein, and John Morris. Screenplay by Anders and Morris.

Sex Drive is an exercise in versatile vulgarity. The actors seem to be performing a public reading of the film's mastery of the subject. Not only are all the usual human reproductive and excretory functions evoked, but new (and I think probably impossible) ones are included. This movie doesn't contain "offensive language." The offensive language contains the movie.

Was I offended? I'm way over that. I was startled. The MPAA ratings board must have been scribbling furiously in the dark, to come up with: "Rated R, for strong crude and sexual content, nudity, language, some drug and alcohol use, all involving teens." What did they forget? Violence. Nothing much blows up real good, and there is a lack of vivisection and disembowelment.

The plot involves Ian (Josh Zuckerman), who is that tragic creature, a virgin eighteen-year-old boy, deeply fascinated by an online girlfriend who calls herself Ms. Tasty (Katrina Bowden). This suggests several topics: (1) Since when is an eighteen-year-old's virginal status *automatically* assumed to be tragic? Never mind. Forget about it. I was going to dig up some statistics proving many eighteen-year-olds are virgins, but when I Googled the topic, the top hits involved eighteen-year-olds complaining about it. (2) Most of the people you meet in chat rooms are much older than they claim, of a different gender, a cop, or your so-called buddy who is goofing on you, ha ha. (3) Every female named Ms. Tasty is either a hooker or take your choice from (2).

Ian has a best buddy suitably named Lance (Clark Duke), who is pudgy, has zits, and only has to smile at a girl to have her offer herself. This is not unrealistic. The unrealistic part is that Ian himself is not pudgy and does not have zits. The two friends live in Wisconsin, and Ms. Tasty, who lives in Tennessee, wants Ian to drive down for guaranteed sex. Personal to Ian: When having sex with anyone named Ms. Tasty, in addition to a nice block of smoked cheddar, take along protection. Ian is in love with a hometown girl named Felicia (Amanda Crew), who is in love with Lance, as all females are. She comes along for the ride, essentially because she is needed to allow the in-car triangle to function.

Ian steals his brother's most prized possession, a perfectly restored 1969 GTO, to impress Ms. Tasty. Ian, Ian, Ian! Anyone calling herself Ms. Tasty who promises you sex doesn't *have* to be impressed. As they motor south, they pass through Amish country. Luckily it's the day of the annual Amish sex orgy, and Ian meets sexy Mary (Alice Greczyn), who falls in love with him, flashes her boobs, etc. The director, Sean Anders, should be ashamed of himself. Lucky the Amish don't go to movies, or he'd be facing a big lawsuit. Better be nice to the Amish. In a year we'll be trading gold bars for their food, ha ha.

What happens in Tennessee, stays in Tennessee. The movie has some laughs, to be sure, even a few big ones, but is so raunchy and driven by its formula that you want to cringe. Let's see. What else . . . Oh, I just noticed the pun in the title, ha ha.

Shall We Kiss? ★ ★ ½
NO MPAA RATING, 102 m., 2009

Virginie Ledoyen (Judith), Emmanuel Mouret (Nicolas), Julie Gayet (Emilie), Michael Cohen (Gabriel), Frederique Bel (Caline), Stefano Accorsi (Claudio), Melanie Maudran (Penelope), Marie Madinier (Eglantine). Directed by Emmanuel Mouret and produced by Frederic Niedermayer. Screenplay by Mouret.

The characters in *Shall We Kiss?* are attractive, wear impeccable clothes, and move easily through minimalist rooms, hotel lobbies, social gatherings, restaurants, and their lives. The sound track is by Schubert and Tchaikovsky. There are discreet paintings on the walls and drawings of composers. They are French, articulate, composed, and dumber than a box of rocks.

That is the only way I can account for their behavior, and since their behavior is the subject of the film, that must be counted as a flaw. They approach the subjects of sex and romance with a naivete so staggering it must be an embarrassment in the greater world. Inside their hermetically sealed complacency, I suppose it's a little exciting.

Gabriel and Emilie are strangers when they have a chance encounter in Nantes. Their eyes meet, there is a connection, they have dinner, and when Gabriel moves as if to kiss Emilie she seems willing, but then pulls back. She is afraid to kiss. Why? She will tell him a story.

Flashbacks to the story involve most of the film, with occasional returns to Emilie (Julie Gayet) relating it to Gabriel (Michael Cohen) in her hotel room. It is about her friends Judith (Virginie Ledoyen) and Nicolas (Emmanuel Mouret, the film's director). They have been best friends since childhood. Judith is happily married. Nicolas has just broken up with a lover of some duration. He is unhappy because he believes he is incapable of fully entering into physical love.

Judith suggests . . . a prostitute? Nicolas tried that. She was perfectly nice but wouldn't kiss him, and without kissing, his engine refused to turn over. What to do? He appeals to Judith. As a dear friend, his very dearest, would she consider . . . you know . . . to . . . She

does. They proceed with the shy hesitation of a first game of spin-the-bottle. May I feel? asks he. May I touch here? And here? Shall we undress? I am on record as calling for more foreplay in the movies, but this isn't foreplay; it's the whole spring training season. And the problem is, they both enjoy it. That won't do. The answer is to do it again right away, roughly, on the floor, to break the spell. They enjoy that even more.

Now *Shall We Kiss?* enters into a complex plot involving deception, role-playing, her husband, his new girlfriend, and a twist I won't even hint at. All performed without the slightest concession to actual human nature as many of we humans understand it. In its long, exploratory conversations, the movie plays very much like a film by Eric Rohmer, who, having now allegedly retired at eighty-eight, has left the field free. But Rohmer used artifice to find truth, and Mouret uses it to find artifice.

You say, but perhaps the French—they are like that? And I reply, nooo, I don't think so. What do I really know about French attitudes toward such matters? Very little, although I once knew a French girl who talked no end about romance. We weren't even in spring training. We seemed to be in the Little League. If actual sex had ever entered the picture, I am convinced she would have regarded it as more than a theoretical exercise in platonic friendship.

Is *Shall We Kiss?* without merit? Not entirely. It has a grace, a languid charm, a pictorial elegance. The plot, when it winds up and unwinds, is ingenious. But are we expected in any sense to find these people realistic? What do we learn from them? All I learned was that that will never work. I already knew that.

Shine a Light ★ ★ ★ ★
PG-13, 122 m., 2008

Featuring Mick Jagger, Keith Richards, Ron Wood, Charlie Watts, Buddy Guy, Christina Aguilera, Jack White, and Bill Clinton. A documentary directed by Martin Scorsese and produced by Steve Bing, Michael Cohl, Zane Weiner, and Victoria Pearman.

Martin Scorsese's *Shine a Light* may be the most intimate documentary ever made about a live rock 'n' roll concert. Certainly it has the best coverage of the performances onstage. Working with cinematographer Robert Richardson, Scorsese deployed a team of nine other cinematographers, all of them Oscar winners or nominees, to essentially blanket a live September 2006 Rolling Stones concert at the smallish Beacon Theater in New York. The result is startling immediacy, a merging of image and music, edited in step with the performance.

In the brief black-and-white footage opening the film, we see Scorsese drawing up shot charts to diagram the order of the songs, the order of the solos, and who would be where on the stage. This was the same breakdown approach he used with his documentary *The Last Waltz* (1978), which he hoped would enable him to call his shots through the earpieces of the cameramen, as directors of live TV did in the early days. The challenge this time was that Mick Jagger toyed with the song list in endless indecision; we look over his shoulder at titles scratched out and penciled back in, and hear him mention casually that of course the whole set might be changed on the spot. Apparently after playing together for forty-five years, the Stones communicate their running order telepathically.

This movie is where Scorsese came in. I remember visiting him in the postproduction loft for *Woodstock* in 1970, where he was part of a team led by Thelma Schoonmaker that was combining footage from multiple cameras into a split-screen approach that could show as many as three or four images at once. But the footage they had to work with was captured on the run, while *The Last Waltz* had a shot map and outline, at least in Scorsese's mind. *Shine a Light* combines his foreknowledge with the versatility of great cinematographers so that it essentially seems to have a camera in the right place at the right time for every element of the performance.

It helped, too, that the Stones' songs had been absorbed by Scorsese into his very being. "Let me put it this way," he said in a revealing August 2007 interview with Craig McLean of the *London Observer*. "Between '63 and '70, those seven years, the music that they made I found myself gravitating to. I would listen to it a great deal. And ultimately, that fueled movies like *Mean Streets* and later pictures of

mine, *Raging Bull* to a certain extent, and certainly *GoodFellas* and *Casino* and other pictures over the years."

Mentioning that he had not seen the Stones in concert until late 1969, he said the music itself was ingrained: "The actual visualization of sequences and scenes in *Mean Streets* comes from a lot of their music, of living with their music and listening to it. Not just the songs I use in the film. No, it's about the tone and the mood of their music, their attitude. . . . I just kept listening to it. Then I kept imagining scenes in movies. And interpreting. It's not just imagining a scene of a tracking shot around a person's face or a car scene. It really was [taking] events and incidents in my own life that I was trying to interpret into filmmaking, to a story, a narrative. And it seemed that those songs inspired me to do that. To find a way to put those stories on film. So the debt is incalculable. I don't know what to say. In my mind, I did this film forty years ago. It just happened to get around to being filmed right now."

The result is one of the most engaged documentaries you could imagine. The cameras do not simply regard the performances; in a sense, the cameras are performers, too, in the way shots are cut together by Scorsese and his editor, David Tedeschi. Even in their sixties, the Stones are the most physical and exuberant of bands. Compared to them, watching the movements of many new young bands on Leno, Letterman, and *SNL* is like watching jerky marionettes. Jagger has never used the mechanical moves employed by many lead singers; he is a dancer and an acrobat and a conductor, too, who uses his body to conduct the audience. In counterpoint, Keith Richards and Ron Wood are loose-limbed and angular, like way-cool backup dancers. Richards in particular seems to defy gravity as he leans so far over; there's a moment in rehearsal when he tells Scorsese he wants to show him something, and leans down to show that you can see the mallet of Charlie Watts's bass drum, visible as it hits the front drumhead. "I can see that because I'm down there," he explains.

The unmistakable fact is that the Stones love performing. Watch Ron lean an arm on Keith's shoulder during one shared riff. Watch the droll hints of irony, pleasure, and quizzical reaction shots, which so subtly move across their seemingly passive faces. Notice that Keith smokes onstage not simply to be smoking, but to use the smoke cloud, brilliant in the spotlights, as a performance element. He knows what he's doing. And then see it all brought together and tied tight in the remarkably acrobatic choreography of Jagger's performance. I've seen the Stones in Chicago in venues as large as the United Center and as small as the Double Door, but I've never experienced them this way, because the cameras are as privileged as the performers onstage.

And the music? What do I have to say about the music? What is there *left* to say about the music? In that interview, Scorsese said, "'Sympathy for the Devil' became this score for our lives. It was everywhere at that time; it was being played on the radio. When 'Satisfaction' starts, the authority of the guitar riff that begins it is something that became anthemic." I think there is nothing useful for me to say about the music except that if you have been interested enough to read this far, you already know all about it, and all I can usefully describe is the experience of seeing it in this film.

Shoot 'Em Up ★ ★ ★ ½
R, 93 m., 2007

Clive Owen (Mr. Smith), Paul Giamatti (Mr. Hertz), Monica Bellucci (DQ), Daniel Pilon (Senator Rutledge). Directed by Michael Davis and produced by Rick Benattar, Susan Montford, and Don Murphy. Screenplay by Davis.

I don't need a lot of research to be confident in stating that never before have I seen a movie open with the hero delivering a baby during a gun battle, severing the umbilical cord with a gunshot, and then killing a villain by penetrating his brain with a raw carrot. Yes, a carrot will do that in this movie. It will do a lot of things.

Shoot 'Em Up, written and directed by the gung-ho Michael Davis, is the most audacious, implausible, cheerfully offensive, hyperactive action picture I've seen since, oh, *Sin City*, which in comparison was a chamber drama. That I liked *Shoot 'Em Up* is a consequence of a critical quirk I sometimes notice:

I may disapprove of a movie for going too far and yet have a sneaky regard for a movie that goes much, much farther than merely too far. This one goes so far, if you even want to get that far, you have to start halfway there, which means you have to be a connoisseur of the hard-boiled action genre and its serio-comic subdivision (or subbasement).

The film opens in one of those grimy cityscapes where a little graffiti might brighten things up. A man with a ten o'clock shadow (Clive Owen) sits on a bench eating a carrot. A pregnant woman is chased past him by men intent on murdering her. "Bloody hell," says the man, a phrase I find so much more elegant than, "What the foosball underwater clockmaker kitchen," if you enjoy creating acronyms. He defends the woman in a hail of gunfire, while delivering her baby, ramming the carrot into his victim's cranium, and finding himself on the run with an infant in his arms, which is how Owen spent much of *Children of Men*, also with people shooting at him, so you could say he looks right at home.

The Owen character is named Mr. Smith. The leader of his enemies is Mr. Hertz (Paul Giamatti). No Mr. Brown around anywhere, but Tarantino seems to hover over the action like a guardian skycam. I am not sure why Mr. Smith is so capable during acts of violence, but it may be because Owen practiced up while he was being considered for the role of James Bond. Yes, that might explain the scene where he continues a gun battle while jumping out of an airplane without a parachute.

That was probably one of the scenes Michael Davis drew by hand, thousands of drawings to give the illusion of animation when he made his pitch to the studio. This is a determined guy. I remember ten years ago he wanted me to see his *Eight Days a Week* at the Slamdance film festival. I was covering Sundance, which is itself three full-time jobs, but he kept after me, ominously brandishing a carrot. I made the trek uphill in the snow to a hotel lobby where his film was being shown and found a spot on a sofa. And the movie was a wonderful comedy about a kid so in love with a girl that he sets up camp and lives in her front yard a whole summer before she finally agrees to go out with him. So there's your auteur theory at work: Davis likes movies about men who will go to any lengths for a woman.

Comedy is a tricky genre to give an unknown indie his start, however, so Davis switched to the usual indie port of entry, horror, making among others a movie about roadkill that wants to kill you. That's the kind of movie you want to back up and run over again.

Shoot 'Em Up will become, I suspect, some kind of legend in the murky depths of extreme action. What elevates it from the depraved to the deserving is a sense of style, a sense of warped humor, and the acting. Clive Owen brings what credibility there could possibly be to his character, and makes us believe it as much as we possibly can (not much, in both cases, but points for effort). Paul Giamatti, Hollywood's favorite nerd, is surprisingly, teeth-gnashingly evil. And Monica Bellucci is DQ, the hooker with the heart of gold, who becomes Mr. Smith's partner and the baby's surrogate mother. I thought and thought about what "DQ" could possibly stand for, and finally had my eureka moment: Dairy Queen.

The plot (two words that should be followed by a hollow laugh) involves Mr. Hertz being hired by Senator Rutledge (Daniel Pilon), political party unspecified, who is running for president but learns he is dying and can only be saved by the bone marrow of infants. In the old days, when political campaigns didn't run so long, there would have been no time to impregnate surrogate volunteers and harvest their offspring, another argument against the extended presidential campaign season.

Man, am I gonna get mail from people who hate this picture. I'll fall back on my stock defense: Did I, or did I not, accurately describe the film? You have been informed. Now eat your carrots.

Shotgun Stories ★ ★ ★ ★
PG-13, 92 m., 2008

Michael Shannon (Son Hayes), Douglas Ligon (Boy Hayes), Barlow Jacobs (Kid Hayes), Michael Abbott Jr. (Cleaman Hayes), Travis Smith (Mark Hayes), Lynnsee Provence (Stephen Hayes), David Rhodes (John Hayes), Natalie Canerday (Nicole Hayes), Glenda Pannell (Annie Hayes). Directed by Jeff Nichols and produced by David Gordon Green, Lisa Muskat, and Nichols. Screenplay by Nichols.

Jeff Nichols's *Shotgun Stories* is shaped and told like a revenge tragedy, but it offers an unexpected choice: The hero of the film does not believe the future is doomed by the past. If it were, most of the key characters would be dead by the end, an outcome that seems almost inevitable. Here is a tense and sorrowful film where common sense struggles with blood lust.

The movie takes place in a "dead-ass town" where three brothers exist. "Hang out" is the only term for what they do. They were named Son, Kid, and Boy by an alcoholic father and, in Son's words, "a hateful woman." Son (Michael Shannon) sprinkles the feed at a local fish farm and loses all his money trying to perfect a "system" he thinks can beat the local casino. His wife has just walked out, taking their son. His brother Kid (Barlow Jacobs) would like to get married, but "I worry about taking care of her. I mean, I don't have a truck. I don't have a house. I sleep in a damn tent." The youngest, Boy (Douglas Ligon), lives in his van and is struggling to beat the heat by persuading a home air conditioner to run off his cigarette lighter.

If this sounds like the setup for a redneck joke, it isn't. The brothers are quiet, lonely, still suffering from abusive childhoods. And consider the remarkable scene where their mother knocks on the door to tell them their father, now married to another woman and with four more sons, has died.

"When's the funeral?" Son asks.

"You can find out in the newspaper."

"You going?"

"No."

Son, Kid, and Boy attend. Since abandoning them, their father had sobered up in rehab, found Jesus, and started a prosperous middle-class family. Now Son chooses to say a few words over the coffin before spitting on it, and a fight breaks out. This fight will escalate into a blood feud in which lives are lost and blood is shed, and yet the enemies are so unprepared that after one buys a shotgun in a pawn shop, he has to be shown how to assemble and load it.

The film is by no means entirely grim and implacable. There are moments of quiet humor, as when Boy finally figures out a way to run the air conditioner off his car battery, and rigs it to blow at him on a river bank and to run a blender for his margaritas. Annie (Glenda Pannell) is fed up with Son's gambling habit but is a gentle woman who loves him. Son himself has hopes for his own son and wants to break the cycle of violence. So does the oldest son of the other family, although the dead father seems to have done a better job of raising those boys than the first three.

Jeff Nichols, the writer and director, is working in the same world where David Gordon Green sets his films; indeed, Green is a coproducer of this film, which uses his cinematographer, Adam Stone. The photography, of course, is wide-screen; these people live surrounded by distant horizons, the vista broken only by the occasional tree or broken-down tractor. Like Green, Nichols uses sleight of hand to sneak in plot details; *Shotgun Stories* uses the most subtle dialogue I can imagine to reveal, by implication, that Boy has, or had, an African-American wife, or girlfriend.

This film has literally been saved by the festival circuit. After being rejected by major distributors, it found a home in smaller festivals, where word of mouth propelled it into its current wider release. It has qualities that may not come out in a trailer or in an ad, but that sink in when you have the experience of seeing it. Few films are so observant about how we relate with one another. Few as sympathetic.

The film is as spare as the landscape. Classical drama comes condensed to a harshness: "You raised us to hate those boys, and we do. And now it's come to this." In a movie where so much violence obviously takes place, we actually see very little of it. Nichols sidesteps the problem of the intrinsic interest of violence by looking away from it and focusing on its effect. We don't get to know the second family very well, but Son, Kid, and Boy are closed up within their melancholy. Although some orange flowers and gentle music try to do their work at the end, we can only hope Son finds the life he desires for his own son.

Shrek the Third ★ ★ ½
PG, 92 m., 2007

With the voices of: Mike Myers (Shrek), Eddie Murphy (Donkey), Cameron Diaz (Princess Fiona), Antonio Banderas (Puss in Boots), John Cleese (King Harold), Julie Andrews (Queen Lillian), Rupert Everett (Prince Charming), Eric Idle (Merlin), Justin Timberlake (Artie). Directed by Chris Miller and produced by Aron Warner. Screenplay by Jeffrey Price, Peter S. Seaman, and Jon Zack, inspired by the book by William Steig.

Shrek the Third is a damped-down return to the kingdom of Far Far Away, lacking the comic energy of the first brilliant film and not measuring up to the second. From the thrills of dragon slaying and damsel rescuing, Shrek's challenges have been reduced to a career decision: Should he become the king?

The movie is as visually enchanting as the first two in the series, and the big green ogre (voice by Mike Myers) is as gentle and lovable, but the movie settles for action that it trusts is funny, instead of aiming for comedy itself. Another peculiarity is that the plot will probably not be engaging for younger audience members, who understand dragons but don't care that heavy lies the head that wears a crown. Shrek spends too much time in lachrymose conversation with his bride, Fiona (Cameron Diaz), and pondering the challenge of fatherhood, and not enough time being an ogre.

Indeed, Shrek is the only character in the movie who makes a big deal about his ogrehood. The king and queen (John Cleese and Julie Andrews) have long since embraced their son-in-law, and on his deathbed the frog king reveals that Shrek is an heir to the throne—one of two, including the feckless Artie (Justin Timberlake). Shrek demurs, preferring life back in the swamp in what Fiona describes as his "vermin-filled shack."

Why would Fiona, raised as a princess, accept life in such a dreary mire of despond? Recall from *Shrek* (2001) that she was a conventional princess only by day and became an ogre after nightfall. When Shrek's kiss rescued her from marriage to Lord Farquaad, she became an ogre full-time. Before that she was a human, I guess, although her father was a frog. Interspecies reproduction is so common in Far Far Away that it makes irrelevant such questions as whether Kermit and Miss Piggy ever had sex. Remember that the dragon and

Donkey fell in love in the first film. For someone like me who has never understood how birds and snakes do it, thoughts of their marital adventures boggle the mind.

Back again this time are the two supporting stars from the earlier films, Donkey (Eddie Murphy) and Puss in Boots (Antonio Banderas). But they're reduced to being friends and traveling partners and are never really "foregrounded." At one point, magically, they switch bodies and talk in each other's voices, but that's what it amounts to: They talk in each other's voices. Such a thing is not intrinsically funny, unless it is plot- or character-driven. Little really depends on it or comes from it, except for a weak little sight gag at the end. Since Murphy's vocal riffs and improvisations have been so inspired earlier in the series, we want more of him this time, not less.

Shrek, Fiona, Donkey, and Puss have to sail to the land of Worcestershire to find Artie, and they encounter Prince Charming (Rupert Everett), who is reduced from princehood to (in an opening scene) performing in dinner theater. Fairly arbitrary developments produce a team of heroines (Cinderella, Snow White, Sleeping Beauty) who are sort of Charlie's Angels, I guess, although they provide the movie with too many characters and not enough for them to do. In the first film, they were a sly DreamWorks dig at Disney and were dumped as obsolete in Shrek's private swamp.

Indeed, the movie practices such economy of characters that the Gingerbread Man and the Three Blind Mice turn up again—unwanted, if you ask me. What's the use of three blind mice if you can't see them run? And although I have been trained to accept talking animals, living pastries fail to engage me.

I learn from *Variety* that there will be a fourth *Shrek* and a Broadway musical, and I hope both turn for their inspiration to the original *Shrek*. That film did so much with the outsider status of an ogre and Shrek's painful uncertainties about his role in non-ogre society. It involved intolerance and prejudice and courage, and had real stakes. And it was funny and had great action scenes, like Shrek's rescue of Fiona. Now everybody in the land of Far Far Away acts as if we (and they) have seen the first two films.

The movie's a pleasure to watch for its skilled animation. But it lacks truly interesting challenges. It makes the mistake of thinking slapstick action is funny for its own sake, a mistake made by a lot of Saturday-morning TV cartoons. True, characters zooming and bouncing around are easy to write because no creative invention is required to set them in motion. But so what?

Shuttle ★
R, 107 m., 2009

Peyton List (Mel), Cameron Goodman (Jules), Tony Curran (Driver), Cullen Douglas (Andy), Dave Power (Matt), James Snyder (Seth). Directed by Edward Anderson and produced by Mark Williams, Todd Lemley, Allan Jones, Michael Pierce, and Mark Donadio. Screenplay by Anderson.

Why do I have to watch this movie? Why does anyone? What was the impulse behind this sad, cruel story? Is there, as they say, "an audience for it"? I guess so. The critic *Tex Massacre* at bloodydisgusting.com rates it four skulls out of five and says, "While gorehounds might not be doing back flips over the blood loss, they should appreciate that director Edward Anderson makes the kills relatively painful and wholly grounded in reality."

I'm not sure if the gorehounds will think there is too much blood loss or too little. Never mind. At least the killings are relatively painful. There's that to be said for it. But I think it's a cop-out to review this movie only as an entry in the horror/slasher genre and not pull back for a larger context. Do images have no qualities other than their technical competence?

Shuttle opens with two young women arriving at an almost empty airport at 2 a.m. It's raining. They can't get a cab. A guy in a van says he'll take them downtown for fifteen dollars. He already has one passenger. Now two young guys also want a ride. Guy says, nothing doing. One girl says, they're with us. Two guys get on board.

Under the driver's window is painted, "No more than three stops." That's strange. Looks like there's room for sixteen, twenty people in the van. The driver takes them on a strange route into no-man's land, pulls a gun, takes all five passengers hostage. OK, so far we're in standard horror territory.

It's what comes next that grows disturbing. The women, played by Peyton List and Cameron Goodman, are resourceful and try to fight back. The young guys help but are neutralized. The other passenger is a crybaby. The film seems set up to empower women. I won't say more about the plot except to say that it leads to utter hopelessness and evil.

That things happen as they do in *Shuttle* I suppose is true, however rarely. But a film can have an opinion about them. This one simply serves them up in hard, merciless detail. There is no release for the audience, no "entertainment," not even much action excitement. Just a remorseless march into the dark.

There is good work here. Peyton List, now twenty-two, working on TV since 2000, is effective as Mel, the more resourceful of the girls. She has a Neve Campbell quality. Tony Curran, as the driver, isn't your usual menacing monster but has more of a workaday attitude inflicting suffering. And the writer-director, Edward Anderson, is reasonably skilled at filmmaking, although it becomes a major distraction when he has the van drive through miles of empty streets when, as the plot reveals, there is little reason.

Last week I reviewed the latest version of *The Last House on the Left*. It had qualities, too, including more developed characters and more ingenious action sequences. But *Shuttle* is uninterested in visual style; it wants to appear nuts-and-bolts, unsentimental, pushing our faces in it. I know the horror genre is a traditional port of entry for first-time directors on low budgets, and I suppose that is Anderson's purpose. All right, he has proven himself. Now let him be less passionately infatuated with despair.

Note: The R *rating proves once again that it is impossible for a film to be rated* NC-17 *on violence alone.*

Sicko ★ ★ ★ ½
PG-13, 124 m., 2007

A documentary directed by Michael Moore and produced by Moore and Meghan O'Hara. Screenplay by Moore.

If you heard the story, you remember it. A woman bled to death in an emergency room while her husband and a bystander both called 911 to report she was being ignored. They were ignored. She was already in the ER, wasn't she?

Her death came too late to be included in *Sicko*, Michael Moore's litany of horrors about the American health-care system, which is run for profit, and insurance companies, who pay bonuses to employees who are successful in denying coverage or claims.

But wait a minute. I saw the movie almost a year to the day after a carotid artery burst after surgery and I came within a breath of death. I spent the next year at Northwestern Memorial Hospital, the Rehabilitation Institute of Chicago, and the Pritikin Longevity Center, and I still require the daily care of a nurse.

I mention this to indicate I am pretty deeply involved in the health-care system. In each and every case, without exception, I have been cared for by doctors who are kind, patient, painstaking, and expert, and by nurses who are skilled, wise, and tireless. My insurance has covered a small fortune in claims. My wife and I have also paid large sums from our own savings.

So I have only one complaint, and it is this: Every American should be as fortunate as I have been. As Moore makes clear in his film, some fifty million Americans have no insurance and no way to get it. Many of the insured discover their policies are worthless after insurance investigators reel off an endless list of conditions and procedures that are not covered, or discover "preexisting conditions" the patients "should" have known about. One woman, unconscious when she is put into an ambulance, is billed for the trip because her insurer says it was not preauthorized. How could she get authorization when she was out cold on the pavement?

We also learn a lot about drug companies and HMOs in the film. It is an item of faith in some circles that drug companies need their profits to finance research and development. Out of a dollar of profit, what percentage would you guess goes to R&D, and what percentage goes to advertising and promotion, multimillion-dollar executive salaries, corporate jets, palatial headquarters, bonuses, and stockholders?

Moore plays 1971 tapes from the Oval Office as Nixon discusses the original Kaiser plan for an HMO. "It's for profit," Nixon says admiringly. Have you ever understood exactly what benefit it is that an HMO provides, while it stands between you and the medical care system and acts as a toll bridge? Do its profits not depend on supplying as little health care as possible, at the lowest possible price?

Moore visits the countries of Canada, England, France, and Cuba, all of which have (1) universal health care, and (2) a longer life expectancy and lower infant mortality than America. In France, he drives with one of the many doctors kept on full-time house-call duty. Of course we have heard all about "socialized medicine," which among many evils denies you freedom of choice of hospitals and doctors. Hold on: That's the free-enterprise HMO system.

Moore sails to Cuba with three boatloads of sick people, some of them 9/11 volunteers who have been denied care for respiratory and other problems because they were—well, volunteers. Unlike firemen and policemen, they had no business being there, I guess. One woman is on $1,000-a-month disability, and needs $240 a month for her inhaler medication. Moore's gimmick (he always has one, but this one is dramatic) is to take her to a Cuban hospital where she finds that her $120 medication costs 5 cents in Cuba. At least that R&D money is helping Cubans.

Moore's original purpose in sailing south was to seek medical care for his passengers at the Guantanamo Bay prison base. He is turned away, of course, but not before observing that accused al-Qaeda terrorists get better (free) medical attention than 9/11 volunteers.

It's a different Michael Moore in *Sicko*. He still wears the baseball cap, but he's onscreen less, not so cocky, not going for so many laughs. He simply tells one story after another about Americans who are sick, dying, or dead because we have an undemocratic, profit-gouging health-care system. Moore's films usually make conservatives angry. This one is likely to strike home with anyone, left or right, who has had serious illness in the family. Conservative governments in Canada, England, and France all support universal health care; America is the only developed nation without it.

Yes, nitpickers can find fault with any attack on our system. There are four health-care lobbyists for every congressman. But there's room for irony when the owner of an anti-Moore Web site can't afford to maintain it when his wife gets sick. And room for tears, when a claims investigator for an insurance company tells Congress she knows she was her company's instrument for denying clients care they needed that might have saved their lives.

Silent Light ★ ★ ★ ★
NO MPAA RATING, 136 m., 2009

Cornelio Wall Fehr (Johan), Miriam Toews (Esther), Maria Pankratz (Marianne), Peter Wall (Padre), Elisabeth Fehr (Madre), Jacobo Klassen (Zacarias). Directed by Carlos Reygadas and produced by Reygadas and Jaime Romandia. Screenplay by Reygadas.

Sometimes we are helpless in the face of love, and it becomes a torment. It is a cruel master. We must act on it or suffer, and sometimes because we act, others suffer. *Silent Light* is a solemn and profound film about a man transfixed by love, which causes him to betray his good and faithful wife.

How he fell into this love, we do not know. Certainly Johan isn't the kind of man to go straying. Nor is Marianne, the woman he loves, a husband stealer. That they are both good to the core is the source of their pain. Yes, Johan and Marianne have sex, but it is the strength of the film that not for a second do we believe they are motivated by sex—only by love.

Esther, Johan's wife and the mother of their six children, knows Marianne and knows about the affair. Johan has told her. He is a religious man and has also confessed to his father and his best friend. There is the sense that he will never leave Esther and never stop loving Marianne. He and Esther say they love each other, and they mean it. You see how love brings its punishment.

The director Carlos Reygadas sets this story among the one hundred thousand or so Mennonites living in Mexico. He does not choose such a sect casually. His story involves people who deeply hold their values and try to act upon them and yet who do not seem to be zealots. (It says much about the Mennonites that their clergy are unpaid.) In fact, the film never mentions the word "Mennonite," there are no church services, and all the characters act from their hearts and not simply their teachings.

Reygadas cast the film entirely from the actual Mennonite community, which I believe will feel he played fair with them. If you didn't know these were untrained actors, you would assume they had years of experience. There is not a false instant in the film, and the performances assume an almost holy reality. Cornelio Wall Fehr as Johan, Miriam Toews as his wife, and Maria Pankratz as Marianne are so focused they gather interior power. They take a story of extreme emotions and make it believable. The father (Wall's real father), the friend, all of the actors, are unshakable.

Silent Light has a beauty based on nature and the rhythms of the land. It opens with a sunrise and closes with a sunset, both in long-held shots, and we see corn being gathered by a harvester, wheat being stacked, long dusty roads between soy fields. The cinematographer, Alexis Zabe, evokes some of the unadorned beauty of a film by Bresson or Bergman, and of the Dreyer film this one in some ways resembles, *Ordet*. He keeps a distance that sometimes suggests awe. When Marianne comes to Johan at a critical time near the end, the camera sees them as distant figures across a field. It is not a time for close-ups.

And look at a scene where Marianne tenderly kisses Esther. First we see them from the side, Marianne bending over. Then from directly overhead. When Marianne stands, the camera remains fixed on Esther's face, and we, but only after a time, see that there is a tear on her cheek. Marianne's. What actually happens next is open to discussion. I was reminded of a similar puzzle in Bergman's *Cries and Whispers*.

This film is not short, and it is not fast. There is no score, location sounds seem hard-edged, and when a hymn is sung, it is not a tune but a dirge. The film's rhythm imposes itself. Curious, how a slow and deep film can absorb, and a fast and shallow one can tire us.

"The world is too much with us," Wordsworth says. "Late and soon, getting and

spending, we lay waste our powers: little we see in nature that is ours." It is Reygadas's inspiration to set this film among a people whose ways are old and deeply felt, and to cast it with actors who believe in those ways. To set it in "modern times," most places in today's world, would make it seem artificial and false. What the film is really about is people who see themselves and their values as an organic whole. There are no pious displays here. No sanctimony, no preaching. Never even the word "religion." Just Johan, Esther, and Marianne, all doing their best.

Silk ★ ★
R, 110 m., 2007

Keira Knightley (Helene Joncour), Michael Pitt (Herve Joncour), Koji Yakusho (Local Overlord), Alfred Molina (Baldabiou), Mark Rendall (Ludovic), Sei Ashina (The Mistress). Directed by Francois Girard and produced by Niv Fichman, Nadine Luque, Domenico Procacci, and Sonoko Sakai. Screenplay by Girard and Michael Golding, based on a novel by Alessandro Baricco.

Silk is a languid, too languid, story of romantic regrets, mostly ours, because romance is expected to carry the film without explaining it. It is told as a mournful flashback, narrated by a man who has been in love with two women, or maybe it was one all the time. He is a young Frenchman as his story begins circa 1860, who falls in love with a local girl, marries her, and then is sent to Japan and falls in love again.

The Frenchman is named Herve, played by Michael Pitt as the passive, soft-spoken plaything of every circumstance he falls into. His complaint seems to be that his life has happened to him. His wife is Helene (Keira Knightley), whom he truly loves, and who truly loves him, but cannot give him a child, although this plays less like a tragedy than just one of those things.

His father is a rich businessman, perhaps the mayor (I could not be sure), who takes the counsel of an entrepreneur, or maybe his employee (I could not be sure), named Baldabiou (Alfred Molina) that they revive the local silk mills. All goes well until disease attacks the silkworms. Then Baldabiou decides to send

Herve to Japan to obtain uncontaminated silkworm eggs.

This journey, by carriage, train, ship, caravan, and horseback, takes him to a small Japanese village where the fearsome man in charge (Koji Yakusho) sizes him up, agrees to sell him eggs, and introduces him, in a way, to his beautiful mistress (Sei Ashina). Their eyes meet, and something happens between them, or Herve is sure it does. He returns to France and his wife with the eggs, which make them all rich. But he is obsessed by thoughts of the woman, and that inspires two more trips to Japan and certain undercurrents in his marriage to the wife he still loves.

There are some mysteries in the storytelling, a central one being the night he is told by a Dutch trader that the mistress "is not what she seems." How so? "She is not Japanese." Then what is she? The IMDb has no doubts, reporting that she is "European," which she is certainly not. My guess is Korean or Chinese, but since the question remains unanswered, one wonders why it was introduced. (Find out on the IMDb, which will correct this error the moment they learn about it.)

Another mystery is how long silkworm eggs can survive during a journey back to France, since their fortunes seem to have no relationship to the nature of the journeys. But never mind. Herve's problem is, when he's not with the one he loves, he loves the one he's with, and is sincere about that at all times.

Our problem, on the other hand, is that we don't care. Michael Pitt almost whispers his way through the film, reveals not passion but damp-eyed self-pity, and (given the language barrier) has no reason to be in love with the Japanese woman except for the movie's blatant exoticism, which argues: Why would you be satisfied with a high-spirited, beautiful wife like Helene, who shares jolly tumbles in the sack, when you could have a Japanese woman who kneels submissively before you, takes forever to serve you tea, looks soulfully into your eyes, speaks not a word, and touches you only once (although we know that, not Herve, who is blindfolded at the time).

There are additional unforgivable plot elements that I dare not reveal, meant to be much more stirring than, under the circumstances, they can possibly be. And a piano score that weeps under many a scene. And a lot of beautiful photography. And then everything is brought together at the end in a flash of revelation that is spectacularly underwhelming.

The Simpsons Movie ★ ★ ★
PG-13, 86 m., 2007

With the voices of: Dan Castellaneta, Julie Kavner, Nancy Cartwright, Yeardley Smith, Harry Shearer, Hank Azaria, and A. Brooks. Directed by David Silverman and produced by James L. Brooks, Matt Groening, Al Jean, Richard Sakai, and Mike Scully. Screenplay by Brooks, Groening, Jean, Scully, Ian Maxstone-Graham, George Meyer, David Mirkin, Mike Reiss, Matt Selman, John Swartzwelder, and Jon Vitti.

The Simpsons are fairly surprised to find themselves in a movie; they can't believe "anyone would pay to see what we did on TV for free." But I suspect a lot of people will. Here is a feature-length version of what *Time* magazine, no less, called "the 20th century's best television series." That may say more about *Time* magazine and the twentieth century than it does about the Simpsons, but never mind: The movie is funny, sassy, and intelligent in that moronic Simpsons way.

There is a plot, sort of, involving Homer's role in polluting the lake in Springfield, which calls down the wrath of the federal bureaucracy and leads to dire consequences for his fellow citizens. The Simpsons' guilt is counterbalanced by poor, idealistic Lisa, who goes door-to-door collecting signatures for her environmental crusade, only to get every door slammed in her face. One house even flees.

This story allows room for the sorts of political asides the Simpsons are famous for; not broadsides, but sideswipes. When the feds finally succeed at something in the movie, they're as surprised as everybody else.

For me, the three biggest laughs in the movie (I won't spoil them) were a plug for the Fox network, a skateboarding sequence inspired by *Austin Powers*, and a unique way to go fishing. Those, and the peculiar everyday lives of the closely knit Simpsons, fill in the gaps in the plot, along with a devout neighbor who, considering what Homer puts in his mailbox, is more sinned against than sinning.

The movie sets some kind of record by crediting no less than eleven writers (James L. Brooks, Matt Groening, Al Jean, Ian Maxstone-Graham, George Meyer, David Mirkin, Mike Reiss, Mike Scully, Matt Selman, John Swartzwelder, and Jon Vitti). That's not the usual case of endless tinkering, but an example of devotion; *Variety* says all eleven produced episodes for the TV show at one time or another. The genius of the series is that it has tapped some of the best offbeat comic talent instead of settling for the TV animation groove. Consider James L. Brooks and voice talent A. (for Albert) Brooks. These people work outside the box.

I'm not generally a fan of movies spun off from TV animation. The Flintstones and Ninja Turtles moved me only marginally. But there's something about the Simpsons that's radical and simple at the same time, subversive and good-hearted, offensive without really meaning to be. It's a nice balancing act. And it finally settles the controversy over what state Springfield is in; it is bordered, we learn, by Ohio, Nevada, Maine, and Kentucky. So you can figure it out right there.

If *The Simpsons* is indeed the best television series of one hundred years (almost half of them, to be sure, without television), I guess I shouldn't be surprised to visit the Internet Movie Database and discover that the movie has been voted the 166th best film of all time, seven places above *The Grapes of Wrath* and ten ahead of *Gone with the Wind*.

That's all the more remarkable because it was first screened for critics on July 24, has had no sneak previews I've heard about, and got 81.4 percent perfect "10" votes. Only 4.5 percent voted "9." That's funny, since you'd think more people would consider it really good but not great. Do you suppose somehow the ballot box got stuffed by Simpsons fans who didn't even need to see the movie to know it was a masterpiece? D'oh.

Sin Nombre ★ ★ ★ ★
R, 96 m., 2009

Paulina Gaitan (Sayra), Edgar Flores (Willy/Casper), Kristyan Ferrer (Smiley), Tenoch Huerta Mejia (Lil' Mago), Diana Garcia (Martha Marlene), Luis Fernando Pena (Sol), Hector Jimenez (Leche/Wounded Man). Directed by Cary Fukunaga and produced by Amy Kaufman. Screenplay by Fukunaga.

El Norte. The North. It is a lodestar for some of those south of our border, who risk their lives to come here. *Sin Nombre*, which means "without name," is a devastating film about some of those who try the journey. It contains risk, violence, a little romance, even fleeting moments of humor, but most of all it sees what danger and heartbreak are involved. It is riveting from start to finish.

The film weaves two stories. One involves Sayra (Paulina Gaitan), a young woman from Honduras who joins her father and uncle in an odyssey through Guatemala and Mexico intended to take them to relatives in New Jersey. The other involves Casper (Edgar Flores), a young gang member from southern Mexico who joins with his leader and a twelve-year-old gang recruit to rob those riding north on the tops of freight cars. Their paths cross.

This is an extraordinary debut film by Cary Fukunaga, only thirty-one, who shows a mastery of image and story. He knows the material. He apparently spent time riding on the tops of northward trains; hundreds of hopeful emigrants materialize at a siding and scramble onboard, and the railroad apparently makes little attempt to stop them. He is also convincing about the inner workings of the terrifying real-life gang named Mara Salvatrucha.

Before turning to the story, I want to say something about the look and feel of the film. It was photographed by Adriano Goldman, who used not hi-def video as you might suspect, but 35 mm film, which has a special richness. Fukunaga's direction expresses a desire that seems to be growing in many young directors to return to classical compositions and editing. Those norms establish a strong foundation for storytelling; no queasy-cam for Fukunaga. Bahrani is another member of the same generation whose shots call attention to their subject, not themselves.

The story of Sayra, her father, and her uncle is straightforward: They are driven to improve their lives, think they have a safe haven in New

Jersey, and want to go there. Some elements of their journey reminded me of Gregory Nava's great indie epic *El Norte* (1983). The journey in that film was brutal; in this one, it is forged in hell.

That hell is introduced by Fukunaga in the club rooms of the gang, whose members are fiercely tattooed, none more than Lil' Mago (Tenoch Huerta Mejia), the leader, whose face is covered like a war mask. Casper is a member of the gang, more or less by force; he brings twelve-year-old Smiley (Kristyan Ferrer) to a meeting, and the kid is entranced by the macho BS. The three board one of the northbound trains to rob the riders, and that's when Casper meets Sayra and their fates are sealed.

Smiley, so young, with a winning smile, is perhaps the most frightening character because he demonstrates how powerful an effect, even hypnotic, gang culture can have on unshielded kids. In his eyes Lil' Mago looms as a god, the gang provides peer status, and any values Smiley might have had evaporate. The initiation process includes being savagely beaten and kicked by gang members, and then proving himself by killing someone. Smiley is ready and willing.

There are shots here of great beauty. As the countryside rolls past and the riders sit in the sun and protect their small supplies of food and water, there is sometimes the rhythm of weary camaraderie. I was reminded of Hal Ashby's *Bound for Glory*. Kids along the tracks are happy to see the riders getting away with something, and at one place throw them oranges. At stations, the riders jump off and detour around the guards to board the train again as it leaves town.

Sin Nombre is a remarkable film, showing the incredible hardships people will endure in order to reach El Norte. Yes, the issue of illegal immigration is a difficult one. When we encounter an undocumented alien, we should not be too quick with our easy assumptions. That person may have put his life on the line for weeks or months to come here, searching for what we so easily describe as the American Dream. What inspired Fukunaga, an American, to make this film, I learn, was a 2003 story about eighty illegals found locked in a truck and abandoned in Texas. Nineteen died.

The Sisterhood of the Traveling Pants 2 ★ ★ ★
PG-13, 117 m., 2008

America Ferrera (Carmen), Alexis Bledel (Lena), Blake Lively (Bridget), Amber Tamblyn (Tibby), Rachel Nichols (Julia), Tom Wisdom (Ian), Leonardo Nam (Brian), Michael Rady (Kostas), Blythe Danner (Greta), Jesse Williams (Leo). Directed by Sanaa Hamri and produced by Debra Martin Chase, Kira Davis, Denise Di Novi, Broderick Johnson, and Andrew A. Kosove. Screenplay by Elizabeth Chandler, based on the novels by Ann Brashares.

The Sisterhood of the Traveling Pants 2, which you will agree has one of the more ungainly titles of recent years, is everything that *Sex and the City* wanted to be. It follows the lives of four women, their career adventures, their romantic disasters and triumphs, their joys and sadness. These women are all in their early twenties, which means they are learning life's lessons; *SATC* is about forgetting them.

The traveling pants, you will recall, are a pair of jeans that the four best friends tried on in a clothing store in the 2005 movie. Magically, they were a perfect fit for all four. So they agree that each one can wear the jeans for a week of the coming summer and then FedEx them to the next name in rotation. Following the jeans, in both movies, we follow key moments in the girls' lives.

Carmen is my favorite. Played by the glowing America Ferrera (*Real Women Have Curves*), she has followed her tall blond friend Julia (Rachel Nichols) to Vermont, where Julia will spend the summer at the Village Playhouse. Carmen sees herself as a stagehand but is dragged into an audition by a talented British actor named Ian (Tom Wisdom) and amazingly gets the female lead in *A Winter's Tale*. Not so amazingly, she falls in love with Ian, and the jealous Julia tries to sabotage her happiness. Meanwhile, her remarried mother produces a baby brother for her.

Alexis Bledel plays Lena, spending the summer at the Rhode Island School of Design and still in love with the Greek guy she met in the previous picture. Amber Tamblyn is Tibby, possibly the most contentious video store clerk in history. She's going through a shaky

401

period in her romance with Brian (Leonardo Nam). Blake Lively is Bridget, who goes on an archaeological dig in Turkey, adopts the supervising professor (Shohreh Aghdashloo) as a mother-figure, then flies home to seek out her grandmother (Blythe Danner) and learn for the first time the details of her own mother's death. It's worth noticing that all four heroines are involved in relationships that are cross-cultural and/or interracial.

The movie intercuts quickly but not confusingly from one story to another, is dripping with seductive locations, is not shy about romantic clichés, and has a lot of heart. These women are all sincere, intelligent, vulnerable, sweet, warm. That's in contrast to *SATC* with its narcissistic and shallow heroines. The *SATC* ladies should fill their flasks with Cosmopolitans, go to see *The Sisterhood of the Traveling Pants 2*, and cry their hearts out with futile regret for their misspent lives.

Because the four leads spend the summer in different places, the movie has an excuse to drop in interesting supporting characters. Blythe Danner is splendid as the Alabama grandmother who knows the whole story of Bridget's mom. Leonardo Nam is a kind and perceptive boyfriend for Lena, Shohreh Aghdashloo (*The House of Sand and Fog*) is a role model for Bridget, Kyle MacLachlan has fun as the wine-sipping director of the summer playhouse, Tom Wisdom does a lot with the small role of the playhouse star. And Rachel Nichols as Julia proves a principle that should be in the Little Movie Glossary: If a short, curvy, sun-kissed heroine has a tall, thin blonde as a roommate, that blonde is destined to be a bitch. No way around it.

As for the pants themselves, they've gathered a lot of patches and embroideries over the three years since the last installment, and they still fit. But not so much is made about them in this film, and by the end they've disappeared, sparing us *The Sisterhood of the Traveling Pants 3* and *The Sisterhood of the Traveling Pants 4*. The movies are inspired by the novels of Ann Brashares, but this one, I learn, combines plot details from novels 2, 3, and 4, and so the sisters can go their separate ways, no doubt keeping in touch by e-mail and congratulating themselves on being infinitely better than the Ya-Ya Sisterhood.

Sita Sings the Blues ★ ★ ★ ★
NO MPAA RATING, 82 m., 2009

Directed, written, and produced by Nina Paley.

I got a DVD in the mail, an animated film titled *Sita Sings the Blues*. It was a version of the epic Indian tale of Ramayana set to the 1920s jazz vocals of Annette Hanshaw. Uh, huh. I carefully filed it with other movies I will watch when they introduce the eight-day week. Then I was told I *must* see it.

I began. I was enchanted. I was swept away. I was smiling from one end of the film to the other. It is astonishingly original. It brings together four entirely separate elements and combines them into a great whimsical chord. How did Paley's mind work?

She begins with the story of Ramayana, which is known to every schoolchild in India but not to me. It tells of a brave, noble woman who was made to suffer because of the foibles of an impetuous husband and his mother. Paley depicts this story with exuberant drawings in bright colors. It is about a prince named Rama who treated Sita unfairly, although she loved him and was faithful to him. There is more to it than that, involving a monkey army, a lustful king who occasionally grows ten heads, synchronized birds, a chorus line of gurus, and a tap-dancing moon.

It coils around and around, as Indian epic tales are known to do. Even the Indians can't always figure them out. In addition to her characters talking, Paley adds a hilarious level of narration: Three voice-over modern Indians, Desis, ad-libbing as they try to get the story straight. Was Sita wearing jewelry or not? How long was she a prisoner in exile? How did the rescue monkey come into the picture? These voices are as funny as an *SNL* skit, and the Indian accent gives them charm: "What a challenge, these stories!"

Sita, the heroine, reminds me a little of the immortal Betty Boop, but her singing voice is sexier. Paley synchs her life story and singing and dancing with recordings of the American jazz singer Annette Hanshaw (1901–1985), a big star in the 1920s and 1930s who was known as "the Personality Girl." Sita lived around 1000 BCE, a date that inspires lively debate among the three Indians discussing her. When her husband outrageously accuses her of adultery and kicks her on top of a flaming pyre, we know exactly how she feels when Annette Hanshaw sings her big hit, "Mean to Me."

There is a parallel story. In San Francisco, we meet an American couple, young and in love, named Dave and Nina, and their cat, named Lexi. Oh, they are in love. But Dave flies off to take a "temporary" job in India, Nina pines for him, she flies to join him in India, but he is cold to her, and when she returns home she receives a cruel message: "Don't come back. Love, Dave." Nina despairs. Lexi despairs. Cockroaches fill her apartment but she hardly notices. One day in her deepest gloom she picks up the book *Ramayana* and starts to read. Inspiration begins to warm the cold embers of her heart.

There are uncanny parallels between her life and Sita's. Both were betrayed by the men they loved. Both were separated by long journeys. Both died (Sita really, Nina symbolically) and were reborn—Sita in the form of a lotus flower, Nina in the form of an outraged woman who moves to Brooklyn, sits down at her home computer for five years, and creates this film. Yes, she reveals in her bio that her then-husband "terminated" their marriage while he was in India. No ex-husband has inspired a greater cultural contribution since Michael Huffington.

One remarkable thing about *Sita Sings the Blues* is how versatile the animation is. Consider Sita's curvaceous southern hemisphere. When she sings an upbeat or sexy song, it rotates like a seductive pendulum. Look at those synchronized birds overhead. When they return they have a surprise, and they get a surprise. Regard the marching graybeards. Watch Hanuman's dragging tail set a palace on fire.

The animation style of the scenes set in San Francisco and Brooklyn is completely different, essentially simple line drawings alive with personality. See how Paley needs only a few lines to create a convincing cat. Paley works entirely in 2-D with strict rules, so that characters remain within their own plane, which overlaps with others. This sounds like a limitation. Actually, it becomes the source of much amusement. Comedy often depends on the device of establishing unbreakable rules and then finding ways to break them. The laughs Paley gets here with 2-D would be the envy of an animator in 3-D. She discovers dimensions where none exist. This is one of the year's best films.

Sixty Six ★ ★ ★
PG-13, 94 m., 2008

Helena Bonham Carter (Esther Rubens), Eddie Marsan (Manny Rubens), Gregg Sulkin (Bernie Rubens), Peter Serafinowicz (Uncle Jimmy), Catherine Tate (Aunt Lila), Ben Newton (Alvie Rubens), Richard Katz (Rabbi Linov), Stephen Rea (Dr. Barrie). Directed by Paul Weiland and produced by Tim Bevan, Eric Fellner, and Elizabeth Karlsen. Screenplay by Peter Straughan and Bridget O'Connor.

The year 1966, as few Americans can be expected to know, is the year England won the World Cup. It is also the year that twelve-year-old Bernie Rubens is going to be celebrating his bar mitzvah in London. This will be an event lasting two days, his blind rabbi tells him. He will become a man, catch the eye of God, be showered with presents, and climax when he is the center of the universe at his own party. In what the director, Paul Weiland, calls "a tru-ish story" based on his own life, Bernie has the rotten luck to select for his party July 30, 1966, the day England won the World Cup.

Of course, England has no chance to get into the finals, right? They're like the Cubs. But in 1966, against all odds, England somehow did win the final game, and as for the Cubs, who knows? Bernie is placed in the peculiar position of being the only person in the nation who hopes England loses. Devout Jew that he is, he sneaks in a book of heathen chants and spells and evokes demon spirits against the national team.

Sixty Six is a warmhearted story about a boy coming of age in a particularly tragic way: Who in the world would rather come to his party than watch the final match on the telly? Bernie is crushed. He has always been the underdog, the last to be picked, the one with glasses, the butt of jokes by his brother Alvie.

Before he discovers the fateful date coincidence, he maps out his party: a formal dinner for 350, a full orchestra. He even invites Frankie Vaughan to sing (for free, I think), and writes to the famous criminals the Kray brothers for their assistance. Then bad luck steps in. His father, Manny (Eddie Marsan), and Uncle Jimmy (Peter Serafinowicz) are forced to sell their grocery store when a supermarket opens next door. A fireworks rocket set off after an England victory starts a fire in the Rubenses' attic and burns up his dad's life savings. The party has to be scaled way back, held at home, and catered by his aunt, who makes a canapé they cannot identify as potato, chicken, or fish.

Yes, the movie is predictable. England will play in the final game, and the party will be far from Bernie's dreams. But Weiland somehow extracts the real meaning of a bar mitzvah from the wreckage. Central to the whole story is the love of Bernie's mother, Esther (Helena Bonham Carter, surprising us by seeming born to the role). She encourages her hangdog husband during a series of setbacks. She puts a good face on things. And she unveils an astonishing vocabulary as one family friend after another telephones with a bogus excuse for not being able to attend.

The story line sounds plain and simple, but the movie is enlightened by Bernie's impassioned narration and by a gallery of small comic details. While Manny is a morose loser, for example, his brother Jimmy is a popular back-slapper and specialist in Jewish humor. Example: "Ask me how I am." "How are you?" "Don't ask!" The blind rabbi (Richard Katz) excels at answering Bernie's questions about God's position on the World Cup ("I don't think it's covered in the Old Testament"). And Stephen Rea, as Bernie's asthma doctor, has a nice scene where he and Bernie puff through straws at a tabletop soccer ball, and their game is intercut with a real one.

Sixty Six isn't a great movie, but it's confident of its material and lucky in its casting. Eddie Marsan, for example, has more ways of looking discontented than most repertory companies. One question: Bernie is a bright kid. Why doesn't he shift the date of his party?

Sleuth ★ ★ ★

R, 86 m., 2007

Michael Caine (Andrew Wyke), Jude Law (Milo Tindle). Directed by Kenneth Branagh and produced by Jude Law, Simon Halfon, Tom Sternberg, Marion Pilowsky, Branagh, and Simon Moseley. Screenplay by Harold Pinter, based on the play by Anthony Shaffer.

When *Sleuth* premiered at the 2007 Toronto Film Festival, a great many critics (including me), writing in advance about it sight unseen, described it as a "remake" of the 1972 film based on Anthony Shaffer's stage play. The festival program was more accurate, describing it as "a fascinating transformation." So it is. Do not make the mistake of thinking that if you've seen the earlier play or film, you've got this one covered. Yes, one of the plot gimmicks is the same, but be honest: If you saw the original, you'd already heard about the gimmick anyway, hadn't you? Only the London opening night audience *possibly* experienced it as a surprise.

The story isn't about the gimmick, anyway. It's about the vicious verbal duel that two men perform one edgy night. Andrew Wyke (Michael Caine), a millionaire thriller novelist, receives a very late visitor: Milo Tindle (Jude Law), who is having an affair with Wyke's wife. The weathered exterior of his country estate belies the interior, an alarming display of metal, glass, crystal, modernist sculpture, and an advanced spy-cam security system. This is not a house to be lived in but to be shown through. It's hard to say which would be more terrifying, the notion that Wyke did the interior design or that his wife did. I vote for the wife. Every real man needs a La-Z-Boy *somewhere*.

Wyke starts in right at the door, asking Tindle, "Is that your car?" Well, there are only two cars parked in the drive, and since the other is Andrew's, why, yes, it is Milo's. "Your car is smaller than my car," Wyke says. Is this remark juvenile or advanced adult cruelty, a comment so gauche it is intended as an insult to the listener? We ask questions like that all through the movie, which is based on a new screenplay by Harold Pinter, the Nobel laureate playwright. True, Pinter is now seventy-seven, and we know from the journals of his friend Simon Gray that he has been ill, but is the great man now reduced to rewriting old country-house mysteries?

Not at all. He has written a new country-house mystery, which is not really a mystery at all in terms of its plot and eerily impenetrable in its human relationship. What is really at stake between Andrew and Milo? Does either one love the wife? Do both? Would Andrew be just as happy to get her off his hands, or does he want to keep her just to prove there is a reason he has the bigger car? The suspense in the film is not about who gets the wife, but about who wins the conversation. Assume someone who has never heard or seen the original *Sleuth* but is familiar with the work of Pinter. That would include a lot of English professors. Attending only to the dialogue, they would find the film pure Pinter.

And that is what you should do. Cast out all thoughts of wives, adultery, disguises, accents, ploys, surprises, and denouements, and simply listen to the words and watch Caine and Law at work. You will observe the Pinteresque interplay of paradox and contradiction, the answers that didn't quite seem to hear the question, the statements of matters so obviously true that perhaps something else altogether is meant by them. In Pinter, the most banal dialogue can carry disturbing insinuations.

Then try to decide when the characters (not the actors) are acting and when they are not. Do they mean what they say? Do they feel what they do? There is a third act development that is entirely absent in the original. What does it mean? Which man takes it seriously? Both? Neither? Each one calling the other's bluff? When Pinter saw or read the original material, I wonder if he thought: "What this needs is the Pinter touch."

The director is Kenneth Branagh, himself a master of stagecraft and a lover of theatrical gesture. How brilliant he was in his film *Hamlet* (1996) to have the prince address his great soliloquy to his own reflection in a mirror. Look again at his underrated *Dead Again* (1991) and see his joy in dazzling effect. In *Sleuth* what he celebrates is perplexing, ominous, insinuating material in the hands of two skilled actors. Law, interestingly, takes the role played by Caine in 1972, and Caine fills the role played then by Laurence Olivier. Caine, who has never been much for the stage, is a superb screen actor, so good his master classes on acting for the camera are on DVD. Here, dry and clipped, biting and savage, he goes for the kill. Jude Law does a plucky job with Milo Tindle, but isn't it one of the laws of drama that characters named Milo Tindle never have a chance?

Now, all of that said, why do I give the movie three stars, instead of more? Curiously enough, because in its strength is its weakness. It is so much about dialogue and performance that I, at least, found myself thinking more about the actors than the characters. All the same, as exactly what it is, it's fascinating.

Slipstream ★ ★ ★
R, 110 m., 2007

Anthony Hopkins (Felix Bonhoeffer), Stella Arroyave (Gina), Christian Slater (Ray), John Turturro (Harvey Brickman), Michael Clarke Duncan (Bartender), Camryn Manheim (Barbara), Jeffrey Tambor (Geek), S. Epatha Merkerson (Bonnie), Fionulla Flanagan (Bette Lustig), Gavin Grazer (Gavin), Kevin McCarthy (Himself). Directed by Anthony Hopkins and produced by Stella Arroyave and Robert F. Katz. Screenplay by Hopkins.

Leave it to a sixty-nine-year-old actor to make the year's most experimental film. Anthony Hopkins's *Slipstream* is an attempt to represent what goes through the mind of a dying man, although you wouldn't guess that from its official plot summary on the Internet Movie Database, which thinks it's about a screenwriter "on the verge of implosion." So have I revealed a plot point? No, because it's clearly stated in the movie's first line of dialogue and repeated in the last.

I have grown so wise, however, only after viewing the movie a second time. When I wrote my interview with Hopkins, I shared the general opinion: Felix, the writer in the film, I wrote, "is confusing reality with illusion. His characters appear in his life, his life appears in the movie, and mostly he looks on uncertainly while both real and imaginary people do all the loving, living, and dying." All true enough in a way, but beside the point.

There is no direct line through the story, which portrays the way a man might think if he had received a sudden shock, was under heavy sedation, and was combining recent experiences with current ones. He doesn't *confuse* his fictional characters with real people; he sees them interchangeably. Let's say he based a character on his wife (Stella Arroyave). Sometimes the character looks like his wife, sometimes his wife looks like the character, sometimes he thinks she's in the room, sometimes he thinks she's on the set, sometimes he thinks they're together in a third place. It's dream logic, and the movie offers a clue by quoting Edgar Allan Poe:

All that we see or seem,
Is but a dream within a dream.

In the overarching action of the movie, Felix has written a screenplay that is being filmed in the Mojave Desert. Gavin Grazer, who plays the director, is said to have a big-shot producer brother whose shadow he tries to escape. Indeed, Gavin is the brother of big-shot producer Brian Grazer, and that's the kind of connection that might occur in the screenwriter's mind and be assigned as a throwaway line to a character in his fantasy. The movie within the movie involves a couple of tough guys (Christian Slater and Jeffrey Tambor) who terrorize a roadside diner after Slater has put a bullet into the head of a bartender (Michael Clarke Duncan). The diner scene owes much to old crime movies; Felix has lived those movies so intently that one of his favorites, the original *Invasion of the Body Snatchers,* produces the real Kevin McCarthy, whom Felix imagines he is driving with through the desert.

Later imaginations fill his computer screen with a screaming studio boss (John Turturro) who is allegedly inside his hard drive, and there are shots in which Duncan (head still oozing with blood) and the movie's continuity girl (Camryn Manheim) complain to him that their characters have not only been killed but shortchanged on some of their lines. One of the movie's most natural examples of dream logic is when Felix asks a Dolly Parton look-alike her name, and she replies, "Dolly Parton Look-alike." Of all the characters, the only one who doesn't seem to fall into dreaminess is the waitress played by S. Epatha Merkerson, maybe because she is the most like who she really is.

Now is *Slipstream* worth seeing? I think so, if you'll actively engage your sympathy with Hopkins's attempt to do something tricky and difficult. If you want to lie back and let the movie come to you, you may be lying there a long time. But I think Hopkins does an impressive job of creating the kind of dream-drug-reverie state people can go through.

I trust you enough, dear reader, to tell you something I should keep private: During a period after my surgical emergency, when I was on what Mr. Limbaugh so usefully describes as prescription medications, I had dreams more real than my waking moments. Then the fog cleared, my health returned, the medication stopped, and I resumed writing brilliant and lucid reviews like this one. But I know Hopkins gets it right, because I've been there. What he gets right is made clear at the end. No, I do not refer to the last appearance of the red convertible, but to the sequence following that, and then the closing dialogue.

Hopkins himself has wisely declined to "explain" his film, going so far at Sundance as to say, "I did it as a little joke." That's the thing about Brits (and the Welsh, in this case). They tend to be pathologically modest, and understatement is their style. Let's apply the statement "I did it as a little joke" to *Grindhouse,* a film that *was* done as a little joke, and see how the same dialogue would translate into the speech of an American director, such as Quentin Tarantino: "This isn't some *Twilight Zone the Movie* f———g thing. This is not a faux double feature. This is two f———g movies for the price of one! Your ten dollars will be well spent at *Grindhouse,* baby!"

And perhaps as well spent at *Slipstream,* although the two films have been made for altogether different audiences, and I anticipate little overlap.

Slumdog Millionaire ★ ★ ★ ★
R, 116 m., 2008

Dev Patel (Jamal Malik), Freida Pinto (Latika), Madhur Mittal (Salim Malik), Anil Kapoor (Prem), Irrfan Khan (Inspector). Directed by Danny Boyle and produced by Christian Colson.

Screenplay by Simon Beaufoy, based on the novel *Q&A* by Vikas Swarup.

Danny Boyle's *Slumdog Millionaire* hits the ground running. This is a breathless, exciting story, somehow heartbreaking and exhilarating at the same time, about a Mumbai orphan who rises from literal rags to literal riches, all on the strength of his lively intelligence. So universal is the film's appeal that it will present a portrait of the real India to millions of moviegoers for the first time.

The real India, supercharged with a plot as reliable and eternal as the hills. The film's surface is so dazzling that you hardly realize how traditional it is underneath. But it's the buried structure that pulls us through the story like a big engine on a short train.

By the real India, I don't mean an unblinking documentary like Louis Malle's *Calcutta* or the recent documentary *Born Into Brothels*. I mean the real India of social levels that seem to be separated by centuries. What do many people think of when they think of India? On the one hand, Mother Teresa, *Salaam Bombay!* and the wretched of the earth. On the other, the Masterpiece Theater–style images of *A Passage to India, Gandhi,* and *The Jewel in the Crown.*

The India of Mother Teresa still very much exists. Because it is side by side with the new India, it is easily seen. People living in the streets. A woman crawling from a cardboard box and adjusting her sari. Men bathing themselves at a fire hydrant. Men relieving themselves at the roadside (you never see women doing that—where do they go?). You stand on one side of the Hooghly River, a branch of the Ganges that runs through Kolkata, and your friend tells you, "On the other bank millions of people live without a single sewer line."

On the other hand, the world's largest middle class, mostly lower-middle, but all the more admirable. The India of *Monsoon Wedding.* Millionaires. Mercedes Benzes and Audis. Traffic like Demo Derby. Luxurious condos. Comfortable suburbs. Exploding education. A computer segment that supplies the world with programming, researchers, and educators. A fountain of medical professionals. So much of the most exciting mod-ern English literature. A Bollywood to rival Hollywood.

Slumdog Millionaire bridges these two Indias by cutting between a world of poverty and the Indian version of *Who Wants to Be a Millionaire.* It tells the story of an orphan from the slums of Mumbai who is born into a brutal early existence. A petty thief, impostor, and survivor, mired in the most dire poverty, he improvises his way up through the world and remembers everything he has learned.

His name is Jamal (played as a teenager by Dev Patel). He is Oliver Twist. High-spirited and defiant in the worst of times, he survives. For example, he scrapes out a living at the Taj Mahal, which he did not know about but discovers by being thrown off a train. How? He pretends to be a guide, invents *facts* out of thin air, advises tourists to remove their shoes, and then steals them. He eventually finds a bit part in the Mumbai underworld and even falls in idealized romantic love, that most elusive of conditions for a slumdog.

His life until about the age of twenty is told in flashbacks intercut with his appearance as a contestant on the quiz show. Pitched as a slumdog, he supplies the correct answers to question after question and becomes a national hero as the suspense builds. The flashbacks show why he knows the answers. He doesn't volunteer this information. It is beaten out of him by the show's security staff as he stands poised on the eve of winning the top prize. They are sure he must be cheating.

The film uses dazzling cinematography, breathless editing, driving music, and headlong momentum to explode with narrative force, somehow stirring in a romance at the same time. For Danny Boyle, it is a personal triumph. If you have seen some of his earlier films (*Shallow Grave, Trainspotting, 28 Days Later,* the lovable *Millions*), you know he's a natural. Here he combines the suspense of a game show with the vision and raw energy of *City of God* and never stops sprinting.

When I saw *Slumdog Millionaire* at Toronto, I was witnessing a phenomenon: dramatic proof that a movie is about how it tells itself. I walked out of the theater on the second day of the festival and flatly predicted it would win the Audience Award. Seven days later, it did. And that it was a definite possibility for an

Oscar best picture nomination. We will see. It is one of those miraculous entertainments that achieves its immediate goals and keeps climbing toward a higher summit.

The Soloist ★ ★ ½
PG-13, 117 m., 2009

Jamie Foxx (Nathaniel Ayers), Robert Downey Jr. (Steve Lopez), Catherine Keener (Mary Weston), Tom Hollander (Graham Claydon), Lisa Gay Hamilton (Jennifer Ayers-Moore). Directed by Joe Wright and produced by Gary Foster and Russ Krasnoff. Screenplay by Susannah Grant, based on the book by Steve Lopez.

The Soloist has all the elements of an uplifting drama, except for the uplift. The story is compelling, the actors are in place, but I was never sure what the filmmakers wanted me to feel about it. Based on a true story, it stars Jamie Foxx as Nathaniel Ayers, a homeless man who was once a musical prodigy, and Robert Downey Jr. as Steve Lopez, the *Los Angeles Times* columnist who writes about him, bonds with him, makes him famous, becomes discouraged by the man's mental illness, and—what? Hears him play great music?

"Explaining madness is the most limiting and generally least convincing thing a movie can do," Pauline Kael once wrote. *The Soloist* doesn't even seem sure how to depict it. Unlike Russell Crowe's mathematician in *A Beautiful Mind*, whose madness was understood through his own eyes, the musician here seems more of a loose cannon, unpredictable in random ways. Yes, mental illness can be like that, but can successful drama? There comes a point when Lopez has had enough, and so, in sympathy, have we.

That is no fault of Jamie Foxx's performance creating a man who is tense, fearful, paranoid, and probably schizophrenic. We can almost smell his terror, through the carnival clown clothing and hats he hides behind. When Foxx learned of this role, he might reasonably have sensed another Academy Award. Unfortunately, the screenwriter and director don't set up a structure for Oscar-style elevation, nor do they really want to make a serious and doleful film about mental illness. But

those are the two apparent possibilities here, and *The Soloist* seems lost between them.

As the film opens, Lopez is troubled. His marriage has problems, he feels burned out at work, he's had a bike accident. He encounters Ayers almost outside the *Times* building, attracted by the beautiful sounds he's producing on a violin with only two strings. The man can play. Lopez tries to get to know him, writes a first column about him, learns he once studied cello at Juilliard. A reader sends Lopez a cello for him (this actually happened), and the columnist becomes his brother's keeper.

This is a thankless and possibly futile task. *The Soloist* does a very effective job of showing us a rehab center on Skid Row, and the reason so many homeless avoid such shelters. It's not what happens inside, but the gauntlet of street people necessary to run just to get to its doors. Indifference about adequate care for our homeless population was one of the priorities of the Selfish Generation.

As a mentally ill man, Ayers is unpredictable and explosive, yes, but almost as if responding to the arc of the screenplay. Characters have arcs in most movies, but the trick is to convince us we're watching them really behave. Here Foxx is let down, and the disappointment is greater because of the track records of director Joe Wright (*Atonement*) and writer Susannah Grant (*Erin Brockovich*). We see a connection between the two men, but not communication.

As a newspaper columnist, Downey is plausible as his overworked, disillusioned character, finding redemption through a story. And Catherine Keener, like Helen Mirren in *State of Play*, convinces me she might really be an editor. Both actresses bring a welcome change of pace from the standard Lou Grant type. Talk about disillusionment; the old-timers can't believe their eyes these days. The *Los Angeles Times* of this movie is at least still prospering.

As for the music, Beethoven of course is always uplifting, but the movie doesn't employ him as an emotional show-stopper, as Debussy's "Clair de Lune" is used in *Tokyo Sonata*. There's no clear idea of what it would mean should Ayers triumph in a public debut; would it be a life-changing moment or only an anomaly on his tragic road through life? Can he be salvaged? Does he want to be? Or will he always be a soloist, playing to his demons in the darkness under a bridge? ☞

Son of Rambow ★ ★ ★
PG-13, 96 m., 2008

Bill Milner (Will Proudfoot), Will Poulter (Lee Carter), Jessica Stevenson (Mary), Neil Dudgeon (Brother Joshua), Jules Sitruk (Didier Revol), Ed Westwick (Laurence Carter), Anna Wing (Grandmother). Directed by Garth Jennings and produced by Nick Goldsmith. Screenplay by Jennings.

The two friends in *Son of Rambow* hang out in a backyard shack that rewards close study. It's made of rough lumber, hammered together into not quite parallel lines; it's out of plumb. It could be drawn, but not easily built. Since the eleven-year-old hero, Will Proudfoot (Bill Milner) is himself a cartoonist and sketch artist, his inventions seem to be seeping into his life. He leads an existence that's strictly limited by his family's religious sect, making him a vacuum for fantasy and escapism, and when his friend Lee Carter (Will Poulter) shows him a pirated copy of *First Blood*, the adventures of Rambo ignite him like fireworks whose time have come.

Set in an English village in the early 1980s, *Son of Rambow* is a gentle story that involves a great deal of violence, but mostly the violence is muted and dreamy, like a confrontation with a fearsome scarecrow that looks horrifying but is obviously not real—or real enough, but not alive. The two boys meet one day in the corridor outside their grade school classroom. Will has been sent there because his religion forbids him to watch TV, even educational videos (it also forbids music, dancing, and so on). Lee has been booted out of his classroom, spots Will, and immediately beans him with a hard-thrown tennis ball. This is the beginning of a strange but lasting friendship.

Lee takes Will into his garage, which looks like a toolkit for inventive kids. A rowboat hangs suspended from the ceiling, and there's equipment for pumping out videotape copies of the movies that Lee pirates at the local cinema, while puffing somewhat uncertainly on a filter-tip (yes, you could smoke in the movies in England in those days).

Electrified by his introduction to Rambo, Will joins Lee in making their own home video remake of the film. This involves Will enacting literally death-defying stunts: He's catapulted high into the air, for example, and swings on a rope to drop into a lake, neglecting to tell Lee he can't swim. The special effects are cobbled together from household items, purloined booty, and Will's sketches and flip-book animation.

All is not well at home, where Will lives with his mom (Jessica Stevenson), a sister, and his drooling grandma (Anna Wing). There's an unwelcome visitor in the house most of the time, Brother Joshua (the perfectly named Neil Dudgeon), who covets the role of Will's absent father and enjoys being stern and forbidding to the lad. The intimacy of his relationship with the mother seems limited mostly to significant nods when he says good-bye at the end of the evening.

Will and Lee find their world unsettled when a busload of French exchange students descends on their school, and Didier (Jules Sitruk) captures their admiration. Taller and older, he takes charge of their indie production and their lives. Meanwhile, their stunt work escalates: They steal a life-sized dog from the Guide Dogs for the Blind people, hook it to a parasail, and inadvertently set off fire alarms at their school. And a runaway Jeep causes a load of scrap metal to fall on Will and Lee, with surprisingly limited results.

All of this takes place in a pastoral countryside and a benign city, where the boys move more or less invisibly. They're not simply growing up, but expanding: their horizons, their imaginations, their genius for troublemaking. Since it is made clear at the start that little fatal or tragic is likely to happen, the movie becomes like a fable—maybe too fabulous for its own good. The plot unspools with nothing really urgent at stake, the boys live in innocence and invulnerability, and the settings and action have a way of softening the characters.

I liked *Son of Rambow* in a benign sort of way, but I was left wanting something more. Drama, maybe? No, that would simply be manufactured. Comedy? It is technically a comedy, although the limited laughs are incredulous. Fantasy? That it is, in a bittersweet way. After the movie, I imagined its

409

writer-director, Garth Jennings (*The Hitch-hiker's Guide to the Galaxy*), being more than a little like Will, and the movie uncannily similar to one of Will's comic epics.

Soul Men ★ ★ ★
R, 103 m., 2008

Samuel L. Jackson (Louis Hinds), Bernie Mac (Floyd Henderson), Sharon Leal (Cleo Whitfield), Adam Herschman (Phillip Newman), Sean Hayes (Danny Epstein), Affion Crocket (Lester), Jennifer Coolidge (Rosalee), Isaac Hayes (Himself), John Legend (Marcus Hooks). Directed by Malcolm D. Lee and produced by Charles Castaldi, David T. Friendly, and Steve Greener. Screenplay by Robert Ramsey and Matthew Stone.

Soul Men is the one that's really going to make you miss Bernie Mac. He's so filled with life and energy here that it's hard to believe . . . well, anyway. It will make you miss him. He found his comfort zone in mainstream comedies, of which I have liked nine of twelve. When an edgy director like Terry Zwigoff came into the picture with *Bad Santa* (2003), he allowed Bernie Mac a little more depth.

In *Soul Men,* there are scenes that hint at what he might have done in a dramatic role. It's a formula comedy, but there are real feelings here that we suspect would exist in this troubled struggle between musicians who haven't played together in twenty years. In the end credits, there are generous tributes to Bernie Mac and Isaac Hayes, also in the film, both gone from us within two days last August. Bernie gets the last, touching word. And you know, even if I mentioned a possible heavy dramatic role, I never felt he was a comedian with a sad man inside. In the credit cookies, he talks about his good luck while thanking a theater audience (of extras) for his career, and we believe him. He seems like a comedian with a happy man inside.

Anyway, years ago Louis (Samuel L. Jackson), Floyd (Bernie Mac), and Marcus (John Legend) were a trio of big-time musicians. But Marcus split for superstardom, and the other two took separate paths to relative anonymity. Now Marcus has died, and Floyd and Louis are desperately needed to appear in a memorial concert at the Apollo in Harlem. They're not even speaking to each other. Fight over a woman.

For the money, Louis agrees to join Floyd in a cross-country road trip to New York. That's the formula: two incompatible guys, long trip, one car. *Planes, Trains and Automobiles,* etc. It's Floyd's car. An El Dorado convertible. But of course it is. Ever notice how often cross-country road trips in the movies involve classic convertibles? Two reasons: The rag top makes it easier for the camera to see them, and recent cars don't look like cars.

In the 1950s, kids used to stand on the corner and spot cars approaching from one or two blocks away. First kid to ID one scored a point. Chevy. Dodge. Chrysler Imperial. Studebaker. Ford. That far away and they could even ID the model: Rocket 88. Fairlane. Golden Hawk. To kids today from a block away, unless it's a Hummer, all cars look the same. Camry. Camry. Camry. Fifty years from now, movie characters will be crossing the country in one-hundred-year-old cars.

Floyd and Louis rehash all their old differences and encounter some remarkably friendly women (including Jennifer Coolidge, Stifler's mom). They have adventures. The beloved Caddy, with absolute inevitability, is damaged. Their spirits lift, and they do one of their old routines. The trio is re-formed by adding a young singer, Cleo (Sharon Leal), who may have more to do with the trio's history than anybody realizes. At the Apollo, the reunion with Marcus and their big stage entrance are interestingly linked.

This movie has a lot of good music in it, some on the sound track, some on the screen. Jackson and Bernie Mac have enormous fun doing intricate dance moves together. Isaac Hayes has a farewell role worthy of our memories. Of the actors, only John Legend is a little stiff, although he goes through a timeline of costumes and hairstyles in the flashbacks. You want a good time? *Soul Men* will provide it. You want to say good-bye to Bernie Mac? He wants to say good-bye to you.

Southland Tales ★
R, 144 m., 2007

Dwayne Johnson (Boxer Santaros), Seann William Scott (Roland/Ronald Taverner), Sarah

Michelle Gellar (Krysta Kapowski/Krysta Now), Curtis Armstrong (Dr. Soberin Exx), Joe Campana (Brandt Huntington), Nora Dunn (Cyndi Pinziki), Michele Durrett (Starla Von Luft), Beth Grant (Inga Von Westphalen). Directed by Richard Kelly and produced by Sean McKittrick, Bo Hyde, Kendall Morgan, and Matthew Rhodes. Screenplay by Kelly.

After I saw the first cut of Richard Kelly's *Donnie Darko* (2002), I was left dazed and confused but somehow convinced that I might have seen *something*. After I saw the director's cut (2004), which was twenty minutes longer, I began to comprehend some of what I had seen, and it became more interesting, even though I still didn't entirely understand it. It even nudged itself up into a favorable review.

After I saw the first cut of Kelly's *Southland Tales* at Cannes 2006, I was dazed, confused, bewildered, bored, affronted, and deafened by the boos all around me at the most disastrous Cannes press screening since, yes, *The Brown Bunny*. But now here is the director's cut, which is twenty minutes shorter, lops off a couple of characters and a few of the infinite subplots, and is even more of a mess. I recommend that Kelly keep right on cutting until he whittles it down to a ukulele pick.

Yes, I admire Kelly's free spirit. In theory. He is a cinematic anarchist, but the problem is, he's throwing bombs at his own work. He apparently has no sympathy at all for an audience unable to understand his plot, and every scene plays like something that was dreamed up with little concern for what went before or would follow after. It's like the third day of a pitch session on speed. What does he imagine an audience feels like while watching this movie? Did his editor ever suggest that he might emerge with a more coherent product if he fed the footage through a revolving fan and spliced it together at random?

The time is the Future: one year from now. By the time the DVD comes out, the time will be the Present. Two Texas towns have been nuked, including Abilene, the prettiest town that I've ever seen. America is in a state of emergency. A left-wing revolution is being masterminded from Venice Beach and the Santa Monica Pier against the oppressive right-wing government. A Schwarzeneggerian actor, related to a political dynasty, has been kidnapped, replaced with a double, and—I give up. A plot synopsis would require that the movie have a plot.

The dialogue consists largely of statements that are incomprehensible, often delivered with timing that is apparently intended to indicate they are witty. All of the actors seem to have generated back stories for their characters that have nothing to do with one another. Only Wallace Shawn emerges intact, because he so easily can talk like that, but a spit curl does not become him. Justin Timberlake is the narrator, providing what are possibly quasi-rational explanations for movies in other time dimensions.

The population of America consists entirely of character actors with funny names. I'm not sure that by the end of the movie they have all met one another, even the ones in the same scenes together. I haven't committed all of *Ebert's Little Movie Glossary* to memory, but I'm pretty sure it contains a Law of Funny Names, which instructs us that funny names are rarely funny in the movies, especially if they are not borne by Groucho Marx or W. C. Fields.

When I tell you I am helpless to describe the plot, perhaps you will have pity on me if I tell you it involves characters named Boxer Santaros; Krysta Kapowski, aka the porn star Krysta Now; Dr. Soberin Exx; Starla Von Luft; Inga Von Westphalen, aka Marion; Dion Warner, aka Dion Element; Nana Mae Frost; Baron Von Westphalen; and Simon Theory. Boxer Santaros is played by Dwayne Johnson, who used to be billed as the Rock and should have led a movement among characters to change their names.

These people mostly seem to have dressed themselves earlier in the day at a used-costume store, although from the Cannes version I particularly miss a character played by Janeane Garofalo, who apparently used the Army surplus store. She was some kind of guerrilla general operating out of what I vaguely recall as a Venice Beach head shop, or maybe it was a bookstore. What a comedown from her great performance in nearby Santa Monica in *The Truth About Cats and Dogs*.

Note to readers planning to write me

messages informing me that this review was no more than a fevered rant: You are correct.

Space Chimps ★ ★ ★
G, 80 m., 2008

With the voices of: Andy Samberg (Ham III), Cheryl Hines (Luna), Omid Abtahi (Titan Jagu), Jeff Daniels (Zartog), Kristin Chenoweth (Kilowatt), Stanley Tucci (Senator). Directed by Kirk De Micco and produced by Barry Sonnenfeld and John H. Williams. Screenplay by De Micco and Robert Moreland.

Space Chimps is delightful from beginning to end: a goofy space opera that sends three U.S. chimptronauts rocketing to a galaxy, as they say, far, far away. Although it's aimed at a younger market and isn't in the same science fiction league as *WALL-E,* it's successful at what it wants to do: take us to an alien planet and present us with a large assortment of bug-eyed monsters, not to mention a little charmer nicknamed Kilowatt who lights up when she gets excited, or afraid, or just about anything else.

The story starts with the circus career of the chimp Ham III (voice by Andy Samberg), the grandson of the first chimp launched by NASA into space (and, yes, that first chimp really was named Ham). Ham III works at being shot out of a cannon and never quite landing where he should. Once, when he goes really high, he considers the beauty of the moon and outer space, and has a *Right Stuff* moment, of which there are several. He feels keenly that he hasn't lived up to the family tradition.

Meanwhile, the U.S. space program faces a crisis. One of its deep space probes has disappeared into a wormhole. It is perhaps a measure of the sophistication of younger audiences that no attempt is made to explain what a wormhole is. Perhaps that's because wormholes are only conjecture anyway, and if you can't say there is one, how can you say what it is?

What with one thing and another, Ham III finds himself enlisted in the crew of a space flight to follow the probe into the wormhole and see what happened to it. Joining the mission is a big chimp named Titan (Patrick Warburton) and the cute (in chimp terms) Luna (Cheryl Hines). Hurtling through what looks like a dime-store version of the sound-and-light fantasy in *2001,* they land on a planet where the local creatures are ruled by a big, ugly tyrant named Zartog (Jeff Daniels).

He has commandeered the original NASA probe and uses its extendable arms to punish his enemies by dipping them into a supercold bath so they freeze in an instant. This is a cruel fate, especially since the eyeballs of his victims continue to roll, which means they must be alive inside their frozen shells, which implies peculiarities about their metabolism.

The chimps, of course, have lots of adventures, including being chased through a cave by a monster of many teeth and being rescued by the plucky Kilowatt, who eventually sees more of the monster than she really desires. Then there's a showdown with Zartog, some business about the planet's three suns (night lasts only five minutes), and a most ingenious way to blast off again.

On Earth, there's an unnecessary subplot about an evil senator (Stanley Tucci) who wants to disband the space program and replace it with something you really have to hear to believe. On second thought, maybe the subplot is necessary, just so we get to hear his idea.

I ponder strange things during movies like this. For example, there seem to be only five forms of life on the planet. Zartog is one, his obedient subjects are another, some flying creatures are a third, the toothy monster is the fourth, and Kilowatt is the fifth. I suppose a planet where evolution has produced only five species is possible. But what do they eat? The planet looks like Monument Valley, is covered with sand, and has no flora or fauna. Could they all be silicon-based? And since Zartog, the tooth monster, and Kilowatt each seem to be one of a kind, who do they mate with? Or do silicon beings need to mate? And have they invented the hourglass?

Spider-Man 3 ★ ★
PG-13, 139 m., 2007

Tobey Maguire (Peter Parker/Spider-Man), Kirsten Dunst (Mary Jane Watson), James Franco (Harry Osborn), Thomas Haden Church (Flint Marko/Sandman), Topher Grace (Eddie Brock/Venom), Bryce Dallas Howard (Gwen

Stacy), James Cromwell (Captain Stacy), Rosemary Harris (Aunt May), J. K. Simmons (J. Jonah Jameson). Directed by Sam Raimi and produced by Laura Ziskin, Avi Arad, and Grant Curtis. Screenplay by Sam Raimi, Ivan Raimi, and Alvin Sargent, based on the comic books by Stan Lee and Steve Ditko.

The great failing of *Spider-Man 3* is that it failed to distract me from what a sap Peter Parker is. It lingers so long over the dopey romance between Peter and the long-suffering Mary Jane that I found myself asking the question: Could a whole movie about the relationship between these two twenty-somethings be made? And my answer was: No, because today's audiences would never accept a hero so clueless and a heroine so docile. And isn't it a little unusual to propose marriage after sharing only one kiss, and that one in the previous movie, and upside-down?

Faithful readers will recall that I found *Spider-Man 2* (2004) the best superhero movie since *Superman* (1978). But I made the mistake of declaring that was because "the movie demonstrates what's wrong with a lot of other superhero epics: They focus on the superpowers, and short-change the humans behind them." This time, I desperately wanted Peter Parker to be short-changed. If I argued earlier that Bruce Wayne and Clark Kent were boring human beings, I had no idea how Peter would begin to wear on my nerves.

And what's with Mary Jane? Here's a beautiful, (somewhat) talented actress good enough to star in a Broadway musical, and she has to put up with being trapped in a taxi suspended eighty stories in the air by alien spiderwebs. The unique quality of the classic comic books was that their teenagers had ordinary adolescent angst and insecurity. But if you are still dangling in taxicabs at age twenty, you're a slow learner. If there is a *Spider-Man 4* (and there will be), how about giving Peter and Mary Jane at least the emotional complexity of soap opera characters?

Superhero movies and James Bond movies live and die by their villains. Spidey number two had the superb Doc Ock (Alfred Molina), who is right up there with Goldfinger and the Joker in the Supervillain Hall of Infamy. He had a *personality*. In Spidey number three we

have too many villains, too little infamy. Take the Sandman (Thomas Haden Church). As an escaped con and the murderer of Uncle Ben, he has marginal interest at best. As the Sandman, he is absurd. Recall Doc Ock climbing buildings with his fearsome mechanical tentacles, and now look at this dust storm. He forms from heaps of sand into a creature that looks like a snowman left standing too late in the season. He can have holes blown into him with handguns but then somehow regains the bodily integrity to hammer buildings. And how does he *feel* in there? Molina always let you know precisely how Doc Ock felt, with a vengeance.

Then there is the black microorganism from outer space, which is not a villain but plays one in the movie. It arrives on Earth in a meteorite that lands, oh, maybe twenty yards from Peter and Mary Jane, but this impact somehow escapes notice by the fabled Spidey-sense. Then it produces little black beasties that look like squids crossed with licorice rope. They not only coat people with a way-cool black, glossy second skin, but specialize in spray-painting Spidey and Spidey wannabes. No ups, no extras.

We know that Spider-Man's powers do not reside in his red suit, which lives in a suitcase under his bed. So how do fake Spideys like Venom gain their powers when they are covered with the black substance? And how does a microorganism from outer space know how to replicate the intricate pattern-work of the Spidey costume, right down to the chest decoration? And to what purpose from an evolutionary point of view? And what good luck that the microorganism gets Peter's rival photographer, Eddie Grace, to infect, so that he becomes Venom! And how does Eddie know who he has become?

Another villain is Harry Osborn, aka the New Green Goblin (James Franco), son of the interesting original (Willem Dafoe), but not a drip off the old gob. While the first GG had the usual supervillain motivations (malevolence, envy, twisted abilities), his son is merely very angry and under the misapprehension that Peter/Spidey murdered his old dad. And *then* Peter and Harry have a *fist fight* when they should be doing Spidey and Goblin stuff.

Yes, there are some nice special effects in the movie. I liked the collapsing construction crane sequence. But the damsel in distress that time was not Mary Jane but Gwen Stacy (Bryce Dallas Howard), the sexy blond lab partner Peter has somehow neglected to mention to Mary Jane, causing her heartbreak because at a civic ceremony he kisses her with "our kiss," i.e., the upside-down one. While Peter goes through a period of microorganism infection, he combs his hair forward, struts the streets, attracts admiring glances from every pretty girl on the street, and feels like hot stuff. Wait until he discovers sex.

Spider-Man 3 is, in short, a mess. Too many villains, too many pale plot strands, too many romantic misunderstandings, too many conversations, too many street crowds looking high into the air and shouting "oooh!" this way, then swiveling and shouting "aaah!" that way. And saints deliver us from another dinner date like the one where Peter plans to propose to Mary Jane. You know a movie is in trouble when the climactic romantic scene of the entire series is stolen by the waiter (Bruce Campbell). And poor Aunt May (Rosemary Harris). An actress of Harris's ability, asked to deliver a one-note performance, and that single note is fretting.

How could Sam Raimi, having gone so right with *Spider-Man 2*, have gone so wrong with *Spider-Man 3*? Did the $250 million budget paralyze him? Has the series grown too heavy on its feet? How many times can we see essentially the same romantic scenario repeated between Peter and Mary Jane? How much dangling in the air can one girl do? And how does Spidey keep his identity a secret anyway, when there are more arrivals and departures through his apartment's window than on a busy day at LaGuardia? ☞

The Spiderwick Chronicles ★ ★ ★ ½
PG, 96 m., 2008

Freddie Highmore (Jared/Simon Grace), Mary-Louise Parker (Helen Grace), Nick Nolte (Mulgarath), Joan Plowright (Aunt Lucinda), David Strathairn (Arthur Spiderwick), Seth Rogen (Hogsqueal), Martin Short (Thimbletack/Boggart), Sarah Bolger (Mallory Grace). Directed by Mark Waters and produced by Karey Kirkpatrick, Mark Canton, Larry Franco, and Ellen Goldsmith-Vein. Screenplay by Kirkpatrick, David Berenbaum, and John Sayles, based on the books by Tony DiTerlizzi and Holly Black.

The Spiderwick Chronicles is a terrific entertainment for the whole family, except those below a certain age, who are likely to be scared out of their wits. What is that age? I dunno; they're your kids. But I do know the PG classification is insane, especially considering what happens right after a father says he loves his son. This is a PG-13 movie for sure. But what will cause nightmares for younger kids will delight older ones, since here is a well-crafted family thriller that is truly scary and doesn't wimp out.

Based on a well-known series of five books, the movie involves a soon-to-be divorced mom and her three children who come to live in a creepy old mansion. This is Spiderwick, named after her great-uncle, Arthur Spiderwick, who disappeared under mysterious circumstances. The house itself is one of the stars of the movie, looking Victorian Gothic with countless nooks and crannies and shadows and scary sounds. Is it haunted? Nothing that comforting. It's . . . inhabited.

The mother is Helen Grace (Mary-Louise Parker), who is battling with the rebellious Jared (Freddie Highmore), one of her twin sons. He doesn't like being away from his dad, is homesick, doesn't want anything to do with this dusty and spiderwebby old ruin that was left to his mom by her aunt. Jared's brainy twin, Simon, looks remarkably identical, no doubt because he is also played by Freddie Highmore, born 1992, a gifted young actor best known for *Finding Neverland, August Rush,* and *The Golden Compass.* The twins' sister is the plucky Mallory (Sarah Bolger), a fencer who seldom goes anywhere without her sword, which is just as well in this movie. You may remember how good she was in *In America* (2002).

Jared is the kind of kid who is always getting blamed for everything. When stuff starts disappearing, for example, he gets the rap. When he hears noises in the wall and punches holes in it, he's being destructive. But he's brave, and when he finds a hidden dumbwaiter, he hauls himself up to a hidden room—his grandfather's study, left undisturbed after all these years. This room fairly reeks of forbidden secrets.

Don't read further unless you already know, as the Web site makes abundantly clear, that he finds a "field guide" to the unseen world left by his great-great-uncle (David Strathairn), and that with its help and a Seeing Stone, Jared can see goblins, sprits, hobgoblins, ogres, trolls, and griffins, which themselves can take many shapes. Some of them are amusing, like Thimbletack (voice by Martin Short), some alarming, like Boggart (Short again), some helpful but undependable, like Hogsqueal (voice by Seth Rogen). And some of the newly visible creatures are truly alarming, like Mulgarath. The credits say his voice is by Nick Nolte, but I gotta say that all of Mulgarath looks a lot like the real Nick Nolte to me.

Anyway, Jared finally convinces his brother, and then his sister and mother, that what he reports is real, and then, after pages from the field guide get into Mulgarath's hands, the Circle of Protection around the house is threatened, and the Graces are faced with dire threats. This is all done with a free mixture of lighthearted action, heavy action, and some dramatic scenes that, as I said, are pretty heavy going for younger imaginations. The movie is distinguished by its acting, not least by the great Joan Plowright as old Aunt Lucinda. Strathairn is completely credible as a spirit-world investigator, although exactly where the sparkling points of light take him, and what he does there, is a little murky.

They say be careful what you ask for because you might get it. I've often hailed back to the really creepy moments in Disney classics, like what happens to Dumbo and Bambi and the witch in *Snow White,* and I've complained that recent family movies are too sanitized. This one, directed by Mark Waters (*The House of Yes, Freaky Friday*), doesn't skip a beat before its truly horrific moments, so if you're under eight or nine years old, don't say you weren't warned.

The Spirit ★
PG-13, 102 m., 2008

Gabriel Macht (The Spirit), Samuel L. Jackson (The Octopus), Eva Mendes (Sand Saref), Scarlett Johansson (Silken Floss), Jaime King (Lorelei), Sarah Paulson (Ellen), Dan Lauria (Commissioner Dolan), Paz Vega (Plaster of Paris). Directed by Frank Miller and produced by Deborah Del Prete, Gigi Pritzker, and Michael E. Uslan. Screenplay by Miller, based on the comic book series by Will Eisner.

The Spirit is mannered to the point of madness. There is not a trace of human emotion in it. To call the characters cardboard is to insult a useful packing material. The movie is all style—style without substance, style whirling in a senseless void. The film's hero is an ex-cop reincarnated as an immortal enforcer; for all the personality he exhibits, we would welcome Elmer Fudd.

The movie was written, directed, and fabricated largely on computers by Frank Miller, whose *300* and *Sin City* showed a similar elevation of the graphic novel into fantastical style shows. But they had characters, stories, a sense of fun. *The Spirit* is all setups and posing, muscles and cleavage, hats and ruby lips, nasty wounds and snarly dialogue, and males and females who relate to one another like participants in a blood oath.

The Spirit (Gabriel Macht) narrates his own story with all the introspection of a pro wrestler describing his packaging. The Octopus (Samuel L. Jackson) heroically overacts, devouring the scenery as if following instructions from Gladstone, the British prime minister who attributed his success to chewing each bite thirty-two times. The Spirit encounters a childhood girlfriend, Sand Saref (Eva Mendes), pronounced like the typographical attribute, who made good on her vow of blowing off Central City and making diamonds her best friend. The Octopus has an enigmatic collaborator named Silken Floss (Scarlett Johansson), pronounced like your dentist.

These people come and go in a dank, desolate city, where always it's winter and no one's in love and their duty is to engage in impossible combat with no outcome, because The Octopus and The Spirit apparently cannot slay each other, for reasons we know (in a certainty approaching dread) will be explained with melodramatic, insane flashback. In one battle in a muddy pond, they pound each other with porcelain commodes and rusty anchors, and The Spirit hits The Octopus in the face as hard as he can twenty-one times. Then they get on with the movie.

The Octopus later finds it necessary to bind The Spirit to a chair so that his body can be sliced into butcher's cuts and mailed to far-off zip codes. To supervise this task, he stands in front of a swastika attired in full Nazi fetishwear, whether because he is a Nazi or just likes to dress up, I am not sure. A monocle appears in his eye. Since he doesn't wear it in any other scene, I assume it is homage to Erich von Stroheim, who wasn't a Nazi but played one in the movies.

The objective of Sand Saref is to obtain a precious vial containing the blood of Heracles or Hercules; she alternates freely between the Greek and Roman names. This blood will confer immortality. Fat lot of good it did for Heracles or Hercules. Still, maybe there's something to it. At one point, The Spirit takes three bullets in the forehead, leans forward, and shakes them out. At another, he is skewered by a broadsword. "Why, oh why, do I never die?" he asks himself. And we ask it of him.

I know I will be pilloried if I dare end this review without mentioning the name of the artist who created the original comic books. I would hate for that to happen. Will Eisner.

Standard Operating Procedure ★ ★ ★ ½
R, 121 m., 2008

A documentary written and directed by Errol Morris and produced by Morris and Julie Bilson Ahlberg.

Errol Morris's *Standard Operating Procedure*, based on the infamous prison torture photographs from Abu Ghraib, is completely unlike anything I was expecting from such a film—more disturbing, analytical, and morose. This is not a political film or yet another screed about the Bush administration or the war in Iraq. It is driven simply, powerfully, by the desire to understand those photographs.

There are thousands of them, mostly taken not from the point of view of photojournalism, but in the spirit of home snapshots. They show young Americans, notably Lynndie England, posing with prisoners of war who are handcuffed in grotesque positions, usually naked, heads often covered with their underpants, sometimes in sexual positions. Miss England, who was about twenty at the time and weighed scarcely one hundred pounds, often has a cigarette hanging from her mouth in a show of tough-guy bravado. But the effect is not to draw attention to her as the person who ordered these tableaux, but as a part of them. Some other force, not seen, is sensed as shaping them.

This invisible presence, we discover, is named Charles Graner, a staff sergeant Lynndie was in love with, who is more than fifteen years her senior. She does what he suggests. She doesn't question. But then, few questions are asked by most of the Americans in the photographs, who are not so much performing the acts as being photographed performing them.

"Pictures only show you a fraction of a second," says a Marine named Javal Davis, who was a prison guard but is not seen in any of them. "You don't see forward, and you don't see backward. You don't see outside the frame." He is expressing the central questions of the film: Why do these photos exist, why were they taken, and what reality do they reflect? What do we think about these people?

Those are the questions at the heart of many of Morris's films, all the way back to his first, *Gates of Heaven* (1978), in which to this day I am unable to say what he feels about his subjects or what they think of themselves. The answers would be less interesting anyway than the eternally enigmatic questions. Morris's favorite point of view is the stare. He chooses his subjects, regards them almost impassively, and allows their usually strange stories to tell themselves.

There is not a voice raised in *S.O.P.* The tone is set by a sad, elegiac, sometimes relentless score by Danny Elfman. The subject, in addition to the photographs, is Morris's interview subjects, seen in a mosaic of close-ups as they speak about what it was like to be at Abu Ghraib. Most of them speak either in sorrow or resentment, muted, incredulous. How had they found themselves in that situation?

Yes, unspeakable acts of cruelty were committed in the prison. But not personally, if we can believe them, by the interviewees. The torturers seem to have been military intelligence specialists in interrogation. They, too, are following orders and choose to disregard the theory that the information is useless since if you torture a man enough he will tell you anything.

I cannot imagine what it would be like to be suspended by having my hands shackled behind my back so tightly I might lose them. Or feeling I am being drowned. And so on—this need not be a litany of horrors.

More to the point of this film is that the prison wardens received their prisoners after the tortures were mostly committed, and then posed with them in ghastly "human pyramids," in "dog piles," or in scenes with sexual innuendo. Again, why? "For the picture." The taking of the photos seems to have been the motivation for the instants they reveal. And, as a speaker observes in the film, if there had been no photos, the moments they depict would not have existed, and the scandal of Abu Ghraib would not have taken place.

Yes, some of those we see in *Standard Operating Procedure* were paid for their testimony. Morris acknowledges that. He did not tell them what to say. I personally believed what they were telling me. What it came down to was, they found themselves under orders that they did not understand, involved in situations to provide a lifetime of nightmares.

They were following orders, yes. But whose? Any orders to torture would have had to come from those with a rank of staff sergeant or above. But all of those who were tried, found guilty, and convicted after Abu Ghraib were below that rank. At the highest level, results were demanded—find information on the whereabouts of Saddam Hussein (whose eventual capture did not result from any information pried loose by torture). At lower levels, the orders were translated into using torture. But there was a deliberate cutoff between the high level demanding the results and the intermediate level authorizing the violation of U.S. and international law by the use of torture.

At the opening of the film, Defense Secretary Donald Rumsfeld is seen, his blue blazer hooked over one shoulder, his white dress shirt immaculate, "touring" Abu Ghraib.

He is shown one cell, then cancels his tour. He doesn't want to see any more.

And so little Lynndie England is left with her fellow soldiers as the face of the scandal. And behind the photos of her and others lurks the enigmatic figure of Sergeant Charles Graner, who was not allowed by the military to be interviewed for this film. I imagine him as the kind of guy we all knew in high school, snickering in the corner, sharing thoughts we did not want to know with friends we did not want to make. If he posed many of the photos (and gave away countless copies of them), was it because he enjoyed being at one remove from their subjects? The captors were seen dominating their captives, and he was in the role, with his camera, of dominating both.

Remember the photo of Lynndie posing with the prisoner on a leash? His name, we learn, was Gus. Lynndie says she wasn't dragging him: "You can see the leash was slack." She adds: "He would never have had me standing next to Gus if the camera wasn't there."

Stardust ★ ★ ½
PG-13. 122 m., 2007

Claire Danes (Yvaine), Charlie Cox (Tristan), Sienna Miller (Victoria), Ricky Gervais (Ferdy the Fence), Jason Flemyng (Primus), Rupert Everett (Secundus), Peter O'Toole (King of Stormhold), Robert De Niro (Captain Shakespeare), Michelle Pfeiffer (Lamia), Ian McKellen (Narrator). Directed by Matthew Vaughn and produced by Vaughn, Lorenzo di Bonaventura, Michael Dreyer, and Neil Gaiman. Screenplay by Jane Goldman and Vaughn, based on a novel by Gaiman.

A fantasy, even a comic fantasy, needs above all to be lean and uncluttered. Only reality is untidy. The classic fantasy structure involves the hero, the quest, the prize, and what stands in the way. It is not a good sign that almost the most entertaining element of *Stardust* is Captain Shakespeare, appearing from the skies in his dirigible pirate ship. Shakespeare, played by Robert De Niro as a transvestite swashbuckler (swishbuckler?), is wonderful, but he should be forced to wear a badge saying, "Hi! I'm the deus ex machina!"

There are lots of other good things in the movie, but they play more like vaudeville acts than part of a coherent plot. It's a film you enjoy in pieces, but the jigsaw never gets solved. I liked it, but *The Princess Bride* it's not.

The plot, by Neil Gaiman, based on his novel: England is separated from the fantasy kingdom of Stormhold by a wall. Outside the wall, in an English village conveniently named Wall, lives a plucky lad named Tristan (Charlie Cox), who is in love with a lass named Victoria (Sienna Miller). He fears to lose her to a rival, but one night they see a shooting star fall beyond the wall, and he vows to retrieve it for her.

It is not very hard to get through the wall, which is an example of Stormhold's crumbling infrastructure. Tristan's father was once able to bound through a gap in the wall, but Tristan has more trouble with an ancient guard and employs a magic candle which, by definition, works its magic. Inside Stormhold, he discovers that the star is, in fact, a beautiful girl with long blond tresses named Yvaine (Claire Danes). I think her name makes her a sort of vain Yvonne. She possesses such secrets as eternal life, which are worth having, and so there's a rivalry for her powers.

In this corner: Three Macbethesque witches (Gaiman is a fan of Shakespeare), led by Lamia (Michelle Pfeiffer), who believe Yvaine can restore their beauty. In the other corner: The Learesque king of Stormhold (Peter O'Toole), who has three living sons and four dead ones, who appear in black and white as Hamlet's fatheresque ghosts. (Note to editors: Why *can't* that be a word?) The dying king believes Yvaine can restore his throne to his living sons, although let's hope he doesn't try dividing the kingdom among them.

Tristan is on his own among these scoundrels. At least he has Yvaine's sympathy. As the only one who doesn't want to rip out her heart and eat it, he has much to recommend him. Lamia, meanwhile, begins by looking like Michelle Pfeiffer, but the more she employs her black magic, the more she looks like Peter O'Toole, who has already gone about as far as he can go.

Meanwhile, Captain Shakespeare sails in like an outtake from *The Adventures of Baron Munchausen* and hopes to pillage, plunder, and provide comic relief. The movie becomes very busy at this point, and Tristan's quest to win Victoria's heart is upstaged by everybody else's quest to eat Yvaine's.

Still, Gaiman has many admirers, they will be familiar with the material and find their way around, and director Matthew Vaughn lays on the special effects; the movie is not boring, just cluttered and not focused enough. There is a kind of narrative flow that makes you want to be swept along and another that's just one thing after another. *Stardust* is fun enough the first time through, but it doesn't pass the Derek Malcolm Test: "A great movie is a movie I cannot bear the thought of never seeing again."

Starting Out in the Evening ★ ★ ★ ★
PG-13, 111 m., 2007

Frank Langella (Leonard Schiller), Lili Taylor (Ariel Schiller), Lauren Ambrose (Heather Wolfe), Adrian Lester (Casey Davis). Directed by Andrew Wagner and produced by Nancy Israel, Fred Parnes, Wagner, Jake Abraham, and Gary Winick. Screenplay by Fred Parnes and Wagner.

Do you sometimes feel like you're the last serious reader left? Do you remember when the *New York Times* best-selling novels were by Faulkner, Mailer, Updike, Cheever, Welty, or O'Hara? Do you thank heaven when Oprah chooses a great novel like *A Fine Balance*? Have you noticed that people have stopped obsessing about J. D. Salinger's disappearing act? Have you never found a later novelist as entertaining as Dickens? Did you study English in college and carry around Shakespeare a little conspicuously?

Oh, and do you ever wonder if you will ever find a soul mate? Here's a movie made for you. *Starting Out in the Evening* is a film about people who think literature is worth devoting a lifetime to. People who think great novelists are a species of saint. It honors values that seem obsolete in our trashy popular culture, obsessed with the sex lives of vacuumheads.

The story involves a seventy-year-old novelist named Leonard Schiller (Frank Langella) and a twenty-five-ish graduate student named Heather Wolfe (Lauren Ambrose). He wrote four books that were acclaimed as important and still are, although he's not much read anymore. He's been working on a fifth novel for a decade. She plays a graduate student who wants to write her thesis about him and has hopes that she may inspire a revival of interest in his work and maybe blast that fifth novel out of his grip.

They are not alike. He puts on a coat and tie to sit down at his desk and write. He speaks with care and reserve. She is filled with all of the brashness and confidence of youth and believes she's just what the doctor ordered. He almost recoils under her first onslaught, but she is bright and verbal and, let it be said, attractive, and he doesn't send her away.

Soon she is discovering what every interviewer learns from every novelist: He doesn't know what anything in his books "stands for," he doesn't know where he gets his ideas, he doesn't think anything is autobiographical, and he has no idea what his "message" is. I am no novelist, but I am a professional writer, and I know two things that interviewers never believe: (1) the muse visits during, not before, the act of composition, and (2) the writer takes dictation from that place in his mind that knows what he should write next.

Leonard has a forty-ish daughter named Ariel (Lili Taylor). She wants to have a baby and hears her clock ticking. She broke up with a longtime boyfriend named Casey (Adrian Lester) because he had no interest in children, but now they are seeing each other again. They know each other so well, they talk together so readily, that it is tempting to fall into the old ways. Their relationship is portrayed almost as fully as the one between Leonard and Heather, and we realize that everyone in the movie hears a clock ticking for some reason.

The Langella performance deserves an Oscar nomination. This is the man who appeared upside-down outside a window in (the very good) *Dracula* (1979), and here he is as a reserved, solitary intellectual, twenty years a widower, confronted by a maelstrom in his life. And there is another matter, too: the question of whether they will fall in love. No, no, not have an affair: fall in love. Leonard is far past the appetite for affairs. How the movie handles this question is one of the most delicate and subtle things about it, and there is a fully clothed scene of intimacy between them that is as warm as a dozen sex scenes.

Lauren Ambrose's Heather has that superficial charm that masks deep wells of instinct and feeling, and Leonard gradually comes to see that she is more than she seems. Along the way, the film provides unusually intelligent discussion of books and careers, shows some social climbing, and depicts the daughter Ariel as conflicted: She has no objection to her father doing whatever he chooses in theory, but practice is more complicated.

The screenplay, by Fred Parnes and the director, Andrew Wagner, is based on a novel by Brian Morton, unread by me but not for long. Wagner is the man whose first film was the remarkable *The Talent Given Us* (2005), a pseudo-documentary starring his own family in a cross-country trip. One superficial similarity, or perhaps it goes deeper than that, involves the romantic feelings of older men. The movie is carefully modulated to draw us deeper and deeper into the situation and uses no contrived plot devices to superimpose plot jolts on what is, after all, a story involving four civilized people who are only trying, each in a different way, to find happiness.

Star Trek ★ ★ ½
PG-13, 126 m., 2009

Chris Pine (James Tiberius Kirk), Zachary Quinto (Spock), Leonard Nimoy (Spock Prime), Eric Bana (Captain Nero), Bruce Greenwood (Captain Christopher Pike), Karl Urban (Leonard "Bones" McCoy), Zoe Saldana (Uhura), Simon Pegg (Montgomery "Scotty" Scott), John Cho (Sulu), Anton Yelchin (Chekov), Ben Cross (Sarek), Winona Ryder (Amanda Grayson). Directed by J. J. Abrams and produced by Abrams and Damon Lindelof. Screenplay by Roberto Orci and Alex Kurtzman.

Star Trek as a concept has voyaged far beyond science fiction and into the safe waters of space opera, but that doesn't amaze me. The Gene Roddenberry years, when stories might play with questions of science, ideals, or philosophy, have been replaced by stories reduced to loud and colorful action. Like so many franchises, it's more concerned with repeating a successful formula than going boldly where no *Star Trek* has gone before.

The 2009 *Star Trek* film goes back eagerly to

where *Star Trek* began, using time travel to explain a cast of mostly the same characters, only at a younger point in their lives, sailing the starship *Enterprise*. As a story idea, this is sort of brilliant, and saves on invention because young Kirk, Spock, McCoy, Uhuru, Scotty, and the rest channel their later selves. The child is father to the man, or the Vulcan, and all that.

Don't get me wrong. This is fun. And when Leonard Nimoy himself returns as the aged Spock, encountering another Spock (Zachary Quinto) as a young man, I was kind of delighted, although as customary in many sci-fi films, nobody is as astonished as they should be. "Holy moley! Time travel exists, and this may be me!" It's more like a little ambiguous dialogue is exchanged and they're off to battle the evil Romulan captain Nero (Eric Bana).

Time travel, as we all know, is impossible in the sense it happens here, but many things are possible in this film. Anyone with the slightest notion of what a black hole is, or how it behaves, will find the black holes in *Star Trek* hilarious. The logic is also a little puzzling when they can beam people into another ship in outer space, but they have to physically parachute to land on a midair platform from which the Romulans are drilling a hole to Vulcan's core. And after they land there, they fight with two Romulan guards using fists and swords? The platform is suspended from Arthur C. Clarke's "space elevator," but instead of fullerenes, the cable is made of metallic chunks the size of refrigerators.

But stop me before I get started. I mention these details only to demonstrate that the movie raises its yo-yo finger to the science, while embracing the fiction. Apart from details from the youths of the characters and the Spock reunion, it consists mostly of encounters between the *Enterprise* and the incomparably larger and much better armed Romulan spaceship from the future. It's encouraging to learn that not even explosions and fires can quickly damage a starship. Also that lifeboats can save the crew, despite the vast distance from home base.

That would be because of warp speed, which for present purposes consists of looking through an unnecessary window at bright lights zapping past. This method of transportation prevents any sense of wonder at the immensity of outer space and is a convenience not only for the starship but also for the screenwriters, who can push a button and zap to the next scene. The concept of using warp speed to escape the clutches of a black hole seems like a recycling of the ancient dilemma of the rock and the hard place.

There are affecting character moments. Young Spock is deliberately taunted in hopes he will, as a Vulcan, betray emotion. Because Zachary Quinto plays him as a bit of a self-righteous prig, it's satisfying to see him lose it. Does poor young Spock realize he faces a lifetime of people trying to get a rise out of him? Nimoy, as the elderly Spock, must have benefited because he is the most human character in the film.

Chris Pine, as James Tiberius Kirk, appears first as a hot-rodding rebel who has found a Corvette in the twenty-third century and drives it into a pit resembling the Grand Canyon. A few years later, he's put in suspension by the academy and smuggled on board the *Enterprise* by "Bones" McCoy (Karl Urban) before he becomes the ship's captain. There are times when the command deck looks like Bring Your Child to School Day, with the kid sitting in Daddy's chair.

Uhura (Zoe Saldana) seems to have traveled through time to the prefeminist 1960s, where she found her miniskirt and go-go boots. She seems wise and gentle and unsuited to her costume. Scotty (Simon Pegg) seems to have begun life as a character in a Scots sitcom. Eric Bana's Nero destroys whole planets on the basis of faulty intelligence, but the character is played straight and is effective.

The special effects are slam-bam. Spatial relationships between spaceships are unclear because the Romulan ship and the *Enterprise* have such widely unmatched scales. Battles consist primarily of jumpsuited crew members running down corridors in advance of smoke, sparks, and flames. Lots of verbal commands seem implausibly slow. Consider, at light-warp speeds, how imprecise it would be to say, "At my command . . . three . . . two . . . one."

I understand that *Star Trek* science has never been intended as plausible. I understand that this is not science fiction but an ark movie using a starship. I understand that the character types are as familiar as your favorite slippers. But the franchise has become much of a muchness. The new movie essentially intends to reboot the franchise with younger characters and carry on as before. The movie deals with narrative housekeeping. Perhaps the next one will engage these characters in a more challenging and devious story, one more about testing their personalities than reestablishing them. In the meantime, you want space opera, you got it. ☞

Star Wars: The Clone Wars ★ ½
PG, 98 m., 2008

With the voices of: Matt Lanter (Anakin Skywalker), James Arnold Taylor (Obi-Wan Kenobi), Ashley Eckstein (Ahsoka Tano), Catherine Taber (Padme Amidala), Anthony Daniels (C-3PO), Christopher Lee (Count Dooku), Nika Futterman (Asajj Ventress), Tom Kane (Yoda), Ian Abercrombie (Palpatine), Samuel L. Jackson (Mace Windu). Directed by Dave Filoni and produced by Catherine Winder. Screenplay by Henry Gilroy, Steve Melching, and Scott Murphy.

Has it come to this? Has the magical impact of George Lucas's original vision of *Star Wars* been reduced to the level of Saturday morning animation? *Star Wars: The Clone Wars,* which is a continuation of an earlier animated TV series, is basically just a ninety-eight-minute trailer for the autumn launch of a new series on the Cartoon Network.

The familiar *Star Wars* logo and the pulse-pounding John Williams score now lift the curtain on a deadening film that cuts corners on its animation and slumbers through a plot that (a) makes us feel like we've seen it all before, and (b) makes us wish we hadn't. The action takes place between the events in the "real" movies *Episode II: Attack of the Clones* and *Episode III: Revenge of the Sith.* The Republic is still at war with the Separatists, its access to the Galactic Rim is threatened, and much depends on pleasing the odious Jabba the Hutt, whose child has been kidnapped— by the Jedi, he is told.

It's up to Anakin Skywalker and his new Padawan pupil, Ahsoka Tano, to find the infant,

as meanwhile Obi-Wan Kenobi and Yoda lead the resistance to a Separatist onslaught. And if all of this means little to you, you might as well stop reading now. It won't get any better.

This is the first feature-length animated *Star Wars* movie, but instead of pushing the state of the art, it's retro. You'd think the great animated films of recent years had never been made. The characters have hair that looks molded from Play-Doh, bodies that seem arthritic, and moving lips on half-frozen faces—all signs that shortcuts were taken in the animation work.

The dialogue in the original *Star Wars* movies had a certain grace, but here the characters speak to each other in simplistic declamation, and Yoda gets particularly tiresome with his once-charming speech pattern. To quote a famous line by Wolcott Gibbs, *Backward ran sentences until reeled the mind.*

The battle scenes are interminable, especially once we realize that although the air is filled with bullets, shells, and explosive rockets, no one we like is going to be killed. The two armies attack each other, for some reason, only on a wide street in a towering city. First one army advances, then the other. Why not a more fluid battle plan? To save money on backgrounds, I assume. The trick that Anakin and his Padawan learner use to get behind the enemy force field (essentially, they hide under a box) wouldn't even have fooled anybody in a Hopalong Cassidy movie—especially when they stand up and run with their legs visible but can't see where they're going.

Ahsoka Tano, by the way, is annoying. She bats her grapefruit-sized eyes at Anakin and offers suggestions that invariably prove her right and her teacher wrong. At least when we first met Yoda, he was offering useful advice. Which reminds me, I'm probably wrong, but I don't think anyone in this movie ever refers to the Force.

You know you're in trouble when the most interesting new character is Jabba the Hutt's uncle. The big revelation is that Jabba has an infant to be kidnapped. The big discovery is that Hutts look like that when born, only smaller. The question is, who is Jabba's wife? The puzzle is, how do Hutts copulate? Like snails, I speculate. If you don't know how snails do it, let's not even go there. The last thing this movie needs is a Jabba the Hutt sex scene.   ☞

State of Play ★ ★ ★
PG-13, 127 m., 2009

Russell Crowe (Cal McAffrey), Ben Affleck (Stephen Collins), Rachel McAdams (Della Frye), Helen Mirren (Cameron Lynne), Robin Wright Penn (Anne Collins), Jason Bateman (Dominic Foy), Jeff Daniels (George Fergus). Directed by Kevin Macdonald and produced by Tim Bevan, Eric Fellner, and Andrew Hauptman. Screenplay by Matthew Michael Carnahan, Tony Gilroy, and Billy Ray, based on the BBC series created by Paul Abbott.

State of Play is a smart, ingenious thriller set in the halls of Congress and the city room of a newspaper not unlike the *Washington Post*. It's also a political movie, its villain a shadowy corporation that contracts with the government for security duties and mercenaries in Iraq. The name is PointCorp. Think Blackwater. If an outfit like that would kill for hire, the plot wonders, would it also kill to protect its profits?

Here is Russell Crowe playing an ace investigative reporter for the *Washington Globe*. All the cops and most of the people on Capitol Hill seem to know him; he's one of those instinctive newsmen who connect the dots so quickly that a 127-minute movie can be extracted from a six-hour BBC miniseries. This keeps him so occupied that he has little time for grooming, and doesn't seem to ever wash his hair.

Crowe stepped into the role after Brad Pitt dropped out. Pitt, I suspect, would have looked more clean-cut, but might not have been as interesting as Crowe in this role, as Cal McAffrey, a scruffy hero in a newspaper movie that is acutely aware of the crisis affecting newspapers. He becomes part of a team that involves not two experienced reporters, as in *All the President's Men*, but Della (Rachel McAdams), one of the paper's plucky bloggers. He tries to teach her some ancient newspaper wisdom, such as: If you seem to be on the edge of uncovering an enormous political scandal, don't blow your cover by hurrying online with some two-bit gossip.

In a short span of time, a man is shot dead in an alley, a passing bicyclist, also a witness, is killed, and a woman is shoved or jumps under a subway train. Cal, of course, covers all of these deaths in person. The dead woman was a researcher for Representative Stephen Collins (Ben Affleck), who breaks into tears during a congressional hearing into Point-Corp and confesses to conducting an affair with her. His wife, Anne (Robin Wright Penn), plays the brave politician's wife and says their family will stay together. Anne and Cal were lovers in college. The dead man turns out to be carrying a briefcase stolen from PointCorp. Now we connect the dots.

There are many other surprises in the film, which genuinely fooled me a couple of times and maintains a certain degree of credibility for a thriller. The implication is that Point-Corp and the administration are locked in an unholy alliance to channel millions of taxpayer dollars into unsavory hands. That this can all be untangled by one reporter who looks like a bum and another who looks like Rachel McAdams (which is no bad thing) goes with the territory.

An important role in their investigation is played by the *Globe*'s editor, Cameron Lynne (Helen Mirren). The paper's new corporate owners are on her neck to cut costs, redesign the venerable front page, get more scoops, and go for the gossip today instead of waiting for the Pulitzer tomorrow. There is, in fact, an eerie valedictory feeling to the film; mother of God, can this be the last newspaper movie? (The answer is no, because no matter what happens to newspapers, the newspaper movie is a durable genre. Shouting, "Stop the presses!" is ever so much more exciting than shouting, "Stop the upload!")

It is a reliable truth that you should never ask an expert how a movie deals with his field of knowledge. Archaeologists, for example, have raised questions about *The Mummy: Tomb of the Dragon Emperor*. When Cal races out of the office at deadline and shouts over his shoulder, "Tell Cameron to kill the story," it is just possible that she would tear up the front page, if the story was so important the paper could not risk being wrong. But when Cal and his sidekick the perky blogger solve the mystery and are back in the office and it is noted, "Cameron has been holding the presses four hours!"—I think her new corporate bosses will want to have a long, sad talk with her, after which she will discover if the company still offers severance packages.

State of Play, directed by Kevin Macdonald (*The Last King of Scotland*), is well-assembled and has some good performances. Crowe pulls off the Joaquin Phoenix look-alike; McAdams doesn't overplay her blogger's new-bieness; Helen Mirren convinced me she could be a newspaper editor. Robin Wright Penn always finds the correct shadings. If Ben Affleck, as he plays this role, were to have his face carved into Mount Rushmore, people would ask which was the original.

The thing is, though, that the movie never quite attains altitude. It has a great takeoff, levels nicely, and then seems to land on autopilot. Maybe it's the problem of resolving so much plot in a finite length of time, but it seems a little too facile toward the end. Questions are answered, relationships revealed, and mysteries solved too smoothly. If a corporation like PointCorp could have its skullduggery exposed that easily, it wouldn't still be in business.

Step Brothers ★ ½
R, 95 m., 2008

Will Ferrell (Brennan Huff), John C. Reilly (Dale Doback), Mary Steenburgen (Nancy Huff), Richard Jenkins (Robert Doback), Adam Scott (Derek Huff), Kathryn Hahn (Alice Huff). Directed by Adam McKay and produced by Jimmy Miller and Judd Apatow. Screenplay by McKay and Will Ferrell.

When did comedies get so mean? *Step Brothers* has a premise that might have produced a good time at the movies, but when I left I felt a little unclean. The plot: Will Ferrell and John C. Reilly play Brennan and Dale, two never-employed fortyish sons who still live at home, eating melted cheese nachos and watching TV. When their parents (Mary Steenburgen and Richard Jenkins) get married, they become stepbrothers and have to share the same room. This causes them to inflict agonizing pain upon each other and use language that would seem excessive in the men's room of a truck stop.

Is this funny? Anything can be funny. Let me provide an example. I am thinking of a particular anatomical act. It is described in explicit detail in two 2008 movies, *Step Brothers* and *Tropic Thunder*. In *Step Brothers* it sounds dirty and disgusting. In *Tropic Thunder,* described by Jack Black while he is tied to a tree and undergoing heroin withdrawal, it's funny.

Same act, similar descriptions. What's the difference? It involves the mechanism of comedy, I think. The Jack Black character is desperately motivated. He will offer to do *anything* to be released. In *Step Brothers,* the language is simply showing off by talking dirty. It serves no comic function and just sort of sits there in the air, making me cringe.

I know, I know, four-letter language is the currency of a movie like this and many of the other films Judd Apatow produces. I would be lying if I said I was shocked. I would also be lying if I said I had no taste or judgment of comic strategy. I'm sure I've seen movies with more extreme language than *Step Brothers,* but here it seems to serve no purpose other than simply to exist. In its own tiny way, it lowers the civility of our civilization.

Now what about the violence? These two adult children do horrible things to each other. The movie must be particularly proud of one scene because they show part of it in the trailer. Dale thinks he has killed Brennan by slamming him with the cymbal of his drum set. He rolls him in a rug and prepares to bury him in the lawn. Brennan comes to, bangs Dale with the shovel, and starts to bury him alive.

I dunno. Maybe it sounds funny when you read it. Coming at the end of a series of similar cruelties, it was one living burial too many. There is also an attempted drowning. And never mind.

Mary Steenburgen and Richard Jenkins, two gifted actors, do what they can. They despair of their grown-up, unemployed brats. They lay down the law. They realize their sons are destroying their marriage. But they exist in another dimension than Brennan and Dale—almost in another movie. Their reaction shots are almost always curious because the only sane reaction would be sheer horror, followed by calls to the men with the butterfly nets.

423

Sometimes I think I am living in a nightmare. All about me, standards are collapsing, manners are evaporating, people show no respect for themselves. I am not a moralistic nut. I'm proud of the x-rated movie I wrote. I like vulgarity if it's funny or serves a purpose. But what is going on here?

Back to the movie. I suppose it will be a success. Will Ferrell and John C. Reilly have proven how talented they are in far better movies. If it makes millions, will they want to wade into this genre again? I hope not. Ferrell actually cowrote the movie with Adam McKay, the director. Maybe he will. But why not a comedy with more invention, with more motivation than hate at first sight? There is one genuinely funny moment in the movie: The blind man who lives next door has a guide dog that misbehaves, snarls, and bites people. Bad taste, yes. But . . . I'm desperate here. Do you see why the dog doing it is funny, but Will Ferrell doing it to John C. Reilly is not funny?

Stephanie Daley ★ ★ ★ ½
R, 92 m., 2007

Tilda Swinton (Lydie Crane), Timothy Hutton (Paul Crane), Denis O'Hare (Frank), Jim Gaffigan (Joe), Melissa Leo (Miri), Amber Tamblyn (Stephanie Daley). Directed by Hilary Brougher and produced by Sean Costello, Lynette Howell, Samara Koffler, and Jen Roskind. Screenplay by Brougher.

At a high school ski outing, a trail of blood is visible in the snow. The trail is left by Stephanie Daley, a sixteen-year-old girl, whose stillborn baby is found in a toilet. The girl claims she didn't know she was pregnant, but the "ski mom" case becomes a sensation. She is charged with murder and before her trial is sent for sessions with a forensic psychologist named Lydie Crane.

Stephanie (Amber Tamblyn) has an imperfect understanding of the realities of pregnancy. She had sex only once, at a party, with a young man who told her not to worry; he withdrew in time. Obviously, he did not. Why didn't she realize she was pregnant? It can happen. But confusing evidence suggests the baby may not have been dead at birth, although it was barely long-term enough to live. Did she kill it, or was it already dead?

The psychologist, Lydie Crane (Tilda Swinton), had a miscarriage of her own. Now she is expecting again—about as pregnant as Stephanie was. Their conversations are almost in code, with much silence. The girl is inarticulate, guilt-ridden ("I killed her with my mind"), and confused. The psychologist deals with her personal conflicts over the case. Swinton is an ideal choice for the role, because when she needs to, few actors can be more quiet, empathetically tactful.

There are courtroom scenes, but this is neither a whodunit, a what-was-done, or a moral or political argument from any position. It simply, sympathetically, sees how real life can be too complicated to match with theories.

I personally believe the body of a stillborn infant deserves respect. It should not be found in a toilet. But we learn that the psychologist herself threw away the ashes of her own stillbirth. Heartless? Depends on the thinking at the time. Scattering someone's ashes can be a loving and spiritual act. A libertarian, on the other hand, might reasonably argue that while a living baby has full human rights, a stillborn baby does not, and remains, in a sense, the property of the mother. In this film, that argument grows cloudy because it is unclear when and how the baby died.

We read about cases like this and think the mothers are monsters. If their babies are alive and found in a Dumpster, certainly they exist outside decency and morality, or their values are corrupted. But what led them to that decision? What did they know? What were they taught? What did they fear? I feel it is the responsibility of parents to raise children who know they can tell their parents anything and go to them for help. If a girl cannot tell her parents she is pregnant, something bad is likely to happen.

Yet *Stephanie Daley* goes even deeper: Did she know she was pregnant? As the psychologist struggles with this baffling girl, she feels her own powerlessness. And the movie invites us into her pity and confusion. Written and directed by Hilary Brougher, it has the courage and integrity to refuse an easy conclusion. When I saw it, some audience members said they were unhappy with the ending. What they meant was, they were unhappy about having to think about the ending.

What would a satisfactory ending be? Guilty? Innocent? Forensic revelations? We have been tutored by Hollywood to expect all the threads to be tied neatly at the end. But real life is more like this movie: Frightened and confused people are confronted with a situation they cannot understand, and those who would help them are powerless. Some cases should never come to trial because no verdict would be adequate. You are likely to be discussing this film long into the night.

The Stoning of Soraya M. ★ ★ ★
R, 114 m., 2009

Shohreh Aghdashloo (Zahra), Mozhan Marno (Soraya), Jim Caviezel (Sahebjam), Navid Negahban (Ali), Parviz Sayyad (Hashem), Ali Pourtash (Mullah), David Diaan (Ebrahim). Directed by Cyrus Nowrasteh and produced by Stephen McEveety and John Shepherd. Screenplay by Cyrus Nowrasteh and Betsy Griffen Nowrasteh, based on the book by Freidoune Sahebjam.

The Islamic practice of stoning women and the Christian practice of burning them as witches are both born not from religious reasons but of a male desire to subjugate women and define them in terms of sexuality. Is this in dispute? Are there any theologians who support such actions? Of all the most severe punishments of both religions, this is the one most skewed against women, and the one most convenient for men.

To be sure, no witches have been burned at the stake in many long years, and few ever were. But women are still stoned to death in some Islamic countries, including Iran, where this film is set. The practice survives in backward rural areas, and the law turns a blind eye. It is rare, and Iran denies it, but French journalist Freidoune Sahebjam's best-selling *The Stoning of Soraya M.* (1994) appears to be quite authentic. A woman really was stoned to death on trumped-up adultery charges, brought for the convenience of her husband who desired to marry a young girl.

Cyrus Nowrasteh's *The Stoning of Soraya M.* does not dramatize this story in a subtle way. You might argue that the stoning of a woman to death is not a subtle subject. But it would be helpful to have it told in a way that shows how almost the entire population of a village allows it to happen, even though most of them know of the woman's innocence and her husband's vile motives. How does a lynch mob form? Instead, we're given a village populated primarily by overacted villains and moral cowards.

Against them is one strong voice: the widow Zahra, Soraya's aunt. She's played by Shohreh Aghdashloo, the Oscar nominee from *House of Sand and Fog* (2004). She knows all the players and all the motives and publicly calls them on it, to no avail. She's a "crazy woman," says the husband, Ali (Navid Negahban). The phrase "crazy woman" can fall easily from the tongue, and it's worth remembering that in Victorian England a wife could be locked in an asylum for life on only her husband's signature (see the great novel *The Quincunx*).

Ali the husband is an immoral monster. His intended child bride has not been asked if she wants to marry him; the marriage has been arranged. The village mullah goes along because Ali threatens to blackmail him about an old prison sentence. The mayor knows it is wrong and doubts Allah desires it, but lacks the courage to do much more than mutter.

The stoning sequence itself is one of the most unbearable experiences I have had at the movies. I learn it lasts nearly twenty minutes. Soraya is buried in a hole up to the waist. Village boys collect stones of a good throwing weight in a wheelbarrow. We see blow after blow, as blood pours from her face and body. She accepts this as her fate, as indeed it is. She did nothing that was not innocent and kind.

The stoning took place in 1986, after the Islamic Revolution. Fundamentalists were in power and enforced their strictures; the measures they introduced are being challenged today in the streets of Iran, and similar extremism is the practice in our dear friend Saudi Arabia. Those with objections fear crushing reprisal. The enforcers have power, position, and wealth to gain, and dare their enemies to go against what they say is God's will.

The message is that if a religion requires practices that seem evil to its members, they should resign from that religion. If it condones a death penalty that is visited unequally on members of a specific gender, race, or class, it is immoral. There cannot be a reward for following it blindly because only a thoughtful choice has meaning. At heaven's gate you cannot say, "I always followed the herd."

The Stoning of Soraya M. has such a powerful stoning sequence that I recommend it if only for its brutal ideological message. That the pitiful death of Soraya is followed by a false Hollywood upbeat ending involving tape recordings and silliness about a car that won't start is simply shameful. Nowrasteh, born in Colorado, attended the USC Film School. Is that what they teach there? When you are telling the story of a woman being stoned to death, you may not be able to use everything you learned in class.

The Strangers ★ ½
R, 90 m., 2008

Liv Tyler (Kristen McKay), Scott Speedman (James Hoyt), Gemma Ward (Dollface), Kip Weeks (Man in the Mask), Laura Margolis (Pin-Up Girl), Glenn Howerton (Mike). Directed by Bryan Bertino and produced by Doug Davison, Roy Lee, and Nathan Kahane. Screenplay by Bertino.

My mistake was to read the interview with the director. At the beginning of my review of *The Strangers,* I typed my star rating instinctively: "One star." I was outraged. I wrote: "What a waste of a perfectly good first act! And what a maddening, nihilistic, infuriating ending!" I was just getting warmed up.

And then, I dunno, I looked up the movie on IMDb, and there was a link to an interview with Bryan Bertino, the writer and director, and I went there, read it, and looked at his photo. He looked to be in his twenties. This was his first film. Bertino had been working as a grip on a peanuts-budget movie when he pitched this screenplay to Rogue Pictures and was asked to direct it. He gave a friend his grip tools and thought: "Cool, I'm never going to need this anymore! I'm never using a hammer again." Then he tells the interviewer: "I still had to buy books on how to direct."

So I thought, Bryan Bertino is a kid, this is

his first movie, and as much as I hate it, it's a competent movie that shows he has the chops to be a director. So I gave it 1½ stars instead of one. Still harsh, yes. I think a lot of audience members will walk out really angry at the ending, although it has a certain truthfulness and doesn't cheat on the situation that has been building up. The movie deserves more stars for its bottom-line craft, but all the craft in the world can't redeem its story.

Yes, Bertino can direct. He opens on a dark night in a neighborhood of deserted summer homes with two people in a car. These are Kristen (Liv Tyler) and James (Scott Speedman). They are coming from a wedding reception. They go inside James's summer home. We learn that he proposed to her, but she "isn't ready." The camera focuses on a 33 rpm turntable that, along with their Volvo, are the easiest two props I can imagine to create a 1970s period look.

I am intrigued by these people. Will they talk all night? Will they do things they'll regret forever? Will they . . . *there is a knock on the door!* Not the sound of a human hand hitting wood. The sound of something hard hitting wood. It is very loud, and it echoes. To evoke an infinitely superior film, it creates the same sense of alarm and danger as the planks do, banging against each other in *Le Fils* (*The Son*), by the Dardenne brothers.

They open the door and find a young girl. They tell her she has the wrong house. She goes and stands in the yard. And then, all night long, their sense of security is undercut by more knocks, breaking glass, scraping, smashing. The sound track is the third protagonist. After a time, Bertino creates an empty space in one of his compositions, and it attracts a . . . figure . . . that casually fills it, wearing a mournful, shroudlike mask. We will see the mask again. Also two figures wearing little-doll masks that are not sweet, but ominous. We recall the opening credits telling us, "This film is inspired by true events." Never a good sign.

Is *The Strangers* inspired by other movies? Asked by Moviesonline.ca if he was influenced "by the film" (never named), Bertino answers, as only someone young and innocent could answer: "I don't *necessarily* think that I looked at it, you know." The *necessarily* is a masterstroke. He adds: "I'm definitely influenced by, like, '70s genre stuff in general, structure wise. . . . I read *Helter Skelter* when I was, like, eleven. That was where I first started getting interested in the idea of people just walking into a house that you didn't know. I lived in a house in the middle of nowhere in Texas on this road where you could call out in the middle of the night and nobody would hear you."

There have been great movies about home invasion, like *In Cold Blood,* that made more of it than gruesome events. *The Strangers* is a well-shot film (the cinematographer is the veteran Peter Sova). It does what it sets out to do. I'm not sure that it earns the right to do it. I will say that Bertino shows the instincts and choices of a good director; I hope he gets his hands on worthier material. It's a melancholy fact that he probably couldn't have found financing if his first act had lived up to its promise. There's a market for the kind of movie that inspires the kinds of commercials and trailers that *The Strangers* inspires, ending with a chilling dialogue exchange:

"Why are you doing this to us?"
"Because you were home." ☞

Strength and Honour ★ ★ ½
R, 104 m., 2007

Michael Madsen (Sean Kelleher), Vinnie Jones (Smasher O'Driscoll), Patrick Bergin (Papa Boss), Richard Chamberlain (Denis O'Leary), Luke Whelton (Michael Kelleher), Michael Rawley (Chaser McGrath), Gail Fitzpatrick (Mammy). Directed, produced, and written by Mark Mahon.

Within the first five minutes, we know precisely how *Strength and Honour* is going to end. The rest is in the details, which are sometimes pretty good. The movie is about a boxer named Sean Kelleher who retires forever from the ring after killing his brother-in-law in a sparring match, and returns only to win the money for a $250,000 heart operation for his young son.

Wait, we're not finished yet. How could he win so much money for his first bout? Because he is fighting bare-knuckled for the title of King of the Travelers (also known as gypsies). His arch-foe in the championship bout is a vicious, mean, hard man named Smasher

O'Driscoll, played by the British soccer star Vinnie Jones, but what do you think the odds are that Sean will lose his fight and his son will die? I should explain that this all takes place in County Cork and stars Michael Madsen, who is a good deal gentler and more loving than you may remember him from *Kill Bill.*

The movie is much about the travelers on a hilltop outside town. Sean is not a traveler, but after his wife dies and he is forced to sell their house to pay medical bills, he buys a caravan and moves in next door to the earth mother Mammy (Gail Fitzpatrick), whose son Chaser (Michael Rawley) lives nearby and begins to think of Sean as a father figure. Sean's financial crisis in the movie, by the way, should be reported to Michael Moore; Irish medical care seems mighty expensive.

This is melodrama mixed with formula and a great deal of tear-jerking, but Madsen plays the character straight down the center and has considerable authority; he doesn't ask for sympathy, doesn't accept favors lightly, says nothing when the travelers accept his $10,000 deposit on the prizefight, pocket the money, and tell him he's not qualified because he's not of the blood. He needs the $250,000 too much to complain. This and other matters are settled among the gypsies around a small bonfire, which provides warm, flickering light for many a conversation. Eventually he's allowed to fight and in the final bout faces the fearsome, animalistic Smasher, who knocks out people just for knocking at his door.

Sharp eyes among you are wondering how they have dollars in Ireland. They do not. They had the Irish pound (in Gaelic, the punt) until they switched to euros in 2002. Why nobody in the film knows this is a mystery; less so perhaps with Sean, who is an American who moved to Cork with his Irish wife.

There is some nice character work in the movie. Richard Chamberlain plays the manager of a boxing gym and Sean's manager and adviser. Michael Rawley is persuasive as the young acolyte. And Gail Fitzpatrick steals scenes with the sheer ferocity of her passion for justice; it's pretty clear that she and her neighbor Sean may be linking up in a double-wide before long.

But the movie, written and directed by

first-timer Mark Mahon, follows so resolutely in the footsteps of so many, many other sporting movies that we're way ahead of the story arc. One novelty is the violence of the bare-knuckle fights, which take place within a ring of savagely shouting men, although it's a puzzle why the prize fight is less well-attended than the opening bouts. If you want to see a predictable boxing movie with a kinder, gentler Michael Madsen who's really quite convincing, here's your movie. But I'd like to see this side of Madsen developed in a better screenplay.

Sugar ★ ★ ★ ½
R, 118 m., 2009

Algenis Perez Soto (Miguel Santos), Rayniel Rufino (Jorge Ramirez), Andre Holland (Brad Johnson), Michael Gaston (Stu Sutton), Jaime Tirelli (Osvaldo), Jose Rijo (Alvarez), Ellary Porterfield (Anne Higgins), Ann Whitney (Helen Higgins), Richard Bull (Earl Higgins). Directed by Anna Boden and Ryan Fleck and produced by Paul Mezey, Jamie Patricof, and Jeremy Kipp Walker. Screenplay by Boden and Fleck.

Sugar approaches with tender care the story of a kid from the Dominican Republic who has a strong pitching arm and a good heart. Miguel Santos, known as "Sugar" because of his sweet personality, is recruited from the fields of dreams in his homeland by Major League Baseball and assigned to an Iowa farm club that is very, very far from home.

I thought I could guess the story. But I couldn't. There isn't a single scene in this film where it really matters which side wins a game, and it doesn't end with a no-hitter. It looks with care at Sugar, and there are a thousand Sugars for every Sammy Sosa. Probably more. Baseball players have become an important export for the Dominican Republic, and poor families like Miguel's dream of the day when sons will be sending home paychecks. A minor league salary represents wealth.

The film is knowledgeable about how the system works. American teams maintain elaborate training facilities in the D.R., send talent scouts to local leagues, and keep recruits under close watch: Room and board is provided, there are security guards to enforce discipline, the kids get a few days off once in a while. This is heaven for them. For years their dreams have been filled with visions of big-time baseball.

Sugar isn't filled with melodramatic developments and a hard landing on American soil. Baseball seems, in fact, a friendly if realistic destination, an income where there was none before. If very few players ever make it into a major league starting lineup, well, they know that going in. What's special about the film—and this is a very special film—is how closely it observes the emotional uncertainties of a stranger in a strange land, not speaking the language, not knowing the customs, beset with homesickness and the dread of disappointing his family.

Algenis Perez Soto, a young baseball player in his acting debut, embodies Sugar with a natural sincerity. The movie regards him with sympathy. Sugar isn't "torn with conflict," as movie ads like to say, but weighed with worry. He finds himself boarding in the friendly Iowa farm home of Helen and Earl Higgins (Ann Whitney and Richard Bull), who have taken in a generation of new players for the local farm club. They know their baseball ("You've been dropping your arm," Helen tells him, and Sugar doesn't disagree).

There is also the presence of their granddaughter Anne (Ellary Porterfield), who sends out mixed messages; she's obviously attracted to him and invites him to meet her friends, evangelicals who would like to get him on board. On the team, he bonds with Jorge (Rayniel Rufino), a more seasoned player from the Republic, and Brad Johnson (Andre Holland), who is the same color but from a different world; if baseball doesn't pan out, he'll go back for an advanced degree from Stanford.

For Sugar, who mumbles he's had "a little" high school, everything depends on baseball panning out. On their regular phone calls, his mother fears she can sense something troubling in his voice. He finds the farm system is supportive, and he gets help from coaches who care, but there is always another player waiting behind him in line.

Anna Boden and Ryan Fleck, who wrote

and directed *Sugar,* are serious filmmakers who have no desire to make a "sports movie." They've obviously done their research on the major league farm system and the men who pass through it; at some level, this entire tryout process is for the benefit of a fan in the grandstands with a wise-ass opinion about the "new kid." Remembering a day when Sammy Sosa was booed at Wrigley Field, I see it now in a wholly new light.

The true subject of *Sugar* is the immigrant experience in America. Boden and Fleck are interested in newcomers to this country, doing what they can to make a living and succeed. Whether this happens for Sugar, or how it might happen, you will see for yourself. The filmmakers are too observant to settle for a quick, conventional payoff. For them this film is a chapter in the more interesting story of the lifetime Sugar has ahead of him. Algenis Perez Soto plays the character so openly, so naturally, that an interesting thing happens: Baseball is only the backdrop, not the subject. This is a wonderful film.

Note: The R *rating is for relatively inconsequential reasons.*

Summer Hours ★ ★ ★

NO MPAA RATING, 103 m., 2009

Juliette Binoche (Adrienne), Charles Berling (Frederic), Jeremie Renier (Jeremie), Edith Scob (Helene), Dominique Reymond (Lisa), Isabelle Sadoyan (Eloise), Kyle Eastwood (James). Directed by Olivier Assayas and produced by Marin Karmitz, Nathanael Karmitz, and Charles Gillibert. Screenplay by Assayas.

Sometimes what holds a family together is custom and guilt. *Summer Hours* begins on the seventy-fifth birthday of Helene, a woman who is joined in the French countryside by her three children and their families. Much of the talk is about how far two of the children had to travel—one from New York, the other from China—and there's the sense they're eager to be going home. Sure, they love their mother. They really do. But you know how it is. They visit less because they should visit more.

Helene understands this. She understands a great deal. She pulls aside Frederic (Charles Berling), her only child still living in France,

to talk about the handling of her estate. This makes him unhappy, but she produces an inventory of the sort women often keep, of her valued possessions. Tea sets, vases, paintings.

The house belonged to her uncle, a fairly well-known painter. She has kept it unchanged since his death, as almost a shrine. She has little of his work, but many of his valuable pieces, including a desk. In less than a year, she's dead, and the children gather again. She predicted to Frederic that the house would have to be sold—indeed, she knew them all well enough to foresee everything—but he assumes his sister, Adrienne (Juliette Binoche), and brother, Jeremie (Jeremie Renier), will want to keep it in the family.

He is wrong. Adrienne is getting married to her New York boyfriend (Kyle Eastwood). Jeremie has been offered a promotion in Hong Kong. The film, which has no false sentimentality, is matter-of-fact about how the valuable works are disposed of. They're all sorry they couldn't keep and maintain the house, but, well . . .

There are two long-standing facts of the family that are discussed, really, for the first time. What exactly was the nature of the long relationship between Helene and her uncle? And how is Eloise to be treated—Eloise, the family's cook and housekeeper since time immemorial? Olivier Assayas, the writer-director, doesn't treat these subjects as melodrama but as the sorts of things adult children naturally discuss. They're much more effective that way.

What happens is that the film builds its emotional power by stealth, indirectly, refusing to be a tear-jerker, always realistic, and yet observing how very sad it is to see a large part of your life disappear. A parent, for example. In Errol Morris's *Gates of Heaven,* these perfect words are spoken: "Death is for the living, and not for the dead so much."

The actors all find the correct notes. It is a French film, and so they are allowed to be adult and intelligent. They are not the creatures of a screenplay that hurries them along. The film is not about what will happen. It is about them. The recent American film that most resembles this one is Jonathan Demme's *Rachel Getting Married.* Some audience members didn't know what to think of it because it didn't tell them. Sometimes you just have to figure out what you think for yourself. *Summer Hours* ends on the perfect note, the more you think about it.

Sunshine ★ ★ ★
R, 107 m., 2007

Cillian Murphy (Capa), Chris Evans (Mace), Rose Byrne (Cassie), Michelle Yeoh (Corazon), Hiroyuki Sanada (Kaneda), Cliff Curtis (Searle), Troy Garity (Harvey), Benedict Wong (Trey). Directed by Danny Boyle and produced by Andrew Macdonald. Screenplay by Alex Garland.

As a permanent winter settles upon Earth, a spaceship is sent on a desperate mission to drop a nuclear device into the sick sun and "reignite" it. To name the ship *Icarus I* seems like asking for trouble in two ways, considering the fate of the original Icarus and the numeral that ominously leaves room for a sequel. Indeed, the first ship disappears. As *Sunshine* opens, the *Icarus II*, with seven astronauts on board, is approaching Mercury, protected by a shield that keeps it from incinerating.

Considering that the movie is set only fifty years in the future, the sun seems to be dying several billion years prematurely, especially in a "hard" (i.e., quasi-plausible) science fiction film. Man, am I glad I didn't go off on a rant about that before learning that the film's science adviser, Dr. Brian Cox of CERN (Conseil Europeen pour le Recherche Nucleaire [European Laboratory for Particle Physics]), thought of it, too.

The sun is not "dying in the normal sense," IMDb.com reports, but in the Cox scenario "has instead been 'infected' with a 'Q-ball'—a supersymmetric nucleus left over from the big bang . . . that is disrupting the normal matter. This is a theoretical particle that scientists at CERN are currently trying to confirm—the film's bomb is meant to blast the Q-ball to its constituent parts, which will then naturally decay, allowing the sun to return to normal."

I'll buy that. Blasting a Q-ball to its constituent parts sounds normal to me, but then I read every sci-fi magazine published during my adolescence, and my hero was John W. Campbell Jr., editor of *Astounding/Analog*, who insisted his fiction not be preposterous

but sensible and possible, such as a mission to the sun to blast a Q-ball to pieces.

But enough about me. What about the Q-ball? It's a "non-topological soliton," Wikipedia explains before grumbling in a related article that "it is not easy to define precisely what a soliton is." Don't you love this stuff? Isn't it better than a lot of analysis of the psychological interactions among the crew? The movie was written by the sci-fi novelist Alex Garland, whose *28 Days Later* made a scary film, and directed by Danny Boyle, whose work ranges widely from the world's filthiest toilet (in *Trainspotting*) to a young boy who chats with the saints (in *Millions*).

But enough about them. Perhaps I skated too quickly over those psychological interactions. There is a subgenre that assumes that when a crew is shut up in a spaceship in utter isolation, they will start to get on each other's nerves. This would seem to be a waste of time aboard the *Icarus II*, since it's essentially a kamikaze mission; the crew members must presumably share the fate of the Q-ball and be blasted into their own constituent parts, but the difference is, the Q-ball likes it.

The interactions are the weakest elements in *Sunshine*, which is strongest when it focuses on the sheer enormity of the mission and its consequences. Sean Penn is needed on board to utter "Awesome!"

One crew member asks the onboard computer to let him see what the sun really looks like, and the computer's answer is a variation on kids warning each other that staring at the sun can make you go blind.

This is even truer when you are millions of miles closer to the sun, unprotected by an atmosphere and wearing only Ray-Bans.

I don't want to reveal too much of the plot, but there is a nice twist, on the way past Mercury, when they pick up a distress signal from, yes, *Icarus I*. As John W. Campbell Jr. would have known, the *last* thing you want to do while passing Mercury is respond to a distress signal from a ship that should not be there and—well, anyway, they do, which leads to trouble, but also leads to a very effective scene dealing with how long the human body might be able to survive in the cold of outer space (which, as the good doctor Isaac Asimov once explained, is longer than you might think).

The actors (Michelle Yeoh, Cillian Murphy, Chris Evans, Troy Garity, Rose Byrne, Cliff Curtis, Benedict Wong, and Hiroyuki Sanada) are effective by trying not to be too effective; they almost all play professional astronaut/scientists, and not action-movie heroes. The design of the ship itself is convincing; it looks like the inside of a computer used as the bunkhouse at a boys' camp. The special effects in outer space are convincing and remorseless. The drummed-up suspense at the end is not essential, since Boyle and Garland seem more interested in the metaphysics of the voyage; Tarkovsky's *Solaris* demonstrated that if you go all the way with the implications of such a situation, it's more interesting than using plot devices.

So anyway, younger girls won't like this picture, unless they know what happens under an automobile hood. Younger boys won't like it because the only thing that's possibly going to blow up real good is the sun. But science fiction fans will like it, and brainiacs, and those who sometimes look at the sky and think, man, there's a lot going on up there, and we can't even define precisely what a soliton is.

Sunshine Cleaning ★ ★

R, 102 m., 2009

Amy Adams (Rose Lorkowski), Emily Blunt (Norah Lorkowski), Alan Arkin (Joe Lorkowski), Jason Spevack (Oscar Lorkowski), Steve Zahn (Mac), Mary Lynn Rajskub (Lynn), Clifton Collins Jr. (Winston). Directed by Christine Jeffs and produced by Glenn Williamson, Jeb Brody, Marc Turtletaub, and Peter Saraf. Screenplay by Megan Holley.

Sunshine Cleaning is a little too sunny for its material. Its heroine, Rose, is a single mom in desperate need of income, trapped in a one-way affair with her high school boyfriend, who fathered her son but married someone else. Her son is always in trouble at school. Her sister, Norah, is a hard-living goofball. Rose starts a new business cleaning up messy crime scenes.

Does this sound sunny to you? The material might have promise as a black comedy, but its attempt to put on a smiling face is unconvincing. That despite the work by Amy Adams

as Rose and Emily Blunt as Norah, two effortless charmers who would be terrific playing these characters in a different movie. And Alan Arkin is back, and engaging, in what is coming dangerously close to "the Alan Arkin role." He's their father, Joe, forever hatching new get-poor-quick schemes.

Rose is a good mom. She understands her seven-year-old son, Oscar (Jason Spevack), who is not really troubled but simply high-spirited. I wonder how many little boys are accused of misbehaving simply because they are boys. Why does she still sleep with Mac, the faithless high school quarterback (Steve Zahn) who seduced and abandoned her? She asks herself the same question.

It's Mac, at least, who tips her off on a possible business. He's a cop and notices that people get paid well for mopping up after gruesome murders. So is born Rose and Norah's Sunshine Cleaning, which will clean up the rugs and scrape the brains off the wall, etc. This job by its nature allows them to witness the aftermath of lives unexpectedly interrupted; an ID in a dead woman's purse leads them to make an awkward new acquaintance.

This is promising material. Gene Siskel loved movies about what people actually do all day long. There is even a documentary subject here. But not this film that compromises on everything it implies, because it wants to be cheerful about people who don't have much to be cheerful about. How can you make a feel-good movie about murder-scene cleanups? "Life's a messy business," the poster says. Yes, and death is messier.

There are times when the movie works, but those are the times it (and even we) forget what it's really about. If you could plot it on a curve, it might look like a cross-section of a roller-coaster. The poster also evokes *Little Miss Sunshine*, by the same producers, also with Alan Arkin, and the presence of Amy Adams evokes the sublime *Junebug*. Those were both movies with more consistent tones and, although based on contrivance, felt more natural.

There's one element in the film that does work, and it's sort of off to the side, apart from the rest of the plot. It involves Winston (Clifton Collins Jr.), a one-armed hardware store owner, who babysits Oscar in an

431

emergency and provides an oasis of warmth and common sense. You may remember him as Perry, one of the killers Truman wrote the book about in *Capote* (2005). An actor like this works a lot but doesn't always get ideal roles. Now he's beginning to emerge, with seven more films in postproduction.

You won't have a bad time seeing *Sunshine Cleaning*. You may get a little frustrated waiting for it to take off. It keeps heading down different runways. There's a movie here somewhere. Not this one.

Superbad ★ ★ ★ ½

R, 112 m., 2007

Jonah Hill (Seth), Michael Cera (Evan), Christopher Mintz-Plasse (Fogell), Seth Rogen (Officer Michaels), Bill Hader (Officer Slater), Martha MacIsaac (Becca), Emma Stone (Jules). Directed by Greg Mottola and produced by Judd Apatow and Shauna Robertson. Screenplay by Seth Rogen and Evan Goldberg.

Superbad is a four-letter raunch-a-rama with a heart and an inordinate interest in other key organs. It is autobiographical, I suspect, inspired not just by the lives of the cowriters, Seth Rogen and Evan Goldberg, who named the two leads after themselves, but possibly by millions of other teenagers. The movie is astonishingly foul-mouthed, but in a fluent, confident way where the point isn't the dirty words, but the flow and rhythm, and the deep, sad yearning they represent.

The movie involves best friends Seth (Jonah Hill) and Evan (Michael Cera), who have been inseparable in high school mainly because they were equally unpopular, and now face the ordeal of attending different colleges. It is three weeks until the end of the high school year, bringing to mind the ancient truism that if you haven't had sex yet and you don't have it soon, you will never have had sex in high school. Such deprivation used to be commonplace; I am of the opinion that only about two members of the Urbana High School graduating class of 1960 had experienced sex, but I'll double-check at our next reunion. I will say, though, that at the end of senior year, third base was seeing a lot of traffic.

Seth is the pudgy, curly-haired one, and Evan is thin and has worried eyes. They have a sidekick named Fogell (Christopher Mintz-Plasse), who is so unpopular he is unpopular even with them. They all feel lust for every girl in the school but are so stuck for conversation that sometimes they simply say what time it is, as if they've been asked. To their wonderment, Seth, Evan, and even Fogell are invited to a party on the last night by the uber-popular Jules (Emma Stone), who belatedly explains that it's not a BYO party, but a BYOAEE party (bring your own and everybody else's).

Their attempts to buy booze while underage are more bizarre than some I have witnessed, involving Fogell's production of an ID card claiming he is "McLovin." And they discover that being the guys who bring the booze is a powerful deterrent to unpopularity. (Note: Underage drinking is *wrong*.) Jules is very happy to see the three friends and their brown paper bags, and Evan is amazed that even the fragrant Becca (Martha MacIsaac) has a smile for him and lots else.

To be sure, the lads are not seeking perfect love. They have heard about girls who get drunk and sleep with the wrong guy, and their modest ambition is simply to be the wrong guy. (Note: There is a thin line between being the wrong guy and being a criminal.) Fogell, for that matter, would be happy to even be the *wrong* wrong guy. (Note: Let's stop these notes and make a blanket announcement: This movie was made by professionals. Do not attempt any of this behavior yourself.)

But back to Fogell. What strange ability do teenagers have to always choose the school's future millionaire brainiacs and call them by their last names? For Fogell, poor wretch, there is nothing left in life but to found Microsoft, so to speak. The actor in the role, Christopher Mintz-Plasse, is an actual highschooler who got the job at a casting call, and it may be a star maker. I am informed by *Superbad* expert David Plummer: "There are already T-shirts being sold with 'I Am McLovin' printed on them."

Anyway, two cops (Bill Hader and coauthor Seth Rogen, in what I assume is a *non*autobiographical role) bust the party, and so original is this film that they are not the usual bullies, but young enough that when a door opens upon the likes of Jules and Becca and the brown paper bags, they begin to lean eagerly over the doorsill.

The movie reminded me a little of *National Lampoon's Animal House,* except that it's more mature, as all movies are. It has that unchained air of getting away with something. In its very raunchiness it finds truth, because if you know nothing about sex, how can you be tasteful and sophisticated on the subject?

In its treatment of adolescent sexual yearning, *Superbad* remembers not only the agony but the complete absence of the ecstasy. I remember in eighth grade, some kid asked how long you could entertain an impure thought before it got upgraded from a venial to a mortal sin. "There aren't rules for things like that," the sister explained, "but I'd say that after five seconds, you're asking for it." The kid and his buddy went down to his basement to study his dad's collection of *Playboy*s, and he got a stopwatch and had his buddy punch him in the arm every four seconds.

Surfwise ★ ★ ★
R, 93 m., 2008

A documentary directed and narrated by Doug Pray and produced by Graydon Carter, Tommy Means, Matthew Weaver, and Jonathan Paskowitz.

Surfwise sounds, of course, like a surfing documentary. It contains surfers and surfing all right, but in fact it's about the strange and problematical Paskowitz family, "the first family of surfing." We meet Dorian "Doc" Paskowitz at eighty-five years old, doing exercises in the nude and then providing a full body inventory: arthritis, muscular degeneration, but nothing that keeps him from surfing. "And I don't take a single pill!" he boasts. This from a 1940s graduate of the Stanford Medical School.

Young Dr. Paskowitz was on a standard post-college career track, I guess, through two failed marriages. Then he sold everything, went on a quest for meaning, found that he loved surfing more than anything else, introduced the sport to Israel, and took to himself a wife named Juliette, with whom he had eight sons and a daughter. These eleven people lived a nomadic life together in a twenty-four-foot camper during the years when the kids were growing up.

We see the campers—there were three, all purchased used, all the same size. A little crowded for two people. Not for the Paskowitz family. As Doc drove from one surfing mecca to another, they crowded in the back, slept together "like puppies," had to listen to their parents make loud, energetic love every single night, ate a lot of gruel and organic soups, and had just about enough clothing to muster eight clothed children, but not always nine. There was nothing at all like formal education.

What are we to make of this existence? Doc sees himself as a messiah of surfing, clean living, and healthy exercise. We might be more inclined to see him as a narcissistic monster, ruling his big family with an iron fist. Sounds like fun, driving from one beach to another, unless you're crowded in the back of the camper with eight other kids and not much of a view. One son recalls the day he discovered other people had eggs for breakfast.

Doc finally found a more stable way to support his family by starting a surfing camp near San Diego. Graydon Carter, editor of *Vanity Fair* and one of the producers of this film, was an early camper. The Paskowitz Surfing Camp inspired devotion, although one of Doc's children after another drifted away from the camper "home." Doc saw each bail-out as treachery.

Remarkably, the film's director, Doug Pray, has been able to track down each and every Paskowitz child, and he weaves their memories together with old home movies, still photos, and news clippings to create an evocative portrait of their lives. The kids are no more screwed up than any other nine kids—maybe less so. They have survived the absence of formal education. One says, "I love my father, but I don't understand him." And at the end they all bury their differences and gather for a family reunion in Hawaii (staged at least in part for the camera, one suspects). In the center of everything, there's Doc, his weather-beaten skin now a deep bronze, and his wife, Juliette, kissing and hugging and looking completely serene about the lives they built for themselves and their children.

433

Sweeney Todd: The Demon Barber of Fleet Street ★ ★ ★ ★

R, 117 m., 2007

Johnny Depp (Sweeney Todd), Helena Bonham Carter (Mrs. Nellie Lovett), Alan Rickman (Judge Turpin), Timothy Spall (Beadle Bamford), Sacha Baron Cohen (Adolfo Pirelli), Jayne Wisener (Johanna), Jamie Campbell Bower (Anthony Hope), Edward Sanders (Toby), Laura Michelle Kelly (Beggar Woman). Directed by Tim Burton and produced by John Logan, Walter Parkes, Laurie MacDonald, and Richard D. Zanuck. Screenplay by John Logan, based on the musical by Stephen Sondheim and Hugh Wheeler, adapted from the play by Christopher Bond.

For many a poor orphan lad
The first square meal he ever had
Was a hot meat pie made out of his dad
From Sweeney Todd the Barber.

Tim Burton's film adaptation of *Sweeney Todd: The Demon Barber of Fleet Street* smacks its lips at the prospect of such a meal, and so it should. In telling this story, half-measures will avail him nothing. It is the bloodiest musical in stage history, now become the bloodiest in film history, and it isn't a jolly romp either, but a dark revenge tragedy with heartbreak, mayhem, and bloody good meat pies.

But we know that going in and are relieved that Burton has played true to the material. Here is one scenario that is proof against a happy ending. It has what is much better, a satisfactory mixed ending, in which what must happen, does. Along the way, with merciless performances by Johnny Depp, Helena Bonham Carter, and Alan Rickman; a brooding production design by Dante Ferretti; and the dark shadows of Dariusz Wolski's cinematography, it allows Burton to evoke the nineteenth-century London of Henry Mayhew's *London Labour and the London Poor*, which reported on the dregs of London and greatly influenced Charles Dickens. The worst you've heard about Calcutta would have been an improvement on London poverty in those days.

And yet there is an exhilaration in the very fiber of the film because its life force is so strong. Its heroes, or antiheroes, have been wounded to the quick, its villains are vile and heartless, and they all play on a stage that rules out decency and mercy. The acting is so good that it enlists us in the sordid story, which even contains a great deal of humor—macabre, to be sure. As a feast for the eyes and the imagination, *Sweeney Todd* is—well, I was going to say, even more satisfying than a hot meat pie made out of your dad.

The story: In London years earlier lived a barber named Benjamin Barker (Johnny Depp) and his sweet young wife and child, and he loved them. But the vile Judge Turpin (Alan Rickman) sentenced Barker on trumped-up charges and transported him to Australia, meanwhile capturing the wife and child. Turpin ravishes the wife, destroying her life, and the girl, Johanna (Jayne Wisener), grows up to become the judge's ward and prisoner.

As the film proper opens, Benjamin has escaped from prison down under and sails into London in the company of young Anthony Hope (Jamie Campbell Bower). He races through the streets to his former barbershop, where the landlady is still the dark-eyed beauty Mrs. Lovett (Helena Bonham Carter), who sells the worst meat pies in London. She tells him about the fate of his family. He moves upstairs to his former barbershop, now a ruin, changes his name to Sweeney Todd, and sets up in business again. But so deep is his rage that he makes an architectural improvement: a sliding chute that will drop his customers straight into the basement after he slits their throats, so Mrs. Lovett can cut them up and bake them into her pies. Now she offers the meatiest and most succulent meat pies in London; business booms, and sometimes satisfied customers go upstairs for a haircut and a quick recycling.

Burton fashions his musical in what can almost be described as an intimate style. No platoons of dancers in London squares, as in *Oliver!* This is a London of narrow alleys, streets shadowed by overhangs, close secrets. The Stephen Sondheim songs don't really lend themselves to full-throated performance, although that has been the practice on the stage. They are more plot-driven, confessional, anguished. Depp and Bonham Carter do their own singing, and very well, too, and as actors they use the words to convey meaning as well as melody. There are also star turns by Sacha Baron Cohen, as the rival Italian barber Pirelli, whose singing career ends dramatically rather early in the film. And by Rickman as the judge and the invaluable Timothy Spall as Beadle Bamford, his flunky. And by the barber's daughter, Jayne Wisener, and his fellow traveler, Jamie Campbell Bower, who become lovers and provide some consolation after the last throat has been slit.

To an unusual degree, *Sweeney Todd* works on a quasi-realistic level and not as a musical fantasy. That's not to say we're to take it as fact, but that we can at least accept it on its own terms without the movie winking at us. It combines some of Tim Burton's favorite elements: the fantastic, the ghoulish, the bizarre, the unspeakable, the romantic; he finds a perfect instrument in Johnny Depp, an actor he has worked with since *Edward Scissorhands*. Helena Bonham Carter may be Burton's inamorata, but apart from that, she is perfectly cast, not as a vulgar fishwife type, but as a petite beauty with dark, sad eyes and a pouting mouth and a persistent fantasy that she and the barber will someday settle by the seaside. Not bloody likely.

Swing Vote ★ ★ ★
PG-13, 119 m., 2008

Kevin Costner (Bud Johnson), Madeline Carroll (Molly Johnson), Paula Patton (Kate Madison), Kelsey Grammer (Andrew Boone), Dennis Hopper (Donald Greenleaf), Nathan Lane (Art Crumb), Stanley Tucci (Martin Fox). Directed by Joshua Michael Stern and produced by Jim Wilson and Kevin Costner. Screenplay by Stern and Jason Richman.

Kevin Costner's new movie is about a presidential election that literally comes down to one man, one vote. The vote belongs to Bud Johnson, an alcoholic egg inspector from New Mexico, who finds himself the focus of the eyes of the world. Costner plays him as a hungover loser who cares about only one pair of eyes, those of his twelve-year-old daughter, Molly. When he realizes he has become an embarrassment to her, he begins to change.

The idea of an entire election coming down

to one man's vote is admittedly just a tad difficult to accept. But the movie makes a plucky stab at explaining how it comes to happen—and it almost sounds plausible. Everything depends on Molly. From the opening scene (Bud too hungover to get Molly to school) we see she's trying her best to be loyal to him, although he's a daily problem. This day, as it turns out, is Election Day, and she is determined at all costs that her dad will turn up at the polling place and vote.

It doesn't turn out that way. Bud gets laid off at the egg works, gets drunk, passes out. Molly waits impatiently at the polling place, where he promised to turn up on time. He doesn't, but an ingenious plot strategy makes it appear that he did, and that his vote was not counted, and when the whole election comes down to that one vote in New Mexico, which is tied, well, then you've got your movie.

The media descend on the town like a locust swarm. TV cameras and reporters are camped permanently outside the Johnson house trailer. Molly, who knows what really happened, keeps it to herself. And we meet people like Kate Madison (Paula Patton), the ace TV reporter who makes friends with Molly, and Sweeney (George Lopez), who will do anything for a scoop.

We also meet the two presidential candidates. Yes, they both fly to New Mexico to court Bud Johnson's decisive vote, and promise him the sun, the moon, and the stars. Kelsey Grammer is the Republican incumbent, President Andrew Boone. Dennis Hopper plays the Democratic challenger, Donald Greenleaf. Each has a campaign manager: Nathan Lane for the Democrat, and Stanley Tucci for the Republican. Oddly enough, there are times when the managers seem to have more ethics than the candidates.

The movie is a genial comedy, but it has significant undertones. Like some of Frank Capra's pictures (*Mr. Smith Goes to Washington* comes to mind), it shows a little guy up against the establishment—except this time it's a little girl, encouraging her dad to do the right thing. This works, because if there's one thing Bud Johnson doesn't want to do, it's embarrass Molly.

It all comes down to a crucial speech before his deciding vote. It's a Capraesque speech, incorporating big ideas into everyday language, and Costner delivers it with dignity, avoiding various pitfalls easily imagined. The speech doesn't make anyone very happy, but that's the idea. Kevin Costner makes a convincing everyman, even handling the transition from drunk to diplomat in one week flat. The turning point comes when he and the president relax in lawn chairs, contemplating Air Force One, and Bud pours out a margarita instead of drinking it. Sober, he turns out to be a pretty smart guy.

Molly always knew that. Young Madeline Carroll is splendid in the role, which during some stretches of the film is really the lead. She's clear-eyed and outspoken, has faith in her dad, and despite his drinking loves living with him. Once we get a glimpse of her mom (Mare Winningham), we understand why. The whole film is strongly cast, and I especially liked Stanley Tucci as a campaign manager who has steered one campaign after another into defeat.

The movie is determined to be bipartisan. It doesn't take sides. Both candidates would sell their mothers to win the election. That's the message, really: Our political system doesn't encourage politicians to tell the truth, but to say what they think voters want to hear. And the press assists them in that process. The movie is actually surprisingly realistic in portraying reporters on the campaign trail. They're a bunch of jackals, with the exception of sweet Kate Madison, who sacrifices the scoop of a lifetime because she has a good heart. That's one detail I really couldn't believe. ☞

Synecdoche, New York ★ ★ ★ ★
R, 124 m., 2008

Philip Seymour Hoffman (Caden Cotard), Samantha Morton (Hazel), Michelle Williams (Claire Keen), Catherine Keener (Adele Lack), Emily Watson (Tammy), Dianne Wiest (Ellen/Millicent), Jennifer Jason Leigh (Maria), Hope Davis (Madeleine Gravis), Tom Noonan (Sammy Barnathan). Directed by Charlie Kaufman and produced by Sidney Kimmel, Anthony Bregman, Ray Angelic, and Spike Jonze. Screenplay by Kaufman.

I think you have to see Charlie Kaufman's *Synecdoche, New York,* twice. I watched it the first time and knew it was a great film and that I had not mastered it. The second time because I needed to. The third time because I will want to. It will open to confused audiences and live indefinitely. A lot of people these days don't even go to a movie once. There are alternatives. It doesn't have to be the movies, but we must somehow dream. If we don't "go to the movies" in any form, our minds wither and sicken.

This is a film with the richness of great fiction. Like *Suttree,* the Cormac McCarthy novel I'm always mentioning, it's not that you have to return to understand it. It's that you have to return to realize how fine it really is. The surface may daunt you. The depths enfold you. The whole reveals itself, and then you may return to it like a talisman.

Wow, is that ever not a "money review." Why will people hurry along to what they expect to be trash, when they're afraid of a film they think may be good? The subject of *Synecdoche, New York,* is nothing less than human life and how it works. Using a neurotic theater director from upstate New York, it encompasses every life and how it copes and fails. Think about it a little and, my god, it's about you. *Whoever* you are.

Here is how life is supposed to work. We come out of ourselves and unfold into the world. We try to realize our desires. We fold back into ourselves, and then we die. *Synecdoche, New York,* follows a life that ages from about forty to eighty on that scale. Caden Cotard (Philip Seymour Hoffman) is a theater director, with all of the hang-ups and self-pity, all the grandiosity and sniffles, all the arrogance and fear typical of his job. In other words, he could be me. He could be you. He could be Joe the Plumber. The job, the name, the race, the gender, the environment all change. The human remains pretty much the same.

Here is how it happens. We find something we want to do, if we are lucky, or something we need to do, if we are like most people. We use it as a way to obtain food, shelter, clothing, mates, comfort, a First Folio of Shakespeare, model airplanes, American Girl dolls, a handful of rice, sex, solitude, a trip to Venice, Nikes, drinking water, plastic surgery, child care, dogs, medicine, education, cars, spiritual solace, whatever we think we need. To do this, we enact the role we call *me*, trying to brand ourselves as a person who can and should obtain these things.

In the process, we place the people in our lives into compartments and define how they should behave to our advantage. Because we cannot *force* them to follow our desires, we deal with projections of them created in our minds. But they *will* be contrary and have wills of their own. Eventually new projections of us are dealing with new projections of them. Sometimes versions of ourselves disagree. We succumb to temptation—but, oh, father, what else was I gonna do? I feel like hell. I repent. I'll do it again.

Hold that trajectory in mind and let it interact with age, discouragement, greater wisdom, and more uncertainty. You will understand what *Synecdoche, New York,* is trying to say about the life of Caden Cotard and the lives in his life. Charlie Kaufman is one of the few truly important writers to make screenplays his medium. David Mamet is another. That is not the same as a great writer (Faulkner, Pinter, Cocteau) who writes screenplays. Kaufman is writing in the upper reaches with Bergman. Now for the first time he directs.

It is obvious that he has only one subject, the mind, and only one plot, how the mind negotiates with reality, fantasy, hallucination, desire, and dreams. *Being John Malkovich. Eternal Sunshine of the Spotless Mind. Adaptation. Human Nature. Confessions of a Dangerous Mind.* What else are they about? He is working in plain view. In one film, people go inside the head of John Malkovich. In another, a writer has a twin who does what he cannot do. In another, a game show host is, or thinks he is, an international spy. In *Human Nature,* a man whose childhood was shaped by domineering parents trains white mice to sit down at a tiny table and always employ the right silverware. Is behavior learned or enforced?

Synecdoche, New York, is not a film about the theater, although it looks like one. A theater director is an ideal character for representing the role Kaufman thinks we all play. The magnificent sets, which stack independent rooms on top of one another, are the compartments we assign to our life's enterprises. The actors are the people in roles we cast from our point of view. Some of them play doubles assigned to do what there's not world enough and time for. They have a way of acting independently, in violation of instructions. They try to control their own projections. Meanwhile, the source of all this activity grows older and tired, sick and despairing. Is this real or a dream? The world is but a stage, and we are mere actors upon it. It's all a play. The play is real.

This has not been a conventional review. There is no need to name the characters, name the actors, assign adjectives to their acting. Look at who is in this cast. You know what I think of them. This film must not have seemed strange to them. It's what they do all day, especially waiting around for the director to make up his mind.

What does the title mean? It means it's the title. Get over it.

T

Take ★ ★
R, 99 m., 2008

Minnie Driver (Ana), Jeremy Renner (Saul), Bobby Coleman (Jesse), Adam Rodriguez (Steven), David Denman (Marty Nicols). Directed by Charles Oliver and produced by Chet Thomas. Screenplay by Oliver.

Well, you can't fault the actors. That must mean it's the fault of the writer and director. *Take* is a monotonous slog through dirge land, telling a story that seems strung out beyond all reason, with flashbacks upon flashbacks delaying interminably the underwhelming climax.

Minnie Driver and Jeremy Renner star, and both of their performances would distinguish a better screenplay. She is Ana, a house cleaner, the wife of an elementary school-teacher, the mother of a hyperactive little boy named Jesse (Bobby Coleman). Renner plays Saul, a loser at a very low level, who owes two thousand dollars to a lowlife and works for a storage company. He gets fired by stealing possessions from one locker and planting them in a locker where the contents will be auctioned. He pockets the extra cash. Neat, right? I don't know how the boss finds out about it. Just Saul's rotten luck.

It's one of those days for him. After getting fired, he splits his knuckles while breaking the window of his car, which won't start. Then he begs a pal for the two thousand dollars, and is lent a car and assigned to steal a Range Rover. Then the owner of the Range Rover beats him to a pulp. He finds a gun in the loaner car, slips it in his pocket, and goes to a drugstore to get his ailing dad's prescription filled. Seeing the cashier's window, he decides on the spot to rob the store, and in the process shoots the cashier and takes little Jesse as hostage. If only he hadn't been fired, a lot of people would have been saved a lot of trouble.

These events are doled out parsimoniously by Charles Oliver, who wrote and directed, intercutting with Ana driving her own broken-down car and towing a trailer. She is driving to the prison where Saul is scheduled to be executed, and wants to talk to him before he dies.

Although there is an enigmatic phone call over the opening credits that may explain this, I am not at all sure how by this point she seems to have misplaced her husband.

Meanwhile (the whole movie takes place meanwhile), we see Saul sitting chained to a chair, being walked down corridors, being prepared for death, and then having a long theological chat with the prison chaplain. The chaplain is certainly a good sport, trying to convince the murderer that everything is part of God's plan. Saul is not too bright, but he cannot quite see how what he has done and what is being done to him represent good planning.

Ana and Saul do indeed meet and talk, but if you're hoping for a conversation along the lines of *Dead Man Walking*, you'll be disappointed. I spent more time wondering how long it takes to try to execute a prisoner in whatever state this is, since Saul still has a not-quite healed scar from the Range Rover beating, and a Band-Aid from the window smashing.

One critic of the movie accuses it of having a sneaky ending that suggests it might all have been a dream. I guess that would explain the emphasis placed on close-ups showing Ana and Saul staring at each other's ID patches on their uniforms. Maybe they imagined each other's lives? But then why would they meet? The backseat shot that may have misled the critic is obviously only in Ana's imagination. Little Jesse can't really be there. After all that's happened, do you think she would walk off and leave her son unattended in a prison parking lot?

Taken ★ ★ ½
PG-13, 91 m., 2009

Liam Neeson (Bryan Mills), Famke Janssen (Lenore), Maggie Grace (Kim). Directed by Pierre Morel and produced by Luc Besson. Screenplay by Besson and Robert Mark Kamen.

If CIA agents in general were as skilled as Bryan Mills in particular, bin Laden would have been an American prisoner since late September 2001. *Taken* shows him as a one-man rescue squad, a master of every skill, a laser-eyed, sharpshooting, pursuit-driving, pocket-picking, impersonating, knife-fighting, torturing, karate-fighting killing machine who can cleverly turn over a petrol tank with one pass in his car and strategically ignite it with another.

We meet Mills (Liam Neeson) in "sort of retirement" in Los Angeles, grilling steaks with old CIA buddies and yearning to spend more time with his seventeen-year-old daughter, Kim (Maggie Grace). Kim now lives with her mom, Mills's ex-wife (Famke Janssen), and her effortlessly mega-rich husband (Xander Berkeley), whose idea of a birthday present is giving Kim, not a pony, but what looks like a thoroughbred.

Mills has seen action in Afghanistan and apparently everywhere else and knows it's a dangerous world for a naive teenage girl. He is against Kim spending the summer in Paris with her girlfriend, even though "cousins" will apparently chaperone. He's right. Kim and her pal succeed in getting themselves kidnapped the afternoon of the same day they get off the plane, although Kim has time for one terrified phone call to Dad before she's taken.

Now listen to this. Using CIA contacts at Langley, Mills is able to use his garbled tape of their conversation to determine the name of his girl's kidnapper (Marko), that he is Albanian, that his ring kidnaps young tourists, drugs them, and runs them as prostitutes; the virgins are auctioned off to Arab sheiks and so on. Headquarters also tells Mills he has ninety-six hours to rescue his daughter before she meets a fate worse than death, followed by death.

With this kind of intelligence, the CIA could be using bin Laden's Visa card in every ATM in Virginia. It's the setup for a completely unbelievable action picture where Mills is given the opportunity to use one element of CIA spy craft after another, read his enemies' minds, eavesdrop on their telephones, spy on their meetings, and, when necessary, defeat roomfuls of them in armed combat. At one point a former colleague in the Paris police says he has left seven bodies behind. Mills is just getting warmed up. How this man and his daughter could hope to leave France on a commercial flight doesn't speak

highly of the French police—and the new *Pink Panther* doesn't open for a week. Oh, why does he have only ninety-six hours? To provide the movie with a handy deadline, that's why.

It's always a puzzle to review a movie like this. On the one hand, it's preposterous. But who expects a Bourne-type city-wrecking operative to be plausible? On the other hand, it's very well made. Liam Neeson brings the character a hard-edged, mercilessly focused anger, and director Pierre Morel hurtles through action sequences at a breathless velocity. If Kim is an empty-headed twit, well, she's offscreen most of the time, and the villains are walking showcases for testosterone gone bad. The only tiny glitch is that if one chase scene doesn't use the same ramp down to a construction site that the opening of *Quantum of Solace* did, it sure looks like it does.

The film reopens a question I've had. A lot of movies involve secret clubs or covens of rich white men who meet for the purposes of despoiling innocent women in despicable perversity. The men are usually dressed in elegant formal wear, smoke cigars, and have champagne poured for them by discreet servants. Do such clubs actually exist? Since every member would be blackmailable, how can they survive? If you lost everything in a Ponzi scheme, would you betray your lodge members? Just wondering.

The movie proves two things: (1) Liam Neeson can bring undeserved credibility to most roles just by playing them, and (2) Luc Besson, the cowriter, whose action assembly line produced this film, turns out high-quality trash, and sometimes much better (*The Fifth Element, Taxi, The Transporter, La Femme Nikita,* even *The Three Burials of Melquiades Estrada*). The bottom line is, if you can't wait for the next Bourne thriller, well, you don't have to. I can easily wait, but Truth in Reviewing compels me to confess that if the movie I was describing in the first paragraph sounded as if you'd like this, you probably will. ☞

The Taking of Pelham 1 2 3 ★ ★ ½
R, 106 m., 2009

Denzel Washington (Walter Garber), John Travolta (Ryder), John Turturro (Camonetti),

439

Luis Guzman (Phil Ramos), Michael Rispoli (John Johnson), James Gandolfini (Mayor). Directed by Tony Scott and produced by Scott, Todd Black, Jason Blumenthal, and Steve Tisch. Screenplay by Brian Helgeland, based on the novel by John Godey.

There's not much wrong with Tony Scott's *The Taking of Pelham 1 2 3* except that there's not much really right about it. Nobody gets terrifically worked up except the special effects people. Oh, John Travolta is angry and Denzel Washington is determined, but you don't sense passion in the performances. They're about behaving, not evoking.

The story, you already know from cable reruns. There are a few changes: The boss hijacker is now an ex-con instead of a former mercenary. The negotiator is now a transit executive, not a cop. The ransom has gone up from $1 million to $10 million. The special effects are much more hyperkinetic and absurd than before, which is not an improvement. When a police car has a high-speed collision, the result is usually consistent with the laws of gravity and physics. It does not take flight and spin head over heels in the air.

The Washington and Travolta roles were played the first time around by Walter Matthau and Robert Shaw. They fit into them naturally. Matthau in particular had a shaggy charm I am nostalgic for. Shaw brought cold steel to the film. Denzel is . . . nice. Sincere. Wants to clear his name. Travolta is so ruthless it comes across as more peremptory than evil.

Since time immemorial, Vehicular Disaster Epics have depended on colorful and easily remembered secondary passengers: nuns with guitars, middle-aged women with swimming medals, a pregnant woman about to go into labor, etc. This time the passengers on the Pelham line disappoint. There's a nice woman who's worried about her child, and an ex–Army Ranger who comes to her aid. That's about it. Few of the juicy ethnic stereotypes of the original.

In fact, the whole film is less juicy. The 1974 version took place in a realistic, well-worn New York City. This version occupies a denatured action movie landscape, with no time for local color and a transit system control room that humbles Mission Control. That

may also explain its lack of time to establish the supporting characters, even Travolta's partners. These sleek modern actioners don't give the audience credit for much patience and curiosity. One star or the other has to be on the screen in almost every scene. The relentless pace can't be slowed for much dialogue, especially for supporting characters. It all has to be mindless, implausible action.

Say what you will about the special effects of the 1970s, at least I was convinced I was looking at a *real train*. Think this through with me: Once you buy in to the fact that the train is *there*, the train becomes a given. You're thinking, ohmygod, what's going to happen to the train? With modern CGI, there are scenes where a real train is obviously not on the screen, at least not in real time and space, and you're thinking, ohmygod, real trains can't go that fast. And when cars crash, cars should crash. They shouldn't behave like pinballs.

Note: Here's an interesting thing. Looking up my 1974 review, I found that four of the characters were named Blue, Green, Grey, and Brown. Could it be that when Quentin Tarantino was writing about Mr. White, Mr. Orange, Mr. Blonde, and Mr. Pink in Reservoir Dogs, *he was . . . naw, it's gotta be just a coincidence.*

The Tale of Despereaux ★ ★ ★
G, 93 m., 2008

Matthew Broderick (Despereaux), Dustin Hoffman (Roscuro), Emma Watson (Princess Pea), Tracey Ullman (Miggery Sow), Kevin Kline (Andre), William H. Macy (Lester), Stanley Tucci (Boldo), Ciaran Hinds (Botticelli), Robbie Coltrane (Gregory). Directed by Sam Fell and Rob Stevenhagen and produced by Gary Ross and Allison Thomas. Screenplay by Ross, based on the book by Kate DiCamillo.

The Tale of Despereaux is one of the most beautifully drawn animated films I've seen, rendered in enchanting detail and painterly colors by an art department headed by Olivier Adam. A story centering around a big-eared little mouse named Despereaux, a sniffy rat named Roscuro, and various other members of the animal and vegetable kingdoms, it is a joy to look at frame by frame, and it would be worth getting the Blu-ray to do that.

I am not quite so thrilled by the story, which at times threatens to make *Gormenghast* seem straightforward. There are three societies with interconnections (mouse, rat, and human), plus a man made of vegetables who possibly runs his social life out of the produce market, and maybe dates dates. Very old joke:

"You got dates?"

"I got no dates, mister."

"Then you got nuts?"

"Hey, mister! If I had nuts, I'd have dates!"

Roscuro (with a Ratso voice by Dustin Hoffman) is first on the scene, racing from a ship in port to sniff at the kingdom's annual spring festival, celebrated by the royal chef Andre (Kevin Kline) by creating a new soup to be shared by every citizen. Alas, Roscuro falls in the soup of the queen, who then falls in the soup herself and puts the king in mourning. He then banishes soup and rats from his realm, which is little matter to the rats, who have a highly evolved civilization somewhere below stairs.

The movie then intercuts between the plights of Princess Pea (Emma Watson) and the wretched scullery maid Miggery Sow (Tracey Ullman) upstairs; the big-eared Despereaux and his parents and teacher midstairs; and a rivalry between Roscuro and the scheming Botticelli (Ciaran Hinds) in the cellars.

Their antagonism leads to a gladiatorial combat, suggesting that the rats have a history as rich as the humans, and also that by this point some kids are going to want the nice mouse back again. The movie is based on a Newbery Award–winning novel by Kate DiCamillo, unread by me, but somehow puts me in mind of another wonderful mouse story, *Ben and Me,* by the great Robert Lawson.

I suppose the plot will be easier for DiCamillo's readers to untangle, and that those too young or too old to have read it will nevertheless appreciate the look of the film. What I'd like to see is this same team take on a better-organized screenplay. Has anyone read the *Gormenghast* trilogy? There's a classic that would seem just about right with this look.

Talk to Me ★ ★ ★ ½
R, 118 m., 2007

Don Cheadle (Petey Greene), Chiwetel Ejiofor (Dewey Hughes), Cedric the Entertainer ("Nighthawk" Bob Terry), Taraji P. Henson (Vernell Watson), Mike Epps (Milo Hughes), Martin Sheen (E. G. Sonderling), Vondie Curtis Hall (Sunny Jim Kelsey). Directed by Kasi Lemmons and produced by Mark Gordon, Sidney Kimmel, Joe Fries, and Josh McLaughlin. Screenplay by Michael Genet and Rick Famuyiwa.

The story of Petey Greene was a movie waiting to be made. Greene came out of prison to become, literally overnight, a popular and influential deejay. He was on WOL, a Washington, D.C., station that was looking for a morning man to connect with its African-American audience and got more than it bargained for. Don Cheadle gives a fascinating performance as a man able to step out of a cell and into a broadcast booth, but not sure where to step next.

The movie, directed by Kasi Lemmons (*Eve's Bayou*, best movie of 1997), remembers a time in the 1960s when the word "Negro" was replaced by "black," when R&B performers like Sam Cooke redefined popular music, when the civil rights movement brought enormous change, and when the assassination of Dr. Martin Luther King Jr. brought despair and anger. The man on the radio in the morning in Washington would stand at the center of these events.

The movie begins with a whirlpool of comedy and manic energy and then grows, as it must, more serious and introspective. Cheadle, that superb actor, embodies the complexities of Petey Greene in a performance that goes from high through second into low (that's harder and more interesting than the usual shifting). When we first meet him, he's a deejay in prison, pumping R&B and his colorful vocabulary out to his fellow inmates. He seems incapable of uttering a boring word.

WOL program director Dewey Hughes (Chiwetel Ejiofor), visiting his brother Milo (Mike Epps) in prison one day, hears Petey and meets him. He casually asks Petey to look him up when he gets out, possibly picturing Petey sorting a stack of mail or emptying wastebaskets. Petey doesn't see it that way. A self-described con man, he talks his way out of prison and into Dewey's office, demanding the deejay job he thinks (or pretends) he has

441

been offered. Helping him charge over the office staff on his way to the inner sanctum is his girlfriend, Vernell, played by Taraji P. Henson as an unstoppable force and immovable object rolled into one.

Of course Petey is not hired as a deejay. And then of course eventually he is. This happens to the amazement of Sunny Jim, the current morning man (Vondie Curtis Hall), another deejay (Cedric the Entertainer), and WOL's owner (Martin Sheen). Petey's progress provides a roll of high comedy; it's remarkable to see the somber, courageous Don Cheadle of *Hotel Rwanda* take flight here like Chris Rock or Jim Carrey. Picture by picture, he is showing us he can do just about anything.

It would be hard to believe that an ex-con could go to work almost immediately in a coveted time slot, but the movie, based on fact, shows how it happened, and Cheadle is convincing as a man who could win the instant trust and affection of his listeners. Petey was manifestly the real thing, and Cheadle, whether or not he listened to tapes from that time, persuades us. Chiwetel Ejiofor plays a balancing act as Dewey the program director; caught between his cautious, fearful boss (Sheen) and a talent on fire, he improvises with the anarchic situation. Michael Genet, the film's cowriter, is Hughes's son and must be retailing lots of family memories.

The film's turning point comes with the shooting of Dr. King. A wave of disbelief and grief sweeps the land, and the young and angry make a reality of James Baldwin's prediction, "the fire next time." Going on the air the next morning, Petey does not precisely cool the anger of his listeners; he speaks reasonably, from the heart and from his life, of the uselessness of violence. It is his finest moment, a historic one. This unexpected angle on the King assassination, focusing on the pain of the living, is handled by Lemmons with deep feeling. She takes an event of enormous, almost incomprehensible tragedy and focuses it on Petey Greene's personal transformation.

The last third of the film follows Greene's life as Hughes tries to manage him into a career as a standup. It is brave and honest of Lemmons and her writers to follow Petey into deep waters, and there is a television appearance that I felt in the pit of my stomach. When

you're lucky enough to do what you're born to do, you can hardly fail. Petey Greene was born to be a talk radio star. But Dewey doesn't understand that it stops there.

The fame of broadcast personalities is by its nature transient. How many people remember Petey Greene? Or, under a certain age, have heard of him? Jay Leno could go on a Jaywalk for miles and not find anybody who has heard of Arthur Godfrey. We labor through life sweeping our memory ahead of us into the dustbin of oblivion. But someone like Petey Greene made a difference and made a mark, and broadcasting is better because of his transparent honesty. He helped transform African-American stations more, probably, than their mostly white owners desired. And talk talents like Howard Stern, whether or not they know who he was, owe him something.

Taxi to the Dark Side ★ ★ ★ ★
R, 106 m., 2008

Featuring Alex Gibney (Narrator), Moazzam Begg, William Brand, Jack Cloonan, Damien Corsetti, Ken Davis, Carlotta Gall, Tim Golden, Scott Horton, Tony Lagouranis, Carl Levin, Alfred McCoy, Alberto Mora, Anthony Morden, Glendale Walls, Lawrence Wilkerson, Tim Wilner, John Yoo. A documentary written and directed by Alex Gibney and produced by Gibney, Eva Orner, and Susannah Shipman.

"We have to work the dark side."

So said Dick Cheney a few days after 9/11, discussing the war on terror. Is this what he meant? In December 2002, an Afghan named Dilawar had scraped together enough money to buy a taxi. He was fingered by a paid informant as a terrorist connected with a rocket attack. Taken to the American prison at Bagram, he was tortured so violently that he died after five days. An autopsy showed that his legs were so badly mauled they would have had to be amputated, had he lived. Later, the informant who collected U.S. money for fingering him was proven to be the terrorist actually responsible for the crime the innocent Dilawar was charged with.

An official report said Dilawar died of "natural causes." The *New York Times* found an autopsy report describing the death as a homicide. After a belated investigation, a few U.S. soldiers were accused of the murder. No officers were involved. Dilawar was the first casualty after we started to work the dark side. In all the torture scandals since, few officers have ever been charged. If all of these crimes took place without their knowledge, they would appear to be guilty of dereliction of duty, if nothing else.

Alex Gibney's horrifying documentary *Taxi to the Dark Side* uses the death of Dilawar as an entry point into a remorseless indictment of the Bush administration's unofficially condoned policy of the torture of suspects, which is forbidden by American constitutional and military law and international agreements, but justified under the "necessity" of working the dark side. Gibney interviews U.S. soldiers who participated in such torture sessions (under orders, they thought, although their superiors claimed innocence, all the way up to Bush, who claimed ignorance of torture even after he had seen official Pentagon and intelligence reports). They seem sorry, sobered, and confused.

The film, one of this year's Oscar nominees for best documentary, has TV footage of administration officials demonstrably lying about what they knew and when they knew it. And it leads to Gibney's conversation with his own father, who was an interrogator of prisoners in World War II, and says not only was such behavior forbidden, but it wouldn't have worked anyway. If you torture a man long enough, he will tell you anything to make you stop. If you act on that "information," you are likely on a fool's errand.

Gibney is the same filmmaker who made the merciless *Enron: The Smartest Guys in the Room* (2005), a documentary where he produced actual tape recordings of Enron operatives *creating* the California "power shortage" by ordering power plants shut down and joking that a few grandmothers might have to die without air conditioning in order for Enron to make more millions. By the same logic, lives may have to be lost to torture to produce intelligence, although there is precious little evidence that the strategy has worked. And besides, is that what we do, as Americans? Are those our values? Then what do we stand for?

Gibney widens the net to include the illegal detainees at Guantanamo, most of whom have never been charged with any crime. He talks with former administration officials and spokesmen who didn't like what they were seeing and resigned. His conversations with the American torturers themselves are the most heartbreaking; young kids for the most part, they thought they were doing their duty. And he includes never-before-seen photos and images of torture at work. One tactic: Prisoners have their hands tied above their heads and are made to balance on boxes in pools of electrified water. Would they really be electrocuted if they fell off? Would you like to try? John McCain, who endured unimaginable torture, is among the most outspoken critics of this strategy.

There are those, their numbers shrinking every day, who would agree we have to "work the dark side." Growing numbers of us are yearning for the light. This movie does not describe the America I learned about in civics class or think of when I pledge allegiance to the flag. Yet I know I will get the usual e-mails accusing me of partisanship, bias, only telling one side, etc. What is the other side? See this movie and you tell me.

Tell No One ★ ★ ★ ½
NO MPAA RATING, 125 m., 2008

Francois Cluzet (Alexandre Beck), Andre Dussollier (Jacques Laurentin), Marie-Josee Croze (Margot Beck), Kristin Scott Thomas (Helene Perkins), Nathalie Baye (Elysabeth Feldman), Francois Berleand (Eric Levkowitch), Jean Rochefort (Gilbert Neuville), Guillaume Canet (Philippe Neuville), Gilles Lellouche (Bruno), Marina Hands (Anne Beck). Directed by Guillaume Canet and produced by Alain Attal. Screenplay by Canet and Philippe Lefebvre, based on a novel by Harlan Coben.

Tell No One will play as a terrific thriller for you if you meet it halfway. You have to be willing to believe. There will be times you think it's too perplexing, when you're sure you're witnessing loose ends. It has been devised that way, and the director knows what he's doing. Even when it's baffling, it's never boring. I've heard of airtight plots. This one is not merely airtight, but hermetically sealed.

The setup is the simple part. We meet a married couple, sweethearts since childhood: Alex (Francois Cluzet) and Margot (Marie-Josee Croze). They go skinny-dipping in a secluded pond and doze off on a raft. They have a little quarrel, and Margot swims ashore. Alex hears a scream. He swims to the dock, climbs the ladder, and is knocked unconscious.

Flash forward eight years. Alex is a pediatrician in a Paris hospital. He has never remarried and still longs for Margot. Two bodies are found buried in the forest where it is believed she was murdered, and the investigation is reopened. Although Margot's case was believed solved, suspicion of Alex has never entirely died out. He was hit so hard before falling back into the water that he was in a coma for three days. How did he get back on the dock?

Now the stage is set for a dilemma that resembles in some ways *The Fugitive*. Evidence is found that incriminates Alex: a murder weapon, for example, in his apartment. There is the lockbox that contains suspicious photographs and a shotgun tied to another murder. Alex is tipped off by his attorney (Nathalie Baye) and flees out the window of his office at the hospital just before the cops arrive. "You realize he just signed his own confession?" a cop says to the lawyer.

Alex is in very good shape. He runs and runs, pursued by the police. It is a wonderfully photographed chase, including a dance across both lanes of an expressway. His path takes him through Clignancourt, the labyrinthine antiques market, and into the mean streets on the other side. He shares a Dumpster with a rat. He is helped by a crook he once did a favor for; the crook has friends who seem to be omnipresent.

Ah, but already I've left out a multitude of developments. Alex has been electrified by cryptic e-mail messages that could only come from Margot. Is she still alive? He needs to elude the cops long enough to make a rendezvous in a park. And *still* I've left out so much—but I wouldn't want to reveal a single detail that would spoil the mystery.

Tell No One was directed and coscripted by Guillaume Canet, working from a novel by American author Harlan Coben. It contains a rich population of characters but has been so carefully cast that we're never confused. There

are Alex's sister (Marina Hands), her lesbian lover (Kristin Scott Thomas), the rich senator whose obsession is racehorses (Jean Rochefort), Margot's father (Andre Dussollier), the police captain who alone believes Alex is innocent (Francois Berleand), the helpful crook (Gilles Lellouche), and the senator's son (Guillaume Canet himself). Also a soft-porn fashion photographer, a band of vicious assassins, street thugs, and on and on. And the movie gives full weight to these characters; they are necessary and handled with care.

If you give enough thought to the film, you'll begin to realize that many of the key roles are twinned, high and low. There are two cops closely on either side of retirement age. Two attractive brunettes. A cop and a crook who have similar personal styles. Two blondes who are angular professional women. Two lawyers. One of the assassins looks a little like Alex but has a beard. Such thoughts would never occur during the film, which is too enthralling. But it shows what love and care went into the construction of the puzzle.

One of the film's pleasures is its unexpected details. The big dog Alex hauls around. The Christian Louboutin red-soled shoes that are worn on two most unlikely occasions. The steeplechase right in the middle of everything. The way flashbacks are manipulated in their framing so that the first one shows less than when it is reprised. The way solutions are dangled before us and then jerked away. The computer technique. The tortuous path taken by some morgue photos. The seedy lawyer, so broke his name is scrawled in cardboard taped to the door. Alex patiently tutoring a young child. That the film clocks at only a whisper above two hours is a miracle.

And then look at the acting. Francois Cluzet is ideal as the hero: compact, handsome in a fortyish Dustin Hoffman sort of way, believable at all times (but then, we know his story is true). Marie-Josee Croze, with enough psychic weight she's present even when absent. Kristin Scott Thomas, not the outsider she might seem. Legendary Jean Rochefort, in a role legendary John Huston would have envied. Legendary Francois Berleand as a senior cop who will make you think of Inspector Maigret. And legendary Andre Dussollier sitting on the bench until the movie needs the bases cleared. Here is how a thriller should be made.

Terminator: Salvation ★ ★
PG-13, 115 m., 2009

Christian Bale (John Connor), Sam Worthington (Marcus Wright), Anton Yelchin (Kyle Reese), Bryce Dallas Howard (Kate Connor), Moon Bloodgood (Blair Williams), Common (Barnes), Jadagrace Berry (Star), Helena Bonham Carter (Dr. Serena Kogan), Jane Alexander (Virginia). Directed by McG and produced by Moritz Borman, Jeffrey Silver, Victor Kubicek, and Derek Anderson. Screenplay by John Brancato and Michael Ferris.

One of Hollywood's oldest axioms teaches us: The story comes first. Watching *Terminator Salvation,* it occurred to me that in the new Hollywood, the story board comes first. After scrutinizing the film, I offer you my summary of the story: Guy dies, finds himself resurrected, meets others, fights. That lasts for almost two hours.

The action scenes, which is to say, 90 percent of the movie, involve Armageddon between men and machines ten years in the future. The most cheerful element of the film is that they've perfected Artificial Intelligence so quickly. Yes, Skynet is self-aware and determines to wipe out humankind for reasons it doesn't explain. A last-ditch resistance is being led by John Connor, or "J.C." for you Faulkner fans.

Christian Bale plays the role of Connor, in a movie that raises many questions about the lines between man and machine. Raises them and leaves them levitating. However, it has many fights between a humanoid cyborg and robotic Skynet men made of steel. How do these antagonists fight? Why, with their fists, of course, which remains a wonderfully cinematic device. They also shoot at each other, to little effect. In fact, one metal man is covered in molten ore and then flash-frozen, and keeps on tickin'. And listen, Skynet buddies, what Bale thought about that cameraman is only the tip of the iceberg compared to what he thinks about you.

There is nothing visible in this world but a barren wasteland. No towns, no houses, no food, no farms, no nothing. Maybe they live on Spam. The Resistance is run from a submarine commanded by General Ashdown (Michael Ironside), who wants to destroy Skynet and all of its human POWs. Connor, who is not even human, vows to save them. Wait. That's Marcus Wright (Sam Worthington), the guy from the past, who looks so much like Connor that maybe he only thinks he's Wright. Marcus is a convicted murderer from the past, awakened from cryogenic sleep.

I know with a certainty approaching dread that all of my questions will be explained to me in long, detailed messages from *Terminator* experts. They will also charge me with not seeing the movie before I reviewed it. Believe me, I would have enjoyed traveling forward through time for two hours, starting just before I saw the movie. But in regard to the answers to my questions: You know what? I *don't care.*

I regret (I suppose) that I did not see the first *Terminator* movie. *Terminator 2: Judgment Day* (1991) was a fairly terrific movie, set in the (then) future, to prevent the nuclear holocaust of 1997. You remember that. It was *about something.* In it, Edward Furlong was infinitely more human as John Connor than Christian Bale is in this film. Think about that.

Schwarzenegger, indeed, reappears in this fourth film, thanks to a body double and a special effects face, which makes him, I think, a cyborg of a cyborg. His famous line "I'll be back" is uttered by one John Connor or another, and I hope it draws more chuckles than it did at the screening I attended. Why, those immortal words are chiseled into granite, or at least into the lobby floor at the AMC River East theaters.

If there is one wholly sympathetic character in this film, that would be Blair Williams, played by the fragrant Moon Bloodgood. She murmurs some tender words at the forty-five-minute mark, representing the most complex dialogue up to that point. Dr. Serena Kogan (Helena Bonham Carter) has a longer speech, but you can't be sure it's really her, and she may have been lying.

Anyway, most of the running time is occupied by action sequences, chase sequences, motorcycle sequences, plow truck sequences, helicopter sequences, fighter plane sequences, towering android sequences, and fistfights. It

445

gives you all the pleasure of a video game without the bother of having to play it. ☞

Tetro ★ ★ ★

NO MPAA RATING, 127 m., 2009

Vincent Gallo (Tetro), Alden Ehrenreich (Bennie), Maribel Verdu (Miranda), Klaus Maria Brandauer (Carlo/Alfie), Carmen Maura (Alone). Directed, written, and produced by Francis Ford Coppola.

Tetro may be the most autobiographical film Francis Ford Coppola has made. He said at Cannes, "Nothing in it happened, but it's all true." I guess I know what that means. He could be describing any "autobiographical" film or novel. The pitfall is in trying to find parallels: Coppola had a father who was a famous conductor, he has a brother he has sometimes argued with, his sister Talia Shire somewhat resembles the heroine of this film, his nephew Nicolas Cage somewhat resembles the character Tetro, and on and on. All meaningless.

Better to begin with a more promising starting point: The film is boldly operatic, involving family drama, secrets, generations at war, melodrama, romance, and violence. I'm only guessing, but Coppola, considering his father and his Italian-American heritage, may be as opera-besotted as any living American director, including Scorsese. His great epic *Apocalypse Now* is fundamentally, gloriously operatic. The oedipal issues in the *Godfather* trilogy are echoed again in *Tetro*. The emotions are theatrical, not realistic.

For that, he has the right actor, Vincent Gallo, who devotes himself to the title role with heedless abandon. There is nothing subtle about his performance, and nothing should be. He is the son of a famous conductor, he lives in exile in Buenos Aires, he has a wife who loyally endures his impossibilities. There are events in his past that damaged him, and he is unhappy that his younger brother, Bennie (Alden Ehrenreich), knocks unexpectedly at the door. He never wanted to see him again.

Tetro's wife, Miranda (Maribel Verdu), welcomes the young man, who works as a waiter on a cruise ship now in port for repairs. She wishes she knew more about Tetro's family and the reasons for his unhappiness. Tetro is uniformly hostile to almost everyone except Miranda, perhaps because he needs at least one person to speak with. Bennie bunks down in their apartment, is kept at arm's length from Tetro, is left alone in the flat, finds an unfinished play by Tetro, finishes it, and submits it to a festival run by the nation's most powerful critic, Alone (Carmen Maura). Argentina here is a nation that still has a powerful critic.

All hell breaks loose with Tetro, inspiring a series of flashbacks involving his father, Carlo (Klaus Maria Brandauer), a conductor who carries himself as a grand man. There are, of course, terrible secrets in the family past, known to Tetro but not to Bennie, and they are revealed in a final act worthy of Verdi.

Coppola and his cinematographer, Mihai Malaimare Jr., have photographed the central story in black and white, which made me hopelessly desire that more features could be made in this beautiful format. People who dislike b&w movies are, in their sad way, colorblind. The flashbacks are in color, presided over by Brandauer, as a sleek and contended reptile. In a way, this is what his amoral character in *Mephisto* could have turned out like. Without straining or being given a lot of evil dialogue, he communicates egomania and selfishness.

Bennie has always idealized his older brother, picturing him as a brilliant writer in a faraway land, and is shaken to find the reality; Tetro's first entrance, on crutches, flailing at the furniture, is not promising. Gallo is not naturally given to playing ingratiating characters. He brings an uneasy edge to his work, and it's valuable here in evoking the deep wounds of his youth. Alden Ehrenreich, the newcomer playing Bennie, in his first major role, is confident and charismatic, and inspires such descriptions as "the new Leonardo DiCaprio," which remind me of the old showbiz joke.

Perhaps it was because of the b&w photography, but while watching the film I was reminded for the first time in years of Sidney Lumet's *A View from the Bridge* (1962) and Raf Vallone. It has the same feel of too much emotion trapped in a room, and Gallo channels Vallone's savage drive. It was a good memory. Here is a film that, for all of its plot, depends on characters in service of their emotional turmoil. It feels good to see Coppola back in form.

Theater of War ★ ★ ½
NO MPAA RATING, 96 m., 2009

Featuring Meryl Streep, Tony Kushner, George C. Wolfe, Kevin Kline, Jay Cantor, Austin Pendleton, Barbara Brecht-Schall, Oskar Eustis, Jeanine Tesori, Carl Weber. A documentary directed by John Walter and produced by Nina Santisi.

Meryl Streep strikes me as one of the nicest people you'd ever want to meet. Also one of the great actresses, but her down-to-earth quality is what struck me in *Theater of War*, a documentary about the Public Theater's 2006 production of Bertolt Brecht's *Mother Courage and Her Children* in Central Park. She rehearses, she works with the composer, she never raises her voice, she endures full-dress rehearsals during a heat wave. The only complaint she has is that it's not a good idea for audiences to see a performance in "process" because the work looks like "bad acting."

Theater of War, directed by John Walter, does have access to all the rehearsals and intercuts them with documentary material about Brecht, his theatrical career, his life in exile, and his adventures with the House Un-American Activities Committee. There are also interviews with Streep, translator Tony Kushner, Brecht's daughter Barbara Brecht-Schall, and the director George C. Wolfe, a friend of Brecht's, who witnessed the historic 1949 production in East Berlin.

All of this makes an interesting, if not gripping, film about the play, the playwright, and the lead-up work to a stage production. It also leaves me wanting a great deal more. Perhaps in an attempt to emulate Brecht's antiwar theme, Walter devotes too much screen time to footage of antiwar protests during Vietnam, the Israeli invasion of Lebanon, and the war in Iraq. TV news footage means little and still less when it is sometimes seen integrated into graphics representing 1950s all-American families. Nor do we need to see again that familiar footage of U.S. schoolchildren practicing "duck and cover" in case of a nuclear attack.

Walter is trying to make an antiwar doc on top of his primary subject. Not needed, not effective. There could be more of Streep actually changing a stage moment in rehearsal. More from her costar Kevin Kline. Another costar, Austin Pendleton, appears in many shots but is not even mentioned—and he, I believe, would have talked more openly about "process."

The film recounts Brecht's development as a Marxist playwright who deliberately avoided engaging the audience on an emotional level or encouraging it to identify with his characters. He wanted them to rise above the immediate experience to the level of thought and ideology. We are to realize: "War is bad and everyone loses!" At this he is so successful that I suspect the play is impossible to make truly involving. It is sort of a passion play of the left, a work that inspires more piety than enthusiasm.

One peculiar element involves college lectures on Marxism by the novelist Jay Cantor (*The Death of Che Guevara*). If it is explained why he was necessary in the film, I missed it. His comments are generalized and not pertinent. But, oddly, his students are always seen with black bars over their eyes, like patrons being arrested in a brothel. Brecht was famous for distancing strategies that prevented audiences from getting so swept up in his stories that they didn't focus on their messages. Perhaps these distracting and seemingly unnecessary black bars are, dare I say, a Brechtian device?

The doc lacks the usual scene of the company gathered to read their reviews; just as well, because the production was not well received. Oskar Eustis, artistic director of the Public Theater, has said *Mother Courage and Her Children* is the greatest play of the twentieth century. My money's on *Waiting for Godot*.

There Will Be Blood ★ ★ ★ ½
R, 158 m., 2008

Daniel Day-Lewis (Daniel Plainview), Paul Dano (Paul/Eli Sunday), Kevin J. O'Connor (Henry), Ciaran Hinds (Fletcher), Dillon Freasier (H. W. Plainview). Directed by Paul Thomas Anderson and produced by Anderson, JoAnne Sellar, and

Daniel Lupi. Screenplay by Anderson, based on the novel *Oil!* by Upton Sinclair.

The voice of the oil man sounds made of oil, gristle, and syrup. It is deep and reassuring, absolutely sure of itself and curiously fraudulent. No man who sounds this forthright can be other than a liar. His name is Daniel Plainview, and he must have given the name to himself as a private joke, for little that he does is as it seems. In Paul Thomas Anderson's brutal, driving epic *There Will Be Blood*, Plainview begins by trying to wrest silver from the earth with a pick and shovel, and ends by extracting countless barrels of oil whose wealth he keeps all for himself. Daniel Day-Lewis makes him a great, oversize monster who hates all men, including, therefore, himself.

Watching the movie is like viewing a natural disaster that you cannot turn away from. By that I do not mean that the movie is bad, any more than it is good. It is a force beyond categories. It has scenes of terror and poignancy, scenes of ruthless chicanery, scenes awesome for their scope, moments echoing with whispers, and an ending that in some peculiar way this material demands because it could not conclude on an appropriate note—there has been nothing appropriate about it. Those who hate the ending, and there may be many, might be asked to dictate a different one. Something bittersweet, perhaps? Grandly tragic? Only madness can supply a termination for this story.

The movie is very loosely based on *Oil!*, Upton Sinclair's 1927 novel about a corrupt oil family—based so loosely you can see the film, read the book, and experience two different stories. Anderson's character is a man who has no friends, no lovers, no real partners, and an adopted son he exploits mostly as a prop. Plainview comes from nowhere, stays in contact with no one, and when a man appears claiming to be his half brother, it is not surprising that they have never met before. Plainview's only goal in life is to become enormously wealthy, and he does so, reminding me of *Citizen Kane* and Mr. Bernstein's observation, "It's easy to make a lot of money, if that's all you want to do, is make a lot of money."

There Will Be Blood is no *Kane*, however.

Plainview lacks a "Rosebud." He regrets nothing, misses nothing, pities nothing, and when he falls down a mine shaft and cruelly breaks his leg, he hauls himself back up to the top and starts again. He gets his break in life when a pudding-faced young man named Paul Sunday (Paul Dano) visits him and says he knows where oil is to be found and will share this information for a price. The oil is to be found on the Sunday family ranch, where Standard Oil has already been sniffing around, and Plainview obtains the drilling rights cheaply from old man Sunday. There is another son, named Eli, who is also played by Paul Dano, and either Eli and Paul are identical twins or the story is up to something shifty, since we never see them both at once.

Eli is an evangelical preacher whose only goal is to extract money from Plainview to build his church, the Church of the Third Revelation. Plainview goes along with him until the time comes to dedicate his first well. He has promised to allow Eli to bless it, but when the moment comes, he pointedly ignores the youth, and a lifelong hatred is founded. In images starkly and magnificently created by cinematographer Robert Elswit and set designer Jack Fisk, we see the first shaky wells replaced by vast fields, all overseen by Plainview from the porch of a rude shack where he sips whiskey more or less ceaselessly. There are accidents. Men are killed. His son is deafened when a well blows violently, and Plainview grows cold toward the boy; he needs him as a prop, but not as a magnet for sympathy.

The movie settles down, if that is the word, into a portrait of the two personalities, Plainview's and Eli Sunday's, striving for domination over their realms. The addition of Plainview's alleged half brother (Kevin J. O'Connor) into this equation gives Plainview, at last, someone to confide in, although he confides mostly his universal hatred. That Plainview, by now a famous multimillionaire, would so quickly take this stranger at his word is incredible; certainly we do not. But by now Plainview is drifting from obsession through possession into madness, and at the end, like Kane, he drifts through a vast mansion like a ghost.

The performance by Day-Lewis may well win an Oscar nomination, and if he wins, he should do the right thing in his acceptance speech and thank the late John Huston. His voice in the role seems like a frank imitation of Huston, right down to the cadences, the pauses, the seeming to confide. I interviewed Huston three times, and each time he spoke with elaborate courtesy, agreeing with everything, drawing out his sentences, and each time I could not rid myself of the conviction that his manner was masking impatience; it was his way of suffering a fool, which is to say, an interviewer. I have heard Peter O'Toole's famous imitation of Huston, but channeled through O'Toole he sounds heartier and friendlier and, usually, drunk. I imagine you had to know Huston pretty well before he let down his conversational guard.

There Will Be Blood is the kind of film that is easily called great. I am not sure of its greatness. It was filmed in the same area of Texas used by *No Country for Old Men,* and that is a great film, and a perfect one. But *There Will Be Blood* is not perfect, and in its imperfections (its unbending characters, its lack of women or any reflection of ordinary society, its ending, its relentlessness) we may see its reach exceeding its grasp. Which is not a dishonorable thing.

Things We Lost in the Fire ★ ★ ★
R, 112 m., 2007

Halle Berry (Audrey Burke), Benicio Del Toro (Jerry Sunborne), David Duchovny (Brian Burke), Alison Lohman (Kelly), Omar Benson Miller (Neal), John Carroll Lynch (Howard Glassman), Alexis Llewellyn (Harper Burke), Micah Berry (Dony Burke). Directed by Susanne Bier and produced by Sam Mendes and Sam Mercer. Screenplay by Allan Loeb.

There is one man at the wake who doesn't seem to belong. Scruffy, unshaven, smoking, uncomfortable with himself, he draws aside from the affluent friends of the deceased. Yet he was the dead man's best friend. Jerry Sunborne (Benicio Del Toro) was never approved of by Audrey Burke (Halle Berry), the new widow, but she has invited him to the funeral all the same. She knows her husband would have wanted her to.

As *Things We Lost in the Fire* opens, Audrey was married for eleven years to Brian Burke (David Duchovny, seen in several flashbacks), and they were happy years, giving her two children and a big house in an upscale suburb. Brian was a "genius" at real estate deals, her lawyer tells her, and she has inherited a fortune. But her loneliness haunts her. In a way, it was Jerry's "fault" that her husband died, because Brian visited Jerry's flophouse on his birthday and was killed in a senseless street crime while trying to stop a stranger from beating his wife.

But that was just like Brian, being loyal to his friend and playing a good Samaritan. Jerry and Brian were friends from childhood; Jerry became a lawyer and then a drug addict, and is now trying to get clean and sober at Narcotics Anonymous. And Audrey surprises herself by inviting him to come and live with them, in a room in the garage. No, she's not thinking of falling in love with Jerry—far from it—but she knows her husband would be pleased to see his friend in a safe place, and after all, Audrey and Jerry loved Brian more than anyone else in the world.

The film, directed by the talented Danish filmmaker Susanne Bier, centers on these two damaged people, who do not precisely help each other to recover but at least to not feel so alone. The screenplay by Allan Loeb is a first feature effort, but he has six more films in the works, including one announced by Ang Lee. He is good at following the parallel advances and setbacks of his characters, and especially good at depicting how the children, ten-year-old Harper (Alexis Llewellyn) and six-year-old Dony (Micah Berry, no relation), relate to the newcomer with resentment, then dependence, then uncertainty. The movie also accurately watches how a twelve-step group works, especially in the character of the member Kelly (Alison Lohman), who keeps an eye on Jerry and alerts Audrey to a relapse. Another affecting supporting performance is by John Carroll Lynch, as a tactful neighbor who steers Jerry toward a Realtor's license.

The key performance in the film is by Del Toro, who never overplays, who sidesteps any temptation to go over the top (especially in scenes of his suffering), and whose intelligence as a onetime lawyer shows through his street-worn new reality. He is puzzled and

449

surprised that Audrey invites him into her home, but with his options, it's the best offer he'll ever receive. There is only one scene between them that is ill-advised, and indeed unbelievable, and you'll know the one I mean.

Susanne Bier has made two films I greatly admired, *Open Hearts* (2002) and *Brothers* (2005), but in her American debut she gets a little carried away with style, especially with close-ups, and very especially with close-ups of eyes. I've never see this many great big eyes in a film: Berry's beautiful, Del Toro's bloodshot, the kids' twinkling or doubtful. The human face is the most fascinating subject for the camera, as Ingmar Bergman taught us, but its elements out of context can grow lonely.

I suppose we could be dubious about a great beauty like Halle Berry seeming to be unaware of the strangeness of asking a heroin addict to live in her garage. But I accepted her decision as motivated by a correct reading of what her husband might have wanted her to do. That question settled, the movie is an engrossing melodrama, and it has its heart in the right place.

30 Days of Night ★ ★ ½

R, 113 m., 2007

Josh Hartnett (Eben), Melissa George (Stella), Danny Huston (Marlow), Ben Foster (The Stranger), Mark Boone Junior (Beau). Directed by David Slade and produced by Sam Raimi, Rob Tapert, and Joe Drake. Screenplay by Steve Niles, Stuart Beattie, and Brian Nelson.

A gaunt stranger haunts the streets of Barrow, Alaska, warning: "That cold ain't the weather. That's Death approaching." Since Barrow is said to be the northernmost town in America, three hundred miles of roadless wilderness from its closest neighbor, and thirty days of continuous sunless night are commencing, I expected someone to reply: "You could have fooled me. I thought it was the weather."

But, yes, it is Death, which is very cold. In *30 Days of Night*, Barrow will soon be invaded by vampires, who have apparently trekked across the three hundred miles of roadless ice and snow wearing their street clothes. You'd think they could find easier blood to drink in Fairbanks or Anchorage, but sunlight is fatal to

vampires, and so the month of perpetual night in Barrow lures them like Canadians to Florida.

Their method of attack is the standard one in creature features. They move with loud *whooshes* at lightning speed when you can't quite see them and with ungainly lurches when you can. They are a miserable lot. Count Dracula at least had style and a sense of personal destiny; these guys are merely obsessed with their next meal. They don't even speak that elegant Hammer Films English; they talk like a garbled transmission played backward: *"Qwe!nt raqulo*gg brop#sith!"* The movie, which speaks their language, helpfully provides subtitles. It is intriguing to think of newly converted vampires attending language classes at Berlitz, since I do not think Chomsky's theories of speech apply to the Undead.

But I could go on like this all day—or night, that is. Something about vampire movies brings out the one-liners in me, unless they are directed by Dreyer, Murnau, or Herzog. The fact is, David Slade's *30 Days of Night* is a better-than-average example of the genre, even if it follows the time-honored pattern of supplying a macho man who gathers a hardy band in hiding while the vampires snuffle about. Josh Hartnett plays the local sheriff, who teams up with his estranged wife, Stella (Melissa George), another law enforcer, who missed the last flight out of town. (Planes can't land in Barrow at night. Don't ask me why.)

The survivors hide in an attic, plunder a supermarket, and scheme and plot to outwit the vampires; this time, at least, there is no crusty old-timer to say he's going to make a run for it, because of the three hundred miles of snow, etc. The vampires stalk the frigid streets led by Marlow, played by Danny Huston, who is actually quite convincing in the role. I know he is called Marlow because of the movie's credits; in the film I believe he is referred to as *Sxzé&vw#ich.*

The most interesting aspect of the movie is Barrow itself. Folks are drawn closer together when they live in such extreme circumstances, although how they support themselves is a mystery to me. No mention of drilling for oil, maintaining the pipeline, guarding against missile attacks, hunting whales, carving scrimshaw, etc. They seem to have settled there out of sheer perversity, and I guess they support themselves by selling stuff to one another. Consider that every knife, fork, spoon, and pickup truck had to come in by air transport.

I award the movie two and a half stars because it is well-made, well-photographed, and plausibly acted, and is better than it needs to be. The director, David Slade, previously made the stunningly good *Hard Candy*. Although his vampires quickly disable the town generators, there seems to be a full moon for all thirty days, bathing the streets in a cold light. Otherwise, this would be a radio play.

I have pretty much reached my quota for vampire movies, but I shouldn't hold that against this one. If you haven't seen too many, you might like it. If you are a horror fanboy, you will love it. And in the interest of equal time for the defense, I close with evocative prose by the critic Undeadmin from his five-dagger (out of five) review on DreadCentral.com: "grabs this hoary monster by the throat, pumps it full of the thick rich blood of life, and shoves it out to greet you, eat you, and coat you in glorious mists of red firing from oh-so-many newly exposed arterial sprays."

This Christmas ★ ★ ★

PG-13, 120 m., 2007

Loretta Devine (Shirley Ann "Ma Dear" Whitfield), Delroy Lindo (Joseph Black), Idris Elba (Quentin Whitfield), Regina King (Lisa "Sistah" Moore), Sharon Leal (Kelli Whitfield), Lauren London (Mel Whitfield), Columbus Short (Claude Whitfield), Chris Brown (Michael "Baby" Whitfield), Laz Alonso (Malcolme Moore), Keith Robinson (Devean Brooks), Mekhi Phifer (Gerald), David Banner (Mo). Directed by Preston A. Whitmore II and produced by Whitmore and Will Packer. Screenplay by Whitmore.

I'm not going to make the mistake of trying to summarize what happens in *This Christmas*. If you see it, you'll know what I mean. I'm not even talking about spoilers; I'm talking about all the setups as the Whitfield family gathers for the first time in four years. Everybody walks in the door with a secret, and Ma Dear (Loretta Devine), the head of the family, has two: She has divorced her husband and is living with her boyfriend, Joseph (Delroy Lindo). Almost everyone in the family secretly knows her secrets, but nobody knows most of the others'.

That makes *This Christmas* a very busy holiday comedy, where plot points circle and land on an overcrowded schedule. Once I saw what was happening, I started to enjoy it. Preston A. Whitmore II, the writer and director, must have sat up for long hours into the night in front of hundreds of three-by-five-inch index cards tacked to a corkboard to keep all this straight.

Ma Dear has, let's see—a son who is secretly married to a white woman (whoops, forgot to mention the Whitfields are African-American), a daughter who thinks she's better than everyone else, a daughter who thinks she's in love but may be mistaken, a daughter whose husband fools around on her, a son who owes money big-time to a couple of guys who yearn to break his legs, and a youngest son named "Baby" who is afraid to tell her about his deepest dream.

Ma Dear is played by the irreplaceable Loretta Devine (*Grey's Anatomy, Dreamgirls, Down in the Delta*). In order, the children I listed are played by Columbus Short, Sharon Leal, Lauren London, Regina King, Idris Elba, and Chris Brown. A strong cast, and we do begin to feel a sense of family, because for all their problems, they love one another and accept weaknesses they cannot ignore. They all talk so much, though, that they should get extra credit for having any secrets at all. You tell one person something in this family, and you might as well announce it on *Oprah*.

Every single cast member, and a few I didn't mention, such as wives, boyfriends, and hoodlums, has a couple of big scenes as problems are revealed, reach crisis proportions, and are healed in one way or another. There is also a lot of eating going on, which is necessary at Christmastime, although this isn't a movie like *Soul Food* where everyone is a champion cook.

But what I think audiences will enjoy most is the music. Baby Whitfield's big secret from his mother is—don't tell anyone—he wants to be a singer. She already has one musician son, the one being chased by gamblers, and wants her youngest to do something more respectable.

451

Baby is played by Chris Brown, who is only eighteen and has already sold millions of albums, and who is a hip-hop artist who can actually sing a traditional song in a classic and beautiful style, as he proves on the occasion when his mother finds out his big secret. At a church, gospel artist DeNetria Champ has another showstopper. And the sound track is alive.

This is a movie about African-Americans, but it's not "an African-American movie." It's an American movie, about a rambunctious family that has no more problems than any other family but simply happens to discover and grapple with them in about forty-eight hours. What's surprising is how well Whitmore, the director, manages to direct traffic. He's got one crisis cooling, another problem exploding, a third dilemma gathering steam, and people exchanging significant looks about secrets still not introduced. It's sort of a screwball comedy effect, but with a heart.

This Is England ★ ★ ★ ½
NO MPAA RATING, 98 m., 2007

Thomas Turgoose (Shaun), Stephen Graham (Combo), Jo Hartley (Cynth), Andrew Shim (Milky), Vicky McClure (Lol), Joseph Gilgun (Woody). Directed by Shane Meadows and produced by Mark Herbert. Screenplay by Meadows

A burning need is the first thing we see in Shaun's eyes. He needs a father, he needs to be taller and stronger, he needs to dress like the other kids dress, he needs to fit in somewhere. Shaun, played by Thomas Turgoose in one of those performances that seem more like self-discovery than an act of will, is twelve years old and lives at the shabby end of a town in Yorkshire, not far from the sea. It is July 1983, and his father has been killed in the Falklands War; he takes the death as a kind of betrayal.

There isn't much money in the family. His mother (Jo Hartley) throws up her hands when he complains about his lack of Doc Martens shoes, without which a boy his age might as well stay home. She sacrifices to buy him some look-alikes, and when he complains they're not the real thing, she says they're better: "These are from *London!*" All the same.

Shaun is always getting beaten up and picked on, until one day he cuts through an underpass and meets a gang of skinheads led by Woody (Joe Gilgun). Woody is friendly. Cheers him up. Tells him he can come around again. Soon Shaun has a surrogate family and a new social group and a better self-image, especially when one of the gang girls shaves off his curly hair.

His mother is horrified. She marches Shaun down to the café where the gang hangs out, wants to know who did this to her son, and asks, "Don't you think he's a little young to be hanging around with you lot?" Then, curiously, she leaves Shaun in their care. You could spend a lot of time thinking about why she does that.

Shane Meadows's *This Is England* focuses on a specific tipping-point in the history of English skinheads. As we meet the gang, it is somewhat benign and not racist (Milky, played by Andrew Shim, is Afro-Caribbean). Shaun has, in a sense, a new family, and even gets his first kiss from a goth girl who likes him. Then Combo (Stephen Graham) is released from prison, and with the lessons he learned there he teaches them violence, looting, and racism. When the gang splits in two, Shaun makes the mistake of following Combo, maybe because he is more impressed by his strength than Woody's friendship.

All of this takes place nearly twenty-five years ago in England, but it could take place today in any American city. Poverty, absent fathers, and dangerous streets make gang membership seem like a safe haven, and soon Shaun is aping the bigger guys, swaggering around, disregarding his mother, getting in trouble.

Meadows knows this world. The director of such films as *Once Upon a Time in the Midlands* (2003), a portrait of working-class life, he says he was a skinhead at about Shaun's age. Other films, like Alan Clarke's *Made in Britain* (1982), with its early Tim Roth performance, also show the strange attraction to violence that grows in such gangs: Do they hurt and get hurt out of hatred, alienation, fear, or a compulsion to fit into the gang? When two gangs fight, is that essentially a mutual initiation ceremony? In England, certainly at that time, handguns were not easy to own, so at least the body count was low. Guns and cars make accidental drive-by killings common in Chicago, where the gangs have it easy; when you're on foot, it's rare to murder a six-year-old girl when you're really after her neighbor.

The movie is taut, tense, relentless. It shows why Shaun feels he needs to belong to a gang, what he gets out of it, and how it goes wrong. Without saying so, it also explains why skinheads are skinheads: Any threatened group has a tendency to require its members to adopt various costumes, hair, or presentation styles that mark them as members, so they can't deny it or escape it, and the group can exercise authority even at a distance.

What happens at the end is part of history: Skinheads became allied with the neo-Nazi National Front. They became violent toward nonwhites and immigrants. It wasn't so much that they hated them, perhaps, as that they needed an enemy to validate themselves because they felt as worthless as they said their opponents were. Whenever you see one group demonizing another group, what they charge the others with is often what they fear about themselves. For Shaun, this is more than he was looking for. Better to be lonely than to be deprived of the right to be alone.

A Thousand Years of Good Prayers ★ ★ ★ ½

NO MPAA RATING, 83 m., 2008

Henry O (Mr. Shi), Faye Yu (Yilan), Vida Ghahremani (Madame), Pasha Lychnikoff (Boris). Directed by Wayne Wang and produced by Wang, Yukie Kito, and Rich Cowan. Screenplay by Yiyun Li, based on her short story.

I suppose you could say that Wayne Wang is our leading Chinese-American filmmaker, but I despise categories like that. He's a fine filmmaker, no labels needed. I bring it up only because his new film, A Thousand Years of Good Prayers, is the first Wang movie since 1997 to deal with Chinese themes. His previous feature, Last Holiday (2006), was the lovable comedy starring Queen Latifah at a posh Czech spa.

When I asked Wang about this hiatus in subject matter, he said: "I'm sorry that over the last ten years, the kinds of films that the audience likes to watch have changed, but I will continue to make these films about Chinese-Americans, and in my own way." And that is what he has done in A Thousand Years of Good Prayers.

The critic Todd McCarthy is correct in calling the film Ozu-like. It is an intensely observed, small-scale family drama, involving disagreement between generations. A father from China arrives in America for his first visit in years with his daughter. Their values have grown apart, their lifestyles are opposite, they suppress what they're feeling. This in microcosm is Ozu's Tokyo Story, the only film I ever showed my film class that made some of them cry.

Mr. Shi (Henry O) gets off his flight in San Francisco and looks around for a daughter who should be waiting for him. Yilan (Faye Yu) is a little tardy. She has not seen her father in years, yet does not kiss him. She takes him home to her antiseptic condo. As they have dinner, silences threaten to overwhelm them. He is reluctant to pry too much. She is guarded.

As the film develops, he will pry more, and she will reveal some long-hidden feelings. He will begin to shop for food and cook meals, as an attempt to turn her apartment into a place that feels more like home. She will find excuses to be absent more and more. He will wander around and try to have conversations in his imperfect English.

We see this corner of America through his eyes. He speaks to people he finds around the condo pool and is surprised they don't have to go to work. They are courteous to him, but uninterested. They have never met a "real" Chinese person in their lives, and so what? One day on a park bench he strikes up a conversation with Madame (Vida Ghahremani). She is about his age, is from Iran, which she thinks of as Persia, and is living with her Iranian-American daughter.

Her English is a little better than Mr. Shi's. But they speak the same language, of people who grew up in cultures that value, even venerate, the older generation. Families stayed together across the years. Parents lived at home until they died. Their children did not have "sex lives" until they were in an approved marriage. It was like this here in North America until two or three generations ago. It would have been unthinkable for my Grandmother Anna to live in a nursing home. She lived with a son and a daughter, and her other children visited regularly, my mother every day.

The legendary professor Howard Higman of Boulder once described to me the difference between American and European society: We are horizontal; they are vertical. An American spreads widely into his own generation and times. A European is more conscious of his place on the family tree. Of course, consumerism and television and a laundry list of other factors are making the developing world more horizontal every day.

A Thousand Years of Good Prayers has moments of truth that should have taken place years earlier. They solve almost nothing. How could they? Mr. Shi is genuinely worried about his daughter's happiness. She grows defensive, even angry, when he gives voice to his concerns. So do we all. Quit prying into my life. You don't understand. This is my life, and it's none of your business. "But I'm only trying to help." I don't need any help. I know what I'm doing. Leave me alone.

In observing the reality of this relationship, Wang contemplates the "generation gap" in modern societies all over the world. His film quietly, carefully, movingly observes how these two people of the same blood will never be able to understand each other, and the younger one won't even care to. The term "generation gap" was not used until the 1960s. It hasn't been very helpful. As Wordsworth wrote:

> The world is too much with us; late
> and soon,
> Getting and spending, we lay waste our
> powers;
> Little we see in Nature that is ours;
> We have given our hearts away, a sordid
> boon!

3:10 to Yuma ★ ★ ★ ★
R, 117 m., 2007

Russell Crowe (Ben Wade), Christian Bale (Dan Evans), Logan Lerman (Will Evans), Ben Foster (Charlie Prince), Peter Fonda (Byron McElroy), Vinessa Shaw (Emmy Roberts), Alan Tudyk (Doc Potter), Gretchen Mol (Alice Evans), Dallas Roberts (Grayson Butterfield). Directed by James Mangold and produced by Cathy Konrad. Screenplay by Michael Brandt, Derek Haas, and Halsted Welles, based on a short story by Elmore Leonard.

James Mangold's *3:10 to Yuma* restores the wounded heart of the Western and rescues it from the morass of pointless violence. The Western in its glory days was often a morality play, a story about humanist values penetrating the lawless anarchy of the frontier. It still follows that tradition in films like Eastwood's *Unforgiven,* but the audience's appetite for morality plays and Westerns seems to be fading. Here, the quality of the acting and the thought behind the film make it seem like a vanguard of something new, even though it's a remake of a good movie fifty years old.

The plot is so easily told that Elmore Leonard originally wrote it as a short story. A man named Dan Evans (Christian Bale), who lost a leg in the Civil War, has come to the Arizona territory to try his luck at ranching. It's going badly, made worse by a neighboring bully who wants to force him off his land. The territory still fears Indian raids, and just as much the lawless gang led by Ben Wade (Russell Crowe), which sticks up stagecoaches, robs banks, casually murders people, and outguns any opposition. Through a series of developments that seem almost dictated by fate, Dan Evans finds himself part of a posse sworn in to escort Wade, captured and handcuffed, to the nearby town of Contention, where the 3:10 p.m. train has a cell in its mail car that will transport Wade to the prison in Yuma and a certain death sentence.

Both Dan and Ben have elements in their characters that come under test in this adventure. Dan fears he has lost the confidence of his wife, Alice (Gretchen Mol), and teenage son, Will (Logan Lerman), who doubt he can make the ranch work. Still less does Alice see why her transplanted eastern husband should risk his life as a volunteer. The son, Will, who has practically memorized dime novels about Ben Wade, idealizes the outlaw, and when Dan realizes the boy has followed the posse, he orders him to return home. "He ain't following you," Wade says. "He's following me."

That's an insight into Wade. He plays his persona like a performance. He draws, reads, philosophizes, is incomparably smarter than the scum in his gang. Having spent untold time living on the run with them, he may actually find it refreshing to spend time with Dan, even as his captive. Eventually the two men end up in a room in the Contention hotel, overlooking the street, in earshot of the train whistle, surrounded outside by armed men who want to rescue Ben or kill him.

These general outlines also describe the 1957 version of *3:10 to Yuma*, directed by Delmer Daves, starring Glenn Ford and Van Heflin in the roles of the rancher and the outlaw. The movie, with its railroad timetable, followed the slowly advancing clock in *High Noon* (1952) and was compared to it; when I saw it in 35 mm at Telluride in the 1980s, I thought it was better than *High Noon*, not least because of the personality shifts it involves.

Mangold's version is better still than the 1957 original because it has better actors with more thought behind their dialogue. Christian Bale plays not simply a noble hero, but a man who has avoided such risks as he now takes, and is almost at a loss to explain why he is bringing a killer to justice, except that having been mistreated and feeling unable to provide for his family, he is fed up, and here he takes his stand. Crowe, on the other hand, plays not merely a merciless killer, although he is that, too, but a man also capable of surprising himself. He is too intelligent to have only one standard behavior that must fit all situations, and is perhaps bored of having that expected of him.

Westerns used to be the showcases of great character actors, of whom I was lucky enough to meet Dub Taylor, Jack Elam, Chill Wills, Ben Johnson, and, when she wasn't doing a million other things, Shelley Winters. *3:10 to Yuma* has two roles that need a special character flavor and fills them perfectly. Peter Fonda plays McElroy, a professional bounty hunter who would rather claim the price on Ben Wade's head than let the government execute him for free. And Ben Foster plays Charlie Prince, the second in command of Wade's gang, who seems half in love with Wade, or maybe Charlie's half-aware that's he's all in love. Wade would know which and wouldn't care, except as material for his study of human nature.

Locked in the hotel room, surrounded by death for one or the other, the two men begin to talk. Without revealing anything of the plot, let me speculate that each has found the first man he has met in years who is his equal in conversation. Crowe and Bale play this dialogue so precisely that it never reveals itself for what it really is, a process of mutual insight. One test of a great actor is the ability to let dialogue do its work invisibly, something you can also see in *In the Valley of Elah* with Tommy Lee Jones and Charlize Theron. Too many actors are like the guy who laughs at his own joke and then tells it to you again.

James Mangold first came into view with an extraordinary movie named *Heavy* (1995). His *Walk the Line* (2005) won an Oscar for Reese Witherspoon. To remake *3:10 to Yuma* seems an odd choice after such other modern films as *Girl, Interrupted*, but the movie itself proves he had a good reason for choosing it. In hard times, Americans have often turned to the Western to reset their compasses. In very hard times, it takes a very good Western. Attend well to Ben Wade's last words in this movie, and whom he says them to, and why.

Timecrimes ★ ★ ★

R, 88 m., 2009

Karra Elejalde (Hector), Candela Fernandez (Clara), Barbara Goenaga (Girl), Nacho Vigalondo (Scientist). Directed by Nacho Vigalondo and produced by Esteban Ibarretxe, Eduardo Carneros, and Javier Ibarretxe. Screenplay by Vigalondo.

Time travel in the movies is always about paradox. And it always drives me nuts. Sometimes I enjoy that, in the same way I enjoy chess—and that's a compliment. My mind gets seduced in chess by trains of thought that are hypnotic to me but, if they could be transcribed, would be unutterably boring to anyone else, since you always think of a chess piece in terms of its function, not its name: If this goes here and he moves there and I take that and he takes me back, and I reveal the check and he. . . . And if you're a grand master, I don't imagine you think in many words at all. It's more like, "Hmmmm . . . aha!"

Timecrimes is like a temporal chess game

with nudity, voyeurism, and violence, which makes it more boring than most chess games, but less boring than a lot of movies. It begins by introducing us to an ordinary sort of Spanish guy named Hector (Karra Elejalde), who is sitting on the lawn of his country place using his binoculars and sees a babe stripping in the woods. Now this is important. What he is witnessing is the outset of an event he has already participated in because of time travel. And when he goes to investigate, he runs the risk of running into himself, which, for paradoxical reasons, he already knows. Not this "he." The other "he."

I guess you can make up the rules of time travel as you go along, but whatever they are, they have to be inexorable, and there have to be dire consequences when a mere mortal rips the fabric of the space-time continuum. The reason we don't get more warnings of this danger, you understand, is that travelers into the past tend to do things that inalterably change the future, so that their present no longer exists for them to return to. I love this stuff.

Hector has a main squeeze named Clara (Candela Fernandez), but leaves her to go into the woods and find the Girl (Barbara Goenaga), who has been assaulted by a certain someone—don't get ahead of me here—and then a little later he meets the Scientist (Nacho Vigalondo, the movie's director), who puts him into what turns out to be a time travel machine, which had earlier or maybe later—now you're getting behind me—done something to lead Hector to sit on the lawn, or maybe see himself sitting on the lawn, or maybe—but now I'm ahead *and* behind—and now (earlier or later?) Hector wraps his bloody head (which I have explained in a review I still haven't written) so he will not be recognized by two of the three Hectors, although I am not sure whether this is Hector One, Two, or Three.

I apologize for the 147-word sentence. In time travel, bad things can happen if you stop for very long. One of the crucial requirements is apparently not to meet yourself coming or going, although if you are physically present twice at the same time, what difference does it make if you see yourself, unless it drives you mad? If I were to see myself walk into this room right now, I would simply nod to myself and ask, "Have you finished writing that review yet?" If I replied no, then I would say, "Well, I have, so why don't we eliminate the middle man and you kill yourself?"

That's not too harsh, because I would only be dying in the past of the unfinished review, see, and be here with my work all done. But then again, in that case, how could I have written it before walking into the room in the first place? I couldn't have, that's how, so that means I couldn't walk into the room, and I would continue writing the review just as I am now, which means the paradox would be solved because nothing happened, which, as nearly as I can tell, would be positive proof that time travel exists.

These problems are dealt with in *Timecrimes* in a thrilling scenario involving possible death by falling off of a roof after getting up there in an unorthodox way, and trying to save the life of a woman one of them loves, maybe two, maybe all three. This is all done in an ingenious and entertaining way. As you might imagine, *Timecrimes* is not a character study. Hector doesn't have the time for that, ha ha. In a time travel saga, by the way, it is considered bad form to wonder what makes somebody tick.

(If, after watching *Timecrimes*, you have the strangest feeling that you have seen some of these problems explored before, you are (a) merely experiencing deja vu, which is the low-cost and safe alternative to time travel, or (b) remembering Shane Carruth's splendid *Primer* (2004), which, if it didn't drive you nuts, this one will, or has, or vice versa.)

Tokyo! ★ ★ ½
NO MPAA RATING, 112 m., 2009

A film in three segments: *Interior Design,* with Ayako Fujitani, Ryo Kase, and Ayumi Ito. Directed by Michel Gondry. Screenplay by Gondry and Gabrielle Bell. *Merde,* with Denis Lavant. Directed by Leos Carax. Screenplay by Carax. *Shaking Tokyo,* with Teruyuki Kagawa, Yu Aoi, and Naoto Takenaka. Directed by Bong Joon-ho. Screenplay by Bong.

Three directors, three films, three reasons to rethink moving to Tokyo: You can't find a place to live, there are earthquakes, and a weird goblin may leap from a sewer and grab your sandwich. *Tokyo!* assigns the French filmmakers Michel Gondry and Leos Carax and the Korean Bong Joon-ho to create their own visions of the megalopolis, which would seem to spawn oddly adapted inhabitants.

The best of the three is *Merde*, the centerpiece by Carax, a director whose films are willfully, sometimes successfully, odd. He stars Denis Lavant as a haywire subterranean denizen who pops off a sewer lid, scrambles to the sidewalk, lurches down the street, and rudely assaults pedestrians. He grabs cigarettes, sandwiches, and arms, alarms a baby, terrorizes the populace, and disappears into another manhole.

He is captured and hauled into court, where a translator is found who allegedly speaks his unknown language. Here he wickedly reviles Japan, its citizens, and specifically its women. It remains unclear why he has chosen to live in sewers. This segment is, oddly enough, similar to some Japanese reality shows, such as *The Screamer,* where a man with an ear-piercing scream is photographed by hidden cameras while he sneaks up behind people and lets loose. What a scream.

Shaking Tokyo, directed by Bong Joon-ho, stars Teruyuki Kagawa as a *hikikomori,* a type so familiar the Japanese have a name for it. A hikikomori, usually male, decides to stay inside one day and essentially never leaves. Some have been reported as hermits for up to ten years, living mostly on pizza deliveries. In America we call these people "software engineers." One day the hero is jarred loose from his isolation by a pretty pizza delivery girl, not to mention an earthquake, which sends others into the unpopulated and barren streets for the first time in months.

Michel Gondry's *Interior Design,* an only slightly more conventional tale, stars Ayako Fujitani and Ryo Kase as young lovers new in Tokyo, who undergo personal and physical changes during the ordeal of apartment hunting. Much more I should not say.

Do these films reflect actual aspects of modern Tokyo? The hikikomori epidemic is apparently real enough, but the other two segments seem more deliberately fantastical. The

entertainment value? Medium to high (*Merde*). Tokyo? Still standing.

Tokyo Sonata ★ ★ ★ ½
PG-13, 119 m., 2009

Teruyuki Kagawa (Ryuhei Sasaki), Kyoko Koizumi (Megumi Sasaki), Yu Koyanagi (Takashi Sasaki), Kai Inowaki (Kenji Sasaki), Haruka Igawa (Kaneko), Kanji Tsuda (Kurosu), Koji Yakusho (Thief). Directed by Kiyoshi Kurosawa and produced by Yukie Kito and Wouter Barendrecht. Screenplay by Kurosawa, Max Mannix, and Sachiko Tanaka.

Just as the economic crisis has jolted everyday life, so it shakes up *Tokyo Sonata*, which begins as a well-behaved story and takes detours into the comic, the macabre, and the sublime. All you know about three-act structure is going to be useless in watching this film, even though, like many sonatas, it has three movements.

It opens on a note of routine, of a family so locked into their lives that they scarcely know one another. Ryuhei is a salaryman in a management job. His wife, Megumi, is a source of predictable domesticity, centering on cleaning, sewing, and the preparation of meals. His older son, Takashi, and younger son, Kenji, are filled with unhappiness but seemingly well-disciplined, although Kenji gets in trouble at school: The teacher unfairly blames him for passing along a manga, or graphic novel, and Kenji defiantly says he saw the teacher reading a porno manga on the train. Many men in Japan do the same, no big deal, but hypocrisy is the point.

In the opening scene, Ryuhei (Teruyuki Kagawa) is fired. He comes home, hands over his week's wages, says nothing. He is an autocratic father, filled with anger. The older son, Takashi (Yu Koyanagi), announces he has enlisted for the U.S. Army as a way to gain citizenship, as he sees no future for himself in Japan. His father forbids him.

Unable to lose face by admitting his job loss, Ryuhei leaves "for the office" every day and lingers in a cheerless concrete oasis with other jobless men. There is a soup kitchen. His wife sees him there, knows everything, stays quiet. Young Kenji (Kai Inowaki), no longer attending school, spends his money on piano lessons with the beautiful Kaneko (Haruka Igawa). His father, breaking with the Japanese tradition of encouraging children to study, has already forbidden piano lessons. Why? Perhaps he feels so inadequate he's threatened by any success involving his family.

What we seem to have are the outlines of a traditional family drama, in which tensions are bottled up, revelations will occur, and a crisis will result in either tragedy or resolution. But that's not what we're given by director Kiyoshi Kurosawa, best known for upscale horror films. He almost misleads us in the early scenes, by framing the family dinners in sedate and orderly compositions. We believe we know where *Tokyo Sonata* is going. We are wrong.

No, it doesn't turn into another horror film, or a murder-suicide. It simply shows how lives torn apart by financial emergencies can be revealed as being damaged all along. Unemployment is the catalyst—an unspoken reality that makes everyone in the family angrier than they already are. All of the performances have perfect pitch; the young son engages us in the same way as the hero of Truffaut's *The 400 Blows*.

The directions the film takes I should not reveal. But notice how Kurosawa (no relation) allows his train to leave the tracks. Dramatic events occur that demonstrate how a routine, once broken, cannot easily be repaired. The entrance of a completely unexpected character results in an instinctive acceptance of the new situation, providing a sad payoff to what at first seems merely arbitrary.

At the same time, Kurosawa observes the agony of unemployment in Japan, which, like the United States, has been beset by outsourcing to cheaper labor pools. (The day when China and India begin outsourcing will be a historic turning point.) Ryuhei joins hopeless queues at an employment office. He finds work cleaning toilets in a shopping mall. His humiliation is underlined when all maintenance workers must change into one-piece coveralls at lockers in full view of passing customers. He has an encounter at work that is bizarre.

And then the film finds a form of release in another unexpected scene. Watch it play out. We are blindsided by its beauty. An extended passage is held in a medium-long shot in which nobody moves, and the effect is uncanny. Is there a happy ending? Nothing as simple as that. Simply a new beginning. Debris has been cleared. Old tapes have been destroyed. Freedom has been asserted. Nothing is for sure.

A sonata is a classical form in which two musical ideas are intercut. In the beginning, they are introduced. In the following sections, they are developed in passages revealing the secrets or potentials of both. The conclusion does not resolve them; instead, we return to look at them, knowing what we know now. The "themes" in this movie are the father and his family. At the end they feel the same tensions as at the beginning, but the facade has been destroyed, and they will have to proceed unprotected.

Toots ★ ★ ★
NO MPAA RATING, 84 m., 2008

A documentary directed by Kristi Jacobson and produced by Jacobson, Whitney Dow, and Alicia Sams.

Toots Shor. For twenty years, the most famous saloonkeeper in the world. A huge, towering man with a sloppy grin, a bear hug, a big laugh, a big gut, and a lot of friends. His restaurant at 51 West 51 in Manhattan was where you had to be for the action. The regulars included Jackie Gleason, Sinatra, Mickey Mantle, DiMaggio and Monroe, Babe Ruth. Mobsters like Frank Costello. Boxers like Rocky Graziano and Tony Zale. Walter Cronkite, Mike Wallace, Bogart and Bacall, Hemingway, Yogi Berra, and John Wayne. He wasn't a regular, but Richard Nixon came when he was in town.

A critic trying to explain Astaire and Rogers once said, "He gives her class. She gives him *sex*." That's how the saloon worked. There was no VIP area. Everybody stood at a big circular bar or was clearly visible in booths. Sinatra was maybe a little pleased to nod to Costello, who ran the mob in Manhattan. Costello was maybe pleased to nod back. They were big guys, but they were maybe impressed. It made Costello classier to hang out with Sinatra. It made Sinatra sexier to be the drinking buddy of a godfather. Toots Shor provided a stage for the road company of Damon Runyon's imagination.

New York had eleven newspapers in those days, and all the columnists made a nightly stop. Ed Sullivan, Earl Wilson, Walter Winchell. The best movie ever made about a newspaper columnist, *The Sweet Smell of Success,* was shot on location at Toots Shor. Sportswriters were the newspaper superstars. They sat down with Yogi, Mickey, DiMaggio, Whitey Ford, Frank Gifford. Sportswriters in those days, we learn, were paid as much as the players and could meet them on equal terms. "One of today's baseball stars," Gifford muses in the movie, "makes as much in two weeks as Mickey Mantle made in his entire career."

Toots evokes the era with seductive charm; it's a fascinating memory of a time past, directed by Kristi Jacobson, Toots's granddaughter. She has access to all the archives—an eighteen-hour tape of Shor's memories, video of him on *This Is Your Life* and *What's My Line* and being interviewed by Edward R. Murrow and Mike Wallace, newsreels, photos, newspaper clippings. She draws heavily on eyewitness accounts by Ford, Gifford, Cronkite, Gay Talese, and many others. Her doc plays like a film noir version of *Entertainment Tonight.*

One thing I noticed is that all of the regulars seem to have witnessed famous moments or think they did. They were all there when Toots challenged Gleason to a race around the block, one going one way, one going the other. Gleason lost and paid Toots one thousand dollars. Then he said, "Wait a minute! We never passed each other going around! You stayed right here!" Good story, but then someone says, "Toots took a cab." Unlikely, when he *could* have stayed right there. And very unlikely that these two men, three hundred pounds or up, would have agreed to race around the block, and that all those famous people just happened to be there that afternoon.

But there were lots of famous people and lots of afternoons. Toots drank with them and then with the evening crowd. His loyal bookkeeper complains that in an evening Toots would pick up thousands of dollars of tabs. A veteran waiter remembers that many of the freebie big shots wouldn't even leave a one-dollar tip. Big shots love to be validated by their friendly saloonkeeper, especially if they're both drunks and he calls you "crumb-bum." He even talked to the mob that way.

It came to an end. In 1970, Toots sold his lease for $1.5 million, and a year later opened a new, larger Toots Shor with a loan from the Teamsters. The old mob had lost power with the rise of independent drug dealers. The new gangsters were not by Damon Runyon, but by Martin Scorsese. People no longer drank all night. They went to discos or the Village. Celebrities no longer liked to be on display. Gone were the days when DiMaggio and Monroe left the restaurant and DiMaggio drove them home *himself.* Toots went broke, the money disappeared, he lived another fifteen years, and he was a ghost of the past. The drinking caught up with him, as it had to. Nobody can really hold his liquor; some just do a better job of standing up and going through their acts.

You see *Toots* and you wish you had been there. The Pump Room was something like that in Chicago, or the old Fritzel's and Riccardo's, with Kup the occupant of Booth No. 1. The columnists from the *Trib, Daily News,* and *American*—let 'em sit in the back. For many of us in the 1970s, O'Rourke's on North Avenue was the place where you didn't want to miss anything. Toots would have never understood O'Rourke's. But the night Charlton Heston autographed Michaela Touhy's bra, that he would have understood.

Towelhead ★ ★
R, 128 m., 2008

Aaron Eckhart (Travis Vuoso), Toni Collette (Melina Hines), Maria Bello (Gail Monahan), Peter Macdissi (Rifat Maroun), Summer Bishil (Jasira Maroun), Chris Messina (Barry). Directed by Alan Ball and produced by Ball and Ted Hope. Screenplay by Ball, based on the novel by Alicia Erian.

Towelhead presents material that cries out to be handled with quiet empathy, and hammers us with it. I understand what the film is trying to do, but not why it does it with such crude melodrama. The tone is all wrong for a story of child sexuality and had me cringing in my seat. It either has to be a tragedy or some kind of dark comedy like Kubrick's brilliant *Lolita,* but here it is simply awkward, embarrassing, and painful.

It tells the story of Jasira, a thirteen-year-old Lebanese-American girl with an obsession about her emerging sexuality. Well, all thirteen-year-olds feel such things. That's why so many of them stop talking to us. They don't know how to feel about themselves. Jasira thinks she does. She's turned on by taxi ads for showgirls, by sexy photos, by her own body. She discovers masturbating more or less by accident, likes it, precociously discusses orgasms.

Her American mother (Maria Bello) lives in Syracuse. Her Lebanese father (Peter Macdissi, of *Six Feet Under*) works for NASA in Houston. Neither is the parent of the year in any conceivable year. Her mother discovers her own boyfriend carefully shaving Jasira's pubic hair and is angry with the girl, not the boyfriend. She ships Jasira off to her father in Houston. He can seem cheerful and ingratiating, but slaps her for wearing a T-shirt to the table, forbids her to wear tampons ("only whores and married ladies wear them"), and is boiling with rage—partly because some of his neighbors think he is an Arab, and he is a Lebanese Christian who hates Saddam even more than they do.

Jasira starts babysitting the younger kid next door, who turns her on to his dad's porno magazines. His dad, known only as Mr. Vuoso, is played by Aaron Eckhart, who was brave enough to take on this slimy role. He actually begins with a variation on the ancient theme "come sit over here on the bed next to me," and escalates to rape. That Jasira is fascinated and to some degree encourages him is meaningless; she knows little about what she is encouraging, and apparently thinks of having sex with an adult as merely the sort of thing her reactionary dad would slap her for.

The progress of her journey involves bloody tampons and other details that could be relevant if handled with more sensitivity. She has sex with an African-American fellow student, who seems polite and nice but is experienced enough to know he is doing wrong. Her dad forbids her to see him because he is

black. Meanwhile, Mr. Vuoso's son calls her a towelhead, a camel jockey, and worse. Racism is everywhere here.

The movie was written and directed by Alan Ball, who also wrote *American Beauty.* Two movies, two suburban men obsessed with underage beauties. Is there a pattern here? Ball also created and has directed *Six Feet Under,* which specializes in acute embarrassment and spectacular misbehavior. So does the director Todd Solondz, whose *Welcome to the Dollhouse* (1995) also dealt with a troubled adolescent girl. But Solondz knew how to do it, what his intentions were, how to challenge us and yet involve our sympathy. Ball seems to be merely thrashing about in a plot too transgressive for his skills.

The actors were courageous. Another key role is played by Toni Collette, as a pregnant neighbor who suspects what's going on and tries to help Jasira and offer her refuge from both her father and Mr. Vuoso. Trouble is, Jasira thinks she doesn't want to be rescued and has come to love orgasms, as is not uncommon. She's played by an appealing young actress named Summer Bishil, who certainly looks as if she were thirteen, but was eighteen when the film was made. Without showing nudity, Ball plays tricks with lighting and camera angles that sometimes regard her like a cheesecake model. I didn't enjoy that feeling. When Billy Wilder's lighting gives Marilyn Monroe a teasingly low neckline in *Some Like It Hot,* that's one thing. When Ball's framing provides one for a child, that's another.

Yes, the sexual abuse of children is a tragedy. Yes, there are adults who need to be educated, enlightened, warned, or thrashed and locked up. This is not the film to assist that process. The actors labor to be true to their characters and sincere in their work, and they succeed. The movie lets them down. It is more clueless than its heroine.

Trade ★

R, 120 m., 2007

Kevin Kline (Ray), Cesar Ramos (Jorge), Alicja Bachleda-Curus (Veronica), Paulina Gaitan (Adriana), Marco Perez (Manuelo), Kate Del Castillo (Laura). Directed by Marco Kreuzpaintner and produced by Roland

Emmerich and Rosilyn Heller. Screenplay by Jose Rivera, based on an article by Peter Landesman.

Trade is a movie about trade in human beings, in this case, a thirteen-year-old Mexican girl who is kidnapped and brought to New Jersey, where her virginity will be auctioned on the Internet for an expected $50,000. Chillingly, the movie is based on fact, on an article by Peter Landesman in the *New York Times Magazine*. And it's not an isolated case.

The girl, named Adriana (Paulina Gaitan), is handed off in a smooth cross-country operation. She finds only one friend along the way, a kidnapped older Polish woman named Veronica (Alicja Bachleda-Curus). Their transportation is handled by Manuelo (Marco Perez), a cruel man with a deeply buried streak of morality that begins to trouble him along the road.

The trip from Mexico to New Jersey turns into a chase, although Manuelo and his captives don't know it. Adriana's seventeen-year-old brother, Jorge (Cesar Ramos), sees her (against all odds) kidnapped in Mexico City and follows Manuelo's car all the way to the border by one means or another (against even greater odds). At a crucial moment near the border, he meets a Texas Ranger named Ray (Kevin Kline), and after some verbal scuffles, they join forces to follow Manuelo, rescue his captives, and penetrate to the heart of the slave-smuggling operation.

A nasty, vile business made more slimy because the director, Marco Kreuzpaintner, doesn't trust the intrinsic interest of his story and pumps it up with chase details, close calls, manufactured crises, and so many scenes of the captives being frightened and abused that they begin to seem gratuitous, even suspect. Yes, it is evil that these heartless gangsters, connected with the Russian Mafia, terrorize young women and sell them as objects. But is it not also evil that the film lingers on their plights with almost as much relish as the camera loved the perils of Pauline tied to the railroad tracks?

My description makes the film sound more urgent than it is. The German director seems to have fallen in love with the American genre of the road picture, and there are altogether too many shots of the trip itself, the land it covers, the roadside civilization, the open spaces.

What is fascinating, in a scary way, are the details of the Internet auction business and how it works and the money made in it. When I watch those TV shows where pedophiles are pounced on by cops, I think "entrapment," but you know what? Some people are asking to be entrapped. How about that Florida federal prosecutor who flew to Michigan hoping to meet a five-year-old girl? Your rights to do what you want in your sex life run into a dead end, I believe, when they involve others doing what they don't want.

All obvious, although not to some deranged creeps. But what is the purpose of this movie? Does it manipulate its subject matter a little too much in its quest to be "entertaining"? Why *should* this material be entertaining? Anything that holds our interest can be entertaining, in a way, but the movie seems to have an unwholesome determination to show us the victims being terrified and threatened. When I left the screening, I just didn't feel right.

Traitor ★ ★ ★
PG-13, 113 m., 2008

Don Cheadle (Samir Horn), Guy Pearce (Roy Clayton), Neal McDonough (Max Archer), Said Taghmaoui (Omar), Mozhan Marno (Leyla), Jeff Daniels (Carter), Archie Panjabi (Chandra), Aly Khan (Fareed). Directed by Jeffrey Nachmanoff and produced by Don Cheadle, David Hoberman, Jeffrey Silver, and Todd Lieberman. Screenplay by Nachmanoff.

Traitor weaves a tangled web of conspiracy and intrigue, crosses politics with thriller elements, and never quite answers its central question: In the war between good and evil, how many good people is it justifiable for the good guys to kill? Maybe that question has no answer. It is probably not "none."

The film stars Don Cheadle, an actor who excels at inner conflict, as Samir, born in Sudan, later an undercover special op for the United States. As a youth, he witnessed his father killed by a car bomb. For me, at least, it was not immediately clear who was responsible for the bomb, although his father was a committed Muslim. Was he killed by Muslim haters or by Muslims who opposed his politics? That ambiguity works in the film's favor. As Samir enlists on the American side and then is seen as a remarkably effective agent for terrorist jihadists, we are kept wondering where his true loyalties lie.

The film makes it a point that Samir is devout in the practice of his religion. He often quotes the Quran, is observant, seems to have true spirituality in his soul. He is not pretending. Of course, the great majority of Muslims are against terrorism and any form of murder. Others, as we have seen, are not. In paying attention to this division, *Traitor* establishes the mystery of which side Samir is a traitor to. Is he a double agent for the United States or a triple agent?

The film, written and directed by Jeffrey Nachmanoff, uses locations in Africa, the Middle East, Europe, and America, and provides an inside view of both the jihadists and a special FBI counterterrorism unit. Guy Pearce and Neal McDonough play FBI agents who disagree about the handling of the case; Jeff Daniels is a CIA agent who approaches the plot obliquely. Said Taghmaoui is very effective as Omar, leader of a terrorist group that has grave suspicions about Samir, until Samir is able to disprove them by being jailed, escaping with Omar, providing bomb-building expertise, and creating a chilling scenario for a terrorist attack in the United States.

The movie proceeds quickly, seems to know its subject matter, is fascinating in its portrait of the inner politics and structure of the terrorist group, and comes uncomfortably close to reality. But what holds it together is the Cheadle character, whose true motives remain opaque to the terrorists, the Americans, and the audience.

As we have learned from the spies of Graham Greene and John LeCarre, and from countless police movies, to be effective, an undercover agent must to a considerable degree cooperate with those he is targeting. Sometimes transference takes place. He begins to think like his enemies, to sympathize with them. Since working convincingly for either side requires a capacity for the fanatical, agents can grow confused about where their loyalties lie. It is this confusion that makes *Traitor* effective, except for those who like their moral choices laid out in black and white.

That's what makes the film's pure thriller elements work so well. Even in violent action scenes, the participants are forced to make instant decisions, or discoveries, about loyalties. We know from other movies how the violence will unfold, but neither we nor the combatants are sure which side everybody is on. That is true even of the urbane Omar, who is definitely a jihadist, but whose motives and their effect are paradoxical.

Don Cheadle is such a good actor. If he were more of a showboat, he would be a bigger star. But he remains the go-to man for a film like this. Except in his work like the *Ocean's* pictures or his heroic work in *Hotel Rwanda*, we cannot often be certain what we are to think of his characters. He effortlessly seems too intelligent, too complex, to be easily categorized. Perhaps my doubt about the motives of Samir's father's killers was due only to confusion on my part. Even so, who would witness the death of his father by a bomb and then be driven to become a builder of bombs? And why? It is an uncertainty potent enough to drive the entire movie.

Transformers ★ ★ ★
PG-13, 140 m., 2007

Shia LaBeouf (Sam Witwicky), Megan Fox (Mikaela Banes), Josh Duhamel (Sgt. Lennox), Tyrese Gibson (Tech Sgt. Epps), Rachael Taylor (Maggie Madsen), Anthony Anderson (Glen Whitmann), Jon Voight (John Keller), John Turturro (Agent Simmons). Directed by Michael Bay and produced by Steven Spielberg, Bay, Brian Goldner, and Mark Vahradian. Screenplay by Alex Kurtzman and Roberto Orci.

Now I have fans who say, "We are so sorry, Michael Bay, you still suck, but we love you."

That's what the director of *Transformers* told Simon Ang during an interview in Seoul. He could have been speaking for me. I think Michael Bay sometimes sucks (*Pearl Harbor, Armageddon*), but I find it possible to love him for a movie like *Transformers*. It's goofy fun with a lot of stuff that blows up real good, and it has the grace not only to realize how preposterous it is, but to make that into an asset.

The movie is inspired by the Transformer toys that twist and fold and double in upon themselves, like a Rubik's Cube crossed with a contortionist. A yellow Camaro unfolds into a hulking robot, helicopters become walking death monsters, and an enemy named Megatron rumbles onto the screen and, in a voice that resembles the sound effects in *Earthquake,* introduces himself: "I—AM—MEGATRON!!!"

I think that's the first time I've used three exclamation points. But Megatron is a three-exclamation-point kinda robot. He is the most fearsome warrior of the evil Decepticons, enemies of the benevolent Transformers. Both races (or maybe they're brands) of robots fled the doomed planet Cybertron and have been drawn to Earth because Megatron crash-landed near the North Pole a century ago and possesses the Allspark, which is the key to something, I'm not sure what, but since it's basically an alien MacGuffin it doesn't much matter. (Note to fanboys about to send me an e-mail explaining the Allspark: Look up "MacGuffin" on Wikipedia.)

The movie opens like one of those teen comedies where the likable hero is picked on by bullies at school, partly because he didn't make the football team, and mostly because he doesn't have a keen car. Sam Witwicky (Shia LaBeouf) talks his dad into buying him one, and he ends up with an old beater, a yellow Camaro, that is actually the Transformer named Bumblebee and gets so mad when his paint job is insulted that it transforms itself into a shiny new Camaro.

This is more than a hot car. It plays the sound track to Sam's life. It helps Sam become visible to his sexy classmate Mikaela (Megan Fox), who says, "Do I know you?" Sam mentions casually that they take four classes together and have been in the same school since first grade. The high school stuff, which could be a teenage comedy on its own, segues into the battling robot stuff, and there is some low-key political satire in which the secretary of defense (Jon Voight) runs the country, while the president (not even credited) limits himself to a request for a Ding-Dong.

Voight sends the armed services into action, and we see a lot of Sergeant. Lennox (Josh Duhamel) and Tech Sergeant Epps (Tyrese Gibson). They and their men labor during much of the movie under the optimistic impression that a metal robot the size of a ten-story building can be defeated by, or even brought to notice, automatic weapon fire. Sam and Bumblebee are crucial to the struggle, although a Secret Ops guy (John Turturro) asks the defense secretary, "You gonna lay the fate of the world on a kid's Camaro?"

Everything comes down to an epic battle between the Transformers and the Decepticons, and that's when my attention began to wander, and the movie lost a potential fourth star. First let me say that the robots, created by Industrial Light and Magic, are indeed delightful creatures; you can look hard and see the truck windshields, hubcaps, and junkyard stuff they're made of. And their movements are ingenious, especially a scorpion-like robot in the desert. (The little spider robots owe something to the similar creatures in Spielberg's *Minority Report,* and we note he is a producer of this movie.) How can a pickup truck contain enough mass to unfold into a towering machine? I say if Ringling Bros. can get fifteen clowns into a Volkswagen, anything is possible.

All the same, the mechanical battle goes on and on and on and on, with robots banging into each other and crashing into buildings, and buildings falling into the street, and the military firing, and jets sweeping overhead, and Megatron and the good hero, Optimus Prime, duking it out, and the sound track sawing away at thrilling music, and enough is enough. Just because CGI makes such endless sequences possible doesn't make them necessary. They should be choreographed to reflect a strategy and not simply reflect shapeless, random violence. Here the robots are like TV wrestlers who are down but usually not out.

I saw the movie on the largest screen in our nearest multiplex. It was standing room only, and hundreds were turned away. Even the name of Hasbro, maker of the Transformer toys, was cheered during the titles, and the audience laughed and applauded and loved all the human parts and the opening comedy. But when the battle of the titans began, a curious thing happened. The theater fell dead silent.

463

No cheers. No reaction whether Optimus Prime or Megatron was on top. No nothing. I looked around and saw only passive faces looking at the screen.

My guess is, we're getting to the point where CGI should be used as a topping and not the whole pizza. The movie runs 140 minutes. You could bring it in at two hours, by cutting CGI shots, and have a better movie.

Transformers: Revenge of the Fallen ★
PG-13, 149 m., 2009

Shia LaBeouf (Sam Witwicky), Megan Fox (Mikaela Banes), Josh Duhamel (Captain Lennox), Tyrese Gibson (USAF Tech Sergeant Epps), John Turturro (Gent Simmons/Jetfire), Ramon Rodriguez (Leo), Kevin Dunn (Ron Witwicky), Rainn Wilson (Professor Colan), Julie White (Judy Witwicky), Hugo Weaving (Megatron). Directed by Michael Bay and produced by Ian Bryce, Tom DeSanto, Lorenzo di Bonaventura, and Don Murphy. Screenplay by Ehren Kruger, Roberto Orci, and Alex Kurtzman, based on Hasbro's Transformers action figures.

Transformers: Revenge of the Fallen is a horrible experience of unbearable length, briefly punctuated by three or four amusing moments. One of these involves a doglike robot humping the leg of the heroine. Such are the meager joys. If you want to save yourself the ticket price, go into the kitchen, cue up a male choir singing the music of hell, and get a kid to start banging pots and pans together. Then close your eyes and use your imagination.

The plot is incomprehensible. The dialogue of the Autobots, Deceptibots, and Otherbots is meaningless word flap. Their accents are Brooklynese, British, and hip-hop, as befits a race from the distant stars. Their appearance looks like junkyard throw-up. They are dumb as rocks. They share the film with human characters who are much more interesting, and that is very faint praise indeed.

The movie has been signed by Michael Bay. This is the same man who directed *The Rock* in 1996. Now he has made *Transformers: Revenge of the Fallen*. Faust made a better deal. This isn't a film so much as a toy tie-in. Children holding a Transformer toy in their hand can invest it with wonder and magic, imagining it doing brave deeds and remaining always their friend. I knew a little boy once who lost his blue toy truck at the movies and cried as if his heart would break. Such a child might regard *Transformers: Revenge of the Fallen* with fear and dismay.

The human actors are in a witless sitcom part of the time, and a lot of the rest of their time is spent running in slo-mo away from explosions, although—hello!—you can't outrun an explosion. They also make speeches like this one by John Turturro: "Oh, no! The machine is buried in the pyramid! If they turn it on, it will destroy the sun!" "Not on my watch!" The humans, including lots of U.S. troops, shoot at the Transformers a lot, although never in the history of science fiction has an alien been harmed by gunfire.

There are many great-looking babes in the film, who are made up to a flawless perfection and look just like real women, if you are a junior fanboy whose experience of the gender is limited to lad magazines. The two most inexplicable characters are Ron and Judy Witwicky (Kevin Dunn and Julie White), who are the parents of Shia LaBeouf, who Mephistopheles threw in to sweeten the deal. They take their son away to Princeton, apparently a party school, where Judy eats some pot and goes berserk. Later they swoop down out of the sky on Egypt, for reasons the movie doesn't make crystal clear, so they also can run in slo-mo from explosions.

The battle scenes are bewildering. A Bot makes no visual sense anyway, but two or three tangled up together create an incomprehensible confusion. I find it amusing that creatures that can unfold out of a Camaro and stand four stories high do most of their fighting with fists. Like I said, dumber than a box of staples. They have tiny little heads, except for Starscream, who is so ancient he has an aluminum beard.

Aware that this movie opened in England seven hours before Chicago time, and the morning papers would be on the streets, after writing the above I looked up the first reviews as a reality check. I was reassured: "Like watching paint dry while getting hit over the head with a frying pan!" (Bradshaw, *Guardian*); "Sums up everything that is most tedious, crass and despicable about modern Hollywood!" (Tookey, *Daily Mail*); "A giant, lumbering idiot of a movie!" (Edwards, *Daily Mirror*). The first American review, however, reported that it feels "destined to be the biggest movie of all time" (Todd Gilchrist, Cinematical). It's certainly the biggest something of all time.

Transporter 3 ★ ★ ½

PG-13, 105 m., 2008

Jason Statham (Frank Martin), Natalya Rudakova (Valentina), Francois Berleand (Tarconi), Robert Knepper (Johnson), Jeroen Krabbe (Vasilev). Directed by Olivier Megaton and produced by Luc Besson and Steve Chasman. Screenplay by Besson and Robert Mark Kamen.

Transporter 3 is a perfectly acceptable brainless action thriller, inspiring us to give a lot of thought to complex sequences we would have been better off sucking on as eye candy. Consider this ingenious dilemma faced by the Transporter. He cannot remove a bracelet that is linked to a mighty bomb in his Audi A8. If he goes more than seventy-five feet from the car, the explosion kills him. He and the car and the girl are trapped on a bridge by men with machine guns. He releases the girl. The men are shooting at him. How can he escape?

Remember, this is the Transporter. He completes 100 percent of his deliveries. If he told you his FedEx tracking number, he would have to kill you. Because we know it's impossible to kill an action hero with machine gun fire, no matter how many rounds, he is in no real danger. But as men advance on him from both ends of the bridge, he has to do *something* to keep up appearances. He can't just sit there and wait for them to fire on him point-blank.

For that matter, the bad guys *know* their machine guns are impotent because they have both ends of the bridge blocked and haven't been hit by one another's bullets. But what does the Transporter do? Steers hard to the left, drives through the bridge rail, and plunges into the lake. Now we're talking real trouble. If he swims for the shore, the bomb will kill him. The only answer is to take the car to the shore with him, while holding his breath.

He improvises a way to get air underwater. It's clever but, thinking it over, I wouldn't advise you to try it while underwater. Anyway, the plot involves bad guys who want to bring eight container ships of toxic poisons into a Ukrainian harbor. Odessa has a beautiful harbor, with some nice steps leading down to the water. But the Ukrainian minister (Jeroen Krabbe) doesn't want to give his permission. Meanwhile, the bad guys kidnap the girl (Natalya Rudakova), and the Transporter's job is to transport her for the bad guys, although he violates his policy and begins to care for her.

Rudakova is no Bonnie Hunt when it comes to personality. She skulks, pouts, clams up, looks out the window, and yet falls in love with the Transporter and is able to ask him, "Kiss me—one last time!" Not the words you want to hear when you release her and people start shooting at you. Some perfectionists will no doubt criticize her acting. I say the hell with her acting. Look at those freckles. I can never get enough of freckles. In the movies, they're usually limited to a sprinkling on either side of a moppet nose. When you see beautiful freckles, as for example with the adorable actress Julianne Nicholson, you rejoice.

The director of *Transporter 3*, Olivier Megaton, is named after the bomb at Hiroshima, which was dropped on his birthday. Named not by his parents (the Fontanas) but by himself. French. (The Transporter's real name is the anticlimactic Frank Martin.) Anyway, although Megaton's CGI fight scenes are every bit as chopped up and incomprehensible as the current norm, he mostly avoids the queasy-cam and uses a stable camera while only the *action* moves. How about that.

He also succeeds in clearing every highway in every chase scene so the road is held only by the chasers and the chasees. Except, of course, when two monster trucks are required to speed this way, in which case, although there has been no traffic since the border, they are required to pass each other, and of course loudly toot their Klaxons—ooo-gaah! ooo-gaah!—as if you don't see them.

This movie is not boring. Jason Statham is a splendid action hero, steely eyed, muscular, taciturn, a close-lipped know-it-all with the official three-day stubble. He could do the snowmobile race with two broken arms. The bad guys are suitably reprehensible, the photography is expert, and when you see the Transporter thinking his way out of that problem on the bottom of the lake, you're amazed that later he restarts the engine and uses it to drive onto the top of a speeding train, and then ingeniously calculates a way to use the train's speed to save . . . but see for yourself. That A8, what a car. Solar panels to run the heat and A/C.

Transsiberian ★ ★ ★ ½
R, 111 m., 2008

Woody Harrelson (Roy), Emily Mortimer (Jessie), Kate Mara (Abby), Eduardo Noriega (Carlos), Thomas Kretschmann (Myassa), Ben Kingsley (Grinko). Directed by Brad Anderson and produced by Julio Fernandez. Screenplay by Anderson and Will Conroy.

Transsiberian is—how shall I put this?—one hell of a thriller. It's not often that I feel true suspense and dread building within me, but they were building during long stretches of this expertly constructed film. It takes place mostly on board the Transsiberian Express from Beijing to Moscow, at eight days the longest train journey in the world. And it uses the train as an asset: The characters all have to be on here somewhere, don't they?

The movie stars Emily Mortimer as Jessie and Woody Harrelson as her husband, Roy. They've just finished working with poor kids in China on behalf of their church group. Roy is a train buff. I've known a couple and they're exactly like this: thinking nothing of going out in the minus twenty-three-degree cold of Siberia to check out an old steam engine. Jessie, we learn, was a wild child when younger but is now clean and sober. Roy is a straight arrow. They love each other.

On board the train they meet another couple. Abby (Kate Mara) is a confused twenty-year-old runaway from Seattle. Carlos (Eduardo Noriega), ten or fifteen years older, is a charming Spanish traveler who knows a lot about customs and passports.

From the moment Carlos sees her, he has his eyes on Jessie. She knows this. When they all get off the train, Roy and Carlos go to look

at the steam engine, and Carlos fingers a long iron rod. Back on the train again, Jessie is startled to find her husband not on board. In a panic, she gets off at the next stop to wait for him, hoping he only missed the train. Carlos and Abby get off to be with her.

Already I'm feeling the fears of a stranger in a strange land. Tourists in Russia are welcomed where tourists go, but the Russians they meet in this movie are poor, bitter, and hostile, starting with the venomous woman who is the "hostess" on their railcar. While they're all waiting together at the next town, Carlos persuades Jessie to take a bus ride with him. Then they trek through a deserted, snowy landscape to see an abandoned but indeed pretty Orthodox church. What happens there you will not learn from me, nor will I say much about later events.

Turns out Roy did merely miss the train. While laid over, he made friends with the Russian narcotics detective Grinko (Ben Kingsley, expanding his repertoire of ethnic characters). Grinko is friendly and confiding. But then certain questions arise, and Jessie is shaky at answering them.

The movie, cowritten and directed by Brad Anderson (*The Machinist, Next Stop Wonderland*), is constructed with many of the devices and much of the skill of a Hitchcock. There is an interesting twist on Hitch's *The Lady Vanishes*. Instead of one or more passengers disappearing, most of the train disappears. Jessie gets up, heads for the rear of the train and almost falls out the back door to her death. From overhead shots we know the train is very long. What happened to all the other cars?

This is one of those trips after which you post dire warnings on the Net and file lawsuits—if you survive. The movie's secrets are manipulated into a clockwork mechanism that grinds to crush Jessie and Roy, and Jessie keeps right on saying the wrong things. She is warned by Grinko: "In Russia, we say that with lies you may go forward in the world, but you may never go back." Eventually, lies are no longer even the point.

Her performance is yet another surprise from Emily Mortimer, that English rose who here comes across as an American survivor of a long, strange trip. She hangs onto her sobriety like a life raft, but she still has a reckless streak. Harrelson, an actor of so many notes, is here earnest and sincere, and too trusting. Kingsley bites like a knife. Noriega persuasively plays Carlos with all of his secrets, and Mara is a wounded runaway who Jessie believes is a "good person."

Although the movie has several action sequences, not one is put in for effect. They all grow from the plot and drive it—even, I would argue, the concluding train sequence, which is certainly improbable but makes a certain sense. Like all the best suspense movies, *Transsiberian* starts in neutral, taking the time to introduce its characters, and then goes from second into high like greased lightning. I was a little surprised to notice how thoroughly it wound me up. This is a good one.

Tropic Thunder ★ ★ ★ ½
R, 106 m., 2008

Ben Stiller (Tugg Speedman), Jack Black (Jeff Portnoy), Robert Downey Jr. (Kirk Lazarus), Nick Nolte (Four Leaf Tayback), Steve Coogan (Damien Cockburn), Danny McBride (Cody), Brandon T. Jackson (Alpa Chino). Directed by Ben Stiller and produced by Stuart Cornfeld, Eric McLeod, and Stiller. Screenplay by Stiller, Etan Cohen, and Justin Theroux.

The documentary *Hearts of Darkness* is about the struggles of filming the great Vietnam War movie *Apocalypse Now*. Ben Stiller's *Tropic Thunder* plays like the doc's nightmare. A troupe of actors, under the impression they're making a Vietnam War movie, wanders dangerously in the jungle and is captured by a gang of drug lords who think the actors are narcs.

The movie is a send-up of Hollywood, actors, acting, agents, directors, writers, rappers, trailers, and egos, much enhanced by several cameo roles, the best of which I will not even mention. You'll know the one, although you may have to wait for the credits to figure it out.

All but stealing the show, Robert Downey Jr. is not merely funny but also very good and sometimes even subtle as Kirk Lazarus, an Australian actor who has won five Oscars and has now "surgically dyed" his skin to transform himself into a black man. So committed is he to this role that he remains in character at all times, seemingly convinced that he is actually black. This exasperates his fellow actor Alpa Chino (Brandon T. Jackson), a rapper who was born black and blasts Lazarus for his delusions. Alpa Chino (say it out loud) is like many rappers and promotes his own merchandise, notably Booty Sweat, an energy drink that keeps him going in the jungle.

If Chino doesn't buy the Lazarus performance, Lazarus is critical of Tugg Speedman (Stiller), who stars in *Simple Jack*, a movie about a mentally challenged farmer who thinks animals can understand him. Ironically, it is this role that saves their lives when they're taken prisoner. The bored drug lords have only one video, an old *Simple Jack* tape, and think Speedman is Jack himself. In a brilliant comic riff by Downey, Lazarus critiques Speedman's work as over the top: The really big stars, he observes, "never go full retard" when playing such roles.

The movie opens with trailers establishing three of the characters—not only Lazarus and Speedman, but Jeff Portnoy (Jack Black), whose specialty is fart humor. Portnoy is a heroin addict who is in withdrawal for much of the trek through the jungle, and has a funny scene after he begs to be tied to a tree and then begs to be set loose.

The setup involves the actors, director Damien Cockburn (Steve Coogan), and burned-out screenwriter Four Leaf Tayback (Nick Nolte) in the jungle with a huge crew and explosives expert Cody (Danny McBride). When one of the explosions goes off prematurely (think the opening of *The Party*), Speedman, acting as producer, fires the crew and announces he will direct the movie himself. He explains that hidden cameras have been placed in the jungle and will record everything that happens. Uh, is that possible, especially when they get lost? These actors, even the five-time Oscar winner, almost seem to believe so, a tribute to their self-centered indifference to technical details.

Intercut with the jungle scenes are Hollywood scenes featuring an agent and a studio executive. The movie, written by Justin Theroux, Stiller, and Etan Cohen, is familiar with the ordeals of filmmaking and location work, and distills it into wildly exaggerated scenes that have a whiff of accuracy. Especially interesting is the way the director, Damien Cockburn, leaves the picture, which perhaps reflects the way some actors feel about some directors.

The movie is, may I say, considerably better than Stiller's previous film *Zoolander*. It's the kind of summer comedy that rolls in, makes a lot of people laugh, and rolls onto video. It's been a good summer for that; look at *Pineapple Express*. When it's all over, you'll probably have the fondest memories of Robert Downey Jr.'s work. It's been a good year for him, this one coming after *Iron Man*. He's back, big time. ☞

Trouble the Water ★ ★ ★ ★
NO MPAA RATING, 93 m., 2008

A documentary featuring Scott Roberts and Kimberly Rivers Roberts. Directed and produced by Carl Deal and Tia Lessin.

Do you know what it means? To miss New Orleans?
—lyrics by Louis Armstrong

As I write, the hell storm Ike is battering Texas. I hear of evacuation buses, National Guard troops, emergency supplies, contraflow, Red Cross volunteers, helicopter rescues. It is a different world from the world after Katrina hit New Orleans. Yes, there were noble rescue efforts, but too little and too late, and without enough urgency on the part of the federal ("You're doin' a great job, Brownie!") government.

If you could have witnessed Katrina at ground zero, your blood would have boiled at the treatment of U.S. citizens. The extraordinary documentary *Trouble the Water* had an eyewitness in the city's Ninth Ward, *during* the storm. Her name was Kimberly Roberts. She was twenty-four. A week earlier, she had purchased a video camera from a street hustler for twenty dollars a week. She used it to film the experiences of her family before, during, and after the storm.

Her footage is surrounded by professionally filmed material that deepens and explains what happened. But the eyewitness footage has a desperate urgency that surpasses any other news and doc footage I have seen. Using lessons learned from TV news, she interviews her family, friends, and neighbors, does voiceovers while making shots, even signs off with her stage name as a rapper: "This is Black Kold Madina from the Ninth Ward."

We see the prologue to the storm. Residents have been urged to evacuate, but many do not have the means or the ways to get to evacuation centers, buses, or trains. If they have cars, they don't have gas money. They hunker down and hope to live through it. Kimberly warns a homeless man: "You better take care of yoself or the storm gonna WHUP yo ass!"

Drops of rain start to fall. They watch the TV news. Katrina worsens. Power goes out. The levee near their house is breached. Waters rise. They take refuge in their attic, in pitch darkness. We hear their call to 911. They have women and children up there, even a baby. They're trapped. They're told no rescue teams are working "at this time"—or not for days, in their neighborhood. They escape, helped by a muscular Good Samaritan who found a boat drifting past. Eventually they retreat to shelter in Alexandria, Louisiana, where the makers of this film, Carl Deal and Tia Lessin, found them and her footage. Her film changed all their plans for their film.

The documentary shows outrageous behavior, none more so than when they and many others are directed to a nearby navy base for refuge. The base is being closed. It has an empty housing unit in plain view with hundreds of beds. The gates are locked. They are turned away at gunpoint by sailors with M-16s (who were commended for their "bravery" in guarding the base).

Roberts needs more practice at holding the camera steady and framing shots. It doesn't matter. We feel her footage at the base of our spines. Sometimes she says nothing, just points the camera, and the images speak for themselves. Carl Deal and Tia Lessin, who have worked with Michael Moore, augment her eyewitness account with footage from TV news showing New Orleans mayor Ray Nagin, Louisiana governor Kathleen Babineaux Blanco, and shots of the breached levees and the panorama of destruction.

The film is about Katrina, and even more about the human spirit. Kimberly and her husband, Scott, are the life force personified: smart, funny, undefeated, indignant, determined. Kimberly sings three songs on the sound track. We see her performing one of them. That scene reportedly won a standing ovation at Sundance 2008, where the film won the Grand Jury Prize as best documentary.

Charges were made after Katrina that the federal response was lacking because so many of the victims were poor and black. "We feel like we're not U.S. citizens," Kimberly says at one point. At another, she rails against George Bush in language I will spare you. One of the most affecting scenes is when Kimberly, Scott, and their dog wander down the streets of their neighborhood, remembering: "There was an old lady living in that house. Always on her porch, saying hello to everybody." Her good cheer disappears when she learns that the man she warned was killed. The storm whupped his ass. That was his own fault. What happened to the residents of the Ninth Ward was not their fault.

Roberts was pregnant when she and Scott went to the Sundance premiere. On Monday, January 21, 2008, at the Park City hospital, she gave birth. It was Martin Luther King Jr. Day.

Tru Loved ★
R, 104 m., 2008

Najarra Townsend (Tru), Jake Abel (Trevor), Matthew Thompson (Lodell), Tye Olson (Walter), Bruce Vilanch (Daniel/Minister), Alexandra Paul (Leslie), Cynda Williams (Lisa), Nichelle Nichols (Grandmother). Directed by Stewart Wade and produced by Wade, Antonio Brown, and David Avallone. Screenplay by Wade.

Tru Loved as a movie is on about the same level as a not especially good high school play. Student directors could learn from it. I'm sure its heart is in the right place, but it fails at fundamentals we take for granted when we go to the movies. By lacking them, it illustrates what the minimum requirements are for a competent film. Yes, you can clearly see and hear them, especially when they're missing.

1. Line readings. That's what they sound like, readings. Classroom readings. The actors lack the knack of making their dialogue sound spontaneous and realistic. They sound like

bright English students who have memorized their lines but find themselves onstage without having had much experience or training.

2. Body language. One of the first things an actor learns is not to gesture to emphasize lines unless the lines really call for it. Insecure actors often seem to punch up dialogue physically as a sort of insurance policy.

3. Framing. When you have five characters at a picnic table, you don't (necessarily) want to block those on the other side with the bodies of those on this side. There are ways to do that or fudge it. Or forget it. But don't have those on side A separated so we can see those on side B centered between persons 1 and 2, and 2 and 3, and then in the reverse shot separate those on side B so we can see those on side A.

4. Don't let the dialogue scream, "I paid attention in Gay Lit class!" When a kid comes home from Walt Whitman High School, don't make a point of establishing a lesbian connection to a name.

> Grandmother: *Tru? What kind of a name is that?*
> Lodell: *Short for Gertrude. As in Stein. She's a writer.*
> Grandma: *I know who Gertrude Stein was. "A rose is a rose is a rose."*
> Lodell: *Yeah. Whatever.*

After bringing up the sainted Gertrude, why does Lodell immediately reject her? "Whatever," when used by a teenager to an adult, is a way of dismissing what has been said. Lodell is a bright kid. Since he has *just now come* from a class studying *Romeo and Juliet, maybe* he might have replied, "And by any other name it smells as sweet as sweet as sweet." Grandma seems as if she'd like that.

5. Daydreams. Can be annoying, especially when absurdly stagy. Even more especially when the daydreams are in soft focus and then we cut frequently to the heroine in sharp focus, looking at scenes in her own daydreams and nodding and smiling.

6. Speech patterns. It's my impression most gay men do not "sound like gay men." But we all know exactly what I mean by sounding like gay men. The other side of the rule is, many men who sound gay are gay, and in many cases intend to sound gay. Don't get all homophilic on me. You know I'm right.

469

7. Cameo appearances. Their use must be carefully controlled to avoid breaking a film's mood with the "Hey! There's Donald Trump!" Syndrome. That is doubly true when the cameo star is famous and appears in a double role, as does Bruce Vilanch, from *Hollywood Squares*. Here he plays "Daniel" and "the Minister." Senator, I know Bruce Vilanch, and he's no Minister.

8. Music. Not necessary to blast in with literal and urgent punch lines and transitions.

The movie is about how Tru moves from idyllic San Francisco to conservative suburbia with her lesbian mothers. This just in: Except for some jocks and those who doth protest too much, today's suburban teens are mostly cool with people who are gay, except in the Palin Belt.

Full disclosure: I lifted the words "San Francisco to conservative suburbia with her lesbian mothers" straight from the plot summary on IMDb.com, because I stopped watching the movie at the 00.08.05 point. IMDb is also where I found out about Bruce Vilanch's dual role. I never did see the lesbian mothers or my friend Bruce. For *Tru Loved*, the handwriting was on the wall. The returns were in. The case was closed. You know I'm right. Or tell me I'm wrong.

> Q: *How can you give a one-star rating to a movie you didn't sit through?*
> A: *The rating only applies to the first eight minutes. After that you're on your own.*

Tulpan ★ ★ ★ ★
NO MPAA RATING, 100 m., 2009

Askhat Kuchinchirekov (Asa), Samal Yeslyamova (Samal), Ondasyn Besikbasov (Ondas), Tulepbergen Baisakalov (Boni), Bereke Turganbayev (Beke), Mahabbat Turganbayeva (Maha). Directed by Sergey Dvortsevoy and produced by Karl Baumgartner and Thanassis Karathanos. Screenplay by Dvortsevoy and Gennady Ostrovskiy.

Tulpan is an amazing film. It shows such an unfamiliar world it might as well be Mars. This is a world where the horizon is a straight line against the sky in every direction. There are no landmarks, no signs, no roads. No vegetation grows much more than a foot or two high. It is dry, dusty, cold, and windy, and nothing seems to be green. This is the world *Tulpan* takes place in, and I can think of only one other story that would feel at home there: *Waiting for Godot*.

Yet the people love it. They are yurt dwellers in Kazakhstan, the largest landlocked nation on earth. They live on what is named in the credits as the Hungersteppe and raise sheep. We meet a young sailor named Asa, discharged from the Russian navy, who has come here to live with his sister Samal, her husband, Ondas, and their children. As the story opens, Asa, Ondas, and his buddy Boni are negotiating with a poker-faced man and his hostile wife for the hand of their daughter, Tulpan ("Tulip").

Asa enthralls them with tales of the seahorse and octopus. They offer ten sheep and a chandelier. It is to no avail; Tulpan, peeking through the doorway curtains, thinks his ears are too big. There is not one single other potential bride in the district, and how is a man to live here without a wife?

These people are quite familiar with what we call civilization. Their children have been deserting to the cities for years. They do not have electricity, and water must be trucked in. I assume they eat a lot of mutton, and there is a man with an ungainly jeeplike vehicle who comes around selling cucumbers, and, I hope, other vegetables. They have a battery-powered radio, which one of the sons listens to eagerly, racing into the yard to announce: "Breaking news! Earthquake in Japan! Seven on the Richter scale!"

They are alarmed that many baby lambs are stillborn. They call out the vet, whose teeth do a thing with his cigarette it is difficult to describe. He travels with a sick baby camel in his motorcycle sidecar. His diagnosis is simple and almost obvious. Asa eventually argues with his taskmaster brother-in-law and walks away from the farm. This consists of disappearing into the void; how do people avoid getting lost here? When Ondas scans the horizon with his binoculars, everything looks the same.

There is humor in the film, some of it involving the cucumber salesman, and tenderness, as when Samal sings a bedtime lullaby to her tired husband and their children. Stark reality, in the difficult birth of a lamb that lives. A shot, long held, of Samal's face, which tells us everything we can ever hope to know about her situation. The film's closing shot is epic in its meaning and astonishing in its difficulty.

This is the first feature by Sergey Dvortsevoy, forty-five, born in Kazakhstan, whose documentaries have been about people in the old Russian republics living between tradition and the future. What does it sound like to you? Ethnographic boredom? I swear to you that if you live in a place where this film is playing, it is the best film in town. You'll enjoy it, not soon forget it, and you'll tell your friends about it and try to convince them to go, but you'll have about as much luck with them as I'm probably having with you. Still, there has to come a time in everyone's life when they see a deadpan comedy about the yurt dwellers of Kazakhstan.

Note: This was the winner of the Un Certain Regard prize at Cannes 2008.

12 ★ ★ ★ ½
PG-13, 153 m., 2009

Sergey Makovetsky (Engineer), Nikita Mikhalkov (Foreman), Sergey Garmash (Cabbie), Valentin Gaft (Elderly Jewish Man), Alexey Petrenko (Transit Worker), Yuri Stoyanov (TV Producer), Sergey Gazarov (Surgeon), Mikhail Efremov (Traveling Actor), Alexander Adabashian (Bailiff), Apti Magamaev (Chechen Accused Man). Directed by Nikita Mikhalkov and produced by Mikhalkov and Leonid Vereschagin. Screenplay by Mikhalkov, Vladimir Moiseenko, and Alexander Novototsky-Vlasov, based on the screenplay by Reginald Rose.

Twelve Angry Men remains a monument of American filmmaking, and more than fifty years after it was made its story is still powerful enough to inspire this Russian version—not a remake, but a new demonstration of a jury verdict arrived at only because one of the men was not angry so much as worried. *12* by Nikita Mikhalkov is a powerful new film inspired by a powerful older one.

You know the story. A jury is sequestered. The men are hot and tired, and impatient to go home. It is assumed that the defendant, a young man accused of murder, is guilty. A quick vote is called for. The balloting shows eleven for convicting, one against. This generates a long and dogged debate in which the very principles of justice itself are called into play.

Perhaps Russia got this film when it needed it. Reginald Rose's original screenplay was written for the CBS drama showcase *Studio One* in 1954 and presented live. Franklin Schaffner (*Patton*) was the director. The telecast took place during the declining days of the hearings held by Senator Joseph McCarthy. CBS also broadcast the army-McCarthy hearings and Edward R. Murrow's historic takedown of the alcoholic witch-hunter. The great film by Sidney Lumet, made in 1957, currently stands at number nine on IMDb's poll of the greatest films, ahead of *The Empire Strikes Back* and *Casablanca*.

If the original story argued for the right to a fair trial in the time of McCarthy's character assassinations, the Russian version comes at a time when that nation is using the jury system after a legacy of Stalinist purges and Communist Party show trials. It also dramatizes anti-Semitism and hatred for Chechens; the youth on trial is newly arrived in Moscow. The issue of overnight Russian millionaires in a land of much poverty is also on many of the jurors' minds.

None of the jurors is given a name, although director Mikhalkov gives himself the role of the jury foreman. One by one, every member of the jury tells a story or reveals a secret. Their set pieces do the job of swaying fellow jurors to reconsider their votes but are effective on their own as essentially a series of one-man shows. There is not a weak member in the cast, and it's a tribute to the power of the actors that the 2½-hour running time doesn't seem labored. The jury is sequestered in the gymnasium of a school next to the courtroom, and they never leave it, but their stories are performed so skillfully that in our minds we envision many settings; they're like radio plays.

Lumet famously began his film with the camera above eye level and subtly lowered it until the end, when the characters loomed above the camera. Mikhalkov, with a large open space to work in, uses camera placement and movement instead, circling the makeshift jury table and following jurors as they wander the room. A sparrow flies in through a window, and its fluttering and chirping is a reminder that the jurors, too, feel imprisoned.

Going in I knew what the story was about, how it would progress, and how it would end. Mikhalkov keeps all of that (writer Rose shares a screen credit), but he has made a new film with its own original characters and stories, and after all, it's not how the film ends, but how it gets there.

Twilight ★ ★ ½
PG-13, 122 m., 2008

Kristen Stewart (Bella Swan), Robert Pattinson (Edward Cullen), Billy Burke (Charlie Swan), Peter Facinelli (Dr. Carlisle Cullen), Elizabeth Reaser (Esme Cullen), Nikki Reed (Rosalie Hale), Ashley Greene (Alice Cullen), Jackson Rathbone (Jasper Hale), Kellan Lutz (Emmett Cullen). Directed by Catherine Hardwicke and produced by Mark Morgan, Greg Mooradian, and Wyck Godfrey. Screenplay by Melissa Rosenberg, based on the novel by Stephenie Meyer.

If you're a vampire, it's all about you. Why is Edward Cullen obsessed to the point of erotomania by Bella Swan? Because she smells so yummy, but he doesn't want to kill her. Here's what he tells her: He must not be around her. He might sink his fangs in just a little and not be able to stop. She finds this overwhelmingly attractive. She tells him he is the most beautiful thing she has ever seen. I don't remember Edward ever saying that to her. Maybe once. He keeps on saying they should stay far, far apart because he craves her so much.

Should a woman fall in love with a man because he desires her so much? Men seem to think so. It's not about the woman; it's about the man's desire. We all know there is no such thing as a vampire. Come on now, what is *Twilight* really about? It's about a teenage boy trying to practice abstinence, and how, in the heat of the moment, it's really, really hard. And about a girl who wants to go all the way with him and doesn't care what might happen. He's so beautiful she would do anything

for him. She is the embodiment of the sentiment "I'd die for you." She is, like many adolescents, a thanatophile.

If there were no vampires in *Twilight*, it would be a thin-blooded teenage romance, about two good-looking kids who want each other so much because they want each other so much. Sometimes that's all it's about, isn't it? They're in love with *being* in love. In *Twilight*, however, they have a seductive disagreement about whether he should kill her. She's like, I don't especially want to die, but if that's what it takes, count me in. She is touched by his devotion. Think what a sacrifice he is making on her behalf. On prom night, on the stage of the not especially private gazebo in the public gardens, he teeters right on the brink of a fang job, and then brings all of her trembling to a dead standstill.

The movie is lush and beautiful, and the actors are well-chosen. You may recall Robert Pattinson (Edward) as Cedric Diggory, who on Voldemort's orders was murdered in a graveyard in *Harry Potter and the Goblet of Fire*. Maybe he was already a vampire. Pattinson is not unaware of how handsome he is. When Bella and Edward, still strangers, exchange stern and burning looks in the school cafeteria, he transfixes her with a dark and glowering—nay, penetrating—stare. I checked Pattinson out on Google Images and found he almost always glowers at the camera 'neath shadowed brow. Kristen Stewart's Bella, on the other hand, is a fresh-faced innocent who is totally undefended against his voltage.

Bella has left her mom and stepdad in hot Arizona, clutching a potted cactus, to come live in the clammy, rainy Pacific Northwest, home of Seasonal Affective Disorder. Her dad (Billy Burke) is the chief of police of the very small town of Forks, Washington (population 3,120). His greatest asset: "He doesn't hover." At high school, she quickly notices the preternaturally pale Cullen clan, who in some shots seem to be wearing as much Max Factor Pancake White as Harry Langdon. Edward is 114 years old. He must be really tired of taking biology class. Darwin came in during his watch and proved vampires can't exist.

There are other strange youths around, including American Indians who appear not too distantly descended from their tribe's ancestors, wolves. Great tension between the wolves and vampires. Also some rival vampires around. How small is this town? The Forks high school is so big, it must serve a consolidated district serving the whole table setting. The main local Normal Kid is a nice, sandy-haired boy who asks Bella to the prom. He's out of his depth here, unless he can transmogrify into a grizzly. Also there are four gray-bearded coots at the next table in the local diner, who eavesdrop and exchange significant glances and get big, significant close-ups, but are still just sitting significantly nodding, for all I know.

Edward has the ability to move as swiftly as Superman. Like him he can stop a runaway pickup with one arm. He rescues Bella twice that I remember, maybe because he truly loves her, maybe because he's saving her for later. She has questions. "How did you appear out of nowhere and stop that truck?" Well might she ask. When he finally explains that he is a vampire, he goes up from eight to ten on her Erotometer. Why do girls always prefer the distant, aloof, handsome, dangerous dudes instead of cheerful chaps like me?

Twilight will mesmerize its target audience, sixteen-year-old girls and their grandmothers. Their mothers know all too much about boys like this. I saw it at a sneak preview. Last time I saw a movie in that same theater, the audience welcomed it as an opportunity to catch up on gossip, texting, and laughing at private jokes. This time the audience was rapt with attention. Sometimes a soft chuckle, as when the principal Indian boy has well-developed incisors. Sometimes a soft sigh. Afterward, I eavesdropped on some conversations. A few were saying, "He's so hot!" More floated in a sweet dreaminess. Edward seemed to stir their surrender instincts.

The movie, based on the Stephenie Meyer novel, was directed by Catherine Hardwicke. She uses her great discovery, Nikki Reed, in the role of the beautiful Rosalie Hale. Reed wrote Hardwicke's *Thirteen* (2003) when she was only fourteen. That was a movie that knew a lot more about teenage girls. The girl played by Reed in that movie would make mincemeat of Edward. But I understand who *Twilight* appeals to, and it sure will.

Note: Now playing around the country is the much better and more realistic teenage vampire movie Let the Right One In, *a Swedish import scheduled to be Twilighted by Hollywood. In this one, the vampire girl protects the boy and would never dream of killing him. That's your difference right there between girls and boys. Warning: This is very* R-*rated.*

2 Days in Paris ★ ★ ★
R, 96 m., 2007

Julie Delpy (Marion), Adam Goldberg (Jack), Daniel Bruhl (Lukas), Marie Pillet (Anna), Albert Delpy (Jeannot), Alexia Landeau (Rose), Adan Jodorowsky (Mathieu), Alex Nahon (Manu). Directed by Julie Delpy and produced by Christophe Mazodier and Thierry Potok. Screenplay by Delpy.

I once gave flowers to a French girl and was told they were "flagrant." When Marion, the character played by Julie Delpy in *2 Days in Paris*, makes mistakes like that, she knows what she's doing. If her relationship with her lover, Jack, is coming apart at the seams, that's her with a little thimble and needle, pulling out the stitches. The movie covers the end of a European vacation that was intended to mend their relationship, and the holiday has gone badly. Sometimes when you want to know, really know somebody, you find out that actually you'd rather not.

Jack (Adam Goldberg) had a bad time in Venice. How can that be? Was it Woody Allen who said the worst sex he ever had wasn't that bad? Same with bad trips to Venice. Jack got severe diarrhea and tried Marion's patience by taking photos of everything, apparently, except the diarrhea itself. Has he never heard of Imodium, that word along with "taxi" and "OK" that gets most Americans around the world? And did he think he was needed to remedy the world's tragic shortage of photos of Venice?

But never mind. The last two days of the holiday are to be spent in Paris, Marion's hometown, before they return to New York, where they now live. They move in upstairs from Marion's parents, Anna and Jeannot (played by Delpy's real parents, Marie Pillet and Albert Delpy). Culture shock sets in at the first meal, braised rabbit. You'd think Anna and Jeannot could try the merciful American tactic of calling it "chicken," but perhaps when you serve the rabbit head along with its eyeballs, it looks like a chicken that has been fed too many hormones.

Marion and Jack wander about Paris, talking in that way that lovers have when they're beginning to get on each other's nerves. But, no, this is not a retread of Richard Linklater's *Before Sunset* (2004), in which Delpy and Ethan Hawke walked and talked around Paris. It is a contemplation of incompatibility, as Paris brings out a side of Marion that Jack has never quite seen: Is she a radical political activist and a shameless slut, or does she only act like one? She runs into old boyfriends so often it makes Paris seem like a small town, and attacks one of them in a restaurant for taking a sex vacation to Thailand.

At home, her father quizzes Jack on French culture, and her mother is so eager to wash and press his clothes that he barely has time to get out of them. Both of Delpy's parents are professional actors, and so these are only performances, I hope. In addition to casting her parents, Delpy puts her mark on this film in many other ways: She starred, directed, wrote, edited, coproduced, composed the score, and sang a song. When a woman takes that many jobs, we slap her down for vanity. When a man does, we call him the new Orson Welles.

Delpy in fact has made a smart film with an edge to it; her Jack and Marion reveal things about themselves they never thought they'd tell anybody, and we wonder why they ever went out on a second date. Much has been made of the similarities between Delpy here and Diane Keaton in *Annie Hall,* but if Delpy's character found a spider as big as a Buick in the bathroom, she'd braise it and serve it up for lunch.

Which is an oblique way of saying that Julie Delpy is an original, a woman who refuses to be defined or limited. Her first great roles were in Bertrand Tavernier's *Beatrice* (1987), Agnieszka Holland's *Europa Europa* (1990), and Krzysztof Kieslowski's *White* (1994); she was in Linklater's *Before Sunrise, Waking Life,* and *Before Sunset*; and she dumped Bill Murray at the beginning of Jim Jarmusch's *Broken Flowers* (2005). In between, she studied film at NYU and made herself available for thirty student productions.

What she has done here is avoid all temptation to recycle the usual lovers-in-Paris possibilities and create two original, quirky characters so obsessed with their differences that Paris is almost a distraction. I don't think I heard a single accordion in the whole film.

Two Lovers ★ ★ ★ ½
R, 110 m., 2009

Joaquin Phoenix (Leonard Kraditor), Gwyneth Paltrow (Michelle Rausch), Vinessa Shaw (Sandra Cohen), Moni Monoshov (Reuben Kraditor), Isabella Rossellini (Ruth Kraditor), John Ortiz (Jose Cordero), Bob Ari (Michael Cohen), Julie Budd (Carol Cohen), Elias Koteas (Ronald Blatt). Directed by James Gray and produced by Gray, Donna Gigliotti, and Anthony Katagas. Screenplay by Gray and Richard Menello.

I believe Sandra senses something is damaged about Leonard. *Two Lovers* never puts a word to it, although we know he's had treatment and is on medication. It's not a big, showy mental problem; lots of people go through life like this, and people simply say, "Well, you know Leonard." But Sandra does know him, and that's why she tells him she not only loves him but wants to help him.

Leonard (Joaquin Phoenix) is focused on his inner demons. His fiancée left him—dumped him—and he has moved back to his childhood room, still with the *2001* poster on the wall. He makes customer deliveries for his dad's dry cleaning business. Sandra (Vinessa Shaw) is the daughter of another dry cleaner in the same Brighton Beach neighborhood of Brooklyn. Her father plans to buy his father's business, and both families think it would be ideal if Sandra and Leonard married.

But Leonard meets Michelle (Gwyneth Paltrow) and is struck by the lightning bolt. She's blond, exciting, and in his eyes sophisticated and glamorous. She seems to like him, too. So a triangle exists that might seem to be the makings of a traditional romcom from years ago.

James Gray's *Two Lovers* is anything but traditional, romantic, or a comedy. It is a film of unusual perception, played at perfect pitch by Phoenix, Shaw, Paltrow, and the other actors.

It is calm and mature. It understands these characters. It doesn't juggle them for melodrama, but looks inside.

Michelle is the kind of person many of us become fascinated with at some unwise point in our lives. She has enormous charm, a winning smile, natural style. But she is haunted. Leonard is blindsided to discover she has a married lover and that she uses drugs. He is able, like so many men, to overlook these flaws, to misunderstand neediness for affection, to delude himself that she shares his feelings. Sandra, on the other hand, is pretty and nice, but their families have known each other for years, and Michelle seems to offer an entry into a new world across the bridge in Manhattan.

The particular thing about *Two Lovers,* written by Gray and Richard Menello, is that it utterly ignores all the usual clichés about parents in general and Jewish mothers in particular. Both Leonard and Sandra come from loving families, and both of them love their parents. Although Leonard sometimes seems to contain muted, conflicting elements of Travis Bickle and Rupert Pupkin, he tries to get along with people, to be polite, to be sensitive. That he is the victim of his own obsessions is bad luck. It's painful watching him try to lead a secret life with Michelle outside his home, especially when her emergency demands come at the worst possible times.

Leonard's parents are Ruth and Reuben Kraditor (Isabella Rossellini and Moni Monoshov), long-married, staunchly bourgeois, reasonable. Ruth, of course, wants Leonard to find stability in marriage with a nice Jewish girl like Sandra, but her love for him outweighs her demands on him—rare in the movies. Reuben is more narrow in his imagination for his son but not a caricature. And Sandra's father (Bob Ari) wants to buy the Kraditor business and likes the idea of a marriage but would never think of his daughter as part of a business deal. Everyone in the film wants the best for their children.

So the drama, and it becomes intense, involves whether Leonard's demons will allow him to be happy. Michelle represents so many problems she should almost dress by wrapping herself in the yellow tape from crime scene investigations. She has a gift for attracting enablers. We meet her married lover (Elias Koteas), who turns out not to be an old letch, even if he is an adulterer. He's essentially another victim, and a short, tense scene he has with Leonard provides private insights.

Here is a movie involving the kinds of people we know or perhaps have been. It's the third film in which James Gray has directed Joaquin Phoenix (after *The Yards* and *We Own the Night*) and shows them working together to create a character whose manner is troubled but can be identified with. The whole movie is so well-cast and -performed that we watch it unfolding without any particular awareness of "acting." Even the ending, which might seem obligatory in a lesser film, is earned and deserved in this one.

Tyson ★ ★ ★ ★
R, 90 m., 2009

Featuring Mike Tyson. A documentary directed by James Toback.

Some kids beat him up once, and he couldn't stop them. Another kid killed one of his homing pigeons, and he fell upon him with fury. And that is the backstory of Mike Tyson, a boxer known as the Baddest Man on the Planet. When he went into the ring, he was proving he would never be humiliated again and getting revenge for a pigeon he loved. I believe it really is that simple. There is no rage like that of a child, hurt unjustly, the victim of a bully.

James Toback's *Tyson* is a documentary with no pretense of objectivity. Here is Mike Tyson's story in his own words, and it is surprisingly persuasive. He speaks openly and with apparent honesty about a lifetime during which, he believes, he was often misunderstood. From a broken family, he was in trouble at a tender age and always felt vulnerable; his childhood self is still echoed in his lisp, as high-pitched as a child's. It's as if the victim of big kids is still speaking to us from within the intimidating form of perhaps the most punishing heavyweight champion of them all.

Mike Tyson comes across here as reflective, contrite, more sinned against than sinning. He can be charming. He can be funny. You can see why Toback, himself a man of extremes, has been a friend for twenty years. The film contains a great deal of fight footage, of Tyson hammering one opponent after another. We also see a TV interview, infamous at the time, of his ex-wife, Robin Givens, describing him as abusive and manic-depressive. Even then I wanted to ask her, "And who did you think you were marrying?"

Tyson freely admits he has mistreated women and says he regrets it. But he denies the rape charge brought against him by Desiree Washington, which led to his conviction and three years in jail. "She was a swine," he says. He also has no use for boxing promoter Don King, "a slimy reptilian (bleeper)." His shining hero is his legendary trainer Cus D'Amato, the man who polished the diamond in the rough from his early teens and died just before the first heavyweight crown.

"Before the fight even starts, I've won," Tyson says. From Cus he learned never to take his eyes from his opponent's face from the moment he entered the ring. So formidable was his appearance and so intimidating his record that it once seemed he would have to retire before anyone else won the title. But he lost to Buster Douglas in Japan in 1990—the result, he says, of not following Cus's advice to stay away from women before a fight. He went

into the ring with a case of gonorrhea. Later losses he attributes to a lack of physical training at a time when he signed up for fights simply for the payday. And there was drug abuse, from which he is now recovering.

This is only Toback's second doc, in a career of directing many fine films (*When Will I Be Loved, Harvard Man, Fingers*). In 1990, he was sitting next to a businessman on a flight and convinced him to finance *The Big Bang*, in which he would ask people about the meaning of life, the possibility of an afterlife, and what they believe in. "Tell me again why I'm financing this cockamamie thing," the man asks him. Toback says, simply, that the film will be remembered long after both he and the man are gone.

Toback is remarkably persuasive. He was offering immortality. It is a tempting offer. In ancient Egypt, an architect named Toback must have convinced a pharaoh to erect the first pyramid. What he offered Tyson was the opportunity to vindicate himself. There is no effort to show "both sides," but, in fact, the case against Tyson is already well-known, and what is unexpected about Tyson is that afterward we feel sympathy for the man, and more for the child inside.

U

The Uninvited ★ ★ ★
PG-13, 87 m., 2009

Emily Browning (Anna), Elizabeth Banks (Rachel), David Strathairn (Steven), Arielle Kebbel (Alex), Maya Massar (Mom), Kevin McNulty (Sheriff), Jesse Moss (Matt), Dean Paul Gibson (Dr. Silberling). Directed by Charles Guard and Thomas Guard and produced by Walter F. Parkes, Laurie MacDonald, and Roy Lee. Screenplay by Craig Rosenberg, Doug Miro, and Carlo Bernard.

Emily Browning's face helps *The Uninvited* work so well. She's a twenty-year-old actress from Australia and has a lot of experience, but looks about fourteen. She makes an ideal heroine for a horror movie: innocent, troubled, haunted by nightmares, persecuted by a wicked stepmother, convinced her real mother was deliberately burned to death. She makes you fear for her, and that's half the battle. Yet she's so fresh she's ready for a Jane Austen role.

I recoiled twice in the opening minutes of *The Uninvited,* and that's a good sign. This is a well-crafted first feature by the Guard brothers (Charles and Thomas) from Britain that weaves a story not as predictable as it might seem. Browning plays Anna, who when we meet her is finishing a stay at a psychiatric clinic under the care of chubby, paternal Dr. Silberling (Dean Paul Gibson). Her dad (David Strathairn), darkly ambiguous, drives her home to be welcomed by his girlfriend, Rachel (Elizabeth Banks), who is all sunshine and false friendliness.

But Anna yearns only to see her older sister, Alex (Arielle Kebbel). They dive off from their boathouse, make sister-talk on the raft, and then Alex swims away as young Matt (Jesse Moss) arrives on his grocery delivery boat. Matt, the boy who was getting too insistent with Anna when they were making out at the beach campfire. And that was the night her sick mother died, burned up in the boathouse, which had been converted into a sick room, and now, as Anna has just seen, been rebuilt.

What really happened that night? How did Rachel start as her mother's nurse and be-come Anna's new stepmom? Don't Rachel and her dad know how it disturbs the girls to see them smooching? And who is Rachel, really? Is that her real name? Google can be an insidious resource.

And more about the story I really cannot say. *The Uninvited* gets under your skin. The cinematography has that classy-horror-movie look, the overhead shots of a lonely car driving through ominous trees, the interiors sometimes shadowed, sometimes uncannily sunny, and the—presences—as Emily Dickinson would punctuate, that are half-seen in a half-sleep.

David Strathairn is well-cast. Nobody can seem more open and affable, and suggest such hooded menace. Who else is so good at telling his daughter there's nothing to worry about, and making us worry? Elizabeth Banks, as Rachel, is almost convincing when she tells Anna she hopes they can be friends. Almost. Hard to imagine that Banks played Laura Bush *and* Miri of Zack and Miri, but that's acting for you. Here she has moments balanced on a knife edge between being cheerful and being a little too quick to start issuing mom-type orders, like telling Matt not to come to the house anymore.

The Uninvited begins with a classically Freudian situation, moves directly into dream analysis, has blood coming from keyholes and corpses speaking from the grave, and is all set, of course, in a huge, rambling New England shore house with gables, attics, long corridors, and places where anyone, or anything, could be hiding. When a movie like this is done well, it's uncommon. *The Uninvited* is done well.

Note: I'm a little surprised by the PG-13, *more evidence the MPAA awards the rating for what a movie doesn't have (nudity, language, sex) than what it does have, images that could be very troubling for some younger viewers.*

The Unknown Woman ★ ★ ★
NO MPAA RATING, 118 m., 2008

Xenia Rappoport (Irena), Michele Placido (Mold), Claudia Gerini (Valeria Adacher), Pierfrancesco Favino (Donato Adacher),

Margherita Buy (Irena's Lawyer), Alessandro Haber (Doorman), Piera Degli Esposti (Gina), Clara Dossena (Thea Adacher), Angela Molina (Lucrezia). Directed by Giuseppe Tornatore and produced by Laura Fattori. Screenplay by Tornatore.

The Unknown Woman contains so many secrets that without revealing a few I cannot write a review. Yes, the blond prostitute in the flashbacks is the dark-haired housemaid in the present. Yes, she has a passionate reason for wanting to go to work for the Adacher family. Yes, there is something deeply strange about her behavior toward their little girl, Thea.

The movie was written and directed by Giuseppe Tornatore, still best known for *Cinema Paradiso* (1990). *The Unknown Woman* (*La Sconosciuta*) is being hailed as his best since then and swept Italy's Donatello Awards for best film, actress, director, cinematographer, music, you name it. It's a spellbinder with a lot of Hitchcock touches and an Ennio Morricone score to match. But does it play fair with us?

I have given the plot a lot of thought. I think I know how and why Irena (Xenia Rappoport) arrives in a northern Italian city with a big roll of cash in her pocket, her bankroll already in place before she begins her mysterious surveillance of an apartment across the road from hers. No, it's not a chronological impossibility, given all we later discover. I even think I know what crime (there is a choice) she goes to prison for.

I do not know who rigged the brakes on Mrs. Adacher's car, but I doubt it was Irena because the evidence looks planted. I don't know why Irena was having Gina, the former maid, sign those papers. I don't know how much Gina understood of what Irena was telling her. I believe that DNA testing could resolve a crucial identity in the movie, but if it has, what are we to make of a long, significant glance Irena exchanges with a man late in the film? I don't know if the man is who she thinks he is. I also don't know how anyone could survive those stabbings with the biggest pair of scissors I have ever seen.

These may be questions you share with me, or you may be sure of your answers. I suppose the smiles in the last shot convey nothing but simple human joy and answer nothing. Maybe it doesn't matter, since the film's construction is skillfully devised to prolong suspense as long as possible—maybe too long. It has to sidestep so many questions that it's as much an exercise in footwork as storytelling. But it uses the devices of melodrama to haul us helplessly along, and has a fascinating gallery of characters, beginning with Irena.

She is from the Ukraine. Her twenties were lost in sexual slavery. It is no accident she gets the job with the Adachers, though an accident leads to it. I believe, because I must, that the bald sadist Mold (Michele Placido) had a way to track her and get her cell number. I suspect, but do not know, that he was one of the two Santas who beat and kicked her on Christmas Eve. Doesn't Mold know if he scares her away, he'll never get what he wants? Does Mold know if what she believes about the Adacher family is true?

These questions build as she steals the Adachers' house keys and security beeper, and goes through every space in the house, even the hidden safe (which has combination numbers big enough to be seen through a keyhole). There are a lot of questions during the disturbing and brutal way she "teaches" little Thea to deal with her rare disease (so rare I have never encountered it, even in fiction, where it is mighty handy). Anyway, all the questions are answered (seemingly, anyway) by the end.

There are a lot of things I can say about *The Unknown Woman*, but I cannot say I was bored or ever let off the hook. Stephen Holden in the *New York Times* questions its integrity. I don't think it has a shred of integrity. Few films of this nature can afford to. It works. Is that enough for you? For me, in a movie like this, it is.

Untraceable ★ ★ ★
R, 100 m., 2008

Diane Lane (Jennifer Marsh), Billy Burke (Detective Eric Box), Colin Hanks (Griffin Dowd), Joseph Cross (Owen Reilly), Mary Beth Hurt (Stella Marsh). Directed by Gregory Hoblit and produced by Tom Rosenberg, Gary Lucchesi, Howard Koch Jr.,

Steven Pearl, and Andy Cohen. Screenplay by Robert Fyvolent, Mark R. Brinker, and Allison Burnett.

Untraceable is a horrifying thriller, smart and tightly told, and merciless. It begins with this premise: A psychopath devises ways to slowly kill people online, in live streaming video. The more hits he gets, the further the process continues, until finally his captive is dead. "You're setting a new record!" he tells one agonized victim, as we see the total growing on a hit counter. Trying to find and stop him are the Cyber Crimes Division of the FBI and the Portland police.

His means of torture and death are sadistic nightmares. Why are so many of us fascinated by horrors in the movies (because, without question, we are)? Maybe it's for the same reason we slow down when we drive past a traffic accident. Maybe because someone else's tragedy is, at least, not ours. It may be hardwired in human nature. I don't have the slightest doubt that if a person were being killed on the Internet, it would draw millions of hits. An FBI spokesman holds a press conference to solemnly warn people that if they log on, they're accessories to murder. Of course that only promotes the site and increases visits.

Diane Lane plays Agent Jennifer Marsh, head of the FBI Portland Cyber Crimes unit. Her partner is Griffin Dowd (Colin Hanks, Tom's son), and her liaison with the Portland police is Detective Eric Box (Billy Burke). They're up against a hacker who uses captive computers of people all over the Net to forward his output and conceal his origins. When you give it a moment's thought, it's sort of a coincidence he's right there in Portland. Maybe that's plot-functional because he can become a threat to Marsh, her daughter, Annie (Perla Haney-Jardine), and her mother (Mary Beth Hurt).

The computer tech jargon in the movie sounds convincing. Whether it's accurate, I have no way of knowing—but that's beside the point, of course. What's ironic is that the key to cracking the case turns out to depend on perhaps our earliest and most basic form of digital communication between remote locations. Diane Lane can play smart, and she does, convincing us she knows her job, while at the same time being a convincing widow, mother, and daughter. The movie is lean and well-acted.

Certain logical questions arise. The killer's ingenuity and unlimited resources are dubious, especially considering what a short turnaround he has between crimes. He has the usual movie villain's ability to know more than he should, move more invisibly than he could, anticipate more than is possible. I think that goes with the territory. Lane's FBI superior is the usual obtuse publicity seeker, making wrong calls. But the through-line of the plot holds firm.

Of course the question occurs: Will the movie inspire copycats? I'm agnostic on this issue. I think a subset of hackers has already demonstrated how ingenious they are at thinking up evil all by themselves, and I doubt a cyber criminal could conceal himself online this successfully: Witness the routine busts of child porn rings.

One detail the movie gets just right. As the current victim dies and the hit-count climbs, we see a scrolling chat room onscreen. The comments are cretinous, stupid, ugly, divorced from all civilized standards. How people with the mentality of the authors of such messages are intelligent enough to get online in the first place is a puzzle. But they do. All you have to do is visit the wrong chat room or bulletin board and see them at their dirty work.

Is there a reason to see this movie? Was there a reason to see *Saw*, or *Se7en*? The purpose and function of the violent movie thriller remains a subject of debate. Yes, I watched fascinated. No, it wasn't art. Its message is visceral. Some people will think: "This is wrong." Others will think: "This is cool." It is the same in countless areas of society.

The movie is made with intelligence and skill. It is a dramatization of the sorts of things that the anonymity of the Internet makes possible, or even encourages. I know that if I learned of a Web site like this one, I, for one, would certainly not log on to it. On the other hand, what did I just do? Type in www.killwithme.com. I found what I expected. But why did I need to find that out? Now what will you do?

Up ★ ★ ★ ★
PG, 96 m., 2009

Edward Asner (Carl Fredricksen), Christopher Plummer (Charles Muntz), Jordan Nagai (Russell), John Ratzenberger (Tom), Bob Peterson (Dug). Directed by Pete Docter and produced by Jonas Rivera. Screenplay by Docter and Bob Peterson.

Up is a wonderful film, with characters who are as believable as any characters can be who spend much of their time floating above the rain forests of Venezuela. They have tempers, problems, and obsessions. They are cute and goofy, but they aren't cute in the treacly way of little cartoon animals. They're cute in the human way of the animation master Hayao Miyazaki. Two of the three central characters are cranky old men, which is a wonder in this youth-obsessed era. *Up* doesn't think all heroes must be young or sweet, although the third important character is a nervy kid.

This is another masterwork from Pixar, which is leading the charge in modern animation. The movie was directed by Pete Docter, who also directed *Monsters, Inc.,* wrote *Toy Story,* and was the cowriter and first director on *WALL-E* before leaving to devote himself full time to this project. So he's one of the leading artists of this renaissance of animation.

The movie is in 3-D in some theaters, about which I will say nothing except to advise you to save the extra money and see it in 2-D. One of the film's qualities that is likely to be diminished by 3-D is its subtle and beautiful color palette. *Up,* like *Finding Nemo, Toy Story, Shrek,* and *The Lion King,* uses colors in a way particularly suited to its content.

Up tells a story as tickling to the imagination as the magical animated films of my childhood, when I naively thought that because their colors were brighter, their character outlines more defined, and their plots simpler, they were actually more realistic than regular films. It begins with a romance as sweet and lovely as any I can recall in feature animation.

Two children named Carl and Ellie meet and discover they share the same dream of someday being daring explorers. In news-reels, they see the exploits of a daring adventurer named Charles Muntz (Christopher Plummer), who uses his gigantic airship to explore a lost world on a plateau in Venezuela and bring back the bones of fantastic creatures previously unknown to man. When his discoveries are accused of being faked, he flies off enraged to South America again, vowing to bring back living creatures to prove his claims.

Nothing is heard from him for years. Ellie and Carl (Edward Asner) grow up, have a courtship, marry, buy a ramshackle house and turn it into their dream home, are happy together, and grow old. This process is silent except for music (Ellie doesn't even have a voice credit). It's shown by Docter in a lovely sequence, without dialogue, that deals with the life experience in a way that is almost never found in family animation. The lovebirds save their loose change in a gallon jug intended to finance their trip to the legendary Paradise Falls, but real life gets in the way: flat tires, home repairs, medical bills. Then they make a heartbreaking discovery. This interlude is poetic and touching.

The focus of the film is on Carl's life after Ellie. He becomes a recluse, holds out against the world, keeps his home as a memorial, talks to the absent Ellie. One day he decides to pack up and fly away—literally. Having worked all his life as a balloon man, he has the equipment on hand to suspend the house from countless helium-filled balloons and fulfill his dream of seeking Paradise Falls. What he wasn't counting on was an inadvertent stowaway—Russell (Jordan Nagai), a dutiful Wilderness Explorer Scout, who looks Asian-American to me.

What they find at Paradise Falls and what happens there I will not say. But I will describe Charles Muntz's gigantic airship that is hovering there. It's a triumph of design and perhaps owes its inspiration, though not its appearance, to Miyazaki's *Castle in the Sky.* The exterior is nothing special: a really big zeppelin. But the interior, now, is one of those movie spaces you have the feeling you'll remember.

With vast inside spaces, the airship is outfitted like a great ocean liner from the golden age, with a stately dining room, long corridors, a display space rivaling the Natural History Museum, and attics spacious enough to harbor fighter planes. Muntz, who must be a centenarian by now, is hale, hearty, and mean, his solitary life shared only by dogs.

The adventures on the jungle plateau are satisfying in a *Mummy/Tomb Raider/*Indiana Jones sort of way. But they aren't the whole point of the film. This isn't a movie like *Mon-sters vs. Aliens* that's mostly just frenetic action. There are stakes here, and personalities involved, and two old men battling for meaning in their lives. And a kid who, for once, isn't smarter than all the adults. And a loyal dog. And an animal sidekick. And always that house and those balloons. ☞

V

Valentino: The Last Emperor ★ ★ ★
NO MPAA RATING, 96 m., 2009

Featuring Valentino Garavani, Giancarlo Giammetti, and Matteo Marzotto. A documentary directed by Matt Tyrnauer and produced by Tyrnauer and Matt Kapp.

To be sure, we see Valentino only at times of great stress, while he is designing a new collection, presenting it in Paris, and preparing for a monumental Roman celebration of his career. But as seen in this film, he seems to suffer from anhedonia, the inability to feel pleasure. He is a multimillionaire, has ruled his profession for forty-five years, has a personal and business partner who has been with him all that time, has every whim attended to. But he seems gnawed by dissatisfaction.

Valentino: The Last Emperor is a documentary with privileged access to the legendary designer in his studio, workshop, backstage, his homes, even aboard his yacht and private jet (which he shares with his matched pugs). It is clear that he does not enjoy being filmed and regrets ever having agreed to it. That gives the film an innate fascination. I know next to nothing about haute couture, but I became involved in the buried drama: Valentino, at seventy-seven, with his world of elegant dresses being destroyed by the branded marketing of—belt buckles! purses! sunglasses!—is clearly at the end of his career.

Nobody will ask him about anything else. Whenever he appears in public, he is surrounded by reporters chanting, "When will you retire?" What are the odds Valentino will announce his retirement right there on the sidewalk to a baying pack of vultures?

But Valentino is coming to the end, all the same. His company has been purchased by an Italian millionaire named Matteo Marzotto, and a multinational is currently buying up its stock. I once bought a pair of sweat pants at Marshall Field's with a Pierre Cardin label. Crummy pants. The only labels I trust are Brooks Brothers and L.L. Bean. But sunglasses with a sequined "V" on them are so close Valentino can smell them. He wants out first.

He works very hard. His head seamstress drives a team of skilled dressmakers. No sewing machines for Valentino. Every stitch by hand. Always at his side is Giancarlo Giammetti, his business partner and onetime lover, who guesses they haven't been apart two months in forty-five years. Valentino was hopeless at business; Giammetti was not. Right at the start Valentino dressed Jackie Kennedy, and his name was made. "I know what women want," he says. "They want to be beautiful." There is a forty-fifth anniversary exhibit of his iconic dresses. To my eye, they look timeless and lovely.

But I am looking at Valentino. He carries himself like an emperor. He walks and stands as if always on stage. He speaks and everyone listens. In photos, he poses as if above the rabble. He is surrounded by much taller women, and treats them as if they are invisible. He relates to his models as if they were mannequins; there is no interaction, nothing personal. Even Giancarlo receives only an official hug, an occasional very quiet "Thank you."

I have the impression Giancarlo is the only one licensed to tell Valentino the truth. "How did I do?" he asks in the backseat of their limousine.

"Great."

"Tell me the truth."

"A little too tan," Giancarlo says. This to a man who looks deep orange. How can he design such dresses and not see himself in the mirror? Surely there is a browner spray-on?

Valentino as a boy idolized the goddesses of the silver screen. All he ever wanted to do was dress them, and that is all he has ever done. The sets and spectacles for his forty-fifth anniversary celebration in Rome resemble, he complains, Cirque du Soleil. They do. The models fly high above the crowd. Everyone is there. The film is crowded with stars, and they're all in the background: Sophia, Gwyneth, Mick, Elton, Princess This, Countess That.

But when he appears at the end of a show, watch him walk out only halfway and give his cursory little wave. No big smile. No blowing kisses. No hands up in triumph. Why isn't he happier? Is he driven by a work ethic that gives him no mercy? Is he . . . shy?

Valkyrie ★ ★ ★
PG-13, 120 m., 2008

Tom Cruise (Colonel Claus von Stauffenberg), Kenneth Branagh (Major General Henning von Tresckow), Bill Nighy (General Friedrich Olbricht), Tom Wilkinson (General Friedrich Fromm), Carice van Houten (Nina von Stauffenberg), Thomas Kretschmann (Major Otto Ernst Remer), Terence Stamp (Ludwig Beck), Eddie Izzard (General Erich Fellgiebel), Jamie Parker (Lieutenant Werner von Haeften), Christian Berkel (Colonel Mertz von Quirnheim). Directed by Bryan Singer and produced by Singer, Christopher McQuarrie, and Gilbert Adler. Screenplay by McQuarrie and Nathan Alexander.

Valkyrie is a meticulous thriller based on a large-scale conspiracy within the German army to assassinate Hitler, leading to a failed bombing attempt on July 20, 1944. At the center of the plot was Colonel Claus von Stauffenberg, played here by Tom Cruise as the moving force behind the attempted coup, which led to seven hundred arrests and two hundred executions, including von Stauffenberg's. Because we know Hitler survived, the suspense is centered in the minds of the participants, who call up the reserve army and actually arrest SS officials before discovering that their bomb did not kill its target.

Considering they were planning high treason with the risk of certain death, the conspirators seem remarkably willing to speak almost openly of their contempt for Hitler. That may be because they were mostly career officers in the army's traditional hierarchy and hated Hitler as much for what he was doing to the army as for what he was doing to the country. Realizing after the invasion of Normandy that the war was certainly lost, they hoped to spare hundreds of thousands of military and civilian lives. Von Stauffenberg was known to be "offended" by the Nazi treatment of Jews in the 1930s, and considered the *Kristallnacht* a disgrace to Germany, which possibly disturbed him as much as the fate of its victims. In any event, little is said among the conspirators about the genocide then under way— although, being alienated from the SS, perhaps they didn't know what was happening. Perhaps.

They repeatedly tell one another that even should they fail, at least the world would know that not all Germans supported Hitler. And so it does. And whatever their deepest motives, they gave their lives in trying to kill the monster. The film, directed by Bryan Singer (*The Usual Suspects*), works heroically to introduce us to the major figures in the plot, to tell them apart, to explain their roles, and to suggest their differences. The two best supporting performances are by Kenneth Branagh, as a general who smuggles a bomb into Hitler's inner circle and then must smuggle it out again, and Tom Wilkinson, as a general who artfully plays both sides of the fence, treating the plot with benign neutrality while covering himself should it fail.

Tom Cruise is perfectly satisfactory, if not electrifying, in the leading role. I'm at a loss to explain the blizzard of negative advance buzz fired at him for the effrontery of playing a half-blind, one-armed Nazi hero. Two factors may be to blame: (a) Cruise has attracted so much publicity by some of his own behavior (Oprah's couch as a trampoline) that anything he does sincerely seems fair game for mockery, and (b) movie publicity is now driven by gossip, scandal, and the eagerness of fanboys and -girls to attract attention by posing as critics of movies they've almost certainly not seen. Now that the movie is here, the buzz is irrelevant but may do residual damage.

If I say that Cruise is not electrifying, I must add that with this character, in this story, he cannot and should not be. This is a film about veterans of officer rank, with all the reserve and probity that officers gather on the way up. They do not scream or hurry and do not care to be seen that way. They have learned not to panic under fire, and they have never been more under fire than now.

A key element of their plot is to use Hitler's Valkyrie plan against him. The reserves were held back to defend Berlin and Hitler in case of an Allied assault, so von Stauffenberg conceived the strategy of killing Hitler, ordering up the reserves to ensure stability, and making the first order of business the immobilization of the SS. We see that the plan might well have worked. Indeed, it did—until the news arrived that Hitler was alive. So much did the führer command the fanatical loyalty of troops and civilians with an almost mystical grip, that merely his voice on the radio could defeat the plot, even with Germany clearly facing ruin.

The July 20 plot is an intriguing footnote to history, one of those "what if" scenarios. If it had succeeded, one of the hopes of the conspirators was said to be an alliance with the Allies against Russia. Given the political realities of the time, when Russia was seen as our ally, that would have been insane, but it shows the plotters continuing to dream of a reborn professional German army with roles for them. The question of the liberation of the death camps is a good one. Even the Allies did not bomb the rail lines leading to them. There were so very, very many people who did not know. ☞

Vanaja ★ ★ ★ ★
NO MPAA RATING, 111 m., 2007

Mamatha Bhukya (Vanaja), Urmila Dammannagari (Rama Devi), Ramachandriah Marikanti (Somayya), Krishnamma Gundimalla (Radhamma), Karan Singh (Shekhar), Bhavani Renukunta (Lacchi), Krishna Garlapati (Ram Babu), Prabhu Garlapati (Yadigiri). Directed by Rajnesh Domalpalli and produced by Latha Rajendra Kumar Domalpalli. Screenplay by Rajnesh Domalpalli.

Vanaja, a beautiful and heart-touching film from India, represents a miracle of casting. Every role, including the challenging central role of a low-caste fourteen-year-old girl, is cast perfectly and played flawlessly, so that it is a renewing pleasure to see these faces on the screen. Then we learn their stories: The actors, naturally and effortlessly true, are all nonprofessionals who were cast for their looks and presence and then trained in an acting workshop set up by the director, Rajnesh Domalpalli. He recalls that his luminous star, Mamatha Bhukya, an eighth-grader, was untrained and had to learn to act and perform classical Indian dances—during a year of lessons set up in his family's basement!

But this movie is not wonderful because of where the actors started. It is wonderful because of where they arrived and who they became. Bhukya is a natural star, her eyes and smile illuminating a face of freshness and de-

light. And the other characters are equally persuasive, especially Urmila Dammannagari, as the district landlady, who has to negotiate a way between her affection for the girl and her love for her son.

But why are you reading this far? An Indian film? Starring Mamatha Bhukya and Urmila Dammannagari? Lesser readers would already have tuned out, but you are curious. And so I can promise you that here is a very special film. It was made by the director as part of his master's thesis in the film department at Columbia University, shot over a period of years on a $20,000 budget, and all I can say is, $20,000 buys a lot in India, including a great-looking, extraordinary film.

Let me tell you a little of the story. In a rural district of South India, a fourteen-year-old girl named Vanaja (Bhukya) lives with her shambling, alcoholic father. Life is bearable because she makes her own way, and when we first see her she's in the front row of a dance performance with her best friend, Lacchi, where they're giggling like bobby-soxers (a word that will mystify some of my Indian readers, but fair's fair). What beautiful girls these are, and I mean that not in a carnal but a spiritual sense. The sun shines from their skin.

Vanaja's father takes her to the local landlady, Rama Devi (Dammannagari), and asks for a job for her. Rama Devi, in her late forties, is not a stereotyped cruel landowner, but a strong yet warm woman with a sense of humor, who likes the girl's pluck during their interview and hires her—at first to work with the livestock. But Vanaja dreams of becoming a dancer and persuades Rama Devi to give her lessons.

As we know from Satyajit Ray's *The Music Room*, many rural landowners pride themselves on their patronage of the arts; to possess an accomplished dancer in her household would be an adornment for Rama Devi. The lessons go well, and there are dance scenes that show how much the actress learned during her year of basement lessons, but there are no Bollywood-type musical scenes here; indeed, the film industry of this district not far from Hyderabad is known as Tollywood, after the Teluga language. It is also a status symbol to speak English, which Vanaja has never been very good at.

The landlady's twenty-three-year-old son, Shekhar (Karan Singh), returns from study in America, prepares to run for office, and notices the new beauty on his mother's staff. And although you may guess what happens next, I won't tell you, except to observe something that struck me. Although there is usually no nudity or even kissing in Indian films (and there is none here), the screenplay is unusually frank in dealing with the realities of sexual life.

Vanaja becomes fifteen, then sixteen. She grows taller. She will be a great beauty. But her lower-caste origins disqualify her for marriage into Rama Devi's family, her drunken father is a worry and burden, the local post-boy is fresh with her, and although the landlady is very fond of her and covets her dancing, her son will always come first. Vanaja's only real allies are her childhood friend and Radhamma (Krishnamma Gundimalla), the landlady's cook and faithful servant.

In any Indian film many of the pleasures are tactile. There are the glorious colors of saris and room decorations, the dazzle of dance costumes, and the dusty landscape that somehow becomes a watercolor by Edward Lear, with its hills and vistas, its oxen and elephants, its houses that seem part of the land. In this setting, Domalpalli tells his story with tender precision and never an awkward moment.

The plot reminds me of neorealism crossed with the eccentric characters of Dickens. The poor girl taken into a rich family is also a staple of Victorian fiction. But *Vanaja* lives always in the moment, growing from a simple story into a complex one, providing us with a heroine, yes, but not villains so much as vain, weak people obsessed with their status in society. When the final shot comes, we miss the comfort of a conventional Hollywood ending. But *Vanaja* ends in a very Indian way, trusting to fate and fortune, believing that there is a tide in the affairs of men, which—but you know where it leads. Let's hope it does.

Vicky Cristina Barcelona ★ ★ ★

NO MPAA RATING, 96 m., 2008

Javier Bardem (Juan Antonio), Rebecca Hall (Vicky), Scarlett Johansson (Cristina), Penelope Cruz (Maria Elena), Patricia Clarkson (Judy Nash), Kevin Dunn (Mark Nash), Chris Messina (Doug). Directed by Woody Allen and produced by Letty Aronson. Screenplay by Allen.

The thing about a Woody Allen film is, whatever else happens, the characters are intriguing to listen to. They tend to be smart, witty, not above epigrams. A few days before seeing *Vicky Cristina Barcelona*, I viewed his *Hannah and Her Sisters* again. More than twenty years apart, both with dialogue at perfect pitch. Allen has directed more than forty movies in about as many years and written all of them himself. Why isn't he more honored? Do we take him for granted?

Vicky Cristina Barcelona is typical of a lot of his midrange work. It involves affluent characters at various levels of sophistication, involved in the arts and the intrigues of love. They're conflicted about right and wrong. They're undoubtedly low-level neurotics. In addition, they are attractive, amusing, and living lives we might envy—in this case, during a summer vacation in Barcelona.

Allen's discovery of Europe (of London, Paris, Venice, Barcelona) has provided new opportunities for the poet of Manhattan (and *Manhattan*). In this film we meet two best friends, Vicky (Rebecca Hall) and Cristina (Scarlett Johansson), who decide to spend July and August in the Barcelona home of Vicky's relatives Judy and Mark (Patricia Clarkson and Kevin Dunn). We're briefed by a narrator that Vicky values stable relationships and is engaged to marry Doug (Chris Messina) when she returns. Cristina is more impulsive, more adventurous, not afraid to risk a little turmoil.

Vicki, we learn, is majoring in "Catalan studies," which makes the capital of Catalonia a perfect destination for her. "What will you . . . do with that?" Mark asks over lunch. "Oh," says Vicky, who clearly has no answer. "Maybe teach, or . . . work for a museum?" Her Spanish, it can be observed, could use some work.

They all go to an art gallery show, and Cristina wonders who the man in the red shirt is. Judy explains that he is Juan Antonio (Javier Bardem), an abstract artist, and there was a scandal over his divorce when he tried to kill his wife or she tried to kill him . . . the details are muddled. At midnight in a restaurant

485

(a conventional dinner hour in Barcelona) the two girls see him across the room. "He keeps looking at us!" Cristina says. "That's because you can't take your eyes off of him," says Vicky. He approaches their table, and in quiet, measured tones, offers to fly them in his plane to an interesting city, see the sights, and sleep with him. Both of them.

Vicky is astonished and offended. Cristina accepts, of course, "with no guarantees." Juan Antonio has, in his own words, made a polite, frank, and straightforward offer. And then the film lingers in the complications of the relationships between these three people before introducing a fourth element: the former wife Maria Elena (Penelope Cruz). The tragedy is, she and Juan Antonio are still deeply in love with each other—but they can't live together without violence flaring up. A *ménage à quatre* takes shape—shaky, but fascinating.

Allen is amusing when he applies strict logic to the situation. If everybody knows and accepts what everybody is doing, where's the harm? Cristina is predisposed to such excitement, and Vicky's love for the stable, responsible, absent Doug begins to pale in comparison with this bohemian existence. Judy, the relative, discovers Vicky's secret and urges her to go with her heart, not her prudence. Vicky and Cristina have conversations in which they show they are open-minded, but perhaps not very prudent. There are unexpected arrivals and developments.

And by now we're engrossed in this comedy, which is really a fantasy—beginning with Juan Antonio, who is too cool and good to be true. All the time, Allen gives us a tour of the glories of Barcelona, the city of Gaudi and Miro, the excuse being that Juan Antonio is showing the girls the sights. As Hollywood learned long ago, there's nothing like a seductive location to lend interest to whatever is happening in the foreground.

More surprises than this I must not describe. It is all fairly harmless, although fraught with dire possibilities. Allen has set out to amuse and divert us and discover secrets of human nature, but not tragically deep ones. He is a little like Eric Rohmer here. The actors are attractive, the city is magnificent, the love scenes don't get all sweaty, and everybody finishes the summer a little wiser and

with a lifetime of memories. What more could you ask?

The Visitor ★ ★ ★ ½
PG-13, 103 m., 2008

Richard Jenkins (Walter Vale), Haaz Sleiman (Tarek), Danai Gurira (Zainab), Hiam Abbass (Mouna). Directed by Tom McCarthy and produced by Mary Jane Skalski and Michael London. Screenplay by McCarthy.

Richard Jenkins is an actor who can move his head half an inch and provide the turning point of a film. That happens in *The Visitor*, where he plays a man around sixty who has essentially shut down all of his emotions. A professor, Walter has been teaching the same class for years and cares nothing about it. He coldly rejects a student's late paper without even inquiring about the "personal problems" that made it late. He makes an elderly piano teacher figure out for herself why she will not be needed again. His lips form a straight line that neither smiles nor frowns.

He is forced to travel from his Connecticut campus to New York, to present an academic paper he coauthored. At least he is honest. Protesting the assignment, he tells a colleague he agreed to put his name on the paper as a favor, has not read it, is not competent to present it. He has to go anyway.

He keeps an apartment in Manhattan. Lets himself in. The naked African girl in his bathtub screams. Her boyfriend appears from somewhere. The interlopers are ready to call the police when he explains it is *his* apartment. They'd been renting it from a crafty opportunist. These "roomers" are Tarek (Haaz Sleiman), from Syria, and his girlfriend, Zainab (Danai Gurira), from Senegal. They immediately pack to leave. He sees them out, then appears at the top of the stairs to tell them they can stay the night. During the film, he will change his mind and appear at the stair-top three times, each time crucial.

Tarek is a virtuoso on an African drum. Walter's late wife was a famous pianist. He loves music but has failed at learning the piano. One day Walter is walking through Washington Square Park and hears two young black boys drumming on the bottoms of plastic buckets. He stops to listen. After a while his head begins to move side to side, half an inch at a time, in response to the rhythm. There you are.

Of course the film, written and directed by Tom McCarthy, is about a great deal more—about illegal U.S. residents and stupid bureaucrats and drums and love and loss. A fourth major character appears, Mouna (Hiam Abbass), who is Tarek's mother and lives in Michigan. She hopes to help her son after he is arrested in an innocent subway incident and threatened with deportation. Walter has already hired a lawyer. He's no bleeding heart, makes no speeches, barely displays emotion, but now for the first time since his wife died, he is feeling things deeply.

This is a wonderful film, sad, angry, and without a comforting little happy ending. But I must not describe what happens because the whole point of serious fiction is to show people changing, and how they change in *The Visitor* is the film's beauty. So much goes unsaid and unseen. Events in Walter's professorial job happen offscreen. We are left to listen to the silences and observe the spaces.

All four actors are charismatic, in quite different ways. Hiam Abbass is one of those actresses who respects small gestures; she knows that when a good cook is using an unfamiliar salt shaker, she shakes the salt first into her hand, and *then* throws it into the pot. And she has other small gestures here that are much more fraught with meaning. Haaz Sleiman and Danai Gurira, as a musician and a jewelry-maker, are young, in love, and simply nice people. The less complicated they are, the better the characters work. And as Walter, Jenkins creates a surprisingly touching, very quiet character study. Not all actors have to call out to us. The better ones make us call out to them.

W

W. ★ ★ ★ ★
PG-13, 131 m., 2008

Josh Brolin (George W. Bush), Elizabeth Banks (Laura Bush), Ellen Burstyn (Barbara Bush), James Cromwell (George H. W. Bush), Richard Dreyfuss (Dick Cheney), Scott Glenn (Donald Rumsfeld), Toby Jones (Karl Rove), Stacy Keach (Reverend Earle Hudd), Bruce McGill (George Tenet), Thandie Newton (Condi Rice), Jeffrey Wright (Colin Powell), Ioan Gruffudd (Tony Blair). Directed by Oliver Stone and produced by Bill Block, Moritz Borman, Paul Hanson, and Eric Kopeloff. Screenplay by Stanley Weiser.

Oliver Stone's *W.*, a biography of President Bush, is fascinating. No other word for it. I became absorbed in its story of a poor little rich kid's alcoholic youth and torturous adulthood. This is the tragedy of a victim of the Peter Principle. Wounded by his father's disapproval and preference for his brother Jeb, the movie argues, George W. Bush rose and rose until he was finally powerful enough to stain his family's legacy.

Unlike Stone's *JFK* and *Nixon,* this film contains no revisionist history. Everything in it, including the scenes behind closed doors, is now pretty much familiar from tell-all books by former Bush aides and reporting by journalists such as Bob Woodward. Although Stone and his writer, Stanley Weiser, could obviously not know exactly who said what and when, there's not a line of dialogue that sounds like malicious fiction. It's all pretty much as published accounts have prepared us for.

The focus is always on Bush (Josh Brolin): his personality, his addiction, his insecurities, his unwavering faith in a mission from God, his yearning to prove himself, his inability to deal with those who advised him. Not surprisingly, in this film, most of the crucial decisions of his presidency were shaped and placed in his hands by the Machiavellian strategist Dick Cheney (Richard Dreyfuss) and the master politician Karl Rove (Toby Jones). Donald Rumsfeld (Scott Glenn) runs an exasperated third.

But what made *them* tick? And what about Colin Powell (Jeffrey Wright) and Condoleezza Rice (Thandie Newton)? You won't find out here. The film sees Bush's insiders from the outside. In his presence, they tend to defer, to use tact as a shield from his ego and defensiveness. But Cheney's soft-spoken, absolutely confident opinions are generally taken as truth. And Bush accepts Rove as the man to teach him what to say and how to say it. He needs them and doesn't cross them.

In the world according to *W.*, Bush always fell short in the eyes of his patrician father (James Cromwell) and outspoken mother (Ellen Burstyn). He resented his parents' greater admiration for his younger brother Jeb. The film lacks scenes showing W. as a child, however—probably wisely. It opens at a drunken fraternity initiation, and "Junior" is pretty much drunk until he finds Jesus at the age of forty. He runs through women, jobs, and cars at an alarming speed and receives one angry lecture after another from his dad.

While running for Congress for the first time, he meets pretty Laura (Elizabeth Banks) at a party, and love blossoms. She was a Gene McCarthy volunteer. Did she turn conservative? I imagine so, but the movie doesn't show them discussing politics. She is patient, steadfast, loving, supportive, and a prime candidate for Al-Anon, the twelve-step program for friends and family of alcoholics. After Bush quits cold turkey, the movie shows him nevertheless often with a beer in his hand, unaware of the jocular AA curse for someone you hate: "One little drink won't kill you." (In an interview, Oliver Stone told me that Bush was not drinking real beer in the later scenes, but the non-alcoholic O'Doul's.)

Dried out, Bush is finally able to hold down jobs. The movie is far from a chronological record, organizing episodes to observe the development of his personality, not his career. Even several spellbinding scenes about the run-up to the Iraq war are not so much critical of his decisions as about how cluelessly, and yet with such vehemence, he stuck with them through thick and thin. At a top-level meeting where he is finally informed that there are no WMDs in Iraq and apparently never were, he is furious for not being informed of this earlier. Several people in the room tried to inform him but were silenced. Colin Powell spends a lot of time softly urging caution and holding his tongue. There is no indication that he will eventually resign.

The movie's Bush is exasperating to work with. At his Texas ranch, he takes the inner circle on a march through the blazing sun, misses a turn, and assures them it's only a half-mile back. Cheney, after three heart attacks, and Rice, wearing inappropriate shoes, straggle along unhappily. His parents are apparently even more disturbed by his decision to run for governor of Texas than by his drinking. Cheney is lectured at a private lunch to remember who is president. He quietly forgets.

Many of the actors somewhat resemble the people they play. The best is Dreyfuss as Cheney, who is not so much a double as an embodiment. The film's portrait of George Senior is sympathetic; it shows him giving Junior the cufflinks that were "the only real thing" his own father, Senator Prescott Bush, ever gave him. The name and the Oedipal Complex were passed down the family tree.

One might feel sorry for George W. at the end of this film, were it not for his legacy of a fraudulent war and a collapsed economy. The film portrays him as incompetent to be president and shaped by the puppet-masters Cheney and Rove to their own ends. If there is a saving grace, it may be that Bush will never fully realize how badly he did. How can he blame himself? He was only following God's will.

The Wackness ★ ★ ★
R, 95 m., 2008

Josh Peck (Luke Shapiro), Ben Kingsley (Dr. Squires), Olivia Thirlby (Stephanie), Method Man (Percy), Mary-Kate Olsen (Union), Famke Janssen (Kristin), Talia Balsam (Mrs. Shapiro), David Wohl (Mr. Shapiro). Directed by Jonathan Levine and produced by Keith Calder, Felipe Marino, and Joe Neurauter. Screenplay by Levine.

The Wackness, which is set in 1994, contains so many drugs it could have been made in the 1970s, along with *Panic in Needle Park* and other landmarks of the psychotropic genera-

tion. The big difference is that drugs have progressed in the years between from cutting-edge material to background music. Both its hero, who has just graduated from high school, and his shrink, forty years his senior, are so constantly stoned that pot and pills are daily, even hourly, fuel.

What saves this from being boring are performances by two actors who see a chance to go over the top and aren't worried about the fall on the other side. Luke Shapiro (Josh Peck) is a college-bound student who deals bushels of marijuana from a battered ice cream pushcart from which no one even attempts to purchase ice cream. Dr. Squires (Ben Kingsley), his psychiatrist, accepts payment in grams and enthusiastically counsels Luke that he needs to get laid. Only when Luke tries to fill the prescription with the doc's stepdaughter Stephanie (Olivia Thirlby, Juno's friend) do ethics come into question.

Peck's performance, for that matter, could have been inspired by Ellen Page's work in *Juno*, assuming he saw the film once and wasn't paying attention. He is cool beyond cool, except when his heart is broken, which happens after he makes the mistake of telling Stephanie he loves her. This is, like, *so* not cool. Meanwhile, Squires's own marriage with Kristin (Famke Janssen) is on the rocks, although both are so spaced out that they don't much care. That leaves space in the story for one meaningful relationship, which is between Luke and Squires.

The Luke character we've seen before, usually not played this well. The psychiatrist is more original. Kingsley, at first unrecognizable with lanky locks and an outdated goatee, is a seriously addicted man, which he must know better than anybody. There's no evidence he has any clients other than Luke, and much of the time he's asking Luke for help. His belief system seems founded on the Beat Generation, and he's acting out his own desires through the younger man. He wants—a laundry list. He wants to be younger, more potent, happily married. He wants to score with hippie chicks (one is played in the movie by Mary-Kate Olsen, who is a superb example of what he has in mind as a hippie chick). He wants to be loved. He wants to love. Everything going wrong in Luke's life right now has been going wrong in the doctor's life for forty years.

It's impossible to not pity this man and carry a reluctant affection for him. He's so screwed up. As a smart, addicted, self-analyzing, secular Jewish intellectual, he could be born of Philip Roth's nightmares. Luke, on the other hand, appears to be a drug-abusing slacker but is, in fact, an *ambitious* drug-abusing slacker, who thinks he might study psychiatry in college. He's in inner turmoil because of problems at home, where the best-laid plans of his father (David Wohl) have run ashore, and the family is being evicted. One motive for Luke's drug-selling spree toward the end of the summer is to bail out his dad, although it appears he would have to turn over the national product of Colombia to succeed.

There's an undeniable pleasure in wallowing in other people's seamy, if entertaining, problems. Even Dr. Squires's descent into despair is accompanied by one-liners and a great sound track (Luke, so retro he's still into cassettes, is always trading custom tracks with both the doctor and his daughter). Toward the end, when Luke summons up the nerve to confess what he truly believes, he has a kind of triumph, heavily laden though it is with qualifiers and apologies. It takes a certain heroism to admit to high feelings and noble instincts of the heart. Drugs are supposed to make that unnecessary, so Luke, I guess, scores more than he realizes. As for the doctor, he achieves all of the benefits of committing suicide, yet suffers none of the drawbacks.

Note: The Wackness *won the audience award at Sundance 2008.*

Waiting for Dublin ★ ★
NO MPAA RATING, 83 m., 2009

Andrew Keegan (Mike), Jade Yourell (Maggie), Hugh O'Conor (Twickers), Guido De Craene (Kluge), Britta Smith (Mrs. Kelleher), Des Braiden (Father Quinlan), Karl Sheils (Vito). Directed by Roger Tucker and produced by Paul Breuls. Screenplay by Chuck Conaway.

As nearly as I can tell, *Waiting for Dublin* is having its world premiere on March 13 in (can you guess?) Chicago, Boston, and New York.

The timing could not be better. The St. Patrick's Day parades will be over in time for an afternoon matinee. And if you are the kind of person who marches in or attends the parade, you may enjoy this film. Other kinds of people, not so much.

Waiting for Dublin is like a time capsule, a film that, in every detail, could have been made in the 1940s and starred Bing Crosby, Pat O'Brien, Maureen O'Hara, and Edmund Gwenn as dear old Father Quinlan, who has the narcolepsy something fierce. It takes place in an Irish hamlet that has one telephone, in the post office that is also the pub. A horse and cart is the favored mode of transport, especially because there is no petrol in wartime.

The time is 1945. The hero is Mike (Andrew Keegan), an American pilot. He and his copilot, Twickers (Hugh O'Conor), run out of fuel and make an emergency landing in Ireland, where they are taken in, given lodging, and welcomed at the pub. The village has another guest, the German pilot Kluge (Guido De Craene). Ireland is officially neutral, and so such visitors are welcome, so long as they are not English, of course.

The town is inhabited, as the old movie rules required, by only colorful eccentrics, who spend all of their time in the pub waiting to be entertained by strangers. They move as a unit, decide as a unit, observe as a unit, and go to Sunday Mass as a unit to see whether Father Quinlan can get as far as *"Introibo ad altare Dei"* before falling asleep.

They quickly grow sympathetic to Mike's plight. Back home in Chicago, he made a $10,000 bet that he would shoot down at least five German fighter planes in the war. He needs one more, the war is about to end, and there is another problem: He made the bet with Al Capone's nephew, who in the movie is named Vito but in real life was named Ralph (Risky) Capone Jr. The movie was wise to change his name; in Chicago, you probably wouldn't make a bet you couldn't cover with a man named Risky Capone.

Mike is desperate—to make a fifth kill and to have sex with the lovely local lass Maggie (Jade Yourell), who says nothing doing unless he proposes marriage and means it. He comes up with a plan to get his fifth kill, and how he does that and with which weapons, I will leave for you to discover, pausing only to wonder how petrol was obtained. His solution and how it plays out is of course utterly preposterous, beginning from the moment Twickers begs off because he has a "cold."

Look, this is a perfectly sweet and harmless film, and if it were in black and white on TCM on St. Paddy's Day, you might watch it. It's so old-fashioned it's almost charming. It is constructed entirely with clichés and stereotypes, right down to the brotherhood of pilots, which was not original when Jean Renoir used it in *The Grand Illusion* (1937). The actors are pleasant, the locations (County Galway) are beautiful, but the movie is a wheeze.

The Walker ★ ★ ★ ½
R, 108 m., 2007

Woody Harrelson (Carter Page III), Kristin Scott Thomas (Lynn Lockner), Lauren Bacall (Natalie Van Miter), Lily Tomlin (Abigail Delorean), Ned Beatty (Jack Delorean), Moritz Bleibtreu (Emek Yoglu), Willem Dafoe (Larry Lockner). Directed by Paul Schrader and produced by Deepak Nayar. Screenplay by Schrader.

Carter Page III likes to tell his friends: "I'm not naive; I'm superficial." His easy, ingratiating manner is ideal for his vocation, which is to act as the unpaid companion of rich society ladies as they attend events without their husbands. Quietly gay, he adores his ladies as friends and sponsors a weekly canasta game for them, which turns into a gossip fest. Paul Schrader's *The Walker* shows him moving smoothly through Washington, D.C., where his father was a senator who investigated Watergate; his mild southern drawl reflects Carter's heritage as the grandson of a tobacco tycoon and the great-grandson of a slave owner. Apparently supported by an inheritance, he is content to be well-dressed, witty, and good company.

Woody Harrelson, who usually plays much rougher types like the bounty hunter in *No Country for Old Men,* inhabits this character as comfortably as an old shirt. His Carter is a character, but not too much of a character. A star in his circle, but in a supporting role. A man who knows his place and treasures it. Schrader says one inspiration for the character was Jerry Zipkin, an escort for Nancy

Reagan, Pat Buckley, and Betsy Bloomingdale. *Women's Wear Daily* coined the term *walker* to describe him, thus identifying a social category. Truman Capote also comes to mind. Unlike the Richard Gere character in Schrader's *American Gigolo,* Carter pleasures his women with company, not sex, and loves doing it.

His three steady "girls," all of a certain age and formidable instincts, are Lynn Lockner (Kristin Scott Thomas), Abigail Delorean (Lily Tomlin), and Natalie Van Miter (Lauren Bacall), who observes that the difficulty with marrying a rich man is that you don't get to have the money, you only get to look at it. Carter is the model of discretion, so much so that Lynn Lockner, the wife of a senator (Willem Dafoe), trusts him to drive her to her weekly meetings with a paid male prostitute in Georgetown. Nobody will recognize his car. He waits outside.

One afternoon she returns to the car almost immediately, trembling. She has discovered her lover stabbed to death. She can't report the murder without involving herself and her husband in scandal. Carter instinctively steps up and takes the hit like a southern gentleman: He tells the police he discovered the body and so becomes their leading suspect. As Carter looks into the crime, the murky undergrowth of Washington corruption begins to exude aromas, and Carter involves his own lover, a young Turk named Emek Yoglu (Moritz Bleibtreu), in their own investigation to save his skin.

The Walker is a quietly enthralling film because it contains the murder and the investigation within Carter's smooth calm. He has practiced for a lifetime at concealing his emotions, first, no doubt, from his father. He is even able to absorb the hurtful fact that his society "friends" drop him like a hot potato. He only wanted to be nice to them; he had no other angle. He enjoyed being on the inside, looking on, overhearing, knowing the real dish. Now he faces murder charges just because he was a good guy.

The Walker is the third of Schrader's "man in a room" films, after *American Gigolo* (1980) and *Light Sleeper* (1992), which starred Willem Dafoe as an upscale drug dealer who tries to get one of his clients off drugs. All three movies involve employment by wealthy older women. Schrader extended the "man in a room" theme to his longtime collaborator Martin Scorsese in his screenplays for *Taxi*

Driver and *Raging Bull*. There is always the same signature: the man in his private space, preparing himself to go out into public. Both *Gigolo*'s Richard Gere and *The Walker*'s Woody Harrelson play men who take elaborate pains with their appearance when it is their reality they should be concerned about.

I have heard complaints that the film "drags in" the murder plot. This is nonsense. All three films involve their heroes in a crime they did not commit, and all three show them trapped as a consequence of their occupations. There is a deep morality at work here, as often in Schrader's work. Also, of course, without the crime as a plot engine, the movie might be only a character study ending on a bittersweet minor chord. I found it fascinating to see Carter Page III discovering under fire that he is, after all, a more loyal friend than his famous father, and a better man.

Walk Hard: The Dewey Cox Story ★ ★ ★
R, 96 m., 2007

John C. Reilly (Dewey Cox), Jenna Fischer (Darlene Madison), Tim Meadows (Sam), Kristen Wiig (Edith), Raymond J. Barry (Pa Cox), Harold Ramis (L'Chai'm), Margo Martindale (Ma Cox), Chris Parnell (Theo), Matt Besser (Dave). Directed by Jake Kasdan and produced by Judd Apatow, Kasdan, and Clayton Townsend. Screenplay by Apatow and Kasdan.

John C. Reilly was appearing on stage in Chicago the other night as Dewey Cox, and the act may be something to fall back on if he ever gives up the daytime job. Apart from anything else demonstrated by *Walk Hard: The Dewey Cox Story*, the movie shows that he can do plausible versions of Johnny Cash, Elvis, Bob Dylan, Roy Orbison, and on and on. He's like a kid who locked himself in his room singing along with his record collection and finally made it pay off.

The movie is a spoof of rock-star biopics, most obviously *Walk the Line*, from which it borrows the wife at home and the affair with the backup singer on the road. There's also a lift from *Ray*, who, you may remember, was blamed for letting his little brother drown. Dewey Cox is out in the barn playing with

machetes with his own brother one day when he inadvertently slices him in half. Fatally? The doctor observes: "It's a particularly bad case of somebody being cut in half."

Life after that is never quite right for Dewey, whose father turns up at every triumph to remind him, "The wrong brother died." He develops into a musical prodigy who masters an instrument almost as soon as he picks it up, and segues effortlessly from one genre to another in order to stay on top of the charts. Soul music? Bubblegum rock? Acid rock? Surfin' songs? Folk rock? He does it all.

And all the time he's on a downward spiral, tempted by Sam, the drummer in his band (*SNL*'s Tim Meadows). Dewey is forever opening a door and finding Sam behind it with cute backup singers, sampling a drug that Sam warns him he is under no circumstances to ever, ever try. He always tries it and cycles through rehabs like a city inspector. His marriage (with Kristen Wiig) breaks up, he falls in love with his backup singer Darlene (Jenna Fischer), travels to India with the Beatles, crosses paths with Buddy Holly and Elvis Presley, and meets Jackson Browne and Lyle Lovett, playing themselves. And all leads to doom because he keeps finding Sam behind another door.

The movie, directed by Jake Kasdan, was cowritten by Kasdan and the producer Judd Apatow (*Superbad*), and they do an interesting thing: Instead of sending everything over the top at high energy—like *Top Secret* or *Airplane!*—they allow Reilly to more or less actually *play* the character, so that, against all expectations, some scenes actually approach real sentiment. Reilly is required to walk a tightrope; is he suffering or kidding suffering, or kidding suffering about suffering? That we're not sure adds to the appeal.

Note: I must mention one peculiar element in the film. As Reilly is having a telephone conversation, a male penis is framed in the upper right corner of the screen. No explanation about why, or whom it belongs to, or what happens to it. Just a penis. I think this just about establishes a standard for gratuitous nudity. Speculate as I will, I cannot imagine why it's in the film. Did the cinematographer look through his viewfinder and say, "Jake, the upper right corner could use a penis?"

Walking to Werner ★ ★ ★
NO MPAA RATING, 93 m., 2007

Featuring Linas Phillips and Werner Herzog.
A documentary directed by Linas Phillips and
produced by Dayne Hanson.

The free spirit Werner Herzog, whose *Rescue
Dawn* is now a considerable success, likes to
walk. He has inspired at least two would-be
filmmakers to follow in his footsteps. Faithful
readers will know that I value Herzog's films
beyond all measure and never tire of telling
the famous story of the time he learned his
dear friend, the film historian Lotte Eisner,
was dying in Paris. Thereupon he set off to
walk from Munich to Paris, convinced she
would not die before his arrival, and he was
quite right.

Another time, he walked completely
around Albania ("Because at that time, you
could not enter Albania"). When I invited him
to my film festival a few years ago, he was lowered from a plateau in a South American rain
forest, made his way by log canoe and trading
skiff to a pontoon plane that took him to a
boat, etc. "He came because it was so difficult,"
his wife, Lena, told me. "If Werner had been in
Los Angeles, it would have been too easy, and
he might not have made the journey."

His friend Dusan Makavejev tells in the
new book, *The Cinema of the Balkans,* that
Werner once came looking for an ancestor in
Croatia and followed his footsteps up a Serbian mountain, hoping to help end the war
raging around him. "The essential things in
life," Herzog has said, "I would cover on foot,
regardless of the distance."

Herzog, his films, and his walking inspired
the filmmaker Linas Phillips to make *Walking
to Werner,* the story of his walking 1,200 miles
from Seattle to Los Angeles to meet the great
man. Another film is by Herzog admirer
Lee Kazimir of Chicago, who walked from
Madrid to Kiev. In a message to me, Kazimir
quoted Herzog: "If you want to make films
you should skip film school. Instead, you
should make a journey of five thousand kilo-
meters alone, on foot. While walking you
would learn more about what cinema truly
means than you would in five years of sitting
in classrooms."

Herzog doesn't encourage these journeys
when he is the destination. He warned Phillips
that he would not be at home when the young
man arrived, because he would be in Laos,
Burma, and Thailand filming *Rescue Dawn.*
Phillips persisted. Kazimir wrote asking his
blessing, and Herzog told me: "I had instant
hesitations, and told him so, as he was going to
make his voyage a public event. Traveling on
foot was, in my understanding, a thing you had
to do as a man exposing yourself in the most
direct way to life, to *pura vida,* and this should
stay with oneself." Kazimir also persisted.

Walking to Werner is the first of these films
to open but doesn't steal the thunder of the
second because both will be about the
trekkers and not Herzog. The real interest in
the film is not the journey or even Linas
Phillips (who comes across a little like Timothy Treadwell, the hero of Herzog's *Grizzly
Man*), but the people he meets on the way.

Some of them look like you might want to
cross the road to avoid them, but with one
hostile exception and one sad exception they
are all sane, friendly, cheerful, and encouraging. I was particularly moved by Robert, a
laid-off Boeing worker in Seattle who sees
Phillips in a bar and tells him, "Don't end up
like me." Phillips asks him to voice the title of
the movie for him and requests his blessing at
the start of the walk.

Another, Eli, was walking without food because "he no longer saw the worth of life and
was too cowardly to kill himself." Phillips, who
discovers "when you travel on foot, there's no
small talk," meets another man who tells him,
"I have no soul." Five miles down the road, the
man catches up with Phillips and corrects
himself: "I do have a soul."

These encounters are supplemented by
Phillips's narration and by the voice of Herzog, often taken from Les Blank's amazing
documentary *Burden of Dreams,* the record of
Herzog filming *Fitzcarraldo.* That was the film
when Herzog, shunning special effects, hauled
a real steamboat over a real hill between two
river systems. "Moviegoers have to be able to
trust their eyes," he explained.

With his long blond hair flowing from
beneath his Tilley hat (the hiker's friend),
Phillips is once mistaken for a woman and
firmly corrects the impression. His face turns

red and weathered, his toes develop blisters, and although he often stays in motels he has a disconcerting tendency to walk late into the night and the rain. He looks exhausted much of the time; did he train for this walk? As gigantic trucks roar past, he calculates the odds of one of them killing him.

One reason for his long hair may be that, in 2003, he performed a one-man show, *Linas as Kinski*, in New York. Having embodied the look and spirit of Klaus Kinski, the temperamental subject of Herzog's documentary *My Best Fiend*, Phillips still seems to be in costume.

He communicates with Herzog by e-mail. "If you want to walk, do it for some other reason," the director advises him. When Phillips speculates about going on to Thailand to film a meeting to end his film, Herzog replies, "An interview would be a cheap end to your film."

WALL-E ★ ★ ★ ½
G, 98 m., 2008

With the voices of: Ben Burtt (WALL-E), Elissa Knight (Eve), Jeff Garlin (Captain), Fred Willard (Shelby Forthright), John Ratzenberger (John), Kathy Najimy (Mary), Kim Kopf (Hoverchair Mother), Garrett Palmer (Hoverchair Son), Sigourney Weaver (Ship's Computer). Directed by Andrew Stanton and produced by Jim Morris. Screenplay by Stanton and Jim Reardon.

Pixar's *WALL-E* succeeds at being three things at once: an enthralling animated film, a visual wonderment, and a decent science-fiction story. After *Kung Fu Panda*, I thought I had just about exhausted my emergency supply of childlike credulity, but here is a film, like *Finding Nemo*, that you can enjoy even if you've grown up. That it works largely without spoken dialogue is all the more astonishing; it can easily cross language barriers, which is all the better, considering that it tells a planetary story.

It is the relatively near future. A city of skyscrapers rises up from the land. A closer view reveals that the skyscrapers are all constructed out of garbage, neatly compacted into squares or bales and piled on top of one another. In all the land, only one creature stirs. This is WALL-E, the last of the functioning solar-powered robots. He (the story leaves no doubt about gender) scoops up trash, shovels it into his belly, compresses it into a square, and climbs on his tractor treads up a winding road to the top of his latest skyscraper, to place it neatly on the pile.

It is lonely being WALL-E. But does WALL-E even know that? He comes home at night to a big storage area, where he has gathered a few treasures from his scavengings of the garbage and festooned them with Christmas lights. He wheels into his rest position, takes off his treads from his tired wheels, and goes into sleep mode. Tomorrow is another day. One of thousands since the last humans left Earth and settled into orbit aboard gigantic spaceships that resemble spas for the fat and lazy.

One day WALL-E's age-old routine is shattered. Something new appears in his world, which otherwise has consisted only of old things left behind. This is, to our eye, a sleek spaceship. To WALL-E's eyes, who knows? What with one thing and another, WALL-E is scooped up by the ship and returned to the orbiting spaceship Axiom, along with his most recent precious discovery: a tiny, perfect green plant, which he found growing in the rubble and transplanted to an old shoe.

Have you heard enough to be intrigued, or do you want more? Speaking voices are now heard for the first time in the movie, although all on his own WALL-E has a vocabulary (or repertory?) of squeaks, rattles, and electronic purrs, and a couple of pivoting eyes that make him look downright anthropomorphic. We meet a Hoverchair family, so known because aboard ship they get around in comfy chairs that hover over surfaces and whisk them about effortlessly. They're all as fat as Susie's aunt. This is not entirely their fault, since generations in the low-gravity world aboard the Axiom have evolved humanity into a race whose members generally resemble those folks you see whizzing around Wal-Mart in their electric shopping carts.

There is now a plot involving WALL-E, the ship's captain, several Hoverpeople, and the fate of the green living thing. And in a development that would have made Sir Arthur Clarke's heart beat with joy, humanity returns home once again—or is that a spoiler?

The movie has a wonderful visual look. Like so many of the Pixar animated features, it finds a color palette that's bright and cheerful, but not too pushy and a tiny bit realistic at the same time. The drawing style is comic-book cool, as perfected in the funny comics more than the superhero books: Everything has a stylistic twist to give it flair. And a lot of thought must have gone into the design of WALL-E, for whom I felt a curious affection. Consider this hunk of tin beside the Kung Fu Panda. The panda was all but special-ordered to be lovable, but on reflection I think he was so fat, it wasn't funny anymore. WALL-E, on the other hand, looks rusty and hardworking and plucky, and expresses his personality with body language and (mostly) with the binocular video cameras that serve as his eyes. The movie draws on a tradition going back to the earliest days of Walt Disney, who reduced human expressions to their broadest components and found ways to translate them to animals, birds, bees, flowers, trains, and everything else.

What's more, I don't think I've quite captured the enchanting storytelling of the film. Directed by Andrew Stanton, who wrote and directed *Finding Nemo*, it involves ideas, not simply mindless scenarios involving characters karate-kicking each other into high-angle shots. It involves a little work on the part of the audience and a little thought, and might be especially stimulating to younger viewers. This story told in a different style and with a realistic look could have been a great science-fiction film. For that matter, maybe it is.

Note: The movie is preceded by Presto Chango, *a new Pixar animated short about a disagreement over a carrot between a magician and his rabbit.* ☞

Waltz with Bashir ★ ★ ★ ½
R, 87 m., 2009

With the voices of: Ari Folman, Ori Sivan, Ronny Dayag, Shmuel Frenkel, Zahava Solomon, Ron Ben-Yishai, Dror Harazi, Boaz Rein-Buskila, Carmi Cna'an. Directed by Ari Folman and produced by Folman, Yael Nahlieli, Bridgit Folman, Serge Lalou, Gerhard Meixner, and Roman Paul. Screenplay by Folman.

Waltz with Bashir is a devastating animated film that tries to reconstruct how and why thousands of innocent civilians were massacred because those with the power to stop them took no action. Why they did not act is hard to say. Did they not see? Not realize? Not draw fateful conclusions? In any event, at the film's end, the animation gives way to newsreel footage of the dead, whose death is inescapable.

The massacre, well documented, took place during Israel's 1982 invasion of Lebanon. The victims were in Palestinian refugee camps. They were killed by a Christian militia. Israelis were in nominal control of the militia but did not stop the massacre. Blame has never been clearly assigned. Certainly the Christians pulling the triggers were guilty. Were the Israelis enablers?

In war, they say, no one sees the big picture, the men at the top least of all. *Waltz with Bashir* opens with a recurring nightmare had by a friend of Ari Folman, who wrote and directed the film. It is described to Folman in the course of his attempt to reconstruct what actually happened during days when he was present; he has the confused impression that the truth of those days was just outside his grasp. He sets out to interview Israeli army friends who were also there, and his film resembles *Rashomon* in the way truth depends not on facts but on who witnessed them and why.

Folman is an Israeli documentarian who has not worked in animation. Now he uses it as the best way to reconstruct memories, fantasies, hallucinations, possibilities, past and present. This film would be nearly impossible to make any other way. Animation will always be identified, no doubt, with funny animals, but is winning respect as a medium for serious subjects. Consider the great success of *WALL-E*, which was greatly entertaining, yet a radical critique of the consumer society.

The film is structured like a conventional documentary, with Folman visiting old army friends and piecing together what they saw and remember. The freedom of animation allows him to visualize what they tell him— even their nightmares. The title refers to an Israeli soldier losing it and firing all around himself on a street papered with posters of the just-assassinated Lebanese president-elect Bashir Gemayel—thus, waltzing with Bashir.

Folman gradually fits together a puzzle with the massacre at the center and his witnesses in concentric rings at various distances. Who knew what was happening? Which Israeli commanders were in a position to stop it? After it was over, it became simply a thing that had happened, seemingly without decision or choice. Had anyone in fact ordered the Christian militia to shoot or had they spontaneously agreed to kill?

It is impossible to pin down the answers. My impression is that some knew, some could have stopped it, but the connections between the two are uncertain. That is almost always the case with genocide. At this moment, for example, the world fully knows that ethnic slaughter is taking place in the Congo. The world stands aside. Eventually we will regret not having acted, as we regret Rwanda, Bosnia, Somalia, and indeed the Holocaust. Those pulling the triggers are the immediate murderers. Those in charge of them are morally guilty. Those who could stop them, even more so. That means us.

The debate still continues about the inaction of the Allies in not bombing the rail lines leading to the death camps, although there were bombs to spare for bombing German civilians. Now *Waltz with Bashir* argues that Israel itself is not guiltless in acts of passive genocide, an argument underlined by the disproportionate Israeli response to the provocations of Hamas. We may be confronted here with a fundamental flaw in human nature. When he said "The buck stops here," Harry Truman was dreaming. The buck never stops.

Wanted ★ ★ ★
R, 110 m., 2008

James McAvoy (Wesley Gibson), Morgan Freeman (Sloan), Terence Stamp (Pekwarsky), Thomas Kretschmann (Cross), Common (The Gunsmith), Angelina Jolie (Fox). Directed by Timur Bekmambetov and produced by Marc Platt, Jim Lemley, Jason Netter, and Iain Smith. Screenplay by Michael Brandt, Derek Haas, and Chris Morgan.

Wanted slams the pedal to the metal and never slows down. Here's an action picture that's exhausting in its relentless violence and its ingenuity in inventing new ways to attack, defend, ambush, and annihilate. Expanding on a technique I first saw in David O. Russell's *Three Kings,* it follows individual bullets (as well as flying warriors) through implausible trajectories to pound down the kills.

The movie is based on comic books by Mark Millar and J. G. Jones. Their origin story involves an anxiety-ridden, henpecked, frustrated office worker named Wesley (James McAvoy), whom you might have glimpsed in a bogus YouTube video trashing his office. In the movie he gets the opportunity to trash a lot more than that. In a plot development that might have been inspired by James Thurber's *The Secret Life of Walter Mitty* (but probably wasn't, because who reads that great man anymore?), Wesley gets the opportunity to find revenge on his tormentors and enter a fantasy world where he can realize his hidden powers as a skilled assassin.

This happens after he is picked up in a bar by Fox (Angelina Jolie), who confides that he is now a member of The Fraternity, a thousand-year-old secret society of assassins who kill bad people. I suppose a lot of people, if they were picked up in a bar by Angelina Jolie, would go along with that story. Although The Fraternity's accuracy rate can be faulted (it missed on Hitler and Stalin, for example), its selection methods must be Really Deep, since orders are transmitted through The Loom of Fate. As demonstrated in the film, if you look at a cloth really, really, *really* closely, you can see that every once in a while a thread is out of line. These threads represent a binary code that is way deeper than my old Lone Ranger Decoder Ring. They also raise questions about the origin, method, and reading of themselves, which are way, way too complicated to be discussed here, assuming they could be answered, which I confidently believe would not be the case.

Never mind. Wesley leaves his office life for a hidden alternative existence in which he masters skills of fighting (by hurtling hundreds of feet) and shooting (around corners, for example). And he is introduced to Sloan (Morgan Freeman), who, the moment I mentioned Morgan Freeman, you immediately knew was deep and wise and in charge of things. He lives in a book-lined library (but Wesley, to my intense regret, never asks him, "Have you really read all these books? Anything by Thurber?"). Sloane explains that Wesley's father was a member of The Fraternity, killed years ago by the man Wesley is now destined to kill. This is Cross (Thomas Kretschmann), who lurks in Europe, where Wesley also meets Pekwarsky (Terence Stamp), another fraternity brother. (Do you suppose The Fraternity's secret handshake is fatal? If brothers give it to each other, do they both die?)

I'd guess there are, oh, ten or fifteen shots in this entire movie without special effects. The rest of the time, we're watching motion-capture animation, CGI, stuff done in the lab. A few of the stunts look like they could not have been faked, but who knows? What do you think your chances are when you run on top of a speeding train? For that matter, if you were assigned to kill someone in Chicago, could you figure out a better way to do it than by standing on top of an El train while it raced past your target's office window? And how did The Fraternity know he would be visible through that window? And how . . . oh, never mind.

Wanted, directed by a hot Russian action-meister named Timur Bekmambetov, is a film entirely lacking in two organs I always appreciate in a movie: a heart and a mind. It is mindless, heartless, preposterous. By the end of the film we can't even believe the values the plot seems to believe, since the plot is deceived right along with us. The way to enjoy this film is to put your logic on hold, along with any higher sensitivities that might be vulnerable, and immerse yourself as if in a video game. That *Wanted* will someday be a video game, I have not the slightest doubt. It may already *be* a video game, but I'm damned if I'll look it up and find out. Objectively, I award it all honors for technical excellence. Subjectively, I'd rather be watching Danny Kaye in the film version of *The Secret Life of Walter Mitty.*

Note: I learn that The Secret Life of Walter Mitty *will be remade next year and will star Mike Myers. Having seen Myers's* The Love Guru, *I think I can predict one of Walter's big secrets.*

War, Inc. ★ ★
R, 106 m., 2008

John Cusack (Brand Hauser), Hilary Duff (Yonica Babyyeah), Marisa Tomei (Natalie Hegalhuzen), Joan Cusack (Marsha Dillon), Dan Aykroyd (Ex–Vice President), Ben Kingsley (Walken/Viceroy), Lubomir Neikov (Omar Sharif). Directed by Joshua Seftel and produced by Les Weldon, Danny Lerner, John Cusack, and Grace Loh. Screenplay by Cusack, Mark Leyner, and Jeremy Pikser.

War, Inc. is a brave and ambitious but chaotic attempt at political satire. The targets: the war in Iraq and the shadowy role of Vice President Cheney's onetime corporate home Halliburton in the waging of the war. Dan Aykroyd plays an "ex–vice president," unmistakably Cheney, issuing orders to CIA hit man Brand Hauser (John Cusack) to assassinate a Middle Eastern oil minister (named Omar Sharif, not much of a joke) whose plans to build a pipeline in his own country run counter to the schemes of the supercorporation Tamerlane.

Hauser is an intriguing character, seen chugging shot glasses of hot sauce for reasons that are no doubt as significant as they are obscure. "I feel like a refugee from the island of Dr. Moreau," he confides at one point to the onboard computer on his private plane, a sort of sympathetic HAL 9000. Arriving in the country of Turaqistan, he finds warfare raging everywhere except within a protected area known as the Emerald City, for which of course we are to read Baghdad's Green Zone. Here American corporations are so entrenched that Hauser reaches the secret bunker of the Viceroy (a Tamerland puppet) through a Popeye's Fried Chicken store.

That sort of satire runs through the movie, which is neither quite serious nor quite funny, but very busy with trying to be one or the other. Lots of other brand names (in addition to *brand* Hauser) appear in connection with an expo being staged by public relations whiz Marsha Dillon (Joan Cusack), who becomes Hauser's cynical adviser. Among her plans for the expo: the televised wedding of Middle Eastern pop superstar Yonica Babyyeah (Hilary Duff, but you won't recognize her).

Arriving in Turaqistan at about the same

time as Hauser is Natalie Hegalhuzen (Marisa Tomei), a reporter for liberal magazines, whose character and others in the film illustrate my First Law of Funny Names, which teaches us that they are rarely funny. She is a warm, pretty woman who quickly appeals to Hauser, already having second thoughts about his hit-man role. She's smart, too, with an occasional tendency to talk like she's writing (she describes Yonica as "a sad little girl who's been pimped out into a pathetic monstrosity of Western sexuality").

All of the story strands come together into a bewildering series of solutions and conclusions, in which the fictional heritage of the name "Emerald City" plays a prominent role. But the intended satire isn't as focused or merciless as it could be and tries too hard to keep too many balls in the air. The movie's time period is hard to nail down; the opening titles refer to the "21st century," but of course that's the present, and current names are referred to (McLaughlin, Anderson Cooper, Cheney, Katie Couric, 50 Cent, etc). One particularly brilliant invention is Combat-O-Rama, which is a version of a Disney World virtual reality thrill ride allowing journalists to experience battle through what I guess you'd call "virtual embedding."

John Cusack is the power behind the film, as star, top-billed writer, and one of the producers. He deserves credit for trying to make something topical, controversial, and uncompromised. The elements are all here. But the parts never come together. Cusack has made fifty-six films and is only forty-two years old, and his quality control is uncanny. He shies away from unworthy projects and is always available to take a chance. A project like *War, Inc.* must not have been easy to finance, shows a determination to make a movie that makes a statement, and is honorable. Sometimes the best intentions don't pay off. I wanted to like it more than I could.

Watchmen ★ ★ ★ ★
R, 163 m., 2009

Malin Akerman (Laurie Jupiter/Silk Spectre II), Billy Crudup (Jon Osterman/Dr. Manhattan), Matthew Goode (Adrian Veidt/Ozymandias), Carla Gugino (Sally Jupiter/Silk Spectre), Jackie Earle Haley (Walter Kovacs/Rorschach), Stephen McHattie (Hollis Mason/Nite Owl), Jeffrey Dean Morgan (Edward Blake/The Comedian), Patrick Wilson (Dan Dreiberg/Nite Owl II). Directed by Zack Snyder and produced by Lawrence Gordon, Lloyd Levin, and Deborah Snyder. Screenplay by David Hayter and Alex Tse, based on the graphic novel by Alan Moore and Dave Gibbons.

After the revelation of *The Dark Knight,* here is *Watchmen,* another bold exercise in the liberation of the superhero movie. It's a compelling visceral film—sound, images, and characters combined into a decidedly odd visual experience that evokes the feel of a graphic novel. It seems charged from within by its power as a fable; we sense it's not interested in a plot so much as with the dilemma of functioning in a world losing hope.

That world is America in 1985, with Richard Nixon in the White House and many other strange details; this America occupies a parallel universe in which superheroes and masked warriors operate. The film confronts a paradox that was always there in comic books: The heroes are only human. They can only be in one place at a time (with a possible exception to be noted later). Although a superhero is able to handle one dangerous situation, the world has countless dangerous situations, and the super resources are stretched too thin. Faced with law enforcement anarchy, Nixon has outlawed superhero activity, quite possibly a reasonable action. Now the murder of the enigmatic vigilante the Comedian (Jeffrey Dean Morgan) has brought the Watchmen together again. Who might be the next to die?

Dr. Manhattan (Billy Crudup), the only one with superpowers in the literal sense, lives outside ordinary time and space, the forces of the universe seeming to coil beneath his skin. Ozymandias (Matthew Goode) is the world's smartest man. The Nite Owl (Patrick Wilson) is a man isolated from life by his mastery of technology. Rorschach (Jackie Earl Haley) is a man who finds meaning in patterns that may exist only in his mind. And Silk Spectre II (Malin Akerman) lives with one of the most familiar human challenges, living up to her parents, in this case the original Silk Spectre (Carla Gugino). Dr. Manhattan is both her lover and a distant father figure living in a world of his own.

These characters are garbed in traditional comic book wardrobes—capes, boots, gloves, belts, masks, props, anything to make them one of a kind. Rorschach's cloth mask, with its endlessly shifting ink blots, is one of the most intriguing superhero masks ever, always in constant motion, like a mood ring of the id. Dr. Manhattan is contained in a towering, muscular, naked blue body; he was affected by one of those obligatory secret experiments gone wild. Never mind the details; what matters is that he possibly exists at a quantum level, at which particles seem exempt from the usual limitations of space and time. If it seems unlikely that quantum materials could assemble into a tangible physical body, not to worry. Everything is made of quantum particles, after all. There's a lot we don't know about them, including how they constitute Dr. Manhattan, so the movie is vague about his precise reality. I was going to say Silk Spectre II has no complaints, but actually she does.

The mystery of the Comedian's death seems associated with a plot to destroy the world. The first step in the plot may be to annihilate the Watchmen, who are All That Stand Between, etc. It is hard to see how anyone would benefit from the utter destruction of the planet, but in the movie's world there is a nuclear standoff between the United States and the Soviet Union that threatens exactly that. During the Cuban missile crisis, remember "Better Dead Than Red"? There were indeed cold warriors who preferred to be dead rather than red, reminding me of David Merrick's statement: "It's not enough for me to win. My enemies must lose."

In a cosmic sense it doesn't really matter who pushed the Comedian through the window. In a cosmic sense, nothing really matters, but best not meditate on that too much. The Watchmen and their special gifts are all the better able to see how powerless they really are, and although all but Dr. Manhattan are human and back the home team, their powers are not limitless. Dr. Manhattan, existing outside time and space, is understandably remote from the fate of our tiny planet, although perhaps he still harbors some old emotions.

Those kinds of quandaries engage all the

Watchmen and are presented in a film experience of often fearsome beauty. It might seem improbable to take seriously a naked blue man, complete with discreet genitalia, but Billy Crudup brings a solemn detachment to Dr. Manhattan that is curiously affecting. Does he remember how it felt to be human? No, but hum a few bars. . . . Crudup does the voice and the body language, which is transformed by software into a figure of considerable presence.

Watchmen focuses on the contradiction shared by most superheroes: They cannot live ordinary lives but are fated to help mankind. That they do this with trademarked names and appliances goes back to their origins in Greece, where Zeus had his thunderbolts, Hades his three-headed dog, and Hermes his winged feet. Could Zeus run fast? Did Hermes have a dog? No.

That level of symbolism is coiling away beneath all superheroes. What appeals with Batman is his humanity; despite his skills, he is not supernormal. *Watchmen* brings surprising conviction to these characters as flawed and minor gods, with Dr. Manhattan possessing access to godhead on a plane that detaches him from our daily concerns—indeed, from days themselves. In the film's most spectacular scene, he is exiled to Mars and in utter isolation reimagines himself as a human and conjures (or discovers? I'm not sure) an incredible city seemingly made of crystal and mathematical concepts. This is his equivalent to forty days in the desert, and he returns as a savior.

The film is rich enough to be seen more than once. I plan to see it again, this time on IMAX, and will have more to say about it. I'm not sure I understood all the nuances and implications, but I am sure I had a powerful experience. It's not as entertaining as *The Dark Knight,* but like the *Matrix* films, *LOTR,* and *The Dark Knight,* it's going to inspire fevered analysis. I don't want to see it twice for that reason, however, but mostly just to have the experience again. ☞

The Water Horse: Legend of the Deep ★ ★ ★ ½

PG, 111 m., 2007

Alex Etel (Angus MacMorrow), Emily Watson (Anne MacMorrow), Ben Chaplin (Lewis

Mowbray), David Morrissey (Captain Hamilton), Brian Cox (Old Angus), Priyanka Xi (Kirstie MacMorrow), Marshall Napier (Sergeant Strunk), Joel Tobeck (Sergeant Walker), Erroll Shand (Lieutenant Wormsley). Directed by Jay Russell and produced by Robert Bernstein, Douglas Rae, Barrie M. Osborne, and Charlie Lyons. Screenplay by Robert Nelson Jacobs, based on the book by Dick King-Smith.

If you can't think of three more endearing recent family movies than *My Dog Skip*, *Babe*, and *Millions*, then here's another title to add to the list. *The Water Horse: Legend of the Deep* is based on a book by the author of *Babe*, made by the director of *My Dog Skip*, and stars the hero of *Millions*, and it fully lives up to its lineage. It opened just in the nick of time on Christmas Day to save parents from having to take the kids to *Alvin and the Chipmunks*.

The movie, set in Scotland but wonderfully photographed in New Zealand, tells the story of a twelve-year-old named Angus (Alex Etel), who finds a curious egg on the beach, brings it home, and is astonished to see it hatch a cute little amphibian with a big appetite. He names it Crusoe and conceals his new pet in the work shed, where it doesn't remain a secret for long, particularly since it seems to double in size every day or so. One day it's terrified by the family bulldog, and a day later the bulldog is terrified by it.

The time is World War II. Angus lives with his mother, Anne (Emily Watson), and older sister, Kirstie (Priyanka Xi), and keeps a bulletin board with news and memories of his beloved father, who is away fighting the war. He tries his best to be "the man of the family," per his father's final instructions, and there is another man around, Lewis Mowbray (Ben Chaplin), who helps out with barnyard duties and general repairs.

Lewis becomes pals with Angus and Kirstie, and helps them keep the secret of Crusoe from their mother, who might not approve of the pet, especially as it balloons to twice Angus's size, and then three times, and then four times, until it grows so big that there is nothing to be done but move it from the work shed to the nearest large body of water, which is, you guessed it, Loch Ness.

We learn the legend of the water horse. In all the world, only one is alive at a time. Before it dies, it lays an egg, which will produce the next water horse. As it reaches maturity, it looks like a jolly sea serpent with certain characteristics reminding us of Shrek and E.T., especially in its playful nature, humanlike expressions, and inadvertent gift for comedy.

The farm has been commandeered as a posting for a British artillery unit, charged with placing a submarine net across the mouth of the loch. The unit commander, the supercilious Captain Hamilton (David Morrissey), seems certain this is where German U-boats will first land on British soil. Some of his men are equally certain that Hamilton drew this cushy assignment as a way of staying out of action. Anne is courted by the slick officer, who goes out of his way to insult Lewis, the man-of-all-work. But all is sorted out with a vengeance, as Angus gradually comes to accept that his father may not be coming home.

Like most British family films, *The Water Horse* doesn't dumb down its young characters or insult the intelligence of the audience. It has a lot of sly humor about what we know, or have heard, about the Loch Ness Monster and various frauds associated with it, and fills the edges of the screen with first-rate supporting performances. Imagine a family film with actors the caliber of Emily Watson, Ben Chaplin, and Brian Cox as an old-timer who spins stories in the local pub.

Will younger kids be a little scared as Crusoe approaches the dimensions of a whale? Maybe, maybe not. Kids seem harder to scare these days, although I'm afraid some of them will find themselves taken to *Sweeney Todd*, which is definitely not for under-thirteens. What kids will love is Angus's thrilling bareback ride on Crusoe. And viewers of all ages will appreciate that *The Water Horse*, despite its fantasy, digs in with a real story about complex people and doesn't zone out with the idiotic cheerfulness of Alvin and his squeaky little friends.

Wendy and Lucy ★ ★ ★ ½
R, 80 m., 2009

Michelle Williams (Wendy), Will Patton (Mechanic), John Robinson (Andy), Larry Fessenden (Man in Park), Will Oldham (Icky),

Walter Dalton (Security Guard). Directed by Kelly Reichardt and produced by Neil Kopp, Anish Savjani, and Larry Fessenden. Screenplay by Reichardt and Jon Raymond, based on the story "Train Choir" by Jon Raymond.

I know so much about Wendy although this movie tells me so little. I know almost nothing about where she came from, what her life was like, how realistic she is about the world, where her ambition lies. But I know, or feel, everything about Wendy at this moment: stranded in an Oregon town, broke, her dog lost, her car a write-off, hungry, friendless, quiet, filled with desperate resolve.

Kelly Reichardt's *Wendy and Lucy* is another illustration of how absorbing a film can be when the plot doesn't stand between us and a character. There is no timetable here. Nowhere Wendy came from, nowhere she's going to, no plan except to get her car fixed and feed her dog. Played by Michelle Williams, she has a gaze focused inward on her determination. We pick up a few scraps: Her sister in Indiana is wary of her, and she thinks she might be able to find a job in a fish cannery in Ketchikan, Alaska.

But Alaska seems a long way to drive from Indiana just to get a job in a cannery, and this movie isn't about the unemployment rate. Alaska perhaps appeals to Wendy because it is as far away she can drive where they still speak English. She parks on side streets and sleeps in her car, she has very limited cash, her golden retriever, Lucy, is her loving companion. She wakes up one morning somewhere in Oregon, her car won't start, and she's out of dog food, and that begins a chain of events that leads to wandering around a place she doesn't know looking for her only friend in the world.

When I say I know all about Wendy, that's a tribute to Michelle Williams's acting, Kelly Reichardt's direction, and the cinematography of Sam Levy. They use Williams's expressive face, often forlorn, always hopeful, to show someone who embarked on an unplanned journey, has gone too far to turn back, and right now doesn't care about anything but getting her friend back. Her world is seen as the flat, everyday world of shopping malls and storefronts, rail tracks, and not much traffic, skies that the weatherman calls "overcast." You

know those days when you walk around and the weather makes you feel in your stomach that something is not right? Cinematography can make you feel like that.

She walks. She walks all the way to the dog pound and back. All the way to an auto shop and back. And back to what? She sleeps in a park. The movie isn't about people molesting her, although she has one unpleasant encounter. Most people are nice, like a mechanic (Will Patton), and especially a security guard of retirement age (Walter Dalton), whose job is to stand and look at a mostly empty parking lot for twelve hours, to guard against a nonexistent threat to its empty spaces.

Early in the film, the teenage supermarket employee (John Robinson) who busts Wendy for shoplifting won't give her a break. He's a little suck-up who possibly wants to impress his boss with an unbending adherence to "store policy." Store policy also probably denies him health benefits and overtime, and if he takes a good look at Wendy, he may be seeing himself, minus the uniform with the logo and the name tag on it.

The people in the film haven't dropped out of life; they've been dropped by life. It has no real use for them and not much interest. They're on hold. At least searching for your lost dog is a consuming passion; it gives Wendy a purpose and the hope of joy at the end. That's what this movie has to observe, and it's more than enough.   ☞

We Own the Night ★ ★ ★
R, 117 m., 2007

Joaquin Phoenix (Bobby Green), Mark Wahlberg (Joseph Grusinsky), Eva Mendes (Amada Juarez), Robert Duvall (Burt Grusinsky), Antoni Corone (Michael Solo), Moni Moshonov (Marat Bujayev), Alex Veadov (Vadim Nezhinski), Tony Musante (Jack Shapiro). Directed by James Gray and produced by Mark Wahlberg, Joaquin Phoenix, Nick Wechsler, and Marc Butan. Screenplay by Gray.

We Own the Night was the slogan of the New York police in the 1980s, painted on the sides of their squad cars as a promise to take back the night from the drug trade. It might have been premature. In James Gray's new film by the same name, the battle for control of the night is undecided, and brothers from the same family find themselves on opposite sides.

Joaquin Phoenix plays Bobby Green, not his real name, the manager of a thriving Brooklyn nightclub, moving smoothly through the crowds every night, meeting and greeting, keeping an eye on everything, loved by a beautiful girlfriend (Eva Mendes). The club is owned by a Russian émigré named Marat Bujayev (Moni Moshonov), whose smile seems sincere but who is said to control the area's drug traffic. Bujayev's nephew Vadim (Alex Veadov) is a dealer, using the club as his base of operations. Bobby himself is not involved and adopts a don't ask, don't tell position. His job is just to run the club.

Bobby Green's father is Burt Grusinsky (Robert Duvall), the district police chief. His brother is Joseph Grusinsky (Mark Wahlberg), serving as a top cop under his father. If it were known that Bobby is related to them, his life would be in danger.

Everything comes to a head. Vadim asks Bobby to join him in the drug trade at the same time the chief orders a crackdown. Joseph is the point man for the cops. A police raid busts the club, and there are reprisals involving the near-murder of both the chief and the cop. Bobby's father asks him to work undercover for them, promising, "We'll watch your back." Excellent, but who was watching the chief's back?

This is not precisely original material. James Gray himself has made two earlier films involving Russian crime syndicate members in New York: *Little Odessa* (1994) and *The Yards* (2000, which also starred Phoenix and Wahlberg). The first won the Silver Lion at Venice. The second, and this one, were accepted by Cannes. But *We Own the Night* seems less original than the first two, maybe because Russian gangsters have become the villains du jour (see them portrayed more urgently in David Cronenberg's *Eastern Promises*).

Still, the film is made with confidence and energy and is well-acted by the principals. One unexpected touch is that the very sexy Amada Juarez (Mendes) is in it for the love, not the money, really cares for Bobby, gives him good advice, isn't the standard two-timing dame. Her feelings bring an additional depth to Bobby's danger.

Bobby himself is a puzzle. He likes the recognition and status that comes with his job but doesn't want to accept the consequences. He has severed connections with his family, partly out of prudence, partly out of murky deeper motives. But when his side starts shooting at his father and brother, there is an indelible loyalty that is touched.

I have some questions. In the small world of Brooklyn cops and robbers, wouldn't a lot of people who grew up with them know Bobby was related to Joseph and Burt? Can you just change your name and lose your identity? Don't cops watch their own backs when they know they've been targeted? Elements in the plot are less than plausible.

But this is an atmospheric, intense film, and when it's working it has a real urgency. Scenes where a protagonist is close to being unmasked almost always work. The complexity of Bobby's motives grows intriguing, and the concern of his girlfriend, Amada, is well-used. *We Own the Night* may not solve the question of ownership, but it does explore who lives in the night, and why.

Whatever Works ★ ★ ★
PG-13, 92 m., 2009

Larry David (Boris Yellnikoff), Evan Rachel Wood (Melody), Patricia Clarkson (Marietta), Ed Begley Jr. (John), Conleth Hill (Leo Brockman), Michael McKean (Joe). Directed by Woody Allen and produced by Letty Aronson and Stephen Tenenbaum. Screenplay by Allen.

Woody Allen said in *Manhattan* that Groucho Marx was first on his list of reasons to keep on living. His new film, *Whatever Works*, opens with Groucho singing "Hello, I Must Be Going" from *Animal Crackers*. It serves as the movie's theme song, summarizing in five words the worldview of his hero, Boris Yellnikoff.

Yellnikoff, played with perfect pitch by Larry David, is a nuclear physicist who was once almost nominated for a Nobel Prize, a statement so many of us could make. His field was quantum mechanics, where string theory can be described in the same five words. He's retired now, divorced from a rich wife who was so perfect for him he couldn't stand it. He lives in a walk-up in Chinatown and works part time as a chess instructor to little "inch worms," whom he hits over their heads with the board.

Mostly what he does is hang out at a table in a coffee shop and kvetch with old pals. These scenes seemed perfectly familiar to me because of my long honorary membership in a group centering on Dusty Cohl at the Coffee Mill in Toronto. Boris doesn't talk with his friends; he lectures them. His speeches spring from the Jewish love of paradox; essentially, life is so fascinating he can't take it any longer.

Midway in his remarkable opening monologue, David starts speaking directly to the camera. His friends think he's crazy. He asks them if they can't see the people out there— us. Allen developed as a standup comic, and the idea of an actual audience often hovers in his work, most literally in *The Purple Rose of Cairo*, where a character climbs down from the screen and joins it.

Boris gets up from the table and walks down the sidewalk, continuing to hector the camera about his own brilliance and the general stupidity that confronts him. It is too great a burden for him to exist in a world of such morons and cretins. He hates everyone and everything—in a theoretical way, as befits a physicist. Later that night he is implored by a homeless waif to give her something to eat, tells her to be about her business, and then relents and invites her in.

This is Melody St. Ann Celestine (Evan Rachel Wood), a fresh-faced innocent from a small town down south, who still believes in the world she conquered in beauty pageants. I've seen Wood in a lot of performances, but nothing to prepare me for this one. She's naivete on wheels, cheerful, optimistic, trusting, infectious. Reader, she wins the old man's heart—and wants it! She proposes marriage, and not for cynical or needy reasons. She believes everything he says, and is perhaps the first person he has ever met who subscribes fully to the theory of his greatness.

This sets in rotation a wheel of characters who all discover for themselves that in life we must accept whatever works to make us happy. Boris and Melody accept each other. Then her parents separately find their way to New York in search of her, and they accept what they discover. They are Marietta (Patricia Clarkson), who is Melody made middle-aged and churchgoing, and John (Ed Begley Jr.), to whom the National Rifle Association ranks just a smidgin higher than the Supreme Court. They are appalled at this human wreckage their daughter has taken to her side.

But whatever works. Both Marietta and John are transformed by the free spirits of New York, as so many have been, although not, it must be noted, Boris Yellnikoff. The New Yorker and the southerners have never met anyone remotely like one another, but the southerners are open to new experiences. More than that I cannot explain.

It might be complained that everything works out for everyone a little too neatly. So it does, because this is not a realistic story but a Moral Tale, like one of Eric Rohmer's. Allen seeks not psychological insight but the demonstration of how lives can be redeemed. To do this he uses Clarkson's innate exuberance and Begley's congenital probity to get them to where they're going. Once they are free to do so, Marietta indulges her feelings, and John reasons it out.

Larry David is the mind of the enterprise, and Evan Rachel Wood is the heart. David is a verbal virtuoso, playing the "Woody Allen role" but with his personal shtick. He'd be lonely if he couldn't confide in his invisible listeners. His opening monologue would be remarkable from any actor, let alone one without training or stage experience. Wood prevents the plot from descending into logic and reason with her character's blind faith that everything is for the better. *Whatever Works* charts a journey for Allen, one from the words of Groucho to the wisdom of Pascal, who informs us, as Allen once reminded us, that the heart has its reasons.

What Just Happened? ★ ★
R, 107 m., 2008

Robert De Niro (Ben), Catherine Keener (Lou Tarnow), Sean Penn (Sean Penn), John Turturro (Dick Bell), Robin Wright Penn (Kelly), Stanley

Tucci (Scott Solomon), Kristen Stewart (Zoe), Michael Wincott (Jeremy Brunell), Bruce Willis (Actor). Directed by Barry Levinson and produced by Mark Cuban, Robert De Niro, Art Linson, and Jane Rosenthal. Screenplay by Linson, based on his book *What Just Happened: Bitter Hollywood Tales from the Front Line.*

Julia Phillips's famous autobiography was titled *You'll Never Eat Lunch in This Town Again.* Barry Levinson and Art Linson will. At this point, if you're going to make a film about Hollywood greed, hypocrisy, and lust, you have to be willing to burn your bridges. There's not a whole lot in *What Just Happened?* that would be out of place in a good *SNL* skit.

Linson is an A-list producer (*Fight Club, Into the Wild*) who wrote this screenplay based on his memoir, subtitled *Bitter Hollywood Tales from the Front Line.* He knows where the bodies are buried and who buried them, but he doesn't dig anybody up or turn anybody in. If you want to see a movie that Rips the Lid Off Tinseltown, just go ahead and watch Robert Altman's *The Player* (1992). Altman took no hostages. He didn't give a damn. And the book and screenplay he started with were by Michael Tolkin, who was closer to the front line and a lot more bitter. He didn't give a damn, either.

What Just Happened? stars Robert De Niro as a powerful Hollywood producer who has two troubled projects on his hands and a messy private life. De Niro warmed up for this film in *The Last Tycoon* (1976), in a role inspired by Irving Thalberg. That screenplay was by Harold Pinter, based on the novel by F. Scott Fitzgerald. Levinson himself directed the brilliant *Wag the Dog* (1998), where De Niro played a political spin doctor assigned to fabricate reasons for a war.

Mamet wrote that screenplay, which was astonishingly prescient. The movie, which premiered on December 17, 1997, gave us a U.S. president accused of luring a "Firefly Girl" into an room near the Oval Office and presenting her with unique opportunities to salute her commander in chief. The first hints of the Monica Lewinsky scandal became public in January 1998. For the White House

methods used to invent reasons for a phony war, Mamet was six years ahead of Iraq.

So what am I saying? Should Mamet have written *What Just Happened?* Why not? For Mamet's *Heist*, produced by Linson, he gave Danny DeVito one of the funniest lines ever written: "Everybody loves money! That's why they call it money!" For that matter, *Variety*'s Todd McCarthy thinks some of the characters in this film are inspired by the making of Linson's *The Edge*, also written by Mamet. A pattern emerges. But everything I think of is luring me farther away from *What Just Happened?*

Anyway, Ben, the De Niro character, has just had a disastrous preview of his new Sean Penn picture, *Fiercely.* The audience recoils at the end, when a dog is shot. The problem with the footage of *Fiercely* we see is that it doesn't remotely look like a real movie. Meantime, Ben is trying to get his next project off the ground. It will star Bruce Willis as an action hero, but inconveniently Willis has put on a lot of weight and grown a beard worthy of the Smith Brothers.

Ben is still in love with Kelly, his ex-wife number two (Robin Wright Penn), but they just haven't been able to make it work and are now immersed in something I think is called Break-Up Therapy. And their daughter Zoe (Kristen Stewart) is having anguish of her own, which goes with the territory for a rich kid from a shattered home in 90210. And Lou Tarnow (Catherine Keener), Ben's studio chief, is scared to death that *Fiercely* will tank. And the film's mad-dog British director (Michael Wincott) defends the dog's death as artistically indispensable. And the writer of the Bruce Willis thriller (Stanley Tucci) is having an affair with Ben's ex-wife number two.

This isn't a Hollywood satire—it's a sitcom. The flywheels of the plot machine keep it churning around, but it chugs off onto the back lot and doesn't hit anybody in management. Only Penn and Willis are really funny, poking fun not at themselves but at stars they no doubt hate to work with. Wincott is great as the Brit director who wants to end with the dead dog; one wonders if Linson was inspired by Lee Tamahori, the fiery New Zealand director of *The Edge*, who stepped on the astonishing implications of Mamet's brilliant last scene by fading to black and immediately popping up a big credit for Bart the Bear.

When Did You
Last See Your Father? ★ ★ ★
PG-13, 92 m., 2008

Colin Firth (Blake Morrison), Jim Broadbent (Arthur Morrison), Juliet Stevenson (Kim Morrison), Gina McKee (Kathy Morrison), Elaine Cassidy (Sandra), Claire Skinner (Gillian), Matthew Beard (Blake, Teenager), Sarah Lancashire (Auntie Beaty). Directed by Anand Tucker and produced by Elizabeth Karlsen and Stephen Woolley. Screenplay by David Nicholls, based on the memoir by Blake Morrison.

"It's stupid, really," Blake Morrison tells his wife. "You spend a lifetime trying to avoid talking to someone, and then all of a sudden it's too late." He has returned to the Yorkshire town where he was born, and where his father is dying. Surely, his wife says, this is the right time? "He's too doped up."

When Did You Last See Your Father? is based on a 1990s best-seller by Morrison, who redefines the question as, "When did you last *really* see him?" He arrives at an answer for himself, but we're left realizing that he never did really see his father. He was too blinded by anger, and it is only after his death that he forgives him and sees him as a *father*, and not as the focus of resentment.

His father is Arthur (Jim Broadbent), who shares a practice with his wife, Kim (Juliet Stevenson), also a doctor. The son is played by Colin Firth, and it is startling in some scenes how much the two men resemble each other. In an opening where Arthur talks their way into reserved seats at a speedway, Blake tells us his father was a charmer who could talk his way into or out of anything.

The old man does it by bluster, expansive cheerfulness, and bluff. There's a lot of ground to cover. Blake correctly suspects that Arthur is having an affair with his Auntie Beaty (Sarah Lancashire), and even in later years Arthur is able to out-charm his son in the pursuit of a woman they both covet. Blake hated his father for treating his mother so badly, although there are few scenes showing son and mother as particularly close. The per-

son he does confide in is his first love, the family's maid, Sandra (Elaine Cassidy).

The film moves from the 1950s, when Blake is played by Bradley Johnson, to the 1960s, when he's played as a teenager by Matthew Beard. It's episodic, remembering a time when father and son went camping and found that a stream had overflowed into their tent, and a time when Arthur taught Blake how to drive. They make big circles on a deserted beach in the family's elegant Alvis convertible, and the scene ends with smiles on both men's faces.

We see lots of pairs of faces, but they're rarely smiling. The director, Anand Tucker (*Hilary and Jackie*), uses mirrors repeatedly throughout the movie, perhaps as a way of suggesting there's more than one way to see something or someone. The Arthur we see at least has more vitality than his son and wife, who grow increasingly glum. Poor Blake has his own libidinous feelings constantly interrupted by his father, whom he refers to as the "sex police." Why should his dad get away with everything and he with nothing?

It's a sad movie, with a mournful score, romantic landscape photography, and heartbreaking deathbed scenes (his mother weeps while changing the sheets). But it's not very satisfying. Blake and Arthur never really did talk man-to-man, and Arthur had a strange way of showing affection to "Fathead," as in a scene where he embarrasses his son by switching his drink at a party. "April Fool's!" he chortles, and his laugh grows so harsh it seems to be echoing in memory.

The real Blake Morrison was the literary editor of the *Observer*. Among his resentments were that his father did not respect the literary life and considered it a waste of time and money to study literature at university. His father "never read a single book all the way through," he says. He's been reading *Death on the Nile* for the last forty-two years. That has the sound of an epitaph long rehearsed.

If there is a genre for this sort of film, surely it demands a reconciliation, a moment of truth-telling, an expression of long-delayed love. Although Blake is told by Auntie Beaty that his father worshipped his family, Arthur never says it, and Blake never asks. He has questions still unvoiced near the end of the

505

film, and the way they are finally answered for him is, in a way, perfectly appropriate.

The film did not provide me with fulfillment or a catharsis. Apparently the memoir wouldn't have, either. That's fair enough. How many unanswered questions are we all left with? I have some. This is a film of regret, and judging by what we see of the characters, it deserves to be.

The Whole Shootin' Match ★ ★ ★ ★
NO MPAA RATING, 101 m., 1979 (rereleased 2007)

Lou Perry (Loyd), Sonny Davis (Frank), Doris Hargrave (Paulette), Eric Henshaw (Olan), David Weber (T. Frank), James Harrell (Old Man). Directed by Eagle Pennell and produced by Pennell and Lin Sutherland. Screenplay by Pennell and Sutherland.

Eagle Pennell died a "hopeless drunk," according to a memorial article in the *Austin Chronicle* by his friend Louis Black. His other friends would have sadly agreed with that. He was forty-nine at the time of his death, in 2002. Twenty-three years earlier, in 1979, he wrote and directed a film named *The Whole Shootin' Match* that you may never have heard of, but which had a decisive influence on American independent film.

When Robert Redford saw it at the Park City Film Festival, it awoke him to the possibilities of low-budget indie filmmaking. He started the Sundance Institute, and soon after, the Park City festival became the Sundance festival. When Richard Linklater, then living in Eagle's hometown of Austin, Texas, saw it, he decided to become a filmmaker himself, and his *Dazed and Confused* owes a lot to Pennell.

When I saw the movie at Telluride in 1980, I went for a walk on the mountainside with Eagle and mentioned that he had made a film about alcoholism. He said that had never occurred to him, although he thought I was right. His characters drink in almost every shot of the film. In the last years of his life, Black reports, Eagle spent every dollar he could beg or borrow on booze. He lived on the streets or on the sofas of his shrinking number of friends. He made other films, one of them the very good *Last Night at the Alamo* (1983). It

was not about John Wayne's Alamo but about a bar in Austin. The line on the poster read: "Some face the future head on. Tonight the boys at the Alamo face it dead drunk."

Now *The Whole Shootin' Match* is getting an almost miraculous new chance at finding an audience. The few surviving prints were battered and beaten, but a good print turned up a couple of years ago in Germany and has been lovingly restored by Mark Rance of Watchmaker Films.

Rance screened it for a few Chicago film types in the loft of Chicago projection genius James Bond. It was like a reunion of some of those who had loved the film the first time around, including Chicago underground filmmaker Tom Palazzolo and Facets founder Milos Stehlik. The print was so sparkling in crisp black-and-white that it played like a new film, a lovable, low-key tragicomedy about a couple of good ol' boys who live on their pipe dreams. As I wrote the first time the film played at the Film Center, in 1980:

"Loyd and Frank live down around Austin, Texas, where they spend most of their time drinking booze and thinking up new ways to get rich quick. By the time the movie opens, they've already lost small fortunes (very small fortunes) as frog farmers, flying squirrel ranchers, and suppliers of polyurethane to rich hippies. But now they stand on the brink of a really big thing. Loyd has invented something called the Kitchen Wizard, which combines all the worst principles of a mop, a floor polisher, and a vacuum cleaner, and they've sold the rights for $1,000 to a patent attorney: Gray skies are gonna clear up."

That suggests the humor of the film, but not its heart. Played by Lou Perry and Sonny Davis, Loyd and Frank are goofballs, yes, but their struggle has a certain heroism to it, especially since they're drunk or hung over almost all of the time. There is an undertone of unspoken, maybe unrealized, despair beneath their daily adventures.

The film shows that Eagle was a born story spinner and creater of characters. If you Google him and read the tributes and memories in the *Chronicle* and other Texas papers, you'll find that many Texans believe he came closer to capturing the blue-collar spirit of their state than anyone else. I know my friend

Molly Ivins thought so. But Eagle *could not* sober up; Louis Black remembers times when he went off to rehab, got drunk on the flight home, turned up at the *Chronicle* to borrow money to pay for the taxi from the airport and more money for another binge. His life must have been torture. But he left behind some lovely work, and *The Whole Shootin' Match* is priceless. I rated it at three stars on its first release. What was I waiting for? Do I ever change a rating? Hell, yes. I'd give it four today, and you'll see why.

The Witnesses ★ ★ ★

NO MPAA RATING, 112 m., 2008

Johan Libereau (Manu), Michel Blanc (Adrien), Emmanuelle Beart (Sarah), Sami Bouajila (Mehdi), Julie Depardieu (Julie). Directed by André Téchiné and produced by Said Ben Said. Screenplay by Techine, Laurent Guyot, and Viviane Zingg.

Michel Blanc is that middle-aged French actor with the round bald head and (often enough) round eyeglasses who has played dozens of engaging roles, most notably in Patrice Leconte's masterpiece *Monsieur Hire*. In Andre Techine's *The Witnesses*, he plays Adrien, a doctor, one of an ensemble of five major characters. They are more or less balanced in importance and screen time, but somehow he draws our attention to himself. He doesn't "steal" scenes; what he does simply seems more urgent, more passionate, more driven.

Early in the film, we see him cruising a Paris late-night rendezvous for gays, picking up a young guy and then stalking away from him in anger when he's asked how old he is. The younger man goes into the shrubbery in search of another partner, but first asks Adrien to hold his coat because he's afraid of it being stolen. "I might steal it myself," Adrien says. "I'd be very surprised," says Manu (Johan Libereau). His instinctive trust generates a connection between the two men, but it doesn't blossom into a sexual coupling. It becomes a friendship that will be greatly tested by the end of the story.

The movie begins in 1984 and has sections set in the following year. This is the time that AIDS begins to be recognized in France, and having sex with strangers in the park will soon lack the illusion of safety. Manu is not sexually interested in Adrien anyway, although Adrien is desperately in love with him. Yet Blanc never turns Adrien's love into something needy and pathetic; he shows Manu around Paris, he confides in him, he glows in his company, they grow close as friends.

Manu lives with his sister, Julie (Julie Depardieu), an aspiring opera singer who has no interest in much of anything beyond her work. We also meet Adrien's friend Sarah (Emmanuelle Beart), a wealthy author of children's books, and her husband, Mehdi (Sami Bouajila), who is a policeman and head of a vice squad that targets prostitution. They've just had a baby; Sarah learns through the experience that, despite her books, she does not like children. Her husband despairs when she neglects the child, does what he can to fill in, and sometimes parks the child with his parents.

Now all the pieces are in place for a momentous weekend when Sarah and Mehdi invite Adrien and Manu to her mother's house at the seaside. The two younger men go swimming in the sea, Manu finds himself in trouble, and he nearly drowns. The policeman saves his life, and in pulling him to shore finds to his surprise that he has an erection. The two men, one of whom has never thought of himself as gay, plunge into a physical relationship that becomes all-consuming.

That Mehdi is being unfaithful to Sarah (whether with a man or a woman) is of little concern to her; they have an "open" marriage, which in her case seems to translate into not caring what anyone else does as long as they leave her alone to write her books. One day Adrien sees telltale lesions on Manu's chest and diagnoses him as a victim of the mysterious new disease he has started to see in his practice. Now consider the ramifications of this infection for all five characters, and you have the driving structure of the story.

I will not reveal details. I would rather focus on the Michel Blanc performance. His Adrien is not a perfect man or a noble doctor, but he is a good man who has the courage to do good, although difficult, things. He has been deeply wounded by Manu's "abandoning" him for

507

Mehdi, and is outraged that Mehdi cheated on his wife with, of all people, the man Mehdi knows the doctor loves. Adrien is even the godfather of the child. This outrage leads to a scuffle that is brief, confusing, violent, and without a "winner," revealing how hurt Adrien really is, and how near his emotional wounds are to the surface of his bland exterior.

Adrien becomes a leader in a gay doctors' crusade against AIDS, meanwhile privately taking on Manu's treatment. Mehdi also doesn't shun his friend when he hears the news, although he is terrified that he has AIDS and cannot bring himself to tell his wife. All of this captures the dread and paranoia of the early AIDS years; none of the characters has the benefit of foresight, and even a kiss or a drink from the same water bottle appears as a possible danger.

Techine tells the story with comic intensity for the first hour, and then aching drama. The possibility of having a disease of this sort, especially when you are married, allegedly straight, and even an anti-gay enforcer for the cops, creates secrecy and shame, and can lead to much worse than simply facing the truth. And it is that pain of the double life that concerns Techine in his later scenes.

Johan Libereau, as Manu, does a completely convincing transformation from an effortless young charmer to a dying man; he wasn't meant to die young like this, he despairingly tells Adrien; in fights at school, he didn't even bruise. Beart is mysterious as a remote, cold woman who likes physical sex but not much else apart from her writing. The cop is deeper and more sensitive than the situation might suggest; when he does the laundry for Manu, it is uncommonly touching, especially when the film notices how staring at an automatic washer can become a form of meditation.

But it is, again, Blanc who fascinates. His face, so often used for comedy or parody, here reflects intelligence, concern, and quiet sadness. His love is real enough, but to no purpose. His attempts to replace Manu are depressing even to himself. *The Witnesses* doesn't pay off with a great, operatic pinnacle, but it's better that way. Better to show people we care about facing facts they care desperately about, without the consolation of plot mechanics.

The Women ★ ★ ★
PG-13, 114 m., 2008

Meg Ryan (Mary Haines), Annette Bening (Sylvie Fowler), Eva Mendes (Crystal Allen), Debra Messing (Edie Cohen), Jada Pinkett Smith (Alex Fisher), Carrie Fisher (Bailey Smith), Cloris Leachman (Maggie), Debi Mazar (Tanya), Bette Midler (Leah Miller), Candice Bergen (Catherine Frazier), India Ennenga (Molly Haines). Directed by Diane English and produced by English, Victoria Pearman, Mick Jagger, and Bill Johnson. Screenplay by English, based on the play by Clare Booth Luce.

What a pleasure this movie is, showcasing actresses I've admired for a long time, all at the top of their form. Yes, they're older now, as are we all, but they look great and know what they're doing. *The Women* is not, as it claims, "based on the play by Clare Booth Luce." The credits should read "inspired by." Nor does it draw from the screenplay of the 1939 film, although it also has no males on the screen.

The film revolves around four close friends, one married with four kids, one married with one kid but being cheated on, one a high-profile professional woman, one a lesbian. Sound a little familiar? But these woman are wiser, funnier, and more articulate than the *SATC* team, and their lives are not as shallow. Maybe it helps that there aren't a lot of men hanging around and chewing up screen time. There are two husbands and a boss, but we only hear this end of the telephone conversations.

The movie is a comedy, after all, and we're not looking for deep insights, but writer-director Diane English (one of the creative forces behind *Murphy Brown*) focuses on story and character, and even in a movie that sometimes plays like an infomercial for Saks Fifth Avenue, we find ourselves intrigued by these women.

Meg Ryan and Annette Bening get top billing as Mary, the wife of a Wall Street millionaire, and Sylvie, editor of a fashion magazine. They've long been best friends, but complications involving Mary's husband and Sylvie's job drive them apart. Then Sylvie, who has never been a mother, finds herself acting as one for Mary's precocious daughter Molly (India Ennenga). A scene where she gives the young girl direct, honest advice about sex is one of the best in the movie. And there's another striking scene when Mary's own mother (Candice Bergen) gives her brutally frank advice about how to deal with a cheating husband.

Debra Messing, from *Will & Grace,* plays Edie, the mother of four. And (spoiler) I will have to reveal that she gives birth to a fifth, in order to observe that she finds a way to distinguish the obligatory childbirth scene. She does some screaming that, in its own way, equals Meg Ryan's famous restaurant scene in *When Harry Met Sally.* As for the fourth friend, Alex Fisher (Jada Pinkett Smith), she's a lesbian and, well, that's about it. She does what she can with the role, but there's not much to do. Her current lover, a supermodel, is introduced for a few pouts and hustled off-screen. In one scene with peculiar staging, Alex walks down a sidewalk *behind* Mary and Sylvie and never has one word of dialogue. What's with that?

There's strong comedic acting in some of the supporting roles, including Cloris Leachman as Mary's housekeeper, Eva Mendes as the bombshell "spritzer girl" at the Saks perfume counter, Bette Midler as a jolly Hollywood agent, and Debi Mazar as a talkative manicure girl from Long Island. Carrie Fisher gets points for playing her entire scene while furiously pumping a workout machine.

George Cukor's 1939 version of *The Women* remains a classic. It played like a convention of Hollywood's top female stars (Norma Shearer, Joan Crawford, Rosalind Russell, Paulette Goddard, Joan Fontaine). This 2008 version also brings together stars, but in a way that illuminates a shift in the Hollywood sensibility. Is there an actress today of the mythical stature of those five?

Meryl Streep, you say? A better actress than any of them, but does she sell tickets in a market dominated by action pictures and comic book superheroes? Angelina Jolie? Big star, but too old for the perfume girl and too young for the others. Nicole Kidman? She gets a nod in the dialogue. The novelty in 1939 was seeing so much star power in a single movie (also true of *Grand Hotel*). Here what we're seeing is an opportunity to regret that we didn't see more of these actresses in roles deserving of them. The old MGM would have kept them busy.

The Women isn't a great movie, but how could it be? Too many characters and too much melodrama for that, and the comedy has to be somewhat muted to make the characters semi-believable. But as a well-crafted, well-written, and well-acted entertainment, it drew me in and got its job done. Did I say that there are no males at all in the movie? True, except for one shot.

The Wrestler ★ ★ ★ ★
R, 109 m., 2008

Mickey Rourke (Randy "The Ram" Robinson), Marisa Tomei (Cassidy), Evan Rachel Wood (Stephanie Robinson). Directed by Darren Aronofsky and produced by Aronofsky and Scott Franklin. Screenplay by Robert Siegel.

The Wrestler is about a man who can do one thing well, and keeps on doing it because of need, weary skill, and pride. He wrestles for a living. Pro wrestling is a fake sport, right? Yes, but as an *activity,* it's pretty real. I watch it on TV with fascination. It's scripted that the villain sneaks up on the hero, who pretends not to see him, and pushes the hero over the ropes and out of the ring. Fake. But when the hero hits the floor, how fake is that? "Those guys learn how to fall," people tell me. Want to sign up for the lessons?

Mickey Rourke plays the battered, broke, lonely hero, Randy "The Ram" Robinson. This is the performance of his lifetime, will win him a nomination, may win him the Oscar. Like many great performances, there is an element of truth in it. Rourke himself was once young and glorious and made the big bucks. He did professional boxing just for the hell of it. He alienated a lot of people. He fell from grace and stardom, but kept working because he was an actor and that was what he did. Now here is his comeback role, playing Randy the Ram's comeback.

This is Rourke doing astonishing physical acting. He has the physique of a body builder, perhaps thanks to some steroid use, which would also be true of Randy. He gets into the ring and does the work. Rourke may not be physically performing every single thing we see, including the leaps off ropes and ladders and the nasty falls. Special effects have robbed movies of their believability. But I've seen a lot of F/X, and I have to say it looked to me like he was really doing these things.

Not that it matters. It appears that he is, and his ring performances and the punishment he takes supply the bedrock for the story, which involves his damaged relationship with his daughter, Stephanie (Evan Rachel Wood), and what he hopes will become a relationship with the stripper Cassidy (Marisa Tomei). Except for his backstage camaraderie with other wrestling old-timers, Randy has burned all his bridges in life. Stephanie is far, far from happy to see him at her door again. And he doesn't quite believe Cassidy, whose real name is Pam, when she carefully explains that she is not available.

Here is the irony, which he won't accept. Cassidy is as much a performer as Randy. He is a ring worker. She is a sex worker. They put on a show and give the customers what they want. It pays the rent. There is always a chasm between pros and their audiences. That's why so many showbiz people marry one another. Magicians say, "The trick is told when the trick is sold." Think about that.

But Randy has grown a little wiser with the years, less blinded by stardom, more able to admit emotional need. Maybe, too, he was using more drugs in those days, and they always take first place before relationships. (He gets a sales pitch from a fellow wrestler who seems to stock more drugs than Walgreen's.) Randy has a residual charm and sentimentality, which helps him and also deceives him. He makes some small progress with his daughter. And as for Cassidy—have you ever seen Marisa Tomei play a bitch? I haven't. I don't know if she can. She seems to have something good at the heart of her that endows this stripper with warmth and sympathy. Not that Randy should get his hopes up.

The most fascinating elements in Darren Aronofsky's film is the backstage detail about wrestling. He does this so well yet has never made a film even remotely like this before. In the snow and slush of New Jersey, Randy and his opponents make the rounds of shabby union halls, school gyms, community centers, and Legion halls, using whatever they can find for dressing rooms, taping their damaged parts, psyching themselves up and agreeing beforehand on the script. We learn before-hand how they make themselves bleed, prepare for violent "surprises," talk through each match. And then they go out and do it. As nearly as I can tell, their planning only means that they get hurt in the ways they expect and not in unforeseen ways.

I cared as deeply about Randy the Ram as any movie character I've seen this year. I cared about Mickey Rourke, too. The way this role and this film unfold, that almost amounts to the same thing. Rourke may not win the Oscar for best actor. But it would make me feel good to see him up there. It really would.

Note: This is one of the year's best films. It wasn't on my "best films" list for complicated and boring reasons. ☞

Wristcutters: A Love Story ★ ★ ½
R, 92 m., 2007

Patrick Fugit (Zia), Shea Whigham (Eugene), Shannyn Sossamon (Mikal), Tom Waits (Kneller), Will Arnett (Messiah), Leslie Bibb (Desiree). Directed by Goran Dukic and produced by Tatiana Kelly, Adam Sherman, Chris Coen, and Mikal P. Lazarev. Screenplay by Dukic, based on the short story "Kneller's Happy Campers" by Etgar Keret.

Imagine that after you kill yourself you don't go to heaven or hell but to an industrial waste-land where nothing works right, there are no good jobs, the fast food is generic, and every-body else who lives there committed suicide, too. Oh, and it doesn't look like anyone has sex, either, perhaps for theological reasons: Could a child be born in the land of the dead? How would you like to have a dad with a hole in his head? Think of Parents' Day.

Wristcutters: A Love Story stars Patrick Fugit as Zia, who has evolved from *Almost Famous* to almost dead. He has been forsaken by his girlfriend, Desiree (Leslie Bibb), and slashed his wrists. That'll show her. Apparently fate has designed a macabre punishment for those who commit the sin of suicide: You don't die, but linger forever in a life like the one you had before, but worse, and surrounded by suicidal people.

And what kind of a name is Zia, anyway? A zia is a brachiopod, and Wiki reports that "99 percent of [this] lampshell species are both fossils and extinct." Read that again. *Both* fossils *and* extinct. Sounds like your neighbors in Wristcutterland. Zia makes a friend named Eugene (Shea Whigham), who, as you have probably guessed from his name, was a Russian rock singer. Pissed off at the audience one night, he electrocuted himself onstage. That showed them.

Zia hears from a recent arrival from the Other Side that Desiree killed herself, too. Assuming she must be on This Side somewhere, he convinces Eugene to drive around looking for her, which begins them on a journey like the ones people are always making in Dead Teenager Movies, the ones with gas stations run by Toothless Doom-Mongers. They acquire a cute hitchhiker named Mikal (Shannyn Sossamon), who is looking for someone to complain to because she got a raw deal. She didn't kill herself, but only accidentally overdosed, so I guess at least she should get free laundry.

Along the road to nowhere, they come across a sort of outcast commune (how do you drop out of a society of suicides?). It is run by just the man for the job, Tom Waits, although my vote would have gone to Keith Richards. And they find Desiree, but how much of the story do you need to know, anyway?

This idea of an afterlife for suicides is intriguing. They thought they were ending their misery, and it was just beginning. That'll show them. Zia gets a job at a place called Kamikaze Pizza, which only scratches the surface of the possible jokes. I can't imagine why this movie is opening at Halloween time, although actually it's opening two days after Halloween, which is par for the course in Wristcutterland. But don't get the wrong idea: The movie isn't laugh-out-loud funny, under the circumstances, but it is bittersweet and sort of wistfully amusing; the actors enjoy lachrymosity, and we witness the birth of a new genre, the Post-Slasher Movie.

X

The X-Files: I Want to Believe ★ ★ ★ ½
PG-13, 104 m., 2008

David Duchovny (Fox Mulder), Gillian Anderson (Dana Scully), Amanda Peet (Dakota Whitney), Billy Connolly (Father Joe), Alvin "Xzibit" Joiner (Agent Drummy). Directed by Chris Carter and produced by Carter and Frank Spotnitz. Screenplay by Carter and Spotnitz.

The X-Files: I Want to Believe arrives billed as a "stand-alone" film that requires no familiarity with the famous television series. So it is, leaving us to piece together the plot on our own. And when I say "piece together," trust me, that's exactly what I mean.

In an early scene, a human arm turns up, missing its body, and other spare parts are later discovered. The arm is found in a virtuoso scene showing dozens of FBI agents lined up and marching across a field of frozen snow. They are led by a white-haired, entranced old man who suddenly drops to his knees and cries out that this is the place! And it is.

Now allow me to jump ahead and drag in the former agents Mulder and Scully. Mulder (David Duchovny) has left the FBI under a cloud because of his belief in the paranormal. Scully (Gillian Anderson) is a top-level surgeon, recruited to bring Mulder in from the cold, all his sins forgiven, to help on an urgent case. An agent is missing, and the white-haired man, we learn, is Father Joe (Billy Connolly), a convicted pedophile who is said to be a psychic.

Scully brings in Mulder but detests the old priest's crimes and thinks he is a fraud. Mulder, of course, wants to believe Father Joe could help on the case. But hold on one second. Even assuming that Father Joe planted the severed arm himself, you'll have to admit it's astonishing that he can lead agents to its exact resting place in a snow-covered terrain the size of several football fields with no landmarks. Even before he started weeping blood instead of tears, I believed him. Scully keeps right on insulting him right to his face. She wants *not* to believe.

Scully is emotionally involved in the case of a young boy who will certainly die if he doesn't have a risky experimental bone marrow treatment. This case, interesting in itself, is irrelevant to the rest of the plot except that it inspires a Google search that offers a fateful clue. Apart from that, what we're faced with is a series of victims, including Agent Dakota Whitney (Amanda Peet) and eventually Mulder himself, who are run off the road by a weirdo with a snowplow.

Who is doing this? And why does Father Joe keep getting psychic signals of barking dogs? And is the missing agent still alive, as he thinks she is? And won't anyone listen to Mulder, who eventually finds himself all alone in the middle of a blizzard, being run off the road, and then approaching a suspicious building complex after losing his cell phone? And how does he deal with a barking dog?

I make it sound a little silly. Well, it is a little silly, but it's also a skillful thriller, giving us just enough cutaways to a sinister laboratory to keep us fascinated. What happens in this laboratory you will have to find out for yourself, but the solution may be more complex than you think if you watch only casually. Hint: Pay close attention to the hands.

What I appreciated about *The X-Files: I Want to Believe* was that it involved actual questions of morality, just as *The Dark Knight* does. It's not simply about good and evil, but about choices. Come to think of it, Scully's dying child may be connected to the plot in another way, since it poses the question: Are any means justified to keep a dying person alive?

The movie lacks a single explosion. It has firearms, but nobody is shot. The special effects would have been possible in the era of *Frankenstein*. Lots of stunt people were used. I had the sensation of looking at real people in real spaces, not motion-capture in CGI spaces. There was a tangible quality to the film that made the suspense more effective because it involved the physical world.

Of course, it involves a psychic world, too. And the veteran Scottish actor Billy Connolly creates a quiet, understated performance as a man who hates himself for his sins, makes no great claims, does not understand his psychic powers, is only trying to help. He wants to believe he can be forgiven. As for Duchovny and

Anderson, these roles are their own. It's like they're in repertory. They still love each other and still believe they would never work as a couple. Or should I say they want to believe?

The movie is insidious. It involves evil on not one level but two. The evildoers, it must be said, are singularly inept; they receive bills for medical supplies under their own names, and surely there must be more efficient ways to abduct victims and purchase animal tranquilizers. But what they're up to is so creepy, and the snow-covered Virginia landscapes so haunting, and the wrongheadedness of Scully so frustrating, and the FBI bureaucracy so stupid, and Mulder so brave, that the movie works like thrillers used to work, before they were required to contain villains the size of buildings.

X-Men Origins: Wolverine ★ ★
PG-13, 107 m., 2009

Hugh Jackman (Wolverine), Liev Schreiber (Sabretooth), Taylor Kitsch (Gambit), Daniel Henney (Agent Zero), Danny Huston (General William Stryker), Kevin Durand (The Blob), will.i.am (Wraith). Directed by Gavin Hood and produced by John Palermo, Lauren Shuler Donner, Ralph Winter, and Hugh Jackman. Screenplay by David Benioff and Skip Woods.

X-Men Origins: Wolverine finally answers the burning question, left hanging after all three previous *Wolverine* movies, of the origins of Logan, whose knuckles conceal long and wicked blades. He is about 175 years old, he apparently stopped changing when he reached Hugh Jackman's age, and neither he, nor we, find out how he developed such an interesting mutation.

His half brother was Victor (Liev Schreiber). Their story starts in "1840—the Northwest Territories of Canada," a neat trick, since Canada was formed in 1867, and its Northwest Territories in 1870. But you didn't come here for a history lesson. Or maybe you did, if you need to know that Logan and Victor became Americans (still before they could be Canadians) and fought side by side in the Civil War, World War I, World War II, and Vietnam. Why they did this, I have no idea. Maybe they just enjoyed themselves.

Booted out of the army in Vietnam, Logan/Wolverine joined a secret black ops unit under General Stryker (Danny Huston), until finally, in Nigeria, he got fed up with atrocities. Nevertheless, he was recruited by Stryker for a *super* secret plan to create a mutant of mutants, who would incorporate all available mutant powers, including those of the kid whose eyes are like laser beams. He wears sunglasses. Lotta good they'll do him.

Am I being disrespectful to this material? You bet. It is Hugh Jackman's misfortune that when they were handing around superheroes, he got Wolverine, who is, for my money, low on the charisma list. He never says anything witty, insightful, or very intelligent; his utterances are limited to the vocalization of primitive forces: anger, hurt, vengeance, love, hate, determination. There isn't a speck of ambiguity. That Wolverine has been voted the number one comic book hero of all time must be the result of a stuffed ballot box.

At least, you hope, he has an interesting vulnerability? I'm sure X-Men scholars can tell you what it is, although since he has the gift of instant healing, it's hard to pinpoint. When a man can leap from an exploding truck in midair, cling to an attacking helicopter, slice the rotor blades, ride it to the ground, leap free, and walk away (in that ancient cliché where there's a fiery explosion behind him but he doesn't seem to notice it), here's what I think: Why should I care about this guy? He feels no pain, and nothing can kill him, so therefore he's essentially a story device for action sequences.

Oh, the film is well made. Gavin Hood, the director, made the great film *Tsotsi* (2005) and the damned good film *Rendition* (2007) before signing on here. Fat chance *Wolverine* fans will seek out those two. Why does a gifted director make a film none of his earlier admirers would much want to see? That's how you get to be a success in Hollywood. When you make a big box-office hit for mostly fanboys, you've hit the big time. Look at Justin Lin with *The Fast and the Furious.*

Such films are assemblies of events. There is little dialogue, except for the snarling of threats, vows, and laments, and the recitation of essential plot points. Nothing here about human nature. No personalities beyond those hauled in via typecasting. No lessons to learn. No joy to be experienced. Just mayhem, noise, and pretty pictures. I have been powerfully impressed by film versions of Batman, Spider-Man, Superman, Iron Man, and the Iron Giant. I wouldn't walk across the street to meet Wolverine.

But wait! you say. Doesn't the film at least provide a learning experience for Logan about his origins for Wolverine? Hollow laugh. Because we know that the modern Wolverine has a form of amnesia, it cannot be a spoiler for me to reveal that at the end of *X-Men Origins: Wolverine*, he forgets everything that has happened in the film. Lucky man.

XXY ★ ★ ★ ½
NO MPAA RATING, 91 m., 2008

Ines Efron (Alex), Martin Piroyanski (Alvaro), Ricardo Darin (Kraken), Valeria Bertuccelli (Suli), German Palacios (Ramiro), Carolina Peleritti (Erika). Directed by Lucia Puenzo and produced by Luis Puenzo and Jose Maria Morales. Screenplay by Lucia Puenzo, based on a short story by Sergio Bizzio.

Alex was born with both male and female sex organs. Although "reassignment" surgery was considered after birth, she has lived as a woman until the age of fifteen, when *XXY* takes up the story. She uses hormones to subdue her male characteristics, but now she has become unsure how she really feels. Alex is neither a man in a woman's body nor a woman in a man's body, but both, in the body of a high-spirited tomboy who broods privately in uncertainty and confusion.

"Hermaphrodite" is no longer the PC term for such people, who prefer "intersex," although it seems to me that they are not so much between the sexes as encompassing them. Their stories are often exploited in lurid, sensationalistic accounts. Lucia Puenzo's *XXY* is the first film I've seen on the subject that is honest and sensitive—indeed, the only one. It is not a message picture, never lectures, contains partial nudity but avoids explicit images, and grows into a touching human drama. It will be described in terms of Alex's sexual ambiguity, but that would simplify it, and this is not a simple film but a subtle and observant one.

Alex (Ines Efron) is the child of a Marine biologist named Kraken (Ricardo Darin) and his wife, Suli (Valeria Bertuccelli). They have moved their family from Argentina to an island off the shore of Uruguay, where Kraken can study specimens and Alex can grow up more privately. That has not been easy. "I'm sick of doctors and changing schools," she tells her mother. Since other kids somehow sense something strange about her, she cannot easily keep her secret. Recently she has stopped taking the hormones. Perhaps (Alex never says) it will be easier to account for a penis if she does not live as a girl.

Guests arrive on the island: a plastic surgeon named Ramiro (German Palacios), his wife, Erika (Carolina Peleritti), and their son, Alvaro (Martin Piroyanski), about Alex's age. Suli has invited them so the doctor can "get to know Alex" and tells her husband she has not told them about their child's secret. Alex and Alvaro are attracted to each other, and together have what is possibly the first sexual experience for either. This is shown with great dramatic impact, but not with graphic intimacy; the point is not what they do, but how they feel about it.

The film gives full weight to all of the characters. When Kraken first saw his newborn infant, "I thought she was perfect." He wants to give Alex the right to make her own decision about having surgery. His wife thinks Alex's penis should be removed, but is not shrill or insistent. Both in their different ways love and care for their child.

In contrast, the surgeon is brutally cruel in a conversation with his own son, who may possibly be starting to realize he is gay and may be attracted to the androgynous Alex for that reason. Alex and Alvaro sense some sort of unstated, even unconscious, common bond. There are problems on the island. Alex has broken the nose of her boyfriend, possibly (I'm not sure) because he wanted to explore her body. And local teenagers chase Alex on the beach and pin her down to settle the mystery of her physiology.

I am making the film sound too melodramatic. The shots are beautifully composed, the editing paces the process of self-discovery, the dialogue is spare and heartfelt, the performances are deeply human—especially by

Efron, who I learn was twenty-two when the film was made, but never looks it.

Nor does she look too distractingly male or female, and so is convincing as both. The film accumulates its force through many small moments and some larger ones. It assembles its story as a careful novelist might, out of many precise, significant brush strokes. And Efron finds a sure line through the pitfalls of her role, succeeding in playing not girl or boy, but—Alex. We understand that Alex is in despair, and we see it reflected in a sketchbook she has drawn. She is weary of being poked and prodded by the unhealthy curiosity of society, weary of being considered a freak. She wants to be accepted as herself, but isn't sure who that is. In wanting her to find happiness, her parents provide a refuge, even though they hardly even discuss her intersexuality with her in so many words. And finally that's why this film can avoid a "solution" and yet end with a bittersweet glow.

Note: XXY *won the top prize in Critics' Week at Cannes 2007.*

Y

Year One ★
PG-13, 100 m., 2009

Jack Black (Zed), Michael Cera (Oh), Oliver Platt (High Priest), David Cross (Cain), Hank Azaria (Abraham), Juno Temple (Eema). Directed by Harold Ramis and produced by Judd Apatow, Clayton Townsend, and Nicholas Weinstock. Screenplay by Ramis, Gene Stupnitsky, and Lee Eisenberg.

Harold Ramis is one of the nicest people I've met in the movie business, and I'm so sorry *Year One* happened to him. I'm sure he had the best intentions. In trying to explain why the movie was produced, I have a theory. Ramis is the top-billed of three writers, and he is so funny that when he read some of these lines, they sounded hilarious. Pity he didn't play one of the leads in his own film.

As always, I carefully avoided any of the movie's trailers, but I couldn't avoid the posters or the ads. "Meet Your Ancestors," they said, with big photos of Jack Black and Michael Cera. I assumed it was about Adam and Eve. Cera has smooth, delicate features, and with curly locks falling to below his shoulders, I thought: "Michael Cera in drag. I wonder where Harold will take that?"

But no, even though Cera is sometimes mistaken for a woman, he's all primitive man, banging women on the head. Then he and Black eat of the forbidden apple and make a leap from tribal "hunter-gatherers" (a term they enjoy) to royal security guards. Everyone throughout the film talks like anyone else in a Judd Apatow comedy, somewhere between stoned and crafty.

It must be said that Jack Black and Michael Cera were not born to be costars. Black was fresh and funny once, a reason then to welcome him in a movie, but here he forgets to act and simply announces his lines. Cera plays shy and uncertain, but then he always does, and responds to Black as if Jack were Juno and a source of intimidating wit.

Another leading role is taken by Oliver Platt, as an extremely hairy high priest, who orders Cera to massage his chest with oil. The close-up of Cera kneading his matted chest foliage is singularly unappetizing. There are several good-looking babes in the city (did I mention it is Sodom?), who, as required in such films, all find the heroes inexplicably attractive. Cera and Juno Temple have a good exchange. She plays a slave. "When do you get off?" he asks. "Never."

That and several other of the film's better moments are in the trailer, of which it can be said, if they were removed from the film, it would be nearly bereft of better moments. The movie takes place in the land now known as Israel (then too, I think), although no one does much with that. The Sodomites include in their number Abraham, Cain, and Abel; it's surprising to find them still in action in the Year One, since Genesis places them—well, before the time of the Year One. Sodomy is not very evident in Sodom, perhaps as a result of the movie being shaved down from an R to a PG-13.

The film has shaggy crowds that mill about like outtakes from *Monty Python and the Holy Grail,* and human sacrifice in which virgins are pitched into the blazing mouth of a stone ox, and a cheerful turn when the gods more appreciate a high priest than a virgin. But *Year One* is a dreary experience, and all the ending accomplishes is to bring it to a close. Even in the credit cookies, you don't sense the actors having much fun.

Yella ★ ★ ★ ½
NO MPAA RATING, 89 m., 2008

Nina Hoss (Yella), Devid Striesow (Philipp), Hinnerk Schoenemann (Ben), Christian Redl (Yella's Father). Directed by Christian Petzold and produced by Florian Koerner von Gustorf. Screenplay by Simone Baer and Petzold.

Yella is a reserved young woman with unrevealed depths of intelligence, larceny, and passion. Their gradual revelation makes this more than an ordinary thriller, in great part because of the performance of Nina Hoss in the title role. Soon after we meet her, she's followed down the street by her former husband, Ben (Hinnerk Schoenemann), who will stalk her throughout the film. Partly to escape him, she leaves her small town in the former East Germany and goes to Hanover to take a job.

Her mistake is to accept a ride to the train station from him. He declares his love, accuses her of betrayal, moans about his business losses. "What time is your train?" he asks. When she says "8:22," he knows her destination. Shortly after, he drives his SUV off a bridge and into a river. Miraculously, they escape. Soaking wet, she runs to the train station and catches the 8:22. Yella has pluck.

That the man who hired her in Hanover has been fired and locked out of his office is the first of her discoveries about the world of business. That night in her hotel lobby, she meets Philipp (Devid Striesow), who sees her looking at his laptop and asks, "You like spreadsheets?" She does. She trained as an accountant.

He asks her to go along with him to a business meeting, carefully coaching her about when to gaze at the spreadsheet, when to gaze at the would-be client, and when to lean over and whisper in his ear—a lawyer's strategy he learned from Grisham movies. She does more than that. She actually reads the spreadsheet and boldly points out deceptions and false assets. She controls the meeting.

Philipp, who now respects her, brings her along to more meetings during which she figures out for herself what he eventually confesses to her: "I cheat." She doesn't mind. And then the film enters more deeply into one particular deal involving shaky patent rights and potential fortunes. Her career seems on an upswing, if it were not that Ben has followed her to Hanover.

All of this time, there are eerie episodes when her ears ring, she hears the harsh cry of a bird, and she seems able to intuitively understand things about people. These episodes remain unexplained until the last minute of the film. And just as well. Nina Hoss is an actress who rewards close observation; she is often seen in profile as a passenger in Philipp's car, her eyes observing him carefully, her expression neutral, then sometimes smiling at what he says, and sometimes only to herself. One of the pleasures of the film is trying to read her mind.

The writer-director, Christian Petzold, uses a spare, straightforward visual style for the most part, except for those cutaways to trees blowing in the wind whenever we heard the harsh bird cry. He trusts his story and characters. And he trusts us to follow the business deals and become engrossed in the intrigue. I did. I could see this being remade as one of those business thrillers with Michael Douglas looking cruel and expensive and finding his female equal. I'm not recommending that, just imagining it.

The male leads have an unsettling similarity in physical presence. You can't say she's attracted to the type, since she's fleeing from Ben and meets Philipp by accident. But they're both ruthless in their way, and Philipp is uncannily effective at imagining things about her that turn out to be pretty accurate. Maybe one thing he senses is that she would be a willing partner in crime. He sets a trap for her, to see if she will return an extra 25,000 euros he entrusted to her. That she would have kept the money angers him at first, but later he apparently decides that by being willing to steal it, she actually passed his test.

There are surprises along the way. One involves the key executive of a company they're dealing with, and is handled with a creepy beginning and a poignant ending. Another surprise in the film I will not even hint at, except to say that I could happily have done without it. It has all the value of the prize in a box of Cracker Jack: worthless, but working your way down to it is a lot of fun.

Yes Man ★ ★
PG-13, 104 m., 2008

Jim Carrey (Carl Allen), Zooey Deschanel (Allison), Bradley Cooper (Peter), John Michael Higgins (Nick), Rhys Darby (Norman), Terence Stamp (Terrence Bundley). Directed by Peyton Reed and produced by Richard D. Zanuck, David Heyman, and Jim Carrey. Screenplay by Nicholas Stoller, Jarrad Paul, and Andrew Mogel.

Jim Carrey made a movie in 1997 titled *Liar Liar* in which his character is a lawyer who suddenly finds he cannot tell a lie. Now here is *Yes Man*, with Carrey playing a bank loan executive who cannot say no. If the movie had been made just a little later to take advantage of the mortgage crisis, it could have been a docudrama.

Carrey begins as a recluse mired in depression, a man named Carl who has been avoiding his friends and not returning his messages for three years, all because his great love walked out on him. His negative stance makes it easy to do his job, which amounts to denying loan applications. He's so indifferent to this work that he isn't even nice to his boss, who desperately wants to make friends. For Carl, it's just up in the morning and no, no, no all day.

Saying no all the way, he's dragged to a meeting of Say Yes!, which is one of those con games that convince large numbers of people to fill hotel convention centers and enrich those who have reduced the secrets of life to a PowerPoint presentation. The Guru of Yes is named Terrence Bundley, and is played by Terence Stamp, whose agent didn't wonder about the extra R. Stamp's message is: Turn your life around by saying yes to everything. This could be dangerous. Anyone who could word the questions cleverly could get you to do anything. For example, "Will you give me all of your money?"—an example used in the film.

The problem with the premise is that the results are clearly telegraphed by the plot. When Carl meets a beautiful girl named Allison (Zooey Deschanel), for example, he is clearly destined to fall in love with her. And when he encounters his sex-mad, toothless, elderly neighbor (Fionnula Flanagan), he is fated to—I wish the movie hadn't gone there. I get uncomfortable seeing reenactments of the dirty jokes we told when we were twelve.

Carrey performs some zany physical humor in the movie, including a drunken bar fight with a fearsome jealous boyfriend who, like all fearsome jealous boyfriends in the movies, stands tall and has a shaved skull. Remember when baldness was a sign of the milquetoast and not the bruiser? I like that phrase "stands tall." Makes me think of John Wayne, who was bald enough, but came along before Mr. Clean.

Every time there's a setup in *Yes Man* we know what must happen. If a homeless guy comes along and asks for a midnight ride to a forest preserve, of course Carl must say yes.

We can also foresee what will happen when Allison doubts his love because maybe he only said yes because of his vow. Allison's doubts come perfectly timed to supply the movie's third act crisis. In fact, the whole story plays as if written by a devout student of the screenplay guru Robert McKee, who also fills rented ballrooms but has the advantage of being smarter and more entertaining than the Guru of Yes. Also, I think you will make more money by saying yes to *Casablanca* than to everything else.

Jim Carrey works the premise for all it's worth, but it doesn't allow him to bust loose and fly. When a lawyer *must* tell the truth and wants desperately not to (even pounding himself over the head with a toilet seat to stop himself), it's funny. When a loan officer must say yes and *wants* to, where is the tension? The premise removes all opportunity for frustration, at which Carrey is a master, and reduces Carl to a programmed creature who, as long as he follows instructions, lacks free will.

As I watched *Yes Man*, I observed two things: (1) Jim Carrey is heroic at trying to keep the movie alive, and succeeds when he is free to be goofy and not locked into yes-and-consequences. (2) It is no news that Zooey Deschanel is a splendid actress and a great beauty, but this is her first movie after which two of my fellow critics proposed marriage to the screen. And I thought they only sat in the front row to better appreciate the film stock.

You Don't Mess with the Zohan ★ ★ ★
PG-13, 113 m., 2008

Adam Sandler (Zohan), John Turturro (The Phantom), Emmanuelle Chriqui (Dalia), Nick Swardson (Michael), Lainie Kazan (Gail), Rob Schneider (Salim), Michael Buffer (Walbridge). Directed by Dennis Dugan and produced by Adam Sandler and Jack Giarraputo. Screenplay by Sandler, Robert Smigel, and Judd Apatow.

The crowd I joined for *You Don't Mess with the Zohan* roared with laughter, and I understand why. Adam Sandler's new comedy is shameless in its eagerness to extract laughs from every possible breach of taste or decorum, and why am I even mentioning taste and decorum in this context? This is a mighty hymn of and to vulgarity, and either you enjoy it or you don't. I found myself enjoying it a surprising amount of the time, even though I was thoroughly ashamed of myself. There is a tiny part of me that still applauds the great minds who invented the whoopee cushion.

Sandler plays an ace agent for the Mossad, the Israeli secret police, who has no interest in counterterrorism and spends as much time as possible hanging out with babes on the beach. Known as The Zohan, he has remarkable physical skills—and equipment, as his bikini briefs and the crotches of all his costumes make abundantly clear. The laws of gravity do not limit him; he can travel through cities like Spider-Man, but without the web strings. He can simply jump for hundreds of feet.

The Zohan harbors one secret desire. He wants to be a hairdresser. His equivalent of pornography is an old Paul Mitchell catalog, and one day he simply cuts his ties with Israel and smuggles himself into the United States in a crate carrying two dogs whose hair he does en route. In America, he poses as an Australian with a very peculiar accent and, asked for his name, combines the names of his airborne flight buddies: Scrappy Coco-man. His auditions in various hair salons are unsuccessful (in a black salon, he attacks a dreads wig as if it were a hostile animal), until finally he is hired by the beautiful Dalia (Emmanuelle Chriqui), a Palestinian.

This plot is simply the skeleton for sight gags. Early on, we saw how much pain he could endure when he dropped a sharp-toothed fish into the crotch of his bikini swimming trunks. Now we see such sights as his sexual adventures with old ladies in the salon. In my notes, I scribbled in the dark: "An angel with the flexibility of a circus freak," adding, "he tells old lady," although maybe the old lady told him. At home with his new friend Michael (Nick Swardson), he effortlessly seduces the friend's mother (the zaftig Lainie Kazan).

His archenemy, the Palestinian agent known as The Phantom (John Turturro), is also in New York, and they make war. The Phantom's training regime is severe. He takes eggs, cracks them, and live chicks emerge. These he puts in a glass and chugs. He punches not only sides of beef but a living cow. Like The Zohan, he is filled with confidence in his own abilities, and

with reason (he can cling to ceilings). Their confrontation will be a battle of the Middle Eastern superheroes.

Now creeps in a belated plot, involving a shady developer (Michael Buffer, of "Let's get ready to rumble!" fame). He wants to tear down a street of Arab and Israeli electronics stores and falafel and hummus shops to put up a mall. This would be a terrible thing, particularly given the prominent role that hummus plays in the film. Opposition to the mall unites the Israelis and Arabs, unconvincingly, on the way to peace and brotherhood at the end.

There are scenes here that make you wince. One involves a savage game of hacky-sack using not a hacky-sack bag but a living cat. Only the consolation that it's done with special effects allows us to endure the cries of the cat. Mariah Carey appears, starts to sing "The Star-Spangled Banner," and somehow survives a cameo with the mall builder. (Maybe his contract says Buffer appears in all movies involving the national anthem.) And something must be said about The Zohan's speech, which in addition to the broad comic accent involves the word "no" in a series that can run from two ("no-no!") to his usual five ("no-no-no-no-no!") to the infinite.

Sandler works so hard at this, and so shamelessly, that he battered down my resistance. Like a Jerry Lewis out of control, he will do, and does, anything to get a laugh. No thinking adult should get within a mile of this film. I must not have been thinking. For my sins, I laughed. Sorry. I'll try to do better next time.

Youth Without Youth ★ ½
R, 125 m., 2007

Tim Roth (Dominic Matei), Alexandra Maria Lara (Veronica/Laura), Bruno Ganz (Professor Stanciulescu), Andre Hennicke (Dr. Josef Rudolf), Marcel Iures (Professor Tucci), Alexandra Pirici (Woman in Room 6), Adrian Pintea (Pandit), Florin Piersic Jr. (Dr. Gavrila). Directed and produced by Francis Ford Coppola. Screenplay by Coppola, based on the novella by Mircea Eliade.

Youth Without Youth proves that Francis Ford Coppola can still make a movie, but not that he still knows how to choose his projects. The film is a sharp disappointment to those who have been waiting for ten years since the master's last film. The best that can be hoped is that, having made a film, Coppola has the taste again and will go on to make many more, nothing like this.

His story involves Dominic (Tim Roth), a seventy-year-old Romanian linguist who fears he will die alone and with his life's work unfinished, so he decides to kill himself. Before he can do that, he is struck by a bolt of lightning that should have turned him into a steaming puddle, but instead lands him in a hospital, burned to a crisp. Then a peculiar process begins. He starts to grow younger. His hair thickens and loses its gray. His rotten teeth are pushed out by new ones. His skin heals. His health returns.

It is the eve of World War II, and Dominic becomes of intense interest to the scientists of the Third Reich. Perhaps Hitler thinks his wounded soldiers can be made whole, or that he himself can turn back the march of time. Dominic, now hale and hearty, finds himself in Switzerland being seduced by a sexy German spy, when one day he sees, or thinks he sees, a woman on a mountain hike who resembles Laura, the lost love of his youth. This is Veronica (Alexandra Maria Lara), who is, wouldn't you know, struck by lightning and starts to grow older. In the process, she regresses backward in linguistic time and begins speaking Sanskrit, Babylonian, and perhaps even the Ur language from which all others descended.

This is exciting beyond all measure to Dominic, who has researched the origins of language, but it is also heartbreaking, because he seems to have had his lost love restored to him, only to be taken away by the implacable advance of age. Coppola found this story in a novella by the Romanian Mircea Eliade, for many years a professor of history of religions at the University of Chicago. It is possible to see how it might have been simplified and clarified into an entertainment along the lines of *Time After Time*, but Coppola seems to positively embrace the obscurity and impenetrability of the material.

There is such a thing as a complex film that rewards additional viewing and study, but *Youth Without Youth*, I am afraid, is no more than it seems: a confusing slog through metaphysical murkiness. That it is so handsomely photographed and mounted, and acted with conviction, only underlines the narrative confusion. We know from interviews that the story means a great deal to Coppola, at the same age as his protagonist. But his job is to make it mean a great deal to us. He is a great filmmaker, and I am sure this film is only a deep, shuddering breath before he makes another masterpiece.

Z

Zack and Miri Make a Porno ★ ★ ★
R, 101 m., 2008

Seth Rogen (Zack), Elizabeth Banks (Miri Linky), Craig Robinson (Delaney), Jason Mewes (Lester), Jeff Anderson (Deacon), Traci Lords (Bubbles), Katie Morgan (Stacey), Ricky Mabe (Barry). Directed by Kevin Smith and produced by Scott Mosier. Screenplay by Smith.

Kevin Smith begins with the advantage of being raised with deeply embedded senses of sin and guilt. He's thirty-eight, and he still believes sex is dirty and that it's funny to shock people with four-letter words and enough additional vulgarisms to fill out a crossword puzzle. This is sort of endearing. It gives his potty-mouth routines a certain freshness; we've heard these words over and over again, but never so many of them so closely jammed together. If you bleeped this movie for broadcast TV, it would sound like a conga line of Iron Men going through a metal detector.

Zack and Miri Make a Porno, as the title hints, is about Zack (Seth Rogen) and Miri (Elizabeth Banks) making a porno. "I don't know bleep about directing," Smith once confided to me. "But I'm a bleeping good writer." He is. Since he likes to eat, I will describe him in food terms. He isn't a gourmet chef, supplying little nuggets of armadillo surrounded by microscopic carrots and curlicues of raspberry-avocado-mint juice. He's the kind of chef I've valued for a lifetime, the kind you see behind the ledge in a Formica diner, pulling down new orders from revolving clips. The kind of diner where the waitresses wear paper Legionnaire hats, pop their gum, and say, "What ya havin' today, hon?"

In Kevin Smith's fantasy diner, the waitresses at this joint strip naked and have noisy lesbian sex, and then Jose the busboy joins in the fun. They all scream loudly: "Bleep, you bleeping bleep! I bleep your bleep! Bleep! Bleep! I'm bleeping bleeping!" *Variety*, the showbiz bible, trains its critics as keen observers of detail, and their alert senior critic Todd McCarthy observes: "There's scarcely a line of dialogue that doesn't feature the F-word, A-word, one of the C- or P-words or some variant of them."

Zack and Miri are poverty-row roommates who have lived together for years, I guess, but never have sex because you might feel funny around a good friend if you bleeped them, and a good friend is so much harder to come by than a bleep. Now they face eviction and ruin, and might have to become bleeping sidewalk-mates. After some little jerk videotapes them—not bleeping but looking like (B)ILFs—they become superstars of the nether lands of YouTube, and have a brilliant idea: They'll cash in on their fame by making a porn film.

Of course, this will require them to bleep on camera, a sacrifice they are willing to make, as long as what happens in the porno, stays in the porno. They enlist aid from a kid (Jeff Anderson) who videos football games, the abundantly tumescent Jason Mewes (Silent Bob's friend Jay), and the well-known Traci Lords, who at last is the only grown-up in a movie.

As they edge uneasily toward their big scene, Miri and Zack pull off the complex feat of being unfaithful to each other with themselves, who they meet on the set. This does not happen easily, and is accompanied by a flood of scatological humor. Their producer is Delaney (Craig Robinson), a guy Zack works with at a Starbucks wannabe, and who is funny as he tries to responsibly perform duties he knows only in theory.

And, of course, awwww, Zack and Miri admit they've been in love along, and achieve something you *never* see in a porn film, lovemaking with barely visible sex and very genuine romance. Seth Rogen and Elizabeth Banks make a lovable couple; she's pretty and goes one-for-one on the bleep language, and Rogen, how can I say this, is growing on me, the big lug.

Will this movie offend you? Somehow Kevin Smith's very excesses defuse the material. He's like the guy at a party who tells dirty jokes so fast, Dangerfield-style, that you laugh more at the performance than the material. He's always coming back for more. Once during a speech at the Indie Spirits, he actually sounded like he was offering his wife as a door prize. Anything for a laugh. Nobody laughed. They all looked at one another sort of stunned. You can't say he didn't try.

Zodiac ★ ★ ★ ★
R, 165 m., 2007

Jake Gyllenhaal (Robert Graysmith), Robert Downey Jr. (Paul Avery), Mark Ruffalo (Davd Toschi), Anthony Edwards (Bill Armstrong), Brian Cox (Melvin Belli), Elias Koteas (Jack Mulanax), Chloë Sevigny (Melanie). Directed by David Fincher and produced by Cean Chaffin, Brad Fischer, Mike Medavoy, Arnold Messer, and James Vanderbilt. Screenplay by Vanderbilt, based on the books by Robert Graysmith.

Zodiac is the *All the President's Men* of serial killer movies, with Woodward and Bernstein played by a cop and a cartoonist. It's not merely "based" on California's infamous Zodiac killings, but seems to exude the very stench and provocation of the case. The killer, who was never caught, generously supplied so many clues that Sherlock Holmes might have cracked the case in his sitting room. But only a newspaper cartoonist was stubborn enough, and tunneled away long enough, to piece together a convincing case against a man who was *perhaps* guilty.

The film is a police procedural crossed with a newspaper movie, but free of most of the clichés of either. Its most impressive accomplishment is to gather a bewildering labyrinth of facts and suspicions over a period of years and make the journey through this maze frightening and suspenseful. I could imagine becoming hopelessly mired in the details of the Zodiac investigation, but director David Fincher (*Se7en*) and his writer, James Vanderbilt, find their way with clarity through the murk. In a film with so many characters, the casting by Laray Mayfield is also crucial; like the only eyewitness in the case, we remember a face once we've seen it.

The film opens with a sudden, brutal, bloody killing, followed by others not too long after—five killings the police feel sure Zodiac committed, although others have been attributed to him. But this film will not be a bloodbath. The killer does his work in the earlier scenes of the film, and then, when he starts sending encrypted letters to newspapers, the police and reporters try to do theirs.

The two lead inspectors on the case are David Toschi (Mark Ruffalo) and William Armstrong (Anthony Edwards). Toschi, famous at the time, tutored McQueen for *Bullitt* and was the role model for Eastwood's Dirty Harry. Ruffalo plays him not as a hotshot but as a dogged officer who does things by the book because he believes in the book. The Edwards character, his partner, is more personally worn down by the sheer vicious nature of the killer and his taunts.

At the *San Francisco Chronicle*, although we meet several staffers, the key players are ace reporter Paul Avery (Robert Downey Jr., bearded, chain-smoking, alcoholic) and editorial cartoonist Robert Graysmith (Jake Gyllenhaal). These characters are real, and indeed the film is based on Graysmith's books about the case.

I found the newspaper office intriguing in its accuracy. For one thing, it is usually fairly empty, and it was true on a morning paper in those days that the office began to heat up closer to deadline. Among the few early arrivals would have been the cartoonist, who was expected to work up a few ideas for presentation at the daily news meeting, and the office alcoholics, perhaps up all night or already starting their recovery drinking. Yes, reporters drank at their desks forty years ago, and smoked and smoked and smoked.

Graysmith is new on the staff when the first cipher arrives. He's like the curious new kid in school fascinated by the secrets of the big boys. He doodles with a copy of the cipher, and we think he'll solve it, but he doesn't. He strays off his beat by eavesdropping on cops and reporters, making friends with the boozy Avery, and even talking his way into police evidence rooms. Long after the investigation has cooled, his obsession remains, eventually driving his wife (Chloë Sevigny) to move herself and their children back in with her mom. Graysmith seems oblivious to the danger he may be drawing into his home, even after he appears on TV and starts hearing heavy breathing over the phone.

What makes *Zodiac* authentic is the way it avoids chases, shoot-outs, grandstanding, and false climaxes, and just follows the methodical progress of police work. Just as Woodward and Bernstein knocked on many doors and made many phone calls and met many very odd people, so do the cops and Graysmith walk down strange pathways in their investigation. Because Graysmith is unarmed and a civilian, we become genuinely worried about his naivete and risk taking, especially during a trip to a basement that is, in its way, one of the best scenes I've ever seen along those lines.

Fincher gives us times and days and dates at the bottom of the screen, which serve only to underline how the case seems to stretch out to infinity. There is even time-lapse photography showing the Transamerica building going up. Everything leads up to a heart-stopping moment when two men look, simply look, at one another. It is a more satisfying conclusion than Dirty Harry shooting Zodiac dead, say, in a football stadium.

David Fincher is not the first director you would associate with this material. In 1992, at thirty, he directed *Alien 3*, which was the least of the Alien movies, but even then had his eye (*Alien 3* is one of the best-looking bad movies I have ever seen). His credits include *Se7en* (1995), a superb film about another serial killer

with a pattern to his crimes; *The Game* (1997), with Michael Douglas caught in an ego-smashing web; *Fight Club* (1999), beloved by most, not by me; the ingenious terror of Jodie Foster in *Panic Room* (2002); and now, five years between features, his most thoughtful, involving film.

He seems to be in reaction against the slice-and-dice style of modern crime movies; his composition and editing are more classical, and he doesn't use nine shots when one will do. (If this same material had been put through an Avid to chop the footage into five times as many shots, we would have been sending our own ciphers to the studio.) Fincher is an elegant stylist on top of everything else, and here he finds the right pace and style for a story about persistence in the face of evil. I am often fascinated by true crime books, partly because of the way they amass ominous details (the best I've read is *Blood and Money* by Tommy Thompson), and Fincher understands that true crime is not the same genre as crime action. That he makes every character a distinct individual is proof of that; consider the attention given to Graysmith's choice of mixed drink.

The Best Films of 2008

December 12, 2008—In these hard times, you deserve two "best films" lists for the price of one. It is therefore with joy that I list the twenty best films of 2008, in alphabetical order. I am violating the age-old custom that film critics announce the ten best films, but after years of such lists, I've had it. A best films list should be a celebration of wonderful films, not a chopping process. And 2008 was a great year for movies, even if many of them didn't receive wide distribution.

Look at my twenty titles and you tell me which ten you would cut. Nor can I select one to stand above the others, or decide which should be number seven and which should be number eight. I can't evaluate films that way. Nobody can, although we all pretend to. A "best films" list, certainly. But of exactly ten, in marching order? These twenty stood out for me, and I treasure them all. If it had been nineteen or twenty-one, that would have been OK. If you must have a Top Ten List, find a coin in your pocket. Heads, the odd-numbered movies are the ten. Tails, the even-numbered are.

I have composed a separate list of the five best documentaries. They each may also be described as "one of the year's best." And this year's Special Jury Award goes to Guy Maddin's *My Winnipeg*, which stands between truth and fiction, using the materials of documentary to create a film completely preposterous and deeply true. Another of "the year's best."

1. *Ballast*

A deep silence has fallen upon a Mississippi Delta family after the death of a husband and brother. Old wounds remain unhealed. The man's son shuttles uneasily between two homes, trying to open communication by the wrong means. The debut cast is deeply convincing, and writer-director Lance Hammer observes them with intense empathy. No, not a film about poor folks on the Delta; they own a nice little business but are paralyzed by loneliness. At the end, we think, "Yes, that is what

would happen, and it would happen exactly like that."

2. *The Band's Visit*

A police ceremonial band from Egypt, in Israel for a cultural exchange, ends up in a desert town far from anywhere and is taken mercy on by the bored, cynical residents. A long night's journey marked with comedy, human nature, and bittersweet reality. Richly entertaining, with sympathetic performances by Sasson Gabai as the bandleader and Ronit Elkabetz as the owner of a local café. Written and directed by Eran Kolirin. Was at Ebertfest 2008.

3. *Che*

The epic journey of a twentieth-century icon, the Argentinean physician who became a comrade of Fidel Castro's in the Cuban revolution and then moved to South America to support revolution there. Benicio del Toro is persuasive as the fiercely ethical firebrand in a film that includes unusual and unfamiliar chapters in Che's life. Steven Soderbergh's film is 257 minutes long, but far from boring.

4. *Chop Shop*

The great emerging American director Ramin Bahrani finds a story worthy of *City of God* in a no-man's land in the shadow of Shea Stadium, where a young boy and his sister support themselves in a sprawling, off-the-books auto repair and scrap district. Alejandro Polanco and Isamar Gonzales seem to live their roles, in a masterpiece that intimately knows its world, its people, and their survival tactics. Was at Ebertfest 2009.

5. *The Dark Knight*

The best of all the Batmans, Christopher Nolan's haunted film leaps beyond its origins and becomes an engrossing tragedy. The "comic book movie" has at last reclaimed its deep, archetypal currents. With a performance by Heath Ledger as The Joker that will surely win an Oscar, a Batman by Christian Bale who is tortured by moral puzzles, and a district attorney by Aaron Eckhart forced to make impossible choices.

6. *Doubt*

A Catholic grade school is ruled by the grim perfectionist Sister Aloysius (Meryl Streep), whose draconian rule is challenged by Father Flynn (Philip Seymour Hoffman). A young nun (Amy Adams) is caught between them, as the film shows how assumptions can be doubted, and doubted again. Viola Davis, as the mother of the only black student, has one significant scene, but it is long, crucial, and heartbreaking. Davis goes face-to-face with Streep with astonishing conviction and creates reasons for doubt that may be more important than deciding the truth. John Patrick Shanley directed and adapted his Tony Award–winning play.

7. *The Fall*

Tarsem's film is a mad folly, an extravagant visual orgy, a free fall from reality into uncharted realms. A wounded stunt man circa 1914 tells a story to a four-year-old girl, and we see how she imagines it. Vast romantic images so stunning I had to check twice, three times, to be sure the film actually claims to have *absolutely no* computer-generated imagery. None? What about the Labyrinth of Despair with no exit? The intersecting walls of zigzagging staircases? The man who emerges from the burning tree? Filmed over four years in twenty-eight countries. Was at Ebertfest 2009.

8. *Frost/Nixon*

The story of a duel between a crafty man and a persistent one. How many remember that the "lightweight" British interviewer David Frost was the one who finally persuaded Richard Nixon to say he had committed crimes in connection with Watergate and let his country down? With his own money riding on the interviews, Frost (Michael Sheen) is desperate after Nixon finesses him in the early sessions, but he pries away at Nixon's need to confess. Frank Langella is uncanny as RMN. Ron Howard directs mercilessly.

9. *Frozen River*

Melissa Leo should be nominated for her performance. She plays an hourly employee in a discount store, struggling to support two kids and a rundown trailer after her husband deserts them with their savings. After making an unlikely alliance with the Mohawk woman (Misty Upham) who was stealing her car, she finds herself a human trafficker, driving Chinese across the ice into America. A spellbinding thriller, yes, but even more a portrait of economic struggle in desperate times. Written and directed by Courtney Hunt. Was at Ebertfest 2009.

10. *Happy-Go-Lucky*

Here's another nominee for best actress: Sally Hawkins, playing a cheerful schoolteacher who seems improbably upbeat until we win a glimpse into her soul. No, she's not secretly depressed. She's genuinely happy, but that hasn't made her stupid or afraid. Mike Leigh's uncanny ability to find drama in ordinary lives is used with genius, as the teacher encounters a driving instructor (Eddie Marsan) as negative as she is positive. Not a feel-good movie. Not at all. But strangely inspiring.

11. *Iron Man*

Like *Spider-Man 2* and *The Dark Knight,* another leap forward for the superhero movie. Robert Downey Jr. and director Jon Favreau reinvent Tony Stark as a conflicted, driven genius who has a certain plausibility, even inundated by special effects. So successful are they that in the climactic rooftop battle between two towering men of steel, we *know* we're looking almost entirely at CGI, and yet the creatures embody character and emotion. Downey hit bottom, as everyone knows. Now he has triumphantly returned.

12. *Milk*

Sean Penn, one of our greatest actors, locks up an Oscar nomination with his performance as Harvey Milk, the first self-identified gay man elected to U.S. public office. At forty, he determined to do "something different" with his life. He's open to change. We see how the everyday experiences of this gay man politicize him, and how his instincts allow him to become a charismatic leader, while always acknowledging the sexuality that society had taught him to conceal. One of the year's most moving films.

13. *Rachel Getting Married*

People told me, "I wanted to attend that wedding," or "I wish I'd been there." It's that involving. Jonathan Demme doesn't lock down one central plot, but considers the ceremony as a wedding of close and distant family, old and new friends, many races, many ages, many lifestyles, all joined amid joyous homemade music. His camera is so observant, we feel like a guest really does feel. Rosemarie DeWitt as Rachel and Anne Hathaway as her sister generate tricky sibling tension.

14. *The Reader*

A drama taking place mostly within the mind of a postwar German who has an affair at fifteen with a woman he later discovers is a war criminal. Her own secret is so shameful she would rather face any sentence than reveal it. About the moral confusion felt in those who came after the Holocaust but whose lives were painfully twisted by it. With David Kross as the younger protagonist, and Kate Winslet and Ralph Fiennes as the older ones. Directed by Stephen Daldry.

15. *Revolutionary Road*

The Man in the Gray Flannel Suit and his wife find hell in the suburbs. Kate Winslet and Leonardo DiCaprio, in two of the best performances of the year, play a young married couple who lose their dreams in the American corporate world and its assigned roles. Sam Mendes reads minds when words aren't enough and has every detail right—including the chain-smoking by those who find it a tiny consolation in inconsolable lives.

16. *Shotgun Stories*

You'll have to search for it, but it's worth it. In a "dead-ass town," three brothers find themselves in a feud with their four half-brothers. Told like a revenge tragedy, but the hero doesn't believe the future is written by the past. Written and directed by Jeff Nichols, it avoids the obvious and shows a deep understanding of the lives and minds of ordinary young people in a skirmish of the class war. The dialogue rings true; the camera is deeply observant. The audience favorite at Ebertfest 2008.

17. *Slumdog Millionaire*

Danny Boyle's improbable union of quiz show suspense and the harrowing life of a Mumbai orphan. Growing from a garbage-pit scavenger to the potential winner of a fortune, his hero uses his wits and survival instinct to struggle against crushing handicaps. A film that finds exuberance in spite of the tragedy it also gives full weight to. The locations breathe with authenticity.

18. *Synecdoche, New York*

The year's most endlessly debated film. Screenwriter Charlie Kaufman (*Adaptation, Being John Malkovich*), in his directing debut. Stars Philip Seymour Hoffman as a theater director mired in a long-running rehearsal that may be life itself. Much controversy about the identities and even genders of some of the characters, in a film that should never be seen unless you've already seen it at least once.

19. *W.*

To general surprise, Oliver Stone's biography of George W. Bush is empathetic and understanding, perhaps because Stone himself was a blueblood Ivy League graduate who could never quite win his father's approval. Josh Brolin in a nuanced portrayal that seems based on the known facts, showing the president as subservient to Vice President Cheney and haunted by old demons.

20. *WALL-E*

The best science-fiction movie in years was an animated family film. WALL-E is a solar-powered, trash-compacting robot, left behind to clean up the waste after Man flees into orbit. Hugely entertaining, wonderfully well-drawn, and, if you think about it, merciless in its critique of a global consumer culture that obsesses on intake and disregards the consequences of output.

* * *

Every year I name a winner of my Special Jury Prize, so named in honor of the "alternative first prize" given by juries at many festivals. This year (roll of the drums) the honored film is:

My Winnipeg

Guy Maddin's latest dispatch from inside his imagination is a "history" of his hometown, which becomes a mixture of the very slightly plausible, the convincing but unlikely, the fantastical, the fevered, the absurd, the preposterous, and the nostalgic. Oddly enough, when it's over, you have a deeper and, in a crazy way, more "real" portrait of Winnipeg than a conventional doc might have provided—and certainly a far more entertaining one. Was at Ebertfest 2009.

* * *

Five documentaries in equal first place:

1. *Encounters at the End of the World*

Werner Herzog moseys around to see whom he will meet and what he will see at the South Pole. The population here seems made of travelers beyond our realm, all with amazing personal histories. In a spellbinding film, Herzog finds a great deal of humor, astonishing underwater creatures, permanent occupants such as seals and penguins, and the possibility of a bleak global future.

2. *I.O.U.S.A.*

A film to make sense of the current economic crisis. The U.S. national debt has doubled in the last eight years, we can't make the payments, the world holds our mortgage, and it can't afford for us to default. So the same unsupported currency seems to circulate one step ahead of disaster. Not a partisan film. Experts of all political persuasions look at our bookkeeping and agree it is insane.

3. *Man on Wire*

On August 7, 1974, a Frenchman named Philippe Petit, having smuggled two tons of equipment to the top of the towers of the World Trade Center, strung a wire between them and walked back and forth *eight* times.

Combines period footage and re-created scenes to explain how he did it and, mystically, why. We know he made it, so how does this film generate such suspense?

4. *Standard Operating Procedure*

About what photographs are and how we see them, focusing on the infamous prison torture photographs from Abu Ghraib. Errol Morris's scrutiny reveals what was really happening and why, and how the photographs do not always show what they seem to. He introduces the name of Charles Graner, who always stayed in the shadows, but without whom there might have been no photos at all.

5. *Trouble the Water*

A few days before Hurricane Katrina hit New Orleans, a young couple from the Ninth Ward named Scott and Kimberly Rivers Roberts bought a camcorder. As the rains began to fall, they began to film, even while trapped by rising waters inside their attic. Their astonishing footage, unlike any other, is incorporated by Carl Deal and Tia Lessin into a documentary that shows why Brownie was not doing a great job, not at all. Was at Ebertfest 2009.

* * *

Looking back over the list, I think most moviegoers will have heard of only about eleven, because distribution has reached such a dismal state. When I wrote to a reader about *Shotgun Stories,* "I don't know if it will play in your town," she wrote back, "How about my state?" This is a time when home video, Netflix, and the good movie channels come to the rescue. My theory that you should see a movie on a big screen is sound, but utopian.

The Best Foreign Films of 2008

December 19, 2008—It was not a great year for foreign films. In America, that is. Or, more exactly, in that America between New York and Los Angeles. Distributors, even those specializing in indie films, have grown shy of movies that look like tricky sales, and with the economic downturn, the situation has grown more depressing. I saw subtitled films that would be great in any year, however, and they are on this list.

Although I missed Cannes this year, I did attend the Toronto festival and saw good foreign films that will not open until 2009, including the Cannes winner *The Class, O'Horten,* and *Waltz with Bashir.* Of those that did open, all are terrific entertainments, which is probably why they won distribution.

Looking over my earlier list of the year's twenty best, I see no thrillers nearly as exciting as *Tell No One* and *Transsiberian.* Indeed, I see no thrillers at all. There is only one human comedy to rival *In Bruges,* and no vampire film even remotely as good as *Let the Right One In.*

These best ten are arranged alphabetically, and all should be considered on a par with the earlier twenty, and can be described as "one of the year's best films" (the only real value of such lists is to help worthy films find audiences). I add some further observations at the bottom of the list.

1. *4 Months, 3 Weeks, and 2 Days*

A harrowing, yet sometimes strangely comic, Romanian film about an utterly clueless young woman (Laura Vasiliu) who begs her roommate (Anamaria Marinca) to help her find an abortion. The roommate does everything but have the abortion herself. A journey of frustration, stupidity, duplicity, cruelty, and desperation, set against a background of a nation where, in the late 1980s, if it weren't for the black market, there would have been no market at all.

2. *A Christmas Tale*

Unlike any movie you can imagine about a dying mother (Catherine Deneuve) and her extended family at Christmastime. Director and cowriter Arnaud Desplechin gracefully moves among the family members, all of whom seem to be more preoccupied with their own troubles than hers. What shines through the movie is the mother's serenity. Desplechin's playful approach subtly shows more than one way to handle this material.

3. *The Duchess of Langeais*

About two elegant aristocrats whose compulsions eat them alive. They're bullheaded to the point of madness. Guillaume Depardieu plays a famous general who sees the duchess (Jeanne Balibar) at a ball and begins a courtship that seems to have no end. Jacques Rivette, now eighty, shows their fruitless romantic duel as a series of conversations that drift away from the passion of sex and into the passion of winning, in a series of almost hypnotic tableaux. Sadly, Guillaume, son of Gerard, died at thirty-seven in October 2008 after mounting health problems.

4. *Edge of Heaven*

Surprisingly powerful for a movie telling interlocking stories, which sometimes go astray. Involves an old Turkish man in Bremen, Germany, a middle-aged Turkish prostitute he meets there, her daughter and his son in Turkey, and the strands they may not realize connect them. Works so well not because of those strands, but because of who they are, and the way writer-director Fatih Akin understands them.

5. *A Girl Cut in Two*

At seventy-eight, another New Wave director still in top form. Claude Chabrol's film plays like a triangular romantic comedy, until we discover that all three of the lovers are hurtling headlong to self-destruction. Even then it's comedic, in a macabre, Hitchcockian way. Ludivine Sagnier as the girl, young and ambitious. Benoit Magimel as an insufferably spoiled rich kid. Francois Berleand as a famous author, older. Based on a famous American triangle I will not name.

6. *I've Loved You So Long*

Kristin Scott Thomas is a long-imprisoned woman who returns to her family but still lives with a cloud of shame and secrecy. Acting in French, she warms, is more free with emotions, more easily reaches joy and sorrow. Watch her at a dinner party as a guest takes sadistic pleasure in asking her questions it is clear she cannot answer. Written and directed by Philippe Claudel.

7. *The Last Mistress*

An astonishing performance by Asia Argento, playing the most famous courtesan in Paris, who loses her lover (Fu'ad Ait Aatou) to marriage and does everything she can to win him back—not for love, but for her reputation. Directed by Catherine Breillat, famous for her explicit eroticism; a film of shocking psychological combat, somewhat similar in period and theme with *The Duchess of Langeais*, but its emotional opposite.

8. *Let the Right One In*

A powerful reminder that vampires, if there were vampires, would not be a joke. They might have been victimized young, stuck at that age into immortality, be poor, be lonely. A boy named Oskar (Kare Hedebrant), shared between indifferent parents, is befriended by the kid next door named Eli (Lina Leandersson). "Are you a vampire?" he asks. Yes. But one who likes him and is protective, in a poignant and sometimes blood-drenched story. Not for fans of *Twilight.*

9. *Tell No One*

Spellbinding. Deserves comparison with Hitchcock. A man goes on a midnight swim with his wife, he is struck unconscious, she disappears, suspicion hangs over his head, and several years later he begins to receive e-mails that could only be from her. The scene of their planned rendezvous in a park is masterful. Starring Francois Cluzet Marie-Josee Croze and (again in French) Kristin Scott Thomas. Directed by Guillaume Canet.

10. *XXY*

Starring Ines Efron as Alex, born with both male and female sex organs and who, at fifteen, is a high-spirited tomboy who broods privately about the choices ahead. During a summer holiday on an island, Alex meets both a surgeon who may have suggestions and the surgeon's son; they are attracted to each other. Not a sensational telling of this story, but a sensitive and romantic one, well acted. From Argentina, written and directed by Lucia Puenzo.

* * *

All film festivals give an award to a special favorite of the jury that somehow doesn't fit in the main categories. In my earlier Top Twenty list, I named *My Winnipeg*, which fits halfway between fiction and documentary. Among the foreign films, I name a wonderful human comedy about two Dublin hit men who are fish out of water in a film that surrounds them with French and Flemish in a city nothing like their own.

In Bruges

Colin Farrell is a young hothead who has no use for foreign lands. Brendan Gleeson is older, more curious, enchanted by this medieval city in Belgium where they have been sent to lie low after a messy murder gone wrong. They're visited by their boss (Ralph Fiennes), who observes, killing a priest may be business, but "blowing a kid's head off just isn't done." Has the kind of humor that grows from close observation of human nature. Written and directed by Martin McDonagh.

* * *

Some Observations

One: Although I have long defended celluloid projection over digital, the time has come for me to relent. Digital projection is now excellent; it was not in earlier years, even though its proponents claimed it was. I still prefer film, but I think the time is approaching when an original promise of digital can come true. If distributors of foreign and indie films are able to beam a digital signal directly to theaters, the cost savings on the manufacture and distribution of prints would be enormous, and allow wide simultaneous openings even in smaller cities. It's clear something has to be done, and maybe this is it.

Two: I am sure to get complaints pointing out that *The Band's Visit*, one of the films on my other list, is a foreign film, having been made in Israel. Yes, that is true. But the Egyptian and Israeli characters in it do not speak a word of one another's languages, and are forced to communicate in English. In a decision of remarkable stupidity, the Academy said the movie had too much English to qualify as a foreign film. So I am observing their ruling as a sort of protest.

That leaves *In Bruges,* on this list, as a film of English speakers in a foreign land. Another fence-sitter. So it gets the Jury Prize because,

like *My Winnipeg,* it falls outside easy categorization. If you think my reasoning is goofy, let me say I agree. But there would have been an Internet uproar of titanic proportions if I had issued two lists, one with eleven titles and one with nine. The anal-retentive enforcers of movie critic rules become hyperactive at annual list time. So maybe one of my motives is to demonstrate my belief that ranking movies in lists has only one point: to honor good films I hope you would admire.

Interviews

Ramin Bahrani

March 24, 2009—Ramin Bahrani is the new great American director. After three films, each a masterwork, he has established himself as a gifted, confident filmmaker with ideas that involve who and where we are at this time. His films pay great attention to ordinary lives that are not so ordinary at all. His subjects so far have been immigrants, working hard to make a living in America. His fourth film, now in preparation, will be a Western. His hero will be named Tom. Well, he couldn't very well be named Huckleberry.

The Old West, too, was a land of immigrants, many of them speaking no English. But Bahrani never refers to his characters as immigrants. They are new Americans, climbing the lower rungs of the economic ladder. There is the Pakistani in *Man Push Cart,* who operates a coffee-and-bagel wagon in Manhattan. The Latino kid in *Chop Shop,* surviving in a vast auto parts bazaar in the shadow of Shea Stadium. The taxi driver from Senegal in *Goodbye Solo,* who works long hours in Winston-Salem, North Carolina. These people are not grim and depressed but hopeful when they have little to be hopeful about. They aren't walking around angry. Wounded, sometimes. They plan to prevail.

Bahrani doesn't categorize his characters. I called them outsiders in one of our conversations at Toronto 2008, and he said he liked that.

"It's not just 'immigrant.' It's different. Their lives are asking, How should I be as a person, how should I be behaving, why is the world this way? You could put me in a room full of people who look just like me, and I would feel like I don't understand." Those are the questions. It's in every Herzog film: How do you live in this world? How is the world like this? What else is there to think about?

Bahrani was born in Winston-Salem. His parents immigrated from Iran.

"Growing up, it was mainly black, white, and me and my brother," he says. His father was a psychiatrist, working much among poor whites and blacks. After graduating from Columbia University, he went for a few weeks' visit to his parents' homeland, and found himself staying several years. He was an outsider there, too.

Coming home, he knew he had to make films. *Man Push Cart* was made for a few tens of thousands, a small crew, no permits, and the catering often consisted of coffee and pastries from the cart. When it looks like his hero is pushing the heavy cart, that's because he is. In Pakistan he was something of a rock star. He is trying his fortune in America.

I saw that film at its world premiere at Sundance 2006. Low-budget, unheralded. I felt strongly that I was seeing the work of a great director. I felt the same way after seeing Scorsese's first film. There was an artistic intelligence alive beneath the immediate vision. The images were of real lives on real streets (mean streets, Scorsese would call them, quoting Raymond Chandler).

In an article about Bahrani and his contemporaries in the latest *New York Times Magazine,* A. O. Scott calls them neo-neorealists. Well, OK. Neorealism was the Italian postwar movement that argued that everyone has one role they are perfect for—themselves. And stories that are perfect for them, about how they live in this world.

Bahrani has very rarely used professional actors; none in his first two films, only two in *Goodbye Solo.* They are not playing themselves, but they're playing people they might have been. Consider the leads in *Goodbye Solo.* We meet Solo, the North Carolina taxi driver from Senegal (Souleymane Sy Savane). By nature he is cheerful, warmhearted. He is married to a Mexican-American woman and dotes on her daughter. He observes people and cares about them.

One day a white man named William (Red West), about seventy, gets into his cab and offers a deal: He'll pay Solo $1,000 if, in ten days, he'll give him a ride to the top of a nearby mountain and leave him there. Solo isn't sure he likes the sound of this.

Souleymane Sy Savane is from the Ivory Coast. Red West is from Memphis. We believe it. They fit into their roles like hands into gloves. You look at Red West and think, this man has been waiting all his life to play this role. He is seventy-two, stands six foot two. You may have heard the name. He was a member of Elvis Presley's Memphis Mafia, a friend, driver, and bodyguard starting in 1955, who appeared in bit parts in sixteen Elvis movies. Since then he has worked for such directors as Robert Altman and Oliver Stone.

"I wanted a real Southerner," Bahrani told me after the film's premiere at Toronto 2008. "I wanted the accent, I wanted the mentality of the South. He sent a video of himself doing a reading of the first scene. I think I watched it for three seconds; I hit pause and said, this is the guy that I wrote about. This is the guy.

"I called him; I said, 'Red, can you not point when you do the reading?' And I gave him one other direction, just to see, would he hear what I said and would he do it? He did it, he taped it, he sent it back; he had listened to everything I said. I brought the guy in and, I mean, there was just no doubt about it. He was the man."

Bahrani asked him only once about Elvis. He told a great story. "I think it was Elvis's cousin that was bringing drugs to him in the end, and Red didn't like it, which was one of the big conflicts of their falling-out. He said, the guy brought drugs, and he broke his foot and said, 'I'll work my way from your foot up to your face.'

"The whole movie is in Red's face. Especially that lifestyle, you know. The strange thing is he's really friendly, and he loves doing comedic things. He used to apologize to Solo when he was getting mad at him, like, 'I'm sorry, Solo, I have to do it for the film.' Only by the fourth week—we did five weeks—did I start to tell him he was doing really good. He knew it by then; he knew he was up to something. After we shot the finale, I had to leave him alone. He went up into that forest and he cried for almost an hour. He was very affected by it. I think he's great. 'I'm gonna be discovered at the age of seventy-two!' he tells me.

"Solo, he just walked in one day. Didn't know me, did not know about my films. Just like he's in the film; charming, warm, open. I liked him immediately. I learned he had been a flight attendant for two years for Air Afrique. I said, 'Do you smoke pot?' He said yes. I said, 'Do you like reggae music?' He said yes. I said this has gotta be the guy. Of course, I put him through seven months of hell before I said yes."

Working with him for months, that's a key to Bahrani's approach. His films may feel like scenes from real lives, but they're meticulously crafted. He doesn't make them up as he goes along.

Before *Chop Shop,* he hung around for a year in that strange alternate New York that the fans in Shea Stadium never see: blocks upon blocks of shabby buildings with auto repair and salvage shops. Preparing for *Goodbye Solo,* Bahrani rode around Winston-Salem for six months with a real cab driver from Africa: charming, friendly, giving—everything that kinda inspired the character.

Goodbye Solo seems to be about what William will finally do. But the movie is about what happens before. The daily life of Solo. The sealed-off life of William. Solo's partner and her daughter. William's lonely moviegoing. Solo's concern. William's hostility toward it. Racism has nothing to do with them. It doesn't in Bahrani's films. His characters are wholly absorbed in how they live in this world.

"Of course I was always an outsider in Winston-Salem. Increasingly, I see how my parents are outsiders, how they really don't seem to belong there. They get along with everyone, everyone gets along with them; there's never been any instance of latent racism toward them, never. They were always accepted.

"They love my dad in the community. He's a psychiatrist. He never saw wealthy people; he came from Iran with nothing. He'd mainly see the mountain people and the very poor, some poor whites and a lot of poor blacks. They loved him. But I can see how my parents don't belong and how they're getting isolated there."

Bahrani went to Columbia University as an undergraduate. "Then I worked at the North Carolina School for the Arts for one and a half years on staff. I didn't know how I was gonna get to make a film, so I went back to Winston-Salem and thought I should figure it out while I'm writing scripts and things. I worked there on staff at the same time David Gordon Green was there, Craig Zobel, and all these other great people."

Then he moved back to New York and now teaches a graduate course at Columbia on film directing. One of his tools is to go through the films of his students a shot, sometimes even a frame, at a time.

"I tell students the difference between me and you is I made the film and you didn't. You can make a movie right now with just this hi-def camera and your computer. If it's gonna be good, I don't know. That's a whole different story; that's a different game."

I sense that every film, for Bahrani, is like the man pushing the cart. It's hard to find financing, and sometimes he has had to shut down to raise funds. He's not making his latest project. He's deciding how he will live for a couple of years. Yet every film looks beautiful. He works with the cinematographer Michael Simmonds. They compose elegantly. You can see their mastery of film grammar. There is never a shot only for style; every shot engages their characters. They are not calling your attention to the film but to its story.

"After finishing this film," he said, "I was very just depressed, and I didn't understand what was going on in the film industry, or how do you make a film. I was very dark for two or three months; I was like, what am I gonna do? And then I read that Herzog interview, where he told you that if the world were ending tomorrow, he would start a film. And I said I'm gonna make a film."

It is a tonic to talk with Ramin Bahrani. He has none of the zealous ego of some filmmakers. No matter what he says, he has found a way to live in this world. He speaks like a friendly young teacher; I'm sure his students regard him as a mentor. Sometimes you hear a faint whisper of a Southern accent, but you have to listen for it. What I hear is the casual friendliness of someone who grew up in Middle America and is driven, not by ambition, but by optimism.

On that afternoon in Toronto, he told me: "I'm starting to realize that no matter if they say film is dying—no matter if they're telling me you have to do this, you have to do that—I think they're wrong. I think the more you risk, the better.

"Did you like the Darren Aronofsky film, *Pi*? Because it risked everything. What the hell is it? I mean, who came up with this thing? The more you risk, the better. You just have to

find someone who is going to believe, who will put the money up, because it's usually the opposite of what they tell you you have to do. How many people told me 'no' to *Goodbye Solo*? How many people told me, 'No, no money, no, no, no'? Finally, a handful of people said 'yes.' They already made their money back at the Venice film festival because I made it so inexpensively. I thank all those people who told me 'no.' The more they tell me 'no,' the happier I become. It makes me angry, and I make the movie."

Daniel Craig

November 9, 2008—"I just don't believe a man who kills for a living doesn't have nightmares." —Daniel Craig

He is more analytical about James Bond than the other Bonds I've met. The earlier 007s spent a lot of time thinking about him as a character, but Daniel Craig approaches him as a comforting concept in an uncertain world. He asks himself, as some of the Batman actors have started to do, what it might be like for a real man to live the life of a fantasy hero.

Craig, who took over the role with *Casino Royale* in 2006, was visiting Chicago to promote *Quantum of Solace*—the twenty-second title in the series, which began with *Dr. No* in 1962, six years before Craig was born. He is a calm, self-possessed man, eyes as blue as Paul Newman's, seeming not so much pumped up as coiled. For his inspiration in the role, he said, he drew on Ian Fleming's original novels.

"The original Bond was always in turmoil with himself, always questioning," he said. "Maybe he got smoother as the books went on. But going back to the beginning, it's the way I approach my work. I'm aware it's a Bond movie and always remains a Bond movie. I've just always felt there should be an element of truth or emotion in a movie, so that the audience can hook in. If it's only action, then it's not the complete picture."

Bond's super-villains were often comic characters with movie-set headquarters inside mountains or on the moon. Now that the world has actual villains hiding inside mountains, or somewhere, it has grown more complex for Bond villains, who often seemed to belong in a comic book, anyway. The villain's specialty in *Quantum of Solace,* a film in preparation for more than two years, is surprisingly current: global financial manipulation.

"The world is rapidly changing," Craig said. "Natural resources and the global economy are going to play a major role in the future. Over the last couple weeks with the way people have been running from banks and running from investment and showing their true colors, anything is possible. So the simple answer is, there will always be a need for a hero or a heroine. He will last as long as you keep the films good and they explore subjects that we see around us."

When you think of Bond, you think of stunts, particularly the spectacular opening sequences that have no connection whatsoever with the remainder of the plot. In the early years, Bond used countless stuntmen and traditional special effects. There was a tangible feel to stunts like Bond skiing off a mountainside and parachuting to safety. We thought to ourselves, some guy really did that!

Now, in the era of computer-generated imagery, anything is possible. When an actor like Christian Bale insists on personally jumping off the Sears Tower, he uses safety wires and nets, but there is a word for what he's doing, and that word, in my opinion, is "insane." As Bond, Craig performs many or most of his own stunts, and you can't safely assume you're looking at CGI. I asked him about the arm sling he was wearing. He laughed. "Not a stunt. Old rotator cuff injury."

"Of course, when it comes to doing a sequence in an airplane, the best way is always going to be CGI," Craig said. That would be the sequence where he pilots a classic propeller job through a very unlikely crisis.

"It was always about trying to marry CGI and real actors so a scene is as seamless as it can possibly be. The majority of our CGI work in this movie is about painting stuff out. Look at the roof chase sequence in Sienna (Italy). There are four cranes constantly out there because there were cameras on wires—they're called skycams; they use them in football games here—and they fly overhead. I'm wired on the back, and occasionally there'll be a rigger holding something up. CGI replaces everything we don't want you to see."

And it looks like you doing the rooftop jumps.

"I didn't make every jump, but the danger is really so minimal. You can twist your ankle walking down the street. I had eight stitches and lost a chunk of my finger on the sound stage doing the most inane thing. But in the jumps from the buildings and the big crashes I didn't hurt myself at all. We worked so hard in rehearsal before we started. The only thing that concerned me was getting them right, because you've got four cameras and lots of people looking at you, and they're cold and they're wet. One of the stuntmen got very badly injured on this film. He's made a full recovery, but there are risks."

Conspicuously missing from the film are two standbys from the past: Q and Miss Moneypenny. The role of M (Judi Dench) has, on the other hand, been much expanded.

"His relationship with M is important because the film was about knowing who your friends are, who to trust, where your allegiances lie. The next time around, I have lots of ideas; I'd love to get Q back involved, and I'd certainly like to have Moneypenny back. But we need to introduce them in their own right. To ask an actor to just come in and do a Moneypenny, or do a Q, is offensive."

And terrorists? The villains du jour?

"The fear of terrorism has always been in my life. I grew up in Ireland during the IRA, and that battle was fought very much on British and Irish soil. Terrorism is too loose a subject. We have to think smarter than that, and we have to keep Bond apolitical. We're not making political movies; we're making Bond movies."

Craig is classically trained; his London stage debut was in Shakespeare, and he's made very serious films. I asked him how he's facing the phenomenon of the Bond image that sticks to an actor.

Craig smiled. "Philosophically speaking, there are worse things. I can't do things as a reaction to Bond. I can't go and deliberately play a part that is the antithesis of Bond. It's one of those high-class problems I'll have to try and deal with."

Doing a Web search for Craig is entering a minefield of attacks on his casting as Bond. He admitted to some surfing himself.

"Don't you know," I asked, "that those flame wars are maintained by fanboys crouching in their basements with way too much time on their hands?"

"You said it," he said. "I'm no enemy of the Internet, but that way for me madness lies. It started for me on *Casino Royale* very early on. It suddenly exploded because the stuff spread everywhere. I made the mistake of going online and looking. I've had bad reviews in newspapers, but these were very strange personal attacks. I can't enter into the argument. All you're gonna do is get into the same language if you're not careful, and the same language is gonna be, 'I hate you!' 'No, I hate you.' There are better things to do."

Neil LaBute

September 16, 2008—Neil LaBute made three tightly wound films about gender wars, and now he's made a fourth, *Lakeview Terrace,* with race added to the battlefield. Like his other films, it involves close scrutiny of the behavior of men in conflict and women in between.

This one is a thriller, on top of everything else. It stars Samuel L. Jackson as a black cop who doesn't like it when an interracial couple moves in next door. He glowers out the window at a black wife (Kerry Washington) and her white husband (Patrick Wilson). And then he begins an alarming harassment, beginning with floodlights through their windows and building into psychological warfare.

LaBute and I discussed the film one day in Chicago; he lives in the suburbs.

"Actually, I think any number of actors from different races could have played that part," he said. "But when we say race relations, we often tend to think black and white immediately. We start the film from Sam's perspective. He's not a bad cop; he's a cop who has lived in the tinderbox of Los Angeles, trying to raise two children. It was important for him not to be just a bad guy. The producers were always looking at it as a thriller, and we were trying to subvert the thriller by asking, how do we tell this from everybody's side?"

It ends in a thriller situation nevertheless, but LaBute has prepared the ground so carefully that the climax seems justified and still depends on psychology as much as a showdown. He doesn't have a simplistic view of the characters. Washington and Wilson are happy together at the beginning, but Jackson's hostility drives a wedge between them, with complex emotional results.

"If you watch the trailer," he said, "you wouldn't know what's going on between Patrick and Kerry. But I think that's a really satisfying side of the story—the pressure upon this young couple. That's the kind of stuff that attracts me. There's a scene we had to cut to get the PG-13 rating. They've moved in their stuff, and we see them kissing and starting to make love, and then we cut to the night where they first see the lights outside. I thought it showed a solid bond between this couple. You remove that and you have precious little between them before the conflict starts."

Enough, I think, to see they love each other. But is the husband ready to protect his home and marriage? LaBute said the Wilson character is "one of those guys I've focused on a lot, the boy-men who don't want to grow up too quickly. From my point of view, I think I was more interested in that. I wanted him to have a solid relationship which, because of the pressure from Jackson, starts to crumble. And I wanted the ending to be ambiguous. I didn't want them to fall into each other's arms. I didn't cut to her in a conventional way. I stayed off her face. When he says, 'We're a family now,' she doesn't respond; she just looks at him and then the ambulance pulls away. I don't think that you can go through something like that and a minute later, all is well. I mean, their life has been dumped upside down."

LaBute created a similar boy-man situation in his first film, *In the Company of Men* (1997), where a dominant and aggressive male coerced a weaker male to join him in playing a cruel trick on a deaf girl. The weaker man and the girl began to like each other, and then the alpha male pulled out the rug, and the weak guy didn't fight. This time, it's not that simple, and there's ambiguity even in the buried motives of the Jackson character. We get two possible, even plausible, explanations for his behavior, and they contradict each other.

I appreciate the ambiguity, I told him. It works like all of your films to pose moral puzzles for the audience.

"Yeah, I think that's true. I hope so, anyway. I'm never as comfortable the day we're smashing a car as when a man and a woman start screaming at each other. I think I grew up around more people screaming at each other than cars crashing. That might be it. So I understand the battlefield a little better. But I'm just drawn to that world, that complex universe of people trying to get along with each other.

"Take the question that's posed by Rodney King, whose story began on a different Lake View Terrace: 'Can't we all just get along?' I think the answer, as I came to making this movie was, just barely, and only if you work at it every day. I think today it's more acceptable to do whatever you feel like. People dispose of relationships more quickly. That we build a fence next to our neighbor. That we say, 'We should get a divorce.' That we go online to meet people so that it's easier to get rid of them when we're through with them. All we do is just click a button and those people are gone. I think people don't like to work as much to forge a good friendship or good relationship. I think on a lot of levels this film wasn't just about black and white, but it was about blue collar versus white collar, and men versus women, and older versus younger."

Samuel Jackson's character has scary depths, I said.

"He comes with a sense of cool. It's nice to see him play the bad guy. And yet he brings a kind of heartbreaking quality to it. He's imposing, and in most movies, it's all for the good. But to see him turn that with just the flicker of an eye. I've seen a lot of Sam Jackson movies, and there's a moment where the husband finally confronts him and says, 'You need to back off. You need to get out of my life.' And Sam smiles at him, and he has a face that I've never seen Sam do, and it just felt so scary. And the scene where he was in the bar, talking about his own wife, and there was just one take where we just went, 'Let's not even talk about it. Let's walk away. That's a perfect take.'

"He's that kind of actor. He really understands the camera and understands his size and how it works, and he's very comfortable with himself. He breathes a lot of life into that role and yet remains a frightening person. The uniform helps, as well. I think we're just always nervous around policemen. I tend to turn my radio off in the car when I see the police. They carry a lot of weight with them."

Spike Lee

Toronto, Canada, September 23, 2008—When he was a kid in Brooklyn, Spike Lee said, he and his brothers loved war movies: "Three little boys, so it was fun to see the Germans get shot and blown up and stuff like that. But even as a kid, I knew that black people were involved in the war because my father's two older brothers were in World War II."

Later, as an adult, he found out more about America's black GIs.

"I think it takes even more of a patriot to fight when you're still being lynched in the Jim Crow South. These black men weren't enlisted; they signed up. You want to fight for the red, white, and blue, and most of the black troops were trained in the South. You're being trained to kill Nazis. On the same base where you're being trained, you see Nazi POWs who are getting better housing, better food, and better health care. Wow, how'd that make you feel?"

Those are some of the points he makes in his new film *Miracle at St. Anna*, focusing on four GIs behind enemy lines in Italy. It premiered here at the Toronto Film Festival. It's not *just* about those points, of course; in almost all of his films, Lee focuses equally on whites, and this one even has a moral Nazi. But after meeting with several of the surviving black veterans, Spike felt their feelings:

"They still have this bitterness. They still think about how they were treated, and thank God for Eleanor Roosevelt, because if it wasn't for her prodding FDR, black soldiers would never have been allowed to fight in World War II. That was her kicking FDR's ass every night in the White House saying, 'You have to let these Negro soldiers fight!' That was Eleanor Roosevelt."

The film is based on a novel by James McBride.

"He had an uncle," said Lee, "that when he used to get drunk, he'd started talking all these crazy tales about, 'We were treated like kings in Italy.' So when he was looking for an idea for his second book, he thought about this crazy uncle he had who fought in World War II, and that's how he started doing research on the 92nd Division, the Buffalo Soldiers."

Two of the soldiers argue about race and the war.

"For me," Lee said, "Derek Luke's character in the film thinks like Dr. King. Michael Ealy's character is more like Malcolm X. You're always gonna have those two philosophies that clash."

Luke's character says he's fighting for his children and grandchildren. Ealy is much angrier.

Two other performances create the most touching relationship in the film, between a towering GI and a small Italian boy whose life he saves. The GI is played by Omar Benson Miller, who also stars in the forthcoming movie *The Express,* as the best friend of Ernie Davis, the first black Heisman Trophy winner. Lee said he thought of casting a basketball player or a football player, "but then I said, this role's too important to do that. So my great casting director, Kim Coleman, said I should think about Omar.

"I'd seen Omar in *8 Mile.* I hadn't seen the film in a while, but I remembered he was bigger than everybody else in the film. His audition was wonderful. I said, 'You got the role, man, but here's the date, and if you can't lose sixty pounds by this date, we're goin' to Italy without your ass.' And thank God, he wanted the role."

And the boy is played by Matteo Sciabordi, one of a thousand kids who turned up for Lee's Italian auditions. Lee's casting people selected one hundred, and when he saw Matteo on tape, he had a feeling he'd get the role: "I think his performance is just as good as the kid in *Bicycle Thief.*"

The film was shot on location in Italy, showing the soldiers surviving a bloody battle when they are wading across a river and are attacked by both sides. First, by Nazis concealed on the other bank. Then by American artillery after they radio the Nazis' position and the racist officer in charge ignores the coordinates because he can't bring himself to believe that African-Americans could possibly have advanced that far that fast. The battle is based on history.

"It was great to shoot in the actual locations where these events took place," Lee said. "The opening, the battle, the Serchio River, that took place. And it was very spooky to shoot this thing in the village of Sant'Anna di Stazzema. We shot at the actual location where that massacre took place on August 12, 1944. There were 560 innocent Italian men and women, elderly men and women, children, slaughtered by the 16th Division of the SS, and I've never, ever felt, I've never, ever shot a scene like that before where you could feel the spirit and the ghosts of those murdered people there.

"Everybody felt it, and it was hard to do. The hardest shot in the film, we had to bayonet a baby. That was rough. The Italian stuntman who played that Nazi, his name is Georgio, he's Italian, he's one of the lead stuntmen. That whole day, all the Italian extras, they hated him. They were spitting at him and he was like, 'I'm just an actor!'"

Mike Leigh

October 16, 2008—For years he was the consummate outsider in the world of British film. Now he's hailed as one of the United Kingdom's greatest directors. He is still an outsider, but things are looking better.

"I think I've probably progressed," Mike Leigh told me, "from being the outsider's outsider to perhaps, in fact, being the insider's outsider."

This was in September at the Toronto Film Festival, where Leigh's wonderful new film *Happy-Go-Lucky* was playing. It also played in the Chicago Film Festival, where his entire career got its start in 1971, and he was awarded CIFF's Lifetime Achievement Award.

Leigh spent seventeen years between his great first theatrical film, *Bleak Moments,* and his second, *High Hopes* (1988). Since then, he's made eight more films, all of them vibrating with his peculiarly engaging characters and liberated plots. He's probably best known for *Secrets & Lies, Topsy-Turvy,* and *Vera Drake.* During the seventeen-year drought, he worked steadily writing and directing theater and making films for the BBC. But the working method he insists on made it impossible to find financial backing.

Although there is an impression in some circles that Leigh films are improvised, they are actually tightly scripted. It's how they get that way that scares backers. He starts with a notion for a story and some actors he admires. Together, they define characters and "devise" improvised situations for them, and a screenplay emerges. Leigh refuses to show backers a script in advance, will accept no consultation on his choice of actors, and demands final cut.

Still, I can't understand why investors are shy of him: What do they really know about movies? They often end up backing trash and losing money. What other director do you know who has never made a bad film, has been nominated for three Oscars, and whose films have oodles more nominations?

Sally Hawkins deserves a nomination for her virtuoso work in *Happy-Go-Lucky*, where she plays an unflaggingly cheerful schoolteacher of around thirty whose life takes a bizarre turn when she signs up with the wrong driving instructor. The instructor is played by the British comedian Eddie Marsan, in anything but a funny role.

"Initially our improvisations involved having the actual car," Leigh told me, "and going around the streets and actually improvising the situation from the word go, the actors not having met each other in character, and me lying in the backseat with the hilarity of what was going on, and trying to control myself, and then the dreadful London street, which the rear suspension of a Ford Focus is hardly the answer for. We worked very thoroughly to get those complex scenes right. And these guys would leave no stone unturned. It's about the truth of the moment. It's 'moments' again."

So okay, you've sunk your money into the production and Leigh is driving around lying on the backseat. What did he start with?

"What I did," he said, "is collaborate with actors to create characters, and somehow two things came together. One was that, having worked with Sally Hawkins in the last two films and gotten to know her, I felt now was the time to make a film that would put her at the center and to create something extraordinary. The other was, I wanted to make a film that I could call an 'anti-miserableist' film. A celebratory film, because there is a massive amount for us to be gloomy about in 2008. There are people out there who get on with it, not least amongst whom are teachers, who are by definition cherishing, nurturing the future. I knew that Sally and I could create a character who was explosive and energetic and positive."

And they did. It's impossible for you not to smile along with her, unless you hate her, of course.

"It's interesting that there's a reaction," he said, "a minority one, but nevertheless a constituency that reacts to *Happy-Go-Lucky* by very unequivocally saying, 'I can't stand this woman. By the end I wanted to kill her.' It's quite a number of British critics, and there have

been some of those responses here at Toronto. I just don't get it. It comes from a way of looking at movies, which is more about looking in terms of movie language than about looking in terms of people and the world out there. It's insular and cynical."

Every Leigh film takes a detour into an unexpected direction. In this one, the heroine has a conversation with a shabby homeless man who seems to have nothing to do with anything, but turns out to be emotionally invaluable to the scenes that follow.

"She has great empathy, she's open, she listens," Leigh said. "I mean, she's walking about, and she hears this strange chant and comes across this tramp, and she's open, she's nonjudgmental."

I loved that scene, I said. She listens to him, asks him if he's hungry. She isn't afraid; she's worried about him. I think he's aware of that, and it soothes him. It is possible nobody has spoken to him in days or weeks.

"Absolutely," he said. "Again there's a constituency of people who said: 'I just don't understand that scene. It's out of style with the rest of the film. It's a red herring.' I've been encouraged to cut it at certain stages. It beggars belief, but there it is.

"There are important things about this scene. You see her walking about in a kind of park. She's in her own space, in a quiet place. She comes across this guy, asks him how-do-you-do, goes back to her apartment, and never says where she's been. It isn't a kind of a plot thing, you know. It's just that some things are private, some things you kind of just hang on to."

The thing about Mike Leigh is that, using his method, he figures out where the private things are, and goes there.

Michael Mann

June 24, 2009—Michael Mann saw the Biograph Theater at 2433 N. Lincoln for the first time while riding past it on a streetcar when he was eight or nine. His mother, Esther, told him, "That's the old Biograph Theater where they killed Dillinger." She took a bow from the audience at the Chicago premiere of his movie *Public Enemies*, which ends with a corpse on the Biograph sidewalk.

After he graduated from film school in London, Mann moved to Webster Street, a few blocks away from the theater. "I used to go there when it was an art theater," he told me. The theater then and now figured on anyone's tour of historic Chicago sites; the legend of John Dillinger and the Lady in Red is woven into the city's memory.

When Mann rebuilt two blocks of Lincoln Avenue for his film, even laying down the streetcar tracks, "These forensics experts from the Chicago Police Department came to our set and they rolled out this long piece of paper, and it was every foot of the eighty-eight feet he walked from there to here where he got shot. So when Johnny Depp gets shot in our movie and he goes down and his head hits the ground, he's looking at the exact brick wall and that old wooden telephone pole that Dillinger looked at when Dillinger was down. Dillinger lived for about three minutes after he was shot. And what was in Dillinger's eyes was in Johnny Depp's eyes, and it became somewhat magical."

Same thing way north in Manitowoc, Wisconsin, where Mann filmed at the original Little Bohemia Lodge, scene of the bungled attempt by the FBI to capture the Dillinger gang. They got away, but innocent civilians were killed.

"Went to the real Little Bohemia," Mann said. "I was surprised it was still there and unchanged. So the room that Johnny Depp is in is Dillinger's bedroom, and it was that bed, and when he puts his hand on the doorknob, that's the doorknob that John Dillinger used. Even the toilet fixtures are unchanged. Everything was exactly the same. And we used the exact route that Dillinger broke out of. They went across through a red bedroom, and they got out that window over the roof and down and escaped to the north along the bank of the lake, and Baby Face Nelson went up south. If there'd been a better way to do it, I probably would have used it, but there wasn't. The way they suppressed the FBI assault and then escaped out the back and scooted off in the woods was brilliant.

"We even had his clothes, by the way. We had his clothes, his shaving kit, everything he abandoned in Little Bohemia."

For Mann, Public Enemies was a homecoming. His first theatrical feature, made after much work for television, was the powerful Thief (1981), starring James Caan. He filmed it in Chicago. Since then he has established himself as an important director of intelligent action-oriented films, most notably The Last of the Mohicans (1992), Heat (1995, with the first pairing of De Niro and Pacino), The Insider (1999, seven Oscar nominations), the ambitious biopic Ali (2001), and Collateral (2004).

For this film, he drew information from a well-regarded book by Bryan Burrough, Public Enemies: America's Greatest Crime Wave and the Birth of the FBI.

"What mystified me," Mann said, "was that Dillinger had no idea of a future. Not even a concept of future plans. You just go and do what you're gonna do for as long as you can do it, and it may be short and sweet, but one hell of a ride."

Mann was in a room in the Peninsula Hotel, talking now about the man who has occupied his thoughts for four years. He is known for preparing a film meticulously.

"They were there for the intensity of the ride. The grimness he came from was so extreme he never even questioned the bountifulness of the moment. If you're lucky enough to have a job in 1933, you're making five hundred dollars a year. They were kings; they put their hands in their pockets and they had twenty thousand dollars in cash in there. They believed in fate. Expressions like 'There's a bullet with your name on it,' or 'When your time's up, your time's up.' In other words, a kind of Calvinism without God—of predetermination."

Popular fancy made Dillinger a sort of Robin Hood, an antiestablishment outlaw in the Great Depression. The banks were failing. Dillinger was robbing banks? Good for him.

"I don't think he was Robin Hood," Mann said, "unless Robin Hood is defined as 'steal money from the rich to keep it all for yourself.' People cheered at who he was taking the money from. I think he was superb at managing his public image. He was great at it, and it was all very conscious and tactical by design. He knew how to behave. He was really charming. The newspaper accounts of that period, they're shocked at how well-spoken he is, how charismatic, how he cracked jokes. People would say that after being in his presence for two or three minutes you thought he was your best friend. This was all manipulative. There was nothing that wasn't self-serving or designed."

In working on Dillinger's manner, Mann and Johnny Depp benefited from the single news account that discussed his speaking style. It was written by a photographer.

"Martie Sanders, the Chicago actress who played the cashier at the Biograph—she gave me an article written by her husband's grandfather. He was a photographer named Sol Davis who worked for the old *Chicago Times*. He read that Dillinger had been arrested in Tucson and was gonna be flown to Crown Point, Indiana, and he knew they'd obviously land in Chicago because in those days commercial air travel was only four years old. And there were seventeen stops from Tucson, and one of the stops was St. Louis.

"So Sol Davis took the train to St. Louis and he bought a ticket on the airplane, a commercial airplane, so he and his camera could get on the flight from St. Louis to Chicago with Dillinger. And he shot all the famous pictures of Dillinger where you see him handcuffed in his seat on the airplane with a blanket around his shoulders and taking a nap. And he did the only interview with Dillinger in which someone wrote down Dillinger's speech patterns; the only place we really have Dillinger actually speaking and it being recorded is in Sol Davis's article."

Depp also conveys a coldness and steel core beneath the popular exterior.

"I think Dillinger had an invincible spirit. One of the things I marveled at about him, with all the attrition of all the people who were close to him, with the devastation all around him, was that he never gave up. Dillinger was a guy who was just so tough, mentally tough, not just physically tough, but mentally so tough. He was five foot eight; he wasn't a giant, but just so strong-willed and of an indomitable spirit."

He was toughened in the Indiana State Prison, Mann found.

"They had institutionalized forms of torture, of beatings, suffocation of people in straitjackets—it was horrendous, it was a hellhole. And he survived that at the top tier of that kind of population, so this was a tough, tough guy."

He also got his education there.

"These are guys who could plan in exquisite detail very disciplined robberies and getaway routes. There was a whole system invented by a guy named Herbert K. Lam, from who the expression 'on the lam' comes from. He influenced Butch Cassidy and Sundance Kid. He'd been in the Prussian military, and he applied military tactics to the science of robbing banks. He mentored Walter Dietrich, and Walter Dietrich mentored John Dillinger, and that's where John Dillinger got his skills. So the time in prison was a postgraduate course in bank robbery—how you're gonna employ the methodology.

"They'd lay on a score for two weeks before they'd take it down. It was very strict; they had caches of gasoline on three different escape routes. They had a detailed tenths-of-a-mile list on the dashboard, and they would take one route or another, and everybody had their appointed job. One guy was Red, who's driving the getaway car, and all he cares about is driving that getaway car. The lobby man, Pete Pierpont, he's controlling the lobby, and he's not gonna worry about anything coming at him from outside because the outside man, Homer Van Meter, he will take care of everything on the outside. The vault man doesn't worry about the lobby or the outside and the tellers because he's just looking at the vault because Charles Mackley is taking all the cash from the tellers. So it was a disciplined, small unit, and they were in and out as fast as possible."

That's where the mystifying part came in.

"With all this planning," Mann said, "it never occurred to these guys to steal $250,000 and then go to Brazil. There was no idea of the future; just this intense, white-hot burning drive. And in Dillinger's case, he lived his whole life in thirteen months, that's it. He hits a bank, gets shot up, gets wounded, gets patched up, and all that occurs in ten days. They go to Sioux Falls—no, Mason City, Iowa, then they're suddenly in Wisconsin, then they decide to go to Florida. And everything is happening in days and weeks, and it's all this insane ride. It's only when Billie Frechette (Marion Cotillard) enters his life that, for obvious reasons, he starts to have even the idea that there's something beyond the immediate right now."

Dillinger shares the spotlight in *Public Enemies* with the legendary FBI agent Melvin Purvis, who became famous for Dillinger's killing, although the case may eventually have driven him to taking his own life in 1960.

"Melvin Purvis left the FBI," Mann said.

"Hoover hounded him. It was like a personal form of blacklisting. He wrote letters to whatever job Purvis had. Hoover expected to get the benefit of killing Public Enemy Number One. Purvis got the credit. Dick Tracy is kind of modeled on Melvin Purvis. So Hoover sidelined him, kicked him out of the FBI, and then hounded him.

"The FBI was totally cooperative with us about this. They had no sensitivity about Hoover at all—zero. In Washington they said, 'Is there anything else you'd like?' And I said, Yeah, pull out the Melvin Purvis file. They went to get the file. There's one sheet of paper in it. One sheet of paper. His employment application. That was it. They were stunned. It was like Stalin erasing all these pictures of the politburo with Trotsky. Same thing. Hoover erased Melvin Purvis."

Philippe Petit

August 5, 2008—*Man on Wire,* one of the most talked-about documentaries of the year, tells the story of how a young Frenchman named Philippe Petit illegally walked on a tightwire between the two towers of the World Trade Center on August 7, 1974. It won the audience award and the best documentary prize at Sundance 2008, and is a superb film that works like a thriller.

But what kind of man would be brave enough, or foolish enough, or confident enough, to attempt such a feat? As someone who is himself afraid of heights, I wanted to ask Philippe Petit, and I did. My questions are pretty obvious. His replies are remarkable for their thoughtfulness and poetry of expression.

RE: You would have achieved your objective by crossing once between the two towers. Why did you do it eight times?

PP: My objective was not to cross once between the two towers. My objective was to venture through the negative space offered by the two towers and discover what kind of ephemeral, improvised theater I could write in the sky. My audience? Taken by surprise. My performance? A dot in the sky.

Why did I cross eight times? I did not plan to cross eight times. I was called by the towers, by the void, by my instinct to perform one more crossing . . . and one more . . . and one more. My friends, watching from the street, told me

later: "You stayed on that wire for forty-five minutes. You did eight crossings." I didn't have a pedometer. I didn't carry a watch. Actors who rely on those impediments should be thrown off the stage!

RE: Have you ever been blown off a wire by high winds or been injured in a fall? How or when?

PP: If I had, I wouldn't be here to answer the question! As a high-wire walker, I do not allow myself to "leave the wire" during a performance. However, during the months of apprenticeship (I was a self-taught wire walker at seventeen) and during the years of practicing, I have had numerous "defeats" on the wire, and that's good. That's how one learns.

On a very long and very high wire, I will not hope to not be blown off by high winds. I will have the certitude that such could not happen. By practicing for months before the event on a low wire oriented along the axis of the predominant winds, I put Aeolus on my side. I am not up there by chance. I am there by choice. And I know the wire. And I know my limits. And I am a madman of details. And to use one of your words, I cannot "fall."

RE: The film does a remarkable job of seamlessly merging actual and re-created footage. What was your contribution to this undertaking?

PP: Thank you for your opinion. My contribution was to try to have the re-created footage reflect the truth of my story. I failed!

RE: The film speaks of the intense concentration in your face during a crossing. Is this a Zen-like state of concentration? What are you thinking about?

PP: It's always easy to describe something complex by applying to it an already known label. So, the "Zen-like state of concentration" is what people are inclined to say about my state of focus. But I would rather struggle for my description, to be honest.

What I am thinking about is, I am not thinking. I am tremendously focused. I have reduced the universe to the state of nonexistence. Only me and the wire. Except, my concentration carries no horse blinders. I have to feel, see, taste, hear, touch, and smell everything to the utmost, so I can catch any sign of threat before any threat appears.

RE: Is there a challenge still before you?

PP: I use the word "challenge" only when referring to intellectual challenge, to artistic creation. Physical challenges do not interest me if they are not mingled with individual expression. What interests me is to inspire the onlooker. So yes, there are a thousand intellectual challenges still before me. I continue to street juggle, I continue to wire walk, to write books, to lecture around the world. As you can see, I don't like to give one-liners as answers in interviews!

RE: Would you describe your emotions on the day the towers fell?

PP: I prefer not to. It's too personal.

Steven Soderbergh

May 22, 2009—In the late months of 2008, while the economic storm was gathering, Steven Soderbergh made a film about buying and selling. *The Girlfriend Experience* follows a high-priced escort named Chelsea as she interacts with clients, many of them regulars, all of them wealthy. It stars Sasha Grey, twenty-one, who in real life has made more than 150 porn films. This is her second film role that doesn't involve explicit hard-core sex.

The title refers to the abbreviation "GFE," shorthand in sex ads for escorts who offer something more than simple sex. They talk, they confide, they provide companionship—they actually kiss, which is where most prostitutes draw the line. Sometimes no sex is involved, although it's permitted.

This is a film for the times we live in. The call girl and her clients are engaged in the same occupation: selling something they don't want in order to buy things they do. The difference is that the prostitute is selling a tangible service, while the financial traders are dealing in abstractions. They all want to talk with Chelsea about her business. They offer financial advice as a way of feeling more important to her. They all think they have a special relationship. They arguably find the hours they spend with her more absorbing and valued than the many hours they spend at work.

It was a coincidence that the economic crisis played such a big part in his story, Soderbergh told me via e-mail: "The outline was written in the spring of 2006, before anyone was talking seriously about a crisis (and also before the

Eliot Spitzer story broke)." The shooting took sixteen days in October 2008, "when everyone was worried about money."

He said he used actors playing characters like themselves: "Meaning the financial guys were financial guys, the Web guy was a Web guy, and so on. I'd give them a basic goal for the scene like, 'Don't let him sell you a package of workout sessions,' and turn them loose. I'd say 95 percent of the film is made up of first or second takes. They were controlled improvisations where the actors were encouraged to speak freely about themselves and as themselves. Therefore, naturally, the meltdown turned out to be a constant topic of conversation. This is probably because most of the johns who see women like Chelsea are from the finance world. This was discovered through our interviews with real escorts."

I think Sasha Grey plays the role about as well as it can be played. It's always a balancing act, offering an illusion of intimacy while maintaining Chelsea's privacy. She may be a porn star, but so what? She owns the character, and it's hard to imagine anyone else playing it. That's what every director is looking for. But why a porn star in the first place?

"You're right, the role wouldn't seem to require an adult film star, but at the beginning I didn't know how explicit the movie would be. Also, I wanted someone who would appear, in a sexual situation, to be completely in control and comfortable. I love the way she watches the jeweler disrobe in the last scene—she's totally calm and free of anxiety, almost Zen-like. I didn't audition anyone else.

"In discussing the role, I tried to keep our conversations very practical; I don't want the performers thinking too much."

The film doesn't involve a conventional three-act story arc. It stays resolutely in Chelsea's present tense. Her life is a continuum, although sometimes something happens to break the pattern, as when her live-in boyfriend gets too curious about a client.

Although Soderbergh has made films closely tied to plots (the three *Ocean's* pictures, *Erin Brockovich*), he said he's getting "a bit tired of traditional setups and payoffs when it comes to storytelling in movies. That doesn't mean I think we should dispense with narrative, but I'm more interested in how something feels than how it's constructed. I think you learn more from what people *do* than from what they say, or feel, or say they feel. In this case, that meant staying focused on what Chelsea *does* day-to-day. It's easy to be brave about that when your budget is $1.6 million."

With *The Girlfriend Experience,* he said, he deliberately avoided any kind of a background for Chelsea. "She hints in the restaurant with her girlfriend that she left home because she didn't want to be dependent on her parents for money. Beyond that, I didn't really have a desire to go into her backstory because I knew people would be looking for 'reasons' why she became a call girl, and I didn't want her judged like that.

"Sasha Grey is very ambitious and wants to make her own films, so I would think she saw this as a learning experience. Although what she learned—you'd have to ask her."

What do you hope she learned?

"You can get what you want without ever raising your voice."

Oliver Stone

October 16, 2008—Oliver Stone says he believes First Lady Laura Bush, Secretary of State Condoleezza Rice, and presidential adviser Karen Hughes play like "a trinity of Macbeth witches" in the life of George W. Bush, "in the sense that they are totally enablers." But Stone's new film *W.* leaves that conclusion to the viewer. "The film foregrounds Bush, and everyone else is shown more or less as we already see them," he told me in an e-mail exchange.

"Rice has no record that we were able to find where she contradicts either Rumsfeld or Cheney, or even does much really to help Powell. She doesn't seem to do much to bring alternative points of view to Bush's attention. But an enabler? Yes. If she had threatened him, perhaps she wouldn't have had the job."

And Laura Bush would not have had her job, either, Stone believes, "had she been more critical of him."

The Oscar-winning director of *Platoon, JFK,* and *Nixon* devoted a great deal of time to researching the development of the president's character and working with his screenwriter, Stanley Weiser. In the end, he said, "This is centrally the story of a man, more than a formal, broad history."

Stone believes the president's life falls into three acts, which his film focuses on, while not following such subjects as his elections or 9/11: "Act One is his youth, intermingled with Act Three, his presidency, and that interconnects with Act Two, his successful middle years. I think overall the most fascinating thing about this incredible president is that he lives up to the American concept of the second chance, and that the second act of his life seems to redeem the first act. The twist on it, to me, is the third act, which becomes a sinister coda to the inauthenticity of his existence."

Stone was so stung by criticism of his alternative assassination explanation in *JFK* that he edited a massive book attempting to document it. Telling Bush's story, he stays fairly close to the generally perceived facts, while adding psychological undercurrents such as Bush's "muscular response to his father as a weak man, and his muscular response to any kind of threat."

And Laura Bush? "I think the more obvious cliché would be that she was the nagging wife about the drinking, but she doesn't seem to have been. There is no real evidence of that except Bush saying at one point that it was either him or the Jack Daniel's that would have to go. Therefore, we went with the idea that she would forgive him, and that would enable him even more. She would be totally psychologically the supportive wife. Detached? Absolutely. Wouldn't you be if you had to always play a role like that in your husband's life?

"In the end," he said, "she is almost the ultimate perfect first lady. I don't think there's been someone like her around since Bess Truman. She seems to make no mistakes, which is eerie."

Bush's lack of attention to detail, he says, is underlined in a scene where he is briefed by Vice President Dick Cheney. Looking at a document, he says, "Only three pages! Good."

I asked Stone: "Born into a patrician family, educated at Andover and Yale, Bush frequently makes elementary grammatical errors, such as using 'is' before a plural. How do you account for this?"

"Perhaps a reading disability, or ADD," he said. "I'm not sure. No one can be in this case, unless he undergoes some kind of medical psychiatric examination, but he seems to be quite disdainful of 'psychobabble.' Certainly, his impatience clearly stretches into the way he talks and acts."

In Act One, beginning with his youth at Yale and continuing during his early days in Texas, Bush is shown as a practicing alcoholic. Fraternity brothers pour Jack Daniel's down his throat through a funnel. In scenes after he is "born again," the film seems to show him continuing to drink beer, but Stone explains: "He's drinking a known nonalcoholic beer. One of the brands we use is O'Doul's."

Did he find anything to back up Bush's alleged cocaine use?

"I certainly believe that he used it from what accounts I've read, but no one inside that group seems to be willing to talk. Kitty Kelley chased it and so did Hatfield in *Fortunate Son*. We couldn't prove it, and so why go there? We already expect minor details to be attacked by the members of the administration in some way in the next few days. By his own admission, Bush established himself as a reckless young person, and that is the image we sought to create without undue malice."

Bush's first secretary of state, Colin Powell, is seen as expressing many doubts, but no outspoken dissent.

"Jeffrey Wright [who plays Powell] studied it at length, and we discussed it many times. Jeffrey is of the opinion, and I agree, that in the end he was 'the good soldier,' which is to say, you follow your commander and fall on your sword if need be. Ultimately, he was not, as a black man, able to resist the white man's final authority. (Incidentally, he did show up in the My Lai investigation as one of the officers who derailed the investigation in 1969.)"

Where would you place Bush on the list of forty-three presidents?

"I really can't say, because I didn't live through them all. But definitely his are the worst eight years of leadership and responsibility that I have seen in my sixty-two years. And that means he surpasses Harry Truman and Richard Nixon."

James Toback

May 5, 2009—Mike Tyson is philosophical. Thoughtful. Self-critical. Vulnerable. There are times when you feel sympathy for the Baddest Man on the Planet. There are times when you . . . like him.

These are things James Toback reveals in his documentary *Tyson*, which presents the heavyweight champion in a new light. This is the man who knocked out his opponents in his first nineteen pro fights, twelve of them in the first round.

"I think he has never escaped from the sense that he is a short, fat, pushed-around kid and that everyone is aware of it and ready to bully him again," Toback told me. "'Fear' is the word that comes up most of all. He keeps saying, 'I was afraid, I was so afraid, I was afraid of this, I was afraid of that.' I've never heard anyone talk about fear so much as a defining reality of his consciousness.

"He dealt with fear by first admitting it, and then deciding he was gonna fortify himself against anyone who's gonna exploit it by becoming homicidally enraged. Managing his rage so he can literally destroy the person who's trying to exploit his fear seems to be the whole center of his life and personality."

Toback and Tyson were born to meet each other and make this extraordinary film. Tyson you know about, or think you do. Toback is a wild child of modern American movies, willing to confess the most alarming details about himself. Both men have records of rampaging promiscuity. Tyson is proud he has recently been faithful to one woman for four months; Toback once inspired a four-page *Spy* magazine fold-out chart chronicling his approaches, pitches, and histories with women during a single year—and those were only the women the magazine found out about. He was married once, to Consuelo Sarah Churchill Vanderbilt Russell, daughter of Lady Sarah Churchill, about whom he has not said one word to me.

Toback and Tyson have been engaged in a dialogue for more than twenty years over the Meaning of It All.

"The turning point in our relationship came on the first night we met," Toback said. "We walked through Central Park and we talked about many things, including my LSD flip-out and what madness was, which he couldn't quite understand, not having experienced it."

But after his prison sentence for rape, Tyson told Toback, "When I was in solitary confinement about nineteen months into my incarceration, I was sitting alone in the corner of my cell and all of a sudden I said to myself, 'This is what

Toback was talking about that night when he was describing madness; I am now insane.'

"He had snapped," Toback said, "and the fascinating thing to me was that the first thing he thought about when the madness clicked in was our conversation twelve years ago. I think he sort of goes back and forth with it. I mean, unlike me, he didn't get an intravenous antidote from the guy who synthesized LSD in Switzerland in 1938 at Sanders Laboratory. And without that, I would have been dead."

That's James Toback for you. He tells you about Tyson going mad in solitary and tops it with a story about himself.

I first met him in 1974, when he was thirty and had written the screenplay for the great James Caan film *The Gambler*. He was already famous within a small world. He came from blue blood; his mother, Selma Judith Toback, president of the League of Women Voters, moderated debates on NBC. His father, Irwin, was a vice president of Dreyfus. James had graduated summa cum laude from Harvard, then headed down as fast as he could because of a gambling addiction, to which he added women, drugs, alcohol, food, and a restless creativity.

He was nominated for his screenplay for *Bugsy*. His debut as a director was with Harvey Keitel's brilliant performance in *Fingers* (1978). He made the (toned-down) autobiographical film *The Pick-Up Artist* (1987) and six other features; the most recent, *When Will I Be Loved* (2004), with Neve Campbell, received four stars from me. In that film, and in *Black and White* (1999), Tyson played small supporting roles. But the Toback film that suggests *Tyson* is his documentary *The Big Bang* (1989), in which he asks people to explain their ideas of life, death, and the universe.

That's also really what he's asking Iron Mike.

"Tyson's mind is endlessly analytical and confessional," he said. "His primary subject of philosophical analysis is himself and his perceptions of the world, but he doesn't take any of them at face value; he's always scrutinizing them. He does it with other people, too. He starts with the concrete and goes to the general.

"For instance, he was fascinated when Joe Frazier did a mike check and instead of counting down five, four, three, two, one, he said, 'Smoking Joe Frazier will shock and amaze you, he'll defeat Ali, he'll beat Ali, he's greater than Ali ever was.' And Mike said: 'Can you believe how pathetic that after all this time, his only identity is his relationship with Ali? That's what gives him a place on Earth. And the reason is, that Ali took away his social standing. Joe Frazier had a place in the world and Muhammad Ali altered it completely, and Frazier's never been able to accept that. He doesn't understand how Ali made his identity permanently something else, and he can't adjust to it, he can't forgive him, he can't forget it. It's still eating away at him.'"

Toback's approach was not the usual Q&A interview. He sat off-camera behind Tyson and let him talk:

"I didn't really question him. I raised subjects. I thought that this voice behind him triggering thoughts, stimulating the unconscious, would be better than specific questions that would tend to limit his scope of answering. I started the first day by asking him to talk about his earliest memories. That was it. For forty minutes we just let two cameras run even though there were long gaps of silence, which I didn't mind at all because of his expressive face.

"One of the things that enabled him to open up was that he knew he was talking to someone who would understand everything he was saying and not take it in the wrong way or exploit it. Although he was shocked at some of the things he said. When he first saw it, he said: 'It's like a Greek tragedy. The only problem is, I'm the subject.' He was watching himself almost as if not remembering he said those things because he was in a quasi-psychoanalysis. I was standing behind him and I was just a kind of voice, and he was sitting there on the couch allowing all of his repressed voices to come out."

As he was editing the film, Toback said, he began to suspect it might appeal to women.

"So I picked women who said they didn't like boxing or Mike Tyson. I'd say: 'Come to the editing room and if after five minutes you want to leave, I'll give you $100. But if you stay, I won't give you anything and you have to tell me what you thought about the movie when it's over.'

"Every single woman, thirty-five out of thirty-five, stayed, and in every case were moved to tears, were fascinated by how it held them. I realized something special was going on. I told Mike, and he said, 'Who are these women? Save their numbers for me.'"

Wayne Wang

October 8, 2008—Wayne Wang has made eighteen films since *Chan Is Missing* in 1982. I have seen fourteen of them and admired all but one. He's had big box-office successes like *The Joy Luck Club, Maid in Manhattan,* and *Last Holiday,* and hasn't made a film primarily about Chinese characters since *Chinese Box* (1997). Now he arrives with two midlength films about changes that set Chinese-Americans apart from their roots.

His sadly observant *A Thousand Years of Good Prayers* stars Feihong Yu of *Joy Luck* as a thoroughly Americanized Chinese-American, and the veteran actor Henry O as her seventy-ish father, who comes to visit her. They find a cultural divide between them that seems impossible to bridge.

It's the kind of quiet, thoughtful movie that involves an audience by drawing it in, not slamming it with action. The kind of film it's growing harder to find. "I'm sorry that over the last ten years, the kinds of films that the audience likes to watch have changed," Wang told me, "but I will continue to make these films about Chinese-Americans, and in my own way."

Here's the exchange we conducted via the Internet:

RE: *A Thousand Years of Good Prayers* seems so intimate and insightful that even though it is based on writings by Yiyun Li, I assume the film is also inspired by your personal thoughts and observations. True?

WW: I identified quite a bit with Yilan, the daughter. I came to the U.S., and like her, learned a new language and a new culture, and became a different person. So much so that the conflicts between my father and me grew deeper. When he finally came over to visit me for the first time since I came to the U.S., our dinners together became quite unbearable. I felt I had little in common with my father and that most of my Americanized opinions about life/love/politics were at odds with his. Like in the film, our dinners grew to become silent and filled with unspoken tension, and I always made an excuse to get out of the house immediately afterward and went to see a movie.

RE: Many contemporary films would view the story from the POV of the daughter, even making the father an object of (affectionate, I hope) humor. You stay with him almost every second. You are not sorry for him; you are focused on his implied evaluation of an unfamiliar society.

WW: These days no one will make a film focusing on an older man as the leading character. So I made a conscious decision to focus on Mr. Shi, every frame of the film. It was not easy to convince an investor about that, especially since the character speaks mostly Chinese and had to be subtitled. But Henry O inspired me to be more insistent about this because he brought such a wise yet innocent quality to everyone he encountered, a bit like what the Dalai Lama projects in his personality.

RE: It strikes me that many of the younger Chinese we glimpsed during the Olympics, while certainly not representative of the whole population, would have felt more at home in the U.S. than Mr. Shi did.

WW: The younger Chinese generation who live in the cities of China grew up watching American TV and reading Western magazines. And most of them speak pretty good English. Actually, most of Asia is a bit like that. In fact, my other new film, *The Princess of Nebraska,* is very much about this younger generation and how Westernized they are. But the older generation, especially if they come from outside the cities, are more traditional, non-English-speaking, and very much like Mr. Shi.

RE: Are the "developed" segments of all nations being shaped by the same consumerist model?

WW: Yes, very much so. I'd say more consumerist than the rest of the world. In China, because they had so little for so long, they now want everything. Big labels such as Louis Vuitton, etc., make a good part of their profits from the Chinese market.

RE: I was touched by Mr. Shi's relationship with the Iranian woman on the park bench. From such different cultures, they instinctively share the loss of traditions that would have more valued them.

WW: I love that part, too. The funny thing about those scenes is that Henry O is an obsessive actor who plotted out his bad English very precisely. Then Vida (the Iranian actress) came to the set and improvised everything and threw Henry O completely off balance.

Luckily, Henry O always recovered enough to make the scene work. The end result turned out better because there was an organic, unrehearsed energy about them. On a personal level, both of them have gone through deep losses and tragedies, during the Cultural Revolution and the Eight Years War between Iran and Iraq, respectively, that their shared loss came through their humor!

RE: Mr. Shi is deeply concerned about his daughter's romantic situation. If she were still in China, I imagine she would feel his concerns more urgently. Has she lost that part of her emotional equipment or suppressed it?

WW: Recently I invited some women from China the same age as Yilan to one of my private screenings. Afterward they told me how much they identified with Yilan's character. They told me that during the Cultural Revolution, there were so many lies and betrayals among neighbors, coworkers, and within the community that the relationships within families were always based on half truths, denials, and suspicions. These women felt very sympathetic to the daughter and understood her distance toward her father. They felt that she never could communicate with him and never knew what he said was true or not. She grew up isolated from her father, and when she moved here she became freer to become independent from that patriarchal control.

RE: An eighty-three-minute film is on the edge of distribution difficulties. My mantra is, "No good film is too long; no bad film is short enough." I should modify that with, "All good films are the right length." Does the length present distribution challenges to you?

WW: So far it hasn't. These days theaters and distributors don't mind a shorter film as they can have more screenings per day and make more money.

RE: This and your *Princess of Nebraska*, which I haven't seen, are your first films in ten years to concern Chinese characters. Not for one second is that intended as criticism; you must and should make the films you feel moved to make. It is simply an observation.

WW: You should see *Princess of Nebraska*. It is a diptych to *Thousand Years*. It focuses on the younger generation in China who grew up with little knowledge of the Cultural Revolution and

the Tiananmen Square massacres. They hardly have any knowledge of their own past and don't really know themselves other than their urge to make money and consume. Whereas Yilan from *Thousand Years* is trying to forget her past and move on to a new life. The irony is that she ends up repeating the history of her father . . . falling into an illicit affair with a married person.

RE: Was it a challenge to juxtapose the different personal styles of the characters Mr. Shi and Yilan?

WW: Not so much their personal styles, but rather working with them to do *less*. They both come from a tradition of melodramatic Chinese acting: Henry O on stage and Faye (Feihong Yu) in soap operas. They both felt that they weren't doing enough unless they were acting more dramatically. I told them to understand their character's motivation and simply *be* them!

RE: I heard you felt some kind of epiphany when you discovered Henry O.

WW: I was having a tough time casting his character. Then I met Henry O and heard him talk about all the persecutions he went through during the Cultural Revolution. I also learned about his personal and emotional dealings with his daughter, who is forty and unmarried. I knew immediately I had found my man. Then he told me that he's one of the few who dared to threaten Tony Soprano and lived to tell about it! He played the Buddhist priest who sued Tony!

Just one more note: In my first film, *Chan Is Missing* (1982), I quoted a Chinese saying: "What is unsaid or what is not seen can be just as important as what is said or what is seen." In *A Thousand Years of Good Prayers* I was interested in telling a story about how the Cultural Revolution affected a father-daughter relationship. In the film, we never see the Cultural Revolution or talk about it, and the father says, "It's enough just to survive all that." Yet we see how it has affected their relationship so powerfully after all these years.

Note: Wayne Wang has the movies in his heritage. His father named him after John Wayne.

Essays

Lost Scenes from *Metropolis* Found!

August 5, 2008—It is the most sensational find in recent film history. A nearly complete print of Fritz Lang's *Metropolis* (1927) has been discovered in Buenos Aires, eighty years after it was thought a quarter of the film was lost forever. Called by many the most important of German films, one of the landmarks of silent Expressionism, its plot had several loose ends that will now be repaired.

The find was made by Paula Felix-Didier, director of the cinema museum in Buenos Aires. Her story is told in an article in Germany's *Zeit* magazine, which traces the print from its arrival in Argentina in 1928. It found itself in the collection of a local film critic, who sold it to the National Art Fund in the 1960s, the magazine says. It arrived in the Museo del Cine in 1992.

Felix-Didier's ex-husband, director of the film department of the Museum of Latin American Art, "had heard from the manager of a cinema club, who years before had been surprised by how long a screening of this film had taken. Together, [they] took a look at the film in her archive—and discovered the missing scenes." Their print has been examined by experts in Berlin, where the film had its 1927 premiere. They agree it is authentic. After a restoration, the Murnau Foundation, owner of the rights, will release it to festivals, theaters, and DVD.

Lang (1890–1976) was a prominent director in Germany who had the power to finance *Metropolis,* one of the two or three most expensive silent films ever made. With a huge cast of extras and astonishing sets, he told the story of an underground city of workers and a city on the surface for those who benefited by their work. The film was followed by *M* (1931), starring Peter Lorre as a child murderer.

Leaving Germany at the rise of Hitler, Lang moved to MGM in Hollywood, where Expressionism was having an influence on the developing genre of film noir. His American movies included *The Big Heat, Scarlet Street, Ministry*

of Fear, and *You Only Live Once.* A scene in *M* of ranks of criminals arrayed above their boss at a dark subterranean meeting, their faces emerging from darkness, is visually quoted in the great *Dark City* (1998), a film much influenced by Lang.

M and *Metropolis* are in the top one hundred of IMDb.com's list of the greatest films of all time. Both of those films and *The Big Heat* (with its famous scene of Lee Marvin throwing a pot of coffee in Gloria Grahame's face) are in my Great Movies Collection at rogerebert.com. I am looking forward to rewriting the *Metropolis* review.

The *American Idol* Candidate

September 10, 2008—I think I might be able to explain some of Sarah Palin's appeal. She's the *American Idol* candidate. Consider. What defines an *American Idol* finalist? They're good-looking, work well on television, have a sunny personality, are fierce competitors, and so talented, why, they're darned near the real thing. There's a reason *American Idol* gets such high ratings. People identify with the contestants. They think, "Hey, that could be me up there on that show!"

My problem is, I don't *want* to be up there. I don't want a vice president who is darned near good enough. I want a vice president who is better, wiser, well traveled, has met world leaders, who three months ago had an opinion on Iraq. Someone who doesn't repeat bald-faced lies about earmarks and the "bridge to nowhere." Someone who doesn't appoint Alaskan politicians to "study" global warming, because—hello!—it *has* been studied. The findings are convincing enough that John McCain and Barack Obama are darned near in agreement.

I would also want someone who didn't make a teeny little sneer when referring to "people who go to the Ivy League." When I was a teen I dreamed of going to Harvard, but my dad, an electrician, told me, "Boy, we don't have the money. Thank your lucky stars you were born in Urbana and can go to the University of Illinois right here in town." So I did, very happily. Although Palin gets laughs when she mentions the "elite" Ivy League, she sure did attend the heck out of college. Five different schools in six years. What was that about?

And how can a politician her age never have gone to Europe? My dad had died, my mom was working as a bookkeeper, and I had a job at the local newspaper when, at nineteen, I scraped together $240 for a charter flight to Europe. I had Arthur Frommer's *$5 a Day* book under my arm, started in London, even rented a Vespa and drove in the traffic of Rome. A few years later, I was able to send my mom, along with the *$15 a Day* book.

You don't need to be a pointy-headed elitist to travel abroad. You need curiosity and a hunger to see the world. What kind of a person (who has the money) arrives at the age of forty-four and has only been out of the country once, on an official tour to Iraq? Sarah Palin's travel record is that of a hopeless provincial.

But some people like that. She's never traveled to Europe, Asia, Africa, South America, or Down Under? That makes her like them. She didn't go to Harvard? Good for her! There are a lot of hockey moms who haven't seen London, but most of them would probably love to, if they had the dough. And they'd be proud if one of their kids won a scholarship to Harvard.

I trust the American people will see through Palin, and save the Republic in November. The most damning indictment against her is that she considered herself a good choice to be a heartbeat away. That shows bad judgment.

An Epistle to St. Paul

You wild, beautiful thing. You crazy handful of nothin'.
　　　—Dragline, speaking of Cool Hand Luke

September 29, 2008—After she read my obituary of Paul Newman, my wife, Chaz, asked me, "Why didn't you write more about his acting?" She was right. Why didn't I? I've been asking myself that. Maybe I was trying to tell myself something. I think it was this: I never really thought of him as an actor. I regarded him more as an embodiment, an evocation of

something. And I think that something was himself. He seemed above all a deeply good man, who freed himself to live life fully and joyfully and used his success as a way to follow his own path and to help others.

If Newman was that kind of person, so, too, was his wife of more than fifty years, Joanne Woodward. Too little attention was paid to her in the appreciations. They grew old and fine together. None of us can ever know the truth of another life. But to the degree that we can guess it, I believe that Joanne and Paul shone upon each other, agreed on the fundamentals, expressed the same fusion with acting, did good, were happy in a way that brings contentment.

How did he embody and evoke? I learn that several Jesuits use *Cool Hand Luke* in classes about film and theology. In this reading, Luke is Jesus, of course, and Dragline is Peter, who sits down with new prisoners after Luke's death and begins, "Let me tell you about Luke." You can work out his mother, Mary, and Judas Iscariot for yourself. Someone should count the inner circle of prisoners who always seem to gather around him. Although Luke could choose to end his suffering by bowing to the cruel prison wardens, he continues to absorb it without complaining, perhaps using nonviolent resistance as an example to the others. Consider the conversion of Dragline. In my recent rereview of the film, I ask what other actor could have so successfully played Luke.

In the obituary, I wrote that I had interviewed him many times. Not true. It only seemed that way. I met him three times, once as he campaigned for Eugene McCarthy in the 1968 Wisconsin primary, once for a few days in 1969 on the set of *Butch Cassidy and the Sundance Kid*, the third time in New York to discuss *Nobody's Fool* (1995). Maybe his films expanded in my mind to make it seem that I knew him better. I could see no division between the man and the actor.

That's not to say he always played himself. He was expert at crafting roles. It's more to say that there was no filter, veneer, or visible style to his acting. You saw him as if through a glass, clearly. He was not "naturalistic," but natural. He was at ease within himself. He didn't seem to "create" characters but more to embrace them, love them, speak for them. I am aware I

549

sound almost foolish here. But that's the way I see it.

It was the summer of 1969 when I visited the set of *Butch Cassidy* on the back lot at 20th Century-Fox. I had been a movie critic for two years. I was working on my first assignment from *Esquire* magazine, which was still celebrating the New Journalism. I was heavy with responsibility to live up to the magazine's requirements and nervous about applying them to Newman. The Wisconsin piece had been straight journalism. This had to be more. He was a movie star. My definition of a movie star was, and is, someone you regard as a magnificent adult when you are not yet one yourself. "Stars" of your own age and younger never have the same psychic force. In 1969, there were very few stars as "major" as Paul Newman.

I walked into his trailer. He did not regard me as an intruder, a possible source of irritation, someone who was invading his private time. He casually welcomed me to the flow. He looked at me openly and accepted that we were talking with each other, and that such a thing was natural. There was no "getting to know you" process with Newman. He acted as if he already knew you. I am not naive. I don't believe I have ever truly known an actor—or a director either, with a few exceptions. When you approach them as a journalist, they are there and you are here. But sometimes they can act as if the line isn't there. Lee Marvin was that way, too. Martin Scorsese. Meryl Streep. Robert Altman. Werner Herzog. Tilda Swinton. Paul Schrader. Joan Allen. Gregory Nava. Mike Leigh. And others, but my list is limited.

Never mind what happened in 1969. I'll dig up the old magazine and put it on the Web site. Let's move forward to 1995, and listen very carefully. When I walked into his room, he said, "Aw . . . it's you again." The point is *not* that he remembered me. The point is how he said, "Aw . . ." It evoked feelings hard to express in words. The "Aw" wasn't "Oh, no," as it sometimes can be. To me it translated as, "Aw, it's that scared kid, grown up." Whatever it meant, it put me right at home.

We linger on such moments because movie stars are important to us. They represent an ideal form we are deluded to think exists inside of us. Paul Newman seemed to represent the best of what we could hope for. He was handsome, yes. He had those blue eyes, yes. Helpful in making him a star, but inconsequential to his ultimate achievement.

What he expressed above all was grace and comfort within his own skin. If he had demons, he had faced them and dealt with them. Is this my fantasy? Of course. That's what movie stars represent, our fantasies. His wife, children, and grandchildren knew him, and which of us would not hope to receive such a loving tribute after we're gone? ("Our father was a rare symbol of selfless humility, the last to acknowledge what he was doing was special. Intensely private, he quietly succeeded beyond measure in impacting the lives of so many with his generosity.")

Humility. Yes. I rode around with him for a day during that Wisconsin primary. No movie star attitude. He plunged right into crowds. Played a game at a pool hall. I remember him starting every speech the same way: "I'm Paul Newman, and first off I want to apologize for making *The Silver Chalice*."

I've read over this piece, I realize it's growing too long, and I *still* haven't discussed Paul Newman's acting. Or maybe I have.

The New Kids on the Block

November 28, 2008—Sometimes I realize something and it astonishes and delights me. I was admiring the key performance of a young Aboriginal boy named Brandon Walters in the new film *Australia,* and I got to thinking about how child actors can sometimes embody a directness and clarity that is beyond the reach of even the best adult actors because it never seems premeditated. It seems as if it's being filmed as it happens.

I know that isn't the case. I know they get coaching and direction, and I don't believe they make their impressions without hard work. But maybe they free up under the camera, or maybe a character for them has the same mesmerizing reality as the cowboys we played walking home from the Saturday matinee.

I came home and kept on thinking about Brandon Walters, and I looked over the titles of the 190 or so films I've reviewed so far in 2008. Then I started making a list. There have been twenty-one films with the lead or a very important character played by an actor between the ages of about four and sixteen. I may have missed one or two. Every one of those performances was exceptional. Every one came effortlessly to memory. Every one in one way or another made the film possible.

The best young performances of the year were in Ramin Bahrani's *Chop Shop*, by a twelve-year-old boy named Alejandro Polanco and a sixteen-year-old girl named Isamar Gonzales. They share a tiny room above a shabby shop in a Queens auto-repair ghetto in the shadow of Shea Stadium. This is great filmmaking and great acting on the run as the two improvise a living where none is to be found.

The work of twelve-year-old Dillon Freasier as the son of Daniel Day-Lewis was crucial to Paul Thomas Anderson's *There Will Be Blood*. The character is cruelly lied to and crudely behaved toward, and somehow finds the reserves to carry on. A lesser actor might not have been able to stand up to Day-Lewis's power.

Fans are lined up around the block for *Twilight*, all unaware of a far superior Danish film about even younger vampires, Tomas Alfredson's *Let the Right One In*. It's already number 115 on IMDb's 250 best films list. Kare Hedebrant is a boy of twelve, befriended by a girl vampire (Lina Leandersson) who has been about his age "for a very long time." The film considers vampirism as if it were real, and dreadful, and a test for the good natures of both characters. No letting the audience off easy. This vampire isn't a vegetarian.

Asa Butterfield plays the eight-year-old hero of Mark Herman's *Boy in Striped Pajamas*, as the son of a Nazi commandant who runs a facility his child doesn't understand. Jack Scanlon, about the same age, is a prisoner in the facility. Neither child is quite able to comprehend the horror they see and rely on friendship to comfort them. Neither gives a hint of realization, and that is crucial.

Charlie McDermott, at about sixteen, plays the son of a desperate mother in *Frozen River*. Meals in their house trailer consist of microwave popcorn and Tang, after the cereal runs out. He cares for his little brother, he wants to help his mother, he does what he can while she resorts to human trafficking: bringing Chinese across the Canadian border to the United States by driving a car across the ice. He is precisely right.

Now consider James (JimMyron Ross), the twelve-year-old boy in Lance Hammer's *Ballast*. He lives with his mother next door to his uncle. The adults are not speaking after the death of his father. Hungry for attention, he tries to find it in the wrong way, and his need slowly opens up his depressed uncle. All of the lead performers in this wonderful film set in the Mississippi Delta are making their acting debuts, but you would never, ever guess that. James is the moving part in a situation otherwise mired down by old wounds.

Catinca Untaru, then eight, plays the little girl in Tarsem's visual masterpiece *The Fall*, and is told legends by a wounded soldier, which she translates into her own fantasies. She embodies a purity, a naivete, and an affectlessness beyond description. You can't understand why she is so perfect. Then you discover that she didn't even speak English and is speaking after phonetic coaching. Her impact transcends language.

Danny Boyle's *Slumdog Millionaire* centers entirely on the growth of an orphaned slum child from scavenging on a garbage heap to becoming a finalist on the Indian version of *Who Wants to Be a Millionaire?* Three different actors play the boy at various ages, all of them convincingly bright, resilient, vulnerable, and tough. The movie is his story, and they make it so.

Dakota Fanning, just turned fourteen, started acting on TV in 2000 and became a film star after *I Am Sam* (2001), second billed opposite Sean Penn. He was a mentally disabled man fighting for the custody of his seven-year-old daughter. Think about that for a movie debut. This year she had two roles observing the gradual onset of adolescence. In *Hounddog*, she had a layabout dad and was raped by a local boy. In *The Secret Life of Bees*, she helped her nanny and only friend escape from her abusive father and found them shelter in a household ruled by Queen Latifah. Dakota Fanning is gifted, professional, and sensible, on the right track to become another Jodie Foster.

That's eleven films, counting two for Fanning. Space prevents describing another ten, with no less assured performances by young actors. Alphabetically, they are *Changeling*, *Fugitive Pieces, Gran Torino, Kit Kittredge, Miracle at St. Anna, Sixty-Six, Swing Vote, Henry Poole Is Here, Towelhead,* and *XXY*.

Remembering these performances, I fell to thinking there should be a special Oscar category for young actors. I pictured two or three of them making their acceptance speeches, and that was pleasant, but then I realized what a terrible idea I'd had. We should preserve for them the pleasure of performance, instead of encouraging them to think about Oscars. That could inspire Oscar campaigns and competition and all the rest of it, and wreak upon their lives a horror like modern Little League. It would be like telling them there is a Santa Claus after all.

Where does the magic come from? How do directors and casting directors make these discoveries? What instinct inspires directors to bet their entire film on an untried and inexperienced child? What would happen if an adult actor could somehow still channel that clarity and affectless truth? Can we think of one who does? Some come very close, and indeed in many cases such notes are not required in a performance.

If I knew the answer to these questions, I would be much wiser than I am. For the present, all I can do is express my gratitude.

Rags-to-Riches *Slumdog* Wins Gold

February 23, 2009—The slumdog didn't stop at winning a million but zoomed straight on up to Oscar gold Sunday night. *Slumdog Millionaire,* perhaps the most literal rags-to-riches story ever told, swept the evening, winning the Academy Award as the best picture of 2008 and seven more Oscars.

Proud and elated Indians formed a parade to the podium as producer Christian Colson and director Danny Boyle called them on stage at the end; there was a radiant smiling close-up of Ayush Mahesh Khedekar, who played the film's hero at his youngest.

The win came at the end of the most entertaining and innovative Oscarcast I've seen, which put the orchestra upstage, moved the front rows close and did it all under a glittering arch inspired by the old Coconut Grove, where the first Oscars were held. Hugh Jackman joked, sang, and danced through the emcee duties and moved up several levels in global stardom.

Sean Penn won as best actor for *Milk,* the story of the nation's first openly gay man

elected as a public official. "For those who saw the signs of hatred as our cars drove in tonight," he said, "I think this is a good time for them to reflect on their shame." The category was widely thought to be a showdown between Penn and Mickey Rourke in *The Wrestler.* Penn closed by saying: "Mickey Rourke rises again, and he's my brother."

Kate Winslet's victory as best actress for *The Reader* was joyfully hailed by the audience; it came after five earlier nominations. "I would be lying," she said, "if I didn't admit I gave my first version of this speech when I was eight years old, standing in front of the mirror with a shampoo bottle." She asked her dad to whistle so she could wave to her parents from the stage.

Best supporting actor went, as widely expected, to the late Heath Ledger, for his astonishing work as the Joker in *The Dark Knight.* His father, mother, and sister accepted on his behalf. There were tears in the eyes of some of the watchers. *The Dark Knight* won one other Oscar, for sound editing, but was additionally consoled recently by passing the $1 billion mark at the box office.

Penelope Cruz was named best supporting actress for her role as a woman who schemes to keep her man in Woody Allen's *Vicky Cristina Barcelona.* Growing up in Spain, she said, she thought the Oscar night ceremony "was a moment of unity for the world because art, in any form, is and has been and will always be our universal language."

The award came as the Academy unveiled a heartwarming new format to present the acting nominees: Five of the former winners in each category singled out the nominees for praise— much better than just reading out their names—and the reaction shots of the nominees in the first row were touching. The star power on stage was dazzling. This new approach was a masterstroke.

Those presentations, Hugh Jackman's virtuoso opening act, and the device of a script typing itself to introduce presenters Steve Martin and Tina Fey for the screenwriting category, achieved something no previous show has ever done for me. I found myself actually expecting to have a great time and wondering what other devices had been invented to intro categories.

The best original screenplay was by Dustin Lance Black, for *Milk,* who said its subject "might want me to say to all of the gay and lesbian kids out there tonight, who have been told that they are 'less than' by their churches, by the government, or by their families, that you are beautiful, wonderful creatures of value."

Best adapted screenplay was by Simon Beaufoy, for *Slumdog Millionaire,* the first of its eventual eight wins. He adapted it from the international best-selling novel *Q and A* by Vikas Swarup, who has been an Indian diplomat in England, the United States, and South Africa.

WALL-E, about a lovable robot trash collector, was another widely predicted winner, for best animated feature. That category was introduced as WALL-E itself found and viewed a video of the nominees in a trash heap. Its director, Andrew Stanton, followed an ancient Oscar tradition by thanking "my high school drama teacher Phil Perry for twenty-eight years ago casting me as Barnaby in *Hello, Dolly!*"

Departures, from Japan, was the somewhat surprising winner of the foreign film category. Unseen in America except at the 2008 Hawaii Film Festival, where it won the Audience Award, it tells the story of an unemployed cellist who finds work as a funeral expediter and counselor. Credit for the award is perhaps due to an Academy reform that requires all voters to have seen every film in the category.

French wire walker Philippe Petit was on stage to accept the Oscar for *Man on Wire,* the documentary about his walk between the World Trade Center towers. He promised the shortest speech in Oscar history ("Yes!") and then kept right on talking, made a coin disappear, and balanced the Oscar in his chin.

The Curious Case of Benjamin Button, at one point a top contender for best film, won awards only in the technical categories, including its art direction and its virtuoso use of makeup and visual effects.

The Duchess, a gorgeous period picture starring Keira Knightley, won for costume design.

Jerry Lewis drew a standing ovation for his Jean Hersholt Humanitarian Award. He looked his age (eighty-two), and sounded slightly winded, but after his twenty-year ordeal of health troubles, he was still filled with spirit and still with the *Bellboy* haircut.

Writing about the Indie Spirits award, I mentioned its goof of Joaquin Phoenix's bearded hip-hop act and said that was some-thing you'd never see at the Oscars. This reinvented show proved me wrong, as a bearded Ben Stiller came out with Natalie Portman and mumbled his lines.

Queen Latifah elevated the annual "In Memoriam" segment with a tender rendition of "I'll Be Seeing You." It ended with perfectly chosen dialogue by Paul Newman. The late Gene Siskel was not included ten years ago (Whoopi Goldberg ad-libbed his name) because all the departed were required to be Academy members. This year, in a surprising departure from policy, the montage included beloved film critic and artist Manny Farber.

Slumdog's eight Oscars included Danny Boyle for best director, and also adapted screenplay, cinematography, original score, original song, sound mixing, and editing. It was a popular winner. A project passed over by many major studios, it won the hearts of moviegoers and was a good winner in industry terms because infrequent moviegoers will now see it and be rewarded by an uplifting experience.

In the streets of Mumbai, where there had been public prayer vigils on behalf of the film, there was rejoicing. The young Indian actors who starred in the film's early scenes were in the audience after starring earlier in their red carpet arrivals.

"This is history being handed over to me," said Resul Pookutty, the *Slumdog* winner for sound mixing, dedicating the award to India, home of Bollywood, the world's largest film industry. Thanking his Mumbai collaborators, Danny Boyle said, "You beautify the sky."

Academy Awards Bombshell

June 26, 2009—In a stunning surprise, the number of Best Picture nominees was increased from five to ten on Wednesday by the Motion Picture Academy. No, Wednesday was not April 1.

"The Academy is returning to some of its earlier roots, when a wider field competed for the top award of the year," said Sid Ganis, outgoing Academy president. In 1934 and 1935 there were twelve nominees, and from 1935 to 1943 there were ten.

The announcement, which came without advance rumor, was greeted with questions, criticism, and little immediate praise. It raises three obvious questions: (1) Will the annual

Oscar telecast now routinely run longer than four hours? (2) Will this increase pressure on the Academy to allow Best Picture nominations for animated films? (3) If animated films stay in a segregated category, will five films now be permitted there, instead of three?

"This is the direct result of intense lobbying by the major studios," writes Nikki Finke, the widely read blogger whose inside sources are among the best in the industry.

Finke charged: "It's no secret that the studios have grown increasingly frustrated that their mainstream fare—the four-quadrant films, the family-oriented toons, the superhero actioners and the high-octane thrillers—have not been able to garner enough Best Picture nods in recent years while the art house offerings of the rapidly dwindling specialty divisions and indie prods dominate the process. That, in turn, has hurt the Oscar broadcast ratings as little-seen and often little-known films compete with one another while blockbuster hits are left out of the Academy Awards show."

On the other hand, the result may not be more mainstream nominees. As the number of Academy voters has grown, they have been increasingly willing to step outside the mainstream. While this would mean a highly regarded hit like *The Dark Knight* would almost certainly be nominated, the new *Transformers* film, which could become this year's biggest blockbuster, would have no chance even if the category grew to twenty films. Taste does remain a factor.

There will be one obvious beneficiary: The trade papers, which get pages of Oscar advertising every year. "This will be a critical—perhaps business-saving—moment for *Variety*," wrote David Poland of the influential MovieCityNews.com. He added: "I'm not crying, as a businessman, either."

He wrote that "there was serious consideration of dumping the Best Animated Feature category, given that the *Up*s of the world should now be mortal locks in a group of ten. But not this year. If *Up* doesn't get a BP nod as a result, I think you can be sure that the category will be gone next year."

What will be the consequences for the annual Oscarcast? I asked Marsha Jordan, for twenty-five years the producer of Oscar coverage for ABC7/Chicago.

"It's great to have extra movies in play," she said, "but the competition just increases with less chance to win. The one thing the Golden Globes do well is separating genres, so that comedies and musicals have a chance. Take a year like 1994. *Schindler's List* won the Globes for best drama. *Mrs. Doubtfire* won for comedy or musical. How do you put them up against each other? That's also a *long* close of a *long* show, with the finale still being a couple of geeky producers center stage."

Thinking it through, I suspect (1) that next year's ten nominees will definitely include *Up*, which may mean the death knell for a separate Animated category; (2) that more indie films will be nominated than the Academy expects; but (3) that the larger field will fragment the vote, so that the (somewhat devalued) Best Picture winner will be a major studio picture. But it's almost always like that anyway. The only recent smaller pictures that won were *Chariots of Fire* (1981), *Annie Hall* (1977), and *Slumdog Millionaire* (2008).

The slumdog may have been the straw that broke the camel's back. Know what? In a field of ten, I think it would have been the winner. On the other hand, three of the other BP nominees were smaller films: *Frost/Nixon, Milk,* and *The Reader.* The only big-time production that made the cut was *The Curious Case of Benjamin Button.*

In Memoriam

Manny Farber

Manny Farber has died. The great iconoclast of American film criticism was ninety-one. He coined the term "underground film," contrasted "termite art" with "white elephant art" in a way that started you thinking about movies in such terms, and once described the auteur theory thusly (I quote from memory): "A bunch of guys standing around trying to catch some director pushing art up into the crevices of dreck."

Never known to the great masses of filmgoers, he started reviewing movies in the *New Republic* in the 1940s, the *Nation* in the 1950s, many other magazines in the 1960s, and finally settled at *Artforum* magazine in 1967, where he referred to the film I wrote as *Beyond the Volleyballs*. He published one collection of his reviews, first titled *Negative Space*, later expanded with *Manny Farber on the Movies*.

He was an advocate of smaller, tougher, moxier movies. "White elephant art," he said, referred to vast and vacuous studio productions that look big and can't be ignored, but contain little of real interest. In contrast, Wikipedia quotes him: "Termite-tapeworm-fungus-moss art goes always forward eating its own boundaries and, like as not, leaves nothing in its path other than the signs of eager, industrious, unkempt activity."

He appreciated that. He liked movies that forged ahead in their own obsessive way, looking to neither side, intent at arriving at no place more grandiose than their endings. Even before the auteur critics of France, he championed such muscular American directors as Howard Hawks.

Once when Russ Meyer and I were in San Diego, working on a screenplay, we had lunch with Manny and the love of his life, Patricia Patterson. He regarded the King of the Nudies with a quizzical, not unfriendly, grin, and said, "So you make the whole movie yourself, by hand?"

Although many film critics read and loved Farber, most of us knew only vaguely of the other side of his work. He was a highly regarded painter, once referred to by the *New York Times* as the finest still-life painter of his time. I went to one of his exhibitions and thought I saw termite art in practice. He often took an overhead view of an assortment of odd little objects, seen against a semi-abstract field. There was wit and playfulness in everything he painted.

I met Manny and Patricia for the first time at the 1972 Venice Film Festival, where, typically for Manny, he had arrived not having bothered to tell anyone he was coming or obtaining any credentials. There they were, getting off the vaporetto at the Lido pier and looking around for the festival. How did we know each other? We may have been introduced by Michael Kutza, director of the Chicago festival. I took him to the press office and announced, "You must give this man a pass because he is the most important film critic in America." My word carried no weight other than getting the Farber name passed along to the festival director, who knew of Farber and came bustling out, apologizing for "misplacing" his application.

At Venice, we spent a lot of time with John Gillet of London's National Film Theater, sitting in beach cafés talking about nothing I can now remember, other than Bobby Fischer and the world chess championship then being played. We had a little portable set and played through the games from the daily paper. I remember one expedition into Venice along with the Yugoslavian director Dusan Makavejev and his wife. We landed at a pizzeria in Piazza San Giacomo, where it became clear that Makavejev fit safely in the termite category.

Manny and Patricia went to Telluride one year, where I had been asked to interview James Stewart onstage about his Anthony Mann Westerns. I told Telluride directors Tom Luddy and Bill Pence that this was a mistake, because Farber had all but put the Stewart/Mann films on the map of critical praise. Manny took my place. I wish I had a transcript. My memory is that his oblique, idiosyncratic questions were unlike anything Stewart had ever been asked before by anyone, and he was greatly amused, even challenged, in replying to them. Farber created a mood in which the two men, within a decade of the same age, were conspirators.

In addition to films, Farber was a critic of art, books, music, anything. Ken Tucker at ew.com says he has this Farber quote taped to his wall: "I get a great laugh from artists who ridicule the critics as parasites and artists manques—such a horrible joke. I can't imagine a more perfect art form, a more perfect career than criticism. I can't imagine anything more valuable to do."

Farber (born 1917) died August 17, 2008, in San Diego, where for many years he was a professor at San Diego State. If you have never read Farber, as many have not, *Negative Space* is in print, and it is never too late to start.

Michael Jackson

June 26, 2009—Michael Jackson was so gifted, so lonely, so confused, so sad. He lost happiness somewhere in his childhood, and spent his life trying to go back there and find it. When he played the Scarecrow in *The Wiz* (1978), I think that is how he felt, and Oz was where he wanted to live. It was his most truly autobiographical role. He could understand a character who felt stuffed with straw but could wonderfully sing and dance and could cheer up the little girl Dorothy.

We have all spent years in the morbid psychoanalysis of this strange man-child. Now that he has died we will hear it all repeated again: the great fame from an early age, the gold records, the world tours, the needy friendships, the painful childhood, Neverland, the eccentric behavior, plastic surgery, charges of child molestation, the fortunes won and lost, the generosity, the secrecy, the inexplicable marriage to Elvis's daughter, the disguises, the puzzling sexuality, the jokes, and on and on.

I never met him. My wife, Chaz, did, a long time ago when she was part of a dance troupe that opened some shows for the Jackson Five. What she remembers is that he was . . . a kid. Talented, hardworking, but not like other kids. That's what he was, and that's what he remained. His father, Joseph, was known even then as a hard-driving taskmaster, and was later described by family members as physically and mentally abusive, beating the child, once holding him by a leg and banging his head on the floor. Michael confided to Oprah that sometimes he would vomit at the sight of the man.

Families are important to everyone, and to African-Americans they are the center of the universe. A census is maintained that radiates out to great-nieces and -nephews, distant cousins, former spouses, honorary relatives, all the generations. Communication is maintained, birthdays remembered, occasions celebrated. Important above all are parents and grandparents. Family was a support system from a time when slave-owning America refused to recognize black families. Family was the rock.

Michael Jackson doesn't seem to have had that rock. His father seems to have driven him to create an alternative universe for himself, in which somewhere, over the rainbow, he could have another childhood. He named his ranch Neverland, after the magical land where Peter Pan, the boy who never grew up, enacted his fantasies with the Lost Boys. I wonder if we ever really understood how central that vision was to Jackson, or how literally he tried to create it.

I have no idea whether Michael abused the children he "adopted." It is possible those relationships were without sex; he seemed frozen at a time before puberty. Whether he touched them criminally or not, it is easy to see what he sought: to create, with and for these Lost Boys, a Neverland where they could imagine together the childhood he never had.

Mixed with that was perhaps a lifelong feeling of inadequacy, burned in by the cruelty of his father. That might help explain the compulsive plastic surgery, the relentless rehearsal, the exhausting tours, the purchase of expensive toys, the giving of gifts.

The scene everyone remembers from *The Wiz* is Dorothy and the Scarecrow, the Tin Man and the Cowardly Lion dancing and singing down the Yellow Brick Road. They were off to see the Wizard, and a wonderful Wizard he was, because of the wonderful things he does.

In the story, the Wizard is a lonely little man hiding behind a curtain, using his power to create a wonderland. Now Michael Jackson will never be able to tell us what he was hiding behind his curtain. But because of his music, we danced and sang.

Karl Malden

Karl Malden, who won an Academy Award for one of the best American films and became a household name for a TV commercial, is dead at ninety-seven. He died of natural causes on July 1, 2009, at home in Brentwood, according to his family.

Malden won his Oscar for the film adaptation of Tennessee Williams's *A Streetcar Named Desire* (1951), playing opposite Marlon Brando and Vivien Leigh. He acted with Brando again in *On the Waterfront* (1954), for which he was nominated. He and Brando had started on Broadway together in 1945.

His toughest physical acting challenge, he once told me, came during the filming of *On the Waterfront*, in a scene where he plays a priest standing in the cargo hold of a ship, trying to bring peace to a labor dispute. The screenplay called for him to be hit in the head with a beer can. Director Elia Kazan called for more than one take.

"It had to be a full beer can because an empty one would bounce wrong," he said during an onstage discussion at the USA Film Festival in Dallas. "It didn't feel real good bouncing off my skull. Father Barry has no way of knowing he's about to be hit. Of course I knew, because the cue was a particular word of dialogue. I found it incredibly hard to keep my face blank before the can hit. Next to that, the acting part was easy."

Malden, reminding viewers, "Don't leave home without it," starred in a popular series of TV commercials for the American Express card in the 1970s and 1980s.

"After fifty years of doing all those other things in the business," he once told the *Los Angeles Times*, "wherever I go, the one thing people will say to me is, 'Don't leave home without it.' What am I going to say? It's kind of frustrating in a way, but at the same time, American Express has been very good to me, and it's given me independence. I don't have to jump at anything and everything that comes my way."

He was born named Mladen Sekulovich on March 22, 1912, in Chicago, the son of a Czech mother and a Serbian father. The family moved to Gary, Indiana, where his father worked in the steel mills and then became a milkman. Malden himself was a steelworker from 1931 to 1934. He was asked to shorten his name by his first drama company and said he always regretted that. As an in-joke, he succeeded in working the name Mladen Sekulovich into the screenplays of *On the Waterfront, Birdman of Alcatraz, Fear Strikes Out,* and *Patton,* in which he played General Omar Bradley. In the popular TV series *The Streets of San Francisco,* his character employed an assistant with the name.

Having started acting in high school, in 1937 he moved to New York to try his luck on Broadway. In the 1930s there was a market for proletarians who looked like they'd knocked around a little, and he was accepted into Lee Strasberg's Group Theater. He served in World War II as a noncommissioned officer in the Eighth Air Force. His first significant movie role was in *The Gunfighter* (1950), and he often played in Westerns, film noir, and realistic dramas—and even in a musical, *Gypsy.*

In addition to his more famous films, he excelled in Hitchcock's *I Confess* (1953); Preminger's *Where the Sidewalk Ends* (1950); Kazan's *Baby Doll* (1956); *One-Eyed Jacks* (1961), the only film Brando ever directed; and Ford's *Cheyenne Autumn* (1964).

He was a president of the Academy of Motion Picture Arts and Sciences, and was proud of his service until this year on a U.S. Postal Service citizen's advisory board recommending subjects for U.S. stamps.

Malden was a much-loved, straightforward, plain-spoken family man who rarely made a gossip column and was married since 1938 to Mona Greenberg, who survives him. It was one of Hollywood's longest running marriages. He is also survived by daughters Mila and Carla, three grandchildren, and four great-grandchildren.

His film career bridged seven decades. "People have told me that I came to this industry at its Golden Age," he once said. "But when I was there, it was just an age."

Paul Newman

Paul Newman, a sublime actor and a good man, is dead at eighty-three. The movie legend died September 26, 2008, at his home in Connecticut, a family spokeswoman said. The cause of death was lung cancer. Newman reportedly told his family he chose to die at home. He lived a long and active life, encompassing acting and directing for stage and screen, philanthropy, political activism, auto racing, and the Newman's Own line of foods.

After serving in World War II as a tail gunner, including missions in the Pacific from an aircraft carrier, Newman studied acting at Kenyon College and quickly found stardom on the stage. His Broadway career began in 1953, costarring in the hit play *Picnic*, and as recently as this spring he was planning to direct a summer theater production of *Of Mice and Men*, until illness prevented him.

In 1954, he made his first film, *The Silver Chalice*, for which it amused him to apologize, and for more than fifty years, Newman ruled as one of Hollywood's most-loved stars. There was scarcely a time when he did not have top billing. He was one of the heirs of Marlon Brando and the other late-1940s Method actors, but his acting seemed more naturalistic and less stylized. In midcareer, he played more antiheroes than heroes. He made the transition quickly from a young heartthrob to one of the aristocrats of his profession.

He made some sixty films. He was nominated for nine Academy Awards and won for *The Color of Money* (1986). He also won the Academy's Honorary Award in 1986 and its Jean Hersholt Humanitarian Award in 1994. His Oscar came for playing the character Fast Eddie Felson, a pool hustler. He was also nominated for the film that introduced the character, *The Hustler* (1961). He made five films as a director, including four starring his wife of fifty years, Joanne Woodward. One of them, *Rachel, Rachel* (1968), won Woodward a nomination for best actress and her husband one for best director.

In addition to acting, Newman found success in auto racing, food retailing, and political activism. His last work as an actor came this year, appearing in the INDYCar series season preview. Ironically, this most graceful of actors called racing "the first thing I found I had any grace in." He started racing professionally in 1972, was still racing in 1995, and was anything but a gentleman amateur: In 1979, he finished second at Le Mans.

In 1982, he began a line of food products under the label Newman's Own, starting with his own recipe for a salad dressing and adding spaghetti sauce, salsa, and, of course, popcorn.

"The embarrassing thing is that my salad dressing is out-grossing my films," he told the *Times* of London earlier this year.

All profits, recently passing the $250 million mark, went to charity. They helped him and Woodward to establish the Hole in the Wall Gang summer camps for sick children. There are now camps in Connecticut, Ireland, France, and Israel. His company's motto: "Shameless exploitation for the common good."

An outspoken liberal, Newman placed nineteenth on Richard Nixon's "enemies list," and cited that as one of his proudest achievements.

How can you choose Newman's best roles? He almost always had his choice of films, working with such directors as Martin Scorsese, Sidney Lumet, Martin Ritt, Richard Brooks, Otto Preminger, Arthur Penn, Alfred Hitchcock, George Roy Hill, Robert Altman, and the Coen brothers.

He had a huge hit in *Butch Cassidy and the Sundance Kid* (1969), costarring with Robert Redford. They teamed again in *The Sting* (1973). His acting nominations came for *Cat on a Hot Tin Roof* (1958), *The Hustler* (1961), *Hud* (1963), *Cool Hand Luke* (1967), *Absence of Malice* (1981), *The Verdict* (1982), *The Color of Money* (1986), *Nobody's Fool* (1994), and *Road to Perdition* (2002).

Other important performances were as Rocky Graziano in *Somebody Up There Likes Me* (1956), as Billy the Kid in *The Left-Handed Gun* (1958), *Exodus* (1960), *Torn Curtain* (1966), *Slap Shot* (1977), *Fat Man and Little Boy* (1989), as Huey Long in *Blaze* (1989), with Woodward in *Mr. and Mrs. Bridge* (1980), and the Coens' *Hudsucker Proxy* (1994).

His last major film role was in *Road to Perdition* (2002), filmed in Chicago. He played a mob boss, costarring with Tom Hanks, who told me he was intimidated: "Oh, lordy! You can't have a history of going to the movies and not be. Seeing his movies was a big time for me. So to be there on the set with him. . . . Number one, he's much taller than you think he's going to be. And number two, those eyes. The first take on the first day, I'm not thinking about my work, I'm thinking, 'Holy cow! I'm in a movie looking into Paul Newman's eyes. How did this happen?'"

Newman did some TV work and voice-overs for animation before announcing his retirement from acting in 2007, telling ABC: "You start to lose your memory, you start to lose your confidence, you start to lose your invention. So I think that's pretty much a closed book for me."

I met him several times, most memorably in 1968, on the set of *Butch Cassidy*. Yes, his eyes were blue. Very blue. He was genial, relaxed; it felt more like hanging out than doing an interview. Between scenes, he held court in his trailer, sometimes sipping a beer. He was not closed off and self-protective like many superstars, not seeming overly impressed with himself. One reason he and Woodward lived in Connecticut, he often said, was to have a more normal life than was possible in Hollywood.

It was that sense of accessibility that audiences responded to. In a reconsideration of *Cool Hand Luke,* I observed: "Could another actor than Paul Newman have played the role and gotten away with it? Of the stars at the time, I would not be able to supply one. Warren Beatty? Steve McQueen? Lee Marvin? They would have the presence and stamina, but would have lacked the smile. The physical presence of Paul Newman is the reason this movie works: the smile, the innocent blue eyes, the lack of strutting. Look at his gentle behavior in the touching scene with his mother (Jo Van Fleet). Both know they will never see each other again, and in a way are apologizing." The movie's hardened character Dragline describes Luke as "you wild, beautiful thing." Could he have described Marvin that way?

Newman didn't do much publicity compared to most actors, and once described it to me this way: "It's kind of an . . . well, not an ordeal, exactly, but doing so many interviews is like double parking in front of a whorehouse; scant satisfaction to both parties."

Newman was born in 1925 in Shaker Heights, Ohio. From 1949 to 1958 he was married to Jackie Witte. They had a son, Scott, and daughters Susan and Stephanie. His son died of a drug overdose in 1978, and in his memory Newman started a drug abuse center. He married Woodward in 1958. They had three daughters, Elinor, Melissa, and Claire.

Newman was known for his modesty. He once said he could envision these words on his tombstone: "Here lies Paul Newman, who died a failure because his eyes turned brown."

In a book about the actor, the writer Lawrence J. Quirk quotes Newman: "I'd like to be remembered as a guy who tried—tried to be part of his times, tried to help people communicate with one another, tried to find some decency in his own life, tried to extend himself as a human being. Someone who isn't complacent, who doesn't cop out."

Natasha Richardson

March 20, 2009—I didn't write an obituary about Natasha Richardson. I didn't write an appreciation. I didn't write anything. When I learned of her death, I thought: This is wrong. I could not bring myself to go through the business of listing her best roles and describing her life.

At first there was only the information that she had been injured and taken to hospitals in Montreal and New York. The words "brain dead" raced into the news, quoting "friends of the family." No family needs friends like those. I did not want to hear this news.

Did I know her? No. Journalists rarely get to "know" many of their subjects. I had been around her and her husband, Liam Neeson. Nice people. You can tell those things. Oddly, the first memory that came to mind was an inconsequential one that had waited dormant for years. Once in Los Angeles, Chaz and I found our car next to theirs at a traffic light. We exchanged some jolly small talk. I've interviewed them, but those few seconds were the ones summoned. There was a feeling about them.

This is not important for you to hear. My job should be to tick off her roles and dates, her lineage, her statements about this and that. But I couldn't bring myself to do that, because her young death was so WRONG. So sudden, so nonsensical, in the fullness of life. Taking a skiing lesson with her son. Her husband in Toronto making a movie. The sunshine, the fresh air, the laughter, then the tumble on the snow and laughing off any concern.

Her mother, Vanessa Redgrave, was the first movie star I ever met. It was on the set of *Camelot* in 1967. I wasn't yet a movie critic. Her aunt Lynn was the first movie star whose home I ever visited. Natasha was a little girl then. I thought of her in a particular way. I was . . . proud of her. Does that sound possible? She was so good in films like *The White Countess,* *The Comfort of Strangers,* and *Patty Hearst,* but

I didn't think of her objectively, as a figure up there on the screen. I thought of her as . . . Natasha. It is a mysterious quality of some movie stars that we feel protective.

Gene Siskel

February 20, 2009—Gene Siskel and I were like tuning forks. Strike one, and the other would pick up the same frequency. When we were in a group together, we were always intensely aware of each other. Sometimes this took the form of camaraderie, sometimes shared opinions, sometimes hostility. But we were aware. If something happened that we both thought was funny but weren't supposed to, God help us if one caught the other's eye. We almost always thought the same things were funny. That may be the best sign of intellectual communion.

Gene died ten years ago on February 20, 1999. He is in my mind almost every day. I don't want to rehearse the old stories about how we had a love-hate relationship, and how we dealt with television, and how we were both so scared the first time we went on Johnny Carson that, backstage, we couldn't think of the name of a single movie, although that story is absolutely true. Those stories have been told. I want to write about our friendship.

Once Gene and I were involved in a joint appearance with another Chicago media couple, Steve Dahl and Garry Meier. It was a tribute to us or a tribute to them, I can't remember. They were pioneers of free-form radio. Gene and I were known for our rages against each other, and Steve and Garry were remarkable for their accord. They gave us advice about how to work together as a successful team. The reason I remember that is that soon afterward, Steve and Garry had an angry, public falling-out that has lasted until this day.

Gene and I would never, ever have had that happen to us. Unthinkable. In my darkest and moodiest hours, when all my competitiveness and resentment and indignation were at a roiling boil, I never considered it. I know Gene never did either. We were linked in a bond beyond all disputing. "You may be an asshole," Gene would say, "but you're my asshole." If we were fighting, get out of the room. But if we were teamed up against a common target, we were fatal. The first time we were on his show, Howard Stern never knew what hit him. He picked on one of us, and we were both at his throat.

We both thought of ourselves as full-service, one-stop film critics. We didn't see why the other one was quite necessary. We had been linked in a Faustian television format that brought us success at the price of autonomy. No sooner had I expressed a verdict on a movie, *my verdict,* then here came Siskel with the arrogance to say I was wrong or, for that matter, the condescension to agree with me. It really felt like that. It was not an act. When we disagreed, there was incredulity; when we agreed, there was a kind of relief. In the television biz, they talk about "chemistry." Not a thought was given to our chemistry. We just had it, because from the day the *Chicago Tribune* made Gene its film critic, we were enemies. We never had a single meaningful conversation before we started to work on our TV program. Alone together in an elevator, we would study the numbers changing above the door.

Making this rivalry even worse was the tension of our early tapings. It would take eight hours to get one show in the can, with breaks for lunch, dinner, and fights. I would break down, or he would break down, or one of us would do something different and throw the other off, or the accumulating angst would make our exchanges seem simply bizarre. There are many witnesses to the terror of those days. Only when we threw away our clipboards and three-by-five cards did we get anything done; we finally started ad-libbing and the show began to work. We found we could tape a show in under an hour.

People started recognizing us out of town. "Life is going to change," Gene said. Joe Antelo, the producer who brought us into syndication, took us to NAPTE, the annual convention of TV syndicated shows, and forbade us to walk around the floor unless we were together. "Together, you're an advertisement," he explained. "Apart, you're tourists." People would ask, "Aren't you those two guys?" Once when we were on an elevator, some ladies started whispering to one another and when we got off, Gene looked back and said, "We're those two guys."

Both of us were obsessed with our newspaper jobs. That was our identity. TV was part-time. We were competitive but not equally competitive. Gene was the most competitive man I have ever met. Everything was an opportunity. At PBS, the camera crew played with one of those toy gambling games where you threw little metal pigs on the floor and saw how many of them landed on their feet. Something like that. I never understood it. They gambled for nickel stakes.

One day Gene said, "Let's make it more interesting," and suggested raising the stakes to a quarter. Then he started to win. There was no way he was cheating. Gene had taken the pigs home with him and *mastered the game.* Another time on an airline flight, we were sitting next to each other playing gin rummy, and for once I succeeded in making the right play and Gene threw his cards down on his tray table so hard they flew all over the aisle. We never played gin again.

Gene had only scorn for games of chance. We went to Vegas a lot and I never saw him play a single one. He would gamble in only two ways: poker and horse racing. He went to the track and to off-track parlors in Chicago and claimed he was a net winner. I found that unlikely. His horse-betting buddy was Johnny Morris, the Chicago Bears star who worked with him at Channel 2. Morris was also said to be a gifted bettor. I learned from a third party that they were both, in fact, successful. I reported this to Gene and asked him what his rules were. "Roger," he said, "there is only one rule: *Never play a hunch.*"

In Vegas, I played the five-dollar poker tables, but Gene was over in the pricier section of the room. At his bachelor party, he swept the tables with his winnings. At my bachelor party, he was a big loser. I asked him what went wrong. "What went wrong," he said, "is that your friends don't know how to play poker. A good player can never win against someone who makes a bet just for fun."

He hadn't been a big sports fan before Michael Jordan started playing for the Bulls. What drew him to the team was the totality of Jordan's competitiveness. Gene began to follow Jordan and the Bulls with a passionate intensity. He and Marlene even bought front-row season tickets—not cheap, but more important to Gene than a car. He was a fan but not a mindless fan. He became a student of the game.

He looked in basketball for the kinds of "tells" a poker player looks for. He said Jordan was better at reading another player's tells than anybody else in the game.

He asked the coach, Phil Jackson, "Why does Dennis Rodman always miss the first free throw?"

Jackson said, "Why do you think?"

Gene said, "For some reason, he thinks he has to."

Jackson nodded thoughtfully.

"He didn't tell me what he thought," Gene said. "A good coach would never do that."

Gene was formidably well-informed. It was a sort of armor. He made it his business. He knew the best restaurants, but that was child's play. He knew fine art and antiques. He knew things like the best chicken-salad sandwich in Los Angeles (the Apple Pan) or the best Italian beef sandwich in Chicago (Mr. Beef). We agreed that Father & Son made the best thin-crust pizza in Chicago. We agreed that deep-pan "Chicago style" pizza wasn't worth the time of day. Gene knew the safest family cars, and those were the only ones he drove. He knew the best schools for his children. He knew the best condo buildings in Chicago. I never thought of buying a place to live without checking with him. When Chaz and I were looking at a house on Astor Street, we asked him to look it over.

He walked through briefly and said, "Don't buy it."

We asked why not. "I don't like the skylight," he said.

What's wrong with it? "From their windows," he said, "your neighbors will be able to see you walking to the bathroom."

He was a bachelor when I first met him, living in an apartment that was said to resemble a bachelor's nightmare. I never saw it. Few did. When he got serious about Marlene and realized he would sooner or later have to take her there, he asked his sister to clean it up "just enough so I can have a cleaning person come in." I gather it wasn't filled with rotting Kentucky Fried Chicken or anything. It was simply filled with everything he had ever brought home and put down, still wherever it landed, and had never been dusted. He and Johnny Morris made a bet once with a TV set as the wager. When Johnny lost, he got a giant old console set and had it delivered to Gene's apartment. The delivery guys dumped it inside the door. It was never moved, and from then on the door never opened all the way.

There was always a little of the Yale undergraduate in Gene. Tim Wiegel, his roommate there, later a sportscaster, told me Gene was famous for wearing a Batman costume and dropping out of trees. He studied philosophy, considered law school, decided to take some time off first. "I told my dad I thought I'd like to try a job in newspapers," Gene said. "He said he'd give me a ride downtown. We had always been a *Sun-Times* family. For some reason, I never knew why, he dropped me off in front of Tribune Tower." Less than a year after walking in the door, he was the Tribune's film critic.

He got his second job, as the movie critic of the CBS Chicago news, because the newscast was bring reformatted to resemble a newspaper city room. Van Gordon Sauter, the executive producer, recruited Gene on the theory, "Don't hire someone because they look good on TV; hire them because they cover a beat and are the masters of it." Gene said that was the reason for the success of our show: We didn't look great on TV, but at least we sounded as if we might know what we were talking about.

Gene met Marlene Iglitzen when she was producing that CBS news show in Chicago. "We fought like cats and dogs," she told me. She moved to CBS in New York. He started to see her in New York, and when she was visiting her family in Chicago he would bring her to screenings. I don't recall him ever bringing any other dates to screenings. She was the one. I remember once we were all in a car in New York, and Gene said he wanted to show me the holy place where he had proposed marriage to Marlene. I think this was on Second Avenue.

"There it is, right on the corner," Gene said, taking Marlene's hand.

"The Pizza-Fotomat?" I said.

"My darling Gene," Marlene said.

He had discovered the right woman. I am going to violate a confidence. Thea Flaum was the person who formed our show on PBS and guided us through our rocky first years. She said to me not so long ago, "You know that Gene could sometimes he difficult to deal with. Well, you both were. Marlene is a smart woman, she worked in TV news, I wondered how it would work for her being married to

Gene. Rog, after I saw them together for a while, I came to the realization that in the most important ways they were the same person."

Marlene kept her name. "When I introduced Marlene Iglitzen to Mel Brooks," Gene said, Mel asked her, "What was it before you changed it?" They had two daughters, Cate and Callie, and a son, Will. The girls were flower girls at my wedding. They followed him to Yale, and Will seems to be headed there. The Siskels threw a party for us before Chaz and I were married. I remembered the party before Gene was married. There was a mentalist who told me everything in my own wallet. This was astonishing to me; I knew my wallet had been in my pants during the whole party.

"How does he do that?" I asked Gene.

"I don't know, but I'll tell you one thing," Gene said. "He couldn't tell *me* what was in *my* wallet." Score one.

Once we were invited to speak to the Harvard Law School Film Society. We walked into their mock trial courtroom armed with all sorts of notes, but somehow got started on a funny note, and the whole appearance became stand-up comedy. Separately or together, we were never funnier. Even the audience questions were funny. Roars of laughter for ninety minutes. I'm not making this up. I don't know what happened. Afterward Gene said, "We could do this in Vegas. No, I'm serious." He was always serious about things like that.

That night we had dinner together in a hotel in Cambridge and had our longest and deepest philosophical discussion. We talked about life and death, the cosmos, our place in the grand scheme of things, the meaning of it all. There was a reason Gene studied philosophy: He was a natural.

He spoke about his Judaism, which he took very seriously. His parents had started the first synagogue on the North Shore after World War II. "I had a lot of long talks with my father about our religion," Gene told me. "He said it wasn't necessary to think too much about an afterlife. What was important was this life, how we live it, what we contribute, our families, and the memories we leave." Gene said, "The importance of Judaism isn't simply theological or, in the minds of some Jews, necessarily theological at all. It is that we have stayed together and respected these things for thousands of years, and so it is important that we continue." In two sentences, he had given me the best definition of Judaism I have ever heard.

In late 1997, I noticed that Gene sometimes began to get things out of order; strange, for a man who was always so alert and precise. We emceed an awards show with a dozen categories, all with the same onstage routine, and Gene asked me to brief him every time before we went on stage. In March of that year, we were the guests of honor at a benefit gala for Chicago's Museum of Broadcasting. It marked the twenty-third anniversary of the show. "Why the twenty-third?" I asked Chaz. "Why not the twenty-fifth?" We decided maybe the museum needed the money.

That night, Gene addressed a lot of his remarks to his family, seated at a table right in front of the stage. He told them things they should be sure to tell Will when he grew older. He mentioned some of his values. He spoke of their educations and the importance of finding a job you love. I took quiet notice of that. Not long after, Jay Leno brought his show to Chicago. In the limo going out to the Rosemont Horizon, Gene said he had an unbelievable headache. Backstage, they found a darkened room and a cool cloth for his eyes, and gave him some Advil. He asked me to come in and tell him what we were supposed to do, which was judge a contest of Jay lookalikes.

"My headache is too bad to focus on it," he told me. "You do it and I'll go on agreeing with everything you say. You can look amazed. We can make it a shtick."

After the show, Stuart Cleland, our executive producer, said, "Gene, I'm taking you to a hospital." Gene was adamant. "Nothing doing. I'm going to the Bulls game." They were in the playoffs. Chaz and I watched the game on TV, and saw Gene in his usual seat on the floor. A day or two later, we heard that Gene had gone into Northwestern Hospital for some tests. We flew to the Cannes festival, and Stuart called us in France: "Gene is having surgery." We wanted to call and send him flowers. "I don't know where he is," Stuart said. "He didn't tell me."

We later found out it was Sloan-Kettering in New York. The announcement was that Gene had some tests and was recovering after a small procedure. That remained the family's official statement. Gene took some time off (together, we chose Tom Shales of the *Washington Post* to sit in for him). When he returned to the show, he was obviously ill but we never discussed his health, except to agree that he was recovering— recovering from what was never said.

I understood this at the time and understand it better now. Gene was a competitor, and now he faced the possibility of defeat. He knew all about odds, and they were against him. But from that summer through the following February, he continued to attend screenings and do the show. He was often in his seat at Bulls games. His step slowed and his mind was not always as lightning fast as usual. What he went through, only Marlene knows. He spoke to his family about his illness, but to no one else, not even his best friends. He was unhappy when the *Tribune* ran an item saying his recovery was "on schedule." He asked, "What schedule? Whose schedule?"

Before his final shows, the studio was cleared so that his nephew could help him walk onto the set and take his seat. No mention was made of his illness. He taped his last program a week or two before his death. His pain must have been unimaginable. But he did it, and I never admired him more. Our eyes would meet, unspoken words were between us, but we never spoke openly about his problems or his prognosis. That's how he wanted it, and that was his right. In a way we'd had our talk on that night in Cambridge. We talked about what mattered.

We once spoke with Disney and CBS about a sitcom to be titled *Best Enemies*. It would be about two movie critics joined in a love-hate relationship. It never went anywhere, but we both believed it was an idea. Maybe the problem was that no one else could possibly understand how meaningless was the hate, how deep was the love.

Studs Terkel

Take it easy, but take it.
　　　　—Studs Terkel's sign-off
　　　　on every WFMT radio show

November 3, 2008—So there wasn't a World Series in Chicago, and Studs missed the 2008 presidential election. Other than that, Louis (Studs) Terkel did everything possible in ninety-six years.

Was he the greatest Chicagoan? I cannot think of another. For me, he represented the joyous, scrappy, liberal, generous, wisecracking heart of this city. If you met him, he was your friend. That happened to the hundreds and hundreds of people he interviewed for his radio show and twenty best-selling books. He wrote down the oral histories of those of his time who did not have a voice. In conversation he could draw up every single one of their names.

Studs said many times in these last years, "I'm ready to check out." He hadn't been in any hurry until a fall in late August slowed him down. At the time of his ninety-third birthday, we had dinner with him a few days before he was having a heart bypass. He was looking forward to it.

"The docs say the odds are four to one in my favor," he said, with the voice of a guy who studied the angles. "At age ninety-three, those are pretty good odds. I'm gonna have a whack at it. Otherwise, I'm Dead Man Walking. If I don't have the operation, how long do I have? Six months, maybe. That's no way to live, waiting to die. I've had ninety-three years—tumultuous years. That's a pretty good run."

It was a run during which his great mind never let him down. "This is ironic," he told me. "I'm not the one who has Alzheimer's. It's the country that has Alzheimer's. There was a survey the other day showing that most people think our best president was Reagan. Not Abraham Lincoln. FDR came in tenth. People don't pay attention anymore. They don't read the news."

Studs read the news. He sang with Pete Seeger: "I sell the morning papers sir, my name is Jimmy Brown. Everybody knows that I'm the newsboy of the town. You can hear me yellin' *Morning Star*, runnin' along the street. Got no hat upon my head no shoes upon my feet."

Studs knew jazz inside out, gospel by heart, the blues as he learned them after being raised in the transient hotel run by his mother on Wells Street. He wasn't the only man who had a going-away party when he left to fight in World War II. He might have been the only one to have Billie Holiday sing at his party.

He was never a communist. He was a proud man of the Left. He was blacklisted by McCarthy, and as a result he lost one of the first national sitcoms in TV history. "I was happy to do it," he said. Every single day of his life he wore a red or red-checked shirt and bright red socks. Of course he smoked a cigar. He liked a drink, too, and loved to hang out in newspaper bars and in ethnic neighborhoods with his pals. I never saw him drunk, and believe me, I had plenty of opportunities to.

He visited me in the hospital more times than I visited him. We received bulletins from those who loved him and cared for him. This was the stunner, from his dear friend Sydney Lewis, on September 11, 2008: "After hearing his very clear wishes, [his son] Dan called hospice. The admissions nurse, a lovely woman, said in her many years of doing this work she'd never seen a person more at peace over the decision. Really, all he wants is for JR [his caregiver JR Millares] and Dan to be around and never again to have to leave his house."

He had been in touch through the summer by e-mail. He wasn't receiving a lot of visitors. He never mentioned his health. He was online encouraging me. That was so typical of him. After I broke my hip, he e-mailed me but never mentioned the hip. He said: "You have added a NEW VOICE, a new sound, to your natural one. This—what you write now—is a richer one—a new dimension. It's more than about movies. Yes, it's about movies but there is something added: A REFLECTION on life itself."

I thought twice about quoting that, because he says nice things about me. I hope you will understand why I did. It is the voice of Studs Terkel's love. Of Studs reaching outside his failing body and giving encouragement, as he has always done for me and countless others. He couldn't have written a shelf of books after listening to hundreds of people and writing down their words if his heart had not been unconditionally open to the world.

An e-mail on September 15, 2008, from Sydney: "When I got here today he was gloomy and hadn't eaten. He said he's half interested in leaving, half in staying. After I printed out the great *Booklist* review of his new book *P.S.*, he perked up, we talked about the election, and before I knew it he'd polished off some meat loaf and grapes and was demanding more grapes! So it goes. I suggested he hang around for at least a few things: book publication, World Series, election, and Garry Wills's Terkel retrospective for *New York Review of Books*. He's agreed to try."

On October 23, 2008, his friend Andrew Patner e-mailed: "The man with the greatest spirit known to man is sitting up and taking nourishment. Swallow coaching, even some (cut-up) meat. Gained back a few pounds. Opining on the election (surprise!), the World Series (surprise!), how lousy his new book is being marketed (surprise!). He's looking now to New Year's Eve ('Why not?'), but pulling at least for Election Day ('I can't miss it!')."

He was the most widely and deeply loved man I ever hope to know. He was married for decades to Ida, whose heart filled a room. After the Freedom of Information Act was passed, he was devastated to find that Ida's FBI file was thicker than his own. J. Edgar Hoover thought he was a subversive. Hoover, he said, had a lifelong suspicion of those who thought the Constitution actually meant something.

Studs was a contented, not an outspoken, atheist. "When I go," he told us, "my ashes will be mixed with Ida's and scattered in Bughouse Square." In his next-to-last memoir, he remembered Ida's last words as they wheeled her away toward surgery: "Louis, what have you gotten me into now?" There will be no tombstone, although being Studs, he has written his epitaph: "Curiosity didn't kill this cat."

Film Festival

Cannes Film Festival
Up, Up, and Away, in My Beautiful, My Beautiful Balloon

Cannes, France, May 11, 2009—As I have so often said, if Cannes ever opens its festival with a 3-D animated feature, I'll believe houses can fly. I am a doubter no longer. Cannes 2009 awarded the honor of its opening night, which traditionally goes to a French film, to Pixar's 3-D *Up.* I would have given anything to be there for the morning press screening, to witness the world's movie critics, festival programmers, cineastes, and academics fitting on their XpanD Series 101 3D Active Glasses, which are "a stylish, eco-friendly, and completely immersive stereoscopic 3D experience."

Alas, I was not at that screening. Our flight arrival was a day later. But I *have* had the great pleasure of seeing *Up* in 2-D, which is how most people will see it. Faithful readers will know that I don't at all miss seeing the 3-D version. All I really miss is seeing the Cannes crowd put on the glasses. At the black-tie evening screening, all the top design houses in Paris will have their handmade gowns and formalwear complemented by the stylish and eco-friendly XpanD eyewear.

This is a wonderful film. It tells a *story.* The characters are as believable as any characters can be who spend much of their time floating above the rain forests of Venezuela. They have tempers, problems, and obsessions. They are cute and goofy, but they aren't cute in the treacly way of little cartoon animals. They're cute in the human way of the animation master Hayao Miyazaki.

That means they're earnest and plucky, and one of them is an outright villain—snaky, treacherous, and probably mad. Two of the three central characters are cranky old men, which is a wonder in this era when the captain of the Starship *Enterprise* must be three years out of school, lest fans be asked to identify with a veteran officer. *Up* doesn't think all heroes must be young or sweet, although the third important character is a nervy kid.

The movie was directed by Pete Docter, who also directed *Monsters, Inc.,* wrote *Toy Story,* and was the cowriter and first director on *WALL-E* before leaving to devote himself full-time to this project. So he's one of the leading artists of this renaissance of animation, which has limitless possibilities if it is not derailed by Hollywood's mass corporate delusion about 3-D.

No, this will not be an entry about 3-D. It's about *Up.* But let me gently mention one of the film's qualities that is likely to be diminished by 3-D: Its subtle and beautiful color palette. *Up,* like *Finding Nemo, Toy Story, Shrek,* and *The Lion King,* uses colors in a way particularly suited to its content. It may be that the wonderful new glasses are unlike all other 3-D glasses and are perfectly transparent, but given their purpose, how can they be? Unlike the tinted glasses used for most 3-D glasses, which cost a dollar or less, these babies use lenses that flicker open and closed at the shutter rate of the projector. They cost around $25, and have to be recycled. Don't look for them in your local theater anytime real soon.

I'll have to see *Up* in 3-D to experience their effectiveness. I'm afraid the brightness and delicate shadings of the color palate will become slightly dingy, slightly flattened out, like looking through a window that needs Windex. With standard 3-D movies, take off the glasses and see how much brighter the *real* screen is. I predict the Cannes screening will look better than almost every U.S. screening.

There is also the annoyance of 3-D itself. It is a marketing gimmick designed (1) to justify higher ticket prices, and (2) to make piracy harder. Yet as most of the world will continue to use 2-D, pirated prints will remain a reality. The effect of 3-D adds nothing to the viewing experience, and I have never once heard an audience member complain that a movie is *not* in 3-D. Kids say they *like* it, but kids are inclined to say they *like* anything that is animated and that they get to see in a movie theater. It is the responsibility of parents to explain this useful truth: If it ain't broke, don't fix it. Every single frame of a 3-D movie gives you something to look at that is not necessary.

Now, then. Back to the *true* film, the 2-D version of *Up*. Find a theater showing it, save yourself some money, and have a terrific visual experience. This is a story as tickling to the imagination as the magical animated films of my childhood, when I naively thought that because their colors were brighter, their character outlines more defined, and their plots simpler, they were actually *more* realistic than regular films.

Up begins with a romance as sweet and lovely as any I can recall in feature animation. Two children named Carl and Ellie meet and discover they share the same dream of someday being daring explorers. In newsreels, they see the exploits of a daring adventurer named Charles Muntz (Christopher Plummer), who uses his gigantic airship to explore a lost world on a plateau in Venezuela and bring back the bones of fantastic creatures previously unknown to man. When his discoveries were accused of being faked, he flies off enraged to South America again, vowing to bring back living creatures to prove his claims.

Nothing is heard from him for years. Ellie and Carl (Ed Asner) grow up, have a courtship, marry, buy a ramshackle house and turn it into their dream home, are happy together, and grow old. This process is silent except for music (Ellie doesn't even have a voice credit). It's shown by Docter in a lovely sequence, without dialogue, that deals with the life experience in a way that is almost never found in family animation. The lovebirds save their loose change in a gallon jug intended to finance their trip to the legendary Paradise Falls, but real life gets in the way: flat tires, home repairs, medical bills. Then they make a heartbreaking discovery. This interlude is poetic and touching.

The focus of the film is on Carl's life after Ellie. He becomes a recluse, holds out against the world, keeps his home as a memorial, talks to the absent Ellie. One day he decides to pack up and fly away—literally. Having worked all his life as a balloon man, he has the equipment on hand to suspend the house from countless helium-filled balloons and fulfill his dream of seeking Paradise Falls. What he wasn't counting on was an inadvertent stowaway—Russell

(Jordan Nagai), a dutiful Wilderness Explorer Scout, who looks Asian-American to me.

What they find at Paradise Falls and what happens there I will not say. But I will describe Charles Muntz's gigantic airship that is hovering there. It's a triumph of design, and perhaps owes its inspiration, though not its appearance, to Miyazaki's *Castle in the Sky*. The exterior is nothing special: a really big zeppelin. But the interior, now, is one of those movie spaces you have the feeling you'll remember.

With vast inside spaces, the airship is outfitted like a great ocean liner from the golden age, with a stately dining room, long corridors, a display space rivaling the Natural History Museum, and attics spacious enough to harbor fighter planes. Muntz, who must be a centenarian by now, is hale, hearty, and mean, his solitary life shared only by dogs.

The adventures on the jungle plateau are satisfying in a *Mummy*/*Tomb Raider*/Indiana Jones sort of way. But they aren't the whole point of the film. This isn't a movie like *Monsters vs. Aliens,* that's mostly just frenetic action. There are stakes here, and personalities involved, and two old men battling for meaning in their lives. And a kid who, for once, isn't smarter than all the adults. And a loyal dog. And an animal sidekick. And always that house and its balloons.

I haven't spoken to Pete Docter since we met on a Disney cruise ship, where he was maybe getting inspiration for the airship interior. I know some things about his work. He likes for his films to contain some sorts of life lessons. Like Walt Disney, he doesn't mind if sometimes they're scary. In *WALL-E,* he incorporated a pointed critique of consumer excess. In *Up,* his whole film is an oblique rebuke to those who think action heroes have to be young.

Is this a daring choice for the opening night at Cannes? Not if you've seen it. Is it a significant choice? Yes, conferring the festival's august prestige upon animation. Will it be a great experience for the 2,246 members of the audience? Yes, except for that damned 3-D.

Fings Ain't Wot They Used t'Be

May 15, 2009—I want things to stay the way they always were. This is insane, because they weren't that way in the first place. I see friends who have grown older, and I want them to grow younger. In Cannes, I look around and see a new building where an old one was. A new franchise store where once there was a bookshop, or a little café, or a woman who thought she could make a living selling flowers. Here was a store where I bought my papers every morning, and Tintin comics so I could improve my reading French. Now it is a Häagen-Dazs, which has splendid ice cream but is a company name made of words in no known language.

I would take my newspapers to a little café nearby named Le Claridge. That was when all the action in Cannes was down at the other end of the Croisette, huddled in the shadow of the old Palais. Now there is a new Palais. The dusky wooden interior of Le Claridge, where you can imagine Inspector Maigret ordering a beer and filling his pipe, is a bright new brasserie, stainless steel and glass, no smoking. In the old days you could read your paper and be left alone.

I have to stop thinking like this. It will turn me into a disgruntled old man before my time. People tell me Carl Fredricksen, the grumpy hero of *Up,* looks like me. Like me? That old blockhead? I was thinking of myself more as Russell, the plucky kid who kept ringing Carl's bell and insisting on helping him across the street. I was forever driving the neighbors crazy with my retail obsessions. I'd be ringing their doorbells selling greeting cards, magazine subscriptions, the World's Finest Chocolate, even midget fire extinguishers for next to the stove, ferchristsakes. What other eleven-year-old do you know who subscribed to *Successful Salesmanship* magazine? Now I'm the old fart in *Up* who doesn't want to move to make way for skyscrapers?

I look around this town or every town I know, and it's as if architectural shape shifters have been operating overnight. No wonder *Dark City* rang a bell. Low becomes high, old becomes new, quaint becomes crass, tradition becomes the future of Tomorrowland. It's getting to where the oldest thing you can find is a monorail. Disney World may tear it down and replace it with traffic congestion. On the pedestrian market street in Cannes, I want that little rubber stamp store to still be there. You never know. I may have to buy some more rubber stamps. I got a handsome stamp there once in the shape of an upturned thumb. In those days I sent out snail mail. I rubber-stamped my envelopes with the thumbs-up, and they were all Returned to Sender. Funny. That's what thumbs-down means.

One of my difficulties is that often enough I like the new things. When the hulking new Palais was constructed, the old Palais stayed standing for a few years, housing the Directors' Fortnight. The old Palais was a decent ugly building, looking like it could have housed the Congress of Workers in a Soviet state. The new Palais was immediately nicknamed the Death Star. "A machine-gun emplacement," declared the architectural critic Billy ("Silver Dollar") Baxter. Then the old Palais was torn down and replaced by an indecent ugly building, the Noga Hilton ("the Naugahyde Hilton," said Billy). One-upping the old Palais, the Noga located the Directors' Fortnight in a subterranean cavern, so far down there were seven flights of echoing concrete stairs to scale after a movie before you were disgorged into daylight. There were elevators, but moviegoers couldn't use them; we were barred by security guards ("gorillas") employed at great expense to prevent sensible people from doing logical things.

Now I actually like the new Palais, which is approaching thirty. The Grand Theatre Lumière, with three thousand seats, is the best place in the world to see a movie. The sound is so good it's almost disturbing. In the old Palais, I saw *Apocalypse Now* and the helicopter gunships seemed to roar overhead while the "Ride of the Valkyries" played. Today, in the new Palais, I saw Jane Campion's *Bright Star,* the story of John Keats and Fanny Brawne, and when Fanny fell under the spell of Keats's romanticism and started a butterfly farm in her room, I could hear their little wings fluttering.

I had a bit of an adventure today. We were walking over to the American Pavilion, behind the Palais, and thought to use an interior shortcut that bypasses three blocks of crowds and barricades, and aims directly from the front of Palais to the left side rear of the building. This passage was built for pedestrians. Gorillas had locked the doors with padlocked chains. You might also think to go up an escalator and walk through the lobby of the Theatre Lumière and down the steps on the other side, but of course that's also forbidden. We asked instructions, but no one employed in the building knows how to get out of it. Maybe that's why they keep their jobs.

Before the morning projection, they played the same tape they've been using for years, asking people to turn off their cell phones. I happen to know that the warm, rich voice belongs to Mrs. Storer, who with her husband runs the Cannes English Language Bookshop, on the well-named rue de Bivouac Napoléon. I hope she still runs it, that is. Last time I was there, they were looking to sell it. If they have succeeded, whatever is at that address is almost certainly not another English-language bookshop.

Behind the old Palais, on the rue d'Antibes, there stood for years Le Petit Carlton, a brasserie that was the headquarters of the Left Bank of Cannes. There the New Wave got plastered and issued its manifestos. There, night after night in the 1970s, Rainer Werner Fassbinder could be seen after midnight with his coterie, dressed in leather, denim, ambition, and discontent. It was only a small, inexpensive street-corner hangout. But the first time I went to Cannes, Michael Kutza, founder of the Chicago International Film Festival, briefed me it was the place where the action was. A thousand movies were launched or torpedoed there. Now it is gone, replaced by some goddamned boutique.

And on and on. And not just in Cannes, but all over the world. In these days, traditional values have been replaced by bottom-line values. The pleasure of people who live in a place is second to the pleasure of people who invest there. In Billy Baxter's *Diary of the Cannes Film Festival* TV special, Rex Reed's narration tells us a "quaint Mediterranean fishing village is transformed once a year by the Cannes Film Festival." These days, a major Mediterranean tourist and shopping center is replaced once a year by the quaint festival.

What Were They Thinking Of?

May 16, 2009—There are few prospects more alarming than a director seized by an Idea. I don't mean an idea for a film, a story, a theme, a tone, or any of those ideas. I'm thinking of a director whose Idea takes control of his film and pounds it into the ground and leaves the audience alienated and resentful. Such a director is Brillante Mendoza of the Philippines,

and the victim of his Idea is his Official Selection at Cannes 2009, *Kinatay*. Here is a film that forces me to apologize to Vincent Gallo for calling *The Brown Bunny* the worst film in the history of the Cannes Film Festival.

After extensive recutting, the Gallo film was redeemed. I don't think editing is going to do the trick for *Kinatay*. If Mendoza wants to please any viewer except for the most tortured theorist (one of those careerists who thinks movies are about arcane academic debates and not people), he's going to have to remake his entire second half.

The sad thing is, the opening scenes in his film give promise of being absorbing and even entertaining. The film opens as the story of Peping, a young man seen taking his girl and their baby to be married in Manila in a jolly group wedding. Mendoza establishes Peping's world as a crowded jumble of street markets, open-air food stands, and people who seem to know each other. He picks up cash sometimes by doing odd jobs for local criminals. He will need more funds as a young married man and is offered a higher paying job.

It is unlikely you will ever see this film, but if there's a possibility, know that spoilers follow.

Peping joins a group of other professional criminals assigned to teach a lesson to a thirtyish prostitute who owes money because of drugs. She is bound, gagged, and thrown into the back of a van. Now commences the Idea. It is Mendoza's conceit that his Idea will make a statement, or evoke a sensation, or demonstrate something—if only he makes the rest of the film as unpleasant to the eyes, the ears, the mind, and the story itself as possible. This he succeeds in doing beyond his wildest dreams.

For at least forty-five minutes, maybe an hour, maybe an eternity, Mendoza gives us Queasy-Cam shots, filmed at night in very low light, of the interior and exterior of the van as they drive a long distance outside Manila to a remote house. The woman is thrown on a bed, she pleads for her life, she is eventually murdered, her body is hacked into pieces, the pieces are wrapped in plastic, and the body parts are thrown out of the van at intervals during the return journey. No drama is developed. No story purpose is revealed. The woman cannot pay at a later date. She has learned her lesson, but to what avail? There is little dialogue.

Peping did not know the woman would be murdered.

On the sound track, there are traffic noises, loud bangings, clashings, hammerings, and squealings of tires. They continue on and on and on. They are cranked so high we recall the guitar setting of "11" in *This Is Spinal Tap.* They are actively hostile. They are illustrated by murk. You can't see the movie and you can't bear to listen to it. Much later, Peping is deposited back in Manila by the van and hails a taxi. We get incessant sights and sounds of the taxi driving, as the night gives way to pale shades of dawn. The taxi blows a tire. The driver gets out to change it. Peping stands on the curb, trying to find another taxi. Loud, real loud, traffic noises. The tire is changed. The taxi driver asks him to get back in the cab. Peping doesn't want to. Finally he does. Some shots of meat being chopped for food, and of his wife and baby. The movie is over. I should add that the movie is based on current events, that some of the vivisectionists are policemen, and that it cannot be shown in the Phillippines.

This is an Idea. An idée fixe, as the French so usefully put it. As Pierre Henri Castel observes, "*Au sens banal, idée fixe est l'équivalent d'obsession.*" Poor Mendoza knows that his strategy is alienating, his scenes unpleasant and painful, his audience recoiling. That is the Idea. You tell me why. Oh, someone will. You mark my words. There will be critics who fancy themselves theoreticians, who will defend this unbearable experience and lecture those plebians like me who missed the whole Idea. I will remain serene while my ignorance is excoriated. I am a human being with relatively reasonable tastes. And in that role, not in the role of film critic, I declare that there may not be ten people in the world who will buy a ticket to this movie and feel the money was well spent.

But there is no reasoning with a man with an idée fixe. He knows with a deep certainty that he is right. He will demonstrate that to us. He is an auteur. Surely we will recognize his inspiration and applaud his bravery. He has filled his own bucket with wet cement and stepped into it. For a time he could wriggle his toes. But now the cement has set, and he is frozen in place with the results of his decision. He will sink or swim.

I've seen several other films here already, but *Kinatay* seized my attention. I was talking the other day with Thierry Frémaux, the director of the festival, and I mentioned that he has many big names among the directors of this year's Official Selections. "Yes," he said, "but not every great director makes only great films. And we cannot show only great films, although every film is one we believe deserves to be seen." Frémaux knows his films, his festival, his audience. His taste is exceptional. He was not, of course, referring to any particular films or directors. I quote him because some of my film critic colleagues, staggering out into the light after *Kinatay,* were banging their palms against their foreheads and crying out, "What got into them when they programmed this film?" To them I say, "Now, now. They can't only show great films."

* * *

One of the best films I've seen here is Lee Daniels's *Precious,* the story of a physically and mentally abused poor black girl from the ghetto, who summons the inner strength to fight back for her future. It contains two great performances, by Gabourey "Gabby" Sidibe, in the title role, and Mo'Nique as her pathetic mother. Sidibe is the life force personified. Mo'Nique has a closing monologue that reduced some of us to tears.

Even Now Already Is It in the World

May 17, 2009—There's electricity in the air. Every seat is filled, even the little fold-down seats at the end of every row. It is the first screening of Lars von Trier's *Antichrist,* and we are ready for anything. We'd better be. Von Trier's film goes beyond malevolence into the monstrous. Never before have a man and woman inflicted more pain upon each other in a movie. We looked in disbelief. There were piteous groans. Sometimes a voice would cry out, "No!" At certain moments there was nervous laughter. When it was all over, we staggered up the aisles. Manohla Dargis, the merry film critic of the *New York Times,* confided that she left softly singing "That's Entertainment!"

Whether this is a bad, good, or great film is entirely beside the point. It is an audacious spit in the eye of society. It says we harbor an undreamed-of capacity for evil. It transforms a psychological treatment into torture undreamed of in the dungeons of history. Torturers might have been capable of such actions, but they would have lacked the imagination. Von Trier is not so much making a film about violence as making a film to inflict violence upon us, perhaps as a salutary experience. It's been reported that he suffered from depression during and after the film. You can tell. This is the most despairing film I've ever seen.

If, as they say, you are not prepared for "disturbing images," I advise you to just stop reading now.

The film involves a couple, He and She, whose infant child falls out a window and smashes to the pavement while they are making explicit love. They feel devastating grief. He, a psychologist, takes She off medications, and they go to live in their secluded hideaway in the forest, a cottage named Eden.

He subjects her to probing questions and the discussion of the Meaning of It All, which must affect her like a needle stab to an inflamed tooth. He is quite intelligent and insightful, and brings passive aggression to a brutally intimate level. Then she wounds him, and while he's unconscious she drills a hole through his leg and bolts a grindstone to it. He drags himself into the forest and tries to hide in an animal burrow. She finds him, and pounds him with a shovel to force him deeper. Then she tries to bury him alive. I won't mention two gruesome scenes involving the genital areas.

What does this metaphor (with a prologue, an epilogue, and four chapters) mean? The dinner conversations all over town must not have been appetizing. Some read it this way: Perhaps the world began with man evil instead of good, guilty instead of innocent. That the Garden of Eden was visited by the Antichrist, not the Lord. That man's Original Sin was not eating from the Tree of Knowledge, but not vomiting forth knowledge and purging himself.

This will all be discussed at great length. What can be said is that von Trier, after what many found the agonizing boredom of his previous Cannes films *Dogville* and *Manderlay*, has made a film that is not boring. Unendurable, perhaps, but not boring. For relief I am looking forward to the overnight reviews of those who think they can explain exactly what it means. In this case, perhaps, a film should not mean, but be.

* * *

You see strangely assorted films all in a row here. The first eight Cannes films I've seen have been: (a) a Pixar animated comedy about a man who ties balloons to his house and floats into the rain forest; (b) a film about the young love of the doomed John Keats; (c) a devastating African-American drama about an abused fat girl; (d) a Korean film about a mother defending her dimwitted son against a murder charge; (e) a Filipino film with forty-five minutes of an impossible-to-see, too-loud-to-listen-to kidnapping; (f) a Hong Kong film about a French chef's violent revenge; (g) a French bourgeois family drama about a bankrupt movie producer; and (h) *Antichrist*. First thing tomorrow, the new Almodóvar film, about a film director who loses his eyesight and the love of his life. At least there will be Penelope Cruz to look at, if only he could see her.

* * *

Cannes has always cast a wide net. It was here I first began to learn more about violent Asian films that were not "chop-socky" trash but in fact polished genre exercises with their own auteurs. After seeing my first Takeshi Kitano film in the awesome Lumière, I began to suspect he might become one of my favorite directors. The legions of Western fans for Hong Kong films, in particular, may have Cannes to thank.

Speaking of Western fans, this morning I saw a classic Western named *Vengeance*. There were certain parallels with Clint Eastwood's *The Unforgiven;* it had gunslingers striding down streets deserted by the townspeople and a score (guitars and lonely flutes) that Sergio Leone might have envied. Was this film set in Durango or Tombstone? No, it was set in modern-day Macao, the Las Vegas of China. Was the hero played by Eastwood? No, he was played by the sixty-five-year-old Johnny Hallyday, known as "the French Elvis." Who was the hero of this Western? Was he named Slade or Cain or Shane? No, he had a good French name, Costello. Who was the film directed by? Johnnie To, who has also made *The Heroic Trio, My Left Eye Sees Ghosts, Running on Karma,* and forty-six other films since 1986.

This was really a good film. The plot is off the shelf: Costello's family is murdered, and he vows revenge. But the "twists," now, that's where the pleasure comes. And the acting, dead serious and low-key, but with some jovial fat men allowed. And a stunning visual sense. And pacing that made it compulsively watchable—just the curative for me after the previous evening's excruciating *Kinatay.*

This is not the place for my review. Let me just mention two details. If you know Johnny Hallyday, picture him standing over a dying crime boss in the street. He has plugged him with about a dozen rounds. And before firing a final fatal round, he thoughtfully and quite seriously observes, "That's your coat."

And then imagine a gunfight in a vast open field, seen from a high angle. Three men surrounded by enemies. The field containing for some reason tightly compacted bales of waste newsprint, almost as high as a man. The three in the center using three bales as cover. The dozens around advancing in a wall of forward-tumbling bales, and firing from behind them. Words do not convey the macabre visual effect of this scene.

The film involves professional killers quite prepared to sacrifice their lives for their values. No, not for their criminal code. For their deep human values. They are craftsmen who respect their work. They will perform it well and faithfully even if the man who hired them knows nothing of it and is away playing with some little children on the beach. These are values that could come from . . . a Western. And recall that the Western began with Greek drama.

A Devil's Advocate for *Antichrist*

May 19, 2009—Lars von Trier's new film will not leave me alone. A day after many members of the audience recoiled at its first Cannes showing, *Antichrist* is brewing a scandal here; I am reminded of the tumult following the 1976 premiere of Oshima's *In the Realm of the Senses* and its castration scene. I said I was looking forward to von Trier's overnight reviews, and I haven't been disappointed. Those who thought it was good thought it was very, very good ("Something completely bizarre, massively uncommercial and strangely perfect" —Damon Wise, *Empire*), and those who thought it was bad found it horrid ("Lars von Trier cuts a big fat art-film fart with *Antichrist*" —Todd McCarthy, *Variety*).

I rarely find a serious film by a major direc-

tor to be this disturbing. Its images are a fork in the eye. Its cruelty is unrelenting. Its despair is profound. Von Trier has a way of affecting his viewers like that. After his *Breaking the Waves* premiered at Cannes in 1996, Georgia Brown of the *Village Voice* fled to the restroom in emotional turmoil and Janet Maslin of the *New York Times* followed to comfort her. After this one, Richard and Mary Corliss blogged at Time.com that *Antichrist* presented the spectacle of a director going mad.

Enough time has passed since I saw the film for me to process my visceral reaction and take a few steps back. I can understand why this confrontational film has so sharply divided its early critics. It is fascinating to me that there's a sharp divide between American, Canadian, and British critics monitored by the Tomatometer, and a cross-section of French critics monitored by *Le Film Français,* a French equivalent to *Variety,* which is published daily at the festival. Reflect that French critics are often noted for more intellectual, theoretical reviews, and American critics are more often populist. Which group hated or approved of the movie more?

Think again. A surprising 44 percent of the early Tomatometer critics gave positive reviews. *Le Film Français* asks its national panel to vote on every film in the Official Selection and the Un Certain Regard section. They can vote as follows: (1) Must win the Palme d'Or; (2) Three stars ("Passionately"); (3) Two stars ("Good"); (4) One star ("One likes it a little"); or (5) *Pas de tout* ("Not at all"). The French critical consensus for *Antichrist* is . . . *Pas de tout.* I can't recall when another Official Selection by an important director has been disliked so strongly.

* * *

A reader signing himself Scott D posted this comment on my blog after my first entry on the film: "If it is in fact the most despairing film you've ever seen, shouldn't it be considered a monumental achievement? Despair is such a significant aspect of the human condition (particularly in the modern Western world) so how can this not be a staggeringly important film, given your statement?"

There is truth to what Scott D says. In the first place, it's important to note that *Antichrist* is not a *bad* film. It is a powerfully made film that contains material many audiences will find repulsive or unbearable. The performances by Willem Dafoe and Charlotte Gainsbourg are heroic and fearless. Von Trier's visual command is striking. The use of music is evocative; no score, but operatic and liturgical arias. And if you can think beyond what he shows to what he implies, its depths are frightening.

I cannot dismiss this film. It is a real film. It will remain in my mind. Von Trier has reached me and shaken me. It is up to me to decide what that means. I think the film has something to do with religious feeling. It is obvious to anyone who saw *Breaking the Waves* that von Trier's sense of spirituality is intense, and that he can envision the supernatural as literally present in the world. His reference is Catholicism. Raised by a communist mother and a socialist father in a restrictive environment, he was told as an adult that his father was not his natural parent, and he renounced that man's Judaism to convert, at the age of thirty, to the Catholic Church. It was at about the same age that von Trier founded the Dogma movement, with its monkish asceticism.

If you have to ask what a film symbolizes, it doesn't. With this one, I didn't have to ask. It told me. I believe *Antichrist* may be an exercise in alternative theology: von Trier's version of those passages in Genesis where Man is cast from Eden, and Satan assumes a role in the world.

The prologue, a masterful sequence of lovely black-and-white slow motion, shows a couple, He and She, making love while their innocent baby becomes fascinated by the sight of snow falling outside an open window, climbs up on the sill, and falls to his death. This is Man's Fall from Grace. Consequently, She (Charlotte Gainsbourg) falls into guilt and depression so deep she is hospitalized. That is one-half of Original Sin. The character named He (Willem Dafoe) insists she cut off her medication. He will cure her himself. That is the other half. Her sin is Despair. His is Pride. These are the two greatest sins against God.

He and She go to their country home, named Eden. He subjects her to merciless talk therapy, relentlessly chipping away at her rationalizations and defenses, *explaining* to her why she is wrong to feel the way she does. I suspect many of the reviews will focus on the

physical violence She inflicts upon He in the next act of the film. It is important to note that the earlier psychological violence He inflicts is equally brutal. He talks and talks, boring away at her defenses, tearing at her psyche, exposing her. Listen to Dafoe's voice in the trailer. It could be used for Satan's temptation of Christ in the desert.

There is little sense at Eden of real lives together; He and She are locked in combat that seems their inescapable destiny after the loss of their child. The violence in the film is explicit, but is it intended to be realistic? I don't believe you can have a hole drilled clean through your leg, an iron bar pushed through it, and a grindstone bolted to it, and do much other than be in agony. That He can even speak, let alone crawl into the woods, contend with her, and defend himself, is remarkable. I think the violence illustrates the depth of her venom and that She, like He, will stop at nothing.

Images suggesting Bosch are evoked toward the end of the film. Human limbs rise up to grasp He and She as they have sex. There is a talking dog, bluebirds, a deer, inhabiting the world of Man. At the end He stands atop a hill while a legion of unnatural humans ascends toward him, evoking *Night of the Living Dead.* The suggestion is biblical, but not from the Bible we know. The human figures are not naked, climbing toward birth, but clothed, climbing toward death. After their fall in the Garden of Eden, Adam and Eve learned shame and covered their nakedness. In this evil world, they are created covered, and by their sins are cast out into nakedness.

Von Trier's original intention, it's said, was to reveal at the end that the world was created by Satan, not God: that evil, not goodness, reigns ascendant. His finished film reflects the same idea, but not as explicitly. The title *Antichrist* is the key. This is a mirror world. It is a sin to lose Knowledge rather than to eat of its fruit and gain it. She and He are behaving with such cruelty toward each other not as actual people, but as creatures inhabiting a moral mirror world. As much as they might comfort and love each other in *our* world after losing a child, so to the same degree in the mirror world they inflame each other's pain and act out hatred. This would be the world created by Satan.

If I am right, then von Trier has proceeded

with perfect logic. Just as a good world could not contain too much beauty and charity, an evil world could not have too much cruelty and hatred. He is making a moral statement. I'm not sure if he's telling us how things are or warning us of what could come. But I am sure he has not compromised his vision. He has been brave and strong and made a film that fully reflects the pain of his own feelings. And his actors have been remarkably courageous in going all the way with him.

In his own defense here at Cannes, von Trier has described himself "the greatest director in the world." Well, if *Le Film Français* says he is merde, what can he be expected to say? He is certainly one of the most heroic directors in the world, uncompromising, resolute. He goes all the way and takes no prisoners. Do I believe his film "works"? Would I "recommend" it? Is it a "good" film? I believe von Trier doesn't care how I or anyone else would reply to those questions. He had the ideas and feelings, he saw into the pit, he made the film, and here it is.

Tarantino the Glourious Basterd

May 20, 2009—Leave it to Quentin Tarantino to find a climax unique in the history of war movies. Also trust QT to get away with a war movie that consists largely of his unique dialogue style, in which a great deal of action is replaced by talk about the possibilities of action. His *Inglourious Basterds,* which premiered Wednesday morning here at Cannes, is a screenplay eight years in the writing, and you can't fill 148 minutes with descriptions of special effects. At least not if you're a motor-mouth like Tarantino.

My review will await the film's August 21, 2009, opening. I know, I wrote a lot about *Antichrist,* but with this one I'd like to hold out until opening day. No, that doesn't mean I disliked it. It means it inspired other kinds of thoughts—about Cannes, Tarantino, and the way the movie industry seems to be going these days.

"Why, Mr. Tarantino," he was asked at the press conference after the film, "did you choose to bring the film to Cannes?" In other words, why didn't you open it with another one of those god-awful junkets where entertainment reporters are plied with chilled shrimp and cycled through three-minute sound-bite ops in a Four Seasons somewhere? You know, a con-trolled environment designed to churn out mindless publicity? Why expose it to the glare of Cannes and to the baying of the hounds of hell, otherwise known as the world's film critics? A place where there are more questions at a press conference for the director of a film than for the stars?

"I make movies for Planet Earth," Tarantino answered, "and Cannes represents that." Not Planet Hollywood (whose branch here has long since closed). He said it never occurred to him to open his film anywhere else. His shooting schedule was under the gun of today's Cannes deadline. "We started talking about the film in August," Brad Pitt said, "and he said he would be here in May. And here we are."

I remember Tarantino the first time he came to Cannes in May 1992, with *Reservoir Dogs.* Chaz and I had him all to ourselves at lunch down on the beach. We picked up the check. When he came in 1994 with *Pulp Fiction,* there was a party that took up most of the top floor of the Carlton. In other words, "something happened," and it wasn't that the freeloaders got chilled lobster. What happened was that Tarantino took his place in the Cannes pantheon. It really does mean more to win the Palme d'Or than the Oscar for best film. It means more for the director, for sure. Hell, the best film Oscar is accepted by the *producer.*

QT is sometimes criticized for including too many references (some say whole scenes) from other movies in his own work. There are legends about his days as a video store clerk, memorizing B movies from the $1.99 bin. But the borrowed, or repurposed, or inspired, or quoted movie material in his films is there not because he lacks imagination but because he has too much. He loves movies with a fervor that inspires him to absorb us not only in his films but in the films he loves. His arms are wide and gather us in.

Inglourious Basterds is, I believe, the only war movie with its climactic scene set in a movie theater. The only war movie with a critical last-minute confrontation in the projection booth. The only war movie with a lecture on the fire hazard of nitrate film stock. The only one that pays much attention to the names of such great directors as Pabst and Clouzot. Tarantino's hero, played by Brad Pitt, is named Lt. Aldo Raine, which is as close as you can get to

Aldo Ray, the star of *Battle Cry* (1955), which costarred Van Heflin, who also gets a shout-out in *Basterds.*

Cannes has become, in a way, the sundowner party of *Day of the Locusts.* There was once a world, much deprecated at the time, of patriarchal studios, star machines, genre movies, fan magazines, searchlights, and filmmakers who wanted their movies to play big to everybody all over the world. Now what survives of that old world, hunched and inward, is no longer show business but just—business. A screenplay is evaluated for its demographic appeal, its video game possibilities, its spin-offs, its potential for commercial tie-ins. The suspense of its premiere is diluted by pale gnomelike creatures hunched over computers down in their parents' basements, busy as bees ripping off video copies of new films and posting them on the Internet, to be downloaded by thieves who get more of a thrill out of stealing a film than by watching it. At least when there's a premiere at Cannes, you know it's a premiere. Some of the entries don't even have complete IMDb entries yet. Fans by the thousands cheer the arrivals. The red carpet becomes a fashion show staged by the Paris design houses, with the world watching on cable.

The critics here are not on junkets. Many of them paid their own way, because if you're a movie critic, baby, this is where you gotta get your ass. Back home, most editors care more about Brad Pitt than Quentin Tarantino. That would be all right if they cared about Pitt for the right reasons. But the American press has been dumbed down so much that some papers seem edited for an audience that does most of its reading off of TV screens. I ran into an old friend who has freelanced for *USA Today.* "Yesterday, Lars von Trier's *Antichrist* was the big story," he told me. "*USA Today* featured coverage of Jim Carrey as Ebenezer Scrooge, arriving at the Carlton Hotel with Jenny McCarthy in a horse-drawn carriage."

There can be news value in such events. Consider the crowds Jerry Seinfeld drew when, dressed as a bee, he slid down a wire from the roof of the Carlton to promote *Bee Movie.* To be sure, much of the press just wanted to have someone on the scene if the cable snapped. Now that *would* be newsworthy, a photo of a crumpled and bloody bumblebee suit.

Cannes behaves as if such a world doesn't exist. Today the talk is about Tarantino. Yesterday it was about Lars von Trier. Here it doesn't matter if you liked his new film. *At least you've heard of him.* There are students here waiting tables in the beachfront pavilions to finance their stays, their hopes of "networking" and making their own films someday. Here there is a young man named Scott Collette who e-mailed me saying, "I am at the greatest film festival in the world, and it looks like I won't be able to get into a single film." He has a festival job with a distributor renting space across the street from the Palais. I advised him to try what worked for our granddaughter Raven—stand in front of the Palais holding a sign saying "Invitation!" and hope someone will give them a ticket.

After *Inglourious Basterds* today, Scott introduced himself outside on the sidewalk. I asked if he'd seen any films. "Not yet. And I got my boss's pass confiscated for using it to try to sneak in." I guess he doesn't look much like the ID photo of a middle-aged distributor. Chaz told him she had heard stories of people with the wrong passes being taken down into the bowels of the Palais and lectured sternly by security.

It happened that at the Tarantino press conference, we were seated near Harvey Weinstein, who with his brother Bob is releasing the movie. The Weinsteins were once kids here without a ticket. "We were hanging around the stage door, hoping to get in and make our way around to the front," Harvey told me. "An official festival limo pulled up, and Clint Eastwood got out. We probably looked needy. He sized us up, held open the door, and let us in. To this day, we both make it a point to let someone into the Palais."

Note to Scott Collette: Someday when you are a big-time distributor with an office across from the Palais, you will remember this story and do the right thing.

Oh, the Days Dwindle Down, to a Precious Few . . .

May 22, 2009—I think I may have just seen the 2010 Oscar winner for Best Foreign Film. Whether it will win the Palme d'Or here at Cannes is another matter. It may be too much of a *movie* movie. It's named *A l'origine,* by

Xavier Giannoli, and is one of several titles I want to discuss in a little festival catch-up. Based on an incredible true story, it involves an insignificant thief, just released from prison, who becomes involved in an impromptu con game that results in the actual construction of a stretch of highway. At the beginning he has no plans to build a highway. He simply sees a way to swindle a contractor out of fifteen thousand euros. He is sad, defeated, unwanted, apart from his wife and child, sleeping on a pal's sofa. What happens is not caused by him or desired by him. It simply happens to him.

This is one of those movies that catches you in its spell. It's a hell of a story. There's a difference between caring what happens in a movie and merely waiting to see what will happen. The hero, who calls himself Phillip, ends by bringing about an enterprise involving millions of euros, hundreds of workers, and tons of massive earth-moving machinery, falling in love with the lady mayor, and becoming a good man, all without ever saying very much. I was reminded of Chance the Gardener in *Being There*. Phillip is shy, socially unskilled, inarticulate, apparently the opposite of a con man. To repeat: There is a true story involved here. Some facts are offered at the end. The highway, which the workers essentially built on their own, with the con man as "management," was completed on time, under budget, and up to code.

The character is played by the veteran French star François Cluzet, who played the lead in last year's *Tell No One*, the top-grossing foreign film in the North American market. That was the superb thriller about the dead wife who wasn't dead. A handsome, undernourished-looking man in his fifties, with a pleasantly lined face, looking something like Dustin Hoffman, Cluzet costars with Emmanuelle Devos, whom you will recognize from a dozen French films. Gerard Depardieu has an important, if overbilled, supporting role. Cluzet's performance is the key. He never says much, allows people to assume things he has not claimed, allows them in a sense to con themselves. He's more fascinating than the impostor in Spielberg's *Catch Me If You Can*.

It has been a very good year for French films at Cannes. One of the most-loved has

been *Les Herbes Folles* (*The Wild Grass*) by Alain Resnais, whose *Last Year at Marienbad* (1961) was one of the founding films of the New Wave. Now eighty-six, looking fit and youthful on the red carpet, he has made one of those films perhaps only conceivable in old age. It is about an unlikely and fateful chain of events that to a young person might seem like coincidence but to an old one illustrates the likelihood that most of what happens in our lives comes about by sheer accident. To realize this is to become more philosophical; the best-laid plans of mice and men are irrelevant to the cosmos.

To explain how this could all possibly happen would be not wild (*folles*) but a folly (*une folie*). Here is how it begins: The heroine Josepha (Sabine Azéma) decides one day to buy a pair of shoes. That leads to her purse being snatched. That leads to Georges (André Dussollier) finding her wallet. That leads to everything else. Resnais uses an omniscient narrator, as he must, because only from an all-knowing point of view can the labyrinth of connections be seen. He films in a colorful, leisurely style; not taking even the most serious things too very seriously, because, after all, they need never have happened.

Le Père des mes Enfants (*The Father of My Children*) belongs to the genre of the country house movie, French division. British country house movies are a mix of Jane Austen, Agatha Christie, and Evelyn Waugh, with Wodehouse as the mixologist. French country house movies tend to tell bourgeois family stories, including children of all ages, and they tilt toward the pastoral. This film, the third by Mia Hansen-Løve, only twenty-eight and a rising star of French cinema, stars Louis-Do de Lencquesaing as a movie producer who is willing to take chances on serious auteurs and is currently deep in debt, not least because of his backing of a temperamental perfectionist not a million miles separated from Lars von Trier. The story is said to be inspired by the real-life producer Humbert Balsan, who made von Trier's *Manderlay* (2005).

The producer is a nice man. Too nice. Too loving, too loyal, too driven. We begin by following him through desperate attempts to keep his company afloat, and then watch as his wife (Chiara Caselli) and children try to deal with the impossibilities he has created. Some of this happens in Paris, much of it happens in his country house, and the focus is not on film production but on family. I was reminded of two other recent French films: the current *Summer Hours,* about an old lady leaving a legacy for her family to deal with, and last year's *A Christmas Tale,* with Catherine Deneuve as a mother less worried about her death than her children are.

Los Abrazos Rotos (*Broken Embraces*) is the much-awaited new Pedro Almodóvar collaboration with his recent muse, Penelope Cruz. It's about an old man remembering a woman he loved. Lluís Homar (*Bad Education*) plays a director who went blind in an auto accident that killed his love (Cruz), who was his secretary, and whom he met as a call girl. Now he works as a successful screenwriter, using touch-typing. One day he's approached by an ambitious young filmmaker named Ray X (Ruben Ochandiano), who he suspects is the son of the evil millionaire he holds responsible for the woman's death.

As always with Almodóvar, it isn't nearly as simple as that. Using interlocking flashbacks, the film reconstructs what actually happened in a combination of overwrought Sirkian melodrama and Hitchcock. The music, indeed, pays homage to Bernard Herrmann's work, particularly his score for Hitchcock's *Vertigo,* and the film's romantic entanglements pay homage to Almodóvar's own pansexual stories. Cruz is a life force, but Homar's work is the film's engine.

It must be a year for movies about old men remembering lost parents and lovers. One of the more unexpected successes here is *The Time That Remains,* a deadpan Palestinian comedy written by, directed, and starring Elia Suleiman. Read that again: *a deadpan Palestinian comedy.* And not especially political, although almost all stories set in Israel must be political to one degree or another.

The film, dedicated to the memory of Suleiman's parents, shows his father as a firebrand gun maker, gradually aging into an old guy who sits outside a café with his pals, smokes, smokes, smokes, and drinks coffee as if he has kidneys of steel. This family lives in a small but pleasant flat with a nice view of Nazareth; they're part of a friendly community.

The film consists of fairly self-contained vignettes of human nature, reminding me curiously of the Czech New Wave comedies. The character played by Suleiman, satire linked with autobiography, a solemn, silent figure with dark shadows under his eyes, is pokerfaced and never speaks. He simply stands and regards all that happens for sixty years. I don't know what that makes it sound like to you. I was surprised by how it grew on me. The karaoke scene is unreasonably funny.

Irène, by Alain Cavalier, seventy-seven, a frequent Cannes winner and nominee, is a personal, subjective, experimental meditation on the 1972 death of the actress and beauty pageant winner Irène Tunc. Unlike Cavalier's conventional narrative films (*Thérèse*), this one actually shows very few speaking actors. It is almost all done with his own first-person narration, and a handheld camera that examines diaries and other relics of a life ended but not forgotten. More than half of Cavalier's own lifetime has passed since Irene died, and his old-man attempts at amends are very touching. The film received an unfairly dismissive review from *Variety.*

One of the final Official Selections, Gaspar Noé's *Enter the Void,* is a nearly unendurable in-depth investigation of a very shallow idea. The camera positions itself close behind the head of a callow youth, jug-eared and crew-cut, as he films with his video camera and then *becomes* the camera as the remainder of the film is seen from his POV. The hero, an orphaned American, lives with his sister in Tokyo, where she is a nude dancer and possibly a hooker, and he is a druggie and possibly a dealer. If they don't practice incest, you could have fooled me.

After he dies in a shooting at a nightclub named the Void, we live through subjective scenes intended as what he sees after death. They involve flashbacks, replays of what has already happened, and hovering above what's happening now. In Noé's view, the soul does survive the body, which for much of this time has been cremated. These scenes are spaced out with sound and light abstractions resembling 1960s underground films past their shelf life. If Noé's camera plunges into a vortex once, it does so a hundred times: Into white holes, black holes, psychedelic kaleidoscopic holes, over and over and over again, representing the delightful diversity of the Void. The visuals might have been juicier if he had known about fractals. The film includes obligatory genitals of both genders, and one of the voids the POV plunges into is the mess in a stainless steel pan after an abortion.

Looking for Eric, by the great British director Ken Loach, is a disappointment, his least interesting work. It involves a hapless man named Eric, from Manchester, whose life takes a turn for the better after the spirit of Eric Cantona, the great star footballer for Manchester United, materializes in his bedroom. Cantona plays himself, produced the film, and may have been involved in the financing, which could explain how it came to be made. What I can't explain is why Loach chose to make it. Maybe after so many great films he simply wanted to relax with a genre comedy. It has charm and Loach's fine eye, and the expected generic payoff.

But I had a problem I'm almost ashamed to admit. Loach has always made it a point to use actors employing working-class accents, reflecting the fact that accent is a class marker. I've always been able to understand them—it's the music as much as the words, and then I start to hear the words. This time, his star Steve Evets uses an accent so thick many of the English themselves might not be able to understand it. Ironically, the Frenchman Eric Cantona is easier to understand.

* * *

The streets of Cannes, a madhouse a week ago, have grown strangely quieter. The press screenings have empty seats. The daily festival newspapers have called it a wrap. Old friends who have been racing against time all week are now finally making plans to meet at dinner. There are a few films still to play, and some to be repeated. Then the jury will appear on stage in the Auditorium Lumière and reveal its awards, and there will be cheers and boos and a big party under an enormous tent for about one thousand of the survivors. Sometimes I feel I have spent my whole life at Cannes, and the rest is just trips out of town.

* * *

Now for something completely different. I was attending the first Cannes screening for *Le Père de mes Enfants.* Before the film began, Thierry Frémaux, director of the festival, appeared onstage and introduced Mia Hansen-

Løve and her entire cast, and they walked down a side and ascended to the stage. Then they did something unexpected and rather beautiful. They didn't line up in a row and face the audience. That's what a movie cast always does. I've seen it dozens, maybe hundreds, of times. You have, too. With perhaps an older actress holding hands with a little one. They file on, they file off.

What these actors did was make a statement with body language. They *stood around.* They behaved as if they were really there. They took possession. As if they were at a cocktail reception. None of them faced the audience while standing at attention. They relaxed. Some stood a little forward, others a little behind. Some looked offstage, or at a friend in the audience, or at one another. They spoke a little among themselves. They didn't ignore the audience, nor were they very aware of it. They were relaxed and at all times graceful. Annie Leibovitz couldn't have arranged them any better for a *Vanity Fair* cover. Whether this was planned I have no idea. I doubt it. It felt natural and instinctive. That's all. I just thought I'd mention it.

"I Got In!" and Other Tales

May 23, 2009—Michael Barker is not only a prime moving force in indie film distribution but also one of the funniest raconteurs alive. He and Tom Bernard, also a funny man, have been the copresidents of Sony Pictures Classics since 1992, which qualifies them as the Methuselahs among studio heads. Their films have won 24 Academy Awards and 101 nominations. He knows everybody and takes little mental notes, resulting in an outpouring of stories I could tell you, but then I would have to shoot you.

Like many funny people, he exerts a magnetic attraction for funny experiences. He attracted one just the other day, when he went to see the new Paul Verhoeven film. "I'm looking at the screening schedule and I can't believe my eyes," he was telling us the other night. This was at dinner on the Carlton Terrace with Richard and Mary Corliss, Chaz, and our granddaughter Raven. "I'd never heard anything about this. I mean, Verhoeven just made *The Black Book,* for chrissakes!

"It's titled *Teenagers,* and it's screening in one

of those little marketplace theaters in the Palais. I figure it must be a rough cut under another title or something. The place is jammed. People are fighting to get in. I'm able to get a seat. There are people sitting in the aisles, standing against the wall, flat on their backs on the floor in front of the screen. You can't breathe.

"The lights go down, they have some titles with names I've ever heard of, except for Paul Verhoeven. The movie starts, and a kid takes off his shirt. This is not the Paul Verhoeven I know. There's a stampede for the exit. People on the floor are almost trampled. I finally get out and the director is standing by the door. Sure enough, it says Paul Verhoeven on his badge. I ask him to his face if he stole the badge.

"You're thinking of the other Paul Verhoeven," he says. "He's my cousin."

* * *

It's been a slow year for sales, what with the economy and all, but Barker and Bernard bought the rights to Jacques Audiard's *A Prophet,* Michael Haneke's *The White Ribbon,* and Jan Kounen's *Coco Chanel and Igor Stravinsky.* They were up-front investors in *Broken Embraces* by Pedro Almodóvar, his ninth film they've released.

* * *

We have our first winners. The jury for the Un Certain Regard section, which votes a day ahead of the Palme jury, has given its Grand Prix to *Dogtooth,* by Giorgos Lanthimos of Greece, about three children raised by their parents in a house behind a wall and taught to remain childish, fear the outside world, and learn nothing about it.

The Jury Prize went to *Police, Adjective,* by Corneliu Porumboiu of Romania, more evidence of the remarkable recent renaissance in Romanian cinema. It's about a cop who is reluctant to destroy a life by making a marijuana arrest.

There was a Special Prize for *No One Knows About Persian Cats,* by Bahman Ghobadi of Iran, about two hip-hop musicians in Tehran who scheme to gain passports to Europe even though they have prison records. Another Special Prize went to *Le Père de mes Enfants* (*Father of My Children*), by Mia Hansen-Løve.

The Iranian film has generated much discussion simply because it is from Iran, a nation with a great cinematic richness that is much more diverse and complex than many Americans realize.

* * *

Faithful readers will recall that after I filed an earlier report from Cannes, I received this message from a reader named Scott Collette:

"I am currently in Cannes, working out of an office on the Croisette across from the Palais. Work ends Tuesday/Wednesday and I am here until the end of the festival and I am very worried that when all is said and done, I will have attended the largest film festival in the world and will have not seen any films. This is already probably the longest I have gone in my life and I'm going through withdrawals. I have no credentials as they are very expensive."

I took sympathy. No reader of mine should come to Cannes and return home empty-handed. Cannes is not a public festival but a business convention. However, our granddaughter Raven blogged about getting a ticket to a screening in the Lumière. She joined the throngs of hopefuls outside the Palais at every screening, holding up signs saying: "*Invitation, si'l vous plait!*"

Saturday afternoon, Chaz, Carol Iwata, and I were leaving after the screening of *Map of the Sounds of Tokyo.* Standing there in the lobby was Scott Collette, proudly holding up his ticket. "I got in!" he said. I asked him how. "What Raven did," he said. "I begged."

* * *

Newcomers to screenings in the Auditorium Debussy may be puzzled by an event that frequently takes place just after the lights go down. A voice, sounding like a dog baying at the moon, cries out despairingly: "Raoul! Raooouuulll!"

It is possibly a different person every time. This is an ancient Cannes tradition. Legend had it that one day in the infancy of the festival, a guy was saving a seat for his pal Raoul. The screening was packed and he was having trouble defending the seat. In desperation, he called out.

The fact that this practice has survived for thirty-five years that I know about, kept alive by people who have never met one another, explained to each curious new festivalgoer, is an excellent demonstration of the Richard Dawkins theory of memes. A meme is an idea, phrase, cliché, or tune that leaps from one mind to another in its attempt to survive, just as genes leap from body to body.

Someday years from now, somebody reading this will call out for "Raoul" at a festival. Who knows. Maybe it will be Scott Collette. Remember: Only the Debussy. Never the Lumière. I can't begin to explain how gauche that would be.

And, at Last, the Winners Are . . .

May 24, 2009—Now I understand why Cannes 2009 opened with Pixar's *Up*. They knew what was coming. Has there ever been a more violent group of Official Selections? More negative about humanity? More despairing? With a greater variety of gruesome, sadistic, perverted acts? You know you're in deep water when the genuinely funniest film in the festival is by a Palestinian in today's Israel, whose material includes a firing squad, a mother with Alzheimer's, and a hero with dark circles under his eyes who never utters a single word.

And most of these films were not over quickly. Not that there's anything wrong with a film running over the invisible 120-minute finish line, if it needs to, and is a good film. I regret that not all the twenty-one films in this year's selection were good. And that's not just me. The daily critics' panel for *Le Film Français* was as negative as I've seen it, even giving a *Pas de tout* ("Not at all") to a film I would defend, von Trier's extreme but courageous *Antichrist*.

In the past I have felt the elation of discovery at Cannes, seeing for the first time films like Kieslowski's *Red*, Lee's *Do the Right Thing*, Coppola's *Apocalypse Now*, Spielberg's *E.T.*— and premieres by Kurosawa, Fellini, Bergman, Chen Kaige, Fassbinder, Altman, Herzog, Scorsese. Titans bestrode the earth in those days. This year the only ecstatic giants, love them or hate them, were Lars von Trier and Quentin Tarantino.

Yes, there were great directors on the list: Michael Haneke, Jane Campion, Ken Loach, Ang Lee, Alain Resnais, Pedro Almodóvar, Marco Bellocchio. But with the exception of Lee, they all chose material of a sort they've mastered. Where were the obsessions, the wild inspirations, the films beyond our imaginings? I hope to be shaken in my bones at least once a year at Cannes. I know the von Trier was hated,

and I've hated some of his films myself, but he was hurling lightning bolts.

* * *

The 2009 feature film jury awarded some reasonable prizes and then lost its mind. In my opinion, the Mendoza film *Kinatay* deserved no award, and *Le Film Français* panel agreed with me (*Pas de tout*). But why in heaven's name would you give him the award for best *direction*? The second half of his film is an illustration of directorial monomania—a willingness to drive audiences from the theater not so much by the violence (rape, beheading, vivisection) but by the *directorial style* itself. You want to depict human atrocity, look to the von Trier.

Or, if you want to award a director in the grip of the relentless execution of an obsession, at least go for broke and give a prize to *Enter the Void*, by Gaspar Noé (*Pas de tout*). At least you could *see* what was happening in his film. Or honor a director who dealt with a human life at length and depth, like Jacques Audiard (*The Prophet*). Or Jane Campion, who handles the enigmatic and apparently chaste love affair of young John Keats as a balancing act between romanticism and genteel derangement. Or give it to Resnais. Now there's a director with a light and wise touch in a whimsical story of fate dealing out what fate always deals. Death, you know.

You want a violent film, honor Johnnie To's *Vengeance*, with Johnny Hallyday as a father who swears a blood oath and then loses his focus in the fog of old age. It played by the rules of film noir and Hong Kong cop thrillers. It didn't insanely slash and burn. You want an existential hit man? Try a woman, the fish market girl played by Rinko Kikuchi in Isabel Coixet's lovely *Map of the Sounds of Tokyo*—a film that evoked some of the same mood as *Hiroshima, mon Amour*. Or go with Almodóvar, even though *Broken Embraces* was minor Almodóvar, just as *Looking for Eric* was minor Loach, and (so most people thought) *Taking Woodstock* was minor Ang Lee.

On the third day of the festival, I made an obvious sort of observation to its director, Thierry Frémaux, about the many important filmmakers in his selection. "Yes, but . . . you know, a great director doesn't always make a great film. We choose from what each year brings us." Was he trying to tell me something?

I should mention the two acting awards, to Charlotte Gainsbourg for *Antichrist* and Christoph Waltz for *Inglourious Basterds.* Gainsbourg and her costar, Willem Dafoe, were truly heroic in meeting the challenge set for them by von Trier. And Waltz, I suspect, won for just plain old-fashioned *acting,* in a Tarantino script that required his character to be many things to many people, including himself.

Before the festival, it was much commented upon that Isabelle Huppert was only the fourth Madame President in Cannes history, and that her jury was the first ever to have a 5–4 female majority. What would this mean?—we all asked. Would the women send a message? Make a statement? Reveal the differences in female values? After the awards, such questions inspire only a hollow laugh. If a male-dominated jury had read out this winners list, there would have been hell to pay.

* * *

The 2009 Cannes festival was heavily tilted toward films that were long and shocking. The awards ceremony Sunday night was concise, elegant, and, for some, equally shocking. I haven't heard more booing at the prize list in some years.

The Palme d'Or went, however, to the generally admired *The White Ribbon,* by Michael Haneke. Set before World War I and filmed in black and white, it tells of a rural German community plagued by a series of inexplicable deaths and other events.

The Grand Prix, essentially second place, went to Jacques Audiard of France, for *The Prophet,* also well-received. It follows a young Arab through the French prison system, which educates him and unwittingly allows him to learn the criminal trade from a Sicilian godfather. Both of the top winners were purchased during the festival for North American release by Sony Pictures Classics.

There was a prolonged standing ovation when the jury awarded a lifetime achievement award to Alain Resnais, eighty-six, one of the founders of the French New Wave, generally credited for launching the modern era of filmmaking.

It has been exactly fifty years since Resnais's classic *Hiroshima, mon Amour* was nominated for the Palme d'Or, and forty-one years since he led a directors' strike that shut down the festival in a protest against its conservative tastes in film. In this year's festival, Resnais's latest film, *Les Herbes Folles,* was a popular favorite. It shows how a series of accidental events determine the paths of lives.

Another popular winner, for the Camera d'Or, or best first film, was Warwick Thornton's *Samson and Delilah,* the first film by and about Aborigines selected by Cannes. It's about a desert journey by two teenagers.

The acting awards went to performances in two of the festival's highest profile films. Best actress was Charlotte Gainsbourg, who underwent and inflicted brutal punishment in Lars von Trier's *Antichrist,* a film in which the Garden of Eden seems to be hell, not heaven. Best actor was Christoph Waltz, as a snaky Nazi SS leader in Quentin Tarantino's *Inglourious Basterds,* about a scheme to attack the Third Reich from behind enemy lines. "You gave me my vocation back," he said to Tarantino from the stage.

Those awards were perhaps not expected, but were well-received. Then the jury started springing surprises that didn't go over as well.

The biggest was the Best Director Award to Brillante Mendoza of the Philippines, for the very violent *Kinatay,* one of the worst-received films of the festival. It involves the kidnapping, torture, rape, beheading, and dismemberment of a woman by members of the police force.

The announcement was greeted by loud booing as the festival's press corps watched on closed-circuit TV in the Auditorium Debussy, next door to the Lumière, where the ceremony was held.

There were also boos for the winner of the Best Screenplay award, Mei Feng, who wrote Ye Lou's *Spring Fever,* from Hong Kong, about a man hired to spy on a love affair; and for Chan-Wook Park's *Thirst,* a vampire film from South Korea. *Thirst* shared the Jury Prize with *Fish Tank,* a story of a troubled teenage boy, by Andrea Arnold of the United Kingdom.

None of these films was booed in the Lumière, but reflect that most of the press would have seen all the films, and most of the black-tie Lumière audience would not have.

Ebert's Journal

Triumph Over *Triumph of the Will*

June 18, 2008—I've just finished viewing Leni Riefenstahl's *Triumph of the Will* (1935) for the second or third time and it will be a Great Movie published June 27, 2008. Whether it is truly great or only technically qualifies because of its importance is the question. As faithful readers will know, I have been avoiding this particular opportunity with dread. I felt it would involve grappling with the question of whether evil art can be great art. Since moral art can obviously be bad art, the answer to the flip side would seem to be clear enough, but it took me a fearsome struggle to thrash out *Birth of a Nation,* even though many more excuses (of time, place, and context) can be offered for Griffith than for Riefenstahl.

As it turned out, *Triumph of the Will* turned out to be a relatively easy assignment for me. The film itself informed me how I was to review it, and this process took place during the act of viewing. I wrote about what I saw, and how I felt when I saw it. I decided not to devote long paragraphs to rehearsing the evils of Nazism, as if that subject was not already pretty well settled. I was not pious in my denunciations, as if I had something to prove. I simply wrote about the sounds and the pictures.

That's the approach I long used in the "shot-by-shot" film analysis sessions that I conducted annually for more than thirty years at the Conference on World Affairs at the University of Colorado, and also for many assorted years at the Hawaii, Virginia, and other festivals, and in classes at the University of Chicago. I recommend the approach to any film enthusiast. The film teaches itself to you.

I began in about 1970, on the advice of John West, a Chicago film exhibitor, teacher, and historian. "You know how coaches use a stop-action 16 mm projector to go through game films?" he asked. "Do the same thing with a feature movie. You don't stop after every frame, of course, but you stop at anything interesting,

and discuss it, and you can back up and look at it a frame at a time."

This I did, to begin with, during U of C classes. The rules were simple: Anyone in the audience shouted out "Stop!" and we did, and discussed why they wanted us to stop. Beginning with Hitchcock, who remains the most fruitful director for such analysis, I worked my way over the years through the work of Welles, Buñuel, Bergman, Herzog, Truffaut, and many others. I found that with a large group, there would always be one member with the expertise to settle the question at hand: a Hungarian speaker, for example, or a psychiatrist, or a specialist on Japanese medieval history. The Colorado groups often numbered one thousand students and locals, and over the years we formed a community.

Of course, the introduction of the laser disc, and later the DVD, made this process infinitely easier.

When I was asked by Criterion to do a shot-by-shot commentary of Ozu's *Floating Weeds,* I almost balked. (In his late work, Ozu's camera never moves. He always cuts between static setups. What would I analyze?) I had, in fact, been through the film a shot at a time at the side of Donald Richie, the greatest English-language expert on the Japanese cinema, at Hawaii, but that had been years ago. All the same, I proposed *Floating Weeds* at Colorado one year, and the discoveries we made there were so fruitful that I modestly believe the resulting commentary track is superb. The greater the artist, the more deeply you can look, and the more you will find.

Viewing *Triumph of the Will* a shot at a time would be a relentless and harrowing experience, and that realization gave me my angle in writing about the film. I did not have to settle vast questions of good and evil. I simply had to look at what has been frequently called "the greatest documentary ever made." But to look slowly, and carefully, and at the screen, not the reputation.

O, *Synecdoche,* My *Synecdoche*!

November 10, 2008—Fair warning: I begin with a parable, continue with vast generalizations, finally get around to an argument with *Entertainment Weekly,* and move on to Greek gods, *I Love Lucy,* and a house on fire.

The parable: The lodestars of John Doe's life are his wife, his children, his boss, his mistress, and his pastor. There are more, but these will do. He expects his wife to be grateful for his loyalty. His children to accept him as a mentor. His boss to value him as a worker. His mistress to praise him as a sex machine. His pastor to note his devotion. These are the roles he has assigned them, and for the most part they play them.

In their own lives, his wife feels he has been over-rewarded for his loyalty, since she has done all the heavy lifting. His children don't understand why there are so many stupid rules. His boss considers John Doe as downsizable and fears he may also get the ax. His mistress asks herself why she doesn't dump this creep and find an "available" man. His pastor has a pretty good idea what goes on during the other six days of the week.

This dynamic radiates out into every other life on Earth and down through time, shading gradually into other religious or irreligious value systems. Every other life relates to those encounters in the same way, depending on local conditions. Life's a stage, and we bit players upon it. Charlie Kaufman's *Synecdoche, New York* is a film that boldly tries to illustrate this universal process by using a director immersed in a production of indefinite duration on a stage representing his mind.

The film is confused, contradictory, and unclear, so I am informed by those unmoved by it. Owen Gleiberman of *Entertainment Weekly* grades it "D plus" and has what I agree is a reasonable reaction to this film: "An artist makes a movie that is so labyrinthine and obscure, such a road map of blind alleys, such a turgid challenge to sit through that it sends most people skulking out of the theater—except, that is, for a cadre of eggheads who hail the work as a visionary achievement."

I imagine he speaks for a majority opinion on this film. I am resigned to belonging to a cadre of eggheads hailing *Synecdoche,* although I have praised many a film, like *The Golden Compass,* that Gleiberman dismissed as not "great trash" but the compacted variety. "Naya, naya, naya! Who's the egghead now?" But Owen is a terrific chap and we like each other, especially when we find ourselves enlisted in the same cadre.

He cites *Last Year at Marienbad* (1961) as another example of obscure obfuscation. How clearly I remember seeing that film in the early 1960s at the University of Illinois. My reaction was precisely the same as the one I felt after seeing *Synecdoche.* I watched it the first time and sensed it might be a great film and that I had not mastered it. We all met with Gunther Marx, a professor of German. We sat over coffee in the Illini Union, late on that rainy night in Urbana. "I will explain it all for you," he said. "It is a working out of the anthropological archetypes of Claude Lévi-Strauss. We have the lover, the loved one, and the authority figure. The movie proposes that the lovers had an affair, that they didn't, that they met before, that they didn't, that the authority figure knew it, that he didn't, that he killed her, that he didn't. Any questions?"

We gaped at him in awe. I was instructed long ago by a wise editor, "If you understand something you can explain it so that almost anyone can understand it. If you don't, you won't be able to understand your own explanation." That is why 90 percent of academic film theory is bullshit. Jargon is the last refuge of the scoundrel. Yes. But if a work seems baffling yet remains intriguing, there may be a simple key to its mysteries. I doubt that James Joyce's *Ulysses* had a big opening weekend. You start reading it and start it and start it, and you shore up in uncertainty and dismay. Then someone tells you, "It's an attempt to record one day in the life of some people in Dublin, mostly focusing on Leopold Bloom. It uses or parodies many literary styles and introduces a new one, the stream of consciousness, which defines itself. Try finding somebody Irish to read the tricky bits aloud. Voilà!" And now we celebrate Bloomsday on June 16.

For thousands of years, fiction made no room for characters who changed. Men felt the need for an explanation of their baffling existence, created gods, and projected onto them the solutions for their enigmas. These gods, of course, had to be immutable, for they stood above the foibles of men. Zeus was Zeus and Apollo was Apollo and that was that. We envisioned them on mountaintops, where they were little given to introspection. We took the situation as given, did our best, created arts that were always abstractions in the sense that they existed outside ourselves. Harold Bloom believes Shakespeare introduced the human personality into fiction. When Richard III looked in the mirror and asked himself what role he should play, and Hamlet asked the fundamental question "To be, or not to be," the first shoe was dropped, and *Synecdoche* and many other works have dropped the second shoe.

Sometimes the most unlikely seeming films will slot right into this groove of projection, strategy, and coping, as they involve the achievement of our needs and desires. You could put Harold Ramis's *Groundhog Day* (1993) on the same double bill with *Synecdoche*. Bill Murray plays a weatherman caught in a time loop. As I wrote at the time: "He is the only one who can remember what happened yesterday. That gives him a certain advantage. He can, for example, find out what a woman is looking for in a man, and then the 'next' day he can behave in exactly the right way to impress her."

Not science fiction. How the world works. On *I Love Lucy*, even ditzy Lucy understood this process: I will act as if I am the kind of woman Cary Grant would desire. We all live through *Groundhog Day*, but it is less confusing for us because one day follows another. Or seems to.

My first time through *Synecdoche*, I felt a certain frustration. The plot would not stay still. It kept running off and barking at cats. The second time was more soothing. I knew what was going on. It is what goes on every day of our lives, made visual by the inspired set design, rooms on top of rooms, all containing separate activities, with the protagonist trying to satisfy, or direct, or obey, or evade, or learn from, or receive solace from, the people in all of the rooms.

Jerry Lewis's *The Ladies' Man* (1961) does the same thing, with a famous set that must have been an inspiration for *Synecdoche*. Maybe that's another film I need to see again. Those French, what philosophers. Jerry Lewis, shake hands with Alain Robbe-Grillet. The French are correct that Jerry is funnier.

It occurs to me that many movies tell the stories of pre-Shakespearian gods. The hero is introduced, remains constant throughout the movie, behaves as he can and must, and wins at the end. That is comforting for us and one reason we go to the movies. Imagine that *The Dark Knight* was exactly similar, frame by frame, from beginning to end, but has a brief extra scene at the end where Batman slips on a wet floor in the Batcave, hits his head on the floor, and is killed. Then the camera slowly pulls back to show the dead caped crusader in the gathering gloom and then up in an invisible wipe to the moon over Gotham City. What's your best guess? Final gross over a billion?

Yes, Owen, I think *Synecdoche, New York* is a masterpiece. But here I've written all this additional wordage about it, and I *still* haven't reviewed it. How could I? You've seen it. How could I, in less time than it takes to see the movie, summarize the plot? I must say that in your finite EW space, you do a heroic job of describing what happens. But what happens is not the whole point. The movie is about how and why the stuff that happens—happens. Might as well try to describe the plot of *Ulysses* in eight hundred words or less. All you can do is try to find a key. Just in writing that, I think I have in a blinding flash solved the impenetrable mystery of Joyce's next novel, *Finnegans Wake*. It is the stream of conscious of a man trying to write *Ulysses* and always running off to chase cats.

Note: Comparable to great fiction? Yes, with the same complexity and slow penetrability. Not complex as a strategy or a shortcoming. Complex because it interweaves and cross-refers, and every moment of apparent perplexity leads back somewhere in the movie to its solution. Some great fiction, like Ulysses *or* The Sound and the Fury *or* The Golden Bowl, *was hypertext when hypertext wasn't a name, but only a need. Henry James seems the steadiest of hands, but underneath, his opening chapters are straining to touch the closing ones, and the middle hides concealed loyalties. And when he writes "intercourse," you never quite know what he means. Very hypertextual.*

Why is the house always on fire, but nobody seems to notice it? Don't unhappy homes always seem like that? Aren't people always trying to ignore it?

The voice-over. Maybe the only time I've heard coughing in a voice-over.

That matte painting. Right. It moves.

What does the title mean? In my review, I wrote: "It means it's the title. Get over it." Not so fast there, Mickey Spillane. As I should have positively known in a Charlie Kaufman screenplay, it is a word that has a meaning. Wikipedia informs me:

Synecdoche (pronounced "si-nek-duh-kee," from Greek sinekdohi (συνεκδοχή), meaning "simultaneous understanding") is a figure of speech in which:

- *a term denoting a part of something is used to refer to the whole thing, or*

- *a term denoting a thing (a whole) is used to refer to part of it, or*

- *a term denoting a specific class of thing is used to refer to a larger, more general class, or*

- *a term denoting a general class of thing is used to refer to a smaller, more specific class, or*

- *a term denoting a material is used to refer to an object composed of that material.*

In other words, the playwright's life refers to all lives, and all lives refer to his life. So Kaufman gives the whole thing away right there in his title. Talk about your spoilers.

Win Ben Stein's Mind

December 3, 2008—I've been accused of refusing to review Ben Stein's documentary *Expelled*, a defense of creationism, because of my belief in the theory of evolution. Here is my response.

Ben Stein, you hosted a TV show on which you gave away money. Imagine that I have created a special edition of *Who Wants to Be a Millionaire* just for you. Ben, you've answered all the earlier questions correctly, and now you're up for the $1 million prize. It involves an explanation for the evolution of life on this planet. You have already exercised your option to throw away two of the wrong answers. Now you are faced with two choices: (A) Darwin's theory of evolution, or (B) intelligent design.

Because this is a special edition of the program, you can use a hotline to telephone every scientist on Earth who has an opinion on this question. You discover that 99.975 percent of them agree on the answer (A). A million bucks hangs in the balance. The clock is ticking. You

could use the money. Which do you choose? You, a firm believer in the Constitution, are not intimidated and exercise your freedom of speech. You choose (B).

Squaaawk!!! The Klaxon horn sounds. You have lost. Outraged, you file suit against the program, charging it is biased and has denied a hearing for your belief. Your suit argues that the "correct" answer was chosen because of a prejudice against the theory of intelligent design, despite the fact that .025 of 1 percent of all scientists support it.

You call for (B) to be discussed in schools as an alternative theory to (A).

Your rights have been violated. You're at wit's end. You think perhaps the field of indie documentaries offers you hope. You accept a position at the Institute of Undocumented Documentaries in Dallas, Texas. This institute teaches that the rules of the *$64,000 Question* are the only valid game show rules. All later game shows must follow them literally. The *$64,000 Question* came into existence in 1955. False evidence for earlier game shows has been refuted by scientists at the institute.

You look for a documentary subject. You know you cannot hope to find backing from the mainstream media, because they all fear reprisals from the powerful game show establishment. You seek a cause that parallels your own dilemma and also illustrates an offense against the freedom of speech. Your attention falls on the persecution of intelligent design advocates like you, who have been banished from mainstream academia.

This looks like your ideal subject. But where can you find financing for such a documentary? You discover a small, promising production company named Premise Media. You like the sound of that word "premise." It sounds like a plausible alternative to the word "theory." To confirm this, you look both up in your dictionary:

Premise (noun). A previous statement or proposition from which another is inferred or follows as a conclusion: If the premise is true, then the conclusion must be true, e.g., if God exists, then he created everything.

Theory (noun). A system of ideas intended to explain something, especially one based on general principles independent of the thing to be explained, e.g., Darwin's theory of evolution.

Your point exactly! You do a Web search for Premise Media. Its cofounder Walt Ruloff has observed, "The scientific and academic communities were deeply resistant to innovation, in this case innovation that might revise Darwin's theory that random mutation and natural selection drive all variation in life forms." You could not agree more. Darwin's theory has been around for 150 years and is stubbornly entrenched. This is a time for innovation, for drawing on fresh theories that life and the universe were intelligently created in recent times, perhaps within the last ten thousand years. How to account for dinosaur fossils? Obviously, dinosaurs walked the earth at the same time as human beings.

Ben Stein, you are growing more excited. You continue your research into Premise Media. Its CEO, A. Logan Craft, once observed that questions about the origin of Earth and its life forms "are answered very differently by secularists and people who hold religious beliefs." Can you believe your eyes? Craft has depended upon one of your own favorite logical practices, the principle of the excluded middle! This is too good to be true.

By his premise, no secularists believe in intelligent design, and no people with religious beliefs subscribe to Darwin's theory. If there *are* people with religious beliefs who agree with Darwin (Catholics, Jews, Protestants, Mormons, Hindus, Muslims, and Buddhists, for example), they are mistaken because they do not subscribe to A. Logan Craft's religious beliefs.

He is certainly right about secularists. You think it's a shame he's right, because then the 1968 Supreme Court decision was correct, and Tennessee's antievolution law was "an attempt to blot out a particular theory because of its supposed conflict with the Biblical account, taken literally." Therefore, according to the court, ID was a religious belief and did not belong in a science classroom but in a theology classroom. This clearly would be wrong, because the new approach to teaching ID in schools omits any reference whatsoever to religion. It depends entirely on the findings of scientists who are well-respected within A. Logan Craft's religious tradition. These scientists, of course, are perfectly free to be secularists, although almost every single one seems to be a fundamentalist Christian. This is America.

You meet with the people at Premise Media. It is a meeting of the minds. At a pitch meeting, they are receptive to your ideas, although with the proviso that you should change the proposed title of your film, *From Darwin to Hitler,* because that might limit the market to those who had heard of neither, or only one.

You and Premise Media agree that the case for ID had not always been argued very well in the past. For example, a photograph of a human footprint overlapping a dinosaur track (proof that man walked the earth side by side with dinosaurs) has been questioned by secularists, who say the footprint looks more like the print of a running shoe. If you studied it carefully, it could be argued that they had a point, although skewed by their secularist bias.

What was needed was better use of photographic evidence. For example, in your film, *Expelled: No Intelligence Allowed,* you document the story of Guillermo Gonzales, who was denied tenure at Iowa State because of his personal premises, after four hundred professors signed a petition opposing "all attempts to represent intelligent design as a scientific endeavor." Gonzales was forced to accept employment at Grove City College, an evangelical Christian school in Grove City, Pennsylvania.

In documenting the secularist hysteria and outrage against Gonzales, you use more convincing photographic evidence than the footprint. For example, you use footage showing a newsstand selling copies of the *New York Post* with this front-page headline:

CRISIS:
1. CREATIONIST ON THE LOOSE
2. SUPPORT THE PETITION
3. STOP GONZALES

The typographical design of the *New York Post* logo, the cars and store signs in the background, and the clothing of the people in the street establish without question that this footage was filmed in the late 1940s. Gonzales was born in 1963. So your film would prove beyond doubt that his enemies walked the earth with his parents.

Gonzales, trained as an astronomer, cited as proof of intelligent design that "Earth is in a prime location for observing the universe." Thus he refutes the theory of elitist secularist academia that the universe "does not have an edge nor center, just as the earth's surface does not have an edge or center." Since all you have to do is look up at the sky to realize that the whole universe is right up there to be seen, the secularists fly in the face of common sense. Yet, for stating such an obvious premise, Gonzales was opposed for tenure at Iowa State. That hit home, Ben Stein. He was a victim like you.

You release your film *Expelled*. As you fully expect from all your experience, it is rejected almost unanimously by the MSM. It receives an 8 percent rating on the TomatoMeter, earning it a place on the list of the worst-reviewed films of all time. In a review not catalogued by Rotten-Tomatoes, ChristianAnwers.net writes that your film "has made Ben Stein the new hero of believers in God everywhere, and has landed a smart right cross to the protruding jaw of evolution's elite."

Again, the useful excluded middle. Those for whom Ben Stein is not a hero are not believers in God. It also follows that the phrase "believers in God everywhere" does not extend to believers in God who agree with Darwin. So ChristianAnswers has excluded two middles at one fell stroke.

Let's hope that word doesn't get back to the bosses of the critic named "Yo" at hollywoodjesus.com. Yo takes a chance by saying: "This creator could have been anything of intelligence, including aliens. Intelligent Design is a scientific movement, not a religious one, a fact stated more than once in interviews in this film. Unfortunately, those statements are constantly ignored as *Expelled* continually brings up the question of God's existence and thereby equates the movement with a belief in God."

And right there, Ben Stein, we can clearly see Yo's error. He has included the middle.

Here is Stein's most urgent question: "How does something that is not life turn into something that is?"

Stein poses this stumper to a jolly British professor who seems direct from Monty Python. He thinks there's a "very good chance" that life might have started with molecules on crystals, which have a tendency to mutate. Cut to a shot of a turbaned crystal-ball gazer. Stein dubs them "joy-riding crystals." He wonders what the odds would be of life starting that way. "You would have to have a minimum of 250

proteins to provide minimal life functions," an ID defender explains. We see an animated cartoon of the Darwinian scientist Richard Dawkins pulling at a slot machine and lining up—"three in a row!" Not so fast there, "Lucky" Dawkins! The camera pulls back to show one-armed bandits stretching into infinity. To win, he'd have to hit the jackpot about a gazillion times in a row. An intelligent design advocate estimates a streak like that would take a trillion, trillion, trillion tries. (That number is a fair piece larger than three trillion.)

Quite a joy ride. ID's argument against the crystal theory seems like a new version of its classic argument "How could an eye evolve without knowing there was anything to see?" Very easily, apparently, because various forms of eyes have evolved twenty-six different times that scientists know about, and they can explain how it happened. So can I. So can you if you understand Darwinian principles.

Anyway, the slot machine conundrum is based on an ignorance of both math and gambling. From math we know that the odds of winning a coin toss are exactly the same every time. The coin doesn't remember the last try. Hey, sometimes you get lucky. That's why casinos stay in business.

The odds of winning on a single number at roulette are 37 to 1. The odds of winning a second time in a row are also 37 to 1, because the table doesn't know who you are. Every single winning roll beats the odds of 37 to 1. And on and on. The more times in a row you win, the more times you face 37 to 1 against you. If Russian roulette were played with a gun containing 37 bullets and one empty chamber, it would quickly lose most of its allure—by a process explained, oddly enough, by Darwin. (See note.)

Still, in July 1891 at Monte Carlo, the same man broke the 100,000 franc bank at a roulette table three times. Wikipedia reports, "A man named Charles Wells won 23 times out of 30 successive spins of the wheel. . . . Despite hiring private detectives the casino never discovered Wells's system. Wells later admitted it was just a lucky streak. His system was the high-risk martingale, doubling the stake to make up losses."

The odds against Wells doing that are pretty high. But as every gambler knows, sometimes you do actually hit a number. You don't have to do it a trillion trillion trillion times to be a winner. You only have to do it once. This is explained by Darwin. If you are playing at a table with other gamblers and you win $100 and none of them do, you are just that much better able to outlast them as competitors. When the casino closes, one person at that table must have won more than any of the others. That's why casinos never close. Of course if you gamble long enough, you will eventually lose back more than the others. Your poor spouse tells you this. You know it is true.

But tonight you feel lucky. If you leave the table still holding your pot, you could become as rich as Warren Buffett. Somebody has to. Look at Warren Buffett. Evolution involves holding on to your winnings and investing them wisely. You don't even have to know how to hold on to your winnings. Evolution does it for you; it is the bank in which useful genetic mutations deposit themselves. There is a very slow rate of return, but it's compounded. At the end of one eon, you get your bank statement and find your pittance has grown into an orangutan. At the end of the next eon, it has grown into Charles Darwin. Scientists, at least 99.975 percent of them, believe that in the long run only useful mutations deposit in this bank. Those mutations with no use, or a negative effect, squander their savings in a long-running bunko game and die forgotten in the gutter.

The assumption of *Expelled* is that no one could possibly explain how Professor Monty Python's molecules and their joy-riding crystals could possibly produce life. As luck would have it, at about the same time the film was being made, teams of scientists at the universities of Oregon and North Carolina explained it. They "determined for the first time the atomic structure of an ancient protein, revealing in unprecedented detail how genes evolved their functions."

"This is the ultimate level of detail," said the evolutionary biologist Joe Thornton. "We were able to see exactly how evolution tinkered with the ancient structure to produce a new function that is crucial to our own bodies today. Nobody's ever done that before." Unfortunately, this momentous discovery was announced almost too late to be mentioned in Ben Stein's film. It wasn't *totally* too late, but it

would have been a great inconvenience for the editor.

What tools did the scientists use? Supercomputer programs and, I quote, "ultra-high-energy X-rays from a stadium-sized Advanced Photon Source at Argonne National Laboratory near Chicago to chart the precise position of each of the 2,000 atoms in the ancient proteins." What did you expect? They put a molecule under a microscope and picked off bits with their tweezers?

Intelligent design "scientists" in *Expelled* are offended by being called ignorant. When Stein points out that "Catholics and mainstream Protestant groups" have no problem with the theory of evolution, he is informed by an ID advocate, "Liberal Christians side with anybody against creationists." Now we have the smoking gun. It is the word "liberal." What is the word "liberal" doing here? The theory of evolution is neither liberal nor conservative. It is simply provable or not.

Besides, I would not describe the Vatican as liberal. Look how cautiously it approached Galileo. He claimed only that the earth revolved around the sun. No big deal like the earth being ideally placed in the universe. There are millions of conservative scientists, and only a tiny handful disagree with evolution, because rejecting scientific proof is not permissive conservative behavior. In that one use of the word "liberal," the creationist religious agenda is peeking through. I would translate it as "Evolutionists side with anybody against a cherished Evangelical belief." Why are they always trying to push evolutionists over the edge, when they're the ones clinging by their fingernails?

Scientists deserving of the name would share the delight of 99.975 percent of their colleagues after learning of the Oregon–North Carolina findings. Then, if they found a plausible reason to doubt them, they would go right to work hoping to win fame by disproving them. A theory, like a molecule, a sea slug, and a polar bear, has to fight it out in the survival of the fittest.

Expelled is not a bad film from the technical point of view. It is well photographed and edited, sometimes amusing, has well-chosen talking heads, gives an airing to evolutionists however truncated and interrupted with belittling images, and incorporates entertainingly unfair historical footage, as when it compares academia's rejection of creationism to the erection of the Berlin Wall.

Hilariously, the film argues that "evolutionists" cannot tolerate dissent. If you were to stand up at a "Catholic and mainstream Protestant" debate and express your support of creationism, you would in most cases be politely listened to. There are few places as liberal as Boulder, Colorado, where I twice debated a creationist at the Conference on World Affairs, and yet his views were heard politely there. If you were to stand up at an evangelical meeting to defend evolution, I doubt if you would be made to feel as welcome or that your dissent would be quite as cheerfully tolerated.

In the film, Ben Stein asks predictable questions and exploits an unending capacity for counterfeit astonishment. Example:

Scientist: "But Darwin did not title his book *On the Origin of Life*. He titled it *On the Origin of Species*."

Ben Stein (nods, grateful to learn this): "I see!"

The more you know about evolution, or simple logic, the more you are likely to be appalled by the film. No one with an ability for critical thinking could watch more than three minutes without becoming aware of its tactics. It isn't even subtle. Take its treatment of Dawkins, who throughout his interviews with Stein is honest, plainspoken, and courteous. As Stein goes to interview him for the last time, we see a makeup artist carefully patting on rouge and dusting Dawkins's face. After he is prepared and composed, after the shine has been taken off his nose, here comes plain, down-to-earth, workaday Ben Stein. So we get the vain Dawkins with his effete makeup, talking to the ordinary Joe.

I have done television interviews for more than forty years. I have been on both ends of the questions. I have news for you. *Everyone* is made up before going on television. If they are not, they will look like death warmed over. There is not a person reading this right now who should go on camera without some kind of makeup. Even the obligatory "shocked neighbors" standing in their front yards after a murder usually have some powder brushed on by the camera person. Was Ben Stein wearing makeup? Of course he was. Did he whisper to

his camera crew to roll while Dawkins was being made up? Of course he did. Otherwise, no camera operator on Earth would have taped that. That incident dramatizes his approach throughout the film. If you want to study "Gotcha!" moments, start here.

That is simply one revealing fragment. This film is cheerfully ignorant, manipulative, slanted, cherry-picks quotations, draws unwarranted conclusions, makes outrageous juxtapositions (Soviet marching troops representing opponents of ID), pussyfoots around religion, segues between quotes that are not about the same thing, tells bald-faced lies, and makes a completely baseless association between freedom of speech and freedom to teach religion in a university class that is not about religion.

And there is worse, much worse. Toward the end of the film, we find that Stein actually *did* want to title it *From Darwin to Hitler*. He finds a creationist who informs him, "Darwinism inspired and advanced Nazism." He refers to advocates of eugenics as "liberal." I would not call Hitler liberal. Arbitrary forced sterilization in our country has been promoted mostly by racists, who curiously found many times more blacks than whites suitable for such treatment.

Ben Stein is only getting warmed up. He takes a field trip to visit one "result" of Darwinism: Nazi concentration camps. "As a Jew," he says, "I wanted to see for myself." We see footage of gaunt, skeletal prisoners. Pathetic children. A mound of naked Jewish corpses. "It's difficult to describe how it felt to walk through such a haunting place," he says. Oh, go ahead, Ben Stein. Describe. It filled you with hatred for Charles Darwin and his followers, who represent the overwhelming majority of educated people in every nation on Earth. It is not difficult for me to describe how you made me feel by exploiting the deaths of millions of Jews in support of your argument for a peripheral Christian belief. It fills me with contempt.

Note: My statement is correct as far as it goes, but a reader, Steve Vanden-Eykel, supplies a much clearer explanation of the principle. He writes me:

"Imagine flipping a coin over and over. For each toss, the odds are 50-50 that it will come up heads (a 1-in-2 chance). The odds of getting two heads in a row is a 1-in-2-to-the-power-of-2 chance, or 1 in 4. Five heads in a row is 1:2⁵, or 1

in 32. A hundred heads? 1:2^{100}, or roughly 1 in 1.3 trillion trillion trillion (thank Gates for the little calculator program on my computer). A creationist would claim that all the lucky chances that evolution requires is like getting not one, not five, but millions upon millions of heads in a row.

"But the creationists are forgetting something. Evolution isn't random, as they often claim. It's selected. You can't really blame creationists for missing this fact. . . . Darwin cleverly concealed it from view by calling his theory 'natural selection.' Let's return to our coin-tossing example, this time including the principle of selection. What if, after every toss, we had the option of not counting it? What if we were allowed to simply discard every toss that came up tails? Now, given the ability to select, how long would it take to rack up a hundred heads in a row? About two hundred throws.

"Once you understand the concept of selection, and how it applies to evolution, you realize that what was thought to be vanishingly unlikely actually becomes virtually inevitable."

We're All Puppets, Laurie; I'm Just a Puppet Who Can See the Strings

March 4, 2009—Inside many superhero stories is a Greek tragedy in hiding. There is the godlike hero, and he is flawed. In early days his weaknesses were simplistic, like Superman's vulnerability to Kryptonite. Then Spider-Man was created as an insecure teenager, and comic books began to peer deeper. Now comes the Watchmen, with their origins as 1940s goofballs, their development into modern costumed vigilantes, and the laws against them as public nuisances. They are human. Although they have extraordinary physical powers, they aren't superheroes in the usual sense. Then everything changes for Jon Osterman, remade after a nuclear accident as Dr. Manhattan. He isn't as human as Batman, but that can be excused because he isn't human at all.

He is the most metaphysically intriguing character in modern superhero movies. He not only lives in a quantum universe but is aware that he does and reflects about it. He says, "This world's smartest man means no more to me than does its smartest termite." He lives outside time and space. He explains that he doesn't see the past and the future, but he does see his own past and his own future. He can apparently go anywhere in the universe and take any shape. He can be many places at the same time, his attention fully focused in each of those places. He sees the big picture, and it is so vast that it's hard for him to be concerned about the fate of the earth. I wonder how many audience members will know much about quantum mechanics. Some will interpret it simply in terms of Dr. Manhattan's powers. It's one of those story devices like the warp drive in *Star Trek*. Dr. Manhattan, however, views it in a much more complex way, from the inside, and apparently in terms consistent with current science. So let's ask what we understand about quantum mechanics. We'll start with me. I understand nothing.

Oh, I've read a lot about it. Here is what I think I know: At a basic level, the universe is composed of infinitesimal bits, I think they're called strings, which seem to transcend our ideas about space and time. One of these bits can be in two places at once, or, if two bits are at a distance, can somehow communicate with each other. Now I have just looked it all up in Wikipedia, and find that not only don't I understand quantum mechanics, I don't understand the article either. So never mind. Let's just say my notions are close to the general popular delusions about the subject, and those are what Dr. Manhattan understands.

So. I've just come from seeing *Watchmen* a second time, this time on an IMAX screen, which was an awesome experience. Not having read the graphic novel, I found my first viewing somewhat confusing. There were allusions and connections I suspected I was missing. I had to think back and take inventory of the characters. On the second viewing I was better prepared and found the movie does make perfect sense on the narrative level. It takes place in 1985 in an alternate timeline, where Richard Nixon is still president, we won in Vietnam, Dr. Manhattan took the photo of Aldrin and Armstrong planting the American flag on the moon, and so on. When the helicopters made their fateful flight to "March of the Valkyries" in *Apocalypse Now*, Dr. Manhattan was there, too.

The plot (very) briefly. In 1985, America and the USSR are at the brink of nuclear war. Perhaps the Watchmen could save the planet. But someone seems to be trying to kill them, retired though they may be. This danger inspires them to reunite for the first time in years. On the second viewing, I realized something I missed the first time through: The Watchmen assassination plot makes no sense, because the only Watchman who could possibly save the planet is Dr. Manhattan, and his disinterest is cosmic. There is only one of the other Watchmen who might possibly persuade him.

The second time through I found myself really *listening* to what Manhattan says, and it is actually thought provoking. I didn't care as deeply about the characters on the human level as I did with those in *The Dark Knight,* but I cared surprisingly about the technically inhuman Manhattan. He doesn't lack emotion as the alien did in the recent remake of *The Day the Earth Stood Still.* He has simply moved far, far beyond its reach. From where he stands, he might as well be regarding a termite. Why does he even bother to make love with Laurie Jupiter? Not for his own pleasure, I'm convinced. And not to father a Little Manhattan, either, because as I understand his body he would ejaculate only energy. Could be fun for Laurie, but no precautions needed, except not to be grounded at the time.

SPOILER WARNING: At the end of *The Day the Earth Stood Still,* the alien decides not to destroy life on Earth because he is convinced that humans do love one another. Nothing that sentimental motivates Manhattan. Listen carefully to what he says. He tells Laurie she exists because, "Your mother loves a man she has every reason to hate, and of that union, of the thousand million children competing for fertilization, it was you, only you, that emerged. To distill so specific a form from that chaos of improbability, like turning air to gold!" He is intellectually amazed by her uniqueness and by the workings of genetics. Her father and mother were the last two people you expect, and from their unlikely coupling Laurie, specifically Laurie and no one else, was created. Manhattan is not saying he may save the planet because Laurie is so wonderful. He is saying he may save the planet because of the sheer wonder of the workings of DNA.

Safe now to read again. The next detail is not important to the plot of *Watchmen,* but I found it fascinating: Manhattan thinks he might leave this planet altogether, travel to a distant galaxy, and there, he suggests, might try his hand at creating some life himself. He would then, would he not, be the intelligent designer of life in that place?

Left unanswered is the question of how life was created here on this planet, and indeed the question of whether Manhattan as he now exists constitutes life. Always remaining is the much larger question, "Why is there something instead of nothing?" These are questions Manhattan might fruitfully meditate upon, although if you exist on a quantum level, as he himself observes, life and nonlife are all the same thing, just nanoscale bits of not much more than nothing, all busily humming about for reasons we cannot comprehend. As he puts it, "A live body and a dead body contain the same number of particles. Structurally, there's no discernible difference. Life and death are unquantifiable abstracts. Why should I be concerned?"

Whoa. I have come all this way and forgotten all the things I meant to say about *Watchmen,* its visual strategy, its acting, and so on. I know from many reports that the film is unusually faithful to the graphic novel written by Alan Moore and drawn by Dave Gibbons, importing some dialogue and frames literally. Faithfulness in adaptation is not necessarily a virtue; this is a movie and not a marriage. But I think it has use here, because it helps to evoke the film noir vision that so many comic-based movies inhabit. Looking at page grabs from the book, I can see Gibbons's drawing style is often essentially storyboarding.

The acting? Very effective. Yes, these characters are preposterous, beginning with their need to wear costumes and continuing with their willingness to retire them. But within the terms of the story and the screenplay by David Hayter and Alex Tse, the performances create a certain poignancy. These are not superheroes with human flaws. They are flawed humans all the time—some of them possibly mad (Rorschach is "crazier than a snake's armpit," a cop says).

You can see Matthew Goode, as Ozymandias, using an interesting tactic: He adopts a manner that leads us to think one thing about him at the first, and another thing later. Jackie Earle Haley, as Rorschach, the raspy narrator, is tortured both in and out of his mask. Patrick Wilson (Nite Owl) needs his costume to really even possess a personality. And so on, including Malin Akerman as Laurie, whose affection for Manhattan seems oddly plausible under the circumstances.

Zack Snyder's *300* (2006) showed a similar mastery of CGI imagery as *Watchmen* does. Most of both films is not really there. But *300* struck me as fevered overkill, literally; there wasn't a character I cared about. It involved, I wrote, "one-dimensional caricatures who talk like professional wrestlers plugging their next feud." In *Watchmen*, maybe it's the material, maybe it's a growing discernment on Snyder's part, but there's substance here.

On a conventional screen *Watchmen* will have considerable power, so don't be at all reluctant to see it that way. If there was ever a film not intended to be seen for the first time on DVD, this is that film. But IMAX intensifies Snyder's visual strategy and the cinematography of Larry Fong. In its sometimes grungy way, it's beautiful. And look at the way Snyder creates its most spectacular artifact, Manhattan's crystal structure on Mars that seems to be a timepiece without hands—or time. Of course it's made with CGI and of course it looks phony. But after all, it isn't really there.

A Roll of Whose Dice?

March 18, 2009—Is the universe deterministic or random? Not the first question you'd expect to hear in a thriller, even a great one. But to hear this question posed soon after the opening sequence of *Knowing* gave me a particular thrill. Nicolas Cage plays Koestler, a professor of astrophysics at MIT, and as he toys with a model of the solar system, he asks that question of his students. Deterministic means that if you have a complete understanding of the laws of physics, you can predict with certainty everything that will happen after (for example) the universe is created in the big bang. Random means you can't predict anything. "What do you think?" a student asks Koestler, who says, "I think . . . shit just happens."

He is soon given reason to doubt his confidence. (From this point on, there are spoilers.) *Knowing* begins fifty years ago with a classroom assignment; grade school children are asked to draw pictures of what the world will look like in the future. Most draw rocket

ships. Lucinda covers her page with row after row of deeply etched numbers. All the pages are buried in a time capsule, and when the future comes around, Lucinda's sealed envelope ends up in the hands of Caleb, Koestler's young son.

The page seems meaningless, a work of madness. But by chance Koestler notices these numbers in a row: 91120013239. Koestler sees 9/11/2001, and when he Googles 9/11 he finds that 3,239 people were killed. The numbers were written down in 1959. In a fever, the scientist extracts other numbers and finds the precise dates and fatalities of major catastrophes during the previous five decades.

How can this be? By now Koestler is in the state of mind that Nicolas Cage evokes so perfectly: profound, heartsick worry. He turns to his MIT colleague, a cosmologist named Beckman (Ben Mendelsohn). Beckman thinks he must be mad and warns against the superstition of numerology. But when recent numbers turn out to be correct predictions, and when Koestler realizes that some of the numbers are coordinates of latitude and longitude, it is impossible to dismiss the sheet of paper. It poses a threat to our very understanding of the universe. Shit doesn't just happen.

As I watched these scenes, I became aware of synchronicity in my own life. It happens that I am still immersed in the never-ending debate about evolution vs. intelligent design on my Ben Stein blog entry (currently 1,530 comments and counting). Only a day or two earlier, a reader named Randy Masters asked me what, in my mind, would constitute "proof" of intelligent design. Fair question. I replied: "I wouldn't expect the Big Banger to manifest in the skies like the Four Horsemen or anything. I would expect him to enlighten scientists so they would learn how to find evidence of his working."

Now, in this movie, a secularist scientist is apparently being furnished with such enlightenment—for how else to explain the numbers? There must be a design. We learn Koestler is long estranged from his father, a clergyman who serenely believes he will be in heaven with his wife. Aren't these numbers evidence of a higher power? More important, what do they mean for the lives of Koestler and Caleb? And for Diana (Rose Byrne), the daughter of Lucinda, and Abby, the granddaughter (Lara

Robinson)? Koestler has tracked them down with feverish intensity.

Knowing is a superbly crafted thriller in any event, but that it brings basic philosophical questions into view was more than I could have hoped for. The film is by Alex Proyas, whose *Dark City* (1998) was also about the hidden nature of the world men think they inhabit. *Knowing*, which could not be a more different film, seems to reveal a similar secret. In Proyas's *I, Robot* (2004), a robot, whose programming is rigidly deterministic, evolves to the point where it is able to ask, "What am I?"—which of course leads to a discovery of the true nature of the world it inhabits.

Of course, it isn't that simple. The professor offered a false choice to his class. No one thinks the universe is random, except possibly at a quantum level, and let's not go there. Gravity doesn't randomly switch off. Light doesn't randomly alter its speed. The classical philosophical choice is between determinism and *free will*. Is the future already predestined, or do we have a role in the outcome? Can lower orders like dogs have degrees of free will? Is it already written when the dog will bark, or is it only strongly suggested by its instincts?

The numbers on Lucinda's page are rigidly deterministic: On this date, in this place, this many people will die, and there is nothing to be done—a fact illustrated when Koestler tries to prevent a subway tragedy and fails spectacularly. From this I believe supporters of intelligent design will take comfort; it appears that Koestler has been given the sort of proof I requested.

But it's not quite that simple. For one thing, how do you conveniently get an exact count on a death toll via a cable news flash? It often takes days to find bodies (after an earthquake, for example), and some victims may linger for weeks. And were the numbers dictated by a supernatural power or by a higher order of natural power? That leads directly to a question at the end of the film.

As you know, there have been appearances all through *Knowing* of mysterious figures standing at a distance. Men in overcoats, alone or in groups of four, regarding the children who can hear them "whispering" in their ears. At the climax, these figures manifest at the site of the house trailer Lucinda lived in as an adult.

At first they seem to be human, but then they divest themselves of human appearance and become glowing, transparent figures of energy and nerves. They beckon Caleb and Abby to follow them as they enter a shimmering vessel that seems to vaguely suggest a geodesic dome or elements of the Martian crystal structure in *Watchmen*.

The vessel takes off, and we see that it is joined by other vessels from all over the globe. Then the sunburst takes place, and the special effects are merciless as the firestorm rips across the planet. The two children are deposited by the vessel in a sun-washed wheat field, join hands, and run toward the only tree on the horizon. A new Adam and Eve in a new Garden of Paradise?

At the moment the mysterious figures cast away their humanity, I fully expected them to sprout wings and manifest as angels, etc. But no. They seem to belong to the natural world, in a form we cannot imagine. The fact that their vessels take off from Earth and physically move through space seems to indicate they are meant to be real, no matter what worm hole they may use to arrive at the new planet. (Or do they travel back through time, and start the process on Earth all over again?)

If we assume the aliens are real in some tangible sense, how did they produce the numbers? Is Lucinda's sheet of paper proof that the universe is deterministic, and that the aliens simply possess the intelligence and information to predict the future, as in theory they could? And if so, isn't their existence a "refutation" of the existence of God? Strict determinism implies an absence of free will, and free will is a necessary component of all spiritual belief systems.

In this scenario, the aliens would have known they would dictate the numbers to Lucinda, that Caleb would be given them, that Koestler would have behaved exactly as he did, and that the outcome would have been exactly as it was. No suspense for them. And the aliens and all of *their* actions would have been foreordained from the instant of the creation of the universe. That leaves the possibility that a higher power created the universe but denies that power any role in its subsequent behavior.

My guess is that many audience members will experience the film as an affirmation of religious belief. Few will bother to think through the implications, which seem to make religion irrelevant—except as a comfort to those like Koestler's clergyman father.

All of my considerations are probably irrelevant to enjoyment of the film. But the film inspired me to think in these ways, and not many films do. It was exciting while watching *Knowing* and while trying to puzzle it out. Just on the fundamental level of a moviegoing experience, I think Proyas's film is a great entertainment, one of those Bruised Forearm Movies where you're always grabbing the friend next to you. Nicolas Cage, a remarkably versatile actor, embodies the role. He internalizes doubt and fear, until they gnaw at his character. He plays a man of action always fearful of inadequacy, a hero by the seat of his pants. The young actors Chandler Canterbury and Lara Robinson (who plays both little girls) are uncommonly good at projecting deep solemnity, not easy for children. *Knowing,* as I sometimes like to say, is what going to the movies is all about.

Note: The names of the characters inspire some associations. Koestler: For Arthur Koestler, of course. After Koestler wrote such novels as Darkness at Noon, *Wikipedia notes, "mysticism and a fascination with the paranormal imbued much of his later work." His* Roots of Coincidence *is "an overview of the scientific research around telepathy and psychokinesis and compares it with the advances in quantum physics at that time."*

Lucinda Embry: Lucinda, to quote from thinkbabynames.com, *is based on Lucine, the Roman goddess of childbirth, giver of first light to the newborn. Her surname "Embry" needs only one more vowel.*

Caleb: Is of Hebrew origin, and its meaning is "dog." In the Bible, Caleb, a companion of Moses and Joshua, was noted for his astute powers of observation and fearlessness in the face of overwhelming odds. And "dog" spelled backward is . . .

Angels: The alien beings do, I now realize, have wisps of wings that nevertheless doesn't necessarily make them supernatural.

Vincent P. Falk and His Amazing Technicolor Dream Coats

June 4, 2009—You might never have heard of Vincent P. Falk, but if you've been a visitor to Chicago you may well have seen him. He has performed for the patrons on every single tour boat cruising the Chicago River. And he is known to every viewer of the NBC/5 morning news, and the ABC/7 afternoon news. He's the smiling middle-aged man with a limitless variety of spectacular suits. He stands on the Michigan Avenue or State Street bridges, showing off his latest stupefying suit. He flashes the flamboyant lining, takes it off, spins it in great circles above his head, and then does his "spin move," pivoting first left, then right, while whirling the coat in the air. Then he puts it on again and waves to the tourists on the boat, by now passing under the bridge, always wearing a suit for the occasion: shimmering black for Kwanzaa, red for Christmas, neon green for St. Patrick's Day so blinding Mayor Daley wouldn't have the nerve to wear it.

For ABC/7, he stands outside the big windows of the news studio, which open onto State Street. You can't miss him. For NBC/5, he's worked his way up to regular Friday morning appearances. The station's news studio overlooks Pioneer Court Plaza, and when the anchors go outside to chat with people, there's Vincent. He's agreed to appear exclusively on the Channel 5 early news, where I have never seen him, because his usual spin on Fridays is just before the 6 a.m. sign-on of the *Today* show.

He also does radio; WGN talker John Williams does his show in a Tribune Tower studio with a window on Michigan Avenue. "I make it a point to not interact with people who try to get my attention," he says. "But Vincent . . ." It's possible Vincent's eyesight is so bad he can't even see Williams behind tinted glass in the daytime, but he knows the studio is there, just as he seems to know a lot of other things.

He's well-informed on the personnel of the TV news operations, for example, recently writing me: "For months, Channel 7 has been cutting me out of the crowd shots. But, recently, I've been getting in the shots on weekends. This is when Michael Wall is usually the director. But I'm still being cut out of the shots all the time on weekdays, when Jef Kos is usually the director." How many viewers with 20/20 vision know those names?

You might be forgiven for suspecting that

Vincent is a few doughnuts short of a dozen. I know I did. Then I saw a remarkable new documentary by Jennifer Burns named *Vincent: A Life in Color,* which unfolds into the mystery of a human personality. His life is one that Oliver Sachs, the poet of strange lives, might find fascinating. Considering that Vincent has been showing up for years and performing his "show" with flamboyant new suits, would it surprise you to learn that he is a college graduate? A computer programmer? A former deejay in gay North Side discos? Owns his own condo in Marina City? Buys his own suits? Legally blind?

All of these things are true. I can easily believe he buys his own suits. What I can hardly believe is that they are sold. We accompany him on a visit to his customary clothing store, which perhaps caters otherwise to members of the world's second oldest profession. Surely he's their best customer; I don't recall ever seeing the same suit twice in the film.

Jennifer Burns, who both produced and directed the film, says that like most Chicagoans, she'd seen Vincent and his colorful suits around for years. How could she not? Then one day she was looking out her office window, watching him performing for a tour boat, "and I was struck by the look of sheer joy I saw on his face. I thought to myself, whatever else you have to say about this guy, he has figured out what makes him happy and he does it, regardless of what anyone else thinks." She approached him, and he agreed to be the subject of a film—not surprising, since his pastime is drawing attention to himself. The subtext of the film is how differently life could have turned out for Vincent.

What Burns discovered was not quite the story we might have expected. Vincent, whose surname comes from one of his foster families, was an orphan abandoned by his mother and raised at St. Joseph's Home for the Friendless. He was already blind in one eye, and glaucoma was dimming the sight in his other. After eight years he was placed in a foster home with Clarence and Mary Falk, who he considers his father and mother; he has had a star named after her. In the documentary, Sister Bernadette Eaton, who taught him as a boy, says at first she didn't realize he could read.

I e-mailed Vincent: "I'm missing something here. The nun says she was 'surprised' to learn you could read. So she didn't teach you. Did you teach yourself?" He responded quickly with an e-mail that was articulate and friendly. That was a surprise, because in the film he has some difficulty in expressing himself. His words don't flow smoothly, he repeats himself, gets tangled up, deflects questions with a joke. A coworker in the doc says if you ask him something, he'll patiently respond, and then he's outta there. No small talk.

Vincent wrote: "I really don't remember who would have taught me to read. Maybe one of the other nuns. Maybe when I started going to school. I went to pre-school (they didn't have Kindergarten), 1st grade, and 2nd grade at St Joseph's. Then, I started 3rd grade my first school year after moving in with the Falks. And, I did attend all those grades at the proper time, with respect to my age (they didn't see a need to hold me back a year or so before starting me in 1st grade, or anything like that)."

I asked Burns what she thought. "I'm sorry this wasn't more clear in the film. Sister Anna Margaret (who declined to be interviewed) recognized that Vincent's problem wasn't intellectual but visual and taught him to read, along with the rest of the class, making sure he was always pushed up against the blackboard so he could see. It was the administration, who had previously written him off as incapable of learning, who were surprised to learn that Vincent could read."

In high school he was picked on; a classmate recalls students would sneak up behind him, tap him on the shoulder, and jump away before he could whirl and try to see them. He began to defend himself with humor, especially with puns, which are still an addiction. He didn't want to be considered blind any longer, Burns says, so he stopped using a cane. He was a member of the National Honor Society, the chess club, the debate team . . . and the diving team, luckily never diving into a pool without water. We meet his diving coach, who was as surprised as we are. It was in high school that he started wearing colorful suits, for reasons he does not explain. My theory: Being the class clown was better than being the class misfit.

Vincent reads with his left eye held less than an inch from a book or computer screen. He uses a monocular telescope for spotting approaching tour boats. His optometrist says he has severe tunnel vision; his good eye is a fraction of normal, and the visible image is like an iris shot surrounded by blur. He walks freely all over the Chicago Loop, often running a few steps or even skipping, so high are his spirits. The movie uses graphics to represent what he can see; it is terrifying to think of him crossing a street.

On his Web site (www.vpfalk.net), he does report one injury: "For the six week period from February 1, 2003–March 8, 2003, there were no pictures posted to this site. This hiatus was caused by personal injury, due to being hit by a taxicab on January 29, 2003 (specifically, a Ford Crown Victoria). The accident occurred on Clark St. right by Quaker Tower."

Vincent, a bright student, was accepted at the Illinois Institute of Technology, studying aeronautical engineering. Yes. After two years he transferred to the University of Illinois, where he planned to study computer science in a program where admission standards are ruthless. At Urbana he became fascinated by audio equipment, not unusual among the visually impaired, "but my parents didn't like that, and hauled me back up to Chicago. They boxed up all my audio stuff and put it in the garage."

He got back into the audio field, and became a popular deejay, first for the go-go boys at Stage 618, and then at the gay disco Cheeks. He didn't exactly fit the image, his old boss recalls, and he held the albums an inch from his face, but he was a great spinner. It was during this time he concluded he was gay. For the past twenty years, he's been a computer programmer for Cook County, helping to track billions of dollars in tax revenue. "He's one of the most brilliant programmers I've ever met," his current boss says.

All of which is admirable, but how does it explain the suits? Having worn them since he was a teenager, he says he gave his first Chicago River bridge performance around 2000, adding the "spin move" about a year later. He knows the times when every tour boat passes his bridges, and the guides know his name and point him out as a landmark somewhere between the Wrigley Building and Marina City. To the guides on the Mercury boats, he is "Riverace" (rhymes with "Liberace"). The captain of one of the Wendella boats says you can set your watch by him. His bridges and the TV studios are within a short walk of his home.

There is a great deal of discussion in the documentary about Vincent's motivation. It explains nothing. Vincent himself will say only that he likes to entertain people, to cheer them up a little. One person in the doc speculates that Vincent has spent a lot of his life being stigmatized and isolated, and the suits are a way of breaking down barriers. I confess that the first time I saw him, I saw a man with unfocused squinting eyes and a weird suit, and leaped to conclusions. But by the time I saw this documentary, things had changed in my life. Anyone seeing me walk down the street would notice an unsteady gait, a bandage around my neck, and my mouth sometimes gaping open. If they didn't know me, they might assume I was the Village Idiot. You can easily imagine Vincent becoming an isolated agoraphobe, locked onto a computer screen. But he spends hours every day in the fresh air and sunshine, picking up that tan and getting lots of exercise.

That's why I respond to Vincent and applaud him. If people take one look at me and don't approve of what they see, my position is "Fuck 'em if they can't take a joke." So here is a man who likes to wear pimp suits and wave them at tour boats. So why not? What are the people on the boats so busy doing that they don't have time for that? I suspect something like 99 percent of them are more entertained by Vincent than by the information that Ludwig Mies van der Rohe designed the IBM Building.

Vincent: A Life in Color played the Wisconsin Film Festival in Madison in April 2009, where Vincent brought along his orange and blue Illinois suit, to compete with Wisconsin's red, black, and gold. Jennifer Burns says she plans a limited run in a Chicago indie house sometime this summer, as a help to a distribution deal. She deserves one. The film gathers an impressive array of people who have had roles in Vincent's life, including a lifelong friend who was another foster child with the Falks. It is beautifully photographed by Patrick Russo, who contrasts Vincent's life in color with the looming riverside architecture and its busy sidewalks. Vincent will never be mistaken for a man in the crowd.

On his Web site, Vincent has photos of himself with virtually every one of the cows that were on display on Chicago sidewalks in 1999, and with many of the subsequent sidewalk globes, bobbleheads, and couches. His suits always match the artwork. He takes his own self-portraits, using a camera on a tripod and an auto timer. On the film's own Web site (www.zweeblefilms.com), you can find the column Neil Steinberg wrote for the *Sun-Times* about Vincent in 2005. It was Neil who sent me his DVD of this film.

Vincent writes me: "For your enjoyment, I have some Blagojevich humor (I'm sure you've heard of him). Recently, he wanted to go to Costa Rica to be on the TV reality show. This makes me think of someone who buys some very, very, very expensive cologne or perfume, and then splashes way too much of it on himself or herself. He or she would truly be a cost-a reekin!!!!??"

Note: Correcting the article, Vincent writes me: "First, NBC5. I'm no longer there on Fri AM. The producers took away my 'spin spot' in Oct. 2007. You can still see me at Studio 5 once in a (great) while in the background during one of the evening news casts (usually the 6PM news).

"As for the bridges, my bridges of choice are Michigan Av and State St (not Wabash). But, I may temporarily move from Michigan Av to Columbus Dr. Apparently, the Bureau of Bridges is starting a repainting project on the lower level of Michigan Av Bridge. Today (Sunday), the north approach to the bridge was closed off due to the painting. I went to the other end of the bridge, and slipped around the barrier, so I could get on the bridge deck for my fashion shows. (Don't worry, the Bureau of Bridges WILL get over it!!!!??!) But, if the painting work moves onto the bridge itself, I won't be able to do that, so it's over to Columbus.

"In a related thing, you can thank the recession of the mid 1970's for the fact that I became a disco DJ. It's been said that the 1970's recession was the 2nd worst in the last 50 years, or so. Second only to the current recession. It was my inability to get a programming job in the period of 1974-1976 that caused me to wind up in the DJ booth.

"Neil Steinberg wrote his article back in 2005, not last year as you said. It was written shortly before Jennifer started shooting her film. About a year earlier, an article was written in the Tribune. That's the one that was regionalized (it was seen only by people within the city, itself).

They also took a photo of me in a bright, shiny, peach colored suit, and printed it in black and white (the nerve of them)!! There was an article about me last year, but that was the good Tribune article, written by Colleen Mastony.

"And, for your benefit and/or enjoyment, did you know that basketball is the perfect game for a gay accountant to play?? If he launches the ball on a perfect trajectory, where it goes through the hoop and touches nothing but fabric, the ball does tend to go swish. He will achieve his net result."

The Fall of the Revengers

June 24, 2009—The day will come when *Transformers: Revenge of the Fallen* will be studied in film classes and shown at cult film festivals. It will be seen, in retrospect, as marking the end of an era. Of course, there will be many more CGI-based action epics, but never again one this bloated, excessive, incomprehensible, long (149 minutes), or expensive (more than $200 million). Like the dinosaurs, the species has grown too big to survive and will be wiped out in a cataclysmic event, replaced by more compact, durable forms.

Oh, I expect the movie will make a *lot* of money. It took in $16 million just in its Wednesday midnight opening. Todd Gilchrist, a most reasonable critic at Cinematical, wrote that it feels "destined to be the biggest movie of all time." I don't believe *Titanic* and *The Dark Knight* have much to fear, however, because (1) it has little to no appeal for non-fanboy or female audiences, and (2) many of those who do see it will find they simply cannot endure it. God help anyone viewing it from the front row of a traditional IMAX theater—or even from the back row. It may benefit from being seen via DVD, with your "picture" setting dialed down from Vivid to Standard.

The term "assault on the senses" has become a cliché. It would be more accurate to describe the film simply as "painful." The volume is cranked way up, probably on studio instructions, and the sound track consists largely of steel crashing discordantly against steel. Occasionally a Bot voice will roar thunderingly out of the left-side speakers (1) reminding us of surround sound, or (2) reminding the theater to have the guy take another look at those right-side speakers. Beneath that is boilerplate hard-pounding action music, alternating with deep bass voices intoning what sounds like Gregorian chant without the Latin, or maybe even without the words: just apprehensive sounds, translating as "Oh, no! No! These Decepticons are going to steal the energy of the sun and destroy the earth!" The hard-pounding action music, on the other hand, is what Hollywood calls "Mickey Mouse music," so named because, like the music in a Mickey Mouse cartoon, it faithfully mirrors the movements on screen. In this case, it is impatient and urgent. I recommend listening to it on your iPod the next time you have difficulty at the doctor's office filling the little plastic cup.

The action scenes can perhaps best be understood as abstract art. The Autobots and Decepticons, which are assembled out of auto parts, make no functional or aesthetic sense. They have evolved into forms too complex to be comprehended. When two or more of the Bots are in battle, it is nearly impossible to distinguish one from the other. You can't comprehend most of what they're doing, except for an occasional fist flying, a built-in missile firing, or the always dependable belching of flames. Occasionally one gets a hole blown through it large enough to drive a truck through, pardon the expression.

You want to talk about incredible? I think it's incredible that *any* of the tiny flesh-and-blood human beings are still alive at the end of the story. As is conventional in action epics about gigantic monsters, the creatures seem to exist on a sliding scale—always possible in theory, I suppose, for a Bot, but disorienting for the audience. On the one hand, you have Bots large enough to rip the top off the Great Pyramid with its bare hands, and on the other, small enough to fit in the same frame with a human, and this movie is widescreen (2:35:1). To be sure, a Bot can lean down to talk to a human. But when they're seen standing up there's a problem. Their heads are small to begin with, and the effect of perspective from the human eye level makes many of them unfortunately look like pinheads.

I didn't have a stopwatch, but it seemed to me the elephantine action scenes were pretty much spaced out evenly through the movie. There was no starting out slow and building up to a big climax. The movie is pretty much all climax. The Autobots and Decepticons must not have

read the warning label on their Viagra. At last we see what a four-hour erection looks like.

The action is intercut with human scenes that seem dragged in kicking and screaming from another movie. There are broad sitcom situations and dialogue as Shia LaBeouf goes off to Princeton, and comic relief from his madcap mother (Julie White), who actually plays the most entertaining character in the movie. Then some romances that cement emotional bonds with the speed of Quick Glue and are well within the PG-13 guidelines. Kevin Dunn and Miss White, as Mr. and Mrs. Witwicky, are the only characters allowed the slightest dimension, confirming my suspicion that the most interesting conversation at a high school dance is likely to be had with the chaperones.

As is frequent in CGI action, the younger women are made to behave like he-men with boobs. College girls are able to turn instantly into combat-ready participants, except when they have to be dragged to safety by boys. They can outrun explosions with the best of them. Their hair, after countless explosions and long days in the desert heat, is always perfect enough for a shampoo commercial. I suspect many young lads prefer their women like this—at arm's length, if you see what I mean.

Much of the dialogue falls under the category of "Look out!" It's necessary in the editing of a film like this to punctuate the action with reaction shots. You're not really able to cut away to another Bot, because their heads are so tiny and so high up there, who knows what they're thinking? You need humans, who react to a blue screen or to a point in space and shout warnings and commands. Acting in a film like this is a season in hell, plus paycheck.

At almost two and a half hours, the film is unreasonably long. Since it's impossible to imagine a studio applauding the extra length and thus greater expense, the running time can possibly be attributed to the ego of Michael Bay, the director: If it is indeed destined to be the biggest movie of all time, who cares how long it is? I suspect it will be trimmed down to under two hours in some overseas markets, and if it is, the human scenes will be the easiest to cut. Then the luckless foreigners will be left with an unremitting assault on the senses.

Michael Bay is obviously under the impression that whatever he was doing deserved a 149-minute canvas to do it on. He *likes* doing this stuff. One pities the hapless animators, peering at their monitors far into the night, trying to distinguish one Bot's hubcap from another's. What we may see at work here is the paradox of rising expectations and diminishing returns

Michael Bay is only forty-four, and I hope he tires of this nonsense and returns to making real movies. He was only thirty-one when he made *Bad Boys* in 1995, and thirty-two when he made *The Rock*. He had been in TV for years. He was a prodigy, like Steven Spielberg. But Spielberg was forty-seven when he directed *Schindler's List*. Michael Bay seems to be evolving in the wrong direction.

So is the hyperactive blockbuster CGI action genre. If there is one thing everyone in Hollywood thinks they know for sure, it's that the three most important words in movie development are *story, story, story.* This is not a story: "A group of inconsequential human characters watch animation."

The very best films in this genre, like Christopher Nolan's *The Dark Knight* and Sam Raimi's *Spider-Man 2,* had compelling characters, depended on strong human performances, told great stories, and skillfully integrated the live-action and the CGI. I've been making a list of my favorite robots, those few that evoked wonder and sympathy and were not simple attacks of sound and images. I think of the gentle, lovable *Iron Giant* (1999) by Brad Bird. And the genius of Jon Favreau's *Iron Man* (2008), with its final battle we really got involved in. And I think of another robot whose body was made of junkyard parts. Its name was WALL-E. That was the 2008 film by Andrew Stanton that some people believe was robbed of a Best Picture nomination by the creation of the animation category.

Transformers: Revenge of the Fallen will no doubt gross many millions. There will no doubt be a sequel. But when audiences feel hammered down by a film, they are less likely to fall for another marketing campaign. If Hollywood wants the *Transformers* franchise to endure, maybe they should hire one of those directors. They still know how to make a movie.

I'm a Proud Brainiac

July 5, 2009—"Roger Ebert is a moron! Transformers 2 is the best action movie ever. Don't listen to that moron! He is only into slow boring romantic movies. That is his type of movies. Michael Bay did a great good. Roger . . . your an old fart!" —John C.

Having now absorbed all or parts of 750 responses to my complaints about *Transformers,* I suppose I shouldn't be surprised that most of those writing agree with me that it is a horrible movie. After all, look where they've chosen to comment. There have, however, been some disagreements that I thought were reasonable. These writers mostly said they had a thing about the Transformers toys of their childhoods, or liked the animation on TV, or like to see stuff blowed up real good. In that case. Michael Bay is your man. If you enjoyed the movie, there is no way I can say you're wrong. About yourself, anyway.

Another common line of attack was disturbing. It came from people who said I was out of touch with the tastes of the audience. That the movie's detractors (lumped together as "the critics") like only obscure movies that nobody else does—art films, documentaries, foreign films, indies, movies made fifty years ago—even, God forbid, "classics." One poster argued that *Transformers* was better than that boring old movie *Casablanca*.

I was informed I didn't "get" Michael Bay. I was too old, "of the wrong generation," or an elitist or a liberal—although not, I was relieved to find, a "liberal elitist." It seems to me *Transformers* also qualifies for conservative scorn. It is obliviously nonpartisan. Yet one said I hated the movie because it was an attack on President Obama. I was afraid to say I hadn't noticed that, because then I would be told I hadn't even seen the movie. It is possible to miss plot points but strange in a movie with so few of them. Veiled in-jokes about politicians and famous people, popular in animation and mass market movies, come with the territory. I enjoy them. The apparent reference to Obama was no big deal, although a reader from Germany told me the actual name "Obama" was used in the German dub. That possibly didn't happen without Bay hearing about it.

But am I out of touch? It's not a critic's job to reflect box office taste. The job is to describe my reaction to a film, to account for it and evoke it for others. The job of the reader is not to find his opinion applauded or seconded, but to evaluate another opinion against his own. But you know that. We've been over that ground many times. What disturbs me is when I'm specifically told that I know too much about movies, have "studied" them, go into them "too deep," am always looking for things the average person doesn't care about, am always mentioning things like editing or cinematography, and am forever comparing films to other films.

I've "forgotten what it's like to be a kid," another poster told me. One of the most-admired contributors to my blog, who signs herself "A Kid," is twelve years old. She hasn't forgotten. Neither have many other readers of middle school age. Their posts give me hope for the future. For them, to be a kid is not to be uncritical or thoughtlessly accepting. They seek magic and don't find it in the brutal hammering of *Transformers.*

A reader named Jared Diamond, a senior at Syracuse and sports editor of the *Daily Orange,* put my disturbance eloquently in a post asking: "Why in this society are the intelligent vilified? Why is education so undervalued and those who preach it considered arrogant or pretentious?" Why, indeed? If sports fans were like certain movie fans, they would hate sports writers, commentators, and sports-talk hosts for always discussing fine points, quoting statistics, and bringing up games and players of the past. If all you want to do is drink beer in the sunshine and watch a ball game, why should some elitist play-by-play announcer bore you with his knowledge? Yet sports fans are proud of their baseball knowledge and respect commentators who know their stuff.

It's true that many Americans have an active suspicion and dislike of the "educated." They ask, "What makes you an expert?" when they're really asking, "What gives you the right to disagree with me?" The term "college graduate" has become in some circles a negative. Hostility is especially focused on the "Eastern elite," to the chagrin of we Midwestern elitists. To describe someone as a "Harvard student" is to dismiss them as beneath consideration. You can often hear the words "so-called" in front of such words as "scientist," "educator," "philosopher." I don't believe this is intended to imply

that the person involved is not a scientist, etc., but to suggest that no one calling himself such a thing is to be trusted—because he is, no doubt, many other undesirable things.

While I am eager, in the words of my alma mater's song "Illinois Loyalty," to "back you to stand, against the best in the land," I envy the hell out of anyone who has gotten himself into Harvard, especially with his mind and not his parents' clout. Some people believe it is the best university in America. Why must that be a mark of shame?

I never took a film class. I will not bore you with yet another recitation of my rags-to-riches saga, my hard-won film education, and blah, blah, blah. Let's just say I started out with a lot to learn and am still trying to learn as much of it as I can. There are people who know so much more about film than I do, it makes me all but weep with gratitude when they deign to speak with me. Two words: David Bordwell. That he speaks to everyone in clear and eloquent prose speaks for itself. It isn't that he "thinks he knows more than anybody else." It's that he does. It's like he happens to know a lot of interesting stuff and is happy to share it with you.

Now about those who sincerely believe *Transformers* is a good, even a great, film. I sincerely believe they are wrong. I don't consider them stupid—at least, not (most of) the ones who write to me. Some of the posters at certain popular Web forums are nine blooms short of a bouquet. But, on the other hand, look at the spirited discussions on the movie forums of the all-Transformers-all-the time Seibertron.com, where a Paramount exit poll showing "90 percent of those polled thought the second film was as good or better than the first one" has been received with ridicule. Significantly, those are moderated forums.

So let's focus on those who seriously believe *Transformers* is one of the year's best films. Are these people "wrong"? Yes. They are wrong. I am fond of a story I tell about Gene Siskel. When a so-called film critic defended a questionable review by saying, "After all, it's opinion," Gene told him: "There is a point when a personal opinion shades off into an error of fact. When you say *The Valachi Papers* is a better film than *The Godfather,* you are wrong." Quite true. We should respect differing opinions up to a certain point, and then it's time for the wise to blow the whistle. "Sir, not only do I differ with what you say, but I would certainly not fight to the death for your right to say it. Not me." You have to pick your fights.

What I believe is that all clear-minded people should remain two things throughout their lifetimes: curious and teachable. If someone I respect tells me I must take a closer look at the films of Abbas Kiarostami, I will take that seriously. If someone says the kung-fu movies of the 1970s, which I used for our old "Dog of the Week" segments, deserve serious consideration, I will listen. I will try to do what Pauline Kael said she did: Take everything you are, and all the films you've seen, into the theater. See the film, and decide if anything has changed. The older you are and the more films you've seen, the more you take into the theater. When I had been a film critic for ten minutes, I treated Doris Day as a target for cheap shots. I have learned enough to say today that the woman was remarkably gifted.

Those who think *Transformers* is a great or even a good film are, may I tactfully suggest, not sufficiently evolved. Film by film, I hope they climb a personal ladder into the realm of better films, until their standards improve. Those people contain multitudes. They deserve films that refresh the parts others do not reach. They don't need to spend a lifetime with the water only up to their toes.

Do I ever have one of those days when, the hell with it, all I want to do is eat popcorn and watch explosions? I haven't had one of those days for a long time. There are too many other films to see. I've had experiences at the movies so rich, so deep—and yes, so funny and exciting—that I don't want to water the soup. I went to *Transformers* with an open mind (I gave a passing grade to the first one). But if I despised the film and it goes on to break box office records, will I care? No. I'll hope, however, that everyone who paid for a ticket thought they had a good time, because it was their time and their money.

The opening grosses are a tribute to a marketing campaign, not to a movie no one had seen. If two studios spend a ton of money on a film, scare away the competition, and open in 4,234 theaters before the Fourth of July, *of course* they do blockbuster business. The test is: Does the film have legs?

Major-league Hollywood seems completely dominated by the belief that money can buy anything and justify anything. When a reader wrote to inform me that Michael Bay paid $8 million to the "writers of the screenplay," I very much doubted it. Turns out that figure is correct. With numbers like that representative of big-time Hollywood, I observe with Yeats that the best lack all conviction, while the worst are full of passionate intensity. No wonder. It pays better.

Questions for the Movie Answer Man

Age Differences

Q. Regarding the age differences of on-screen parents and their children, the most egregious recent example I can think of was in *Alexander* (2004) where Angelina Jolie (twenty-nine) played the mother of Colin Farrell (twenty-eight).

—Tina Scuccimarri, Midhurst, Ontario

A. This is becoming the Question That Will Not Go Away. Other readers write:

Devin Tuffy, San Francisco, California: One of the most obvious cases would be brothers Groucho and Zeppo Marx playing father and son in *Horse Feathers.*

Daniel Lyons, Canton, Michigan: In the film *The Apostle,* June Carter Cash (born 1929) plays the mother of Robert Duvall (born January 1931).

Chris Meadows, Springfield, Missouri: In *Indiana Jones and the Last Crusade,* Sean Connery was (and still is) only twelve years older than Harrison Ford. And in *Drunken Master II* (aka *Legend of the Drunken Master*), Anita Mui plays Jackie Chan's mother but is actually nine years *younger* than he is.

David Teigland, Salt Lake City, Utah: I always think of Angela Lansbury and Laurence Harvey in *The Manchurian Candidate.* Lansbury was only two years older than Harvey. Her performance, though, made the relationship completely believable.

Ali Arikan, Istanbul, Turkey: In *Hamlet,* Laurence Olivier was born in 1907, yet Eileen Herlie, who played Gertrude, was born in 1920! And here is an interesting postscript: Herlie also played Gertrude in a 1960 Broadway production of *Hamlet* with Richard Burton in the titular role, and she was younger than him, too (by five years, in fact).

Alternate Endings

Q. What is your opinion of the growing trend for movies to include "alternate" endings on their DVD releases? While I'm reasonably comfortable with a different presentation of the ending from that originally conceived (for example, *Training Day*), it seems that to offer a different *outcome* is an admission of failure on the part of the director. If the movie is well structured, shouldn't the outcome follow inevitably and essentially from the plot and characters depicted? Even in movies famous for the twist in their tales, the ending is compelling at the very least in retrospect (for example, *The Sixth Sense, The Crying Game, Memento*). To me, an alternate ending sends the message that the director lacks commitment to or faith in his material. I give a pass here to movies where a director restores his or her preferred ending in the director's cut over one that was handed down by "creative executives" (for example, *Blade Runner*), but I've never felt that watching a movie should be an exercise in choosing the ending that makes you feel most comfortable.

—Carl Zetie, Waterford, Virginia

A. In the case of a movie not worth taking seriously in the first place, alternate endings can be fun. Otherwise, I agree with you.

Beards

Q. I've detected prejudice in your writings regarding facial hair. In your review of *The Illusionist,* you describe Ed Norton as having "the lower half of his face masked behind an impenetrable Van Dyke." More recently, in your review of *The Girlfriend Experience,* you describe the role of sex in an escort-client relationship as "the beard," by which I assume you mean something to hide one's true motivations behind. And there have been others.

I have facial hair, mainly because I like the way it looks and the shape it gives to my face. Also because I hate shaving. I don't think it hides much, except maybe a double chin. My emotions and personality tend to express themselves through my eyes and mouth, words and actions. You seem to think that the chin is the window to the soul. Is it so? Do you universally ascribe obfuscator motives to men with long whiskers? Does it depend on the whiskers or on the man? Do you consider invention of the razor a historic advance in honesty? In short, do you have a metaphysical problem with beards?

—Robert McLendon, Altadena, California

A. Some of my best friends have beards. Others of my best friends are beards.

Before the Devil Knows You're Dead

Q. We recently saw *Before the Devil Knows You're Dead.* In your review of that film, you said Marisa Tomei "just keeps on getting sexier as she grows older so very slowly." Is it possible that hormones compelled you to say that, considering she was in some state of undress in half her scenes? Also, why was the opening scene necessary? In my advancing age, I'm more and more repelled by such scenes. Also, as long as I've been reading this column, I've never seen anyone ask how they do such scenes. Can you safely do that in this column? I'm baffled how they could fake that opening scene.

—Chris Baecker, San Antonio, Texas

A. Let's face it. Convincingly faking sex is done all the time, and not just in the movies. The opening scene was perhaps necessary to establish the characters, but it wasn't exactly essential.

Che

Q. After watching both parts of *Che* yesterday at the Landmark Theater in Chicago, I noticed that the light in each part was different. In the first part, in Cuba, the light was warm and the colors were rich. Yet in part two, in Bolivia, the light is harsh and the colors always looked washed out. Why? Was this on purpose? Was this simply a function of the time of year the movie was filmed and the angle of the sun? For example: I notice in winter the light in Florida is warm and colorful due to the angle of the sun being low on the horizon. Yet go back to Florida in the summer, when the sun is directly overhead, and the light looks harsh and washed out, not as warm.

—Stuart Bagus, Chicago

A. I believe it was deliberate—Steven Soderbergh subtly indicating a time when things went right for Guevara and a time when they went wrong. One reason for the intermission between the two halves is that audiences do not notice (except unconsciously) that the two parts were filmed with separate aspect ratios: part one in 2.35:1, and part two in 1.85:1, limiting the space around Che visually as it was also actually closing in.

Comics to Movies

Q. With so many films being drawn from TV series lately (*Get Smart, Sex and the City, The X-Files*) and comics (too many to mention), I've heard quite a few debates about which films best handle the transfer. It seems that the winners are most often the films that are either most faithful to the original creation (*The Dark Knight,* thematically and stylistically, though hardcore fans may disagree), or the least faithful (*Get Smart, From Hell*). Would this suggest that brave filmmaking is more likely to succeed critically? If so, is this strange, since a risk is supposed to be risky? That is, has Hollywood been so careful in recent years that we're just happy to see someone going all out for it, skewing genuine criticism?

—John Collins, Melbourne, Australia

A. What's in the middle? The sort-of-faithful? The good films you mention leap beyond their origins; the lesser ones, like *SATC,* simply try to repeat them.

Crash

Q. I noticed that *Crash* is listed as the number one most-rented movie on Netflix, ahead of Scorsese's number two *The Departed,* and number three *The Bucket List.* I know you picked *Crash* as the number-one film of 2004, but does this surprise you?

—Charlie Smith, Chicago

A. Yes. I took a lot of heat for that choice at the time. I did some Googling and discovered an article by Robert K. Elder in a Chicago newspaper published not a million miles from this one. He reports that *Crash* claimed the number-one spot in September 2005, and has been there *every single week since.* He quotes a Netflix spokesman: "More people have now seen *Crash* via Netflix than saw it in theaters," even though it won the Oscar for best film of the year.

What do I make of this? First, it's self-fulfilling. A lot of people must see it at number one and place it in their queues. Also, many Netflix rentals are inspired by users recommending titles to their lists of friends. When we do that, we're proselytizing: We think our friends *should* see it. That may have something to do with the human emotion named Elevation, which I have written about.

In an America learning to be a diverse society, there is a feeling among many people that we must look beneath group stereotypes and see the real people there. *Crash* shows an interlocking group of characters who are forced through a series of coincidences to do that. The insights they gain are deeply moving, or sad, or joyful. You feel as if you've shared something.

I'm glad you didn't ask about *The Bucket List*.

Critics Eating Candy

Q. In his review of *Daylight*, Gene Siskel wrote: "As a measure of my boredom, about a half hour into this picture I became fixated on the critic down the row from me eating some candy. It wasn't Roger. It was John Petrakis from the *Chicago Tribune*, and I tried to guess the candy he was eating by the sounds he was making." Do you remember this? Did you join in?

—Jerry Roberts, Birmingham, Alabama

A. I remember the review. What I have always wondered is, do different candies make different sounds? I am sitting here trying to imagine. I think most of the sounds are inside your head. The M&M's crunch, for example, or the Red Hots slosh. Notice that Gene doesn't say what he concluded. If he listened, even though he couldn't tell, he must have thought the movie was *really* bad.

The Curious Case of Benjamin Button

Q. While I loved the book *Marley and Me*, I found the movie to be a typical "zany" Hollywood comedy. On the other hand, *The Curious Case of Benjamin Button* had me

bawling throughout. You write: "But it's so hard to care about this story. There is no lesson to be learned. No catharsis is possible." That is simply the reason why the movie works so well. The viewer knows there is no happy ending here. Hell, the ending is only the worst possible thing to happen. I think you are incorrect in assuming people will not go see this movie twice. I saw it tonight and plan on going later in the week to pick up any nuances I may have missed. I think a review that drives home the point of the movie has been written by Capone over at Ain't It Cool News.

—Neal Greenberg, Freehold, New Jersey

A. Well, at least you chose another one of our excellent Chicago critics. I gave *Marley* a half star more than *Benjamin*, although, of course, star ratings are relative, not absolute, and are nonsense either way.

Q. Have you seen anyone's analysis of the extensive self-plagiarism screenwriter Eric Roth exhibits in his new film? I've compiled a list of parallels between his *Forrest Gump* and *The Curious Case of Benjamin Button* on my blog: http://madeinhead.org/anism/?p=369.

—Jason Preston, Junction City, Kansas

A. Many people have noted parallels, but your blog is pretty much a slam dunk. In rewriting, Roth plugged the Fitzgerald short story into *Gump*.

Q. Like most people, I knew the CGI in *The Curious Case of Benjamin Button* was groundbreaking, but I had no idea of the extent of the achievement: Aside from one brief appearance in an early scene, the real Brad Pitt literally does not appear in the first fifty-two minutes of the film. Even experienced CGI artists are impressed by this milestone achievement. And while I personally think *Benjamin Button* is somewhat overrated, it will be scandalous if it doesn't win the Oscars for FX and makeup.

Regarding the widely reported similarities between his screenplays *Forrest Gump* and *Benjamin Button*, it's obvious that Eric Roth has been creatively lazy, but he's also deviously clever: After all, if he sues himself for plagiarism, he wins either way.

—Jeff Shannon, Seattle

A. Of course, Brad Pitt had to do enormous amounts of acting and body movement to provide a baseline for the CGI, and that is thankless but skilled work. And Roth had to write *Forrest Gump* as a baseline for *Button.*

Q. Your review of *Benjamin Button* observes that fiction, generally, should have a *forward flow* for time (flashbacks and -forwards notwithstanding). As an exception to this, might I suggest Martin Amis's novel *Time's Arrow*? While the focus of his story differs from the Fitzgerald and film versions of Button, it does consistently show the flow of time backward and, in my opinion, works well.

—Paul D'Amboise, Saint-Hubert, Quebec

A. If you didn't believe or *know* that time flowed forward, could you distinguish it from backward time? If a participant saw one of his tasks coming undone (a painting unpainting itself, for example), would it seem subjectively to him that he had painted it first? We assume time flows from past to future, but physicists assure us that it's relative. When the universe finishes expanding, maybe time flips and it flows backward to its beginnings. Stop me before I start babbling.

Dark City

Q. I know you are a huge fan of Alex Proyas's wonderful film *Dark City.* I consider it one of my favorites. I was curious if you had the opportunity to see the director's cut and what your thoughts are on this new version of the film.

—Kevin Kluck, Cincinnati

A. I think the changes are improvements, particularly the decision to let us find out for ourselves who and what the Strangers are. On a personal note, I am pleased that they include the original version with my commentary track, and that they have used that and additional material I recorded to create a commentary on the director's cut.

Q. I just read your review of Proyas's *Dark City* in your Great Movies section. My question is: Was this movie ruined by a "Hollywood executive"? Now, I love *DC*. It's one of my favorite movies. However, the first time I saw it, I entered the theater a bit late, and so missed the opening narration explaining the Strangers, the city, etc. I walked in right when the protag-

onist wakes up in the tub. As a result, the movie was much more mysterious to me, and I only slowly discovered what I had missed in the opening—like the hero. I feel that without that opening narration, the movie was, in fact, much better; more suspenseful by far. I know it's hard to measure such a thing—the second time I saw it, I, of course, already knew the plot, but I still felt the opening narration spoiled the film quite a bit. I envision some Hollywood suit saying: "People won't have the patience to endure what they don't understand for that long. Better give away most of the secrets via a narration in the beginning," and forcing Proyas into it. Am I right?

—Colin Prepscius, New York

A. The director's cut by Alex Proyas on the most recent DVD suggests you are 100 percent correct. By the way, this is one of the movies Blu-ray was made for.

The Dark Knight

Q. I was so impressed with *The Dark Knight* I saw it again, just to make sure my appreciation hadn't been influenced by all the hype. I went the second time with entirely my own eyes, and to test my theory that so much of its success is the result of the Answer Man's fellow Chicagoan, the cinematographer Wally Pfister. Everything about this movie—the writing, the direction, the performances, and even before that, the courage to set out in such an unorthodox direction—is as great as it is only as a result of the cinematography. My question then: Do you think the cinematographer, in this particular alchemy, could have been anyone other than Pfister?

—Jimmy Jacobs, Columbia, South Carolina

A. There are a lot of great cinematographers, but Pfister has worked with director Christopher Nolan three previous times (*Memento, Batman Begins, The Prestige*) and is on the A-plus list. He and Nolan obviously have a deep rapport.

Q. In your review for *The Dark Knight,* you say that the Joker is a product of his father's poor treatment, but that's just one story he uses to explain his scars. Another is that he did it for his wife, and Batman interrupts before he offers a, most likely, different story. I think the point was that he doesn't have a cause. Who's wrong here?

—Samy Amanatullah, San Diego

A. I am. I should have mentioned all of his dubious stories, instead of sampling.

Q. SPOILER WARNING: The Joker poses a dilemma for Batman in *The Dark Knight* that forces Batman to choose between saving two people. If Batman has an actual choice about who to save, then the moral consequences of that decision rest with him. However, the Joker lies about who is where, and only by choosing to attempt to save either person does Batman get an opportunity to save the other person. Doesn't the Joker's lie defeat the purpose of transferring any responsibility of a death to Batman? More precisely, doesn't the Joker's lie exist only for the purpose of fooling the audience, paradoxically removing Batman of any culpability for who dies? If the Joker wants only to be senselessly cruel to Batman, he has got to bet that Batman cares a lot more about one person than the other. Seems like a lot of effort for not such a sure thing. Unfortunately, he gets lucky.

—Steve Sherry, Washington, D.C.

A. I rather like the Joker's deception. It provides another turn of the screw. Batman is forced to choose, and the Joker ensures that his choice is futile.

Q. I wonder if the writers of *The Dark Knight* meant to imply that Batman's only moral solution to the Joker's dilemma is to flip a coin.

—Ben Shin, New York

A. Since no choice could be logically defended, that's as good a way as any.

David Attenborough

Q. The narrator of the original *Planet Earth* BBC series was David Attenborough, not Patrick Stewart. I'm probably not the first person to e-mail about this, nor am I likely the first to complain that they have taken the greatest documentary series that I have ever seen and cut it up into a feature length film.

—Brandon Budelman, Albany, New York

A. And Sigourney Weaver did the American version. I am happy to run this correction

to my review of *Earth,* because it provides an excuse to supply the greatest statement I have ever overheard in a public place. This was in the Academy Club in London, run by Auberon Waugh, and as it happens Sir David was at the next table with a friend. He said, "So there we were, off the coast of Syria, surrounded by copulating whales, with guided missiles staring down our throats, and what do you think happens but . . ."

Death Race

Q. Now that you have seen just how awful a *Death Race* movie can be, is there any chance that you might go back and retroactively give the original a higher rating than your original zero stars condemnation? I know that the star ratings are essentially meaningless, but as is, it suggests that the new one is better than the original and, good Lord, not even [name deleted] would say something that insane.

—Peter Sobczynski, eFilm critic.com, Chicago

A. I wrote back to you explaining that the lowest rating a movie can receive for being bad is one-half star. To receive no stars, it must be, in my opinion, somehow immoral. In *Death Race 2000* (1975), cross-country racers received 100 points for every wheelchair they mowed down, 70 points for the aged, 50 points for kids, etc. I considered that immoral.

But you, Peter, with your mastery of debate, which I have come to admire over the years, responded: "I agree on your point. However, I would argue that the obviously satirical nature of the material and the subtext commentary about the increasingly debased and violent nature of popular entertainment elevates it from being completely immoral. By not having any of that subtext, I would argue that the new one is far more immoral than the original in addition to all of its other artistic sins. Additionally, while the notion of extra points for running over people in wheelchairs is a nasty one indeed, the punch line of the scene is that Frankenstein avoids hitting the old people when he comes across them and instead mows down the people who deliberately wheeled them out in the street to die."

Quite true. Now I can only fall back on my long-standing decision not to revise past reviews, because I think they should remain as I originally wrote them, and because with more than eight thousand reviews on the Web site that would commence a never-ending task.

Defiance

Q. In your review of *Defiance*, you mentioned the character Shamon Haretz, who tells the group he is an intellectual. You wrote, "This is no use to the partisans, although he is allowed to stay. . . . I thought, I'm also an . . . intellectual. Of what use would I be in the forest?" This reminded me of a comment by John W. Campbell Jr., science fiction writer and editor of *Astounding/Analog* magazine. Campbell threw this provocative thought at his readers: "It has yet to be proven that intelligence is of any survival value." That shook up a lot of his readers. He then went on to explain, by way of example, that if a group of intellectuals and strong men were trapped in a cave by falling boulders, that no amount of logical thought would move those boulders an inch. Obviously, Campbell was not abandoning logic (he codified Asimov's "Three Laws of Robotics") but pointing out that it had limits. To me, it suggested that it would be a good idea to build body and mind!
—Mike Reese, Chicago

A. Of course, intelligence would be useful in knowing survival skills, such as how to tell direction or start a fire. But as several reality shows have demonstrated, it is of no use in becoming a TV star.

Dining with Lefty

Q. I'm reading your new book about Scorsese and had a question. In the section introducing *Casino*, you mention that you spotted Frank "Lefty" Rosenthal in Florida at a restaurant. Did you ever talk with him or discuss *Casino*?
—Joseph O'Driscoll, Salt Lake City

A. I didn't dare. It was in Joe's Stone Crabs in Miami Beach, and he was pointed out to me by the owner, Joanne Bass (the third-generation Joe). She said he had lunch there almost every day, usually alone, usually at the same table. This showed his good sense. As Gene Siskel once told me, "Roger, everything there is good. Everything. Not just the entrees. The potatoes. The coleslaw. The onion rings. The spinach. The key lime pie. The bread basket." I wouldn't violate Joanne's confidence by sharing this if Mr. Rosenthal were still alive, but he died on October 13, 2008. It was enough for me to simply see him. I was reminded of a story about William Faulkner, who spent a semester as a writer in residence at a famous university. He was asked by a pal, "What do you do?" His reply: "I walk across the campus twice a day so the students can say, 'There he goes.'"

Downsizing IMAX

Q. After I went to see *Watchmen* earlier this year in the supposedly IMAX format, I realized I might need a primer on what true IMAX and the true cinema experience entails. As I usually see movies in "normal" format, I wasn't particularly impressed by the IMAX format and decided never to pay that premium again. Maybe a Theater Wall of Fame (always remain positive) could be added to your Web site? It might prove a great reference for those on the lookout for a good theater nearby at which they know the films are portrayed in the best possible way.
—Volkert Doop, Washington, D.C., and Norway

A. It is ironic that IMAX, a company founded to provide a top-quality alternative to standard projection, has lowered its traditional standards and the value of its famous name. A true IMAX film is in 70 mm and is seen on a vast 72-by-53-feet screen, with all stadium seating. Now theaters advertised as "IMAX" are occupying modified multiplexes, where their standard screen has been only somewhat enlarged and the projection is digital. To charge extra for this "IMAX" experience is false advertising. A true IMAX theater is still a great place to see films such as *The Dark Knight*. If the IMAX theater you're considering has opened somewhat recently, check it out carefully.

DVDs

Q. This may be some sort of marker of our times: Doc Films at the University of Chicago ends its synopses of certain films with the words: "This film does not exist on DVD." Directors include D. W. Griffith, Carl Dreyer, Fritz Lang, Jean Renoir, Ernst Lubitsch, Raoul Walsh, André de Toth, Douglas Sirk, Yasujiro Ozu, and Kenji Mizoguchi.

—Bill Stametz, Chicago

A. Astonishing. It says something about DVD producers, but even more about Doc Films, the nation's oldest film society.

Q. Why do some movies come on DVD with "embedded" subtitles, i.e., without the possibility of turning these subtitles off? I've recently experienced this, trying to watch the French version of *The Diving Bell and the Butterfly*. The subtitles, when unwanted, can be very distracting.

—Mario Ouellet, Ottawa, Ontario

A. I've never encountered a DVD like that, but I completely agree with you. What the French call the "VO" (*version originale*) should always be offered, with subtitles optional.

Q. You recently dealt with a question about DVDs with "embedded" subtitles (I believe the term would be "hard coded"). I've seen this a couple of times, along with supposedly widescreen DVDs that are actually sending a letterboxed 4:3 signal, meaning it will display with black bars even on an HDTV. In general, they tend to either be discs from early in the DVD era, or niche/obscure/low-budget titles—in other words, either made before people knew what they were doing or made now by people with not enough experience and/or money to do it properly.

—Christopher Wells, Louisville, Kentucky

A. Now that I have a new digital HD set, I've become more sensitive to such issues than ever. The good news is that I think the DVD manufacturers have, too.

Fanboys

Q. As a high school teacher, father, husband, and *Star Wars* fan, I must register my offense at your *Fanboys* review. My involvement with the *Star Wars* fandom lifestyle has brought me countless memories and friendships. It has opened the door to relationships with my students and colleagues I would oth-

erwise have been ignorant of. I am among a legion of *Star Wars* fans. It's time you stopped posing for your fellow critics. You've obviously caught a lot of flak for your favorable review of *Star Wars—Episode I: The Phantom Menace*. Perhaps you're slinging mud at what appears to be an easy target as a means of earning back some credibility. Look at the breadth and depth of the community you alienate. We are doctors, lawyers, teachers, priests, authors, actors, accountants, custodians, social workers, construction workers, and more. We are too big to be dismissed.

—Matthew Schnaare, via e-mail

A. I have received a lot of unhappy feedback from that review, in which I wrote: "Anyone who would camp out in a tent on the sidewalk for weeks in order to be first in line for a movie is more into camping on the sidewalk than movies." I have now learned many things about myself, most of which I cannot print here, although they solved the puzzle of what I would do with a third thumb. I was unfair in referring to all fans, when the ones I was thinking of were the heroes of *Fanboys*.

Q. After reading your *Fanboys* review, I was upset and angry. As a diehard *Star Wars* "fanboy" who is far from "socially inept," I must say that if you think that the film is a "celebration of an idiotic lifestyle," then you should go to a *Star Wars* convention and say that to every single person there, and let's see what they'll say to you. If you have a good reason for saying what you said, feel free to reply.

—Alex D. Geslin, Greeley, Colorado

A. Well, the film *is* a celebration of an idiotic lifestyle. To me, that would involve driving to California to break into Skywalker Ranch and steal a print of the new *Star Wars* movie but first making a detour to Iowa to have a rumble with some detested *Star Trek* fans. That's the film. As for real life, I now know from countless readers that *Star Wars* fans devote much of their time to raising funds for sick kids. I hadn't realized that, and I applaud it. I reserve the right to consider it idiotic to live in a tent on a sidewalk for several weeks to be first in line for the next *Star Wars* movie.

Q. At the age of twelve, I was livid while reading your trashing of my favorite blockbusters. I've outgrown those days. I read your review of *Fanboys* and, for the first time, was struck hard enough to comment: Absolutely spot on! What struck me was the insightful glance at the current trend in our culture toward groupthink. It's everywhere—music, television, fashion, business. The arts scare me the most. Too much energy is being wasted on fruitless endeavors and trivia. A quick glance at one of innumerable fan message boards will reveal the emotion and time invested in fandom. In the search to be different the fans become the same—a tired cliché taking pride in their uselessness. *Get a life* indeed! I congratulate you on the tone of your review. I can only hope that someone hates it enough to start listening to what you have to say!

—Daniel Bauer, Ontario

A. Fanboys were intensely unhappy with that review and have let me have it. To what I've said already, I'll add: It's fine to have fun as a fan, but to *define* yourself as a fanboy—to offer that as the reply to "What are you?"—is sad.

Fast and Furious

Q. I am disappointed by your review of *Fast and Furious*. You gave away the fact that Michelle Rodriguez dies early in the movie. Seeing that she died within the first twenty minutes, it was kind of ruined for me. Given that she is billed fourth on IMDb, I would not have expected her to die so soon. She is also all over the trailers and even the ad on your Web site calling her one of the "original cast," thus I believe this was a faux pas on your part, in revealing her death is the reason he returns to L.A. I believe you could have said he returns for the death of a friend but not a character that is plastered on all of the movie posters for the movie.

—Kyle Cieply, Greenville, South Carolina

A. You make a good point. On the other hand, the advertising gave you the wrong impression. If her early death had been a surprise, like the top-billed Janet Leigh in *Psycho*, that would have been a real spoiler. But if they bring her in for a bit part . . .

Film Critic Crisis

Q. Around the first of the year, responding to the plague of newspaper downsizing,

David Poland of Movie City News ran a list of movie critics with full-time jobs in the United States. It had 144 names on it. Now it's down to 141. Your reaction?

—David Manning, Los Angeles

A. I was cast into a well of depression until I received this message from Joe Leydon of Houston, who reviews for *Variety*, the Moving Picture Blog, and other publications:

"Wouldn't you agree that, as late as the early '80s, and maybe later, there really weren't that many full-time film critics in the U.S.? I remember at the time I finally got my full-time gig—in 1982, for the *Houston Post*—someone pointed out to me that more people were full-time pro baseball players than there were full-time film critics."

Ebert again: I am now advising aspiring movie critics to go into baseball.

Foreign Films for Kids

Q. I came across a foreign movie I thought my wife and kids would like: *CJ7*. They loved it! So I have been trying to find other foreign films for kids that are not animation. Do you have a list you can think of at the top of your head that would be okay for kids nine and up?

—Anthony Thacher, Corona, California

A. Here are a few: *Children of Heaven*, *King of Masks*, *Millions*. Useful guides are screenit.com, with detailed information for parents, and Nell Minow at http://blog.beliefnet.com/moviemom/.

Get Smart

Q. Although there are rare times when a remake is justified, such as when the world has greatly changed and it would be relevant to see how such events would affect precise film characters, I'm greatly annoyed at Hollywood's lack of creativity. If I see one more film version of a '60s or '70s TV show (now we have *Get Smart* to deal with), I'm going to puke.

—Richard Voza, Mickleton, New Jersey

A. You may have to lay in a supply of sick bags. With its $38 million opening weekend, *Get Smart* looks like the launch of a franchise. And it will justify the filming of still more old TV retreads, although the bottom of the barrel must be approaching. All hail to Kevin

Costner, who refuses to do sequels. On the other hand, how much work has that cost him compared to Harrison Ford; their career paths have crossed many times, but Ford is notably receptive to sequels.

Q. In your review of the spy spoof *Johnny English,* you said "Can we all pretty much agree that the spy genre has been spoofed to death?" I noticed that you gave *Get Smart*—a spy spoof that, based on the trailer and outside reviewers, seems pretty mediocre—a whopping 3.5 stars. What do you feel sets *Get Smart* ahead of similar films like *Johnny English,* since both seem so heavily reliant on slapstick and silliness?

—Adam Fangman, Omaha

A. I begin with the advantage of having seen both films. But I nevertheless feel the spy genre has been pretty much spoofed to death.

The Girlfriend Experience

Q. Regarding your review of *The Girlfriend Experience*: Prostitutes in movies are never used for what they provide in real life, which is sex. In movies, prostitutes are paid for anything and everything but the thing they actually provide. See *Pretty Woman, The Girlfriend Experience,* and countless others. Eliot Spitzer or any other man never paid large amounts of money to talk to a woman.

—Eric, Meriden, Connecticut

A. Although it may have turned out that way.

Goodbye Solo

Q. I found it interesting in your glowing review of *Goodbye Solo* that you described the story as about two people, one of whom has possible suicidal ideas. I remember your negative review of the critically acclaimed Iranian film *Taste of Cherry.* Wasn't there a similar plot in both movies? Interesting, because both films are by those of Iranian heritage.

—Ali Hirji, Edmonton, Alberta

A. Ramin Bahrani, director of *Goodbye Solo,* has great admiration for the films of Abbas Kiarostami, the director of *Taste of Cherry,* and acknowledges the similar plot lines. But few films are more different.

Gran Torino

Q. I object to this statement in your review of *Gran Torino*: "What other figure in the history of the cinema has been an actor for fifty-three years, a director for thirty-seven, won two Oscars for direction, two more for Best Picture, plus the Thalberg Award, and at seventy-eight can direct himself in his own film and look meaner than hell? None, that's how many." John Huston should be considered in the same league as Eastwood. A first-rate actor, an award-winning director, even directing his own father to a Best Supporting Oscar. On any list of the best in cinema, there will be multiple Huston movies, perhaps giving Clint a run for his money. We can only hope Clint's career will last as long.

—Maggie Sorrells, Williston, North Dakota

A. Technically, my statement is correct. But you are quite right that Huston is the only name that belongs on the same list.

Q. In your review of *Gran Torino,* you write: "When he gets to know Thao, the teenage Hmong who lives next door, he takes him down to his barber for a lesson in how Americans talk. He and the barber call each other a Polack and a dago and so on, and Thao is supposed to get the spirit. I found this scene far from realistic and wondered what Walt was trying to teach Thao. Then it occurred to me Walt didn't know it wasn't realistic."

You'll be amused to read what was reported in the local paper about Ted Widgren, the ninety-year-old owner of the shop used in the movie. Widgren watched some of the filming from the back of his shop—and at one point, they had to briefly halt production when Widgren was caught talking under his breath after the barber swore at Eastwood in one scene. "I was most surprised with the barber," he said. "I wouldn't say that."

—Douglas Mooney, Detroit

A. On the other hand, maybe Walt Kowalski's barber knew him so well he was just humoring his favorite customer. It sounded like they'd done that routine before.

Great Moviegoing

Q. I didn't like the film *Little Miss Sunshine* at all, until my grandmother watched it after suffering a stroke last year. She'd lost almost all ability to communicate, but her mind was still sharp, and her nonverbal response to that film revealed an astonishing amount about the power of the medium. I was ashamed that I'd ever been so pedantic in my criticism. You've mentioned watching *City Lights* outdoors in the Piazza San Marco in Venice as one of the great moviegoing experiences in your life. Have you ever had a great moviegoing experience with a film you didn't think was all that good?

—Chi Laughlin, Clyde, Ohio

A. Yes, but not in the sense you mean. It would have been the morning press screening at Cannes of Vincent Gallo's movie *The Brown Bunny*. Europeans are not shy about booing. Never have I heard so many boos, whistles, hoots, and snorts. When anybody got up to leave, their chair snapped back with a pop. At times the theater sounded like microwave popcorn. As you may know, I thought Gallo's re-edited version was significantly better.

The Hangover

Q. I don't know about you, but it bothers me when I watch a movie trailer only to find that some footage is not found in the actual movie. They did this with *Orange County* and now *The Hangover*. It almost feels like false advertising in a way.

—Travis Dockweiler, Kalamazoo, Michigan

A. It's not done deliberately. The marketing houses assemble trailers from a rough cut of the film, because studios like to release them quite a while in advance of the opening date. It's like not having to wait for the DVD to see a deleted scene.

The Happening

Q. I've noticed some reviewers complaining about the twist ending to M. Night Shyamalan's *The Happening*. What twist ending? A twist ending redefines everything that came before it; the ending to *The Happening* implies that the events in the story are not yet over. In fact, *28 Weeks Later* had an almost identical ending and I don't recall any reviewers referring to it as having a "twist" ending. It makes me wonder if *The Happening* would be

viewed differently had it been directed by someone else.

—Adam Greenbrier, Colorado Springs, Colorado

A. Quite likely. There isn't a twist, but there is a big poke in the ribs.

Q. Would it serve Mr. Shyamalan better to try different types of movies? His movies always take place in or near Pennsylvania and seem to be some type of supernatural movie. *The Happening* seemed to be very similar to *Unbreakable* or *Signs* or any other movie he's done. I like his style but it's getting old.

—Derek Pencak, Kenosha, Wisconsin

A. Shyamalan has complained that the studios typecast him, but, in fact, *The Happening* is not supernatural. I would, however, like to see a straight drama from him.

Q. I understand your review of *The Happening* as a study of the reaction to an unknown threat by the masses. However, I left the theater feeling sick after all of the graphic, depraved suicides. Please comment on the value of the continuous death scenes and why you chose not to acknowledge that M. Night Shyamalan felt that it was necessary to video a man start a lawn mower, watch it roll around, lay down in front of it, and then get gored by the mower when the audience knew full well what the man intended to do.

—Jed Nolan, Morgantown, West Virginia

A. You could argue that at the point when he did that, the man was no longer himself but had lost his sense of reason. That could be symbolic of the planetary suicide that the movie says we are currently committing.

Hellboy II: The Golden Army

Q. In your review of *Hellboy II: The Golden Army,* you justly praise the film for director Guillermo del Toro's fantastic visual imagination in populating his world with unique monsters. But can these things exist only in the realm of computer-generated bits and bytes? You call the Hellboy character "CGI for the most part" and say the film's sights were "created by CGI, of course, but how else?" I was delighted when watching the credits to see whole teams of artists who brought the movie to life with special effects makeup, prosthetics, and animatronics (just like the original inhabitants of the Mos Eisley Cantina). After reading an article in the *Los Angeles Times,* I learned that some of the film's best fantasy visuals, such as the multi-ocular Angel of Death, were created and puppeted in the *real* world and captured that way in Del Toro's camera lens. CGI is, of course, just another kind of paint on a filmmaker's palette. But let's not forget the hard work and tremendous artistry of those who continue to push the limits of what can be achieved the old-fashioned way.

—Alex Meeres, Regina, Saskatchewan

A. I wrote hastily and overlooked Del Toro's love of the whole vast craft of traditional special effects.

Q. During the fight with the elemental god in *Hellboy II,* I couldn't shake the idea that the creature was inspired by the Forest God from Hayao Miyazaki's brilliant *Princess Mononoke.* The moment Selma Blair said that the elemental god could "give and take life," I began to recall Miyazaki's film, whose own elemental god has that exact ability. I couldn't get *Princess Mononoke* out of my thoughts; the way the spirit grows into the night, the cruel and violent way it meets its fate, etc. It all reminded me of *Mononoke*'s Forest God. Any doubts I had were dispelled by, as you describe it, what *Hellboy*'s elemental god turns itself into. Remember the ending of *Princess Mononoke*? Remarkably similar, no?

—John Bell, New Bedford, Massachusetts

A. I think you're right on the money. SPOILER WARNING: The monster becomes a tree, surrounded by a sylvan forest glade.

How Long Is a Movie?

Q. As a reviewer and a fan of film in general, what is your opinion on knowing the running length of a film that you're watching? Would it be best for viewers to not know how much is left in a film or how long they've been watching? I know I am guilty of checking my watch when I am seeing movies, but I feel like it can really ruin the suspense of a movie if we know things must be resolved in the next five minutes.

—James Pooley, Bedford, Massachusetts

A. Can't you sort of sense when the movie's at that point anyway? I proudly wear the Official Movie Critics' Watch, the Timex In-

diglo with large numbers in the New York typeface, I believe. Kenneth Turan of the *Los Angeles Times* turned me on to it.

I Love You, Man

Q. In his novel *This All Happened,* Newfoundland writer Michael Winter has a character point out that two males cannot tell each other they love each other unless they follow it with "man." You seem to have intuited the same thing in your review of *Pineapple Express.* Weird, huh?

—Mike Spearns, St. John's, Newfoundland

A. Really weird, man. Now give me a hug. Not too affectionate.

IMDb Top Film Votes

Q. Am I alone in thinking that in recent years the Internet Movie Database voting system has been skewing its Top 250 list to the relative detriment of the world's great classic films? Specifically, and to be blunt, I'm talking about what seems to be ballot stuffing on the part of a predominantly buzz-motivated teen population for certain fashionable fanboy films.

Short of scrapping the voting system altogether, I wonder if it wouldn't be more fair for the IMDb to begin an entirely new count and then put a moratorium on the polling of any new film for, say, at least one year from its release date. Keeping any candidate beyond the Academy Awards' marketeering season would mitigate the temporal zeal and level the playing field somewhat. *Casablanca* had to wait and work to build its reputation. Why shouldn't *WALL-E*? I have doubt the IMDb will act on this as the all-American obsession with "the best of tops" is firmly part of their bread and butter, but perhaps with petition we could move the gods.

—Soren Rasmussen, Paris, France

A. Keith Simanton, IMDb's managing editor, replies: "Our Top 250, as voted by users, is just that, a list of the Top 250 films as voted on by our users. It's not a classic (ah, there's a subjective term!) list by any measure, nor is it a critic's list. We leave that to the professionals. We do get bouts of irrational exuberance for some titles. I rather like it and find it analogous to my own experience. I've often felt more fondly about a film upon leaving the theater than my tempered opinion of it as the weeks and months pass. Our 'this, too, shall pass' approach has proved itself out as this inflation value of the new is not a recent phenomenon.

"In 1991, *Beauty and the Beast* was the number one title on the Top 250 and now it's not even in the chart; great movie though it is, things do tend to balance out over time. At any moment there are always some recent titles in the list but they do find their level eventually. Some of them even continue to maintain a high level, one I personally would not have accorded them. We do appreciate the suggestion, however, as we're always looking for ways to improve the service and this kicked off a great internal debate."

The Incredible Hulk

Q. I'm still wondering why it's so tough for Marvel to reconcile psychological extrapolation and pure action with the Hulk. Having seen both incarnations, they're vastly different movies, and I'm still curious why it's so tough to dabble in the middle rather than one or the other. I still prefer Lee's version, when all is said and done, even if the new version was fun.

—Felix Vasquez Jr., New York

A. The original comics were good at meeting in the middle, but movie audiences, I think, want to jump one way or the other.

Q. I agree with pretty much everything you said in your *Incredible Hulk* review, but I thought I'd give you some additional info about the plot. The plan of General Ross is not to create Hulk soldiers but to use Hulk to create "Super Soldiers," which Blonsky became on their second meeting (the serum didn't look to me like it needed much improvement, but what do I know?). That means, in comic book geek language, that he wants to create a bunch of Captain Americas.

—Alexandre Rowe, Montreal

A. I have read this three times and am still not sure of its meaning. But I confess I do not speak comic book geek.

Joaquin Phoenix

Q. Has Joaquin Phoenix lost it, or what?

—Greg Nelson, Chicago

A. I watched him on *Letterman* and was appalled. There are theories that he was deep in character in his new hip-hop persona, behaving strangely for his buddy Ben Affleck's new documentary, channeling Andy Kaufman, or whatever. I doubt if that particular hip-hop personality is going to inspire many fan clubs.

More seriously: He was on the show to *promote* his new film *Two Lovers*. All he did was ensure that his bizarre behavior was referred to in most of the reviews of the film. He had no right to do that. Independent, original films have a hard enough battle without their stars putting on psycho shows. He had no right to do it to James Gray, who directed it and cowrote it with Ric Menello. No right to do it to his fellow actors Gwyneth Paltrow, Vinessa Shaw, Isabella Rossellini, and the others. No right to distract from the film itself, which was selected for the official competition at Cannes and is running at 83 percent on the Tomatometer. I don't care if he did it deliberately or mistakenly. He should have stayed at home.

Knowing

Q. SPOILER WARNING: In your blog entry on *Knowing* you stated, "At the moment the mysterious figures cast away their humanity, I fully expected them to sprout wings and manifest as angels, etc." Actually, they did, or at least were beings that mankind interpreted as angels. Movie designers based the appearance of the four strangers on the biblical prophet Ezekiel's description of "four beings" in human form. The blue mist given off by their bodies resembled wings, and Ezekiel recorded the spaceship as having "wheels within wheels," just as it looked in the movie.

—Mike Cloud, Houston

A. So I was informed on about half of the nearly six hundred comments that entry has inspired. The wings are wispy streams of light. I must have been expecting traditional feathered wings and was distracted by the shimmering wheels within wheels. The movie obviously contains biblical imagery, but my

613

readers disagree fiercely about whether the figures are supernatural, or real aliens.

Q. I went to see *Knowing* only because of your review. I really enjoyed it. When I saw all the negative reviews on Rotten Tomatoes (only 15 percent on the Tomatometer), I was surprised. I felt like they weren't reviewing the movie as much as the premise behind it. I don't agree with the premise, but I thought it was a really good movie. I even paid the way for many of the students in my ethics class to see it. They *loved* it. Critics are still free to write whatever they want; however, I feel that they should review the movie and not judge it on its theological/philosophical premise. Would you agree? Do you feel frustrated or intimidated when you are out there by yourself?

—Cal Ford, Corsicana, Texas

A. Not when I'm right. I am heartened that a lot of moviegoers seem to agree with me. *Knowing* has passed $70 million at the box office and is holding up well. I wrote a blog entry about it that so far has attracted 812 comments, all of them literate and intelligent (a rarity on a blog), and a large majority of them are favorable. The premise is, of course, preposterous, but that's hardly a first for a sci-fi thriller. The Tomatometer, by the way, has doubled to 34 percent.

Last Chance Harvey

Q. In the new movie *Last Chance Harvey,* Emma Thompson is reading and carrying around a book and Dustin Hoffman even refers to it. At one point she sort of flashes the cover, as if it's an inside reference. What was the book?

—Charlie Smith, Chicago

A. I'm always trying to identify the books in movies. The one she's holding seemed to be by Anita Harmon, but a search at alibris.com finds no books at all by that name. Either I saw it wrong, or the director wasn't playing fair.

Lee vs. Eastwood

Q. Recently there has been a press argument between Spike Lee and Clint Eastwood. I'm wondering what you think of Lee's accusations. Spike Lee is a talented, original voice in American filmmaking, but what he has to say about *Flags of Our Fathers* seems to be a little off the mark. Your thoughts?

—Nathan Marone, Chicago

A. Lee believes that Eastwood should have shown some African-American soldiers in his depiction of the battle of Iwo Jima. Eastwood counters that there were no African-Americans involved. An article in the *New York Times* concludes that there were African-Americans involved in the battle, but (because of racial discrimination) they were in the supply lines, not the front lines. Both directors have a point. It is certainly true that black characters for years were underrepresented in Hollywood movies about World War II. The Tuskegee Airmen are an example.

Q. Did Clint Eastwood say there were no African-Americans involved in the Iwo Jima campaign? Or did he say that there were none included in his *Flags of Our Fathers* story? Which there weren't. There were about nine hundred African-American Marines on the island at the time. And there were African-American soldiers and sailors on duty there, too. I don't have the numbers for the army or navy. But Bill Madden, the primary source for my novella *Iwo Blasted Again,* landed on Iwo Jima in the first wave with Easy Company, Second Battalion, Fifth Marine Regiment, and said his amtrac had a black sailor at the helm. Beyond that, it seems that Lee's comments had a great deal to do with publicizing his new movie, *The Miracle at St. Anna.*

—Ray Elliott, Champaign, Illinois

A. As former president of the James Jones Literary Society, you have studied WW2 extensively. It may be that no African-Americans were directly involved in the flag-raising story that Eastwood set out to tell, but certainly he could have shown them in the wide-scale scenes of invasion and landing. Eastwood is certainly not racist. I suspect this was the result of oversight.

Q. Regarding the Spike Lee–Clint Eastwood flap, I'm getting so tired of this. If Spike Lee wants more blacks in WWII films, why doesn't he make a film about the Tuskegee Airmen? Their heroism, the racism they had to endure . . . this is a film he could really put his heart into. And I would love to see it. I've been hearing about the Tuskegee Airmen for years but don't know much about them.

—Kathleen Church, Chicago

A. HBO made a widely seen 1995 film on the airmen, starring Laurence Fishburne, Andre Braugher, Cuba Gooding Jr., Mekhi Phifer, and John Lithgow. It's on DVD.

Let the Right One In

Q. Do you agree with the Film Threat comment that kids should watch *Let the Right One In*? On a base level, the supposed heroes of our story are vengeful, violent kids. Don't you think more children will come away from this thinking extreme acts of violence are okay? Do you really want little girls finding a new hero in Eli? I found the movie a bit troubling and can't say that I'd recommend *any* parents showing it to their tween or young teenagers.

—Kevin Mendonca, Hollywood

A. For kids, no. For teenagers, it depends on the level of maturity. If nothing else, the movie provides a real cinematic experience in contrast to the fantasy of *Twilight*.

Q. There's been a lot of negative buzz among bloggers about the poorly translated subtitles on the DVD and Blu-ray release of the acclaimed Swedish vampire film *Let the Right One In*. The distributor, Magnet Home Entertainment, released the discs with subtitles that were "dumbed down" compared to the more informative and accurate translation provided by the film's theatrical release subtitles. Magnet has fixed the problem, and subsequent pressings will include the theatrical subtitles, with "theatrical subtitles" indicated on the packaging. Kudos to them for correcting the problem, but still, it seems like a mistake to even consider the misguided "benefit" of dumbed-down subtitles that eliminate subtleties of character and dialogue.

—Jeff Shannon, Seattle

A. Mike Cucinotta of iconsoffright.com seems to have broken the story, and uses lots of screen grabs to document the tone-deaf dumbing-down. For example: Oskar, a twelve-year-old boy, sees Eli, a girl about his age, standing outside on a winter night without a warm coat. She's balanced on a jungle gym.

Oskar: "Do you live here?"

Eli: "Yeah. I live right here, in the jungle gym."

Oskar: "Seriously, where do you live?"

Eli: "Next door to you."

Oskar: "How do you know where I live?"

In the dumbed-down version, these are the subtitles for the same conversation:

Oskar: "Where do you live?"

Eli: "I live here. Next to you."

Cucinotta says Magnet is restoring the original subtitles in discs now being released. Look for those crucial words "theatrical subtitles." The whole story is here: http://iconsoffright.com/news/2009/03/let_the_wrong_subtitles_in_to.html

Lives Lost to Movies

Q. In the review that you and Siskel did of *I Still Know What You Did Last Summer*, you said the movie drained years, even centuries, out of the human "time pool." I did some calculations and learned that it's worse than you feared.

Let's say a bad movie makes $50 million. I'll round the ticket price out to $10. I suppose that's 5 million people who saw it. If the movie is 90 minutes, then 7,500,000 hours are wasted. A *year* is only 8,760 hours. So, the bad movie has wasted 856 years. The average lifespan in the U.S. is a mere 75 years. Therefore, the equivalent of 11 entire lives are completely wasted away because of this movie. This is a low example. Many movies make far more than $50 million, are longer than 90 minutes, and are watched repeatedly on DVD. Ticket prices are usually under $10. So in conclusion, not only does making a bad movie vaporize years of potential community service, it is mathematically equivalent to committing mass murder.

—Will Lugar, Tulsa

A. The horror! The horror!

Mae West

Q. I recently read an article in the paper that attributed the following quote to Jean Harlow: "Is that a pistol in your pocket or are you just glad to see me?" My sister says this is an exact quote from a movie and she thinks Mae West said it, but we couldn't find anything on the Internet. Do you know the quote, who said it for sure, and what movie this comes from?

—Janice Moore, Arlington Heights, Illinois

A. It was indeed the very same woman who said, "Beulah, peel me a grape." Mae West first uttered the immortal pistol line in *She Done Him Wrong* (1933). Her double entendres helped inspire movie censorship, of which she said: "I believe in it. I made a fortune out of it." She got away with saying incredible things in general-audience movies. For example, "A hard man is good to find." "Anything worth doing is worth doing slowly." "The only good woman I can recall in history was Betsy Ross. And all she ever made was a flag."

Magnolia

Q. I read your Great Movies review of *Magnolia* and asked myself why the film was titled like that and thought of all the different characters, all beautiful blossoms, alone, but connected at the root of one great magnolia. I see *Magnolia* as a story about redemption. The film so closely observes its sinners, and we suffer as we watch them trapped in their self-made cages of misery. But all along a change is coming; from the very outset something is in the air. The religious allegory here is about receiving a second chance.

—Shawn Inlow, Osceola Mills, Pennsylvania

A. That's certainly one meaning. The IMDb user swlf63 adds on a message board: "(1) Magnolia Blvd. is a street in the San Fernando Valley where the film takes place. Some of the characters in the film I believe drive down this street; (2) 'Magnolia' sounds similar to 'Magonia,' a term created by Charles Fort (who wrote about strange phenomena and is referenced in the film's closing credits), which is an alleged place in the sky where things are kept until they fall from it, which might explain the rain of frogs; (3) 'Magnolia' is an eight letter word with 2 a's, being the 2nd and 8th letters. This is an odd coincidence which relates back to the numbers 82 featured frequently in the film as a reference to Exodus 8:2: 'If you do not let them go, I will send a plague of frogs.' "

Mamma Mia!

Q. I went to see *Mamma Mia*, and as a sixty-five-year-old ABBA fan, I loved it. It was

refreshing. No violence. Loving, exciting, entertaining, what a movie should be. Don't berate a movie just because you don't like it. As a critic, you should be intellectually honest and not self-serving.

—Tom Kilpatrick, Nashville

A. But that's exactly what I do: berate a film because I don't like it. Would it be more intellectually honest for me to lie and say I did?

Man on Wire

Q. Will *Man on Wire* be prevented from being nominated as Best Documentary because part of the film was reenacted, like *The Thin Blue Line*?

—Carol Iwata, Chicago

A. I asked Bruce Davis, executive director of the Academy, who responds: "Since 2004, when several prominent nonfiction films raised questions about whether certain practices should be ruled beyond the documentary pale, the Academy's Documentary branch has used an interesting approach to eligibility. Recognizing that doc filmmakers themselves have varying degrees of tolerance toward reenactments (asking real people to do things that they had done in the past over again for the camera), actments (employing actors to re-create events), stock footage, distressed footage (manipulating images to make them appear 'historic'), scripted sequences, and computer-generated images, the rules now place those kinds of eligibility questions in the laps of the individual nominations voters.

"No film is disqualified for using any of those elements—in fact, the rules explicitly permit them. But the director is now required to identify if and where such elements have been used in his film, on a form that is distributed to each nominations voter. If a particular Doc branch member feels that a contending film has made excessive use of, say, reenactments (and a purist may regard any such use as excessive), she is free to penalize it on her ballot. Indications to date have been that the branch is tolerant of minor amounts of any of these elements, so long as they are not employed misleadingly."

Marley and Me

Q. How can you be so dead-on correct about 99 percent of the movies you review, but be 100 percent off about a piece of crap like *Marley and Me*? Boring material, terrible script, and totally misleading advertisement—worse than a Lifetime cable movie! We took our five-year-old to what was supposed to be a fun family movie about a dog, not a slice of life from a totally uninteresting family. I won best jazz guitarist in all the major guitar magazines for two years in a row. I'm not perfect and neither are you, but I've never made a piece of music that's as horrible and dead wrong as your review.

—Scott Henderson, Los Angeles

A. You are the only person who has ever said I'm dead-on correct 99 percent of the time, so thank you. But—weren't you just a little fascinated by the sheer insanity of the Grogans continuing to live in the same house with Marley? I'm guessing—no, you weren't. I love dogs, but Marley is scary. I guess your child didn't like the movie either. I suspect in a lot of families, the kids will love Marley, but the parents will look at each other and communicate telepathically: "Not in our house, Marley won't."

Metropolis

Q. About a year ago it was reported that the original full-length version of Fritz Lang's silent film *Metropolis* (1927), including lost footage, had been found in a South American film vault. When will this film be made available?

—Ed Carty, St. Louis

A. This was one of the great film archival discoveries. The film is still in the process of being restored; one scene, at a reel end, is so badly damaged it is almost unusable. A restoration is hoped for by the end of 2009.

Moon

Q. So, how coincidental is this? The movie *2001: A Space Odyssey* includes a character named Dr. Heywood Floyd. The new movie *Moon* evokes *2001* powerfully for you and is directed by someone whose birth name is Duncan Zowie Heywood Jones. Heywood isn't exactly a common name. Maybe he was born to direct this movie.

—John Wilson, Ottawa, Ontario

A. Jones was born in 1971, when *2001* was at the height of its fame, and is the son of David Bowie, who I think we can be sure saw it, who was famous as Ziggy Stardust, who played an alien in *The Man Who Fell to Earth*, and who is only four degrees of separation from Kevin Bacon. Cue *Twilight Zone* theme.

Music in Movies

Q. I was watching *The Thing* the other day and started to think. There are movies that engross you and you don't think about anything else. With *The Thing*, what does it for me is the music. At the beginning there is a simple "dunn, dunn" sound repeated over and over that creates tension throughout the whole opening that caused me to get lost in the sequence. Is there one thing that tends to do that for you?

—Jeff Schindler, Durham, North Carolina

A. You're right, it's often the music, reaching us below conscious thought. I was looking at the new version of *Last House on the Left* the other day and I realized I was already feeling uneasy and all I'd seen were some trees.

North Carolina

Q. I'm a student at the University of North Carolina. I aspire to become a filmmaker. Lately, however, I've been feeling film is going down the tubes. We have a generation of actors and directors making remakes so horrible I feel that they're taking down the magic and beauty of cinema. Sometimes when I see movies like *Slumdog Millionaire*, *The Dark Knight*, and *WALL-E*, I am given a sense of hope. I feel I have to save film and it's been an overwhelming feeling that has gotten me depressed and agitated. Do you think film is still good, and that it will continue to inspire filmmakers to come?

—Tallman Boyd, Chapel Hill, North Carolina

A. Living in North Carolina, you can take heart that two of the truly great younger American directors, Ramin Bahrani (born there) and David Gordon Green (graduate of the North Carolina School of the Arts), have deep North Carolina connections. Green's *George Washington* and Bahrani's *Goodbye Solo* were both shot in and around Winston-Salem; Bahrani won the Critic's Prize at Venice 2008. See their works to witness brilliant, wonderfully photographed films made on limited budgets. You may be inspired.

Nothing but the Truth

Q. Thank you for your heads-up regarding Rod Lurie's *Nothing but the Truth*, but I have to cringe in anticipation of Kate Beckinsale's character. If she is indeed meant to be Judith Miller, I dearly hope she is not portrayed as some saintly, sympathetic figure. The real Judith Miller carried so much water for Bush's attack on Iraq that some of us may never forgive her. I hope her role in the rush to war is not forgotten in the emanation she may get from this movie.

—Bob Koelle, Wilmington, Delaware

A. This is a powerful film that has not yet been released for tangled reasons having to do with the Hollywood economic crisis. It portrays Miller in a generally favorable light but is not about Iraq, on which I suspect Lurie agrees with you. It deals specifically with the fact that she indeed went to prison rather than reveal her sources as a journalist.

Objectively Wrong

Q. A few minutes ago I read Stephen Hunter's 2001 review of *2001: A Space Odyssey* and almost vomited. Here's an excerpt: "Now, seen in the actual 2001, it's less a visionary masterpiece than a crackpot Looney Tune, pretentious, abysmally slow, amateurishly acted and, above all, wrong." A crackpot Looney Tune? Amateurishly acted? Wrong? What does that even mean, "wrong"? Wrong about what? Is this guy seriously criticizing this 1968 film for not exactly predicting all of the inventions of the new millennium? How could a Pulitzer Prize–winning critic miss the point so badly?

—Robert Ford, Coquitlam, British Columbia

A. I don't ordinarily print letters disagreeing with other critics, and Stephen Hunter is one whose work I respect. Disbelieving what you quoted, I went to the *Washington Post* Web site and found a page for the review, but no review. The quote you supply is also used on Metacritic.com, so it's apparently accurate.

If so, it reminds me of a helpful lecture I supplied to a young film critic for a Chicago TV station who was new at the job: "Film criticism is all opinion, and always subjective.

There is no right and no wrong. That having been said, Phil, it is nevertheless *wrong* for you to state that *The Valachi Papers* is a better film than *The Godfather*."

Pauline Kael

Q. I am a big fan of *Last Tango in Paris* and would like to read the famous review by Pauline Kael. I have searched the Internet and a few journals and cannot find a copy of the review anywhere. Do you have a copy you could post a link to or e-mail to me, or do you know how I can get a hold of it?

—Jennifer O'Donnell, Oaxaca City, Mexico

A. The absence of Pauline Kael's film criticism on the Web is a continuing disgrace. You will find that review, however, and many more of her reviews of key films, in her book *For Keeps*. All of Kael's books can be purchased used, but apparently none are currently in print.

Q. Regarding your lament that Pauline Kael's reviews are not available on the Web: Dennis Cozzalio has a link to all her reviews on his blog, named Sergio Leone and the Infield Fly Rule.

—Ali Arikan, Istanbul, Turkey

A. The direct link is http://geocities.com/paulinekaelreviews. I went there with great eagerness, but it appears to me the site uses only about half her capsule reviews from the *New Yorker* (which were collected in *5,001 Nights at the Movies*), and not her famous full-length reviews. This situation should be remedied.

Q. Your Answer Man item this week about the availability of Pauline Kael's criticism reminded me that I hadn't brought you up to date about our looking into a reprint of *Going Steady*. Our paperback editor checked out the situation regarding her work, and it appears that the small British firm of Marian Boyars Publishers, Ltd., now has rights to most of her titles. Just talked with our paperback editor, and she confirmed that Little, Brown (the original publisher of *Going Steady*) had directed her to Kael's literary agency in England, Curtis Brown, Ltd., since rights had reverted to Kael in 1988. Hardcover or paperback editions of the following Kael titles are still available from Marion Boyars in the U.K.: *Going Steady, Deeper Into Movies, Kiss Kiss Bang Bang, I Lost It At the Movies, Reeling, Raising Kane and Other Essays,* and *Hooked,* and I believe there are editions of her other books as well from Marion Boyars that are still available in the used market. These are also sold via Amazon (and its related sellers) in the U.S. (other than in the used book market). *5,001 Nights at the Movies* is still in print in the U.S. and is "available at better bookstores," but of course it's essentially a video guide and doesn't contain any complete essays. I expect it may take a well-selected Library of America volume to get her principal pieces widely available again in the U.S. With rights for the individual volumes apparently still held by Marion Boyars, I doubt that any U.S. publisher would be able to issue reprints in the near term. I wish the situation looked more promising, but for now it looks as if we'll have to make do with *5,001 Nights at the Movies* and whatever else can be ordered, either used or new, online.

—Rodney Powell, University of Chicago Press

A. I went to amazon.co.uk and found virtually all of her titles, as you report. I have often ordered books from them and know they accept American orders. But the American situation is dire. I agree she is abundantly deserving of the honor of a Library of America title.

Q. Glad to see the Answer Man item concerning Pauline Kael this week. Given that the Library of America has published a volume of James Agee's movie criticism, as well as two volumes of Edmund Wilson's critical work, a volume of Kael may not be too far-fetched a notion. In any case, two other interesting volumes of "Kaeliana" that are still available are the collection of interviews published by the University Press of Mississippi in 1996, *Conversations with Pauline Kael,* and the little volume by Francis Davis published after her death, *Afterglow: A Last Conversation with Pauline Kael.*

—Rodney Powell, University of Chicago Press

A. I agree. This Library of America volume is a book that needs to exist.

Paul Newman

Q. In your recent Great Movie review of *Cool Hand Luke* you note: "But such a film could not possibly be made in more recent decades, not one starring Brad Pitt or Tom Cruise or other actors comparable to Paul Newman's stature. It is simply too painful. I can imagine a voice at a studio pitch meeting: 'Nobody wants to see that.'" However, I think *The Shawshank Redemption* had plenty of punishment for its main character: prison rape, beatings, solitary confinement. True, there's maybe a bit more hope to that particular character's struggle, but all in all I think the characters in that film suffer quite a bit more than in *Cool Hand Luke* (and it was made less than fifteen years ago). What do you think?

—Patrick Naugle, Elgin, Illinois

A. Yes, but Tim Robbins doesn't have the iconic immunity of a Pitt or Cruise, and the movie ended ambiguously but happily.

Pineapple Express

Q. Like you, I enjoyed *Pineapple Express.* And like you, I think David Gordon Green is a poet of film. As much a departure as *Pineapple* is for Green, you can still see his poetry. It's subtle and washed over by the action and buffoonery, but it's there. It's in how things are juxtaposed, and not just the images. It's also in the absurdity and in other places of which I'm less certain. That said, I was surprised so many critics disliked it. I shouldn't have been, I know, but I was.

—Jimmy Jacobs, Columbia, South Carolina

A. I liked it first of all because I found it funny. Second, it's well directed. We are going to be hearing a lot more about Green. *Pineapple Express* was not a "personal" film as his other works have been, but it sure does demonstrate he can do a doper buddy genre picture and make it good. I imagine he can do about anything.

Playing Buster Keaton

Q. Bill Paxton has a dream project: to direct Jimmy Fallon in "the ultimate Buster Keaton biopic." Cameron Crowe cast Fallon in *Almost Famous,* and that worked out pretty well. Fallon's partial resemblance to Buster is noteworthy, so this suggests an intriguing gambit similar to casting Robert Downey Jr. in *Chaplin*. Paxton directed *Frailty*, to which you gave a four-star rating. So what do you think? Should a risk-taking studio make Paxton's dream come true?

—Jeff Shannon, Seattle

Q. With Paxton and Fallon involved, assuming it's a good script, I don't see the risk on a studio's part. The risk on their part is that some executives have probably never heard of Buster Keaton, the greatest actor-director in the history of the cinema, and that includes Orson Welles, who they also haven't heard of. I read an article by Ralph Keyes saying journalists should cut back on their "retro talk" because younger readers are not familiar with their references, like Beaver Cleaver. If writers had never mentioned names I'd never heard of, what would I have ever learned? So here, in defiance, are two names in retro talk: Buster Keaton. Orson Welles. Believe me, I could go on.

Playing the Stooges

Q. The cast for the upcoming Farrelly brothers Three Stooges film at MGM is just about set! *Variety* reports: "Studio has set Sean Penn to play Larry, and negotiations are under way with Jim Carrey to play Curly, with the actor already making plans to gain 40 pounds to approximate the physical dimensions of Jerome (Curly) Howard. The studio is zeroing in on Benicio Del Toro to play Moe." What do you think?

—Lara Golubowski, Chicago

A. I found this amazing sentence in the story by Michael Fleming: "The quest by Peter and Bobby Farrelly to harness the project spans more than a decade and three studios. They first tried at Columbia, again at Warner Bros., and finally at MGM." What the H-e-double-hockey-stick??? The Farrellys (*There's Something About Mary*) had *trouble* floating a Three Stooges movie? Either studio executives (a) had never heard of the Three Stooges, or (b) were troubled by their own similarities to Larry, Curly, or Moe. What about the cast? The Farrellys are making wise choices: Get real actors to play comedy. They'll have to play it straight to make it work. No winking at the audience.

The Prestige

Q. I just read your review of the film *The Prestige* (2006). In it you mention Harry Houdini and say that you "read anything you could lay your hands on" about the man. Maybe you know the story (as I have read it somewhere) of what led to his death. Please correct if I am wrong. As I remember, Houdini was in a dressing room after a performance, when some students came in the room. Houdini asked volunteers to punch him in the solar plexus with all their might. It was a show of strength, plain and simple. The students considered themselves strong and wanted to see whether they could "lick" Houdini, who was, of course, completely unprepared (he didn't have time to tighten his stomach muscles). When struck by one of the fellows, he barely acknowledged the tremendous blow by the thoroughly prepared and "pumped-up" student. However, the blow had ruptured some internal organ and he died a few weeks later. Perhaps you could set me straight if I'm wrong.

—Goran Ingvarsson, Sweden

A. That is certainly the most widely heard version. However, Wikipedia offers a more detailed story. His assailant was a McGill University student named J. Gordon Whitehead, who struck Houdini many times. Wikipedia continues: "Although in serious pain, Houdini nonetheless continued to travel without seeking medical attention. Harry had apparently been suffering from appendicitis for several days and refusing medical treatment. His appendix would likely have burst on its own without the trauma."

Projection

Q. Los Angeles, home to the film industry, employs some of the least competent projectionists I've encountered anywhere in the world, and I'm getting tired of getting up mid-movie to complain that the picture is out of focus (the problem even surfaces in press and festival screenings!). If presented with the option of watching films on the big screen or at home on DVD, I choose the theater every time, but it's hard to deny that one advantage of owning an HD set and Blu-ray player is that I can always count on the clearest possible image. Between focus problems and the reduced bulb levels you're frequently writing about (not to mention crying babies, poor cell phone etiquette, rising ticket prices, and so many other factors), do you think today's projectionists may be undercutting the advantage of experiencing films in theaters?

—Jeff Joseph, Los Angeles

A. It's not only Los Angeles. I've gone out to the lobby many times to complain about bad focus, bad sound, a dim bulb, or improper framing. The most common reply: "That's how they made it." We Chicago critics see most of our films in a screening room run by Steve Kraus. I have never seen a projection error there. Perfection is possible, if the projectionist loves his job.

Prop Placement

Q. In your review of *The Love Guru*, you once again credit Mike Myers with creating peek-a-boo prop placement in the Austin Powers films. I think it's past time that we all acknowledge, as Myers himself has, that he stole the whole idea from the late, great Benny Hill, whose TV shows he saw growing up in Canada, years before they were shown in the United States. I'll note here that Hill never overdid it to the degree that Myers does.

—Mike Doran, Oak Lawn, Illinois

A. Credit given. I think "prop placement" is an excellent term for the technique you refer to, which involves using props on the screen to conceal a moving object, such as Austin Powers's whatchamacallit.

Ratings Systems

Q. I came across an item stating that Edgar Rice Burroughs's *John Carter of Mars* novels are being filmed. I looked forward to it until I read that the rating target is PG-13. The novels can easily be set to R. I feel disenfranchised from current studio movies by not getting adult-level entertainment—and I don't mean pornographic. To me and many of my friends, PG-13 means marketing and video games. I stopped seeing James Bond films as they became too kiddified. There is a level of content an adult desires, and most of today's PG-13s don't hit the mark. The most recent R-rated adult fantastic, for me, was *Watchmen*.

Do you think a return to R-level content based on adult concepts will ever happen?

—Todd A. Kennard, Imlay City, Michigan

A. There's a theory that the surprisingly soft box office figures for Sam Raimi's *Drag Me Down to Hell* are explained by the insistence of the distributors on cutting the film for a PG-13, which Sam Raimi fans sensed was just not right. As mass market "tent-pole" movies are increasingly tailored for the younger teenage audience, a demographic is being lost. Although distributors know that many theaters do a laughable job of policing the ratings, they are haunted by nightmares of a single sixteen-year-old being turned away. Strange, how many under seventeens somehow found a way to see *Watchmen* and *The Taking of Pelham 1 2 3*.

The Reader

Q. Why has no acclaim gone to David Kross, who brilliantly played the young Michael Berg in *The Reader*? The courtroom scene when he realizes what Hanna has done, tears streaming down his face, is heartbreaking. Yet he's received virtually no mention. It's as if Kate Winslet did the movie by herself. She was great, there is no doubt; this young man was so moving and went through so many emotions on screen, but he has not once been mentioned.

—Natasha Davidson, Los Angeles

A. Yes, he was the other actor in many of the scenes Kate Winslet won the Oscar for, and he was very gifted. Only seventeen when filming began, he had to learn English for the role. As a German actor, he may not have inspired U.S. distributors to push his career with an Oscar campaign.

Remaking *True Grit*

Q. There has been a lot of publicity surrounding the announcement that the Coen brothers are set to produce and direct the remake of the 1969 classic *True Grit*. Much of the publicity focuses on the point that the new film will, "unlike the original," be told from "the girl's POV" and that the remake will be closer to the novel. Having reread your review of *True Grit*, I think you hit it spot on when you said it was "one of the most delightful, joyous scary movies of all time." Has no one seen the original? Despite Wayne's Oscar-winning performance, *True Grit* was told entirely from Kim Darby's POV (Wayne didn't even appear in the first fifteen minutes). And the original was pretty close to the novel. What are your thoughts on the remaking of *True Grit*?

—Steven Matthews, Santa Monica, California

A. My hunch is that the Coens didn't write the press release. When some directors announce a remake, you know they're not going to do an actual remake but will move in a new and unanticipated direction. That would include the Coens. Also Werner Herzog, who is in postproduction on *Bad Lieutenant* after completing a shoot in New Orleans. He'll have Nicolas Cage in the title role, which was played by Harvey Keitel in the 1992 Abel Ferrara film. Asked about the Herzog film at a Cannes 2008 press conference, Ferrara confided: "I wish these people die in Hell. I hope they're all in the same streetcar, and it blows up." Herzog's response: "Let him fight the windmills, like Don Quixote." My guess: The two films could play on the same double feature, and the only similarities you'd notice would be in their titles.

Sasha Baron Cohen

Q. What's your take on the new subgenre of mockumentaries made by Sacha Baron Cohen, such as *Borat* and *Bruno*? I've gotten into debates with several friends about the people he chooses to interview in character. Sometimes his interview subjects are ordinary people who, either out of deep-seated bigotry or a desire to play along with the interviewer, express appalling prejudices on camera. Many people are troubled by this aspect of Cohen's work, arguing that the mockery of ordinary people smacks of elitism. My view is that Cohen is doing society a service by revealing just how easily average people will express shocking and hateful views on camera to a total stranger. Many of the people he interviews do come off looking spectacularly foolish, but it's hard for me to sympathize with them too much since they did sign a release allowing the footage to be used.

—Donald White, Falls Church, Virginia

A. It is astonishing to me how some people are willing to have themselves viewed in public. Cohen's recruits, Jay Leno's jaywalkers, Jerry Springer's guests—you'd think they'd cringe being seen that way. Apparently (a) they don't know how they come across, (b) they don't care, or (c) they'll do anything for their fifteen minutes of fame. If they really said it and signed a release, I say it's okay for us to laugh at them saying it. Is it elitist? Of course it is. Show me a man who doesn't want to be seen as elite, and I'll show you one who doesn't have to worry.

The Searchers

Q. I've long suspected that not so deeply layered in the John Wayne and John Ford film *The Searchers* is the idea that Debbie isn't Ethan's niece—she is his daughter. Ethan's sister-in-law Martha (Dorothy Jordan) is clearly in love with Ethan (Wayne), by the way she treats him, and by the way she holds his clothes close to her when she believes no one is looking. The sheriff (Ward Bond) pointedly ignores what is going on behind him when Ethan and Martha interact. Her daughter, Debbie (Natalie Wood), is the apple of Ethan's eye.

Ethan's reactions are driven by something deeper than a man's unrequited love for the woman who married his brother, seen in his pursuit to at first rescue Debbie, and then to kill her to save her from a "fate worse than death." If Ford did intend to hint at this, then the story takes on a deeper and more awful meaning. I guess the wonderful thing about art is that it can be interpreted in many ways.

—Stephen Sheehan, Omaha

A. I found your idea intriguing and turned for help to people who know more about films than just about anybody else: the legendary critic Andrew Sarris and his wife, the equally legendary Molly Haskell, and the noted University of Wisconsin scholar and author David Bordwell.

Molly tells me: "Although that interpretation is certainly possible, Andrew and I both felt it to be improbable; it just doesn't belong in the Fordian universe. The feelings between the two are palpable, but never (it seems to both of us) overtly expressed. That tacit love is quite sufficient to explain Ethan's special feeling for his niece."

David writes: "In grad school long ago we

talked about this; good to know that some people are still doing so. Still, I'm skeptical, since there's little evidence of the sort that I guess lawyers call 'probative.' Ethan loves Debbie, true, but his expression of affection is typical of how you'd treat a child; he's quite affectionate to little Lucy, too. Of course Martha is in love with Ethan, but there's no direct evidence that that love has been consummated. Ward Bond does avert his eyes, but that's just as likely because a moment of tenderness between Martha and Ethan would be something he'd overlook out of gallantry in any event.

"Ethan's reactions are driven by something deeper than revenge for the death of his brother and his family, but there is evidence that that something is racism—as indicated in his comments, before the attack, about the obvious Indian ancestry of Martin Pawley. Finally, if Ethan were trying to save Debbie from rape at the hands of the Comanche, several characters point out that he's long since failed; she's obviously come of age and probably has become a warrior's wife. It's that state of sexual maturity, at least according to the orthodox reading, that impels the later years of his quest: Martin (Jeffrey Hunter) is convinced that Ethan means to kill her for becoming defiled, and his struggle to keep Ethan from doing so is the engine driving the last portion of the film.

"All of this is more interesting, at least to me, than some hidden blood tie. It presents a more complex portrait of a man so blinded by codes of honor, family loyalty, masculine pride, sexual jealousy, and racial prejudice than would a reading that indicates he's out to rescue his daughter. This mix alone is extraordinarily edgy for an American movie. It seems to me that everything we see in the film supports this interpretation. I think we'd need some anomaly or extra clue to infer that Debbie is Ethan's child.

"And the context of Ford's other work doesn't suggest the hidden-affair account: Think of the unrequited yearning of Maureen O'Hara and Walter Pidgeon in *How Green Was My Valley,* or Wyatt Earp and the schoolmarm in *My Darling Clementine,* or even Lincoln and Ann in *Young Mr. Lincoln.* For Ford, as for many of his contemporaries, it seems

that unconsummated love is deeply poignant. Something else we've lost, maybe."

17 Again

Q. Just writing to correct an error in your recent review of the movie *17 Again.* You said: "She (Scarlett) thinks it's strange that he looks exactly like the boy she married at seventeen. He explains he is the son of an uncle, who I guess would have to be Old Mike's brother, so it's curious Old Scarlett never met him, but if she doesn't ask that, why should I?" This is incorrect. Actually what he says is that he is (Uncle) Ned's son and that it had been a surprise to Ned as well to find out that he had a son.
—Monica Drake, Georgetown, Ontario

A. To those who haven't seen the film: Matthew Perry, whose marriage to Scarlett (Leslie Mann) has failed, magically finds himself in the present time but inhabiting his seventeen-year-old body (Zac Efron). Eager to mend his marriage, he poses as his son's new friend from school. He looks exactly like the boy Scarlett married, because he is the boy Scarlett married. Monica Drake has explained why Scarlett didn't know her husband's Uncle Ned had a son. This explains everything except what Uncle Ned will say when Scarlett calls him to chat about his son.

The Seven Up Series

Q. You love the Seven Up series. Spanish beach real estate has collapsed worse than anywhere. I fear Tony, one of the subjects of the films, has been wiped out. I don't want to wait till *56 Up* is released to find out if my guess is correct. Do you know how Tony is doing?
—David Williams, Bellingham, Washington

A. The Seven Up series of documentaries by the great British director Michael Apted, which I consider a noble use of the time-traveling nature of film, has visited the same group of subjects every seven years since they were seven in 1964. Tony Walker was the young boy who dreamed of growing up to be a jockey, achieved his dream for a time, then became an often-recognized London cabbie and even played one in a few British TV shows. He was able to move his family to a beach resort in Spain.

I have no doubt that Apted knows how Tony is doing, but I am reluctant to ask him. The next movie, *56 Up*, is due in 2012, and it's part of the fascination of the series to wait seven years between installments. The project is about the mystery of time's passage in human lives and is the opposite of the breathless updates on reality TV. Seeing what can happen after years is the kind of wake-up call you get at your high school reunion.

Silent Horror

Q. I was lucky to be raised by a father with a deep love of cinema. So, I was able to see movies like *Nosferatu* and other silent films when I was fairly young. They held a spell over me. Reading your Great Movie review of *The Cabinet of Dr. Caligari* reminds me that as great as some modern horror films are, nothing, in my mind, has ever compared to those silent classics. I didn't get to see *Caligari* until a film class in college, but I remember the class, full of twenty-somethings who all thought they were film experts, spellbound. The sets, the images, were haunting, terrifying, and just dazzling. To me, true horror works when it haunts you long after the movie.

Modern movies go for the jumps and scares. Of course, some more modern horror films like *Psycho* stay with you, but nothing can give me chills like seeing that scene of the Somnambulist carrying the woman over those bizarre peaks and rooftops. Or the scene of the vampire standing up out of the coffin in *Nosferatu*. I sometimes fear modern moviegoers will miss these classics. Still, I do run into lovers of cinema who are younger than myself, in college as I was, and they have a thirst to learn. I hope that is always the case, and I hope these films are around forever.

—Bryan W. Alaspa, Chicago

A. In a strange sense, silent horror films can somehow seem almost real. The format creates a reverie state, and horror at that time was intended to disturb and frighten, not simply to shock. Those sad people who say they "don't like" silent or black-and-white films, or "old movies" in general, are simply saying "I don't want to see thousands of the greatest movies ever made."

Skydiving

Q. You know the action sequence involving the freefall without a parachute where one person catches up to another? The first time I saw it was in *Moonraker,* and many times since, including *Point Break, Shoot 'em Up,* and *Crank*. But is it accurate that when freefalling, you can change the velocity to which you are approaching the earth *that dramatically,* that by closing your arms and legs together, you could catch up to someone flailing their arms and legs?

—Tor Ramsey, Shelby, North Carolina

A. For an answer, I turned to computer columnist Andy Ihnatko of Boston, who somehow always knows about stuff like this. He replies:

"Yes, it is absolutely true. The short answer is to think about how fast a skydiver falls before and after the chute deploys. Same man, same parachute; after he pulls the rip cord, he's exposing more surface area to the onrushing air. Simple. Or, you can take a look at a YouTube video, which you can find by searching for 'indoor skydive.' It shows a static skydive attraction where a huge turbofan in the floor blows upward at the same force as you'd encounter after jumping from a plane. The person in 'freefall' position perpendicular to the oncoming air is hovering four feet above the floor. The person who's presenting the lowest profile can stand in place like nothing unusual is going on."

The Soloist

Q. Regarding *The Soloist,* Lopez [the columnist played by Robert Downey Jr.] couldn't fix this homeless musician and did not understand him, and his wife said "Just be his friend." For me, this was a perfect description of the entire movie. No, we do not understand Nathaniel's mental state. Yes, there will most likely be no major change to his mental health in his or our lifetime. He is what he is without explanation. He is odd, scary, interesting, and an incredible musician. Music seems to absorb him and bring him joy and some level of peace. Music can do that for some and Lopez seems to also be one of those beings. So as to your question as to why Lopez hasn't had enough: Nathaniel (Jamie Foxx) really has become a friend, someone worth Lopez's time, energy, and caring, a fellow human being with much to offer. I am so sorry that you did not think Nathaniel was worth his or our time. I think that was the crux of this movie.

—Sandra Donahue, Quincy, Illinois

A. I regret it if I gave that impression. Nathaniel is worth the columnist's time and our time, but I am not sure the movie found a successful way to demonstrate that.

Spider-Man 3

Q. Even though Spider-Man is Marvel's creation and property, on film Spidey belongs to Sony. But since Marvel Studios is trying to regain control of its characters (watch the postcredits scene in *Iron Man* and the last one in *Incredible Hulk*) for an Avengers film, why would they have set *Incredible Hulk*'s climax in New York City? It's obvious Spider-Man, Marvel's biggest moneymaker, should've been around for that final face-off, so why not just pick another city?

—Bernardo Ratto, New York

A. Either (a) Spider-Man will not appear in any Avengers film, or (b) such a film would have to be a Sony-Universal-Marvel coproduction. Either possibility allows the choice of NYC in *Hulk*. If they choose (a), I suggest it open with Spidey mysteriously missing and end with the Avengers failing to find him.

Star Ratings

Q. I have followed with no small amount of amusement your discussions of the star ratings provided on your reviews, but your disregard for such has never seemed more pronounced than recently. You provided *The Haunting in Connecticut* with two stars while praising its actors and technical credits. Meanwhile, *Monsters vs. Aliens* received a half star more while you lambasted its technical merits. Have you completely abandoned any sort of decision-making system for the stars, resorting instead to an entirely arbitrary one? In my mind's eye, I see you with a blindfold, a dartboard, and a fistful of annoyance. That thought, when I had it, provided me with the heartiest chuckle I've experienced all morning.

—Duell Aldridge, Muscle Shoals, Alabama

A. My stars are not absolute but relative, somewhat reflecting what a film intends to do and how well it succeeds. I didn't lambaste the technical merits of *Monsters vs. Aliens* but its 3-D, which I found an annoying distraction, dimming a screen intended to be bright.

Star Trek

Q. I disagree with much of your *Star Trek* review, but for a reason more related to the origin of this entire film *species*. While this latest effort pays homage to the earliest of the Star Trek series, let's not lose sight of the origin of so much of that series—*Forbidden Planet* (1956). The captain, doctor, and engineer are all ripped from that seminal movie, as are facets of the ship, especially the transporters (which began as stasis fields to cushion the crew during deceleration from warp speed). Even the banter between characters and Kirk's womanizing, McCoy's fondness for drink, and Scotty's ability to accept impossible tasks are all borrowed from *Forbidden Planet*, as are the grand vistas, meaningful plots, lost civilizations, and invincible enemies. So, let's enjoy this latest (and yes, perhaps the best) sequel to the 1950s' best space saga.

—George L. Curran III, Harrisonburg, Virginia

A. Also, Robby the Robot introduced the concept of robots with personalities, grandfathering R2D2, C3PO, and WALL-E.

Q. I hope you were not holding too much of the science against *Star Trek*, especially since some of the science problems seem to be based on your own misunderstandings. It should be pretty obvious that if you want to stop a warp-speed starship with any precision, a computer is going to have to do it, and "three . . . two . . . one" is just counting down how long until the computer stops the ship. And I don't see how a space elevator fits into the film at all. A space elevator sits in geosynchronous orbit above a planet's equator, so it stays above the same point on the planet's surface, allowing an ultralight cable to be dropped to the surface to haul stuff up. Such a device would be useless if you want to suspend something above plot-convenient points like San Francisco that don't happen to be on the equator. For that, you'd need an attachment to a ship moving with the planet's rotation. I don't know what kind of alloys they have in the 24th century, but a chain might very well fit the bill. Using warp speed to escape the clutches of a black hole makes science fiction sense. What doesn't make sense is no one being even slightly perturbed when they almost get sucked into a black hole while their captain is trash-talking.

—Christopher Raehl, Chippewa Falls, Wisconsin

A. In other words, the computer is controlling warp-speed autopilot, and the human countdown is simply to keep the crew informed? (1) Why couldn't the computer speak that? (2) Why does the crew need to know? It's not like they experience annihilating G-forces or anything. But I grant your point.

About the geosynchronous orbit, no matter where above a planet the platform is suspended, don't you think the cable would have to be made from an ultralight buckyball thread as Clarke suggested, and not from a metal chain, which would weigh millions of tons and require more matter than the Romulus ship contains?

Q. I would like to inform you what parts of your *Star Trek* review make it lesser than anyone else and just seem to be drivel that stings the eyes when read. You write, "Anyone with the slightest notion of what a black hole is, or how it behaves, will find the black holes in *Star Trek* hilarious." Damn it man, you're a film critic, not an astro-physicist!

"The logic is also a little puzzling when they can beam people into another ship in outer space, but they have to physically parachute to land on a platform in the air from which the Romulans are drilling a hole to the Earth's core." Your logic is puzzling. When the drill is active, all communications and transporter capabilities are disabled. Thirdly, they didn't parachute to land on the platform when it was drilling the Earth's core; that was on Vulcan.

"Chris Pine, as James Tiberius Kirk, appears first as a hot-rodding rebel who has found a Corvette in the 23rd century and drives it into the Grand Canyon." Though I can understand that you were trying to help others picture the scene in their minds, it was merely a borrow pit that had been dug throughout the years. They're all over the Midwest.

—Joel Gainey, New Orleans

A. Thanks for your corrections. I got carried away with the Grand Canyon, which,

after checking with Google Earth, I find is not located in Iowa. Regarding the astrophysics: I have never seen a black hole and am not sure if one can be seen, since even light cannot escape from it. But if I could see one, I doubt it would be on such a scale that it and the *Enterprise* could fit into the same frame.

Q. I believe the film did try to address the issue of why the characters "have to physically parachute to land on a platform." If I'm not mistaken, it is mentioned that the drill is interfering precisely with the function of the beam; the drill must therefore be disabled manually before the beam can be used. In this case, then, the logic may not be entirely puzzling.

—Andrew Wang, Los Angeles

A. I missed that detail, perhaps because I was astonished that three men would attempt to parachute from Earth orbit and zero in on a platform so small one of them misses it. And then I got caught up in their battle with the Romulans, which involves a duel with swords and a fistfight, although I was relieved to find such weapons are still used in the 25th century.

Q. I was lucky enough to see *Star Trek* this past Saturday with my husband, mother, and father, who is a diehard fan of the original series and idolizes William Shatner to a degree that is not at all weird. My real criticism (besides the shaky camera work, as I'm approaching twenty-nine and apparently can't handle movies the way I used to) was that Shatner wasn't included. I'm sure there's a story there, and I don't think anyone, even my dad, expected him to have a large role. But we all agreed that they could have at least had him voice the "Space, the final frontier" monologue, topping off what was, to me, a surprisingly good movie.

—Rachel Dixon, St. Louis

A. Shatner himself thought he should have been in it, since Nimoy was, but according to Fred Topel at starpulse.com, he and Nimoy shook and made up after Nimoy pointed out that Shatner was in *Star Trek: The Next Generation,* so now they were even. Director J. J. Abrams told Topel that he wanted to use Shatner, but "His character died on screen in one of the films. When we tried to figure out a way to put him in, every time we did it, it was a gimmick."

However, your idea of using him for the final voice-over is brilliant. Voice-overs by dead characters have been used before. Look at *Sunset Boulevard.*

Q. So, to paraphrase: *Star Trek* is an action adventure movie (rather than true science fiction, like *Knowing*)? Apart from grousing about script details your only gripes seemed to be that this is mainly a setup movie for the next one (which is a fair comment), and that it wasn't as filled with hot air as previous installments. But it didn't read as a thumbs-down, "don't see this" review. So are you telling folks not to bother? Or did you just want to stay far away from the *Trek* love-in? When I read a review telling me to stay away from a flick, I want to know why (if I was Stephen Hawking, maybe the dissing of black holes would be enough). And, by the way, how wrong is *Star Trek* about its black holes?

—Jason Tchir, Toronto

A. *Star Trek* was very wrong about black holes. (1) You can't see them. (2) One in the center of Vulcan would disappear the planet and everything else in the vicinity, including spaceships. (3) If you're being sucked into one, it's way, way too late to get out. There's a good discussion about the science of *Star Trek* by *Discover* magazine's "Bad Astronomy" blogger, Phil Plait, here: http://blogs.discovermagazine.com/badastronomy/. He loves the film.

What did 2.5 stars mean? They meant I couldn't recommend it, but it was funny anyway. *Knowing* was a much better, more stimulating, more intriguing movie. The science in both films was preposterous.

Star Wars: The Clone Wars

Q. As you said yourself, *The Clone Wars* is "basically just a 98-minute trailer for the autumn launch of a new series on the Cartoon Network." From a review standpoint, does it not matter in the least that this *movie* is, in all truth, three Saturday morning cartoon episodes shown back to back? Is there no regard for whether or not the movie achieves what it desires for its target audience, children?

—Eric Furtado, Foster City, California

A. I believe that, if anything, children deserve better entertainment than adults. They're instinctively smart until a diet of wretched movies like this pounds them down. I would infinitely prefer a child see something like *Finding Nemo* or *The Thief of Bagdad.*

The Strangers

Q. Allow me to liken *The Strangers* to *Hamlet,* if you will. What made the sad ending of 1997's *Hamlet,* to which you awarded four stars, so much more redeeming than that of *The Strangers*? Both movies featured complicated, multidimensional, and human characters that, through trials and tribulations, suffered and ultimately were killed. Both films were superbly acted, filmed, and directed, and I find the endings to be very similar. So what about the end of *The Strangers* made it a 1.5-star movie while *Hamlet* got four? Wasn't *The Strangers* also more about the feelings of the two main characters and the wrenching sympathy to be felt for them?

—Kyle Strand, Louisville, Colorado

A. I think it had a lot to do with everything that happened before the ends of the two films.

Swing Vote

Q. I thought your question to Kevin Costner (whether he could envision casting Dennis Hopper as the Republican candidate and Kelsey Grammer as the Democrat in *Swing Vote* instead of the other way around) was interesting, especially since Costner said he could not imagine that casting. However, I remember seeing a Hopper interview years ago with Mike Wallace, in which Hopper confirmed that he is, in fact, a loyal Republican. When the interviewer asked how it was possible that a poster boy for the '60s counterculture grew into a man who voted twice for George W. Bush, Hopper replied, "I got sober, man."

—Harris Fleming Jr., Waldwick, New Jersey

A. Like, wow, man!

Taken

Q. I have not seen *Taken,* but I would like to briefly comment on your assertion that if CIA agents were as skilled as the Liam Neeson character, bin Laden would have been in custody in September 2001. On an episode of *60 Minutes* from a few months ago when they interviewed a Delta Force commander, he said he and his troops have twice been within three hundred yards or less of bin Laden only to have their operation impaired by the "forces that be" of their supposed Afghan escort. I submit, there has been no sincere effort to capture or kill bin Laden.

—James B. Bolen, Memphis

A. Did the Afghan "impairment" involve threats of violence? There's a scandal here.

Terminator: Salvation

Q. In your review of *Terminator: Salvation,* you mentioned John Connor's initials in writing, "led by John Connor, or 'J.C.' for you Faulkner fans." I'm familiar with some of the religious symbolism in the *Terminator* series (e.g., J.C., the savior of humanity), and I'm at least somewhat familiar with Faulkner's work, but I didn't catch this reference. What does the "J.C." mean or call attention to?

—Brian, Orlando

A. In Faulkner's novel *Light in August,* the hero is named "Joe Christmas," and is thought to be a reference to Jesus Christ. John Connor seems doomed to die again and again and again for our sins.

The Thief of Bagdad

Q. Thanks for including *The Thief of Bagdad* in your Great Movies collection. This is one of my family's favorite movies, bar none. When we were kids, WPIX in New York used to show it every year on Thanksgiving morning, followed by *Babes in Toyland,* the one with Stan and Ollie. Problem is, some years they showed this 100-minute movie in a 90-minute slot, leaving out large chunks of film. My response to the edited version was a line borrowed from Jaffar's death sentence pronouncement upon the shackled future Mr. and Mrs. Ahmad. He saith thus, "In the morning they die the death of one thousand cuts." So does this movie, says I, when shown in this truncated fashion. Thank God cable came along, and home video.

How crazy is our family for this movie? We saw this in a theater when it first came to

America in the late '50s. Then we went to another showing, recently, of a clean, color-fixed copy that was playing at the revival house Loew's in Jersey City. And while we are normally well-mannered, polite moviegoers who usually demonstrate proper theater etiquette, we almost got thrown out because we kept speaking the dialogue. Perfectly, with the proper inflections, too. (My favorite lines came from Rex Ingram.) Boy, if they ever showed *Thief* and the original *Producers* on the same bill here, my cousin and I would be banned for life. Maybe even executed.

—Richard T. Hajeski, Elmwood Park, New Jersey

A. It should be as popular as *The Wizard of Oz,* another film of the same vintage.

300

Q. A lot of the reviews of *300* (2006) cast it as some kind of modern propaganda. I think the framing sequence (from David Wenham, sometimes on screen, sometimes off) tells us that the story is propaganda, but it's propaganda by ancient Greeks, featuring ancient Greeks fighting Persians, concocted specifically to get a different set of ancient Greeks to go and fight the Persians again. I don't know if that's what first Frank Miller and then Zack Snyder were shooting for. It'd be a good question for Herodotus.

—David F. Wall, Waltham, Massachusetts

A. Herodotus, as you know, wrote one of the lines of the dialogue: "Before battle was joined they say that someone from Trachis warned him how many Persians there were by saying that when they fired their bows, they hid the sun with the mass of arrows. Dianeces, so the story goes, was so dismissive of the Persian numbers that he calmly replied, 'All to the good, my friend from Trachis. If the Persians hide the sun, the battle will be in shade rather than sunlight.'"

I knew, of course, that Persia is modern-day Iran. But I didn't want to go there, because I'm not sure Frank Miller could have foreseen the current situation.

Q. Re your *300* review: I discussed this film with my political communication students as an example of how oral history and legends are created. You mention the Schwarzeneggerian biceps all Spartans seem to have, the logistical problems of a huge Persian army, and their eight-foot-tall king. Preposterous, I grant you that, but isn't that how the ancient Spartans would have told the legend to their children? I doubt they would have constructed their oral history around skinny warriors standing up to a small and famished army led by a physically unimpressive foreign tyrant. The film simply wanted to retell the legend as the Spartans did for centuries.

—Salvador Monroy, Mexico City

A. True enough, I suppose, but would anyone even then have believed the scope of the carnage in *300*? You have to admit that the film piles it on pretty heavily.

Tropic Thunder

Q. I saw *Tropic Thunder* tonight and read your review afterward. I was curious when you said it was "much enhanced by several cameo roles, the best of which I will not even mention. You'll know the one, although you may have to wait for the credits to figure it out." I didn't stay for the credits and don't know which cameo you are speaking of.

—Paul Gowan, Chico, California

A. SPOILER WARNING: Maybe I was simply dense, but I, for one, did not recognize Tom Cruise.

2009 Oscars

Q. Jack Nicholson is usually front and center at the Oscars. Where was he for the 81st Academy Awards?

—Doug Dobbs, Kingfisher, Oklahoma

A. Well, the winner of the most male acting Oscars in history is not sick, if that's what you're thinking. Tom O'Neil of the *Los Angeles Times* speculates he was at home watching the Lakers. Might have been unseemly if he had been seen at the game.

Q. The discussion continues about why Jack Nicholson didn't attend the Oscars this year. Jack might have skipped because Heath Ledger was nominated for a role they both played, the Joker in *The Dark Knight*. Jack's presence would have prompted questions from every journalist seeking quotes about how he compared his performance in the 1989

Tim Burton film to Ledger's. And the cameras would be on him as the award was announced, looking for his reaction. I think he would have wanted to avoid that, for personal reasons and to keep the focus on Ledger, as it should be.

—Harry Thomas, *San Antonio Express-News*

A. This makes perfect sense to me.

Q. On the Oscars, the camera's constant movement during the "In Memoriam" segment was obnoxious and distracting, and it prevented the TV viewing audience from seeing the faces and names of those who had passed. Why not stick to the usual format and give the audience the chance to reflect on those we've missed?

—Joe Pezzula, Los Angeles

A. Some loved the Oscarcast, some hated it, but *everyone* agreed the "In Memoriam" segment was a train wreck, even if Queen Latifah gave a lovely singing performance. As one bizarre camera angle followed another, viewers could not even see some of those being remembered. The show director, Roger Goodman, should have realized his mistake, bailed out of his game plan, and cut to the full screen.

Tyler Perry

Q. I read an article about Tyler Perry's Madea films being a social phenomenon among black people. The critics hate them but their audience loves them. *All* of Perry's films have earned less than a five-star rating on IMDb, which is not critic-driven, yet most of them have been box office hits. How do you explain this? Is it that reviewers are mostly white so they just don't "get it"? Or are these films just a pretext for black people to gather as a community and see themselves in a mirror that Hollywood has refused them for too long? Is it phase two of blaxploitation?

—Benoit Methot, Montreal, California

A. Actually, a fair number of black critics also dislike them. I gave a one-star review to *Diary of a Mad Black Woman* and was branded as a racist on two Chicago radio stations, apparently by callers who had never read another of my reviews about films with black actors or themes. (Five of my "best films of the year" in the decade before the movie fell into that category.) I knew nothing about the character of Madea and nothing of Tyler Perry's enormous popularity, and maybe I didn't "get it," but I thought it was a bad movie. *Madea Goes to Jail* has so far grossed nearly $70 million despite its 27 percent (one-star) rating on the Tomatometer. Here's what I think. I love the movies, and if people spending their money have a good time, that makes me happy.

Up

Q. In the movie *Up,* I noticed that the later scenes showed close-ups of the main character (Carl Fredricksen) in which he is clearly unshaven, which is logical considering several days have passed in the movie's time line since he took off from home. Funny that this should happen in an animated movie as opposed to any live action ones where the characters' beards never grow, or if they start off as two to three days' growth they mostly stay the same way throughout the film.

—Gerardo Valero, Mexico City

A. Your observation is on the money. I'm trying to think of the last action movie I saw with realistic facial hair. I sometimes wonder how these guys go through days of unremitting action while still finding time off to use an electric shaver on the stubble setting. What ever happened to the old cliché of the clean-shaven hero?

Q. In your Answer Man section, Gerardo Valero from Mexico City said that Carl from *Up* had an unshaven beard at the end of the film. You said you couldn't remember the last action movie that shows an action hero progressing through the film with his facial hair growing longer. As I was watching *Deja Vu,* the 2006 Denzel Washington movie, I noticed that Val Kilmer's character went through the movie without shaving. In fact, the effect of the unshaven beard makes the character look tired and beaten up.

—Alex Hagani, New York

Q. An exception that proves the rule. I noted that most action heroes, even in the midst of nonstop action, somehow find time to maintain their beards at the official length established by *Miami Vice.* This has the

benefits of signaling their high testosterone levels, shadowing any signs of a double chin, and saving time on makeup.

Valkyrie

Q. Regarding your *Valkyrie* review and the negative buzz Tom Cruise has been receiving since the "couch incident," I'm at a loss to understand how the most irrelevant of happenings could damage such a big career so badly while, for example, Robert Downey Jr. is on the brink of being canonized for his comeback year (*Iron Man, Tropic Thunder*) after years of wasting his life in prison and drugs. Nothing against either of these two actors, who seem like nice enough people and whose movies are pretty good. I'm just wondering who exactly is behind this war against Tom Cruise. Personally I feel sorry watching him on TV these days going out of his way trying to be nice to everybody and getting hammered on a constant basis, and it's not like I've even yet seen *Valkyrie* or give a care about Scientology.

—Gerardo Valero, Mexico City

A. Gossips are bullies who like to pile on. They do little real reporting but take cues from one another and apply them to new developments.

Video Games

Q. While I agree with your review of *Terminator: Salvation,* and, unlike you, hope what was once a great franchise can finally die in peace, I take offense to this sentence in particular: "It gives you all the pleasure of a video game without the bother of having to play it." I know of your view on video games, being a fan of yours to some extent, and I must protest. I know that you're too old to learn about the world of video games, Roger, but that doesn't mean slights against them are appropriate. There is a greater world to video games than *Call of Duty* and *Grand Theft Auto,* shallow, superficial excuses for games churned out to the same dumb, mindless male audience as the very film you review. I encourage you to not blanket all of the industry and the works therein with the idea that video games cannot be moving experiences and fall only under the moniker of cheap male masturbatory action experiences such as the aforementioned games.

—Garrett Cosgrove, Battle Creek, Michigan

A. My good young man, I am not too old to learn about video games, but I'm old enough to know better. Life is too short, and it always has been. But please, be my guest. Shoot your rosebuds while ye may.

WALL-E

Q. Did you notice that the WALL-E robot bears a striking resemblance to the robot in *Short Circuit,* a movie reviewed unfavorably by both you and Gene Siskel at the time? Although *WALL-E* is the better movie (I liked *Short Circuit,* too, as a child), I would think that *Short Circuit* deserves credit as the inspiration.

—Willy Yu, Los Angeles

A. The robots certainly resemble each other in their personalities, tank treads, and binocular optical equipment, although Robot Number 5 has a laser beam and electronic gizmos where WALL-E has a trash compactor. But, yes, they seem to spring from the same evolutionary tree.

Variety reporter Peter Debruge, who did a story on the comparison, writes me: "Just thought I'd share a *WALL-E* insight: Pixar's been hearing the *Short Circuit* comparison a lot, but one thing director Andrew Stanton tried hard to avoid was the dude in a suit performance style for the character (or puppet-style "Fozzie Bear acting"). So yes, they both have binocular-style eyes and tank treads for mobility, but that's more coincidence than influence (if anything, they kept those features in spite of the fact that they'd been featured in a corny Steve Guttenberg comedy from the '80s). Basically, Stanton and company tried to design WALL-E to fit his function. Look how his arms work, for instance: He doesn't have shoulders or elbows, although he's flexible enough to do far more than scoop up trash. EVE's resemblance to Apple i-devices, on the other hand? Definitely not an accident."

Watchmen

Q. It's my understanding that the Ozymandias character in *Watchmen,* whose "real" name is Adrian Veidt, was named after Conrad Veidt, though I can't find any source on this. I also seem to recall Rorschach, who is named Walter Kovacs, was named for Ernie Kovacs. Any truth to these?

—Chris Swanson, Phoenix

A. I can't find any evidence that author Alan Moore named him after Conrad Veidt. Still, he must have known about the actor, famous as Major Strasser in *Casablanca.* The actor changed Weidt to Veidt to make it easier for non-Germans to pronounce. (A Hollywood sales pitch helped: "Women fight for Conrad Veidt!") And there's a certain facial similarity between the actor and Matthew Goode, who plays Ozymandias. A more direct superhero connection is between Batman's enemy the Joker and Veidt's performance in the silent classic *The Man Who Laughs.* Legend has it that Batman creator Bob Kane was inspired by Veidt's makeup in that film, which is in my Great Movies collection. Ernie Kovacs? Can't find proof.

Q. The Vulture blog at *New York* mag surveys the *Watchmen* critics who mention the size of Dr. Manhattan's you know what. You called it "discreet." Are you trying to send a message?

—Ronny Barzell, Los Angeles

A. Not the one you got. I was referring to the way it blends perfectly with his blue color scheme. I don't know what Peter Travers of *Rolling Stone* was smoking when he wrote of Manhattan "flashing a few yards of giant blue wiener." Zack Snyder, director of the film, likens it to a "bell clacker." My own opinion? Manhattan has ceased to exist as flesh and blood and has reconstituted himself as quantum energy. He controls every detail of his appearance and manifests as a blue giant. How many men could resist the opportunity to do a little tweaking?

Q. After reading your *Watchmen* review, there's a vital piece of information I feel you left out: Have you read the graphic novel? When it comes to reviews for movies that appeal to both the geek masses and the mainstream, knowing the reviewer's familiarity with the source material can be helpful to both camps. For instance, when the *Lord of the Rings* movies were released, I preferred reading reviews from critics who had not read the books (and thus entered the theater with the same knowledge that I would). Of all other reviews of *Watchmen* I've read, there's a common bond: those who had read the novel previously could follow along. Those who hadn't found themselves at a loss to explain what was going on.

—Erik Dresner, Elmhurst, New York

A. I have been told I must in maybe a third of the almost five hundred *Watchmen* comments on my blog. Over and over again I have been told. I purchased the book but have decided not to say if I've read it, because, frankly, it has been scrutinized in such minute detail by its admirers that I fear becoming mired in a quicksand of debate. A film critic, of course, is writing for readers who must not be presumed to have read the book.

Wendy and Lucy

Q. I was anticipating *Wendy and Lucy* for months. It didn't disappoint; I got to look at Michelle Williams for ninety minutes, which was the basis of my anticipation in the first place, but, ironically, don't you think that despite her marvelous performance she was too good-looking for the part? The attempt to take the shine off of her was doomed to failure, and the number of male volunteers to halt her floundering would have filled Soldier Field. Perhaps the point was to emphasize the character's relentless self-reliance, but we all have a breaking point.

—Joel Ostrow, Deerfield, Illinois

A. Two opinions: (1) Most movie stars are too good-looking for their roles. (2) A homeless, penniless, clueless woman far from home represents an opportunity to help, not an opportunity to date. A "male volunteer" thinking of anything else should be ashamed of himself.

What's That Film?

Q. Years ago I saw a movie involving a captive in a shed fed each day by a guard. The captive finds a bullet and makes a hole in the heavy door. He places the bullet in the hole and when the guard unlocks the door he hits the primer of the bullet, which fires and hits him in the chest, killing him. The captive escapes. I saw this movie only once, probably in the early '60s. Any ideas of the title? We need more like it.

—David R. DeSau, Neskowin, Oregon

A. How many more like it do you think we need, before we start groaning, "Oh, no! Not again! The old bullet-in-the-door routine."

Q. What is the title of the horror movie where a vampire is impaled by a cello endpin through the heart? Where might I get a copy?

—James Kjelland, Evanston, Illinois

A. I don't know, but we need more like it.

Wilhelm Scream

Q. I have been an Indy fan for as long as I can remember; I grew up on the movies. I thought *The Kingdom of the Crystal Skull* was a fantastic movie, and I sat through the movie with the biggest grin on my face. And it wasn't just because the movie itself was great. As I was watching, I noticed that the same sound effects were used from the other three movies for the punches in the fights. Also, the same ambient jungle sounds from *Raiders* were used. Hearing these sounds put together with different pictures and sequences made the movie truly special for me. Did you pick up on this reuse as you were watching the film? And if so, did it have a similar effect on you?

—Jonathan Furr, Concord, North Carolina

A. Sound effects experts often recycle existing sounds from other movies. At rogerebert.com, look up the "Wilhelm Scream" in the Answer Man archive for another example of sounds that live on long after they were first used. First used in 1951, the scream is still being employed today.

The Wrestler

Q. I would like to lodge a formal complaint against you for your deceptive review of *The Wrestler*. You should be forced to paper-cut Mickey Rourke with a thirty-pound printout of your review. You have given a slew of misguiding four-star reviews. Exhibits A–C this year alone are *In Bruges*, *The Dark Knight*, and *Taxi to the Dark Side*. But *The Wrestler* is worse. It is a siren among songbirds. A grizzly among goldfish. It is not permissible for an

Ebert review to segregate a brilliant *acting* performance from the underlying ocean of clichéd compost. How did it come to pass that you gave a perfect score to a horse-poopy film based on Mickey playing Rourke? Mr. Ebert, thou hadst erred.

—Helga Mohammed el-Salami,
Beverly Hills

A. I have self-administered one hundred lashes with a wet noodle.

Q. At the end of your review of *The Wrestler,* you said that it was not on your year's best list for long and complicated rea-sons. If you have some time to spare to share these reasons with a fellow movie geek, I would love to know them.

—Dmitry Voronov, Toronto

A. Of course I do consider *The Wrestler* to be one of the year's best films and said so in my review. It was not on my list for reasons having to do with a mistake I made using the cut and paste feature of my word processor. That's the boring part. How I did that, since I am a word processing whiz, would be the complicated part, but I don't think you have time for it.

Ebert's Little Movie Glossary

These are the year's new contributions to my glossary project. Hundreds of entries were collected in *Ebert's Bigger Little Movie Glossary,* published in 1999. Contributions are always welcome.

* * *

And the Winner *Actually* Is . . . When a movie depicts a life-and-death fight between a main character and a lesser one, and it occurs off-camera, the second character will be the first one shown emerging from it, apparently the winner. Then he will suddenly collapse, and the real victor, the main character, will come into frame immediately after.

—Geraldo Valera, Mexico City

Anticlimactic Rescue Journey. If a horror movie periodically cuts to a lesser character slowly making his way to the scene of the crime with the hope that he alone can save the day, he will instead get killed abruptly upon arrival. (See *The Shining, Friday the 13th*, and *Misery*.)

—David VanCouvering, Davis, California

Cellular Follies. When the plot calls for it, the characters won't be able to dial out on their cell phones because of no coverage, even if earlier in the same film they dialed in from the dark side of the moon. On the other hand, if a character is trapped at the bottom of a collapsing mine shaft, etc., searchers will still be able to talk to him via cell phone, reception be damned!

—Ashley Riddell, Tønsberg, Norway

The Cocky Credits Rule. Movies that know they're good always end with a stylized image of the movie title before the main credits. (See *The Dark Knight, Children of Men, If . . .*, and *Slumdog Millionaire*.) Movies that know they aren't good gently fade to the tech credits, hoping you'll forget the movie title and won't be able to warn people against it.

—Rhys Southan, Brooklyn, New York

Diagnosis: Death. Whenever a character sneezes or coughs for no apparent reason, they will die. There are no exceptions.

—Agatha Jadwiszczok, New York

Don't Count on It. When a movie villain is powerful, relentless, or indestructible throughout the course of the film, you can never be 100 percent convinced that he's really a goner if he meets his demise. (See *Terminator 2: Judgment Day, The Hitcher*, and *Cape Fear*.)

—Adam Rurik, Mount Pearl, Newfoundland

The Encore! Rule. In any film that culminates in a concert by the characters, the concert audience will go wild with appreciation even though the "concert" is only one song long.

—Jon Jerome, Lake Villa, Illinois

The FBI/Local Police Incompetence Rule. If both the FBI and the local police appear in the same movie, one group or the other can be competent investigators, but never both. Either (1) the FBI will be arrogant prima donnas who deal with a real crisis (*Die Hard*), while the local cops, although unshaven and unkempt, are more street-savvy and do whatever it takes to bring the bad guys to justice; or (2) the FBI agents are sophisticated investigators, thoroughly professional, and cool under pressure, while the local police are a bunch of incompetent yahoos (*Silence of the Lambs*).

—Dallas Dodge, West Hartford, Connecticut

The Fuller (Closer) Brush Man. In any war movie where you get to know a character who isn't the hero, he gets killed.

—Legendary director Sam Fuller, 1980

George Carlin's Toilet-Head Syndrome. Have you noticed that in the movies lately a popular thing to do is stick someone's head in the toilet and flush the toilet repeatedly? Where did that come from? They never used to do that. You never saw Spencer Tracy stick Henry Fonda's head in the toilet. Maybe Katharine Hepburn's, but not Henry Fonda's.

—George Carlin, from the book *Napalm and Silly Putty,* contributed by Andrew Polino

He Was Dying Anyway. Many lead characters who martyr themselves for a cause or someone they love are shown to be dying from cancer in order to ease the blow of their death. Audience members will be heard to say, "Well, he was dying anyway" as they leave the theater. Key clues will be the "coughing up blood" and "Your test results came back" scenes. See Clint Eastwood in *Gran Torino* and Tommy Lee Jones in *Space Cowboys*. Also known as the "Altruism Is Dangerous to Your Health Rule."

—Fred Decker, Apex, North Carolina

"Hold Your Fire" Music Cue. When one character is considering shooting another, and there's a close-up of the would-be shooter's finger tightening on the trigger (and a tense crescendo on the sound track), that gun is *not* going to be fired.

—Tom Hill, Portland, Oregon

The House with the Unstable Nut. Whenever movie characters escape from a catastrophic world crisis (or merely a perilous situation) and end up in an individual's home by random chance, they will invariably choose one that an unstable nut inhabits, which will only complicate an already difficult scene. (See the crazy woman in *The Happening*, Tim Robbins's basement in *War of the Worlds*, the sadomasochists in *Pulp Fiction*, the plastic surgeon in *Minority Report*, and the Steve Buscemi character in *The Island*.)

—Geraldo Valera, Mexico City

May–December Archaeologists. Archaeologists in movies always work in pairs: a beautiful young woman and a grizzled old man. No movie ever made has featured a grizzled old woman and beautiful young man.

—Keith Hiatt, Emeryville, California

The Mostly Male Hell Rule. Hell must be depicted with a large, even 100 percent, population of males, rather than females.

—Robert Tan, Taoyuan City, Taiwan

Noisy Predator Fallacy. In any movie where the heroes are being stalked by predators, the creature will show its presence with a low, rumbling growl, even if it is not a creature that normally growls or is even an alien. Any predator that hopes to be successful keeps silent before it strikes.

—Jonathan Langley, Minneapolis

"Oh, Danny Boyle, the Pipes, the Pipes Are Flowing" Scene. Any moment in a Danny Boyle film where the hero's prized objective can be achieved only by complete immersion of the main character in a lagoon of excrement.

—Greg Hill, Boston, Massachusetts

The Plot in the Title. Any movie with "Beverly Hills" in it (*Beverly Hills Cop, Beverly Hills Ninja, Troop Beverly Hills, Down and Out in Beverly Hills, Slums of Beverly Hills*) will feature a fish-out-of-water scenario, in which a poor, uncouth, or slovenly main character tries to fit in with the rich, elitist, and snobby citizens of 90210.

—Joshua Finkelstein, New York

The Ponderosa Effect. When the film frame is caught in the path gate of a projector and is too close to the light source, it becomes stuck and does not advance. The result is that frame burns through the center and expands into total destruction, not unlike the territorial map of the Ponderosa ranch during the credit sequence of the television series *Bonanza*.

—Charles Coleman, Chicago

Preemptive Confession. When a character intends to confess something and says, "There's something I have to tell you," the other person immediately confesses, "I have something to tell you first," prompting the original character, after hearing it, to say, "Never mind."

—Mike Smith, Pittsburgh

Rule of Risky Pickups. When a high school or college boy is attempting to chat up a drunken girl at a party in the hopes of getting lucky, she will invariably vomit all over him.

—John Morton, New York

Rule of Spectral Verticality. In movies, ghosts pass through all walls whether they want to or not, no matter what the walls are made of. They never, however, fall through floors.

—Steve Paulson, Arlington Heights, Illinois

Through a Glass Safely. People who fall through plate glass often suffer severe lacerations, but the protagonist in an action movie can bust through (or be thrown through) plate glass and emerge unscathed. (See *Beverly Hills Cop, Total Recall,* and *Resident Evil: Apocalypse*.)

—Andy Hutton, Fremont, California

Upper Bunk Rule. Any scene in which two adults are sleeping on a bunk bed will inevitably result in the top bunk collapsing onto the bottom bunk. (See *Black Sheep* and *Step Brothers*.)

—Mitchell Schnurbach, Montreal

The View from the Bridge. When a character is attempting to escape across a bridge, there will be a convenient boat passing under the bridge at exactly the right time for our character to jump to safety. There is a slight variation on this in *In Bruges*, where a character jumps from a balcony onto a passing canal boat. Another example is in *The Bourne Supremacy*.

—David Mullen, Carlow, Ireland

Water, Water Everywhere! Rule. When a character is really, really thirsty, maybe after wandering days through the desert, and gets to drink some water, the water has to drip all over out of the actor's mouth. If it is the last precious container of water in the desert, at least half of it has to fall to the ground.

—Nestor Ares, Potomac, Maryland

What Is a Helicopter For? A helicopter has the ability to hover. Many action movies do not realize this. They have their helicopters perform "strafing runs" against ground targets instead of assuming a relatively stationary hover, thus making an otherwise trivial shooting job much more difficult. (See *From Russia with Love*, *The Thing*, and *Blue Thunder*.)

—Andy Hutton, Fremont, California

Who's Your Daddy? Whenever a couple very much in love is separated by circumstance *and* happen to make love the night before they split, they will invariably conceive a child whose paternity will never be obvious to the father once they, inevitably, meet again. (See Keri Russell and Jonathan Rhys Meyers in *August Rush*, Robert Redford and Glenn Close in *The Natural*, Tom Hanks and Robin Wright Penn in *Forrest Gump*, Jim Caviezel and Dagmara Dominczyk in *The Count of Monte Cristo*, and Linda Hamilton and Michael Biehn in *Terminator*.)

—Geraldo Valera, Mexico City

Index